Encyclopedia of American Humorists

Garland Reference Library
of the Humanities
(Vol. 633)

Encyclopedia of American Humorists

Edited by
Steven H. Gale

Garland Publishing, Inc.
New York & London • 1988

Library of Congress Cataloging-in-Publication Data

Encyclopedia of American humorists.

   (Garland reference library of the humanities ;
vol. 633-   )
   Includes index.
   1. American wit and humor—History and criticism.
2. American wit and humor—Bio-bibliography.
3. Humorists, American—Biography—Dictionaries.
4. Authors, American—Biography—Dictionaries.
I. Gale, Steven H.   II. Series: Garland reference
library of the humanities ; v. 633, etc.
PS430.E53 1988   817'.009   87-8642
ISBN 0-8240-8644-9 (alk. paper)

Printed on acid-free, 250-year-life paper

Manufactured in the United States of America

To Kathy, Shannon, Ashley, and Kristin,
and to my sister, Norma, and my mother and father,
and in memory of my brother, Bill,
once more and as always,
with all my love and thanks

Contents

Pseudonyms

Pen Name

Allen, Woody	Allen Stewart Konigsberg
Arp, Bill	Charles Henry Smith
Crayon, Geoffrey	Washington Irving
De Quille, Dan	William Wright
Doesticks, Q.K. Philander	Mortimer Neal Thomson
Dooley, Mr.	Finley Peter Dunne
Douglas, Jack	Jack Crickard
Downing, J., Major	Charles Augustus Davis
Downing, Jack	Seba Smith
Forester, Frank	Henry William Herbert
Kerr, Orpheus C.	Robert Henry Newell
Knickerbocker, Diedrich	Washington Irving
Langstaff, Launcelot	Washington Irving
Ockside, Knight Russ	Mortimer Neal Thomson
Oldstyle, Jonathan	Washington Irving
Nasby, Petroleum V.	David Ross Locke
Quad, M.	Charles Bertrand Lewis
Ross, Leonard Q.	Leo Rosten
Solitaire	John S. Robb
Suggs, Simon	Johnson Jones Hooper
Tenn, William	Philip Klass
Tensas, Madison	Henry Clay Lewis
Twain, Mark	Samuel L. Clemens

Acknowledgments

In an undertaking as massive as compiling a 135-entry encyclopedia of American and Canadian humorists, the number of people who helped with the project is in itself nearly overwhelming, and I regret that I cannot acknowledge individually the help that literally hundreds of my colleagues provided in the way of suggestions for subject entries or for scholars who might be particularly appropriate to write on those subjects. I hope that those who offered suggestions understand how deeply appreciative of their help I am.

Among those who deserve special recognition is Gary Kuris, the editor at Garland Publishing who invited me to edit this encyclopedia and who was extremely helpful and understanding during the entire process, which took nearly three years. I also appreciate the help and careful attention given the volume by the editorial and production staffs at Garland, especially Pam Chergotis in editorial. In addition, the reference staff at the Spiva Memorial Library at Missouri Southern State College, Gay Pate and David Reiman in particular, deserve a thank you for their help, as do the reference librarians under Joan Banks at the Joplin Public Library.

The work that I did on the *Encyclopedia of American Humorists* was made immeasurably easier by the contributions of my associate editors, Doug Robillard, David Sloane, George Test, and Kenny Williams. The amount of time and worry that they saved me made the task a lot easier to face. Along the same line, I truly appreciate the work of the individual scholars whose essays are contained in this volume—they labored hard and enthusiastically. In addition, Gail Demery did yeoman work helping me check footnotes, and Paige Stansberry, serving as an editorial assistant, saved me uncountable hours by contacting contributors when there were questions to be answered or factual information needed to be confirmed.

Finally, and as always, I owe a tremendous debt of thanks and appreciation to my wife, Kathy, and my three daughters, Shannon, Ashley, and Kristin, who supplied support and encouragement throughout. Kathy and Shannon also helped in the indexing and proofing of the manuscript, and Ashley and Kristin assisted in the manuscript preparation as well; their backup was especially valuable to me. Without the love and understanding of my family, this encyclopedia would not have come into being.

Preface

In December 1984, I was working on *S.J. Perelman: An Annotated Bibliography*, which was published by Garland Publishing the following fall. At the Modern Language Association Convention in New York, I stopped by the Garland booth to give editor Gary Kuris an update on the status of the project. He had been waiting for me with a pleasant surprise; he invited me to edit an encyclopedia of American humorists. The project excited me, and I immediately began work on it.

During the last three years, I have had a number of experiences, some pleasurable and some extremely frustrating. I first had to define the contents of the volume. I wanted to include all major (that is, the best and most important) and representative American humorists from the beginnings of American literature to the present. Identifying those writers is not as easy as it might at first seem to be, though. The most important question that arose was, what is the definition of a humorist? For the purpose of *Encyclopedia of American Humorists* I had to make some arbitrary decisions—otherwise the volume would have been endless. (Some of the determining factors are discussed in the Introduction.) One of my first decisions was to include only those writers who are known primarily as humorists. Even such major humorists as James Thurber and Perelman did not write exclusively humorous material, of course, but their reputations are based on their humorous writings. Many major American authors, on the other hand, utilize humor in their work but are not recognized for this aspect of their canon above all others—William

Faulkner and Edgar Allan Poe come to mind. Rather than include entries on these writers in *Encyclopedia of American Humorists*, I decided to hold them for a proposed second volume that will involve "serious" literary artists who use humor effectively.

There are two kinds of exceptions to the limitations implied by the above definitions. First, there are a few authors such as Oliver Wendell Holmes, whose main body of work was not humorous but who wrote humorous works. In these cases only the humorous works have been examined. Second, there are some authors who have been considered in studies of the American humor tradition whom I would not consider humorists. These include local colorists such as Bret Harte, and they are included primarily because researchers will probably expect to find entries on them in the encyclopedia.

Once the definition of my subjects was set, I contacted over 200 American literature scholars (primarily in America, although I also communicated with a couple in Great Britain and in France) and supplied them with a list of approximately 150 names to be considered for inclusion in the encyclopedia. I asked them to let me know which names they thought would be appropriate (or inappropriate) for inclusion; I welcomed their suggestions of additional names to be considered, and I asked if they were interested in writing an entry or if they could recommend anyone else who would be especially well suited to write an entry on a particular author. I ended up with over 200 possible entries.

Over a period of two years, the list of

subject authors was refined and writing assignments were made. Scholars were instructed in the format—which was to include biographical and bibliographical information (primary sources and annotated secondary sources) for easy, quick reference and a detailed literary analysis for in-depth study that would be useful to either laymen or established scholars in the field. Occasionally an entry does not fit this format exactly. A few scholars felt that their subject author's life or work could be better understood if minor variations from strict categorization were allowed, and in several instances certain information simply was not available. The themes and techniques of the subject's best and most representative works were to be examined, and there was to be a brief summary that included an assessment of the importance and influence of the subject in the area of American humor. By and large, the length of the entry reflects the importance of the subject author, though this is not always true, especially if the scholar who wrote the entry felt that the subject had not received an appropriate amount of attention previously.

The final choice of subject authors also included another important aspect. I was looking for scholars to write on each subject who had some expertise on the subject and who were recognized as good writers. This means that not every subject author whom I would have liked to include in *Encyclopedia of American Humorists* is included because I chose in a few instances not to include an entry if I could not count on its being as well written as possible, and I did not want to seek out someone to write on a humorist who did not already have an interest in the writer simply to be able to include another entry. John

Brougham, Dan Greenberg, Lewis Grizzard, and Shepherd Mead are examples of this unfortunate situation. Conversely, some lesser writers were included because of the enthusiasm of an expert on that specific entry and because of my desire to expose a wider audience to a figure who has heretofore been neglected. Interestingly, America has always been blessed with talented authors who write humor columns for local newspapers (the *Gainesville* [Florida] *Sun*'s Bill Henderson and the *Joplin* [Missouri] *Globe*'s Marti Atoun are fine representatives of this fraternity), but obviously it would be impossible to include every writer of humor in the nation's history in this encyclopedia. I hope that, for whatever reason, I did not leave out anyone's favorite American humorist.

Part of the joy of working on this project came from the enthusiasm and careful work of the many scholars whose essays appear in the volume. Most tried religiously to meet their deadlines (several even used overnight express mail deliveries to ensure that they would do so) and to create entries that go beyond simple, shallow summaries of other people's research. Their willingness to contribute original scholarship was admirable. As would be expected, some entries are better than others, but I was pleased, too, by the consistently high quality of the submissions.

Part of the disappointment and frustration came from the inability of a number of respected scholars to participate because of prior commitments— though many still found the time to make recommendations as to whom they thought might be able to write in their stead. Other disappointments involved people who agreed to contribute an essay but who later begged off, often well after the due date for their work had passed. There were also several people who became ill or otherwise incapacitated for a while but who managed eventually to turn in their work. Unfortunately, one contributor died after completing two essays, but his family was unable to find the manuscripts.

In any event, the result of all of the above is the *Encyclopedia of American Humorists*, which is intended to be the most comprehensive and up-to-date reference text on American and Canadian humorists ever published. There are scholarly articles on 135 authors from the colonial period through today, including all of the major humorists as well as a wide range of the best and most representative of the rest. These essays represent the efforts of scholars from an extremely diverse field of disciplines: English departments, naturally, but also American studies, economics, education, film, history, humanities, journalism, library, literature and language, journalism, and women's studies departments, and several independent scholars. This diversity suggests that the subject of American humor is one that appeals to a wide range of people and that this volume will not only fill a reference need but will also be of interest to those who enjoy humor for its own sake.

Joplin, Missouri

Introduction

Our sense of humor defines us as Americans far more accurately than does our sense of tragedy.

Humor has been present in American literature from the very beginning, of course, even before there was an America *per se*. As has been demonstrated in a number of excellent scholarly studies, including those by Constance Roarke, Thomas Masson, Moody Boatright, Louis Rubin, Walter Blair, Jessie Bier, Norris Yates, Hamlin Hill, Thomas Inge, Arlin Turner, and scores of others, American humor has developed characteristics that reflect our character, both regional and national to some extent. Until relatively recently, though, scholars have tended to treat American literature as inferior to British literature—and American humor has been paid even less attention and respect than mainstream American literature. That situation has been changing, and from the number of books that have been published on humor and humorists in the last several years, it appears that a wave of interest in the subject is building in academe. There has always been a large popular audience for the genre.

Some critical reservations about humorists derive from the fact that it is difficult to evaluate humor in spite of the fact that most of the critics named above have developed their own definitions of humor (some of them are rather elaborate). In addition, humor is used for so many different purposes that often it is not easy even to define what is humorous and who is a humorist. Authors as divergent in purpose and style as Seba Smith, James Augustus Longstreet, Mark Twain, S.J. Perelman, Henry Kuttner, Erma Bombeck, and Andy Rooney are "humorists." So what is it that they have in common that allows us to call them humorists? As with many literary definitions, categorization may be based on the author's intent as much as anything else. These writers intend to amuse their audiences. But, as is true of other important literary figures, the humorists in *Encyclopedia of American Humorists* composed literature that enlightens as well as amuses. Their primary works are humorous or their reputations are based on the humor in their writing, yet there is an important social element underlying that humor; they are trying to expose the foibles and foolishnesses of our society and the individuals who compose it. It is the manner in which these authors try to accomplish this end, then, that determines whether they appear in this volume. It does not matter whether a reader (only literary humorists are included, not comedians or other performers—unless that is merely a tangential aspect of their work) smiles at the satire of Art Buchwald or laughs at the amusing incidents that James Thurber insightfully recalls from his youth; in both cases the writer is trying to tell us something about ourselves or our culture by drawing our attention to the subject in a way that we will find funny.

In perusing the writings of all of the authors included in this volume, a reader would be likely to conclude something that leads us back to our opening statement about the character of American humor. The best humor has at its base a ready understanding of human nature. In June 1986, when A. Bartlett Giamatti left the presidency of Yale University to become the president of the National Baseball League, Andy Rooney suggested in his nationally syndicated newspaper column that baseball manager Billy Martin might be considered as president of Yale. That is an amusing reversal of perspective. Two months earlier, in April, Rooney had devoted a column to the televised broadcast of Vladimir Horowitz's return piano concert in Moscow, a moving event reported in a moving article. Without the ability to feel the significance of the Horowitz recital and to share its emotional impact with a Soviet citizen who was in attendance, Rooney could not have written the piece on Giamatti and Martin.

The Humorists

Adams, Franklin Pierce

Born: Chicago, Illinois, on November 15, 1881

Education: University of Michigan (1 year)

Marriages: Minna Schwartz, divorced; Esther Sayler Root; four children

Died: March 23, 1960

Biography

Franklin Pierce Adams, or F.P.A. as he identified himself in his long-running newspaper column, "The Conning Tower," grew up in Chicago, Illinois, where he was born on November 15, 1881. The son of Moses and Clara Schlossman Adams, he attended public schools there and graduated from the Armour Scientific Academy in 1899. He then attended the University of Michigan for a year.

In 1903, Adams began writing features for the *Chicago Journal*. Later he moved to New York to write a column, "Always in Good Humor," for the *Evening Mail*. He joined the *New York Tribune* in 1913, naming his new column "The Conning Tower." He took the "Conning Tower" with him when he went to work for subsequent newspapers, and the column ran until 1941. During this time and through 1956, he also contributed frequently to such popular magazines as *Literary Digest, Ladies' Home Journal, Good Housekeeping, Collier's, Harper's,* and *Atlantic.* From 1938 to 1948, he was a regular participant on the radio quiz show, *Information Please*, which was also televised for thirteen weeks in 1952. According to the *New York Times*, the television version failed because "the erudition of men like Mr. Adams, Clifton Fadiman, and John Kieran tended to militate against it as a source of 'light entertainment.'"

A prolific writer, Adams wrote and edited over twenty-five books in addition to his regular column. However, he now may be best known for having been a founder and sort of dean of the Algonquin Club, a group of witty, sophisticated, often-cynical writers, actors, editors, agents, and other creative talents, including Robert Benchley, Ring Lardner, George S. Kaufman, Harpo Marx, Herman Mankiewicz, Noel Coward, Paul Robeson, and Dorothy Parker. Beginning in 1919 and throughout the 1920s, this group met regularly for lunch at the Algonquin Hotel's Rose Room, where the owner, Frank Chase, gave them their own table (The Round Table), a private waiter (Luigi), and free relish trays.

There the group sported, often making up word games to allow themselves to shine. According to Margaret Chase Harriman, Frank Chase's daughter, Adams invented "I-Can-Give-You-a-Sentence," one of the group's more renowned games. In it, the would-be wit must furnish a sentence that plays on the sound of a particular word assigned to him or her. Asked to provide a sentence with "meretricious" in it, Adams wished everyone "a meretricious and a Happy New Year." Dorothy Parker, however, later brought the game to its zenith with her sentence for "horticulture": "You can lead a horticulture, but you can't make her think."

In general, the intent of these games and of the luncheon conversation was to revel in spirited wit, though this inevitably opened the doors for cutting, sarcastic, and cynical observations. For example, to Alexander Woollcott's boast, "What is so rare as a Woollcott first edition," Adams replied, "A Woollcott second edition." Another time he observed, "Everything is lower in price. Even the $5 silk shirts are down to $8.50, reduced from $13.50." Despite Dorothy Parker's pet name for the luncheon group, The Vicious Circle, the witticisms could sometimes be warm instead of barbed. Of Parker, who occasionally contributed light verse to "The Conning Tower," Adams boasted that he had raised her from a couplet. By the early 1930s, however, the Algonquin Club began to dissipate, though many of its members went on to make considerable contributions in their fields. Adams continued writing his column, books, and magazine articles, editing volumes of light verse, and appearing on radio and later on television. Thus, his death in 1960 still merited front page coverage in the *New York Times*.

Literary Analysis

Adams published his first book, *In Cupid's Court*, in 1902 while he was still living in Chicago. His last published volume was *The F.P.A. Book of Quotations*, which he edited in 1952. He contributed to prominent magazines as late as 1956. In a writing career that spanned some fifty-four years, including two world wars, periods of economic booms and busts, and a cold war, Adams's style of humor understandably underwent significant changes. Like the humor of other early twentieth-century humorists, Adams's comes mostly from the tradition of the mid-nineteenth-century literary comedians, who used quick wit, wordplay, and self-conscious parody, often for satiric purposes.

Like many of his contemporaries, such as Clarence Day, Dorothy Parker, Morris Bishop, and Gelett Burgess, Adams wrote for an erudite audience that could identify and respond to classical and neoclassical allusions and literary forms. His early work, especially, includes parodies of or responses to the odes of Horace, Catullus, and other Roman poets. For example, *Tobogganing on Parnassus* (1912), whose very title comically deflates the home of the Muses, contains a verse, "Catullus, Considerable Kisser." The poem begins as a poem by Catullus might, "How many kisses, Lesbia, miss, you ask would be enough for me?" and it continues for several lines in a traditional vein. However, the final two lines undercut both the classical pretentions and the romantic sentiment: "Come, Lezzy, please add all of these, until the whole amount of 'em/ Will sorely vex the rubbernecks attempting to keep count of 'em." "Help: The Passionate Householder to His Love" parodies Christopher Marlowe's Renaissance poem, "The Passionate Shepherd to His Love." Instead of Marlowe's "Come live with me and be my love," Adams writes, "Come live with us and be our cook." This kind of play with classical and established materials, which he deflates by pairing incongruous levels of formality in diction, tone, and sentiments, is typical of Adams's earlier work.

As the United States prepared to enter World War I, Adams's poetry became more pointed and political. He railed against German brutality:

> *I'm Captain Hans of the submarines*
> *I feed the sea with human be'n's;*
> *I do not care about the means—*
> *I'm in the German navy.*
>
> (from *Weights and Measures*)

But, he also attacked American capitalists who fulminated against the Germans while profiteering or abusing their workers. "The Indignant Captain of Industry" lambasts a factory owner who, while the women working in his garment shop toil in a building devoid of sunlight or ventilation, indignantly decries the Prussians' use of poison gas, and "The Patriotic Merchant Prince" features another industrialist who during the day adulterates his product to enhance profits and in the evening makes speeches about how "The honor of the Stars and Stripes [Applause] must be defended."

During this period Adams was not entirely preoccupied with politics, though, nor did he lose his sense of playfulness and irony. *Weights and Measures* (1917), for example, also features "Ballade of a Traveller's Jinx" (the refrain of which is "Mine is the trunk that goes astray)," several more parodies of Roman poets, "The Ballade of Schopenhauer's Philosophy," "Lines to a Beautiful and Busriding Lady," and "If Poets Had Feared the Advertisers." By pointing out discrepancies between the noble times past and the mundane present, Adams generates humor, but in a way which, like Parker, James Thurber, and Robert Benchley, reveals a hardened, somewhat cynical view of contemporary society, one in which he is forced to acknowledge how advertising impinges on every aspect of daily life and how our lady loves are daily degraded by mass transit. This outlook characterized much of Adams's humor, as indeed it characterized much of the wit of the Algonquin Club.

Adams's postwar humor remains cynical, although it never becomes bitter. *Half a Loaf* (1927), composed mostly of excerpts from "The Conning Tower" published during the height of the Roaring Twenties and the heyday of the Algonquin Club, casts a doubtful eye on this era of good feeling. Adams respectfully takes issue with General Pershing's assurance that "we are moving forward in the direction of good-will." Adams's own perception of the times is that "in a good-will race with a glacier, the best we could hope for would be to finish as runner-up." Other social commentary includes his nomination of the *Herald-Tribune* for the year's Half-Truth Prize, for its observation that "Big wars are very costly to the losers." And Adams sees the irony that an American public that remained blasé in the face of the Teapot Dome oil scandals became outraged because Shoeless Joe Jackson and Eddie Cicotte accepted bribes for throwing the 1919 World Series.

The style of Adams's comic verse is somewhat less formal in the postwar era. In general, among comic writers from the period there are far fewer allusions to classical and neoclassical poetry and verse forms, and more to Romantic and post-Romantic poets, even while T.S. Eliot was using his considerable authority to cast aside the Romantics and resurrect such highly structured poets as John Donne and others schooled in the classical traditions. Yet, arguably, both Eliot and Adams saw their time as one in which conventional forms of order and authority failed.

Eliot's response was to try to impose order through intricately structured poems that harken back to more stable and ordered eras. Adams, on the other hand, seems to sense the inappropriateness of classical forms that do not ring true to the postwar world, and, hence, he largely abandons them. So, instead of parodying Horace, he speculates "If Rudyard Kipling Had Been Dorothy Parker." Adams, in Parker's persona, concludes:

If you can dodge the Menace of the Years;
If you can look at life nor let it task you,
If you can fry in hell, yet rise above it—
Well, if you can, or if you can't, I ask you
What of it?

(Half a Loaf)

Adams's later humor continued in much the same style: he wrote a considerable amount of comic verse; some poems were pointed and satiric, others were simply playful. His sort of nonsensical, light verse offered appealing diversion for Depression-era readers, who made the Marx Brothers box-office successes. Occasionally, though, Adams would still address issues head-on. In "I Remember, I Remember," the narrator recalls his childhood, when his father was able to pay the rent and still have something to spare: "But now 'tis little joy/ To know I'm farther off from riches/ Than when I was a boy" (*The Melancholy Lute: Selected Songs from Thirty Years*, 1936).

Summary

Overall, Franklin P. Adams's career must be deemed successful. Through "The Conning Tower" he had a daily forum for some twenty-eight years for his ideas, observations, and bursts of comic creativity. Several of his books went through multiple editions; he was a major player in a legendary gathering of talented, creative, and somewhat influential people, and for a decade he appeared regularly on a popular radio show.

One suspects, however, that Adams, like Parker and perhaps some other members of the Algonquin Club, was undone by his own cynicism. For all of his talent, insight, and wit, he remained emotionally aloof, settling for the occasional brilliant insight and *bon mot* but never truly sustaining a work of power and imagination—comic or otherwise. Whether in response to personal, cultural, or other cataclysms, the Algonquin group used their cleverness to insulate themselves from cynicism or even despair. Unable not to see through the veneer of good times during the Roaring Twenties to the corruption and disharmony lurking beneath, they translated their insights into wordplay that at once allowed them to acknowledge unpleasant sights but still to remain aloof from them. Perhaps, had their cynicism not been so strong, Adams, Parker, and some of the others might have gone on to merge their astute observations about their world with emotional power, thereby creating something truly exceptional. As it was, though, they largely kept themselves at arm's distance from their work and produced literature that is entertaining and astute but that does not ultimately aspire to very great heights.

Selected Bibliography

Primary Sources

Books

In Cupid's Court. Evanston, Ill.: W.S. Lord, 1902.
Tobogganing on Parnassus. Garden City, N.Y.: Doubleday, Page, 1911.
In Other Words. Garden City, N.Y.: Doubleday, Page, 1912.
By and Large. Garden City, N.Y.: Doubleday, Page, 1914.
Among Us Mortals. Boston and New York: Houghton Mifflin, 1917. Pictures and legends by W.E. Hill; text by F.P.A.
The Conning Tower; June 1914–October, 1917. New York: 1914–1917 Scrapbook of clippings from *New York Tribune*.
Weights and Measures. Garden City, N.Y.: Doubleday, Page, 1917.
Something Else Again. Garden City, N.Y.: Doubleday, Page, 1920.
Women I'm Not Married To. Garden City, N.Y.: Doubleday, Page, 1922.
Overset. Garden City, N.Y.: Doubleday, Page, 1922.
So There! Garden City, N.Y.: Doubleday, Page, 1923.
So Much Velvet. Garden City, N.Y.: Doubleday, Page, 1924.
The World, New York. New York: Macy-Masius, 1926.
Half a Loaf. Garden City, N.Y.: Doubleday, Page, 1927.
The World, New York: The Second Conning Tower Book. New York: Macy-Masius, 1927.
Column Book of F.P.A. Garden City, N.Y.: Doubleday, Dorn, 1928.
Christopher Columbus and Other Patriotic Verses. New York: Viking, 1931.
Diary of Our Own Samuel Pepys: 1914–1935. New York: Simon and Schuster, 1935.
The Melancholy Lute: Selected Songs of Thirty Years. New York: Viking, 1936.
Nods and Becks. London and New York: Whittlesey House, McGraw-Hill, 1944.
The Servants (with Genuflections to Kipling's "The Ladies"). New York: Close, Graham and Scully, n.d.

Anthologies, Edited Works, Forewords

The Book of Diversion. Compiled by Adams, Deems Taylor, and Jack Bechdolt. New York: Greenberg, 1925. Revised and enlarged as *The Weekend Companion*. New York: World, 1941. Verse, songs, epigrams.
Answer This One: Questions for Everybody. Compiled by Adams and Harry Hansen. New York: E.J. Clode, 1927.
Poems, by Bernice Dewey. Ed. Adams. New York: Galleon, 1933.
Percy Hammond: A Symposium in Tribute by F.P.A., John Anderson, and Others. Garden City, N.Y.: Doubleday, Dorn, 1936.
Dunne, Peter F. *Mr. Dooley at His Best*. Foreword by Adams. New York: Scribner's, 1938.
Heywood Broun As He Seemed to Us. New York: Random House, 1940. Essays by F.P.A., John L. Lewis, Herbert B. Swope, et al.

Congreve, William. *Love for Love.* Introduction by Adams. New York: Scribner's, 1940.

Innocent Merriment: An Anthology of Light Verse Selected by F.P.A. New York and London: Whittlesey House, McGraw-Hill, 1942.

The F.P.A. Book of Quotations. New York: Funk and Wagnalls, 1952.

Newspaper Columns

Chicago Journal, 1903.

"Always in Good Humor." *New York Evening Mail,* 1904–1913.

"The Conning Tower." *New York Tribune,* 1913–1922: *The World,* 1922–1931; *The Herald-Tribune,* 1931–1937; *The Evening Post,* 1938–1941.

Secondary Sources

The Algonquin Wits. Ed. Robert E. Drennan. Secaucus, N.J.: Citadel, 1968, pp. 1–38.

Blair, Walter, and Hamlin Hill. *America's Humor: From Poor Richard to Doonesbury.* New York: Oxford University Press, 1978, pp. 409–411.

Harriman, Margaret Case. *The Vicious Circle: The Story of the Algonquin Round Table.* New York: Rinehart, 1951.

Van Doren, Carl. "Day In and Day Out." *Century,* 107 (December 1923): 308–315.

———. Review of *Diary of Our Own Samuel Pepys: 1914-1934. The Nation,* 141 (December 11, 1935): 687–689.

Richard Alan Schwartz

Ade, George

Born: Kentland, Indiana, on February 9, 1866
Education: Purdue University, B.S., 1887
Died: May 16, 1944

Biography

George Ade was born on February 9, 1866, in the small village of Kentland, Indiana, the son of pioneer parents. His father, John, had emigrated from England at age 12; his mother, Adeline Bush, was Ohio-born of Scots extraction (clan Adair). The pair had married in 1851, and moved to frontier Indiana two years later; they settled in Kentland in 1860. George was the fifth of six children.

While Kentland was only 80 miles south of Chicago, it bordered on open prairie, and George spent a farm boyhood. It was also one of material comfort; John was a bank cashier and Republican notable. George, too, was a lifelong Republican; William Howard Taft began his 1908 campaign at Ade's 400-acre estate. Neither George nor his father were primarily farmers,

and George, in fact, hated farm life, which he considered depressing, ugly, and exhausting. He preferred reading and composition and convinced the family to send him to Purdue University, from which he graduated in 1887. Here he met his lifetime friend, cartoonist John T. McCutcheon, who would help him get his first job in Chicago journalism.

Meanwhile, he held a number of writing positions in Lafayette, Indiana, first for the *Morning News,* later for the *Evening Call,* and finally as a patent medicine ad writer. In 1890, he joined McCutcheon in Chicago, Illinois, as weather reporter for the *Morning News.* Quickly he became an understudy to the whole *News* staff; he covered city hall, the police beat, ethnic and labor gatherings, and sports and the theater, building a far-reaching acquaintance with Chicago's famous and notorious and an intimate knowledge of the streets and ordinary folk that would characterize his early stories. In 1893, Ade transferred to the *News's* evening paper, the *Record,* where he would establish his reputation as an essayist and short-story stylist and remain until 1900.

His first "Stories of the Streets and of the Town" column appeared in 1893, and its popularity encouraged the Chicago News Company to publish selections in booklets regularly after 1894. Eight collections would appear. In 1895, Ade created the slang-talking "Artie" Blanchard whose adventures in book form (1896) resulted in Ade's discovery and promotion by William Dean Howells. "Artie" was quickly followed by the "Pink Marsh" and "Doc' Horne" series, also highly popular and successfully published, accompanied by McCutcheon's cartoons and illustrations. Although neither man received title page credit, their work was identifiable. In 1897, Ade produced his first "Fables in Slang," which permanently established his fame and wealth. Howells, Mark Twain, Brander Mathews, and William Allen White praised them, and the first book-length collection in 1900 sold 69,000 copies within a year. The "Fables" were syndicated, at first through R.H. Russell and later by a number of other publishers. Over the next 30 years Ade wrote more than 500 "Fables," half of which were collected in eleven books. When he left the *Record,* his salary jumped from $65 to $1,000 weekly. Later, theater royalties would bring him $5,000 weekly during the height of his career as author and playwright.

While many of Ade's plays are unpublished (some have been lost, and some were never copyrighted), he combined the success and sales of his vernacular tales with a decade of fascination with and production for the stage. Writing not only the fables and his full-length and one-act plays, but occasional verses and jingles, Ade was prolific between 1890 and the 1920s; Dorothy Ritter Russo's standard bibliography lists at least 2,500 entries, and more have been discovered. The financial returns were great, and Ade spent his later years enjoying them. He endowed Purdue liberally (the football stadium was named for him) and acted as godfather to his old fraternity, Sigma Chi. He bought his estate, Hazelden, near Brook, Indiana, where he wined and dined thousands as an old bachelor. His gradually decreasing popularity by the 1930s disturbed him only slightly. Ade died in Brook, on May 16, 1944.

Literary Analysis

George Ade wrote for a generation of rural-born Americans undergoing the shock of urbanization. He both reflected and shared their anxieties as he tried to interpret modern society for them. Giving the people "what they thought they wanted," he produced stories, fables, plays and movies about the conflict between traditional copybook maxims and real life. Essentially a cynic, he created characters of misplaced hopefulness or stoic endurance rather than anomie. He loved to ridicule but could feel for his plodding nobodies. His outbursts were always modified into acrid burlesque; Ade was incapable of truly savage or vulgar satire.

His earliest "Stories of the Streets and of the Town" were largely reassuring vignettes of life in the interstices of Metropolis. He explored alleys, ethnic neighborhoods, and survivals of small-town Chicago. One of his best stories, "Effie Whittlesy," dealt with a woman who had unknowingly become a servant to a former hometown friend. To the wife's consternation, the husband refuses to treat Effie as a domestic. They discuss the homefolks, share reminiscences; he disappears with her into the kitchen. Reluctantly concluding that he is too embarrassed to employ her, he convinces her that economic misfortune need not reduce self-respect.

Ade's first sustained character, "Artie" Blanchard, at first glance seems a shallow lout. Modeled after a newspaper officeboy, Charles Williams, a repository of vainglory, "Artie" was a boisterous, pugnacious hustler who spouted colorful street argot, but he was endearing, earnest, and had a kind heart. "Artie was the embodiment of 'Young Chicago,' precisely the kind of American boy that every American girl wants a crack at reforming."[1] The "Artie" character was followed by Ade's second sustained protagonist, "Pink Marsh," a middleaged black who shined shoes. "Pink" was in part a Zip Coon stereotype, a malaprop, and ludicrous schemer, but he, too, was viewed sympathetically as an example of proletarian survival, and his white "Morning Customer" was a supercilious tormentor. Finally,

Ade created "Doc' Horne," a genial liar who reminds one of Gene Ahearn's later "Major Hoople" of *Our Boarding House.*[2] He and his disbelieving audience lived in a cheap hotel filled with life's losers, but they kept their dreams and dignity intact, if not their veracity.

Ade is best remembered for his "Fables in Slang." Prolifically produced, the fables were written in what Ade preferred to call colloquial style; "slang" sounded both vulgar and sub-literary, and he maintained the distinction between suitable and unsuitable argot. Nor were all the fables heavily laden with verbal shockers, although some titles could be eye-poppers (e.g., "The Fable of the He-Flirt who was very Jimpsey in the Hotel Office but a Phoney Piece of Work when Turned Loose in a Flat"). They did all incorporate vivid expression, both neologism and argot, and unusually juxtaposed words, and Ade's unconventional and unsystematic capitalization made the reader stop and savor the unfolding of his amorality plays.

Ade's readers were impressed by the Aesopian form as well as eccentric language of the fables. Jarring incongruities and ironic inversions were Ade's forte, and the use of an archaic form to portray modern norms was arresting. In concise, economically concentrated narratives (1500–2000 words), he presented cautionary tales of greed, loneliness, self-delusion, and bumptiousness. Most of them treated the inadequacy of traditional values in a changing world satirically through parody, pun, anticlimax, wisecrack, or non sequitur. "The Fable of Sister Mae, Who Did as Well as Could Be Expected" dealt with two sisters, one of whom parlayed good looks into a rich marriage while her industrious but lumpy sister wound up a domestic in "Mae's" mansion. "The Fable of the Reckless Wife Who Had No One to Watch Her" told of a "young Couple who sat and looked devouringly at each other for the first six months of the Life Sentence and finally it became rather trying on the Eyes."[3] He finds happiness in bachelor-style dissipations; she in the company of a girlchum in sloppily stuffing herself, in deshabille. A clergyman preaches gobbledygook to appreciative congregations, a man who suffers the aftereffects of gargantuan indulgence blames the last four grapes, another pays to be flattered outrageously and transparently by a phrenologist, a W.C. Fieldsian druggist suffers a day of petty indignities from non-customers—such folk, along with lonely young women and inept do-gooders, reappeared in Ade's writing for a generation. The world of these fables is one of the difference between aspiration and likelihood, the sufficiency of a "good front" and occasionally of momentary resentment, as in "The Fable of the Caddy Who Hurt His Head While Thinking" of his father's hard lot compared to those of the swells who employed him.

Most fables end with an ironic moral; the "lesson" of "Sister Mae" is given as "Industry and Persistence bring a sure Reward." To the person who blamed those last four grapes for his indigestion, Ade advises: "Avoid Fruit." Ade seldom created his Fables to express or create anger; he was simply wry, and his victims settled for what life handed them.

In his other works Ade similarly sought popularity through superficial ridicule. Some of these pieces were brief burlesques, such as "Mrs. Peckham's Carouse" (1898), which is about the inadvertent drunkenness of a teetotaler, or "Il Janitorio" (1896), a parody of life's little irritations treated as grand opera. Some were studies of hypocrisy and pose: "The Mayor and the Manicure" (1912) was a racy, one-act play about blackmail, bluff, and the "main chance." Some were simply escapist, as *The Slim Princess* (1907), a short novel about Graustarkian court intrigues. The best-received, however, were those theater pieces about small-town characters and life, with sardonic rustics, chaste romance, football and college color, and family scenes. Some were perfect vehicles for Will Rogers, such as "The County Chairman," a slangless play about midwestern town politics which ran for several years and became an amateur and summer-stock favorite, or "Father and the Boys," a tale of a money-hungry widower who neglects his children's moral education, to everybody's comic discomfort.

In 1898, Ade travelled with the Ringling Brothers circus to research a series of columns; that same year his actress friend May Irwin had made "Mrs. Peckham's Carouse" into a vaudeville staple. Ade was inspired to write a series of light operas and comedies. "The Sultan of Sulu," based on a contemporary news item about a local Philippine ruler, was produced in 1902. By 1910, he had written ten others: "The County Chairman" and "Peggy from Paris" in 1903, "The Sho-Gun" and "The College Widow" in 1904, "Just Out of College" (1905), "The Bad Samaritan" (1906), "Artie" (1907), "Father and the Boys" (1908), "The Fair Coed" (1909), and "The Old Town" (1910). "The College Widow," "The County Chairman," and "Just Out of College" eventually became motion pictures. "The College Widow" in particular would periodically reappear; Jerome Kern and P.G. Wodehouse adapted a musical version, "Leave It to Jane," which was revived in 1959. Dozens of his fables were made into movie shorts by Essanay, and during the 1920s Ade wrote three works expressly for motion pictures: "Our Leading Citizen," "Back Home and Broke," and "Woman Proof."

Because Ade was so enamored with vignettes and wisecracks, not all of his plays were successful; brilliantly polished miniatures and jests could not be sustained through three acts. "Just Out of College," "Artie," "The Bad Samaritan," and "Peggy from Paris" were poorly received slaps at modern pretensions because the parade of characters and types became repetitive and the bustle obscured the plot. Ade's two comments on American imperialism, "The Sultan of Sulu" and "The Sho-Gun," were musical comedies; his serious points were swallowed up in a profusion of silly jingles, scenery, costume, and plot complications among pasteboard characters.

One analyst has judged Ade a "literary Rotarian" who wrote too quickly and in too many genres to sustain quality or depth of characterization.[4] Because he produced so much dross along with the finer short essays and tales and because his style and social tone seemed unacceptably innocent to a post–World War I generation, Ade came to be a purveyor of nostalgia and sentimentality rather than the tough realist an earlier generation perceived. In obscurity by his death, his work by mid-century was known only to a few aficionados even though it influenced such writers as S.J. Perelman. Recently, scholarly interest in Ade has revived, but critical appraisal of his work is mixed and largely dependent on the critic's particular focus. Literary realists relish his stories and disparage most else. Linguists and punsters admire the fables and find the stories lightweight. Social historians see useful material in those tales realized on the screen by Thomas Meighan and Will Rogers but hardly consider them serious literature. Almost no one reads his plays or occasional magazine articles.

Summary

George Ade never aspired to more than contemporary popularity, nor did he have the patience to create more than a rapid series of facile, if entertaining, cynical anecdotes and wisecracks. Many of his works for the stage were slapdash, and even the sparkling vernacular fables have a sameness when read in bulk. By now, much of his once-striking language seems dated or contrived. Even at his angriest about life, he rarely could summon up more than a sardonic shrug; his satire seems timid in comparison to that of James Thurber, Ring Lardner, or Sinclair Lewis.

While Ade never achieved major stature and is now known largely as a crossword puzzle entry, his work still is interesting to students of American literature and popular culture. Extraordinarily popular in his own time, his humor synthesized the frontier tall tale that exaggerated in order to flatten pomposity and the Yankee moral jest. His stories were excellent local-color portraits of city-dwellers. In his many fables he sought to free his generation of false expectations that could cripple their ability to negotiate life, and the best of the fables are both gritty and witty. The more successful plays are pageants of a vanished society and provided his audiences an alternative to dialect burlesque, pratfalls, and sexual innuendo.

Current devotees, such as Jean Shepherd and Shel Silverstein, have been greatly influenced by his ironic style and inversion of clichés. Along with Eugene Field and Finley Peter Dunne, George Ade helped create and establish a distinctively midwestern genre of American humor.

Notes

1. Lee Coyle, *George Ade* (New York: Twayne, 1964), p. 34.
2. Maurice Horn, ed., *World Encyclopedia of Comics* (New York: Chelsea House, 1976), pp. 532–533.
3. Jean Shepherd, ed., *The America of George Ade, 1866–1944* (New York: Putnam, 1960), pp. 155–156.
4. Coyle, p. 137.

Selected Bibliography

Primary Sources

Anthologies and Letters

Chicago Stories. Ed. Franklin J. Meine. Chicago: Regnery, 1963; published as *Stories of the Streets and of the Town*, Chicago: Caxton Club, 1941.
The Permanent Ade. Ed. Fred C. Kelly. Indianapolis: Bobbs-Merrill, 1947. Includes two of Ade's plays: *Marse Covington* and *The Sultan of Sulu.*
The America of George Ade, 1866–1944. Ed. Jean Shepherd. New York: Putnam, 1960.
The Letters of George Ade. Ed. Terence Tobin. West Lafayette: Purdue University Press, 1973. A selection from the chief depository of Ade manuscripts.

Fables and Short Story Collections

Artie. Chicago: Herbert S. Stone, 1896.
Doc' Horne. Chicago: Herbert S. Stone, 1899.
Fables in Slang. Chicago: Herbert S. Stone, 1900.
More Fables in Slang. Chicago: Herbert S. Stone, 1900.
The Girl Proposition. New York: R.H. Russell, 1902.
Breaking into Society. New York: Harper and Brothers, 1904.
Knocking the Neighbors. New York: Doubleday, Page, 1912.

Essays

In Pastures New. New York: McClure, Phillips, 1906; Upper Saddle River: Literature House, 1969. Ade's European travels.
The Old-Time Saloon. New York: Long and Smith, 1931.

Secondary Sources

Bibliography

Russo, Dorothy Ritter. *A Bibliography of George Ade.* Indianapolis: Indiana Historical Society, 1947. Painstakingly conscientious; about 2,500 entries.
Stronks, James, "Supplement to the Standard Bibliographies of Ade, [etc.]." *American Literary Realism* 1870–1910, 16 (1983): 272–277. Five additions to the Russo catalogue.

Biographies and Monographs

Coyle, Lee. *George Ade.* New York: Twayne, 1964. The first full-length assessment; it stresses his career as a playwright. Numerous examples excerpted.
Kelly, Fred Charters. *George Ade, Warmhearted Satirist.* Indianapolis: Bobbs-Merrill, 1947. The standard biography, by a friend; anecdotal and uncritical.

Articles and Chapters in Books

Brenner, Jack. "Howells and Ade." *American Literature*, 38 (May 1966): 198–207. Describes William Dean Howells's early support but subsequent disappointment.
Daniels, R. Balfour. "George Ade as a Social Critic." *Mississippi Quarterly*, 12 (Fall 1959): 194–204. Ade as a critic of the *nouveau riche*, social pretensions, courtship, and marriage.
De Muth, James. *Small Town Chicago.* Port Washington: Kennikat, 1980. Comparative analyses of Ade, F.P. Dunne and Ring Lardner; concise and very thoughtful.
Duffey, Bernard. *The Chicago Renaissance.* Westport, Greenwood, 1972; 1954. A chapter on the newspaper work of Eugene Field, Ade, and Dunne.
Gianakos, Perry. "George Ade's Critique of Benevolent Assimilation." *Diplomatic History,* 7 (1983): 223–237. Regarding Ade's attack on our Philippine policy, in the Chicago *Record* in 1899.
Hoffa, William W. "George Ade." In *Dictionary of Literary Biography.* Vol. 11. *American Humorists 1800–1950.* Ed. Stanley Trachenberg. Detroit: Gale, 1982, pp. 3–11.
Kolb, Harold H., Jr. "George Ade." *American Literary Realism 1870–1910,* 4 (Spring 1971): 157–169. Historiography of Ade criticism, with an annotated bibliography.
Rubin, Louis D., ed. *The Comic Imagination in American Literature.* New Brunswick: Rutgers, 1973. Ade's work discussed within essays by Bernard Duffey ("Humor Chicago Style") and C. Hugh Holman ("Anodyne for the Village Virus").
Trimmer, Joseph F. "Memoryscape: Jean Shepherd's Midwest." *Old Northwest,* 2 (December 1976): 357–369. Ade's impact on the style and temper of Shepherd's earlier works.

Dissertations

Byrne, Archibald John. "The American Adam: Chicago Style." Ph.D. dissertation, Harvard University, 1967. Discusses the newspaper collaboration of Ade and John T. McCutcheon.
Nordhus, Philip B. "George Ade: A Critical Study." Ph.D. dissertation, State University of Iowa, 1957. Traces the genres that most influenced Ade's style, imagery, and language.
Sims, Norman H. "The Chicago Style of Journalism." Ph.D. dissertation, University of Illinois, Champaign-Urbana, 1979. Demonstrates Ade's contribution to a distinctive period.

Kalman Goldstein

Allen, Woody [Allen Stewart Konigsberg]

Born: Brooklyn, New York, on December 1, 1935

Education: Midwood High School, Brooklyn, diploma, 1953
New York University and City College of New York, briefly in the early 1950s; no degree

Marriages: Harlene Rosen, 1954, divorced, 1960; Louise Lasser, 1963, divorced, 1969

Biography

Norman Mailer once introduced Woody Allen to a gathering of distinguished writers as *"l'auteur des auteurs cinématiques."* No one else in American film approaches him in originality, in interest, or in being an *author*, in the traditional sense of that term. If Allen did not control his films from start to finish, he would not make them. With each film, he says, "I want to say something." Although he has become a brilliant stylist, he still insists that it is content that makes or breaks a film. He is open about the fact that he has a point of view that he keeps "hammering away at all the time—my affection for New York, my lack of it for the West Coast, my attitude toward God, family, and human relationships."[1] His vision and unique authority have allowed him to create a vital body of work that reflects not only his ongoing concerns and his growth and development as an artist but also the preoccupations of twentieth-century, middle-class, urban life. A midwestern audience can have problems with Allen's metropolitan and sometimes self-centered eccentricities and may find his films strange and disjointed. Molly Haskell has said that he uses the medium as his "private sandbox," a criticism that he specifically answers during the famous sequence outside the New Yorker theater in *Annie Hall* (1977), where he refers to Federico Fellini, another major filmmaker who has been accused of the same thing.

Like many foreign and so-called "art" films, Allen's movies do not make a great deal of money. *Annie Hall* was one of the lowest-grossing film ever to win an Academy Award for Best Picture, and as is true with Jerry Lewis, with whom Allen is otherwise not easily compared, his work tends to be more popular in Europe than in America. But, this is fine with Allen, who says that he is uncomfortable with popularity because it stems from a reinforcement of middle-class prejudice: "If that many people like a picture, maybe I'm becoming part of the establishment and not challenging anyone."[2]

Although in many ways he may be the most successful filmmaker in America, Allen shuns Hollywood, mocking the health-crazed, golden glow of California in films such as *Annie Hall* and exalting instead the black-and-white majesty of a city that he admits he romanticizes. *Manhattan* (1979) begins with the following voice-over narration: "He adored New York City. He idolized it all out of proportion." Personally, Allen says, "I don't think I could live beyond a thirty-mile radius of the Russian Tea Room," and he confesses that he enjoys going to watch the New York Knicks play because he does not have to cross a bridge to get there.

It was 1941 when he first crossed a bridge to get to Manhattan from Brooklyn where he was born Alan Stewart Konigsberg on December 1, 1935, the son of a jewelry engraver who took him to Times Square when he was six years old. Allen provides glimpses of what his childhood was like when in *Annie Hall* he juxtaposes the chaotic, noisy gesticulations of his Jewish family, obsessed with guilt and death, with the clean, American refinement of Annie's midwestern, ham-eating upbringing. In what is probably a more autobiographical portrait, Paul, in Allen's play, *The Floating Lightbulb* (1981), does not "apply" himself in school and escapes academic routine and the drudgery of life in a decaying apartment in Brooklyn by practicing magic. But unlike Paul, Allen in real life was very good at sports, especially baseball, as well as magic, and he did not retreat to his room, too scared and insecure to perform or create in public. To the contrary, there is a story that at his bar mitzvah he donned blackface and did an imitation of Al Jolson, and by the time he was sixteen he was selling jokes and one-liners to columnists Earl Wilson and Walter Winchell.

After an undistinguished career at Midwood High School, he changed his name to Woody Allen and acquired a $25.00-a-week contract with the David O. Alber public relations firm to create as many as fifty jokes a day for such clients as Bob Hope, Arthur Murray, and Guy Lombardo. He also spent one semester at New York University, failed a film course, tried night courses at City College of New York, and married his high school sweetheart, Harlene Rosen, a seventeen-year-old philosophy major at Hunter College. At nineteen he was sent to Hollywood as the youngest member of NBC's Writers' Development Program. There he learned his craft under the tutelage of Danny Simon, Neil Simon's brother: "I've learned a couple of things on my own since and modified things [Simon] told me, but everything, unequivocally, that I learned about comedy writing, I learned from him."[3] By the time he was in his early twenties, Woody Allen was making as much as $1,700 a week writing material for nightclub acts, Broadway revues, and such television performers as Sid Caesar, Garry Moore, Herb Shriner, and Jack Paar. His work was used regularly on "The Ed Sullivan Show," and "The Tonight Show," but by 1960 he was ready to handle his own material. Encouraged by the two men who are still his managers, Jack Rollins and Charles H. Joffe, he made his club debut with a young singer named Cass Elliot at a Greenwich Village nightspot called The Duplex. He soon became a regular stand-up comic at such Manhattan clubs as The Bitter End, The Village Vanguard, and The Blue Angel. The primary influences on Allen as a stand-up comic, by his own admission, are Mort Sahl for his "jazz-like" style and Bob Hope for his timing. He also admits that he adores the Marx Brothers, who are a central icon of meaning in *Hannah and Her Sisters* (1986), and that he learned the importance of fast-pacing from them. He has also spoken about S.J. Perelman's influence on his prose style.

Literary Analysis

Allen's nightclub routines, like the films that followed, embodied the concerns and fads of his generation. Although not strictly autobiographical, his work grows out of his own life, personal anxieties about love and sex and death reflecting an insecure world. When he and Harlene divorced in 1960, he included in his routine the idea of a couple choosing divorce over a Bermuda holiday because "the vacation is over in two weeks, but a divorce is something you always have." During the early 1960s Allen gained a national reputation as a stand-up comic. He had developed the persona of the alienated "schlemiel," the self-absorbed little guy, the urban misfit with glasses and delusions of "scoring big," a Jewish amalgamation of Harold Lloyd and Charlie Chaplin with some of the zaniness of the Marx Brothers thrown in. But, just as he had wanted to go beyond writing material for others, now he was ready to expand his talents and move into writing short stories, plays, and films.

In 1964, he travelled to Europe for producer Charles Feldman, to write and perform in *What's New Pussycat?* with Peter O'Toole and Peter Sellers. He claims that he was interested in writing for the theater, but "got sidetracked" into films.[4] His first three features were not entirely satisfying for him because he did not have complete artistic control. *What's Up, Tiger Lily?* (1966) and *Casino Royale* (1967) are both spoofs of the popular James Bond series. His part in *Casino Royale* as Jimmy Bond is small,

but in *Tiger Lily* he is given credit as re-release director. The film takes the visuals of a Japanese Kung-fu spy thriller that was already a Bond parody and dubs it over in English with Woody Allen-type dialogue. The incongruity between the visuals and the dialogue pokes fun at a popular film genre. The international intrigue at the basis of this plot is an attempt to retrieve the world's best egg salad recipe. But, Allen thought that the other writers who were brought in added stupid jokes to his lines, and he disowned the film and even tried to block its release.

In the meantime, however, his first play, *Don't Drink the Water*, was produced at the Morosco Theatre in New York in 1966. Narrated by a priest named Father Drobney, it is about a New Jersey caterer and his wife and daughter who are forced to take refuge in an American embassy "somewhere behind the Iron Curtain" for innocently snapping a picture of what turned out to be a top secret Communist military location. Directed by Stanley Prager, it was a big hit and remains one of the most frequently performed plays in American amateur theater. A filmed adaptation was made in 1969, but Allen was not involved with it.

With his next play, *Play It Again, Sam* (1969), Allen wrote the lead for himself, basing the situation loosely on his second divorce, this time from Louise Lasser, whom he had married in 1963. Allan Felix is a film critic whose wife, Nancy, leaves him. With the help of his friends, Linda and Dick Christie, he tries to pull his life together, especially sexually. His imaginary mentor is his screen idol, Humphrey Bogart, to whom he turns for advice about women. Almost without knowing it, Allan and Linda fall in love. The parting of Rick and Ilsa at the end of *Casablanca* is the model for the conclusion as Allan renounces his love for Linda and sends her off on a plane to join Dick in Chicago. Were this a somewhat later Allen creation, it would probably end here—conclusions in midlife are rarely happy—but early in his career, the tone is lighter and the ending happy, a positive vision that Allen again seems to have discovered now that he has passed the age of fifty. But *Play It Again, Sam* ends as Felix goes back to his apartment to meet a beautiful girl who has just moved in next door.

Allen's career as a playwright has not been as prolific as his career in films, nor as his career as a writer of essays and short stories. His only other full-length play so far is *The Floating Lightbulb*, which was first produced at Lincoln Center in 1981, though he has written several one-acts, including "Death Knocks" (published in *Getting Even* in 1971), a mock-heroic version of the traditional Christian allegory where death appears as a grim, darkly robed figure to play what is usually a game of chess for the life of a man. In Allen's version, which seems, like *Love and Death* (1975), to owe much of its serious source material to Ingmar Bergman's *The Seventh Seal*, a stocky, middle-aged dress manufacturer named Nat Ackerman plays a homey game of gin rummy for the life-or-death stakes. A companion piece to "Death Knocks," "Death" (published in *Without Feathers* in 1976) has a salesman named Kleinman search for a killer whom he discovers is Death.

"Query," which was first published in *The New Republic* on September 18, 1976, dramatizes several functions of comedy, while "God" (published in *Without Feathers*, 1976) explores exactly what its title indicates, using the familiar metaphor of "all the world's a stage," but the actors' roles and lines are uncertain, and there may be no audience. Blanche DuBois from *A Streetcar Named Desire* (she came up in *Sleeper*, 1973) wanders in and is chased off by Allen's favorite comedian, Groucho Marx. The play ends much as it began, with its characters looking for an ending. Throughout, it centers on that familiar question that underlies all of Allen's work: where is meaning to be found? One of his characters, a Brooklyn co-ed named Doris Levine, sums up the dilemma:

> But without God, the universe is meaningless. Life is meaningless. We're meaningless. (Deadly pause) I have a sudden and overpowering urge to get laid.

In the late 1960s, Allen began contributing comic essays and short stories to national magazines such as *Life* and *Esquire*, and during the 1970s he frequently published in both *The New Yorker* and *Playboy*. Many of these essays, short stories, and one-act plays have since been published in three volumes by Random House, *Getting Even* (1971), *Without Feathers* (1975), and *Side Effects* (1980). "How Bogart Made Me the Superb Lover I am Today" (*Life*, March 21, 1969, pp. 64-67) is typical of this work, a tongue-in-cheek confession that is supposed to explain the genesis of *Play It Again, Sam*. "The Kugelmass Episode," first published in *The New Yorker*, and reprinted in *Side Effects*, is perhaps Allen's best-known short story and won the O. Henry Award for 1977. It is the literary version of a theme that he was to explore a few years later on film in *The Purple Rose of Cairo* (1985): the use of art (books or movies) to escape the drab depression of routine reality. In *The Purple Rose*, Mia Farrow, as Cecilia, finds refuge from her brute of a husband by going to the movies. It is 1930s Depression America, and Cecilia finds herself enamored of a handsome

second male lead, Tom Baxter, played by Jeff Daniels. Magically, the feeling seems to be mutual, so that at about the fifth viewing of a minor screwball adventure—Allen's film takes its title from this film within the film, *The Purple Rose of Cairo*—Baxter steps down off the screen and he and Cecilia go off together. Illusion and reality have merged. The characters on screen, now without one of their co-stars, become angry and begin fighting among themselves. Then the audience, watching those bickering characters, becomes angry that their mindless bit of Hollywood entertainment has become more like a Michelangelo Antonioni movie. The complications multiply in a kind of surreal game that strikingly illustrates the degree to which we are, in fact, unable to distinguish between illusion and reality. This particular film of Allen's is often compared to Buster Keaton's *Sherlock, Jr.*, but it owes more to "The Kugelmass Episode" where Kugelmass, an unhappily married humanities professor at City College, escapes his drab reality by entering the magic cabinet of the Great Persky to be whisked away from the twentieth century to dine by candlelight with Gustave Flaubert's Emma Bovary. Enter this cabinet with the novel of your choice, and it is possible to live *in* that novel for as long as you want. This device leads to complications as Kugelmass has Persky reverse his magic and bring Emma Bovary out of Flaubert's novel for a weekend affair at the Plaza Hotel. The problem is then how to get Emma back into her book, as the problem in *Purple Rose* becomes how to get Tom back onto the screen. "The Kugelmass Episode," like most, if not all, of Allen's work, explores the essential fact of post-edenic existence that the ideal and the real rarely, if ever, meet in a world where what is and what ought to be are like oil and water.

In films, it may be necessary to go back to Chaplin and Keaton—men totally responsible for their best movies—to find anyone comparable to Allen. Instinctively these artists recognized that comedy, as opposed to tragedy, is a means of triumphing over death, and that it is, as François Truffaut once said, "the most serious business in the world." For stories about the small daily problems of men and women—catching a lobster or going to the dentist—for an open-hearted look at the human predicament, Allen is linked to Chaplin, to whom he admits a great debt. The Little Tramp and the good-hearted, but victimized Jewish "schlemiel," have a lot in common, emphasizing, through the exploration of their loss, basic, moral, American values, especially the importance of family. But, from a more modernist perspective, Allen may be linked to Keaton, the stone-faced survivor who knows that existence precedes meaning and whose art explores the nature of the creative process. This is the area of "meta-film," anxiety-of-influence movies whose subtext is the medium itself. Although a common practice among European filmmakers, especially those with whom Allen likes to identify himself—Bergman, Fellini, and Truffaut—a self-conscious manipulation of genre and form in order to defamiliarize and reinvest content with meaning is not common among mainstream American filmmakers. A crucial connecting element in Allen's work as it has evolved over the years has been an obsession with reworking, reinventing, and thereby revitalizing familiar forms.

Allen's first film as a director, *Take the Money and Run* (1969), spoofs gangster films, bio/pics, and the fashionable *cinéma-vérité* problem documentary that grew out of the activist liberalism of the 1960s. His Virgil Stockwell is hopelessly unredeemable, and the solemn pretense of the film to trace his career only points to the danger of taking social regeneration too seriously. *Bananas* (1971), released the year that Salvador Allende came to power in Chili and just after the peak of antiwar activity in America, parodies political commitment in general and Latin American politics in particular. Allen uses sports commentator Howard Cosell to give a play-by-play of the action in the tiny banana republic of San Marcos, thereby linking athletic events, war, and sex, putting all three of them on about the same level, much as the Marx Brothers did in *Duck Soup*, a film that will reappear significantly in *Hannah and Her Sisters*.

In the episodic *Everything You Ever Wanted To Know About Sex* (*but were afraid to ask)* (1972), Allen begins his conscious experiments with image. With his first two films he says he "just wanted to get on the boards. I wanted to be funny, and I couldn't have cared less how they looked."[5] In *Sex* he became more concerned with form. Each of the seven episodes mimics a different style: horror films, particularly of the *Frankenstein* sort, historical dramas, "art" films, particularly the Italian form as practiced by Antonioni, and science fiction, as Allen employs a facsimile of Stanley Kubrick's launch pad in *2001* to explore "What Happens During Ejaculation." The film that followed, *Sleeper* (1973), picks up the science fiction idea but is far more visually sophisticated than anything that Allen had done before, with long, fluid takes, and a deliberate use of color that again recalls the work of Antonioni. Miles Monroe, the Allen character, is a clarinet player (as is Allen in "real" life), who ends up two hundred years in the future and is forced to confront "modernity" carried to an extreme. This is the first script collaboration between Marshall Brickman and Allen, and the result is a new sense of social satire that will lead

eventually to *Annie Hall* and *Manhattan*. Allen takes a familiar genre and infuses it with self-reflexive references. The emphasis is on road movie romances and early film comedy with Laurel and Hardy pie-fights, Mack Sennett chases, and the brilliant mechanical transformations of a Keaton. The deliberate evocations are a loving tribute and a reminder that the future grows from the past.

Allen's most audacious and technically innovative cinematic experiment is probably *Zelig* (1983), a radical revision of his usual struggles to define and establish identity. Skillfully blending historical footage from the 1920s with new material, the film is on one level a playful commentary on Warren Beatty's intensely serious, documentary-style *Reds*, and on another, like the earlier *Take the Money and Run*, a further questioning of the whole idea of documentary "truth." *Zelig* depicts a man with no identity of his own. "It's about the kind of personality that leads to fascism," Allen says, a chameleonlike personality that gives up its own identity into order to be part of the crowd.[6]

After *Love and Death* in 1975, a reverential take-off on nineteenth-century Russian life, literature and the films of Sergei Eisenstein and Ingmar Bergman, increasingly serious subjects become the basis of Allen's comedy. In 1978, after starring in *The Front*, a film about the Hollywood blacklist of the 1950s, he made *Interiors*, his only non-comic film, an intense, Bergmanesque drama about the emotional entanglements of a family of three sisters. It was not a success and the consensus of public opinion was that Allen should stick to comedy and not try "to out-Bergman Bergman." But, public opinion does not seem to affect what Allen does, and since the mid-seventies, certainly since *Annie Hall* in 1977, he has resisted the impulse toward easy jokes and the frenetic comic action of his earlier work. In 1986, when he released *Hannah and Her Sisters*, he confessed that *Interiors* now seemed "a bit cool," but its subject continued to fascinate him. Allen has sometimes been compared with George Cukor as a "woman's director." His own explanation is simply that he comes from a family where he was always surrounded by women. His mother had seven sisters who had female children, so he has many female cousins, and also one sister, with whom he is still very close. She, along with his ex-girlfriend, Diane Keaton, and current one, Mia Farrow, remain his closest advisors on ideas and scripts. *Hannah and Her Sisters*, which Allen admits "is about personal concerns of mine," in many ways takes the three girls from *Interiors*—Renata, Flynn, and Joey—and allows them to develop into their own women. Starting out as a "serious" film, it is only with the addition of

Mickey, played by Woody Allen, that it becomes comic in the familiar Allen vein. Over the years, he says, "I've tried to get more and more serious and rounded," aspiring to make a film he can really respect, such as Vittorio DeSica's *Bicycle Thief*, Bergman's *Persona*, or Jean Renoir's *Grand Illusion*.

Although his films have always, to some degree or another, been quite personal, with *Annie Hall*, the warm comedy loosely based on his own romance and break-up with Diane Keaton, Allen emerged as a major comic artist, using a unique vision to convey universal human experience. The film began as a novel, *Anhedonia*, a reference to the central character's inability to experience pleasure, but Allen changed the title so that the emphasis would be on the development of Diane Keaton's character, Annie. The opening monologue is a voice-over narration by Allen or his character, Alvy Singer (the distinction is purposely blurred) in which he cites Sigmund Freud's *Wit and Its Relation to the Unconscious*, stressing the underlying seriousness of this comedy. Maurice Yacowar has suggested that its primary theme is "the power of art to compensate for the limitations of life."[7] At one point in the film, after making love to Annie, Alvy exclaims, "As Balzac said, 'There goes another novel.'" The idea, formally articulated in the book that Alvie gives to Annie, Ernest Becker's *The Denial of Death*, is one that Allen has continued to explore in *Interiors, The Purple Rose of Cairo*, and his more recent work—that man's essential activities are a response to his inevitable death, and that art in particular is a means, however limited, of transcending this mortality. Within the film, Alvy, a writer, makes art out of life in the form of a play based on his relationship with Annie (as Allen made a movie based on his relationship). The film's non-linear structure, its uniquely cinematic manipulation of time and space so that characters can speak as children of what they are doing as grown-ups or watch themselves as they were at ten or be two places at the same time, is a deliberate slap in the face at the plodding chronological line humans face as they march from birth to the grave. The structures of Allen's films, from *Annie Hall* on, are designed to employ the language of film in asserting the power of art to transcend the vagaries of life and love.

As Renoir does, Allen seems to look at life from one perspective, but then turns around and looks at it from another, saying "Yes, but. . . ." His Alvy Singer may write a successful play, but then there are all the pathetic, struggling entertainers who never make it. Alvy is hired by one of them to write gags, and a later film, *Broadway Danny Rose* (1984), lovingly focuses on a number of showbusiness has-beens—a one-

legged tap dancer, a blind saxaphonist, even a parrot that sings "I Gotta Be Me"—devoted, but unsuccessful performers whose most exciting moment each year may be the TV dinners that they can look forward to at Thanksgiving (a favorite Allen holiday around which he has structured not only *Broadway Danny Rose* but also *Hannah and Her Sisters*) at the apartment of their loyal agent, Danny Rose, played by Allen. In other films, it is the Allen character who achieves success, wins the woman, or learns a lesson about himself. But, in *Broadway Danny Rose*, the problem is not in Rose's personality—his belief in his role as a personal manager does not change, nor does he ever manage a commercial success—rather it is in the character of Tina Vitale (Mia Farrow), who struggles with her identity and her feelings. The ambiguous ending (does Danny forgive her because he is in love with her or because he never gives up on anyone?) is as typical of Allen as the happy ending of *Hannah and Her Sisters* or the sobbing disillusionment of Cecilia's hopeless life in Depression-era New Jersey that concludes *The Purple Rose of Cairo*.

Of his own films, Allen's favorite is *Stardust Memories* (1980), which is about a filmmaker—much like Allen—who yearns to do serious work, but his public resists his somber side, and adoring fans tell him, "We like your films—particularly the earlier, funnier ones," which was exactly Allen's experience with *Interiors*. *Stardust Memories* is in many ways like Fellini's *8 1/2*, a film that it deliberately echoes. Both heroes, Sandy Bates and Guido, are middle-aged filmmakers who, on the verge of nervous breakdowns, temporarily abandon their everyday routines and undergo forms of self-exploration that allow them at the end to return to their lives and their art reconciled to the limitations of reality, and in the case of Bates to the big advantage of not being dead.

A reconciliation with the compromises demanded by life seems to have helped Allen settle as a mature artist of an "age of anxiety." A line from *Hannah and Her Sisters*—"the heart is an amazingly resilient little muscle"—reflects the calm and self-assurance that infuse his recent work. He can enjoy making a light-hearted romp, such as *A Midsummer Night's Sex Comedy* (1982), with its tribute not only to Shakespeare, but once again, to Bergman and his *Smiles of a Summer Night*. This film, he admits, is "good for little wisps of fun," but he looks forward to making others with "ideas to chew over in them."[8] From the Allen of the past, we know that these ideas will have to do with questions that do not have easy answers, questions such as, "Where is meaning to be found?," but the Allen of the present, with a large body of creative work behind him, seems more willing to live without answers. A world that can produce the Marx Brothers cannot be all bad, and with friends and family, even a man who must ultimately face death alone does not have to suffer life in similar isolation.

Summary

The closing lines of the early film, *Sleeper*, pinpoint what have remained Allen's primary concerns. When asked what he believes in, Miles Monroe answers, "Sex and death. Two things that come once in a lifetime. But at least after death you're not nauseous." Allen has always been obsessed with death, even as a child, doubting the existence of God and afraid of nuclear annihilation. In *Annie Hall*, young Alvy Singer is in despair because he is convinced that the universe is going to expand and blow apart. To his biographer, Eric Lax, Allen has said, "Any man over thirty-five with whom death is not the main consideration is a fool."[9] The key question explored in almost all of his work is simply, "If there is no God and no afterlife, what is the point of living?" Until *Hannah and Her Sisters* in 1986, he seemed unable to find a satisfactory answer. Playing Boris in *Love and Death*, Allen is shot by a firing squad for a crime that he did not commit, and after yelling to Sonia that the worst that can be said about God is that he is "an under-achiever," he dances away with a white-shrouded figure in a playful inversion of the conclusion of *The Seventh Seal*. By the time he makes *Hannah*, Allen seems to have found firmer footing. Although there are still echoes of Freud, Nietzsche, and Socrates, and the inevitable cerebral conclusion that "the only knowledge attainable by man is that life is meaningless," the Allen persona asks a new question and gains a new insight into the essential nature of existence. He recalls a botched suicide attempt: "In a godless universe, I didn't want to go on living." Then he asks, "But what if I were wrong?" His temporary solution is to go to the movies where he watches the Marx Brothers in *Duck Soup* sing "Hail, Freedonia!" and their chaos, joy, and anarchic exuberance puts everything in perspective. According to Allen, all of *Hannah* leads to that sequence, where Mickey realizes that he will never know whether life has meaning, but maybe it is worth living after all: "*Maybe* life isn't meaningless, and that's the best you can do." This may not be a great affirmation, but it seems to be a mature artist's recognition of both possibility and limitation. Chaplin once said, "As a man grows older, he gains a sad dignity, and that is fatal to a comic." It may have been fatal to Chaplin, but Allen has found in dignity a new dimension for comedy, a balance of distance and compassion that allows him to look at human frailties with both laughter and love.

Notes

1. Bernard Drew, "Woody Allen Is Feeling Better," *American Film* (December 1977), p. 13.
2. Caryn James, "Auteur Auteur!," *The New York Times Magazine*, January 19, 1986, p. 26.
3. Diane Jacobs, *. . . But We Need the Eggs: The Magic of Woody Allen* (New York: St. Martin's Press, 1982), p. 9.
4. Ibid., p. 33.
5. Ibid., p. 70.
6. James, p. 27.
7. Maurice Yacowar, *Loser Take Tall* (New York: Ungar, 1979), p. 179.
8. James, p. 30.
9. Eric Lax, *On Being Funny: Woody Allen and Comedy* (New York: Charterhouse, 1975), p. 227.

Bibliography

Primary Sources

Films

What's New, Pussycat?, screenplay, 1965.
What's Up, Tiger Lily?, re-release director, 1966.
Casino Royale, actor, 1967.
Don't Drink the Water, based on Allen's stageplay, 1969.
Take the Money and Run, 1969.
Bananas, 1971.
Play It Again, Sam, based on Allen's stageplay, actor, 1972.
Everything You Always Wanted To Know About Sex* (**but were afraid to ask*), 1972.
Sleeper, 1973.
Love and Death, 1975.
The Front, actor, 1976.
Woody Allen: An American Comedy, documentary narrated by Allen, 1977.
Annie Hall, 1977.
Interiors, 1978.
Manhattan, 1979.
Stardust Memories, 1980.
A Midsummer Night's Sex Comedy, 1982.
Zelig, 1983.
Broadway Danny Rose, 1984.
The Purple Rose of Cairo, 1985.
Hannah and Her Sisters, 1986.
Radio Days, 1987.

Plays

Don't Drink the Water, 1966.
Play It Again, Sam, 1969.
Death, 1975.
God, 1975.
The Query, 1976.
The Floating Lightbulb, 1981.

Books

Getting Even. New York: Random House, 1971.
Without Feathers. New York: Random House, 1975.
Side Effects. New York: Random House, 1980.

Secondary Sources

Books

Adler, Bill, and Jeffrey Feinman. *Woody Allen: Clown Prince of American Humor*. New York: Pinnacle Books, 1975.
Benayoun, Robert, *The Films of Woody Allen*, Trans.

Alexander Walker. New York: Harmony Books, 1986.

Brode, Doug. *Woody Allen, His Films and Career.* Secaucus, N.J.: Citadel Press, 1983.

de Navacelle, Thierry. *Woody Allen on Location.* New York: William Morrow, 1987.

Hirsch, Foster. *Love, Sex, Death and the Meaning of Life.* New York: McGraw-Hill, 1984.

Jacobs, Diane. . . . *But We Need the Eggs: The Magic of Woody Allen.* New York: St. Martin's Press, 1982.

Lax, Eric. *On Being Funny: Woody Allen and Comedy.* New York: Charterhouse Press, 1975.

Yacowar, Maurice. *Loser Take All.* New York: Frederick Ungar Publishing Co., 1979.

Articles

Dempsey, Michael. "The Autobiography of Woody Allen." *Film Comment,* May-June, 1977, pp. 9-16.

Drew, Bernard. "Woody Allen Is Feeling Better." *American Film,* December 1977, pp. 10-15.

Farber, Stephen. "Woody." *Moviegoer,* May 1985, pp. 14-19.

Geist, William E. "Woody Allen: Everything You Always Wanted to Know About the Woodman." *Rolling Stone,* April 9, 1987, pp. 38-51, 84-88.

Gittelson, Nathalie. "The Maturing of Woody Allen." *The New York Times Magazine,* April 22, 1979, pp. 30-32, 102-107.

Halberstadt, Ira. "Scenes from a Mind." *Take One,* November 1978, pp. 16-20.

James, Caryn. "Auteur! Auteur!" *The New York Times Magazine,* January 19, 1986, pp. 18-30.

Klein, Joe. "Woody on the Town." *Gentleman's Quarterly,* February 1986, pp. 172-175, 242-243.

Lerman, Leo. "Woody the Great." *Vogue,* December 1972, pp. 144-151.

Maltin, Leonard. "Take Woody Allen—Please!" *Film Comment,* March-April 1974, pp. 42-45.

Rich, Frank. "Woody Allen Wipes the Smile off His Face." *Esquire,* May 1977, pp. 72-76, 148-149.

Rose, Lloyd. "Humor and Nothingness." *Atlantic Monthly,* May 1985, pp. 94-96.

Schickel, Richard. "The Basic Woody Allen Joke." *The New York Times Magazine,* January 7, 1973, pp. 10, 33-37.

Shales, Tom. "Woody: The First Fifty Years." *Esquire,* April 1987, pp. 88-95.

Joanna E. Rapf

Armour, Richard [Willard]

Born: San Pedro, California, on July 15, 1906

Education: Pomona College, A.B., 1927; Harvard University, A.M., 1928; Harvard University, Ph.D., 1933

Marriage: Kathleen Fauntleroy Stevens, December 25, 1932

Biography

Richard Armour, one of the most prolific American humorists of the twentieth century, was born on July 15, 1906, in San Pedro, California, the only child of Harry Willard and Sue Wheelock Armour.

As Armour describes it in his nostalgic autobiography, *Drug Store Days,* his childhood was secure and peaceful. "I could never see what was so bad about being an Only Child," he wrote. "I was never bossed or beaten by an older brother or sister and I was never punished for having bossed or beaten a younger brother or sister."[1] While Armour had no siblings, he did share his youth with an assortment of colorful relatives, including a mother who dressed her embarrassed son in lace collars, a maternal grandmother who sewed sheets for the Ku Klux Klan during the Civil War, and a fraternal grandmother so domineering and physically immense that she held virtually the entire Armour family in the palm of her hand. Armour's father, a druggist, managed family businesses both in San Pedro and in Pomona, California, where the family moved in 1912.

In the early 1920s Armour entered Pomona College and worked during his summer vacations as a tour guide in Europe. After his graduation in 1927, he began graduate studies at Harvard, where he received his M.A. in 1928 and his Ph.D. in English philology in 1933. Armour was an active member of the Army Reserve from 1927 to 1937 and served in both World War II and the Korean War. He was twice awarded the Legion of Merit. He also worked for the U.S. government from 1964 to 1970 as an overseas American specialist for the State Department.

Most of Amour's professional life has been devoted to his twin loves, teaching (his areas of specialization are Romantic poetry and Chaucer) and writing. In the course of his academic career Armour has taught at such institutions as Northwestern University, the University of Texas, the College of the Ozarks, Wells College, the Claremont Graduate School, Whittier College, the University of Hawaii, and California State University. He was Dean of Faculty at Scripps College from 1961 to 1963 and was named Professor Emeritus there in 1966. As a guest lecturer Armour has appeared at over 200 colleges and universities.

Armour's career as a popular writer began propitiously in 1937 when his first two submissions to national magazines—*The New Yorker* and *The Saturday Evening Post*—were both accepted. During the next five decades Armour's essays and verse appeared in over 200 American and British magazines; in all, he has published over 6000 pieces of prose and poetry. He has also written more than fifty books of satire, children's literature, light verse, and general nonfiction. Armour's academic output, in contrast, has been sparse; his scholarly books include *Barry Cornwall: A Biography of Bryan Waller Procter* (1935) and *Coleridge the Talker* (1940).

Armour's first book of student-oriented satire, *It All Started with Columbus*, was published in 1953 and set the pattern for most of those that followed. In a mock-scholarly format, it covered the fundamentals of American history at approximately the same intellectual depth that one might expect from a high school textbook, but with liberal puns, tongue-in-cheek commentary, and humorous footnotes. Later books used a similar approach to deal with such topics as Shakespeare, Marxism, medicine, art, sex, sports, warfare, and education.

Armour also published collections of his comic verse and a series of autobiographical books clearly aimed for an older audience. *Drug Store Days* recalled Armour's childhood in southern California, *My Life with Women* recounted his experience with love and marriage, *Through Darkest Adolescence* described the trials of being a parent, and *Going Like Sixty* contained relevations and advice for those entering later middle age. In these books, Armour used puns and satiric broadsides less frequently, concentrating instead on gentle reminiscences punctuated with liberal doses of light verse.

Many of Armour's books have been commercial if not critical successes; the most popular and well received of his satires, *It All Started with Columbus*, has sold over one million copies. Armour's guide to punctuation, *On Your Marks*, was made into an award-winning children's film in 1971, and *Going Around in Academic Circles* was produced as a musical in 1976.

Armour has been married to his childhood sweetheart, the former Kathleen Fauntleroy Stevens, since December 25, 1932. They have two children, Geoffrey Stevens and Marin Elizabeth, and several grandchildren. Now retired from academic life, Armour occasionally lectures, writes a syndicated feature for *Family Weekly*, is a member of the editorial board of *The Writer*, and serves as department editor for both *Quote* and *The Weekly Digest*.

Literary Analysis

Although he has written a prodigious number of books, many of them best-sellers, and has published light verse in such prestigious magazines as *The New Yorker*, Richard Armour is not generally regarded as an important or influential American humorist, and is seldom included in serious studies of comic writing.

Given his tremendous productivity and durability, why isn't Armour more favorably received by scholars? One answer is that Armour's books are targeted for audiences far different from the urban critics who review his prose and poetry. His parodies and satires, which are pseudo-academic in tone and subject, are most popular among junior and senior high school students. His autobiographical books, which deal with the problems and rewards of love, marriage, children, and aging, find their most ardent fans among middle-American parents and grandparents. New York critics, who typically belong to neither of these groups, have frequently been unreceptive or even hostile to Armour's brand of satire. Typical is David Dempsey's review of *It All Started with Eve*:

> Mr. Armour's spoofing is a sort of reflex action rather than a cerebral activity, and it is executed in a whinny of self-congratulation. He has an uncanny knack for never missing an obvious joke, and a rare facility for belaboring with a pike-staff what he should be nicking with a rapier.[2]

Nor are such attacks entirely undeserved. Armour's "obvious jokes" generally take the form of puns; in almost all of his satires, they follow a strict formula and can be spotted a mile away:

> The first time Helen [of Troy] was abducted she was only about ten years old. In view of her age, some have referred to this as an *abductio ad absurdum*.[3]

> Having finished *David Copperfield*, how do you feel? Full of the Dickens?[4]

> Anyone hacked up by a scimitar was carried off to the nearest burial ground, or scimitary.[5]

> But let me take another tack, or possibly nail.[6]

This comic device, while amusing at first, quickly become tedious with repetition. When carried on for hundreds of pages, it can be excruciating. Armour's style, which resembles the rapid one-liner delivery of stand-up comedians, is best appreciated in small doses, not in a sustained, critical reading. Armour's fans, who most likely read bits and pieces of his books in their spare moments, do not experience the overkill that critics cannot escape in their rushed readings. Small wonder, then, that many of Armour's books have been savaged by critics as predictable and formulaic while applauded by readers as enjoyable and refreshing.

Armour has taken the criticism in stride, conceding that his use of wordplay is sometimes excessive but arguing that his young fans seem to enjoy it and that many of his books (including his favorite, the autobiographical *Drug Store Days*) conatin no puns at all. Given his success, it is difficult to argue that he has misjudged the tolerance of his readers. And it is true that Armour's prose is not entirely dependent upon wordplay. He less frequently uses such comic devices as understatement, irony, faint praise, and mock naivete, and takes particular delight in reading literal interpretations into idiomatic expressions.

Armour's books have frequently been compared to those of Will Cuppy, another American humorist whose prose is characterized by obscure scholarly minutiae, heavy footnoting, and mock pedantry. Given the two writers' superficial similarities of style and their frequent agreement on specific subjects, such comparisons were probably inevitable. Witness Armour's and Cuppy's observations on Alexander the Great:

> Alexander's generals . . . fought each other . . . until things were pretty much as they were before Alexander started, except for more tombs.[7]

> Alexander's empire fell to pieces at once, and nothing remained of his work except that the people he had killed were still dead.[8]

A closer examination of the two writers, however, reveals significant stylistic and substantive differences between them. First of all, Cuppy never allowed his humor to overshadow the fundamental purpose of his work—to confront mankind with its own selfishness and stupidity. Armour's prose, in contrast, is characterized by a tendency to go for big punchlines at the expense of more subtle insights. As Dempsey put it, "What Cuppy possessed—and what Richard Armour . . . does not—was the capacity for an endless refinement of style, a gentle and effortless sense of the absurd."[9] Armour's books are so packed with trivial wordplay, in fact, that his larger message is often obscured. This, unfortunately, is a stylistic weakness that Armour has been unable to either recognize or rectify. Although it is difficult to believe, he has insisted that his model for *It All Started with Stones and Clubs*, a frivolous, pun-oriented "attack" on war,

was Jonathan Swift's brilliant *A Modest Proposal.* (*Stones and Clubs*, interestingly, was purchased by all 4,000 libraries of the U.S. Army, indicating that its anti-war message may not have been as convincingly presented as Armour might have wished.)

Second, Cuppy's effectiveness as a humorist derives from his ability to tell undistorted but absurd truths in a straightfaced and understated way. Cuppy believed that people and institutions were inherently hilarious; it was rarely necessary for him to exaggerate human behavior to make it appear foolish. Armour, in contrast, frequently sacrifices truth for laughs, an odd predilection for one whose avowed purpose is "taking the dullness out of study, [and] making learning fun."[10] This tendency to blend fact with fiction is particularly troubling when Armour does not make it clear that he is just kidding. One wonders how many unsophisticated adolescents trusted Armour enough to believe that:

> One of the leading scholars was Tom S. Aquinas. Those who believed his theories were known as Tomists; those who weren't quite sure were called Doubting Tomists. Superficial students, who only skimmed his works, were referred to as Peeping Tomists.[11]

Critics are generally much kinder to Armour when reviewing his light verse, perhaps because of its folksy wisdom and unlabored easy-going style:

Middle Age

As I often remark when I'm low as can be,
It's a terrible rat race I'm in,
And what is still worse, I'm beginning to see,
The rats are quite likely to win.[12]

Armour's poetry is also appealing because it rarely uses puns for comic effect. When Armour does use wordplay in his humorous verse, it is generally limited to the kind of inventive rhyming characteristic of Ogden Nash. One of his most well-known poems, in fact, is often mistakenly attributed to Nash:

Going to Extremes

Shake and shake
The catsup bottle.
None will come,
And then a lot'll.[13]

This type of humor is more likely to provoke smiles than outright laughter, but, as Armour might ask, so what? While it is difficult to be awed by such poetry, it is almost impossible to be offended by it. Critics therefore tend to be tolerant or even grudgingly admiring of Armour's verse. Lewis Nicholas, in reviewing *Light*

Armour, wrote, "There is a merry band whose verse should be treated in the fashion of thoughtful cook with the shad—keep the roe and throw away the fish. Keep, among a number of other good eggs, Richard Armour."[14]

Summary

While Richard Armour's brand of satire has been treated harshly by critics, many of whom are unable to understand his considerable appeal to adolescent students, his light verse and autobiographical prose are frequently praised for their wit and relaxed style. True, it is unlikely that Richard Armour will ever be put in the same class as Will Cuppy, but it is equally unlikely that Armour, who is devoted to his young fans and satisfied with their enthusiastic praise, will really mind.

Notes

1. Richard Armour, *Drug Store Days* (New York: McGraw-Hill, 1959), p. 24.
2. David Dempsey, "Too Broad An Approach," *New York Times Book Review*, November 18, 1956, p. 16.
3. Armour, *It All Started with Eve* (New York: McGraw-Hill, 1956), p. 27.
4. Armour, *The Classics Reclassified* (New York: McGraw-Hill, 1960), p. 146.
5. Armour, *It All Started with Stones and Clubs* (New York: McGraw-Hill, 1967), pp. 59-60.
6. Armour, *Going Like Sixty* (New York: McGraw-Hill, 1974), p. 2.
7. Armour, *It All Started with Stones and Clubs*, p. 35.
8. Will Cuppy, *The Decline and Fall of Practically Everybody* (New York: Henry Holt, 1950), p. 45.
9. Dempsey, "Too Broad An Approach," p. 16.
10. "Richard Armour," *Contemporary Authors: A Bio-Bibliographical Guide to Current Authors and Their Works* (Detroit: Gale Research), New Rev. Ser., Vol. 4, p. 30.
11. Armour, *It All Started with Europa* (New York: McGraw-Hill, 1955), p. 47.
12. Armour, *Going Like Sixty*, p. 27.
13. Armour, *Light Armour* (New York: McGraw-Hill, 1954), p. 67.
14. Lewis Nicholas, "Rhyming Universals." *New York Times Book Review*, October 3, 1954, p. 14.

Selected Bibliography

Primary Sources

Humorous Prose and General Nonfiction

Golf Bawls. New York: The Beechhurst Press, 1946.
Writing Light Verse. Boston: The Writer, Inc., 1947.
For Partly Proud Parents. New York: Harper, 1950.
It All Started with Columbus. New York: McGraw-Hill, 1953.
It All Started with Europa. New York: McGraw-Hill, 1955.
It All Started with Eve. New York: McGraw-Hill, 1956.
Twisted Tales from Shakespeare. New York: McGraw-Hill, 1957.
It All Started with Marx. New York: McGraw-Hill, 1958.
Drug Store Days. New York: McGraw-Hill, 1959.
The Classics Reclassified. New York: McGraw-Hill, 1960.
Pills, Potions and Granny. London: Hammond, Hammond, 1960.
A Safari into Satire. Los Angeles: California Library Association, 1961.
Armour's Almanac; or, Around the Year in 365 Days. New York: McGraw-Hill, 1962.
Golf Is a Four-Letter Word. New York: McGraw-Hill, 1962.
The Medical Muse, or What to Do unitl the Patient Comes. New York: McGraw-Hill, 1963.
Through Darkest Adolescence. New York: McGraw-Hill, 1963.
American Lit Relit. New York: McGraw-Hill, 1964.
Going Around in Academic Circles. New York: McGraw-Hill, 1966.
It All Started with Hippocrates. New York: McGraw-Hill, 1966.
It All Started with Stones and Clubs. New York: McGraw-Hill, 1967.
My Life with Women. New York: McGraw-Hill, 1968.
A Diabolical Dictionary of Education. New York: World Publishing Co., 1969.
English Lit Relit. New York: McGraw-Hill, 1969.
A Short History of Sex. New York: McGraw-Hill, 1970.
Writing Light Verse and Prose Humor. Boston: The Writer, Inc., 1971.
All in Sport. New York: McGraw-Hill, 1972.
Out of My Mind. New York: McGraw-Hill, 1972.
It All Started with Freshman English. New York: McGraw-Hill, 1973.
The Strange Dreams of Rover Jones. New York: McGraw-Hill, 1973.
The Academic Bestiary. New York: Morrow, 1974.
Going Like Sixty. New York: McGraw-Hill, 1974.
The Spouse in the House. New York: McGraw-Hill, 1975.
The Happy Bookers: A History of Librarians and Their World. New York: McGraw-Hill, 1976.
It All Started with Nudes. New York: McGraw-Hill, 1977.
Anyone for Insomnia? A Playful Look at Sleeplessness. Santa Barbara, Calif.: Woodbridge Press, 1982.
Educated Guesses: Light-Serious Suggestions for Parents and Teachers. Santa Barbara, Calif.: Woodbridge Press, 1983.
Pieces of Posthumous Prose. Santa Barbara, Calif.: Woodbridge Press, date not set.

Light Verse

Yours for the Asking. Boston: B. Humphries, Inc., 1942.
Privates' Lives. Boston: B. Humphries, Inc., 1944.
Leading with My Left. New York: Beechhurst Press, 1946.
Light Armour: Playful Poems on Practically Everything. New York: McGraw-Hill, 1954.
Nights with Armour: Lighthearted Light Verse. New York: McGraw-Hill, 1958.
An Armoury of Light Verse. Boston: International Pocket Library, 1964.
Punctured Poems. Englewood Cliffs, N.J.: Prentice-Hall, 1966.

Children's Books

(with Leonard E. Fisher.) *Our Presidents*. New York: Norton, 1964.

The Year Santa Went Modern. New York: McGraw-Hill, 1964.

The Adventures of Egbert the Easter Egg. New York: McGraw-Hill, 1965.

Animals on the Ceiling. New York: McGraw-Hill, 1966.

A Dozen Dinosaurs. New York: McGraw-Hill, 1967.

Odd Old Mammals. New York: McGraw-Hill, 1968.

On Your Marks: A Package of Punctuation. New York: McGraw-Hill, 1969.

All Sizes and Shapes of Monkeys and Apes. New York: McGraw-Hill, 1970.

Who's in Holes? New York: McGraw-Hill, 1971.

Strange Monsters of the Sea. New York: McGraw-Hill, 1979.

(with P. Galdone.) *Insects All Around Us*. New York: McGraw-Hill, 1981.

Have You Ever Wished You Were Something Else? Easy Reading Picture Books, 1983.

Drama

(with Bown Adams.) *To These Dark Steps*. New York: The New York Institute for the Education of the Blind, 1943.

Biography and Literary Criticism

"The Life and Works of Bryan Waller Procter (Barry Cornwall) With a Collection of His Unpublished Letters." Doctoral dissertation, Harvard University, 1933.

Barry Cornwall: A Biography of Bryan Waller Procter. Boston: Meador Publishing Co., 1935.

The Literary Recollections of Barry Cornwall. Boston: Meador Publishing Co., 1936.

Coleridge the Talker. Ithaca, New York: Cornell University Press, 1940.

Edited by Armour

Young Voices: A Book of Wells College Verse. Aurora, New York: Wells College Press, 1941.

Secondary Sources

Contemporary Authors: A Bio-Bibliographical Guide to Current Authors and Their Works. New Rev. Ser., Vol 4, pp. 29–31. A good summary of critical reaction to Armour's poetry and prose, along with an extended interview with the author.

Dempsey, David. "Too Broad An Approach." *New York Times Book Review*, November 18, 1956, p. 16. A scathing critique of *It All Started with Eve* in which Dempsey compares Armour unfavorably to Will Cuppy.

Gilroy, Harry. "Van Buren Was a Panic." *New York Times Book Review*, May 17, 1953, p. 14. A sarcastic review of *It All Started with Columbus*, heavily laced with damning excerpts.

McDowell, Edwin. "A Game of Authors." *New York Times Book Review*, October 23, 1960, p. 18. In this highly favorable article, McDowell praises *The Classics Reclassified* as "sprightly satire."

Nichols, Lewis. "Rhyming Universals." *New York Times Book Review*, October 3, 1954, p. 14. A perceptive and generous analysis of *Light Armour*.

Who's Who in America, 1986–1987. 44th edition, Vol. 1 (A–K). Chicago: Marquis Who's Who, 1986, p. 85. Standard biographical information.

C.J. Bartelt

Bagby, George William

Born: Buckingham County, Virginia, on August 13, 1828

Education: University of Pennsylvania, M.D., 1849

Marriage: Lucy Parke Chamberlayne, 1863, eight children

Died: November 29, 1883

Biography and Literary Analysis

In his preface to the 1910 edition of George William Bagby's sketches, Thomas Nelson Page observed that Bagby had presented antebellum rural Virginia "with a sympathy, a fidelity and an art which may be found nowhere else. . . ." Page described Bagby's techniques as realistic, but today one would feel compelled to enter a caveat against this judgment for many of Bagby's descriptions of Virginia, particularly in his later essays, are colored with a sentimentality that strikes a contemporary reader as blatant and excessive. Yet, though Bagby's view of his native state was at times blurred by sentiment and nostalgia, a number of his descriptions of plantation life in the Old Dominion before the Civil War are more vivid, pungent, and accurate in detail than those of any other Virginia writer of the period.

Bagby was well prepared by experience and environment to describe rural Virginia. He was born on the Buckingham County plantation of his maternal grandfather and spent the first and most impressionable years of his life in south central Virginia. His mother, Virginia Evans Bagby, was forced by a frail constitution and poor health to move to the town of Covington, where she died when George was eight years old. Bagby's father, who owned a general merchandise store in Lynchburg, sent George and his sister to live on the Cumberland County plantation of their aunt, Elisabeth Hobson. George later looked back with fondness on the years spent with his aunt and associated them with pleasant memories of bountiful good food and exciting adventures with slave children in the countryside. "The Great Mother," he afterwards reflected, "first laid her hand, omnipotent and warm, upon me in the midst of the soughing pines on the Cumberland hillsides." His early acquired sensitivity to the minutiae of natural life would later inform many of his successful essays, including the beautifully crafted "Fishing on the Appomattox" (1860).

After attending several of the "Old Field" schools in Buckingham and Prince Edward Counties, Bagby was sent, at the age of ten, to the Edgehill School in Princeton, New Jersey. After two years he transferred to the Hurlbut School in Philadelphia, and in 1843, at the age of fifteen, he entered Delaware College. Academic work at Delaware was followed, in 1846, by studies in medicine at the University of Pennsylvania. In 1849 young Dr. Bagby returned to Virginia, a state from which he had been largely absent for eleven years. Although his allegiance to the Old Dominion was not seriously compromised by his years of residence in the north, he did acquire, as he admitted in his introduction to "The Old Virginia Gentleman," a keener sense of the defects of his native state. This objectivity would result in the genial but telling satire of such essays as "My Uncle Flatback's Plantation" (1863) and "Bacon and Greens" (1866).

Bagby may have studied medicine to satisfy his father's wishes. It is clear that he made little or no attempt to establish a practice in Lynchburg, to which he moved after his graduation from the University of Pennsylvania; for by 1853 he had joined a close friend, George Woodville Latham, in the publication of the *Lynchburg Express*. For the rest of his life he would devote himself exclusively to journalism and to the writing of essays. Even after the failure of the *Express* in 1856 he continued to write for a number of local newspapers. Of special significance were his initial contributions to *Harper's* magazine. One of these sketches, entitled "The Virginia Editor" (December 1856), was a keen-edged portrait of a Virginia journalist, a "young, unmarried, intemperate, pugnacious, gambling gentleman" who ends his life with "half an ounce of lead . . . 'honorably and satisfactorily adjusted' in his heart or brain. . . ." So successful was the sketch that Bagby received a challenge from an offended Virginia editor, a duel that was barely averted by the intercession of a mutual friend.

From 1857 until 1859 Bagby resided in Washington, D.C., where he served as correspondent for a number of Southern newspapers. During this period, in 1858, he sent the first of eight "Mozis Addums" letters to the *Southern Literary Messenger* in Richmond. Modeled on the speech of backwoods characters he had known as a youth in Southside Virginia and influenced by the well-established tradition of Southwest dialect humor, these letters of a semi-literate rural Virginian addressed to a friend named "Billy Ivvins" in "Curdsville, Va.," were an immediate success and added, in Bagby's words, "several hundred names to the subscription list of the *Messenger*." Although Bagby later came to resent the lasting popularity of Mozis, complaining that for many years the name made him "a little sick wherever I heard it," the enormous popularity of his character was no doubt partly responsible for his being named editor of the *Messenger* in 1860, succeeding John R. Thompson.

The call to Richmond was no doubt gratefully received by Bagby, for he had come to feel increasingly alienated by the anti-slavery fervor of many of Washington's politicians. Perhaps as a reaction to the increasingly abolitionist political atmosphere, Bagby's pro-slavery attitude became more and more intransigent. Under his editorship the *Messenger* was transformed into a frankly partisan publication. In the December 1860 issue, for example, Bagby praised South Carolina for withdrawing from the Union and sarcastically asked this question of his native state: ". . . is she [Virginia] stricken with the palsy of fear?" In January 1861, he called for the fifteen stars of the South to be torn from the flag and arrayed in a Southern Cross. Under this holy and sublime banner the South would, he argued, "fight for our wives, our children, and our aged sires, whom the mercenary hordes of the North would fain deliver over to the sword of the invader and the pike of the negro insurrectionist." The succession which Bagby so fervently desired came, but the ensuing war had a disastrous effect on his magazine. After struggling for over three years to keep the *Messenger* alive in the face of dwindling paper and ink supplies and gradually shrinking subscriptions, Bagby resigned his position as editor in January 1864. Five months later the magazine ceased publication.

Poor health, including chronic dyspepsia that afflicted him from the year of his graduation from medical school until his death, forced Bagby to withdraw from the Confederate Army after the Battle of Manassas. But, his fortunes were so closely tied to the Confederacy that he fled Richmond with Jefferson Davis's entourage one day before the city fell to Union troops. He left behind a wife (Lucy Parke Chamberlayne of Richmond, whom he had married in 1863) and an infant daughter. Within a month, however, he had returned to the ruined capital, where he tried to support his family with his writing. Insufficient work drove him to New York, the heart of the northern capitalistic empire that he had so despised; but after a few months a severe eye infection forced him to return to Richmond.

Faced with rent of sixty-five dollars a month for a two-and-a-half-room apartment and the expenses of supporting a second child, Bagby turned in desperation to lecturing. His oration on "Bacon and Greens" (1866) was a great success in Lynchburg, Richmond, and other Virginia towns. Bagby's premise in "Bacon and Greens" (the greens referred to in this lecture are cabbage) is a potent example of his audacious wit and humor: ". . . While other people eat bacon and greens (and thereby become very decent people indeed), the only perfect bacon and the only perfect greens are found in Virginia; and hence it follows, as the night the day, not that the Virginians are the only perfect people, but that they are a peculiar and a very remarkable people." In spite of the success of this lecture, admission at twenty-five cents a person did not produce enough revenue to enable Bagby to meet the financial needs of his family. By 1867 he was over $1,000 in debt, and additional expenses had been incurred by the death of his first son and the birth of a second.

In 1867 Bagby was offered a partnership in a newly established newspaper named the *Native Virginian* in Orange Court House. From November of that year until 1870 he struggled unsuccessfully, first in Orange and later in Gordonsville, to keep his paper going in the midst of war-impoverished rural Virginia. In 1870 he gratefully accepted an appointment as Assistant Secretary of the Commonwealth, acting as custodian of the State Library. This position afforded him eight years of relative financial stability, but his personal fortunes were marked during this period by further problems, including bad eyes, chronic dyspepsia, the death in 1873 of his third son, and the birth in 1875 of twins. Bagby's humorous account of their birth, "Meekins's Twinses," became a popular lecture and was the last of the Mozis Addums pieces.

If the years following the Civil War were difficult ones for Bagby, they were also the years during which many of his most famous essays were written. Of these essays without doubt the most popular was "The Old Virginia Gentleman." Written for the lecture circuit in 1877, this essay has served as the title for the three collections of his essays that have been published in this century. "The Old Virginia Gentleman" illustrates as vividly as any of Bagby's later works the curious mixture of precisely observed realistic detail with a tone that frequently lapses into emotional panegyric.

The plantation described in this essay is much like that of Bagby's earlier and more realistic description, "My Uncle Flatback's Plantation." In describing the drive that leads to the Big House through miles of slash pine and scrub oak, Bagby's meticulous narrative does not fail to note the numerous potholes "that make every vehicle, but chiefly the bug-back carriage, lurch and careen worse than a ship in a heavy sea." Threading through such realistic descriptions, however, is a strongly elegiac note for a vanished way of life. In the last analysis it is this mourning for a lost time—for ". . . a beauty, a simplicity, a purity, an uprightness, a cordial and lavish hospitality, a warmth and grace which shine in the lens of memory. . . !"—that turns "The Old Virginia Gentleman" into an unabashed celebration of the perfection of antebellum Virginia.

The men and women of Bagby's plantation are idealized romantic stereotypes. The plantation matron is placed upon a pedestal as "mother, mistress, instructor, counsellor, bene-factress, friend, angel of the sick room." The Virginia gentleman is a representative of a glorious race of men, of a "breed of human animals" as fine as any the world has ever seen, characterized by courage, pride, honesty, honor, and integrity of character. This gentleman becomes inextricably identified with a belated and defiant justification for the plantation system: "If it [slavery] accompanied here, as in Greece, the development of a splendid breed of animals, say so; if it helped that development, say so fearlessly." The destruction of the plantation system, in Bagby's view, ended Virginia's Golden Age and rendered inexpedient the noble virtues that once characterized her ladies and gentlemen.

Looking over the whole of Bagby's output, one is struck by a recurring tension in his essays between the impulse to see precisely and accurately and the impulse to sentimentalize and mythologize. This tension is revealed in the letters Bagby wrote to the Richmond *State* during the final years of his life. On one hand he is capable of flying "into a violent passion about our Virginia laziness, our ignorance and indifference in regard to the arts or ornamentation." Still, Bagby also is convinced that plain industry and Yankee earnestness will not restore Virginia to its antebellum state of grace. ". . . Were the Commonwealth one solid mass of factories from Alexandria to the Carolina line," he observes, "it would not require the loss of men like Patrick Henry and John Randolph of Roanoke." This tension between Bagby the realist and Bagby the romantic, between Bagby the astute critic of Virginia foibles and Bagby the celebrator of the Old Dominion's mythical past, is never resolved in his writing.

Summary

On November 29, 1883, George W. Bagby died at his home in Richmond on Grace Street next to St. Paul's Church and was buried in Shockoe Hill Cemetery. He left behind a number of finely written essays informed by a whimsical and sometimes outrageous humor that reminds one of the early writings of Mark Twain. Bagby was not altogether free of a certain flaw that he attributed to his friend and fellow Virginian, John Esten Cooke. In an essay written in 1859 he had good-humoredly accused Cooke of too often looking back at Virginia's past rather than forward toward its future and of viewing that past through rose-tinted glasses. In a number of his essays, the same charge could be made against Bagby. At his best, however, his observations of Virginia plantation life are shaped by an admirable blending of accuracy and objectivity with genuine affection for his subject. A number of his essays—"My Uncle Flatback's Plantation," "Fishing on the Appomattox," and "Corn-Field

Peas," for example—have held up well over the passing of a century. They should survive as long as a southern consciousness and a Virginia consciousness survive that are capable of appreciating and drawing spiritual nourishment from those cultural anomalies that make the region unique.

Selected Bibliography

Primary Sources

What I Did with My Fifty Millions. Philadelphia: J.B. Lippincott and Company, 1874.

Meekins's Twinses: A Perduckshun uv Mozis Addums. Richmond, 1877.

Original Letters of Mozis Addums to Billy Ivvins. Richmond: Clemmit and Jones, 1878.

Selections from the Writings of Dr. George W. Bagby. 2 vols. Richmond: Whittet and Shepperson, 1884. Thirty-seven essays and sketches, the most complete collection of Bagby's work. Includes a biographical sketch by Bagby's friend, Edward S. Gregory.

The Old Virginia Gentleman and Other Sketches. Ed. Thomas Nelson Page. New York: Charles Scribner's Sons, 1910. Includes sixteen sketches and essays, a preface by editor Page, and the biographical sketch by Edward Gregory.

The Old Virginia Gentleman and Other Sketches. Ed. Ellen M. Bagby. Richmond: The Dietz Press, 1938. Twenty-seven of Bagby's writings, with the Page preface and an introduction by Douglas Southall Freeman. Bibliography by Ellen Bagby.

The Old Virginia Gentleman and Other Sketches. 4th ed. Ed. Ellen M. Bagby. Richmond: The Dietz Press, 1943. Identical to the 1938 edition but with one additional sketch, "The Southern Fool."

Secondary Sources

Freeman, Douglas Southall, "George W. Bagby, Patriot." In *The Old Virginia Gentleman and Other Sketches.* Ed. Ellen M. Bagby. Richmond: Dietz Press, 1938, pp. xvii–xxvii.

Gregory, Edward S. "George William Bagby." In *Selections From the Miscellaneous Writings of Dr. George W. Bagby.* 2 vols. Richmond: Whittet and Shepperson, 1884, pp. xiii–xxxvii. Also included in the 1910 collection of Bagby's writings.

Hubbell, Jay B. "George William Bagby." In *The South in American Literature.* Durham: Duke University Press, 1954, pp. 680-683. The fullest recent treatment of Bagby's work.

King, Joseph Leonard. *Dr. George William Bagby: A Study of Virginia Literature.* New York: Columbia University Press, 1927. The only full-length biography of Bagby. Bibliography of Bagby's writings included.

Page, Thomas Nelson. "A Virginia Realist." In *The Old Virginia Gentleman and Other Sketches.* New York: Charles Scribner's Sons, 1910, pp. v–xiii.

Richie D. Watson

Baker, Russell Wayne

Born: Loudoun County, Virginia, on August 14, 1925

Education: Johns Hopkins University, B.A., 1947

Marriage: Miriam Emily "Mimi" Nash, March 11, 1950, three children

Biography

In his "Observer" column in the *New York Times* Russell Baker offers biting satire and wry humor about the cares of daily life. Drawing from personal background and current events, he has established himself as a philosopher *par excellence* of the human experience.

Baker was the son of Benny Baker, a stonemason from the Virginia mountains, and Lucy Elizabeth Baker, a Tidewater schoolteacher. Until he was five he and his family lived in Morrisonville, but after Benny Baker's death in 1930, his mother moved Russell and his sister to Newark, New Jersey. There the family endured the struggles of the Depression era.

In hopes of improving their living conditions, Lucy moved the family to Baltimore, but betterment came slowly. Her eventual remarriage stabilized the financial situation. Receiving a scholarship, Russell entered Johns Hopkins University in 1942. After an interruption due to a tour of duty in the Navy, he graduated with the Bachelor of Arts from that institution in 1947. Following his graduation, he worked for the *Baltimore Sun*, first as police reporter and later as general assignments reporter. He left the *Sun* in 1954 to join the Washington bureau of the *New York Times*. In 1972 he began his "Observer" column, which he continues to write.

Johns Hopkins, Hamilton College, Franklin Pierce College, Princeton University, Union College, and Wake Forest University granted Baker honorary degrees. A member of the American Academy and Institute of Arts and Letters, he accumulated several other awards: the Frank Sullivan Memorial Award (1976), the George Polk Award for Commentary (1979), the Pulitzer Prize for Distinguished Commentary (1979), the Elmer Bobst Prize for Nonfiction (1983), and the Pulitzer Prize for Biography (1983).

Literary Analysis

As a high schooler, Baker found writing exciting; however, he foresaw little hope of earning a livelihood with the craft. A third-year English writing exercise in the informal essay marked a major victory for the budding journalist. From a list of topics Baker chose "The Art of Eating Spaghetti," which evoked fond memories of a happy meal with his family in New Jersey. Baker then proceeded with a reminiscence that would "violate all the rules of formal composition I'd learned in school" (*Growing Up*, p. 188). He spent so much time writing out of self-gratification that he had to turn in his essay as homework. Baker feared failure; instead he received an A-plus. In his autobiography he reflects: "In the eleventh grade, at the eleventh hour as it were, I had discovered a calling" (pp. 188–189). Mr. Fleagle, an English teacher considered dull by most, set Baker onto his career path.

Subsequently, the informal essay became Baker's bread-and-butter, and as he did in the spaghetti essay, he writes generally of the "warmth and good feeling" (p. 188) of a situation. In its traditional context the informal essay should entertain rather than instruct. Baker follows this prescript with his familiar and free style, yet he heightens the genre by adding a bit of lesson-teaching. Never didactic, the journalist gently chides the reader into seeing the foibles of members of his society. Baker successfully balances good humor and mild reproof.

The talents of the writer before he began the "Observer" column emerge in *An American in Washington* (1961), and the work foreshadows the sort of humor Baker would rely on regularly. His tongue-in-cheek depiction of life in the nation's capital covers the people and their society, emphasizing the political structure. "Why the Cocktail Party?," a satirical look at an American institution, typifies the work. In a style reminiscent of H.L. Mencken, Baker remarks: "The guest list frequently seems to have been drawn up by the Mad Hatter. The connoisseur of the cocktail circuit will delight in noting the number of people he meets whom he had thought dead for years" (pp. 38-39). In this brief treatise Baker effectively portrays a sham society.

The "Observer" column provides a steady supply of rich material for Baker's other works. An early collection, *No Cause for Panic* (1964), contains such sections as "The American Way of Life," "People," "The Losers," and "Looking for America." He tends to draw upon common experiences, as when he employs the press conference format for "The Big Wheel," another of his irreverent looks at politics. The essay begins:

> Ladies and gentlemen, the Big Wheel of the United States.
>
> Thank you. Please be bucket-seated.

> (p. 37)

Baker's wordplay borders on the mundane, but it works. This familiar kind of humor may account for some of his popularity.

Baker is, however, capable of more sophisticated humor, as demonstrated by his essay on William Shakespeare. Baker contends that had

sixteenth-century critics lavished more praise on Shakespeare we would not have to study him today. He envisions the playwright's winning the Pulitzer Prize for *Titus Andronicus* and becoming so enthralled with the publicity that he does not find time to produce his great works.

The adaptability of Baker's *New York Times* offerings was demonstrated when he gathered fifty essays in *Poor Russell's Almanac* (1972), a well-wrought parody of Benjamin Franklin's famous almanac. The journalist imitates his predecessor well, and his effort testifies to his ability to employ a variety of styles.

So This Is Depravity (1980) perhaps best exemplifies Baker's brand of sarcasm. In the essay, "Asylum," the writer observes: "Recently I discovered that I was going sane" (p. 1). For this condition he sought the counsel of a doctor who warned: "If you permit yourself to sink into sanity . . . you will be unfit to function in American society." Seeing the craziness of his environment, Baker chooses to expose universal *faux pas*.

In his autobiography, *Growing Up* (1982), Baker uses the anecdotal style characteristic of his essays to describe the happiness and hardship of his early life. His *bildungsroman* chronicles the Depression era extremely well, but the author's keen wit keeps the work from becoming maudlin. Baker introduces many of his family members in *Growing Up* and offers more anecdotes about them in *The Rescue of Miss Yaskell and Other Pipe Dreams* (1983), another compilation of his journalistic work.

Summary

With his sardonic wit, Russell Baker touches on universal human experiences: eccentric relatives and politicians, taxes, hometowns, and daily irritants. The "insanity" of American society constantly offers him a variety of subjects, and with his fertile imagination and rich humor he transforms them into masterpieces.

Selected Bibliography

Primary Sources

An American in Washington. New York: Alfred A. Knopf, 1961.

No Cause for Panic. Philadelphia and New York: J.B. Lippincott, 1964.

Poor Russell's Almanac. Garden City, N.Y.: Doubleday, 1972.

So This Is Depravity. New York: Congdon and Lattès, 1980.

Growing Up. New York: Congdon and Weed, 1982.

The Rescue of Miss Yaskell and Other Pipe Dreams. New York: Congdon and Weed, 1983.

Secondary Sources

Sheppard, R.L. "Daily Sanity." *Time,* January 17, 1972, p. 63. Reviews and praises Baker's "Observer" column in the *New York Times,* suggesting that

Baker's often cynical view of the world offers a beneficial outlet for the frustration of humanity. Testifies to Baker's "therapeutic" effects.

Skow, J. "Good Humor Man." *Time,* June 4, 1979, pp. 48–49. Praises Baker's style of writing and philosophies of life.

Trillin, C. "Uncivil Liberties." *Nation,* September 1, 1984, p. 136. Responds to a Baker column concerning a reckless bicyclist. Writing in a Bakeresque style, Trillin confesses to being the "homicidal" bicyclist who almost ran over Baker.

E. Kate Stewart

Baldwin, Joseph Glover

Born: Friendly Grove Factory, Virginia, on January 21, 1815
Education: English School of Staunton Academy, Staunton, Virginia
Marriage: Sidney White, ca. 1840, several children
Died: September 30, 1864

Biography

Joseph Glover Baldwin was born at Friendly Grove Factory, Virginia, on January 21, 1815. He left the English School of Staunton Academy at the age of fourteen, when he took employment in the office of the chancery clerk in the Virginia county of which he was a native. He later worked with his brother editing a newspaper, and in 1836 he moved to DeKalb, Mississippi, where he continued his journalistic endeavors and read law. Admitted to the bar, he practiced as an attorney in Mississippi and Alabama. At the time of his marriage to Sidney White in 1840, he took residence in Alabama. While in Livingston, Baldwin contributed frequently to the *Southern Literary Messenger.* In 1853, *Flush Times in Alabama and Mississippi: A Series of Sketches* was published; the next year *Party Leaders* appeared. Baldwin and his family moved to California where he took a seat on the supreme court of that state for a four-year period that began in 1858. He died on September 30, 1864.

Literary Analysis

Baldwin's notoriety as an author, particularly as a humorist, derives from *Flush Times in Alabama and Mississippi,* a compilation of essays first published in the *Southern Literary Messenger.* The more serious *Party Leaders* purports to be a political biography of Thomas Jefferson,

Alexander Hamilton, Andrew Jackson, Henry Clay, and Edmund Randolph; however, it lacks the "dignity" becoming a work of its genre because its composition appears journalistic in style. Baldwin attempted to repeat his earlier, more successful work in *Flush Times in California,* a fragmentary work, uncompleted at the death of its author.

The biography and social comment that constitute Baldwin's non-humorous composition never enjoyed the popularity of the 1853 *Flush Times* sketches. However, the *Richmond Examiner* reviewed *Flush Times* so favorably that its reviewer called Baldwin superior to Herman Melville in talent, and almost fifty years later, in 1901, *Flush Times* was the focus of a laudatory article in the *Sewanee Review.*

From his early years Baldwin was famous as a raconteur. Bent on entertaining attorneys who traveled from courtroom to courtroom, he told stories that were lawyer-centered. Although he added humorous incidents to his accounts, his work bears few marks of the oral tradition. Instead, he writes in an essay form that reflects the method of Samuel Johnson, Charles Lamb, Oliver Goldsmith, or Washington Irving. He alludes to well-known works or characters of literature frequently; among his favorites are William Shakespeare's Falstaff and Prince Hal. Although Baldwin's narratives attend more often to character than story, they seldom employ dialogue.

In content *The Flush Times of Alabama and Mississippi* consists of the biographical "Hon. S.S. Prentiss" and the serious discussion of law on the frontier, "The Bar of the South-West," as well as the other, lighter essays. Legal proceedings, particularly those perpetrated by semi-literate lawyers, and the language of the law appear often. The horse-swap motif appears in "An Equitable Set-Off" and "A Hung Court." Baldwin begins "Simon Suggs, Jr., Esq.; A Legal Biography" with references to a character from a work by Johnson Jones Hooper, where the consequence of a horse trade is a suit filed by the injured party, and the son of Hooper's Simon Suggs becomes a lawyer.

Judges, attorneys, clients, and testimony during litigation form much mataral for Baldwin's humor; consequently, twentieth-century readers, especially those with little contact with court proceedings, often encounter difficulty with Baldwin's free use of Latin, his allusion to contemporaneous court cases, and his use of attorneys' cant. The phrase *to take water,* for example, constitutes the sole basis for humor in "A Cool Rejoinder." In it, an attorney "in the habit of *imbibing* pretty freely" announces that his client chooses not to pursue the cause before the court; he states, "I will take water." To this declaration of a non-suit, the judge declares that such an action will greatly astonish the lawyer's stomach. A full appreciation of another of the *Flush Times* sketches, "Examining a Candidate for Licensure," depends upon the reader's knowing the meanings of *liable, in action, in possession,* and *fee simple,* among other legal principles.

Baldwin proves that he can employ social comment lightly too. In "Samuel Hale, Esq." a frank-talking lawyer frightens a schoolmistress not a little inclined towards abolitionism back to her home in Connecticut. Parochialism and provincialism become concerns in "Justification after Verdict," in which a Tennesseean "considered Knoxville at once the Athens and Paris of America." In this story Baldwin places the man in unfamiliar surroundings and leaves him to bring ridicule upon himself.

Summary

A lesser-known figure of American letters, Joseph Glover Baldwin wrote most of his work while a native of Mississippi and Alabama, and thus critics group him with Johnson Jones Hooper, Davy Crockett, Augustus Baldwin Longstreet, George Washington Harris, and Thomas Bangs Thorpe—all of the Old Southwest. His reputation rests chiefly on *Flush Times in Alabama and Mississippi,* a collection of shorter pieces. Although Baldwin's humor is lively and unrestrained in its colorful portrayal of life on the southern frontier, it is markedly set in time and regionalism.

Selected Bibliography

Primary Sources
Flush Times in Alabama and Mississippi: A Series of Sketches, 1853. Rpt. Gloucester, Mass.: Peter Smith, 1974.
Flush Times in California. Rpt. Athens: University of Georgia Press, 1966.
Party Leaders, 1855. Rpt. Freeport, N.Y.: Books for Libraries, 1972.

Secondary Sources
Bain, Robert. "Baldwin, Joseph Glover." *Dictionary of Literary Biography.* Vol. 3. *Antebellum Writers in New York and the South,* 1979. Highlights life and works, bibliography included.
Current-Garcia, Eugene. "Joseph Glover Baldwin: Humorist or Moralist?" *Alabama Review* 5 (1962): 122-141. Departing from the long-held view of Baldwin solely as humorist, treats him as a writer who seeks to instruct.
Farish, Hunter Dickson. "An Overlooked Personality in Southern Life." *North Carolina Historical Review* 12 (1935): 341-353. Appears as a "re-discovery" of Baldwin; the work has been superseded by others.
Lynn, Kenneth. *Mark Twain and Southwest Humor.* Boston: Little, Brown, 1959. Notes Baldwin and his contemporaries in the region as literary precursors of Mark Twain.

Stennis, Roderick. "The Reputation of Joseph Glover Baldwin." Thesis, University of Mississippi, 1974. An assessment of Baldwin's work with emphasis on *Flush Times in Alabama and Mississippi;* includes biography.
Stewart, Samuel Boyd. "Joseph Glover Baldwin." Diss. Vanderbilt University, 1941. Treating life and writings, the most thoroughly researched and detailed of Baldwin studies.

Thomas H. Stewart

Bangs, John Kendrick

Born: Yonkers, New York, on May 27, 1862
Education: Columbia College, Ph.B., 1893; spent one year in Columbia Law School
Marriage: Agnes Hyde, 1886, three children
Died: January 21, 1922

Biography

John Kendrick Bangs was born in Yonkers, New York, on May 27, 1862, the gifted descendant of prominent New Englanders whose occupations included evangelism, soldiering, writing, and education. It is no wonder, then, that John Kendrick was able to poke pleasant fun at a vast array of beliefs and attitudes. Bangs's grandfather, Nathan Bangs, was a Methodist preacher and had been president of Wesleyan University, and his father, Francis Bangs, was a quick-witted New York City lawyer who played a decisive part in founding the Bar Association of New York City. It is probable that from these two, John learned not only to strive for success but also to see things in a humorous way and, therefore, to transcend the common view of life, death, and society. During his youth, Bangs read widely in the classic British novels and poetry and also such American authors as George Horatio Derby, Artemus Ward, and Mark Twain. This exposure would flower in his most popular farces in the 1890s.

While at Columbia College, Bangs became involved in a variety of extracurricular activities. The most important, as far as his later career is concerned, was his time spent on the literary magazine *Acta Columbia*. He became known as one of the "University Wits" and contributed under the names Shakespeare Jones, T. Carlyle Smith, and the Collegiate Vituperator. These writings caused a mild stir among professors and area magazines, including *Puck,* which denounced them as juvenile (ironically, Bangs was contributing to *Puck* at the time). The social graces of New York City were a prime target in these works, the poetry of which reflected in tone the verses of Gilbert and Sullivan.

Bangs received his Ph.B. in Political Science at Columbia College in 1893. His attempt at law school lasted only one year, after which he devoted his complete attention to writing. Two years after becoming the literary editor of *Life*, a magazine that he had helped to found, Bangs published his first book. *The Lorgnette* (1886) was a batch of satirical sketches, many of which had been previously printed in *Life*. *New Waggings of Old Tales* (1888) followed two fairly unsuccessful volumes, and first demonstrated the technique of satirizing famous lecturers and authors that Bangs would soon hew to a fine art, presenting for the reader's enjoyment conversations between William Shakespeare, Dr. Johnson (accompanied by James Boswell of course), Homer, and among others, Baron Munchausen. Bangs left *Life* in 1888 but continued to contribute to it and many other magazines, including *Puck* and *Judge*. He became the primary contributor and editor to the "Editor's Drawer" section of *Harper's Monthly*, and through the late 1880s, 1890s, and into the first decade of the twentieth century, he added to his list of accomplishments the editorship in various departments of *Munsey's Weekly*, *Harper's Bazaar*, *Harper's Young People*, and *Puck* (which had decidedly changed its attitude concerning the humorist). Most of these contributions would find their way into the many books to follow.

Bangs's first national best seller was *Coffee and Repartee* (1893), which was his first volume to include a character known as "The Idiot," who would become the focus of several later books. Also in the 1890s, Bangs became very interested in the social and political affairs of Yonkers and nearby Manhattan. He joined several social clubs and even ran unsuccessfully for mayor of Yonkers; a description of this went into a political treatise on how to lose votes in Bangs's book, *Three Weeks in Politics* (1894). His most popular books stem from the late 1890s and include *The Houseboat on the Styx* (1896) and *The Pursuit of the House-Boat* (1897).

The last 15 years of Bangs's life, with approximately 56 books of fiction, poetry, and humorous drama to his credit, were spent in lecturing, although he abandoned New York City and urban life by moving to Maine. Content to live his last years in peaceful semi-retirement, he died on January 21, 1922, at the age of sixty.

Literary Analysis

A collector of all types of folklore and fairy tales, Bangs became a veritable Lewis Carroll to his three boys. The tales that he invented for them came into print as *Tiddledywink Tales* (1891),

The Tiddledywink's Poetry Book (1892), *In Camp with a Tin Soldier* (1892), *Half-Hours with Jimmieboy* (1893), and *The Mantel-Piece Minstrels* (1896). These books incorporate on the child's level the same quick wit and imagination found in Bangs's novels for adult readers, which include *The Water Ghost and Others* (1894) and its companion piece, *Ghosts I Have Met* (1898), and are accounts of encounters between Bangs and supernatural spirits. It is interesting to note that over and over again Bangs protests against the Gothic tradition in these writings. He goes to some length to explain that an encounter took place in broad daylight and not at the traditional December evening at midnight. Of course, after Bangs pledges himself to the truth, a spirit enters and imagination takes over. But, like his character based on Baron Munchausen, Bangs always assures the reader of the story's authenticity. As is true with most good storytellers, by the end of the tale it makes little difference whether the events actually took place. In fact, to understand Bangs's work, it is necessary for the truth to be reshaped, stretched to encompass the dead as well as the living in a world that only a child may believe in. In this way the glimpses of reality that are ever present in Bangs's world shine through.

After the success of *Coffee and Repartee* Bangs developed his character "The Idiot" and published *The Idiot* (1895), *The Idiot at Home* (1900), *The Genial Idiot* (1908), and *Half Hours with the Idiot* (1917). The books are comparable to Socratic dialogues discussing current events and the myths of the American culture. For example, in one chapter of *The Genial Idiot* there is a discussion of what makes an ideal husband between the Idiot, Mr. Pedagog, Mr. Brief, Mrs. Pedagog, the Lawyer, and Mr. Bibliomaniac. Obviously, these characters represent, if not actual celebrities, different points of views of the time. Much more successful and interesting are his books dealing with Hades.

Bangs was willing to try his luck with new ideas, no matter how unbelievable the ideas might be. In *The Houseboat on the Styx*, *The Pursuit of the House-Boat*, and *The Enchanted Typewriter* (1899), he portrays in a semi-realistic way what life is like for an assortment of famous shades who frequent a club on the river Styx. After hiring Charon for a "janitor," the group argues politics, ethics, art, and the nuisance of poets. In one chapter, Hamlet enters and is found even more melancholy than usual. He relates that his depression has been brought on by the way actors are portraying him on the other side of the Styx. After an interruption by Boswell, who is bodily thrown out by an enraged Dr. Johnson, Shakespeare (who, it is hinted throughout, did not really write any plays at all) decides to write a new play in which Hamlet himself plays the actors who have wronged the poor prince. He can now strut idiotically about the stage and feel no remorse whatsoever. Charles Aram proposes the title of "Irving" and Charles the First volunteers as understudy. The farce continues until one day when all the shades are away watching a prize fight between Samson and Goliath, the women of Hades take over the boat and are kidnapped by Captain Kidd and his band of pirate shades.

Females rarely play enviable parts in Bangs's books about the supernatural. Xanthippe and Mrs. Noah (two very disagreeable sorts) represent the females of the underworld and no doubt reflect Bangs's attitude toward feminism around the turn of the century. Inevitably, Captain Kidd finds himself no match for a boat full of historical females, and when a plan to leave them stranded on an eternal shopping spree in Paris fails, he gives himself up to Sherlock Holmes, who is hot on his trail. *The Enchanted Typewriter* is a slight variation in that Bangs himself becomes involved in the fun. He finds that an old typewriter is typing by itself and, after investigation, Boswell makes his presence known; so begins a friendship that soon leads to a tale about a trolley full of ghosts, two rows of invisible shades at the theater, and a bicycle built for twenty with Bangs, the only visible rider, in the second seat. *Mr. Munchausen* (1901) is yet another book in the same vein. Munchausen calls from Hades and dictates to Bangs's stenographer a novel's worth of outrageous tales.

A book that is only slightly related to the series on Hades is *Mr. Bonaparte of Corsica* (1895), and indeed it may well have given Bangs the idea for the *Houseboat* creations. In this humorous account of the life of Napoleon, the reader follows Mr. Bonaparte from his strategic birth (it is noted that his brother was born first to scout out the territory) to his demise, after which he goes to Hades and leads a revolt with Caesar to take over the throne. Amusingly, a historical mistake seems to occur when Napoleon mentions an event which has yet to happen, but then a soldier close at hand promptly corrects the emperor.

In 1899, Bangs published *Peeps at People*, which involves a series of satirical views of famous people at home, including Emile Zola, Andrew Lang, Rudyard Kipling, and others. A prying journalist discovers in one chapter that Lang is playing golf in the country while his literary corporation of 900 workers are busy in London writing his massive output of "647,000,000" words and are also translating Shakespeare, Burns, Boswell, and others into Lang's own style. Perhaps because he was not one of the literati himself, Bangs was able to see the men of great literature not as statues of perfection but as actual men. By exaggeration, he could show them as human. Although the humor may get tedious at times for the modern reader, the originality and imagination found in these books demand a place for Bangs in studies of American humor.

Besides his many novels, Bangs also published several plays (most dealing with drawing room humor) and much verse, which is, in contrast with his short stories and novels, at best mediocre and often sentimental.

Summary

Bangs was an entertainer, not a reformer. He is supposed to have loathed the regional humor of local color popular at the time. In addition, he never reached the misanthropic stages of other humorists such as Mark Twain. He tended to avoid altogether the darker aspects of humor and to strike at social follies of the natural and supernatural world with a pen and not an axe. Although virtually forgotten now, when publishing he was well received. The books involving the famous shades of Hades remain his most interesting and humorous.

Selected Bibliography

Primary Sources

The Lorgnette. New York: George Coombes, 1886.

Roger Camerden, A Strange Story. New York: George Coombes, 1887.

Katharine, A Travesty. New York: Gilliss Brothers and Turnure, Art Age Press, 1887.

(co-written by Bangs, Frank Dempster Sherman, and Oliver Herford.) *New Waggings of Old Tales by Two Wags.* Boston: Ticknor, 1888.

Mephistopheles, A Profanation. New York: Gilliss Brothers and Turnure, Art Age Press, 1889.

Tiddledywink Tales. New York: Russell, 1891.

The Tiddledywink's Poetry Book. New York: Russell, 1892.

In Camp with a Tin Soldier. New York: Russell, 1892.

Coffee and Repartee. New York: Harper, 1893.

Toppleton's Client, or A Spirit in Exile. London: Osgood, McIlvaine, 1893; New York: Webster, 1893.

Half-Hours with Jimmieboy. New York: Russell, 1893.

Three Weeks in Politics. New York: Harper, 1894.

The Water Ghost and Others. New York: Harper, 1894.

The Idiot. New York: Harper, 1895.

Mr. Bonaparte of Corsica. New York: Harper, 1895.

The Bicyclers and Three Other Farces. New York: Harper, 1896.

A Rebellious Heroine, A Story. New York: Harper, 1896.

The Mantel-Piece Minstrels, and Other Stories. New York: Russell, 1896.

The Houseboat on the Styx, Being Some Account of the Divers Doings of the Associated Shades. New York: Harper, 1896.

The Pursuit of the House-Boat, Being Some Further Account of the Divers Doings of the Associated

Shades, Under the Leadership of Sherlock Holmes, Esq. New York: Harper, 1897.

Paste Jewels, Being Seven Tales of Domestic Woe. New York and London: Harper, 1897.

Ghosts I Have Met and Some Others. New York and London: Harper, 1898.

Peeps at People, Being Certain Papers from the Writings of Anne Warrington Witherup. New York and London: Harper, 1899.

The Dreamers, A Club. Being a More or Less Faithful Account of the Literary Exercises of the First Regular Meeting of That Organization. New York and London: Harper, 1899.

Cobwebs from a Library Corner. New York and London: Harper, 1899.

The Enchanted Type-Writer. New York and London: Harper, 1899.

The Booming of Acre Hill and Other Reminiscences of Urban and Suburban Life. New York and London: Harper, 1900.

The Idiot at Home. New York and London: Harper, 1900.

Over the Plum Pudding. New York and London: Harper, 1901.

Mr. Munchausen, Being a True Account of Some of the Recent Adventures Beyond the Styx of the Late Hieronymous . . . Baron Munchausen. Boston: Noyes, Platt, 1901.

Uncle Sam Trustee. New York: Riggs, 1902.

Olympian Nights. New York and London: Harper, 1902.

Bikey the Shicycle and Other Tales of Jimmieboy. New York: Riggs, 1902.

Mollie and the Unwiseman. Philadelphia: Coates, 1902.

Emblemland. New York: Russell, 1902.

The Inventions of the Idiot. New York and London: Harper, 1904.

The Worsted Man, A Musical Play for Amateurs. New York and London: Harper, 1905.

Mrs. Raffles, Being the Adventures of an Amateur Cracks-Woman Narrated by Bunny. New York and London: Harper, 1905.

R. Holmes & Co., Being the Remarkable Adventures of Raffles Holmes, Esq., Detective and Amateur Cracksman by Birth. New York and London: Harper, 1906.

Andiron Tales. Philadelphia: Winston, 1906.

Alice in Blunderland, An Iridescent Dream. New York: Doubleday, Page, 1907.

Potted Fiction, Being a Series of Extracts from the World's Best Sellers Put Up in Thin Slices for Hurried Consumers. New York: Doubleday, Page, 1908.

The Genial Idiot, His Views and Reviews. New York and London: Harper, 1908.

The Real Thing and Three Other Farces. New York and London: Harper, 1909.

The Autobiography of Methuselah. New York: Dodge, 1909.

Songs of Cheer. Boston: French, 1910.

Mollie and the Unwiseman Abroad. Philadelphia and London: Lippincott, 1910.

Jack and the Check Book. New York and London: Harper, 1911.

Echoes of Cheer. Boston: French, 1912.

A Little Book of Christmas. Boston: Little, Brown, 1912.

A Line o' Cheer for Each Day o' the Year. Boston: Little, Brown, 1913.

A Chafing Dish Party. New York and London: Harper, 1913.

The Foothills of Parnassus. New York: Macmillan, 1914.

From Pillar to Post, Leaves from a Lecturer's Notebook. New York: Century, 1916.

Half Hours with the Idiot. Boston: Little, Brown, 1917.

The Cheery Way, A Bit of Verse for Every Day. New York and London: Harper, 1919.

Secondary Sources

Articles and Books

Bangs, Francis Hyde. *John Kendrick Bangs.* New York: Knopf, 1941.

———. "John Kendrick Bangs and the *Acta Columbiana*." *Columbia University Quarterly*, March 1936, pp. 1–17.

———. "John Kendrick Bangs, Humorist of the Nineties." *Yale University Library Gazette*, January 1933, pp. 53–76. Bangs's son has published the only biography of his father. It is a major resource for Bangs scholarship although, as might be expected, Francis Hyde Bangs is not as critical of the author as other scholars might be. The two articles are simply early versions of what would be included in the biography.

Blanck, Jacob. "Bangs, John Kendrick, 1862–1922." *Bibliography of American Literature.* Vol. 1. New York: Yale University Press, 1955. Blanck gives a complete bibliography of Bangs's work.

Eichelberger, Clayton L. *Harper's Lost Reviews: The Literary Notes by Laurence Hutton, John Kendrick Bangs, and Others.* Millwood, New York: Kraus-Thomson, 1976.

Hoffa, William W. "John Kendrick Bangs." *Dictionary of Literary Biography.* Vol. 11. *American Humorists, 1800–1950.* Ed. Stanley Trachtenberg. Detroit: Gale, 1982, pp. 17–21. Hoffa's interesting article synthesizes the biography of Bangs and includes a bibliography of his works.

Stronks, James B. "John Kendrick Bangs Criticizes Norris's Borrowings in *Blix*." *American Literature*, 42 (November 1970): 380–386. Stronks states that Bangs's article, which first appeared in *Literature* in 1899, is the first adverse criticism of Norris. Stronks sees this attack as one against the realists as a whole.

Dissertation

Cox, Virginia L. "John Kendrick Bangs and the Transition from Nineteenth to Twentieth-Century American Humor." Ohio State University, 1971. Cox asserts that although Bangs's humor is out of date and is rarely rated along with the better-known masters of the genre, his work is a true reflection of his age.

Michael Pettengell

Barthelme, Donald

Born: Philadelphia, Pennsylvania, on April 7, 1931

Education: University of Houston, 1950–1957 (no degree)

Biography

Donald Barthelme was born in Philadelphia, Pennsylvania, on April 7, 1931, the oldest of five children of Donald and Helen Bechtold Barthelme. Barthelme's father, Donald, Sr., was an architect, and received his B.Arch. from the University of Pennsylvania in 1930. In 1933, the entire family moved to Houston, Texas, where Barthelme's father designed an office. In addition to working as an architect, he also accepted a teaching post at the University of Houston.

Barthelme remembers his childhood as rather average, although his father's interest in architecture made the family somewhat out of place among their Texas neighbors. Barthelme's father designed the house they lived in, and the house's unusually modernistic design became something of a local point of interest. Barthelme, however, spent most of his time going to the movies, summering with his grandfather in Galveston, and reading whatever books he could find around the house.

According to Lois Gordon, in her volume *Donald Barthelme*, Barthelme decided to be a writer at the age of ten, and "that was that." He edited and wrote for numerous grade school and high school newspapers and literary magazines, including the Lamar High School *Sequoyah* in 1948–1949, and later the University of Houston *Cougar* from 1950–1951. He entered the University of Houston in the fall of 1950, but skipped spring, 1951, and then went to school erratically (with time out for military service) through 1957. When he quit, he was still a junior in college.

In 1951, while still sporadically attending college, Barthelme went to work for the *Houston Post*. In 1953, he joined the Army and was shuffled from Fort Polk to Japan and Korea, where he worked on various Army publications as a writer and editor. Discharged from the Army in 1955, he went back to work for the *Post*, but soon quit for a job on the University of Houston News Service, where he worked under Farris Block. In 1956, Barthelme replaced Block as the editor of *Acta Diurna*, a weekly in-house newsletter of the University of Houston. Also in 1956, he became editor of *Forum*, a small arts journal that he founded, and published works by Alain Robbe-Grillet, Leslie Fiedler, Jean-Paul Sartre, and others. He also did a great deal of reading during this period and considerably expanded his cultural horizons.

In 1959, Barthelme became involved with the Contemporary Arts Museum in Houston and by 1961 he had advanced to the position of acting director. In 1962, he became the full-time director of the museum. But, as he had many times before, Barthelme abruptly resigned this position to move to New York City and pursue a career as a writer. In that same year, he edited *Location*, an art and literary review founded by Tom Hess and Harold Rosenberg, and published reviews in *Harper's*. In 1963, *The New Yorker* accepted his short story, "L'Lapse," and in 1964, his first book, *Come Back, Dr. Caligari*, was published. This began a steady outpouring of work, the most recent example of which is his collection of short pieces, *Overnight to Many Distant Cities* (1983, G. P. Putnam's Sons). In 1973, he served as a Visiting Professor at Boston University, and he also teaches at City College in New York. Today, Donald Barthelme lives quietly with his wife, in Greenwich Village in New York City, where he works on his various literary projects in a quiet, methodical manner.

Literary Analysis

Donald Barthelme is, of course, an excellent writer, and his critical reputation, as evidenced by the extensive bibliography of critical works at the end of this piece, is assured. Most of these critics do not consider him primarily as a humorist, yet humor is a major element in his writing, even though it is dark, brooding, convoluted, deeply personal, and often anguished humor. Certainly his approach to humor differs from that of most of the other writers included in this volume.

Barthelme's early passion for film, evidenced in the numerous film reviews that he wrote for his high school, college, and home-town paper, came to the fore in the first story he sold to *The New Yorker*, "L'Lapse." The two principal characters in the piece, Marcello, a film critic, and Anna, a cold young blonde, speak to each other in the artificially stylized jargon of an early script by Michelangelo Antonioni. The title of the story itself is a punning reference to Antonioni's first major success as a filmmaker, *L'Avventura*. As with Antonioni's films, the major subject matter of Marcello and Anna's conversation is boredom, the impossibility of communication. Furthermore, their entire vocabulary seems composed of junk phrases, cast-off slogans and old advertisements. Anna declares, "I want my life to be *really* meaningless." Marcello counters that, as a critic, he must strive for a style of "brilliant boredom" where the ultimate object of his writing will be the glorification of emptiness. Further, in the story, Barthelme continually blurs the line between the conversation of the characters and a film script within which the characters may be operating, complete with background directions. After a time it seems as if the characters are operating entirely within a group of filmic conventions, or clichés, peculiar to Antonioni's films. "L'Lapse" thus sets up a situation which is central to Barthelme's view of the world: while his characters may have some freedom of action within certain strictly defined limits, they are also simultaneously fictional constructs, and the "reality" of their extended existence may be foreshortened at any time. Whether the constricting conventions are filmic, literary, or the result of a world lived according to advertisements, Barthelme's characters walk or struggle toward their individual destinations with the shared constant of an extremely tenuous existence.

Other stories, such as "The Teachings of Don B.: A Yankee Way of Knowledge" (which parodies the writings of Carlos Castenada); "Swallowing" (which disguises a meditation on the Vietnam War and political corruption with a surrealistic narrative involving a starving young artist who is given some fetid cheese to eat by a group of governors who are simply getting rid of something they do not want), and "The Young Visitirs" [sic] (which attacks Washington society and the shallowness of Presidential politics) all follow the same general rules of construction. The nebulousness of Barthelme's narrative voice in his opening, and the difficulty of locating this voice properly within any ordinary narrative structure, is another of author's trademarks. "Swallowing," for instance, starts off as a sermon, or editorial, or perhaps a newspaper opinion column, in which Barthelme observes that the American people have "swallowed" a great deal of misinformation. After this brief introduction, Barthelme's narrative voice proposes to make the problem of "swallowing" clear with an instructive fable of a 4,000-pound cheese left over from the 1960 New York World's Fair, and how a group of governors gave the rotting cheese to a starving artist. The artist eats the cheese whole, and in doing so, is transformed into a successful poet, a poet who is, in fact, perhaps *too* successful. Indeed, Barthelme suggests that the poet will now become one of the same corrupt class as the governors, and he characterizes the poet's new work as a group of "things."

What sets Barthelme's stories apart from other political satires and satirists is their resolutely fabulistic tone. If Barthelme's characters inhabit a world in which they may have the material underpinnings pulled out from under them at any time, they also inhabit a world which owes a strong debt to the nursery tale or fable. But, this fabulistic sense is transmogrified by the continual updating of these myths to the present, as seen in Barthelme's later short novel, *Snow White.* A supreme ironist, Barthelme is also a moralist, and his tone is mordant and almost Calvinistic, as in "The Palace," a short story that is really a meditation on the inequities of the class system and the effects of a held-over feudalistic culture in modern America. Barthelme makes it very clear which side he is on: if he identifies with any of his phantasmal characters, it is most strongly with those who represent (or are seen to represent) the servile classes. In all of the stories mentioned above, Barthelme is also extremely wary of the influences of power; it is not the governors in "Swallowing" who are corrupt, it is the power that has made them so which is corrupt. Because of this, when the artist eats the cheese, he assumes and subsumes their characteristics and becomes a societal "poet laureate."

At the same time, formal matters of syntax and sentence structure are among Barthelme's concerns as a writer. "An Hesitation on the Bank of the Delaware" is on one level a parodistic account of the exploits of George Washington and his attempts to collect numerous houses all over the United States as part of his personal property, but it is also a deft parody of the writing and typographical structures employed in the eighteenth century. Thus, "house" becomes "houfe" and "horse" becomes "horfe," and Barthelme takes full advantage of the confusions that arise as a result. In this respect, Barthelme's piece resembles John Barth's epic picaresque novel, *The Sot Weed Factor,* which is a bizarre mixture of sitcom humor and Henry Fielding-like elements mixed together in an overtly political allegory.

These short stories are playful, indirect, and full of sly puns and allusions, but they are also deadly serious in their commentary on contemporary social structures and the ways in which these structures enslave and delude the mostly unsuspecting public. Barthelme enjoys himself immensely at the typewriter, of this there can be little doubt, and at the bottom of each of his works is a constant undercurrent of "humor as salvation and mediating force," but in his longer works, Barthelme becomes more obviously serious. Although, on one level, his novel *Snow White* can be seen as simply a slapstick, Vonnegutesque variant on the classic fairy tale, Barthelme, in fact, is using the story as a vehicle for his true concerns. His Snow White is a young lady of the 1960s who must fend for herself in an indifferent and often hostile world of landlords, teachers, and books and magazines that continually remind her that she must seek a stronger identification with the traditional role of women or else strike out in the direction of the New Feminism. However, Snow White remains more buffeted than seduced by these forces, and the entire novel can be seen as an attempt by Barthelme to discern and discuss women's roles in relation to the assembly line of anonymous men with whom she lives (The Seven Dwarfs). As critic Lois Gordon notes, "Snow White knows she needs a *real* liberation," but in the world of Barthelme's fiction none is forthcoming. Instead, there is a continual "shaping" of the individual by the forces and tides of mass culture, so the characters in *Snow White* become simply empty vessels waiting to be filled. Yet, when filled with the stuff of 1960s pop culture, they still feel profoundly empty. Barthelme underscores this by showing the "unreliability" of myths and fairy tales: there is no happy ending in this book, no prince coming to Snow White's rescue; indeed, the plot, such as it is, and the identities of the protagonists (blurred and shared within the seven men with whom Snow White lives) remain, until the last, defiantly unclear. Snow White constantly berates the author of the text for these shortcomings, calling them a "failure of the imagination." In fact, the novel is about Snow White's own failure of imagination and how believing in artificially predestined conclusions traps one in a web of unsatisfying and unfulfilled role and gender expectations.

Like all of Barthelme's other works, *Snow White* is a pastiche, and it is appropriate that he should rise to prominence as a writer during the pop, recyclable decade of the 1960s, when Andy Warhol and Robert Rauschenberg in the visual arts were reusing and reshaping pop artifacts in their own work, simultaneously acknowledging and rejecting the banality of twentieth-century Western culture. From 1967 to 1983, in his most recent collection of stories, Barthelme's quicksilver approach to his material has changed little. The early stories and one short novel can serve as useful emblems for his later work, which continue to explore the difficulties of perceiving things as they are rather than as they seem to be, the use of ancient and popular myths as a vehicle for other (often political or social) moral insights, the blurring of actual dialogue, and a playful interest in syntactical and narrative structure. While Barthelme's humor may seem too convoluted and self-referential, there can be little doubt that he is one of the twentieth century's most enterprising and entertaining wordsmiths.

Summary

Donald Barthelme's style is a unique amalgam of shifting narrative loci, pop imagery, recycled myths and fairy tales, an often intrusive narrative voice, and a questioning of the ordinary narrative format of most humorous writings. Dark, sardonic, and occasionally quite bitter,

Barthelme's style not only makes him one of the late twentieth century's best humorists but also one of the few humorists to achieve renown as a serious literary artist.

Selected Bibliography

Primary Sources

Novels

Snow White. New York: Atheneum, 1967; London: Cape, 1968.

The Dead Father. New York: Farrar, Straus and Giroux, 1976. London: Routledge and Kegan Paul, 1977.

Collections of Stories and Short Works

Come Back, Dr. Caligari. Boston, Mass.: Little, Brown, 1964. London: Eyre and Spottiswoode, 1966.

Unspeakable Practices, Unnatural Acts. New York: Farrar, Straus and Giroux, 1968; London: Cape, 1969.

City Life. New York: Farrar, Straus and Giroux, 1970; London: Cape, 1971.

The Slightly Irregular Fire Engine. New York: Farrar, Straus and Giroux, 1971.

Sadness. New York: Farrar, Straus and Giroux, 1972; London: Cape, 1973.

Guilty Pleasures. New York: Farrar, Straus and Giroux, 1974.

Amateurs. New York: Farrar, Straus and Giroux, 1976; London: Routledge and Kegan Paul, 1977.

Great Days. New York: Farrar, Straus and Giroux, 1979; London: Routledge and Kegan Paul, 1979.

Overnight to Many Distant Cities. New York: G.P. Putnam's, 1983.

Periodical Publications

"The Emerging Figure." *Forum*, 3 (Summer 1961): 23–24.

"The Case of the Vanishing Product." *Harper's*, 223 (October 1961): 30–32.

"After Joyce." *Location*, 1 (Summer 1964): 13–16.

"The Tired Terror of Graham Greene." *Holiday*, 39 (April 1966): 146, 148–149.

Untitled commentary on "Paraguay." In *Writer's Choice*. Ed. Rust Hills. New York: David McKay, 1974, pp. 25–26.

(With William H. Gass, Grace Paley, and Walker Percy.) "A Symposium on Fiction." *Shenandoah*, 27 (Winter 1976): 3–31.

Uncollected Short Stories

"Man's Face." *New Yorker*, May 30, 1964, p. 29.

"Then." *Mother*, November–December 1964, pp. 22–23.

"Blue Flower Problem." *Harvest*, May 1967, p. 27.

"Philadelphia." *New Yorker*, November 30, 1968, pp. 56–58.

"Newsletter." *New Yorker*, July 11, 1970, p. 23.

"Adventure." *Harper's Bazaar*, December 1970, pp. 92–95.

"The Story Thus Far." *New Yorker*, May 1, 1971, pp. 42–45.

"Natural History." *Harper's*, August 1971, pp. 44–45.

"The Mothball Fleet." *New Yorker*, September 11, 1971, pp. 34–35.

"Alexandria and Henrietta." *New American Review* 12 (1971): 82–87.

"Edwards, Amelia." *New Yorker*, September 9, 1972, pp. 34–36.

"Wrack." *New Yorker*, October 21, 1972, pp. 36–37.

"Over the Sea of Hesitation." *New Yorker*, November 11, 1972, pp. 40–43.

"A Man." *New Yorker*, December 30, 1972, pp. 26–27.

"Three." *Fiction*, no. 1 (1972), p. 13.

"The Inauguration." *Harper's*, January 1973, pp. 86–87.

"The Bill." *Viva*, Novembr 1973, n.p.

"The Bed." *Viva*, March 1974, pp. 68–70.

"The Dassaud Prize." *New Yorker*, January 12, 1976, pp. 26–29.

"Monumental Folly." *Atlantic*, February 1976, pp. 33–40.

"The Great Debate." *New Yorker*, May 3, 1976, pp. 34–35.

"Presents." *Penthouse*, December 1977, pp. 106–110.

"Momma." *New Yorker*, October 2, 1978, pp. 32–33.

"Captain Blood." *New Yorker*, January 1, 1979, pp. 26–27.

"Conversations with Goethe." *New Yorker*, October 20, 1980, p. 49.

"The Farewell Party." *Fiction*, 6, no. 2 (1980): 12–16.

Secondary Sources

Aldridge, John W. "Donald Barthelme and the Doggy Life." *Atlantic*, 222 (July 1968): 89–91. Rpt. *The Devil and the Fire*. New York: Harper's Magazine Press, 1972, pp. 216–266.

Bocock, Maclin. "'The Indian Uprising'; or Donald Barthelme's Strange Object Covered with Fur." *Fiction International* 4–5 (1975): 134–146.

Critique, 16, 3 (1975). Special Barthelme issue.

Davis, Robert Con. "Postmodern Paternity: Donald Barthelme's *The Dead Father*." *Delta*, May 8, 1979, pp. 127–140.

Dervin, Daniel A. "Breast Fantasy in Barthelme, Swift, and Philip Roth: Creativity and Psychoanalytic Structure." *American Imago*, 33 (1976): 102–122. An interesting examination of varying uses of the female breast as an iconic and/or metaphoric device in the work of the three authors mentioned; the piece seems occasioned by the publication of Roth's *The Breast*.

Dickstein, Morris. *Gates of Eden: American Culture in the Sixties*. New York: Basic Books, 1977, passim. An excellent overview of the numerous changes in literary style and cultural values that came with the 1960s in America; Barthelme's fiction is just one of many topics considered by the author.

Ditsky, John M. "'With Ingenuity and Hard Work, Distracted.' The Narrative Style of Donald Barthelme." *Style* 9 (Summer 1975): 388–400. A discussion of the prose narrative style typically exhibited in Barthelme's work; Ditsky finds it difficult but rewarding, repaying numerous re-readings.

Federman, Raymond. *Surfiction*. Chicago: Swallow Press, 1975.

Gass, William H. "The Leading Edge of the Trash Phenomenon." *New York Review of Books*, 10 (April 25, 1968): 5–6. Rpt. in *Fiction and the Figures of Life*, New York: Knopf, 1970, pp. 97–103. Written when "pop" fiction was still in its infancy, Gass's essay is not exactly sympathetic to Barthelme's concerns, but is valuable for the perspective it gives on contemporary critical responses to Barthelme's work.

Gillen, Francis. "Donald Barthelme's City: A Guide." *Twentieth Century Literature*, 18 (1972): 37–44.

Gilman, Richard. "Donald Barthelme." *Partisan Review*, 39 (Summer 1972): 382–396. The first really serious, extended, and sympathetic examination of Barthelme's work in any depth or detail; the excellence one would expect from *The Partisan Review*.

Glicksberg, Charles I. "Experimental Fiction: Innovation versus Form." *Centennial Review*, 18 (Spring 1974): 127–150.

Gordon, Lois. *Donald Barthelme*. Boston: Twayne, 1981. Fine overview of Barthelme's life and work, and invaluable for those who want to get a general grasp of the writer's accomplishments and priorities.

Guerard, Albert J. "Notes on the Rhetoric of Anti-Realist Fiction." *TriQuarterly*, 30 (Spring 1974): 3–30.

Hassan, Ihab. *Paracriticisms*. Urbana: University of Illinois Press, 1975.

Johnson, R.E., Jr. "Bees Barking in the Night: The End and Beginning of Donald Barthelme's Narrative." *Boundary*, 2, 5 (1977): 71–92.

Kinkowitz, Jerome. "Donald Barthelme." *Literary Disruptions*. Urbana, Ill.: University of Illinois Press, 1975, pp. 62–81, 212–217.

——. "Donald Barthelme." *Dictionary of Literary Biography*. Vol. 1. Detroit, Mich.: Gale, 1978, pp. 34–39.

Leland, John. "Remarks Re-marked, Barthelme: What Curios of Signs!" *Boundary*, 2, 5 (Spring 1977): 795–811.

Longleigh, Peter. "Donald Barthelme's Snow White" *Critique*, 11, 3 (1969): 3–34. Astute and detailed examination of Barthelme's novel *Snow White*; discusses Barthelme's appropriation of the classic fairy tale for his own subtextual concerns.

McCaffery, Larry. "Barthelme's *Snow White*: The Aesthetics of Trash." *Critique*, 16, 3 (1975): 19–32.

Malory, Barbara. "Barthelme's *The Dead Father*." *Linguistics in Literature*, 2 (1977): 44–111.

Rother, James. "Parafiction: The Adjacent Universe of Barth, Barthelme, Pynchon and Nabokov." *Boundary*, 2, 5 (1977): 21–43. This is a fine and serious piece of work, comparing numerous points of shared ground in their works, but feels that despite their common reflexivity, each displays a unique and vigorous fictive voice.

Schmitz, Neil. "Donald Barthelme and the Emergence of Modern Satire." *Minnesota Review*, 1 (Fall 1971): 109–118.

Scholes, Robert. "Metafiction." *Iowa Review*, 1 (Fall 1970): 100–115.

Spencer, Sharon. *Space, Time and Structure in the Modern Novel*. Chicago: Swallow, 1971.

Stevick, Philip. "Lies, Fictions, and Mock-Facts." *Western Humanities Review*, 30 (Winter 1976): 1–12.

Stott, William. "Donald Barthelme and the Death of Fiction." *Prospects*, 1 (1975): 369–386.

Tanner, Tony. *City of Words*. New York: Harper and Row, 1971.

Weixlmann, J., and S. Weixlmann. "Barth and Barthelme Recycle the Perseus Myth." *Modern Fiction Studies*, 25 (Summer 1979): 191–207.

Whalen, Tom. "Wonderful Elegance." *Critique*, 16, 3 (1975): 44–48.

Wilde, Alan. "Barthelme Unfair to Kierkegaard: Some Thoughts on Modern and Postmodern Irony." *Boundary*, 2, 5 (1977): 45–70.

Zavarzaden, Mas'ud. *The Mythopoeic Reality*. Urbana: University of Illinois Press, 1976.

Wheeler Dixon

Behrman, S[amuel] N[athaniel]

Born: Worcester, Massachusetts, on June 9, 1893

Education: Clark College, Worcester, 1912–1914; Harvard University, B.A., 1916; Columbia University, M.A., 1918; honorary degree, Clark College, 1949

Marriage: Elza Heifetz, 1936, one child

Died: September 9, 1973

Biography

The son of conservative Jewish immigrants, Samuel Nathaniel Behrman was born in Worcester, Massachusetts, on June 9, 1893. There is, however, some doubt as to the accuracy of this date; in his book-length study of Behrman, Kenneth T. Reed suggests that Behrman "arbitrarily selected" the date, as no record of his birth appears to exist.[1] In his *People in a Diary* (1972), Behrman recalls his upbringing in a "poverty-stricken" home in the "Providence Street ghetto" section of Worcester, a predominantly Jewish neighborhood in which his father's Talmudic scholarship accorded his family a status in the local "theological aristocracy" that money could not buy. Nevertheless, the difficulty of these early days exerted a marked influence on Behrman, as he was "haunted by dreams of poverty" all of his life.[2] Most of Behrman's best-known work was written between 1927 and 1940, a period of harsh economic reality after the stock market crash of 1929, and his comedy often concerns matters of capital: acquiring it, desiring it, marrying for it, or—a common activity of Behrman's younger, socialist characters—denouncing it.

Behrman entered Clark College in 1912 and studied there until 1914, though he was suspended twice for failure to attend classes in physical education. He then attended Harvard University, enrolling in George Pierce Baker's English 47 playwriting course. After graduating from Harvard in 1916, Behrman enrolled the following year at Columbia University, where he studied French drama under Brander Matthews and from which he received a Master of Arts degree in 1918. While a student at Columbia, he sold an essay and several works of short fiction to *The New Republic*, *The Smart Set*, *The Liberator*, and other periodicals.[3] After graduation, Behrman worked for the *New York Times*, at first typing and classifying want ads and later managing a "Queries and Answers" column. In *People in a Diary*, he also recalls other "sleazy jobs" that he held before the Theatre Guild's production of his first successful play, *The Second Man*, in April 1927. These jobs included writing publicity for a Texas oilman, serving as a press agent for a New York producer, and collaborating on plays and works of short fiction with J. Kenyon Nicholson. Kenneth Reed asserts that, after Behrman descended to what he himself termed a "low point in my material condition and morale" in 1925, he reached a "turning point" in his career: collaboration with Owen Davis on a successful play and arrangement for a pre-Broadway tryout of *The Second Man*.[4] From this point until his death, Behrman was a successful and prolific writer of fiction, essays, screenplays, and sophisticated comic drama. The 1930s were, if nothing else, his most hectic decade as a writer, as he travelled back and forth from New York to Hollywood. From 1927 to 1939, 10 of Behrman's plays opened on Broadway and 16 films on which he worked were released. In addition, in 1938 Behrman, Maxwell Anderson, Sidney Howard, Elmer Rice, and Robert Sherwood founded the Playwrights' Company, which mounted some of New York's most heralded productions, particularly in the 1940s. While Behrman remained interested in the theater throughout his career, his most active years writing for the stage and screen spanned the late 1920s to the early 1940s. Returning occasionally both to the stage and screen in the 1950s and 1960s, Behrman preferred to write non-dramatic prose during his later years, producing 6 full-length works and numerous essays, nearly 40 of which were published in *The New Yorker*.

Literary Analysis

Numerous contributions to *The New Yorker* would seem to validate Reed's thesis that Behrman was "from first to last a prose essayist, notwithstanding his tireless ambitions as a playwright,"[5] though film buffs might remember Behrman as one of many successful eastern writers who, with the advent of sound in the cinema, moved to Hollywood to write for major studios. Especially famous are the several screenplays he wrote for Greta Garbo: *Queen Christina* (1933), *Anna Karenina* (1935), and the controversial

Two-Faced Woman (1941). Regardless of his considerable successes as an essayist and screenwriter, however, Behrman is most often discussed today as a comic playwright. He is, in particular, remembered as the creator of sophisticated and thoughtful comedy in the late 1920s and 1930s and is regularly included along with such contemporaries as Eugene O'Neill, Philip Barry, and Clifford Odets in the syllabi of university courses in American drama. While there is some critical disagreement over the quality of specific plays, there is a broad consensus that Behrman's best, most representative work was produced between 1927 and 1939. Arguing that Behrman's 13 Broadway plays produced after 1936 "deservedly received mixed reactions from the critics,"[6] Reed regards most highly Behrman's work up until that year: *The Second Man* (1927), *Serena Blandish* (1929), *Meteor* (1929), *Brief Moment* (1931), *Biography* (1932), *Rain from Heaven* (1934), and *End of Summer* (1936). For Cyrus Hoy, Behrman's most successful play comes a bit later—*No Time for Comedy* in 1939; and for both Reed and Hoy the much later, bittersweet *The Cold Wind and the Warm* (1958), based on Behrman's reminiscence of his youth published as *The Worcester Account* (1946) and in fragments in *The New Yorker*, stands as the highest dramatic achievement of Behrman's later years.[7] And, though admittedly quite different from his earlier work, *The Cold Wind and the Warm* possesses an intellectual seriousness characteristic of his best comedies.

While nearly every critic mentions the "seriousness" of Behrman's comedies—generally tracing this characteristic to the ominous climate of the 1930s when America attempted to recover from the Great Depression and Europe prepared for World War II—there is considerable disagreement about where to place Behrman's plays within a tradition of comic drama. The most widely-held view of these plays emphasizes their similarity to the Restoration comedy of manners. Opposing this thesis, Gerald Weales urges that Behrman be considered seriously as a "comedian of ideas," not merely as a deflator of hypocritical or excessive manners and tastes.[8] Similarly, Hoy lavishes high praise on Behrman's *Biography* and especially *No Time for Comedy*, citing both as "testimony to a humane and intelligent playwright's attempt to mirror the complexities and anxieties of modern society in one of the most traditional of dramatic forms."[9] Unlike Weales, who recommends a comparison between Behrman's plays and those of Bernard Shaw, Hoy sees resemblances to Anton Chekhov in, among other plays, *End of Summer*.[10] Still another view of this matter has been advanced by W. David Sievers, who places Behrman in the company of both Philip Barry

and Eugene O'Neill as equal contributors to a canon of American psychoanalytic drama: "Although he consistently employs the comedy of manners form rather than expressionism, Behrman possesses a mature awareness of the complexity of unconscious motivation and has been able to reflect this in a number of timely and delightful plays."[11] Sievers's hypothesis gathers support from the generally recognized special interest at Clark College in the writings of Sigmund Freud, who in his only trip to America lectured at the school shortly before Behrman enrolled there, and from Behrman's admitted knowledge of psychoanalytic theory. Thus, defining the nature of Behrman's comic technique is no simple task; nevertheless, each of the above perspectives helps illuminate important aspects of Behrman's best comedies.

Despite Weales's well-taken objections to Brooks Atkinson's labelling of Behrman as the "Congreve of American letters," his dramas often bear comparison both to seventeenth-century comedies of manners and to the more recent dramas of Oscar Wilde and Noel Coward. Admittedly lacking in the romantic intrigues and foppish preoccupations with "genteel" taste upon which comedies of manners are usually constructed, Behrman's comedies typically do concern the romantic dilemmas of at least several characters of means. Still further comparisons might be urged on theatrical grounds. For example, comedies of manners have always been concerned with contemporary fashion and with the ridiculing of some characters' slavish dependence upon the social codes governing fashion. Although not much concerned with the correction of contemporary vulgarity in matters of taste, Behrman nonetheless relies upon beautiful sets and employs fashionable costumes for his roster of memorably strong leading women. The opening scenes of *The Second Man*, *Biography*, and *No Time for Comedy*, for instance, occur in tastefully decorated New York apartments; the first acts of *End of Summer*, *Rain from Heaven*, and *Wine of Choice* (1938) begin on late spring afternoons in the estate-cottages or country homes of wealthy characters. Nancy Baker Traubitz argues that audiences also expected the leading ladies of high comedy to dress with impeccable style, to look as if they had just returned from Paris draped in the expensive clothing modelled in *Vogue* or *Vanity Fair*, and Behrman's leading ladies seldom disappointed.[12] In this respect, Behrman was indeed fortunate to write plays with the likes of Lynn Fontanne, Ina Claire, and Katharine Cornell in mind—all three epitomized style and wit; all three appeared in Behrman's greatest successes. Like Claire, who starred in, among others, *Biography* and *End of Summer*, Marion Froude in the former play is described by Behrman as "one of those women [who] . . . cause foreigners to exclaim enthusiastically that American women are the most radiant in the world."[13] In their unique ways, Behrman's mature women characters, like their counterparts in many Hollywood screwball comedies, are much more than attractive women in chic fashions—they are the centers around which the action in Behrman's plays revolves.

Like comedies of manners or other "high" comedy, Behrman's best plays are marked by clever dialogue and witty repartee, especially between the central romantic pair. *No Time for Comedy*—which in the original Playwrights' Company production featured Laurence Olivier as Gaylord ("Gay") Esterbrook, a successful comic playwright who reviles the very genre to which he owes his considerable acclaim, and Katharine Cornell as Linda Page, Gay's wife and an equally well-known comedienne—provides abundant evidence of Behrman's skill. Throughout much of the play, Esterbrook contemplates leaving his wife for another woman, a woman who has convinced him to write a work of tragic profundity. And, when Esterbrook—the master of clever dialogue—is ready to abandon his craft (and his wife) for self-pity and the other woman, he finds a formidable verbal combatant in Linda:

> Gay: What the hell's the use of kidding myself—I've got nothing to say.
> Linda: But you say it charmingly!
> Gay: To hell with that. I'm sick of that. It's no time for that.
> Linda: Never was such a time. The world's depressed. This is the moment to be gay, if possible.
> Gay: That's like calling for a minuet in a plague town.
> Linda: Why not?

> (pp. 45–46)

From the opening of *The Second Man* in 1927, Behrman's comedies became known for their verbal sophistication and Behrman, to quote from George Jean Nathan's exuberant review of the play, was recognized by many as a writer with a "lively and seeing mind, a good sense of character," and a talent for "whipping the English language into a sparkle."[14]

Nathan's commendation contains also the very factors that cause Behrman's plays to transcend the generic boundaries of the comedy of manners and enter into the more serious arenas of Shavian and Chekhovian drama. Especially in *End of Summer*, Behrman replicates the bittersweet strains of Chekhov's *The Cherry Orchard* (1904): as the seasons change from spring to fall, Leonie Frothingham's mother dies, and Leonie herself finds a new male admirer. An old generation is gone, but new relationships begin both for Leonie and her daughter Paula, whose love is finally accepted by her socialist boyfriend, regardless of the money that may come with the relationship. Certainly the later *The Cold Wind and the Warm*, Behrman's nostalgic return home to Worcester, ends in a similarly tragicomic way. Early in the play Dan Eisner, a young man about to be married, dies of diabetes, and near the end Willie Lavin, the central character's (Tobey Sacher's) best friend, commits suicide. Moreover, the play is built around several relationships marred by unrequited love. Still, like the advice Linda gives her self-pitying husband in *No Time for Comedy*—"There are enough people dying. Living's the stunt. . . . You snap your fingers in its [horror's, death's] face" (p. 48)—the end of *The Cold Wind and the Warm* brings with it an affirmation of life in the face of human misery:

> Tobey: Jim [Nightingale, an old friend], now that I'm back here, the whole past is like a heavy sack around me. All the dead—my father and mother—Dan and Willie—the anonymous dead. What does it all mean anyway?
> Jim: Why does life have to have meaning? It's good in itself. That oboe is good. What Willie gave you was good. Dinner tonight will be good—I hope!

> (p. 142)

Although not always so directly life-affirming as the conclusions of *The Second Man*, *End of Summer*, or *No Time for Comedy*, which promise new or renewed romance, the ends of Behrman's plays at least offer some sense of optimism or acceptance. Binkie in *Wine of Choice* vows never to "acknowledge failure" with Wilda, and Marion in *Biography*, after her relationship with Richard Kurt has fallen apart, is happy to go to China alone as the final curtain falls.

It is hardly conventional that a successful comedy such as *Biography* might conclude with the central character's exuberance over a failed relationship and the prospect of travelling to the Orient by herself (with her maid, of course). Perhaps Behrman *approaches* the Shavian "comedy of ideas" primarily in this depiction of a new "womanly woman": attractive, intelligent, sexually emancipated, and—of course—independent. Yet it is, in the main, difficult to see in Behrman's plays the irreducible iconoclasm of the Shavian play of ideas with its commitment to social and theatrical reform. To be sure, Behrman's plays include debates between the wealthy and their socialist antagonists, between the pessimistic and their optimistic adversaries, between the representatives of a narrow social orthodoxy and those whose lifestyles signal a liberation from such constraint. In his development of rounded, at times deeply troubled characters, characters who at times seem to possess a psychological complexity requiring psychoanalysis, Behrman *does* surpass the merely predictable, much as Shaw did. Still, Behrman is *not* Bernard Shaw. He is, however, a thoughtful comic playwright whose abilities to draw fascinating characters, create entertaining situations, and write clever dialogue have earned him a prominent place in the history of the American theater.

Summary

S.N. Behrman's career as a writer of essays, plays, films, and novels spans a period of over fifty years, from his earliest work as a graduate student to his book of memoirs, *People in a Diary* in 1972. Today he is remembered mostly as a playwright, as a creator of witty and urbane plays for the Broadway stage. Working with some of the best actors of his day, and with the Theatre Guild and his own Playwrights' Company, Behrman brought 20 plays to Broadway, his best coming between 1927 and 1939, with the possible exception of *The Cold Wind and the Warm* in 1958. During this time he was a major contributor to a then amazingly small and undistinguished body of American comic drama, and he remains today as one of the American theater's most prolific talents.

Notes

1. Kenneth T. Reed, *S.N. Behrman* (Boston: Twayne, 1975), p. 19.
2. Ibid., p. 6.
3. Ibid., pp. 19–46.
4. Ibid., pp. 26–27.
5. Ibid., p. 34.
6. Ibid., p. 68.
7. Cyrus Hoy, "Clearings in the Jungle of Life: The Comedies of S.N. Behrman," *New York Literary Forum*, 1 (Spring 1978): 222–227. Also, Behrman, *People in a Diary* (Boston: Little, Brown, 1972), pp. 229–238.
8. Gerald Weales, "S.N. Behrman Comes Home," *Commentary*, 27 (March 1959): 256–260.
9. Hoy, p. 200.
10. Maureen Shea, dissertation, Ohio State University, 1977.
11. W. David Sievers, *Freud on Broadway* (New York: Hermitage House, 1955), p. 322.
12. Nancy Baker Traubitz, dissertation, University of Maryland, 1978, pp. 33–36.
13. Reed, p. 5.
14. Barnard Hewitt, *Theatre U.S.A.* (New York: McGraw-Hill, 1959), pp. 369–370.

Selected Bibliography
Primary Sources
Plays
The Second Man. New York: Doubleday and Page, 1929.
Brief Moment. New York: Farrar and Rhinehart, 1931.
Meteor. New York: Samuel French, 1934.
Biography. New York: Samuel French, 1936.
End of Summer. New York: Random House, 1936.
Rain from Heaven. New York: Samuel French, 1936.
Amphitryon 38. New York: Random House, 1938.
Wine of Choice. New York: Random House, 1938.
No Time for Comedy. New York: Random House, 1939.
The Talley Method. New York: Random House, 1941.
The Pirate. New York: Random House, 1943.
Jocobowsky and the Colonel. New York: Random House, 1944.
Dunnigan's Daughter. New York: Random House, 1946.
I Know My Love. New York: Samuel French, 1949.
Jane. New York: Random House, 1952.
Fanny. New York: Random House, 1955.
The Cold Wind and the Warm. New York: Random House, 1959.
Lord Pengo. New York: Random House, 1963.
But for Whom Charlie. New York: Random House, 1964.

Non-dramatic Works
Duveen. New York: Random House, 1952.
The Worcester Account. New York: Random House, 1954.
Portrait of Max: An Intimate Memoir of Sir Max Beerbohm. New York: Random House, 1960.
The Suspended Drawing Room. New York: Stein and Day, 1965.
The Burning Glass. Boston: Little, Brown, 1968.
People in a Diary. Boston: Little, Brown, 1972.

Secondary Sources
Books, Articles, and Chapters in Books
Hoy, Cyrus. "Clearings in the Jungle of Life: The Comedies of S.N. Behrman," *New York Literary Forum*, 1 (Spring 1978): 199–227. Views Behrman's comedies of the 1930s, especially *No Time for Comedy,* as attempts to affirm "the value of the comic spirit" even in a "time of world crisis."
Reed, Kenneth T. *S.N. Behrman.* Boston: Twayne, 1975. This book-length study provides a useful introduction to Behrman's life and work.
Sievers, W. David. *Freud on Broadway.* New York: Hermitage House, 1955, pp. 322–336. Assesses Behrman's comedies from a Freudian perspective; specific discussion of *The Second Man, Brief Moment* (1931), and *Biography.*
Weales, Gerald. "S.N. Behrman Comes Home." *Commentary*, 27 (March 1959): 256–260. Prompted by a production of *The Cold Wind and the Warm,* Weales discusses Behrman as a Jewish writer.

Dissertations
French, Alice Mae. "The Dramaturgy of the Playwrights' Company," University of Missouri-Columbia, 1974. Traces the 22-year history of the

company with discussion of Behrman's *The Talley Method*, *No Time for Comedy*, and *The Pirate*.

Jorge, Robert Richard. "A Delicate Giant: S.N. Behrman and the Theatrical Compromise: An Investigation into His Last Three Produced Plays," University of Minnesota, 1978. Study of the productions of *The Cold Wind and the Warm*, *Lord Pengo*, and *But for Whom Charlie*.

Shea, Maureen Ann. "The Playwriting Technique of S.N. Behrman: The Theatre Guild Years, 1927–1938," Ohio State University, 1977. Employing notes, drafts, and revisions of plays housed in the Wisconsin State Historical Society, Shea provides a careful textual and influence study of six plays.

Traubitz, Nancy Baker. "'Our Revels Now Are Ended': Comic Closure in Three American Plays of the 1930's," University of Maryland, 1978. A study of *End of Summer*, Robert Sherwood's *Idiot's Delight* (1936), and Philip Barry's *Philadelphia Story* (1939).

Stephen Watt

Benchley, Robert Charles

Born: Worcester, Massachusetts, on September 15, 1889
Education: Harvard, A.B., 1913
Marriage: Gertrude Darling, June 6, 1914, two children
Died: November 21, 1945

Biography

Perhaps to foil biographers and certainly to please himself, Robert Benchley once provided the following account of his life:

> Robert Charles Benchley, born Isle of Wight, September 15, 1807. Shipped as cabin boy on the *Florence J. Marble*, 1815. Arrested for bigamy and murder in Port Said, 1817. Released 1820. Wrote *Tale of Two Cities*. Married Princess Anastasia of Portugal 1831. Children: Prince Rupprecht and several little girls. Wrote *Uncle Tom's Cabin* 1850. Editor of *Godeys Ladies Book*, 1851–1856. Began *Les Miserables* in 1870, finished by Victor Hugo. Died 1871. Buried in Westminster Abbey.[1]

This succinct biography is colorful and impressive. And, of course, as Benchley saw it, too much fact tended to be boring.

The younger of the two sons of Charles Henry Benchley, who came from a prominent New England family, and Maria Jane Moran

Benchley, whose father was a native of Protestant Northern Ireland, Robert Charles Benchley was—in fact—born in Worcester, Massachusetts, on September 15, 1889. After his brother, Edmund Nathaniel, who was thirteen years older, was killed in the Spanish-American War in 1898, young Robert received the concentrated affection of his mother and the attention of Lillian Duryea, his late brother's fiancée. Duryea sent him to Phillips Exeter Academy in 1907 for his last year of high school and then on to Harvard.

The comic and dramatic talent that later made Benchley's reputation was already evident at Exeter. Assigned to write an essay on how to do something practical, he penned "How to Embalm a Corpse." Alternating mock travelogues with parodies of politicians, he was in great demand at Harvard to speak at dinners and to play comic roles in amateur productions. As a senior, he was elected to Hasty Pudding, a social club known for its annual burlesque; the Signet Society, a literary club; and the presidency of *Lampoon*, the college's humor magazine. Benchley had few academic problems at Harvard. An exception was a course in international law; it is said that he discussed a fisheries dispute, one of the main questions on the final examination, from the point of view of the fish. Benchley failed the course and did not graduate with the class of 1912. He received his A.B. the following year. On June 6, 1914, he married a childhood schoolmate, Gertrude Darling, in Worcester; they would have two children, Nathaniel Goddard and Robert.

Benchley held a series of tedious jobs—including secretarial work, public relations, and reporting—in Boston and New York from 1912 to 1916. He considered trivial what little humorous writing he was able to sell (his first humorous piece appeared in October 1914 in *Vanity Fair*). Then, in 1916, Franklin P. Adams made Benchley associate editor of the *New York Tribune*'s Sunday magazine. Benchley produced weekly features such as "Do Jelly Fish Suffer Embarrassment?" In May of 1917, he was fired by the *Tribune*, primarily for not conforming to the paper's interventionist tone. During the next two years, he worked as a producer's press agent, a publicity secretary, the editor of the *Tribune*'s Sunday pictorial supplement, the *Graphic*, and a publicity agent for the Liberty Loan drive.

In May of 1919, Benchley became managing editor of *Vanity Fair*. There he found congenial colleagues in Dorothy Parker and Robert E. Sherwood. Though these three brought new life and wit to the magazine, their irreverence and editorial independence irritated top management. Sherwood and Benchley resigned when

Parker was dismissed in January 1920 for her candid theatrical reviews. Benchley then began writing "Books and Other Things," a column that appeared regularly in the *New York World* for about a year. *Of All Things!*, his first collection of humorous articles, was published in 1921.

Hired as drama critic of *Life*, the humor magazine, in 1920, Benchley would hold this position until 1929. During 1924, he stopped using his middle name. In December of 1925, his first contribution to *The New Yorker* appeared. By 1927, Benchley had developed "The Wayward Press" for *The New Yorker*, a regular feature in which he commented on current events under the pseudonym "Guy Fawkes." Two years later, he became drama critic for *The New Yorker*, where he stayed until 1940. From 1933 to 1936, he also wrote a column of casual humor for King Features Syndicate. Ten collections of Benchley's writings were published between 1921 and 1938.

While working as a humorist and critic, Benchley was also a popular comedian of stage, film, and radio. In 1922, he delivered a monologue, "The Treasurer's Report," in an amateur revue staged by the group of wits that he regularly joined for lunch at the Hotel Algonquin's "Round Table." This skit soon began earning him fame and money. After presenting it in Irving Berlin's *Music Box Revue* of 1923, and then on the Keith vaudeville circuit, he used it in his first film short. Benchley wrote and acted in a small role in *Sport Parade*, a full-length motion picture that appeared in 1932. He began a sequence of "how to" films after his *How to Sleep* for MGM won the Academy Award for best short picture in 1936. Between 1928 and 1945, Benchley made nearly fifty short pictures; he also appeared in a number of feature-length films and collaborated on the scripts of many more. In 1938, he entered radio when he became master of ceremonies of the Old Gold program, which soon rose to sixth place in a national popularity poll.

Though his work as a humorist provided him with an easy source of income, Benchley did not regard his comic talents highly. He spoke of the "serious" writing that he wanted to do, but he never seemed to find the time for it. In 1943, maintaining that few humorists are funny after the age of fifty, Benchley announced that he would write no more. He died in New York City on November 21, 1945.

Literary Analysis

Despite the efforts of such writers as Oliver Wendell Holmes, the literary humor of the sentimental short story and the familiar essay went stale after Washington Irving. Yet from about 1910 to 1930, more and more writers, responding to the frustrations and absurdities of contemporary urban and suburban middle-class life, attempted to enliven American literary humor. Of these writers, Robert Benchley, a superb comic essayist and brilliant parodist, was one of the best known and most effective. He also proved to be a significant influence on younger humorists such as James Thurber, E.B. White, and S.J. Perelman.

In his humorous work, Benchley wrote as the good-hearted and absent-minded Little Man who was often frustrated but firm in his reason and integrity. Benchley's writing rarely achieves the savage irony and range as that of American humorists such as Thurber and Ring Lardner; rather, it recalls the eighteenth-century moderation of the *Spectator*, distinguished but limited by its polite good sense. The success of his first book, *Of All Things!*, in 1921 marked the beginning of a long and prolific career. Though he always searched carefully for the best comic turn of phrase, Benchley nonetheless wrote quickly. He turned out eleven books in seventeen years, weekly drama reviews, many columns for *The New Yorker*, numerous movie scripts, and over 600 essays for magazines—all while leading an active public life.

Mocking logic from the first page, Benchley sets the pattern for his subsequent work in *Of All Things!*, a collection of 22 comic essays and three extended parodies that appeared originally in *Motor Print, Collier's, Life, Vanity Fair*, and the *New York Tribune*. Benchley begins by irrelevantly dedicating the book to Henry Bessemer for having invented the steel converter. In his acknowledgments, he notes that he never asked permission to reprint the pieces, but that the editors of the periodicals in question probably would not mind anyway.

"The Social Life of the Newt," one of Benchley's most hilarious pieces, leads off his first collection and demonstrates two important Benchley techniques: setting a pure nonsensical scene that borders on dadaism, and undercutting his own position by asking a rhetorical question and providing an absurd answer. He parodies both the personifications of the popularizers of science and their efforts to give their prose spurious erudition by citing German sources. In the volume's second essay, "Coffee, Megg, and Ilk, Please," the kindly incompetent appears; he cannot speak up and cringes in abject terror before any workingman.

Inspired by a single disastrous effort to drive a car with no assistance, "Lesson Number One" finds Benchley satirizing the tendency of the common man to parade his half-knowledge and to rationalize his ignorance. Benchley's finest piece in *Of All Things!*, "Christmas Afternoon, Done in the Manner, If Not the Spirit, of Dickens," mixes warmth and absurdity, whimsy and satire. Concerned with abuses of the Christmas spirit, Benchley probably wrote more about Christmas than any other American humorist. In "Christmas Afternoon," the children are little beasts, but the Christmas spirit is impugned no more than it was by Charles Dickens. Elsewhere in his first collection, Benchley writes travesties of authors' letters, renders parodies that turn into sheer nonsense, and has his Little Man fail at gardening. Three parodies of well-known magazines are placed together as "Tabloid Editions."

Benchley's second collection of pieces, *Love Conquers All*, was published in 1922 (actually, many of the selections in the second book were written before some of those in the first). Once again, his narrator is an outsider who is bewildered by committees, summer camp, tennis, gardening, skating, baseball, chess, and bridge. Two essays, "The Tariff Unmasked" and "How to Understand International Finance," satirize the average man's indifference and ignorance. Parody remains Benchley's strong suit. "Opera Synopses" is a good example of his effort to parody suspect art, while "Family Life in America" mocks the naturalistic novel. Though it contains some serious writing and occasionally reveals the darker underpinnings of Benchley's work, *Love Conquers All* is characterized by the self-mockery that informs all of Benchley's books.

By the time Benchley's second collection was assembled, he had fully developed his style and had hit a plateau of quality. He had developed a completely formed and fully characterized fictional mask—the Little Man. Unlike such nineteenth-century humorists as Artemus Ward and Mark Twain, who made distinctions between sane, clear-minded authors and their unsound and sometimes quite mad characters, a modern humorist like Benchley stresses the resemblance of his character to the author. Certainly Walter Blair's profile of Benchley's favorite archetype fits Benchley himself:

> The character he [Benchley] pretends to be time after time is prevented from doing a number of harmless things he would like to do—leave a party when he wants to, smoke a cigarette, wear a white suit, waltz, make faces, pick flowers, and so *ad infinitum*. The frustrations have given this character, so the collected pieces show, a mass of phobias and complexes which he shows at work on innumerable occasions.[2]

Benchley's Little Man is also searching perpetually for his true self, his identity—an important quest throughout the body of American literature.

Insofar as the author measures the world by the standards of the Little Man's common sense—which Benchley often does—his bumbler resembles Mr. Dooley, Abe Martin, and Will Rogers. Donning the mask of befuddlement, Benchley airs numerous opinions about the average American, the family, suburbia, science, nature, politics, business, travel, literature, the fine arts, and humor itself. Through the reactions of the Little Man, he ridicules political commentators, psychoanalysts, physicians, economists, botanists, and zoologists—in short, all of those "experts" who get too abstruse for the moderately intelligent and educated man to follow.

After the publication of *Love Conquers All*, three years passed before Benchley's third collection, *Pluck and Luck*, appeared; but this and subsequent collections do not differ greatly in content or quality from the first two. The 50 pieces that comprise *Pluck and Luck* are parodies. Unflaggingly, Benchley sends up such subjects as Twain's autobiography, Michael Arlen's work, May Sinclair's fiction, a biography of John Keats, linguistics, William Shakespeare, children's books, comic opera, and sex plays. Satirizing both the prudish and the prurient in "Drama Cleansing and Pressing," he avers, "A pretty good way to judge in advance about the intrinsic art of a sex play is to see whether the characters have a good time at it or not. If they get fun out of the thing, then it's a harmful play. If they hate it, it's a work of art."[3] Only one piece in *Pluck and Luck*, "Whoa!," departs from the volume's general warm and optimistic tone. In this selection, Paul Revere has a vision of the future in which he sees millions of young Americans marching off to war and giving their arms and legs and lives for unspecified goals. Ernest Hemingway and John Dos Passos were not more bitter.

A master of the short piece, Benchley attempted some longer, more connected humorous writing in *The Early Worm* (1927). Six of the 46 pieces in this collection make up a parody of travel-adventure writing, "The *Life* Polar Expedition." Tired of the publicity about what he regarded as mainly stunts by Charles Lindbergh and Admiral Byrd, Benchley has a group of bumblers, including himself and "Lieut.-Commander Marc Connelly," set off from New York to the North Pole on bicycles. By week's end, they have reached Westchester County.

Many of Benchley's numerous pieces about nature are parodies of those lecturers and writers whom naturalist John Burroughs had labeled "nature-fakers." Benchley attacks such pseudo-popularizers in passages like the following from *The Early Worm*:

> If you will look at these eggs, you will see that each one is *Almost* round but

not *Quite.* They are more of an "egg-shape." This may strike you as odd at first, until you learn that this is Nature's way of distinguishing eggs from large golf balls. You see, Mother Nature takes no chances. She used to, but she learned her lesson. And that is a lesson that all of you must learn as well. It is called Old Mother Nature's Lesson, and begins on page 145.

Now, these eggs have not always been like this. That stands to reason. They once had something to do with a hen or they wouldn't be called hen's eggs. If they are called duck's eggs, that means that they had something to do with a duck. Who can tell me what it means if they are called ostrich's eggs? . . . That's right.[4]

Benchley wrote much parody of this sort because the popularizers were so vulnerable.

In Benchley's last collection of the 1920s, *20,000 Leagues Under the Sea, or, David Copperfield* (1928), he tends to deal more frequently with domestic and international politics. The confusion of the times is reflected in his social and economic commentaries. Pieces such as "Cease Firing!" and "The Typical New Yorker" reaffirm Benchley's essential stance as a humorist: while accepting and appreciating the normality of Americans, one must nonetheless criticize their frailties of character. Yet, by laughing at himself and casting himself as an archetypal bumbler, he wins the reader to his side. By the late 1920s, the illustrations for Benchley's essays, done by Gluyas Williams, had become integral parts of his work.

Presenting perhaps the finest view of the Benchley character, the title piece of *The Treasurer's Report, and Other Aspects of Community Singing* (1930) appears at the end of the collection. Benchley occasionally placed his monologue in a "frame" in which some background about the speech is provided. An accumulation of clichés and repetitions, "The Treasurer's Report" has a framework that is included in an "Author's Note"; Benchley relates how he happened to improvise the monologue, how he delivered it in the theater until he had grown sick of it, and how he is now purging himself of it by writing it down. There are also comments about the speaker and directions for his actions, the final one being *"Exits, bumping into proscenium."*[5]

Sometimes, Benchley would launch into a dialogue based on an imaginary situation suggested by a news item. The appointment of George W. Wickersham to investigate the non-enforcement of Prohibition and report on law-lessness in general led to "Law-Breaking at Its Source," which appears in *The Treasurer's Report.* The entire Wickersham Commission comes knocking at the door of an average citizen, Mr. Welchman—who, like Wickersham, is referred to as "Mr. W." Mr. Welchman turns the tables on the Commission members and dominates the interview; through him, Benchley makes satirical gibes and establishes his main point regarding the futility of the commission:

> Mr. W: What particular law infractions have you enjoyed most?
>
> Mr. W.: That would be difficult to say, Mr. Wickersham. Sometimes I like one, sometimes another. It all depends on how I happen to be feeling, and on the weather. In summer, for instance, I am rather partial to violating Article 4, Section 6 of the Criminal Code of New York State, but that is because I feel the heat so terribly. In winter I like to devote myself to the Constitutional amendments, although as yet I have never prevented a Negro from voting.
>
> Mr. Baker [former Secretary of War Newton D. Baker]: They tell me that's a lot of fun.[6]

Throughout *The Treasurer's Report*, Benchley's Little Man offers ironic comments on many aspects of American culture; a fool he may be, but he is a good fool.

Benchley's portraits of the loser who battles inanimate objects continue in *No Poems, or, Around the World Backwards and Sideways* (1932). Typewriter ribbons, shoelaces, newspapers, fountain pens, hairbrushes, and suitcases— all spell trouble for the Little Man. One bafflement follows another, as in "Back in Line," where encountering numerous difficulties in mailing a package at the post office comes to represent all struggles with bureaucracy. Although the Little Man remains hopeful, the world of *No Poems* is somewhat grimmer than that of the early works.

In a key essay in *No Poems*, "Mind's Eye Trouble," the fictitious Benchley confesses that a lack of visual imagination causes him to substitute his own boyhood environment for whatever setting a particular author has utilized. For example, regardless of whatever Victor Hugo had in mind, he thinks of Front Street in Worcester, Massachusetts, when he reads *Les Misérables.* Scenes from the works of Lord Byron, Samuel Richardson, Twain, and Hugh Walpole are recreated in the playground of the Woodland Street school or its vicinity. These reworkings of scene are the literary equivalent of Mr. Dooley's checking on the validity of political ideas by seeing how they play on Archey Road. Rightly or wrongly, Benchley's Little Man demands that authors from Julius Caesar to Katherine Mansfield—as the very price of their survival—give him events and people meaningful within his own frame of reference.

With a depressing pun for a title, Benchley's *From Bed to Worse, or, Comforting Thoughts About the Bison* (1934) appeared in the midst of the Great Depression. The more than sixty pieces collected in this volume are still shorter this time; the title reflects the downward spiral of the times. Near the book's end, Benchley even finds himself under attack by pigeons: "God knows that I was decent enough to them in my undergraduate days. . . . But somehow the word got around in pigeon circles that Benchley was anti-pigeon."[7] Various pieces deal with unproductive labor, divorce, vanishing fathers, disease, and assorted crimes. The optimistic, younger satirist has given way to a more pessimistic, middle-aged Benchley who is voicing his concerns and, indeed, fears.

One of Benchley's best parodies, "Love Among the Thinkers," lends its strength to *From Bed to Worse.* Very funny, but also violent, it attacks naturalism, economics, biology, Gestalt psychology, capitalism, and abnormal sexuality. In an introductory note, Benchley sets the scene:

> Let us suppose . . . that [Sinclair Lewis's] *Ann Vickers* meets [H. G. Wells's] *Theodore Bulpington in the moonlight on the Day Nursery roof of the Stuyvesant Industrial Home, and that she feels the Urge to be a Woman, as even a social worker must feel it when June brings the scent of far-off Devon wafting on velvet waves of Night. How would they go about it?*[8]

Benchley continues to poke fun at physicians. In "How to Avoid Colds," he advises: "If you think that you have caught a cold, call in a good doctor. Call in three good doctors and play bridge."[9]

Benchley's last two original collections, *My Ten Years in a Quandary, and How They Grew* (1936) and *After 1903—What?* (1938), contain pieces that tend to be shorter than those in any of his previous books, perhaps because many of them were drawn from a chatty column that he was turning out three times a week for King Features Syndicate from 1933 to 1936. Writing had become a chore for Benchley by the time he dropped the King column, but some of his best paragraphs and quips are found in these two volumes.

My Ten Years in a Quandary includes over a hundred pieces, ten of which feature the laconic MacGregor, who serves as Benchley's sarcastic spokesman. Questions of identity surface in many of these pieces; Benchley's nonsense often approaches outright contempt. More than ever, the individual is caught up by society. Ominous titles pepper the table of contents: "The Evil Eye," "Help!," "Duck, Brothers!," "My Trouble," "Judgment-Day Rehearsal," "Phobias," and "No More Nightmares." Nevertheless, Benchley cannot help being funny as he reproaches himself and his world. If he has a quandary, it is because his humor remains light while shadows lengthen in his view of the world.

Taking on psychoanalysts in "All Aboard for Dementia Praecox" and "Phobias," Benchley assumes the stance of the Sane Neurotic. Though he admits to retarded perception, defective judgment, stupor, and lack of skill in motor performance, he adds: ". . . I can say only that there are hundreds of people willing to bet that I have *never* had my eyes open. I have no proof to the contrary."[10] By implication, psychoanalysts have no proof for their assumptions. In "Duck, Brothers!," Benchley makes his persona very gullible and pompous in foretelling showers of meteorites, thus spoofing writers and readers who take astronomical predictions too seriously. By pretending to be one himself, Benchley criticizes grammarians of the stuffy-genteel sort in "Do You Make These Mistakes?"

The title of Benchley's last original collection, *After 1903—What?* (1938), suggests an even more problematic world. The pieces remain short (again, there are over one hundred in the book), the tone is still harsh, and the humor is more sardonic. Though Benchley did not announce until 1943 that he was through as a writer, this work foreshadows the end of his career as a humorous essayist, presenting a Benchley who is exhausted, world-weary, and dejected.

Adopting an oafish role in "News from Home," Benchley notes that he is a slave to odd bits of news, to the fillers and *curiosa* about zebras with too many stripes, wife-murderers, a man who lost his wooden leg to a beaver while he slept, lazy firemen, Japanese fishermen who use trained birds to dive for fish, and strange weather. As elsewhere, Benchley's comments cut two ways: the Little Man may be an inattentive reader, but the press is cluttered with trivia.

In "My Face," the last piece in *After 1903—What?*, Benchley admits to being fascinated with his personal appearance, his identity. Looking in the mirror at different times, he sees himself as Popeye's friend Wimpy, film star Wallace Beery, or English cartoonist Bruce Bairnsfather's Old Bill. At essay's end, he observes that "whatever is in store for me, I shall watch the daily modulations with an impersonal fascination not unmixed with awe at Mother Nature's gift for caricature and will take the bitter with the sweet and keep a stiff upper lip." And, then, as though the temptation is too great to resist, he adds: "As a matter of fact, my upper lip is pretty fascinating by itself, in a bizarre sort of way."[11]

The posthumously published *Chips Off the Old Benchley* (1949) contains some of Benchley's finest humorous writing. Only five of the pieces had been previously collected; material from *Life* in the 1920s, *Liberty* and *The New Yorker* in the 1930s, and a number of essays—early and late—from *Vanity Fair*, the *New York Mirror*, and news syndicates are included. Frank Sullivan observes in his introduction that Benchley often "dealt with the same common or garden variety of subject other writers tackled, but a subject was rarely the same after Mr. Benchley got through with it." Each Benchley sentence "was apt to become an adventure. You never knew when you started where you would end but then neither did Mr. Benchley."[12]

Benchley parodies postcards, turkish baths, art criticism, radio, and Sir Walter Scott. In "Tiptoeing Down Memory Lane," he mocks collections of literary anecdotes, while "Do I Hear Twenty Thousand?," a dialogue spoof of the great dead authors and book auctions, finds Percy Bysshe Shelley, Jonathan Swift, Alfred, Lord Tennyson, Alexander Pope, Edgar Allan Poe, and others engaged in a heavenly discussion about the prices their books bring on earth. Sculpture and painting are not mentioned often in Benchley's work. He said a little more about classical music, not much of it friendly. In "Music Heavenly Maid," the Little Man is a writer who is trying to work—unsuccessfully—while his neighbors listen to a symphony concert on the radio. Disliking censorship, Benchley parodies military press releases in "À Bas the Military Censor: The Ride of Paul Revere—As It Would Be Featured in Washington Today." He concludes that

> On the whole, it seems lucky that General Washington and the rest of the Boys in Buff handled their own publicity by releasing news to the enemy and the public at the same time, letting nature take its course. It has made history much more intimate.[13]

In 1970, 39 uncollected Benchley pieces from *Liberty* appeared as *Benchley Lost and Found*, with illustrations by Peter Arno and others. Originally published in the 1930s, these "prodigal pieces" provide further examples of the whimsical Benchley who damns with urbane wit and mock anger the discomforts of travel on trains, standing in line at the post office only to find that your package is improperly tied, malicious fogs that obscure the race track during the final lap, sand that gets kicked in your face at the beach, puffery about vitamins, and a host of other annoyances, petty and otherwise.

Three anthologies of Benchley's previously collected essays were published during the 1940s: *Inside Benchley* (1942), *Benchley Beside Himself* (1943), and *Benchley—Or Else* (1947). A fourth, *The Benchley Roundup*, appeared in 1954. The last volume consists of a selection by Nathaniel Benchley of his favorites from about a thousand previously published pieces by his father.

Much of Benchley's writing has never been collected. No volume of his film scripts exists. Though they contain some of his most incisive criticism of writing and current events, Benchley's "The Wayward Press" commentaries for *The New Yorker*, written under the *nom de plume* "Guy Fawkes," have not been collected.

Following a decade of prolific publication, Benchley turned increasingly to movie work after 1935. The shift to films from writing came primarily because movie-making was easy and lucrative, while writing was hard and never as remunerative as working in motion pictures. All of the major subjects in his humorous writings reappear in his movie shorts: self-help lectures, Christmas, domestic afflictions, animals, travel difficulties, and his problems with inanimate objects and machines. It is noteworthy that Benchley was able to translate many of the qualities of the Little Man from the rarefied atmosphere of publications such as *The New Yorker* to the mass media. He managed to walk the tightrope between in-group faddishness and broad appeal.

Examining Benchley's movie career, Robert Redding maintains that when Benchley played the role of a lecturer in his movie shorts, his monologue "invariably took some unexpected and inexplicable turns." Benchley's words or his manner "might betray an awareness that all was not going well, but as often he would briskly proceed, apparently satisfied that his outlandish discourse was altogether lucid and instructive." Redding sees Benchley in other movies assuming the role of "Joe Doakes," "a fumbling, ineffectual, supposedly average citizen, . . . reenacting trivial, everyday humiliations of the sort that, again, most of his viewers could recognize." Viewers watch Benchley "being intimidated, or defeated outright, by supercilious clothing salesmen, uniformed attendants, precocious children, malevolent ironing boards and furnaces and window shades."[14]

During the late 1930s and early 1940s, Benchley found a sympathetic audience among middle-class moviegoers. This popular success suggests that his brand of "sheer madness" was recognizable on many cultural levels in America. Something of the Little Man's futility, lurking terror, glorious confusion, and rather hopeless bravado seemed to strike universal chords. Benchley's subjects were common annoyances. Though his language was formal rather than colloquial, it imitated the informality and hesitancy of spoken English. And, while they often required special knowledge, his allusions did not sail over the common man's head into the stratosphere.

In accounting for Benchley's success with his movie shorts, it must also be remembered that most of his earlier sallies into entertainment were made by way of the stage or platform and that in many of his best essays, he wrote like the actor or monologist that he was at heart. By doing comic impersonations of himself in print as he later did in his films, Benchley linked oral and written humor, thus joining a line of American "performers" that includes George Handel ("Yankee") Hill, Danforth Marble, Bill Nye, Artemus Ward, Twain, Emily Kimbrough, and Cornelia Otis Skinner.

The closest that Benchley came to providing a definition of humor was a hint that it depended on conventions shared with the humorist by his audience. In effect, a joke is funny only if the humorist and his audience think it is. Like Twain, Benchley disliked the role of a mere funnyman whom no one took seriously. On the whole, he preferred metropolitan subtlety to crossroads crudity in his humor. He disliked the reverse anti-intellectual snobbery and crude misuse of words of the crackerbox oracles. Along with Benchley, the contemporary humorists he admired—such as Franklin P. Adams and Stephen Leacock—were attempting to intellectualize the vernacular and, in so doing, broaden the American experience.

Nevertheless, Benchley believed that intellectualized, or "high-brow," humor involved more than simply the use or non-use of the vernacular. In 1924, Gibert Seldes praised George Herriman (the creator of "Krazy Kat"), Joe Cook (the stage comic), Irving Berlin, and Ring Lardner in his book, *The Seven Lively Arts*. Benchley responded to Seldes's views:

> To us it is quite understandable that Mr. Seldes, a highbrow, should revel genuinely and without affectation in the work of Lardner, Cook, Berlin and Herriman, because these gentlemen are Grade-A highbrows themselves. Each has a universal quality which renders him popular, but at his best he is so far over the heads of the average reader and audience that he might as well be working in a foreign medium.
>
> Lardner's entire structure is built on an unsparing and sophisticated exposure of the lowbrow mind, so subtle and delicate that thousands of readers of the *Saturday Evening Post* unquestionably found nothing amusing in it except the quite adventitious misspelling and slang. Messrs. Cook and Herriman are entirely mad at heart, and sheer madness is, of course, the highest possible brow in humor. They have, just as Ring Lardner has, certain fundamental comic elements which make everybody laugh, regardless of brow-elevation, but in the upper reaches of their imagination they are for only the sophisticates.

On the other hand, Benchley classified Russian comedy, Shakespearean comedy, and H.L. Mencken's humor as lowbrow:

> Mr. Mencken, while sophisticated enough for all practical purposes in his mental processes and serious criticism, is, when he wants to be funny, dependent on the extremely lowbrow medium of comic-sounding words like "pish-posh" and "*sitz-platz*," and figures of speech reminiscent of Public School 165 when sitting down heavily and kicking in the seat of the pants were considered good enough fun for anyone. When Mr. Mencken has said something funny to you it is all over your face like a pail of whitewash, and he has nothing left for himself.
>
> The comedy of the Russians and Shakespeare, with its concomitant cheek-blowing and grunting, is comparable with the Mencken method in tonnage, but is without Mr. Mencken's mature intent. It all is derived from the whitewash pail and all is particularly delightful to auditors under eight years of age or their equivalent.[15]

Benchley insisted that humor must convey a sense of spontaneity. It must be fresh, understated, and in one's own language. Whatever his own limitations in theory and practice, Benchley's views on humor link him both with the older humorists of his generation and with such younger contemporaries as S.J. Perelman, E.B. White, and James Thurber who further intellectualized the vernacular.

Though Benchley's popularity could not match that of Will Rogers with his one hundred million or more readers, his syndicated column, which he wrote three times a week in the early 1930s, was carried by 16 mass-circulation newspapers, including the *New York Daily News* and the *Boston Globe*. Four volumes of his selected pieces continue to sell (by early 1963, each had sold an average of 46,000 copies), and many more readers have encountered Benchley's best work by separate pieces scattered in anthologies.

Summary

Robert Benchley began his career as a humorist by writing on collegiate topics for the amusement of his fellow students and alumni. Developing his talent, he eventually enriched the familiar essay with wit, whimsy, suavity, and learning. Though other writers were striving to do the same, Benchley went farthest, building his humorous pieces around a self-caricature of the author, the Little Man or bumbler who was disturbed but unconquered by the modern world.

Notes

1. Babette Rosmond, *Robert Benchley: A Biography* (Garden City, N.Y.: Doubleday, 1970), p. 17.
2. Walter Blair, *Native American Humor* (San Francisco: Chandler, 1960), p. 171.
3. Robert Benchley, *Pluck and Luck* (New York: Holt, 1925), p. 268.
4. Robert Benchley, *The Early Worm* (New York: Holt, 1927), p. 5.
5. Robert Benchley, *The Treasurer's Report, and Other Aspects of Community Singing* (New York and London: Harper, 1930), p. 345.
6. Ibid., p. 154.
7. Robert Benchley, *From Bed to Worse, or Comforting Thoughts About the Bison* (New York and London: Harper, 1934), p. 277.
8. Ibid., p. 189.
9. Ibid., p. 200.
10. Robert Benchley, *My Ten Years in a Quandary, and How They Grew* (New York and London: Harper, 1938), p. 234.
11. Robert Benchley, *After 1903—What?* (New York and London: Harper, 1938), p. 271.
12. Robert Benchley, *Chips Off the Old Benchley* (New York: Harper, 1949), p. xvii.
13. Ibid., p. 353.
14. Robert Redding, *Starring Robert Benchley* (Albuquerque: University of New Mexico Press, 1973), pp. xv–xvi.
15. Robert Benchley, "Pretty Dull Reading," *Life*, 88 (June 19, 1926): 19.

Selected Bibliography

Primary Sources

Of All Things! New York: Holt, 1921; London: Lane/Bodley Head, 1922.
Love Conquers All. New York: Holt, 1922; London: Lane/Bodley Head, 1923.
Pluck and Luck. New York: Holt, 1925.
The Early Worm. New York: Holt, 1927.
20,000 Leagues Under the Sea, or David Copperfield. New York: Holt, 1928.
The Treasurer's Report, and Other Aspects of Community Singing. New York and London: Harper, 1930.
No Poems, or, Around the World Backwards and Sideways. New York and London: Harper, 1932. Republished as *Around the World Backwards and Sideways*, London: Dobson, 1952.
From Bed to Worse, or, Comforting Thoughts About the Bison. New York and London: Harper, 1934; London: Dobson, 1950.
My Ten Years in a Quandary, and How They Grew. New York and London: Harper, 1936; London: Dobson, 1951.
After 1903—What? New York and London: Harper, 1938; London: Dobson, 1950.
Inside Benchley. New York and London: Harper, 1942.
Benchley Beside Himself. New York and London: Harper, 1943.
Benchley—Or Else! New York: Harper, 1947; London: Dobson, 1948.
Chips Off the Old Benchley. New York: Harper, 1949.
The "Reel" Benchley. New York: Wyn, 1950; London: Heinemann, 1951.
The Benchley Roundup. Ed. Nathaniel Benchley. New York: Harper, 1954; London: Cassell, 1956.
Benchley Lost and Found. New York: Dover, 1970.

Movie Shorts (All of these films are taken from Benchley's writings. However, it is not always possible to ascertain for which films he wrote screenplays. This list is based upon information found in Robert Redding, Starring Robert Benchley, pp. 181–188)
The Treasurer's Report, Twentieth Century-Fox, 1928.
The Sex Life of the Polyp, Twentieth Century-Fox, 1928.
Lesson No. 1, Twentieth Century-Fox, 1929.
Stewed, Fried & Boiled, Twentieth Century-Fox, 1929.
Furnace Trouble, Twentieth Century-Fox, 1929.
Your Technocracy and Mine, RKO, 1933.
How to Sleep, MGM, 1935.
How to Behave, MGM, 1936.
How to Train a Dog, MGM, 1936.
How to Vote, MGM, 1936.
How to Be a Detective, MGM, 1936.
The Romance of Digestion, MGM, 1937.
How to Start the Day, MGM, 1937.
A Night at the Movies, MGM, 1937.
How to Figure Income Tax, MGM, 1938.
Music Made Simple, MGM, 1938.
An Evening Alone, MGM, 1938.
How to Raise a Baby, MGM, 1938.
The Courtship of the Newt, MGM, 1938.
How to Read, MGM, 1938.
How to Watch Football, MGM, 1938.
The Opening Day, MGM, 1938.
Mental Poise, MGM, 1938.
How to Sub-Let, MGM, 1939.
An Hour for Lunch, MGM, 1939.
Dark Magic, MGM, 1939.
Home Early, MGM, 1939.
How to Eat, MGM, 1939.
The Day of Rest, MGM, 1939.
See Your Doctor, MGM, 1939.
Inferiority Complex, MGM, 1940.
Home Movies, MGM, 1940.
The Trouble with Husbands, Paramount, 1940.
Waiting for Baby, Paramount, 1941.
Crime Control, Paramount, 1941.
The Forgotten Man, Paramount, 1941.
How to Take a Vacation, Paramount, 1941.
Nothing But Nerves, Paramount, 1942.
The Witness, Paramount, 1942.

Keeping in Shape, Paramount, 1942.
The Man's Angle, Paramount, 1942.
My Tomato, MGM, 1943.
No News Is Good News, MGM, 1943.
Important Business, MGM, 1944.
Why, Daddy?, MGM, 1944.
I'm a Civilian Here Myself, U.S. Navy, 1945.

Secondary Sources

Article

Gibbs, Wolcott. "Robert Benchley: In Memoriam." *New York Times Book Review*, December 16, 1945, p. 3. Biographical material, anecdotes, and critical evaluation by a fellow humorist and friend.

Books and Material in Books

Benchley, Nathaniel. *Robert Benchley: A Biography*. New York: McGraw-Hill, 1955. More reliable than the average "authorized" biography. By Benchley's elder son, a playwright, novelist, and short story writer.

Redding, Robert. *Starring Robert Benchley*. Albuquerque: University of New Mexico Press, 1973. Deals with Benchley's career in Hollywood. Includes "A Survey of Robert Benchley's Motion Picture Work."

Rosmond, Babette. *Robert Benchley: His Life and Good Times*. Garden City, N.Y.: Doubleday, 1970. A chatty biography based in part on interviews with a number of Benchley's friends.

Solomon, Eric. "Notes toward a Definition of Robert Benchley's Humor." *Studies in American Humor*, 3, N.S. (Spring 1984):34–46. Concludes that Benchley was "a humorist for all seasons, theatrical and journalistic, and his critical writing is as valuable as his creative achievement" (p. 45).

Thurber, James. *Credos and Curios*. New York: Harper & Row, 1962, pp. 146–152. Stresses the liveliness of Benchley's style and his influence on Thurber.

Yates, Norris W. *Robert Benchley*. New York: Twayne, 1968. A critical-analytical survey. Includes a discussion of Benchley's theory and practice of humor and a detailed examination of Benchley's humorous techniques.

————. "Robert Benchley's Normal Bumbler." In Yates's *The American Humorist: Conscience of the Twentieth Century*. Ames, Iowa: Iowa State University Press, 1964, pp. 241–261. Emphasizes the sanity of Benchley's humor.

L. Moody Simms, Jr.

Bierce, Ambrose Gwinett

Born: Horse Cave Creek, Ohio, on June 24, 1842
Education: Kentucky Military Institute, 1859–1860
Marriage: Mollie Day, December 25, 1871, three children
Died: 1914 (?) (disappeared in Mexico)

Biography and Literary Analysis

"I was one of those poor devils born to work as a peasant in the fields, but I found no difficulty getting out of it," Ambrose Bierce wrote of his origins. Born on June 24, 1842, in Horse Cave Creek, Ohio, Bierce was the tenth of thirteen children born to a farm couple he described as "unwashed savages" and religious fanatics. Like Mark Twain, William Dean Howells, Bret Harte, Hamlin Garland, Frank Norris, and Theodore Dreiser, apprentice-printer's work and newspaper writing were his real education, for Bierce's formal secondary education consisted of a single year at the Kentucky Military Institute. Then came the Civil War. Bierce's most interesting biographer, Richard O'Connor, notes that in 1861 Bierce "was only one of thousands of restless, disaffected American males who must have heard the echo of Fort Sumter's guns with a feeling almost of relief, of joyous anticipation."[1]

War amazed Bierce, but it did not disappoint him. To Bierce, looking back up at its thrilling intensity from the slough of late middle age, the great Union victory at Shiloh seemed to be the supreme moment of his life: "I will willingly surrender another life than the one I should have thrown away at Shiloh." Both of Bierce's most famous and oft-anthologized short stories are set in the Civil War, and both have savagely ironic trick endings that dramatize war's absurdity. "Chicamauga" presents a silent, horrific version of carnage as seen through the eyes of a deaf child, and "An Occurrence at Owl Creek Bridge" depends for its effect upon one of the most famous of all "surprise endings" in literature, the astonished discovery by the reader that a Confederate patriot's miraculous deliverance from death at the end of a Union hangman's rope is only the last, desperate fantasy of the man's mind during the milliseconds just before his destruction.

No other significant literary imagination in our heritage has experienced more than a fraction of the dangers, terror, irony, and exaltation in warfare that caught up and transformed Bierce just as he reached manhood. He served the Union from the outbreak of hostilities in 1861 until Lee's surrender at Appomattox, fought with great distinction in a half-dozen of the war's most murderous engagements, nearly died of a head wound at the Battle of Kenesaw Mountain, accompanied Sherman's fiery march from Atlanta to the sea, and even played what he described as an "exceedingly disagreeable" role in post-war Reconstruction, serving in Alabama as a Treasury aide whose duties were to confiscate Confederate property as war indemnity. War furnished him a sensibility and material to engage it—a career. He loved war. Finally, he was to die in it. As an old man of 72, famous as a cynic and iconoclast and *enfant térrible* and a guru to younger men like H.L. Mencken who had appointed themselves nay-sayers to an America captivated by Teddy Roosevelt's stagey heroics at San Juan Hill, Bierce visited for a last, elegiac time the battlefields of his young manhood and then disappeared forever into the firestorm of the Mexican revolution of 1913-1914. It was a melodramatic and mysterious death quite worthy of one of the most colorful lives an American writer ever lived. If Hollywood had concocted Bierce's life, the script would have been dismissed as B-movie claptrap. Nor does the fusion of genius with adventure (as in the case of, say, Rudyard Kipling, Jack London, or Ernest Hemingway) usually lead us to expect a reputation for cynical wit and misanthropic satire. But, then, everything about Bierce is a surprise.

A trip to Panama and an expedition to explore and map the Indian-haunted plains and mountains between Nebraska and California (Bierce was now a major in the post-war Army) were Bierce's next adventures after his Civil War years. "I left the one road a few miles out of a Nebraskan village and met the other at Dutch Flat, in California," he wrote. In between, Bierce's mapping party found the West of Sioux, buffalo, and wolves beautiful and exotic, and he fell in love with California once and for all.

Settling in San Francisco in 1866, Bierce began to educate himself by reading the classics; in the next year he was contributing mawkishly romantic poems to newspapers like the *Californian* but soon began imitating Mark Twain and Bret Harte for the *Golden Era, Alta California,* and the satirical weekly *News-Letter.* He emerged as a widely quoted satirical wit when he became the mainstay of the *News-Letter's* "Town Crier" page and the paper's editor, James Watkins, helped polish and sharpen Bierce's style by getting him to read Jonathan Swift, Voltaire, and William Makepeace Thackeray. Watkins insisted that Bierce subdue his tendency toward vulgarity and noisy indignation and find more subtle weapons, and Bierce soon developed the effortless, stainless-steel economy of the brilliant satirist and wit; his streak of morbidity and sadism lent those metallic flashes a startling clarity and quotability: "Woman fell in sewer. Sweets to the sweet." Separated by a typographical device he called "Telegraphical Dottings," Bierce discovered a convenient means to display his wit even as he denied any vestige of logical progression or linkage between items. Thus: "Successful abortion. The woman died.-.-.French priest has abandoned the errors of the Romish for those of the Protestant Church.-.-.Young ruffians insult school girls. School girls like it.-.-.Olympic Club muscle men elected performing and executive apes.-.-.The average morality of the country has increased by the death of two Kentucky sheriffs, killed in action.-.-.Governor Walker of Virginia is inaugurated. There! That's the last we shall hear of him until he is arrested for stealing."

Bierce married Mollie Day, a San Francisco girl of good family, on Christmas Day in 1871, and in 1872 he closed out his "Town Crier" column with advice to his readers not to "trust humanity without collateral security; it will play you some dirty trick" and left for London, the great literary capital of the day.

Buttressed by Mollie's father's money and with Ambrose already known in English literary circles as an impudent wit, the Bierces (two sons, Day and Leigh, and a daughter, Helen, were soon added to the family) spent the years 1872-1875 in London, where Bierce contributed to *Fun* and *Tom Hood's Comic Annual,* edited two issues of a pro-royalist journal called *The Lantern* for the exiled French Empress Eugénie, and published under the pseudonym Dod Grile three collections of vitriolic sketches and witticisms, *The Fiend's Delight* (1873), *Nuggets and Dust Panned Out of California* (the American Wild West was a tremendous hit in Victorian England), and *Cobwebs from an Empty Skull* (1874). The English called him "Bitter" Bierce.

Homesickness (mostly Mollie's) and Bierce's asthmatic condition prompted the family's return to San Francisco in 1875. Bierce could find no writing work so he took a position at the U.S. Mint's assay office (San Francisco was in the toils of a deep recession). In 1877 he finally got back into journalism as associate editor of a newly founded weekly called the *Argonaut.* In this journal Bierce's "Prattle" column, a bath of vitriolic and witty political and literary invective into which every notable writer, politician, and personality on the Pacific Slope sooner or later was doomed to be immersed, made its author famous and feared again and involved Bierce so deeply in local feuds that he took to wearing his army Colt on the street only partly as a publicity stunt. His published wit was audacious to the point of libel. For example, on the death of a prominent Oakland citizen, the author of "Prattle" noted: "The personal property of the late

Anthony Chabot, of Oakland, has been ordered sold. This is a noble opportunity to obtain Senator Vrooman." Half court jester, half scourge, Bierce had become the arbiter of taste and truth for the literate minority of the western United States. Bierce wrote and drank, ignored his children, and tried to avoid his mother-in-law, who spent most of her waking hours under his roof. But, life, as life will, closed in.

In 1880 Bierce caught gold fever and, as O'Connor writes, could not resist the opportunity to strike out for the Dakota badlands and leave his mother-in-law in charge of his family while he put "a few mountain ranges between himself and the dragon on his hearth."[2] The adventure was a fiasco, and Bierce's position as agent for the Black Hills Placer Mining Company turned out to be merely a front for a stock-manipulation scheme. Even if Bierce gained no wealth, though (there was a great deal more fraud than gold in them thar hills), the atmosphere of the place must have had a sardonic appeal for him. One of the most infamous of the hired guns Bierce hired to keep to guard against highwaymen was listed on the company payroll as "Boone May, murderer," and years after the fact Bierce revealed (with more than a hint of grisly pride) that he and Boone had executed with their own *ad hoc* firing squad a bandit who attempted to relieve the company of its payroll while its chief officer was travelling by wagon through the mountain fastness to pay his miners. As his own salary was in arrears and the fraudulence of the company was increasingly evident, Bierce returned to San Francisco and journalism in 1881. He was to be San Francisco's pet curmudgeon for the next decade.

During 1881–1886, Bierce wrote his "Prattle" column for a satirical weekly called *The Wasp*, and in this period he began to precipitate out of his disillusion those crystal darts of wit that became the entries in *The Devil's Dictionary*. In 1887 he began the long and tumultuous association with William Randolph Hearst's *San Francisco Examiner* and the rest of the Hearst publishing empire that was to be the conduit of Bierce's greatest notoriety. Even though the years with Hearst made Bierce famous and modestly well off, and indeed allowed him to perfect what is arguably the most distinctive satirical style in the history of American letters, his personal life was a train of disappointments and tragedy.

In 1888 he was separated from Mollie, and in the following year his first-born son, Day, was killed in a gun duel over a girl. In 1901 his second son, Leigh, died of drink. Bierce's own drinking and his asthma grew worse. Sent to Washington, D.C., by Hearst to head a lobbying effort opposing congressional passage of Collis Huntington's Funding Bill for Central and Southern Pacific Railroads (Bierce was successful in defeating it), he took up residence in the capital, living there with a woman named Carrie Christiansen. Bierce's daughter, Helen, described Carrie as an "extremely plain little person whom he had taken from a dull small town in California," but the little person took Bierce "for one of the gods" and served the master as confidant, nurse, typist, and, no doubt, mistress.

Bierce's most famous short stories are unmistakably written in purple ink on loan from Edgar Allan Poe but they are usually very good examples of their kind. His best collection, *Tales of Soldiers and Civilians*, was published in 1891. *The Monk and The Hangman's Daughter* (1892) is a medieval romance that Bierce translated from the German. *Black Beetles in Amber* (1892) consists of witty verses in a satirical vein; later poems were published in *Shapes of Clay* (1903). *Can Such Things Be?* (1893) was a collection of tales dealing with macabre and magical incidents and set in frontier California and the Civil War. Contemporary political and social issues were satirized in mock-Aesopian style in *Fantastic Fables* (1899), and *The Shadow on the Dial* (1909) consists of essays on the ills of contemporary civilization. In the style of that over-leisured, over-acquiring age, the enormous output of Bierce's lifetime in letters was assembled in no fewer than twelve volumes in 1912. Now a collected author, three score and ten, asthmatic, and with his sons dead before him, Bierce found in the bloodthirsty tumult of the Mexican revolution a convenient means of extinguishing himself. "To be a gringo in Mexico," Bierce wrote just before his final disappearance, "ah, that is euthanasia." He was never heard from again.

Bierce's fame as a humorist depends on the compilation he first titled *The Cynic's Word Book* (1906), later retitled *The Devil's Dictionary*. The critic H. Greenbough Smith points out that Dr. Samuel Johnson was in the habit of occasionally "gingering" his dictionary with a witty epigram or some other "outbreak of petulant wit"; thus, Johnson, in the midst of his sober and painstaking lexicography, would set an entry agleam with a little flash of playfulness, defining, say, "oats" as the food of horses in England but in Scotland that of men. Greenbough suggests that Bierce strove to eliminate the sobriety and "make a whole volume of such coruscations, all satire, sting, and sparkle."[3] Humor is essentially the fulfillment of our logical expectation in a way that we did not expect, and *The Devil's Dictionary* is an example *par excellence* of the practice.

The precision and economy of Bierce's epigrams and comic definitions are unlike anything else in our heritage. In a land that has always said *yes*, Bierce most emphatically says *never*. For example, the entry for "positive" reads: "mistaken at the top of one's voice." An auctioneer is "a man who proclaims with his hammer that he has picked a pocket with his tongue," and "success" is simply "the one unpardonable sin." The precision of Bierce's phrasing is admirable in itself, but, of course, our major delight in his performance proceeds from the comical wisdom frozen inside the crystals of his wit, a wisdom with which we ruefully must agree. Thus, a "year" is "a period of 365 disappointments"; "peace" is "a period of cheating between two wars"; and "prayer" is a request "that the laws of the universe be annuled in behalf of an unworthy petitioner." "Politeness" Bierce defines as "acceptable hypocrisy" and "history" as "an account mostly false of events mostly unimportant, which are brought about by rulers mostly knaves, and soldiers mostly fools." Humor like this demands to be admired *as a performance*; it does not win hearts: Bierce displays; he never shares.

Summary

From Mark Twain to today's television situation comedies, the American comic imagination tends to try to create an atmosphere of pleasant, folksy camaraderie, and the enormous success of humorists and entertainers like Twain, Robert Benchley, George S. Kaufman, Jack Benny, Will Rogers, Bob Hope, Russell Baker, Neil Simon, Johnny Carson, Chevy Chase, Eddie Murphy, and Bill Cosby derives less from their wit than from their companionability. None of these public personas could be described as cynical; all seem knowing and sophisticated without the slightest suggestion of *real* anger or despair. American comedy from Tom Sawyer to Andy Griffith has had nothing to do with rage, nor do our most durable humorists ever bring the foundations of things into question or seem to be giving outrage a savage twist, as Swift does in the greatest and angriest of all satires, "A Modest Proposal." Bierce's cynical wit and unquenchable misanthropic satire stand apart from the mainstream, and we are always aware that he is substituting shafts of wit for the real weapons he wielded in the Civil War. Bierce's, we feel, is a literary imagination gathered about a bottomless darkness. His disciples were Savonarolas like Mencken and Sinclair Lewis who attacked American culture as something essentially diseased and unwholesome, their humor a surgeon's scalpel—or that other sharp instrument of corrective surgery, a guillotine blade. Of all our humorists, Bierce is the most singular, the darkest, the least likely. One can find his legacy in the "black" comedy of Thomas Pynchon, Joseph Heller,

Kurt Vonnegut, Robert Coover, and John Barth, a humor of outrage and counterattack.

Notes

1. Richard O'Connor, *Ambrose Bierce* (Boston: Little, Brown, 1967), p. 19.
2. Ibid., p. 119.
3. Cathy Davidson, *Critical Essays on Ambrose Bierce* (Boston: G.K. Hall, 1982), p. 54.

Selected Bibliography

Primary Sources (contemporary editions only)

Ambrose Bierce's Civil War. Ed. William McCann. New York: Sagamore Press, 1957.

The Collected Writings of Ambrose Bierce. Ed. Clifton Fadiman. New York: Citadel, 1960.

Ghost and Horror Stories of Ambrose Bierce. Ed. E.F. Bleiler. New York: Dover, 1964.

The Enlarged Devil's Dictionary. Compiled and ed. Ernest Jerome Hopkins. Garden City: Doubleday, 1967.

The Complete Short Stories of Ambrose Bierce. Ed. Ernest Jerome Hopkins. Rpt. with foreword by Cathy N. Davidson. Lincoln: University of Nebraska, 1984.

Secondary Sources

Davidson, Cathy N., ed. *Critical Essays on Ambrose Bierce.* Boston: G.K. Hall, 1982. Excellent collection with reviews by Bierce's contemporaries and fourteen essays on his work contributed by critics of today.

———. *The Experimental Fiction of Ambrose Bierce: Structuring the Ineffable.* Lincoln: University of Nebraska, 1984. An intelligent assessment.

Fatout, Paul. *Ambrose Bierce: The Devil's Lexiographer.* Norman: Oklahoma University Press. Special attention to Bierce's *Dictionary.*

Grenander, M.E. *Ambrose Bierce.* New York: Twayne, 1971. Compact biography and assessment.

Hicks, Granville. *The Great Tradition: An Interpretation of American Literature Since The Civil War.* 2nd ed., rev. New York: Macmillan, 1935. Bierce is seen as a gothicist in a classic survey of our literary heritage.

Mencken, H.L. "Ambrose Bierce." In *Prejudices: Sixth Series.* New York: Knopf, 1927. Homage from a disciple. Funny and accurate.

O'Connor, Richard. *Ambrose Bierce.* Boston: Little, Brown, 1967. Charming biography by a Civil War scholar.

Douglas Fowler

Bloomingdale, Teresa

Born: St. Joseph, Missouri, on July 26, 1930
Education: Duchesne College, B.A. in English, 1952; Creighton University, graduate study
Marriage: A. Lee Bloomingdale, 1955, ten children

Biography

Teresa Bloomingdale was born July 26, 1930, in St. Joseph, Missouri, daughter of Arthur V. Burrowes (newspaper editor) and Helen Cooney Burrowes. After receiving her B.A. in English from Duchesne College, Omaha, she worked as a legal secretary at Creighton University School of Law from 1952-1954. From 1954-1955 she taught at Webster School, St. Joseph, Missouri. She was married on July 2, 1955, to A. Lee Bloomgindale, attorney and president of Mutual Protective Insurance Co., Omaha. While actively pursuing a career as writer and lecturer, Teresa Bloomingdale mothered her ten children: Lee, John, Michael, James, Mary, Daniel, Peggy, Ann, Timothy, and Patrick.

Now a grandmother as well as a mother of school-age children, Bloomgindale continues writing "on a very strict schedule, sitting down to the typewriter about 8:30 A.M. (after the children have gone to school) and stopping at 3:30 P.M. when they come home."[1]

Literary Analysis

Teresa Bloomingdale bases her themes on her personal experience: family humor and career humor. (She reports that she is not surprised to find the former more popular than the latter.) Her first three books—*I Should Have Seen It Coming When the Rabbit Died* (1979), *Up a Family Tree* (1981), and *Murphy Must Have Been a Mother* (1982)—talk about her life as a mother and wife. Her fourth book—*Life Is What Happens When You're Making Other Plans* (1984)—claims to emphasize her experiences as author, columnist, lecturer, talk show guest, but it is clear here also that her family is her main concern. Bloomingdale dedicates *Other Plans* to her ten children ("The fortunate results of my making other plans!") and acknowledges the help of her mother and sister in writing the flip little verses preceding each chapter.

Life Is What Happens When You're Making Other Plans lays out Bloomingdale's rules of etiquette for embarrassed career ladies; her pet peeves (such as video games, grocery coupons, and reruns of *Casablanca*); her advice to aspiring authors; her appearance on television talk shows; her visit to her New York publisher with her daughter Mary; her thirties-and-forties vocabulary for Young Americans (including

"Going Steady," "Being Pinned," "Chaperone," and "Boogie-Woogie"); her "Show and Sell" of the family house; her plotting a far-away vacation with her husband; and so on. Reminiscent of her earlier books, there is a chapter on letters that Bloomingdale has composed in her head but has never written—letters to childhood enemies, benefactors, authorities—and even to Paul Newman, who is to pass the letter on to Robert Redford in case he himself isn't interested (*Other Plans*, p. 149). One of the most revealing chapters deals with the journal her eldest daughter persuaded her to keep—like Pepys. Preliminary preparations were exhausting: pen or pencil? what kind? what color ink? when to write? where to keep the journal? The contents turned out to be most prosaic—truly boring—until she made up an entry about Johnny Carson's calling her for his show and about Joanne Woodward's calling to ask whether Paul was there (*Other Plans*, p. 177).

The final chapter of *Other Plans*, "Notes from a Liberated Lady," encapsulates Bloomingdale's view of herself. Though she "rather liked the idea of coming down off [her] lonely pedestal and piddling around with a little career," she absolutely refuses to look under the hood of a car, fill out an income tax return, mow the lawn, or clean the garage:

> God intended for *man* to clean the garage; it says so in the Bible. "Whereas, woman shall dust, and woman shall cook, and woman shall wash the clothes, *woman shall not clean out the garage*; so sayeth the Lord, sayeth She." (*The Book of Betsy*, Chapter IV, verse iii, New Translation).[2]

In subject matter and style, Bloomingdale admits to being influenced by Aloise Buckley Heath, another mother of ten, whose humor Bloomingdale calls "clean and classy, gentle and loving." An even stronger influence was Jean Kerr's *Please Don't Eat the Daisies* (published, coincidentally, about Kerr's four sons under age four the same year Bloomingdale had her fourth son in three-and-a-half years).[3] Although she may be classified with such popular writers of "domestic" female humor as Erma Bombeck and Peg Bracken, Teresa Bloomingdale is more restrictive in her topics and more delicate in her treatment than Bombeck and Bracken, who often range more widely and prod more sharply.

Bloomingdale writes with great affection for her subjects. Her voice is soft, and her words are simple; but they have a charm that can capture quite as effectively as those of her more abrasive literary sisters. Mother of ten and grandmother of two, Teresa Bloomingdale is still actively engaged in writing humorous books, articles, columns, and reviews dealing with domestic female life; in editing, lecturing, and making guest appearances on television and radio. She still has unfulfilled ambitions: to "write a humorous diary for every mother who cannot take" the tour around the world that Bloomingdale would like to take as well as "a murder mystery" and "The Great American Novel."[4]

Notes

1. Letter from Teresa Bloomingdale to Martha A. Fisher, January 12, 1985.
2. *Life Is What Happens When You're Making Other Plans*, p. 213. Bloomingdale adds, "Frankly, I love my husband too much to upset the order of his garage. (Forgive me, sisters; some people are too old to change.)."
3. Letter from Teresa Bloomingdale to Martha A. Fisher, January 12, 1985. Another instance of Bloomingdale's admiration for Kerr is revealed in one of her short pieces, "Mom, I Need a Costume!" (*McCall's*, May 1982, pp. 82, 118, 120). Here Bloomingdale singles out for special praise the chapter in *Please Don't Eat the Daisies* about costuming Kerr's son Christopher as a back tire for his school play.
4. Letter from Teresa Bloomingdale to Martha A. Fisher, January 12, 1985.

Selected Bibliography

Primary Sources

Major Works
I Should Have Seen It Coming When the Rabbit Died. New York: Doubleday, 1979.
Up a Family Tree. New York: Doubleday, 1981.
Murphy Must Have Been a Mother. New York: Doubleday, 1982.
Life Is What Happens When You're Making Other Plans. New York: Doubleday, 1984.
Sense and Momsense. New York: Doubleday, 1986.

As Columnist
Omaha Sun, 1976–1978.
Omaha Metro, 1972–1977.

As Contributing Editor
McCall's, 1982–1984.

As Contributor
Good Housekeeping, Our Sunday Visitor, Catholic Digest, and other periodicals.

Secondary Sources
Interview. *Omaha Magazine*, 1982.
Interview. *Writer's Digest*, February, 1983.
Letter to Martha A. Fisher, January 12, 1985.

Martha A. Fisher

Blount, Roy, Jr.

Born: Indianapolis, Indiana, on October 4, 1941

Education: Decatur (Georgia) High School, 1955–1959; Vanderbilt University, B.A. (*magna cum laude*), 1959–1963; Harvard University, M.A. (English), 1963–1964

Marriages: Ellen Pearson, September 6, 1964, two children, divorced, March 1973; Joan Ackermann, 1976

Biography

A self-styled "Crackro-American" humorist, Roy Blount, Jr., has plied his trade as a sports writer, commentator on contemporary relationships between men and women, and political analyst. He has published a portrait of the Pittsburgh Steelers' 1973 season, a study of Jimmy Carter's presidency, and three collections of essays and light verse. He has served as staff writer and associate editor of *Sports Illustrated*, where he specialized in the offbeat in sports, and more recently as a contributing editor to *The Atlantic*. He has also appeared regularly on televison and radio, notably on *The Tonight Show* and on National Public Radio's *Prairie Home Companion*.

Born October 4, 1941, in Indianapolis, Indiana, Blount (pronounced *blunt*) grew up in Decatur, Georgia, a suburb of Atlanta. His father, Roy Alton Blount, a savings and loan director, was a civic-minded man, active in the Methodist church. His mother, Louise Floyd Blount, he credits with teaching him to read. He and his sister, Susan, were given a "clean and decent" middle-class upbringing.[1] When his dreams of playing professional baseball began fading, he turned in high school to writing. Exhilarated by the success of "Roy's Noise," his column in the Decatur High School newspaper, he decided that "writing Humor was my vocation."[2] His promise as a writer earned him a Grantland Rice sportswriting scholarship to Vanderbilt University, where in addition to writing for the school newspaper, the *Decatur-Dekalb News*, and (during a summer's internship) the *New Orleans Times-Picayune*, he distinguished himself as the alternate mascot (Mr. Commodore) and as a student. Elected to Phi Beta Kappa, Blount graduated magna cum laude in 1963 and won a Woodrow Wilson fellowship to continue graduate study in English at Harvard. (His favorite course was "Difficult Fiction.") In September 1964, he married Ellen Pearson, and with an M.A. in English, he joined the Army, where in two years he earned the rank of first lieutenant, without, as he describes it, seriously harming anyone else or himself. In 1966, he returned to journalism as a writer and columnist for the Atlanta *Journal.* At first he feared that he could not make a living from humor, partly because he was not as good at it as he had imagined he was in high school and partly because of the "historical moment," the 1960s, when humor tended toward "theater of the Absurd and Black Humor, neither of which is funny."[3] Nevertheless, as a *Journal* columnist he discovered a way to be funny and to deal with pressing social and political issues. Frequently using humor, satire, and light verse (especially limericks), he earned a name for himself as a proponent of civil rights and a scourge of "cultural enemies." He also tried teaching for one year as an instructor at Georgia State College (1967-1968) before leaving Atlanta for a position as a staff writer at *Sports Illustrated* in New York City. "Writing for a Georgia outlet," he has said of the move north, "is like putting on skits for your parents: you can only go so far."[4] For several years (1968-74) he regularly wrote for *SI*, and from 1974-75 he served as an associate editor. His first book, *Three Bricks Shy of a Load*, grew out of an *SI* assignment: he "hung out" with the Pittsburgh Steelers during their 1973 season to write an inside account of life in and around professional football. In that year, too, Blount's marriage ended in divorce; in 1976 he married Joan Ackermann, a writer, and moved to Mill River, Massachusetts, a rural town in the Berkshires, some two hours from New York City and near his two children from his first marriage, Ennis and John Kirven. In 1980, he published *Crackers*, a study of Jimmy Carter's presidency, the South entering the 1980s, and his own roots. He also has published three collections of his short pieces, written for an impressive list of magazines, over thirty "pathologically disparate publications"[5] from *The New York Times Book Review* and *The New Yorker* to *Playboy*, *Organic Gardening*, and *Rolling Stone*. Blount admits that magazine writing "wears you down after a while." It is, he has said, "like dating a lot of beautiful women . . . Someday, you've gotta settle down."[6] While he has expressed interest in writing a novel, he admits that his tendency is toward short pieces.

Literary Analysis

Blount might be called a cosmopolitan regionalist. Although he lives in Massachusetts and writes for the best national publications, his values are southern. He may quote Kierkegaard or Sartre, but his standard is what passes muster in the South. While prejudice and ignorance are very much a part of his South, so are common sense and a pleasure in quirkiness, especially in language. Blount explains that in leaving Georgia he left behind the "oral resonance" of the South but also the closemindedness that sees the

Pentagon as "pure needed" and "fatherless babies in the ghetto as cases of threateningly unbridled self-interest."[7] Like Mark Twain, one of his literary heroes, he writes from New England with a southerner's perspective. He quotes approvingly Twain's description of the South: "Ignorance, intolerance, egotism, self-assertion, opaque perception, dense and pitiful chuckleheadedness—and almost pathetic unconsciousness of it all."[8] Blount recognizes, however, that with chuckleheadedness also comes an exuberance rare in an increasingly homogenized America. As a result, he finds his adopted home in Massachusetts to be "generally speaking—more tasteful than Georgia but less tasty."[9] To the editors of *Contemporary Authors* he describes his politics as "Dated white Southern liberalism, with healthy undertones of redneckery and anarchism; nostalgia for Earl Long,"[10] the Louisiana governor whose flights of mental instability were legendary. Southernness, Blount has said, gives him a kind of "ballast"[11] in judging the contemporary scene, but clearly it is an unpredictable ballast.

The southern love of language especially delights Blount. Southerners, he says, "derive energy from figures of speech, as plants do from photosynthesis."[12] One of the South's great virtues is its "way of *personalizing* things. *Literalizing* things."[13] He notes with pleasure that Southern Baptists *"talk to Jesus,"* and that the "sorriest white people" in the South think they can be anonymous by wearing white robes with *points* on them. Blount imagines how refreshing Alabama football coach Bear Bryant's style would be if it replaced educational jargon. Fostering "enhanced positive learning experientialization" would become "What you got to do is, keep your weight low to the ground, get your head in under the student's rib cage, and *thrust* upward."[14]

Blount rejoices in all of those who go against the grain, especially those who joyfully goof up and without a moment's anxiety embarrass themselves. One of the best statements of this credo appears in an essay, "'I Always Plead Guilty,'" the response of Alabama politician Big Jim Folsom to any charge of corruption. Blount praises those spirited enough to make astounding mistakes, a behavior that he calls "celebrative, life-enhancing, go-get'em fucking up."[15] He argues that King Lear and Oedipus had that ability, but too many modern men, Ronald Reagan, Wayne Newton, Alan Alda, among them, lack it. Blount exaggerates his case, but he notes with respect Dr. Martin Luther King, Jr.'s not-dissimilar call for "creative maladjustment."[16] Style that honestly marks one as individual means a lot to Blount, in athletics or in writing. He worries about his own precision and timing, whether swinging a bat against a baseball machine, catching a football from Terry Bradshaw, or crafting a sentence.

Being born in the year that E.B. and Katharine White's *Subtreasury of American Humor* was published (1941) was a happy omen, Blount feels, because *The New Yorker* humorists—Robert Benchley, Ring Lardner, James Thurber, S.J. Perelman—became the "heroes of my adolescence."[17] Still, Blount's grain is southern, and so in "Who is the Funniest American Writer?" he pays homage to Twain, that other "desouthernized Southerner," whose humor is "dark inside but makes you smile profoundly."[18] Blount also acknowledges the influence of his contemporaries, especially Hunter S. Thompson, whose madcap political reporting he admires, and Garrison Keillor, whose sophisticated provincialism he shares. While Blount admits that Nora Ephron is not a stylist, he credits her with bringing the collection of "humor piecework," brief meditations on the ironies of everyday life, back to the top of bestseller lists.

In his first book, *Three Bricks Shy of a Load* (1974), Blount fulfills the boyhood dream of "making it in the NFL," but as a "scribe," a sports journalist just outside the huddle of the Pittsburgh Steelers during their 1973 season. Playing pro football, he concludes, is a "brutal and peculiar line of work," and you have to "be hungry and strange—*missing* something" to undertake it. "But," he adds quickly, "how sensible an occupation is writing?" (p. x). Blount spent six months with the Steelers from training camp through the draft in January. He chose the Steelers because, he says, they had a reputation for eccentricity—"I like to be surrounded by a certain *kind* of decadence . . ." (p. 18). Head coach Chuck Noll lacked Blount's virtue of doing "something crazy" (p. 235), but there were plenty of unpredictable characters among the players, owners, scouts, fans, and referees: a pole-vaulter who dreamt of his pole becoming a rope, a one-eyed center who blocked a referee, a player so slow he "even falls slow" (p. 311), a wife who described her husband's personality as sterling because he never used it, a big running back who could not understand "them audubons" of college football (p. 283). Along the way Blount reveals himself: we learn that he is six feet tall and weighs 200 pounds, that at Harvard he sensed that he was out of his element when critic I. A. Richards swooned while reading Shelley, that he served as a model for a character in Dan Jenkins's novel, *Semi-Tough*. Blount proves that he can be one of the guys, but readers need a liberal education to appreciate his insight fully. Franco Harris's running style he compares to the sculptures of Brancusi, and to analyze other Steelers he quotes such authorities as Schopenhauer, Henry Adams, and Samuel Johnson.

In *Crackers* Blount presents himself as a "Crackro-American" writer, one "*from* Georgia but *outside* Georgia, who could sort of intermediate" (p. 59) and explain the Carter administration to the nation. He addresses the celebrated events of Carter's presidency, the attack by a rabbit, the *Playboy* interview, the failed raid to free the hostages in Iran. Crackers, according to Blount, are *supposed* to bring "rip-roaring red-blooded embarrassment" (p. 189); Southerners are "chosen people," whose duty is "to be out of whack, to hold back, to be unamalgamated" (p. 185). Carter's failure, according to Blount, was not that he was "tacky and awful," but that he wasn't "*profoundly* tacky enough" (p. 53). "Jimmy *moderates* to excess," Blount complains (p. 192). The Southerners whom Blount finds fascinating are earthier men such as Billy Carter, Andrew Young, Big Jim Folsom, Jerry Jeff Walker (a Southerner in spirit). All are capable of "abandon," keeping people off balance; they are funnier, more eloquent, more able "to raise hell" (p. 114) than the first "cracker president." "I don't want people to be *right* all the time," Blount concludes. In rip-roaring contrast to the president's moderation, Blount offers italicized portraits of "More Carters," imaginary but authentic crackers of the clan, such as Velveeta Carter of Bird Swale, Tenn., and A. Don and E. Don Carter, 39, the "Two-Headed Four-Armed Three-Legged Gospel Singing Man" (p. 51).

One Fell Soup (1982) is a collection of essays and light verse on social issues ("Facing Ismism"), language and letters (the glut of special interest magazines such as *Deep End: The Depressive's Companion*), sports (from cricket fighting to batting practice), the eternal verities ("The Socks Problem," on disappearing socks), and sex ("The Family Jewels," "After Pink—What?"). One of the best essays is a spoof on "the new orgasm," published first in *Cosmopolitan*. Blount discusses the "mounting new skepticism toward the orgasm" which has even led to the formation on college campuses of Anti-Excitement Leagues. One critic, V.N. Menander Spurgeon, has discovered that the word *orgasm* derives from "*Orgasmus*, the Greek god of playing with dynamite" (p. 135). Another, M.O. Naseberry, has studied a town of no orgasms, Impassive, Montana, where folks get their thrill with Rototilling. There are also some delightful sports pieces. In "Five Ives Gets Names," a dramatic monologue in the tradition of Lardner, the speaker, a rookie jumped up on 5 milligrams of speed, is called on to bunt but instead homers. In an essay on the difficulty of writing on participation sports such as bowling, Blount renders the sound of a strike: "vum vum rml rml rml rml DEBACLE!" (p. 182). Blount's perspective, that of a learned and astute good old boy, is clear in his suggestion in "The Presidential Sports Profile" that we judge presidents on their ability as athletes or even as fans: "If you have a sense of what it would be like to get stuck watching 'Monday Night Football' with someone . . . you have a sense of what it would be like to get stuck with him as your President" (p. 216). Finally, Blount includes some of his best light verse, such as the couplet "Song Against Broccoli": "The neighborhood stores are all out of broccoli/ Loccoli" (p. 57).

In *What Men Don't Tell Women* (1984) Blount offers a collection of pieces on the contemporary scene held together by "scraps of testimony, from men of many stripes, reveal-ing for the first time the things men don't tell." These revelations he calls "blue yodels" in tribute to the Mississippi Brakeman, country singer Jimmie Rodgers, who "made an art of the pained moaning sound" (p. 8). In Blount's "Blue Yodels," male voices worry over whether high heels are sexy or instruments of bondage, whether the toilet seat should be left up, whether Male Empowerment Workshops can help. The speakers are men befuddled by the opposite sex, men on the defensive. One notes that tears are a woman's terrorism. Another warns that men must hold on to the movie cameras if they want any power over women. "The whole point of being the gender in power," he says, "is that you don't have to be shapely to be attractive" (p. 46). One cannot explain to a woman friend how men can see a "double-edged poignance" in a dirty joke; another laments that women do not know what WD-40 is, so "they don't get about half the remarks in this world" (p. 107). Perhaps the saddest of these fragments of miscommunication is Wes's: "All I know is, living with a woman's love is like swimming with a fish in your arms. You're astonished how you glide. But let your attention dry and the fish will flinch and go deep, and you feel it leave, and you know you didn't hold it right" (p. 157).

In the essays Blount addresses his own quandaries about sex, about his "Pronoun Guilt," for instance: "The careful reader will note that sometimes my pronouns imply that every person in the world is male, and sometimes that he isn't. . . . The question of sexism in pronouns is one that deeply concerns me, since that is the kind of guy I am" (p. 15). He explains "What Authors Do": while the writer candidly confesses, "All I ever wanted was for people not to look at me like I was a dip," the *author* discovers himself recommending Henry James, attending Book and Author Dinners, and chatting on talk shows. One of the best pieces is a portrait of Elvis Presley, "He Took the Guilt out of the Blues," a deed Blount equates with taking "the

smell out of collards" (p. 51). Elvis got white people to "wiggling," and his "historic" grin told young girls everywhere that they had nothing "to feel guilty about but guilt itself" (p. 52). "Why Wayne Newton's is Bigger Than Yours" is a free-wheeling stream of wit touching on salaries, work, Marxism, Freud, Little Richard's love of "bobbycue," and the Fall of Man. (The starting point is the revelation that Newton's yearly earnings expressed in an hourly wage come out to $5,769.23 per hour.) In "How to Sportswrite Good" Blount notes that "Sportswriting is like country music: it is sometimes very good, and sometime when it is really bad it is even better" (p. 158). Two of the best pieces in the collection are on sports, more or less. In "Why Not Active People *in* Beer?" he suggests that advertisers are missing a great opportunity in not emblazoning their ads on the inviting space of tennis courts and hockey ice. In "The Secrets of Rooting," he describes the power of cheerleaders over adolescent males and bemoans the blandness to the adult mind of their cheers and of their national organization, the International Cheerleading Foundation. He remembers a turning point in his life, when as Alternate Mr. Commodore at Vanderbilt, he worked a basketball crowd into a frenzy, racing up and down the sideline, then thrusting a shapely cheerleader in the air. At that moment he realized, however, that with "one more step into the world of pep and spirit and that *kind* of thigh holding, I would never attain intellectual distinction. I would never write for the better magazines." Blount, nonetheless, becomes nostalgic when he notes that his children attend progressive schools where everyone participates in sports and there are no cheerleaders.

In his most recent collection, *Not Exactly What I Had in Mind* (1985), Blount works against the temper of the times and the president for the times, Ronald Reagan, "the most widely beloved American since E.T." (p. xii). In many of the pieces Blount attempts, he says, to "pull against the President's sense of humor without losing hold of mine" (p. xiv). While Reagan uses humor to diminish the seriousness of problems, quipping, for instance, about bombing the Russians, Blount wants humor that ultimately causes us to see ourselves and our foibles more honestly. Blount is especially harsh on what he feels is the president's constituency, the Yuppies. Carl Lewis, for example, exasperates him. Lewis is perfect: a gold medalist in the Olympics, he collects Waterford crystal and carries his own make-up kit. In short, Lewis, the "master of all he deigns to touch" (p. 115), represents a "major affliction" striking "thousands of contemporary Americans" including lawyers, consultants, TV Christians, and Pentagon officials. That affliction, Blount says, has a name in the South: "down home we used to call it Too Stuffed to Jump" (p. 116). American heroes, Blount argues again, should be "out of plumb" (p. 116), and he offers as an example Bill Murray, former star of "Saturday Night Live" and such film comedies as *Ghostbusters.* Murray is a "great kidder" (p. 118), serious about life, yet impishly unpredictable in the way that he lives.

Summary

Blount's books have a conversational flow, one tropic branching into another and another before (usually) returning. Yet, even his collections have a unity of spirit and of device. *What Men Don't Tell Women* is punctuated with "Blue Yodels," moaning voices of contemporary men on their own sex and the other sex. *Crackers* similarly is unified by portraits of "More Carters," those imaginary kinsfolk of the first cracker president. Some insight into Blount's method is suggested by his interest in his compost pile (which he has celebrated in *Organic Gardening*). He sees it as symbolic of his writing: "Compost, to me, is a lot like writing . . . My whole interest is *mix* . . . shredded *Times* . . . etiolated broccoli . . . hair, hulls, worms from Hugh Carter's worm farm, shrimp legs. A *great heterogeneity* of tissues, coming together to create a richness, like unsavory influences forming a style" (pp. 186–187). Blount's humor similarly derives from "mixing things together," the polite and the racy, the learned and the vulgar, and he is not afraid of throwing decorum to the wind. This same pleasure in *heterogeneity* is apparent in his definition of humor, a word that he usually capitalizes: "Whether feverish or laid-back, Humor springs from a certain desperation, which uses jujitsu on looming fear and shame, flirts almost pruriently yet coolly with madness and sentimentality, and fuses horse sense with dream logic."[19]

Notes

1. Roy Blount, Jr., *Crackers: This Whole Many-Angled Thing of Jimmy, More Carters, Ominous Little Animals, Sad-Singing Women, My Daddy and Me* (New York: Alfred Knopf, 1980; rpt. New York: Ballantine, 1982), p. 3.
2. Blount, *Not Exactly What I Had in Mind* (Boston: The Atlantic Monthly Press, 1982), p. 173.
3. Ibid.
4. Blount, *Crackers*, p. 45.
5. Blount, *One Fell Soup, Or I'm Just a Bug on the Windshield of Life* (Boston: Little, Brown, Atlantic Monthly Press, 1982; rpt. New York: Penguin, 1984), p. 7.
6. Ann Evory and Linda Metzger, eds., *Contemporary Authors*, New Rev. Ser., Vol. 10 (Detroit: Gale Research, 1983), pp. 10, 60.
7. Blount, *Not Exactly*, p. xiii.
8. Ibid., p. 159.
9. Ibid., p. 158.
10. Evory and Metzger, *Contemporary Authors*, p. 60.
11. Blount, *About Three Bricks Shy of a Load: A Highly Irregular Lowdown on the Year the Pittsburgh Steelers Were Super but Missed the Bowl* (Boston: Little, Brown, 1974; rpt. New York: Ballantine, 1980), p. 18.
12. Blount, *What Men Don't Tell Women* (Boston: Little, Brown, Atlantic Monthly, 1984; rpt. New York: Penguin Books, 1985), p. 28.
13. Blount, *Crackers*, p. 58.
14. Blount, *Not Exactly*, p. 166.
15. Blount, *What Men*, p. 116.
16. Blount, *Crackers*, p. 237.
17. Blount, *Not Exactly*, p. 171.
18. Ibid., p. 157.
19. Blount, *Not Exactly*, p. 174.

Selected Bibliography

Primary Sources

About Three Bricks Shy of a Load: A Highly Irregular Lowdown on the Year the Pittsburgh Steelers Were Super but Missed the Bowl. Boston: Little, Brown, 1974; rpt. New York: Ballantine, 1980.

Crackers: This Whole Many-Angled Thing of Jimmy, More Carters, Ominous Little Animals, Sad-Singing Women, My Daddy and Me. New York: Alfred Knopf, 1980; rpt. New York: Ballantine, 1982.

One Fell Soup, Or I'm Just a Bug on the Windshield of Life. Boston: Little, Brown and Company, An Atlantic Monthly Press Book, 1982; rpt. New York: Penguin, 1984.

What Men Don't Tell Women. Boston: Little, Brown, An Atlantic Monthly Press, Book, 1984; rpt. New York: Penguin, 1985.

Not Exactly What I Had in Mind. Boston: Atlantic Monthly Press, 1985.

Secondary Source

Contemporary Authors. New Rev. Ser. Vol. 10. Ed. Ann Evory and Linda Metzger. Detroit: Gale Research, 1983.

Grady W. Ballenger

Bombeck, Erma

Born: Dayton, Ohio, on February 21, 1927
Education: Attended Ohio University;
  University of Dayton, B.A. 1949
Marriage: William Bombeck, August 13,
  1949, three children

Biography

Erma Bombeck, humorist and columnist, was born in Dayton, Ohio, on February 21, 1927, to Erma Haines and Cassius Fiste. At fourteen, her mother had married thirty-two-year-old Fiste, and the baby Erma Louise was born two years later. Her father suffered a fatal heart attack on June 4, 1936. After his death, Erma Louise and her mother moved in with her maternal grandmother Haines. The young mother, only twenty-five at that time, found work at Leland Electric factory—a job that required her to report each day for the 7 A.M. shift.[1]

Two years later, when Erma was eleven, her mother remarried. She married Albert "Tom" Harris, a moving-van operator. The little girl found adjustment to a new stepfather difficult but made friends with him after a few months. Hoping to overcome the child's shyness, Erma's mother arranged for her to take tap-dancing lessons. Soon afterward, the mother took Erma Louise for an audition at a local radio station, and the young girl was given a spot with an act that included tap-dancing and singing. She worked at the station for nearly eight years.[2]

Erma Louise attended Emerson Junior High School in Dayton. She began writing (at thirteen or fourteen) a humor column for the school newspaper, *The Owl*, and her interest in singing and dancing diminished as she discovered the challenge of writing.[3]

When she enrolled in Patterson Vocational High School, she took typing and shorthand. Those skills allowed her to get a job as copygirl at the *Dayton Herald*, where she worked after classes every day. By saving her money, she was able to enter Ohio University in Athens, but her funds soon ran out and she went back to Dayton to get a job writing advertising copy, newsletters, and menus for Rike's Department Store. As soon as she began earning money again, she registered at the University of Dayton, a Roman Catholic school, where she earned her B.A. degree in four years, working part time and attending summer school for three summers. She was the first member of her family to earn a college degree.[4]

After graduation she took a full-time job as a reporter for the *Dayton Herald* and renewed her acquaintance with William Bombeck, who had worked as a copyboy for the *Herald* during the time she had worked there as a copygirl. The two fell in love, and they married on August 13, 1949, when Erma was twenty-two.[5]

That year was important for another reason. Bombeck joined the Roman Catholic Church, leaving the United Brethren Church to which all her family had belonged.[6]

After four years of marriage, the Bombecks adopted a little girl, Betsy. Erma gave up her job to stay home with the baby, soon became pregnant with Andrew, and later gave birth to another boy, Matthew. The family moved to Centerville, a tract development a few miles outside Dayton.

Literary Analysis

The years of suburban living were significant for Erma Bombeck. Being caught in the pattern of domesticity with the day-to-day, never-ending chores of cooking, washing, and cleaning gave her insight into the lives of the women around her. She became frustrated over the lack of time and energy for writing and soon realized that the only way to remain sane and deal with her predicament was to laugh at herself and her situation. She did that, and she began to write about her adventures in a way that other housewives and mothers could identify with.

In the early 1960s Erma began writing columns for a suburban weekly, earning three dollars for one column each week. Writing in her bedroom on a desk made of plywood supported by cinder blocks, she was able to do her column while Bill and the children were at school. As time drew near for them to come home, she would put away her work and start dinner for the family.[7] In 1965 the *Dayton Journal* merged with the *Herald*, and Bombeck was invited to write a twice-weekly column. Three weeks later, the *Newsday* syndicate acquired her column, and within a year she found her work appearing in thirty-six newspapers. Doubleday published her first book, *At Wit's End*, in 1967. By that time Bombeck columns were appearing in 200 newspapers across the country. By 1984 almost 900 papers used the columns on a three-times-a-week basis.[8] Six other books have been published. In 1971 Doubleday brought out *Just Wait Until You Have Children of Your Own*, and in 1973 the same firm published another collection of Bombeck columns called *I Lost Everything in the Post-Natal Depression*. Books published since that time have been brought out by McGraw-Hill. They include: *The Grass Is Always Greener over the Septic Tank*, 1976; *If Life Is a Bowl of Cherries, What Am I Doing in the Pits?*, 1978; *Aunt Erma's Cope Book*, 1979; and *Motherhood, the Second Oldest Profession*, 1983.

As the author's books and columns grew in popularity, her career branched out. She became a contributing editor for *Good Housekeeping* magazine and for *Today's Health*.[9] She appears three times a week on the television program, "Good Morning, America."

Honorary degrees have been bestowed upon Bombeck by St. Scholastica College (Duluth, Minnesota), Rosary College (River Forest, Illinois), Bowling Green University (Ohio), The College of Mount St. Joseph on the Ohio, Arizona State University, University of Dayton (her alma mater), Benedictine College (Kansas), and Depauw University. She received a Freedoms Foundation award in 1970.[10] She received the Theta Sigma Phi Headliner Award for outstanding journalistic writing soon after publication of her first book, and this was followed by the Mark Twain Award for humor. The National League of American Pen Women has named her a National Honorary member.

Bombeck's decision to laugh at herself and at the experiences of suburbia has given her a never-ending source of humorous material. The short, good-natured, brown-haired (most of the time) writer says that she spends 90 percent of her time living scripts and 10 percent of her time writing them. Her appeal is universal. She writes about the trauma of keeping house, of rearing children, of living with a husband who is "a football watcher who sits in front of the tube like a dead sponge surrounded by bottle caps."[11]

She is an expert at the art of zeroing in on one or more of the routine domestic bits of housewife drudgery that every reader can identify with. She describes those experiences in terms larger than life and suddenly the reader sees how funny they are. She describes herself as a "nonviolent mother of three unplanned children. I've been married to the same man for thirty-two years, with whom I've never had a meaningful conversation in my entire life. I iron by demand, have a daughter who is twenty-six years old and has no curiosity as to how to turn on a stove. And I have two sons who make Cain and Abel look like Donny and Marie Osmond."[12]

While Bombeck writes on many subjects, most of her columns are concerned with her husband and children. For example, she wrote about her husband, who was content and well in his shady retreat until she goaded him into becoming "The Healthiest-Looking Man in the Doctor's Office." She described her efforts to get Bill Bombeck tanned and after he evidently surrendered to her urging, she closed that column with this statement: "Later as we sat side by side, leafing through a magazine, I tried again. 'I know you don't agree with me now, but believe me when I tell you, you are the healthiest-looking man in this doctor's office.'"[13]

Mothers around the world can identify with the column called "I Dedicated Myself to the Tooth Cult," one of her columns reprinted by request. When braces became the status symbol of the 1960s, her dentist suggested that she take her son to the orthodontist. American mothers were agonizing over the time and expense involved in getting a child's teeth straightened. Bombeck recalls the stories she heard as she sat week after week in the dentist's office. "'You'll make so many trips to this office that your car will come here automatically.' 'You'll buy fifty toothbrushes in a month, which he will lose.' The worst is when you've gone through eight or nine years of straightening his teeth and he enters into a mixed marriage with a girl with an overbite.'"[14]

There is more—hundreds of columns more —each with its own special mood and chuckle-provoking commentary on the foibles of life from the viewpoint of modern woman.

Even the titles of the columns are evocative. In "Everybody Else's Mother," Bombeck says the nameless individual known as everybody else's mother is right out of the pages of Greek mythology—mysterious, obscure, and surrounded by hearsay. She is the answer to every child's prayer. For example, when the traditional mother says, "Have the car home by eleven or you're grounded for a month," everybody else's mother says, "Come home when you feel like it."[15]

"Pacifier Pioneers" was a paean of praise for pacifiers that concluded with Erma's mother warning her: "Do you know that if you keep using this pacifier, by the time the baby is four years old, her teeth will come in crooked and her mouth will have a permanent pout?" Mothers will understand Erma's comment: "Do you know, Mother, that if I do not use that pacifier, I may never permit her to become four?"[16]

Not all of Bombeck's columns are humorous. Perhaps the most serious one written recently is titled: "When Will We Weep for the Phantom Classes?" It concerns the tragedy of teenagers killed in drunk-driving-related accidents.

Erma has been a defender of the housewife since she wrote her first columns. At first she resented the housewife's being excluded from the women's movement. She said: "When did a woman selling orange slices in the dime store become more impressive than a woman who did a good job raising three kids for twenty years?" As the years went by, she became much more supportive of the effort to win recognition of the talents and abilities of women both in the workplace *and* in the home.

Although her decision to become a Catholic carried with it a dedication to the philosophy of that church, she has been troubled by the church's position on birth control. She agrees with the prohibition against abortion but considers family planning an important part of a family's life.[17]

Erma Bombeck continues to direct her exaggerated jibes at the housewife and mother, but she recognizes that the woman's role has expanded to the office, and one of her most amusing columns describes the working mother whose kids call her at the office every five minutes.

Bombeck found encouragement for her humor through reading Jean Kerr, and Kerr's *Please Don't Eat the Daisies* encouraged her to express her own unorthodox look at life. Others, in turn, have been influenced by Bombeck. Among these writers are Carol Dykstra, Sondra Gotlieb (the wife of the Canadian ambassador to the United States), Marilyn Schwartz (a columnist for the Dallas *Morning News* who has never been married), and D. L. Stewart (a liberated husband who writes about life in the bedroom community of Beaverbrook, Ohio). Coincidentally, Stewart writes for the Dayton *Journal Herald*, the same paper that Bombeck wrote for.[18]

Summary

Erma Bombeck has given the world a great gift—a collage of laughter and tears, bordered with a deeper understanding of what it means to be able to laugh at ourselves. She has used her column to let readers see themselves and the daily adventures and misadventures of life.

Notes

1. John Skow, "Erma in Bomburbia," *Time*, July 2, 1984, p. 58.
2. Ibid.
3. Ibid.
4. Diane K. Shad, "The $500,000 Housewife," *Newsweek*, January 2, 1978, p. 60.
5. *Two Thousand Women of Achievement, 1971*, Vol. III (London: Melrose Press, 1971, s.v. "Bombeck, Erma"), p. 84.
6. Skow, "Erma in Bomburbia," *Time*, July 2, 1984, p. 59.
7. John Skow, "Erma Bombeck: Syndicated Soul of Suburbia," *Reader's Digest*, November 1984, p. 45.
8. *Contemporary Biography—Women*, Vol. I, Part II, "Original Profiles" (Tustin, Calif.: American Biography Service, 1983), pp. 42–43.
9. Ibid.
10. Ibid.
11. *Contemporary Biography—Women*, Vol. I, Part II, pp. 42–43.
12. Ibid.
13. Erma Bombeck, "The Healthiest-Looking Man in the Doctor's Office," *Today's Health*, August 1972, p. 46.
14. Erma Bombeck, "I Dedicated Myself to the Tooth Cult," *The Birmingham News*, August 8, 1984, p. 7-G.
15. Erma Bombeck, *Motherhood, The Second Oldest*

Profession (New York: McGraw-Hill Book Company, 1983), p. 25.
16. Ibid., p. 31.
17. Skow, "Erma in Bomburbia," *Time*, July 2, 1984, p. 59.
18. J.D. Reed, "And On Other Home Fronts," *Time*, July 2, 1984, p. 61.

Selected Bibliography

Primary Sources

At Wit's End. Garden City, N.Y.: Doubleday, 1967.
Just Wait Until You Have Children of Your Own. Garden City, N.Y.: Doubleday, 1971.
I Lost Everything in the Post-Natal Depression. Garden City, N.Y.: Doubleday, 1973.
The Grass Is Always Greener over the Septic Tank. New York: McGraw-Hill, 1976.
If Life Is a Bowl of Cherries, What Am I Doing in the Pits? New York: McGraw-Hill, 1978.
Aunt Erma's Cope Book. New York: McGraw-Hill, 1979.
Motherhood, The Second Oldest Profession. New York: McGraw-Hill, 1983.
Numerous syndicated newspaper columns of Bombeck's work.

Secondary Sources

Contemporary Biography—Women. Vol. I, Part II. Tustin, Calif.: American Biography Service, 1983, pp. 42–43.
Reed, J.D. "And on Other Home Fronts," *Time*, July 2, 1984, p. 61.
Shad, Diane K. "The $500,000 Housewife," *Newsweek*, January 2, 1978, p. 60.
Skow, John. "Erma Bombeck: Syndicated Soul of Suburbia." *Reader's Digest*, November 1984.
———. "Erma in Bomburbia," *Time*, July 2, 1984, pp. 56–60.
Two Thousand Women of Achievement, 1971, Vol. III. London: Melrose Press, 1971, p. 84.

Irma R. Cruse

Bracken, Peg

Born: Filer, Idaho, on February 25, 1920
Education: Antioch College, A.B., 1940
Marriages: Roderick Allyn Lull, 1952, one child, divorced, 1964; Parker Ferguson Edwards, 1966

Biography

When she was nine months old, Peg Bracken's family moved from Filer, Idaho, to Duluth, Minnesota, and then to Clayton, Missouri (the McKinleyville of her autobiographical *A Window over the Sink*). Her writing career began at age ten when she produced a serious novel about her mother, *Julie Ruth: A Minister's Daughter*. After the manuscript was rejected by Doubleday, Bracken turned to lighter work. For the Clayton high school paper she wrote a humor column called "Box Pop"; later, at Antioch College, she became editor of *The Antiochian*.

After receiving her A.B. degree in English at Antioch in 1940, Bracken took a job writing advertising copy in Cleveland, Ohio, and in 1942 she went to Portland, Oregon, where she produced advertising copy, radio continuity, and free-lance fashion copy for Jantzen and Pendleton. Between 1942 and 1960 Bracken sold light verse and short humorous pieces to *The Saturday Evening Post*, *Collier's*, *Good Housekeeping*, *The New Yorker*, *Atlantic Monthly*, and other magazines. From 1952 to 1960, she also sold short fiction and long articles to many of the most popular periodicals. Her first full-length book, *The Nine Months' Wonder* (with Helen Berry Moore) was published by Prentice-Hall in 1958. Then followed a series of eight books published by Harcourt (1960-1981), which solidified her reputation as one of America's outstanding female humorists.

Married in 1952 to Roderick Allyn Lull, an editor, Bracken bore a daughter, Johanna Kathleen. Divorced in 1964, she moved to California, where for a time she wrote the humor page for *The Ladies' Home Journal* and a syndicated newspaper column, working on her books at the same time. After a couple of years she quit the newspaper column to write a regular monthly column for *Family Circle*. Each year she made a couple of lecture tours and did considerable commercial TV work.

In 1966 Bracken married artist Parker Edwards and in 1974 they moved to Lahaina, Maui, Hawaii, where she wrote her two latest books. At present, Bracken says she has traded writing for drawing—either temporarily or permanently: "Working on the right side of the brain is a great pleasure after so many years of little black words."[1]

Literary Analysis

Darkest Hour

Oh, life has trials which bruise and blister, and which
Can sear the soul, but this one is the worst:
To start the second half of any sandwich
And find that all your meat was in the first.

—P. Bracken[2]

Readers of America's most popular periodicals between 1942 and 1960 were delighted by such verses as well as by short pieces of humorous prose by P. Bracken. Then in 1960 *The I Hate to Cook Book* exploded from the press, followed by *The I Hate to Housekeep Book* in 1962, *I Try to Behave Myself* in 1964, and *Peg Bracken's Appendix to the I Hate to Cook Book* in 1966. Translated into at least six different languages, these four books established Bracken as supreme champion of the rebellious modern housewife.

This reputation has been a source of dismay ever since, as she would rather be regarded as an essayist, humorist, and satirist than as a purveyor of domestic advice.[3] In *I Didn't Come Here to Argue* (1969) she made an abrupt switch in subject to describe her new life in "Hamlet" (Bolinas, California, across the bay from San Francisco). The sassy voice of the *Hate* books becomes more mellow—at times even lyrical. For instance, Bracken delights in a lagoon which she describes as "still and silver, where there is probably a little boy trying for carp with a trout-size line, and a solemn egret, fragile against the quiet sky, his leg tucked underneath his wing" (*Argue*, p. 27). As a collector of sunrises, she watches the bay before dawn, fuzzy with fog or churning with rain. One morning "it was a surly ocean creaming under a black sky. Then, with great precision, the sun drilled a rosy hole through a cloud bank, and the water was suddenly opal" (*Argue*, p. 45).

In the main, however, *Argue* tackles such prosaic topics as dealing with everyday consumer problems, coping with illness, or taking care of one's books. Bracken's humor here is gentle and bemused, though some of her inquiries are serious. She ponders the problems of marriage, of growing old, and—in her most impressive passage—of succumbing to Sin: "I inherited a conscience that's studded with shoulds and shouldn'ts like a clove-stuck ham, making me feel bad both before and after I've done something, though fortunately not while I'm doing it" (*Argue*, p. 54). There follows a reconsideration of the Ten Commandments, which seem to allow all kinds of horrible transgressions—like pulling wings off robins or dumping "all Boston's garbage into Walden Pond"—so long as they're not done on Sunday. Bracken's humor, in effect, dismisses the problem when she finally decides to make up her own list of 108 sins after the example of the Buddhists' roster of 108, "for which they bong the temple bell 108 times every New Year's Eve" (*Argue*, p. 55). Bracken has broadened the range of her topics and her tone in *Argue*, veering from tender lyricism to a surprisingly sharp satire of contemporary morality.

But I Wouldn't Have Missed It for the World (1973) introduces still another topic—travel. Bracken recounts the joys and hazards she and her husband encountered as they journeyed in Europe, northern Africa, and Japan. With a keen yet affectionate eye she portrays her traveling companions, lodgings, tipping customs, package tours, and—yes—food. She describes several special meals in rapturous detail, supporting her repeated claim that she would much rather eat out than cook. On the whole, Bracken has softened her tone in this account, content to accept the world as she finds it.

Bracken returns to her original topic in *The I Hate to Cook Almanack* (1976), and even in *A Window over the Sink* (1981) food retains a prominent place, though the food references are well integrated in her reminiscences of childhood friends and family.[4] She revels in fond memories of her brother, Jack, and special schoolmates in McKinleyville (Clayton, Missouri, where Bracken's father was superintendent of the school system). She pays loving tribute to her grandparents and to her Aunt Liz Noah, an artist who encouraged the joy in word play that became one of Bracken's chief obsessions.[5] The amusing story of Bracken's "first genuine kiss," administered by a shady character in a forbidden roadhouse, is explicit without sacrificing taste. For all of these memories the initiating framing device is the window over the sink in the new kitchen Bracken and her husband have added to their Hawaiian home.

A Window over the Sink is subtitled *A Mainly Affectionate Memoir*. Bracken says she had not actually planned to write a memoir: "I had really planned to take a literary approach to kitchen and food."[6] But, she is never really sure what a book will be like until it is finished. Bracken admits that organization is not her strong point. She writes from an idea, letting the words suggest new directions. She has read widely, and her work is studded with references to and quotations from such diverse sources as George Washington, Plautus, the New Testament, and Leroy Satchel Paige, yet she manages not to become tiresome or snobbish with all of her namedropping. She snatches the reader away with her for a tantalizing glimpse of each new vista, then leads him gently back to the mainstream.

Bracken has been influenced by such diverse writers as Mark Twain, James Thurber, E.B. White, Katherine Mansfield[7] and Phyllis McGinley (*Argue*, p. 179), among others. *Life* magazine called her "the Jean Kerr of the West Coast,"[8] and she has often been compared to Erma Bombeck. Bracken feels, however, that such a comparison is "unfair to both of them" and adds modestly, "I think [Bombeck is] funnier."[9] Bracken tends less to slapstick than Bombeck does; her quiet meanderings are in distinct contrast to Bombeck's explosive forays into the psyche of the American female. Like Teresa Bloomingdale, Bracken rejects the feminist movement, preferring the advantages that she believes the modern woman already enjoys (*Argue*, pp. 186-197).

Having won a secure place in the kitchens and hearts of housewives over the western world with her cook-and-behave books, Peg Bracken may lead them yet to her view that the real goal of life is to evolve "a self that can be lived with, with reasonable enjoyment; for one is apt to be stuck with it, sooner or later" (*Argue*, p. 182).

Notes

1. Letter from Peg Bracken to Martha A. Fisher, April 2, 1985.
2. In *Writer's Digest*, May 1970, pp. 25-26, Frank Cameron explains that Bracken hated her christened name "Ruth Eleanor." She began to sign her light verse "P. Bracken" so she could assume a persona of either sex. But as her feminine voice could not be hidden, she eventually changed the "P" to "Peg" legally.
3. "My career as a humorist . . . took a sharp turn for the domestic in 1960, when I was talked into writing *The I Hate to Cook Cook*, and I've never been able to get quite out of the kitchen since. I wasn't and am not in any way an expert in home-type or culinary matters (nor in etiquette) but have somehow become a well-known non-expert in them all" (Letter to Martha A. Fisher, April 2, 1985).
4. It is interesting to note the culinary tone of most chapter titles in *Window*: "A Consideration of the Egg," "A Word About Punkin Soup," "Many Ways with Ambrosia," "My Mother Was a Good Plain Cook," "A Pride of Crumpets," "Of Irish Stews and Birthday Cakes."
5. Satirizing the increasing emphasis on the Feminine Mystique, Bracken advises the reader: "Squint just a little and you can see us in our jim-dandy dream homes, shrill with wall-to-wall carping" (*Argue*, p. 186).
6. Betsy Lammerding, "The Bracken Lifestyle: Keep the Flame on Low," *Boston Globe*, July 1, 1981, p. 58W.
7. Frank Cameron, "Peg Bracken: An Exclusive Interview." *Writer's Digest*, May 1970, pp. 24-26.
8. Haskel Frankel, "A Peach Called Bracken." *Saturday Review*, September 5, 1964, pp. 22-23.
9. Lammerding, p. 58W.

Selected Bibliography

Primary Sources

Books

(with Helen Berry Moore.) *The Nine Months' Wonder.* Englewood Cliffs, N.J.: Prentice-Hall, 1958.

The I Hate to Cook Cook. New York: Harcourt, 1960.

The I Hate to Housekeep Book. New York: Harcourt, 1962.

I Try to Behave Myself. New York: Harcourt, 1964.

Peg Bracken's Appendix to the I Hate to Cook Book. New York: Harcourt, 1966.

I Didn't Come Here to Argue. New York: Harcourt, 1969.

But I Wouldn't Have Missed It for the World! New York: Harcourt, 1973.

The I Hate to Cook Almanack. New York: Harcourt, 1976.

A Window over the Sink. New York: Harcourt, 1981.

As Contributor

The Saturday Evening Post, The Ladies' Home Journal, Cosmopolitan, McCall's, The New Yorker, Atlantic Monthly, and other periodicals.

Secondary Sources

Ball, Anne. "Feud with Food Led to World of Words." *Richmond News Leader,* October 28, 1970, p. 37. Bracken explains that she is not a "Ladies Lib Lady."

Cameron, Frank. "Peg Bracken: An Exclusive Interview." *Writer's Digest,* May 1970, pp. 24-26. Cameron presents Bracken as "a constant challenger of notions and ideas . . . the essence of her pointed whimsey."

Frankel, Haskel. "A Peach Called Bracken." *Saturday Review,* September 5, 1964, pp. 22-23. In an interview a "smartly turned out" Bracken debunks her reputation as a cooking and housekeeping authority.

Hoffman, Marilyn. "Peg Bracken: A No-frills Approach to Home, Hearth, and Good Food." *Christian Science Monitor,* September 23, 1981. Bracken describes life in her Hawaiian A-frame house, the setting for her book, *A Window over the Sink.*

Lammerding, Betsy. "The Bracken Lifestyle: Keep the Flame on Low." *Boston Globe,* July 1, 1981, p. 58W. Lammerding labels Bracken's books "lighthearted and witty accounts of common-sense coping with mundane chores such as housekeeping and other situations that all of us face."

Martha A. Fisher

Brackenridge, Hugh Henry

Born: Kintyre, Scotland, in 1748

Education: Slate Ridge School, Peach Bottom Township, Pennsylvania; College of New Jersey (now Princeton), B.A., 1771, M.A., 1774; read law

Marriages: Miss Montgomery, 1785, one child; Sabina Wolfe, 1790, three children

Died: June 25, 1816

Biography

To his contemporaries, Hugh Henry Brackenridge was an eccentric or dangerous character. Judge Brackenridge heard court cases in work boots, feet on his table, shirt open, face unshaven, and hair unbrushed. As an attorney, he chased clients from his office who brought frivolous cases. He defended Indians in court. Riding half-dressed through a rain storm, he explained that he was protecting his clothes. His second wife, an illiterate country girl, caught his fancy by jumping a fence. He sided with farmers in the Whiskey Rebellion and was nearly tried for treason. He ridiculed the genteel practice of dueling but could knock down an antagonist and throw him out of his house.

Brackenridge achieved a reputation as a rough fellow but was well educated and devoted to cultural pursuits, an embodiment of the revolutionary, democratic mythology of self-advancement. Born in Kintyre, Scotland in 1748, he was raised in the Scots-Irish settlement Peach Bottom Township, Pennsylvania. Encouraged in intellectual ambitions, he traded farm chores for tutoring at the Slate Ridge School. At the College of New Jersey, he distinguished himself in oratory and supported himself in part by ghosting compositions. He received a B.A. in 1771. *Father Bombo's Pilgrimage* (written with classmate Philip Freneau) may be the first American novel. His poem, "The Rising Glory of America" (also written with Freneau), was presented at commencement ceremonies. Brackenridge taught school and read divinity, took a master's degree from the College of New Jersey in 1774, and wrote patriotic dramas. He served as a chaplain in Washington's army from 1776 to 1778, moved to Philadelphia to publish the *United States Magazine,* read law under Samuel Chase, was admitted to the Pennsylvania bar in 1780, and moved to Pittsburgh, then a frontier community. In 1785, he married a Miss Montgomery, with whom he had a son, Henry Marie; his second marriage, to Sabina Wolfe in 1790, produced two sons and a daughter.

Brackenridge served one term in the state assembly, from 1786 to 1788, but provoked voters, opposing land ownership bills and approving the federal constitution. He never regained political popularity. Rewarded for work for the Jeffersonian party, he was appointed to the state Supreme Court in 1799. Brackenridge established and contributed to *The Pittsburgh Gazette* (the city's first newspaper) and the *Tree of Liberty*. He founded the first bookstore in Pittsburgh. *Modern Chivalry*, his most famous work, published in installments from 1792 to 1815, comments on contemporary issues. Brackenridge intended to continue the volumes at the time of his death in Carlisle on June 25, 1816.

Literary Analysis

Brackenridge's output was immense and varied: verse drama, hudibrastics, dialect poetry; political essays in newspapers, pamphlets, and handbills; serialized fiction; sermons; and law commentary. While his primary vocation was literature, it became a tool of his political career, and Brackenridge worked a half century before he had a reasonable chance to make a career in letters. His work anticipated frontier humor and local color tales. *Modern Chivalry*, his most important work, dramatized national issues in local controversies, often absurd. He supported democracy, revealing how it might operate foolishly, but he never became disillusioned.

Father Bombo's Pilgrimage (1770) ironically comments on "The Rising Glory." The common theme in Bombo's picaresque travels is his ability to extricate himself from trouble by using his wit to fool whatever ignorant and low types he falls among, changing dialect at will, and misleading people with sham erudition. The victims are mostly European, but the satire is generalized. Everyone is an object of mockery, not least of all the ostentatious colonial Bombo (bombast), a forebear of the frontier sharpers and con men of *Modern Chivalry*. The commonplace detail, low language, and exaggerated physical action also preview frontier humor. The homely *Father Bombo's Pilgrimage*, written when Brackenridge and Freneau were composing a blank verse epic to forecast a glorious cultural awakening in America, exposed man everywhere as a gullible buffoon.

Brackenridge's journalistic effort to promote American literature in 1779, the *United States Magazine*, failed within a year, but he established an ironic voice writing newspaper pieces under assumed characters. In *The Pittsburgh Gazette* he sometimes impersonated readers, using wit rather than dispensing wisdom, and he realized the virtues of using *personae*. Brackenridge believed that literature in a democracy should be educational and that literary art disguised in plain language could reach the mass audience that he sought. "It is Tom, Dick, and Harry, in the woods, that I want to read my book," he wrote in *Modern Chivalry*. "The democrat is the true chevalier." Fictional narrative was itself a reflection of popular taste; the novel was still disreputable and mainly appealed to "feminine" (uncultured) readers. Brackenridge wrote for the mass audience in whom he saw the future of the United States.

Modern Chivalry (1792–1815) is difficult to describe: a picaresque narrative partly didactic, satiric, and realistic. Captain John Farrago, a revolutionary patriot, is the central focus in a farrago of loosely organized travelogue and authorial comment. Brackenridge displays classical allusions and acknowledges his debts to writers like Jonathan Swift, Henry Fielding, and Miguel de Cervantes. He begins "The Modern Chevalier" as hudibrastic couplets in the manner of Samuel Butler, used in Part One of the narrative, though no one writer is primarily important as source for incident, narrative form, or tone. Brackenridge's main source of material was frontier life, and *Modern Chivalry* is notable as the first novel to portray American frontier life following the Revolutionary War. The hodgepodge of material could balance comment and illustration, literary style and colloquialism, and so would be, on whole, neither hectoring nor patronizing. Following eighteenth-century convention, Brackenridge gave his subjects comic epithets instead of actual names, although his people are American settlers: Traddle the weaver (treadle), Drug the doctor, Grab the lawyer, and Harum-Scarum the gamecock. Teague O'Regan, the captain's servant, is a stereotypical illiterate Irish immigrant. He and the captain visit the frontier settlements of Lack-Learning and Madcaps. However, they also visit Philadelphia and meet President Washington. The author insisted on the authenticity of his story: "Should it be considered in the light of burlesque, it must be a very lame one . . . want of probability has not been an observation."

Most of the tall tales in *Modern Chivalry* feature Teague, the object of popular adulation. People want him in the legislature because he is uncorrupted by education; with addition of the title Major, he becomes the most sought-after bachelor to Philadelphia belles. Appointed an excise officer, he is tarred and feathered, taken for a natural curiosity by learned professors, and shipped to Europe, then liberated and made a champion of the *sans culottes*. Repatriated, Teague runs afoul of another community and is voted the Devil by people who want an instant demonic transformation to show the will of the majority (other passionate democrats vote to enfranchise animals and elect them as well).

The satire is double-edged. The low types are fools, but educated people's actions are equally absurd or impractical. Captain Farrago is *raisonneur* only in part, for he, too, becomes foolish in trying to reason with mobs attacking a church, schools, doctors, and lawyers. He must be subtle, telling people not to burn a university because the buildings provide storage and the lessons serve as a harmless diversion until the young are old enough to work. Farrago is a benevolent con man, but there are sharpers aplenty. To secure a bogus treaty and a government pay-off, one sharper tries to make Teague an Indian chief because his Irish brogue can pass for any Indian language. Political demagogues and blackguard journalists threaten social stablity everywhere; people are always willing to believe tales and scurrilous charges no matter how "tall." Sometimes reported fact is as comical as any con game, as when the author describes a frontier wedding behind a deadpan mask: "A *cattle-driver* had come from the *western settlement*, to exchange at the fair, stock, for salt, iron, and *women*. In barter for the last article, a cow was given for a girl."

Modern Chivalry has much that is indelicate, especially in dialogue. Teague calls the captain's Scotsman servant a "son o'd a whore," among other insults. Brackenridge allows his characters their own voice to show prejudice and want of learning or sense, and he imitates Scottish, French, German, Jewish, and slave dialects mostly by capturing the sound, rather than idiomatic expression, and the accents are more nationally distinct than regional. The language is that of an evolving culture in which Old World origins and loyalties are often more evident than the American experience: "The American has in fact, yet, no character; neither the clown, nor the gentleman."

The gamblers, whiskey drinkers, quacks, gamecocks, vigilante mobs, revival preachers, do-gooding reformers, corrupt lawyers, and politicians of western humor and local color inhabit *Modern Chivalry*; however, they live in a real frontier, not an imaginary time past. *Modern Chivalry* shows the coming of civilization, not the wild days gone, with none of the elegaic tone that characterizes some of the anecdotes about Mike Fink and Davy Crockett. Nor does the novel include a consistent framing device to subsume the low types in civilized decorum. Captain Farrago represents history, embodying genteel sanity and moderation, while Teague stands for the new American democrat. Farrago lacks new experience, though possessed of book learning; his practical ignorance and desire to observe the world set him off on his travels. He becomes the governor of a frontier settlement, but he must accommodate an unruly populace.

Throughout *Modern Chivalry* Brackenridge shows his talent for delineating characters through their speech. His own voice as narrator is by no means consistent. He attacks foolishness with sharp criticism. More often, however, his tone is that of Democritus, the "laughing philosopher" to whom he alludes several times, most significantly when he recalls the traditional contrast of the laughing observer with the weeping one: "I think it is as well to laugh; to be Democritus, rather than Heraclitus. But if there is any remedy for this evil, it must be ridicule." One source for the *persona* of Democritus was the French writer Montaigne, whom Brackenridge cites with approval; the ancient Greek philosopher had been a pseudonym for three centuries in England and in America, as in Robert Burton's *Anatomy of Melancholy*, and Brackenridge himself signed "Democritus" to a handbill in 1774 and to a collection of essays entitled *The Standard of Liberty* (1805).

"Democritus" is not a strict rationalist nor one with abstract values against which he measures the follies of man—thus he avoids disillusionment and weeping. He expects to observe folly. *Modern Chivalry* is an "anatomy of democracy" set against the Enlightenment's belief in the efficacy of reason and Romantic notions of the innocence and perfectibility of man. Though his potential increases by freedom, his fundamental nature remains simple: "I mean this as no burlesque on the present generation; for mankind in all ages have had the same propensity to magnify what was small, and elevate the low.... Human nature is the same every where." Thus, the modern chevalier will be led more by his folly than reason as were his ancestors.

Summary

One cannot say for certain that Brackenridge influenced later writers, though his frontier humor anticipated work like the letters of Major Jack Downing and *Georgia Scenes*. In his use of coarse language, Brackenridge was well ahead of other humorists. Ultimately, he stood outside of the political groupings of his own day as well, aiming jests at all parties and social ranks but never losing allegiance to the American experiment in democracy. The Democritian voice warned readers of *Modern Chivalry* not to take him too seriously: "I have been affecting to speak sense, whereas my business is to speak nonsense.... I would as soon please fools as wise men; because the fools are the most numerous, and every prudent man will go with the majority."

Selected Bibliography

Primary Sources

Father Bombo's Pilgrimage to Mecca. Ed. Michael Davitt Bell. Princeton: Princeton University Library, 1975. Only complete text.

Modern Chivalry. Ed. Claude M. Newlin. New York: American Book Company, 1937; rpt. New York:

Hafner, 1968. Part One printed in 1792, 1793, and 1797; Part Two in 1804 and 1805; collected edition, 1815.

Gazette Publications. Carlisle, Pa.: Alexander and Phillips, 1806. A variety of pieces, including dialect poems, essays on the constitution, and Revolutionary War sermons.

A Hugh Henry Brackenridge Reader: 1770–1815. Ed. Daniel Marder. Pittsburgh: University of Pittsburgh Press, 1970. Selections and excerpts of works Marder discusses in his critical biography, cited below.

Secondary Sources

Biography

Marder, Daniel. *Hugh Henry Brackenridge.* New York: Twayne, 1967.

Newlin, Claude Milton. *The Life and Writings of Hugh Henry Brackenridge.* Princeton: Princeton University Press, 1932.

Articles and Chapters in Books

Ellis, Joseph J. *After the Revolution: Profiles of Early American Culture.* New York: W.W. Norton, 1979, pp. 73–110. The failure of democracy to patronize the literary artist is discussed; Brackenridge is called the first American writer to adopt ambivalent attitude toward national ideals.

Gilmore, Michael T. "Eighteenth-Century Oppositional Ideology and Hugh Henry Brackenridge's *Modern Chivalry.*" *Early American Literature,* 13 (1978): 181–192. Background of Brackenridge's politics.

Leary, Lewis. *Soundings: Some Early American Writers.* Athens: University of Georgia Press, 1975, pp. 161–174. Satire of *Modern Chivalry* includes author, Captain Farrago, and all ordinary men; focus not social criticism but "episodes, humorous and humane," in language that is colloquial and coarse.

Lenz, William E. "Confidence Games in the New Country: Hugh Henry Brackenridge's *Modern Chivalry.*" *Colby Library Quarterly,* 18 (1982): 105–112. Comments on the confidence game, style rather than substance, and the satiric paradigm of democratic society found in the novel.

Simpson, Lewis P. "The Satiric Mode: The Early National Wits." In *The Comic Imagination in American Literature.* Ed. Louis D. Rubin, Jr. New Brunswick: Rutgers University Press, 1973, pp. 49–61. Satire of Enlightenment pretense to reason; wit and intellect are central to Brackenridge's view of democracy.

Thomas Pribek

Bruce, Lenny

Born: Long Island, New York, on October 13, 1925
Education: High school dropout
Marriage: Harriet Loyd (Honey), June 15, 1951, one child, divorced January 21, 1957
Died: August 3, 1966

Biography

Considered incredibly outrageous, provocative, sick, and anti-social in his own time, Lenny Bruce appears to us now more as a harbinger of the attacks on middle-class values and mores in the late 1960s and early 1970s than as a solitary voice screaming obscenities into the void of the postwar American consciousness. He fits comfortably into that tradition of harsh social satire whose leading figures include Juvenal and Jonathan Swift (Bruce frequently compared himself to Aristophanes, Rabelais, and Swift in his many legal defenses against obscenity charges). And, like those social satirists who also insisted on acknowledging every aspect of human physicality and behavior and who sometimes tried to shock their audiences into doing likewise, he hoped to change society by forcing it to acknowledge its self-deceptions. Though his work became bitter and preachy toward the end of his life when the police were arresting him on drug and obscenity charges almost wherever he tried to perform, many fans appreciated him for his comedy as well as for his social criticism.

Lenny Bruce was born Leonard Albert Schneider, the son of immigrant Jewish parents, Mickey and Saddie Schneider, who were divorced when Bruce was eight years old. For most of his childhood Bruce lived with his mother, but his father visited him often, bringing him gifts and acting as disciplinarian. In later life Bruce remained close to his mother but was estranged from his father, toward whom he felt considerable bitterness. When he was 16 Bruce dropped out of high school, a move he later regretted, and ran away from home to work on a farm in Long Island. A year later he enlisted in the Navy and served as a shell-passer on a cruiser, the *U.S.S. Brooklyn.* In over three years of wartime duty he took part in four major invasions. He comments upon his wartime experience in his autobiography, *How to Talk Dirty and Influence People*:

> Blood and salt water mixed together looks blue. Eight men followed by twelve, then by about forty more, floated gracefully by the bow of the *U.S.S. Brooklyn.* These dead Air Force men that just a few months ago were

saying . . . "Now listen, Vera, I'm going to put all my stuff in these cardboard boxes, and I'm going to lock them in that closet back of the den. Please don't let anyone touch them . . . I don't want anyone, do you understand, *anyone*, fooling around with my stuff."

His stuff. My stuff. Everyone was worrying about their stuff . . . their papers . . . their possessions.

The bodies continued to float by, their heads bumping the starboard side.

Seeing those pitiful, fresh-dead bodies, I knew what a mockery of life the materialistic concept is. After they got the telegram, someone would go through his "stuff" and try to figure out why in the world he wanted "all that stuff." The stuff that he kept so nice would eventually be thrown out of the basement, for the stuff would now be crap.

"Hey, throw this crap outta here!"

When the war ended Bruce was anxious to be mustered out of the service so he dressed up as a woman and walked around on deck until he was caught. He denied being a homosexual but claimed that he enjoyed wearing women's clothing. He received an undesirable discharge, but a Red Cross lawyer reviewed his case and argued that Bruce had had a good service record and that no charges had been filed against him. Consequently, his discharge was upgraded to honorable status.

After the war Bruce began his career as a standup comic, first acting as a master of ceremonies for vaudeville-type acts and as a contestant in rigged amateur contests. These early experiences allowed Bruce to discover and shape his material and to perfect his style, which was greatly indebted to contemporary Jewish standup comedians who played with the subtleties of language and upon their intimate relationship to a live audience. Ultimately, he worked his way into the night club circuit, and at the peak of his career he performed at several prominent clubs. His arrests for obscenity and drug use, while giving him national notoriety and exposure, sapped his energy and financial resources and adversely affected his career. He felt that the police were persecuting him, and much of his autobiography makes this case. In this context it is perhaps significant that when he was found dead in 1966 the Los Angeles police immediately announced the cause to be a drug overdose, though the subsequent medical report stated that the cause of death was unknown and the medical analysis was inconclusive.

Literary Analysis

Bruce was very attentive to words: their sonorous qualities, their connotations and denotations, their uses and abuses. He recognized the political and social power that language possesses, and many of his comic routines, including most of the ones that were attacked as obscene, demonstrate how language, itself, shapes our view of the world and of what we consider true and moral. He used his comedy to show the extent to which the American middle class responds to words rather than to the underlying realities that they describe and distort. His concern for the power of language puts him in a category with writers like George Orwell and anticipates to some extent not only modern scholarship on the sociology of language but also the language-based political activism of the Yippies and others during the anti-Vietnam War protests, particularly such "radicals" as Jerry Rubin and Abbie Hoffman, who saw the importance of manipulating symbols to counter the "establishment's" control of political terminology and signification.

Many of Bruce's comic routines center on his examination of linguistic qualities. For instance, in his most famous routine, "Religions Incorporated," Bruce applies the language of Madison Avenue advertising and sales to religious evangelism and self-promotion. In this way he makes his point about the commercialism of modern-day religion at the same time that he establishes a comic incongruity between the levels of discourse typically reserved for promoting products and those used for discussing religion. Bruce was arrested in Chicago for performing this routine.

Sometimes Bruce would concentrate on a particular word or phrase. In the account of his World War II experiences quoted previously, for example, he achieves a pointed sort of humor by showing the different meanings "stuff" achieves, ultimately transforming "stuff" to "crap." His routine, "'To' is a preposition; 'Come' is a verb," works on this principle, too. Assuming the role of the male lover, he asks, "Did you come? Good." Merely by altering his vocal inflection he transforms that into a new question, "Did you come good?" Still interested in the verb "come," he assumes the female voice, "Don't come in me," which refrain he then chants to the tune of the "Song of the Volga Boatmen." The routine continues along these lines. Through this routine Bruce achieves comic effects by introducing each new application of the verb "to come" in an unexpected, yet appropriate context. At the same time, he goes beyond linguistic play to real issues in sexual relationships with which many audience members are familiar but few openly acknowledge. This interplay between comic incongruity and social taboo typifies Bruce's humor.

In other situations Bruce exploited words for their shock value, ultimately revealing how we inappropriately deem words offensive or obscene while we accept the behavior they describe. Thus, his routine, "Tits and Ass," points to the incongruity between audiences' outrage over those words and their unquestioning acceptance of Las Vegas shows that exploit those female sexual features. By exposing every socially accepted justification of the nightclub shows as simply an appeal to "tits and ass, and more ass, and tits, and ass and tits and ass and tits and ass," he creates comic incongruities, eliminates the shock value of the words through sheer repetition and rhetorical devices such as assonance and alliteration, and exposes the hypocrisy implicit in condemning the language but condoning the activity.

In a slightly different way he points to the excessive concern paid to using polite language to refer to minority groups, even while underlying attitudes and behaviors fail to accord them genuine respect. Thus, he begins his routine, "Blacks," by asking if there are any niggers in the audience. After then imitating a liberal outraged by his use of the derogatory word, he continues:

> Are there any niggers here tonight? I know that one nigger who works here, I see him back there. Oh, there's two niggers, customers, and ah, *aha*! Between those two niggers sits one kike—man, thank God for the kike!
>
> Uh, two kikes. That's two kikes, and three niggers, and one spic. One spic—two, three spics. One mick. One mick, one spic, one hick, thick, funky, spunky boogey. . . .
>
> Two guineas plus three greaseballs and four boogies makes usually three spics. Minus two Yid spic Polack funky spunky Polacks.
>
> AUCTIONEER: Five more niggers! Five more niggers!
>
> GAMBLER: I pass with six niggers and eight micks and four spics.

The point? That the word's suppression gives it the power, the violence, the viciousness. If President Kennedy got on television and said, "Tonight I'd like to introduce the niggers in my cabinet," and he yelled, "niggerniggerniggerniggerniggerniggernigger" at every nigger he saw . . . till nigger didn't mean anything any more, till nigger lost its

meaning—you'd never make any four-year-old nigger cry when he came home from school.

In addition to examining language Bruce frequently conceived his material in terms of filmic images and staged scenes. As a result, there is a dramatic quality to much of his humor. "Religions Incorporated," for instance, features a board meeting of the major religious leaders, and Bruce sustains this image as he works his way around the table, adding commentary from the rabbis, priests, and ministers. In *How to Talk Dirty and Influence People*, Bruce describes vividly how he arranged for a female wino to appear on a television show, *Your Mystery Mrs.*, a show which, like *Queen for a Day*, had women tell their tales of woe to an audience anxious to feed on their pathos. The entire episode is a charade and fabrication, and Bruce provides a rich account of how the wino staggers onto the stage, pretending that she is a widow. The m.c., thinking quickly, explains her wobbly gait by telling the audience that the Mystery Mrs. has just been released from the hospital. He then asks her about her fictitious late husband, for whom she is supposed to be grieving. "Yeah, he was a hell of a man!" she says; "All of a sudden I [Bruce] saw a cue card that the audience saw, too: 'GET TO THE PRIZES AND GET HER THE HELL OFF!' This certainly confused the studio audience. A brave woman like that, who had just gotten out of the hospital? Is that a way to talk about her?" Significantly, Bruce follows this comic tale of how entrepreneurs exploit a gullible audience's capacity to feel compassion with his account of how he originated the "Religions Incorporated" routine. The juxtaposition invites us to make an equation between the two forms of exploitation. Both routines, like Mark Twain's Duke and Dauphin, who describe themselves in *Huck Finn* as converted pirates from the Indian Ocean, reveal not only the sham of the exploiters but also the perverse fascination with other people's suffering that motivates the exploited audience/Christians.

Bruce justifies comparison with other writers as well. He stands as a kindred spirit to Eugene Ionesco and dramatists in the Theater of the Absurd, to Thomas Pynchon, Kurt Vonnegut, and other black humorists, and to satirists like Garry Trudeau, all of whom were his contemporaries or immediate successors. Perhaps more significantly, he was also a kindred spirit of the counter-culture that sprang up in the middle and late 1960s in opposition to middle-class values and that expressed itself not only through political action but also through such comic/satiric outlets as *The National Lampoon*, the Freak Brothers, "underground" newspapers, comedians like Dick Gregory and George Carlin, and even such rock groups as The Mothers of Invention and the Doors.

Summary

Most of Bruce's comedy centers on the disparity between the way things actually are in America and the way Americans want to think of them as being. Sometimes, particularly in connection with his arrests for obscenity, he exposed what he considered to be overt hypocrisies; other times he revealed to his audiences their own elaborate self-deceptions in personal, sexual, and socio-political relationships. One of the few things that theorists of comedy agree upon is that incongruity is an essential component of humor. The disparities present in our social hypocrisies and self-deceptions provide an immediate opportunity for incongruities to surface. Bruce's genius was to render these incongruities comic and to make them inescapably visible. In so doing he not only raised issues about ethics and morality that were to absorb American society after his death, he also made them funny.

Selected Bibliography

Primary Sources

Books

How to Talk Dirty and Influence People. Chicago: Playboy Press, 1963; revised, 1964.
Stamp Help Out. 1964.
The Essential Lenny Bruce. Ed. and compiled by John Cohen. New York: Ballantine Books, 1967.
The Almost Unpublished Lenny Bruce. Ed. Kitty Bruce. Philadelphia: Running Press, 1984.

Records

Interviews of Our Time. Fantasy Records, 1959.
The Sick Humor of Lenny Bruce. Fantasy Records, 1959.
I Am Not a Nut, Elect Me. Fantasy Records, 1960.
Lenny Bruce: American. Fantasy Records, 1962.
Lenny Bruce: The Berkeley Concert. Bizarre Records, n. d.
What I Was Arrested For. Douglas, 1971 (originally released under the title *"To" Is a Preposition; "Come" Is a Verb.*).
Thank You Masked Man. Fantasy Records, 1972.
The Real Lenny Bruce. Fantasy Records, 1975.

Secondary Sources

Blair, Walter, and Hamlin Hill. *America's Humor: From Poor Richard to Doonesbury.* New York: Oxford University Press, 1978, pp. 499-501, 515-519.
Goldman, Albert. *Freakshow.* New York: Atheneum, 1971, pp. 187-222.
———. *Lenny Bruce!!* New York: Random House, 1971.
Lewis, Anthony. "The Jew In Stand-up Comedy." In *From Hester Street to Hollywood,* ed. Sarah Blacher Cohen. Bloomington: Indiana University Press, 1983, pp. 65-69.
Schaeffer, Neil. *The Art of Laughter.* New York: Columbia University Press, 1981, pp. 59-80.

Related Sources

Barry, Julian. *Lenny.* New York: Grove Press, 1971. A play.
McKendrick, Robert. *Honey: The Life and Loves of Lenny's Shady Lady.* Chicago: Playboy Press, 1976. About his wife.

Richard Alan Schwartz

Buchwald, Art[hur]

Born: Mount Vernon, New York, on October 20, 1925
Education: University of Southern California, 1945-1948
Marriage: Anne McGarry; three children

Biography

Art Buchwald served in the U.S. Marine Corps from 1942 to 1945, during which time he was with the Fourth Marine Air Wing in the Pacific. He worked as a correspondent for *Variety* in Paris in 1948 and was a member of the editorial staff of the Paris edition of *New York Herald Tribune* from 1949 to 1962 when he moved to Washington, D.C. and began writing a column entitled "Art Buchwald." Buchwald's popularity and critical acceptance is reflected in two facts: he is currently syndicated in 550 newspapers, and in 1986 he was formally inducted into the American Academy and Institute of Arts and Letters.

Literary Analysis

Art Buchwald writes topical, social and political satire. He writes about such economic indicators as Alka-Seltzer and Rolaid sales. He says that when the country is doing badly, no one is digging up the streets or drilling steel pilings into the ground early in the morning. When the country is doing well, however, people have less time for personal contacts or for relaxation; so, Buchwald concludes, "The price of a good economy is a breakdown in services that the economy provides." In 1972, Buchwald wrote a short introduction to a collection of Garry Trudeau's cartoons called *Still a Few Bugs in the System.* Buchwald predicted, "As with all anti-establishment figures, Mr. Trudeau will soon be an honored member of the establishment, if he is not already."

Buchwald is a master of parody. His particular type of parody is based on developing an incongruity between the subject and the grammatical framework of the piece. Consider, for example, a piece entitled "Win One for Hoffa," in which the subject is "football," but the grammatical framework is "union negotiations." Like many of his pieces, this one involves social satire:

> "Why did you drop that pass that was right in your arms?" "I caught my quota for the half. If I caught another one, the guys would have thought I was trying to speed up the game." "Well, if you drop another pass, I'm pulling you out of the game and putting Wallnicki in." "You can't do it. I've got three years seniority over Wallnicki. If you pull me out, the entire team walks off the field."

Buchwald is satirizing the confict between labor and management in this piece, and the labor negotiations that result from the conflict.

Buchwald is also a master of political satire. Consider a piece in which Buchwald writes about the 12,654th plenary session of the 17-nation disarmament conference in Geneva, in the year 1994. Ambassador Stone is about to make a statement, but he sneezes instead. The sneeze is interpreted by Ambassador Groanyko as a proposal, and Groanyko is then concerned as to what the Soviet response should be:

> SOVIET ADVISER: We could say "Gesundheit."
>
> GROANYKO: Yes, but how do we know the sneeze wasn't a trap to make us say "Gesundheit."
>
> 2nd SOVIET ADVISER: But if we don't say Gesundheit, and he really sneezed, it could be a big propaganda victory for the West.
>
> GROANYKO: Should we ask time to get instructions from Moscow?
>
> SOVIET ADVISER: No. It would look like we don't have authority to make decisions on our own.
>
> GROANYKO: I think the best thing is to say "Gesundheit" with reservations. If it's a trap we can always renounce it.

Here again the satire and the parody are based on incongruity. This time, however, the incongruity is between the seriousness of the situation (a meeting of super powers), and the triviality of the subject (a sneeze). Buchwald's popularity is based not only on his ability to make shrewd and perceptive observation but also on his ability to develop a superficially sensible but actually ludicrous juxtaposition of two highly incongruent subjects. He is a master of this technique and, therefore, very effective as a social critic.

Buchwald believes that humor is the most acceptable form of hostility. He feels that it is

ironic that he has become such an honored member of the establishment by attacking this same establishment. He once wrote that there was no J. Edgar Hoover—that he had been invented by the *Reader's Digest*.

Buchwald is a master of irony and satire. In an interview on the CBS television program *60 Minutes*, which aired June 12, 1981, Buchwald made the statement that since Henry Kissinger left office, he is the only male sex symbol left in Washington. He has invented a Buchwaldian Washington, D.C., in which accidental peace is a constant threat. In this Buchwaldian Washington, D.C., he claims to have a constant fear that the number of Communists in the United States is decreasing. Buchwald is afraid that the Communist Party in the United States is becoming so infiltrated by U.S. government agents that some day the entire Communist Party will be made up of F.B.I. informants. These F.B.I. informants would pay their party dues, unlike the regular Communist Party members, and in time the Communists might become the leading political party in the country.

Summary

Art Buchwald is the most widely syndicated political satirist in the United States. He is read in 550 American newspapers, and between 1953 and 1984 he authored twenty-nine book-length political satires for major publishers.

Selected Bibliography

Primary Sources

Books

Art Buchwald's Paris. New York: Little, Brown, 1953.
The Brave Coward. New York: Harper, 1955.
More Caviar. New York: Harper, 1957.
A Gift from the Boys. New York: Harper, 1958.
Don't Forget to Write. New York: World, 1960.
How Much Is That in Dollars? New York: World, 1961.
Is It Safe to Drink the Water? New York: World, 1962.
I Chose Capitol Punishment. New York: World, 1963.
And Then I Told the President. New York: Putnam, 1965.
Son of the Great Society. New York: Putnam, 1966.
Have I Ever Lied to You? New York: Putnam, 1968.
The Establishment Is Alive and Well in Washington. New York: Putnam, 1969.
Counting Sheep. New York: Putnam, 1970.
Getting High in Government Circles. New York: Putnam, 1971.
I Never Danced at the White House. New York: Putnam, 1973.
Irving's Delight. New York: David McKay, 1975.
Washington Is Leaking. New York: Putnam, 1976.
I Am Not a Crook. New York: Fawcett, 1977.
The Buchwald Stops Here. New York: Putnam, 1978.
Down the Seine and Up the Potomac with Art Buchwald. New York: Fawcett, 1978.
The Bolo Caper: A Funny Tail for All Ages. New York: Putnam, 1983.

Laid Back in Washington. New York: Berkley, 1983.

While Reagan Slept. New York: Putnam, 1983.

Wilde, Larry; Goodman Ace; Mel Brooks; Art Buchwald; Abe Burrows; Bill Dana; Selma Diamond; Jack Doublas; Hal Kanter; Norman Lear; Carl Reiner; Neil Simon. *How the Great Comedy Writers Create Laughter.* Chicago: Nelson-Hall, 1976. (co-authored with Ann Buchwald.) *Seems Like Yesterday.* New York: Berkley, 1981.

Article

Black, Donald, and Art Buchwald. "2 Experts, Scientific and Wry, Study Laughter." *New York Times,* December 9, 1984, p. 32.

Secondary Sources

Duggan, Ervin S. "The Real Art Buchwald." *Washingtonian,* January 1985, pp. 112-119.

Kinsley, William. *From Aesop to Buchwald: A Review Essay.* Norman, Oklahoma, 1971.

Mintz, Lawrence E. *The Browning of Buchwald. Prospects* (Annual of American Cultural Studies), 1975.

Shanley, Andrew J. "Art Buchwald: Washington's Jester Drops His Mask to Talk Seriously About War, Reagan, and His Other Deepest Worries." *Geography,* January 1984, pp. 12-15.

Wynter, Leon E. "When Is a Computer Not a Computer? When It's a Comic; If Machines Can Write Gags, Will They Perform, Too? Buchwald Seeks Password." *Wall Street Journal,* May 6, 1985, p. 1.

Don L.F. Nilsen

Burdette, Robert Jones

Born: Greensboro, Pennsylvania, on July 30, 1844

Education: Hinman School and Peoria High School, Peoria, Illinois; Cooper Institute, New York, 1868; Theological Seminary of Kalamazoo, D.D., 1906

Marriages: Carrie Garrett, March 4, 1870, one child; Clara Bradley Wheeler-Baker, March 25, 1899

Died: November 19, 1914

Biography

Robert J. Burdette was born in Greensboro, Pennsylvania on July 30, 1844, the second of ten children in the family of Frederick and Sophia (Jones) Burdette. He grew up in Cumminsville, Ohio, and Peoria, Illinois. In Peoria he attended Hinman School, a private boys' academy, which he used later in his career as the setting for many of his humorous sketches about adolescence. By all accounts, Burdette's upbringing was happy and his family life stable.

In 1862 Burdette enlisted with the 47th Illinois regiment. He served on the Tennessee front and in the Vicksburg campaign and saw combat in more than twenty battles, distinguishing himself for leadership and bravery. His years of service were a formative period in his life, serving as a store of imagery and metaphor on which he drew throughout his writing career, and providing material for numerous uplifting sketches about military life which were collected as *The Drums of the 47th* (1914).

Following discharge from the army in 1865, Burdette worked as a country school teacher before entering the Cooper Institute in New York where he briefly studied languages and art. The New York sojourn ended within a year when he sailed for Cuba on a gun-running expedition, during which he was wounded. He returned to Peoria soon after and entered the newspaper trade.

Burdette married Carrie Garrett on March 4, 1870. She was an invalid at the time and never recovered though she was able to bear a son, Robert Jr., in 1877.

Burdette's first newspaper job was with the *Peoria Daily Transcript.* In 1871 he helped found the *Peoria Review,* and upon its demise joined the staff of the *Burlington* (Iowa) *Daily Hawk-Eye,* where he began a biweekly feature titled "Hawk-eyetems of Roaming Robert, the Hawkeye Man." These were gently humorous observations in sketch form on Burlington, Iowa, town life. So quickly were they picked up in the newspaper exchange that the *Hawk-Eye* developed a national reputation within a few years.

Burdette was a gifted extemporaneous speaker, so in response to the national attention he was receiving he turned to public speaking. His first lecture, delivered in Keokuk, Iowa, in December of 1876, was "The Rise and Fall of the Mustache," a rambling, extemporized rhapsody on the joys of parenthood which he claimed, at the end of his career, to have delivered over 5,000 times. So favorable was the response to Burdette's inaugural lecture that he signed with the Redpath Lyceum circuit in 1877. For the next decade he followed a murderous schedule that took him from coast to coast countless times and often had him living on trains for as many as eight or nine months out of the year. He was well rewarded for his efforts, however. "Rise and Fall" became one of the most popular lectures in American history, and Burdette was one of the circuit's biggest attractions, outdrawing even the celebrated Lyceum duo of Mark Twain and G.W. Cable. Burdette counted many friends among the lecturers of the period, including Henry Wheeler Shaw, William Lightfoot Vischer, Bill Nye, Henry Ward Beecher, and in particular James Whitcomb Riley, whom Burdette introduced to Eastern audiences. While lecturing, Burdette continued to write for the papers, sending the *Hawk-Eye* a letter a day until the mid-eighties when, having moved his family from Burlington to Ardmore, Pennsylvania, he began publishing a regular column in the Brooklyn *Eagle* and occasional pieces in the Philadelphia *Times*.

Religion was always a strong force in Burdette's life. While on tours, for example, he was a regular guest preacher, filling what he liked to call "one day" pastorates that were literally spread across the continent. During the final stages of his wife's illness, he spent a great deal of time involved with the Lower Merion Baptist Church in Bryn Mawr and began preaching there following her death in 1884. For the rest of his life he divided his time between lecturing and church-related activities, eventually moving to California when he married a widow, Clara Wheeler-Baker, in 1899, the same year that he accepted the pulpit of the First Presbyterian Church of Pasadena. In 1901 he helped found the Temple Baptist Church in Los Angeles and, following his ordination in 1903, served for six years as its minister, drawing an average Sunday attendance of over 3,000 to hear his sermons. Burdette also served as a City Commissioner in Pasadena and divided his last years among travel, church activities, and occasional writing projects for the *Los Angeles Times Magazine*. A serious injury in 1909 leading to chronic pancreatitis resulted in his death on November 19, 1914.

Literary Analysis

Burdette liked to refer to himself as an author of "humorous philosophy," by which term he meant light entertainment that, while far from didactic, always had a clear moral purpose. His avowed literary model was Charles Lamb, though in reality the exigencies of the newspaper business and the travel schedule of the Lyceum circuit never allowed him to develop a mastery of the formal essay. For the most part he was a paragraphist and occasional verse parodist. His best work tended toward sketches of a thousand words and was seldom thematic. He was a fine wit and a graceful literary stylist, but he never allowed verbal pyrotechnics to carry his writing. Though he occasionally used parody to make light of the popular taste for orientalia, he was not a true satirist. He preferred to sketch life in the manner of a local colorist, emphasizing amiable caricature and homely situations, which he softened with a stylish touch that made his work extremely palatable to the American Victorian sensibility and resulted in a phenomenal popularity. His stature as a popular humorist

is evidenced by the fact that he was exceeded only by Mark Twain in terms of the number of selections included in the 1888 edition of *Mark Twain's Library of Humor.*

Burdette's first collected volume was *The Rise and Fall of the Mustache and Other Hawk-eyetems* (1877), which contained the best examples of his town life sketches. These introduced some of his regular characters, including Master Bilderback, a romanticized version of the bad boys who populated the humor of the period, and the Middlerib family, whose persistent misfortunes foreshadowed the poor souls and perpetual victims of early twentieth-century humor. Burdette's favorite subjects were the mundane complications of a middle-class lifestyle that was neither rural nor urban. Lawn care, pets, school pranks, commercial transactions, house cleaning, and obnoxious neighbors were common topics and placed Burdette in the forefront of a gradually emerging focus on suburban lifestyles in American culture.

Burdette's second volume, *Hawk-Eyes* (1879), contained mostly pieces about train travel and life on the Lyceum circuit, subjects that produced his most memorable humor. He was sensitive to the enforced proximity of life on the road and the embarrassments that ensue from being alone without privacy. In brief sketches drafted without revision and mailed to the *Hawk-Eye*, he recorded these experiences through the eyes of a persona who was wry and aloof, producing humor that clarified Burdette's normally romantic vision with a drop of social realism. Burdette's letters and personal papers from this period, excerpted in *Robert J. Burdette, His Message* (1922), contain some of the most vivid accounts available of the rewards and hardships peculiar to the life of a professional lecturer.

Among Burdette's travel sketches was his one recognized masterpiece of American humor: "The Brakeman at Church," a thousand-word sketch that first appeared in the *Hawk-Eye* as a letter from Lebanon, Indiana, dated December 29, 1879. The piece was a straightforward exercise in extended metaphor, in which a railway veteran surveys the popular Protestant denominations of the day by characterizing each as a type of railroad. The Presbyterian church, for example, was described as "narrow gauge . . . pretty track, straight as a rule; tunnel right through the mountain rather than go around it, spirit-level grade . . . mighty straight road, but the cars are a little narrow, have to sit one in a seat and no room in the aisle to dance." So popular was this piece that it was reprinted by virtually every newspaper of note in the country. The *Hawk-Eye* reissued it as a pamphlet, and it was repeatedly published as a pocket memorandum for advertising purposes by dozens of businesses.

Burdette's subsequent collections—*Schooners That Pass in the Dark* (1894), *Chimes from a Jester's Bells* (1897), *Old Times and Young Tom* (1912)—contained materials culled from earlier volumes interspersed with original domestic sketches more maudlin than humorous. Other literary credits included a collection of verse parodies appropriately titled *Smiles Yoked with Sighs* (1900) and *The Silver Trumpets* (1912), a collection of religious verse.

Summary

Robert J. Burdette was the leading literary comedian of the 1870s and 80s, a newspaper contributor, successful lecturer and Baptist minister, whose humor emphasized genial wit played against sentimentality.

Selected Bibliography

Primary Sources

Humor

The Rise and Fall of the Mustache and Other Hawk-Eyetems. Burlington, Iowa: Burlington, 1877.
Hawk-Eyes. New York: C.W. Carleton, 1879.
Schooners That Pass in the Dark. New York: Dillingham, 1894.
Chimes from a Jester's Bells: Stories and Sketches. Indianapolis: Bowen-Merrill, 1897.
Old Time and Young Tom. Indianapolis: Bobbs-Merrill, 1912.

Poetry

Smiles Yoked With Sighs. Indianapolis: Bowen-Merrill, 1900.
The Silver Trumpets. Philadelphia: The Sunday School Times, 1912.

Miscellaneous

William Penn. New York: Holt, 1882.
The Modern Temple and Templars: A Sketch of the Life and Work of Russell H. Conwell, Pastor at the Baptist Temple, Philadelphia. New York: Silver, Burdette, 1894.
A Little Philosophy of Life. Pasadena: Clara Vista Press, 1914.
The Drums of the 47th. Indianapolis: Bobbs-Merrill, 1914.

Secondary Source

Burdette, Clara B., ed. *Robert J. Burdette, His Message.* Pasadena: Clara Vista Press, 1922. A quasi-biography compiled from extensive selections from Burdette's personal papers with continuity provided by Mrs. Burdette. This is the only book-length text about Burdette's life, highly colored by the editor's family connection.

Gary Engle

Burgess, Frank Gelett

Born: Boston, Massachusetts, on January 30, 1866
Education: Massachusetts Institute of Technology, B.A., 1887
Marriage: Estelle Loomis, 1914, no children
Died: September 18, 1951

Biography

Frank Gelett Burgess, American humorist, novelist, and short-story writer, was born in Boston, Massachusetts, on January 30, 1866. He was the son of Thomas H. Burgess and Caroline Brooks Burgess. He used the middle name, "Gelett," instead of "Frank," all of his life. As he grew up, he spent summers in West Falmouth, not far from Boston. Like most boys, he was of an adventurous nature. He told one interviewer that as a boy in Boston, he climbed to the top of every church steeple. "Always inside," he admitted. In those steeples, he left his mark, a circular combination of Phoenician letters which he adopted as his signature.[1]

Burgess studied civil engineering at the Massachusetts Institute of Technology, thinking that would give him a chance to do sketching.[2] He graduated in 1887, when he was twenty-one.[3] While in college, he edited the *Tech*, the student magazine.[4]

The young college graduate went job-hunting and found a position with the Southern Pacific Railroad as a surveyor. He worked for the firm three years. All that time he was having a conflict between his mathematical nature and his love for art. The artist got the upper hand and he bought a knapsack and started out on a walking and sketching trip through France and Spain.[5]

In 1891 Burgess returned to San Francisco, decided to cross the Bay to Berkeley and was employed as an instructor in topographical drawing at the University of California in Berkeley.[6] He described his teaching career later as a time when for three years he "taught country boys the difference between their hands and their feet."[7]

One of his artistic revolts brought an end to his career as a university instructor. A patent medicine manufacturer, Dr. Cogswell (who was also a temperance advocate), had presented the city of San Francisco with a cast-iron effigy of himself holding a book in one hand and a bottle (out of which water flowed) in the other. The figure jarred on the nerves of Burgess and one night he waded into the basin surrounding the figure and pulled down the statue.[8]

He commented that he thus became the first practical iconoclast in America. The graduating class at the university elected him an honorary member after the escapade became known but, according to Burgess in the interview with S. J. Woolf, "the faculty decided he had better look elsewhere for a job."[9]

Small magazines were springing up in both England and America during this period. *The Chap Book* and *The Wave* were published in Chicago and gained attention among literary figures. However, in San Francisco, where Burgess was looking around for something to do, *The Lark* began publication with the objective of bringing a "new note, some of the joy of morning for the refreshment of our souls in the heat of midday."[10]

Burgess was associated with Bruce Porter in *The Lark*, and the publication lasted for two years, from 1895 to 1897. He began his literary career as both author and illustrator in that magazine, and often wrote entire numbers "from cover design to jocose advertisements."[11]

In the first issue of *The Lark*, Burgess wrote a quatrain called "The Purple Cow" that followed him the rest of his life. The bit of poetry tickled the fancy of readers in a way that the sophisticated readers of the last half of the twentieth century find hard to understand. In that period (the last decade of the nineteenth century), it almost became his trademark. The quatrain was:

> I never saw a Purple Cow,
> I never hope to see one;
> But I can tell you, anyhow,
> I'd rather see than be one.[12]

When Burgess moved to New York in later years, he wrote a sequel to his then-famous quatrain:

> Oh, yes, I wrote the "Purple Cow"—
> I'm sorry now, I wrote it!
> But I can tell you, anyhow,
> I'll kill you if you quote it.

The sequel appeared in *Cinq Ans Après* in 1900.[13]

Among the short poems that caught the fancy of readers of the magazine were the following:

> I wish that my Room had a Floor!
> I don't so much care for a Door,
>   But this crawling around
>   Without touching the Ground
> Is getting to be quite a Bore![14]

Another poem written and illustrated by Burgess was titled "The Invisible Bridge." Two young men were shown groping their way through mid-air, crossing over the heads of people who watched from roof and street:

> I'd never dare to walk across
> A Bridge I could not see,
> For Much afraid of falling off
> I fear that I should be.[15]

Another bit of rhyme, called "The Lamp Post Theory," showed a tall lamp post and two stumpy ones:

> There is a Theory some deny
> That Lamp Posts once were three foot high,
> And a Little Boy was terrible strong,
> And he stretched 'em out to 'leven foot long![16]

In one of the early numbers of *The Lark*, Burgess announced another magazine that he entitled *Le Petit Journal des Refusées*. His announcement claimed that the new journal would accept only articles that were accompanied by a rejection letter from a leading magazine of the literary establishment. In his editorial statement he observed, "There are 63,250,000 people in the United States. Of these, but 50,000 have suffered amputation of both hands. For the remaining 63,200,000 writers, there are today but 7,000 periodicals. . . ." He chose to publish the disappointed writers in a magazine printed on wallpaper, and cut into trapezoid shapes.[17]

While still editing *The Lark*, Burgess turned his attention to fiction. He wrote short stories as well as novels and plays, but continued his adventures with children's books. While he illustrated some of the books, friends illustrated some of the issues of *The Lark*. Among those friends were Bruce Porter (already mentioned as a partner in publishing *The Lark*, who had helped him raise one hundred dollars to publish the first issue of that magazine), Carolyn Wells, Ernest Peixotto, and Florence Lundborg. William Doxey, a San Francisco bookseller, financed publication of *The Lark* after the first issue.[18]

Although *The Lark* was making money after two years, Burgess decided to stop publication. He felt that its popularity had been a product of the times and that what he called "its end of the century madness" would run its course shortly. Soon after he moved from the West Coast to New York. There he published a number of works that were popular for a time. One of those, *Goops and How to Be Them*, published in 1900, proposed to be a manual of manners for Polite Infants and tried to teach by negative example. Throughout the small volume (which he illustrated), he dramatized his controlling theme: "For, although it's Fun to See them, It is Terrible to be them!"

Parents were more impressed by the didactic qualities of the books than were their children, but the Goops became popular and sequels were published. Among the sequels were: *More Goops and How Not to Be Them* (1903); *Blue*

Goops and Red (1909); *The Goop Directory of Juvenile Offenders* (1913); and *New Goops and How to Know Them* (1951). In 1984 Dover Publications published *The Gelett Burgess Coloring Book, The Goops*. The publishing firm noted, "The pictures and verses reproduced here are selections from two works by Gelett Burgess published by Frederick A. Stokes Company: *Goops and How to Be Them* . . . and *More Goops and How Not to Be Them*."[19] Grandchildren and great-grandchildren of the readers of the original books are still finding the poems and illustrations of Gelett Burgess entertaining.

In 1906 Burgess published a work that he titled *Are You a Bromide? or The Sulphitic Theory*. In 1907 *The Maxims of Methuselah* was published. He followed that book with *The Maxims of Noah* in 1913, and in 1941 published *Burgess Unabridged*. While editing *The Lark* in California, the writer had tried his hand at a series of short stories and he had moved in a circle of writing friends called "Les Jeunes." When he established himself in New York, he continued his pattern of avoiding timeworn and mundane approaches to writing and sought always to find fresh creative ways of expression in both writing and art.

In 1914 Burgess married Estelle Loomis, a former actress. He lived in France during World War I but was not involved in the war. In addition to his books, he wrote a number of essays that appeared in *Masses, Companion, American Magazine, Smart Set*, and *Critic*.[20]

After the war, as life settled into so-called normalcy, he continued to write novels, poems, and plays, and to illustrate some of his own work. His popularity faded as years went by, and he went back to the West Coast in 1949. He lived in Carmel during those last years and died on September 18, 1951.

Literary Analysis

Much of Burgess's work is dated now, but in the light of its popularity during the last decade of the nineteenth century and the first decades of the twentieth century, he needs and deserves recognition, particularly because of his innovative approach to each genre of literature. Determined not to bog down in Victorian style, he ventured into new forms of writing and new ideas. At one time when he was hard up for funds, he persuaded the editor of a Sunday paper to give him an advance of $750. With that money he proposed to go to Europe, buy a title, and write about his experiences. He suffered some setbacks when the officials of San Marino raised the price of a title he had hoped to buy there; in a small monarchy where he planned to settle for his adventures, a revolution broke out,

and the monarchy became a republic, defeating that plan.[21]

The short stories that he wrote while editing *The Lark* included a series that was called "The Romance Association," an umbrella title for stories about Robin, the narrator, and his wife, Vivette, who hired themselves out to create scenarios that would bring excitement and unexpected adventures into the lives of clients who were bored with life. As the author described his goal in those works, "instead of set scenes and printed flats, we perform on the picturesque stage of life."[22]

Burgess introduced new words into the vocabularies of his readers. In his work entitled *Are You a Bromide: or The Sulphitic Theory*, he struck a humorous tone as he tried to explain the two basic kinds of human behavior. The term "bromide" is used as a synonym for a bore. The sulphitic person he described as an original thinker. He said that the sulphitic person was one whose actions could never be foreseen, "except that it will be a spontaneous manifestation of his own personality."[23]

A number of words coined by Burgess have become a part of the speech today. Among those words are "blurb," "goop," "bromide," "smagg," and "vram." Several of the words are credited to him in dictionary definitions.[24]

The Maxims of Methuselah was a collection of sharply worded, biting epigrams. His book *Burgess Unabridged* represented the lifelong interest that he had in exploring the sound and meaning of individual words.

Critics vary in their evaluation of Burgess's work. Walter Blair and Hamlin Hill consider *The Lark* to be the predecessor of such publications as *Mad Magazine* and the *National Lampoon*.[25] There was enthusiastic support from those who understood that Burgess was a rebel. Nearly every step of his career revealed that. Others, however, were annoyed by his writing. The *Chicago Journal* said that it was "weary" of the painful attempt to do something new."[26] Readers and critics who disapproved of his obvious rebellion against old, stale approaches often forgot that he had also tried his hand at such pastoral pieces as "The Last Nymph," "Nerea," and "The Ambitious Shepherd," which followed the pattern of sixteenth- and seventeenth-century writers. These efforts were tiresome, but Burgess did not abandon his more scholarly pursuits. In 1948, shortly before he returned to the West Coast, Burgess entered into a serious controversy about the authorship of William Shakespeare's works, that is, whether they were written by some other writer of the period. His articles were printed in the *Saturday Review of Literature*. In October 1948, Burgess commented on an article in the June 5, 1948, issue of *SRL* by a critic named Redman who reviewed *Shakespeare: 23 Plays and the Sonnets*, edited by G.B. Harrison. Burgess disagreed with some of Redman's comments and responded in an article called "Pseudonym, Shakespeare." Another critic, Clark Kinnaird, replied to the Burgess article, and Cranston also wrote a reply. Apparently other writer-scholars became involved in the controversy, for by February 5, 1949, Burgess had prepared a counter-refutation. He ignored Kinnaird's letter but replied in some detail to that of Cranston, and he referred to letters from a Mr. Hoepner and from Mr. Humphrey who also disagreed with his theory about the authorship of the Shakespearean plays.[27]

Burgess even had a definite philosophy about his humor. In his interview with S.J. Woolf, he said: "Humor is the most serious subject in the world and it's almost impossible to discuss it without being solemn."[28] The humorist spent hours revising everything he wrote. He was a purist in the use of the English language. Woolf reported that Burgess once stopped the presses of a magazine to change one single word. He once wrote an entire article in words of one syllable to prove that they have more "might" than longer ones. While the two talked, Woolf sketched a portrait of the humorist. Burgess examined the drawing, then offered to superimpose some sketches of the Goops on the bottom of the picture. However, before doing the drawings he carefully did a sketch of them on another piece of paper, then copied them from that first drawing onto the portrait.[29]

When Robert Van Gelder interviewed Burgess for the *New York Times Book Review* in 1941, while the writer was still living in New York, he preserved for future readers a picture of the man as he looked at that time: "Even a baldish head, elfin eyes that peer through rimless glasses, and a mustache so thin that it might be a misplaced eyebrow, did not dispel a look of gloom."[30] Van Gelder did more than give the description of the man; he told readers what Burgess was like and how he used his time:

> . . . he is almost as invisible as his purple cow. There is a tenuous quality about his conversation that at times blurs outlines. But after all, this is to be expected of a man who spends his spare time constructing complicated machines out of buttons, hairpins, knitting needles, paper clips and toothpicks. . . . He has turned his hotel room into a factory, keeps pliers with his safety razor, and a saw without a handle in one of his shoes.[31]

The reporter said that when Burgess completed one of his machines after months of work, he sat and gloated over it, while Mrs. Burgess fretted and fumed and implored him to build something useful.

In 1937 Burgess wrote a book called *Look Eleven Years Younger*, in which he exhorted readers to give attention to both mental and physical health.[32] One of his most popular articles, published first in *Ladies Home Journal*, April 1943, was reprinted in *Reader's Digest* in May 1966. The article, "Don't Sell Yourself Short," fit well into the then-developing pattern of self-help books.

Summary

Gelett Burgess was a rebel and he introduced new and fresh ways of looking at life through his writing and his illustrations. Perhaps his books for children are his best known, but he wrote something for every age group and for nearly every interest. Although some of his work is dated now and he is seldom read, his place as a writer-humorist is assured. Few people remember his name but practically everyone knows about the "purple cow," "the Goops," and the "bromides." All copywriters use the word "blurb" as a part of their working vocabulary. Best of all, the work of Gelett Burgess reveals an always-young attitude of joy, and delight in the experiences of life.

Notes

1. S.J. Woolf, "Still No Purple Cow," *New York Times Magazine*, June 8, 1941, pp. 16–17.
2. Ibid.
3. John Wenke, "Gelett Burgess," *Dictionary of Literary Biography*,Vol. 11, *American Humorists, 1800-1950*, Part I (Detroit: Gale Research Co., 1983), p. 69.
4. Stanley J. Kunitz and Howard Haycraft, eds., *Twentieth Century Authors* (New York: H.W. Wilson Co., 1942), pp. 219–220.
5. Woolf, *New York Times Magazine*, pp. 16–17.
6. Ibid.
7. Ibid.
8. Kunitz; Haycraft, *Twentieth Century Authors*, p. 219.
9. Woolf, *New York Times Magazine*, p. 17.
10. Ibid.
11. Kunitz; Haycraft, *Twentieth Century Authors*, p. 220.
12. Ibid.
13. Wenke, *Dictionary of Literary Biography*, p. 74.
14. Ibid.
15. Ibid.
16. Ibid.
17. Ibid., p. 74.
18. Ibid., p. 71.
19. Dover Publications, Publisher's Note, 1984.
20. Wenke, *Dictionary of Literary Biography*, p. 76.
21. Woolf, *New York Times Magazine*, p. 16.

22. Wenke, *Dictionary of Literary Biography*, p. 75.
23. Ibid.
24. Webster's *New Collegiate Dictionary*, 1965, shows that "blurb" and "goop" were coined or invented by Burgess. In Webster's *Ninth New Collegiate Dictionary*, "goop" appears but is not credited to Burgess. "Blurb" is "coined by Gelett Burgess" in the Ninth Edition.
25. Wenke, *Dictionary of Literary Biography*, p. 75.
26. Ibid., p. 72.
27. Walter Blair and John Gerber, eds., *The College Anthology* (Chicago: Scott, Foresman and Company, 1949), pp. 125-133.
28. Woolf, *New York Times Magazine*, p. 17.
29. Ibid.
30. Robert Van Gelder, "An Interview with Mr. Gelett Burgess," *The New York Times Book Review*, June 8, 1941, p. 2.
31. Ibid.
32. Burgess, *Look Eleven Years Younger* (New York: Simon and Schuster, 1937).

Selected Bibliography

Primary Sources

Goops and How to Be Them. New York: Stokes, 1900.
The Burgess Nonsense Book. New York: Stokes, 1901; London: Simpkin, Marshall, Hamilton, Kent, 1914.
A Little Sister of Destiny. New York: Houghton Mifflin, 1906.
The White Cat. Indianapolis: Bobbs-Merrill, 1907.
War the Creator. New York: Huebsch, 1916.
Why Men Hate Women. New York: Payson & Clark, 1927.
The Bromide and Other Theories. New York: Viking, 1933.
Two O'Clock Courage. Indianapolis: Bobbs-Merrill, 1934
"Have You an Educated Heart?" *Reader's Digest*, January 1934; rpt. October 1941.
Look Eleven Years Younger. New York: Simon & Schuster, 1937.
"Sympathy Is What You Make It." *Reader's Digest*; rpt. from *Forbes*, April 15, 1942.
The Goops Coloring Book. New York: Dover Publications, 1984.

Secondary Sources

Articles in Books

Blair, Walter, and John Gerber. *The College Anthology*. Chicago: Scott, Foresman, 1949.
Kunitz, Stanley J., and Howard Haycraft, eds. *Twentieth Century Authors*. New York: H.W. Wilson, 1942.
Harris, William H., and Judith S. Levey, *The New Columbia Encyclopedia*. New York: Columbia University Press, 1975.
Webster's Biographical Dictionary. Springfield, Mass.: G. & C. Merriam, Publishers, 1966.
Wenke, John. "Gelett Burgess." In *Dictionary of Literary Biography*. Vol. 11. *American Humorists, 1800-1950*. Part 1. Detroit: Gale Research, 1982, pp. 68-76.

Newspapers and Periodicals

The New York Times, September 18, 1951; September 20, 1951.

Van Gelder, Robert. "An Interview with Mr. Gelett Burgess." *The New York Times Book Review*, June 8, 1941, p. 2.
Woolf, S.J. "Still No Purple Cow." *New York Times Magazine*, pp. 16-17.

Irma R. Cruse

Cerf, Bennett Alfred

Born: New York City, on May 25, 1898
Education: Columbia University, B.A., 1919; Columbia University School of Journalism, Litt.B., 1919
Marriages: Sylvia Sydney, 1935-1936; Phyllis Frazier, 1940, two children
Died: August 27, 1971

Biography

Bennett Cerf was perhaps America's best-known publisher-humorist during the middle part of the twentieth century. His sense of humor made him a popular television personality in middle America, where the names of New York City publishers are not often on everyone's lips. Cerf was a panelist on the television game show, "What's My Line?" Each week, he offered a pun to host John Charles Daly, and all America groaned. A steady audience bought Cerf's collections of puns and riddles, plugged on television every Sunday evening by his presence.

Cerf was the son of Gustave and Fredricka Cerf, and was born in New York City on May 25, 1898. He spent his whole life in the city, save for a few stints elsewhere—as during the First World War, when he served in the United States Army. Educated at Columbia, he earned two degrees before going to work for eccentric publisher Horace Liveright at Boni and Liveright in 1923. Cerf was vice-president of the company when he left it in 1925, buying out Liveright's shares in the Modern Library. With partner Donald Klopfer, Cerf revived the Modern Library, which had an extensive list of inexpensive hardbound editions of literary classics. Cerf and Klopfer also established Random House publishers in 1927. Random House and Alfred A. Knopf (with whom Cerf would form a partnership 30 years later) set the standards for American book publishing during the middle of the twentieth century.

Cerf was an activist publisher. In the early 1930s, when James Joyce's *Ulysses* was banned in the United States, Cerf had a copy smuggled into the country. It was seized (as Cerf had hoped) by customs officials, and the book was put on "trial." The particular book Cerf had arranged to be smuggled had reviews praising it pasted on the inside cover. When the book came to trial, with the pasted-in reviews as part of the evidence, the result was a landmark decision that opened the doors for literary material previously banned because of sexual content. Cerf then happily published *Ulysses* in the United States.

In addition, Cerf's authors included William Faulkner, Eugene O'Neill, Gertrude Stein, William Styron, Truman Capote, Ayn Rand, John O'Hara, William Saroyan, James Michener, and Dr. Seuss. He was an innovative publisher, and besides restoring the Modern Library and developing a stable of great American writers, he was a ground-breaking children's publisher. Random House's Landmark Books of nonfiction for young readers are still regarded as one of the great creations in juvenile publishing.

Cerf was a showman, so it was natural that he would become a regular on a television show. That second career—as a "What's My Line?" panelist—opened doors that would have been closed otherwise. In his autobiography he described the chilly reception he first received from William Faulkner's relatives when he traveled to Oxford, Mississippi, for Faulkner's funeral. But, when he was recognized as Bennett Cerf the famous game-show panelist, the Faulkner relatives suddenly changed their attitudes. He was a regular on the show from 1952 until 1966 and was visible in other ways. He wrote the column, "Cerfboard," in *This Week* through the 1950s and contributed "Trade Winds" to *The Saturday Review* from 1942 to 1957. His humor column, "Try and Stop Me," was syndicated by King Features.

Briefly married to actress Sylvia Sydney, Cerf later married Phyllis Frazier in 1940, in a ceremony performed by New York Mayor Fiorello LaGuardia. He described his marriage as "glorious, just about perfect." According to his autobiography, Phyllis Cerf was nearly a full partner in the Random House enterprise. They had two sons, Jonathan and Christopher.

Cerf died in 1971, and not long after his death the "Trade Winds" column in *The Saturday Review* carried this notice: "He set out to be a book publisher, and he became one of the best. He gave full measure to his profession. Everyone connected with the world of books is in his debt."

Literary Analysis

Cerf was described as a "connoisseur of puns and anecdotes" and a "tireless raconteur whose joke books and anthologies have become best sellers." The pun-of-the-week Cerf would offer the millions of "What's My Line?" fans would often be from the collections of puns, riddles, and anecdotes that he had edited. He published these collections for dual audiences of adults and children:

> Q. What's big and red and eats rocks?
> A. A big, red, rock eater.

After several years as a successful publisher, Cerf put together a collection that he bragged was "crammed with over forty years of stories that I had collected." *Try and Stop Me* was published in 1944 and became a number-one bestseller. As was Cerf's custom (and it became an industry custom), his book was published by a firm other than his own. King Features Syndicate bought the rights to serialize the book, and after excerpts had been drawn from it daily for nearly a year, the book was "used up." But, the public wanted more. King Features asked Cerf to continue the column, which he did, producing two or three anecdotes daily.

Cerf was less an originator than he was a jokester. As a highly skilled joke-teller on television and in print, he served a clearinghouse function. No man could be expected to create the amount of material demanded of Cerf, and one of his particular prizes was the anecdote. As a member of show business and literary society, Cerf heard many stories that he dutifully passed on to his readers. Here is one such:

> Professional comedians rarely appreciate each other's talents, but George Burns and Jack Benny are notable exceptions to the rule. Not only have they been fast friends for thirty-odd years, but Burns can break Benny up by merely sticking his tongue out at him. Benny calls Burns up from all corners of the globe just to gab with him, and keeps yakking so long that Burns usually ends up by hanging up on him.
>
> Benny, in fact, now counts on this so that one day in Hollywood he told an agent named Rubin, "I'm calling George Burns in Chicago in ten minutes and I'll bet you twenty-five dollars he hangs up on me." Rubin accepted the bet. When Benny got George Burns on the wire, their usual kidding, desultory conversation ensued. Finally Benny, sounding puzzled, said, "Well, George, aren't you going to hang up on me in your usual insulting fashion?"
>
> "I certainly am not," declared Burns, then added, "and by the way, Rubin called me and gave me half his bet."
>
> (From *Laugh Day*)

Summary

Bennett Cerf was a major figure in American publishing, and a skilled humorist in his own right. Cerf collected and dispensed anecdotes, puns, and riddles for an audience evenly divided between adults and children.

Selected Bibliography

Primary Sources

The Pocket Book of War Humor. New York: Pocket, 1943.

Try and Stop Me. New York: Simon and Schuster, 1944.

Laughing Stock. New York: Doubleday, 1945.

Anything for a Laugh. New York: Doubleday, 1946.

Shake Well Before Using. New York: Doubleday, 1948.

Laughter, Inc. New York: Doubleday, 1950.

Good for a Laugh. New York: Doubleday, 1950.

An Encyclopedia of American Humor. New York: Doubleday, 1954.

The Life of the Party. New York: Doubleday, 1956.

Reading for Pleasure. New York: Harper, 1957.

Out on a Limerick. New York: Harper, 1960.

The Laugh's on Me. New York: Doubleday, 1960.

Laugh Day. New York: Doubleday, 1964.

A Treasury of Atrocious Puns. New York: Doubleday, 1968.

The Sound of Laughter. New York: Doubleday, 1970.

At Random. New York: Random House, 1977.

Secondary Sources

Current Biography.

Who's Who in America.

William McKeen

Chappell, Fred

Born: Canton, North Carolina, on May 28, 1936

Education: Canton High School, 1954; Duke University, B.A., 1961, M.A., 1964

Marriage: Susan Nicholls, August 2, 1959, one child

Biography

Fred Chappell is a gifted philosophical writer, social critic, humorist, and, above all, a fine poet with a sharp talent for piquant vernacular dialogue and the imagery of nature. He is also a southern writer with a strong sense of place; realizing the importance of the rural mountain country of western North Carolina to this writer is a prerequisite to understanding Chappell's novels, short stories, and poems. As Andrew Harper in Chappell's *Gaudy Place* (1973) says,

the Appalachian sensibility differs from that of the Deep South or even from that of other parts of North Carolina such as the central Piedmont area or the coastal towns along the Outer Banks.

The farms created in Chappell's verse poem, *Midquest* (1981), and those of his own youth were small, and the cultivation of their hilly and rocky soil difficult. Farm life was hard and exhausting, the only diversions being "hardshell Baptist preachers" or the moonshine made in the hills by three hundred-pound Big Mama and her three boys. As J.T. says in *Bloodfire* (1978), "it's good to know/ The eternal verities still hold their own,/ That poverty and whiskey and scratch-ankle farming/ Still prop the mountains up."[1] Like Chappell himself, the autobiographical narrator from *Midquest*, "old Fred," is living at a time when the traditions of mountain life are being leached out of the soil by urban customs and the poverty of farm life. Chappell believes that the uprooting of mountain families led to a dislocation of values.[2] Yet, he also sees that the misery inflicted by poverty has been driving people away from their farms. His thoughts are spoken by Virgil Campbell, the Southwestern wag, who says as he watches his house destroyed by a flood: "'Guy works and slaves and where's/ It get you. . . . A limp dick, gray hairs,/ A pile of debts is all I know.'"[3] One part of mountain life retains its power over Chappell—the Puritan conviction of human damnation and its perspective on life as a struggle between the fallen part of human beings, their desires or "appetites," and the "wills" or minds that give them the illusion of controlling their own lives. In Chappell's work the ancient Manichean struggle (mind-body, good-evil, heaven-hell) is fought in a philosophical battle in which the forces he names the "will" and the "appetite" take on the names of characters and struggle for control of the human psyche. Like Nathaniel Hawthorne's Young Goodman Brown, Chappell's characters see life only in these dualistic terms and throw themselves into a false choice between the blindly self-willed life in which all desires are denied and the despairing and frenzied pursuit of sensation exacerbated by a paralysis of will. The struggle to maintain a balance between will and appetite is the source of tension in everything that Chappell has written, from his undergraduate poetry about his father and grandparents to his most recent novel, *I Am One of You Forever* (1985).

Unfortunately, this balance is never achieved. In most of the novels appetite wins out; it is always a destructive and evil force, never a desire that can be safely or healthily satiated or one that has a right to some satisfaction. To view desire as simply destructive is clearly reactionary, a return to the oppressive concept of original sin and to the conviction that there is a basic evil lurking in each person that, if given freedom, would pervert everything that has a claim on civilization. Chappell's nightmare is given full freedom in his surrealistic novel *Dagon* (1968), an allegory of the unleashed appetite and the abnegated will. *Dagon* was the last novel of this type that Chappell wrote; his subsequent fiction, *The Gaudy Place* (1973), *Moments of Light* (1980), and *I Am One of You Forever* (1985), turns toward more humane and less philosophical concerns and a new appreciation of humor's role in distancing pain.

Emerging from a *purgatorio* in his fiction, Chappell rediscovered detached humor and the sharply comic natural imagery in the language of his family and neighbors who lived in the mountains. He also saw the importance of the stability of life lived with several generations of family on the same land—as he lived during his first eighteen years. He grew up on the family farm surrounded by his grandparents, his mother, Anne Davis Chappell, who was a schoolteacher, and his father, James Taylor Chappell, who was a farmer and schoolteacher. Another source of continuity was that all of Chappell's education took place in North Carolina. He was graduated from Canton High School in 1954 and from Duke University with a B.A. in 1961, and an M.A. in 1964. Chappell married fellow Canton native Susan Nicholls in 1959; they have a son, Heath.

As an adolescent in Canton, Chappell felt trapped in a limited environment, and he and a friend, "Fuzz," formed a cabal against their parochial world.[4] Although their camaraderie led to readings of Baudelaire and Rimbaud, they also fed one another's feelings of frustration and hopelessness. When Chappell matriculated at Duke he began to write poetry seriously; he still considers himself primarily a poet. At Duke Chappell found friends like Reynolds Price who were also talented writers. More important, though, was his contact with William Blackburn, the Duke professor of creative writing who had taught William Styron and Mac Hyman. Blackburn offered encouragement, instruction, and an outlet for publication in the anthology *Under Twenty-Five* (1963), a collection of prose and poetry by Duke undergraduates.

After receiving his degree Chappell entered Duke's M.A. program and began work on a massive thesis, a concordance to Samuel Johnson's poetry. He also began writing fiction and published *It Is Time, Lord* (1963), a novel in which the central character, James Christopher, tries to understand his passivity by delving into the most painful experiences of his childhood but discovers that the self is too precious a resource to spend on the futile effort of fixing an immuta-

ble past. After receiving his M.A. in 1964, Chappell moved to the University of North Carolina at Greensboro to become the writer in residence. In 1964 he published *The Inkling*, a novel that contrasts the powers of the will and the appetite in the form of Jan Andersen, who is "fiercely self-willed," and his insane sister, Timmie, who represents uncontrolled desire.[5] While in Florence on a Rockefeller Foundation grant, Chappell wrote *Dagon*, a novel that takes his obsessive interest in the submerged will to the limits of realism and into a surrealistic surrender to Dagon, the mutilated god whom Leland associates with maimed sexuality and materialism.

Because of philosophical concerns of Chappell's novels it is unlikely that he will ever be a popular writer; his obsession with free will, the past, desire, and the relation of causality and action are highly intellectual concerns. Moreover, his narrative point of view is difficult. He switches narrators frequently (*The Gaudy Place*), uses unreliable narrators (*It Is Time, Lord*), pushes realism into surrealism (*Dagon*) or dream imagery (*It Is Time, Lord* and *I Am One of You Forever*), and uses a time warp to confront the young narrator of *The Inkling* with an older version of himself.

Chappell has written a great deal of fiction, including a collection of short stories, *Moments of Light*, but his best work is his poetry. Since college he has published steadily; a 1983 bibliography lists 178 individual entries for poems.[6] Chappell's first collection, *The World Between the Eyes* (1971), treats the themes of *It Is Time, Lord* in more depth.

During the mid-1970s Chappell labored on his most important work to date, a four-volume examination of his mountain homeland and its people, their values, their humor, their poverty, and their resilience. *Midquest*'s point of departure is the narrator's thirty-fifth birthday—May 28, 1971—the door to middle age. It is a door that he can open into the past and then into the second part of his life. Each of the volumes was published separately as *River* (1975), *Bloodfire* (1978), *Wind Mountain* (1979), and *Earthsleep* (1980) before publication as the tetralogy *Midquest* (1981). Like *Ulysses*, *Midquest* treats one day only, even though it attempts to review Fred's entire past and present.

In 1984 Chappell published another cycle of related poems in *Castle Tzingal*. Tzingal is an imagined kingdom where the king, "an iron and fruitless man," poisons the lives of his queen Frynna, the poet Marco, and the admiral of his navy.[7] The collection is a political satire aimed at those whose values kill the poetic voice. In his most recent collection of poetry, *Source* (1985), the poet returns to his literal source of inspiration in the mountains, where he reaffirms his bond with the Appalachian country. The narrative voice celebrates all forms of natural life around it and tries to become one of them: "Let me lie there too and share the sleep/ Of the cool ground's mildest children."[8] Chappell's talent is flowering and producing fiction and poetry, and since he is still not past the midquest of his own life, we can expect more from him, including a forthcoming short story collection, *Waltzes Noble and Sentimental.*

Literary Analysis

Fred Chappell is a philosophical writer concerned with a number of ontological questions: How much does the past determine us? What is the balance between will and appetite? Is there action without cause? He asks, in addition, about the farmers' closeness to nature and wonders whether a life bonded with the earth obviates the concerns of the alienated and passive man whose father may have been a member of the last generation of farmers. These concerns are predicated on an acceptance of one of the major props to the old farm life, as Chappell remembers it—the religious belief that posits man as "fallen" and inherently evil—a pessimism that shadows most of his work.

Chappell occasionally writes from a "comic," Dantean perspective, which attempts to subsume all of the world's good and evil to a larger and desirable conclusion. There are also moments of laughter in the novels, but it is usually the detached, even humorless reaction of a character realizing the absurdity of his situation. At the end of *The Gaudy Place* Andrew Harper laughs at the distance between his wealthy Uncle Zebulon and the young con man, Arkie. Although Arkie mistakenly shoots Zeb, thinking that he is Clemmie's new pimp, Zeb does carry some responsibility for the shooting since he is a corrupt and greedy landowner in Arkie's rundown Gimlet Street area. In *Dagon* Peter Leland suffers a ritualistic murder as a sacrifice to an omnipotent but inhuman god. After his death Leland reviews his life and laughs without rancor because he has retained his sense of identity. From the vantage of death, "he perceived with a dispassionate humor the whole of human destiny" and laughs (p. 176).

Humor, as opposed to dispassionate laughter, is a major force in Chappell's most recent novel, *I Am One of You Forever*, his collection of short stories *Moments of Light*, and his long tetralogy, *Midquest*, which the poet calls a "verse novel."[9] The poem is based on the four elements: water, fire, wind, and earth and attempts to investigate all of human experience, good and bad, within the confines of one day and the experience of one man, a structure that deliberately follows Dante's *Divine Comedy*, whose narrator also re-

considers his life at age thirty-five. Into this structure Chappell tried to inject humor since it was one of the elements he thought missing in contemporary poetry (Preface, *Midquest*, p. x). The four books of *Midquest* invoke laughter through eccentric "humour" characters like Virgil Campbell and because they remind us of the old definition of "humourous" as referring to the four elements and four physiological fluids that were thought to comprise the universe and the human body. The humorous person was originally one whose disposition led him or her to a quick perception of the laughable.[10]

Midquest is also humorous in the usual sense of provoking laughter. One poem in each volume is devoted to Campbell, who provides the major source of amusement. In these four poems, "Dead Soldiers" (*River*), "Firewater" (*Bloodfire*), "Three Sheets in the Wind" (*Wind Mountain*), and "At the Grave of Virgil Campbell" (*Earthsleep*), Chappell lightens the tetralogy through Virgil, an eccentric, independent, hard-drinking and preacher-cussing mountain shopkeeper.

Virgil comes from the tradition of Southwestern humor: Fred's father, J.T., acts as genteel listener of Virgil's highly flavored vernacular stories and tall tales; and like the ring-tailed roarers celebrated in early nineteenth-century humor, Campbell also exaggerates, drinks, and boasts his independence. David Paul Ragan has established the specific influence of Sut Lovingood in creating a character who is coarse and vulgar but has respect for truth and rebels against intolerance, hypocrisy, and even the uncontrollable forces of nature such as fires and floods.[11] Like Mark Twain, however, Chappell makes us respect his narrator. J.T. and his son, Fred, do not laugh at Virgil; they respect his feelings of independence from the small-mindedness of the local school board and the self-righteousness of the "hillside holies" who proselytize him and "witness at" him for not hiding his drinking from the preachers. Campbell is an older and less naive Huck Finn who lives independently of civilization's rules; thus, humor is often blended with satire.

In *It Is Time, Lord*, Chappell's first novel, Virgil shows his open-mindedness when J.T. loses his job teaching because he was growing alfalfa in a jar to observe paramecia. When his detractors claim that he is blasphemously trying to "create life," J.T. is forced out. Fortunately, Virgil is there to guide him through the ordeal, offering to find him a new job and lending moral support:

> At last my father spoke. "What I suppose you're going to hear is that I said that man is descended from the mon-

keys. Something like that, anyway."

"Hell, I knew that," Mr. Campbell said. "Any damn fool can see that."

(p. 90)

Virgil shows his independence here as well as in "Dead Soldiers," a poem recounting a damaging 1946 flood that threatened to smash the Fiberville bridge. Instead of adopting a fatalistic attitude, Virgil fights back by shooting the scores of whiskey jars (the dead soldiers) that float out of his basement. Fred admires Virgil's courage, his ability to see his house eaten away by the polluted and swollen stream and still jokingly shoot the crumbling bridge, saying "Better put it out of its misery" (*River*, p. 28).

"Firewater" is Virgil's tall tale, told in colorful vernacular, of the one hundredth anniversary of Clay County. The moonshiner Big Mama, whom the deputy has been trying to catch for years, is invited to parade down Main Street with a model still. She consents and brings more than a model with her. The mule walking behind her floats along staggeringly drunk—just on the fumes. The deputy tries to arrest her, but the presence of her three sons' shotguns force him to back down. Virgil laughs at the town's hypocrisy and invites J.T. to have a snort of moonshine with him—their liquid rebellion against the hypocrites.

In "Three Sheets in the Wind: Virgil Campbell Confesses," the shopkeeper tells J.T. about the time he was caught with a "frolic girl" by his wife, Elsie, and a "hardshell Baptist preacher."[12] He does not regret what he did, but instead satirizes the gossips who carried the tale to Elsie:

> You'd think the tale
> Would talk about our diddling, but that wasn't all
> By any means. These snuffbrush gossips hear
> A story, they fix it up till it's as queer
> And messy as the wiring in radios
> And sinful as Nevada.

(*Wind Mountain*, p. 29)

When Virgil and the woman are caught in her bedroom, he escapes, nude, and runs smack into a sheet hanging out to dry, then falls down, knocking himself out. Elsie sews him into the sheet and beats him with a curtain rod; Virgil believes that he has died and gone to hell. He resolves to stop "tomcatting" and live soberly but takes a drink to celebrate the tale. In *Earthsleep*, the volume concerned with death, Chappell's "At the Grave of Virgil Campbell" is more elegiac than humorous, with the narrator looking to Virgil as a guide in the fight against sham and hypocrisy. Fred, half drunk himself in imitation of his guide through the Carolina inferno, complains about the greedy widows in town, the officious preachers, and the conformity among his townsmen. He praises Virgil's honesty and his drinking as the antidotes to the teachers and preachers who make it sinful to think and unlawful to drink. Alcohol becomes the narrator's way of exorcising the bugbear of reactionary conservatism, the Joycean "Raw-Head-&-Bloody-Bones" of Western Carolina.[13]

In *I Am One of You Forever* Virgil is still alive and healthy, drinking and battling the town. The role of blocking authority is considerably lightened, however, and transferred to the narrator's father, Joe Robert, and the young man who helps him on the farm, Johnson Gibbs. Society's rules, as in the Tom Sawyer and Huckleberry Finn tradition, are upheld by the women: "We three males might have been the same age. The women in the family represented good sense and authority and our rebellion against the situation formed us into a tight high-spirited company."[14] The novel is a series of short stories, told from the young narrator's point of view, that flow toward and away from the central sad fact of Johnson Gibbs's death in the army. Despite this focus, there is a great deal of humor and farce in the relationship between Joe Robert and Johnson Gibbs and in the stories about a series of "humour" characters, eccentric uncles and aunts who are tolerated and even loved by the family.

Much of the humor relies on "rusties," or practical jokes. The three boys eat all of the grandmother's fancily-wrapped chocolates that are reserved for the Ladies' Bible Circle and relace each candy with a fragile pullet egg that eventually smears ladylike white gloves. When Uncle Luden visits from California and draws a tremendous number of phone calls from the townswomen (despite his three wives), Joe Robert pretends that a posse of jealous men has arrived at the house and manages to get Luden on the roof and thoroughly soaked with rain before the joke is called off. This is pure Tom Sawyer prankishness, complete with anonymous notes telling Luden to keep away from the women. Uncle Gurton is famous for his forty-year-old, untrimmed beard and for his single phrase uttered at the end of a meal: "I've had an elegant sufficiency; any more would be a superfluity" (p. 51). Joe Robert gives Gurton a sleeping potion and sneaks a look at the beard. When asked by the grandmother if he has seen enough, Joe Robert replies with Gurton's phrase. When Johnson returns from the army to "spark" Laurie Lee, a silly woman who reads movie magazines, Joe Robert is concerned about a "furlough marriage" (he believes that they do not last). After the lovers drive off together, the narrator, young Jess, asks his father where they are going:

> I believe they're headed up the Primrose Path to Sweet Perdition," he said. "With maybe a stop off at Flagrante Delicto."
>
> "I never heard of those places. How do you get there?"
>
> "If Johnson's got any sense, they'll go by way of Rubber Junction," he answered.
>
> (pp. 81–82)

In order to stop the marriage, Joe Robert takes Johnson's perennial chewing gum and replaces it with "Feenamint," a laxative. Johnson and Laurie Lee spend hours in the bathrooms and decide that love is not such an interesting disease after all.

Although the second part of the novel is overshadowed by a telegram announcing Johnson's death, Chappell lightens the narrative by switching to stories about the uncles and aunts. Uncle Zeno starts many stories but never ends them. Uncle Runkin brings his own hand-carved coffin and places the parts of a skeleton about the house, especially in the icebox. Aunt Samantha Barefoot, a country singer, greets Jess's grandmother with a distinctive, earthy voice: "You haven't aged a minute in seven years. It makes me feel like something a possum has pissed on and buried" (p. 167). Although Jess feels close to his father, he also feels like an outsider. He is a dreamer interested in books rather than hunting, farming, and sports. On a hunting trip with Joe Robert, Johnson, and Luden, Jess admits to himself his feeling of alienation. When the men leave the cabin, Jess lags behind, musing about his identity. Johnson returns and asks, "'Well, Jess are you one of us or not?'" (p. 184). The answer is of course provided by the title. The narrator, older now, is bound by memory and choice to the values of his mountains.

Chappell's greatest contribution to the history of American humor is the Southwestern character Virgil Campbell. He is the backwoods rascal who tells his own story with many exaggerated tall tales and much boasting to the incredulous and amused J.T. and Fred. His creative use of language and his reliance for values and imagery on the natural world give him a distinctive and humorous voice. And, while Virgil provides us with amusement, he is also mediator between the laughable and the comic. Campbell, like Dante's Virgil, guides the narrator to a "comic" vision that attempts to incorporate all of life. The narrator of *Midquest*, musing over the grave of Virgil Campbell, concludes that he

has been reborn on this day, his thirty-fifth birthday. He begins the day much like Dante himself: "In the middle of the journey of our life I came to myself within a dark wood where the straight way was lost."[15] At the end of the day he is truly reborn, for his final vision is Dantean. His love for Susan–Beatrice and for the truth-seeking of Virgil Campbell has led him to a vision of greater love and harmony:

> *The love that moves the sun and other stars*
> *The love that moves itself in light to loving*
> *Flames up like dew*
> *Here in the earliest morning of the world.*
>
> (*Earthsleep*, p. 43)

Chappell's reputation as humorous writer and comic artist will ultimately rest on *Midquest* because it molds all of the elements that the poet sought to control, including his ingrained pessimism, into a more hopeful shape.

Summary

Fred Chappell's work is underrated. His finest contribution to American humor is his mastery of the vernacular language and values of the mountain folk of western North Carolina. Chappell captures their voices, their use of images from the natural world and their irreverence for pretension and hypocrisy, in the figure of Virgil Campbell. Virgil is more than a backwoods Sut Lovingood, however, or even an older Huckleberry Finn. He, like Dante's Virgil, leads the narrator of *Midquest*, "Old Fred," back from paralysis of will and hopelessness to a respect for lives lived close to the earth and for the truth, something as natural as the dirt itself.

Notes

1. Fred Chappell, *Bloodfire* (Baton Rouge: Louisiana State University Press, 1978), p. 26.

2. David Paul Ragan, *Dictionary of Literary Biography*, Vol. 6, 2nd ser., ed. James E. Kibler, Jr. (Detroit: Gale, 1980), p. 37. Ragan believes that this dislocation causes the tension in all of Fred Chappell's works. All further references to this work appear in the text.

3. Fred Chappell, *River* (Baton Rouge: Louisiana State University Press, 1975), p. 26. All further references to this work appear in the text.

4. Fred Chappell, "A Pact with Faustus," *Mississippi Quarterly*, 37, no. 1 (1983–1984): 10.

5. Fred Chappell, *The Inkling* (New York: Harcourt, 1965), p. 3. All further references to this work appear in the text.

6. James Everett Kibler, Jr. "A Fred Chappell Bibliography, 1963–1983," *Mississippi Quarterly*, 37, no. 1 (1983–1984): 63–88.

7. Fred Chappell, *Castle Tzingal* (Baton Rouge: Louisiana State University Press, 1984), p. 5.

8. Fred Chappell, *Source* (Baton Rouge: Louisiana State University Press, 1985), p. 5.

9. Fred Chappell, Preface, *Midquest* (Baton Rouge:

Louisiana State University Press, 1981), p. ix. All
further references to the Preface will appear in the
text.

10. C. Hugh Holman, *A Handbook to Literature*,
Fourth Edition (Indianapolis: Bobbs-Merrill,
1980), p. 220.

11. David Paul Ragan, "At the Grave of Sut Lovingood: Virgil Campbell in the Works of Fred Chappell," *Mississippi Quarterly*, 37, no. 1 (1983-
1984): 24.

12. Fred Chappell, *Wind Mountain* (Baton Rouge:
Louisiana State University Press, 1979), p. 124.
All further references to this work appear in the
text.

13. Fred Chappell, *Earthsleep* (Baton Rouge: Louisiana State University Press, 1980), p. 29. All further references to this work appear in the text.

14. Fred Chappell, *I Am One of You Forever* (Baton
Rouge: Louisiana State University Press, 1985),
pp. 9-10. All further references to this work appear in the text.

15. Dante, *Inferno*, trans. John D. Sinclair (New
York: Oxford University Press, 1939; rpt. 1961),
p. 23.

Selected Bibliography

Primary Sources

Fiction

It is Time, Lord. New York: Atheneum, 1963; London:
Dent, 1965; trans. Maurice-Edgar Coindreau as
L'Hamecon d'Or, Paris: Gallimard, 1965.

The Inkling. New York: Harcourt, 1965; London:
Chapman and Hall, 1966; trans. Claude Levy as
Premonitions, Paris: Gallimard, 1969.

Dagon. New York: Harcourt, 1968; trans. Maurice-
Edgar Coindreau as *Le Dieu-Poisson*, Paris: Christian Bourgois, 1970. This translation is important
because Chappell's work has been more popular in
Europe than in the United States.

The Gaudy Place. New York: Harcourt Brace, 1973;
rpt. New York: Manor Books, 1976.

Moments of Light. Los Angeles: New South, 1980.
Foreword by Annie Dillard. A collection of previously published short stories.

I Am One of You Forever. Baton Rouge: Louisiana
State University Press, 1985.

Waltzes Noble and Sentimental. A short story collection that is completed but not yet published.

Poetry (Books)

The World Between the Eyes. Baton Rouge: Louisiana
State University Press, 1971.

River: A Poem. Baton Rouge: Louisiana State University Press, 1975.

Bloodfire: A Poem. Baton Rouge: Louisiana State University Press, 1978.

Wind Mountain: A Poem. Baton Rouge: Louisiana
State University Press, 1979.

Earthsleep: A Poem. Baton Rouge: Louisiana State
University Press, 1980.

Midquest: A Poem. Baton Rouge: Louisiana State University Press, 1981. This is a collection of the four
volumes *River*, *Bloodfire*, *Wind Mountain*, and
Earthsleep. There are no revisions in these poems.

Castle Tzingal. Baton Rouge: Louisiana State University Press, 1984.

Source. Baton Rouge: Louisiana State University Press,
1985.

Poetry (Chapbooks)

The Man Twice Married to Fire. Greensboro, N.C.:
Unicorn Press, 1977.

Awakening to Music. Davidson, N.C.: Briarpatch
Press, 1979.

How I Lost It. Athens, Ohio: Rosetta Press, 1980.

Driftlake: A Lieder Cycle. Emory, Va.: Iron Mountain
Press, 1981.

Interviews

*Kite-Flying and Other Irrational Acts: Conversations
with Twelve Southern Writers.* Ed. John Carr.
Baton Rouge: Louisiana State University Press,
1972, pp. 216-235.

*Craft So Hard to Learn: Conversations with Poets and
Novelists About the Teaching of Writing.* Ed.
George Garrett. New York: Morrow, 1972, pp. 35-
40.

*The Writer's Voice. Conversations with Contempo-
rary Writers.* Ed. John Graham and George Garrett. New York: Morrow, 1973, pp. 31-50.

"William Blackburn and His Pupils: A Conversation."
Ed. James L.W. West, III, and August Nigro. *Mississippi Quarterly*, 31 (Fall 1978): 605-614.

Acts of The Mind. Ed. Richard Jackson. University,
Alabama: University of Alabama Press, 1983,
pp. 153-157.

Secondary Sources

Articles and Chapters in Books

*American Authors and Books: 1640 to the Present
Day.* 3rd rev. ed. Ed. W.J. Burke and Will D. Howe.
New York: Crown, 1972, p. 112. Very brief refer-
ence article.

The Author's and Writer's Who's Who. 6th ed. London: Burke's Peerage, 1971, p. 142. Brief biographical sketch.

Holman, C. Hugh. *A Handbook to Literature.* 4th ed.
Indianapolis: Bobbs-Merrill, 1980. Holman's
articles on wit and humor help in understanding
the "humour" characters in *I Am One of You
Forever.*

International Who's Who In Poetry. 6th ed. Ed. Ernest
Kay. Cambridge, England: International Biographical Centre, 1986, p. 800. Very short biographical
sketch.

Mason, Julian. "Fred Chappell." In *Southern Writers:
A Biographical Dictionary.* Ed. Robert Bain, Joseph
M. Flora, and Louis D. Rubin, Jr. Baton Rouge:
Louisiana State University Press, 1979. A helpful
source of biographical information that lists each
of Chappell's works and provides a short analysis
of them.

Ragan, David Paul. "Fred Chappell." In *Dictionary of
Literary Biography.* Vol. 6, 2nd ser. Ed. James Everett Kibler, Jr. Detroit: Gale, 1980, pp. 36-47. This
excellent article lists all of Chappell's works, provides an overview of his themes, and analyzes each
of the novels. This is the best place to begin research on Chappell.

Rubin, Louis D., Jr., ed. *The History of Southern Literature.* Baton Rouge: Louisiana State University
Press, 1985. This collection of essays has a short
but helpful article on Chappell.

Who's Who in the South and Southwest. 14th ed.

1975-1976. Chicago: Marquis, 1975, p. 121. A brief biography.

Wiloch, Thomas. "Fred Chappell." In *Contemporary Authors.* New Revision Series. Vol. 8. Detroit: Gale, 1962-1983, pp. 94-95. A short but extremely helpful overview of biographical information.

Bibliography

Kibler, James Everett, Jr. "A Fred Chappell Bibliography, 1963-1983." *Mississippi Quarterly*, 37, no. 1 (1983-1984): 63-83. An excellent bibliography covering all of Chappell's works, including listings of individually published poems and stories. Although Chappell has published additional material since 1983, Kibler's is the best starting point for bibliographical information.

Articles and Reviews in Journals

Chappell, Fred. "A Pact with Faustus." *Mississippi Quarterly*, 37, no. 1 (1983-1984): 9-20. Chappell explains his early feelings of alienation growing up in Canton, North Carolina.

Dillard, R.W.H. "Letters From a Distant Lover: The Novels of Fred Chappell." *The Hollins Critic*, 10 (1973): 1-15. Analyzes the major philosophical concerns in Chappell's novels.

Garrett, George. "A Few Things About Fred Chappell." *Mississippi Quarterly*, 37, no. 1 (1983-1984): 3-8. Editorial introducing the *Mississippi Quarterly*'s 1983-1984 special issue on Chappell.

Jones, Rodney. "The Large Vision: Fred Chappell's *Midquest.*" *Appalachian Journal*, 9 (1981): 59-65.

Moore, Edward M. "Some Recent Southern Things." Review of *Dagon*, by Fred Chappell. *Sewanee Review*, 78 (1970): 366-378. Some information about *Dagon*; Moore considers it a "weird" book that does not provide adequate motivation for Leland's degradation.

Morgan, Robert. "*Midquest.*" *American Poetry Review*, 11 (1982): 45-47.

Morrison, Gail M. "'The Sign of the Arms': Chappell's *It Is Time, Lord.*" *Mississippi Quarterly*, 37, no. 1 (1983-1984): 45-54. An excellent article on Chappell's themes, based on several personal interviews conducted by David Paul Ragan and Gail M. Morrison.

Mosby, Charmaine Allmon. "*The Gaudy Place*: Six Characters in Search of an Illusion." *Mississippi Quarterly*, 37, no. 1 (1983-1984): 55-62. Good article that analyzes the illusions held by the major characters in the novel.

Ragan, David Paul. "At the Grave of Sut Lovingood: Virgil Campbell in the Work of Fred Chappell." *Mississippi Quarterly*, 37, no. 1 (1983-1984): 21-29. An excellent article that places Virgil Campbell in the tradition of Southwestern humor.

Root, William Pitt. "The Earth Is Shoving Us to Sea." *Abatis One*, 1983, pp. 46-48.

Secreast, Donald. "Images of Impure Water in Chappell's *River.*" *Mississippi Quarterly*, 37, no. 1 (1983-1984): 39-44. Examines water symbolism.

Smith, Barbara. "Chappell at *Midquest.*" *Abatis One*, 1983, pp. 49-51.

Smith, R.T. "Fred Chappell's Rural Virgil and the Fifth Element in *Midquest.*" *Mississippi Quarterly*, 37, no. 1 (1983-1984): 31-38. Good comparison of Chappell's Virgil and Dante's Virgil.

Stephenson, Shelby. "Fred Chappell's Four-Part Autobiographical Epic." *Pembroke Magazine*, 14 (1982): 11-13.

——— . "Vision in Fred Chappell's Poetry and Fiction." *Abatis One*, 1983, pp. 33-45.

Tillinghast, Richard. "Scattered Nebulae." *Sewanee Review*, 90 (1982): 291-300.

Tucker, Ellen. "Fred Chappell: His Life in Mid-Course." *Chicago Review*, 33 (1981): 85-91.

Volant, Larry P. "Five Novels." *Sewanee Review* 73 (1965): 333-339. Brief mention of *It Is Time, Lord.*

Laura Niesen de Abruña

Clark, Charles Heber

Born: Berlin, Maryland, on July 11, 1841

Education: Grammar school, Georgetown, D.C.

Marriages: Clara Lukens, April 27, 1871, five children; Elizabeth Kille, April 27, 1897

Died: August 10, 1915

Biography

Charles Heber Clark was born in Berlin, Maryland, on July 11, 1841. His father, William J. Clark, was an itinerant Episcopalian minister whose Northern sympathies did not sit well with his pro-slavery, rural Maryland congregations during the years preceding the Civil War. Clark's father resettled the family in Philadelphia when Charles was fifteen. There, following two years of service in the Union army and having had only a smattering of education in the District of Columbia, Charles went to work, first as a scrivener and errand boy for a commercial firm and soon thereafter in the newspaper trade.

In a two-year period with the *Philadelphia Inquirer* Clark served as a local reporter, music critic, book reviewer, editorial writer, and author of literary "sketches." In 1867 he joined the editorial staff of the *Philadelphia Evening Bulletin*, where he began publishing his first humorous sketches. Clark eventually became a partner in the *Bulletin*, then sold his share in 1882 to purchase the *Textile Record*, a trade journal that he published and edited until 1902. Following his retirement, Clark wrote editorials for the *Philadelphia North American*.

Clark made his home in the village of Conshohocken on the Schuylkill River. One of his Sunday school pupils there, J. Elwood Lee, convinced Clark to invest in plans for a factory for the manufacture of medical supplies. This investment proved highly profitable and became the basis of Clark's personal fortune. In 1888 Clark assumed the presidency of the J. Elwood Lee Company. In 1905 the company was consolidated with Johnson & Johnson of Brunswick, New Jersey, of which Clark then became a director.

Clark was a major figure in Philadelphia manufacturing circles. He was an organizer of the Manufacturers' Club and served for ten years as its secretary and editor of its journal. He considered himself a student of political economy, using his considerable editorial influence on behalf of protectionist tariff policies called for by the manufacturing community. There is scant public record of his family life. On April 27, 1871 he married Clara Lukens, who bore him five children. On April 27, 1897, two years after his first wife's death, he married Elizabeth Kille, who survived him. He died on August 10, 1915.

Literary Analysis

Clark's reputation as a humorist rests primarily on his first book, *Out of the Hurly-Burly; or, Life in an Odd Corner* (1874), which included many of his early *Bulletin* sketches. It purported to be a record of the history and current events of the village of New Castle, Delaware, but in fact was a fictionalized celebration of life in Clark's beloved Conshohocken presented in a first-person narrative. Its persona, Max Adeler, was learned, amiable, and modest, and its rambling sketches illustrated the qualities of neighborliness, natural beauty, and suburban serenity that Clark clearly admired. Clark was an excellent stylist, capable of polished and graceful prose. Much of the book's charm stemmed from Clark's talent for comic characterization and his aimless wandering through his material, alternating between sentimental but affecting descriptive passages and humorous dramatic vignettes that portrayed the downside of suburban living. Frequent topics included problems of commuting, the frustrations of gardening and lawn care, the complexities and dangers of home repair, neighborly nosiness, child rearing, and pets. Clark also drew upon his newspaper experiences for occasional scenes set in the editorial offices of the fictional *Morning Argus*. A degree of continuity was provided by a running story about a shy boarder in the Adeler household trying to find the courage to propose to a young woman in the town.

An important distinction of *Hurly-Burly* was that it included roughly 350 woodcut illustrations by Arthur B. Frost. These were Frost's first published works and immediately established him among such notable nineteenth-century American comic illustrators as Felix O. C. Darley, Edward Kemble, and Frederick Burr Opper.

Hurly-Burly was exceptionally popular, eventually selling more than a million copies world wide. It was particularly well received in Great Britain where Clark finally sold the plates for the book. It was also widely translated and earned Clark a gold medal from Emperor Franz Joseph of Austria to whom the author had sent a copy on a whim.

Clark's second volume, *Elbow Room* (1876), was a clear effort to capitalize on the popularity of *Hurly-Burly*. Subtitled "A Novel Without a Plot," it presented itself as a sequel to *Hurly-Burly* and expanded the scale of the Frost illustrations. It was much more tightly structured than its predecessor, being only half as long and lacking the descriptive effusions that encumbered the former book. Clark also evolved a regular cast of characters to populate his village setting. Among these were some of Clark's finest accomplishments, including the Fogg family whose hapless patriarch's answer to the problem of squalling infants was a liberal dose of animal magnetism.

Clark's third volume, *Random Shots* (1879), lacked the unity of the first two but contained some of his most ambitious humor. Among its thirteen lengthy pieces, all illustrated by Frost, were several domestic sketches, an attempt at a tall tale, and two satirical cannons fired in the general direction of such popular targets as Mormonism and Latin American political instability. There were also two romantic stories in the worst maudlin Victorian tradition. Of scholarly interest is the volume's concluding tale, "Mr. Skinner's Night in the Underworld," in which a pragmatic New Jersey entrepreneur and self-made millionaire makes a fantasy trip in the manner of Tannhauser through Horselberg Mountain, meeting along the way numerous characters from German legend and classical mythology. Clark used the premise to satirize simpleminded commonsense and the American business mentality, predating by a decade Mark Twain's application of the technique in *A Connecticut Yankee in King Arthur's Court*.

In his later years Clark was reputedly embarrassed by his reputation as a humorist and tried to establish a serious literary career with two volumes of short stories and three novels. Among the latter, *In Happy Hollow* (1903) is worth noting, containing evidence of Clark's gift for characterization in the figures of Colonel and Mrs. Joseph Bantam, who court each other into their fifth decade of marriage with soul-rending ardor.

Summary

Charles Heber Clark was a leading figure among the Literary Comedians of the 1870s. His early suburban sketches under the name "Max

Adeler" earned him an international reputation that lasted well into the twentieth century.

Selected Bibliography

Primary Sources

Humor .
Out of the Hurly-Burly; or, Life in an Odd Corner. Philadelphia: G. Maclean, 1874.
Elbow Room. Philadelphia: J.M. Stoddart, 1876.
Random Shots. Philadelphia: J.M. Stoddart, 1879.
An Old Fogey and Other Stories. London: Ward, Locke, 1881.

Short Stories
The Fortunate Island and Other Stories. Boston: Lee and Shepard, 1882.
By the Bend in the River: Tales of Connock Old and New. Philadelphia: John C. Winston, 1914.

Novels
Captain Bluitt: A Tale of Old Turley. Philadelphia: H.T. Coates, 1901.
In Happy Hollow. Philadelphia: H.T. Coates, 1903.
The Quakeress, A Tale. Philadelphia: John C. Winston, 1905.

Miscellaneous
The Great Natural Healer. Philadelphia: George W. Jacobs, 1910.

Secondary Sources

Articles
Garrett, C.H. "Max Adeler." *Book Buyer*, September 1902.
Oberholtzer, E.P. "Max Adeler: Reminiscence of Charles Heber Clark." *Book News Monthly*, January 1916.

Biography
Dictionary of American Biography. Vol. 2, 1958.
The National Cyclopedia of American Biography. Vol. 35, 1967.
Who's Who in America, 1914-1915.

Gary Engle

Clemens, Samuel Langhorne [Mark Twain]

Born: Florida, Missouri, on November 30, 1835
Education: Informal
Marriage: Olivia Langdon, February 2, 1870, four children
Died: April 21, 1910

Biography

Samuel Langhorne Clemens, who was to achieve fame as America's greatest humorist, was born to John and Jane Lampton Clemens in Florida, Missouri, on November 30, 1835. John Clemens, a taciturn Virginian, frustrated lawyer and storekeeper, fathered six children and failed at several enterprises before moving his family to Hannibal, Missouri, in 1839, haunted by dreams of wealth from an investment in Tennessee land and eager to lead civic development as "Judge" Clemens. John Clemens's death in 1847 ended young Sam Clemens's "formal" schooling in one-room schoolhouses and brought about his employment and apprenticeship with the *Hannibal Gazette* and *Missouri Courier* for two years under John C. Ament. Clemens's childhood yielded him the rich southern background that colored his major writings about childhood and the Mississippi River and small-town life in developing America. After another year with Ament as a journeyman, Sam worked for his brother, Orion, from 1850 through 1853 on the *Hannibal Journal* and then wandered to Philadelphia, Pennsylvania, and New York in 1854. By this time he had studied the Bible at home, read *Peter Parley's Magazine*, devoured *Don Quixote*, and encountered the legend of Joan of Arc, not to mention the vast amount of patriotic, sentimental, and general literature that he set as an apprentice printer during the pre-Civil War era. He had also seen *The Spirit of the Times*, a major source of regional and southwestern humor, and the Boston *Carpet-Bag*, in which Clemens's "The Dandy Frightening the Squatter" marked his national debut as a humor writer on May 1, 1852.

From 1854 through 1857 he set type and published travel letters in Orion's next venture, the *Muscatine* (Iowa) *Journal*, and in the *St. Louis Evening News*. In 1857, Clemens undertook his second major apprenticeship, this time as a riverboat pilot under master Horace Bixby on the Mississippi River, an experience subsequently immortalized in *Life on the Mississippi*. This period of his life ended with the coming of the Civil War. His service in the war was extremely brief, as he described it twenty-five years later in "The Private History of the Campaign That Failed."

In July 1861, Clemens accompanied his brother to Nevada where Orion was to take up appointment as Secretary of the Territory. At the age of twenty-six, Clemens returned to newspaper work in the booming silver mining country of Nevada, a sojourn punctuated by brief periods of mining when Virginia City (and later San Francisco) became too hot to hold him due to his vitriolic attacks on corrupt businessmen or newspaper rivals. His most important position was as a legislative reporter for the Virginia City *Territorial Enterprise*, which Delancey Ferguson describes as more of a feature-writing than reporting post. Along with Joe Goodman and Dan De Quille (William F. Wright), Twain developed his exaggerated burlesque style, laden with Biblical allusions, overblown sarcasm, and local detail. He also developed a regional reputation as the Moralist of the Main, causing the famous humorist from the East, Artemus Ward, to seek him out while on a comic lecturing jaunt through the West in 1863–1864 and to solicit a story from him a year later for Ward's book of comic adventures among the Mormons. The story arrived late and was independently published in Henry Clapp's New York *Saturday Press* on November 18, 1865, as "The Celebrated Jumping Frog of Calaveras County." Its universal and instantaneous popularity brought Twain national attention.

As Mark Twain (a term meaning "safe water depth," taken from his riverboating days), the maturing humorist wrote for the *San Francisco Call*, the *Californian*, and the *Golden Era*, among others. For the *Sacramento Union*, he travelled to the Sandwich Islands as a reporter, an adventure that served as the source of some of the most charming material in *Roughing It*. The most important development during this period was his contact with the San Francisco *Alta California*, which agreed to sponsor travels across the Isthmus of Panama and to the eastern states and on the *Quaker City* steamer excursion to Europe and the Holy Land in exchange for comic letters written in the "American" western viewpoint. At the same time, on October 2, 1866, Twain began his long career as a comic lecturer, following in Ward's footsteps, with the announcement that the doors would open at seven and the "trouble" would begin at eight.

The voyage on the *Quaker City* provided the final element needed to complete Twain's growth into a national and international comic spokesman for American values. His purpose was to describe Europe and the Holy Land from the viewpoint of an American vandal abroad, the narrow provincial viewpoint of the naive booster. His letters to the *Alta* in 1867 accomplished this and simultaneously laid the basis for further lecturing on his return. More importantly, the letters also provided material for *The Innocents Abroad*, published by Elisha Bliss and the American Publishing Company and sold by subscription. He also met Mary "Ma" Fairbanks, a literary confidante for some years, and Charles Langdon, whose ivory miniature of his sister, Olivia, led Twain to meet her and then to court her for the next three years.

By 1871, Twain, the frontier humorist, was a substantial, married man. *The Innocents Abroad* was successful and remunerative; he was part owner of the *Buffalo Express* through the backing of his father-in-law Jervis Langdon. Family illnesses marred the picture and spurred the family's relocation to Elmira, New York, and then to Hartford, Connecticut, while Twain took to the lecture platform to pay his bills, reading passages from the manuscript of his second major book, *Roughing It* (1871). Mark and Livy soon moved to Nook Farm in Hartford, becoming part of a literary colony including Livy's close friends the Hookers, as well as Charles Dudley Warner, Joseph Twitchell (Twain's minister and later travel companion in *A Tramp Abroad*, published in 1880), and Harriet Beecher Stowe.

Twain's period in Nook Farm was perhaps the happiest in his life. His pessimism and rationalist dissatisfaction with Christianity were held in unstable and stressful equilibrium by the influence of Livy and Joe Twitchell. An infant son died, but three daughters were born. His literary career flowered, and included the development of his friendship with William Dean Howells, who would call him, in *My Mark Twain* (1910), "the Lincoln of our literature." With Warner he wrote *The Gilded Age*, published in 1873. "Old Times on the Mississippi" appeared as a serial in *The Atlantic Monthly* in 1874–1875, advancing his acceptance by the literati of the Northeast; "Old Times" was to be expanded into *Life on the Mississippi* in 1883. *The Atlantic*, under editor Howells, published a number of his best short pieces, including "A True Story." "Cannibalism in the Cars," a burlesque of legislative procedure, appeared in London's *Broadway*, a journal owned by Routledge, Twain's British publisher, in 1868, and Twain, along with Charles Leland and Bret Harte among others, enjoyed tremendous popularity in England and a higher degree of literary respect than he found at home in America. *The Adventures of Tom Sawyer*, based on his Hannibal childhood, appeared in 1876. *The Prince and the Pauper* followed in 1882 and *Adventures of Huckleberry Finn* in 1885. *A Connecticut Yankee in King Arthur's Court* was published in 1889. Throughout this period, Twain lectured and travelled extensively, becoming a champion of international copyright and seeking business investments to assure his economic solidity and the well-being of his family. He was a Victorian family man by training and desire but unconventional in details to the point of affront, sceptical of conventional religions, and critical of social hypocrisy to the point of self-torture, as demonstrated in the previously unpublished writings now appearing in the Iowa-California edition of his complete works.

In 1885, Twain began the publishing firm of Charles L. Webster & Co., and in 1890 he backed financially the development of the Paige typesetting machine. When both ventures failed, Twain suffered near bankruptcy. He undertook a round-the-world lecture tour to pay off his debts in 1895, following publication of *Pudd'nhead Wilson* and *Tom Sawyer Abroad* in 1894 and the "Personal Recollections of Joan of Arc" in *Harper's Magazine* in 1895-1896. Even earlier, however, by the time *The American Claimant* appeared in 1892, Twain had been awarded an honorary degree and entertained by the crowned heads of Europe. He had become an international spokesman for the American viewpoint and for the rights of man against tyranny, inhumanity, and oppression.

Until the death of Olivia in Italy in 1894, much of this period of Clemens's life was spent abroad. Although *A Connecticut Yankee* had damaged Twain's sales in England, his foreign audience remained appreciative, lecturing could be remunerative, and privacy and inexpensive living were both possible to the expatriate. He returned to America immediately after Livy's death, however, and, with the exception of one last triumphal trip to Great Britain and sojourns in Bermuda, remained there. His last years were increasingly bitter as two of his three daughters died before him. He amused himself in 1906-1908 by dictating an unevenly reliable autobiography to Albert Bigelow Paine, his eventual literary executor, and he left a number of unfinished manuscripts and other materials that have emerged over the past half century without diminishing his international stature as a major author and humorist. Twain died on April 21, 1910, going out as he had come in, with Halley's comet, and was buried at Elmira, New York.

Literary Analysis

Mark Twain's humor is central to our estimation of his importance, and no other humorist in America has come to so fully embody the American image. There are two ways of discussing Twain's humor, through content and through form, and both are pertinent. Twain separated himself from other literary comedians of the Civil War period by attempting to avoid the mechanical humor of devices. Tricks of spelling (cacography) that were epidemic among humorists such as Artemus Ward, Josh Billings, and Petroleum V. Nasby are largely absent from his works. Nevertheless, although he was above

spelling "American eagle" as "Amerikun igle," even *Adventures of Huckleberry Finn* shows him leaning deftly on such a device to signalize Huck's view of "sivilization." Likewise, he could use anticlimax, as in his comment that the railroad magnates of the Baltimore and Ohio were not like the wretched Goshoot Indians—there was only a plausible similarity. Even in such one-line jokes the social orientation of Twain's sarcasm seems clear. Sometimes this ability to generate one-liners is enhanced by an involvement in the plot action, as when the Connecticut Yankee looks out over what he will soon know as Camelot and queries his knight-captor, "Bridgeport?," the home of P.T. Barnum's famous castle, Iranistan. The transformed pauper in *Prince and the Pauper* remarks on the death of the King and the laying-over before burial, "'Tis strange folly, will he keep?"—a joke which no amount of lobbying from Twain's supposed censors, his wife Livy and daughters in genteel Nook Farm, could cause Twain to remove from the novel. In each of these jokes, the unromantic spirit of the practical man—the "new man"—as in Henry James's Christopher Newman in *The American*—can be seen at work manifesting the pragmatic ideology of typical middle-class Americans.

In somewhat longer sequences, Twain also appears a master joker. One of the finest jokes in *A Connecticut Yankee in King Arthur's Court* is a brief paragraph included in the Yankee's horrible description of prisoners released from the dungeons of the wicked princess Morgan le Fay. The Yankee says of a prisoner that his crime was committed more in inadvertence than in malice—he had said that Morgan Le Fay had red hair—well, the Yankee continues, she had red hair, but when people are above a certain social grade, their hair is "auburn." All comedians of Twain's era made jokes about redheads, perhaps in part because of the impact of Irish immigration; only Twain used such silliness to develop in comic terms the arbitrary savagery of monarchic absolutism against the defenseless common man. In *The American Claimant*, such jokes grow even more elaborate when the comic figure of Colonel Sellers (revived from *The Gilded Age* of some twenty years earlier) invents a process to bring the dead back to life. Colonel Sellers boasts that he will bring back the greatest statesmen of all time and—at last—get a Congress that knows enough to come in out of the rain. The joke is actually a borrowing from the tradition of Artemus Ward and John Phoenix in the 1850s and 1860s; both earlier humorists told versions of it before Twain. Noteworthy again is the use of American reference points and a focusing on democracy, a focus that is even more obvious in the context of the novel—Sellers goes on to invent plans to free all

Russians from Czardom and transform their nation into a republic.

In longer episodes and in his novels in general, Twain also used humor extensively, both his original jokes and borrowings from the American comic tradition. The influence of Twain's southwestern sources is evident not only in his general handling of melodramatic action but also in some obviously borrowed scenes. "Sicily Burns' Wedding" from *Sut Lovingood's Yarns* by George W. Harris has long been acknowledged as the source of a similar episode in Twain's *Personal Recollections of Joan of Arc*, and "Simon Suggs Attends a Camp Meeting" in Johnson J. Hooper's *The Adventures of Simon Suggs* is almost undeniably the source for the camp meeting flock fleeced by the fraudulent Dauphin in the *Adventures of Huckleberry Finn*. From the Northeast, Twain borrowed such stories as Huck's Pap's tale of Old Hank Bunker who fell off the shot tower and had to be buried between two barn doors; the story was an adaptation from Twain's "The Story of the Old Ram" and before that appeared as a joke in Boston's *Yankee Blade*, a comic paper of the 1840s. Pudd'nhead Wilson got his name "Pudd'nhead" by saying that if he owned half of a barking dog, he would shoot his half. The statement puzzled the fictional southern yokels in the small town but was perfectly funny as a clever story narrated by P.T. Barnum in his autobiography, published in the North in 1855, and a favorite of Twain's during his Hartford years. These larger humorous constructions characterize the Americans who narrate them, tie them to a world where irony is inserted into events as a form of detachment, a form of understanding by the speaker who rises above mere events; it is a paradigm for the unsentimental attitude of the American business corporation— and as such is radically different from the humor of other nations and characteristic of our national psyche.

Lastly, of course, humor permeates entire stories and dominates the plots of Twain's major works, both his fiction and his semi-fictional works of travel (through which Twain earned his first reputation as a sceptical reporter from the West). Even before Twain embarked on the *Quaker City* voyage, he knew that he would report on Europe and the Holy Land from the sceptical viewpoint of a western American—a vandal abroad—brashly ignorant of culture and openly objecting to the commercialization of sublime history. Naturally, he finds a burlesque playbill from the times of the Christian martyrs in the Roman Colosseum and weeps like a baby at the tomb of his first ancestor—Adam—in the Holy Land; America laughed with him, and the Adam piece has continued to be anthologized.

The Gilded Age was a two-volume novel based on a burlesque of parliamentary procedure that Twain had already treated in a short story, "Cannibalism in the Cars." Expanded to novel length, however, the humor became an indictment of the get-rich-quick mentality of a corrupt era in American politics; the play derived from *The Gilded Age* has been revived as recently as 1986. *A Connecticut Yankee* is a book-length burlesque of the Round Table of Arthurian England, and as such it angered many English readers and damaged Twain's book sales in England for decades.

Other portions of Twain's humor register the darker side of human nature. Even "The Celebrated Jumping Frog of Calaveras County" might be said to show a cynical view of man's self-centered naïvete. Its widely remembered tag-line, "I don't see no p'ints about that frog that's any better'n any other frog," showed a false simplicity that caused Jim Smiley to trick himself into losing a bet with a stranger; Smiley gets so excited by the challenge that he loses his self-control and searches the swamp while the stranger disables Smiley's frog. Americans quoted the line for years. In "The Man That Corrupted Hadleyburg," Twain showed greed corrupting all of the virtue in a town because it had not been tested. To demonstrate his belief that virtue must be tested in the real world, Twain set up a comic situation, presided over by a crackerbox philosopher named Jack Halliday, and gave his most sardonic humor free reign in showing the destruction that false virtue achieves. "To the Person Sitting in Darkness," attacking the evils of colonialism, is a grimmer satire of the oppression of native peoples by powerful commercial interests clothed in government powers. "The War Prayer" contains Swiftian anger directed at the war prayers of Christian people for the destruction of their opponents. These darker, bitter humorous writings, like the satires of Swift and Voltaire, provide imposing evidence of their creator's hatred of the vices of mankind and his despair over the possibility of mankind's improvement.

The America into which Mark Twain was born was a bold nation in rapid transition from country and small-town life to the modern industrial age. On the one hand, its concerns were with the teachings of the Bible and on the other with the assertions of a national democratic rhetoric. Twain absorbed one sensibility with his mother's milk and the other from the printer's ink of the 1850's. Even the small midwestern villages of America were current with the literature of the East and shared many ideals of that culture. Frontier life, however, modified behavior in ways that educated men even of the regions themselves found remarkable and which they recorded in a wide range of comedy printed in newspapers and magazines in the 1840s and 1850s. At the more refined end of the spectrum of writers emerging from this background could be found John Hay and Howells, in the middle—mixing sentiment and local color—Edward Eggleston and Bret Harte, and among the writers passed off merely as humorists, John Phoenix, Artemus Ward and other literary comedians, and Mark Twain, prior to his acceptance as a major American writer. All participated in some way in the movements known as "local color" and realism, advancing the interest in American materials derived from the pioneering writings of Washington Irving and the interest in comic local detail made reputable by Oliver W. Holmes's *The Autocrat of the Breakfast Table.*

Samuel L. Clemens absorbed a wide array of literary influences and assimilated them into the personality of Mark Twain. His early writings have been heavily collected. The most juvenile reflect a good sense of comic absurdity. A few pieces in "vernacular" speech and subject matter, as analyzed by Henry Nash Smith, show the important influence of the Southwest in freeing his diction and broadening his range of materials. Undoubtedly, the works of Johnson Jones Hooper, George Washington Harris, Augustus Baldwin Longstreet, and Joseph Glover Baldwin were known to Twain from his early reading, and scenes reflecting some of their works appear in his novels. His legislative reporting for the *Territorial Enterprise* in the early 1860s gives clearest evidence of his extensive reading of the Bible and his skill in absorbing and converting Biblical and political newspaper rhetoric to the purposes of satire and burlesque. The story of Joan of Arc appealed to Twain's Victorian consciousness, but he also claimed to have been most heavily influenced in humor by John Phoenix (the pen name of George H. Derby), and his debt to Artemus Ward in regard to subject matter and manner is also notable, particularly in light of Ward's development of the platform lecture pose that Twain followed.

"The Dandy Frightening the Squatter" (1852) and "The Celebrated Jumping Frog of Calaveras County" (1865) exhibit the "western" attitude toward blind pride. The main figures in these two short stories behave arrogantly and matter-of-fact strangers correct them, in one case through humiliation of greenhorn behavior, in the other through wily but understated chicanery. The nation responded with Jim Smiley's adversary, "I don't see no p'ints about that frog that's any better'n any other frog," as Twain's story circulated through the network of newspaper exchanges that existed before the age of syndicated humor. The refusal to accept pretentiousness was peculiarly American and typical of the attitude that the literary comedians of the Civil War era popularized in response to the established Genteel tradition.

Twain next embodied this attitude in comic newspaper sketches and travel letters to the *Alta California*, the *New York Tribune*, and other papers in San Francisco, New York, St. Louis, and Washington, D.C., throughout the remainder of the 1860s. When honed on the lecture platform and suitably revised for mass subscription sales by the American Publishing Company, these writings matured into *The Innocents Abroad* and *Roughing It*.

The Innocents Abroad burlesqued the commercialized hypocrisy of old Europe that preyed upon untutored Americans who were themselves guilty of the supercilious bad manners of the *nouveau riche*. Since the voyage of the *Quaker City* extended to the Holy Land and Egypt, Twain's itinerary included ancient history and sacrosanct sites as well as Spain, France, and Italy, and the humorist attacked the ignorance of Portuguese Catholicism, the cynicism of Parisian glove-sellers, and the ugliness of Spanish and Italian monasticism. Where the letters had played heavily upon the Barnumization of holy relics, the book emphasized the innocence of the gullible traveler while maintaining the essential message. Twain made fun of the "pilgrims" on the voyage—creating controversies that still erupted a decade later—and mocked Italian guides by asking about a mummy and about Columbus ("Is he dead?"—a borrowing of one of Artemus Ward's best-received jokes from a London travel letter in 1867). In the Holy Land, Twain wept at the tomb of his great lost ancestor—Adam—in a sequence that remained a standard for the humor of the *naif* for the remainder of the century. When the letters were revised into a book, Twain added sublime and ideal descriptions to the attacks on inhumanity and hypocrisy in both the Holy Land and Egypt that allowed for Twain's strongest reportorial sarcasm. *The Innocents Abroad* thus supplied a new kind of travel literature to Americans eager to acknowledge their own scepticism, pragmatism, and originality. Despite its attacks on established religious practices, it was a moral book written from the point of view of a reporter from the American West. It broadened Twain's scope from regional to international and established him as a comic spokesman.

Roughing It was Twain's second semi-fictional travel book, again sold by subscription by the American Book Company of Hartford. The young tenderfoot's trip across the frontier to the mother-lode mining country of Nevada was described with Twain's full play of exaggeration, comic anecdotalism, and social sarcasm. Such sequences as the stagecoach ride, Bemis and the buffalo, the jackass rabbit, and Slade the outlaw were particularly effective. To pad out the volume, Twain included a substantial amount of material on the Mormons, then a topic of great interest and one that had been treated briefly by Ward, Max Adeler, and others. Twain also added a lengthy section covering his adventures in the Sandwich Islands (Hawaii) for the *Sacramento Union* in 1866. Although some of Twain's humor in this portion of the book is among his best as a sarcastic American traveler, some critics see this element as an extrinsic component of the book.

As Twain's output of shorter works continued, he co-authored with Charles Dudley Warner of Nook Farm *The Gilded Age*, subtitled "A Tale of Our Times," in 1873. The authors' intention was to pillory the vices of an age that encouraged get-rich-quick schemes at the expense of honest hard work. Philip Sterling and Harry Brierly represent the two sides of life, with the Quaker Ruth, a medical student, and the beautiful lobbyist Laura, who will be seduced and become a murderess, as their female counterparts. Ruth's family, the Boltons, are honest and sincere in comparison to the robustly fraudulent Colonel Sellers, who typifies the age's expectations of speculative wealth. The nation itself also comes under Twain's sarcastic eye as he takes on Washington, D.C., and the Congress of the United States. Colonel Sellers took on independent life in a play from *The Gilded Age* and in a second novel, *The American Claimant*, published in 1892.

The Adventures of Tom Sawyer appeared in 1876 and immediately took its place as one of America's greatest boy's books, written for children of all ages. The novel completed Twain's identification with the Mississippi River, established successfully with "Old Times in the Mississippi" in the *Atlantic Monthly* in 1875, the same year that he had published his first substantial book of short pieces, *Sketches New and Old*. Aunt Polly, whitewashing the fence, and the adventures in the cave brought both excitement and a sense of local color to readers nostalgic for farm life. The humor of a boy's life, even more boldly drawn than in T.B. Aldrich's *Story of a Bad Boy*, allowed Twain to develop comic incidents such as feeding the cat medicine and teasing the schoolmaster in ways that reflected southwestern roughness. The fence whitewashing has rivalled the "Jumping Frog" story as an example of insightful connivery based on human nature. Edgar Lee Masters rated *Tom Sawyer* above *Huckleberry Finn* as late as 1915, and he was not alone. A year later, Twain once again showed the awkward side of his western background with a burlesque of Ralph Waldo Emerson, Oliver Wendell Holmes, and Henry Wadsworth Longfellow as three tramps in a speech at John Greenleaf Whittier's birthday dinner; Howells later referred to it as "that hideous mistake of poor Clemens," but letters of apology from Twain were kindly received.

A Tramp Abroad, published in 1880, and *The Prince and the Pauper*, in 1882, show important sides of Twain, although they often seem merely stepping stones to *Adventures of Huckleberry Finn*, which appeared in 1884, Twain's greatest work and a masterpiece of world fiction. *A Tramp Abroad* is a comic account based on a walking tour taken by Twain and Twitchell that burlesques standard travel records. However, it contains a number of Twain's best western American stories, which are frequently excerpted. Taken as a whole, though, the book shows the mix of Victorian ideas and experiences characteristic of upper-middle-class social experience—an interesting externalized counterpart to Henry James's highly internalized international novels. *The Prince and the Pauper* was the best loved of Twain's novels written at Nook Farm because of the sweetness of its child portraits and its forthright advocacy of goodness. Sarcasm is relegated to minor figures like Yokel. Melodramatic interplay between soldier Miles Hendon and Tom Canty and between the prince and the band of thieves provides clearly demarcated areas of good and evil. At a time that other humor writers were writing short newspaper pieces, Twain alone generated novels with such dramatic contrasts and moving action.

Adventures of Huckleberry Finn is Twain's outstanding work. It was first published in Great Britain, in 1884, (as were most of his works as a means of protecting the English copyright), and later in America, in 1885. The Mississippi River provided the locale and Twain's childhood provided the characters of Huck Finn, who was based on Tom Blankenship, and Pap Finn, based on a town drunk in Hannibal. Tom Sawyer's adventures provided a springboard, but Huckleberry Finn was unique, frequently highly sceptical of Tom's bookish sentimentalism, and, most importantly, speaking in his own language. Huck's dialect, a blend of regional speech, vulgar or "vernacular" dialect, and the other devices of literary comedy utilized by Twain, announced a new voice in American literature, more pungent in action, more sincere in sentiment, and more ironic in criticism than its predecessors, and so it has been recognized by such critics as H.L. Mencken, Ernest Hemingway, and Henry Nash Smith, a leading Twain scholar–critic. Huck's descriptions of the river thus reach a new level as poetry of the commonplace in realistic descriptions of setting. As opposed to the river, the river towns provided sites for scathing pictures of venality and inhumanity in sequences dealing with feuds, vendettas, fraud, and the ugly instincts of crowds taken in by con-men, titillation and the lynch law. Most important, the trip down the Mississippi River established a new ethic on Huck and Jim's raft in which white and black find true respect for each other above the social conventions of the corrupt shore. Although the extensive use of such epithets as "nigger" and the depiction of slave characteristics have caused some recent critics to label the book racist, the novel clearly represents Twain's depiction of how a boy of "sound heart" could rise above a "deformed conscience," a statement of social and personal growth consistent with Twain's suppressed mechanistic determinism. The last fifth of the novel continues to trouble critics who cannot accept Huck's subordination to Tom Sawyer in an extended burlesque sequence, but to Twain the ending represented the power of social training over personal experience. Banned by the Concord, Massachusetts, library, the book sold excellently and, despite its appearance in comic format with copious illustrations, relatively quickly came to be acknowledged as a major work.

Twain's life became increasingly taken up with public events and his home life. His publishing firm, Charles L. Webster & Co., proudly published *Grant's Memoirs* and provided the widow of the great soldier with a handsome royalty check. In 1889, Twain published *A Connecticut Yankee in King Arthur's Court*, a book that treated the Arthurian roundtable in a burlesque format and permanently damaged Twain's English sales. This novel is an extended farce of the Yankee Barnum type, boosting democracy and technology, opposing slavery, and decrying feudalism in politics as institutionalized forms of inhumanity, particularly in an established church. Hank Morgan, the Yankee picaro, confuses Camelot with Bridgeport, Connecticut, establishes telephones in hermits' caves, and devises a "man factory" to nurture democracy. A blend of high ideals and low entrepreneurialism, the protagonist establishes a family that he leaves fifteen centuries behind upon his long sleep in Merlin's Cave when his "new deal" is destroyed in a brutal battle with the feudal lords and Catholic church.

Pudd'nhead Wilson, published in 1894, is Twain's last classic work though some critics complain about the novel's "jackleg" construction, severed from "Those Extraordinary Twins," a burlesque piece on Siamese twins. However, its hero, David Wilson, a Yankee lawyer named "Pudd'nhead" and isolated by small-town Southerners who misunderstand his sarcasm, develops fingerprinting as a scientific technique to unravel a case of baby-switching between "white" and "black" babies, a case so

tortured and ambiguous that neither child benefits, nor does Roxy the slave mother. Even Wilson's elevation in the eyes of the town is small comfort, and this published work presages Twain's more embittered works, including the previously unpublished "Great Dark Manuscripts" of the Iowa-California edition (1967) and *What Is Man?*, privately printed in 1906. *Personal Recollections of Joan of Arc*, published in 1896, allowed another strand of Twain's Victorian consciousness its fullest expression. *Following the Equator* in 1897 permitted Twain to complete his quest to pay off his debts dollar for dollar. Perhaps more notably, tycoon H.H. Rogers, the manager of Twain's finances, helped engineer the takeover of Twain's titles by Harper & Bros., which brought out the first of many standard editions of Twain's works in 1899.

Later Twain writings were among his most strongly worded as an American critic. "The Man that Corrupted Hadleyburg" developed John Milton's "Areopagitica" into a small-town American short story in 1899. "To the Person Sitting in Darkness," on imperialism in Africa and Asia, appeared in 1901. "The War Prayer" and "King Leopold's Soliloquy" appeared in 1905, along with the sweeter "Eve's Diary," based in his love of Livy Clemens. *Christian Science* and "Captain Stormfield's Visit to Heaven" followed in 1907, along with a Doctor of Letters from Oxford University, after other similar awards in America. The weight of Twain's pessimism became much heavier in his later writings, accounting for numerous unfinished manuscripts, but he remained active as a national humorous spokesman throughout his later years, despite trips abroad, deaths in his family, and his own health problems. His sarcasm became more strongly expressed, and his despair was rampant in the unpublished manuscripts, written with "a pen warmed up in Hell," but to the reading public, his carefully fostered image as the white-suited father of Huckleberry Finn remained dominant. Albert Bigelow Paine's neatly pruned biographical and bibliographical work was intended to sustain this view in the face of questions about Twain's mental tension as a Victorian writer suggested in Van Wyck Brooks's *The Ordeal of Mark Twain* in 1920. The centennial of *Huck Finn* and the anniversaries of Twain's birth and death in 1985 proved that Twain is still front-page news in American newspapers and his depiction of American racism and American humanity continues to be of vital importance.

Summary

Mark Twain—Samuel Langhorne Clemens—remains the greatest American humorist and the spokesman of American beliefs and ideals in the later half of the nineteenth century. After establishing himself as a moralist-humorist in Nevada and California newspapers and with "The Celebrated Jumping Frog of Calaveras County," he rose to national prominence by showing the western attitude toward fraudulent idealism in Europe and the Holy Land in *The Innocents Abroad* in 1869. His novels melodramatized his democratic opposition to corruption and established inhumanity both in America and abroad in *The Gilded Age*, *A Connecticut Yankee in King Arthur's Court*, and *Pudd'nhead Wilson*. *Adventures of Huckleberry Finn*, a sequel to *Adventures of Tom Sawyer*, is Twain's greatest book, using American dialect and an idyllized life on a raft on the Mississippi River to show how people who are socially and racially different can overcome social training. Long after his death, analysts continue to ponder Twain's published and unpublished writings, but his critical reputation continues to grow.

Selected Bibliography

Primary Sources

First American publication date given; other dates and less important publications are found in Jacob Blank's *Bibliography of American Literature* and Merle Johnson's *Bibliography of the Works of Mark Twain, Samuel Langhorne Clemens.*

The Celebrated Jumping Frog of Calaveras County and Other Sketches. New York: C.H. Webb, 1867.

The Innocents Abroad. Hartford: American Publishing Company, 1869.

Roughing It. Hartford: American Publishing Company, 1872.

The Gilded Age, with Charles Dudley Warner. Hartford: American Publishing Company, 1873.

Sketches New and Old. Hartford: American Publishing Company, 1875.

The Adventures of Tom Sawyer. Hartford: American Publishing Company, 1876.

A Tramp Abroad. Hartford: American Publishing Company, 1880.

The Prince and the Pauper. Boston: Osgood, 1882.

The Stolen White Elephant and Other Stories. Boston: Osgood, 1882.

Life on the Mississippi. Boston: Osgood, 1883.

Adventures of Huckleberry Finn. New York: Webster, 1885.

A Connecticut Yankee in King Arthur's Court. New York: Webster, 1889.

The American Claimant. New York: Webster, 1892.

The 100,000 Banknote and Other New Stories. New York: Webster, 1893.

Tom Sawyer Abroad. New York: Webster, 1894.

Pudd'nhead Wilson. Hartford: American Publishing Company, 1894.

Personal Recollections of Joan of Arc. New York: Harper, 1896.

How to Tell a Story and Other Essays. New York: Harper, 1897.

Following the Equator. Hartford: American Publishing Company, 1897.

The Man That Corrupted Hadleyburg and Other Stories and Essays. New York: Harper, 1900.

What Is Man? New York: De Vinne Press, 1906.

Eve's Diary. New York: Harper, 1906.

The $30,000 Bequest and Other Stories. New York: Harper, 1906.

Christian Science. New York: Harper, 1907.

Extract from Captain Stormfield's Visit to Heaven. New York: Harper, 1909.

Mark Twain's Speeches. Ed. F.A. Nast. New York: Harper, 1910.

The Mysterious Stranger. Ed. Albert Bigelow Paine and Fredrick Duneka. New York: Harper, 1916.

The Curious Republic of Gondour and Other Whimsical Sketches. New York: Boni & Liveright, 1919.

Mark Twain's Autobiography. Ed. Albert Bigelow Paine. New York: Harper, 1924.

Mark Twain's Notebook. Ed. Albert Bigelow Paine. New York: Harper, 1935.

Mark Twain in Eruption. Ed. Bernard De Voto. New York: Harper, 1940.

Letters from the Earth. Ed. Bernard De Voto. New York: Harper & Row, 1962.

Note: The Iowa–California edition of Mark Twain's works continues to bring forth significant works by Twain from unreprinted newspaper sources and unpublished manuscripts and will eventually replace the standard editions of Twain's works and the various collections of newspaper writings and other materials published after 1899.

Secondary Sources

Biography

Andrews, Kenneth. *Nook Farm, Mark Twain's Hartford Circle.* Cambridge: Harvard University Press, 1950.

Emerson, Everett. *The Authentic Mark Twain.* Chapel Hill: University of North Carolina Press, 1983.

Ferguson, Delancey. *Mark Twain: Man and Legend.* Indianapolis: Bobbs-Merrill, 1943.

Hill, Hamlin. *Mark Twain: God's Fool.* New York: Harper, 1973.

Kaplan, Justin. *Mr. Clemens and Mark Twain: A Biography.* New York: Simon and Schuster, 1966.

Paine, Albert Bigelow. *Mark Twain, a Biography.* New York: Harper, 1912.

Wecter, Dixon. *Sam Clemens of Hannibal.* Boston: Houghton Mifflin, 1952.

Criticism

Blair, Walter. *Mark Twain and Huck Finn.* Berkeley: University of California Press, 1960.

Branch, Edgar M. *The Literary Apprenticeship of Mark Twain.* Urbana: University of Illinois Press, 1950.

Brooks, Van Wyck. *The Ordeal of Mark Twain.* New York: Dutton, 1920, rev. 1933.

Budd, Louis J. *Our Mark Twain.* Philadelphia: University of Pennsylvania Press, 1983.

Cox, James M. *Mark Twain: The Fate of Humor.* Princeton: Princeton University Press, 1966.

De Voto, Bernard. *Mark Twain's America.* Boston: Little, Brown, 1932.

——— . *Mark Twain at Work.* Cambridge: Harvard University Press, 1942.

Fatout, Paul. *Mark Twain on the Lecture Circuit.* Bloomington: Indiana University Press, 1960.

Foner, Philip S. *Mark Twain: Social Critic.* New York: International Press, 1958.

Ganzel, Dewey. *Mark Twain Abroad.* Chicago: University of Chicago Press, 1968.

Howells, Willliam Dean. *My Mark Twain.* New York: Harper, 1910.

Lorch, Fred W. *The Trouble Begins at Eight: Mark Twain's Lecture Tours.* Ames: Iowa State University Press, 1968.

Lynn, Kenneth S. *Mark Twain and Southwestern Humor.* Boston: Little, Brown, 1959.

Marks, Barry A., ed. *Mark Twain's Huckleberry Finn.* Boston: D.C. Heath, 1959.

Rogers, Franklin R. *The Pattern for Mark Twain's Roughing It.* Berkeley: University of California Press, 1961.

Scott, Arthur L. *Mark Twain: Selected Criticism.* Dallas: Southern Methodist University Press, 1955.

Sloane, David E.E. *Mark Twain as a Literary Comedian.* Baton Rouge: Louisiana State University Press, 1979.

Smith, Henry Nash. *Mark Twain: The Development of a Writer.* Cambridge: Harvard University Press, 1962.

———. *Mark Twain's Fable of Progress: Political and Economic Ideas in "A Connecticut Yankee."* New Brunswick: Rutgers University Press, 1964.

Wagenknecht, Edward. *Mark Twain: The Man and His Work.* New Haven: Yale University Press, 1935.

Walker, Franklin. *San Francisco's Literary Frontier.* New York: Knopf, 1930.

Note: Many valuable books and articles are necessarily omitted from this selected bibliography. The annual publication *American Literary Scholarship* lists new criticism from 1964 on. In addition to Scott's collection of reviews and articles, important compilations have been made by Frederick Anderson, Walter Blair, and Louis Budd. Readers should also consult chapters on Mark Twain in the *Cambridge History of American Literature*, *The Literary History of the United States*, *The Literature of the American People*, and Walter Blair's *Native American Humor*, and other references to be found in specialized bibliographies treating Mark Twain.

David E.E. Sloane

Cobb, Irvin S[hrewsbury]

Born: Paducah, Kentucky, on June 23, 1876
Education: Public school, Paducah, Kentucky
Marriage: Laura Spencer Baker, one child
Died: March 10, 1944

Biography

Irvin Shrewsbury Cobb was born in his maternal grandfather's house in Paducah, Kentucky, on June 23, 1876. The nine years that he lived in that house gave him a profound sense of identification with the community and steeped him in a family tradition of loyalty to the ideal of the Confederacy, on whose behalf members of both sides of his family had fought. Though Cobb eventually wound up a cosmopolite of international renown, his public image and private sense of self were always thoroughly grounded in his southern heritage.

At the age of sixteen, Cobb's promising public school career ended with the sudden collapse of the Cobb family fortune. Cobb left school and went to work, first driving an ice wagon, then as an apprentice on the *Paducah Daily News*.

Over the next twelve years Cobb made a strong impression in Kentucky journalism, starting off at the age of nineteen as editor of the *Daily News* and quickly moving on to serve in reportorial and editorial positions with the *Cincinnati Post*, the *Paducah Daily Democrat*, and the *Louisville Evening Post*. While with this last paper he began to reveal his gifts as a humorist by penning a regular column called "Kentucky Sour Mash."

In 1904, having married Laura Spencer Baker of Savannah, Georgia, Cobb moved to New York City, where he rapidly gained a reputation as a humorist and feature writer for the *Evening Sun*, *Evening World*, and *Sunday World*. During this period, Cobb was considered an integral member of Charles M. Chapin's legendary rewrite team at the *Evening World*. Cobb was extraordinarily prolific, a result of having a photographic memory. By some estimates, for example, Cobb generated over half a million words of copy covering the sensational Stanford White murder trial.

As fine a newsman as he was, Cobb's real talents pushed him in the direction of humor and fictional sketches, outlets for which finally drew him into the magazine field. In 1911, he joined the staff of the *Saturday Evening Post* and entered the major phase of his writing career. The next twenty years were divided between the *Post* and William Randolph Hearst's *Cosmopolitan Magazine*. Among his accomplishments at the *Post* was the publication of numerous "Judge Priest" stories that solidified his national reputation as a humorist.

On behalf of the *Post*, Cobb served as a war corespondent in 1914 and 1915 and again in 1918. Cobb's work during this period was acknowledged by the French Republic in 1919 when he was elected a Chevalier in the Legion of Honor. The war years also gave him a wealth of personal reminiscences on which he based a series of lectures that started him on a career as the foremost after-dinner speaker of his generation. So great was his reputation in the field that his name associated with any published joke books or collections of toastmaster anecdotes could guarantee profitable sales. The number of his speaking engagements and the itinerant nature of his professional life following the war led to numerous travel books and membership in no less than thirteen speakers' clubs and fraternal organizations throughout the country.

There was virtually no literary medium that Cobb did not try during his career, and his success in all of them was notable. In addition to his magazine fiction, familiar essays, and humor columns, he collaborated on five plays between 1907 and 1916, and his skills as a public speaker transferred well to radio.

In 1932, Hollywood began filming a feature based on Cobb's "Judge Priest" stories and starring Cobb's longtime friend, Will Rogers. Cobb moved to California to serve as an advisor on the project and remained there for several years as an active member of the film community. Cobb often made his own appearance a butt of his humor, claiming that he was one of the ugliest men in America. He was tall, heavy set, and basset-faced, characteristics that made him a natural for character roles in film. As early as 1921, he had been playing bit parts in silent films, but it was not until 1934 that he received widespread recognition for his work in the role of a riverboat captain in John Ford's *Steamboat Round the Bend*. In the next four years, Cobb appeared in five more films, his career in the movies coming to an end in 1939 as a result of illness.

In the last years of Cobb's life, poor health severely limited his productivity. His autobiography, *Exit Laughing* (1941), was his last major work. Though his public appearances were curtailed, his fame was not. Among the several tributes that he received were honorary degrees from Dartmouth College and the University of Georgia. He died in New York City on March 10, 1944.

Literary Analysis

Cobb's reputation during his lifetime was based as much on the quantity as the quality of his output. In addition to his grueling speaking schedule, Cobb averaged roughly two books a year, many of which were collections of his magazine pieces. Among his stories, those featuring the character of Judge Priest were deservedly the most celebrated. In the character of Priest, Cobb found a channel for his store of memories of life in Paducah. Based in part on members of Cobb's own family, the Judge was a wise overseer of a post-bellum southern community, and his dry wit and kindly manner wrapped around a shrewd intelligence set the overall tone for the stories. For all of their popularity, the stories were structurally simplistic and perpetuated the conventions of nineteenth-century local color writing.

Cobb's artistry was greater in his travel books, in large part because these gave him the opportunity to exploit first-person narrative and tap the rich public persona that he developed in his speaking career. His first, *Roughing It De Luxe* (1913), as the title indicates, was a straightforward updating of Twain's earlier definitive version of tourism in the West, complete with a naive pilgrim's point of view and containing episodes on topics such as the western landscape, Mormonism, curio vendors, and seasoned trail guides. One of the book's better sections is a satire of California boosterism that served as a model for a later volume, *Some United States* (1926), in which Cobb again toured America through the vehicle of 17 self-contained and comically insightful essays on various regional stereotypes. Cobb's books on European travel, notably *Europe Revised* (1913), tended to mix self-deflating comedy based on the nineteenth-century notion of the American innocent abroad with witty and quite direct criticism of the European tourism industry.

Cobb's most successful work was *Speaking of Operations . . .* (1915). Originally a magazine article describing in a humorously detached tone his surgery to treat a severe gastric hemorrhage, the piece struck so resonant a chord with the public that it was issued in book form and remained in print long after Cobb's death. *Operations* represented Cobb's style of humor at its best. Conversational, witty, and well focused, it offered the author's opinions about those minor details of a hospital stay that most patients overlook but all remember in the recounting.

The majority of Cobb's books of humor, most of which rambled well beyond four hundred pages, tended to be longwinded if gracefully stylized streams of witty opinion touching on a breadth of trivial subject matter that evinced his extraordinary photographic memory. Unlike his close friend, Will Rogers, with whose folksy style Cobb's manner as a public speaker was often compared, he was no pundit. He avoided politics and current events, preferring to cast himself in the role of a humble yet opinionated everyman for whom collar buttons and the Spenserian free-hand method of penmanship instruction loomed as large as the memory of the entire First World War. Whatever the subject, Cobb had a ready wit and a gift for phrases as pungent as his attribution of the prevalence of garlic in Italian cuisine to the dictum "when in Rome be an aroma."

Cobb's reputation did not long survive him. His style, defined by nineteenth-century rhythms of oral delivery, seems dated by mid-twentieth-century standards. Among his contemporaries, H.L. Mencken had been able to deliver opinions about the American character with a degree of acerbity that Cobb, always gentlemanly, seemed incapable of, and Robert Benchley's everyman was closer than Cobb's to the neurotic pitch of absurdity called for by the modern age.

Summary

Irvin S. Cobb, prolific author of humorous short stories, travel books and familiar essays, was America's most famous after-dinner speaker in the first half of the twentieth century. Extremely popular during his own time, his style epitomized the essence of nineteenth-century prose humor.

Selected Bibliography and Filmography

Primary Sources

Fiction

Back Home; Being the Narrative of Judge Priest and His People. New York: George H. Doran, 1912.

The Escape of Mr. Trimm; His Plight and Other Plights. New York: George H. Doran, 1913.

Fibble, D.D. New York: George H. Doran, 1916.

Local Color. New York: George H. Doran, 1916.

Old Judge Priest. New York: George H. Doran, 1916.

Those Times and These. New York: George H. Doran, 1917.

From Place to Place. New York: George H. Doran, 1920.

J. Poindexter, Colored. New York: George H. Doran, 1922.

Sundry Accounts. New York: George H. Doran, 1922.

Snake Doctor, and Other Stories. New York: George H. Doran, 1923.

Goin' on Fourteen. New York: George H. Doran, 1924.

Alias Ben Alibi. New York: George H. Doran, 1925.

On an Island that Cost $24.00. New York: George H. Doran, 1926.

Prose and Cons. New York: George H. Doran, 1926.

Collections of Humor and Travel Books

Cobb's Anatomy. New York: George H. Doran, 1912.

Cobb's Bill of Fare. New York: George H. Doran, 1913.

Roughing It De Luxe. New York: George H. Doran, 1913.

Europe Revised. New York: George H. Doran, 1914.

Speaking of Operations—. New York: George H. Doran, 1915.

Eating in Two or Three Languages. New York: George H. Doran, 1919.

The Life of the Party. New York: George H. Doran, 1919.

The Abandoned Farmers. New York: George H. Doran, 1920.

"Oh Well, You Know How Women Are!" New York: Goerge H. Doran, 1920.

One Third Off. New York: George H. Doran, 1921.

A Plea for Old Cap Collier. New York: George H. Doran, 1921.

A Laugh a Day Keeps the Doctor Away. New York: George H. Doran, 1923.

"Here Comes the Bride"—And So Forth. New York: George H. Doran, 1925.

Many Laughs for Many Days. New York: George H. Doran, 1925.

Some United States. New York: George H. Doran, 1926.

War Reminiscence and Miscellany

Paths of Glory. New York: George H. Doran, 1915.

Speaking of Prussians. New York: George H. Doran, 1917.

The Glory of His Coming. New York: George H. Doran, 1918.

The Thunders of Silence. New York: George H. Doran, 1918.

Stickfuls; Compositions of a Newspaper Minion. New York: George H. Doran, 1923.

Autobiography

Exit Laughing. New York: Bobbs-Merrill, 1941.

Plays

Cobb, Irvin S., and Safford Waters. *Funabashi.* Produced 1907.

———. *Mr. Busybody.* Produced 1908.

Cobb, Irvin S., and Bozeman Bulger. *Sargeant Bagby.* Produced 1913.

Cobb, Irvin S., and Harry Burke. *Guilty as Charged.* Produced 1915.

Cobb, Irvin S., and Roi Cooper Megrue. *Under Sentence.* Produced 1916.

Film Appearances

Pardon My French, 1921.

Peck's Bad Boy, 1921.

The Five Dollar Baby, 1922.

The Great White Way, 1924.

Steamboat Round the Bend, 1934.

Everybody's Old Man, 1936.

Pepper, 1936.

The Arkansas Traveler, 1938.

Hawaii Calls, 1938.

The Young in Heart, 1938.

Secondary Sources

Lieb, Sandra. "Irvin S. Cobb." *Dictionary of Literary Biography.* Vol. 11. *American Humorists, 1800-1950.* Ed. Stanley Trachtenberg. Detroit: Gale, 1982, pp. 82–88. An overview of Cobb's writing in a biographical context.

The National Cyclopedia of American Biography. Vol. 18. Ann Arbor: University Microfilms, 1967, pp. 375–376.

New York Times, March 11, 1944, p. 14. Obituary.

Gary Engle

Connelly, Marc[us Cook]

Born: McKeesport, Pennsylvania, on December 13, 1890
Education: Trinity Hall Preparatory School, Washington, Pennsylvania, no degree
Marriage: Madeline Hurlock, 1930, divorced, 1935
Died: December 21, 1980

Biography

Marcus Cook Connelly was the first son of Patrick Joseph and Mabel Cook Connelly. His father and mother had met while Patrick Joseph toured with a road company as a singer; after their marriage, Mabel Connelly joined her husband onstage. In 1888, a daughter was born while they were on tour. After her death in 1888, the Connellys, wanting another child, quit the stage to settle in McKeesport, Pennsylvania, where Marcus Cook Connelly was born on December 13, 1890

In McKeesport, Connelly's father ran the White Hotel, which hosted many touring companies; contact with the actors and his father's own stage experience helped foster Connelly's ambitions to be an actor himself. In 1902, at age twelve, Connelly was enrolled at Trinity School in Washington, Pennsylvania, a preparatory-boarding school for boys. That same year, his father died. His mother continued to run the hotel.

Connelly left school in 1907, at seventeen, to go to Pittsburgh to become a writer. There he worked on various newspapers for nearly eight years and tried his hand at verse and musical comedy lyrics.

One of these attempts, *The Amber Princess*, for which Connelly had written the book and lyrics, took him to New York City in 1917. The play folded after only fifteen performances; without the train fare home, Connelly remained in New York, to begin about five years of freelance writing, attempts at playwriting, and various odd jobs in the theatre.

During this period he met George S. Kaufman; the two men began a fruitful collaboration in playwriting, from about 1920 to 1924. Their most memorable work together includes *Dulcy* (1921), *To the Ladies!* (1922), *Merton of the Movies* (1922), and *Beggar on Horseback* (1924). In these early years in New York, Connelly also became one of the Algonquin Wits—the famed Round Table and Vicious Circle, whose members included Kaufman, Franklin P. Adams, Deems Taylor, Robert Benchley, Heywood Broun, Alexander Woollcott, Robert E. Sherwood, Dorothy Parker, and Harold Ross. In 1925, Connelly was named to the editorial board

of the newly founded *The New Yorker*, for which he wrote short stories, sketches, essays, and profiles and performed various editorial chores. The following year he had a theatrical success on his own, *The Wisdom Tooth* (1926).

In late 1928, Pulitzer-Prize cartoonist Rollin Kirby called Connelly's attention to Roark Bradford's newly published collection of dialect stories, *Ol' Man Adam and His Chillun*. In 1929, Connelly completed his most famous play, *The Green Pastures*, based on Bradford's stories: he traveled to Louisiana to talk with Bradford and to absorb the local color in his attempt to render milieu and dialogue authentically. Connelly also directed the 1929 production of the play; *The Green Pastures* won a Pulitzer Prize in 1930. That same year, Connelly also received an O. Henry Award for his short story, "Coroner's Inquest." On October 4, 1930, he married Hollywood actress Madeline Hurlock. The couple were divorced in 1935; they had no children.

From 1933 to 1944, Connelly divided his time between New York and Hollywood, writing screenplays for *Cradle Song* (1933); *Captains Courageous* (1937); *I Married a Witch* (1942); and *Reunion* (1942). He also wrote the screenplay for, and directed, the Warner Brothers production of *The Green Pastures* (1936). During this period, Connelly did not abandon live theater; *The Farmer Takes a Wife* (1934), written with Frank B. Elser, had a successful New York run; Connelly also produced, directed, and financed Arthur Kober's *Having Wonderful Time* (1937), rewrote, produced, and directed Arnold Sundgaard's *Everywhere I Roam* (1938), and wrote and staged *The Flowers of Virtue* in New York (1942).

Connelly realized his own acting ambitions in 1944 with the role of Stage Manager in the New York production of Thornton Wilder's *Our Town* and in the London production in 1946. The remaining twenty years of his active career show a happy versatility. In 1947, he became professor of playwriting at Yale University, a post that he held for five years. In 1951, he was appointed the United States Commissioner to UNESCO; that same year *The Green Pastures* was revived in New York City for a limited run. He served as President of the National Institute of Arts and Letters in 1953. In 1958, he directed *Hunter's Moon (There Are Two Points)* in London; the following year, he adapted *The Green Pastures* for broadcast television.

Connelly's last published works are ventures into new territory: his first and only novel, *A Souvenir from Qam*, appeared in 1965, and *Voices Offstage*, a memoir, in 1969. On Connelly's ninetieth birthday, Mayor Ed Koch presented him with a certificate of appreciation for his contributions to theater in New York City;

Connelly died eight days later, on December 21, 1980.

Literary Analysis

Marc Connelly's life as a man of letters spanned over fifty years; his writings include plays, short fiction, screenplays, a novel, and a memoir. Yet Connelly's literary reputation rests primarily on one play, *The Green Pastures* (1929), which won a Pulitzer Prize in 1930. As a humorist and playwright, Connelly deftly portrayed facets of American life between two wars; his work belongs so particularly to the 1920s and 1930s that it is rarely read now.

Connelly's most successful collaborations with Kaufman include the plays *Dulcy, To the Ladies!, Merton of the Movies,* and *Beggar on Horseback.* Both *Dulcy* and *To the Ladies!* poke gentle fun at the conventional American businessman and his household: in *Dulcy,* the husband succeeds in a business venture despite a foolish wife; in *To the Ladies!* the husband succeeds—in a brilliant parody of a businessman's banquet—because of an astute wife. *Merton of the Movies* comments harshly both on the naïvete of the moviegoing public and on the tawdriness of the film world that that public idealizes. The best of the four plays, *Beggar on Horseback,* which borrows its story from Paul Apel's *Hans Sonnenstossers Hollenfahrt,* and its expressionist technique from August Strindberg, satirizes the world of American business and "the aesthetic and domestic standards of entirely commercialized nouveaux riches."[1]

Biting satire is clearly not the major aim of work by Kaufman and Connelly: any potentially harsh social comment in their four plays is mitigated by an easy resolution of the dramatic conflict. Criticism of the utter crassness of the American businessman in *Beggar on Horseback* is considerably muted by the use of the device of a dream sequence. The stultifying vision of middle-class life is made laughable because it is depicted in the protagonist's nightmare; its dangers to his artistic ambitions vanishing on waking. Thus, the dramatic form of all four plays remains close to musical comedy and anticipates the popular romantic movie comedies of the early 1930s. *The Green Pastures,* based on Bradford's dialect stories *Ol' Man Adam an' His Chillun,* is unlike Connelly's previous work in purpose, theme, and execution. According to Connelly, the play "is an attempt to present certain aspects of a living religion in the terms of its believers."[2] Despite that admirably stated intention, it was difficult to find a producer because neither religious plays nor plays with all-black casts had succeeded at the box office; moreover, a black man playing God might offend white religious theatergoers. However, the Broadway production of *The Green Pastures* was a commercial and critical success, accepted as the depiction of a living folk religion. Despite its classification among examples of "regionalism," however,[3] the success of the play demonstrated its transcendence of the limits usually suggested by such a category. It was hailed in the 1930s as twentieth-century kin to medieval religious drama, and as "a vivid resume of folk types and experience."[4] Connelly adapted and directed the Warner Brothers film of *The Green Pastures* in 1936.

Like much of Connelly's work, however, *The Green Pastures* does not wear well. A limited revival in 1951 received a lukewarm reception. In the early 1960s, a black bishop found the play "irreligious" in its perpetuation of "outmoded stereotypes."[5] The bishop's comments are difficult to dispute. Critical discussion focused for a time on whether Connelly's depiction of the rural black's homely anthropomorphism of God was at all just.[6] Eventually, Paul T. Nolan, Connelly's chief literary advocate, admitted that by the early 1970s, the play looked inescapably "behin' de times."[7]

Whatever criticisms of cultural insensitivity can be leveled at *The Green Pastures,* the central theme of the play remains intriguing: God Himself learns, from His creature Man, that mercy is attained through suffering; He is transformed by that knowledge from the wrathful God of the Old Testament to the merciful Lord of the crucifixion and redemption. Humanity as a whole is the protagonist of the play; so, too, is de Lawd Himself. Nevertheless, the dissonance arising from the portrayal of rural black folk increasingly hinders sympathetic identification of audiences with the play; social change has interfered with the successful transmission of its creative thematic innovation.

The degree of topicality of Connelly's short fiction and sketches, most of which appeared in *The New Yorker* in the 1920s, has, unfortunately, made them suffer the same fate; unlike other *New Yorker* fiction of the period, Connelly's work is rarely anthologized now. Although the point of much of Connelly's satire has dulled simply because of the passage of time, his *New Yorker* fiction does illustrate his ability to write vivid dialogue: Connelly renders the upper-middle class couple, the spoiled, rich young bride, and the Midwestern Rotarian with telling accuracy; and, for the most part, he has only to let these people be themselves to make his satiric point. For this reason, he favors the sketch and the monologue over the conventional short story, preferring to show rather than tell.

In "Barmecide's Feast" (1927), for example, Connelly sketches the Christmas Eve of a childless, well-off couple only through their conversation; the meticulously drawn picture of the evening, ironically titled, exposes the emptiness of upper middle-class city life. He satirizes one of his favorite targets, the businessman, in a playlet depicting a Rotary Club meeting at sea in "Luncheon at Sea" (1927); travelling Rotarians have a meeting at which virtually nothing happens. In "An Hour Before Noon" (1928), Connelly allows a modern bride to reveal her own shallow egotism by making the short story an extended monologue, a device effectively used also by his fellow Algonquin Wit, Dorothy Parker, in her fiction.

But, in any extended comparison with his other colleagues at *The New Yorker*—James Thurber, S. J. Perelman—Connelly invariably suffers. No word play or subtle characterization rises to rescue his short fiction from its dependence on topicality and understatement. "The Guest" (1929), for example, features Connelly's Mercer, a forerunner of Thurber's Walter Mitty; but Connelly's meek Mr. Mercer is limited to a one-joke sketch in a hotel room where he is placed at the mercy of malfunctioning machines meant to serve hotel patrons.

A Souvenir from Qam (1965), Connelly's only novel and his last published fiction, might serve as a summary of Connelly's major characteristics as a writer. In form, the novel, like the plays that Connelly co-authored with Kaufman, is much like the romantic movie comedies of the 1930s. Like the hero of *Beggar on Horseback*, Newton Bemis, the protagonist, must struggle against the opportunism of a woman he loves, mistakenly, before he finds a genuine kindred spirit in a fictional Middle Eastern state depicted as the site of the original Garden of Eden. Bemis's idealism triumphs, and any social comment on the materialism of western ways is lost amid the musical-comedy rendition of life in the fictional oil-rich state of Suruk.

Summary

Marc Connelly, journalist, playwright, and *New Yorker* humorist, co-authored, with George S. Kaufman, four successful comedies—*Dulcy, To the Ladies!, Merton of the Movies,* and *Beggar on Horseback.* Connelly showed himself to be a deft portrayer of particular facets of American life between two wars. His plays, and his humorous short fiction and sketches for *The New Yorker*, demonstrate a knack for gentle satire of the urban middle and upper classes, particularly their vulgarity, domestic trappings, and of the American businessman's blindness to the arts and to genuine fun.

Despite the accuracy of Connelly's renditions of the American scene in both drama and short fiction, they are so clearly tied to a particular time and place—urban America, in the 1920s

and 1930s—that they go largely unread today. Connelly's Pulitzer-Prize-winning play, *The Green Pastures*, once hailed as the twentieth-century version of the medieval religious plays, has been similarly neglected: fifty years have significantly altered the status of blacks in America, so that what once seemed an accurate depiction of the living folk religion of rural southern blacks now seems a simplistic stereotype. Though the character of de Lawd learns that He, with man, must suffer to learn to be merciful, the dialect and characterization of the blacks are obstacles to contemporary audiences, who find it difficult to see beyond the historical cultural freight to the play's genuinely universal theme. Connelly's only novel, *A Souvenir from Qam*, is a deftly plotted story reminiscent of the comedies of the 1920s, with its vanquishing of the opportunistic *femme fatale* and the triumph of the naive but pure-minded hero.

Connelly seems to have recognized his own importance in his memoir, *Voices Offstage*—he tells the stories of his contributions to New York popular theater in the 1920s, 1930s, and 1940s. As playwright, producer, and director, he helped to make drama a vital American art form. His other works, popular as they were, remain inextricably tied to their time and place, less interesting to the literary critic than they are to the cultural historian.

Notes

1. Fred B. Millet, *Contemporary American Authors* (New York: Harcourt, Brace, 1940), p. 113.
2. Connelly, *Green Pastures* (New York: Farrar and Rinehart, 1929), p. xv.
3. Op. cit., Millet, p. 117.
4. Edith Isaacs, *The Negro in American Theatre* (New York: Theatre Arts, 1947), p. 88.
5. Paul T. Nolan, *Marc Connelly* (New York: Twayne, 1969), p. 83.
6. Nich Aaron Ford, "How Genuine Is the Green Pastures?" *Phylon*, 20 (1959): 194.
7. Nolan, "The Green Pastures: "Behin' De Times,'" *Dramatics*, 42 (1971): 21.

Selected Bibliography

Primary Sources

Plays

Dulcy. Comedy in three acts by George S. Kaufman and Connelly. New York: G.P. Putnam's Sons, 1921.
To The Ladies! George S. Kaufman and Connelly. *Contemporary American Plays.* Ed. Arthur Hobson Quinn. New York: Charles Scribner's Sons, 1923. New York: Samuel French, 1924.
Merton of the Movies. A dramatization of Harry Leon Wilson's story of the same name. By George S. Kaufman and Connelly. New York: Samuel French, 1925. Included, in abridged form, in *The Best Plays of 1922-1923.* Ed. Burns Mantle. New York: Dodd, Mead and Company, 1922.

Beggar on Horseback. George S. Kaufman and Connelly. New York: Boni and Liveright, 1924. Ed. John Gassner. *Twenty Five Best Plays of the Modern American Theatre. Early Series 1916-1929.* New York: Crown Publishers, 1949.

The Wisdom Tooth. Fantastic comedy in three acts. New York: Samuel French, 1927.

The Green Pastures: A Fable. Suggested by Roark Bradford's southern sketches, *Ol' Man Adam an' His Chillun.* New York: Farrar and Rinehart, 1929. Has been republished in over thirty different editions and anthologies, including: *French's Standard Library Edition,* 1932; *Pulitzer Prize Plays.* Ed. Katherine Coe and William H. Cordell. New York: Random House, 1940; *A Treasury of the Theatre: From Henrik Ibsen to Eugene Ionesco.* Ed. John Gassner. New York: Simon and Schuster, 1960; *The Green Pastures.* Ed. Vincent Long. With critical essays by W.R. Matthews, John Macmurray, and Henry Self. London: Delisle, 1963.

The Farmer Takes a Wife. Connelly and Frank D. Elser. Abridgement in *Best Plays of 1934-35.* Ed. Burns Mantle. New York: Dodd, Mead and Company, 1935.

Short Fiction

"Luncheon at Sea." *The New Yorker,* July 19, 1927, pp. 18-19.

"Gentleman Returning from a Party." *The New Yorker,* November 19, 1927, pp. 24-25.

"Barmecide's Feast." *The New Yorker,* December 24, 1927, pp. 13-15. In *The New Yorker Scrapbook.* New York: Doubleday, Doran, Inc., 1931; and *Short Stories from the New Yorker.* New York: Simon and Schuster, 1940.

"A Dear Old Couple." *The New Yorker,* March 24, 1928, pp. 19-20.

"The Committee: A Study of Contemporary New York Life." *The New Yorker,* April 7, 1928, pp. 22-24.

"An Hour Before High Noon." *The New Yorker,* April 21, 1928, pp. 23-25.

"The Guest." *The New Yorker,* December 21, 1929, pp. 23-24. Rpt. in *Comic Relief: An Omnibus of Modern American Humor.* Ed. Robert Linscott. New York: Blue Ribbon Books, 1942.

"Coroner's Inquest." *Colliers,* February 8, 1930, pp. 23-24; rpt. in *College Omnibus.* Ed. James D. McCullum. New York: Harcourt, Brace and Company, 1933; rpt. in *Fiction Goes to Court.* Ed. A.P. Blaustein. New York: Holt, 1954.

Novel

A Souvenir from Qam. New York: Holt, Rinehart, and Winston, 1965.

Memoir

Voices Offstage: A Book of Memoirs. New York: Holt, Rinehart and Winston, 1968.

Secondary Sources

Books

Bonin, Jane F. *Prize-Winning American Drama: A Bibliographical and Descriptive Guide.* Metuchen, N.J.: Scarecrow, 1973. Includes a scene-by-scene summary of *The Green Pastures,* Pulitzer Prize winner for the theater season of 1929-1930, the theater history of the play, popular response to it, and a brief list of representative reviews. Also includes a brief appraisal of Connelly's literary reputation, emphasizing that his fame rests on *The Green Pastures;* includes references to several critical articles on the play.

Connelly, Marc. *Green Pastures.* With an Introduction and Conclusion by Vincent Long, and Postscripts by the Very Rev. Dr. W.R. Matthews, John Macmurray, and Sir Henry Self. London: Delisle, 1963. Brief critical essays focus entirely on *The Green Pastures* as the expression of an anthropomorphism of God essential to genuine, undogmatic Christianity.

Isaacs, Edith J.R. *The Negro in the American Theatre.* New York: Theatre Arts, 1947. Brief discussion of *The Green Pastures;* the book as a whole helps to set the play in the context of black theater from the nineteenth century to the early 1940s.

Millet, Fred B. *Contemporary American Authors.* New York: Harcourt, Brace, 1940. Factual account of Connelly's literary activities to 1934, with brief discussion of plays written with Kaufman and mention of *The Green Pastures* as an example of regional literature.

Nolan, Paul T. *Marc Connelly.* Twayne's United States Authors Series, no. 149. New York: Twayne, 1969. The only book-length study of Connelly's life and work, with an exhaustive bibliography of Connelly's work, including titles of plays no longer extant or available only in manuscript. Also includes an annotated bibliography of reviews and critical material on Connelly and on American popular theater generally.

Articles

Ford, Nick Aaron. "How Genuine Is the Green Pastures?" *Phylon,* 20 (1959): 67-70, 193-194. Charges that Connelly's "attempt to present certain aspects of a living religion in terms of its believers" is not realized at all in *The Green Pastures.* Basing his assertions on an "informal random poll" of about one hundred students, teachers, ministers, and "untutored citizens," Ford concludes that Connelly misrepresents the unlettered black's conceptions of the physical features of God, his concept of God's moral sensitivity, and his concept of heaven. Thus he finds the play a failure.

Krumpelmann, John T. "Marc Connelly's *The Green Pastures* and Goethe's *Faust.*" *Studies in Comparative Literature.* Ed. Waldo F. McNier. Baton Rouge: Louisiana State University Press, 1962, pp. 199-218. This broad comparison concludes merely that "either directly or indirectly, consciously or unconsciously," Connelly was influenced by Goethe's *Faust.* Direct parallels between the plays do not exist. Krumpelmann can point out only general similarities: Faust's final redemption through love is likened to de Lawd's movement from wrath to an understanding of "mercy through sufferin'"; Goethe's God, like de Lawd, is pleased with His creation; the aging Faust and Moses both fail to attain earthly paradise. Neither play is illuminated by the comparison.

"Marc Connelly." *American Drama Criticism: Interpretations 1890-1977.* Ed. Floyd Eugene Eddleman. 2nd ed. Hamden, Conn.: Shoe String, 1979, pp. 79-81. Complete list of reviews and essays on plays by Connelly and his collaborators.

Nolan, Paul T. "God on Stage: A Problem in Characterization: Marc Connelly's *Green Pastures*." *Xavier University Studies*, 4 (1965): 75–84. Argues that the character of de Lawd is based on a stereotype of the "Good White Man," as he sees himself in relation to the folk, but the identification of the audience with de Lawd shifts at the end of the play to sympathy for Hosea and Hezdrel, who are morally superior to de Lawd, and ultimately, his teachers.

———. "*The Green Pastures*: 'Behin' De Times.'" *Dramatics*, 42 (1971): 17, 20–21. Argues that although *The Green Pastures* may seem dated or condescending because of its portrayal of rural southern blacks, the play should not be devalued. First, Connelly created in the champion Hezdrel a model from whom even de Lawd learns valuable lessons. The comic routines, spirituals, and costumes of the "folk" demonstrate the worth, joy, and spirituality of black Americans, compelling a white audience to participate in human experience much as de Lawd does, and thus to learn mercy through the depiction of suffering. Finally, the message of *The Green Pastures* now seems trite simply because of the passage of time, not because of any problem in the play or in the attitudes of the author.

———. "Marc Connelly's 'Divine Comedy': *Green Pastures* Revisited." *Western Speech*, 30 (1966): 216–224. Nolan finds the secret of popularity of *The Green Pastures* in its mixture of folk materials, religious matter, and its theme: "No one, including God, can judge the human race from the outside, and the only way to join the human race is through suffering." As all folk drama should, the play convinces the audience first of the differences between themselves and the folk, then wins the sympathetic identification of the audience because the audience must finally acknowledge their shared religious history. Thus, the audience realizes, the play is not about rural southern blacks, but about man.

Wilkington, Robert. "Notes on the Corpus Christi Plays and *The Green Pastures*." *Shakespeare Association Bulletin*, 9 (1934): 194–197. Considers performance of *The Green Pastures* as a means to understanding the details of the performance of the Corpus Christi plays; argues that both the older drama and the modern play empoloy an anthropomorphic God and use local color, anachronism, and music to achieve similar effects. Speculates that we may infer from the episodic structure of *The Green Pastures* that medieval audiences regarded individual pageants as dramatic units rather than merely as parts of the entire dramatic cycle.

Carmela McIntire

Conroy, Jack

Born: Monkey Nest mining camp, Missouri, on December 5, 1899
Education: University of Missouri at Columbia, 1920–1921, no degree
Marriage: Gladys Kelly, June 30, 1922, three children

Biography

Uncle Ollie, an eccentric, wily northeast Missouri farmer, Slappy Hooper, whose billboard paintings of stoves warm hoboes in winter, and the Fast Sooner Hound, who outruns the Wabash Cannonball on three legs, are only a few of Jack Conroy's contributions to American humor that are drawn from work situations—for Conroy himself was a worker, an exceptional worker to be sure.[1] In dangerous coal pits, railroad shops, and construction jobs, on auto production lines, wherever, in short, men and women labor for their living, Conroy experienced firsthand how humor lightens the task and brightens people's lives under the dreary, hazardous conditions of industrial work. Conroy's humor delights at the same time that it opens up the world of labor to readers. In revealing the world of actual blue-collar occupations with all its grime, heartache, and frequent comic invention, Conroy shows us universal characteristics that transcend class difference and cultural bias.

John Wesley (Jack) Conroy was born on December 5, 1899, to Irish parents in a tiny Missouri coal mining camp derisively called "Monkey Nest" by miners who toiled and sometimes died there. At age ten Conroy lost his father, killed in a mine explosion; a brother and two half-brothers also died in work-related accidents. Death was always close by when Conroy was growing up, but so were the hollows, woods, and meadows that surrounded the mining camp and its ugly hillock of mine tailings. Conroy could slip away to dream of a natural world and discover odd folk characters like the "Weed King" or "ride shanks' mare" into Moberly to the hitching lot behind the Merchants' Hotel and listen to farmers spin their tales in the droll, skeptical manner that also fascinated young Mark Twain when he visited his uncle in Florida, Missouri. Both Florida and Moberly fall within a region called "Little Dixie" in honor of its stand during the Civil War and the Scots-Irish lineage of southern farmers who first settled there.[2] The Italian, Welsh, Irish, and English miners of Monkey Nest, by contrast, maintained their own ethnic heritage. There as a boy Conroy heard a diversity of ballads and tales and shared in festivities that marked the rude community life of Monkey Nest. One community that was shared by all, however, was the life in the mines and the solidarity of the miners who as union members struck for safer conditions and better pay. Conroy grew up in a folk community that was soon to dissolve under competition from the new technology of oil and the dispersive social forces of industrialization that came late to northern Missouri.

At age fourteen Conroy entered the Wabash railroad shops in Moberly as a laborer. Rising quickly thanks to his literacy and intelligence, he became recording secretary of his union local. Shortly before the Moberly railroad strike in 1922, Conroy had gained the position of apprentice "car toad." He had left his job only briefly in 1920 to study one semester at the state university in Columbia. On the eve of the strike he married Gladys Kelly, a farmer's daughter. The union was defeated in the strike. In the ensuing years, Conroy, with three children and a wife, was forced to work at a series of day jobs, building brick roads, loading cement sacks, operating machinery in a steel mill, and so forth. With the Wobblies and hoboes, Conroy hopped freight cars throughout the Midwest in search of work. In 1927 he found a job in a rubber-heel factory in Hannibal, Missouri, and a year later, following his nephew Fred Harrison, he answered the lure of higher wages in the Willys-Overland factory in Toledo, Ohio.

After assembling autos by day, Conroy wrote drafts of stories by night and sent them to such magazines as H.L. Mencken's *American Mercury*. Mencken was impressed with the freshness, directness, and vitality of Conroy's writing and requested more. Sustaining himself and his family on earnings from Mencken, Conroy edited his own little magazine, *The Rebel Poet*. With the Depression came a sudden flowering of "proletarian" writing portraying the worker's life. The year 1933 was signal for Conroy's burgeoning literary career. In May of that year he founded *The Anvil*, which published "stories for workers," and in November his novel, *The Disinherited*, was published to wide critical acclaim. Conroy was celebrated by conservative and leftist critics alike as a worker–writer of great promise.

Conroy's second novel, *A World to Win* (1935), was considered a failure by those critics who in the wake of the Popular Front embraced established novelists and modernist literature. Conroy, like many other writers on the left, turned toward documentary writing and mined his own experiences for rich sources of folk narrative.

Joining the Federal Writers Project, first in St. Louis, later in Chicago, Conroy collaborated with the black novelist and researcher Arna Bontemps in a project that eventually culminated in *They Seek a City* (1945), an important documentary study of black workers migrating to northern factory cities. In addition, Conroy and Bontemps wrote a series of children's stories based upon Conroy's folk narratives. Supporting himself and his family as a book reviewer and encyclopedia editor (Franklin J. Meine, the noted scholar of American humor, was for a time his boss), Conroy published *Midland Humor* (1947) and *Anyplace but Here* (1965), the latter again a collaboration with Bontemps. Following his retirement to Moberly, Missouri, in 1966, Conroy continued to write stories, all of which appeared in *The Weed King & Other Stories* (1985). Gladys Conroy died in 1983. In his large stone house with the thousands of books he has read over a long life, Conroy receives visitors and friends from all over the world. On May 22, 1984, the people of Moberly honored their best-known writer in a day-long celebration. Conroy has received numerous awards, including an honorary doctorate from the University of Missouri, a Guggenheim Fellowship, the Mark Twain Award (from the Society for the Study of Midwestern Literature), the *Literary Times* award, and the Society of Midland Authors award.[3]

Literary Analysis

The Disinherited, still in print after fifty-two years, is a collection of picaresque narratives based on Conroy's experiences growing up in Monkey Nest, moving about the country in search of work, and returning finally to Missouri during the worst of the Depression. There the narrator, Larry Donovan, finds a new purpose in leading others like himself out of the passivity and defeatism of prolonged unemployment where, through no fault of their own, society had consigned them. It is a story rich in the polyphonic "voices" of the folk whom Conroy had known. The authentic idiom and dispassionate tone of the narrative, together with Conroy's sensitivity to the humorous potential in the absurdities of hardship and fate, make this perhaps the most important novel to emerge from the early years of the Depression.

Conroy perceived how some working people learn to turn hardship into humor through storytelling, identifying their lot with a comic-absurd impulse in the universe, and through the half-bitter, half-joking reflection summarized in folk sayings and locutions. His penchant toward comic self-deflation appears often in Conroy's first novel, as when Larry Donovan, a semi-autobiographical portrait of the author, takes a riveter's job on a high bridge despite his fear of heights—and crawls weakly down to the imprecations of his angry boss. Comic impulse, too, is inherent in the picaresque form of the novel, as Walter Blair points out (pp. 86–87). The grotesque, close at times to the farcical, appears in Conroy's novel, as in the accidental burial of a boy, reported by his half-wit brother. Such grotesque elements appear frequently in folk humor (in Ellis Parker Butler's stories, for instance). Terse images of humiliation and ludicrousness spell out vividly in Conroy's novel the condition of the unemployed: "Nothing impairs morale like the dissolution of a last pair of shoes. Maybe it starts with a little hole in the sole; and then the slush of pavements oozes in, gumming sox and balling between your toes" (p. 234).

The folklorist and western historian J. Frank Dobie admired Conroy's use of folk humor in *The Disinherited*, calling attention to the fact that the "number of words necessary in circumlocution to say that a man pissed is extraordinary."[4] Jokes and pranks are part of the worker's daily fare, a means of breaking monotony and initiating greenhorns to their new roles. *The Disinherited* represents the passing of the frontier point of view in its proper locale and its transplantation to new industrial settings. Rough, homespun humor is grafted onto the caustic good-naturedness of Wobbly laughter in Conroy's writing in appreciation of new political realities affecting the working person faced with an uprooted, proletarian life in factory cities, unemployment, and devastating cultural upheaval. Humor, Conroy shows us, is an enduring staple of a dispossessed people whom it empowers despite their loss of artisanal skills and yeoman self-sufficiency and despite the rising tide of mass culture and passive consumerism. Humor in Conroy, too, is the reagent that permits incongruous elements, both "lowbrow" and "highbrow," to mix, as Constance Rourke points out in her landmark study. Conroy's narratives join people, regardless of education and economic status, in shared laughter, thus inculcating unobtrusively democratic and humanistic values.

This democratic, humanistic impulse, roughly formulated in the slogan attached to his little magazine, "We prefer crude vigor to polished banality," motivated Conroy in his work as editor and collaborator. His literary magazine, *The Anvil*, ran thirteen issues (1933-1935), publishing Richard Wright's first writings and giving space in its pages to many young writers then unknown such as Nelson Algren, Meridel Le Sueur, Erskine Caldwell, and Langston Hughes, among others.

In May 1935, at the first American Writers' Congress, Conroy was celebrated as a worker-writer who, unlike most "proletarian" writers, wrote from first-hand experience. But, his dependence upon the Communist Party for a distribution agency cost Conroy his magazine. Political machinations involving the Party, Conroy's tireless business manager, Walter Snow,

and the editors of *Partisan Review*, Philip Rahv and Wallace Phelps (who later changed his name to William Phillips) in New York City, forced the merger of *The Anvil* and *Partisan Review*. After a few issues this new magazine was suspended. *Partisan Review* re-appeared a year later, devoted to modernist literature and Trotskyist in orientation.[5]

The Communist Party of America was not noted for its humor; in fact, most writers close to the Party found it rather dreary. A number of satires, including Conroy's unpublished "samizdat," circulated among friends, and Will Wharton's mordant poems were first published with Conroy's encouragement as *Graphiti from Elsinore* in 1949.[6] Nonetheless, the Party was keenly interested in promoting manifestations of folk culture to reinforce its identification with the American people after the appearance of the Popular Front in 1935. Thus, six of Conroy's "Uncle Ollie Stories" were published in the Sunday supplement of the *Daily Worker* in 1938-1939.

Based upon northern Missouri farmers he knew, Conroy made Uncle Ollie a composite yet highly individualized figure displaying traits characteristic of a folk type still in evidence today. Uncle Ollie hopes to sell his "mushmelons" at a profit but through a series of misadventures finally decides impulsively to employ them as ammunition against strikebreakers in a nearby canning factory. Uncle Ollie is a lovable though ornery man, impractical in matters such as driving a car or sensing market conditions, but he is instinctively just in his shrewd appraisal of character and application of human standards. Like the direct, vivid language and humor of the Wobbly folk poets, who in song and ballad expressed their resistance to the dehumanizing effects of machine culture, Conroy's "Uncle Ollie Stories" reveal how an individual, however insignificant his economic power may be, is able to fight back against big money and ensconced privilege. Indeed, most of Conroy's Uncle Ollie stories embody the enduring characteristics of rural folk culture and humor in northeast Missouri while addressing themselves to such social and political problems as the exploitation and disenfranchisement of the "little guy."

No better example of this two-fold purpose exists than Conroy's folk narratives, collected and re-cast as written text while Conroy worked on the Illinois Writers Project in Chicago from 1938 to 1941. The best known of these narratives is "The Fast Sooner Hound." Conroy heard the kernel of the story while working in the Wabash railroad shops years before. A precedent for the tale exists in Mark Twain's *Roughing It* in the narrator's description of a "cayote" who can outrun a bullet even before it is fired. A type of animal fable, "The Fast Sooner Hound" is the story of a wonder dog whose native intelligence, loyalty, and resourcefulness make him a folk hero.[7] In Conroy's narrative a boomer fireman is an itinerant stoker on a locomotive who "is never long for any one road." Forbidden by company rules to ride along, the Sooner Hound runs alongside the train. The Roadmaster, skeptical of the Sooner Hound's prowess, challenges the boomer fireman to a race between the dog and the Wabash Cannonball, the fastest locomotive on wheels. Word flies, and people line the tracks for a hundred miles. At full tilt the roadmaster looks back, sure that he has left the Sooner Hound far behind. The Boomer drops his fireman's shovel and looks out the window, whooping, "He's true blue as they come! . . . Got the company interests at heart, too, he's still with us." "What do you mean," says the Roadmaster, "I can't see hide nor hair of him." "We're going so fast," says the Boomer, "half the journal boxes are on fire and melting the axles like hot butter. The Sooner's running up and down the train hoisting a leg above the boxes. He's doing his level best to put out some of the fires. That dog is true blue as they come and he's the fastest thing on four legs, but he's only using three of them now!" (1985, p. 44).

Conroy cast this oral tale into a written narrative, embellished it, and submitted it and seven others to the Illinois Writers Project. It first appeared in B.A. Botkin's classic *A Treasury of American Folklore* (1944). Teaming up with Arna Bontemps, Conroy wrote three children's stories based upon these narratives. *The Fast Sooner Hound*, still in print, has outlived the steam locomotive and the passenger train. Generations have enjoyed the tale, and recently Stephen Wade performed Conroy's "The Fast Sooner Hound," "The High Divers," and "Slappy Hooper" in Wade's long-running show, *Banjo Dancing*, at the Arena Stage Theatre in Washington, D.C. Oral tales in conception, Conroy's humorous folk narratives re-appeared as such in this live performance, calling forth the audience's imaginative participation.

"Slappy Hooper" is the story of a billboard sign painter whose craft, like that of the Greek Apelles, excels mere imitation. In this tale Conroy appears to make fun of Plato's admonishments about the evil social effects of art's illusory reflections. Slappy's first job is a picture of a loaf of bread for a bakery: "It would make you hungry just to look at it. That was the trouble. The birds begin to flying on it to peck at it, and either they'd break their bills and starve to death because they didn't have anything left to peck with, or they'd just sit there perched on the top of the billboard trying to figure out what was the

matter until they'd just keel over." Another tale, "The High Divers," parodies a traditional stunt, listed in the *Guinness Book of Records*, which involves diving from a high platform into a shallow pool of water. The narrator, one such breakneck diver, suspects that he has been cheated by a certain Eddie La Breen, a rival diver, who sneaked around at night to wring out the wet bath mat that served as the pool of water. His bones broken, the narrator asks ruefully: "And if he didn't do it, who did?"

The humor in Conroy's folk narratives lies in part in the absurdity of the situation, in part in the language of its telling. The language is crisp and colloquial, with accented beats like the poetic meters of Old English poetry, as exemplified in "The Demon Bricksetter from Williamson County": "A man that sets brick in a pavement only needs to have a weak mind, a strong back, and a great big hand with long fingers that will stretch and won't strain easy. It ain't no job for a violin player, you can bet your sweet life." This tale, and another entitled "The Sissy from the Hardscrabble County Rock Quarries," are variations of the brag, employing traditional techniques of exaggeration from the frontier humorists. Conroy interprets the Missouri localisms that he employs: "I'm a man as is work-brickle. . . . I'm a man as can't say quit. When I lay a-holt, I'm like a turtle, and I don't let loose till it thunders" ("Demon Bricksetter").[8]

Like the folk storytellers, both black and white, whom he had listened to in Monkey Nest, in the Moberly hitching lot, in the Wabash shops, and in both factories and taverns along Chicago's North Clark Street, Conroy's narrative style appeals to the ear, echoing traditional folk locutions, ballads, sermons, and tall tales, as well as written texts. Less conscious perhaps than George W. Harris was in *Sut Lovingood* of the comic potential in juxtaposing flowery, "bookish" language with folk speech, Conroy faithfully represents in his narratives the speech of the young man such as the narrator of the "Uncle Ollie Stories," who, like himself, grew up in a largely oral, folk community and educated himself through discursive readings in romance and classic literature appearing in "Little Blue Book" editions. Thus, arcane words like "fain" and "dassen't" appear in a context of colloquial expression. The humor of such juxtapositions lies in the incongruity of formal and folk diction, as Conroy says in *The Disinherited*, referring to "Emerson's axiom that an object removed from its habitual environment at once becomes humorous" (p. 126).[9]

If comic deflation and self-directed irony are characteristic of Conroy's own writing, then his appreciation of these techniques applied to maudlin ballads and bawdy songs reveals a writer alert to comic possibility through parody. Possessing a prodigious memory and a sharp eye for the humorous potential of "masterpieces" found in used book bins, Conroy, with help from Wharton and Algren, wrote a play based loosely upon a nineteenth-century melodrama satirizing his old rival, James T. Farrell. *The Drunkard's Warning* played in St. Louis bars and Chicago lofts in order to raise funds for the revived *Anvil* (1938-1940).[10] Acclaimed by literary friends and tavern patrons for his impromptu recitations of maudlin and obscene ballads, Conroy attempted to interest a publisher in an anthology of American sentimental verse entitled *The Rosewood Casket: A Garland of Rue and Lavendar*, but never succeeded in selling the manuscript. In a marathon session, however, in the early 1950s, Conroy recited his large repertoire of traditional bawdy songs, once sung by Monkey Nest miners and barroom bards, to Vance Randolph whose manuscript, "Unprintable Songs of the Ozarks," still rests in the Library of Congress, awaiting a publisher. Both manuscripts deserve publication, for they constitute a legacy of American native humor as legitimate as, though less reputable than, what appears in Walter Blair's anthology, *Native American Humor*.

Conroy's *Midland Humor* is a collection of yarns and poems, beginning with the burlesque frontier sermon, "The Harp of a Thousand Strings," a traditional satire often performed by Win Stracke, founder of Chicago's Old Town School of Folk Music during Conroy's Chicago years. The collection includes both little-known writers such as Robert Jones Burdette and renowned authors such as Twain and Booth Tarkington. Drawing from the rich sources of midwestern humor, Conroy's anthology reflects his personal taste. Published in 1947, it contrasts the robust, anti-authoritarian temper of midwestern humorists with the more refined humor of the East, to which it took exception. As if in rebellion, Conroy explains, against the pretensions of eastern writers and their "smart alecky aspersions" about the rude yokels west of the Hudson, midwestern humorists appear ready to go to extremes to show the superiority of their regional craftiness and physical prowess (p. viii). Midwestern humor entered a more sophisticated phase in the writings of George Ade, Finley Peter Dunne, and Kin Hubbard, whose work is currently enjoying renewed appreciation in new editions.

Now in his eighties, Conroy continues to add reminiscences of his boyhood in a late-frontier mining camp to his "Monkey Nest Tales." Like the comic figure of the "Weed King," who engages in the absurd task of eradicating every weed from his rock-bestrewn field, Conroy's characters are eccentrics in the folk mold. These include Birdie, who pens lovesick poetry secretly to a Syrian peddlar ("The Siren"); the Morphadite, a traditional trickster figure ("The Morphadite"); and Charley, the family's horse, whose habit of breaking wind while pulling the family buggy embarrasses the mother and tickles the children.[11] Comic detachment and intertextual allusion serve in these stories to undercut the sentimentality implicit in reminiscence, imparting a tone of bemused wonderment and affection without altering the severity of the circumstances portrayed. Conroy's vivid imagination, abundant in folk humor and wisdom, gives the reader a feeling of the immediacy of life without the programmatic intent of proletarian writing or the pretentiousness often characteristic of excursions into one's past. Like Tolstoy, Conroy never quite got over his incomparable childhood, both its joys and hardships. His stories help us to remain young in our own hearts.

Summary

Jack Conroy's life and work cover almost the entire span of the twentieth century. He has lived to see the passing of a late frontier in his native Missouri. Little given to sentimentalizing the past, Conroy followed this folk culture into new industrial settings, showing how humor and storytelling continue to exist in cities and factories where people meet, work, and attempt to distract themselves through their own creative resourcefulness. His attitude toward experience seems to be a mixture of wise skepticism and detachment, resolved in rollicking, gusty laughter. Primarily a storyteller, Conroy has drawn most of his narratives from oral memory and observation. He is, in his own words, "a witness to his times." The folk tales he collected and made into literary narrative ("The Fast Sooner Hound," "Slappy Hooper," "The High Divers," "The Type Louse," and others) have become part of the classic legacy of American humor and folklore, providing material for theatrical performance such as Stephen Wade's *tour de force, Banjo Dancing*. Moreover, his *Midland Humor* is the only important work of its kind to attempt to delineate the nature of midwestern humor by example. Finally, his novels and short stories, with their comic-grotesque sense of play, use of folklore intertext, and ineffable qualities of tenderness and humor, provide models for writers interested in tapping the rich stream of American folklife.

Notes

1. For additional detail, see introduction to *The Weed King & Other Stories*.
2. See Howard W. Marshall on "Little Dixie" and its folk cultural scope: *Folk Architecture in Little Dixie: A Regional Culture in Missouri* (Columbia, Mo.: University of Missouri Press, 1981).
3. See articles on Conroy under Secondary Sources.

4. Letter, J. Frank Dobie to Jack Conroy, July 16, 1963.

5. See articles listed in the bibliography: Fabre; Wixson (1984); Conroy (1978).

6. Prairie City, Ill.: Decker Press, 1949.

7. See John W. Roberts, "Folklore of the Precious Canine: Jim the Wonder Dog," *Missouri Folklore Society Journal*, 3 (1981): 59-70.

8. See Walter Blair, *Native American Humor* (New York: American Book Company, 1937).

9. Similarly, Conroy championed the Missouri folk poet, H.H. Lewis, whose folk expressions, neologisms, and earthy images won him the Harriet Monroe Poetry prize in 1937. See Conroy, *Jack Conroy Reader*, pp. 237-242.

10. See Conroy, "Days of the Anvil," *American Book Collector*, 21 (1971): 14-19.

11. These stories are gathered in *The Weed King & Other Stories*. Ed. Douglas C. Wixson (Westport, Conn.: Lawrence Hill, 1985).

Selected Bibliography

Primary Sources

Novels
The Disinherited. 1933. Westport, Conn.: Lawrence Hill, 1982.
A World to Win. New York: Covici-Friede, 1935.

Social History
Bontemps, Arna, and Jack Conroy. *They Seek a City*. Garden City, N.Y.: Doubleday, Doran, 1945.
———. *Anyplace but Here*. New York: Hill & Wang, 1966.

Anthologies
Botkin, B.A. *A Treasury of American Folklore*. New York: Crown, 1944.
Conroy, Jack. *Midland Humor: A Harvest of Fun and Folklore*. New York: Current, 1947.
Conroy, Jack, and Curt Johnson, eds. *Writers in Revolt: The Anvil Anthology, 1933-1940*. N.Y.: Lawrence Hill, 1973.

Children's Books
Bontemps, Arna, and Jack Conroy. *The Fast Sooner Hound*. 1942. Boston: Houghton Mifflin, 1970.
———. *Sam Patch, The High, Wide, and Handsome Jumper*. Boston: Houghton Mifflin, 1951.
———. *Slappy Hooper, the Wonderful Sign Painter*. Boston: Houghton Mifflin, 1946.

Collections of Stories and Prose Writings
The Jack Conroy Reader. Ed. Jack Salzman and David Ray. New York: Burt Franklin, 1979.
The Weed King & Other Stories. Ed. Douglas C. Wixson. Westport, Conn.: Lawrence Hill, 1985.

Secondary Sources
Aaron, Daniel. "Introduction." *The Disinherited*, by Jack Conroy. New York: Hill & Wang, 1963, pp. vii-xiv. One of the best general introductions to Conroy's first novel.
Blair, Walter. *Native American Humor (1800-1900)*. New York: American Book Company, 1937. Blair's introduction is indispensable reading for understanding Conroy's folk narratives.
Bluestein, Gene. *The Voice of the Folk*. Amherst: University of Massachusetts Press, 1972. See Chapter Four, "Folklore and the American Character."

Bridgman, Richard. *The Colloquial Style in America*. New York: Oxford University Press, 1966. See the chapters on "Parts of Speech" and "Henry James and Mark Twain" on the difficulties and achievements in the use of vernacular.
Burke, John Gordon. "A Preliminary Checklist of the Writings of Jack Conroy." *American Book Collector* 21 (1971): 20-24. Contains some errors and omissions, but the most complete up to 1969.
Coffin, Tristram Potter, ed. *Our Living Traditions*. New York: Basic Books, 1968. See Hennig Cohen's useful essay on "American Literature and American Folklore," pp. 238-247. See also Archie Green's "The Workers in the Dawn: Labor Lore," pp. 251-262.
Conroy, Jack. "On *Anvil*." *TriQuarterly*, 43 (1978): 111-129.
———. "Days of *The Anvil*." *American Book Collector*, 21 (1971): 14-19.
———. "H.H. Lewis: Plowboy Poet of the Gumbo." *Jack Conroy Reader*, pp. 237-242.
———. "The Laughing Frontier." *Jack Conroy Reader*, pp. 247-259.
———. "The Literary Underworld of the Thirties." *Jack Conroy Reader*, pp. 151-164.
———. "Memories of Arna Bontemps—Friend and Collaborator." *Jack Conroy Reader*, pp. 281-290.
Dorson, Richard M. *Folklore: Selected Essays*. Bloomington: Indiana University Press, 1972. See Dorson's chapters on "Esthetic Form in British and American Folk Narrative," "Oral Styles of American Folk Narrators," and "History of the Elite and History of the Folk."
Fabre, Michel. "Jack Conroy as Editor." *New Letters*, 39 (1972): 115-137. See Fabre's account of the *Anvil* and its demise.
Fine, Elizabeth C. *The Folklore Text, From Performance to Print*. Bloomington: Indiana University Press, 1984. See Fine's valuable chapter on performance-centered texts for insights into the relation between text and performance in Conroy's folk narratives.
Marshall, Howard W. *Folk Architecture in Little Dixie: A Regional Culture in Missouri*. Columbia, Mo.: University of Missouri Press, 1981. This is the best cultural description of Missouri's "Little Dixie" region available.
Roberts, John W. "Folklore of the Precocious Canine: Jim the Wonder Dog." *Missouri Folklore Society Journal*, 3 (1981): 59-70.
Rourke, Constance. *American Humor, A Study of the National Character*. 1931. Rpt. Garden City, N.Y.: Doubleday, 1953.
Salzman, Jack. "Conroy, Mencken and *The American Mercury*." *Journal of Popular Culture* 7 (1973): 524-528.
Smith, Henry Nash. "A Sound Heart and a Deformed Conscience." *Mark Twain, A Collection of Critical Essays*. Ed. Henry Nash Smith. Englewood Cliffs, N.J.: Prentice-Hall, 1963, pp. 83-100. See Smith's discussion of vernacular protest.
Wixson, Douglas C. "From Conroy to Steinbeck: The Quest for an Idiom of the People in the 1930s." *MidAmerica VIII* (1981): 135-150.

———— . "Introduction." *The Weed King & Other Stories*. Westport, Conn.: Lawrence Hill, 1985, pp. xi-xxxi.

———— . "Jack Conroy, 'The Granddaddy of All Rebel Writers.'" *Tradition*, 1 (Fall 1985): 3; 9.

———— . "Jack Conroy and Industrial Folklore." *Missouri Folklore Society Journal*, 7 (1984).

———— . "Jack Conroy, the Sage of Moberly." *Book Forum*, 6 (1982): 201–206.

———— . "Literature from the Crucible of Experience: Jack Conroy in Ohio, 1927-30." *Midwestern Miscellany*, 8 (1980): 44–60.

———— . "*The Rebel Poet, The Anvil, The New Anvil*." In *American Literary Magazines: The Twentieth Century*. Ed. Edward Chielens. Westport, Conn.: Greenwood Press.

———— . "Red Pens from the Village: *The Anvil* and *The Left*, Midwestern Little Magazines." *MidAmerica XI* (1984): 42–55.

Douglas C. Wixson

Crockett, David [Davy]

Born: Greene County, Tennessee, on August 17, 1786

Education: Less than a year of formal schooling

Marriages: Mary (Polly) Finley, August 14, 1806, three children; Elizabeth (Betsy) Patton, spring or summer of 1816, four children (plus two by Elizabeth's first marriage)

Died: March 6, 1836

Biography

A product of the American frontier and one of its most enduring symbolic embodiments, Davy Crockett was born on August 17, 1786, in Greene County, Tennessee. The grandfather after whom Davy was named had crossed the Appalachians with his family during the preceding decade, only to be killed, along with Davy's grandmother, by a party of Creek and Cherokee Indians in what is now Hawkins County, Tennessee, in 1777. Davy's father, John Crockett, who was fortunate enough not to be at the homestead when the attack took place, married Rebecca Hawkins about three years later and settled in Greene County, then a portion of Washington County, North Carolina. Like his famous son, John was active in local government, serving as constable for three terms, but was none too prosperous. Plagued by debts, some of which resulted from the destruction by floodwaters of a mill that he had helped to build, John occasionally hired out young Davy to help relieve the family's financial problems. One such experience, his work as a cattle drover at about age twelve for a man named Jacob Siler, is mentioned prominently in his autobiography. Siler tried to keep the independent Davy in his service beyond the stipulated period, but Crockett escaped at night through the winter snow, making his way back from Virginia to the Crockett home after a several weeks' journey.

His independence is further illustrated by the quick termination of his first school attendance. After a fight with a fellow student during the fall of 1799, less than a week into his academic career, Crockett skipped school until the schoolmaster, Benjamin Kitchen, inquired about his poor attendance. To avoid his angry father's hickory rod, Crockett ran away from home, working at odd jobs for well over two years. He returned during the spring of 1802 so changed that, by his own account, none of his family at first recognized him.

A year or so after his reappearance, Crockett sought another six months' instruction in reading and writing, apparently because he blamed his rejection by a young Quaker woman on his lack of education. His newly acquired learning failed to win him the heart of his beloved, but he soon shifted his affections to another young woman, Margaret Elton, to whom he became engaged in the fall of 1805. Unfortunately, the allure of a country frolic drew Davy away from Margaret at an inopportune moment, and soon thereafter, she married a rival. Despite his disappointment, Crockett continued his search for a suitable wife, and he married Polly Finley on August 14, 1806. Before her death in 1815, Polly bore him three children: John Wesley, William, and Margaret.

During his marriage to Polly, Crockett supported his family primarily through farming and hunting, but he also served two enlistment terms as a soldier under Andrew Jackson in the Creek Indian War. Polly died soon after his discharge (as fourth sergeant), and he then married a widow, Betsy Patton, who added two children by her previous marriage, George and Margaret Ann, to the Crockett brood and subsequently bore Davy four more children: Robert Patton, Elizabeth Jane, Rebeckah Elvira, and Matilda. In addition, she possessed money and slaves enough to improve the Crockett fortunes considerably, at least for a time.

Late in 1817, Crockett moved his new family to Shoal Creek in the present Lawrence County, Tennessee, where his political career began to prosper. Even before Polly's death, Crockett's compatriots had shown their confidence in him by electing him a lieutenant in the Tennessee militia. After the move to Lawrence County, Crockett was chosen militia colonel and began serving in various civil offices, including justice of the peace and Lawrenceburg town commissioner. In 1821, he was elected to the Tennessee State Legislature for Lawrence and Hickman Counties, and in 1823, following a move necessitated by the flooding of a mill complex that Crockett owned, he was chosen state representative for several sparsely populated counties in far western Tennessee. Despite a defeat in the congressional campaign of 1825, his national political career was launched by his election in 1827 to the United States House of Representatives, a body to which he was reelected in 1829 and 1833. His reelection campaigns of 1831 and 1835 were unsuccessful.

Davy Crockett's political rise was the result of the same phenomenon that carried Andrew Jackson to the Presidency, a shift in power from the established East to the vigorous West and an increasing faith in the capacities of the common man. To an even greater extent than Jackson, Crockett gave the impression of being a man of the people. He was the consummate frontiersman, a hunter-provider without peer, whose native wit made him a formidable opponent for the better-educated rivals who sought to unseat him. Unfortunately for his political aspirations, which included a desire to be President, Crockett shifted his allegiance from the Jacksonian Democrats to the Whigs and thereby lost much of his professional political support. The split with Jackson was caused by Crockett's disapproval of Jackson's centralization of power in the Presidency and by his opposition to Jackson's removal of the federal deposits from the Bank of the United States. Of even greater importance, however, was the Jacksonians' refusal to support Crockett's version of the Tennessee Land Bill, a version which would have secured ownership of extensive tracts of land in west Tennessee for the poverty-stricken squatters who had long occupied them. The failure of the Land Bill and his ill-advised participation in a Whig-sponsored political tour of the East while Congress was still in session cost Crockett the backing of much of his constituency and led to his final defeat by the Jacksonian Adam Huntsman in the 1835 Congressional campaign.

Whether or not he made the embittered statement generally attributed to him that the Tennessee electorate might "all go to hell and I will go to Texas," Crockett set out for Texas in November of 1835. Although his original purpose appears to have been exploration rather than combat, he committed himself to the cause of Texas independence by signing, probably in the village of Nacogdoches, an oath of allegiance to the Texas Republic. He then proceeded to San Antonio, where he died at the Alamo on March 6, 1836.

Literary Analysis

Davy Crockett was an ambitious politician for whom humor was a political tool, a means of winning votes. As a stump orator, he had the ability, which Lincoln would later exploit even more effectively, to use pithy anecdotes, homely metaphors, and homespun jokes to win over a crowd. He was "the gentleman from the cane," the clever but uneducated backwoodsman about whom endless tales were spun by journalists and others (including Davy himself) to illustrate, at one moment, the untutored buffoonery of the frontiersman and, at another, the frontiersman's native shrewdness. The Davy Crockett of public imagination was simultaneously the clown who drank from the fingerbowls at a formal banquet and the sly politician who lured the electorate to the local tavern before his opponent could speak. As one might expect, the more flattering stories were printed by those who agreed with Davy's politics and the less flattering by those who opposed them.

Crockett stories in the periodical press were soon followed by longer works about Crockett or Crockett-like characters, including several plays. The earliest of these, James Kirke Paulding's *The Lion of the West* (1831), contains a "ring-tailed roarer" named Nimrod Wildfire who is reputed to have been modelled primarily after Crockett. Although Paulding's original has been lost, various adaptations of the play's materials by other writers suggest that the humor was largely verbal, resulting especially from Wildfire's absurd use of pseudo-Latinate words (such as "exfluncated" and "te-to-taciously") and his spouting of elaborate frontier brags. Walter Blair quotes such a brag from a Kentucky jest-book of the period:

> My name is Nimrod Wildfire—half horse, half alligator and a touch of the airthquake—that's got the prettiest sister, fastest horse, and ugliest dog in the district, and can out run, out jump, throw down, drag out and whip any man in all Kentuck![1]

Joseph Arpad, citing a letter from Paulding to the oral humorist John Wesley Jarvis, argues that Jarvis contributed a great deal of the humorous material for Paulding's play.[2] At any rate, such material had long existed in the frontier oral tradition and was simply made more familiar and more respectable through its use by Paulding.

In 1833, Matthew St. Clair Clarke anonymously published *The Life and Adventures of Colonel David Crockett of West Tennessee*, a work that reappeared in the same year with the title *Sketches and Eccentricities of Colonel David Crockett of West Tennessee.* Much of the later development of Crockett lore was to involve Davy's transformation into a tall-tale hero of the type exemplified by Paul Bunyan and Pecos Bill, and on the first page of his first chapter, Clarke indicates that that transformation had already begun. Speaking of Davy's childhood, Clarke tells us that "No one, at this early age, could have foretold that he ever was to ride upon a streak of lightning, receive a commission to quiet the fears of the world, by wringing off the tail of a comet, or perform several other wonderful acts." Much of the book is genuine biography (written in a style somewhat reminiscent of James Fenimore Cooper), but elements of humorous extravagance, probably drawn from the popular press and once again from American oral humor, occur throughout. There are, for example, the tales of Davy's selling, stealing back, and repeatedly reselling a coonskin for whiskey money and of Davy's climbing and sliding down a tree over and over again in order to keep from freezing.

Although Clarke's book may have contributed to Crockett's re-election to Congress in 1833, Crockett was displeased enough with the various misrepresentations contained in the *Sketches and Eccentricities* and in a plethora of newspaper articles to take part in the one substantial literary project with which his name has confidently been associated, the publication of *A Narrative of the Life of David Crockett, of the State of Tennessee* (1834). Controversy still exists as to how the book was composed, but the present critical consensus is that Crockett dictated the material to a collaborator, Thomas Chilton, who then polished the book into its final form. How much polishing Chilton found it necessary to perform remains uncertain.

As a number of commentators have pointed out, the *Narrative*, in telling its tale of a poor, unknown boy's rise to prominence, bears a resemblance, probably intentional, to Benjamin Franklin's *Autobiography.* The book also possesses picaresque elements, especially in its earliest chapters, which anticipate Mark Twain's *Huckleberry Finn* (The episodic account of a resourceful young Davy's struggle to maintain his independence in a world dominated by exploitive, authoritarian adults certainly provides a foretaste of Twain's great work). Young Crockett, who shows considerable resistance to formal education, is twice a runaway from adult oppression, and on at least one important occasion, upon his return to his family after an absence of about two years, he conceals his identity, after which he is finally recognized and joyously received by those who thought him forever lost—a trick that Huck will also employ.

The style of the *Narrative* is simple without being boorish; the book contains fewer dialect flourishes than one might expect. Some nonstandard language is included, and many homespun figures of speech occur (for example, "I was certain his anger would hang on to him, like a turkle does to a fisherman's toe."), but the grammar is generally sound and the presentation rather matter-of-fact. Sometimes, however, this very matter-of-factness has a startling effect, as in the following account of an incident from the Creek Indian War:

> It was, somehow or other, found out that the house had a potato cellar under it, and an immediate examination was made, for we were all as hungry as wolves. We found a fine chance of potatoes in it, and hunger compelled us to eat them, though I had a little rather not, if I could have helped it, for the oil of the Indians we had burned up on the day before, had run down on them, and they looked like they had been stewed with fat meat.

The brutality of this passage is a sample of Old Southwest humor, the comic tradition which developed out of the harsh circumstances of frontier life and which the Crockett stories helped establish.

Two subjects that the *Narrative* deals with extensively and that were to remain prominent in later Crockett lore are his electioneering technique and his prowess as a hunter. Of one of his earliest speeches, he gives the following account:

> At last I told them I was like a fellow I had heard of not long before. He was beating on the head of an empty barrel near the road-side, when a traveler, who was passing along, asked him what he was doing that for? The fellow replied that there was some cider in that barrel a few days before, and he was trying to see if there was any then, but if there was he couldn't get at it. I told them that there had been a little bit of a speech in me a while ago, but I believed I couldn't get it out. They all roared out in a mighty laugh, and I told some other anecdotes, equally amusing to them, and believing I had them in a first-rate way, I quit and got down, thanking the people for their attention. But I took care to remark that I was as dry as a powder-horn, and that I thought it was time for us all to wet our whistles a little: and so

I put off to the liquor stand, and was
followed by the greater part of the
crowd.

By contrast, the various descriptions of hunts,
primarily bear hunts, emphasize Crockett's courage and resourcefulness rather than his wit, but
tall-tale elements creep into these hunting narratives frequently enough to foreshadow later
comic developments. The number and size of his
animal quarries sometimes seem exaggerated,
for example, and the tale of repeatedly sliding
down a tree to keep warm is prominently featured.

Several other works that have been attributed
to Crockett's pen are now known not to be his.
*An Account of Col. Crockett's Tour to the North
and Down East* (1835) may contain some genuine Crockett material but is believed to be primarily the work of William Clark, one of Crockett's Whig colleagues. The book narrates the
events of the tour that was eventually to cost
Crockett so dearly and contains many satiric
comments about Andrew Jackson and Jackson's
hand-picked successor, Martin Van Buren. The
touches of dialect humor are at least as frequent
as in the *Narrative*, and the persona of the *Account* bears some resemblance to Twain's persona in *The Innocents Abroad*; Crockett is presented here as the naive traveler whose fresh
reactions to the wonders of civilized life give us
new insights into civilization's strengths and
weaknesses.

The *Account* is an obvious attempt to drum
up support for Crockett and the Whig cause, a
purpose shared by *The Life of Martin Van Buren*
(1835). Laden with anti-Democratic vitriol, *The
Life* was published under Crockett's name but is
now assumed to have been written by Augustin
Smith Clayton, a legal and literary associate of
the Georgia wits Augustus Baldwin Longstreet
and Oliver Hillhouse Prince. Neither work
achieved its purpose, and the next Crockett book
(excluding the almanacs) appeared after his final
Congressional defeat and death at the Alamo.
Composed by Richard Penn Smith, *Col. Crockett's Exploits and Adventures in Texas* (1836) is
presented as though drawn directly from Crockett's own journals, with the last entry dated
March 5, 1836. The *Exploits* begins with a dia-
tribe, full of puns and homespun anecdotes,
against Jackson and Van Buren, modulates into a
poem, "Farewell to the mountains," and then
relates Crockett's journey from Tennessee to the
Texas border and beyond that to the Alamo. As
J.D. Wade has pointed out, one section of the
book is a plagiarized adaptation of Longstreet's
"Georgia Theatrics";[3] the remainder is a hodgepodge of sentiment, adventure, and comic por-

traiture. More obviously fictionalized than the
earlier Crockett books, the *Exploits* includes,
among other things, a sub-plot centering on the
love of a character called "the Bee hunter" for
beautiful Kate of Nacogdoches, accounts of two
hunting expeditions (for buffalo and cougar), a
long conversation with an overly curious inn-
keeper, and (perhaps most successfully) a detailed characterization of a blustering, cowardly
Red River gambler named Thimblerig.

The fictionalization of Crockett's life, which
had begun long before his death and which the
Exploits further encouraged, was carried to
extraordinary lengths in *Davy Crockett's Almanack* (1835-1856) and the many oral tales
about the great frontiersman. One version of
his life

> . . . began by picturing him as a baby
> giant planted in a rock bed as soon as he
> was born and watered with wild buffa-
> lo's milk. Another declared that as a boy
> he tied together the tails of two buffa-
> loes and carried home five tiger cubs in
> his cap. In another he wrung the tail off
> a comet, and announced that he could
> "travel so all lighnin' fast that I've been
> known to strike fire agin the wind."[4]

He was given a consort who wore a hornet's nest
in her hair, and he wandered the world like a
Hercules or a Superman, doing battle with the
elements and conquering every foe.

Two later developments of the Crockett
material should be mentioned in passing. Frank
Murdoch's *Davy Crockett; Or, Be Sure You're
Right, Then Go Ahead* (1872) was staged for
nearly twenty-five years with Frank Mayo in
the title role, and in the 1950s, Walt Disney
brought Davy back into vogue through several
movie and television productions starring Fess
Parker. As Walter Blair and Hamlin Hill indicate, however, the Murdoch melodrama contains hardly a trace of the comic Davy, and the
Disney productions contain only slightly more.[5]
In Disney's three-part Crockett biography, the
comedy is centered in two secondary characters,
Georgie Russell (played by Buddy Ebsen) and
Thimblerig (played by Hans Conried). The tall-
tale Davy is referred to in the "Ballad" sung
at the beginning of each episode (for example,
in the claim that he "Killed him a b'ar when
he was only three") and in an occasional mention of the brag that Davy could grin his prey
into submission. Beyond that, Disney attempted
to capitalize on the Crockett craze by confronting Davy with another tall-tale hero, Mike Fink,
but the Crockett-Fink adventures produced
nothing like the reaction to the Crockett movie
biography.

Summary

Davy Crockett was important to the development of American humor in several ways. He was a comparatively uneducated backwoods politician who demonstrated the power of rough-hewn wit to win over the American electorate. He was also a convenient persona for the several political satirists who published their works under his name. He was the delight of a myriad of popular writers and oral humorists who could attach their traditional or their newly spun tales of the American frontier to the Crockett reputation, tales replete with the colorful speech and the rough-and-tumble humor of the Old Southwest. He was also the extraordinary ordinary man, the naive sage whose tenacious independence foreshadowed the freedom-loving resourcefulness of a Huckleberry Finn and the democratic hero whose survival skills made him fit company for such other humorous demigods as Pecos Bill, Mike Fink, and Paul Bunyan.

Notes

1. Walter Blair, *Horse Sense in American Humor: From Benjamin Franklin to Ogden Nash* (New York: Russell & Russell, 1942), p. 36.
2. Mentioned by Walter Blair and Hamlin Hill, *American Humor: From Poor Richard to Doonesbury* (New York: Oxford, 1978), p. 109.
3. J.D. Wade, "The Authorship of David Crockett's 'Autobiography,'" *The Georgia Historical Quarterly*, 6 (1922): 236.
4. Constance Rourke, *American Humor: A Study of the National Character* (New York: Harcourt, 1959), p. 57.
5. Blair and Hill, 143–146.

Selected Bibliography

Primary Sources

The Life and Adventures of Colonel David Crockett of West Tennessee. Cincinnati: E. Deming, 1833. This work, now attributed to Matthew St. Clair Clarke, was republished later in the same year by J. & J. Harper of New York as *Sketches and Eccentricities of Colonel David Crockett of West Tennessee.*

A Narrative of the Life of David Crockett, of the State of Tennessee. Philadelphia and Baltimore: Carey & Hart, 1834. Put together by Crockett and Thomas Chilton, this is generally considered to be the most factually reliable of the early Crockett books.

An Account of Col. Crockett's Tour to the North and Down East. Philadelphia and Baltimore: Carey & Hart, 1835. The extent to which Crockett may have contributed to this largely political piece remains uncertain, but William Clark is usually cited as its primary author.

The Life of Martin Van Buren. Philadelphia: R. Wright, 1835. Another political piece, Wade and others have argued convincingly for Augustin Smith Clayton's authorship.

Davy Crockett's Almanack. Various cities: various publishers, 1835–1856. First published in Nashville, Tennessee, by Snag & Sawyer, the almanacs are an important repository of Crockett lore, especially of tall-tale material.

Col. Crockett's Exploits and Adventures in Texas. Philadelphia: T.K. & P.G. Collins, 1836. A very influential piece of hackwork by Richard Penn Smith, the *Exploits* has frequently been reprinted with the Chilton *Narrative* and the Clark *Account* as the definitive Crockett *Autobiography.*

Secondary Sources

Albanese, Catherine L. "David Crockett." *Dictionary of Literary Biography: Antebellum Writers in New York and the South.* Ed. Joel Myerson. Detroit: Gale Research, 1979, pp. 94–96. This is a concise account of Crockett's life and literary career.

Blair, Walter. *Horse Sense in American Humor: From Benjamin Franklin to Ogden Nash.* New York: Russell & Russell, 1942. The book's second chapter is dedicated entirely to Crockett. Blair argues that the Crockett lore, including the tall tales, is an expression of America's faith in a common sense approach to coping with life.

Blair, Walter, and Hamlin Hill. *America's Humor: From Poor Richard to Doonesbury.* New York: Oxford University Press, 1978. Blair and Hill give perhaps the best account of the place the Crockett lore occupies in the context of American popular humor.

Clark, William Bedford. "Davy Crockett." In *Dictionary of Literary Biography.* Vol. 11. *American Humorists, 1800–1950.* Part 1: A–L. Ed. Stanley Trachtenberg. Detroit: Gale Research, 1982, pp. 89–94. This is a clear capsule analysis of the comic content of the Crockett books.

Rourke, Constance. *American Humor: A Study of the National Character.* 1931. Rpt. New York: Harcourt Brace Jovanovich, 1959. Rourke does an especially good job of discussing Crockett as a tall-tale hero.

———. *Davy Crockett.* New York: Harcourt, Brace and Company, 1934. This is one of the more appealing of the popular biographies.

Shackford, James. *David Crockett: The Man and the Legend.* Westport, Connecticut: Greenwood Press, 1956. Although new historical material has been unearthed concerning Crockett's life, this remains the definitive biography. It achieves its stated purpose of separating fact from legend surprisingly well.

Wade, J.D. "The Authorship of David Crockett's 'Autobiography.'" *The Georgia Historical Quarterly*, 6 (1922): 265–268. Wade overstates his case for Augustin Smith Clayton's participation in the writing of the Crockett books, but he does establish that Clayton was at least one of those who published under the Crockett name.

Robert H. O'Connor

Cuppy, Will

Born: Auburn, Indiana, on August 23, 1884
Education: University of Chicago, Ph.B., 1905, M.A., 1914
Died: September 19, 1949

Biography

Author, critic, humorist, and self-proclaimed hermit, Will Cuppy holds a unique place in American humor for the prodigious amount of research that preceded each of his works. In a career spanning forty years, he produced only five books, with two more published after his death. Painfully shy, he agreed to the publication of his books only at the urging of his co-worker on the *Herald Tribune*, novelist Isabel Paterson. Yet, all of Cuppy's mature works met with enthusiastic approval from critics and public alike who enjoyed his pessimistic but wildly funny views of mankind and the animal kingdom.

William Jacob Cuppy was born in Auburn, Indiana, on August 23, 1884. His parents, Thomas Jefferson Cuppy and Mary Frances Stahl Cuppy, were descended from pioneers who had come originally from South Carolina. Summers were spent on the South Whitley, Indiana, farm of Cuppy's paternal grandmother, and the author later remembered these months as the happiest of his childhood.

Cuppy attended Auburn High School, and after graduating in 1902, entered the University of Chicago. During his undergraduate days, he lived at the Phi Gamma Delta fraternity house and served as college reporter for several Chicago newspapers. He earned a bachelor's degree in philosophy in 1905 and stayed on at the University for seven more years, enrolling in a wide range of courses and working on his Ph.D. dissertation on Elizabethan prose writers, which he abridged in 1914 in order to receive his master's degree in English.

Cuppy's first book came about at the request of the university administration that he create some traditions for their newly founded fraternity. He imitated the college stories then in vogue and produced *Maroon Tales* (1910), eight tales of football heroes, college romances, and other campus high jinks. While they were obviously immature works, they show inventiveness and flashes of the Cuppy wit that would shine in his next books.

Cuppy headed for New York City and a career in journalism in 1914. During the First World War, he was a second lieutenant in the Motor Transport Corps; following the armistice he worked for the *New York Herald Tribune*. In 1926, he began a weekly column in the newspaper's *Books* supplement in which he reviewed mystery and adventure novels and true crime accounts. Later, in the 1940s, he edited three volumes of mystery stories.

Early in the 1920s Cuppy bought a cabin at Jones's Island, Long Island, where he retired to conduct research and write articles for magazines. Even after the neighboring area became Jones Beach State Park, Cuppy spent most of his time there, although he also kept an apartment in New York. From his adventures in solitary life on the island came his next book, *How to Be a Hermit* (1929).

During the next twenty years, Cuppy painstakingly researched and wrote a series of burlesques of nature guides containing short, fact-filled and humorous sketches of animals. *How to Tell Your Friends from the Apes* (1931) covered birds, mammals, and prehistoric man; *How to Become Extinct* (1941) focused on fish, reptiles, and a range of extinct creatures from the dinosaur to the dodo; and *How to Attract the Wombat* (1949) included mammals, fish, birds, and insects.

Cuppy was a retiring man with an inferiority complex, according to his friend, editor Burton Rascoe. Cuppy never married and lived alone. His hours of writing were erratic; in his book-filled Greenwich Village apartment he would write all night, sending out for food. In ill health for several years, he was found unconscious in his apartment on September 9, 1949, and taken to St. Vincent's Hospital. He died there on September 19 and was interred after cremation in Auburn, Indiana.

After Cuppy's death his friend and literary executor, Fred Feldkamp, produced two more books from the more than 200 card boxes full of notes that Cuppy left. *The Decline and Fall of Practically Everybody* (1950) treated famous historical personages in much the same way that Cuppy had described animals; *How to Get from January to December* (1951) served as a humorous almanac with a comic entry for each day. Although Feldkamp suggested that further books might emerge from the mass of research, no other compilations were ever published.

Literary Analysis

In his writing Cuppy appeared misanthropic. His mock-scientific sketches presented an anthropomorphic view of the animal kingdom, satirizing the human race and its preoccupation with technological trifles and bestial behavior by comparing the doings of his animal subjects with those of his human compatriots. His satire ranged from gentle to vicious, yet his remarkable sense of the absurd, coupled with a simple, staccato writing style, usually prevented his tone from becoming too peevish or ill-tempered.

How to Be a Hermit; or, A Bachelor Keeps House was Cuppy's first major success. A collection of articles previously published in the *Herald Tribune, McCall's,* and elsewhere, the book detailed halcyon days in his cabin on Jones's Island. This modern-day Thoreau, however, does not utilize nature in clever ways to make his stay more comfortable; instead, he maintains a "to hell with it" attitude and lives in wild disorder, dining on canned goods, fish, and whatever he can scrounge from his neighbors. Interspersed with attacks on the necessity of housekeeping and proper etiquette are his favorite hermit recipes and character sketches of the more colorful inhabitants of the area. Only at the conclusion, when Cuppy learns that the island will be turned into a state park, does he rail against the stupidity of his fellow men and the idiocies of modern life.

How to Be a Hermit, highly successful when it appeared, was the only book in which Cuppy extensively used his own character as a persona. His next three books focused on the natural kingdom and described the habits of several of its denizens. The books were set up as field guides, with short essays on each animal and occasional overviews on topics dear to his heart (such as "What I Hate about Spring" and "How to Swat a Fly"). The animals' natural habits and attributes were enumerated in rapid-fire statements, and peppered throughout the essays were footnotes, a few truly scholarly, but most either punchlines or non sequiturs: "The Spectral Tarsier of the West Indies is uncanny. He has huge bug-eyes, elongated ankles and knobby toes. He is sometimes confused with Delirium Tremens" (*How to Tell Your Friends from the Apes,* p. 46). Cuppy was neither sentimental nor charitable when it came to animals; he could be cruel and contemptuous, yet he was never maliciously so.

In *The Decline and Fall of Practically Everybody,* Cuppy turned his attention to famous figures in history, from Cheops to Miles Standish. As in his animal essays, Cuppy mixed biography, odd facts and surmises, and irreverent and sharp comments on his subjects' accomplishments and behavior:

> He is known as Alexander the Great because he killed more people of more different kinds than any other man of his time.[2] He did this in order to impress Greek culture upon them. Alexander was not strictly a Greek and he was not cultured, but that was his story, and who am I to deny it?[3]

> ---
> [2]Professor F. A. Wright, in his *Alexander the Great,* goes so far as to call him "the greatest man that the human race has as yet produced."

> [3]He spoke what was known as Attic Greek.
> (*The Decline and Fall of Practically Everybody,* pp. 38f)

The book was both a popular and critical success.

The second of Cuppy's posthumously published books, *How to Get from January to December,* was the most eclectic of his works, designed as a book of days with short readings for each date. Whether it concerned a person or event connected with the day or a spoof of advice column letters, each entry bore Cuppy's unmistakable terse style and wry sense of humor. The tone was gentler and less caustic, since the emphasis here was not on man's incompetence or animals' bizarre behaviors but rather on supplying and commenting on snippets of arcane information from the world's body of knowledge.

Summary

Will Cuppy was a man of paradoxes. As Fred Feldkamp wrote in his introduction to *The Decline and Fall of Practically Everybody,* "Beneath the gruff exterior he often affected, Cuppy was a thoroughly generous, kindly human being. He pretended he hated people, and, in fact, he was genuinely uneasy about meeting new people— he was afraid they might not like him or that they'd take up a lot of his time" (p. 3). This gruff exterior intruded into his writing as well; often supercritical of the human race, Cuppy mixed an old-fashioned gentility and love of scholarship for its own sake with a very modern acerbity and sense of the ridiculous. In his humor he most resembles Robert Benchley, James Thurber, and Thorne Smith, although a Mark Twain-like misogyny is certainly evident. Cuppy's style, footnotes and all, was later emulated by the equally witty Richard Armour in his mock-scholarly studies of literature and history.

Will Cuppy will be remembered as a crusty but gentle misanthropist, a scholarly humorist who found much to ridicule in both animals and man and who held little hope for the betterment of human existence as long as humans were in control.

Selected Bibliography

Primary Sources

Books

Maroon Tales; University of Chicago Stories. Chicago: Forbes, 1910.

How to Be a Hermit; or, A Bachelor Keeps House. New York: Liveright, 1929.

How to Tell Your Friends from the Apes. New York: Liveright, 1931; London: Methuen, 1934.

How to Become Extinct. New York and Toronto: Farrar and Rinehart, 1941.

The Great Bustard and Other People (containing *How to Tell Your Friends from the Apes* and *How to*

Become Extinct). New York and Toronto: Murray Hill Books, 1944.

How to Attract the Wombat. New York: Rinehart, 1949; London: Dobson, 1950.

The Decline and Fall of Practically Everybody. Ed. Fred Feldkamp. New York: Holt, 1950.

How to Get from January to December. Ed. Fred Feldkamp. New York: Holt, 1951.

Edited by Cuppy

World's Great Detective Stories. New York: World, 1943.

World's Great Mystery Stories. New York: World, 1943.

Murder without Tears. New York: Sheridan House, 1946.

Footnotes by Cuppy

Sellar, Walter Carruthers, and Yeatman, Robert Julian. *Garden Rubbish and Other Country Bumps.* New York: Farrar and Rinehart, 1937.

Secondary Sources

Biography

Banta, Richard E., comp. *Indiana Authors and Their Books 1816-1916.* Crawfordsville, Indiana: Wabash College, 1949. Condensation of article in *Authors Today and Yesterday.*

"*Books* Covers the World of Books." *Publishers Weekly,* September 30, 1939, pp. 1338-1347. Article on the *Herald Tribune's Books* section includes brief interviews with Cuppy and Isabel Paterson.

Kunitz, Stanley, ed. *Authors Today and Yesterday.* New York: H.W. Wilson, 1933, pp. 182-184. Autobiographical sketch.

Kunitz, Stanley J., and Haycraft, Howard, eds. *Twentieth Century Authors.* New York: H.W. Wilson, 1942.

Kunitz, Stanley J., ed. *Twentieth Century Authors, First Supplement.* New York: H.W. Wilson Co., 1955. Similar in content to article in *Authors Today and Yesterday.*

"Will Cuppy." *New York Times,* September 20, 1949, p. 29. Cuppy's obituary notice.

Books

Jitomir, Howard Steven. *Forgotten Excellence: A Study of Thorne Smith's Humor.* Dissertation St. John's University, 1983. Ann Arbor: UMI, 1983. Compares Cuppy's themes with those of Thorne Smith, Robert Benchley, and James Thurber.

Rascoe, Burton. *Before I Forget.* Garden City, New York: Doubleday, Doran, 1937. Description of Cuppy at the University of Chicago and in New York by his classmate and editor.

——— . *A Bookman's Daybook.* New York: Horace Liveright, 1929. Brief reminiscence of a visit to Cuppy's shack on Long Island.

Yates, Norris W. "The Wise Fool as Pedant." Chapter in Yates's *The American Humorist; Conscience of the Twentieth Century.* Ames: Iowa State University Press, 1964. The first major study of Cuppy and his place in American humor.

Articles

Benét, William Rose. "The Phoenix Nest." *Saturday Review of Literature,* October 15, 1949, p. 40. Brief eulogy.

Lieb, Sandra. "Will Cuppy." *American Humorists, 1800-1950.* Ed. Stanley Trachtenberg. Vol. 11 of *Dictionary of Literary Biography.* 2 vols. Detroit: Gale Research, 1982, pp. 94-99. Excellent biographical information and critical analysis of Cuppy's work. Lieb discusses themes, style, and content and provides a bibliography.

Eric W. Johnson

Davis, Charles Augustus ["J. Downing, Major"]

Born: New Jersey, in 1795
Died: 1867

Biography

Charles Augustus Davis was born in New Jersey in 1795. By the time he published his first "J. Downing, Major" letter in 1833, he had become a prominent member of the silk-stocking community in New York City. A cosmopolitan with a keen interest in current affairs and a man of considerable financial experience, he was a partner in the firm of Davis and Brooks, shipping and commission merchants. An enemy of everything democratic, Davis was a wealthy Whig and a close friend of the aristocratic Philip Hone. As a member of New York's elite, he hosted a dinner in honor of the visiting English novelist Charles Dickens and attended balls with the Philip van Rensselaers at Saratoga Springs, New York. Davis was a member of the Bread-and-Cheese Club, organized by James Fenimore Cooper, and the Book Club, along with such notables as Washington Irving.

Davis's J. Downing letters helped solidify his position as a leading conservative Whig in New York. In 1835, he was chosen vice-president of a large, elite anti-abolition meeting. Along with James J. Roosevelt, Jr., Peter Stuyvesant, and others, he was named to the city's Committee on the Erection of Buildings and the Arrangement of the Fire Department. In 1842, Davis was given one of two places of honor among a select group of twenty-four Whigs chosen to host a visit to New York by Daniel Webster. In addition to his Downing letters, Davis is generally recognized as the pseudonymous author of three pamphlets on finance (1844, 1849, and 1857). Davis died in 1867.

Literary Analysis

While Brahmin humorists such as Oliver Wendell Holmes produced patrician humor for New

England highbrows, another group of New England and New York writers—including Asa Greene, George W. Arnold, Seba Smith, and Charles Augustus Davis—were turning out a more popular brand of humor for a wider audience. Predominantly periodical and newspaper humorists rather than authors of books, they still utilized such established literary forms as essays, poems, and letters. However, perhaps because they were aiming at a popular audience, they used homespun rather than learned characters to speak for them, and they did not hesitate to use slang and ungrammatical vernacular language.

The character of Jack Downing was the creation of Seba Smith, a Portland, Maine, newspaperman. Smith's objective in creating the homely character of Downing was not to serve his socially conservative bias but rather to exploit his interest in the mores and speech patterns of the Maine down-easterners among whom he had grown up. Jack Downing marks the emergence and full acceptance in America of the character Jennette Tandy has called the "unlettered philosopher." When Smith decided to make Downing an imaginary associate of Andrew Jackson, his treatment of the President, although humorously satirical, was tempered with a certain kindness and warmth. Both the comic fool and the sage observer, in letters sent back to the eager folks in Downingville, Maine, Smith's Downing exposes the world of political chicanery to which Jackson is an honest exception.

Downing's role as a Presidential advisor awakened another writer whose intention, writes John William Ward, "was not to explore the medium of folk speech and habits but to use the medium as a weapon against Andrew Jackson."[1] During Jackson's tour of the northeastern states in 1833, spurious Downing letters began to turn up in a variety of newspapers. More than one individual tried to cash in on Downing's popularity, but Charles Augustus Davis proved to be Smith's only serious competitor.

No one could have been removed further in social status from Downing than Davis, who began his series of letters to the *New York Daily Advertiser* in June 1833. He scrupulously signed his letters "J. Downing, Major" rather than "Jack Downing," but few readers noticed the difference. As quick to pick up the counterfeits as they were the originals, other newspapers featured "Jack" or "J." indiscriminately. Living in New York, Davis had the opportunity of getting his letters on various national events to the reading public before Smith's letters on similar events could arrive from Maine.

Prior to the 1830s Davis's literary interests were strictly those of a gentleman. He enjoyed essays and poems that exhibited grace and an English flavor; he avoided the homely. Yet, he began writing slapstick letters in the language of a hayseed (as best he could pick it up from his reading) because he despised Andrew Jackson and his plebian political party. Davis's antipathy to Jackson grew out of his own close friendship with Nicholas Biddle, the president of the Bank of the United States; Jackson's opposition to the Bank and his attempts to destroy it were of considerable interest at the time that Davis was writing his Downing letters. The letters quickly became a tool in the campaign by Biddle, Henry Clay, and the Whigs against Jackson's bank policy.

Collected in book form in 1834 (and going through numerous editions by 1836), Davis's letters presented pointed and constructive criticisms of the Jacksonians. With an ease and elaboration never attempted by Smith, Davis attacked the financial problems involved in the destruction of the national bank. He captured the fancy of contemporary newspaper readers by introducing new characters while maintaining the New England atmosphere and by relating popular anecdotes that had an easy vulgarity. Able to lay out complicated concerns in simple terms, he wielded the homely parable as a two-edged sword.

Throughout the letters, Davis's chief humorous device was to depict Downing as extremely naive in political matters. Downing's rustic buffoonery reflects negatively on Jackson, who comes across as arrogant and narrow-minded, because even Downing sees the foolhardiness of destroying the Bank of the United States. Though Davis's Yankee dialect was not as accurate as Smith's, his homespun metaphors are all the more remarkable given his cosmopolitan background.

Summary

Appropriating Seba Smith's Jack Downing, Charles Augustus Davis comically manipulated his "common man" for his own purposes, primarily to attack Andrew Jackson and the Democratic Party. When the Whig Party finally became aware of the appeal of the "unlettered philosopher," it is not surprising that they arranged to have criticism of the Jacksonians expressed in the voice of such folk heroes as "J. Downing, Major."

Notes

1. John William Ward, *Andrew Jackson: Symbol for an Age* (New York: Oxford University Press, 1955), p. 82.

Selected Bibliography

Primary Sources

Letters of J. Downing, Major, Downingville Militia, Second Brigade, to His Old Friend, Mr. Dwight, of the *New York Daily Advertiser*. New York: Harper, 1834.

Secondary Sources

References in Books

Blair, Walter. *Horse Sense in American Humor.* Chicago: University of Chicago Press, 1942, pp. 65–76. A good discussion of Davis's J. Downing. Compares Davis's character with Seba Smith's Jack Downing.

Hone, Philip. *The Diary of Philip Hone, 1828–1851.* Ed. Bayard Tuckerman. 2 vols. New York: Dodd, Mead, 1889. Hone, a good friend of Davis's, includes numerous references to the latter in his diary.

Tandy, Jennette. *Crackerbox Philosophers in American Humor and Satire.* New York: Columbia University Press, 1925, pp. 32–38. In Chapter II Tandy discusses Davis's J. Downing as an "unlettered philosopher" of the 1830s.

Ward, John William. *Andrew Jackson: Symbol for an Age.* New York: Oxford University Press, 1955, pp. 79–91. Good on the political background of the Downing letters.

L. Moody Simms, Jr.

Day, Clarence Shepard, Jr.

Born: New York City, on November 18, 1874

Education: Yale University, B.A., 1896

Marriage: Katherine Briggs Dodge, 1928

Died: December 28, 1935

Biography

In several respects Clarence Day, Jr., mediated between the robust, tall-tale frontier humor of nineteenth-century America and the witty, cynical, self-deprecating humor of twentieth-century urban America. Though his writing reflects a modern, urbane, and sophisticated sensibility, at its best it retains the cheerful vitality and the celebration of life more common to the earlier era.

Born in 1874, Day grew up the eldest of his siblings in a New York City household dominated by his assertive father, Clarence Day, Sr., and by his mother, the former Lavinia Stockwell. After a brief enlistment in the Navy, where Clarence, Jr., contracted what developed into a crippling arthritis, he worked with his father as a stockbroker. Indeed, until his final year, when *Life with Father* proved a smashing financial success, Day earned his living primarily as a stockbroker, an investor, and an entrepreneur in the glove business, not as a writer. Day married Katherine Briggs Dodge in 1928, and they re-

sided in New York for the duration of his life, first in an elaborate Riverside Drive apartment and, after the Wall Street crash of 1929, in less distinguished quarters.

Literary Analysis

Day's writing career spanned from 1920 until his death in 1935. Most of his stories appeared separately in such journals as *The New Yorker, Harper's Magazine, The Outlook, The Saturday Review of Literature, The New Republic,* and the *Literary Review* of the *New York Evening Post.* He later collected these stories into books, which include *This Simian World* (1920), *The Crow's Nest* (1921; revised as *After All,* 1936), *Thoughts Without Words* (1928), *Scenes from the Mesozoic* (1935), *God and My Father* (1935), *Life with Father* (1935), and *Life with Mother* (posthumously, 1937). *In the Green Mountain Country* (1934) is a non-humorous book dedicated to Calvin Coolidge. The books about Father, in particular, were only slightly edited and revised versions of earlier stories that Day literally cut and pasted together to form a manuscript. In fact, according to Day's publisher, Alfred A. Knopf, when the manuscript of *Life with Father* reached the publishing house it was mistaken for garbage and thrown away. Day had kept no copy, and the manuscript was rescued at the last minute from a paper mill in Massachusetts, where it was in the process of being recycled. All but three pages were saved.

Day's earlier work is witty and philosophical; it satirizes human frailties and shortcomings. He was an early contributor to the fledgling *The New Yorker* magazine, whose self-conscious, urban, and sophisticated orientation was especially appropriate for his satiric pieces. When these pieces were collected in such books as *This Simian World, Thoughts Without Words,* and *Scenes from the Mesozoic,* they received substantial critical acclaim but were unsuccessful in the popular market, probably because of the presence of the very elements that made them suitable for *The New Yorker.* In one respect, Day's early pieces continue the tradition of earlier "literary comedians," such as Artemus Ward and George Horatio Derby. Like his predecessors, Day relies on puns, quick incongruities, and clever word play. Initially, he also employed the excessive punctuation and overstatement used by the earlier literary comedians, but he eliminated those devices as his career progressed. Day is perhaps more closely aligned with Gelett Burgess, the editor of and primary contributor to the nonsense magazine, *The Lark.* Like Burgess, Day liked to write short, comic verses and accompany them with his own, exaggerated drawings. And, like Burgess, Day, in his early work, appeals primarily to an erudite audience.

However, while most of Day's comic techniques appear in earlier American literature, especially in American humor written between the Civil War and World War I, the targets to which he applies these techniques represent something significantly different in American humor. While earlier humor might satirize particular types (the Yankee, the Irishman, the backwoodsman, the bumpkin, or the dandy, for example), or criticize particular political views (as did, for instance, James Russell Lowell's attacks on the Mexican-American War or Petroleum Nasby's deflation of the South during the Civil War), it rarely commented on society as a whole or on human nature, per se. These, however, are precisely Day's targets.

Day's satire of human society is the focus of his first book, *This Simian World*. The book's premise is that human nature and society are shaped largely by our simian origins, by the fact that we evolved specifically from apes. How might we be different, individually and collectively, if we had evolved from a different species? Given our descent from monkeys, our interest in vaudeville and spectacle is understandable, even inevitable. A species evolved from eagles, on the other hand, would disdain such antics. Day considers at length what a civilization evolved from felines might be like.

> Don't imagine them as a collection of tigers walking around on their hind-legs. They would have only been like tigers in the sense that we men are like monkeys. Their development in appearance and character would have been quite transforming.
>
> Their mouths would have been smaller and more dignified. Where now they express chiefly savageness, they would have expressed fire and grace.
>
> They would have been courteous and suave. No vulgar crowding would have occurred on the streets of their cities. No mobs. No ignominious subway-jams.
>
> Imagine a cultivated coterie of such men and women at a ball, dancing. How few of us humans are graceful. They would have all been Pavlowas.

The cat race would be rich in hermits and solitary thinkers. They would not have been a credulous people; false prophets and swindlers would have found few dupes. "And what generals they would have made! What consummate politicians!" The cat people would be more intense than we are, but saner. They would require more sanitariums, but fewer asylums. Their hatred would be more violent, their friendships more consuming. The females would be "languorous, slender and passionate. Sleepy eyes that see everything. An indolent purposeful step. An unimaginable grace. If you were her lover, my boy, you would learn how fierce love can be, how capricious and sudden, how hostile, how ecstatic, how violent!"

Day considers races spawned from other species as well. Evolved from cows we could contemplate a single thought for hours or days; our minds would not possess the simian's short attention span. Because we evolved from primates, we are self-aware. This, according to Day, leads to our need for a sense of purpose, thence to religion. Our Satan, he points out, comes in the form of a serpent. Had we derived from chickens, we would have pictured our devil a hawk. Our minds are overactive and distractable, features that remove us spiritually and distance us from Nature.

We also seem to need certainty and to have our truths absolute and final: our inability to accept the relativity of truth reflects our simian heritage. Within this context Day anticipates the relativism of modernism and the understandings, especially evident in post–World War II epistemology, that profound insights and experiences are not translatable to propositional statements and that new paradigms by which we understand ourselves and the world will continuously replace old ones. Day concludes elsewhere that civilization is a matter of self-knowledge. "The test of a civilized person is first self-awareness, and then depth after depth of sincerity in self-confrontation. . . . Unless you are capable of this kind of thinking, what are you? No matter how able or great, you are still with the animals."

While *This Simian World* is essentially a prolonged essay about human nature, *The Crow's Nest, Thoughts Without Words*, and *Scenes from the Mesozoic* are truly more comedic. They also have their bite, though, and reflect some of the themes that Day was most interested in. For example, a drawing in *Thoughts Without Words* shows Adam and Eve looming over the tiny figures of God and Satan, with the accompanying caption, "So Adam created two beings, Jehovah and Satan. Yea, in his own image he created them." Day toys with the story of Eden in his other works, too. In *The Crow's Nest*, "Humpty Dumpty and Adam" purportedly relates the true story of the Fall. While we find earlier comic distortions of the Bible in American humor, only Mark Twain comes to mind as one who anticipates Day by using such comic distortions to challenge traditional, Christian notions of our place in the universe and of religion itself.

Like his contemporaries, James Thurber and Robert Benchley, Day also pokes fun at domestic life. He frequently depicts men as excessively constrained by social obligations and by women. The "Thoughts on Endless Conflicts" section of *Thoughts Without Words*, for instance, contains a piece entitled "The Inspiring Wife." Beneath a drawing of a massive woman, pointing upward and utterly dominating her tiny husband, are the lines, "She told him of a Better Land,/ She tried to give his spirit wings./ But he could never understand/ Her talk of Higher Things." Likewise, *Scenes from the Mesozoic* shows a female dinosaur leaning out the window to address her mate tearfully. The accompanying verse reads, "The parting injunctions/ Of mothers and wifes/ Are one of those functions/ That poison our lives." In the same book there is another poem in which Day characteristically inverts the sentiments of an established author, this time Oliver Goldsmith: "When lovely woman weds a Tartar/ And learns too late that love is grim,/ How sedulously she plays the martyr,/ And meanwhile makes one out of him."

Unlike Thurber and Benchley, though, Day acknowledges that women also suffer at the hands of men. In fact, he was active in the feminist causes of the 1920s, and in 1926 he illustrated Florence Guy Seabury's *The Delicatessen Husband and Other Essays*, a book the *New York Times* described as feminist humor. *Scenes from the Mesozoic* features a drawing of God smirking as a man bites a woman's jugular vein, accompanied by the lines, "'In the Beginning,' saith the law/ (As true today as then),/ 'God looked upon the earth and saw/ That it was good'—for men." And, in *Thoughts Without Words*, Day presents a drawing of a smug little man explaining something to his skeptical wife: "This lady with the stoney eye/ Is listening to an alibi,/ Which its inventor can't conceive/ She'll have the heart to disbelieve."

Some of Day's other humor is less pointed, though still not without a cutting edge. One drawing shows a caricature of a mother pushing a baby in its carriage: "Tender are a mother's dreams./ But her babe's not what he seems./ See him plotting in his mind/ To grow up some other kind." Another picture shows a self-satisfied, bespectacled man standing atop a classical column: "When eras die, their legacies/ Are left to strange police./ Professors in New England guard/ The glory that was Greece."

The general flavor, then, of Day's work, exclusive of the stories about Mother and Father, is satiric, often biting. Those poems, parables, and essays do not let us laugh comfortably; instead, they are calculated to make us reconsider our values, attitudes, and behavior. They frequently invoke literary allusions that are apparent only to those well versed in Western culture. The very title, *Thoughts Without Words*, for example, at once plays off Mendelssohn's cycle, "Songs without Words" and Claudius's lines in Act III of Shakespeare's *Hamlet*, "My words fly above, My thoughts stay below./ Words without thoughts do not to Heaven go." This sort of clever, complex allusion typifies much of Day's work. It is directed at the modern, urban American who has learned to look at his life with a touch of irony. However, like so many of his literary contemporaries, comic and otherwise, Day reflects in these pieces a disenchantment with modern life as well as a need to articulate a sophisticated, essentially modernist outlook.

By contrast, the anecdotes about Mother and Father are affectionate, apolitical, not philosophical, and fully accessible to a general audience that need not be well versed in the cultural traditions of the West. They avoid the puns, the witty ambiguities, and other technical devices of the literary comedians and rely instead primarily upon deftness of characterization and the detailed descriptions of incongruous scenes and episodes. It is not surprising, therefore, that these were the stories that received wide, popular approval and are the ones for which Day is now best known.

God and My Father, *Life with Father*, and *Life with Mother* were extraordinarily successful in their own time and beyond. *Life with Father* was a bestseller, and the 1939 Broadway production of Howard Lindsay and Russell Crouse's play version enjoyed one of the longest runs in history. Perhaps the current decline in the popularity of the Father stories is caused by the fact that the audiences have changed. Essentially reminiscences, these stories appealed to the nostalgia of those who could still remember an America without telephones and with carriages and gaslights and an uptown Manhattan that featured farmlands and dirt roads. For Day's contemporaries his domestic scenes might stir some personal recollections. Living in a different world, we now find these stories basically quaint. Ironically, it is the biting satire of his earlier works that has the most to say to our world of "Saturday Night Live" and post-modernism.

Yet, the Father stories offer us something, in spite of their dated quality. One reason their nostalgia appealed to the audiences of the 1930s and 40s was that by then America had already begun to change substantially, and Father's world—before the Depression, before World War I—had already vanished; in fact, it was already dissolving while Father lived within it. Day uses this fact as the basis of one of his primary comic devices. An incongruity exists throughout the anecdotes: Father's self-assertiveness (his belief that he can understand and control the world, or at least his share of it and his conviction that he knows how things should be), on the one hand, and the view of a world neither easily understood nor controlled, by Father or anyone else. Father's firm belief in reason and in the principles of scientific management, as applied to all facets of life, yield to Mother's peculiar brand of logic, to ignorant and intimidated maids, to creative, adventuresome children, and to random expressions of human nature. We derive humor from these stories through our recognition that stiff, proper, dignified Father is, in fact, not in control. Yet, unlike the "little men" of the era, such as James Thurber's Walter Mitty or even T.S. Eliot's J. Alfred Prufrock, Father is not defeated by his inability to make his world function as it should. He retains his spirit, his self-confidence, and his belief in himself, and so, even in failure, is more to be admired than pitied. Thus, Day has it both ways: he shows the incorrectness and inappropriateness of Father's dogmatic orientation in a changing world, and at the same time, because Father, himself, never truly recognizes his own defeats, Day leaves us on an upbeat note rather than with the despair of a Mitty.

Two of the most popular stories illustrate this formula. In "The Noblest Instrument" Father decides that raising a son in the proper manner includes having him learn to play an instrument. And, because the violin is the noblest of instruments, this is the one that his firstborn son must learn. Father, therefore, buys a violin for Clarence, hires a teacher, and considers the matter settled. He refuses to acknowledge that his son may be devoid of musical aptitude, even when the teacher, the neighbors, and Mother complain to him about how irritating it is to hear Clarence practice. Father blames Clarence for not trying hard enough to learn; he blames the teacher, Herr M., for not teaching well; he accuses Mother of exaggerating Clarence's harmonic deficiencies; he even argues from utility: if Clarence cannot play, then the money spent on the violin will have been wasted. As the story progresses, the discrepancy between Clarence's ineptitude and Father's obdurance becomes more emphatic. The widening of this discrepancy provides the basis of our pleasure, and the story concludes with Clarence receiving permission to forego his lessons, but Father remaining unconvinced that his son is a musical misfit, that the world would permit something so contrary to his notion of the proper order of things. Hence, the story's final line reads, "Father said Herr M. was a failure."

In "Father and His Hard-Rocking Ship" Father asserts his belief that a household should be managed like a business, complete with double-entry ledgers and close accounting of all expenditures. He is, therefore, constantly frustrated by Mother's haphazard record-keeping and her inability to stay within a budget. Once again, the humor comes from the disparity between Father's belief that a rational approach will allow him to control the household and the inadvertent subversion of that process as Mother addresses her day-to-day needs. The high point of the story comes when Father gives Mother six dollars to buy a coffee pot. Mother charges one for five dollars instead, then insists, when he asks her to return the cash, that she has saved him a dollar. Instead of being refunded the six dollars, Father ultimately succumbs to Mother's relentless "logic" and gives her the extra one that she had saved him.

The character sketches of Mother and Father are drawn with affection, and Day treats neither parent condescendingly. Moreover, he provides a view of upper-middle-class New York life during the 1880s and 90s, just as America was preparing to transform into an essentially urban society in which the rules and roles of small town, pre-Civil War life simply do not apply. Even for readers of the 1920s and 30s, then, Father was a throwback to an earlier era. This characteristic gives him his position as a comic figure as well as much of his appeal.

Summary

As different as the Father and Mother stories are from Day's other work, they all share his awareness of a changing world, of the difficulty of adjusting to it, and of the necessity for retaining flexibility and avoiding dogmatism when approaching it. Responding to the same influences affecting the young T.S. Eliot and Sherwood Anderson, among others, Day wrote in his 1917 introduction to W.S. Gilbert's *Mikado* that keeping up the human spirit is "the problem of the age." Day admired Gilbert's characters for accepting their disastrous fates with "aplomb and a wise savoir vivre." In his own writings these traits are ultimately the most outstanding.

Selected Bibliography

Primary Sources

Non-humorous

The Story of the Yale University Press Told by a Friend. New Haven: At the Earl Trumbull Williams Memorial, 1920.

In the Green Mountain Country. New Haven: Yale University Press, 1934.

Humorous

This Simian World. New York: Knopf, 1920; London: Cape, 1920.

The Crow's Nest. New York: Knopf, 1921; revised and enlarged as *After All.* New York and London: Knopf, 1936.

Thoughts Without Words. New York: Knopf, 1928.

God and My Father. New York: Knopf, 1932; republished as *My Father's Dark Hour.* London: Hamilton, 1932.

Life with Father. New York and London: Knopf, 1935.

Scenes from the Mesozoic and Other Drawings. New Haven: Yale University Press, 1934; republished as *Yesterday Is To-day: Drawings and Rhymes.* London: Boriswood, 1936.

Life with Mother. New York and London: Knopf, 1937; London: Chatto & Windus, 1937.

Contributions

Gilbert, W.S. *The Mikado and Other Plays.* Introduction by Day. New York: Boni and Liveright, 1917.

Bennett, Charles A. *At a Venture.* Illustrated by Day. New York: Dutton, 1924.

Dodd, Lee Wilson. *The Sly Giraffe.* Illustrated by Day. New York: Dutton, 1925.

Seabury, Florence Guy. *The Delicatessen Husband and Other Essays.* Illustrated by Day. New York: Harcourt, Brace, 1926.

Colby, Frank. *The Colby Essays.* 2 vols. Selected and ed. Day. New York and London: Harper, 1926.

Secondary Sources

Blair, Walter, and Hamlin Hill, *America's Humor.* New York: Oxford University Press, 1978, pp. 419-421.

Canby, H.S. *American Memoir.* Boston: Houghton Mifflin, 1947, pp. 300-303.

Knopf, Alfred A. "Publishing Clarence Day." *Yale University Library Gazette,* 55 (January 1981): 101-115.

———. "Random Recollections of a Publisher." *Proceedings of the Massachusetts Historical Society,* 73 (1961): 95-98.

Schwartz, Richard Alan. "Clarence Day." In *Dictionary of Literary Biography.* Vol. 11. *American Humorists: 1800-1950.* Ed. Stanley Trachtenberg. Detroit: Gale Research Company, 1982, pp. 108-113.

Yates, Norris W. *The American Humorist: Conscience of the Twentieth Century.* Ames: University of Iowa Press, 1964, pp. 229-239.

Richard Alan Schwartz

Dennie, Joseph

Born: Boston, Massachusetts, on August 30, 1768
Education: Harvard College, B.A., 1790
Died: January 7, 1812

Biography

Born in Boston, Massachusetts, on August 30, 1768, Joseph Dennie was the only child of Joseph and Mary Green Dennie. Dennie first attended school at the age of seven in Lexington, Massachusetts, where his parents had moved during the Revolutionary War. His father was a merchant and his mother's family was connected with publishing. Attempts to turn Dennie toward commerce failed. His father underwent periods of insanity, and Dennie's childhood was not one that encouraged his literary talents. He was permitted to prepare for Harvard under the Rev. Samuel West and graduated, despite periods of illness and one rustication for disputes with authorities, in 1790. He served as a law clerk for three years but practiced little after his admission to the Massachusetts bar after a judge rebuked him in his first case (in 1794) for being overly wordy.

Dennie's literary career began almost simultaneously with his abandoned law career. During his clerkship, he had joined with several bright young professional men writing for New Hampshire newspapers. Dennie participated in literary ventures with his friend, Royall Tyler, as Colon of Colon & Spondee and subsequently began a short-lived periodical named *The Tablet* which lasted for thirteen weekly numbers in 1795. He then moved to Walpole, New Hampshire, where he joined a small group of literati and wits there. As the "Lay Preacher," the conservative Federalist began writing essays for the *Farmer's Weekly Museum* with such success that he became its editor in April 1796. Upon the demise of the paper three years later, Dennie moved for the last time, to Philadelphia, Pennsylvania, where he served briefly as secretary to Timothy Pickering, the Secretary of State under John Adams.

William Cobbett, the notorious "Peter Porcupine," planned to publish an edition of the Lay Preacher's writings, but Cobbett returned to England without completing the project. As soon as he was well established in Philadelphia society, Dennie joined with another publisher, Asbury Dickens, to start his own magazine, *The Port Folio*, a weekly edited by "Oliver Oldschool, Esq." The journal was highly popular during the first decade of its existence and outlived Dennie by fifteen years. His reputation as "The Lay Preacher," many of whose essays from earlier days he now reprinted in his Philadelphia journal for a wider audience, continued well after his death, and his Addisonian prose style was admired by later commentators such as S.A. Allibone, although it was rejected as derivative by R.W. Griswold in *The Prose Writers of North America.* Along with Charles Brockden Brown he was one of the first professional writers in America and was capable of both the elevated humor of Richard Addison and Oliver Goldsmith and sarcastic burlesques of political and social events. His health was never strong nor his finances secure, and he died at forty-four in 1812.

Literary Analysis

Joseph Dennie's reputation lies with his writings as the "Lay Preacher" for the *Farmer's Museum* and as Oliver Oldschool, Esq., for *The Port Folio*. He could be both a witty and sarcastic writer, aware of the rhetorical patterns of Addison and intent on maintaining them in his essays. In politics and social belief, he was a conservative Federalist, suspicious of democracy. After writing as Colon, of Colon & Spondee, in his New Hampshire days with some success, he hoped to start in Boston a periodical of light social criticism and humorous commentary, the four-page *The Tablet*, published by William Spotswood from May 19 through August 11 of 1795. His "Farrago" essays from New Hampshire papers were intended to be the bulwark of *The Tablet*. In a "Farrago" piece that Edmund Clarence Stedman and Ellen MacKay Hutchinson chose for their *Library of American Literature* (New York: Charles Wibster, 1889), for example, Dennie attacks "Silent American Society," decrying the empty heads lying behind so many empty faces: "A modern company of gentlemen and ladies, sitting on both sides of the room, reflecting the rays of each other's eyes, and maintaining a dead silence, reminds one more of a regiment under Prussian discipline, than of social beings, sitting at their ease, and chatting with fluency and good humor." The thirteen essays that appeared in *The Tablet* attacked Harvard University, lampooned the social bon vivant, and applied the gentle humor of Goldsmith and Lawrence Sterne to recollections of his own early years and family relations. He produced roughly thirty Farrago essays through 1802, according to G.F. Whitcher, but they did not sustain his magazine as a commercial venture.

As the "Lay Preacher" for the *Farmer's Weekly Museum*, Dennie wrote a variety of sketches having much in common with the character sketches of the late seventeenth century. Dennie chose topics that had some relation to democratic society or ideology at least tangentially. Many of the "Farrago" and "Lay Preacher" essays were carried to Philadelphia and were printed in *The Port Folio*; Royall Tyler rejoined his friend Dennie in further writings of Colon & Spondee, along with other Philadelphia literary notables. Dennie himself wished to unite the familiarity of Benjamin Franklin with the simplicity of Sterne. So widely did Dennie become known, often being referred to as the "American Addison," that even notable British writers submitted material to *The Port Folio*, and Thomas Moore found Dennie one of the few congenial spirits in America during his visit to the United States.

As editor of *The Port Folio*, Dennie took the pen name of Oliver Oldschool, Esq. Successful from the beginning, the journal was devoted to politics and literature, culling the best from Dennie's previous writings, including his and Tyler's continuation of the Colon & Spondee writings, and adding new contributors from the nation's political and literary capitol at the turn of the century. Its first issue of 1,500 copies had to be reprinted, a major publishing success for that era. Unfortunately for Dennie, full financial success did not result, and he relinquished his partial interest in 1808 and became a salaried editor. *The Port Folio* soon became a monthly. Under Dennie *The Port Folio* was a sophisticated literary journal, capable of praising and reprinting William Wordsworth's *Lyrical Ballads* in one issue and lampooning them in the next. Whimsy, burlesque, and satire were characteristic of the literary humor fostered by Dennie as editor and writer, and he is supposed to have influenced Washington Irving at one time. Dennie was such an egregious verbal attacker of democracy that he was indicted for sedition in 1804, and his inflammatory writing, including sarcastic poetry on Jefferson's alleged affair with a slave woman and other racy topics, made *The Port Folio* spicy reading for its period. The burlesque of "Jack and Jill" in the "modern" critical mode that is often attributed to Dennie is, unfortunately, probably by Nicholas Biddle, briefly the editor of *The Port Folio* after Dennie. Dennie's sarcasm and light irony and his use of language aligned him in his day with Addison, Jonathan Swift, and Sterne but might as easily have linked him with H.L. Mencken in a later period. After 1809, the new owners of *The Port Folio* restricted Dennie to a politically neutral position, and his satire was considerably diminished.

Summary

Joseph Dennie, the "American Addison," was one of the wittiest of the editorial essayists of the early federal period. As "The Lay Preacher" and "Oliver Oldschool, Esq.," his writings were prominent in *The Farmer's Museum* and *The Port Folio*, significant early American humorous literary journals.

Selected Bibliography

Primary Sources

Like many periodical authors, Dennie had trouble deriving books from his collected essays, and readers should consult *The Port Folio*, available in many libraries and on microfilm; *The Tablet* is also available on microfilm.

The Lay Preacher; or Short Sermons for Idle Readers. Walpole, N.H.: David Carlisle, 1796; also *Harrison Hall*, Philadelphia, 1817, collected and arranged by J.E. Hall; rpt. Scholars' Facsimiles and Reprints: New York, 1943, with an introduction by [Harold] Milton Ellis.

The Spirit of the Farmer's Museum, and Lay Preacher's Gazette. Ed. and partially written by Dennie. Walpole, N.H.: Thomas and Thomas, 1801.

The Letters of Joseph Dennie 1768-1812. Ed. Laura G. Pedder. Orono: University of Maine Press, 1936; issued as *The Maine Bulletin*, 38 (January 1936): 6.

Secondary Sources

Ellis, Harold M. *Joseph Dennie and His Circle: A Study in American Literature from 1792 to 1812.* Austin, Tex.: Studies in English, #3; rpt. New York: Johnson Reprint, 1972.

Oberholtzer, E.P. "The Port Folio." In *The Literary History of Philadelphia.* Philadelphia: Jacobs, 1906, pp. 168-188.

Whitcher, G.F. "Joseph Dennie." In *Dictionary of American Biography.* Vol. 3. New York: Charles Scribner's Sons, 1936, pp. 235-237.

David E.E. Sloane

De Quille, Dan [William Wright]

Born: Knox County, Ohio, on May 9, 1829
Education: Extent of formal education unknown
Marriage: Caroline Coleman, 1853, five children
Died: March 16, 1898

Biography

A colleague and perhaps a mentor of Mark Twain,[1] Dan De Quille was a past master of the art of the literary hoax, that deadpan brand of humor that tricks unwary readers into believing a story that is fundamentally implausible but becomes progressively credible. De Quille thus is part of an American tradition that began with the tall tales of the frontier storytellers and was elevated to high art by Mark Twain. Other contemporary practitioners of this form of humor were Ambrose Bierce, Sam Davis, James W. Gally, Fred Hart, and Bret Harte. Like all of these, De Quille was part of the generation of pioneer western writers who came from the East and Midwest but who made their reputations in the newspapers and magazines of the Far West, particularly those of California and Nevada.

"Dan De Quille" was the pen name of William Wright. He was born in Knox County, Ohio, on May 9, 1829, and lived there for twenty years until he moved with his family to a homestead in Iowa. There he married Caroline Coleman in 1853 and fathered five children, two of whom died in infancy, before he left by himself in 1857 to become a miner in California. For two years he was part of the wave of prospectors who, in a backwash from the mining activity of 1849 on the California coast, searched for gold on the eastern slope of the Sierra Nevadas. He moved to the Lake Tahoe region of Nevada in 1859, where he tried his luck at prospecting for another three years without notable success. In 1862, he gave up prospecting for journalism when he joined the *Virginia City Territorial Enterprise*, a daily newspaper that served the population of the Nevada Territory in general and the Comstock Lode area in particular. Under the inspired ownership of Joseph Goodman, the *Enterprise* attracted men of talent and spirit and soon became one of the liveliest and most renowned newspapers in the West. Even after Goodman and most of his distinguished colleagues left the paper and De Quille himself began to freelance for the *Salt Lake City Tribune* and a score of other periodicals across the country, De Quille remained with the *Enterprise* as its most important writer until it suspended publication in 1893, thirteen years after the Comstock region began its sharp decline in profitability and population. He left Virginia City in 1897 old, ill, and poor, to live out the remnant of his life with a daughter in West Liberty, Iowa, where he died and was buried in 1898.

Literary Analysis

Dan De Quille earned several separate but overlapping reputations during his lifetime of writing. One was as an excellent, highly readable, journalist who reported with notable honesty and accuracy the daily affairs of the Comstock. He was especially respected for his expertise in mining and for his encyclopedic knowledge of the history and culture of Nevada and eastern California. This knowledge supplied the material for his many fictional sketches and short stories about the region. It also made him the unofficial historian of the Comstock, especially after the publication of *The Big Bonanza* in 1876. That book immediately became, and remains, the classic contemporary account of that fabulous mining phenomenon from its origin through its heyday. Interfusing all of these other literary activities was his humor, the versatility and excellence of which helped establish him as the area's most popular and beloved writer.

His versatility enabled De Quille to appeal to all levels of readers. Accordingly, sometimes his humor is broad and obvious, as in his sketches of stereotypical Indians, immigrants, uneducated blacks, and simple prospectors. These are heavily dependent for laughs on the use of picturesque vernacular. Of course, almost every other western humorist from Mark Twain down also composed similar sketches and probably for the same reason: to cultivate as large a number of devoted readers as possible. In a middle category are the many conventional anecdotes and short tales of situational comedy, ridiculous exaggeration, or good-natured fun. At the peak of his art, however, are pieces of charming whimsy and delicate subtlety that only a master humorist could create. De Quille at this level has no master.

His humor derives first from a sophisticated imagination. He had a ready native wit that easily and cleverly invented fictitious situations or added a few touches of emphasis or detail that converted what might have appeared as fact into fiction. Next, although little biographical information exists, it quickly becomes apparent to any reader of De Quille that he had somehow acquired an impressive education. His works are often sprinkled with allusions to European culture and classical literature, and he very likely enriched his own fancy with ideas and techniques that he absorbed from these sources.

These enriching elements he added to the vast store of information that he already had about the people, places, and lore of the mining country of the West. No other author of his time and place was better stocked with the raw material of literature and legend. He did not refine it and work it as thoroughly—or to as serious a purpose—as did Mark Twain or Bret Harte; rather, he seemed content to restrict its use to a lighter, gentler, more whimsical end. His humor at its best appeals to the wit rather than to the emotions.

Among the earliest well-known examples of his humor are bantering sallies in the *Enterprise* against his roommate, Twain. On one occasion, for example, when Twain got a swollen nose in a boxing match, De Quille concocted several stories in which Twain's nose enlarged to such monstrous proportions that whole towns turned out to witness the spectacle. These stories, of course, were "in" jokes and depended for their effect upon readers who were familiar with Twain and who had heard of his mishap. Although written in a seemingly serious tone, they eventually betrayed their purpose by gross exaggeration.

But, De Quille quickly progressed to other subjects and more subtle humor when he developed his distinctive adaptations of the tall tale that he called "quaints." These were burlesques of verisimilitude. They were characterized by drollery and made plausible by a wealth of invented corroborative detail, a serious tone, and cleverly specious rationalization. Usually, they were indistinguishable from regular news stories or feature items except that at their core was a preposterous or at least an unlikely claim—a hoax. Everything that followed was designed to enhance their credibility.

Several of the *Enterprise* "quaints" are still remembered. One of them reported "the discovery of the wonderful 'Silver Man'" by some miners in a remote part of Nevada. De Quille's story followed the publication of Twain's 1862 hoax about a petrified man and might have been influenced by it. However, a brief comparison of the two points up some significant differences in the two authors' styles. Twain's article is quite short and its irony, while clever, is also cutting. It was intended in part as a satire of a local coroner and its humor turns on the crude gesture implied by the petrified man's hand. De Quille's article is much longer and elaborately substantiated with pseudo-scientific and historical detail. Its irony is milder, more general, and subtler and is disguised by the apparent endorsement of the "marvel" implied by the narrator's enthusiasm.

Another "quaint" from the mid-1860s introduced the "traveling stones" of the Pahranagat Mountains of Nevada. With scientific exactness De Quille described a recent discovery of certain stones, seemingly with magnetic properties, that would travel up to a yard to connect with other rocks of similar properties. This yarn elicited serious inquiries from scientists in Germany. P.T. Barnum, the great showman famous for his cynical dictum "a sucker is born every minute," was himself duped by the story and reputedly offered De Quille $10,000 for samples.

In 1874, De Quille concocted his most famous "quaint," a delightful account of "solar armor." This story told the "sad fate" of a man who invented something like a diving suit cooled by a portable air-conditioner. The inventor perished when he tested his suit on a walk across Death Valley in the middle of summer; he froze to death "because his armor had worked but too well" and could not be turned off. This story attracted the attention of a London newspaper that reported it and indicated an interest in more details. De Quille promptly invented a sequel that supplied a great many more details, particularly about the chemicals used. It became a favorite of his readers.[2]

Other well-known hoaxes of his include his reporting of the discoveries of a mountain alligator, a five-headed snake, and a species of eyeless fish that lived only in the scalding hot and min-eralized water found in the depths of some Com-stock mines. As De Quille told it, these fish instantly died of chills when they were brought to the surface and transferred to cool, fresh water. All of these inventions evoked serious inquiries from Eastern scientists and other out-siders. They were consequently appreciated all the more by the mining country people who were able to laugh at those supposedly more sophisticated than they.

De Quille's sense of humor attended his writ-ing of *The Big Bonanza*, the book that assured his place in history. Impishly, he slyly and seam-lessly introduced whimsy into factual sections as if it were authentic information. For example, in the midst of a discussion of the healthful climate of Virginia City, De Quille observed that the town's children "grow like mushrooms. This is probably because they have to contend with but a small amount of atmospheric pressure—there is nothing to prevent their shooting up and ex-panding in all directions" (p. 159). Less ob-viously, the story of the traveling stones of the Pahranagat Mountains concludes a chapter inno-cently entitled "Adventures of Early Prospec-tors." Undoubtedly, it was a source of entertain-ment to his contemporaries who knew about the original "quaint," but the hoax is as likely to trap unwary readers of today as it did the German scientists and Barnum.

After *The Big Bonanza* there is little of the inspired wit and elaborate hoaxing that ap-peared in the first half of his career. Nor is this surprising. De Quille was no longer young and the Comstock had begun its steep decline. Still, the love of the gentle hoax did not desert him in his old age. It is evident most notably in his disposition to use autobiographical "I" narrators in the local color short stories that he continued to publish. In these works of the second half of his career he kept his readers guessing: were they true, or not? De Quille delighted his whole life in framing narratives that were lifelike, if not true to life. By all accounts De Quille himself was an exceptionally truthful individual, but in his art he loved to inhabit the borderland be-tween truth and fiction and mischievously blur the boundary line.

Summary

The best of Dan De Quille's humor can be found in the light and witty hoaxes that he passed off as reportage in the first half of his career. Begin-ning with some preposterous notion, he skill-fully made it seem believable by the copious use of invented detail and specious reasoning. His deceits, however, were gently entertaining and not pointed. They can still be appreciated today as the exuberant art of a talented imagination.

Notes

1. De Quille is widely credited by many of his col-leagues on the *Enterprise* and associates on other papers not only with having taught Twain much about journalism but also with having supplied Twain with much of the material that he later perfected.
2. The best presently available source for these "quaints" is C. Grant Loomis's "The Tall Tales of Dan De Quille," *California Folklore Quarterly*, 5 (January 1946): 26-71.

Selected Bibliography

Primary Sources

Books

The Big Bonanza. Hartford, Conn.: American Publish-ing, 1876; rpt. Intro. by Oscar Lewis. New York: Thomas Y. Crowell, 1947.

Washoe Rambles. Intro. by Richard E. Lingenfelter. Los Angeles: Westernlore Press, 1963. Newly col-lected edition of twelve related travel letters to the *Golden Era* of 1861.

Dan De Quille of the Big Bonanza. Ed. with intro. by James J. Rawls, foreword by Oscar Lewis. San Francisco: Book Club of California, 1980. Contains previously uncollected and unpublished articles and stories.

Articles

"The Tall Tales of Dan De Quille." Ed. with intro. by C. Grant Loomis. *California Folklore Quarterly*, 5 (January 1946): 26-71. Excellent collection of material from the *Territorial Enterprise*.

"Salad Days of Mark Twain." Intro. by Lawrence Ber-kove. *Quarterly News-Letter*, 46, no. 2 (Spring 1981): 31-46.

Secondary Sources

Berkove, Lawrence I. "Dan De Quille and 'Old Times on the Mississippi.'" *Mark Twain Journal*, 24, no. 2 (Fall 1986).

———. "The Literary Journalism of Dan De Quille," *Nevada Historical Society Quarterly*, 28, 4 (Winter 1985): 249-261.

Lillard, Richard G. "Dan De Quille, Comstock Re-porter and Humorist," *Pacific Historical Review*, 13 (1944): 251-259.

Lawrence I. Berkove

Derby, George Horatio ["John Phoenix"; "John P. Squibob"]

Born: Dedham, Massachusetts, on April 3, 1823
Education: United States Military Academy at West Point, [B.S.], 1846
Marriage: Mary Angeline Coons, January 14, 1854, three children
Died: May 15, 1861

Biography

George Horatio Derby "has now [wrote John Lang in 1978] slipped into oblivion."[1] Yet in *Mark Twain's Library of Humor* (1888), Derby was described as one of America's most famous writers:

> George H. Derby, the first of the great modern humorists, who made his pseudonym of "John Phoenix" a household word, was born in Norfolk County, Mass., in 1824 [actually 1823], of an old Salem family. He was graduated at West Point (where his peculiar gift frequently showed itself) in 1846, and he saw active service as Captain of Engineers in the Mexican War. He was wounded at Cerro Gordo, and at the conclusion of the war he was stationed in California. It was here that he published (first in the San Diego *Herald*) the humorous pieces which won him immediate celebrity throughout the country.
>
> He was sunstruck while building lighthouses on the Florida coast; softening of the brain ensued, and he died in an insane asylum at New York in 1861.[2]

Except for the inaccurate birthdate and the archaic diagnosis of the cause of death, the sketch presents a reliable outline of Derby's life. More importantly, it records his reputation in his own century as "the first of the great modern humorists" and "a household word."

The Derby wit, George R. Stewart says, "seems established past question" with John Barton Derby, George's father. The son must have received the gift by genetic means, however, for John Barton deserted his family when George had not yet started to toddle, leaving him to be raised by his mother and her two unmarried sisters. Nevertheless, the boy undoubtedly learned that he came from an "old Salem family" which included "bold shipmasters and great merchants, founders of colonies, a governor of Massachusetts Bay, a president of Harvard College," and "great-grandfather Elias Hasket Derby, merchant-prince of Salem, one of America's earliest millionaires."[3]

When he reached the age of ten, the millionaire's great-grandson was packed off to The School for Moral Discipline in Dedham, near Boston. In that rarefied Bostonian atmosphere of Moral Discipline, George established an early reputation as a humorist of the Bad Boy variety by playing pranks that eventually led to his expulsion. Following a pattern typical of Bad Boys, Derby then went from school to school. What may have saved him from some ultimate infraction of the rules was holding jobs (clerking in the Concord of Ralph Waldo Emerson and Henry David Thoreau and teaching at a country school in New Hampshire) that must have taught him much about human nature and society. Having matured sufficiently to enter the United States Military Academy on July 1, 1842, he completed all requirements and graduated in 1846, standing seventh in his class of fifty-nine. However high his standing as a cadet, Derby remained a prankster even at the Academy, establishing "a reputation as a wit and notorious practical joker which remained with him throughout life."[4]

Although it seems an unwise assignment to give to a notorious practical joker, Derby was appointed a second lieutenant of ordnance after his graduation. He served only briefly in that capacity and then was transferred to the Topographical Engineers, a branch of the Army in which he served until his death. On April 18, 1847, he came close to dying in the Mexican War when he was shot in the hip at the battle of Cerro Gordo, but he recovered from the severe wound and was reassigned to the Topographical Bureau, working first in Washington, D.C., and then in 1848 going on an exploring expedition to Minnesota. Early the following year, he was sent to Monterey, California, and for the next seven years he stayed in the West, mostly on the Pacific Coast, conducting exploratory expeditions and writing official reports.

Only occasional sparks of the Derby wit enliven his official writing, but in 1850 he began to write sketches that allowed his sense of humor free play. In 1853, after being sent to San Diego, he became famous almost overnight—partly because of his writing, but also thanks to one of his practical jokes. As George R. Stewart tells it:

> His friend J.J. Ames, editor of the *San Diego Herald*, left town temporarily, putting Derby in unofficial charge of the paper. In the course of a few issues the latter transformed a sober, Democratic, small-town weekly into a riotous conglomeration of wit, burlesque, and satire, devoted to the Whig party. All California laughed, and Derby's out-

bursts were even reprinted in the East. He became immediately the state wit, and humorous stories without number were credited to him.[5]

Derby built on that fame not only with more humorous sketches but also with more ingenious practical jokes, the most notorious being his successful swapping around of all the babies at a Sonoma party. That prank is said to be the prototype of an identical incident that Owen Wister included in *The Virginian* (1902), but as Walter Blair and Hamlin Hill point out, the trick already had a long history stretching back at least as far as the sixteenth century.[6] Before his wedding Derby separately told his mother and his bride-to-be that the other could not hear—then he introduced them. Of course, they began shouting at each other while Derby stood by enjoying the commotion. Writing in the 1930s, Franklin Walker said that "even after nearly a century has passed, men still chuckle over the time Phoenix stopped the driver of the Golden Eagle Bakery wagon to confound him with an order for 'three golden eagles, baked brown and crisp.'"[7]

Sadly, not much remains to be told about Derby's life. Having his sketches published by *The Pioneer* (founded in 1854), he had by 1855 written enough so that his friend Ames could, with Derby's consent, collect the best of his work and publish it as *Phoenixiana; or Sketches and Burlesques* (1855), a book that Stewart says "ranks among the worst-edited books in all literature."[8] Married in California to Mary Angeline Coons of St. Louis, he was transferred to the East in 1856 and died five years later as a result of a sunstroke he had suffered in 1859 in Florida. He was survived by his wife and their three children: Daisy Peyton Derby (born December 3, 1854), George McClellan Derby (born November 1, 1856), and Mary Townsend Derby (born April 23, 1858). Although deranged for the last year and a half of his life, he had already written enough following the publication of his first book to warrant the publication of a posthumous volume: *The Squibob Papers* (1865), a book that John Lang says was "even more poorly edited than [Derby's] first."[9]

Literary Analysis

Although badly edited, Derby's two books attained such great popularity that they were reprinted dozens of times in the nineteenth century, and readers hailed Derby as one of the nation's funniest writers, a leading Western humorist. He did live on the frontier, but Derby was no illiterate. Critics have spotted in his two books allusions to and quotations from the Bible, Sappho, Cicero, Virgil, Horace, Chaucer, Spenser, Shakespeare, Ben Jonson, Cervantes, Milton, Newton, Pope, Swift, Sterne, Goldsmith, Samuel Johnson, Boswell, Hugh Blair, William Herschel, Henry Carey, Thomas Hood, Scott, Byron, John Stuart Mill, Emerson, Longfellow, Poe, Irving, Agassiz, Charles Lever, Richard Henry Dana, G.P.R. James, Thackeray, Macaulay, Dickens, and Harriet Beecher Stowe.

At least half a dozen writers on this list achieved their renown by mastery of the burlesque, an ancient tradition that began with *The Batrachomyomachia* and that had established itself in American literature by the last third of the eighteenth century.[10] Like those who influenced him, Derby used both modes of the burlesque: the high, in which an elevated style is combined with a trivial subject; and the low, which treats a grand subject in a lowly manner.

To effect such mixtures of incongruous styles and subjects, Derby and most of the ironists who influenced him created as their speakers or leading characters "*alazon*-pedants who over the centuries tried to impress others with learning that they didn't have."[11] Derby's most memorable *alazon*, a dentist named Dr. Tushmaker, advances the technology used by his profession when he invents a tooth-extraction machine so powerful that it pulls out the whole skeleton of an old woman, making her thereafter the "India-Rubber Woman" ("Phoenix at Benicia," *Phoenixiana*). The title of one of the thirty-three humorous pieces in *Phoenixiana* suggests how very humorous *alazon*-pedants must have seemed in 1850s frontier California: "The San Francisco Antiquarian Society and California Academy of Arts and Sciences" (the inspiration, perhaps, for the two-member Freethinkers' Society of Dawson's Landing in Mark Twain's *Pudd'nhead Wilson* [1894]).

Even when *alazon*-pedants are little evident in, or even absent from, his burlesques, Derby frequently spoofs scientism (that is, pseudo-science) and absurd technologies. In "A New System of English Grammar," published in *Phoenixiana*, for example, Phoenix applies scientific precision to adjectives and adverbs, indicating by a system of numbering from one to a hundred ("perfection") which degree of the quality the modifier denotes:

> As a 19 young and 76 beautiful lady was 52 gaily tripping down the sidewalk of our 84 frequented street, she accidentally came in contact—100 (this shows that she came in close contact) with a 73 fat but 87 good-humored-looking gentleman, who was 93 (i.e., intently) gazing into the window of a toy-shop.

(p. 39)

In "Sewing Machine—Feline Attachment" (one of the twenty-seven pieces in *The Squibob Papers*), Phoenix explains with elaborate precision how to construct a cat-powered sewing machine, a Rube Goldberg-type contraption with a "living mouse . . . suspended by the tail, within a few inches of the nose of the *motor* [the cat]":

> As the cat springs toward the mouse, the latter is removed, and keeping constantly at the original distance, the machine revolves with great rapidity. The prodigious velocity produced by the rapacity of the cat in its futile endeavors to overtake the mouse, can only be imagined by one who has seen the Attachment in full operation.
>
> (p. 62)

Derby is no easier on his fellow writers than on pseudo-scientists and eccentric inventors. His parodies and travesties of orations, book reviews, newspaper reports, and even poetry deflate presumptions just as humorously and effectively as his thrusts at scientific pretentiousness. Derby's "Fourth of July Oration in Oregon" (*The Squibob Papers*) is "[o]ne of the most elaborate burlesques" among a wealth of similar spoofs by humorists such as Artemus Ward, Bill Nye, Petroleum V. Nasby, and Orpheus C. Kerr.[12] "Musical Review Extraordinary" (*Phoenixiana*) pokes fun not only at inflated reviews but also at the notion of bringing scientific precision to musical composition—in this case, "The Prairie" by Jabez Tarbox, a symphony that reproduces exactly the sounds of oxen lowing and the other noises of an immigrant wagon train. "Illustrated Newspapers" and "The Ladies Relief Society" (*Phoenixiana*) parody news reports of the day, and "The Song of Nothing Shorter" stands out as one of the better take-offs of Longfellow's *Hiawatha*.[13]

Derby's satire, as most of his critics have noted, comes without venom. His attacks on fakery and pretension hit their targets but with an effect surprisingly benign and genial. Beneath the good-natured surface of Derby's humor, however, lie skepticism and irreverence. In "Lectures on Astronomy," for example, we are told that "the death of an individual man on this Earth, though perhaps as important an event as can occur to himself, is calculated to cause no great convulsion of Nature or disturb particularly the great aggregate of created beings" (*Phoenixiana*). "Boston—A Moral City" (*The Squibob Papers*) and "The Literary Contribution Box: Lines to Lola Montez" (*Phoenixiana*) are representative of Derby's irreverence. What makes his skepticism and irreverence so palatable is Derby's style. He lightens and enlivens even the

most pessimistic of observations with his inveterate word play, delighting in puns, "malapropisms, twisted clichés, mangled quotations, and elaborate pseudo-etymologies."[14] In "Phoenix at the Mission Dolores" (*Phoenixiana*), readers are warned not to name a child William, for if they do, they will have a reminder of Bills around the house.

Derby's comic techniques—his word play, his allusiveness, and his mixing of styles and genres—can be found in Menippean satire and the comic diatribes of the Cynic philosophers of Greece. These techniques are endemic to much humor, not just Derby's. Nevertheless, critics have said that along with much of the humor of his precursors, Derby's work anticipates the writing of twentieth-century humorists John Barth, Donald Barthelme, Robert Benchley, S. J. Perelman, and James Thurber. To that list Richard Brautigan's name should be added. But, the most important and most obvious example of Derby's influence, as most of his critics have noted, is Mark Twain. Gladys Bellamy cites textual evidence showing that Derby's influence lasted for at least "forty years of Mark Twain's life as an author."[15]

Although Derby, like Twain, first gained his reputation as a western writer, critics such as John Lang say that Derby "has somewhat erroneously come to be considered a Western humorist."[16] Lang rightly argues that "Derby's roots ran deep into the soil of New England, and much of Derby's writing contains very little Western matter."[17] Indeed, much of what he wrote seems little tied to *any* region. Nevertheless, the boisterous, irreverent atmosphere of the frontier undoubtedly encouraged and inspired Derby; and although his fellow Westerners were, like him, eastern transplants, they were the first to recognize and applaud his comic genius. In that sense, it is not only correct but also instructive to label Derby a western writer.

Summary

Legendary among hs contemporaries as a practical joker, Derby earned a national reputation as one of the West's funniest literary comedians. Using irreverent word play in his five dozen comical sketches and burlesques, he poked fun at pretension and credulity, especially any foolish belief in the omnipotence of scientific method and precision. An engineer himself, Derby understood the science of his day and was thereby able to discern its limitations and the misunderstandings of others. Whether Mark Twain already held such attitudes when he first read Derby's work is beside the point in view of the many obvious parallels between Twain's work and Derby's. Yet, Twain's renown still grows, whereas Derby's "has now slipped into oblivion." Stewart explains the difference in reputations by saying "that to be a great humorist a writer must be something much more, and a humorist secondarily."[18] Still, the difference may have much to do with size of output, although Twain clearly moralizes more than does Derby. Those who read him will discover why Derby exerted such a strong influence on Twain: the best burlesques of John Phoenix delight and instruct.

Notes

1. John Lang, "George Derby and the Language of Reasoned Absurdity," *Publications of the Missouri Philological Association* (1978), pp. 61–70.
2. *Mark Twain's Library of Humor*, ed. Samuel Langhorn Clemens et al. (New York: Charles L. Webster, 1888), p. 31.
3. George R. Stewart, *John Phoenix, Esq.: The Veritable Squibob: A Life of Captain George H. Derby, U.S.A.* (1937); rpt. (New York: Da Capo, 1969), pp. 4–5.
4. ———, "Derby, George Horatio," *Dictionary of American Biography* (1943), p. 251.
5. Stewart, "Derby, George Horatio," p. 252.
6. Walter Blair and Hamlin Hill, *America's Humor from Poor Richard to Doonesbury* (New York: Oxford University Press, 1978), pp. 229–230.
7. Franklin Walker, *San Francisco's Literary Frontier* (Seattle: University of Washington Press, 1969), p. 45.
8. Stewart, *John Phoenix*, p. 169.
9. Lang, "George Horatio Derby (John Phoenix, Squibob)," in *Dictionary of Literary Biography*, Vol. 11, *American Humorists, 1800-1950*, ed. Stanley Trachtenberg (Detroit: Gale, 1982), p. 120.
10. Edwin H. Cady, *The Light of Common Day: Realism in American Fiction* (Bloomington: Indiana University Press, 1971), pp. 53–59.
11. Blair and Hill, p. 232.
12. Barnet Baskerville, "Nineteenth-Century Burlesque of Oratory," *American Quarterly*, 20 (1968): 731–738.
13. Fred Leevis Pattee, *The Feminine Fifties*; rpt. (Port Washington: Kennikat, 1966), pp. 167–176.
14. Lang, "George Derby and the Language of Reasoned Absurdity," p. 64.
15. Gladys Carmen Bellamy, "Mark Twain's Indebtedness to John Phoenix," *American Literature*, 13 (1941): 42.
16. Lang, "George Horatio Derby," p. 114.
17. Ibid.
18. Stewart, *John Phoenix*, p. 201.

Selected Bibliography

Primary Sources

Professional Writings

The Topographical Reports of Lieutenant George H. Derby with Introduction and Notes by Francis P. Farquhar. San Francisco: n.p., 1933.

Humorous Writings

Phoenixiana; or, Sketches and Burlesques. By John Phoenix. New York: Appleton, 185[5].

The Squibob Papers. By John Phoenix. New York: Carleton, 1865.

Secondary Sources

Books

Bangs, John Kendrick. "John Phoenix and His Work." Intro. to *Phoenixiana*. New York: Appleton, 1903, pp. vii–xii. Informative, this six-page introduction shows that almost half a century after Derby's death a leading American humorist still "had a warm spot in [his] heart for the venerable Squibob" (p. viii).

Bier, Jesse. *The Rise and Fall of American Humor.* New York: Holt, Rinehart and Winston, 1968, pp. 78 and 110–111. Very brief discussion of Derby as one of the "literary comedians" of mid-nineteenth-century America.

Blair, Walter, and Hamlin Hill. *America's Humor from Poor Richard to Doonesbury.* New York: Oxford University Press, 1978, pp. 229–237. Lively and comical, but also perceptive and informative, this first-rate discussion stresses Derby's *alazon*-pedants and his debt to eighteenth-century satirists in successfully joking about science.

Cady, Edwin H. *The Light of Common Day: Realism in American Fiction.* Bloomington: Indiana University Press, 1971. Although Cady does not mention Derby, the chapter on "*The Batrachomyomachia* and American Fiction" outlines the history of the tradition that includes Derby.

Hauck, Richard Boyd. *A Cheerful Nihilism: Confidence and "The Absurd" in American Humorous Fiction.* Bloomington: Indiana University Press, 1971, p. 243. Passing mention of Derby as one of the American writers whose humor "is laced with a sense of peril."

Lang, John. "George Horatio Derby (John Phoenix, Squibob)." In *Dictionary of Literary Biography.* Vol. 11, Part 1: A–L. *American Humorists, 1800-1950.* Ed. Stanley Trachtenberg. Detroit: Gale, 1982, pp. 114–123. Analyzing and illustrating Derby's elaborate wordplay, Lang provides an excellent introduction to his subject's life and work.

Pattee, Fred Lewis. *The Feminine Fifties.* 1940. Rpt. Port Washington, N.Y.: Kennikat, 1966, pp. 93, 172, 203, 206–215. Pattee compares Derby's parody of *Hiawatha* with others of the period and declares: "Not much was added to Western humor after Derby" (p. 212).

Stegner, Wallace, ed. *Selected American Prose: The Realistic Movement, 1841-1900.* New York: Holt, Rinehart and Winston, 1958, pp. xvii, 17–20. Identifies John Phoenix's elegy for Jeames Hambrick as a model for similar parodies in Mark Twain's works.

Thorp, Willard. *American Humorists.* University of Minnesota Pamphlets on American Writers 42. Minneapolis: University of Minnesota Press, 1964, pp. 17–19. Thorp says that the humor of the literary comedians "is seldom regional" and that they "relied almost entirely on tricks of language to get laughs."

Walker, Franklin. *A Literary History of Southern California.* Berkeley: University of California Press, 1950, pp. 84–92.

———. *San Francisco's Literary Frontier.* 1939. Rpt. Seattle: University of Washington Press, 1969, pp. 40–45. In both books, Walker summarizes and paraphrases from Stewart's *John Phoenix* (see Biography section below).

Biographies

Delano, Alonzo. "Reminiscences of John Phoenix, Esq., The Veritable 'Squibob.'" *Hesperian*, March 1862, pp. 30–34. Humorous account of the meeting of Derby and Delano, another early California humorist.

Stewart, George R. "Derby, George Horatio." *Dictionary of American Biography.* 1943 ed. Brief biographical sketch.

———. *John Phoenix, Esq.: The Veritable Squibob: A Life of Captain George H. Derby, U.S.A.* 1937. Rpt. New York: Da Capo, 1969. "[W]ritten to display not so much Derby's writings as his personality" (p. vii), Stewart's book nevertheless remains the most complete and detailed critical treatment of Derby's humor.

Articles

Baskerville, Barnet. "Nineteenth-Century Burlesque of Oratory." *American Quarterly,* 20 (1968): 726–743. Derby's "Fourth of July Oration in Oregon" is discussed as "one of the most elaborate burlesques" of patriotic oratory.

Bellamy, Gladys Carmen. "Mark Twain's Indebtedness to John Phoenix." *American Literature,* 13 (1941): 29–43. Bellamy convincingly shows that Derby's humor influenced Twain throughout his writing career.

Lang, John. "George Derby and the Language of Reasoned Absurdity." *Publications of the Missouri Philological Association,* 3 (1978): 61–70. Shows that "Derby's farcical language is inherently iconoclastic" (p. 65), although "his satire is [generally] neutralized by his buffoonery" (p. 67).

Mabbott, T. O. "George H. Derby: A Debt to Poe." *Notes and Queries,* March 10, 1934, p. 171. Cites evidence of Edgar Allan Poe's influence on Derby.

James H. Maguire

De Vries, Peter

Born: Chicago, Illinois, on February 27, 1910
Education: Chicago Christian High School, 1923–1927; Calvin College (Grand Rapids, Michigan), B.A., 1931; Northwestern University, summer 1931
Marriage: Katinka Loeser, October 16, 1943, four children

Biography

In twenty-three novels and two collections of short pieces, Peter De Vries has established himself, according to Kingsley Amis, as the "funniest serious writer to be found on either side of the Atlantic." Born February 27, 1910 to Dutch immigrant parents in Chicago, Illinois, De Vries was raised in the Calvinistic Dutch Reformed Church. He has said that because of the ethnic and religious "insularity" of his childhood he still feels "somewhat like a foreigner."[1] His father, Joost, a model for some of the eccentric fathers in his fiction, owned an ice and coal delivery business that later became a moving van company. De Vries's childhood centered on the church. He attended church three times each Sunday, and he was not allowed to do "anything much that was secular, even on weekdays."[2] When he was thirteen, the death of his older sister greatly affected the family. His father became more religious and melancholic, while his mother, Henrietta, turned from the church. (Transformations from belief to disbelief, or disbelief to belief, recur in his novels.) At parochial schools, Englewood Christian School (1916–1923) and Chicago Christian High School (1923–1927), he was bright and popular. It was his "impulse always to be funny" as a way to win "affection and approval."[3] At Calvin College in Grand Rapids, Michigan, where his parents sent him to prepare for a career in the ministry, he played basketball, edited the monthly student newspaper, and competed successfully in debate and speech tournaments. In 1931, he won the Michigan intercollegiate championship in extemporaneous speaking—a triumph for him because he had stuttered as a child.

After graduating with a B.A. in English in 1931, he edited a community newspaper in Chicago. Failing health led him to seek treatment for tuberculosis in a Denver, Colorado, sanatorium. He returned to Chicago where he became active in reform politics and held simultaneously a number of jobs, including peddling taffy apples, acting on radio, and moving furniture for the family company. De Vries's first publication came in 1934 in a little magazine in Texas. By the end of the decade, he had published short stories and poems in *Story, Esquire,* and *Poetry.* In 1938, he was named an associate editor of

Poetry, and two years later became editor. In October 1943, he married Katinka Loeser, a short story writer and a contributor to *Poetry*. His first novel, *But Who Wakes the Bugler?*, was published with illustrations by Charles Addams in 1940. His second and third novels, issued in 1943 and 1944, received few favorable reviews, and De Vries soon dropped them from his list of publications.

De Vries's career as a literary humorist really began after April 1944, when he invited James Thurber to Chicago to give a benefit lecture for *Poetry*. De Vries's 1943 essay for *Poetry*, "The Comic Prufrock," was the first serious appraisal of Thurber's work, and Thurber, equally taken with De Vries, urged him to move to New York City and write for *The New Yorker*. Editor Harold Ross was at first hesitant about hiring him, but De Vries's clever prose and personal charm won Ross over. Taking Thurber's advice, De Vries turned down a full-time staff position and in September 1944, signed on part-time as a poetry editor, cartoon editor, and caption writer. In 1946, with a $1,000 award from the National Institute of Arts and Letters, he moved from the City to Westport, Connecticut, where he lives today. He turned his attention from poetry to comic fiction, novels and short pieces, or "casuals," for *The New Yorker*, although several poems attributed to characters appear in his novels, and two poems are included in *The Oxford Book of English Light Verse*. He has described himself during these years as a devoted father who enjoyed domestic duties as a break from writing. His first child, Jan, was born in 1945, followed by Peter Jon in 1947, Emily in 1949, and Derek in 1952.

In the 1950s De Vries began to build a loyal readership. In addition to *No But I Saw the Movie* (1952), a collection of short pieces mostly from *The New Yorker*, he published four novels. *The Tunnel of Love* (1954), about the trials in marriage and art of cartoonist Augie Poole, was an Atlantic Book Club Selection and De Vries's first bestseller. With Joseph Fields he adapted it for a year's run on Broadway in 1957, and it later became a movie, the first of three of his novels to be adapted for the screen. *Comfort Me with Apples* (1956), its sequel *The Tents of Wickedness* (1959), and *The Mackerel Plaza* (1958), a favorite of critics, are witty, satirical portraits of suburban Connecticut. In the novels after 1960, when his daughter Emily died of leukemia, De Vries's humor noticeably darkens. Though it has light moments, *The Blood of the Lamb* (1962) closes with a description of a father's helplessness as his daughter dies from cancer. *Reuben, Reuben* (1964), one of De Vries's own favorites, *The Vale of Laughter* (1967), and the interlocking novellas, *The Cat's*

Pajamas & Witch's Milk (1968), have also been called black comedies, a label that De Vries does not like.

In the 1960s he was recognized by *The New York Times Book Review* as the "most reliably funny comic novelist now at large."[4] He was invited to lecture at the University of Virginia (1962), Villanova University (1966), and the University of Michigan (1968), and in 1968 he received an honorary doctorate from the University of Bridgeport. He was elected to the National Institute of Arts and Letters (1961) and the American Academy of Arts and Letters (1983). In his novels in the 1970s and 1980s, notably *I Hear America Swinging* (1976), *Sauce for the Goose* (1982), *Slouching Towards Kalamazoo* (1983), and *The Prick of Noon* (1985), he has examined the dizzying changes in relations between the sexes. He has continued to publish regularly; from 1970 to 1985, ten novels and a second collection of short pieces, *Without a Stitch in Time*, have appeared. In 1985 Viking-Penguin announced the publication of a uniform paper edition of his novels, a move that should further enlarge his audience.

Literary Analysis

De Vries has described himself as "a serious writer of the comic novel."[5] While he satirizes suburban culture, its split-level churches and mate-swapping, he prefers to be labeled a humorist; the satirist, he explains, "shoots to kill while the humorist brings his prey back alive."[6] The tone of what De Vries calls his "charitable" humor is best summed up in the quip that opens *Let Me Count the Ways*: "Man is vile, I know, but people are wonderful" (p. 1). Most of his young male protagonists are drawn directly from his autobiography. They come from "insular" childhoods; indeed many grow up in Dutch Reformed families or have working-class backgrounds they hope to rise above. Eddie Teeters, narrator of *The Prick of Noon*, for example, is from Backbone, Arkansas, a place he has resolved never to be from again. His father has the "grave responsibility" of tending a cemetery, but Eddie, by directing sex films, is determined to make his way into country-club Connecticut and the species "*Homo suburbanitis*" (p. 4). Similarly, Ted Peacham of *Consenting Adults* is embarrassed that his father, a mover by trade, hibernates like a bear during the winter; Ted dreams of hobnobbing with the Lake Shore elite. De Vries admits that "biographical or psychological analysts could make the case that my fascination with the sophisticated and 'worldly' world is a vicarious escape from this (in many ways) painful immigrant childhood, with its sense of exclusion and inferiority, and that my satirizing of the upper crust is, well, a simultaneous appeasement of the household gods being flouted."[7]

De Vries's novels take place in Chicago and the Midwest or in the suburbs of New York City, commuter stops called Avalon, Decency, or Woodsmoke but modeled on Westport, Connecticut. Because of his provincial interest in suburbia, he has jokingly called himself a "regionalist, like Thomas Hardy."[8] His characters are more or less interchangeable among his novels. The residents of Avalon are typical; in *The Mackerel Plaza* they are described as living a "kind of hand-to-mouth luxury, never knowing where the next quarterly instalment of taxes or the payment on a third car is coming from" (p. 6). Comedy, De Vries notes, has always recognized that we "human beings are all absurd variations of one another in any case."[9] His protagonists typically worry about balancing identity and conformity, finding something outside themselves to believe in, and coming to grips with love, courtship, and marriage. They act impulsively, especially in courtship, usually bringing on themselves all sorts of thorny consequences.

De Vries is fond of first-person narrators who either share his quick wit or, like Mrs. Wallop, are malaprops. The worst people in his novels are those who take no pleasure in language or those who abuse wit, using it, for example, for advertising jingles. Word games, parodies, paradoxes, bungled allusions, witty retorts, twisted aphorisms, malapropisms, sudden switches in diction from slangy to formal—these are hallmarks of De Vries's style. He holds the pun particularly dear, and he is a master of comic names: a lusty Scottish-Welsh poet in *Reuben, Reuben*, is named Gowan McGland, and the Marvel family reunion in *Through the Fields of Clover* takes place on the banks of the Spitachunk River.

De Vries learned much about the comedy of the beleaguered middle-class male from *The New Yorker* humorists, particularly S. J. Perelman and Thurber, and his humor suggests a wide reading in literature, humor theory, and philosophy. Reviewing *Slouching Towards Kalamazoo*, *The New Yorker* counted allusions to some 30 authors, including W.B. Yeats (in the title) and Nathaniel Hawthorne (De Vries's seductress emblazons *her* T-shirt with an A+). In addition, De Vries has cited as "main influences" the composers Claude Debussy and Jean Sibelius. From them, he says, he learned the value of "free-form," of an "emphasis on the individual nuance rather than the melodic whole, a chord being its own justification quite apart from any duty to the supporting continuity."[10]

De Vries's plots are rambunctious, full of characters who set up a quip and then are heard from no more. Louis Hasley complains that his novels are "loosely organic" and "too frequently undermotivated." Millicent Bell similarly argues that De Vries's "weakness as a writer of books that are *wholes* may derive from his itch to laugh at anything that he happens to think of along the way" (*New York Times Book Review*, October 11, 1970, p. 4). De Vries admits to "meandering" on occasion but only "like the beagle who rambles in a strict attention to the trail."[11] His world is farcical, and ironic twists in plot are commonplace—a faulty fire alarm causes a house fire; a character attempting suicide fails to asphyxiate himself when his car runs out of gas; a young man is so relieved to learn that his girlfriend is not pregnant that he proposes marriage.

Despite such sudden twists, De Vries's novels do follow a basic structure. A young male narrator or protagonist is introduced (or, in *Sauce for the Goose*, a young feminist writer). We learn his family background, follow his adventures in courtship, and usually watch as he makes a mess of his career and love life. At the end, however, there is usually some return to order. T. Jeff Evans notes that De Vries's protagonist "moves away from conformity and institutions in order to discover the repressed self."[12] Discovering in the process that the "self is false or distorted outside the community," the protagonist usually becomes reconciled to marriage, a convention that inhibits him but also provides him comfort. Though they never give up—Ted Peacham, for instance, tires of a *ménage à trois* only to start a torrid affair with triplets—sexual freedom does not bring De Vries's characters lasting happiness. As one says, "We're no better off with our freedom than the Victorians were with their tyranny" (*Reuben, Reuben*, p. 434). While each of his novels addresses some front in the war between the sexes, an escalating war because of what one narrator calls the "gummed-up first person singular . . . the two I's . . . that can't make a We" (*Clover*, p. 257), De Vries has suggested that what is needed is a "joint submission of both to the hard facts of life."[13] De Vries's own marriage, it is worth noting, has lasted over forty years, making him, in his words, a sort of "underground" in a "supposedly mate-swapping culture."[14]

The Calvinistic teachings of his childhood impressed upon De Vries that man was depraved, yet even as his novels depict human foibles, they affirm basic human values. In his early novel, *The Handsome Heart*, a psychiatrist says, "What Truth is or whether there is any such thing in an absolute sense or personified in a God or what have you, I don't know—and neither do you. But there is a scale of human values by which man lives, a hierarchy so to speak, within which there is much uncertainty and great variation, in the light of each individual case" (p. 205). Even in De Vries's darkest novel, *The Blood of the Lamb*, a child dying of leukemia forces her father to see that in a universe where such a cruel death is possible, the best human values, "reason, courage, and grace," still have meaning.

Frequently De Vries's novels wrangle with the question of what, if anything in this vale of tears, is worthy of laughter. Hank Tattersall in *Cat's Pajamas* argues that humor deals with "that which isn't funny. Or at least isn't funny at the time: broken bones, broken machinery, bad food, hangovers. Husbands. Wives. Brats." Tragedy and comedy, he concludes, "have a common root . . . Desperation" (pp. 61–62). Some of De Vries's comedy is decidedly black—Tattersall dies from exposure after being caught in a pet door; inside his alcoholic dog and his mongoloid stepson are deaf to his pleas for help. In general, however, De Vries seems to share the attitude of Wally Hines, the psychologist in *Vale of Laughter* who studies the theory as well as the practice of humor. Hines describes his "central philosophy" as a "guarded pessimism" (p. 167).

Religious belief is often a key issue in De Vries's novels. When Mrs. Marvel in *Through the Fields of Clover* asks her youngest son, Cotton Marvel, to go to church, he replies, "There is no God." She counters, "Don't split hairs with me, dear." Reverence, she explains, is a "fine thing," and it leads to "*Values*, the kind your father and I have had for forty years" (p. 17). Having himself grown up in a severe Calvinist sect, De Vries frequently satirizes secularized worship. In *The Mackerel Plaza* (1958), for example, the Rev. Mackerel wants to remarry, but his congregation is intent on keeping alive the memory of his dead wife. One member even proposes building a shopping mall, to be named Mackerel Plaza in her honor. Like all of De Vries's protagonists, the Rev. Mackerel has serious concerns, but he is a man of flesh. Caught staring at a girl's legs, he replies, apologetically, "Don't worry ma'am, my thoughts were on higher things" (p. 203). His church, the People's Liberal Church, faithfully displays the latest in ecumenical style. America's first split-level church, it has a designer pulpit that "consists of a slab of marble set on four legs of four delicately differing fruitwoods, to symbolize the four Gospels, and their failure to harmonize" (p. 7). Mackerel's sermons are terse; he is the "Ernest Hemingway of the pulpit." With a text from Havelock Ellis, he wins over his flock with such paradoxes as, "It is the final proof of God's omnipotence that he need not exist in order to save us" (p. 8). Mackerel's hesitancy

about memorializing his wife leads to his being suspected of causing the accident in which she died. Mackerel has a nervous breakdown during which a psychiatrist prescribes as a cure "making a decision for Christ." The novel ends with Mackerel's name cleared, his marriage to his first wife's sister, and his admission that he has lost what little faith he had, a loss he compares to "losing a wooden leg in an accident" (p. 257). Lying close to him in bed, his wife can only suggest a return to the values De Vries frequently reasserts: she urges him "to be as humane as humanly possible" (p. 260).

Reuben, Reuben (1964), the novel that De Vries once called his favorite, is ambitious in structure. There are three interconnected parts. The novel opens with the first-person narrative of Frank Spofford, septuagenarian Yankee chicken farmer and would-be writer. Part two describes the last days of Gowen McGland, a rascally Scottish-Welsh-Irish poet. In the final part we learn the story of Alvin Mopworth, a British radio actor, writing a critical study of McGland. All three men fail in love and in writing. Spofford infiltrates the enemy, the suburbanites, hoping to introduce his granddaughter to them, and incidentally to find material for his new avocation of writing. Before he knows it, he has become a "D.P.," a displaced person, in his own hometown. Infected with suburban values, he is not happy as a yokel, yet the Successful Writers School refuses to admit him because he is too sophisticated. His fellow misfit, the poet McGland, also tries to live off the fat of suburbia, but when he seduces one housewife too many, her husband, a dentist, removes his one remaining sound tooth. Rather than go toothless into old age, McGland commits suicide. In the final section Mopworth energetically pursues women only to be accused by them of overcompensating for latent homosexuality. His life is full of such ironic misinterpretations. Researching a biographical study of McGland, he meets Spofford's granddaughter, Geneva, who, it turns out, was McGland's last mistress. Mopworth marries Geneva, but neither his marriage nor his book is successful. He botches his marriage when he renews an affair with McGland's ex-wife, and others rush to press with better books on the dead poet. At the end of the novel Mopworth, a lonely Englishman in New York, separated from his children and divorced from his wife, is still trying to recover some meaning in his life. Saddened by the "human botch of mating" (p. 433), he is described in the novel's closing line as sitting with a group of strangers talking far into the night about love.

In novels of the 1970s and 1980s De Vries has shown special interest in "liberated" sexuality. Yet, even in describing the sexual calisthenics of blue-movie stuntman Teeters in *The Prick of Noon*, De Vries's prose is decorous. One of his best comic studies of free sex, *I Hear America Swinging* (1976), begins with a parody of Whitman: "I hear America swinging,/ The carpenter with his wife or the mason's wife, or even the mason,/ The mason's daughter in love with the boy next door, who is in love with the boy next door to him,/ Everyone free, comrades in arms together, freely swinging" (p. v). De Vries's swingers, ironically, are farming folk in the American heartland, Middle City, Iowa. Dr. Bill Bumpers, the marriage counselor who surveys all this coupling, actually has a doctorate in English. When the Social Science Department at Demeter University turns down his dissertation on causes of divorce in rural Iowa, he is forced to turn it into a creative dissertation, an "anti-novel." Among his first patients are Heck and Hattie Brown whose farm is called Pretty Pass. Farmer Brown is entranced with "new ideas," particularly about sex. He even practices the "brittle dialogue" (p. 32) of the cultured folk: explaining his new crop of soybeans, he says, "Alfalfa's terribly *démodé*" (p. 57). Group sex at Pretty Pass becomes complicated when Clem, the "hired hand," joins in. With *his* newfound sophistication Clem sets himself up as America's "first primitive critic," "a Grandma Moses of exegesis" for the local newspaper. Bumpers, after experiencing the "moist heap" (p. 121) of an orgy, concludes that a "man should be greater than some of his parts" (p. 153), and he flees this swinging American heartland with his true love, Claire de Lune. In our last view of him, he holds his sleeping bride, as he wistfully—a little too wistfully—recalls the innocence of his first love.

Summary

Asked to comment on one analysis of his humor, De Vries answered, "One just sits in the corner and secretes the stuff. Don't ask a cow to analyze milk."[15] To attain a prose so effortless and striking that Anthony Burgess has ranked him as "one of the great prose virtuosos of modern America,"[16] De Vries revises, usually writing over four to ten drafts, in a process that he has described as "mostly cutting . . . one tenth perspiration and nine tenths condensation."[17] "I don't think about what I am or what I'm trying to do," he told an interviewer, "except to amuse an intelligent reader with what I hope is some truth we both know about life."[18] And, surely, as long as there are suburbs and those who aspire to live in them, easy money, discontented marriages, the sexual itch, and the chill of self-knowledge, De Vries will continue to amuse intelligent readers.

Notes

1. Roy Newquist, "Peter De Vries," *Counterpoint* (Chicago: Rand McNally, 1964), p. 146.
2. Newquist, p. 146.
3. Ben Yagoda, "Being Seriously Funny," *New York Times Magazine*, June 12, 1983, p. 55.
4. William R. Higgins, "Peter De Vries," *American Novelists Since World War II. Dictionary of Literary Biography*. Ed. James E. Kibler, Jr. (Detroit: Gale, 1980), p. 79.
5. Richard B. Sale, "An Interview in New York with Peter De Vries," *Studies in the Novel*, 1 (1969): 364.
6. Newquist, p. 149.
7. Ibid., p. 147.
8. Roderick Jellema, *Peter De Vries* (Grand Rapids, Mich.: William B. Eerdmans, 1966), p. 11.
9. Newquist, p. 149.
10. Ibid., p. 153.
11. Ibid., p. 149.
12. T. Jeff Evans, "Peter De Vries: A Retrospective," *American Humor*, 7, 2 (Fall 1980): 14.
13. Sale, p. 366.
14. Ibid.
15. Newquist, p. 146.
16. Yagoda, p. 42.
17. Sale, p. 364.
18. Newquist, p. 149.

Selected Bibliography

Primary Sources

Novels

But Who Wakes the Bugler? Boston: Houghton Mifflin, 1940.

The Handsome Heart. New York: Coward-McCann, 1943.

Angels Can't Do Better. New York: Coward-McCann, 1944.

The Tunnel of Love. Boston: Little, Brown, 1954.

Comfort Me With Apples. Boston: Little, Brown, 1956.

The Mackerel Plaza. Boston: Little, Brown, 1958.

The Tents of Wickedness. Boston: Little, Brown, 1959.

Through the Fields of Clover. Boston: Little, Brown, 1961.

The Blood of the Lamb. Boston: Little, Brown, 1962.

Reuben, Reuben. Boston: Little, Brown, 1964.

Let Me Count the Ways. Boston: Little, Brown, 1965.

The Vale of Laughter. Boston: Little, Brown, 1967.

The Cat's Pajamas & Witch's Milk. Boston: Little, Brown, 1968.

Mrs. Wallop. Boston: Little, Brown, 1970.

Into Your Tent I'll Creep. Boston: Little, Brown, 1971.

Forever Panting. Boston: Little, Brown, 1973.

The Glory of the Hummingbird. Boston: Little, Brown, 1974.

I Hear America Swinging. Boston: Little, Brown, 1976.

Madder Music. Boston: Little, Brown, 1977.

Consenting Adults, or The Duchess Will Be Furious. Boston: Little, Brown, 1980.

Sauce for the Goose. Boston: Little, Brown, 1982.

Slouching Towards Kalamazoo. Boston: Little, Brown, 1983.

The Prick of Noon. Boston: Little, Brown, 1985.
Peckham's Marbles. Boston: Little, Brown, 1986.

Collections
No but I Saw the Movie. Boston: Little, Brown, 1952.
Without a Stitch in Time. Boston: Little, Brown, 1972.

Drama
(with Joseph Fields.) *The Tunnel of Love. A Play.*
Boston: Little, Brown, 1957.

Secondary Sources

Books
Bowden, Edwin T. *Peter De Vries: A Bibliography.*
The University of Texas at Austin: Humanities
Research Center, 1978. The definitive compilation
of De Vries's publications before 1977.
Bowden, J. H. *Peter De Vries.* Boston: Twayne Publishers, 1983. Biographical chapter and individual
analyses of novels up to *Sauce for the Goose*
(1982).
Jellema, Roderick. *Peter De Vries.* Grand Rapids,
Mich.: William B. Eerdmans, 1966. A booklet in
the series, Contemporary Writers in Christian Perspective, covering the first eight novels.

Articles and Interviews
Evans, T. Jeff. "Peter De Vries: A Retrospective."
American Humor, 7, 2 (Fall 1980): 13–16. Overview of De Vries's comic novels.
Hasley, Louis. "The Hamlet of Peter De Vries: To Wit
or Not to Wit." *South Atlantic Quarterly*, 70
(1971): 467–476. Questions De Vries's overuse of
puns and witty language.
Higgins, William R. "Peter De Vries." In *American
Novelists Since World War II. Dictionary of Liter-
ary Biography.* Vol. 6. Ed. James E. Kibler, Jr. De-
troit: Gale, 1980, pp. 79–83.
Newquist, Roy. "Peter De Vries." In *Counterpoint.*
Chicago: Rand McNally, 1964, pp. 149–154. An
interview that includes questions about De Vries's
Dutch Reformed Church background and his
stance on the "modern Ordeal of woman."
Sale, Richard B. "An Interview in New York with
Peter De Vries." *Studies in the Novel*, 1 (1969):
364–369. Includes questions about black humor and
about writing habits.
Yagoda, Ben. "Being Seriously Funny." *New York
Times Magazine*, June 12, 1983, pp. 42–44. Por-
trait of De Vries and overview of his career.

Grady W. Ballenger

Donleavy, J[ames] P[atrick]

Born: Brooklyn, New York, on April 23,
1926
Education: Trinity College, Dublin, no degree
Marriages: Valerie Heron (later divorced),
two children; Mary Wilson Price, two
children

Biography

J.P. Donleavy is American-born though he has
lived in Ireland for many years and most of his
novels are set in Ireland. His New York background is evident in some of his books, but his
vision of his native country seems to have become almost fantastic in recent years. He has
said that living in Ireland has made America a
land of romance for him. Though not more reclusive than some other writers, Donleavy keeps
the facts of his life private. He has speculated
that "it could be damaging to someone like me
or J.D. Salinger to become famous in the famous
sense of being famous."[1]

Donleavy was born in Brooklyn and reared in
the Bronx. He has described his childhood in
idyllic terms and sometimes seems to regard the
New York of his childhood as almost Arcadian.
His father was an Irish immigrant, but he maintains that he did not grow up in an immigrant
ghetto; his family was middle-class and drove
big, new cars. Having been expelled from one
preparatory school and barely graduated from
another (he claims a "piss-poor high school record") at the time of United States entry into
World War II, he joined the Navy. Apparently
he spent his entire service career in Virginia and
Maryland. After training as a radarman for an
amphibious landing craft, presumably in preparation for the invasion of Japan, he was allowed
to study at the Naval Academy Preparatory
School.

After the war, moved by what he had learned
about Ireland in his reading, his mother's stories
of Dublin, and (he claims) his inability to be
admitted to an American university, he applied
to Trinity College in Dublin. This is probably
the crucial event in Donleavy's life. It introduced
him to Ireland, the scene and perhaps inspiration of his best writing; Dublin and Trinity provided the milieu in which he became an artist;
and people he met there not only helped establish him as a writer but provided the originals of
some of his most memorable characters. Gainor
Crist, on whom Donleavy has written and
spoken eloquently, the original for Sebastian
Dangerfield, the Ginger Man, and an obvious
mentor for Donleavy, was a fellow student at
Trinity. At Trinity the author officially studied

microbiology, but he says that he never intended to take a degree, and spent his time instead painting, writing, drinking, brawling, and talking with friends. At some point in his first Irish sojourn he married Valerie Heron. He also left his lodgings in Dublin and occupied a cottage in Kilcoole, County Wicklow. By this time Donleavy had abandoned painting for writing; in his words, "I decided then to write a novel which would shake the world. I shook my fist and said I would do it. 'That's what I'm going to do, and no one's going to stop me.'"[2] This book turned out to be *The Ginger Man*. Donleavy brought the unfinished manuscript with him to the United States in 1949 or 1950 and worked in solitude, first at his family's home in the Bronx and then in Boston. In 1952 he submitted the completed novel to Scribner's and Random House; both rejected it on account of its obscenity although both publishers recognized its merits. In 1953 Donleavy returned to Ireland. His explanations of this move are fascinating, deeply emotional, and rather theatrical: he felt rejected by America. Returning to Ireland was exiling himself, though he apparently feels that America spurned him. In his article, "An Expatriate Looks at America," Donleavy quotes from one of his own letters of the time, written to Gainor Crist:

> This is not the land of the big noble rich, everyone is screwed. There is a fantastic red scare here, the whole country undergoing a rigorous censorship. I want to go back to Europe where I can regain my dignity. Come if you will but there is no good life here. It is sad and bitter. Where no man has the opportunity to feel any love. This is a land of lies. The whole country is strangling with the tentacles of the Church and various American legions of Decency. It's all vulgarity obscenity and money. A country of sick hearts and bodies. So tragic that I just sit and sit full of pain.[3]

Though the pain seems real, the logic is peculiar. A man who feels strangled by the Church in America probably should not move to Ireland, a nation with, moreover, a vigorous censorship that prevented publication of *The Ginger Man* twenty years after its American debut. Donleavy's preference for Ireland clearly has more to do with his feeling that that country allows him dignity and peace of mind than with objective conditions. He tells us that when he left the United States "I literally couldn't speak for about 10 weeks. I wrote things down on pieces of paper. I was almost dead." Despite fairly frequent trips since then to New York and residences in London, Donleavy has been an Irish resident since 1953, and an Irish citizen since 1967.

Literary Analysis

The Ginger Man, Donleavy's first novel, was published in France in 1955. At Brendan Behan's suggestion, he submitted his manuscript to the Olympia Press, which agreed to bring it out, but Donleavy was unaware that it was to be part of the Traveler's Companion series, a collection of pornographic works. Donleavy later engaged in extensive litigation with the Olympia Press, trying to recover the copyright; this experience has left him with a lasting distrust of lawyers that he frequently incorporates into his novels. Eventually, he bought Olympia Press to end the litigation. *The Ginger Man* appeared, in expurgated form, in 1956 in England and in 1958 in the United States. It was eventually published in unbowdlerized form in 1963 in London and two years later in the United States. Donleavy's explanations of this peculiar publishing history are ambiguous. Though he considered himself driven from America by censors, though he frequently speaks of shaking his fist at the world and defying it to crush his indomitable spirit, he did censor his own book in order to get it published.

The Ginger Man thus spent some years as an "underground" classic, read and admired particularly by the young, praised by other writers; its protagonist, Sebastian Dangerfield, exercised a powerful attraction on many readers (as, for instance, Rodney Dangerfield, the American comedian, whose stage name is a homage to Sebastian). Donleavy was fairly well known, being regularly compared to England's "Angry Young Men" and the early black humorists in this country when at last the complete book became available for the public. Since its publication, Donleavy has been a prolific writer. Though some of his books are reworkings or collections of work done in the 1950s, he has issued a steady stream of novels and other books. They never reach the best-seller list, but they sell steadily and, he has pointed out, are really cumulative best-sellers. Most of his books are still in print, particularly in England, where his readership and reputation seem to be greatest: his books have made him rich and famous.

Donleavy has testified often, and with an unusual urgency, to the importance of wealth and fame as motivations for his work. For instance, in an interview with Molly McKaughan, to the question of his early motivation, he responds, "That was easy. It was simply money and fame."[4] Later, she asks him what drives him to write, and his response, lovingly elaborated, is "Money, above all things. Fame goes, but money never does. It's got its own beauty. It's never gone to ashes in my mouth. I've always exquisitely enjoyed it." Asked if money has affected his writing, he says, "One hundred percent! Totally and absolutely. In fact, I would say that money is everything in my profession. One's mind almost becomes a vast cash register, clicking away (laughs)."[5] In an article called "Writers and Money," Donleavy maintains that "Writing is turning one's worst moments into money. And money is one of the motives for becoming a writer. The others are leisure and money, women and money, fame and money, and sometimes just money all alone by itself."[6] The flauntingly philistine attitude accords queerly with the claim of complete artistic independence, the I-write-for-myself-and-don't-care-who-likes-it stance that he simultaneously maintains.

Despite his long and active career, Donleavy is still most often identified as the author of *The Ginger Man*, his outstanding accomplishment. He told Molly McKaughan, "I knew I had to write a book that would be the best book in the world. It was that simple."[7] The strengths elaborated in this book are the strengths of Donleavy's later work. He has been unafraid of repeating his effects and, to a certain extent, characters and plot developments; his reputation with critics has suffered to the extent that they see him as repeating (but at a lower level of quality) *The Ginger Man* in his subsequent novels.

The most impressive feature of the novel is the energy and indomitable charm of the protagonist, Dangerfield. Donleavy has made it clear that Dangerfield is in some respects a portrait of Crist, his American fellow student at Trinity. Dangerfield is a rogue, or *picaro*, and he has repellent characteristics that should cost him the reader's sympathies. He is an inveterate sponger, a lazy dreamer, a bad student (the only thing that we learn of his supposed studies in the law is that he cheats), a bad husband and father. He neglects his wife except to abuse her, charm her into bed, or cadge money and shelter from her; he has beaten her when she was pregnant; he has neglected his child so badly that she has rickets. He spends the milk money on drink and pawns her pram. He destroys the plumbing in his house and showers his family with excrement.

Completely ignoring his studies while living on the GI Bill in anticipation of money from his father which will eliminate the need to work ever again, Sebastian has plenty of spare time for riotous drinking escapades and becoming involved in affairs with three women. Eventually, his wife and daughter gone, his academic career officially a shambles, he escapes to London with money supplied by his latest girl, Mary, a simple Irish girl of pneumatic build and insatiable sexuality. There he mistreats Mary but, on Christmas, experiences an ambiguously happy conclusion to his mad career.

This account, which omits most of the raucous incidents of the novel, indicates the refractory material that Donleavy works with. Sebastian Dangerfield is a repellent character, yet Donleavy makes readers accede to his claims and accept Sebastian despite his vices. Sebastian carries us with him in part because of his humor and resourcefulness and his occasional generosity, but mostly because the novel successfully presents him as a victim. The title suggests the theme of man running from death, and Sebastian often refers to himself as a victim of a cruel and dangerous world. He dreams of terrible assaults by organized gangs, and his thoughts return to "the fear. It's coming up from my toes and makes me feel empty and sick. I feel I'm standing before a blackness."[8] And, he tells himself, "I may be just a bit younger than Christ when they tacked him up but they've had me outstretched a few times already" (p. 273). Readers validate Sebastian's self-pity, his dramatizing of his unfair situation. More than one critic has described Egbert Skully (the Dangerfields' landlord) as something of a monster; actually, he just wants to be paid his rent and to be compensated for the furniture and fittings that Sebastian has burned or sold.

In addition to creating a powerful *picaro* and launching him in a series of exciting episodes (not really much of a *plot*), Donleavy has used a new and successful technique in this novel. The two most noticeable features of it are the elliptical use of grammar—frequent sentence fragments, particularly phrases founded on participial phrases—and the shifting point of view. The narrative perspective changes fluidly from third person to first person, dramatizing Sebastian's intermittent attempts to objectify himself. It is clearly an important part of the author's success in ensuring identification with Sebastian. This early passage illustrates both of these qualities, as well as Sebastian's violence and the sentimental underlayer:

> And Dangerfield lifting the axe above a wild head, driving it again and again through the pillow. Screams of money, money. Dragging the mattress out the door, along the hall to the kitchen. Up on the table with it. And the axe is right here ready to cleave the first imposter who sets foot in this room. One more good swig of this. I'm sure it's good for the bowels and at least hurry me to bye byes. Left my soul sitting on a wall and walked away, watching me and grew because souls are like hearts, sort of red and warm, all like a heart.

(p. 25)

A final Donleavy characteristic is the use of little verses, often sentimental or inconsequential or picturesquely poetic or jocose, at the ends of many chapters. One chapter ends with:

> *In*
> *Algeria*
> *There is a town*
> *Called*
> *Tit.*

More emotional (the emotion as is often the case is self-regarding pity) is:

> *I set sail*
> *On this crucifixion Friday*
> *With the stormy heavens*
> *Crushing the sea*
> *And my heart*
> *Twisted*
> *With dying.*

The books that have followed *The Ginger Man* have been a fairly uniform collection. Most of them have male protagonists who become involved in improbable, riotous, ribald adventures. The style continues to employ the devices mentioned above, sometimes to excess. These novels are funny and sad. They are frequently set in Dublin and, when they are not, there is an Irish background to the characters' lives. Heroes are always essentially innocent men, subject to Dangerfieldian moments of *angst* and melancholy (as Donleavy himself seems to be). They are irresistible to women; in every Donleavy novel there is a scene where a beautiful woman tells the hero that *he* is beautiful, that she has long desired him (or desired him intensely since meeting him), that he is a sexual partner of rare gifts. Donleavy's novels involve people with funny names; in them, attorneys figure always as malign forces, and there is much exchanging of letters with law firms. One trait that seems to satisfy Donleavy more than most readers are his alliterative titles: *The Beastly Beatitudes of Balthazar B.*; *The Saddest Summer of Samuel S.*; *Meet My Maker the Mad Molecule*; *The Destinies of Darcy Dancer, Gentleman.*

Each new novel by Donleavy has been greeted as something of a disappointment by reviewers, but there have been rare declarations that some of his more recent books may be better than *The Ginger Man*. The reasons for critical dissatisfaction are varied. One is Donleavy's persistence in making his own way, preserving his own idiosyncratic way of writing. His novels *will* include little poems to close chapters; there *will* be alliteration and stylized use of fragmentary sentences. Another objection is that, after Sebastian Dangerfield, he has never created another hero as interesting or as finely balanced between outrageous behavior and victimization by a cruel world. The hero of *The Beastly Beatitudes of Balthazar B.* (1968), a novel certainly in Donleavy's first rank, is charming but too passive. While the protagonist makes his tentative way through the familiar world of Trinity and Dublin, things happen to him but he is unable to act strongly. He becomes engaged only because the woman he loves seduces him, then proposes to him. He eventually marries someone else out of helplessness. Meanwhile, the active, picaresque role that Sebastian played in *The Ginger Man* is here assigned to Balthazar's friend, Beefy, who is fun although often peripheral to the plot. George Smith, the hero of *A Singular Man* (1963), though he is not so passive, is also glum and lacking in vitality; in this book the preoccupation with death that peeps out from behind the humor in *The Ginger Man* pervades the entire book. The mainspring of action here is George Smith's use of money (he is very rich) to shield himself from danger and construct a mammoth mausoleum for himself. Where Donleavy's novels eschew his vigorous humor or simply fail to provide it, they give the reader nothing to compensate for its absence. His serious ruminations, too, often are unconvincing or even bathetic.

The Ginger Man is essentially the only novel in which Donleavy treats low life. From here on the author concentrates on the kind of world to which Sebastian and his friends aspired—the life of the idle rich. Sebastian's father and father-in-law are, in fact, both rich, and he lives in pursuit of a "golden udder" that will remove him to a higher sphere. He is followed by George Smith, a wealthy businessman who throws paper money from balconies; Balthazar B., who has enormous inherited wealth; Darcy Dancer, a poor but aristocratic owner of an Irish estate; and Clayton Claw Cleaver Clementine, the protagonist of *The Onion Eaters* (1971), who is from an old and distinguished family and the owner of a castle with a staff of servants.

Besides *The Ginger Man*, Donleavy's best novels are *A Singular Man, The Beastly Beatitudes of Balthazar B.*, and *The Saddest Summer of Samuel S. The Destinies of Darcy Dancer, Gentleman* has some of his early vitality and humor. His worst novels are *Schultz* (1979), in which he forsakes the Irish and New York scenes and the type of characters he knows how to manage in favor of a theatrical tale set in London and featuring a vulgar Jewish show-business character, and *The Onion Eaters*, a novel without interest, humor, or even coherence. The hero is distinguished by a passivity unusual even for Donleavy's sad heroes and by the possession of three testicles. Much is made of this unfunny detail. There is the usual collection of odd people, the usual sexual license, and the usual Rabelaisian humor, but it is an insignificant apprentice work resurrected for publication.

In addition to his nine novels, Donleavy has also published a nonfiction book called *The Unexpurgated Code: A Complete Manual of Survival and Manners* (1975). It is an odd book which explains how to achieve undeserved social status and how to survive despite being out of your element. In this manual for social climbers, some of the advice is fascinating. For instance, if it is necessary to announce that you do not have long to live: "in broaching the subject the more sensitive of friends will use cowboy parlance reminiscent of the rough out of doors in deference to the fighting spirit they think you want them to think you have."[9] Some of it is absurd in its irrelevance—how to behave at your own execution, including the possibility that your severed head might mouth obscenities. Some of it is coarse without being really funny—advice on nose-picking, on the clap, "Upon Your Spit Landing on Another." Some of the entries (the book is organized as an etiquette book) express real social nihilism. One chapter, "Knowing When You Have Reached the Top," recommends that you climb to a high balcony overlooking a large crowd; then, "commence peeing. If no one tries to rush the hell out of the way of your pissing all over them, you have reached the top" (p. 62). Elsewhere, the author insists that "nobody likes to kick a man when he's down unless it's the only way of keeping him there" (p. 127). *The Unexpurgated Code*, despite some jokes that fail and a general lack of restraint and taste, is a funny book and an interesting departure from routine by Donleavy.

Summary

Donleavy's recent novel *Leila* (1983) is a continuation of *Darcy Dancer*, so it seems likely that he will continue as he has been writing for thirty years. He is an original, inimitable and unimitated except by himself. He is a combination of Henry Miller, the rollicking Irish tradition, and Franz Kafka. Perhaps he may not reach again the level of *The Ginger Man* but one such book is more than most of his contemporaries have produced. *The Ginger Man* is a comic work of near genius and, combined with a sizable body of good work done since then, it places him among the best of the postwar American comic novelists.

Notes

1. Molly McKaughan, "The Art of Fiction LIII: J.P. Donleavy," *Paris Review*, 63 (Fall 1975): 155.
2. Ibid., p. 125.
3. J.P. Donleavy, *The Ginger Man* (New York: Seymour Lawrence/Delacorte, 1965), p. 41.
4. McKaughan, p. 126.
5. Ibid., pp. 141–142.
6. "Writers and Money: Traumas of the Writing Trade," *Saturday Review*, April 15, 1978, p. 66.
7. McKaughan, p. 126.
8. J.P. Donleavy, *The Ginger Man*, p. 128.
9. J.P. Donleavy, *The Unexpurgated Code: A Complete Manual of Survival and Manners* (New York: Delacorte/Seymour Lawrence, 1975), p. 72.

Selected Bibliography

Primary Sources

Novels

The Ginger Man. Paris: Olympia Press, 1955; expurgated edition New York: McDowell, Obolensky, 1958; unexpurgated edition New York: Seymour Lawrence/Delacorte, 1965.
A Singular Man. Boston: Little, Brown, 1963.
The Saddest Summer of Samuel S. New York: Delacorte/Seymour Lawrence, 1966.
The Beastly Beatitudes of Balthazar B. New York: Seymour Lawrence/Delacorte, 1968.
The Onion Eaters. New York: Seymour Lawrence/Delacorte, 1971.
A Fairy Tale of New York. New York: Delacorte/Seymour Lawrence, 1973.
The Destinies of Darcy Dancer, Gentleman. New York: Seymour Lawrence/Delacorte, 1977.
Schultz. New York: Seymour Lawrence/Delacorte, 1979.
Leila: Further in the Destinies of Darcy Dancer, Gentleman. New York: Delacorte, 1983.

Plays

Fairy Tales of New York. New York: Random House, 1961.
The Ginger Man: A Play. New York: Random House, 1961.
A Singular Man: A Play. London: Bodley Head, 1965.
The Plays of J.P. Donleavy. New York: Delacorte/Seymour Lawrence, 1972.

Stories

Meet My Maker the Mad Molecule. Boston: Little, Brown, 1964.

Other

The Unexpurgated Code: A Complete Manual of Survival and Manners. New York: Delacorte/Seymour Lawrence, 1975.
De Alfonce Tennis, The Superlative Game of Eccentric Champions, Its History, Accoutrements, Rules, Conduct and Regimen. New York: Dutton, 1985.
"An Expatriate Looks at America." *Atlantic Monthly*, December 1976, pp. 37–46.
"Writers and Money: Traumas of the Writing Trade." *Saturday Review*, April 15, 1978, pp. 66–73.

Secondary Sources

Books

Masinton, Charles G. *J.P. Donleavy: The Style of His Sadness and Humor*. Bowling Green, Ohio: Popular Press, 1975. Balanced, clear; good on influences; best, perhaps, on Donleavy's use of language.

Bibliography

Madden, David W. "A Bibliography of J.P. Donleavy." *Bulletin of Bibliography*, 39 (1982): 170–178.

Includes primary and scholarly materials and selected reviews of Donleavy's books through 1981.

Biography

Grant, William E. "J.P. Donleavy." In *Dictionary of Literary Biography*. Vol. 6. *American Novelists Since World War II, Second Series*. Ed. James E. Kibler, Jr. Detroit: Gale, 1980, pp. 83-95. A biographical sketch combined with intelligent criticism and some bibliography.

Interviews

Jacobson, Kurt. "An Interview with J.P. Donleavy." *Journal of Irish Literature*, 8 (1979): 38-48. Mostly concerned with background of *The Ginger Man* and the originals for Dangerfield and O'Keefe in that novel.

McKaughan, Molly. "The Art of Fiction LIII: J.P. Donleavy." *Paris Review* 63 (Fall 1975): 122-166. A thorough, wide-ranging, and exceptionally interesting interview. Donleavy discusses his origins as a novelist, his ideas about art, his views of himself, even his views on exercise and Irish drunkenness.

Articles

"The Black Humorists." *Time*, February 12, 1965, pp. 94-96. Considers Donleavy with Friedman, Barth, Heller, Purdy; describes him as "a uniquely modern Aristophanes with an existential horror of death."

Cohen, Dean. "The Evolution of Donleavy's Hero." *Critique*, 12 (1971): 95-109. Study of Sebastian Dangerfield, George Smith, and Samuel S. Makes much of the Gingerbread Man analogy.

Corrigan, Robert A. "The Artist as Censor: J.P. Donleavy and *The Ginger Man*." *Midcontinent American Studies Journal*, 8 (1967): 60-72. Very interesting examination of Donleavy's bowdlerization of his own book to achieve respectable publication. Comparative examples demonstrate precise expurgations.

LeClair, Thomas. "A Case of Death: The Fiction of J.P. Donleavy." *Contemporary Literature*, 12 (1971): 329-344. Anxiety, dread, and horror of death as motivations in Donleavy's first three novels.

Masinton, Charles G. "Etiquette for Ginger Men: A Critical Assessment of Donleavy's *Unexpurgated Code*." *Midwest Quarterly*, 18 (1977): 210-215. Relates *Code* to Donleavy's novels and both to what the author sees as a general decline.

Morse, Donald F. "The Skull Beneath the Skin: J.P. Donleavy's *The Ginger Man*." *Michigan Academician*, 6 (1974): 273-280. Another discussion of the omnipresence of death and Dangerfield's life as a flight from it.

Norstedt, Johann A. "Irishmen and Irish-Americans in the Fiction of J.P. Donleavy." *Irish-American Fiction: Essays in Criticism*. Ed. Daniel J. Casey and Robert E. Rhodes. New York: AMS, 1979, 115-125. Modest but different approach; treats Donleavy's characters as Irish-Americans, focusing needed attention on O'Keefe in Ginger Man; relative degrees of loathing toward Ireland and U.S.

Podhoretz, Norman. "The New Nihilism and the Novel." *Doings and Undoings*. New York: Farrar, Straus, 1964. Good on *The Ginger Man*. Says Dangerfield's claim on our sympathy is his honesty.

Shaw, Patrick W. "The Satire of J.P. Donleavy's *Ginger Man*." *Studies in Contemporary Satire*, 1 (1975): 9-16. Reads *The Ginger Man* as not just picaresque but a satire on society, which inhibits freedom.

Sherman, William D. "Hard Times and the Noble Savage." *The Hollins Critic*, 1 (1964): 1-4, 6-11. Analysis of Donleavy's earlier works primarily in terms of their dramatization of desperate need for money and love.

———. "J.P. Donleavy: Anarchic Man as Dying Dionysian." *Twentieth Century Literature*, 13 (1968): 216-227. Relates *The Ginger Man* to "a literary sensibility which embraces an attitude and response toward life which I shall call 'comic anarchy.'"

Vintner, Maurice. "The Artist as Clown: The Fiction of J.P. Donleavy." *Meanjin Quarterly*, 29 (1970): 108-114. General overview of early work; sees Donleavy as writer who has for years "stood at the edge of greatness."

Weales, Gerald. "No Face and No Exit: The Fiction of James Purdy and J.P. Donleavy." *Contemporary American Novelists*. Ed. Harry T. Moore. Carbondale: Southern Illinois University Press, 1964, pp. 143-154. Astute on Sebastian as victim: he is possible as saint "only if we accept that he makes his own arrows."

Merritt Moseley

Douglas, Jack [Jack Crickard]

Born: 1908

Education: Lynbrook (New York) High School; expelled for hitting the janitor, 1927

Marriages: Three; two divorces, including singer Marion Hutton; last marriage, Reiko, 1960, two children

Biography

Jack Douglas was born in 1908 in Lynbrook, New York. He described the location as rural and generally uninteresting: "About the only fun we had was watching railroad crossing accidents" (*Funny Thing*, p. 14). His mother was English with a theatrical background; his father worked as a cable engineer. Douglas played drums in the high school band, gaining experience that helped him break into show business as a drummer/singer at a dance marathon in Madison Square Garden. He left the entertainment field briefly for a plunge into professional boxing when he became unhappy with his salary: "Rudy Vallee . . . was getting $19,950 a week more than I was" (*Funny Thing*, p. 24). After training seriously in Orangeburg, New York, with Jack Sharkey and other notable fighters, he lost his first bout to an opponent who knocked him down 13 times in 6 rounds: "He won a unanimous decision. Even *I* voted for him" (*Funny Thing*, p. 32).

Soon thereafter he returned to music, drumming with the Al Vann Orchestra. He also worked as a caddy, a stunt flyer, and a messenger boy before leaving the East Coast for California. There he supplemented drumming and singing engagements with radio comedy, teaming with Cliff Arquette and Red Corcoran on a show called *The Franco Hi-Jinks*. In addition, he became a dancing chorus boy and introduced a singing/comedy act at the Cotton Club in Culver City. Then he joined the Buddy Rogers road band for bookings that included the Chicago World Fair. Next came a stand with a Cuban rumba ensemble. Drinking and disorderly behavior tended to limit the length of his affiliation with any single group. In 1939, he successfully toured England as a stand-up comedian.

His first writing job came the following year, when Bob Hope asked him to supply jokes for a new radio program. Hope's belief in competition writing—pitting gagmen against each other to see who could produce the funniest material—provided excellent training in a pressure cooker. Douglas notes that "Hope had an uncanny knack for picking writing talent, including myself. To hell with *modesty*—that's for strip teasers" (*Funny Thing*, p. 53). He went on to write successful radio and television comedy for Ozzie and Harriet Nelson, Dean Martin and Jerry Lewis, Jimmy Durante, Jack Carson, Johnny Carson, Phil Harris, Garry Moore, Danny Thomas, Ed Wynn, Jack Paar, and others. In 1955, he received a comedy-writing Emmy for the extremely popular *George Gobel Show*; his work helped win another Emmy award for Red Skelton. He also wrote and doctored film scripts, including the early "Road" movies of Bob Hope and Bing Crosby.

Douglas was noted for his eccentric lifestyle. While denying rumors that he shot at aircraft flying over his home, he did surround the property with a steel fence and signs identifying it as the "Northridge Lion Farm." After building a new $100,000 house in California, he went on the road with a comedian and never returned to live in it, later explaining: "Sometimes things happen when you're away on the road. Something did. Something blond" (*Funny Thing*, p. 90). Back in the West working with Skelton, he surprised his family one day by acquiring a high-speed Jaguar—"My wife warned me: if I ever raced it, she'd leave me. I raced it. She left me" (*Funny Thing*, p. 103). He raced competi-

tively for several years, reaching tenth in the national ratings before a serious accident at Torrey Pines, California, persuaded him to drop the sport in 1956.

The following year he became a television personality, making the first of more than 50 guest appearances on Jack Paar's *Tonight* show. Although he had given up drinking years earlier, many viewers mistook him for a lush because he spoke with a lazy drawl, "mainly because I drawl and I'm lazy" (*Funny Thing*, p. 147). In 1960 while rehearsing a new night club act, he met Reiko, a young Japanese singer. They married less than seven weeks later despite language difficulties: "My Japanese consisted of two words—'sessue' and 'hayakawa'" (*Funny Thing*, p. 162). Reiko brought stability and a note of contentment into his life. The couple made many television appearances together. They have two sons, Bobby and Timothy.

Literary Analysis

Douglas's popularity as a television personality helped stimulate the publication of his first book, *My Brother Was an Only Child*, in 1959. The material had been created ten years earlier and privately distributed among 500 of the author's acquaintances with the title *No Navel to Guide Him*. It became an underground hit at California cocktail parties, but when Douglas followed friends' advice and tried to publish the work, he received cold and even angry rejections. Only his popularity on *The Tonight Show* led to a publisher's being persuaded to take a chance on it.

The book was as off-beat and full of surprises as its author. There was no plot; its ninety-six pages contained forty-seven chapters of anecdotes, short jokes, and black humor. Some chapters related narratives of zany characters including "George the Toilet Seat," "Of Jones," "Ptarmigan Psmith," "Doctor Murgeon, the Virgin Surgeon," and "Old John," who "wasn't always known as Old John. When Old John was young he was known as *Young* Old John." Chapter Seven offered a "Tim Snopes" story that began: "The last time I saw Old Tim Snopes he was just a shell of his former self. In fact, when you held him up to your ear you could hear the ocean."

Chapter 36 followed the sad demise of barrister "Titus Fenn," a deaf-mute who turned bad when he started talking too much: "He went on and on. No matter what the subject, just mention anything and he'd start running off at the hands." In mixed company, Titus would "put soot on his fingers and tell dirty stories." He finally paid for his indulgences when he called a cab driver a vile name with his index finger: "The driver promptly slammed the taxicab door on it, and to this day that finger has a slight lisp."

Chapters that did not contain narrative surprised readers with a variety of gags. The text of Chapter 19 said only: "To hell with Chapter 19. Every damn book you pick up has a Chapter 19." Chapter 28 read, "For Men Only. (Hold a lighted match behind this page.)" Chapter 32 contained precautionary instructions for "How to Train an Aardvark," while in Chapter 57 readers were told "How to Make a Zombie" (get her drunk).

Heavily plugged by Paar, the book soared onto the best-seller list within a few weeks and remained there for more than six months. Douglas followed it with a popular sequel. *Never Trust a Naked Bus Driver* (1960) came in the same format (116 pages, 47 chapters), with highlights including "The Most Unforgettable Marquis I Ever Met," "Songs My English Mother Thought She Could Sing," "Winners of the 1960 Fortune Cooky Writer's Contest," and "The Golden Book of Sex." In "The Wonderful World of Narcotics," a scholarly Douglas noted the positive effect of drugs on some important artists: "How about Edgar Allan Poe—could he have written *War and Peace* without the use of narcotics? I think not. And how about Tolstoy—without the right needle in the right vein I doubt very much if he would have ever gone near a piano and 'Suwanee River' and 'The Old Folks at Home' would have been lost to the world."

His next book, *A Funny Thing Happened to Me on My Way to the Grave* (1962), offered name-dropping autobiography spiced with anecdotes about show business, California living, auto racing, and women, including an eighty-year-old admirer who wanted to marry him. *The Adventures of Huckleberry Hashimoto* (1964) continued in the autobiographical mode, describing the Douglas family's adventures while traveling to Tahiti, Hawaii, and Reiko's home in Japan. "Huckleberry Hashimoto" was a nickname for his young son, Bobby.

Next came *The Neighbors Are Scaring My Wolf* (1968), an account of the Douglases' attempt to live peacefully in the affluent community of Old New Litchridge, Connecticut. The place was populated with fictitious neighbors including the frightening "Olenka Kloompt" and a ubiquitous set of horseback riders: "The horses seem to be able to control themselves admirably until they reach our place. Then it's bombs away! I've tried following them around with my Little Miss Muffet Manure Spreader, but they kick me. The *riders*—not the horses."

This story line of the family seeking to live happily among unstable and insensitive people established a pattern for Douglas's succeeding books. In *Shut Up and Eat Your Snowshoes* (1970) the clan escaped to an isolated setting in Lost Lake, Ontario, Canada. *What Do You Hear from Walden Pond?* (1971) returned them

briefly to Hollywood while unhappy Jack worked on a made-for-TV movie. In *The Jewish-Japanese Sex and Cookbook and How to Raise Wolves* (1972), they were back in Connecticut with pets that included a Pomeranian, an Alaskan malamute, a mountain lion, and a litter of timber wolves. *Benedict Arnold Slept Here: Jack Douglas' Honeymoon Mountain Inn* (1975) recounted their misadventures as temporary owners of a picturesque but troublesome hotel in Maine. *Going Nuts in Brazil with Jack Douglas* (1977) found the family in South America, witnessing the introduction of condoms among the natives. (The devices were finally accepted in some localities as bus tokens.) And *Rubber Duck* (1979) looked back to Old New Litchridge and "Mrs. Ogelvie," an offensive nurse Reiko found floating dead in the bathtub one Sunday morning.

These later titles attracted little critical attention and failed to achieve the popularity of Douglas's initial works. The gags were still good, but they came embedded in story lines of only mild interest. Douglas shackled his black humor in the service of plots that presented him and his family as isolated rational beings adrift in a mad world. To sustain the illusion he leaned on a supporting cast of cruel lawyers, weak-minded public officials, busty women, and other vulnerable prototypes. Nevertheless, he remained as adept as ever with the outrageous anecdote and the switch. His experience scripting for comedians gave his storytelling a well-tuned sense of rhythm and timing. His best material hinged on key words that were often italicized as if for recitation. Even the carelessly written *Going Nuts in Brazil* contained such unforgettable asides as the following:

> The Cambridges had outdone themselves on this party; Bobby Short was at the piano, entertaining his little heart out. No one was paying any attention to him because no one in Brazil had ever heard of him except a little Jewish couple who had once made a pilgrimage to New York's Carlyle Hotel to hear him. They applauded everything he played. They even applauded when he didn't play. Finally about eleven p.m., Bobby asked them to stop. They didn't, so Bobby told them if they didn't stop overdoing it he would cut off his hands. They didn't stop and you can guess the rest. Bobby's now back playing at the Carlyle, but he sounds kind of *thumpy*.
>
> (p. 163)

Summary

A gifted comedy writer, TV personality, and nightclub performer, Jack Douglas's best books,

My Brother Was an Only Child and *Never Trust a Naked Bus Driver*, combined unplotted collections of anecdotes and gags into volumes of eccentric humor.

Selected Bibliography

Primary Sources

Books

My Brother Was an Only Child. New York: E.P. Dutton, 1959.

Never Trust a Naked Bus Driver. New York: E.P. Dutton, 1960.

A Funny Thing Happened to Me on My Way to the Grave. New York: E.P. Dutton, 1962.

The Adventures of Huckleberry Hashimoto. New York: E.P. Dutton, 1964.

The Neighbors Are Scaring My Wolf. New York: E.P. Dutton, 1968.

Shut Up and Eat Your Snowshoes. New York: G.P. Putnam's Sons, 1970.

What Do You Hear from Walden Pond? New York: G.P. Putnam's Sons, 1971.

The Jewish-Japanese Sex and Cookbook and How to Raise Wolves. New York: G.P. Putnam's Sons, 1972.

Benedict Arnold Slept Here: Jack Douglas' Honeymoon Mountain Inn. New York: G.P. Putnam's Sons, 1975.

Going Nuts in Brazil with Jack Douglas. New York: G.P. Putnam's Sons, 1977.

Rubber Duck. New York: G.P. Putnam's Sons, 1979.

Recordings

Jack Douglas at the Bon Soir. Columbia, 1960.

Secondary Sources

"Gyrations of the Gagmen." *Newsweek*, 53 (June 1, 1959): 83. A brief account of Douglas's dismissal from the writing staff of Jack Paar's *Tonight* show.

"Toynbee Doob's Pal." *Time*, 73 (June 15, 1959): 74. A half-page look at Douglas's eccentric lifestyle stimulated by the popularity of *My Brother Was an Only Child*. Contains a photo.

Stuart Kollar

Dunne, Finley Peter

Born: Chicago, Illinois, on July 10, 1867
Education: West Division High School, Chicago, 1884
Marriage: Margaret Abbott, 1902, four children
Died: April 24, 1936

Biography

Finley Peter Dunne was born Peter Dunne, Jr., in St. Patrick's Parish on Chicago's Near West Side, on July 10, 1867. Finley was his mother's maiden name, which he would adopt shortly after her death from tuberculosis in 1883. He was the fifth of seven children and born a twin (his brother died in infancy) to middle-class Irish immigrants. His father, Peter Dunne, was from Queens (now Laoighis, or Leix) and Ellen Finley was from Kilkenny; she was 25 years younger than her husband, who was a carpenter and real estate owner. Dunne family tradition held that the menfolk should be either carpenters or clergymen; one uncle was Vicar General of the Chicago Diocese, and a Riordan cousin would be Archbishop of San Francisco for thirty years. Finley Peter would break with those traditions: his religion was perfunctory, and early in life he showed talent for writing, debate, and witticism rather than craft. He was not even a consistent Irish-American Democrat in politics and later would count Republicans Theodore Roosevelt and Warren Harding among his closest political friends.

Immediately after graduation from high school in 1884 (he was the only boy of the family to attend), Dunne went to work for the *Chicago Telegram*. Becoming their sports reporter, he was credited with coining the term "southpaw" while covering White Stocking games. In 1888, he moved to the *Times* as political and city editor; 1889 saw him on the *Daily Tribune* staff; in 1890 he became a political reporter for the *Herald*. He began to hit his stride, however, when he joined the *Evening Post* in 1892, for managing editor Cornelius McAuliff encouraged him again to break with tradition and write ironic, satirical editorials rather than the stuffy comments on politics that were expected. Until its sale to zealous Republican Herman Kohlsaat in 1896, the paper was independent and irreverent politically. Throughout the 1890s, whether for the *Post*, or after 1896 for the *Daily Journal*, Dunne wrote scathing, reform-minded satire, lambasting corrupt common councilmen, "Boss" John Powers, traction magnate Charles Yerkes, and George Pullman. He consistently supported the Municipal Reform Association and was credited with especially effective editorials in the crucial 1898 elections. Later, Dunne would be asssociated with noted Progressives Lincoln Steffens, Ray Stannard Baker, Ida Tarbell, and William Allen White on *American* and *Collier's* magazines, although he sometimes made fun of them.

On December 4, 1892, Dunne debuted as a dialect humorist, again due to McAuliff's prompting. The *Evening Post* had a new Sunday edition, and in its second issue Dunne introduced Colonel McNeary, a thin disguise for Dearborn Street tavern owner James McGarry, who ran a saloon for journalists, businessmen, and politicians. McNeary was heckled continuously by John McKenna, a real-life local Republican. While McKenna relished the notoriety and was disappointed when he was eventually replaced in 1896 by Malachi Hennessy as a foil, McGarry complained that his identity had been penetrated and that he was embarrassed at the jibes. Thus, on October 7, 1893, Dunne moved the fictitious saloon to "Archey Road" (Archer Avenue) in Bridgeport, a mostly Irish working-class neighborhood. McNeary was replaced by fellow County Roscommon bartender Martin Dooley. For the rest of the decade, Dooley held forth in working-class brogue on local politics, Irish-American ethnic life, and general social issues.

National politics and American foreign policy at the turn of the century and Dunne's comments on them turned his local audience into a national one. Mr. Dooley's acerbic comments on our imperial adventures and particularly his reaction to "His Cousin George" (Admiral Dewey) in the Philippines made Dunne's fortune. Boston publishers Small and Maynard brought out *Mr. Dooley in Peace and in War*, a collection of pieces from the *Post* and *Journal*, of which half were specifically topical. The volume sold 10,000 copies a month in 1898 and was displaced from the best-seller list only by the second collection, *Mr. Dooley in the Hearts of His Countrymen*, released the next year. Eventually, Dunne published eight collections by Mr. Dooley, which included about one third of the over 700 dialect essays. Americans memorized and recited his tag-lines and made them political currency; three U.S. presidents read his essays and discussed them in Cabinet meetings. Theodore Roosevelt kept up a critical friendship and correspondence with Dunne, reacting to his jibes.

Dunne was now a celebrity, a wealthy man who appreciated luxury and spent his money almost as quickly as it came in. He left the *Journal* and Chicago at the end of 1900 and moved to New York. He travelled to Ireland to visit his parents' home counties, to Italy for an audience with the Pope, and to France where he proposed to socialite Margaret Abbott, whom he married in 1902. Between 1903 and 1910, the couple would have four children, including a set of twins. They settled on Long Island, near Southampton; Dunne became an avid golfer and founder of the National Golf Links of America. William C. and Payne Whitney were among his friends; Payne left him a bequest of $500,000 in 1928 that enabled Dunne to retire.

During the 1900s and 1910s Dunne divided his time among dialect pieces, non-dialect editorials, and essays for a number of magazines. He began to write for *Collier's* in 1902 and edited the *New York Morning Telegraph* from 1902 to 1904. In 1906 he joined a group of Progressives who had left *McClure's* to produce *American* magazine. From 1906 to 1915 he contributed "In the Interpreter's House," which employed symbolic characters such as "Worldly Wiseman" to enunciate a learned and broadly humanistic philosophy toward public affairs. For six months in 1911 he wrote "In the Bleachers" for *Metropolitan*, a right-wing socialist journal. In 1915, he returned to *Collier's* for four years as editor. No Dooley essays appeared after 1916 (their production had dwindled after 1912), although financial need caused their brief reappearance from 1924 to 1926 for the Bell Syndicate and *Liberty* magazine.

After 1926, Dunne ceased writing, except for a series of epistolary memoirs (done at the insistence of his son Philip) while he was terminally ill with cancer. He died in New York on April 24, 1936, and was given a grand funeral in St. Patrick's Cathedral.

Literary Analysis

Mr. Dooley has achieved a firm position in American literature and folklore. His topical and philosophical aphorisms are staples in the repertory of politicians and lawyers, political scientists and historians. Dunne's neighborhood saloonkeeper is godfather to this century's leading political humorists, from Will Rogers to Mort Sahl, Russell Baker, and Art Buchwald. Edward Asner portrayed him before the nation at the 1976 Democratic National Convention. "Dooleyisms" are so imbedded in public discourse that they no longer need their original context. "Hands across the sea and into someone's pocket" has a portable cynicism removed from the debate over the Philippines; "the Supreme Court follows the election returns" has a relevance beyond *Downes v. Bidwell*. Dunne's nonpolitical gag lines have a similar perennial impact: "Not being an author, I'm a great critic," for example, has had usage far beyond its original references to childrearing. Dooley's store of mother-wit as well as topical dissection and his way with a pun or gag made him a giant among humorous creations. It is fitting, if ironic, that

Dunne's creation has swallowed its creator, that many who quote Mr. Dooley have little memory or appreciation of Finley Peter Dunne.

It is fitting, because Mr. Dooley was not simply Dunne's persona; Philip Dunne has rightly argued that he was a special creation, a fully realized character that his father constructed with meticulous care to be true to a fictitious biography, occupation, and social class.[1] Certainly Dooley was not used as a shield behind which Dunne could be outrageous; Dunne was even more outspoken in many of his editorials during the 1890s. (Although it is true that as Dunne mellowed after the 1900s, Dooley became more the genial philosopher than the caustic observer.) The symbolic characters of "In the Interpreter's House," especially Mr. Worldly Wiseman, are generally held to represent Dunne's personality and ideology more clearly than do the inhabitants of the saloon. Furthermore, when Dunne did allow Dooley to step out of character in order to represent the author's anger, as in his sarcasm about the Dreyfus case, the results were weak. While Dunne usually wrote editorials with ease, he sweated and procrastinated over the Dooley pieces in order to be true to his creation as well as to himself. His later inability to imagine himself in Bridgeport once he had become a conservative socialite pained him and eventually helped convince him to stop writing.

If Dooley was a creation, separate and distinct from Dunne, the achievement was all the more impressive. For two dozen years the author evolved and sustained a fictional character whose background and viewpoints were different from his own, though not diametrically so. Martin Dooley was no stage Irishman, capable merely of witty wordplay and vainglory in facing a suspicious America. Instead, while Dunne's inspiration still held, he created a whole human being, as capable as any real person of the gamut of feelings, attitudes, and reactions. "The Sage of Archey Road" enchanted readers because of his believability as well as by his humor.

Dooley's believability was based in great part on language. Dunne "revered the art of saying things perfectly: he hated slovenliness of thought and expression."[2] Dunne's use of dialect may trouble modern readers unfamiliar with the brogue or uncomfortable about its past association with ethnic slurs,[3] but it is essential to grasping Dunne's creativity and the Dooley character. McNeary, as a genteel proprietor with an educated Loop clientele, spoke a generalized Irish-English. Dooley, on the other hand, lived and worked in the predominantly Irish, proletarian Sixth Ward and spoke the brogue of the district and of his social class. Dunne did not simply mispronounce for comedic effect, as had a previous generation of "phunny phellow" humorists; he carefully reproduced the neighborhood argot.[4] Moreover, his early dialect pieces were redolent of Gaelic-American life in the Bridgeport district: sodalities, Irish card games like "45," Gaelic words and expressions, reflections of "old country" parochial rivalries. Dunne, a middle-class, assimilated child of Leinster parents, had to place himself in the mind and speech patterns of a West Country Connaughtman who had come over in steerage, had been a manual laborer, and reflected Roscommon prejudices against people from Limerick, Mayo, Waterford, and Kilkenny (his mother's county). These would have to ring true in a city whose Irish population had recently tripled and now represented over 20% of Chicago. Thus, the dialect provided more than clownish access, a verbal mask, or even "an element of poetry";[5] it created verisimilitude.

The use of dialect and ethnic vignette also enabled Dunne, as a pioneer Irish urban humorist, to point out the successful Irish adjustment and contribution to American life. Dooley was no recent immigrant but a Chicago resident since before the 1871 Fire; he and his people antedated recent native-born migrants. As a property owner and civic leader, no matter how humble, he was a part of urban progress. Bridgeport was a hard-working, proud community whose people had created a successful life. Except perhaps for "Hogan," the snobbish intellectual, none of the Archey Road denizens were portrayed in anything but a sympathetic light. Some, in fact, emerged as quiet, tragic heroes like Shaughnessey, who persevered despite disappointments and stoic lonely old age, or the Irish firemen who performed brave deeds until the last conflagration killed them. Many of the early essays are of this type: homely, toilsome, humble people fight to make a decent life in the industrial slums. The tales are as full of pathos and anger as of humor.

Further, Dunne used the early dialect essays to have Dooley inform non-Irish readers about Irish history and politics, Orangemen and Fenians. He did so in a manner intended to create both sympathy and reassurance: sympathy for Irish oppression and reassurance that Fenians were wordy bumblers rather than alien terrorists. For example, see "On a Plot" (1898) or "The Freedom Picnic" (1899). This humorous treatment of Irish-American nationalism earned Dunne the hatred of Clan-na-Gael extremist John Finerty but enabled Dooley, as a loyal, naturalized citizen, to use his brogue to ridicule the voguish Anglo-Saxon nativism.

Another result of Dunne's using dialect was to highlight the tension between Dooley's worldview and that of a changing America.

James De Muth has noted that "Mr. Dooley warmly affirmed, for Chicago's ordinary citizens, the contemporary relevance of their commonplace, conventional tastes and orthodox morality."[6] This cannot have come easily to one who did not share those "conventional tastes." In fact, one series for the *Ladies' Home Journal* in which Dooley ventured to disparage the feminist "Molly Donahue" was so distasteful to Dunne the reformer that he cancelled it after four stories. Rather than warm affirmation, the Dooley character increasingly represented a link to Chicago's social past, and both the older generation's brogue and his own hermetic life inside the saloon were appropriate to Dooley's increasing skepticism. Just as Dunne gradually became incapable of recreating Dooley's milieu, so the tavernkeeper became estranged from the Archer Avenue of a younger, assimilative generation eager to change the image of the Archey Road. Only Hennessy remained as a steady customer, and even so, the dialect pieces became more monologue than dialogue. Because Dooley was a lifelong working-class Irishman, Dunne could be only tentative about themes of upward mobility central to the humor of the next generation.

A final purpose for dialect humor was democratic reductionism. Dunne excelled at using ludicrous analogy to deflate pretension, and a proletarian brogue provided several tools to this end. Here he continued the tradition of the folk-moralists from Seba Smith on who had used rude manner and vulgar speech to "confidently pierce the complex rationalizations clouding controversial public issues and reduce arrogant public figures to the modest stature of the farmers, clerics, tradesmen, and local politicians they knew so well."[7] Admiral Dewey became "Cousin George" or a ward-heeler uncle, Henry Cabot Lodge "brave Hinnery the moonlighter," and the War Department Strategy Board demented, cracker-barrrel checkers players. McKinley may have been President but so was Dooley (of his liquor store), and neither man could explain our foreign policy. This reductionism via brogue was also an ideal method by which Dunne could entertainingly educate readers about the complex issues themselves. His topical essays in *Mr. Dooley in Peace and in War* and in subsequent books about diplomacy, warfare, national politics and the Supreme Court are full of excellent examples. Homely analogies and brogue conduct the reader through fact-laden, informative journalism; here is one area where Dooley is more persona than character. Finally, the brogue gave Dunne access to puns and ironic turns of phrase that were both funny and pointed. Referring to the United States's behavior toward Filipinos, for instance, "treated" became "threated"; the Jekyl Island retreat of the multimillionaires became "Shekel Island"; the industrialists' and bankers' trusts—"thrusts"!

By the time that a national audience discovered Mr. Dooley in 1898, Dunne had matured and fixed his use of language. The essays continued sharp and tart, impudent, full of the rhythms of democratic discourse, and laden with those bilingual puns or conversational interjections that so attracted and influenced James Joyce and other writers.[8]

Similarly, Dunne had fixed the form in which Dooley presented his views. A newspaper item or a stray remark by Hennessy would provoke a snort from Dooley, who would then launch his monologue. Because both Dunne and Dooley were didactic, the essay would first present opposing views on an issue (fact-laden if political), while the speaker searched for a simile, a metaphor, or an anecdote by which to illustrate or "reduce" the issue. Troubles within the Belgian royal family might reveal the shared experiences of life; life itself might be likened to a Pullman dining car. Dooley might discourse on fame, envy, and debunking by remarking that "if Julius Caysar was alive to-day he'd be doin' a lock-step down in Joliet," or he might reduce the pompous with a well-placed descriptive pun, as when General Funston became General "Fustian." Arriving at a characteristically skeptical conclusion, he would allow Hennessy a comment, then close with a punch line.

While Dooley's form and address would not change, the subjects of his essays would. After 1900, neither Dunne nor Dooley surveyed Chicago politics or the Archey Road. Increasingly, the nonpolitical essays were concerned with larger, less parochial topics: travel, friendship, religion, women, books, children. Critics have been of two minds about Dooley the avuncular philosopher: some see him broadening his understanding, others as having lost his original immediacy. In any case, the change was inevitable as Dunne moved to New York and strove for a broader audience.

Dooley's political focus was also different; national affairs now absorbed his attention. In part, this was due to the success of the Spanish-American War essays and of the new audience for his monologues. In part, too, this arose from the enlarged influence of Finley Peter Dunne. William Gibson has revealed the extent to which Dunne and Theodore Roosevelt corresponded and visited and the extent to which Roosevelt reacted to Dooley essays. While never losing his independent viewpoint, Dunne became a member of the Oyster Bay circle and the President's crowd became a "most cherished source of copy."[9] Dunne was also working closely with noted Progressive writers on *Collier's*, *American*, and *Metropolitan* during the era.

Mr. Dooley could not help but be amused by those slam-bang years. The result was a new series of creative tensions between Dooley and the dialect essayist.

The two were equally disturbed by Rooseveltian foreign policy. Considering U.S. behavior in the Philippines hypocritical bullying, Dooley saved some of his angriest sarcasm for American treatment of small nations. Generally, though, whereas Dunne tended to a deep cynicism about domestic reform, the Dooley essays retained a hope-laden skepticism more in tune with his readers' conceptions of Progressivism.

Dunne thought that some reforms, such as the educational and public health work of the social settlements, were beyond criticism or satire but that most reformers were self-deluded about human nature and institutional change. Worldly Wiseman derided capitalism as well as socialism and was increasingly critical of our culture as a whole. Historians disagree as to whether Dunne created a reading public for exposure journalism, but they agree that he did not believe in muckraking or in formulas for change. Like Brand Whitlock, he inclined toward a philosophical anarchism or fatalism.[10] Dooley, on the other hand, recognized life being bettered even if human nature was intractable. He noted that reform came only through middle-class fright, but it *did* come. In his classic commentary on Progressivism, "National Housecleaning," he reassured Hennessy that "th' noise ye hear is not th' first gun iv a rivolution. It's on'y th' people iv th' United States batin' a carpet. Ye object to th' smell? That's nawthin'. We use sthrong disinfectants here."[11] While complaining that the jabs smarted, Roosevelt considered Dooley a positive force toward progressive change. Dooley, in turn, agreed with the general outlines of the "New Nationalism," especially on the need for government activism to make both labor and capital responsible to the people.[12]

After about 1910, and certainly by World War I, Dunne realized that Dooley was becoming more nostalgic and discursive than sharply observant. Some of this he attributed to his own change in life style, some to generational change, but much to the absence of a hospitable atmosphere for his joshing humor. "Humor," he told his son, "is a privilege of the innocent and the secure. As a nation we have lost both our innocence and our security. . . . Humor is only effective as a political weapon when the victim has enough humor in himself to perceive that he has been wounded."[13] Dooley, typically, was earthier about the matter: "I wuddn't want to have me life prolonged till I become a nuisance. I'd like to live as long as life is bearable to me an' as long afther that as I am

bearable to life, an' think I'd like a few years to think it over."[14]

Summary

Finley Peter Dunne produced brilliant dialect humor in books, magazines, and newspapers for a generation. Both politically influential and acute, he set a standard for later political humorists. He borrowed from a number of traditions to develop Mr. Dooley. His tavernkeeper was a crackerbox philosopher, a dialectician, a tall-tale raconteur, an Irish storyteller with a persistent concern for the sound of the spoken language. His linguistic portfolio included malapropisms, unorthodox spellings, repetition, paradoxical leveling, transformed cliché, absurd juxtaposition, and double entendre. Above all, he endowed Dooley with a keen wit, human concern, a sense of critical observation, and a realistic irony that kept his essays lively. He has been one of the few topical humorists whose material has not quickly become quaint or anachronistic. His work has been a beloved resource not only because it illuminates a period and reflects upon the doings of charismatic leaders or flamboyant villains but because it is still howlingly funny.

Notes

1. Philip Dunn, ed., *Mr. Dooley Remembers* (Boston: Little Brown, 1963), pp. 50–51.
2. Elmer Ellis, ed., *Mr. Dooley at His Best* (New York: Scribner's, 1938), p. xiii.
3. Georg Mann, "Call for Mr. Dooley," *Eire Ireland*, 9 (Autumn 1974): 119–127.
4. Clyde Thogmartin, "Mr Dooley's Brogue: The Literary Dialect of Finley Peter Dunn," *Visible Language*, 16 (Spring 1982): 184–198.
5. Bernard Duffey, *The Chicago Renaissance* (Westport, Conn.: Greenwood, 1972), p. 23.
6. James De Muth, *Small Town Chicago* (Port Washington, N.Y.: Kennikat, 1980), p. 35.
7. James De Muth, "Finley Peter Dunne," *Dictionary of Literary Biography*, Vol. 11: *American Humorists 1800–1950*, ed. Stanley Trachtenberg (Detroit: Gale, 1982), p. 126.
8. Grace Eckley, *Finley Peter Dunne* (New York: Twayne, 1981), pp. 148–150.
9. William H. Gibson, *Theodore Roosevelt Among the Humorists* (Knoxville: University of Tennessee Press, 1980), pp. 46–65.
10. John Harrison, "Finley Peter Dunne and the Progressive Movement," *Journalism Quarterly*, 44 (1967): 475–481; John Semonche, "The *American Magazine* of 1906–1915," *Journalism Quarterly*, 40 (1963): 86.
11. Both this, and "The Food We Eat," two repeatedly anthologized essays on Progressive reform, appeared originally in *Dissertations by Mr. Dooley* (New York: Harper and Brothers, 1906; rpt. Upper Saddle River, N.J.: Literature House, 1969).
12. Ibid., p. 64.
13. Dunne, p. 213.
14. Ellis, p. 245.

Selected Bibliography

Primary Sources

Anthologies

The World of Mr. Dooley. Ed. Louis Filler. New York: Collier, 1962. Includes some nondialect pieces from *American* magazine.

Mr. Dooley on the Choice of Law. Ed. Edward J. Bander. Charlottesville: Michie, 1963. A legal scholar and columnist's specialized selection.

Mr. Dooley and the Chicago Irish. Ed. Charles Fanning. New York: Arno, 1976. An anthology of Dunne's 1890s' *Evening Post* columns on Chicago Irish community life with an important introductory essay.

Mr. Dooley's Chicago. Ed. Barbara C. Schaaf. Garden City: Doubleday, 1977. Dialect columns from the *Evening Post* on Chicago municipal politics with introductions. A solid bibliography on Chicago history and literature. Very valuable.

Memoirs

Mr. Dooley Remembers. Ed. Philip Dunne. Boston: Little Brown, 1963. A series of essay memoirs Finley Peter Dunne wrote while terminally ill, with commentary by his son.

Essays

Mr. Dooley in Peace and in War. Boston: Small, Maynard, 1898; rpt. New York: Greenwood, 1968.

Mr. Dooley in the Hearts of His Countrymen. Boston: Small, Maynard, 1899; rpt. New York: Greenwood, 1969.

Mr. Dooley's Philosophy. New York: R.H. Russell, 1900.

Mr. Dooley's Opinions. New York: R.H. Russell, 1901.

Observations of Mr. Dooley. New York: R.H. Russell, 1902; rpt. New York: Greenwood, 1969.

Dissertations by Mr. Dooley. New York: Harper and Brothers, 1906; rpt. Upper Saddle River, N.J.: Literature House, 1969.

Mr. Dooley Says. New York: Scribner's, 1910.

Mr. Dooley on Making a Will and Other Necessary Evils. New York: Scribner's, 1919.

Secondary Sources

Biographies and Monographs

Bander, Edward J. *Mr. Dooley and Mr. Dunne: The Literary Life of a Chicago Catholic.* Charlottesville: Michie, 1981. Puts creator and character into perspective; collects Mr. Dooley's "best lines." Extended, annotated bibliography, and appendix listing and categorizing the 530 dialect essays Dunne produced for the *Evening Post.* An invaluable research tool.

Brown, Malcolm. *The Politics of Irish Literature.* Seattle: University of Washington, 1972. Background to the ethnic influences in Dunne's style.

Brown, Thomas N. *Irish-American Nationalism 1870-1890.* Philadelphia: Lippincott, 1966. Useful to understand political and historical references in Dunne's earlier pieces.

Eckley, Grace. *Finley Peter Dunne.* New York: Twayne, 1981. Concise, thoughtful examination of Dunne's life and place in American humor and literature, Dooley's pertinence to his time, and the essays' enduring impact.

Ellis, Elmer. *Mr. Dooley's America: a Life of Finley Peter Dunne.* New York: Knopf, 1941. The standard full biography, and likely to remain so, as the author had access to letters and manuscripts since lost or destroyed by the Dunne family.

Fanning, Charles. *Finley Peter Dunne and Mr. Dooley.* Lexington: University of Kentucky, 1978. An important, penetrating monograph on Dunne's Chicago environment and early career, Mr. Dooley's genesis, and the maturation of the dialect essay style.

Articles and Chapters in Books

De Muth, James. "Finley Peter Dunne." *Dictionary of Literary Biography.* Vol. 11. *American Humorists 1800-1950.* Ed. Stanley Trachtenberg. Detroit: Gale, 1982, pp. 123-133.

De Muth, James. *Small Town Chicago.* Port Washington: Kennikat, 1980. Comparative analysis of the comic perspectives of Ade, Dunne, and Lardner. Very perceptive.

Dudden, Arthur P. "The Record of Political Humor." *American Quarterly,* 37 (Spring 1985): 50-70. Special attention given to Dunne and Will Rogers in a survey of trends in American political humor.

Fanning, Charles. "The Short Sad Career of Mr. Dooley in Chicago." *Ethnicity,* 8 (1981): 169-188. The early Dunne pieces as the most complete record of Irish-American working class in 1890s.

Gibson, William M. *Theodore Roosevelt Among the Humorists.* Knoxville: University of Tennessee Press, 1980. Sections on William Dean Howells and Mark Twain as well as Dunne; Dunne's complex friendship with President Roosevelt.

Harrison, John. "Finley Peter Dunne and the Progressive Movement." *Journalism Quarterly,* 44 (1967): 475-481. Argues that Dunne was a philosophical anarchist, similar to Brand Whitlock in his cynicism about contemporary issues and reformism.

Semonche, John. "The *American* Magazine of 1906-1915." *Journalism Quarterly,* 40 (1963): 36-44, 86. Dunne's collaboration with Progressive writers who had left *McClure's.*

Thogmartin, Clyde. "Mr. Dooley's Brogue: the Literary Dialect of Finley Peter Dunne." *Visible Language,* 16 (Spring 1982): 184-198. Dooley's dialect as the spoken English of Chicago working class Irish-Americans of the 1880s and 1890s.

Kalman Goldstein

Evans, Charles Napoleon Bonaparte

Born: Norfolk County, Virginia, on October 18, 1812
Marriage: Elizabeth Clancy, 1836, seven children
Died: March 10, 1883

Biography

Charles Napoleon Bonaparte Evans was born in or near Suffolk in Nansemond County, Virginia, on October 18, 1812. His parents were James E. and Jane Shirley Evans. After leaving home at an early age following the death of his father and remarriage of his mother, Evans learned the printing trade at shops in Virginia, South Carolina, and North Carolina. He became editor of the *Greensborough* (North Carolina) *Patriot* in 1835 and purchased the paper in 1836 shortly before his marriage to Elizabeth Clancy, daughter of his partner. Evans left the *Patriot* in 1840 to purchase the *Milton* (North Carolina) *Chronicle* in Caswell County. It was as editor of the *Chronicle* that he gained his regional celebrity in the course of the next forty-three years. He died on March 10, 1883.

Literary Analysis

Evans began his editorial career as a partisan Whig, but he opened his columns to the views of Democratic and other opponents and, when the Whigs declined, rather easily switched his allegiance to the Democrats. Milton, North Carolina, was a small marketing center on the upper Roanoke River, and Evans was a perennial booster of such projects as boat lines, plank roads, railroads, agricultural fairs, river bridges, or whatever seemed likely to promote the economic interests of the community. As the Civil War approached, he adopted the Union position against secession but became a stalwart Confederate once the die was cast with the secession of North Carolina in May 1861.

The *Chronicle*, though apparently never enjoying a subscription list of more than a few hundred readers, had a popularity considerably larger than those figures suggest. Evans's views on political, social and other issues were not infrequently quoted by other editors of the Piedmont section of North Carolina and parts of Virginia. However, it was not so much the depth and trenchancy of his views as his rollicking good humor that caught the fancy of readers. The marriage of Ebenezer Sweet to Jane Lemon in 1859, for example, evoked from Evans not only an announcement but the happy reflection that

> "How happily extremes do meet
>   In Jane and Ebenezer,
> "She's now no longer sour, but Sweet,
>   And he's a Lemon squeezer!"

By far the most popular of Evans's columns, though, were those that he devoted to a fictitious character known as "Jesse Holmes, the Fool-Killer." The popularity of "The Fool-Killer" reflected the vogue of folk-humor widely found in such literary creations as Hamilton C. Jones's "Cousin Sally Dillard," Johnson Jones Hooper's "Simon Suggs" (both of whom were also North Carolinians), and others. Lacking the stylistic talents of his more polished contemporaries, Evans made a virtue of provincialism by writing about individuals, types, and situations well known to his special audience.

"Jesse Holmes, the Fool-Killer" appeared in a series of letters supposedly written by him to the editor of the *Milton Chronicle* about once a month. As depicted in the woodcut that accompanied each "Fool-Killer" letter, "Jesse Holmes" was a pugnacious little character in a long-tailed coat and floppy hat. He carried a club for chastising malefactors, of whom he was always sure to find numerous specimens in his journeys along the highways and byways of Caswell and adjacent counties.

The victims of the "Fool-Killer's" wrath included various kinds of cheats, cowards, faithless lovers, overbearing parents, heavy drinkers, brutal slave-patrollers, and rascally public officials. While the state legislature and other institutions might come in for their share of cudgeling, it was the "Fool-Killer's" perception of a society in moral decline that gave the column its characteristic pungency. "Editor," writes "Jesse Holmes" in one epistle:

> parents have much to answer for in this world and the world to come, for the training up of their children. You may search the world and where you find one man honest and just from innate principle—from a spontaneous love of right and justice—I'll show you two who are honest and just only from the force of circumstances. That is to say they would cheat, lie and steal at the drop of a hat but for the fear of being found out, and the dread of punishment by the laws of government and society. Now, Editor, when the children are raised up to love honesty, justice and virtue, and to spurn vice, because it is right and proper to do so, even if there were no laws of government or society to punish, then the glorious Millennium will come! when chickens may "roost lower," and bolts and bars to doors may be thrown away, and men's simple words will be far better than many of their bonds are now.

In a typical episode, the "Fool-Killer" encounters a young man who claims to have been asleep in a store when thieves broke in and robbed the place without waking him, but "The plea was too thin! . . . and having heard him at a certain church thanking the preacher (in a voice heard all over the church) for concluding his sermon, I claimed the chap for my meat and mauled the goose grease out of him."

"Send for Jesse Holmes" became a familiar expression within the periphery of the "Fool-Killer's" influence. Other newspapers often reproduced all or parts of the letters detailing Holmes's activities and those of his even more combative associate known as "The Rascal Whaler." Their common aim of ridding society of its fools and miscreants through direct, individual intervention struck a responsive chord in an age when such intervention was increasingly hedged in by institutional restrictions—the frontier ethos lived on in the mid-nineteenth century ethical stance of "Jesse Holmes, the Fool-Killer."

The character created by C.N.B. Evans was resurrected in 1908 by William Sydney Porter ("O. Henry") in his story "The Fool-Killer," which appeared in *The Voice of the City*. Porter, a North Carolinian and cousin of Evans, recalled "Jesse Holmes" as an image "that hung on the walls of my fancy during my barefoot days. . . . To me he was a terrible old man, in gray clothes, with a long, ragged, gray beard, and reddish fierce eyes. I looked to see him come stumping up the road in a cloud of dust, with a white oak staff in his hand and his shoes tied with leather thongs" Twentieth-century incarnations of the "Fool-Killer," including that of "O. Henry" and of Helen Eustis in her 1954 novel, *The Fool Killer*, have transmuted Evans's curmudgeon into a somewhat more benign and lovable figure than the one who earned celebrity in the pages of the *Milton Chronicle*.

Evans sold the *Chronicle* to his son and two partners in 1864 and took over a paper in nearby Danville, Virginia. The *Chronicle* appears to have ceased publication soon afterward, but by about 1868 Evans had revived it and he continued to edit the paper until his death in 1883. In 1882, he won election to the North Carolina Senate but contracted bronchial pneumonia during the session, the disease proving fatal. The *Chronicle* was discontinued shortly after his death.

Summary

Charles Napoleon Bonaparte Evans was a man of little formal education who learned his trade as a printer and a writer while an apprentice and journeyman in Virginia and the Carolinas between about 1825 and 1840. As editor of the *Milton Chronicle* from 1841 to 1883, he earned a measure of regional celebrity with his feisty humor, notably expressed through the fictitious "Jesse Holmes, the Fool-Killer," a character who enjoyed a devoted following among newspaper readers in North Carolina and Virginia. The "Fool-Killer's" ability to take the imparting of justice into his own hands and deal effectively with scoundrels and scapegraces won him the affection of thousands for whom the impersonality of mid-nineteenth century institutions was not yet an acceptable substitute for frontier directness.

Selected Bibliography

Primary Sources

Scattered issues of the *Milton Chronicle* may be found at the libraries of the University of North Carolina at Chapel Hill, the North Carolina Division of Archives and History, and the North Carolina State Library.

Secondary Sources

Hubbell, Jay B. "Charles Napoleon Bonaparte Evans: Creator of Jesse Holmes the Fool-Killer." *South Atlantic Quarterly*, 36 (October 1937): 431–438. Commentary on Evans's life and career.

Parramore, Thomas C. "Discovered: A Sixth Fool Killer Letter." *North Carolina Folklore Journal*, 23 (August 1975): 70–74.

Stokes, Durward T. "Charles Napoleon Bonaparte Evans." *Dictionary of North Carolina Biography*. Ed. William S. Powell. Vol. D–G. Chapel Hill, N.C.: University of North Carolina Press, 1986. Fullest treatment of Evans available.

——— . "Charles Napoleon Bonaparte Evans and the *Milton Chronicle*." *North Carolina Historical Review*, 46 (July 1969): 239–270.

——— . "Five Letters from Jesse Holmes, the Fool Killer, to the Editor of the Milton Chronicle." *North Carolina Historical Review*, 50 (July 1973): 304–321.

Thomas C. Parramore

Feiffer, Jules

Born: Bronx, New York, on January 26, 1929

Education: Art Students League, New York City, 1946; Pratt Institute, New York City, 1947–1948, 1949–1951

Marriages: Susan Sheftel, September 17, 1961, divorced, 1983, one daughter; Jennifer Allen, September 11, 1983

Biography

When notified in 1986 that he had been awarded the Pulitzer Prize for editorial cartooning, Jules Feiffer wryly pointed out that he was happy to receive his first Pulitzer since starting his career in 1956: "I get one every thirty years whether I deserve it or not." In those thirty years Feiffer gained international recognition as a satiric cartoonist, playwright, and writer of novels and screenplays. His absurdist universe, always rooted in the real one, owes a debt to works by Samuel Beckett and Robert Benchley, though other literary and cartoon sources are identifiable in what is finally Feiffer's own, truly original voice.

David and Rhoda (Davis) Feiffer, his parents, immigrated to the United States from Poland as teenagers and raised their son in the Bronx, New York, the city so central to his work and in which he was born on January 26, 1929. Art courses at the Art Students League and Pratt Institute and a variety of art-related jobs (following a hated period—1951–53—in the U.S. Army Signal Corps as a cartoon animator) led to his 1956 appearance in the offices of the *Village Voice* with a batch of cartoon strips. Here began the thirty-year period leading to that first Pulitzer and to the long association with the *Voice* that still continues. His cartoons have been nationally syndicated since 1959 and have appeared in such international newspapers as the London *Observer* and, regularly, in *Playboy Magazine*. By the mid-1960s he had published his first novel, *Harry, the Rat with Women*, and his first important play, *Little Murders*, had been produced on Broadway and by the Royal Shakespeare Company in London. His enormous productivity is reflected in a bibliography that includes numerous collections of his cartoons, three novels, four screenplays, and more than a dozen produced plays. His many awards, in addition to the 1986 Pulitzer, include an Oscar (for *Munro*, an animated cartoon, 1961), the George Polk Memorial Award, 1962, the London Drama Critics Award for Best Foreign Play (*Little Murders*, 1967), and the Outer Circle Drama Critics Awards for 1969 and 1970.

Literary Analysis

Jules Feiffer etches his corrosive portrait of American society through a variety of satirical forms, all of them linked by the nature of the characters who inhabit them. His cartoons burst onto the American scene in 1956 and he has been using this format to dissect contemporary society ever since, flaying scheming presidents and other public figures but most memorably ridiculing average men and women in stages of post-Freudian combat. Feiffer's amalgam of political cartoon and comic strip stands at the satiric center of a tradition that looks back to Al Capp ("Li'l Abner"), Walt Kelly ("Pogo"), and E. C. Segar ("Popeye") and forward to Garry Trudeau ("Doonesbury"), Berke Breathed ("Bloom County") and Jeff MacNelly ("Shoe"). In contrast to earlier cartoonists, who distanced their satire by creating rural or mythical habitats for their characters, Feiffer's America is instantly recognizable and preeminently urban, its citizens educated, middle class, and neurotic, its geographical and satiric locale firmly established as New York City.

In Feiffer's world, sex and friendship, like so many of his men and women, are mutually incompatible. In one strip from the early 1980s, a young man assails his female mate for kissing him on the mouth because "that could lead to other stuff." "What if it does?" she queries. "But you and I are *friends*! We talk all night, we help each other out, we *like* each other," he protests. She, enticingly: "Uh, huh." He: "You can't have sex if you're friends. You screw up a good relationship!"

Feiffer's men and women analyze themselves to death, perpetually taking their mental temperatures as their relationships hurtle toward disaster. Awareness of a direct link between sexual role-playing and political power considerably sharpens the humorist's scalpel. "I consider myself a political moralist," he once told an interviewer. "And sexual relationships are based on power plays, the same as political relationships are." Power plays of all kinds, committed by average people and presidents alike, are thus central to Feiffer's work and are linked, in turn, to the self-conscious projection of a personal or national image to camouflage inadequacy and immaturity. In a 1986 cartoon strip, Feiffer articulates the seasons of a man's life through sketches of his speaker, alternatingly deflated and puffed up, with captions cued to each drawing: "As I entered my adolescence I was miserable, insecure and angry. . . . At 28, I was a winner. . . . At 40, I was depressed, insecure and angry. . . . At 45 I was a powerhouse. . . . At 50, I was morbid, insecure and angry. . . . At 60, I was a patriarch. . . . At 63, I am suicidal, insecure and angry. . . . Maturity is a phase . . . adolescence is forever."

Perpetual adolescence also dominates Feiffer's screenplay for *Carnal Knowledge* (1971), an underpraised and misunderstood film that shows the libidos of its aging heroes isolated from virtually every other aspect of their lives. A complex film both visually (under Mike Nichols's direction) and textually, *Carnal Knowledge* employs elements of Feiffer's cartoons (episodic narrative, minimalist settings, tightly framed talking heads) as structural and thematic devices to alienate the viewer from its two central characters and to ridicule notions of the male sexual fantasy at the film's core.

The ghost of Swedish playwright August Strindberg, whose subjective explorations of the battle of the sexes revolutionized modern drama, hovers over Feiffer's work. However, Strindberg endows his women with wills that generally make mincemeat of their men, attributing their superior strength to an amorality inborn in *all* women—a view derived from his own hideous relationships in a personal life beset by madness; Feiffer turns Strindberg's malice comic and, depending upon the vehicle, directs it against both sexes. Strindberg would be enraged by *Carnal Knowledge*'s vivisection of its abhorrent, deluded heroes whose sex lives Feiffer savagely traces from college age through the mid-life crises of their thirties and forties, transforming them into vehicles for an attack on the male ego in mid-century America. Even Feiffer's screenplay for director Robert Altman's *Popeye* (1980), derived, appropriately enough, from Segar's old comic strip, capitalizes on the notion of a battle of the sexes. On meeting the hero, Olive Oyl exclaims, "Popeye! What kind of name is that?" Popeye replies, "What kind of name is Olive Oyl? It sounds like some kind of lubricant!"

Two plays rank among Feiffer's most important and original work. Prompted especially by the assassination of President John Kennedy in 1963, *Little Murders* (1966) predicts that the violence permeating American society must inevitably filter down to the daily lives of "average" families. In this regard, as in his later, more controlled *Grown Ups*, Feiffer draws upon the psychological familial violence inherent in the dramas of Strindberg's American successors (Eugene O'Neill, Tennessee Williams, Arthur Miller), but in *Little Murders* his satirical style moves toward outrageous absurdist overstatement to reflect the hysteria of random violence in 1960s America. Surviving members of the Newquist Family discover that if you can't lick 'em you may as well join 'em, and gleefully fire rifle potshots from the windows of the New York apartment in which they have been imprisoned by terrorism of the city below.

Traditional comedy ends with reconciliation, with what George Bernard Shaw (in *Man and Superman*) calls "universal laughter." *Little Murders* concludes with (as Feiffer's stage direction describes it) "general merriment," triggered by this family's delight in the increasing accuracy of its aim and the prospect that after dinner Mom, too, will try her skill with the rifle. Feiffer's macabre subversion of dotty family comedy encapsulates a deadly decade in recent American history.

Grown Ups (1981), Feiffer's funniest, most mature, and complex play, rejects the bizarre exaggeration of *Little Murders* and maintains throughout an essentially realistic style and pace. What begins as hilarious, identifiable family comedy erupts into something else as Feiffer incorporates but extends and fleshes out the surface relationships of *Carnal Knowledge*, *Little Murders*, and the cartoon strips. Entirely original yet nurtured by families in O'Neill, Miller and, especially, Philip Roth, the three generations of the family portrayed in *Grown Ups* reveal the little murders performed daily in the name of security and love. Deliberately inviting audience empathy through queries incessantly repeated in family conversations across the land ("So what's new?" "When are you coming to visit?"), Feiffer concentrates upon the domestic circle of manipulation and guilt that travels among the generations: adult children—ironically dubbed "grown-ups"—and their parents; husbands and wives; siblings; parents and young children; grandparents and grandchildren. Moreover, the play concerns American notions of success, typically entwined by Feiffer with ideas of political power. Still called "Sonny Boy" by his parents, Jake—*Grown Ups*'s thirty-five-year-old hero—ultimately rejects the prestige associated with success only as an act of revenge against his castrating mother and father.

The play's realism (especially its rejection of dark Ibsenite secrets of the past to "explain" the present) is heightened by a nearly Pinteresque evasion of communication that functions as a central comic element ("Do you know what she's talking about?" "She doesn't know what she's talking about." "You're over my head."). Though rooted in traditional Feiffer territory—New York City and its environs—the members of this family, like characters in absurdist drama, tell stories that few get to complete and even fewer truly hear. A three-act play, *Grown Ups* gains in intensity and darkness, moving in characteristic Feiffer fashion from family comedy toward Strindbergian nightmare, but one that never fully denies a lacerating comic vision.

Summary

In his cartoons, plays, novels, and screenplays, Jules Feiffer creates a satirical landscape of urban

America, its inhabitants neurotically absorbed in post-Freudian struggles with "relationships" and daily survival. The more they seek self-discovery, the more they lapse further into anxious self-deception (Jonathan in *Carnal Knowledge*; the Newquists in *Little Murders*). Their rhetoric, like that of the doublespeak political figures prominent in his cartoons during the Vietnam (Lyndon Johnson) and Watergate (Richard Nixon) eras, distorts meaning, rationalizing the characters' true motives, enabling them to conduct business as usual. When a rare Feiffer figure (Jake in *Grown Ups*) does successfully confront his true nature, the pain of that discovery prompts an overreaction as destructive as it is unnecessary.

From his story of a four-year-old boy mistakenly drafted into the Army in an early animated film (*Munro*) through the mid-1980s cartoon strips caricaturing the Reagan White House, Feiffer has targeted all bastions of American authority and power, but his work continually stresses the link between organized national and corporate power on the one hand and daily gender games of sexual politics on the other. Feiffer's cynicism occasionally masks the redemptive aim of his work. "There is hope in my plays and in my cartoons," he once said. "By showing certain things, you can institute insights which later can lead to action." Like the best and most astringent satirists before him, Feiffer goads the conscience toward action, holding out the possibility for change even as he scathingly identifies the human impulse to resist it at all cost.

Selected Bibliography

Primary Sources

Cartoon and Related Collections

Sick, Sick, Sick. New York: McGraw Hill, 1958.
Passionella and Other Stories. New York: McGraw Hill, 1959.
The Explainers. New York: McGraw Hill, 1960.
Boy, Girl, Boy, Girl. New York: Random House, 1961.
Hold Me! New York: Random House, 1963.
Feiffer's Album. New York: Random House, 1963.
The Unexpurgated Memoirs of Bernard Mergendeiler. New York: Random House, 1965.
Editor, The Great Comic Book Heroes. New York: Dial, 1965.
The Penguin Feiffer. London: Penguin, 1966.
Feiffer on Civil Rights. New York: Anti-Defamation League of B'nai B'rith, 1966.
Feiffer's Marriage Manual. New York: Random House, 1967.
Pictures as a Prosecution: Drawings and Text from the Chicago Conspiracy Trial. New York: Grove Press, 1971.
Feiffer on Nixon: The Cartoon Presidency. New York: Random House, 1974.
Feiffer's America: From Eisenhower to Reagan. New York: Knopf, 1982.

Plays

The Explainers (musical revue), 1961.
Crawling Arnold (one-act play), 1961. In Best Short Plays of the World 1958-1967. Ed. Stanley Richards. New York: Crown, 1968.
Little Murders, 1966. New York: Random House, 1968.
The Unexpurgated Memoirs of Bernard Mergendeiler, 1967. In Collision Course. New York: Random House, 1968.
God Bless, 1968. In Plays and Players (London), January 1969, pp. 35–50.
Dick and Jane. In Oh! Calcutta!, 1969. New York: Grove Press, 1970.
The White House Murder Case, 1970. New York: Grove Press, 1970.
Watergate Classics, 1973.
Knock, Knock, 1976. New York: Hill and Wang, 1976.
Hold Me!, 1977. New York: Dramatists Play Service, 1977.
Grown Ups, 1981. New York: Samuel French, 1982.
A Think Piece, produced 1982.

Screenplays

Munro (animated cartoon), Rembrandt Films, 1961.
Carnal Knowledge, Avco Embassy, 1971. New York: Farrar, Straus and Giroux, 1971.
Little Murders, Twentieth Century-Fox, 1972.
Popeye, Paramount, 1980.

Novels

Harry, The Rat with Women. New York: McGraw-Hill, 1963.
Ackroyd. New York: Simon and Schuster, 1977.
Tantrum: A Novel-in-Cartoons. New York: Knopf, 1979.

Secondary Sources

Articles

Dudar, Helen. "Jules Feiffer on the Tyranny of Trivia." New York Times, June 20, 1982, sect. 2, pp. 6, 19.
"Jules Feiffer." Film Dope, September 1978, pp. 21–22.
Lahr, John. "Jules Feiffer." Behind the Scenes: Theatre and Film Interviews from the Transatlantic Review. Ed. Joseph F. McCrindle. New York: Holt Rinehart, 1971, pp. 19–30.
McGilligan, Pat. "Feiffer and Popeye." Focus on Film, March 1981, pp. 10–12.
Rich, Frank. "The Case for Keeping Grown Ups Open." New York Times, January 15, 1982, sect. C, p. 3.
Thomas, J.C. "Jules Feiffer: From Cartoons to Carnal Knowledge." Show, November 1979, pp. 31–33.
Weales, Gerald. "Jules Feiffer." Contemporary Dramatists. Ed. James Vinson. 2nd ed. New York: St. Martin's, 1982, pp. 239–241.
Whitfield, Stephen J. "Jules Feiffer and the comedy of Disenchantment." In From Hester Street to Hollywood. Ed. Sarah Blacher Cohen. Bloomington, Ind.: Indiana University Press, 1983, pp. 167–182.

Mark W. Estrin

Field, Eugene

Born: St. Louis, Missouri, on September 3, 1850

Education: Williams College, 1868; Knox College, 1869; University of Missouri, 1870

Marriage: Julia Sutherland Comstock, October 16, 1873, eight children

Died: November 4, 1895

Biography

Eugene Field may be more readily remembered as the author of sentimental poems about children such as "Little Boy Blue" and "Dutch Lullaby" (Wynken, Blynken, and Nod) than as a humorist. Yet Field was a wit who never passed up opportunities to lampoon fellow Missourians, who wrote such popular satire for the *Denver Tribune* that almost overnight he became the best known columnist in Colorado, and who earned such national fame as the author of the witty, sparkling "Sharps and Flats" column in the *Chicago Morning News* that his contemporaries regarded him as the best newspaper humorist in America. Field's paradoxical capacity for both gently sentimental and tough-minded humor was noted by a long-time friend and colleague, Charles H. Dennis: "We found Field to be a surprising paradox—a merciless satirist who loved his fellow man."[1]

The satirist who loved his fellow man was born in a house on Collins Street in St. Louis, Missouri, on September 3, 1850, to Roswell M. Field and Frances Reed. (Eugene's father was the lawyer who initiated legal proceedings on behalf of the slave Dred Scott and thus began one of the most famous legal cases in American history.) Seven years after Eugene's death in 1895 admirers held ceremonies at 634 South Fifth Street (now Broadway) to dedicate the residence as his place of birth. His younger brother, Roswell, observed that the family resided there only after Eugene was born, but the principal speaker for the occasion, Mark Twain, thought the place of birth less important than the fact that the house being dedicated was a genuine, well-known former home of the family.

Boyhood in St. Louis ended after Eugene's mother died in 1856. The following year Eugene and his younger brother, Roswell, were sent to Amherst, Massachusetts, to be raised by their cousin, Mary Field French, who lovingly provided a home and instilled New England virtues in the lively young boys. From 1865 until the fall of 1868, Eugene attended a private academy conducted by the Reverend James Tufts of Monson, Massachusetts. In 1868, he enrolled in Williams College. Temperamentally unsuited for formal education at the time, he was sent home before the year was up, perhaps because he could not restrain his enthusiasm for practical jokes. The following year he enrolled in Knox College (Galesburg, Illinois) but spent his junior (and last) year of college attending the University of Missouri with brother Roswell.

Nothing in Field's education and not much in his early years as a journalist suggest that within the next twelve to fifteen years he would command a national reputation and a national audience. Eugene's father died in 1869, leaving an inheritance that Eugene received at the age of twenty-one and promptly spent travelling in the British Isles and western Europe. Returning to Missouri, he married Julia Sutherland Comstock on October 16, 1873. Eight children were born to them; five survived childhood. Also in 1873, Field began to work for the *St. Louis* (Missouri) *Journal.* He spent the following year with the *Gazette* in St. Joseph, Missouri, and then returned to St. Louis where he was employed by the *Times-Journal.*

Although colleagues discerned only moderate promise in Field as a newspaperman because the particulars of news gathering and newspaper management did not greatly interest him, he progressed steadily to editorial posts on the *Kansas City Times* (1880) and the *Denver Tribune* (1881). The latter hired him as editor to make the *Tribune* a lively newspaper. There is abundant evidence that he succeeded. Two years later (1883) he accepted Melville Stone's offer to write a column for the *Chicago Morning News.* No doubt the offer tempted Field because it would free him from all chores except writing, but the $50 salary per week, a princely sum in Denver, was especially attractive. In Chicago, however, the wage proved to be no financial cure-all. Field had not been in Chicago very long before a daughter's request for a Bible verse to recite in Sunday School inspired him to respond: "The Lord will provide; my father can't."[2]

Field was cursed with a delicate stomach and a lanky body that did not lend itself to vigorous physical activity. He was a man of deep and abiding interests in rare books, Christmas, the Latin poet Horace, fairy tales and other folklore that children delight in, the theater, professional baseball, and people. The interest in Christmas and children, for example, led to some of his best-known pieces. His most constant enthusiasm was for the human comedy around him.

Field's interest in people was evident from his first days as a journalist. His dispatches to the *St. Louis Journal* from the Missouri capital contained little factual information about the legislative session, but he more than compensated for this with the hilarious squibs depicting state officials and legislators in a comic light. The dispatches make clear that he knew the after-hours activities of the capital city and that he already commanded the rhymed barb. In addition, he was a practical joker who acted out whatever zany impulses possessed him. For instance, during U.S. Senator Carl Schurz's reelection campaign in 1874, Field brashly swapped roles with the senator at a political rally when he took advantage of a momentary break in the proceedings to have fun at the expense of Schurz and his loyal German following with this announcement:

> Ladies und Shentlemen, I haf such a pad colt dot it vas not bossible for me to make you a speedg to-night, but I haf die bleasure to introduce to you my prilliant chournalist friend Euchene Fielt, who vill spoke to you in my blace.[3]

An even more vivid instance of theatrical jesting occurred in Denver. Shortly before British playwright Oscar Wilde was to appear, Field dressed up in a spectacularly foppish way and paraded about the city, white lily in hand, playing the part of Wilde to the amazement of townspeople. The prank ended at the *Tribune* office where the pretender announced that he was ready to be interviewed by the editor (Field himself). In Chicago he delighted in donning prison garb and showing visitors about the newspaper office.

Such theatrics were not entirely unexpected from Denver and Chicago's most avid theatergoer. While in Denver, Field wrote most of the drama reviews for the *Tribune*. They reveal an irrepressible wit as well as an astute knowledge of plays and players. *Tribune* readers enjoyed such tart comments as Field's reference to an actor who "played the king as if he was afraid someone would play the ace."[4] Yet because of his genuine love for good plays and actors with talent, theater folk (including his staunch friend, Francis Wilson, whose dramatically expressive legs—Field's notion—inspired hilarious comments in the *Morning News*) tolerated his antics.

Field died in Chicago on November 4, 1895.

Literary Analysis

Eugene Field's irrepressible humor brought him early success that sustains his literary reputation today. His first humorous column was published in the *Denver Tribune* on October 10, 1881. Before the year was out a collection of squibs from these columns was published in a slender book impishly titled *The Tribune Primer*. It contained among other things his witty responses to newspaper life, naughty children, politicians, wayward fathers, and nagging wives. Readers especially appreciated his presentation of the human comedy in a sometimes grim domestic setting. Some pieces are pure mischief:

> See the wasp. He has pretty yellow stripes around his body, and a Darning Needle in his Tail. If you will Pat the Wasp upon the Tail, we will give you a nice Picture Book.[5]

Other pieces foreshadow the "black humor" of today:

> This is a gun. Is the Gun Loaded? I do not know. Let us Find out. Put the Gun on the table, and you, Susie, blow down one barrel, while you, Charlie, blow down the other. Bang! Yes, it was loaded. Run quick Jennie, and pick up Susie's head and Charlie's lower jaw before the Nasty Blood gets over the New carpet.[6]

Paragraphs like these and pieces up to twenty paragraphs long are the contents of the *Primer*, which enjoyed phenomenal popularity with readers and inspired so many imitators—some 20 papers took up the style—that Field abandoned it. Even so, it was the *Primer* that brought Field to the attention of Melville Stone.

In the more sophisticated environment of Chicago, Field's humor changed, becoming less broadly comic and depending more upon understatement, but it continued to reflect the man's irrepressible zaniness. A typical prank was to attribute pieces to others. For example, one of Field's lullabys was attributed to the distinguished minister Henry Ward Beecher. A fine parody of his friend James Whitcomb Riley was attributed to William Dean Howells. There were other kinds of hoaxes. Field wrote at length about a child prodigy who existed only in his imagination. A similar hoax was his review of a non-existent book, the biography, *Florence Bardsley.*

Field's piece on the railroad car magnate George M. Pullman in a "Sharps and Flats" column (a title taken from a play written by his friend and biographer, Slason Thompson) indicates the kind of humor that emerged in Chicago. The event that inspired Field to satirize one of Chicago's richest and most powerful men was King Humbert's awarding of the honorary title of *marchese* to Pullman after the Chicagoan had given the king an opulent sleeping car for his travels. "Never since the great fire of 1871 has Chicago been so powerfully agitated," Field wrote, "as it was when it became noised about that King Humbert of Italy had created our esteemed fellow-townsman Col. George M. Pullman a knight of the first water."[7] Field feared that the stir made in Chicago by the honorary title reflected a hunger for aristocratic status among Chicago's newly rich. The column reveals that Field was determined to unstuff Pullman's shirt and to deflate any popular yearnings for an artificial aristocracy.

Field's comic strategy attacked literary pretensions as well. For example, bogus epigraphs are assigned to Petrarch, Tasso, and Dante. The quotation attributed to Petrarch is a bit of nonsense in Italian (and a comic warning to Chicagoans whose knowledge of European culture might be too thin to distinguish sense from nonsense). The other passages touch humorously upon sleep and, hence, the sleeping-car magnate. "Sleep mocks at death," the quotation attributed to Dante reads, "When weary of the earth,/ We do not die—we take an upper berth" (p. 133). Pullman's title is subjected to various witty modes of deflation. Comic catalogs are used: "Very many of our Irish citizens are of high extraction, . . . descendents of dukes, earls, boyars, barons, and knights" (p. 133). The title of "boyar" is entirely out of place; it identifies an aristocratic order abolished in an earlier era by Peter the Great. Later, associating "booyars" properly with "Roosha," Field shows that he is less interested in making amends to history than creating additional nonsense, for he immediately juxtaposes "booyars" with "flambustules of Siam" (p. 135). According to the satiric logic thus established, titles simply become more nonsense.

There is also a great deal of obvious humor, some of it the misspellings and mispronunciations that were contained in the popular wit of the era. The reader is told that *marchese* is pronounced "mar-kee-sy," a pronunciation thereafter made sport of. A reference is made to the "flat-backed militia" who occupy some Pullman cars—i.e., bed bugs. Then there are the "Pshaw of Persia," and the "bourbons from Bourbon Co., France." *Bon ton* is pronounced as "bong tong." An Irishman named Murphy is referred to as the "Markesy di Potata," and the name given to a putative Italian Legate is "Sig. Pietro Casa del Comma."

The column transcends this low level of humor, however, when Field begins to consider a coat of arms for Pullman. His irrepressible zaniness breaks through, and the Fieldian wit admired by his contemporaries emerges brilliantly:

> This chaste design represents a shield engrailed, bordured, and vert, with a supporting figure at each side; the figures are what in the vernacular of heraldry is called expectant and demand-

ant; the shield dexter is quartered—that is to say, divided into four berths, or compartments, which are left blank for posterity to fill; the shield sinister is decorated with the portraiture of a small feather pillow issuant, this being the heraldic symbol of luxury and ease; upon this pillow appears the personification of indefatigable industry and ceaseless vigilance, rampant, illustrating not only the means by which the markeesy has achieved his noble ends, but also the still nobler teaching of the most wise Solomon, who said, "Go to the ant, you sluggard, or you will go to the dogs."

(pp. 135–136)

Clearly Field has done his homework in heraldic lore. In its context, *rampant* constitutes a brilliant pun. According to heraldry, *rampant* means that an animal such as a horse or lion is represented rearing on its hind legs with its forelegs elevated, the right above the left, the head usually depicted in profile—the creature here is not a noble animal but "indefatigable industry." Another meaning of rampant is thus called to mind: unchecked, unrestrained growth. The social criticism invoked resonates in the cleverly reworked aphorism of Solomon that closes the paragraph.

Field returns to the coat of arms to identify "indefatigable industry" with several insects:

> One correspondent says that the insect is not an ant, but a potato-bug; another declares that it is a busy bee; and still a third maintains that it is neither a chinch-bug, nor a busy bee, nor yet an ant, but one of those predatory vampires known by name only in polite society as "the flat-backed militia."

(pp. 136–137)

Ant, potato bug, bed bug—Pullman and his honorary title are thus reduced by Field to unpleasant minuteness. The piece ends with a bit of barbed verse:

> *When the party is breezy and wheezy,*
> *And palpably greasy, it's easy*
> *   To coax or to wring,*
> *   From a weak-minded king,*
> *The titular prize of markeesy.*

(p. 137)

In a few paragraphs Field has written an effective satire that is particularly brilliant. In this respect it is typical. Both Thompson and Dennis (friends, fellow journalists, and Field's biographers) refer to Field as a "paragrapher" and marvel at his skill. Often "Sharps and Flats" consisted of disparate paragraphs on whatever subjects struck Field's fancy.

Dennis gives a detailed description of how these columns were written. Each required about two hours of intense concentration. Arriving at his office about eleven o'clock, Field would cull articles or bits of articles, a headline, a printed name, or some other fragment that might suggest a paragraph to him and put them in a cigar box. He always perused his favorite newspapers in this fashion (the *New York Sun*, *St. Louis Globe-Democrat*, and *Cincinnati Enquirer*; he responded enthusiastically to satirical editorials in the *Sun* and *Globe-Democrat*, laughing outright). From these Field would construct a typical column. If there were insufficient scraps in the cigar box, he would perform a mental roll call of the states to jog his memory about well-known people residing in them.[8] This daily ritual could have only one result: the contents of most of Field's humorous work are the current events of the 1870s to the mid-1890s, usually structured to fit his daily column. He collected many of the humorous columns in *The Tribune Primer* and *Culture's Garland* (1887). Hence it is fair to say that, except for some comic poems published separately from the column, Field's reputation as a humorist rests mostly upon the contents of these two volumes.

Field is one of those writers whose larger reputation must be taken into account. He is so well known as the children's laureate that readers who come to him as a humorist may be influenced by his larger reputation, which has perhaps been diminished by events after his death. For instance, he wrote a limited amount of vivid bawdy verse.[9] Among the bawdy pieces, "Our Lady Lil" and "The Fair Limousin" still receive notice. Yet one has to wonder about the association some critics make between these instances of bawdy and the poems for children. Poems like "Our Lady Lil" were unpublished in Field's lifetime and clearly written for reading at men-only affairs. A more serious challenge to Field's popular reputation is the emergence of Charles Newton French's claim that he wrote Field's most famous poem, "Little Boy Blue." It is difficult to assess this claim of authorship, though the loss of the poem from Field's oeuvre would not diminish significantly his status as the poet for children.

While Field's bawdy poetry *is* a roguish kind of humor, the parody of *The New England Primer* which brought him his first great success should have been a warning that he was no genteel conformist. There is also a modest amount of verse in the vernacular. When Field's wild imagination is fully engaged, the vernacular poems work, but he found the vernacular poem too easy to write and gave it up. Those most frequently referred to (such as "Casey's Table d'Hote") are not exceptional successes. Field was much better as a parodist, successfully taking off on such subjects as the hymns of Watts and poems by John Greenleaf Whittier, Philip Lanier, James Whitcomb Riley, and Alfred Lord Tennyson. It was typical of Field to attribute a parody of Tennyson to James Russell Lowell.

Summary

Recent scholarship reveals that Field is an important transitional figure in American humor. In *America's Humor from Poor Richard to Doonesbury* Walter Blair and Hamlin Hill define him as a humorist "trying to convert from rusticity to urbanity."[10] The more detailed study of Kenny J. Williams and Bernard Duffy, *Chicago's Public Wits*, also helps to establish Field's historical place. They reprint selections of his prose and verse, including the column on Pullman, a sequence of squibs about literary and theatrical people, a "Chaucerian Paraphrase of Horace," an article on the Hamlin Garland–Mary Catherwood debate over realism and naturalism ("Mr. Garland's *in hoc signo* is a dungfork or butter paddle"), and some of Field's verse, concluding with the fine "Dutch Lullaby." They are thus able to show that Field is indeed an important transitional figure who expressed the broad comedy of Midwest and frontier America in the 1870s and later in Chicago, a humor that presages the sophisticated humor that flourishes in urban America today. There is no question that he has been an important influence. Blair and Hill refer to him as "the spiritual father of Chicago's humorists,"[11] but he is more than that. The "deft urbanity" noted by Williams and Duffy "made him unique in the Chicago newspaper world and marked also a distinct addition to popular humor."[12] The general import of the last words cannot be overlooked because Eugene Field wielded an influence that extended far beyond Chicago. Although he is not a major American humorist, he is a national figure who influenced American humor on a national scale.

Notes

1. Charles H. Dennis, *Eugene Field's Creative Years* (New York: Doubleday, Page, 1924), p. 45.
2. Slason Thompson, *Life of Eugene Field: the Poet of Childhood* (New York: D. Appleton, 1927), p. 98.
3. Thompson, p. 54; Dennis, p. 24.
4. Dennis, p. 36.
5. Copies of *The Tribune Primer* (1881) are rare. The passage cited here may be found in Thompson (p. 73), who describes the *Primer*, pp. 72-74.
6. Cited in Walter Blair and Hamlin Hill, *America's Humor from Poor Richard to Doonesbury* (New York: Oxford University Press, 1978), p. 383.

7. The column on Pullman is available in *Chicago's Public Wits*, edited with commentaries by Kenny J. Williams and Bernard Duffy (Baton Rouge: Louisiana University Press, 1983), pp. 132-137.
8. Dennis, pp. 46-48.
9. Robert Conrow, *Field Days: The Life, Times, and Reputation of Eugene Field* (New York: Charles Scribner's Sons, 1974). Chapter 5, "His Rabelaisian Nature," is devoted to a study of Field's bawdy, pp. 113-137.
10. Blair and Hill, p. 383.
11. Ibid.
12. Williams and Duffy, p. 124.

Selected Bibliography

Primary Sources
Culture's Garland. Boston: Ticknor, 1887.
The Tribune Primer (1881). The first copyrighted edition is *The Complete Tribune Primer.* Illus. Frederick Opper. Boston: Mutual Book Company, 1900.
The Writings in Prose and Verse of Eugene Field. 12 vols. New York: Charles Scribner's Sons, various dates from 1900 to 1920.
Autobiography
Auto-Analysis. Privately printed, 1894. See Slason Thompson, *Life of Eugene Field*, Chapter XIV, pp. 257-275, for best account.

Secondary Sources
Biographies
Conrow, Robert. *Field Days: The Life, Times, and Reputation of Eugene Field.* New York: Charles Scribner's Sons, 1974.
Dennis, Charles H. *Eugene Field's Creative Years.* New York: Doubleday, Page, 1924.
Thompson, Slason. *Eugene Field: a Study in Heredity and Contradictions.* 2 vols. New York: Charles Scribner's Sons, 1901.
――――. *Life of Eugene Field: the Poet of Childhood.* New York: D. Appleton, 1927. Thompson remains Field's principal biographer.

Criticism
Blair, Walter, and Hamlin Hill. *America's Humor from Poor Richard to Doonesbury.* Oxford University Press, 1978. This is a superior work for placing Field in his historical context and evaluating his place in American humor.
Williams, Kenny J., and Bernard Duffy. *Chicago's Public Wits: A Chapter in the American Comic Spirit.* Baton Rouge: Louisiana State University Press, 1983. A critical study and anthology, this book performs its double service admirably.

Clyde G. Wade

Field, Joseph M.

Born: London, England (?), in 1810
Education: Perhaps some legal study
Marriage: Eliza Riddle, 1837, 2 children
Died: January 28, 1856

Biography

Actor, theater manager, playwright, journalist, and editor, Joseph M. Field displayed the versatility characteristic of the nonprofessional literary men who forged the humor of the Old Southwest. Field was born in 1810, but some sources give his place of birth as Dublin, others, London. His father, Matthew Field, was a Catholic publisher and "well-known Irish exile whose property had been confiscated after the Rebellion of 1798."[1] Field's own manuscript sketch of his younger brother, Matthew, suggests that his father moved from Ireland to London shortly after 1803 and thus points to London as his probable birthplace. Exactly when the Fields emigrated to America is also in doubt, but the same sketch suggests that they did so "immediately after the late war [the War of 1812] between England and the United States." The Fields settled in New York City, where Field's father published the first Roman Catholic almanac of America. Joe Field's formal education seems not to have been extensive though he did apparently study law for a time, and he began his acting career early, appearing at the Tremont Theatre in Boston in 1827.

Between 1830 and 1844, Field's professional life was devoted primarily to acting and playwriting. He made his New York debut at the Park Theater in 1830 and by 1833 was touring with Sol Smith through the Southwestern circuit, playing Cincinnati, St. Louis, Mobile, Montgomery, and towns between. On November 6, 1837, Field married Eliza Riddle, the leading lady for the company of Ludlow and Smith. With his wife he continued to play the circuit controlled by Ludlow and Smith: Mobile, St. Louis, and New Orleans. During this period two children were born to the Fields: Kate Keemle (born October 1, 1838), who as Kate Field became a prominent actress, journalist, and lecturer; and a son Matthew (February 1843), who died of cholera as a child. As an actor, Field's forte seems to have been what his manager, Noah Ludlow, called "eccentric comedy," but he did aspire to more heroic parts as well: Romeo, Othello, Lear, Iago, and others. Of Field's acting ability, James Oakes, a Boston journalist, wrote in his obituary: "As an eccentric comedian he had but few superiors on the stage, and in many juvenile tragedy characters achieved excellence; and, indeed, both his literary and dramatic ac-

quisitions were large and varied, while his general intelligence was of no ordinary character."
Field's "literary and dramatic acquisitions" found expression in a series of plays, only one of which, a religious drama called *Job and His Children*, is extant. Most of Field's plays seem to have been farces. *Tourists in America* (1835) may well have been a satire on English literary visitors to America. *Victoria* (1838) was "a burlesque in which James Gordon Bennett, Sr. (played by Field) of the New York *Herald* is shown in a visit to England to interview young Queen Victoria on her future policy toward the United States."[2] *Oregon, or the Disputed Territory* (1846) treated a topical theme by using the allegorical mode, with such characters as John Bull, Uncle Sam, Texas, Oregon, California, and Massachusetts. Field's "big success," however, was *1943: or, New Orleans a Century Hence*, played in 1843 in New Orleans with Field as the Manager.[3] A bill of advertisement for this play, included in Noah Ludlow's history of the frontier theater, *Dramatic Life as I Found It*, gives some indication of the nature of Field's wit. The scene is 1943, at which time Fancy shows the Manager:

> The ladies in power; great political excitement among the dames and dummies; canvassing for the office of mayor; to the polls; *Judge Sally Jones* the candidate of the dames; men in petticoats; women in trousers; auction of old bachelors.

In a later scene, the Manager apparently comes upon a "mermaid's cave," for he finally "bobs" for mermaids and indeed "catches one."[4]
Field's literary ability also led to a career in journalism. About 1839 he began writing humorous topical poems under the name "Straws" for the *New Orleans Picayune*, which sent him to Europe as a correspondent during 1840. In 1844 he established, with his brother Matthew and veteran newspaperman Charles Keemle, the *St. Louis Reveille*. Matthew died shortly after the founding of the paper, but Keemle and Field continued to edit the *Reveille* until 1850. It was during this period, too, that Field became a contributor of frontier humor sketches to the New York *Spirit of the Times*, the country's major outlet for the humor of the Old Southwest, and to his own *Reveille*, itself an important regional publisher of frontier humor. Many of Field's sketches were gathered together in his most significant contribution to American literature, *The Drama in Pokerville; the Bench and Bar of Jurytown, and Other Stories* (1847).
After the sale of the *Reveille* in 1850, Field returned to the theater, especially to managing.

In that year he managed the Mobile Theatre, and in 1852 he opened the Varieties Theatre in St. Louis. Field was unable to make this last theater a financial success, though, and his management ended in November 1853. After closing the Varieties, Field returned to managing in Mobile until his death from consumption on January 28, 1856.

Literary Analysis

Joseph M. Field's importance to American humor lies in three areas: his editorship of the *St. Louis Reveille*, his contribution to the Mike Fink legend, and his authorship of *The Drama in Pokerville*. From 1844 to 1850, the *Reveille*, under Field's editorship, specialized in humorous sketches of frontier life. Among its contributors were Sol Smith, John S. Robb ("Solitaire"), Matt Field, and Field himself ("Everpoint"). In addition, the *Reveille* printed stories and anecdotes by dozens of lesser-known correspondents, flying under such fanciful names as "Wing," "Thunder," "Plume," "Sopht," and "Jo. Bird." The paper abounded in stories of hoaxes, swindles, and eccentric characters; it presented humorous treatments of frontier institutions of all kinds—courtship, marriage, justice, politics, and gambling. These sketches—especially those of Smith, Robb, and Field—comprise a significant part of the body of work known as the humor of the Old Southwest.
Field first contributed to the Mike Fink legend in 1844 when he published "The Death of Mike Fink" in the *Reveille*. Basing his account on information from Keemle, his co-editor at the *Reveille* who had held a military command in the vicinity of Fink's death at Fort Henry, Field wrote with the intention of clearing away the "mythic haze" surrounding Fink's death. In Field's account, Fink was killed by a gunsmith named Talbott, who had defamed Fink after Mike's accidental killing of his young companion, Carpenter. Carpenter had died of Mike's gunshot during one of the frolics for which Fink was famous, that of friends' shooting containers of whisky off each others' heads at forty yards. Talbott made a great deal of noise about Fink's being a murderer; Mike was heard to threaten Talbott's life; Mike came to Talbott to explain; and the gunsmith, "not a coolly brave man," panicked and shot Fink. Thus Mike died, at least in this account.
Field wrote a longer, more romanticized version of Fink's adventures, "Mike Fink: 'The Last of the Boatmen,'" for the *Reveille* in 1847. As Walter Blair and Franklin J. Meine, historians of the Mike Fink legend, have noted, this version "has the form of a melodramatic novel of the day—full of typical claptrap—wild coincidences,

disguises, sentimental characters, and maudlin maunderings." Nevertheless, the story vividly presents the rough, sometimes terrifying comedy of Fink's adventures, as in one scene in which Fink and his boys tar and feather a man and woman who have attempted to drug Mike and kill him. While the terrified man and woman plead for their lives, the boys decide to stage a mock wedding, conducted by the black cook of Mike's keelboat. When the couple is pronounced "bone of one bone," Mike proposes a toast, forcing the conspirators to drink the drugged drink they had prepared for him. The episode closes when the *gens d'armes* arrive, only to be driven into flight by Mike and his crew. Such boisterous comedy runs throughout Field's "Last of the Boatmen," which is noteworthy, too, for its use of vernacular dialect and for one episode's fine mythic confrontation between Mike's keelboat and a Mississippi steamboat. In the latter Mike refuses to move his keelboat out of the path of a steamer, causing a terrible crash, the sinking of both boats, and considerable loss of life among the steamboat's passengers. Here is a tale, note Blair and Meine, worthy to rank with "John Henry's contest with the steam drill" as a representation of American forces, man and machine, in conflict.[5]

Field's other significant contribution to American humor is his volume of frontier sketches, *The Drama in Pokerville* (1847). The book is typical of the humor of the Old Southwest in both subject matter and style. Field especially delights in stories about hoaxes or swindles and in sketches of eccentric characters. He focuses especially on the life of the steamboat, courtroom, and stage. His stories frequently make use of the box-like structure characteristic of southwestern humor. Typically, Field first speaks in his own voice, establishing the background of his tale in standard, grammatically accurate language. Then he recounts a story told him by someone else or presents a dramatic situation in such a way that it tells itself through dialogue. This inner story usually depends heavily on vernacular dialect, the humor of which is increased through the contrast with the formal language of the opening frame.

Among Field's eccentrics are a "fancy barkeeper," Mr. Twirl, whose poetry of motion delights his customers until it is one day discovered to be the result of his being very drunk; Mr. Nobble, the most henpecked of husbands, who endures the abuse of a wife who is always sick or dying; and an Illinois Sucker whose lack of acquaintance with the system of watercocks in a St. Louis bath house results in a very embarrassing predicament. This last figure overfills his tub with boiling hot water and must sing out for help from the very large woman in atten-

dance, whom he calls "old seven hundred weight." His description of what happens next illustrates the wonderful comedy of southwestern dialect humor:

> The cussed cocks *wouldn't* stop, none of 'em; and I was hoppin' about in the water, and had to sing out for old *fatty*, any how! I'd rather a gin a farm, by thunder, but out I sung, and half opened the door 'fore I recollected about my *costoome*! Back went old *fatty* against the centre-table, and broke a pitcher, and I hopped on to a chair, and into my skin; and then I broke for one of the opposite bathing-rooms, and locked myself in, and told the old woman I'd give her ten dollars, if she would swob up, hand me my shirt, and say nothing about it! I dont know whether she did or not, but I almost die a laffin, spite of my sore leg, whenever I think of it.
>
> (p. 102)

The most extended piece in *The Drama in Pokerville* is the title story, a satiric look at the life of a touring theater company like those Field himself played in for years. The pretentiousness of some such companies' managers and of the local aspirants to culture is Field's especial target. Mr. Oscar Dust, "Manager of the Great Small Affair Theatre," announces in his poster that "he has arrived, with the purpose of FOUNDING THE DRAMA in Pokerville!" (p. 9), and the local editor hails "the *dawn* of Thespis" (p. 13) in the town. The central episode in the story describes a dinner given by a pretender to Pokerville aristocracy, Mrs. Major Slope, in honor of the company. The description of the Slope house suggests that of those other frontier "aristocrats," the Grangerfords:

> "*Both* rooms" had been prepared; two extra busts of La Fayette (not a Shakespeare in all Pokerville) being added to the *sculpture*, three highly coloured "American naval victories," completing the walls, and a perfect arabesque of blue and yellow fly-paper netting finishing off the ceiling. Then, of course, on side tables were vases of artificial flowers, infinitely to be preferred to the natural ones without.
>
> (p. 45)

Here the company and local worthies sup heavily on what they believe to be roast pig, but what is actually possum, that a local wag has persuaded the cooks to serve instead. Indeed, the affected Mr. Flush, recently returned from London, declares the meat to be "the very pig which

Chawles Lamb had celebrated" (p. 53). After dinner the hosts and guests outdo one another at "spontaneous eloquence," capped by the leading lady of the Great Small Affair company, Mrs. Oscar Dust herself, who recites a "metrical *impromptu*" as mechanical as those of Emmeline Grangerford:

> Your key-ind *approval to uphold my cause,*
> To gue-ard *the path you crown with your ap-*
> *plause:*
> Ble-you *are the* ske-eyes, *an Eden promise still,*
> *Nor serpent wiles shall tempt from Pokerville.*

(p. 59)

All of this grandeur soon receives a rather dramatic deflation, however, as one of the actors goes into a "downright phrensy, which his potations sometimes induced" (p. 62), and the rest of the guests become ill from too much possum. Such deflation of pretensions is characteristic of Field's best humor. We see it not only in his treatment of theater companies but also in his sketches of law courts, small towns, and American "boosterism" generally. In "An 'Awful Place,'" the leading citizens of progressive Madison, Indiana, persuade the touring General Jackson to leave his tour boat and see their town. When the General reluctantly agrees, he steps "ashore, *up to his knees,* upon the soil that adored him!" (p. 105). In "The Bench and Bar of Jurytown," Judge Frill moves his court into a "grand new room in the great new courthouse," but his audience remains stubbornly unchanged:

> The crowd was dense, the day warm, coat sleeves were numerous, and tobacco abundant. The front spit*tors* in the gallery, under the press, distributed their salivary favours, indiscriminately, below; the spit*tees* below were equally liberal towards each others' legs, and what with the blowing of noses, and a characteristic *bronchitis,* there was the most awful clearing of throats, *hawking,* and horn-blowing that ever Judge Frill had listened to!

(p. 94)

Here, as in much of his best work, Field captures the rough, unvarnished life of the frontier, a life often at odds with American aspirations in a period of change and progress.

Summary

Actor, theater manager, playwright, journalist, and editor, Joseph M. Field made a significant contribution to the humor of the Old Southwest as the editor of the *St. Louis Reveille,* an important outlet for work in the genre, and as the author of two important works on Mike Fink and a collection of frontier sketches and tales, *The Drama in Pokerville; the Bench and Bar of Jurytown, and Other Stories.* Field's works are characteristic of the humor of the Old Southwest; among them are tall tales, stories of hoaxes and swindles, sketches of eccentric characters, and satiric views of the life of the theater, courtroom, and riverboat. The genre is itself important as a truly American kind of comedy and as an influence on such major American figures as Mark Twain and William Faulkner.

Notes

1. Alice Adel Beffa, "Joe Field, A Man of the Forties" (M.A. Thesis, Washington University, 1941), p. 53.
2. Noah M. Ludlow, *Dramatic Life as I Found It.* Ed. Francis Hodge. 2nd ed. (New York: Benjamin Blom, 1966), p. xxvii.
3. Ibid., p. xxvii.
4. Ibid., p. 571.
5. Walter Blair and Franklin J. Meine, eds., *Half Horse Half Alligator: The Growth of the Mike Fink Legend* (University of Chicago Press, 1956), p. 94.

Selected Bibliography

Primary Sources

The Drama in Pokerville; the Bench and Bar of Jurytown, and Other Stories. Philadelphia: T. B. Peterson and Brothers, 1847. Reprinted by Literature House/Gregg Press, 1969.

"Mike Fink: 'The Last of the Boatmen.'" *St. Louis Reveille,* June 8, 9, 10, 11, 12, 13, 15, 18, 19, 20, 1847. Rpt. *Half Horse Half Alligator: The Growth of the Mike Fink Legend.* Ed. Walter Blair and Franklin J. Meine. Chicago: The University of Chicago Press, 1956, pp. 93–142. The Blair-Meine volume brings together all the known accounts of Fink and is a model study of the growth of a legendary figure.

Job and His Children. In *America's Lost Plays.* Vol. 13. Ed. Ralph H. Ware and H.W. Schoenberger. Bloomington: Indiana University Press, 1940, pp. 235–259.

Joseph M. Field Papers. Ludlow–Field–Maury Collection, Missouri Historical Society, St. Louis, Missouri.

Secondary Sources

Dissertations and Books

Beffa, Alice Adel. "Joe Field, A Man of the Forties." M.A. Thesis. Washington University, 1941. A very complete biographical study.

Blair, Walter, ed. *Native American Humor.* San Francisco: Chandler, 1960. Revision of 1937 edition. A standard anthology, with an excellent introduction to southwestern humor by one of the pioneer scholars in the field.

Cohen, Hennig, and William B. Dillingham, eds. *Humor of the Old Southwest.* Athens: The University of Georgia Press, 1975. Revision of 1964 edition. Includes selections by Field, a brief biographical sketch, and an excellent introduction to frontier humor.

King, Grenville Clark. "'Phazma': A Biography of Matthew C. Field (1812–1844)." Dissertation,

University of Illinois, 1975. A biography of Joe Field's brother, with much information on both men's acting careers and work on the *Reveille*.

Ludlow, Noah M. *Dramatic Life as I Found It*. Ed. Francis Hodge. 2nd ed. New York: Benjamin Blom, 1966. The most complete available record of Field's careers as actor and playwright.

Smith, Solomon Franklin. *Theatrical Management in the West and South for Thirty Years*. New York: Harper & Brothers, 1868. Reprinted, with an introduction by Arthur Thomas Tees, by Benjamin Blom, 1968. Contains information on Field's career as an actor for Smith's companies.

Articles

Coad, Oral Sumner. "Joseph M. Field." *Dictionary of American Biography*. Vol. 6. Ed. Dumas Malone. New York: Charles Scribner's Sons, 1935, p. 366. A useful brief sketch.

Oehlschlaeger, Fritz. "A Bibliography of the St. Louis *Daily Reveille*, 1844-1846." Forthcoming in *Studies in American Humor*. Contains publication information on Field's contributions to the *Reveille*.

Spotts, Carl Brooks. "The Development of Fiction on the Missouri Frontier." *Missouri Historical Review*, 29 (1935): 100-108, 186-194. Gives a basic account of Field's career.

Fritz Oehlschlaeger

Ford, Corey

Born: New York City, on April 29, 1902
Education: Left Columbia University in 1923 without taking a degree
Died: July 27, 1969

Biography

The son of James Hitchcock and Adalaide Rickets Ford, Corey Ford was born in New York City on April 29, 1902. He was raised in the city and attended Columbia University where he worked on the staff of the *Jester*, the university humor magazine. Deciding to pursue a career as a writer, Ford left Columbia in 1923 without taking a degree and moved quickly into the circle of humorists who wrote for such magazines as *Life* and *Vanity Fair*. By 1924, Ford was writing regularly for two humor magazines, *Life* and *Judge*. In 1925, Harold Ross, the founder of *The New Yorker*, asked him to do a series of articles for that magazine. Ford began his association with *Vanity Fair* in 1926; a series of "Impossible Interviews" was followed by his monthly John Riddell parodies.

Ford also wrote for the stage, collaborating with Russell Crouse on a comedy, *Hunky Dory*, in 1922, and on a musical comedy, *Hold Your Horses*, in 1933 (both plays had short runs). Losing a great deal of money when the stock market crashed, Ford took a job in 1934 as a screenwriter with RKO Studios in Hollywood. Little came of this association. Ford then travelled for a time, returning in 1938 to Hollywood where he worked for the Hal Roach Studio and enjoyed a close friendship with W. C. Fields. He was also employed by other studios during the late 1930s, receiving screenplay credit for *Zenobia* (United Artists, 1939) and *Remember?* (with Norman Z. McLeod; MGM, 1939).

With the outbreak of World War II, Ford served in the U.S. Army Air Force for a time before joining the Office of Strategic Services. Spending most of the war in the OSS, he attained the rank of colonel. Living in New Hampshire after the war, Ford became increasingly interested in conservation and joined *Field and Stream* as an associate editor. Though humor writing was no longer his major concern, he did write a number of book-length parodies during the 1950s and 1960s. Ford died in Hanover, New Hampshire, on July 27, 1969.

Literary Analysis

Though Corey Ford was a prolific author of humorous material during a long and diverse career, his most important work as a humorist appeared during the 1920s and early 1930s. His peers and contemporaries during this period included Robert Benchley, James Thurber, Frank Sullivan, Donald Ogden Stewart, Don Marquis, and Dorothy Parker. Among this assortment of wags and wits, Ford was the humorist who "aimed at deflation, not annihilation."[1] In 1967, he described his own approach to comedy as well as much of the humor of the era: "Much of it was bigger than life, the flying custard pie, the snowball aimed at the top hat; but it was happy and wholesome, and there was no malice concealed in a joke like a rock in a snowball." "Fun had only one purpose," Ford recalled, "and that was to be funny. Humor was its own excuse."[2]

Ford early demonstrated a talent for parody. Objects of his parodies include such writers as Theodore Dreiser, William Faulkner, Sherwood Anderson, Ernest Hemingway, Eugene O'Neill, Sinclair Lewis, Robert Frost, A. A. Milne, John Galsworthy, Kathleen Norris, and Edward Stratemeyer, the creator of the Rover Boys books, among many others. Ford also parodied other figures who ventured into print, such as Mae West, Rudy Vallee, and Calvin Coolidge. Some, like Hemingway, took umbrage at Ford's jabs; others, like Dreiser, congratulated him on the accuracy of his gibes.

The greatly exaggerated good fellowship of the Rover Boys books provided a natural target for Ford. His popular parodies of these books for *Life* were collected in 1925 as *Three Rousing Cheers for the Rollo Boys*. In 1926, material from *Judge*, *Life*, *Vanity Fair*, and *The New Yorker* was collected in *The Gazelle's Ears*. Mostly brief reflections on contemporary life, these whimsical pieces are related in the first person by a typical Ford narrator who is harassed and somewhat confused. The pieces contributed to *The New Yorker* during its formative years were especially important in helping to establish the tone and style of what was to become America's most important and longest-lived humor magazine.

Ford began writing his John Riddell parodies for *Vanity Fair* in 1927. They proved to be so successful that three collections were published with elaborate frame stories and connecting material: *Meaning No Offense* (1928), *The John Riddell Murder Case* (1930), and *In the Worst Possible Taste* (1932). Essentially playful, these parodies vary in approach—some are rather elaborate jokes or hoaxes, others are literary criticism in parody form. Aiming at such targets as theme, style, and the writer's personality, Ford obviously expected his readers to have some acquaintance with the author and his work. In addition to the satiric jabs contained in his parodies, Ford's humor is conveyed through his sense of the ridiculous and absurd. For example, in "The Bridge of San Thornton Wilder," a takeoff of *The Bridge of San Luis Rey* collected in *Meaning No Offense*, Ford transforms dramatist Thornton Wilder's characters into public figures, including George Jean Nathan (George Jean Estaban) and H.L. Mencken (H.L. Manuel):

> One day twin boys were discovered in the foundlings' basket before the door of the Convent of Santa Borzoi Alfred Samuel de las Blanches. Names were applied to them before the arrival of the wet-nurse, and indeed names have been applied to them ever since. There was no way of knowing who their parents were, but local gossip, noticing as the boys grew older how aloof they held themselves and how smart and cynical they were, declared them to be Germanic and laid them in turn at all sorts of European doorways. As they grew up they gradually assumed the profession of scribe, and made a fair living condemning plays, criticizing books, and publishing a monthly magazine called

> *The Smart Set*, wherein they printed advertisements of the merchants and achieved a reputation of sorts by refusing to approve of anything.[3]

Ford's most successful parody was his book-length *Salt Water Taffy* (1929), which parodied Joan Lowell's *The Cradle of the Deep*. Published in 1929, Lowell's book purported to be an account of her life as a young girl on a trading schooner in the South Seas. *The Cradle of the Deep* was circulated by the Book-of-the-Month Club and praised for its authenticity before being exposed as containing more fiction than fact. In his parody Ford followed the incidents of Lowell's book fairly closely. *Salt Water Taffy* is presented as the "autobiography" of one June Triplett; her father, Ezra Triplett, commands a sailing ship whose name constantly changes. Thirty-two photographic illustrations include some of Ford's friends posing as the characters in his parody. Ford used Triplett and her family again in his 1931 *Coconut Oil*, a parody of African safari books.

No humorous books from Ford's pen appeared during his stints as a screenwriter in the late 1930s and his service with the U.S. Army Air Force and the Office of Strategic Services during World War II. Several of his humor books published after the war are quite short; one of the most popular of these was *How to Guess Your Age* (1950). As an associate editor for *Field and Stream*, Ford produced a column called "Lower Forty" in which he often wrote humorously about the "Lower Forty Shooting, Angling and Inside Straight Club." Some of this material was collected in several books during the late 1950s and 1960s. During the same period, Ford wrote a number of parodies, including *The Day Nothing Happened* (1959), a parody of books like Jim Bishop's *The Day Lincoln Was Shot* (1955), and *Guide to Thinking* (1961), dealing with computers.

Summary

During a career in which he wrote more than 30 books and 500 articles and stories, Corey Ford was a popular parodist both in the United States and Great Britain. Based on careful observation, his parodies consistently exhibited his sense of whimsy and the ridiculous. His goal was to provide his readers with a sense of nonsense, with warm and graceful fun.

Notes

1. Alden Whitman, "The Deflator," *New York Times*, July 28, 1969, p. 31.
2. Quoted in Whitman.
3. Corey Ford, writing as John Riddell, *Meaning No Offense* (New York: Day, 1928), pp. 25–26.

Selected Bibliography

Primary Sources

Three Rousing Cheers for the Rollo Boys. New York: Doran, 1925.

The Gazelle's Ears. New York: Doran, 1926.

(as John Riddell.) *Meaning No Offense: Being Some of the Life, Adventures, and Opinions of Trader Riddell, an Old Book Reviewer.* New York: Day, 1928.

(as June Triplett.) *Salt Water Taffy; or, Twenty Thousand Leagues Away from the Sea.* New York and London: Putnam's, 1929.

(as John Riddell.) *The John Riddell Murder Case, a Philo Vance Parody.* New York and London: Scribners, 1930.

(as June Triplett.) *Coconut Oil, June Triplett's Amazing Book Out of Darkest Africa!* New York: Brewer, Warren and Putnam, 1931.

(as John Riddell.) *In the Worst Possible Taste.* New York and London: Scribner's, 1932.

(with Alastair MacBain.) *From the Ground Up.* New York: Scribner's, 1943.

Short Cut to Tokyo: The Battle for the Aleutians. New York: Scribner's, 1943.

(with Bernt Balchen and Oliver La Farge.) *War Below Zero: The Battle for Greenland.* Boston: Houghton Mifflin, 1944; London: Allen and Unwin, 1945.

(with Alastair MacBain.) *Cloak and Dagger: The Secret Story of the OSS.* New York: Random House, 1946.

(with John Falter.) *The Horse of Another Color.* New York: Holt, 1946.

(with Alastair MacBain.) *The Last Time I Saw Them.* New York: Scribner's, 1946.

(with Alastair MacBain.) *A Man of His Own, and Other Dog Stories.* New York: Whittlesey House, 1949.

How to Guess Your Age. Garden City, N.Y.: Doubleday, 1950.

Every Dog Should Have a Man: The Care and Feeding of Dog's Best Friend. New York: Holt, 1952.

Never Say Diet: How to Live Older and Look Longer. New York: Holt, 1954; London: Allen, 1954.

Has Anybody Seen Me Lately? Garden City, N.Y.: Doubleday, 1958.

You Can Always Tell a Fisherman: The Minutes of the Lower Forty Shooting, Angling and Inside Straight Club. New York: Holt, 1958.

The Day Nothing Happened. Garden City, N.Y.: Doubleday, 1959.

Guide to Thinking. Garden City, N.Y.: Doubleday, 1961.

What Every Bachelor Knows. Garden City, N.Y.: Doubleday, 1961.

Minutes of the Lower Forty. New York: Holt, Rinehart & Winston, 1962.

And How Do We Feel This Morning? Englewood Cliffs, N.J.: Prentice-Hall, 1964.

Uncle Perk's Jug: The Misadventures of the Lower Forty Shooting, Angling, and Inside Straight Club. New York: Holt, Rinehart & Winston, 1964.

A Peculiar Service. Boston: Little, Brown, 1965.

Where the Sea Breaks Its Back: The Epic Story of a Pioneer Naturalist and the Discovery of Alaska. Boston: Little, Brown, 1966; London: Gollancz, 1967.

The Time of Laughter. Boston: Little, Brown, 1967. An autobiographical work, focusing on the humor and humorists of the 1920s.

Secondary Sources

Article

Whitman, Alden. "The Deflator," *New York Times*, July 28, 1969, p. 31. Published in conjunction with an obituary of Ford; a useful brief overview of Ford's career but contains a few inaccuracies.

Books and Material in Books

Bryan, J., III. *Merry Gentlemen (and One Lady).* New York: Atheneum, 1985, pp. 199-226. Biographical information regarding Ford is included.

Kramer, Dale. *Ross and The New Yorker.* Garden City, N.Y.: Doubleday, 1951, pp. 67, 85-86, 208, 280. Material on Ford's association with the beginnings of *The New Yorker.*

Samson, Jack. "Introduction" to *The Best of Corey Ford.* Ed. Samson. New York: Holt, Rinehart and Winston, 1975, pp. xi-xvi. Deals mainly with Ford's work on *Field and Stream* and his "Lower Forty" column.

Weales, Gerald. "Not for the Old Lady in Dubuque." In *The Comic Imagination in American Literature.* Ed. Louis D. Rubin. New Brunswick, N.J.: Rutgers University Press, 1973, pp. 231, 236, 238-239, 241-242. Material dealing with Ford's connection with *The New Yorker.*

L. Moody Simms, Jr.

Freeman, Mary Eleanor Wilkins

Born: Randolph, Massachusetts, on October 31, 1852

Education: High school, Brattleboro, Vermont. Attended Mount Holyoke Seminary, 1870-1871, left because of ill health

Marriage: Dr. Charles Freeman, January 1, 1902, legally separated, 1922

Died: March 15, 1930

Biography

The elder of the two children of Warren and Eleanor Lothrop Wilkins, Mary Ella (later changed to Eleanor) Wilkins was born in Randolph, Massachusetts, on October 31, 1852. Her father, a housepainter, had financial difficulties and the family moved to Brattleboro, Vermont, in 1867. Mary attended Brattleboro High School, graduating in 1870. She then began work at Mount Holyoke Seminary, but ill health forced her withdrawal; her formal education ended after she had taken a few more courses at a girl's seminary in West Brattleboro.

Living at home, she tried teaching in a girl's school and hoped, for a while, to support herself as an artist. In reduced financial condition, the family had to live in a home where the mother served as housekeeper; but her death, in 1880, caused even more troubles for the family, and the death of Anna, Mary's younger sister, in 1876, was a blow to the family. Mary kept house for her father and wrote poetry that was published in the early 1880s. In 1882, her first story, "Two Old Lovers," was accepted by *Harper's Bazar* (its spelling in the nineteenth century), and she began a long and prolific career as a writer of fiction. She was successful from the first; her stories were accepted by the popular magazines. A first collection, *A Humble Romance and Other Stories* (1887), was published by Harper and Brothers. Fourteen more volumes, containing about one hundred and fifty of her stories, were to follow, as well as fifteen novels.

Her life was largely uneventful, a record of hard work and frequent publication. In 1892 she met Dr. Charles Freeman, of Metuchen, New Jersey. They were married in 1902, when she was nearly fifty. Thereafter, she lived in New Jersey and made it as well as her own New England the scene of her fiction. The marriage turned out badly. Freeman, an alcoholic, spent time in sanatoriums and, in 1920, was committed to the state hospital for the insane in Trenton. They were separated in 1922 and Freeman died the next year; his will disinherited her but she was able to contest it successfully. Honors came in her later years: in 1926, she was awarded the William Dean Howells Medal and was elected to the National Institute of Arts and Letters. On March 15, 1930, she died at the age of seventy-seven.

Literary Analysis

Freeman's first collection of short stories was a critical success. A second collection, *A New England Nun and Other Stories* (1891) followed, and she began writing novels as well, with *Jane Field* (1893) and *Pembroke* (1894). For the next decade and a half, her volumes appeared every year. Some of the most notable were *The Portion of Labor* (1901), a novel, and collections such as *Six Trees* (1903) and *The Wind in the Rosebush and Other Stories of the Supernatural* (1903). After this, there was a falling off in the quality of her fiction, though she continued to produce it with great regularity. *The Givers* (1904) and *The Debtor* (1905), both novels, are generally judged harshly by critics. Similarly, further collections of short stories, including *The Copy-Cat and Other Stories* (1914), *The Win-*

ning Lady and Others (1909), and *Edgewater People* (1918) were not well received. In 1927, Henry Lanier edited a volume of *The Best Stories of Mary E. Wilkins*, a solid and influential selection of her finest work in the short story genre.

Some critics have made a case for one or another of her novels, but it is generally conceded that Freeman's genius asserted itself most readily in a good portion of her two hundred short stories. In composing them she placed herself in that school of American fiction called "local color." There is no easy definition of the term, but some characteristics might be named: the author attempts to present an almost photographically realistic picture of ordinary life, and the locale is restricted to a small geographic area, usually rural, of small farms and villages. Dialect, local manners, customs, beliefs, and occupations are rendered in loving detail. The reader gets to know the place and the people intimately, for the author concentrates upon recording the smallest details of daily life—food, work, courtship and marriage, the small quarrels that seem to go on and on. Because it is easy to sentimentalize such lives and the author wishes to avoid sentimentality, descriptions are carefully orchestrated with some irony. Reference to the larger concerns of the outside world is accomplished by synecdoche; the tiny scope of the presented lives implies the larger world we live in.

Josephine Donovan argues cogently that New England local color fiction is a "woman's tradition" in American writing by discussing the writings of a brilliant group, including Harriet Beecher Stowe (1811-1896), Rose Terry Cooke (1827-1892), Elizabeth Stuart Phelps (1844-1911), Sarah Orne Jewett (1849-1909), as well as Mary Freeman, as exemplars of this tradition. She locates the sources of local color in English rural sketches and stories by Mary Russell Mitford (*Our Village*) and Elizabeth Gaskell (*Cranford*) and in the sketches and tales of earlier American woman writers: Catherine Sedgwick's *A New-England Tale*, Sarah Josepha Hale's *Sketches of American Character*, and Caroline Kirkland's *A New Home—Who'll Follow?* In their insistence upon local details, dialect, and creation of humble characters, these earlier writings pointed the way for the local colorists. To that tradition, Freeman and others added a preoccupation with women's issues such as intense relationships between women or between mothers and daughters, self-sacrifice, and the difficulties that characters experience in establishing a proper role as women.

There is considerable room for humor in local color fiction, and Freeman uses some skillful techniques. Characters are presented as typical of their New England background; they tend to be laconic in the extreme, expressing a world of emotion in the briefest of sentences. Old Candace Whitcomb, in "A Village Singer," who has sung in the village church for forty years, is dismissed and replaced by a younger woman with a better voice. The old woman's rage is expressed in her mistreatment of the picture album given her by the congregation and by her stubborn playing and singing from her home next to the church as she tries to drown out her rival. Her bitterness is ill-concealed, and she becomes ill to the point of dying. But, then she seems to moderate her stance, asks for forgiveness, and, as a final gesture of good will, wants the rival to sing at her deathbed. She listens with "a holy and radiant expression," but her final comment, in death, at the end of the story is, "You flatted a little on—soul." This sort of human quirkiness is evident as early as Freeman's first published story, "Two Old Lovers," in which David Emmons has courted Maria for years but never asked the essential question. At the end of the story, on his deathbed, at a time when the reader could expect a resolution, David can only say, "Maria, I'm—dyin', an'—I allers meant to—have asked you—to—marry me."

Freeman delineates her character types with precision and affection. The heroine of "A New England Nun," one of her best-known tales, is Louisa Ellis, who happily leads a spinster's life, glorying in the solitary existence that allows her to have everything just as she wants it. She can do her sewing (sometimes undoing stitches just for the pleasure of redoing them), have fresh currants with her tea, keep her little house neat and orderly, and distill fragrances from the roses and mints in her garden. The story has its mild conflict in the return of an old beau, Joe Daggett, pledged for fourteen years to marry Louisa and now ready, however reluctantly, to redeem his pledge. Both are silently resigned to the dubious happiness they foresee; neither is quite ready to get out of the arrangement, though Joe really loves another woman, and Louisa understands that, in marriage, he will upset her nunlike existence, disarrange her precisely kept belongings, bring in his coarse masculinity, and, worst of all, track dirt into her house. The good luck of being able, finally, to reject Joe as a suitor returns Louisa to the balance of her desired life. As the author puts it, "If Louisa had sold her birthright she did not know it, the taste of the pottage was so delicious."

But, the reader, laughing at such quaint behavior, also notices a rather wonderful quality in these and other characters in the stories. There is genuine pathos in their absolute scrupulousness, their determination to be honest and to do what is right. Louisa Ellis will marry Joe Dag-

gett, if she has to, because she promised to marry him. It is necessary for the author to act as a sort of *deus ex machina* to rescue Louisa from what would have been an unhappy union, one to be borne, no doubt, in humble silence. Likewise, Martha Patch, in the appropriately titled story, "An Honest Soul," is making patchwork quilts to fill some orders. Nearly finished, she notices that she has made a mistake in her matching of the patches, and she takes the quilts apart, a long and tedious task, to repair her error. Unfortunately, she repeats the mistake because she is suffering from hunger and must labor again, for weeks, to set the job right. Here the author speculates, somewhat ambiguously for the reader: "It is a hard question to decide, whether there were any real merit in such finely strained honesty, or whether it were merely a case of morbid conscientiousness." Still, the story, in its plot and characterization, has been unambiguous on this point. Conscientiousness is not morbid. Martha is doing what she knows is right, and she excites sympathy and admiration.

The people in her stories seem gentle and almost silent as they move through their mostly uneventful lives, but they generally possess a quiet tenacity that Freeman chooses to delineate in the humorous turnings of her plots. In "The Revolt of 'Mother,'" another of the frequently reprinted tales, she portrays, in Sarah Penn, one of these admirable persons. The Penn family has a small, rather mean house that the father has been promising for years to replace. Everyone has waited patiently while he has built the farm into a prosperous undertaking, and Sarah has kept house in the little building, making do with what she has, working "like an artist so perfect that he has apparently no art." The crisis comes when Adoniram, the husband, begins to put up another new barn, which may not even be needed, on the site of the long-promised fine new house. Furthermore, he has not consulted with his wife about the project. The issue is clearly drawn: when one pledges something, one should keep the pledge. Sarah speaks to her husband, to hold him to his promise, but he is evasive and she is unsuccessful. When he is away on business, she asserts her strength by moving furniture and family from the inadequate house to the well-built new barn, turning it, at a stroke, into a fine house. Returning, the old husband is thunderstruck at this clear opposition to his wishes and has nothing to say: "Adoniram was like a fortress whose walls had no active resistance, and went down the instant the right besieging tools were used." Freeman's metaphors of walls, buildings, and fortresses serve well as she depicts the quiet war between women and men.

Another device to evoke humor is Freeman's use of commentary upon her stories and upon the characters she is drawing. She likes to nail down a peculiarity with a quick remark and does not often let pass the opportunity of capping a description with an observation. David Emmons, of "Two Old Lovers," is characterized as a tardy lover who has courted Maria Brewster for a quarter of a century without asking for her hand. But, then, he is surely the slowest of all men in the village of Leyden and, as Freeman has it, "there was a standing joke that the meeting-house passed him one morning on his way to the shop." In the story, "A Poetess," Betsey Dole is represented as the author of very poor verse. Asked to write a memorial poem, she is described as sitting and composing it, line by line, looking like the genius of sentimental poetry. This is not quite enough for Freeman, though, who pushes the comedy a bit further by suggesting that a proposed reader could know, without even reading, what the lines of poetry would be like, and that, in them, "flowers rhymed neatly with vernal bowers, home with beyond the tomb, and heaven with even."

Freeman's delineation of the New England character is accompanied by a sharply defined description of setting. The locale of these stories greatly influences their movement, and human traits are shaped by the physical surroundings. The land in Vermont is harsh and difficult; long hours and years of hard work are needed for its people to scrape out a bare living. As a result, the people bear the marks of their labor and near poverty. They must be steadfast to survive, and hence they make a virtue of steadfastness. In "Louisa," for instance, a girl will not marry even though the unwanted marriage might rescue her and her family from hardship. "Sister Liddy" takes place in an almshouse, an unpleasing setting within a village, bare and treeless. Its bareness reflects the lives of the characters: "It seemed like the folks whom it sheltered, out in the full glare of day, without any kindly shade between itself and the dull, unfeeling stare of curiosity."

In stories such as "Sister Liddy," there is little of the humor that Freeman often uses to ease the persistent sense of unfulfillment in some of her other stories. By means of the setting, she conveys a sense of despair among the poverty-stricken inmates of the house. Life is narrow and monotonous, a product of an unyielding environment that can make the characters unyielding. In the "Introductory Sketch" to her novel, *Pembroke*, Freeman comments upon the intractable will of the people and illustrates with an anecdote:

> There lived in a New England village, at no very remote time, a man who objected to the painting of the kitchen floor and who quarreled furiously with his wife concerning the same. When she persisted, in spite of his wishes to the contrary and the floor was painted, he refused to cross it to his dying day and always, to his great inconvenience but probably to his soul's satisfaction, walked around it.

The stubbornness displayed here is damaging to the human spirit, but it is appropriate and comic. Because such obstinacy is necessary even for survival, it becomes a central trait of the characters that the author is creating.

Summary

In her many stories and novels, Mary Wilkins Freeman portrays, with loving care, the small world of her deprived characters. More or less doomed to live within narrow circumstances, they show often their resolve and, sometimes, their harshness. Within the rather small scope she allows herself, the author realistically shows how her people live within the restrictions that govern their lives and frequently seem to overcome them. Given her self-imposed limitation, Freeman is able to depict her characters as individuals struggling against adversity and, sometimes, achieving small triumphs.

Selected Bibliography

Primary Sources

A Humble Romance and Other Stories. New York: Harper and Brothers, 1887.

A New England Nun and Other Stories. New York: Harper and Brothers, 1891.

Pembroke. New York: Harper and Brothers, 1894.

Silence and Other Stories. New York: Harper and Brothers, 1898.

The Love of Parson Lord and Other Stories. New York: Harper and Brothers, 1900.

Understudies. New York: Harper and Brothers, 1901.

The Portion of Labor. New York: Harper and Brothers, 1901.

Six Trees. New York: Harper and Brothers, 1903.

The Wind in the Rose-Bush and Other Stories of the Supernatural. New York: Doubleday, Page and Company, 1903.

The Fair Lavinia and Others. New York: Harper and Brothers, 1907.

The Best Stories of Mary E. Wilkins. Introduction by H.W. Lanier. New York: Harper and Brothers, 1927.

Secondary Sources

Biography and Bibliography

Foster, Edward. *Mary E. Wilkins Freeman.* New York: Hendricks House, 1956. Fullest biography; most complete bibliography available.

Books and Chapters in Books

Donovan, Josephine. *New England Local Color Literature: A Women's Tradition.* New York: Frederick Ungar, 1983. Excellent background material on local color and one chapter on Freeman.

Hamblen, Abigail Ann. *The New England Art of Mary E. Wilkins Freeman.* Amherst, Mass.: The Green Knight Press, 1966. Useful monograph that discusses many of the stories.

Quinn, Arthur Hobson. *American Fiction: A Historical Survey.* New York: Appleton Century, 1936. Brief but helpful account of Freeman's work.

Westbrook, Perry D. *Acres of Flint: Writers of Rural New England, 1870-1900.* Washington, D.C.: The Scarecrow Press, 1951. Studies local color tradition.

Westbrook, Perry D. *Mary Wilkins Freeman.* New York: Twayne Publishers, 1967. The best and fullest critical account of Freeman's fiction.

Douglas Robillard

Friedman, Bruce Jay

Born: The Bronx, New York, on April 26, 1930

Education: University of Missouri, B.A., 1951

Marriage: Ginger Howard, June 13, 1954, three children, marriage dissolved

Biography

The quintessential Bruce J. Friedman protagonist, visible in several of his novels and short stories, is a child of New York, reared in a three-room apartment by a brassy, overpowering mother with vague showbiz connections and enormous vitality, often expressed through sexual display or insult. His father, an inconsiderable nebbish who works faithfully and haplessly at a trade like couch-cutting, hardly figures except as a disappointment to both son and mother. The son attends a large school, vaguely agricultural, somewhere in the Midwest and later serves in the Air Force, in a non-flying role that makes him feel like an impostor. After marriage to a western girl of disturbing sexuality he lives on the East Coast and works in a city as a sort of writer—in public relations for the homicide squad, for instance, or writing product labels. The tension of his life causes an illness. His recovery from it may or may not improve his life.

Friedman has been understandably reluctant to declare that his life is the model for this repeated pattern and, beyond a certain point, it obviously is not. He was, however, born in the Bronx. His mother, remembered by neighbors as a flamboyant woman, had show-business connections that introduced Friedman to Broadway shows as a child. He graduated from DeWitt Clinton High School and went to the University of Missouri. There he majored in journalism and wrote for the university newspaper. In 1951 he entered the Air Force, writing for a magazine called *Air Training.* While in the Air Force, he married Ginger Howard, an actress and model. In 1954 he returned to New York and began a career with Magazine Management Company, for which he edited such magazines as *Man, Male,* and *Man's World.* While trying to get started as a writer of fiction, he professes to have enjoyed his work there, and Mario Puzo, one of his comrades on the men's magazines, has praised his work as an editor.

Although he had sold the short story "Wonderful Golden Rule Days," a rueful short piece about high school disappointment, to *The New Yorker* in 1953, Friedman enjoyed what he calls his "breakthrough" in 1958 when his years of writing at night began to pay off with stories being accepted by *Playboy* and other magazines. In 1962 he published his first novel, *Stern,* which received some good reviews although it sold only 4,000 copies. His next book was a collection of short stories, *Far From the City of Class, and Other Stories* (1963), which contained those of his stories published in the fifties as well as several that obviously represent the beginnings of *A Mother's Kisses* (1964), Friedman's second novel and a best-seller. He began to be solicited by representatives of the theater and Hollywood at this time. In 1966 his second collection of short stories, *Black Angels,* appeared as did a reissue of *Stern* and *A Mother's Kisses* in one volume, and an off-Broadway production of his one-act play, *23 Pat O'Brien Movies,* based on one of the stories in *Far From the City of Class.* His first full-length play, *Scuba Duba: A Tense Comedy,* was produced in 1967 and was a popular success. An article in the *New York Times Magazine* in January 1968· called him "the hottest writer of the year."

Subsequently, Friedman's work has taken a curious turn. His third novel, *The Dick* (1970), was rather harshly received by reviewers. It was followed by another play, *Steambath* (produced off-Broadway in 1970), and then *About Harry Towns* (1974), a collection of loosely related vignettes, originally published as separate stories, concerning a prosperous scriptwriter undergoing a sort of midlife crisis. Harry Towns is unlike earlier Friedman protagonists, and the novel is not very funny. In 1976 Friedman published *The Lonely Guy's Book of Life,* a wry send-up of the self-help genre. His novel *Tokyo Woes* was published in 1985.

The sharply reduced output of fiction since

1970 is apparently related to his increased involvement in the movies. As early as 1971, he wrote the screenplay for *The Owl and the Pussycat*. Since then, he has been involved in screenwriting for *Stir Crazy*, *Splash*, and *Doctor Detroit*. *Doctor Detroit* was based on one of his stories, "Detroit Abe"; another story, "A Change of Plans," was the basis for the movie *The Heartbreak Kid*; and his book *The Lonely Guy's Book of Life* was made into a Steve Martin film called *The Lonely Guy*. Like his screenwriter-protagonist Harry Towns, Friedman is now a bicoastal figure.

Literary Analysis

From the beginning Bruce Jay Friedman has been identified as a "black humorist." Black humor, omnipresent in the sixties as new figures like Joseph Heller, Edward Albee, and Thomas Pynchon, along with Friedman, began to impose their shocking but still funny visions on an unprepared American reading public, is hard to define. Friedman himself edited a collection titled *Black Humor* in 1965. Its introduction provides a few clues—black humorists write about outsiders; their work contains despair of a resilient type; they operate "obliquely, coming at you from somewhere in left field, throwing you some laughs to get you to lower your guard." The humor is outrageous, he decides, because the times are outrageous.[1] Stanley Kauffman succinctly defines black humor as "the perception of what is funny in the terrible . . . the *acceptance* of insanity, putting a fix on it, and attempting to mark out a *cordon sanitaire* of laughter."[2] Friedman, commenting on his own writing in a *New York Times Magazine* profile, insists on its seriousness and continues: "I've never written a line in my life pointed toward satire—or anything else. I don't try to be funny ha-ha and I never laugh at my own writing. Let me tell you right now I don't go in for that sort of thing."[3] Nevertheless, his early novels are, despite the pain of their characters, funny ha-ha. With their mordant outlook on the human predicament, their focus on disturbance and mutilation and embarrassment and all of the things that make people uncomfortable and fearful, they make the reader laugh out loud, continuously.

In some ways *Stern*, Friedman's first book, is his best. In it he achieves his subtlest combination of humor and dread. It is the story of a middle-class Jew who moves from the city of his birth to the suburbs. Having imagined for himself some sort of idyll, he finds instead a nightmare. His house is a malevolent presence, his shrubs wither, his son has no friends and sits in the middle of the blasted lawn, sucking blankets. Stern commutes long distances to his work. On his return each night he is attacked by giant,

mysterious dogs. Worst of all is "the kike man," a neighbor who calls Mrs. Stern a kike and pushes her down, peering at her exposed crotch. The plot details the effects, on Stern, of this challenge to his happiness. The challenge is also, as he constantly feels, to his manhood. He believes that he should confront the kike man and fight him, but he finds reasons not to do so. Eventually his anxiety produces first an ulcer that sends him to a convalescent home and then a nervous breakdown. Recovered, he challenges the kike man to a fight; though his ear is nearly severed by the blow he receives and his own punch comes out "girlish and ineffectual," Stern feels, momentarily, that he has acquitted himself. He finds himself still afraid, though, and contents himself with hugs for his wife and son.

Stern illustrates Friedman's greatest strengths as a writer. One of them is his absolute accuracy in depicting paranoia and worry, particularly the worry of a man unsure if he is fulfilling his obligations as a man. Stern is insecure about his role as worker, as father, as husband. He appreciates any excuse his life may offer him for *not* having to live up to the requirements he acknowledges—and in this sense the ulcer and the nervous breakdown are escapes for him. He seeks ways of validating himself, both to himself and to others. Life is frightening and mysterious for him. He also embodies the peculiar type of Jewishness characteristic of Friedman's character, Jewishness recognized as a stigma (particularly in the suburbs), as a source of nervous joking, but never as a religion. Stern remembers only the mysterious groaning of religious services, the family fighting that always ruined the Seder.

The comedy in *Stern*—and this is true of Friedman's best work generally—is of two sorts, both functions of his rich use of detail. One is his almost limitless ability to create characters and endow them with strange features and convincing, though not really realistic, ways of expressing themselves. Stern's mother and father, his remembered uncles, his doctor, the people he meets at the rest home, all are vivid and memorable. The more important source of comedy is the author's style. Friedman writes a vivid, nervous, excessive style, full of vigorous verbs and heightened figures of speech. For instance, Stern thinks about the kike man, extrapolating wildly from his glimpse of the man's veteran's jacket:

> It meant he had come through the worst
> part of the Normandy campaign, knew
> how to hold his breath in foxholes for
> hours at a time and then sneak out to
> slit a throat in silence. He was skilled as
> a foot fighter and went always with
> deadly accuracy to a man's groin. Stern

pictured him at veteran beer parties, drawing laughs with stories of the kike who'd moved in down the way a mile.

(pp. 52-53)

When Stern encounters a crippled black orderly at the Grove Rest Home, he responds to him in this vividly phrased passage:

Despite his complicated legs, he seemed a terribly strong man to Stern, who felt that even were he to flee to the Netherlands after a milk and cookie infraction, getting a fifteen-hour start, the Negro would go after him Porgy-like and catch him eventually.

Stern and two other patients escape for some fun with a Puerto Rican girl, an escapade in which Stern validates himself by fighting and having sex, and the girl proves to be another of the unusual characters Stern keeps encountering:

Turning to Stern, she said, "He's a natural man. I'd like to feel his energy coursing through my vitals." In the distance, Stern had imagined her hips to be flaring and substantial, but actually they had a kind of diving, low-slung poverty about them. She wore a skintight blue skirt, and Stern wondered whether she hadn't worn it for an entire year and was to wear it the next three until poverty-stricken Puerto Rican underwear came bursting through its fabric.

Friedman's second novel, *A Mother's Kisses*, is funnier than *Stern* but less profound in theme. The protagonist, Joseph, is also a worrier, but less interesting than Stern; his obvious problems (bad summer job, an inability to get into a good college, general adolescent insecurity about life) are subordinated to his increasingly strained relationship to his mother. She is the classic Friedman mother—loud, showy, protective, pushy, more than a little in love with her own son. She accompanies Joseph to summer camp, then to Kansas Land Grant Agricultural University, where she is installed in the Goatback Hotel until he finally makes her leave. Meg is a broad caricature of the Jewish mother and, although much more interesting than Joseph, finally becomes tiresome. Joseph is passive. His story, aside from the Oedipal mother problems, is of encountering a series of amusingly grotesque people. He works at camp with an old man named Lemuel who "spoke with a crooked, snaggletoothed wisdom, tilting his head a little and making learned old seaman's faces." But, the things he says belie the wisdom in his appearance; for instance, he offers this *aperçu*:

"You know what," he said, Ahab now, craftily appraising a squall off the starboard bow.

"What's that?"

"A man sometimes will do a funny thing."

"What do you mean?"

"That's what I mean," he said. "That's just what I mean."

Joseph did not want to hurt his feelings and so he gave his head a little shake as though the thought hadn't quite penetrated just yet, but he was going to go off and do a lot of pondering about it.

Joseph "resolves" his problem with his dominating mother, finally succeeding in sending her back to New York, though not without ambivalent feelings, and makes a modest adjustment to his world. His story, though, is not only less dramatic than that of Stern but simply less interesting as a story. It is enhanced by incidentals and the comic monster, Meg.

Friedman's other major work of the early sixties is included in his two books of short stories, *Far from the City of Class* and *Black Angels*. The first volume contains several stories which in different form are to become part of *A Mother's Kisses*; for instance, "Far from the City of Class" is about a Jewish boy beginning college in the Midwest; "The Trip" is about a mother accompanying her unwilling son to a similar college; in "The Good Time," a Meg-like mother smothers her dominated son (now in the Air Force) with forced fun and vulgar attentions; in "The Canning of Mother Dean," a fraternity housemother, later reincarnated as Mother Gibbons in *A Mother's Kisses*, is fired by Eastern sharpies. Other stories suggest Stern. Perhaps the funniest, "When You're Excused You're Excused," plays on Jewish material: Mr. Kessler takes advantage of a slight illness to excuse himself from Yom Kippur services; now "excused," as he insists, he goes completely wild, moving from workouts at a health club to smoking pot, adultery, and crime. But, he draws the line when one of his new friends reacts slightingly to the name of a Jewish ballplayer. Mr. Kessler explains:

"Maybe I went to Vic Tanny's and shacked up with a girl named Irish and got drunk and ate barbecued ham hocks. Maybe I hid a dead cop and smoked marijuana and went to a crazy party and got kissed by a Negro homosexual ballet dancer. But I'm not letting you get away with something like that. . . . NO SON OF A BITCH IS GOING TO SAY ANYTHING ABOUT POOR 'PHUMBLIN'

PHIL' WEINTRAUB ON YOM KIP-
PUR!"

A third category of stories involves fantasy.
In one a man is addressed directly by a show on
television. In another a man is allowed to go
back in his history and complete all his failed
seductions. Another character finally enjoys a
breakthrough, after years in analysis, by murdering the analyst's wife. Another investigates the
afterlife and decides that the "good" are divided
from the "bad" there by the quality of their
sandals.

The second book of stories, *Black Angels*, has
fewer connections with the novels, though "The
Punch" succinctly addresses a man's need to
punch somebody in order to show his wife that
he is a man and is similar in tone to *Stern*. The
vein of fantasy is strong here. In "The Investor,"
a hospital patient's temperature is tragically
linked to the market price of a volatile stock;
when it splits three for one, his temperature
drops to 52 7/8. In a nice twist, the widow of the
deceased runs off with the doctor. Their conversation is vintage Friedman: When the doctor,
having just told her of her husband's death,
blurts out "You're a doll and have you ever been
to Rochester?" she responds with "My mother
said all doctors were bastardos, and we paid
them in crops, the main one being asparagus
spears. Are you sure you're not saying all of this
because of m'boobs?" In "The Night Boxing
Ended," a boxer literally knocks another's head
off:

> The writers present tended, generally,
> to say it "floated" out into the sixth row
> alongside, where it was caught by a gen-
> tleman in the haberdashery business,
> not, as a matter of fact, a regular fight
> fan. . . . Actually, it sailed out rather
> swiftly, in the style of a baseball hit off
> the end of a cracked bat, not with blind-
> ing speed either, but with a certain
> amount of zip on it.

Both of these collections contain fine fiction;
Friedman is inventive, and his skill at character
creation and his comic style are effective in the
short form. He is a major short story writer.

Friedman's next novel, *The Dick*, is less successful. The main character, a homicide public
relations expert named Kenneth LePeters, is
beset with worries. He isn't really a dick (he has
a half-sized "badgette"). His wife is at first
frigid, then involved in a tempestuous affair
with another detective. He is very insecure in his
suburb, where his daughter is the only white
child in a black school. Perhaps most symptom-
atically, he has a Jewish problem. Originally
Kenneth Sussman, he has changed his name; he

worries when his Jewishness becomes known
and is reluctant to know other Jews. The novel
has a number of funny features and perhaps a
surplus of "characters"—every detective is more
or less made up of comic and grotesque qualities,
including the familiar prosthetic appliances
which amuse Friedman so much. The theme of
dubious manliness is present again, this time
made rather obtrusively phallic (the title, the
assumed name of LePeters, the hero's genital
disorder) and the ending is pat.

About Harry Towns is a hip story of a man
who is lost in the world, but not as unhappy
about his plight as he might be, or as guilty
about his shortcomings as he should be. A bad
son and husband, a patchy father, a drug-user
who is late to his mother's funeral because of a
previous engagement to score cocaine, Harry
lives a life that he often suspects to be wrong,
but despite rather histrionic gestures of self-
reproach, he continues much as he has begun.
He, too, undergoes an altering illness and seems
to have changed his ways, but we see no real
change and reserve judgment on its likelihood.
About Harry Towns is a departure for Friedman
and not a very satisfactory one. He has changed
the milieu of his fiction, changed his protagonist
(Harry is almost nothing like Stern or LePeters),
and reduced the comedy. Most importantly, the
style has become cool, laid-back. The enormous
energy and resulting comedy of the early Friedman style have given way to efficient, sometimes
flat prose.

Friedman's 1976 book, *The Lonely Guy's
Book of Life*, is funny. Not a novel, it is a compendium of advice for lonely guys (essentially
perceived as divorced men living in the city).
The chapters, such as two titled "The Lonely
Guy's Cookbook" and "Sex and the Lonely Guy,"
are short, relatively separable, and jokey. Occasionally they show the slightly manic flair of
early Friedman. Having established that the
lonely guy will take lots of naps so that time will
pass more quickly, he offers tips on napping,
including:

> Nap itches. The veteran napper, of
> course, scratches his in advance. Still
> and all, stubborn ones often slip by and
> should be handled with light, stroking,
> almost Zen-like motions, not clawed at
> with outrage. As for the out-of-the-way
> shoulder-blade itches, the veteran
> napper prepares for these by keeping an
> object with an abrasive surface—such as
> a Brillo pad—in bed with him and back-
> ing his way up on it.

The Lonely Guy envisioned by this book is a
one-dimensional being. He is lonely because he
lives alone. We get no sign here of the deeper

perception Friedman worked into *Stern*, for instance, that a guy can be lonely without being alone, that a core loneliness can tear at him while he is making love with his wife. There has been a simplification of the vision here, and the humor is correspondingly easier. This is a funny book, but it is not black humor. The comedy is without the undertone of dread and despair that deepened Friedman's early books.

In spite of his filmwriting experiences, Friedman has not been ruined by Hollywood; he is still a major humorous writer. But, it is possible to detect certain negative influences of his motion picture career. One is the way that Friedman has turned to a different *milieu*. Compare Harry Towns, screenwriter, in his luxurious apartment of glass and steel high atop Manhattan with his expensive cocaine habit, his casual stewardess and showgirl habit, his jaunts to Vegas, and his expense account trips to the Coast, to Stern or LePeters, miserable in the unexclusive suburbs, worried about elderly Jewish uncles and aunts, unsure about the mortgage, concerned with the children's friends. One body of material is not more valid than another; still, Friedman worked more successfully the vein of lower-middle-class neurosis, no matter what his own circumstances at the time may have been, than the expensive anxieties of rootless cosmopolitans.

Another effect of his screenwriting may be the increasing patness of Friedman's endings. *The Dick* ends with a sequence—LePeters becoming a masterful cop, then renouncing the career, shooting the toes off his wife's lover, then spurning her melting pleas for reconciliation—that, in its staginess and obvious wish-fulfillment, would have worked better as one of Stern's imaginary triumphs or one of the fantasies of *Black Angels*. Finally, it seems possible that writing for the movies has done something to homogenize and detoxify Friedman's humor. His screenwriting credits (*Splash*, *The Lonely Guy*) represent a good-natured, upbeat comedy that emphasizes funny jokes and comic distress that does not last. *Splash* is a boy-meets-mermaid story with a happy ending. *The Lonely Guy*, unlike the book, has a happy, wish-fulfillment twist, with the Steve Martin character writing a best-seller and fending off women who now cannot get enough of him.

Writers must use their experiences, and successful writers write from an experience of successful living. Success can be funny in the same dark way as failure, however. The savage humor of inadequacy and fear that motivated Friedman's *Stern*, *A Mother's Kisses*, the two collections of short fiction and his plays of the 1960s, are simply better than his more recent work. Still, his more recent work is part of an estimable body of writing that makes Friedman one of America's most important living humorists.

Summary

Bruce Jay Friedman is a writer of novels, short stories, plays, various kinds of nonfiction, and (particularly in recent years) screenplays. He became known in the early 1960s as a practitioner of "black humor"—a term usually acknowledged as his own—and as the possessor of a unique slant on the anxieties of middle-class urban family men. Unlike his contemporaries Philip Roth and Joseph Heller, with whom he is frequently compared, Friedman's work, especially in the shorter forms, has mixed comedy, despair, realism, and fantasy in a way that is immediately recognizable and unmistakeably his own. Although his work has moved in different directions since the early 1970s, his best writing is that which exploits the comic side of sickness, uncertainty, and dread.

Notes

1. Bruce Jay Friedman, ed., *Black Humor* (New York: Bantam, 1965), p. xi.
2. Stanley Kauffman, "Frightened Writer," *New Republic*, 155 (October 8, 1966): 20.
3. Josh Greenfield, "Bruce Jay Friedman Is Hanging by His Thumbs," *New York Times Magazine*, January 14, 1968, p. 42.

Selected Bibliography

Primary Sources

Novels

Stern. New York: Simon and Schuster, 1962.
A Mother's Kisses. New York: Simon and Schuster, 1964.
The Dick. New York: Knopf, 1970.
About Harry Towns. New York: Knopf, 1974.
Tokyo Woes. New York: Fine, 1985.

Plays

Scuba Duba: A Tense Comedy. New York: Simon and Schuster, 1968.
Steambath. New York: Knopf, 1971.

Collections of Stories

Far from the City of Class, and Other Stories. New York: Frommer-Pas mantier, 1963.
Black Angels. New York: Simon and Schuster, 1967.

Other

The Lonely Guy's Book of Life. New York: McGraw-Hill, 1976.
Black Humor (editor). New York: Bantam, 1965.

Secondary Sources

Books

Schultz, Max F. *Black Humor Fiction of the Sixties.* Athens: Ohio University Press, 1973, pp. 91–123. Puts Friedman into context of his contemporaries. Useful comparisons with Charles Wright and Joseph Heller.
——— . *Bruce Jay Friedman.* New York: Twayne, 1974. The only full-length treatment. Covers books up through *The Dick* and *Steambath*.

——— . *Radical Sophistication: Studies in Contemporary Jewish-American Novelists.* Athens: Ohio University Press, 1969, pp. 173-197. Considers Friedman specifically as a Jewish novelist and the problems of Jewishness for his protagonists. Particularly good on the function of love and sex in the novels (focuses on *Stern* and *A Mother's Kisses*).

Articles

Algren, Nelson. "The Radical Innocent." *The Nation*, 199 (September 21, 1964): 142-143. Excellent critical introduction; compares Friedman to Samuel Beckett; maintains that "Friedman's craft is in provoking laughter at the same time that the air grows murderous."

Greenfield, Josh. "Bruce Jay Friedman Is Hanging by His Thumbs." *New York Times Magazine*, January 14, 1968, pp. 30-42. Contains useful biographical information, commentary by Friedman on his writing, useful analysis of typical Friedman situations. Particular focus on *Scuba Duba*, Friedman's approach to questions of race.

Kauffman, Stanley. "Frightened Writer." *New Republic*, 155 (October 8, 1966): 20, 37. Intelligent appreciation, good on black humor and on Friedman's style.

Klein, Marcus. "Further Notes on the Dereliction of Culture: Edward Louis Wallant and Bruce Jay Friedman." *Contemporary American-Jewish Literature: Critical Essays.* Ed. Irving Malin. Bloomington: Indiana University Press, 1973, pp. 229-247. Interesting assessment: "Friedman, dancing on the edge of a breakdown, is obsessively funny and vulgar."

Larner, Jeremy. "Compulsion to Toughness." *The Nation* 195 (December 1, 1962): 380-381. A review of *Stern* but contains useful observations on challenge to self-respect and fantasies of violence that are recurrent motifs in Friedman's fiction.

Lewis, Stuart. "Myth and Ritual in the Short Fiction of Bruce Jay Friedman." *Studies in Short Fiction*, 10 (1973): 415-416. A labored argument that Friedman's stories "juxtapose the world of nature myths with our technological society," backed by citations from *The Golden Bough*.

——— . "Rootlessness and Alienation in the Novels of Bruce Jay Friedman." *CLA Journal* 18 (1975): 422-433. Humorless look at the problems of Friedman's protagonists.

Pinsker, Sanford. "The Graying of Black Humor." *Studies in the Twentieth Century*, 9 (1972): 15-33. An interesting analysis of black humor, comparing Friedman unfavorably with Ken Kesey and Joseph Heller and declaring that Friedman's canon demonstrates that black humor alone makes for a limited—and often shaky—foundation on which to build a novel.

Trachtenberg, Stanley. "The Humiliated Hero: Bruce Jay Friedman's *Stern*." *Critique*, 7 (1965): 91-93. Good, though brief, treatment of Stern as victim, placing the novel in the context of "the gloomy introspection of Poe, Hawthorne, and Melville." Shows no awareness that *Stern* is a funny book, however.

Wisse, Ruth R. *The Schlemiel as Modern Hero.* Chicago: University of Chicago Press, 1971. Brief treatment of Friedman, focused on *Stern*.

Merritt Moseley

Geng, Veronica

Born: Atlanta, Georgia, on January 10, 1941
Education: University of Pennsylvania, B.A., 1963

Biography

Born in Atlanta, Georgia, Veronica Geng lived there only briefly and, after a few years in Washington, D.C., where her father's military career took the family, she grew up mainly in Philadelphia. She attended the University of Pennsylvania, majoring in English, and graduated *cum laude* in 1963. Upon graduation she moved to New York and began doing editorial work for textbook publishers. She then became a freelance copyeditor and did some freelance journalism.

In 1975 Geng contributed a parody of film reviewer Pauline Kael to the *New York Review of Books.* This was her first published piece of humor. Following the sale of several humorous pieces to *The New Yorker* in 1976, she joined the staff and served as a fiction editor from 1977 through 1982. During that time, she continued to contribute regular humorous "casuals" to the pages of *The New Yorker.* She still publishes regularly in that journal; in addition, she was a movie critic for the *Soho News* (1980-1981). She has written (and continues to write) about movies for the *New York Review of Books, Film Comment,* and other journals. Besides *The New Yorker,* she has published humor in *The New Republic, American Film, Harper's,* the *New York Times Book Review,* and a book called *The Eighties: A Look Back.* Veronica Geng's first book, *Partners,* was published by Harper and Row in 1984.

Geng's "casuals" are something other than an essay, something other than a short story; they often have a satiric edge, frequently employ parody, and are aimed at deflating pomposity, solemn nonsense, and dishonesty. They are sophisticated, addressed to literate people who appreciate the absurd. She follows in the tradition of the distinguished creators of *The New Yorker's* characteristic short comic piece: Robert

Benchley, James Thurber, S.J. Perelman, and, more recently, Woody Allen.

Literary Analysis

Veronica Geng began with parody, and much of her best work relies on her perfect-pitch ability as a parodist. *Partners* contains such unlikely but funny parodies as "Report from Your Congressman," an only slightly exaggerated simulacrum of the windy self-congratulation in the average report to constituents; "A Man Called Jose," a report on the Russian presence in Cuba in the style of a hard-bitten *New York Daily News* columnist spinning copy out of proletarian sentiments and florid prose ("The guy's name is Leonid Brezhnev and his name is Fidel Castro and by any name he is a gutless thug"); or "Coming Apart at the Semes," a chronicle of representative American families done in the style of a structuralist journal, *AXES*, the "quarterly forum for discourse on artistic praxis and those who praxe it."

"The Sacred Front" is an excellent illustration of how Geng often works by combining two disparate bodies of experience, or two different types of writing. The pun in the title characterizes the piece, which is a story about spies and fellow-travelers, done improbably and delightfully in the style of Henry James. Miss Geng says that she creates best when she "mixes things up together." That her subjects are incongruous, often astonishing, gives them their humor. Often the matter comes from current news; the manner is an accomplished parody of a writer, or a type of writing, that is ripe for parody, though it may or may not have some clear connection with the "plot." "Lulu in Washington" skewers the pretensions of Louise Brooks's autobiography *Lulu in Hollywood* with lines like "My integrity, like my sexual beauty, came so naturally that I was quite mystified by the attention it drew if I happened to mention it." It is a tale of "the Director," J. Edgar Hoover, making a pornographic film to blackmail politicians. Obviously, humor in this Hollywood parody is created by combining two different types of directors, film and F.B.I. "Record Review" is a fantasy review of Richard Nixon's White House tapes—released as records—in the breathless style of a rock critic. "Teaching Poetry Writing to Singles" operates on two cultural excrescences: the singles scene and the Kenneth Koch school of "poetry for everybody." Singles are discouraged from using the term "poem," instead being urged to try to write "words in lines of uneven length on a piece of paper."

The funniest piece in *Partners* may be "James at an Awkward Age," which takes off from a now-forgotten television series called "James at 16," but with Henry James as the awkward teen-

ager. Desperate to know what his father does for a living but too shy and/or circumlocutious to ask comprehensibly, agonizing with a crush on his cousin Minny Temple, young Henry, as Geng renders him, is a clever combination: a successful parody of the James style with teenager slang.

Geng demonstrates when a trend has gone too far by constructing a parody of it which takes it further into absurdity. Following a spate of books by women who had had affairs with famous men—William Faulkner, Dwight Eisenhower, and others—she presents "My Mao," an autobiographical account by a woman who loved Mao Tse-Tung. "Petticoat Power" makes fun of articles telling women how to succeed in the man's world of business by attaching themselves to a mentor and dressing for success. "Buon Giorno, Big Shot" skewers the aggressive style of interviewing made famous by Oriana Fallaci, demanding that her subject declare, for instance, whether he is a Fascist hyena. "Masterpiece Tearjerker" points out the excesses of "Upstairs, Downstairs" and its clones.

One index of genuine quality in parody or satire is that it is capable of amusing a reader unfamiliar with its target. Geng's work meets this standard; this is in part a sign that her parody is of trends, or styles, or intellectual positions (or postures) rather than simply of particular writers. Likewise, though a number of her pieces originate in satire on some contemporary political event or social process, they transcend their occasions. "The Sixth Man," while it alludes to British spies in high places, identifies its suspect through the kind of guilt by association common to all such exposes; that he is identified as "Ernest," that the informant is "Cicely," that the whole thing goes beyond Burgess and Maclean and Blunt into the world of Oscar Wilde, is part of Geng's unusual twist, her way of "mixing things up together."

Though she sometimes plays off political events, Geng hardly writes from a politically committed position. Like any good satirist, she targets folly where she finds it. Ellin Stein, reviewing *Partners* in *Ms.*, was uncomfortable with Geng's artistic detachment, complaining that "this is clearly not 'women's humor'—in fact, there is little to indicate the sex, political persuasion, or anything else about the writer." Stein particularly singles out "Ten Movies That Take Women Seriously" as having gone over her head. This is not surprising since the piece satirizes the kind of solemnity about women sometimes found in *Ms.* What it means to "take women seriously" is obviously the variable; Geng summarizes ten movies, obviously preposterous, which qualify as feminist: Marlo Thomas horsewhips a Samurai because she does not like the cut of his jib, or Jill Clayburgh builds an independent career for herself as a photographer, "taking pictures of a streetcorner where newly divorced women come to vomit." This humor, the opposite of the *engagé*, verges on the absurd.

Geng has said that she is no longer so interested in writing parody because she believes that it is too easy. A number of her pieces, particularly those written after *Partners*, derive their humor from situational incongruity, or from a satiric stance with no obvious single target, or from inspired absurdity. Of a number of pieces about male-female relationships, the funniest is "Lobster Night," which describes a frantic night of agonizing reappraisals, realignments, and confessions between two men and two women who change partners to fulfill all the possible permutations of couples and triangles. The four people all speed around, usually by taxi, from one fashionably unusual cafe to another even stranger—Chez les Cent Un Dalmatiens, Ovos Fervidos, the Cod's Head du Soir; superheated emotional declarations seem to illustrate nothing, though the narrator sees "infidelity to be the act that makes fidelity possible for others." At least three other pieces focus on the relationship of a narrator and "Ed," a relationship fraught with complications, most of which seem to come from the excessive self-consciousness of the participants. "Our Side of the Story" is an attempt to correct mistaken perceptions that have become current. In "The New Thing" the narrator tries to defend herself and Ed against the charge that their relationship is just an imitation of the old "Saturday Night Live" television program.

A final group of Geng's pieces have an almost pure comic quality which is like the best of Benchley. For instance, "More Mathematical Diversions" pretends very loosely to be a column of games based on mathematical principles but is only a collection of very funny jokes. "Love Trouble Is My Business" takes off from the claim by a *Village Voice* columnist that "This may be the only time in history in which the words 'Mr. Reagan' and 'read Proust' will appear in the same sentence." Geng meets the challenge in a "casual" which uses these words in every sentence, in increasingly baroque ways. The speaker, a hard-boiled detective, concludes this way:

> "*Cherchez la femme*," I said to myself—
> a phrase I'd picked up on a case where
> the judge gave clemency to a homicidal
> maniac for having read Proust—and
> then I went out in the rain to a book-
> store where I usually browsed for
> dames, and found one perusing
> Mr. Reagan's latest autobiography. Just

for fun, I looked over her shoulder and read: "For a long time, before I met Nancy, I used to go to bed early."

Summary

Veronica Geng is a prolific and highly accomplished writer. She writes comic "pieces"—short (one or two pages) humorous creations, appearing in magazines. Though the parody genre may be "too easy" to her, hers are consistently accurate and amusing. Her pieces often parody one style of writing while focusing on wildly incongruous content. She represents a continuation of the great tradition of American humor that includes the major nineteenth-century magazine and newspaper humorists and twentieth-century figures like Ring Lardner, Perelman, and Benchley.

Selected Bibliography

Primary Sources
Partners. New York: Harper & Row, 1984.

Secondary Sources
Drexler, Rosalyn. "Bethpage Burdette and Jailhouse Mariachi." *New York Times Book Review*, 89 (July 15, 1984): 12. Brief review, generally favorable.
Givens, Ron. "Truly Tasteful Humor." *Newsweek*, 104 (September 17, 1984): 81-82. Strongly positive review of *Partners* and a Roy Blount, Jr., book; sees them as exceptions to deplorable state of comic writing today.
Stein, Ellin. "*Partners*." *Ms.*, 13 (October 1984): 145. Mixed, puzzled review, lamenting lack of commitment, failure of *Partners* to be more Swiftian.

Merritt Moseley

Gibbs, Wolcott

Born: New York City, on March 15, 1902
Education: The Hill School
Marriage: Elinor Mead Sherwin, 1933, two children
Died: August 16, 1958

Biography

Wolcott Gibbs was born on March 15, 1902 and christened Oliver Wolcott Gibbs after an ancestor, Oliver Wolcott, who signed the Declaration of Independence as a delegate from Connecticut. The "Oliver" was soon dropped. His father, Lucius Tuckerman Gibbs, was an executive with the Pennsylvania Railroad, and his mother came from an old and wealthy New York family, the Duers. He attended the Hill School, from which he was expelled, according to Brendan Gill, for causes unknown.[1] As a consequence, he failed to attend college. Through his father's influence, he got a job on the Long Island Railroad, rising to the rank of brakeman. He married a railroadman's daughter, but the marriage was of short duration.

Gibbs left the railroad after four years, at the urging of wealthy relatives, and, through their influence, obtained a reporter's job on a Long Island weekly. In 1927, he joined a fledgling magazine, *The New Yorker*, thanks to his cousin, Alice Duer Miller, whose name was listed below the magazine's masthead as one of the founding editors. He began as copy reader in 1927, contributing verse and humorous columns; under the direction of Katharine Angell White, he rose to copy editor and soon became what James Thurber later called "the best copy editor the *New Yorker* has ever had."[2] He married a woman who worked in the advertising department but, soon afterward, following a quarrel, she jumped to her death from their Manhattan apartment. In 1933, he won the approval of his *Social Register* relatives by marrying Elinor Mead Sherwin, with whom he had two children.

During *The New Yorker*'s first quarter century, Gibbs was the magazine's most prolific contributor. He wrote verse, "casuals," profiles, comments, and later, book, movie and theater reviews. In 1938, he succeeded E.B. White in writing "Talk of the Town," and when Robert Benchley resigned as drama critic in 1940, Gibbs took over and remained in that post until his death. He contributed to no other publication but *The New Yorker* and seldom traveled beyond the city, except to his beloved summer cottage on Fire Island. There he died of a heart attack on August 16, 1958. He was survived by his wife and two children.

Literary Analysis

In "The Secret Life of Myself" (January 19, 1946), Gibbs's burlesque of Thurber's "The Secret Life of Walter Mitty," a rehearsal of one of "Charles L. Bedrock's urbane and searching studies of a woman's heart" is going badly and the director wishes that he could get the only person who could possibly save it:

> God, he said, I wish Wolcott Gibbs were
> here. He's only a drama critic, but I
> understand he's been called in a couple
> of times—secretly, of course—to advise
> Behrman and Robert E. Sherwood and
> a couple of others. I bet he'd know what
> to do.

> (p. 43)

From the darkened rear of the theater strides Wolcott Gibbs, who instantly dreams up sparkl-

ing lines and even takes over the male lead, thus saving the enterprise. The author's heroic fantasy, unlike Mitty's, proved to be real—and even astonishingly routine. At *The New Yorker*, where founder Harold Ross insisted that accurate and precise phrasing rather than personality counted, Gibbs was the invaluable staffer who could do everything—and do it well. His early years editing anonymously the handiwork of colleagues, and absorbing their styles, turned him into a skilled parodist. He honed his skills by playing off the popular styles of the day. A remark in a religious magazine, "Pastors will do well to watch the methods of the newspaper," inspired "The Story of the Bible in Tabloid" (February 13, 1926), one of his first. It begins: "CHASED FROM LOVE NEST. She Tempted Me" Cries Adam, Blaming Beautiful Snake-Charmer" (p. 39).

Gibbs's keen alertness to stylistic affectation prepared him well to master what soon became a prized feat at *The New Yorker*, puncturing commercial literary genres deemed below the high standards set at the magazine. In "Pal, A Dog" (October 26, 1929), Gibbs deftly mimicked the sentimental style and moralizing tone of formulaic *Saturday Evening Post* stories, telling a fractured anecdote about a man's best friend who got "mixed up with a pack of rather tough rabbits and we never saw him again" (p. 29).

Gibbs's acknowledged mastery of literary impersonation prompted him to try his hand at something book-length, and in 1931, he published *Bird Life at the Pole*, by "Commander Christopher Robin." The book is a broad burlesque of polar expeditions as well as of A. A. Milne's *Winnie the Pooh*. Commander Robin and his crew set out on the ex-battleship *Lizzie Borden* to discover the South Pole but take a wrong turn leaving the Panama Canal and end up at the North Pole instead. There they are met by souvenir hunters brought by Popular Polar Tours, Inc. The idea is more amusing than the voyage itself, which is kept comically afloat by Gibbs's jibes at William Randolph Hearst. "The Antarctic calls," says "Mr. Herbst," the voyage's financial backer; "mankind is ever advancing the frontiers of civilization and the Herbst papers are always to be found in the van. It is our duty to our readers" (p. 20). Herbst wants the mountains and rivers discovered to bear his appointed names and Robin will return to write 400 articles which are "to be thoroughly sound and scientific, and at the same time, so simple that the smallest child can understand them" (p. 21). Gibbs not only attacks Hearst's empire-building and its merchandising, but also his paper's sleazy tabloid style purveyed here by Mr. Mitchell—Walter Winchell, that is, a Hearst staffer particularly loathed at *The New*

Yorker. One of his gossipy dispatches is perfect Hearst hash:

> The Robin Pole Trek has left Gigglewater Gulch, where there is a broken heart for every mazda, and is mal-demering it for the Arctic. . . . Cynera (Jr. League) Svenson is garbo-gilberting with an ostrich. . . .

> (p. 87)

Except for these parodistic diversions, *Bird Life* proved to be a tedious voyage, as reviewers uniformly noted.

In addition to parodying the popular press, Gibbs mimicked current literary celebrities, particularly authors of admirably distinctive styles who, in the view of *The New Yorker*, were given to pretentiousness, such as Aldous Huxley ("Topless in Ilium," August 15, 1936, pp. 25–26) or who had fallen into annoying mannerisms, such as Alexander Woollcott ("Primo, My Puss," January 5, 1935, pp. 28–29). The more compelling the stylist, the more successful Gibbs's impersonation, best illustrated in "Death in the Rumble Seat" (October 8, 1932), a masterful send-up of Ernest Hemingway in his 1930s *machismo* phase. The scene of bravery moves from the romantic bullring to the mundane Merritt Parkway:

> Good drivers go fast too, but it is always down the middle of the road, so that cars coming the other way are dominated, and have to go in the ditch themselves. There are a great many ways of getting the effect of danger, such as staying in the middle of the road till the last minute and then swerving out of the pure line, but they are all tricks, and afterwards you know they were tricks, and there is nothing left but disgust.

> (p. 15)

Gibbs's reputation as a deadly accurate parodist reached a climax of notoriety with his "Profile" of Henry Luce, "Time . . . Fortune . . . Life . . . Luce" (November 28, 1936), written entirely in the *Time* style. It was prompted by an article in *Fortune*, another Luce publication, which was critical of editorial and financial practices at *The New Yorker* and written by Ralph Ingersoll, who had been Ross's managing editor. In retaliation, Ross sought to attack Luce's flagship enterprise by exposing its monied Yale Club atmosphere, its glib assumption of omniscience, and its lack of reverence for sound, clear grammar. Who better to play saboteur than the magazine's all-purpose trouble-shooter and in-house hit-man. Gibbs reproduced Timespeak perfectly—the clipped, over-hyphenated and hyper-ventilating style, the breathless tone, the annoying inversions of subjects and verbs—and carried it to insufferable length until "backward ran sentences until reeled the mind" (p. 21). Ingersoll himself was pilloried as an overpaid but dutiful bureaucrat: "former Fortuneditor, now general manager of all Timenterprises, descendant of 400-famed Ward McAllister. Littered his desk with pills, unguents, Kleenex, Socialite Ingersoll is Time's No. 1 hypochondriac, . . . writes copious memoranda about filing systems, other trivia, seldom misses Yale football game" (p. 23). "Where it all will end," Gibbs concluded with mock gravity, "knows God!" (p. 25).

Luce was outraged by the portrait of him as an arrogant snob and humorless teetotaler. Actually, Gibbs was harsher, implying that Luce was also ruthless and unprincipled. Readers in the know seemed to credit his accuracy since favorite lines were repeated and howled over in magazine offices and social gatherings for weeks afterwards.

Gibbs's sudden notoriety lured him out of the shadows at *New Yorker* headquarters. The following year (1937) saw the publication of his selected *New Yorker* pieces, *Bed of Neurosis*, with illustrations by *New Yorker* cartoonist Rea Irwin. The collection included many parodies but featured Gibbs's "casuals" dealing with the tribulations of assorted hypochondriacs at odds with the hectic pace of modern urban life—hence the book's title—and narrated in the magazine's patented dry, slightly arch, and noncommittal voice. These pithy, often insightful vignettes constitute Gibbs's contribution to the quasi-autobiographical "Little Man" humor perfected at the magazine by Benchley and Thurber, among others. In "Be Still, My Heart" (December 29, 1934), Mr. Cobb, the typically jittery urbanite, seeking a cure for his fear of fainting in public places, finds himself passed from specialist to specialist, each of whom deluges him with the latest medical jargon. Finally, in desperation, he finds old Doctor Hardy, "a soiled and whiskey antique" (*Bed*, p. 52), who tells him straight, "Go right ahead. Faint. It ain't going to hurt you" (p. 53). Public spectacles like Shakespearian plays performed in Yankee Stadium no longer faze Mr. Cobb, but he learns to resent his sudden good health since he is now stripped of his one infallible alibi. Gibbs's shy, easily victimized New Yorker recalls White's Mr. Trexler in "The Second Tree from the Corner," but, Gibbs's neurotics find no solace in their hostile environment, no second tree from the corner. In "The Whizz of Infinity" (February 6, 1932), Mr. Gore finds consolation in an unintelligible philosophy text full of more evidence of the collapse of good sense and the decay of clear style. Gibbs obfuscates expertly: "We are aware of existing; therefore we are merely one. We are conscious of remaining ourselves through inward and outward change; therefore we are not merely diverse" (*Bed*, p. 79). Persuaded to believe that "life is no more than a flash of consciousness in eternity" (p. 79), Gore learns to regard all annoyances as immaterial—including unpaid bills, demanding employers, and finally a policeman giving him a parking ticket. He takes refuge in his comforting fatalism as he returns home and over a stiff drink finds that "the policeman had already ceased to exist, that life was surely just a flash of consciousness in eternity" (p. 84).

The rest of *Bed of Neurosis* is filled out with reminiscences of growing up in suburban Long Island, playing Puck in a school production of *A Midsummer Night's Dream*, and enduring Army basic training. Many pieces remain readable less for their characterizations than for Gibbs's urbane and vivid prose style. Reviewers were laudatory but thought the satire too arcane for anyone but seasoned readers of *The New Yorker*.

After a decade of reviewing Broadway plays, Gibbs created one of his own, *Season in the Sun*, produced in 1950. It was based on autobiographical stories published in *The New Yorker* about a New York writer and his literary friends and situated on Fire Island. The play's hero, George Crane, undergoing a mid-life career crisis, has just resigned from the staff of a weekly humorous magazine, presided over by a hot-tempered and autocratic editor named Dodd. He is full of self-contempt for failing to write more than "a bunch of paragraphs for a 15¢ magazine" (p. 15). With his wife and two children, he has taken a cottage on Fire Island for the summer, where he hopes to complete a novel that will take him beyond New York friends who have become "vacant, used-up people. Exhausted. *Finished*" (p. 21). George's wife, Emily, thinks that his work as a paragrapher is deservedly admired and quotes a passage back to him—an excerpt from a recent Gibbs "Talk of the Town" entry. While George is doubtful that such stuff can sustain him, Emily calls it "neat and funny." Besides, "not many men could do it" (p. 17). George wavers and then succumbs to the temptations of newly arrived old friends, and his high-minded resolve collapses utterly with the arrival of Dodd: "the greatest editor in America" (p. 167)—a stand-in, clearly, for Harold Ross. Dodd thinks that George's prose "sounds like parody" (p. 98), considers his hero but an "animated sermon" (p. 154) and finally labels his sudden artistic zeal as the evasion it is: "What you've tried to do, George, is deny everything you know as an experienced man. That there's no retreat for you into the past, no way for you

to be innocent and protected all over again, at least not this side of senility" (p. 155). Saved from himself, George is ready to return to Manhattan as the best "paragrapher" on the best 15¢ humorous magazine in New York.

Clearly, Gibbs himself was undergoing a career crisis. The play was prompted by a narrow escape from lung cancer. Perhaps, too, he was trying to avoid doing what he felt a mature, but rapidly aging writer should do—break from Ross, that notoriously demanding father-figure—so he compensated for his failure of nerve by writing a mock Oedipal comedy about his inability to do so. Although the play is surprisingly devoid of wit and repartee, it is rich with private jokes, and it was a considerable hit. Its success was probably due less to Gibbs's slight dramatic gifts than to a coterie audience's insatiable curiosity about the private lives of *New Yorker* literati.

Gibbs seems to have agreed with Dodd/Ross, for he spent his last years toiling dutifully, if less prolifically, for Ross and his successor, William Shawn. The success of *Season* and Gibbs's acclaim as *The New Yorker*'s resident dramatic critic justified another collection of pieces, *More in Sorrow* (1958), which included many parodies previously reprinted in *Bed of Neurosis* and some new ones, a few Fire Island stories, profiles, and miscellaneous casuals. The parodies, headed by the Luce piece, appear first, perhaps to acknowledge Gibbs's preeminence in that minor art. Surely the best of the new ones is "Shad Ampersand" (October 27, 1945), in which the overwrought chronicle style of Sinclair Lewis in his dotage (*Cass Timberlane*) is larded with Perelmanesque names, *non sequiturs*, and garbled allusions:

> The city of Grand Revenant, in High Hope County, and the sovereign state of Nostalgia, . . . was founded in 1903, a year that also saw the birth at Kitty Hawk, N.C., of a strange, boxlike contrivance that held the bright seeds of death for Coventry and Nagasaki and other proud cities, half a world away.
>
> Its pioneer settler was old Cornelius Ampersand a prodigious seducer of Indians along the thundering marge of Lake Prolix and on the cold, improbable trails that lead from Baedeker and Larousse to Mount Thesaurus.
>
> (*Sorrow*, p. 37)

A section called "Wounds and Decorations" is composed mostly of reviews of forgettable plays and movies that are notable only for prompting his, and the magazine's, disdain for all goings-on in Hollywood. A morose, embittered spirit shadows these selections, perhaps that of the failed novelist of *Season in the Sun.* The book's elegiac title seems, therefore, apt.

In his last years, Gibbs lamented the sinking of literate wit beneath the suds of television situation-comedy humor. In "A Fellow of Infinite Jest" (April 13, 1957), the "last of the fashionable literary humorists" finds himself dismissed by his own children as out of touch with real life and hence the subject of their mockery. The new TV generation, too preoccupied with being entertained, is not disposed to offer up its ineptitudes to the cause of fine-tuned humor. Consequently, this "Poor Yorick," perhaps Gibbs himself, is left to feel like a discarded object, fit only to prompt glib family musings. At the end, his wife and children are thinking about life insurance for a writer "whose days were numbered" (p. 40).

Summary

Founding editor Harold Ross readily admitted that three writers really created *The New Yorker* in the mid-1920s—Thurber, White, and Wolcott Gibbs. Although he possessed neither Thurber's deep reservoir of nostalgic memories nor White's insatiable curiosity about modern life, Gibbs helped to create the stance and style that Ross envisioned for his enterprise. He was Ross's Henry Fowler (*English Usage*), which made him *The New Yorker*'s conscience on matters of style and correctness. Lamentably, he found no compelling subject on which to bestow his stylistic talents. Again and again, he fell back on parody, which, though it began as a liberating exercise and became a trenchant instrument of literary criticism, proved finally to be Gibbs's accommodation to his own literary failings. Nonetheless, from 1927 to 1957, he was America's Beerbohm, setting the high standards later enforced at *The New Yorker* by parodists from S. J. Perelman and John Updike and Woody Allen to Mark Singer and Veronica Geng.

Notes

1. *Here at the New Yorker* (New York: Random House, 1975), p. 126.
2. *The Years with Ross* (Boston: Little, Brown, 1957), p. 128.

Selected Bibliography

Primary Sources
Bird Life at the Pole. New York: William Morrow, 1931.
Bed of Neurosis. New York: Dodd, Mead, 1937.
Season in the Sun. New York: Random House, 1950.
More in Sorrow. New York: Henry Holt, 1958.
Secondary Sources
Gill, Brendan. *Here at the New Yorker.* New York: Random House, 1975. Only critical comment on Gibbs, calling him a talented writer who poked fun at writers who took big chances and miscarried with them but couldn't himself risk possible exposure.
Kramer, Dale. *Ross and the New Yorker.* Garden City, N.Y.: Doubleday, 1951. Stresses Gibbs's many editorial talents.
Thurber, James. *The Years with Ross.* Boston: Little, Brown, 1957. Personal recollections of Gibbs's eccentric work habits and sour personality.

Thomas Grant

Glass, Montague

Born: Manchester, England, on July 23, 1877
Education: Attended City College of New York from 1891 to 1893; studied law at New York University from October 1895 to February 1897
Marriage: Mary Caroline Patterson, 1907, one child
Died: February 3, 1934

Biography

The son of James David and Amelia Marsden Glass, Montague Marsden Glass was born in Manchester, England, on July 23, 1877. His father owned a prosperous linen and cotton manufacturing concern in Manchester with offices in New York. Though proud of their Anglo-Saxon and Norman blood, Glass's family recognized their Jewish roots and upheld Jewish traditions. Young Glass studied Hebrew with Samuel Green, an Australian who may well have been the source for his large stock of Yiddish stories. In 1890, Glass's family moved to New York City.

After proving inept at business, Glass attended City College of New York from 1891 to 1893 and studied law at New York University from October of 1895 to February of 1897. While at the latter institution, he contributed comic sketches and verse to the school's literary journal, the *Item.* Though never admitted to the bar, Glass worked for a number of years for the law firm of David and Kaufman, where he gathered the real-life material that he later fashioned into *Potash and Perlmutter.*

In 1909, Glass began full-time writing to support himself and his wife, Mary Caroline Patterson Glass, whom he had married in 1907. For several years, he had been writing stories featuring Abe Potash and Mawruss (Morris) Perlmutter, partners in the cloak and suit trade. It was not until two stories, "Taking It Easy" and "The

Arverne Sacque," were published in 1909 in the *Saturday Evening Post*—gaining him regular-contributor status—that Glass achieved wide recognition. His work was soon appearing in such high-circulation magazines as *Life* and *Cosmopolitan.*

Given the appeal the characters Potash and Perlmutter had for the American reading public, Glass's career was marked out for him. His first collection of stories, *Potash and Perlmutter,* appeared in 1910, and its sequel, *Abe and Mawruss,* in 1911. Volume after volume dealing with the same or similar characters followed. The two partners may have won their greatest popularity on the stage—the dramatization of *Potash and Perlmutter* (1913), with Charles Klein, was the first of numerous plays, six of them written with Jules Eckert Goodman. Potash and Perlmutter's adventures also went on in motion pictures, a syndicated column, and a radio serial. Working best under pressure, Glass wrote easily. Enormously profitable, his work sometimes brought him as much as $100,000 a year. His friends characterized him as impulsive, generous, and extravagant. Survived by his wife and a daughter, Glass died at his winter home in Westport, Connecticut, on February 3, 1934.

Literary Analysis

Glass had trouble selling the first stories featuring Potash and Perlmutter because editors were afraid that these one-dimensional ethnic stereotypes might offend Jewish readers and advertisers. Such fears, however, proved groundless. It is true that Glass found a great deal of humor in the manners and speech of Jewish immigrants in the garment trade, but he also revealed a great deal of affection for his characters. Not only did the public laugh at Potash and Perlmutter, they loved them as well.

Many of Glass's previously published stories were collected in 1910 in what is generally considered to be his masterpiece, *Potash and Perlmutter.* In the book's seventeen chapters, Glass traces the adventures of two Jewish partners in a cloak and suit business in New York City's garment district between 1904 and 1909. Calling Potash and Perlmutter "by far the most conspicuous of Mr. Dooley's successors," Jennette Tandy went on to observe that "it is a far cry from the sarcastic brevities of the rustic philosopher to the involved meanderings, the 'olav ha-sholem's of Abe and Mawruss."[1] Undoubtedly, Glass introduced many readers to a new world of social tradition and idiom.

Potash and Perlmutter are a pair of true provincials. Aside from the grotesqueries of their phraseology, their chief charm lies in the naiveté with which they use images drawn from commercial transactions and Jewish family life to transform the events of the world. Glass characterizes the pair through the use of literary dialect, including misspellings, shifts of syntax, apostrophes, and other devices (people drive "oitermobiles" and drink "tchampanyer"). Though sometimes gullible and greedy themselves, Perlmutter, the idealist, and Potash, the pessimist, more often join forces to do battle with competitors and various shysters and con men ranging from insurance salesmen to lawyers. Having worked their way from garment cutters to factory owners, the partners are suspicious of shortcuts to success. In the end, the hardworking and tightfisted morality of Potash and Perlmutter is usually rewarded.

Allen Guttmann finds Glass sharing a common attitude with many other twentieth-century Jewish-American writers: humor is the product of a proud people who are very sensitive about their lowly social status.[2] The typical accents of the Jewish humorist can be found in the various situations in which Glass places Potash and Perlmutter. For example, when Potash dissolves an earlier business relationship with one Pincus Vesell, he observes that he is so sick and tired of partners that he would say no if Andrew Carnegie suggested that he and Potash become partners in the cloak and suit business. To the reader, who may himself have been struggling in business, the very idea of a partnership with Carnegie is laughable and rejecting such an offer even more so.

Glass's *Abe and Mawruss,* a sequel to *Potash and Perlmutter,* appeared in 1911, followed by *Object: Matrimony,* a collection of eleven stories recounting Philip Margolies's love for Birdie Goldblatt, and the novel, *Elkan Lubliner, American,* both in 1912. Glass then joined with Charles Klein to stage *Potash and Perlmutter.* Produced by A. H. Woods, the play—which had an extended run of 441 performances—premiered at the Cohan Theatre in New York on August 16, 1913. "After we had decided on the plot and began to write the scenes," Glass later recalled, "Mr. Klein was approached by some of his Jewish friends, who told him that the play would be offensive to them [because of its ethnic stereotyping] and induced him to abandon it."[3] Klein finished a draft of the play, which Glass polished, after he gave up all payment and had his name removed from the project. After Klein died when the *Lusitania* was torpedoed in May of 1915, Glass made sure that his family would receive royalties by placing his coauthor's name on the play. Opening in England at London's Queen's Theatre on April 14, 1914, the play rolled up over 600 consecutive performances during a two-year period. It was also staged in other parts of England by several touring companies.

Glass next collaborated with Roi Cooper

Megrue on the play *Abe and Mawruss* (1915; retitled *Potash and Perlmutter in Society* for its London release to alert British audiences to the return of the key characters). Both *Potash and Perlmutter* and *Abe and Mawruss* illustrated one of Glass's main themes—the universal brotherhood of mankind. Glass worked with Jules Eckert Goodman on the stage version of *Object: Matrimony* (1916). Their collaboration continued on such later plays as *Business Before Pleasure* (1917), *Why Worry?* (1918), *Present Company Excepted* (1922), *Partners Again* (1923), and *Potash and Perlmutter, Detectives* (1926).

An interest in current events led to Glass's *Worrying Won't Win* in 1918. Having covered the Paris Peace Conference, he published *Potash and Perlmutter Settle Things* (1919), in which the partners comment humorously and practically on postwar settlements. In November 1922, Glass joined his talent with that of Ring Lardner, Heywood Broun, Franklin P. Adams, George S. Kaufman, and Robert Benchley to turn out *The 49ers Review*, a conglomeration of burlesques, satires, and spoken pieces. Glass talked about the parallels between his life and his fiction in one of the pieces that appeared in *The Truth About Potash and Perlmutter* (1924). Abe and Morris are featured in one of the pieces in *Lucky Numbers* (1927), which includes stories about other Jewish businessmen.

Using the pseudonym Theophilus Cossart, Glass had privately printed in 1928 a poetic farce in the spirit of Benjamin Franklin's *Poor Richard*, entitled *A Full and True Account of the Prodigious Experiment Brought to Perfection in Boston at Father Burke's Academy*. The short story collection *You Can't Learn 'Em Nothin'* (1930) demonstrates the fact that Glass's own experiences remained his best source of comedy materials. Written with Dan Jarrett, his last Broadway play, *Keeping Expenses Down*, which premiered at New York's National Theatre on October 20, 1932, ran for only twelve performances, perhaps because the Potash and Perlmutter formula failed when grafted on to new characters. A revival of the play *Potash and Perlmutter* in 1935 lasted less than a month. Perhaps the American public was finding its humorous entertainment increasingly in radio and film and less in the forms of the theater and the short story.

Summary

Though Montague Glass was not a great writer, his dialogue does demonstrate the typical accents of the Jewish humorist. As a humorist, Glass used the characters of Potash and Perlmutter to interpret the Jewish immigrant experience for the American reading and theater-going public. As one of his contemporaries noted, his humor

"softens down one's prejudices, gives one a sort of community spirit with the rest of the world."[4]

Notes

1. Jeanette Tandy, *Crackerbox Philosophers in American Humor and Satire* (New York: Columbia University Press, 1925), p. 163.
2. Allen Guttman, "Jewish Humor," in *The Comic Imagination in American Literature*, ed. Louis D. Rubin, Jr. (New Brunswick, N.J.: Rutgers University Press, 1973), p. 330.
3. Quoted in Thomas L. Masson, *Our American Humorists* (Enlarged ed.; Freeport, N.Y.: Books for Libraries Press, 1966), p. 141.
4. Masson, *Our American Humorists*, p. 136.

Selected Bibliography

Primary Sources

Elkan Lubliner, American. Garden City: Doubleday, Page, 1912.

Object: Matrimony. Garden City: Doubleday, Page, 1912.

Potash and Perlmutter: Their Copartnership, Ventures, and Adventures. Philadelphia: Henry Altemus, 1910; London: Hodder and Stoughton, 1914.

Abe and Mawruss: Being Further Adventures of Potash and Perlmutter. Garden City: Doubleday, Page, 1911; London: Hodder and Stoughton, 1914.

The Impromptu Cousin. New York: Winthrop, 1914.

And The Greatest of These. New York: Winthrop, 1914.

Two Tales of Ingratitude as Related by Montague Glass. New York: Winthrop, 1914.

The Competitive Nephew. Garden City: Doubleday, Page, 1915.

Potash and Perlmutter in Society. London: Hodder and Stoughton, 1917.

Worrying Won't Win. New York and London: Harper, 1918.

Potash and Perlmutter Settle Things. New York and London: Harper, 1919.

The Truth About Potash and Perlmutter and Five Other Stories. Racine, Wisconsin: Whitman, 1924.

Y'Understand. Garden City: Doubleday, Page, 1925; London: Heinemann, 1925.

Lucky Numbers. Garden City: Doubleday, Page, 1927; London: Heinemann, 1927.

You Can't Learn 'Em Nothin'. Garden City: Doubleday, Page, 1930.

As Theophilus Cossart. *A Full and True Account of the Prodigious Experiment Brought to Perfection in Boston at Father Burke's Academy.* New York: Marchbanks, 1928.

Plays

Glass, Montague, and Charles Klein. *Potash and Perlmutter.* New York, Cohan Theatre, August 16, 1913; London, Queen's Theatre, April 14, 1914. Published as *Potash and Perlmutter: A Play in Three Acts.* New York, Los Angeles, and London: French, 1935.

Glass, Montague, and Roi Cooper Megrue. *Abe and Mawruss.* New York, Lyric Theatre, October 21, 1915; produced again as *Potash and Perlmutter in Society*, London, Queen's Theatre, September 12, 1916.

Glass, Montague, and Jules Eckert Goodman. *Object: Matrimony.* New York, Cohan and Harris Theatre, October 25, 1916.

———. *Why Worry?* New York, Harris Theatre, August 23, 1918.

———. *Business Before Pleasure.* New York, Eltinge Theatre, August 15, 1917; London, Savoy Theatre, April 21, 1919.

———. *Present Company Excepted.* New York, Pennsylvania Hotel, January 10, 1922.

Glass, Montague, Ring Lardner, Heywood Broun, Franklin P. Adams, George S. Kaufman, and Robert Benchley. *The 49ers Review.* New York, Punch and Judy Theatre, November, 1922.

Glass, Montague, and Jules Eckert Goodman. *Partners Again.* New York, Garrick Theatre, February 28, 1933.

Glass, Montague, and Dan Jarrett. *Keeping Expenses Down.* New York, National Theatre, October 20, 1932.

Glass, Montague, and Jules Eckert Goodman. *Potash and Perlmutter, Detectives.* New York, Ritz Theatre, August 31, 1926.

Secondary Sources

Adams, Franklin P. *The Diary of Our Own Samuel Pepys.* 2 vols. New York: Simon and Schuster, 1935. There are numerous scattered references to Glass in both volumes of this personal chronicle of the years from 1911 to 1934.

Guttmann, Allen. "Jewish Humor." In *The Comic Imagination in American Literature.* Ed. Louis D. Rubin, Jr. New Brunswick, N.J.: Rutgers University Press, 1973, pp. 329–338. Guttmann finds Glass sharing a common attitude with many other twentieth-century Jewish-American writers: humor that is the product of a proud people who are very sensitive of their lowly social status.

Landa, J.M. *The Jew in Drama.* Port Washington, N.Y.: Kennikat, 1968, pp. 209–214. Landa praises the freshness, the humanity, and the good nature of Glass's play, *Potash and Perlmutter* (1914).

Masson, Thomas L. *Our American Humorists.* Enlarged ed. Freeport, N.Y.: Books for Libraries Press, 1966, pp. 133–144. First published in 1931. Following a brief introduction (in Chapter XIII) in which he notes Glass's encyclopedic knowledge and well-developed sense of humor, Masson reproduces a long letter from Glass recounting his life and literary career.

Sojka, Gregory S. "Montague Glass." *Dictionary of Literary Biography.* Vol. 11. *American Humorists, 1800–1950.* Ed. Stanley Trachtenberg. Detroit: Gale, 1982, pp. 151–155. Discussion of Glass's writing in a biographical context.

Tandy, Jennette. *Crackerbox Philosophers in American Humor and Satire.* New York: Columbia University Press, 1925, pp. 163–164. Tandy calls Glass's characters, Potash and Perlmutter, "by far the most conspicuous of Mr. Dooley's successors" (p. 163).

Yates, Norris. *The American Humorist: Conscience of the Twentieth Century.* Ames, Iowa: Iowa State University Press, 1964, pp. 138, 172, 220, 335. Yates lumps Glass with a number of other "relatiely pale grinders-out of crackerbox humor" in turn-of-the-century America (p. 220).

L. Moody Simms, Jr.

Golden, Harry Lewis

Born: Mikulincz, Austro-Hungarian Empire, on May 6, 1902

Education: City College of New York, B.A., 1923

Marriage: Genevieve Gallagher, 1926, four children

Died: October 2, 1981

Biography

Harry Golden was born Herschel Goldhirsch, on May 6, 1902, in the Galician village of Mikulincz, then part of the Austro-Hungarian Empire. His mother, Anna Klein, was the daughter of a Rumanian grain merchant; his father, Leib, was a teacher, writer, and auxiliary cantor. Later, in America, Leib Goldhurst (immigration officials changed his name) would write the first sports story for a foreign-language newspaper. Leib and the oldest of Herschel's seven siblings emigrated in 1904, settled in New York's Lower East Side, and brought over the rest of the family in 1905. Herschel would spend his childhood in Manhattan (they moved in 1918 to the Bronx), attending Public School 20 with fellow future-celebrities Paul Muni, George Gershwin, Edward G. Robinson, Jacob Javits, and Irving Caesar. Herschel became Harry in high school, which he completed in three years of evening classes. Then he would attend City College of New York evenings, graduating in 1923.

Harry followed the path of most large-family immigrant children: employment by age eleven, full-time work in a hat factory by age fourteen. Working for furrier Oscar Geiger, however, broadened his horizons and reinforced a habit of voracious reading that made his later personal journalism so informed. Geiger, a Single Taxer, tutored young men in literature and social analysis; he introduced Harry to assimilated, middle-class Jews. When Clara Goldhust became one of the pioneering women stockbrokers, her brother acted as assistant and wrote the house newsletter. Harry married Genevieve Gallagher, Clara's stenographer, in 1926, and the couple moved to Larchmont, New York, and later to River Plaza, New Jersey. They had four children; three of the boys would become writers or academics and aid Harry as editors or researchers.

Harry Goldhurst had a short-lived, disastrous career as an independent broker (with Kable and Company), which led to his bankruptcy, a 1929 trial for mail fraud, and a prison term of three years and nine months. Richard Nixon granted him a full pardon in 1973. It was this experience that caused him to become Harry Golden in 1941, when he moved south and entered journalism. Meanwhile, from 1933 to 1938 he managed one of his brother Jacob's hotels, the Markwell, in New York's theater district. Here he encountered more interesting character types: drunken entertainers, cardsharks, Jack Johnson "on his uppers," and accumulated a vast store of anecdotes. He also became deeply involved in Jewish community life and history and began to do some reporting, writing, and promotional work for the *Daily Mirror.*

Golden went south in 1941 looking for steady work. His wife remained in the north; they were legally separated in 1961. Golden spent eight months in Norfolk, Virginia, then settled in Charlotte, North Carolina, working first for the state A.F. of L. *Labor Journal* and, after the death of the publisher, for the *Observer.*

In 1942 Golden began the *Carolina Israelite,* a venture in personal journalism that would earn him an audience and influence. A sixteen-page monthly written entirely by Golden, it consisted of essays of varying length on various subjects— history, reminiscence, social commentary, anecdote, or literature. They ranged in tone from whimsical to pedagogical. The *Israelite* was extensively quoted in the *Congressional Record,* and Golden wrote speeches for Adlai Stevenson as well as liberal southern politicians. He contributed articles on southern Jewry to *Commentary,* had a column on southern affairs in the *Nation* during the 1950s and after 1968, and wrote articles on race relations for *The Crisis* from 1962 to 1966.

The general public best knew Harry Golden from his 17 books, beginning with *Only in America* in 1958. His rapid, phenomenal success encouraged a series of other collections, published generally at eighteen-month intervals. These consisted of compilations from the *Israelite,* plus some original essays, which Harry, Jr., helped him edit. For several years Harry Golden was a focus of popular culture. A racehorse was named "Only in America"; a beer company used "Enjoy, Enjoy!" as an ad slogan; restaurants offered "2¢ Plain"—for thirty-five cents! Profits from his books allowed Golden to take several trips to Europe and Israel and to research and write books of journalistic history and social investigation. He began with a biography, *Carl Sandburg* (1961), and followed this with *Forgotten Pioneer* (about peddlers; 1963), *Mr. Kennedy and the Negroes,* (of which he was most proud; 1964), *A Little Girl Is Dead* (about the Leo Frank case; 1965), *The Israelis* (1971), *The Greatest Jewish City in the World* (1972), *Travels Through Jewish America* (1973), and *Our Southern Landsmen* (1974). His three sons, Harry, Jr., Richard, and William, aided him in research and editing, and Golden credited them as collaborators in his later books.

Golden ceased publishing the *Israelite* in 1968 but continued to write and lecture until his health failed. He died in Charlotte, North Carolina, on October 2, 1981.

Literary Analysis

Harry Golden saw himself primarily as part of a tradition of serious journalists engaged in reform and independent social analysis; he likened himself to Henry Grady, Josephus Daniels, William Allen White, and Oscar Ameringer.[1] Half of his books were straight reportage, as were his articles on social and economic change for the journals of opinion. He began the *Israelite* from a conviction that moderates and liberals would share his view of Jim Crow's anachronism. Demographic, economic, and technological change was upon the South; segregation could not long survive enlightenment, modernization, and increased black purchasing power. His trenchant and courageous stands won the respect of a few; the *Israelite* was known as one of only two southern papers that had supported the 1954 *Brown v. Board of Education* decision.

To reach a larger audience and disarm those who would resent him as a northerner and a Jew, however, Golden chose a light, humorous approach in order to try to touch hostile minds through gentle laughter and folksiness. "I will always believe," he later argued, "that if Galileo had used humor, the Inquisition and the Popes would have left him alone" (Golden, 1969, p. 279). This decision shaped the form, content, and pertinence of his writing and the texture of his humor.

Early in his career Golden was literally a cracker-barrel philosopher. He would jot down ideas, lead sentences, short paragraphs on diverse topics and throw the scraps of paper into a barrel. With a publication deadline looming, he would fish about the barrel, flesh out those scraps that he had blindly chosen, and arrange them in the paper according to length. When success brought him file cabinets and secretaries, Golden still continued to publish unrelated material both in the *Israelite* and in the collections. Even after his sons' editing, Golden's books of essays were catch-alls. Each would contain a section largely of reminiscences and one largely on race or religion in the South, but the remaining sections were a miscellany only vaguely related to the chapter titles. The last chapter was so diverse that it could only be entitled "(More) Complaints and Free Advice" from book to book. Rather than denoting a disordered mind, this clutter of spontaneity reassured his opponents that Golden was a *naif,* not part of the stereotypical New York, liberal-Jewish-Communist conspiracy. To all but the most pronounced racists, Golden could eventually become a fellow Tarheel, a full-fledged, if not beloved, Carolinian.

To his stance as a random raconteur, Golden added reassurance that he realized his "place" in the scheme of things. The very first essay in *Only in America*, "Why I Never Bawl Out a Waitress," set the tone of most Golden soft-pedalling of anger or injury. After considering the cosmos, multiplying planets, suns and galaxies—"When you think of all this, it's silly to worry whether the waitress brought you string beans instead of limas" (Golden, 1958: p. 21). This cosmic deflation could reflect a modest sense of proportion but also suggests that little in this world merits truly angry satire or militancy. Golden was entirely out of temper and humor with 1960s radicals, and this shows plainly in later books like *Ess, Ess, Mein Kindt* and *So Long as You're Healthy*.

Golden's third technique, using ingratiating humor for reform, lay in the gentle ribbing of his often-quoted "Golden Plans." His most famous, the "Vertical Negro Plan," was the answer to lunch-counter segregation. If sit-ins against Jim Crow caused violence, if whites refused to sit with blacks, then everyone should stand! This could be extended to schools, where pupils would work at old-fashioned, seatless bookkeeping desks. Variants included a "carry-the-books" plan whereby schools would be integrated by black children toting books and bundles for whites, or theaters would be integrated by black "nannies" with white babies or lifelike pale dolls. He even had a "Turban" plan which reprised a technique some blacks had already tried: pretend to be an Asian or African and find many Jim Crow rules waived. Here was an absurdist critique of segregation made more palatable by indirect expression.

Harry Golden may be remembered more for his sentimental stories of the Lower East Side than for his civil rights advocacy. All of his books of essays have titles drawn from Yiddish expressions. Golden was a fount of stories and information about his childhood milieu, about loving families and economic struggles. Nostalgic romanticizing of the past was congenial not only to southerners but to his own generation of Jewish-Americans, uncomfortable with their own successes in acculturation. On the one hand, the Jewish story in America was "from *shul* to pool"; Golden the traditionalist mocked those who were discarding their past for trivial acceptance through self-indulgence. On the other hand, Golden stressed the immigrants' drive for assimilation and middle-class acceptance and the redemptive values of adversity. His own life and the repeated variants on "Only in America!" represented the nation as dedicated to and capable of cultural/racial tolerance; clothing his tales in the normative traditional morality that he believed made his message more acceptable to his 1950s audience, though it would increasingly antagonize the younger generation.

In "You're Entitle'" Golden has a vignette about a Gainesville, Florida, hospital emergency room with three thermometers: the oral thermometers are racially segregated, but there is only one marked "rectal." This, to him, was "gradual integration" (Golden, 1962, p. 218). Similarly, he noted North Carolina men's rooms with segregated stalls but only one urinal—was this the inspiration for the "Vertical Negro" plan? In the same collection, Golden advises unmarried couples checking into a hotel to use Jewish names to fool the house detective. Who in the antisemitic South would pretend to *be* Jewish? This final technique, of exposing hypocrisy or absurdity by guffaws, allowed Golden his sharpest outlet for humorous hostility. When heckled about his purpose in the South as a transplanted Yankee Jew, Golden once replied, to great applause: "I am trying to organize a Jewish society for the preservation of Christian ethics" (Golden, 1969, p. 260).

Summary

Contemporary admirers of Harry Golden called him a "Jewish Will Rogers" or even likened him to Montaigne. However, he is represented in the *Dictionary of Literary Biography* today only by a brief obituary, not an essay. His popularity as a writer and wit has been ephemeral largely because his social values and humorous techniques were considered unsuitable in the more rancorous "counterculture" 1960s. When Golden continued to celebrate traditional mores and praised the repressive college president S.I. Hayakawa, when he claimed to prefer the "moral effect of the gutter" (Golden, 1964, p. 42) to school sex education or suggested that one way to discourage robbery was by making it too easy, he seemed both anachronistic and foolishly opinionated. Ill health brought about the *Israelite*'s end but, in part, so did declining readership and the disheartening deaths of those whom Golden had admired (the Kennedys, Stevenson, Sandburg, Martin Luther King, Jr.). He seemed to have nothing acceptable to say to militants, street demonstrators, and racial separatists. To them his old-fashioned gentility seemed too conciliatory, bland, and even complacent. They dismissed him as a writer who had merely tried to convince people that by simply noticing hypocrisy and injustice and laughing at it, they had done sufficient work toward its eradication. One would call him the "court jester of the Eisenhower Age."[2]

Ironically, Golden was proudest of those books of research, reportage, and analysis that were relatively neglected during his own lifetime in favor of his ingratiating humor, and they may have the greatest ultimate value.

Notes

1. Harry Golden, "Last of the Personal Journalists?," *Saturday Review*, 46 (January 12, 1963): 90–91.
2. Theodore Solotaroff, "Harry Golden and the American Audience," *Commentary*, 31 (January 1961): 13. See also reader response to the article, in *Commentary*, 31 (March 1961): 256–258.

Selected Bibliography

Primary Sources

Autobiography
The Right Time. New York: Putnam's, 1969.

Collections
Only in America. Cleveland, Ohio: World, 1958.
For 2¢ Plain. Cleveland: World, 1959.
Enjoy, Enjoy! Cleveland: World, 1960.
You're Entitle'. Cleveland: World, 1962.
So What Else Is New? New York: Putnam's, 1964.
Ess, Ess, Mein Kindt. New York: Putnam's, 1966.
The Best of Harry Golden. Cleveland: World, 1967.
The Golden Book of Jewish Humor. New York: Putnam's, 1972. Jewish jokes which Golden used in his lectures with citations for those previously published by others.
So Long As You're Healthy. New York: Putnam's, 1974.
Long Live Columbus. New York: Putnam's, 1975.

Miscellaneous
Hapgood, Hutchins. *The Spirit of the Ghetto*. Ed. Harry Golden. New York: Funk and Wagnalls, 1965; rpt. of 1902 Funk and Wagnalls edition. Introduction, and running commentary.

Secondary Sources

Articles
Roth, Philip. "The New Jewish Stereotypes." *Response*, 5 (Fall 1971): 88–94. Reprint of an article from *American Judaism*, Winter 1961. Believing Jewish writers should aim higher, Roth attacks Golden and Leon Uris for using Jewish themes to dissipate guilt.
Solotaroff, Theodore. "Harry Golden and the American Audience," *Commentary* 31 (January 1961): 1–13. In regard to both strengths and weaknesses, Golden's humor and phenomenal public acceptance are part of the 1950s cultural and social malaise.

Book Reviews
Corman, Avery. "Review of *Long Live Columbus*." *New York Times Book Review*, March 2, 1975, p. 30. Golden's autobiographical insights and whimsy are entertaining, but the short essay form is tedious.
Haas, Joseph. "Review of *Ess, Ess, Mein Kindt*." *Saturday Review*, 49 (November 12, 1966): 64. Courage and a sense of principle are involved in the Golden volume.
Holden, W. Sprague. "Review of *So Long As You're Healthy*." *Journalism Quarterly*, 47 (Winter 1970): 778–779. Golden is seen as a cross between Will Rogers and Jeremiah.
Johnson, Gerald. "Review of *So Long As You're Healthy*." *New York Times Book Review* September 13, 1970, pp. 22, 24. Speculates on declining readership and impact in late 1960s.
Milch, Robert J. "Review of *The Right Time*." *Saturday Review*, 52 (July 5, 1969): 31. Golden is a mirror of 1950s shallowness, superficiality, and ultimate timidity, not a writer of consequence.

Kalman Goldstein

Greene, Asa

Born: Ashby, Massachusetts, on February 11, 1789
Education: Westford Academy, 1799; Williams College, 1811, B.A.; Brown University medical school, 1813, M.D., 1822
Died: December 31, 1838

Biography

Asa Greene was born in Ashby, Massachusetts, on February 11, 1789. His father, Oliver, was a farmer and a tanner. His mother, Dorothy, had already borne four children, three daughters and a son. The family moved to Westford, near Lowell, when Greene was ten. A few years later, they returned to Ashburnham, in the Ashby area. By then there were three more children. After attending local schools, Greene prepared himself for entrance into the junior class of Williams College with the aid of the Ashburnham minister who was a Harvard graduate. Greene had some knowledge of Latin and a good command of Greek. He was also competent in mathematics, navigation, history, and rhetoric. His two years at Williams College were so successful that he was chosen as one of the public orators for the Commencement Program in September 1813. His wit and talent for writing poetry also made him a popular student. Greene was well-read in English literature, with a special interest in Joseph Addison, Samuel Johnson, Jonathan Swift, and Oliver Goldsmith. However, his schooling left him dissatisfied. He was too close to his provincial background to shake off his Yankee ways of thinking and feared that his education might estrange him from the folk wisdom of his native environment, though he was influenced by Tristram Burgess, a professor of oratory and belles-lettres, which explains his interest in writing fiction. In 1822, Greene attended Brown Medical School in Providence. Greene's medical opinions are expressed in his satire of quacks in *The Life and Adventures of Dr. Dodimus Duckworth A.N.Q.*, especially regarding the controversy about bloodletting. Dr. Duckworth actually contradicts notions that

Greene learned from his teachers. Setting the standard of Brown medical studies against that which prevailed in the communities where Greene later practiced sharpened his awareness of the comic potentialities of the medical profession. Between 1822 and 1825, Greene was a physician in Lunenburg, Townsend, and North Adams, the Berkshires, then became a bookseller in Pittsfield, Massachusetts, and published a weekly, *The Berkshire American*, with advertisements, general notices, an agricultural column, foreign and domestic news, and humorous essays. He moved the paper to North Adams, then an active manufacturing town, in February 1827. His editorial policy was to give a full picture of current events. His articles were racy, ingenious, and of good moral tone, and his paper served as a vehicle for social and moral commentaries. Greene was a serious-minded partisan of good causes and an inspired tongue-in-cheek satirist of lawyers, doctors, and sentimental literature. The last issue of *The Berkshire American* came out on June 18, 1828. Greene was made an honorary M.D. by the Berkshire Medical Institution in September 1827 and a year later Master of Arts by Williams College. He started publication of the *Socialist* in May 1826. Exclusively devoted to essays and literary items, the paper suspended publication on May 22, 1829, due to a lack of subscribers. In November 1829, Greene became editor of the *Constellation*, a New York City four-page weekly whose primary object was to entertain and instruct. In the beginning the *Constellation* recorded many police court cases in order to compete with its rival, the *Sun*, but later emphasized literary material at the expense of news. Greene offered brief comic sketches and vignettes on a variety of subjects in serial form as in the "Israel Icicle" and the "Cornelius Cabbage" stories. His anecdotes and dialogues were topical, didactic, and iconoclastic, and his best satirical material consisted of a series of letters about city life in native idiom. Greene relinquished the editorship of the *Constellation* on September 8, 1832. He subsequently co-edited with Francis Stebbins a daily in New York, the *Citizen*, another shortlived paper.

Greene's lack of success induced him to give up journalism and try his hand at fiction. He published three books in 1833, his *annus mirabilis: A Yankee Among the Nullifiers, The Life and Adventures of Dr. Dodimus Duckworth, A.N.Q.*, and *Travels in America by George Fibbleton*. Then he became the editor of the *Transcript*, a paper that competed with the highly successful *Sun* from 1834 through 1839. Paragraphs of gossip, topical notes, and especially police reports stimulated sales. Greene welcomed in his columns frank, salacious articles on cases of sexual or criminal misconduct. Such an editorial policy averted political quibbles and led him to concentrate on the observation of people and manners in America. The *Transcript* also burlesqued the sentimentality of the period and objected to the derogatory comments of English travelers in America. Greene left the *Transcript* late in 1835 and made his living as a book dealer while writing a guide book entitled *A Glance at New York* (1837). He died in New York City on December 31, 1838.

Literary Analysis

As editor of the *Constellation*, Greene helped portray Down East life at a time when literature was dominated by the more sophisticated writings of James Fenimore Cooper and James Kirke Paulding. He was among the few Yankees such as Horace Greeley and William Cullen Bryant who gained a reputation among the New York literary circles when the *Knickerbocker* was almost omnipotent. Greene's chronicles of Israel Icicle and Cornelius Cabbage seem to echo the much earlier provincial commentaries of Silence Dogood and Poor Richard, whom Benjamin Franklin made stock figures of eighteenth-century humor. There was also in his anecdotes the zest of R.B. Thomas's *Farmer's Almanac*, which indicates Greene's indebtedness to oral lore. In the *Constellation*, he also indulged in parodies of contemporary intellectual pursuits such as phrenology and feminism. For instance, his Mrs. Huckabuck is both pretentious and ignorant while assuming a stance of scientific expertise. A self-styled "belieever in the doctorin of freenullogy," she observes "the noggins on my cranickum thof I say it myself, are a stonishingly developed. And whare there's so much fier you know, there must be a little smoke. I'm pecooliarly struck with my noggins of *intellectuyallity*, whitch you know bein on the frunt parte of the forred, are most cognizable to the vishual site."[1] Making fun of sentimental fiction, Greene characterizes Angellia, the heroine of the Cornelius Cabbage series, with animal and vegetable metaphors suggestive of Royall Tyler's inspiration when he parodied Della Cruscan verse in the *Farmer's Museum* thirty years earlier:

> Her form was not like that of all other heroines, sylph-like and aerial, tall and slender, with such common qualities as may be picked up in every novel. Far from it; she was in stature four feet one, and in circumference about equal to any three heroines of the present degenerate days. Her head was cast in the most delicate mould—being neither so round as a cocoanut, nor so long as a cucumber—and set most appropriately on

a neck of reasonable length and diameter—which neck was situated between her shoulders. What lips she had . . . They were, as all lips should be, well calculated to close her mouth, to help her to eat and to speak, and to hide a set of teeth which were rather uneven and decayed.[2]

It was also in the *Constellation* that Greene portrayed his first Yankee picaro, Enoch Timbertoes, a traveling Downeaster from Massachusetts who writes letters to Tim, a young farmer boy in his native village. Timbertoes's sketches of city life depict tricksters who feign innocence and swindle gullible Yankees. The candid greenhorn also gives vent to his xenophobia by castigating English novels and upbraiding those who do not observe the Sabbath. Averse to "pettifoggers, land sharks, turneys at law and lawers,"[3] Timbertoes offers the traditional point of view of the Yankee bumpkin faced with urban modernity. This burlesque vision of life somehow blunts the satirical edge, for the central character has more comic impact than the scenes of American life that he describes.

Closer to the English picaresque tradition exemplified by Tobias Smollett is *The Life and Adventures of Dr. Dodimus Duckworth, A.N.Q.*, published in 1833. This satire about quack doctors is obviously based on autobiographical data. The title itself indicates the basic intention since it is followed by the notation A.N.Q., *a notorious quack*. The omniscient narrator is Duckworth's biographer who intends to disclose fraudulent practice to the public. Although the quack epitomizes the most invidious Yankee traits, he nevertheless shows the sterling qualities of the new American Adam. A successor to Roderick Random, Duckworth remains an ambiguous figure. Deep-rooted in Yankee soil, the Duckworth family can claim an ancestor whose task was to punish the colonists for non-observance of the Sabbath. Greene mocks antiquated Down-East habits, superstitions, and rituals. He demonstrates that excessive respect for traditions discourages initiative and results in penury: the Duckworths live in a dilapidated house in which ragged shirts serve as curtains. The adventures of young Dodimus actually constitute a grotesque inversion of the American dream. At Dodimus's birth, the awkwardness of the midwife, Mrs. Motherwort, seems to be a bad omen, for the newborn child is expected to be either an idiot or a renegade by his family. Dodimus's mother decides that he will be a doctor when she sees him torturing animals. He learns his trade with Doctor Whistlewind, who generally amputates half a dozen limbs before breakfast. Dodimus shares the cynicism of his fellow quacks when he says, "Well, better die of the remedies than of the disease—or rather, I should say, diseases, because, as I mentioned before, you have a conglomeration of them. It is a principle in the practice of medicine, never to let the patient die of the disease, whatever may happen from the remedies."[4] Greene also blames patients who never tire of being fooled by quacks. The third-person narrative constantly sets the episodes of Duckworth's life in a moralistic perspective. In this respect, another character, Parson Long-Grace, is clearly a replica of Henry Fielding's Parson Trulliber.

Throughout the novel, Greene denounces rampant vanity and hypocrisy. On the other hand, he sometimes assumes a benevolent tone when he describes New England country life. His evocations of Saturday night feasts, huskings, quiltings, and sparkings ring of authenticity, though all of the Yankee characters that he singles out are butts of his satire. Farcical scenes, disparaging imagery, and malapropisms support the ironies in those sketches. Greene's command of the linguistic peculiarities of New England reveals his talent for reproducing dialect in such vernacular phrases as "This-ere tother swarm" (Vol. I, p. 75), "nither make head nor tail on't" (Vol. II, p. 64), and "healing-like" (Vol. II, p. 93). Elsewhere, the aberrations of Dodimus's mind are expressed through malapropisms that cannot be confused with eye-dialect. For instance, he says "coountenance" for "continent" (Vol. I, p. 54), "cartleg" for "cartilage," and "sack-o-rum" for "sacrum" (Vol. I, p. 22). Duckworth's picaresque biography is full of digressions and inconsequential episodes. At first eager to emulate Smollett and Fielding, Greene accumulated many anecdotes to substantiate his view of Yankee rural life, but New England society was not stratified enough to offer enough resistance to the rise of the common quack. Instead of a mock-epic of the American dream, Duckworth's life story often turns out to be an involuntary celebration of energy and shiftiness.

A Yankee Among the Nullifiers was published in 1833, shortly after the Nullification crisis during which John Calhoun and South Carolina were opposed to Andrew Jackson and the Union over the problem of the tariff. In addition to illustrating the conflict between federal power and states' rights, the book is a satire on Southern political ideas and manners as well as a spoof of romantic adventure novels. The dedication to Tristram Burgess, his Brown professor, suggests that, like his master, Greene stood for the Union and a protective tariff. The plot is picaresque: Elnathan Elmwood, a native of Massachusetts and graduate of Harvard, goes south to make his fortune. He tutors Henrietta Harrington, the young daughter of a planter, but takes time to study law. He then runs for Congress in competition with Major Harebrain Harrington, a relative of Henrietta.

The narrator is a Yankee who adopts a neutral pose to disclose southern gullibility. The high-minded, idle planter is constantly set in contrast with the penny-saving, notion-vending peddler. Conventions of southern chivalry are ridiculed, especially when Harebrain challenges Elnathan for the heart of Henrietta. To fight the gentleman, the Yankee appears on the field with a chopping block, a meat barrel, and a half bushel of salt—he thus plans to preserve his antagonist's remains with true Yankee economy. Harebrain spurns the Yankee as a peddler of Latin, and Henrietta's father thinks him a penniless pedagogue. Throughout the novel, Southerners are stereotypes. Both pretentious and naive, they are invariably hoodwinked by Yankees. Greene shows his attachment to the Union, especially in a fable contrasting Jock the Northerner, who manufactures jew's-harps, and Bill the Southerner, who sets monkeys to work on his fields with an orangutan as overseer because harvesting is too much of a chore for him. Eventually Jock and Bill have to harmonize their views in order to survive. Another character, Caesar Johnson, is a tall, stout, middle-aged black with a commanding presence and a dignity that seem to insure the respect and attention of his fellow slaves. Using him as a persona, Greene burlesques the whole concept of Nullification as Caesar explains in dialect the procedure imagined by John Calhoun:

> A Nullifier be a man wat does cisely as he pleases, and no tanks to nobody. He neider obey law nor conseltutiun. He neider pay tax, nor sport Guberment, nor submit to any man, whoeber he be. In a single word, gemmen, de Nullifier is de most indepennent man in de whole world. Wateber he don't like, he Nullify. One State, he Nullify de whole Unitum States, one County, he nullify de whole State, one leetle Town, he nullify de whole County, one wite gemmen, he nullify de whole town, and one brack gemmen, he nullify—look Sambo, and see dat no wite man is listnin.[5]

Aggressive and cowardly Elnathan exemplifies the rise of the common man in the final part of the book. In the meantime, Harebrain is surprised that Yankees should make so much money by hard work, whereas Southerners are doomed to poverty since rank bans labor for them.

Greene finds it hard to assume the same comic distance toward Yankees that he does with Southerners. His regional bias does not, however, preclude a fairly objective treatment of sectionalism. As a humorist, he illustrates the paradoxes and incongruities of the national scene in a way that could temper antagonisms in the minds of the readers.

With *Travels in America by George Fibbleton, Ex-Barber to His Majesty the King of Great Britain*, Greene's outspoken nationalism becomes more biting. This novel countered the accounts of British visitors in the United States. Earlier travelers such as William Cobbett had praised the country for its freedom and prosperity but by 1825 English authors were so derogatory that several American writers felt the need to defend the native character. Such was the case with Paulding, who published *John Bull in America, or the New Munchausen*. In 1832, *Domestic Manners of the Americans* by Frances Trollope was judged to be outrageously slanderous by the national press. A parody of the English novelist's criticism, *Travels in America* was also written by Greene in response to Isaac Fidler's *Observations on Professions, Literature, Manners and Emigration*. Greene ironically emulates Fidler by transforming the candid European observer into a knavish opportunist. Born in England, Greene's Fibbleton hopes to rise from rags to riches in the New World. He becomes a barber, then turns into a jack of all trades who unsuccessfully seeks to marry a wealthy widow. He eventually returns to his former profession, thereby exerting a constant threat to the nostrils of his patrons. Perfidious, ignorant, and arrogant, Fibbleton presents caricatures of the residents of the United States that are so exaggerated that they become grotesque. Accordingly, the reader is primed to refute all such libels on the American character. For instance, Fibbleton says, "New York was founded by an enterprising tribe of the aborigines, known by the name of the Manhater."[6] He expresses his confused though hostile opinions through innumerable malapropisms such as "Knee per Sultan" for "ne plus ultra" and "Palace Aids" for "Palisades." His vision of American history is distorted, too, as exemplified in his version of the Boston Tea Party:

> The women of Boston, which is the metropolis of all New England, refused to make their tea in the manner prescribed by the British Statutes; but must need, in the mere spirit of contradiction, threw it all in common into one huge tea-pot, and made a cold infusion, which so heated His most gracious Majesty, that he sent an army to punish them for their refractory conduct. The husbands of course could do no less than take the

part of their wives, and so the rebellion was got up; such was the effect of our most gracious King's attempt to interpose his rightful prerogative in regulating the tea-tables of the disloyal dames of Boston.[7]

Greene's burlesque of the English vision of America through the eyes of Fibbleton sometimes results in images suggestive of the tall tale tradition as in his description of lodgings in Saratoga: "As many were piled in as could conveniently lie, by placing them like bags of cotton, one atop of the other. For my part, I preferred to take the underside of the bed, for here we only lay two deep."[8]

If *Fibbleton's Travels in America* was aimed at vindicating the American character in the face of foreign judgments, Greene's ultimate full-length fictional work was devoted to a portrayal of New York City life. *The Perils of Pearl Street, Including a Taste of the Dangers of Wall Street*, appeared in January 1834, shortly after *Fibbleton's Travels in America*. A facetious account of mercantile adventures in New York, the work purports to be an autobiography "by a late merchant" and describes the ups and downs of trying to make a fortune in merchandising and banking. Greene creates a burlesque actor-narrator who satirizes the shams and trickeries of New York traders and financiers, but the pseudo-picaresque autobiographer is himself burlesqued from the very beginning. William Hazard, the son of a carpenter, resolves to be a trader. He lives in Spreadaway, an upstate village. After being fired from several firms in New York he speculates in cotton and hops, then starts a lottery, but these risky ventures result in bankruptcy. In order to pay off his obligations, Hazard eventually lectures on bookkeeping and engages in politics. By turns he is a loser and a reliable commentator on mercantile eccentricities. Such characterization is aimed at contrasting village greenhorns with city slickers, but Greene's realistic descriptions of idiosyncrasies blunt his satiric shafts and convert initially ironic portraitures into good-humored observations. Greene is obviously indebted to two humorous traditions. In *The Perils of Pearl Street* characters such as Janus Fairface and Mrs. Callagain are evidence of Charles Dickens's influence. On the other hand, the concomitant use of both dialect and standard American English illustrates the confrontation of two life styles. After Seba Smith's Jack Downing, Greene's William Hazard dimly foreshadows Thomas Haliburton's Sam Slick who appeared as the comic hero of a new business culture in 1835. In the Jacksonian era, Greene could not easily imagine the rise of the common man from rural surroundings to an urban environment without mocking the foibles of Down Easters, yet his caricatures were diversified and suggestive. It took the sophistication of later popular humorists to bring out the comic paradoxes of a society between 1830 and 1837 born from frontier ideals and rife with sectionalism and conflicts.

Summary

Asa Greene was a Yankee "gentleman" who enjoyed deflating contemporary humbugs. Attempting to fuse the English picaresque tradition with Yankee lore, he invented eccentric characters at odds with a chaotic social environment. He concentrated on foibles rather than vices. Based on his experience as editor and publisher, Greene's humorous works constitute a transition between Yankee folk humor and the more ambitious achievements of Thomas Chandler Haliburton and James Russell Lowell. Influenced by Fielding and Smollett, Greene could not free himself from a provincial moralism that prevented a more inclusive vision of the American panorama, yet, he attempted to steer a middle course between the derogatory stereotypes of his fellow citizens offered by British observers and the presentation of native folk demigods by some Americans. He attempted to give to his manifold observations the status of literary achievements. Like Seba Smith in New England and most southwestern humorists of his time, Greene belonged to a generation of educated, gentlemanly observers who adroitly expressed popular opinions. Although he sometimes derided rural manners, his condescension gave way to truculent nationalism when foreign observers gibed at the crude manners of his fellow citizens, and he helped bridge the gap between popular culture and the literature for and by the élite.

Notes

1. The *Constellation*, April 16, 1831.
2. The *Constellation*, June 19, 1830. Royall Tyler and Thomas Green Fessenden were among the prominent humorists who parodied the lyrical outbursts of the American disciples of early romantic poets influenced by Hester Lynch Piuzzi, one of the founders of the Della Cruscan movement in Florence in the late eighteenth century. The *Farmer's Museum* was founded in Walpole, New Hampshire, in 1793. Its early editor was Joseph Dennie.
3. Ibid., January 8, 1831.
4. *The Life and Adventures of Dr. Dodimus Duckworth, A.N.Q.*, (New York: Peter Hill, 1833), vol. 1, p. 224.
5. *A Yankee Among the Nullifiers* (New York: William Stodart, 1833), p. 118.
6. *Travels in America by George Fibbleton* (New York: William Pearson, 1833), p. 30.
7. Ibid., pp. 180-181.
8. Ibid., p. 175.

Selected Bibliography

Primary Sources

A Glance at New York. New York: A. Greene, 1837

A Yankee Among the Nullifiers: An Autobiography by Elnathan Elmwood, Esq. New York: William Stodart, 1833.

The Life and Adventures of Dr. Dodimus Duckworth, A.N.Q., to Which Is Added the History of a Steam Doctor. 2 vols. New York: Peter Hill, 1833.

The Perils of Pearl Street, Including a Taste of the Dangers of Wall Street, by a Late Merchant. New York: Betts and Anstice and Peter Hill, 1834.

Travels in America, by George Fibbleton, Esq., Ex-Barber to His Majesty, The King of Great Britain. New York: William Pearson, 1833.

Secondary Sources

Blair, Walter. *Native American Humor (1800–1900).* New York: American Book Company, 1937. Greene's place is assigned in the tradition of American humor.

Blair, Walter, and Hill Hamlin. *America's Humor, From Poor Richard to Doonesbury.* New York: Oxford University Press, 1978.

Reed, Arthur Lachlan. "Asa Greene, New England Publisher, New York Editor and Humorist, 1789–1838." Dissertation, University of Minnesota, 1953. The only full-length biography. Reed refutes Walter Blair's argument that Greene had not authored the Timbertoes letters.

Royot, Daniel. *L'Humour Américain, des Puritains aux Yankees.* Lyon: Presses Universitaires de Lyon, 1980. Specific studies devoted to Greene's use of the picaresque tradition (pp. 211–217, 246–247, 266–267).

Tandy, Jennette. *Crackerbox Philosophers in American Humor and Satire.* New York: Columbia University Press, 1925.

Daniel G. Royot

Habberton, John

Born: Brooklyn, New York, on February 24, 1842
Marriage: Alice Lawrence Hastings, 1868
Died: February 25, 1921

Biography

John Habberton was born in Brooklyn, New York, on February 24, 1842. After the death of his father (Job John) in 1848, he was taken to Illinois and reared by an uncle. The move made an unforgettable impression on him as western scenery, manners, and colloquial speech contrasted sharply with the land and styles of New York. Habberton began to develop an ear for dialect and an eye for colorful detail that would distinguish his humor.

Sunday School provided another lasting influence. The Bible played strongly upon Habberton's imagination, introducing favorite stories that he would rework in his fiction through the mouths of children, rustics, and hypocrites. His earliest literary ambition—writing biographies of missionaries—embodied a wish to share the adventure that he found between the lines of conventional religious literature. As a boy, he devoted months to writing a hymn, a project of mental anguish that permanently spent his poetic ambition.

But, he remained an avid reader: the most omnivorous in his village, by his own account. When he returned to the East at the age of 16 to learn the publishing trade, he fell under the influence of Charles Dickens's work and dashed off sketches of New York in the light style of *The Uncommercial Traveler.* To his surprise, the pieces were accepted and printed by weekly papers as far away as Boston. While still in his teens Habberton became a published writer.

The Civil War interrupted his publishing activities but not his writing. As a Union private bored with army life, he passed the time by keeping a careful diary that described barracks quarrels, bad food, gossip, and other trivial matters commonly encountered by foot soldiers between battles. Initially he sent his observations home for the amusement of his family. One day, though, a few pages were discovered and read aloud in camp. His comrades enjoyed the performance, and thereafter he wrote to entertain the garrison.

Following discharge with the rank of lieutenant, Habberton secured a position with the publishing house of Harper and Brothers. He married Alice Lawrence Hastings in 1868, and the couple settled in New Rochelle, New York. Habberton enjoyed success in publishing for a few years. Then he decided to establish his own company and quickly went bankrupt. A well-meaning but gullible man, he adopted several children and squandered much of his money. Between 1874 and 1900, a burden of debt forced him to supplement the royalties he earned from writing fiction with employment as an editor and reviewer for such periodicals as the *Christian Union,* the *Outlook,* the *New York Herald, Godey's Magazine,* and *Collier's Magazine.* He died in 1921 at the age of 78 at a Soldier's Home in Kearny, New Jersey.

Literary Analysis

Habberton's first sustained literary effort came in 1872, a gush of realistic short stories inspired by the work of Bret Harte and Edward Eggleston. His vivid boyhood impressions of Illinois, supplemented with extravagant stories supplied by an uncle who had been in California during the Gold Rush, gave him plenty of suitable material. Habberton concentrated on characterization and local color elements. He wrote quickly, sometimes completing several manuscripts in a single week. Considering the tales simple entertainments without literary merit, he used assumed names as he rushed them out to prospective publishers. Almost all were accepted, and soon Frank Leslie's *Illustrated Newspaper*, *Chimney Corner*, and other periodicals were running Habberton's work under by-lines that included H.A. Burton, J.J. Burnham, A.H. Garland, and F.Guernsey.

The stories demonstrate Habberton's ability to depict character through a few lines of dialect. His miners, school marms, law men, widows, and deacons mangle the language, making stronger impressions through their speech than by their actions in such tales as "Old Twitchett's Treasure," "Jim Hockson's Revenge," and "The Meanest Man at Blugsey's." Like Harte, Habberton offers few villains, preferring instead to show the pure heart buried beneath every rough exterior. The cacography he uses to establish realism has a positive secondary effect: a degree of lively verbal burlesque.

His knack for fast writing coupled with keen observation soon enabled him to build a literary reputation upon a single book: *Helen's Babies*. Its conception came about by chance when Habberton scribbled a 10,000-word chronicle of his own children's antics in order to entertain their bedridden mother. Her approval encouraged him to revise the work for publication, masking his identity behind a persona named "Uncle Harry" and changing the boys' names to "Budge" (age five) and "Toddie" (three). Though he detected dialect problems in the first draft, Habberton tired of the story and offered his manuscript to publishers just as it stood, acknowledging its shortcomings by leaving his name off the title page. He planned to polish the book during production, but the proofs arrived just as he was hurrying away on a trip. He made no attempt to correct them. *Helen's Babies* went to press in 1876 virtually as he had drafted it.

If Habberton's "babies" came into the world with faults visible to their author, they had hearts as pure as the western stock populating his earlier tales. Civilized behavior and conventional speech were ideals toward which the two boys struggled with earnest intentions and comic results. With the galloping pace of children at play, they led Uncle Harry through a purgatory of mud pies, poison, and rooftop peril. When he caught up they sat on him, pounded his chest, and made him pray, sing, and tell stories in the manner of their vacationing father. If he grew angry, they found refuge in innocence or tearful repentance, both sugared with baby talk.

Uncle Harry could have no interests of his own; his correct attempts to court a lovely neighbor named "Miss Mayton" were always subject to sabotage. When he tried to make a strong first impression by sending the lady a hat box filled with artfully arranged flowers, she opened it to find his bouquet replaced by Toddie's "dolly," a dirty towel tied in knots. Enraged, he confronted the offender:

> "Toddie," I roared as my younger nephew caressed his loathsome doll, and murmured endearing words to it, "where did you get that box?"
>
> "On the hat-wack," replied the youth, with perfect fearlessness, "I keeps it in ze book-case djawer, an' somebody took it 'way an' put nasty ole flowers in it."
>
> "Where are those flowers?" I demanded.
>
> Toddie looked up with considerable surprise, but promptly replied:—"I froed 'em away—don't want no old flowers in my dolly's k'adle. That's ze way she wocks—see!" And this horrible little destroyer of human hopes rolled that box back and forth with the most utter unconcern, as he spoke endearing words to the substitute for my beautiful bouquet!

Drawing upon his Sunday School lessons, Habberton laced the book with Bible stories, first recounted faithfully by Uncle Harry, and then distorted in retelling by the children. A long treatment of "Jonah" came to its conclusion only after Toddie had thrown up in public and proudly told his brother: "Budgie, down to the village I was a whay-al. I didn't froe up Djonah, but I froed up a whole floor full of uvver fings."

Critics cared little for the material, but readers found it irresistible. *Helen's Babies* sold an astounding 250,000 copies in the United States and became a principal example of the bad-child humor so popular during the latter part of the century. Habberton soon heard acquaintances quoting his book. He was even introduced to a man who modestly acknowledged writing it. When friends finally revealed his true identity to the press, he was deluged with compliments and requests for more manuscripts.

As usual, Habberton produced rapidly. During 1877, he published no fewer than five new books, several of which may have been written prior to *Helen's Babies*. Three dozen of his short stories were collected and issued under the title *Some Folks*. His second novel, *The Barton Experiment*, used well-drawn character sketches to laugh at temperance excitement raging in some parts of the country. *The Jericho Road: A*

Story of Western Life followed the misfortunes of a sickly hero whose few funny moments came when he repeatedly threatened to fall down and die in front of his tormentors. Theology smothered humor in *The Scripture Club of Valley Rest*, which presented long-winded discussions by a group of men who met frequently to debate the Bible. In *Other People's Children*, Habberton created a successful sequel to *Helen's Babies*, with a partisan narrator relating the blameless misdeeds of Budge and Toddie during a visit with their new aunt (the former Miss Mayton) and still-suffering Uncle Harry.

During this period, Habberton became so popular that he expressed guilt about the space his titles were occupying on publishers' shelves. The prominence soon faded, however. He returned to his bad-child formula several more times with diminishing success: in *Just One Day* (1879), *The Worst Boy in Town* (1880), and *Trif and Trixy* (1897), the children fell victim to an excess of nineteenth-century sentimentality, with innocence overshadowing their comic potential. Other efforts included *The Crew of the "Sam Weller"* (1878), *The Bowsham Puzzle* (1884), *Country Luck* (1887), and *The Chautauquans* (1891). Habberton also scripted a successful play, *Deacon Crankett* (1892), and a disappointing biography of George Washington (1894).

His finest humor capitalized upon differences in manners and dialect, contrasting the reasoned behavior and language of a New York journalist with the coarse actions and vernacular of children and rustics. His early experience as a diarist and local colorist helped him develop a talent for fast pacing and clear visual description that complemented his knack for capturing dialect.

Like some other humorists of the 1800s, Habberton was mildly ashamed of his reputation as a comic writer. He considered his most popular books unfinished, pieced together with too little time to demonstrate deeper talents. Wide reading made him hunger for literary eminence, but sentimentality spoiled his serious efforts. He never again approached the achievement of his first book. "I did not want my literary ability to be measured by *Helen's Babies*," he later wrote, "And I confess to periods of discomfort when wiser and better writers seem inclined to hold me . . . in some way responsible for the failure of their own works while mine were selling largely."

Summary

John Habberton was a local colorist who used verbal burlesque and realism to contrast sophisticated behavior with the rude actions of children and Westerners. His first and most important book, *Helen's Babies*, was a popular example of bad-child humor emphasizing the innocence of youth in a world filled with temptation.

Selected Bibliography

Primary Sources

Fiction

Helen's Babies, With Some Account of Their Ways, Innocent, Crafty, Angelic, Impish, Witching and Repulsive. Also, a Partial Record of Their Actions During Ten Days of Their Existence. By Their Latest Victim. Boston: Loring, 1876.

The Barton Experiment. New York: G.P. Putnam's Sons, 1877.

The Jericho Road: A Story of Western Life. Chicago: Jansen, McClurg & Co., 1877.

Other People's Children: Containing a Veracious Account of the Management of Helen's Babies by a Lady Who Knew Just How the Children of Other People Should be Trained. New York: G.P. Putnam's Sons, 1877.

The Scripture Club of Valley Rest; or, Sketches of Everybody's Neighbors. New York: G.P. Putnam's Sons, 1877.

Some Folks. New York: Derby Brothers, 1877.

The Crew of the "Sam Weller." New York: G.P. Putnam's Sons, 1878.

Just One Day. New York: George R. Lockwood, 1879. Also published as *Mrs. Mayburn's Twins, with Her Trials in the Morning, Noon, Afternoon, and Evening of Just One Day.* Philadelphia: T.B. Peterson & Brothers, 1882.

The Worst Boy in Town. New York: G.P. Putnam's Sons, 1880.

The Bowsham Puzzle: A Novel. New York: Funk and Wagnalls, 1884.

Country Luck. Philadelphia: L.B. Lippincott, 1887.

The Chautauquans. New York: Robert Bonner's Sons, 1891.

A Lucky Lover. Boston: Bradley & Woodruff, 1892.

Trif and Trixy. A Story of a Dreadfully Delightful Little Girl and Her Adoring and Tormented Parents, Relations, and Friends. Philadelphia: Henry Altemus, 1897.

Caleb Wright: A Story of the West. Boston: Lothrop, 1901.

Some Boys' Doings. Philadelphia: G.W. Jacobs, 1901.

Drama

Deacon Crankett. 1880.

Miscellaneous

George Washington (1732-1799). New York: H. Holt, 1884.

"My Literary Experiences." In *Lippincott's Magazine*, December 1886, pp. 708-713. A sketchy but revealing account of his writing career with melancholy overtones.

Secondary Sources

"John Habberton Dead." *The New York Times.* February 26, 1921, p. 11. A short obituary.

Stuart Kollar

Haliburton, Thomas Chandler

Born: Windsor, Nova Scotia, on December 17, 1796

Education: King's College, Windsor, Nova Scotia

Marriages: Louisa Neville, 1816, died, 1840; Sarah Harriet Owen, 1856; two children

Died: August 27, 1865

Biography

The man whom Artemus Ward credited with founding the American school of humor was Canadian by birth, English by citizenship, and a staunch anti-republican in training and sentiment. Yet, in his efforts to satirize the American New Englander for purposes of drawing object lessons for his fellow Nova Scotians about the hazards of social democracy, Thomas Chandler Haliburton gave life and international currency to the comic stereotype of the enviably shrewd Yankee peddler, whose spirit courses through such contemporary offspring as the men who hustle used cars and aluminum siding.

Haliburton was born in Windsor, Nova Scotia, on December 17, 1796. He received his education at King's College in Windsor, then followed in the footsteps of his father and paternal grandfather by pursuing a career in public service and the law. He practiced first at the bar at Annapolis Royal, the former capital of Nova Scotia, and served three years as a representative in the Nova Scotian Assembly, then as chief justice of the Court of Common Pleas, and in 1841 accepted an appointment to the Supreme Court of Nova Scotia. Haliburton's public career was defined by an unshakeable Toryism forged of a long family tradition and tempered by his conservative Anglican education.

In 1816, Haliburton married Louisa Neville. He was able to provide a comfortable life for his family through a series of profitable business investments that included numerous retail stores in Windsor, wharf facilities, a quarry, a joint stock company and several land investments. Haliburton's success gave him social and material privileges that ossified his conservative leanings. He was a sensualist who relished the complementary arts of eating, drinking, and conversation. His reputation as a wit far exceeded, by contemporary accounts, his quality as a jurist.

In 1856, the political climate in Nova Scotia had deteriorated, in Haliburton's view, to the point that his rabid anti-republicanism left him an embittered outsider. Haliburton turned his back on his native land and moved to England, taking up residence at Isleworth in Middlesex. In 1859, he married Sarah Harriet Owen (his first wife having died in 1840) and was elected to Parliament, where he served conservative interests until 1865. Though he was honored late in life by Oxford University for his literary accomplishments, Haliburton's parliamentary service was undistinguished, hampered as he was during most of the period by severe gout and a body of class attitudes belonging to an earlier century. Haliburton died at Isleworth on August 27, 1865.

Literary Analysis

In 1823, at the age of 26, Haliburton produced *A General Description of Nova Scotia*, a volume of provincial history that included an account of the British expulsion of the Acadians from which Henry Wadsworth Longfellow is said to have derived his account of the event in *Evangeline*. It was the first of several volumes of history and current events he was to write over the next three decades. But, for all his productivity, Haliburton's reputation as an historian was demolished in 1851 with the publication of *The English in America*, a two-volume work so extensively and identifiably plagiarized that it permanently weakened Haliburton's reputation as a serious scholar.

His reputation as a humorist, however, made him a literary lion on both sides of the Atlantic. As early as 1828, Haliburton began contributing articles to the *Novascotian*, a paper popular among the amateur literati. In these articles Haliburton introduced the character of Sam Slick of Slickville, a Yankee peddler of Connecticut clocks, whose business it was to sweep down on the good folks of rural Nova Scotia and harvest their savings with a sales technique composed of glib flattery (known as "soft sawder") guided by a keen understanding of the parts that greed, envy, and vanity play in human nature.

Haliburton developed a structure for his *Clockmaker* pieces by borrowing the eighteenth-century Addisonian moral essay and refreshing it with the addition of colorful vernacular dialect and pointed characterizations in the manner of the regional American humorists of the mid-nineteenth century. Each piece depended on a contrast between a stodgily urbane narrative persona—the Squire—and Slick, whose outspoken observations about American culture provided the meat of the essays and served as the basis of their appeal. Over time a pattern emerged in which Slick and the Squire roamed back and forth through Nova Scotia in a picaresque fashion that lent itself well to regular collections issued in book form. The first series was published in 1836, followed shortly thereafter by a second and third. In all, Haliburton's humorous works were issued in literally hundreds of editions before the end of the nineteenth century.

Haliburton's satiric intention in the first series of *The Clockmaker* was to underscore the importance of self-help in responding to the financial difficulties of Nova Scotia during the period of decolonialization following the Napoleonic wars. In the second series (1838), his aim was to ridicule the principles underlying the democratic reform movement in Nova Scotia; in the third (1840), addressed exclusively to a British audience, he argued against the movement in England to grant Nova Scotia a degree of self-government.

Though not intended as flattery, Haliburton's portrait of the American Yankee became so popular in Canada, America, and England that Haliburton emerged as the only North American during this period to rival Charles Dickens as an international literary celebrity. Sam Slick was beloved on both sides of the water for his shrewdness, his thrift, and his laconic insights into human nature. So successful was the character that Haliburton eventually sent him overseas in *The Attache; or, Sam Slick in England* (two series, 1843 and 1844), in which the character served as a member of the American legation to the court of St. James. Unfortunately, the humor of *The Attache* suffered from a lack of that intimate sense of place that distinguished the early work. Two subsequent volumes—*Sam Slick's Wise Saws and Modern Instances* and *Nature and Human Nature* (1855)—being simple collections of aphorisms and anecdotes, lacked any of the satiric energy that had inspired Haliburton early in his career.

Haliburton's one other accomplishment in the field of humor was *The Letter-bag of the Great Western; or, Life in a Steamer* (1840), an epistolary account of an ocean crossing loosely imitating Tobias Smollett's *The Expedition of Humphry Clinker*. Its comic spirit resided in Haliburton's fondness for outrageous puns and jokes about bodily infirmities, racial differences, and the grammar of the underprivileged classes—features that offended as many of his contemporaries as they entertained.

Haliburton's position in the history of American humor remains a subject of debate. Canadian critics and scholars continue to see Haliburton as the first world-class author in a Canadian national literature, and they offer as a significant credential his role in popularizing the figure of the comic Yankee. American critics have tended to view him as an imitator of American regional humor, particularly the Jack Downing letters by Seba Smith and the Crockett almanacs. Haliburton did lack the ear for recording subtle differences among regional American dialects, but he wrote with far superior literary effect than his American counterparts. Moreover, his Slick was the first of the many New England Yankees to approach epic stature in the development of an American literary heritage.

Summary

Thomas Chandler Haliburton was the Canadian author of *The Clockmaker* and creator of Sam Slick, the most popular version of the New England Yankee character in all of nineteenth-century literature.

Selected Bibliography

Primary Sources

A General Description of Nova Scotia, Illustrated by a New and Correct Map. Halifax: The Royal Acadian School, 1823.

An Historical and Statistical Account of Nova Scotia. Halifax: n.p., 1829.

The Clockmaker; or, The Sayings and Doings of Samuel Slick, of Slickville. 1st ser. Halifax: n.p., 1836.

The Clockmaker. 2nd ser. London: Richard Bentley, 1838.

The Bubbles of Canada. London: Richard Bentley, 1839.

A Reply to the Report of the Earl of Durham. London: Richard Bentley, 1839.

The Clockmaker. 3rd ser. London: Richard Bentley, 1840.

The Letter-bag of The Great Western; or, Life in a Steamer. London: Richard Bentley, 1840.

The Attache; or, Sam Slick in England. 1st ser. London: Richard Bentley, 1843.

The Attache. 2nd ser. London: Richard Bentley, 1844.

The Old Judge; or, Life in a Colony. London: Henry Colburn, 1849.

The English in America. London: Colburn, 1851.

(ed.) *Traits of American Humor, by Native Authors.* London: Colburn, 1852.

Sam Slick's Wise Saws and Modern Instances; or, What He Said, Did, and Invented. London: Hurst and Blackett, 1853.

(ed.) *The Americans at Home; or, Byways, Backwoods, and Prairies.* London: Hurst and Blackett, 1854.

Nature and Human Nature. London: Hurst and Blackett, 1855.

An Address on the Present Condition, Resources and Prospects of British North America. London: Hurst and Blackett, 1857.

The Season Ticket. London: Richard Bentley, 1860.

Secondary Sources

Blair, Walter. "Down East Humor." In *Native American Humor.* San Francisco: Chandler, 1960, pp. 38-62. Remains the standard twentieth-century critical assessment of Haliburton's reputation from the American point of view.

——, and Hamlin Hill. "The Yankee and the Major." *America's Humor.* New York: Oxford University Press, 1978, pp. 180-186.

Chittick, V.L.O. *Thomas Chandler Haliburton: A Study in Provincial Toryism.* New York: Columbia University Press, 1924. The standard biography; contains the most comprehensive bibliography available. A useful supplement to O'Brien and Cogswell.

Cogswell, Fred. "Thomas Chandler Haliburton." *Dictionary of Canadian Biography.* Vol. 9 (1861-

1870). Toronto: University of Toronto Press, 1976, pp. 348–357. There is no current bibliography. Cogswell's suffices, updating Chittick by mentioning sources of general reference; offers a Canadian cultural context that provides a useful balance for Blair's American view.

The Dictionary of National Biography. Vol. 8. London: Oxford University Press, 1917, pp. 927–928.

The National Cyclopedia of American Biography. Vol. 5. Ann Arbor: University Microfilms, 1967, pp. 353–354.

O'Brien, A.H. *Haliburton: A Sketch and Bibliography.* Montreal: Gazette Printing, 1909.

Watters, Richard Eyre. "Introduction." *The Sam Slick Anthology.* Toronto: Clark, Irwin and Co., 1969, pp. iii–xxix.

Gary Engle

Hargrove, Marion

Born: Mount Olive, North Carolina, on October 13, 1919

Education: Awarded high school diploma, 1946

Marriages: Alison Pfeiffer, December 1, 1942, divorced, May 20, 1950, two children; Robin Edwards Roosevelt, March 17, 1954, four children

Biography

Marion Hargrove, Jr., was born in Mount Olive, North Carolina, on October 13, 1919, to Emma and Marion Lawton Hargrove. Growing up in Charlotte, he attended the local high school, where he became feature writer and editor of the school paper. He was one-half point short of credits for graduation in 1938 when he left (in 1946 the school would award him a diploma based on his Army service). After a series of odd jobs, he became feature editor for the *Charlotte News,* to which he contributed "In the Army Now" after he was drafted in July 1941. These columns became the nucleus of his wartime bestseller, *See Here, Private Hargrove.*

Hargrove was still a "semiskilled cook" at Fort Bragg when the United States entered World War II. But, in February 1942, playwright Maxwell Anderson arrived at the post to research material for *The Eve of St. Mark.* Some of Hargrove's buddies drew the dramatist's attention to their friend, who helped smuggle him into the barracks, provided local color for the play, and collaborated on a radio script, "From Reveille to Breakfast." Anderson, in turn, based the character "Francis Marion" on Hargrove and carried his columns to William Sloane of the Henry Holt publishing house, convincing him to publish them as a book. *See Here, Private Hargrove* was an immediate hit, both hardbound and in the pioneer paperback "pocket" books, selling over two million copies. Metro-Goldwyn-Mayer bought the movie rights to it and to a sequel (*What Next, Corporal Hargrove?*) for a total of $70,000. The Army transferred Hargrove to the magazine *Yank* in New York City, where he served as a feature editor, and promoted him to corporal. Here he met and married his first wife, Alison Pfeiffer, a Smith College student and guest editor at *Mademoiselle,* in December 1942. Anderson helped them find a home in a Nyack, New York, writers' colony. They had two children before their 1950 divorce. Both subsequently remarried: he to Robin Edwards Roosevelt (1954), who had once been married to Franklin Roosevelt's grandson. The second marriage produced four children.

Through the publicity attending his success, Hargrove became a spokesman for the soldier, doing articles for the *New York Times Magazine* on everyday G.I. problems, behavior, and morale. He wrote introductions for George Baker's *The Sad Sack* and Barrie Stavis's *Chain of Command,* and served on the advisory council (with John Hersey and John Mason Brown) for the "G.I. Joe Literary Award." After his discharge, as a sergeant, Hargrove continued in the public eye. He tilted with the National Association of Manufacturers, with Robert Moses over veterans' housing and in opposition to new parkway construction, and appeared frequently on behalf of liberal causes. In 1946, he became commander of a provisional post of the American Legion. The Duncan-Paris Post, the membership of which was composed largely of artists and writers, was accused in those early Cold War years of harboring Communists and "fellow travellers," and Hargrove was involved in acrimonious newspaper exchanges until his resignation. In 1953, he reemerged briefly as a public advocate, campaigning against the unauthorized use of material from *Yank* by profit-making publishers.

By 1948, he had written another novel, *Something's Got To Give,* and he began freelance production of feature articles for a number of popular magazines: *Life, Holiday, Collier's, McCall's, Good Housekeeping, Harper's* and *Atlantic Monthly.* During the 1950s, he was feature editor of *Argosy.*

The 1950s and early 1960s were years of sustained creativity. In 1956, he completed his third novel, *The Girl He Left Behind,* also about Army life and also made into a movie by Warner Brothers. Moving to California, he began to write for television (most notably the comic western series, *Maverick*) and for motion pictures. He provided either the adaptations or screenplays for *Joe Butterfly* (1957), *Cash McCall* (1960), *Boys' Night Out* (1962), *The Music Man* (1962), and *Forty Pounds of Trouble* (1963). His work for *The Music Man* earned him a Writers' Guild Award in 1962.

Marion Hargrove now resides in Santa Monica, California.

Literary Analysis

Fortuitous publication timing and public morale needs help in part to explain the phenomenal success of *See Here, Private Hargrove*. Written largely before Pearl Harbor and published shortly thereafter, the book presented army life as painless and untraumatic, a series of innocuous episodes, experiences divorced from the grimness of war. Parents were reassured that their sons would not be brutalized by the military, that, in fact, they could become more responsible and disciplined. As Hargrove noted elsewhere: "He has been trained to fight but he has chosen to think and feel as he damned well pleases."[1] Hargrove and his buddies engaged in sophomoric hazing, short-sheeting beds and driving frustrated sergeants to exasperation. They spent their days in cleaning garbage cans, wrestling with heavy inanimate objects, and baroquely "shooting the breeze," but eight weeks of basic training and subsequent army life would make these boys into men, proud and self-reliant but essentially conformist. (This message would be repeated even more strongly in Hargrove's other military novel, *The Girl He Left Behind*.) *See Here, Private Hargrove* was also pleasantly didactic; it was the first of a substantial body of literature seeking to accustom civilians to military slang.

The book retained its appeal throughout the war and long afterward; even today it is warmly remembered by people who do not connect Hargrove's name with any other production. This is greatly due to its light tone, as a good-humored army book midway between those that transparently used the "bad example" caricature in order to socialize people to the army,[2] and those, especially by cartoonists, that commented satirically and sometimes bitterly about the injustices of military caste.[3] While Hargrove increasingly aligned himself with those who would press for reforms and testify before the 1946 Doolittle Board, his book was a work of mild iconoclasm.[4]

Neither of his army books was well served by their movie adaptations. Robert Walker, as Hargrove, monotonously and empty-headedly broke regulations; Tab Hunter as Andy Shaeffer in *The Girl He Left Behind* was exaggeratedly spoiled and churlishly sullen. Neither character

realized Hargrove's intentions. The book-version Hargrove usually is an improvident bumbler, but he is also an earnest young man who falls in with a company of uproarious pranksters. Their high-jinks are collegiate rather than mindless, and their dialogue is similar to that of college freshmen endeavoring to appear mature and controlled. The tag-line endings to many episodes reinforce the impression of Hargrove and company as young men trying to understand a radically different environment through irony, not willful disobedience or inherent ineptitude. Andy Shaeffer is a petulant fellow struggling to find self-respect and freedom from overprotective parents. He seeks guidance, first from a goldbricking buddy, then from a moody California "Golden Girl," and finally from a belittling sergeant who becomes his sarcastic but caring parent-surrogate. As witty and slangy as is typical Hargrove repartee, as shallow as the characters are who inhabit the books, there is a serious concern with personal growth and adjustment to the larger society amid the chuckles.

This is also the case with his other novel, *Something's Got to Give*. A satire on radio programming, commercials, and the hypocrisy of postwar materialism, the book clothes some deep criticism of contemporary values with deft wordplay, witty dialogue, and homey, simple characters. Joe and Carolyn Dobbs and Chuck and Betsy Bartlet become involved in a morning show about child-raising, and the narrative contrasts their bemused media success with the deepening chaos of their lives and relationships. They are actually happy when vicious gossip leads to their contract being broken.

One recent critic has argued that Hargrove's books reflect an ambivalence about success and ambition. His heroes are torn between avoiding entanglement in the system and a self-regard that sees irresolution or anonymity as lack of character. Private Hargrove lacked ambition (though surely Marion Hargrove did not) but evolved into a G.I. liaison with the civilian world. The Dobbses and Bartlets suffer from the effects of ambition and withdraw to domesticity. Shaeffer regains his woman and finds a calling only after accepting scorn and responsibility not only for himself, but for others: he becomes a drill instructor![5]

Hargrove's magazine pieces ranged from straight reportage to humorous anecdote, but he usually tried to handle all of his subjects in a light, unassuming, and inoffensive manner. In "Don't Send Souvenirs," a *New York Times Magazine* article about soldier morale and well-meaning families who send the wrong kind of presents, for instance, he combines psychological insight with one-liners like: "It comforts

George like a kick in the short ribs."[6] And, in a straightforward human interest piece about the Travellers' Aid Society, "Somebody's Always Going Away," he begins with an anecdote about an octogenarian who runs away from home every weekend rather than take a bath.[7] Most of his writing for popular magazines is easy reading and informative, if pedestrian.

When Marion Hargrove went to Hollywood, he took a resuscitated "Private Hargrove" persona with him. As well as adapting works from other media for the screen, most notably *The Music Man*, he has written screenplays and television scripts that entertainingly portray irreverent adventures of petty schemers as well as mild burlesques of other shows. *Maverick* was designed as a take-off on "Gunsmoke," and *Boys' Night Out* a mildly leering version of the "young bachelor" movies that were prevalent in the 1950s. When he has occasionally ventured beyond the picaresque into other themes, as in *Forty Pounds of Trouble*, part Runyonesque sentimentality, part promotional tour of Disneyland, he has not been as successful.

When Hargrove's oldest son Christopher entered the army in 1965, the younger man remarked: "I am not a Private Hargrove. I play it safe."[8] Hargrove has been most enjoyable and effective when he has *not* played it safe, when his characters were at odds with, though not at war with, conventionality.

Summary

For over two decades, Marion Hargrove regularly entertained Americans with pleasant, light farce in a variety of media. Whether critically well received or not, most of his writing—novels, articles, screenplays, and television scripts—have been popular. Even critics who pronounce his work thin or glib praise his breezy tone, skill at dialogue and repartee, and ability to delineate personable rogues. Many of his characters have been admirable vehicles for actors like James Garner, who starred in *Maverick* and in three of Hargrove's movies. In both books and movies, Hargrove has shown a talent for ensemble pieces, although some critics argue that his characters are too alike in their wittiness. Moreover, Hargrove has an ear for period adolescent slang, inflated language, and ludicrous conversation, and is an unexpected resource for that aspect of midcentury popular culture. Precisely because much of it is ephemeral, Hargrove's canon can serve the social historian as an example of that midcentury ambivalent iconoclasm so different from the 1960s social satire that was to follow.

Notes

1. Marion Hargrove, "Soldier Salute to U.S.O.," *New York Times Magazine*, May 31, 1942, p. 30.

2. For example, Robert Osborn, *Dilbert*, New York, Coward-McCann, 1943, or David H. Culbert, "Walt Disney's 'Private Snafu,'" *Prospects*, 1 (1975): 81–98.

3. Among others, Bill Mauldin, Edward Baker ("Sad Sack"), Dave Breger ("G.I. Joe"), and Dick Wingert ("Hubert") stand out.

4. For example, Louis Paul, *The Ordeal of Sergeant Smoot* (New York: Crown, 1943); Harry Brown, *Artie Greengroin, PFC* (New York: Knopf, 1945); Brown and Ralph Stein, *It's a Cinch, Private Finch* (New York: Whittlesy, 1943).

5. Robert Secor, "Marion Hargrove," *Dictionary of Literary Biography*, Vol. 11, *American Humorists, 1800–1950*, ed. Stanley Trachtenberg (Detroit: Gale, 1982), pp. 176–179.

6. Hargrove, "Don't Send Souvenirs," *New York Times Magazine*, July 5, 1942, p. 13.

7. Hargrove, "Somebody's Always Going Away," *Collier's*, 125 (May 13, 1950): 20–21, 73–74.

8. *New York Times*, June 19, 1965, pp. 31, 60.

Selected Bibliography

Primary Sources

Books

See Here, Private Hargrove. New York: Holt, 1942.
Something's Got to Give. New York: Sloane, 1948.
The Girl He Left Behind. New York: Viking, 1956.

Magazine Articles

"The Girls We're Going to Marry When the War Is Over." *Good Housekeeping*, 115 (November 1942): 39, 128.
"You'll Never Get Rich, But He Did." *Life*, 21 (December 12, 1949): 11–12, 15–16.
"The Nonsmoker." *Atlantic Monthly*, 194 (August 1954): 89.
"This Is a Television Cowboy?" *Life*, 46 (January 19, 1959): 75–76, 78.

Miscellaneous

Baker, Sgt. George. *The Sad Sack*. Introduction by Hargrove. New York: Simon and Schuster, 1944.
Stavis, Barrie. *The Chain of Command*. Foreword by Hargrove. New York: Ackerman, 1945.

Secondary Sources

Selected Book Reviews

Foell, E.W. Review of *The Girl He Left Behind*. *Christian Science Monitor*, May 17, 1956, p. 7. The novel seen as a thin romance which does not capture the spirit of the peacetime army.
Gehman, Richard. Review of *Something's Got to Give*. *Saturday Review*, 31 (May 1, 1948): 23–24. His first book was amateurish but timely; this one is likeable and fresh but lightweight.
McCutcheon, J.T. Review of *The Girl He Left Behind*. *Chicago Sunday Tribune*, May 27, 1956, p. 4. Amusing and glib repartee are noted, but all of the characters speak like Hargrove.
Wylie, Max. Review of *Something's Got to Give*. *New York Times*, May 9, 1948, p. 17. Hargrove's writing is fast and easy but seems unreal; the author intrudes into the story and dialogue.

Chapters in Books

Secor, Robert. "Marion Hargrove." *Dictionary of Literary Biography*. Vol. 11. *American Humorists*

1800–1950. Ed. Stanley Trachtenberg. Detroit: Gale, 1982, pp. 176–179.

Shivers, Alfred S. *Maxwell Anderson*. Boston: Twayne, 1976. Includes a description of how Anderson discovered Hargrove, who aided him with background material on military life.

Hargrove in Hollywood

Halliwell, Leslie. *Halliwell's Film Guide*. New York: Scribner's, 1983. Includes lists of casts, credits, and capsule critiques of motion pictures to which Hargrove contributed.

Hirschborn, Clive. *The Warner Brothers Story*. New York: Crown, 1979. Brief discussion of the three Warner Brothers movies in which Hargrove was involved.

The New York Times Film Reviews. Multi-volume compendium published by The New York Times Company. A collection of reviews, mostly by Bosley Crowther, of Hargrove's screen credits: "Joe Butterfly," Howard Thompson, reviewer, *New York Times*, May 30, 1957, p. 23, *New York Times Film Review*, Vol. IV, pp. 2988–2989; "Cash McCall," Howard Thompson, reviewer, *New York Times*, January 28, 1960, p. 26, *New York Times Film Review*, Vol. V, p. 3172; "Boys' Night Out," Bosley Crowther, reviewer, *New York Times*, June 22, 1962, p. 15, *New York Times Film Review*, Vol. V, p. 3331; "The Music Man," Bosley Crowther, reviewer, *New York Times*, August 24, 1962, p. 14, *New York Times Film Review*, Vol. V, pp. 3342–3343; "Forty Pounds of Trouble," Bosley Crowther, reviewer, *New York Times*, January 24, 1963, p. 5, *New York Times Film Review*, Vol. V, p. 3372.

Kalman Goldstein

Harris, Joel Chandler

Born: Eatonton, Georgia, on December 9, 1848

Education: No formal education beyond grade school

Marriage: Esther LaRose, April 29, 1873, nine children

Died: July 3, 1908

Biography

For the great majority of his modern readers, Joel Chandler Harris's considerable national and international renown rests primarily on one area of his literary accomplishment, his achievement as the master storyteller who expertly recreated in print the Afro-American fables from the folklore of the pre-Civil War American plantation slave of the deep South. Harris brought forth Brer Rabbit, his friends, and his enemies from their murky ancient origins in the communal memory and oral tradition of southern slave culture. By his unique additions, his skillful recastings of the tales in the frame which featured Uncle Remus, the old black storyteller and his listener, the little white boy from the plantation manor house, Harris gave the fictions a singular life, charm, and energy that has resulted in their enduring fame.

Harris's career, however, encompassed at least four other journalistic or literary vocations in which he distinguished himself. He first became known as a skillful writer of comic "fillers" for Georgia newspapers. Composing humorous bits and shorter pieces—a "paragrapher"—Harris first displayed the sense of humor that was to mark all of his writing. As he advanced from reporter to paragrapher to writer of his own popular signed column and finally to associate editor of the powerful and progressive *Atlanta Constitution*, Harris's comic gift was a singularly valuable asset.

Harris's own purely original fiction gained him another reputation as a short story writer and novelist who took as his most frequent setting the small-town rural South. He distinguished himself as creator of local color fiction that sought to capture the flavor of the region in speech, manners, and attitudes, focusing often on the time preceding, during, and immediately following the Civil War, especially the Reconstruction. Harris hoped to contribute to the healing of wounds of the spirit left by the war for both black and white Southerners. Finally, Harris had yet another successful literary career, writing his purely original non-black-folklore-based children's books.

Given these achievements, Harris must be considered an important American regional writer and certainly the most significant of the varied group identified as southern local colorists before Mark Twain. Harris was in his own time, and remains today, a preeminent figure in American humor.

The man who was to gain this reputation was born to Mary Harris in the little town of Eatonton, Putnam County, Georgia, on December 9, 1848. His father was believed to be an Irish day laborer with whom Mary Harris had fallen in love when he was working near the home of Mary's mother in nearby Newton County. Defying strenuous resistance from her parents, Mary cohabited with him in Putnam County until a short time after their baby's birth, when the Irishman disappeared forever. Mary gave her son her own family name and set about raising him as best she could. She reconciled with her mother and accepted the offer of an Eatonton planter, Andrew Reid, who gave Mary a cottage on his plantation's grounds. In his biography,

Paul Cousins notes that the democracy of mid-nineteenth-century Georgia white society, composed largely of small independent farmers and a small elite of plantation owners, made it not at all unusual for poverty and wealth to live side by side, and the townspeople, knowing Mary to be a gifted seamstress, supplied her with all the work that she needed to support herself and Joel.

When later families, such as Frank Leverette's, came to occupy the main house, the children of these families made a path through the hedge and kept literature-loving Mary Harris supplied with books, newspapers, and magazines. Mary's reading of Oliver Goldsmith's *The Vicar of Wakefield* in the hearing of young Joe Harris left an enduring impression; Harris cited that Goldsmith reading as the beginning of his own desire to write. Mary also stimulated Harris's story-telling ambitions by the tales that she recounted to him. Such was Mary Harris's influence on her son that the prominent place given to fatherless children, households headed by a mother, and strong-minded, independent women in Harris's fiction seems a logical outcome.

In his life in Eatonton, Harris was surrounded by a vigorous society of hard-working small farmers, primarily not slaveholders, much committed to individualism and with the down-to-earth humor often marked by frontier high spirits and violence that marked the southwest humorists. Harris was passionately dedicated to all modes of clowning and pulling of practical jokes as a boy, notes R. Bruce Bickley, including achieving such memorable moments of youthful disturbing-the-peace in Eatonton as the market day when he drove a herd of hogs to panic in the main street.

Andrew Reid sent Harris first to a co-ed private school, Kate Davidson's Academy for boys and girls, then to all-male Hillsborough Academy. The boy was especially careless about attendance at the first school as he found himself too uncomfortable around the female pupils. The prankster's odd shyness in the company of girls is explicable in light of his lifelong attempt to compensate for a number of physical problems. He was quite short, endowed with bright red hair and freckles, and he stammered severely. His sensitivity about his hair was so acute that, as an adult, he always wore a broad-brimmed felt hat even while indoors. He felt great discomfort in public and possessed, in his own words, an "absolute horror" of having to meet new people. He was unable to read his work aloud, even to his children, or to address groups. It may well be, as several scholars of Harris's life have speculated, that these problems resulted from his learning when very young of his illegitimacy. It may well be, too, as

suggested by an insightful interviewer from the *New York Times* in 1909, that his lifelong dedication to humor and his incorrigible commitment to playing tricks on others were, in fact, natural reactions by Harris to his extreme shyness.

In his writing, by concealing himself behind the mask of the comedian, Harris managed to accomplish his comic ends and to pursue his goal of helping right the social wrongs of his time and region without having to reveal himself in the candid directness of confrontation and dialogue.

Harris owed his beginnings in journalism and his chance to commence his literary career to Joseph Addison Turner, whose advertisement for "an active, intelligent white boy . . . to learn the printer's trade" Harris answered in 1862. A planter and lawyer whose true love was literature, Turner was, by the standards of that time and place, a most cultured gentleman. In the practical-minded South, where literature was regarded largely as self-indulgence, Turner aspired, despite all obstacles, to create works that were purely and representatively southern in both theme and style. He sought to create a body of writing that would bring both fame and wealth to him and new prestige to his region. While Turner never achieved his goal, he succeeded admirably in conveying to the thirteen-year-old boy whom he engaged as printer's devil for *The Countryman*, the newspaper that he printed at his plantation, a love for literature that went well beyond humor or efficient journalism. Also, and perhaps most importantly, during the four years that Harris lived at Turner's plantation, Turnwold, he was supplied with a surrogate father who was at once affectionate, supportive, demanding in valuable ways, and filled with humor. Harris was to cite his Turnwold experience as a crucial time in his life, and to admit his considerable debt to Turner repeatedly in later years.

While learning the journalist's trade, Harris regularly published his own writing by working pieces into *The Countryman* while setting Turner's pages in type. Selections included painfully poor puns: "Why do the Yankees delay their attack upon the chief rebel port?" Answer: "Because they find a Charles*ton* too heavy for their gunboats to carry." Harris quickly transcended his journeyman comedian's errors of obviousness, however, and, other papers began to reprint his humorous one-liners.

Less than two years after his arriving at Turnwold, Harris's verses, light philosophical essays, and book reviews began to appear in *The Countryman*. Harris subscribed wholeheartedly to Turner's belief that the South must pay more attention to writers of the region, and in 1864 he wrote a spirited review of Henry Lynden Flash's hyper-romantic poetry, stating that it was time for the South to "atone for her former coldness to her sons of song." This youthful dedication to his region was to be, in its mature form, important throughout Harris's career.

The most valuable education that Harris received at Turner's plantation, however, was of a more informal sort and involved the folktales the young printer's devil heard in the servants' quarters. A range of raconteurs—Uncle George Terrel, Old Harbart, Aunt Crissy—introduced Harris to the rich legacy of black folktales. Harris locked into his memory the folk materials, including the character of a talented and devious rabbit and the narrative techniques of these black folktellers, their gifts for creating empathy with their audiences—the comedy, pleasant fear, and delight they generated by coaxing, taunting, praising, rebuking, occasionally tricking, and otherwise manipulating their audiences as they told their tales. Delaying outcomes, claiming ignorance of what was going to occur next, hiding behind the storyteller's pose and refusing to elaborate—"That's how the story goes"—all of these strategies Harris listened to, memorized, internalized with wonderful fidelity until they would become his own stock in trade through the Uncle Remus stories.

Harris left Turner's service in 1866, when the gracious benefactor's finances collapsed with the fall of the Confederacy. He served briefly as typesetter for the *Macon Telegraph*, then the New Orleans *Crescent Monthly*, and finally the Forsyth, Georgia, *Monroe Advertiser*.

Harris's mounting reputation at *The Advertiser* led, in 1870, to his receiving an offer to become associate editor of the *Savannah Morning News*, a major Georgia paper. His joining this paper was appropriate, for the *News*'s founder-editor was William Tappan Thompson, the Southwest humorist who created the Major Jones stories. Thompson's gentle tone, happy outcomes, and avoidance of violence and harsh language closely paralleled Harris's own emphasis in his general comic writing and non-Uncle Remus local color pieces. Through his writing on the *News*, Harris expanded his reputation well beyond the state, and selections from his column, "Affairs in Georgia," began to be read and appreciated throughout the South.

Harris, together with such other southern wits as Thompson, Twain, and Artemus Ward, had a positive effect in supplying comic relief to an often-troubled region during a time of anxiety and uncertainty. Harris's contribution to the creation of a "New South" of hope, self-confidence, and optimism included both his humor and the steadily upbeat tone of his editorial writing that encouraged southern economic and intellectual progress.

This is not to say that Harris came immediately to this stance, or that he did not suffer early in his career from the enduring effects of southern racism. Bickley notes that the Harris who, in his journeyman newspaper work, wrote, "A Lumpkin negro seriously injured his pocketknife recently by undertaking to stab a colored brother in the head," was to become dedicated to repairing the psychological damage caused by the years of strain between the races.

At the same time that Harris began to make his mark in his career, he also met his wife-to-be, Esther ("Essie") LaRose, the 17-year-old daughter of a French-Canadian steamboat owner, who lived at the same boardinghouse in Savannah in 1872. They were married in Savannah on April 29, 1873. Essie and the happy home that she made were Harris's anchors in his hectic life in journalism. The couple was to have nine children but to lose three of them to disease in early childhood.

When an epidemic of yellow fever paralyzed Savannah in August 1876, Harris and his family fled to Atlanta. This led to his next job, a position with the *Atlanta Constitution* where editors Evan Howell and Henry Grady were eager to engage a talent such as Harris. Grady and Howell were creating a newspaper of considerable influence in a city that was clearly on the rise, and Harris quickly became caught up in the paper's mission, the drive to bring Atlanta, and Georgia, and, indeed, the whole region into the movement to create the "New South." Harris and Grady, as associate editors under Howell, worked well together. Grady spread the gospel of industrial and political cooperation between the North and the South, urging Southerners to exploit their region's natural resources and begin the region's economic revitalization. Harris, though a product of the cultural traditions of the Old South, championed a new literature emancipated from the ultraromantic, oversentimental past, a literature that developed the South's as-yet-untapped reservoirs of purely original literary materials. He lived in Atlanta for 32 years, dying there of uremic poisoning caused by cirrhosis of the liver and acute nephritis on July 3, 1908.

Literary Analysis

It is ironic that, as Harris urged southern writers to create a truly new literary focus, he should base his own greatest creations on the character of an old born-in-slavery southern black man. Harris first wrote from the perspective of Uncle Remus in the fall of 1876 when filling in for Sam Small, a just-resigned staff feature writer who had used Old Si, an old-time Atlanta black, as a spokesman to comment on politics and the local scene. The dialect that Small used for his character was no more than a jumble of exaggerated misspellings resembling the butchery of English used by literary comedians of the time such as Josh Billings and Artemus Ward. Harris's Uncle Remus was a believable, individualized, engaging three-dimensional creation, who held the reader's attention by his character and his narrative style as much as by the yarn he told.

In his first brief attempt at the dialect story, "Markham's Ball," Harris simply carried on Small's tradition to comment humorously on a party celebrating a local political victory, but with the next sketch, "Jeem's Rober'son's Last Illness," Harris introduced Uncle Remus and gave American literature a vital new character and a novel folkloric-fictional mode. Uncle Remus's dialect, demonstrating Harris's fine ear for the rhythms and inflections of black speech, was an accurate reproduction of a living person's spoken language, not a whimsical exaggeration of the coarser peculiarities of a dialect. His yarn, moreover, demonstrates the talent of a master storyteller for rhythm, timing, development, and manipulating his listener. Uncle Remus meets a younger black from a nearby town at the train station, and they discuss Jim Robertson, a mutual friend whom the younger man has not seen for some time. "He ain't down wid de beliousness, is he?" asks the visitor. "Not dat I knows un," Uncle Remus responds in a solemn tone. "He ain't sick, an' he ain't been sick. He des tuckn'n say he wuz gonter ride dat ar roan mule er Mars John's de udder Sunday, an' de mule, she up'n do like she got nudder ingagement." From his rough experience with that same mule in the past, Uncle Remus counsels Jim that "he'd better not git tangled up wid er," but Jim, asserting that he is a "hoss-doctor" and quite up to this challenge in horse discipline, has bridled the mule and mounted. Uncle Remus then narrates the disastrous results of foolhardy Jim's plan to ride this perilous mule.

In this initial appearance of the full-fledged Uncle Remus, the extraordinary departures Harris made from the coarse tradition in black dialect humor is clear. Far from being a caricature, Uncle Remus has genuine human appeal and a natural dignity, making him feel subtly superior to certain blacks and making the others respect his years. To help set the scene, Uncle Remus keeps us aware of the situation in historical perspective, of how close to his thoughts are the past plantation days for the old man who refers automatically to "Mars John."

As Harris wrote more and more Uncle Remus sketches, the old black man evolved from two initial forms into a single final character. There was first an old black man living in the city who appeared at the railroad station and haunted the editorial offices of the *Constitution*. He had much to say—usually to a younger black listener or on occasion to the staff members of the newspaper generally—sometimes involving country humor, as with the fierce mule, sometimes focusing on the unfortunate state of morality in local and national politics, sometimes treating the lack of religious or ethical values in his neighbors' acts and attitudes. He was bitter about his poverty even as he hoped for a handout from the journalists. This Uncle Remus was wistful about having left the country, and his thoughts regularly returned there in speculations that he would be welcomed back at the home of the plantation owners whom he had left.

The second Uncle Remus, he who was to eclipse the first and gain Harris his greatest fame, had either returned to the plantation or never left it and was content to stay there. The strategy of returning Uncle Remus to the plantation was endorsed by Harris's discovery that, when presented by Uncle Remus, the black folktales featuring humanized animals had an immense appeal to readers in other sections of the country. The key to the unsuspected treasures he held in his memory came to Harris when he read, sometime in the 1870s, an article in *Lippincott's Magazine* that discussed the folklore of blacks in the American South and suggested the imaginative richness of this material. "This article gave me my cue, and the legends told by Uncle Remus are the result," he later wrote.

July 1879 saw the first appearance of an Uncle Remus story featuring the old man's accounts of goings-on among the "creeturs," and the reaction of readers to the story in the *Constitution* was extremely enthusiastic. An astonished and delighted Harris watched the tales reprinted throughout the country. In 1880, the publishing house of D. Appleton approached Harris about issuing a collection of the Uncle Remus tales, songs, and aphorisms, and in early 1881 *Uncle Remus: His Songs and His Sayings* appeared. An instant success, the collection sold 7,500 copies in the first month of publication, and the critical response was extremely positive in both the United States and England. The initial success of the first collection of Uncle Remus tales established a popularity that the yarns have maintained to the present day; the works, in various editions, have never been out of print.

The animal stories were in no sense Harris's first experiment in different literary forms. He had published his poetry as early as the *Countryman* days; his essays and book reviews in *The Constitution* had always been well-received;

and in 1878 he tried a novel, when *The Constitution* serialized *The Romance of Rockville*. The novel, however, revealed certain of the difficulties that were always to plague Harris in his attempts at longer, non-folklore-based fiction: lack of a tight, effective plot, an insufficient range of engaging characters, and inadequate suspense.

In the animal tales, however, the plot structures, characterizations, and pacing came to Harris fully formed by the generations of Afro-American story-tellers who had repeated and refined the fables. Indeed, the trickster figure is a well-established fixture in many African oral traditions. However, the narrator, his little boy listener, and the mood of their relationship were the inspired creations of Harris himself. As a number of critics—including Mark Twain—have noted, the stories may be seen as "alligator pears,"' which we eat for the sake of the dressing, so drawn are we to the old man and his auditor.

The setting is the period after the war, though his asides show that Uncle Remus remembers both the time before the conflict and the war years with great fidelity. Uncle Remus is a free man and, more than that, is a force to be reckoned with in the society of the plantation where he has chosen to stay; he is a venerable sage and an educator of the young as well as a would-be counselor, gentle corrector, and helpful critic of the adult society, both black and white.

The scene is a relaxed moment in Uncle Remus's cabin or his garden, where the little boy is visiting, and the old man is regularly engaged in some operation of humble housekeeping—patching a hole in a shirt, nailing up a shelf, cooking a simple meal—and some thought of Uncle Remus's or some comment by the little boy causes the old man to consider how the "doin's" of humans puts him in mind of the goings-on among the "creeturs." Sometimes the activity that prompts the tale involves the little boy misbehaving, performing some forbidden act such as "chunkin' rocks" at the chickens. If so, Uncle Remus calculates his prologue and fable so that it will illustrate the wrongness of such conduct. Criticism and correction accomplished, however, Uncle Remus shows that he feels warmly for the little boy, always, in sin or virtue, and calls him "honey." His cabin is a place of quiet psychological nourishment for both the old man and the child.

The settings of most fables told within this frame are similar. The animals meet each other as they are going along the road or as both have come to another common location—the ferry across the river, going to market, on the way to clear some new land. They exchange friendly greetings. These salutations, though often passed between animals who are in nature the hunter and the hunted, such as Brer Fox and Brer Rabbit, are invariably cordial, in the formula of the stylized cordiality the black slave had to maintain with his master and other white people. Just how thin this veneer of manners is, though, and how deep the resentment is that it masks, quickly becomes apparent as the would-be trickster plays upon the sense of assumed cooperation to set up his intended victim for the harsh trick that he plans—often designed to produce fatal consequences for the victim. Sometimes the pair lay out a project that they will complete together; sometimes they arrange a contest. In proposing the interaction the initiator frequently praises the intended victim, noting his strength, agility, or some other ability that the trickster lacks. The schemer stresses how neighborly and empathic he is in approaching the other creature, how pure his motives are; he suggests that the cooperation might be the commencement of a new, friendly relationship between the creatures. The master trickster of the pair sometimes sets up the trick, but more frequently he sees through the trap that the inferior schemer is trying to lay for him, and he often not only escapes, but turns the scheme back on the would-be trapper. The more gifted tricksters, such as Brer Rabbit and Brer Terrapin, show a marvelous gift for improvising in a tight spot and playing on the coarser intellect of their antagonists, which is crucial to their staying alive, given the number and deadliness of their adversaries.

The stories suggest allegorically the tensions between the races. By illustrating the triumph of the weaker creature over his stronger adversary, using not his strength but his ingenuity, Uncle Remus shows the little boy the wit of the weaker creature and, in an indirect way, the case for realigning the values and the social structure of southern society, as, in each of the stories, the stronger creature comes to a new appreciation of the nerve, daring, and ingenuity of his less physically powerful enemy.

The pattern is seen clearly in the first tale in the 1880 edition of *Uncle Remus: His Songs and His Sayings*, "Uncle Remus Initiates the Little Boy." Here Brer Fox meets Brer Rabbit in the road and states that he wants to try to cultivate better relations between them in response to a wish expressed by Brer B'ar: ". . . he sorter rake me over de coals kaze you en me ain't make fr'ens en live neighborly, en I tole 'in dat I'd see you." Brer Rabbit appreciates the gesture and would indeed like an improvement in relations, yet he has certain unspoken hesitations, and advises the other animal to keep his distance, as, "I'm monstus full er fleas dis mawnin.'"

After Brer Rabbit and his family prepare a

chicken dinner—the consumption of chickens by rabbits creates no problem in the fantastic world of Uncle Remus—to serve Brer Fox to honor the new relationship, the fox fails to show up. Brer Rabbit, however, spots the tip of a fox's tail behind a tree outside his door. Next day, Brer Fox sends word that he had been too sick to come and hopes Brer Rabbit will dine with him at the fox's house to compensate. When he reaches Brer Fox's house, however, Brer Rabbit sees no dinner on the table, but a bowl and carving knife set out, with the fox wrapped up in a flannel blanket sitting next to it, groaning. Using care not to get too far inside, the rabbit tells that fox that he has got so that he can't really enjoy chicken, ". . . ceppin' she's seasoned up wid calamus root." Seeing that Brer Fox does not have any calamus root, Brer Rabbit hurries out to get some. Brer Fox creeps out of the house to close in on Brer Rabbit, but Brer Rabbit has positioned himself well out of the reach of his adversary and sings out, "Oh, Brer Fox! I'll des put yo' calamus root out yer on dish yer stump. Better come git it while hit's fresh."

The allegory suggests that any gesture of supposed friendship on the stronger creature's part might conceal a hostile design toward the weaker, and the weaker must be alert, suspicious, and alive with ingenuity. Brer Rabbit must keep up the front of gracious cooperation even as he expertly turns the tables, illustrating the characteristic mode of unarmed combat through which the weaker creature in these contests must survive.

The Brer Rabbit stories also illustrate certain of the most complex self-criticisms that were a part of the lore of the antebellum slave. The famous story of the tar-baby, with its two episodes, may be the most intricate in its racial implications. In the first part, "The Wunderful Tar-baby Story," the rabbit, full of himself, buoyant with cockiness—"dez ez sassy ez a jaybird"—is posing as a creature of might and dignity himself when he meets the dummy constructed of tar that Brer Fox has left seated at the side of the road. Feeling that the tar baby must be his inferior, Brer Rabbit commences to demand that it demonstrate the proper address, show ". . . how ter talk ter 'spectubble folk," and respond to him with the same sort of required artificial graciousness that the white world demanded of the black. When the dummy will not obey and continues to act "stuck-up," the offended rabbit attacks the silent tar-baby first with his fists, then his feet, and lastly with his head. With all his limbs and head stuck in the tar-baby, Brer Rabbit, the black folk hero, has completely incapacitated himself by attacking not the representation of his masters but the allegorical symbol of his own race while Brer

Fox, the symbol of the master race, laughs at the rabbit's predicament.

In the second story, "How Mr. Rabbit Was too Sharp for Mr. Fox," however, Brer Rabbit escapes the trap into which he has led himself by his own conceit. By appealing to Brer Fox's desire to dispatch his victim in the most excruciating way imaginable, Brer Rabbit frees himself. In a show of psychological manipulation, Brer Rabbit begs the fox to kill him in any way, be it by skinning, burning, or drowning, if only the executioner will refrain from the one intolerable fate—tossing Brer Rabbit into the briar patch. The fox flings Brer Rabbit into the feared tangle of briars, only to be taunted, after several moments pass, by the liberated rabbit, whose cockiness returns instantly, as he pops up out of the briars at a safe distance, seats himself on a log to pick the tar from his fur, and yells, "Bred en bawn in a briar-patch, Brer Fox!"

Even though they recognize that he may be his own worst enemy at times, readers must salute the rabbit and admire his survival skills. There are, however, other tales that illustrate more troubling principles in the requirements for survival in Brer Rabbit's world. The allegory of the weaker animal triumphing over the stronger through guile takes many forms, and often suggests the hazards of absolute, unrestrained deviousness. It may be unsettling to the liberal reader of the tales, who wishes to find a finely sustained and even-handed allegory of the plight of the plantation slave in his subtle and undeclared war with his white masters, to recognize that the weaker critter-protagonist who lives by his wits is not above betraying, manipulating, or lying to any other creature—including those who share his weakness and vulnerability. An example of this trait is found in "Mr. Rabbit Nibbles Up the Butter" (from the first edition of 1881) in which the creatures are in a rare period of concord and Brer Rabbit, Brer Fox, and Brer Possum begin displaying their ultimate trust by storing their food in the same shanty, "sorter bunchin' der perwishuns tergedder." Brer Rabbit fails to take this unusual opportunity to improve relations, unfortunately, but seizes the chance to indulge himself by secretly eating the butter that Brer Fox has brought. When the outraged Brer Fox misses his butter, Brer Rabbit claims innocence, and frames Brer Possum by smearing his paws with the last of the butter while he takes a nap. Panicked, the hapless possum agrees to a strange "trial by fire" contest in which each of the possible thieves attempts to jump over a huge fire, with the assumption that the guilty one's crime will weigh him down. The two more spry creatures vault the blaze, but the earthbound possum is burned to death in the fire. The shocked little boy objects to this injustice, but the old man offers no consolation: "In dis worl', lots er folks is gotter suffer fer udder folks sins. Look like hit's mighty onwrong; but hit's des dat away."

While Harris never commented directly on the symbolic significance of the tales that he recreated so effectively, a number of modern commentators have found much importance in this material. R. Bruce Bickley sees the major thrust of the tales as Harris's endorsing a basic desire for a realignment of values and social structures in white society in the South. Bickley notes that the stronger race learns to respect the weaker. At the same time, it is stressed that Uncle Remus's admiration for his hero was never unadulterated, and that the unrestrained one-upmanship of Brer Rabbit—Bickley sees something of the young Joel Harris here—steadily makes the reader qualify his approval of the rabbit hero. Other critics, notably Darwin Turner, have noted that the folktale triumphs that Brer Rabbit achieves are far from real-life victories of the black slave over the plantation owner but rather a set of fantasy successes, an extended daydream of turning the tables, a way for the powerless black slave to sublimate his frustration and humiliation. Robert Bone and Jesse Bier find the tales harsh specimens of the essential mode of American humor, the world of irony and cynicism. Stressing Brer Rabbit's willingness to do whatever he must to gain his success, Bier underscores the every-man-for-himself battle of wits in which Brer Rabbit has much in common with other famed American humor tricksters such as Sut Lovingood.

The sources of Uncle Remus brought the shy author troubling exposure. A positive outcome of his fame, however, was Harris's meeting, in 1882, with his fellow American humorist, Mark Twain. Their subsequent friendship was to last a lifetime and to prove of enduring profit and pleasure to both men. The two humorists had a great deal in common in their poor rural backgrounds, their chosen materials—especially their mutual debt to southern black folklore— and their sense of empathy with the South's blacks.

Twain was an invaluable counselor in pointing out to Harris strategies for maximizing his financial return from his writings. Twain also urged Harris to expand his cast of human characters, and along with Uncle Remus and the little boy, three new characters appeared in the collection: Aunt Tempy, Tildy, the house girl, and African Jack. Aunt Tempy was intended to act as foil to Uncle Remus and African Jack and to tell the witch tales. Tildy, whom Harris defined as "irreverent, indecorous, pert, careless, and yet capable of believing anything that human lips could tell," was to serve as the wide-eyed listener to complement all three narrators. African Jack tells the coast stories in a Gullah dialect with possibilities beyond that which Uncle Remus' plantation lore and speech could accomplish. As the additions suggest, Harris was constantly modifying and adding new directions in his consequent collections of Uncle Remus tales. This included Uncle Remus's increasing moral emphasis.

At the same time that the series of Uncle Remus collections were gaining great success, Harris was experimenting with another mode of fiction, local color tales of southern life in wartime and Reconstruction to appeal to an older audience. Beginning with *Mingo and Other Sketches in Black and White* of 1884, Harris published seven story collections in this vein that, outside of some shows of clever dialect comedy, have limited interest for modern readers. The failure of these local color tales results largely from the excessive emphasis in the often-sentimental stories on the need for optimism, warm good feeling, forgiveness, and brotherhood among Americans of all colors and political persuasions in the stressful post-Civil War period.

Among Harris's local-color stories, the most celebrated has been "Free Joe and the Rest of the World," which appeared in *Free Joe and Other Georgian Sketches* in 1887. The strain of Reconstruction, particularly that reflected in the less-than-self-reliant former slave, is pictured in a dark light quite unlike Harris's other local color fiction. One begins to wonder at the value and intensity of Joe's suffering, his sense, not of being freed, but of now being slave to every white man. Joe's lonely life culminates in his solitary death, leaving curious and unexpected doubts about not only the virtues of Joe's emancipation but about the slave's character and suggesting that freedom is a curse to those as passive and unfocused as Joe. Other local color tales, such as "Trouble On Lost Mountain" (from the *Free Joe* collection) and "Where's Duncan?" (in the 1891 stories entitled *Baalam and His Master*), also present raw violence and black-white hatred.

The other stories in the *Free Joe* collection are much more optimistic.

In *The Chronicles of Aunt Minervy Ann* (1899), Harris once again considers the tension and anxiety that existed for the races in the South immediately after the war, but, unlike Free Joe, the forceful and self-assured Aunt Minervy Ann is quite unintimidated by freedom. With good humor and sound judgment, she regularly defuses dangerous situations. She knows just who and what she is: Black and proud of it, "Affikin fum way back fo' de flood an' fum de word go."

The up-beat tone typical of the Aunt Minervy Ann tales also appears in two story collections focused on the need for new harmony between the North and South. *Tales of the Home Folk in Peace and War* (1898) is a story sequence that chronicles the inception, growth, and postwar continuation of a warm, communal friendship among a group of northern and Confederate soldiers, suggesting Harris's hopes for a harmonious future. The stories in *On the Wing of Occasions* (1900) presumably chronicle the evidence of Divine intervention and assistance in specific cases during the war. The reader, however, becomes less aware of the guiding Hand of the Almighty than the annoying and constantly present manipulating hand of the author.

One story in the collection, however, features the first appearance of a new character who was to prove of considerable value to Harris, Billy Sanders; he is an earthy, seemingly buffoonish mid-Georgia type, of limited education but great good sense and insight into others' motives. Sanders was to serve Harris well in his later writings, as did Aunt Minervy Ann, supplying unadorned, down-to-earth rural wisdom on race relations, political goings-on both good and bad, and personalities of the time.

Beginning with *On the Plantation* in 1892, Harris turned from his Uncle Remus tales and began to devote his efforts to non-folklore-based children's books. *On the Plantation* describes adventures shared by a mischievous twelve-year-old boy, a younger girl, and their ever-grumbling black nursemaid. The blend of prankishness and shyness seen in the boy, Joe Maxwell, is suggestive of the work's author at the same time of life. While entertaining, the stories have never enjoyed a reputation approaching that of the Uncle Remus tales.

At this time, also, Harris made two serious attempts at novel writing, with very limited success. *Sister Jane: Her Friends and Acquaintances* was published in 1896, and was followed in 1902 by *Gabriel Tolliver: A Story of Reconstruction*. Both novels demonstrate that Harris's particular literary gift was not suited to maintaining an extended narrative. Like *Sister Jane*, *Gabriel Tolliver* suffers from loose organization, poor pacing, and a rambling plot, faults for which neither the fine evocation of place nor the amusing narratives and stunts of Billy Sanders, which appear throughout the novel, can fully compensate.

In 1900 the profits from his writings and the guarantee of a steady income from publishers' contracts permitted Harris to leave the journalism that had long before become more of a labor than a pleasure and to turn his efforts entirely to fiction. In the time that Harris had initially thought of as his retirement, he was much honored by admirers, for through the joint impact of appreciation for Uncle Remus's creator and the positive feeling for the influential editor who had done so much to improve life for both races in the South, Harris had become a southern institution, even a national one.

The last phase of Harris's career, however, was not restricted to leisure and receiving well-deserved accolades. Though very fearful that the adventure was ill-advised, Harris, aged 58, after being steadily, strenuously urged—"bedeviled," in Harris's phrase—by his son Julian and a group of Atlanta businessmen, agreed to become the sole editor of a hazardous experiment in magazine publishing, a literary monthly to be called *Uncle Remus' Magazine*. Never had a monthly magazine attempted to make its editor also its principal writer and drawing card, and never had such a magazine been undertaken in the South. But, Julian Harris was greatly determined, and, once he convinced his father to undertake the magazine, the elder Harris threw himself into the work with the dedication, energy, and enthusiasm that marked all his undertakings. His motto for the magazine was "Typical of the South—National in Scope," and he soon made it clear that *Uncle Remus' Magazine* was to express both his profound love of his native region and his loyalty to the Union. Harris sought to get a steadily upbeat, positive impact and even thought of calling the journal *The Optimist*.

The first number, thanks to the inexperienced staff's errors, was two months late, and printing errors caused thousands of copies to be discarded. Subsequent issues were much better. Harris's magazine lived up to its name, for he personally wrote six of the articles in that first number, and other southern authors, such as associate editor Don Marquis, added additional pieces.

Brer Rabbit stories appeared in the magazine, to keep the Old South flavor, but Harris deemphasized them, seeking to identify the periodical with the present and the future of the South, not its past. Harris's novel, *The Bishop, The Boogerman, and the Right of Way*, was serialized in the magazine, and illustrates Harris's approach. It is an Old-South versus New-South story with a happy ending that particularly appealed to young readers. A younger, more forward-looking Southerner convinces a reactionary plantation owner of the need to permit the railroad to cross his land. The young man causes the older to recognize the need for change and progress, for setting aside the prejudices and fears of the past in general.

Harris wrote the majority of the magazine throughout its brief history, even doing the book reviews (as Anne Macfarland, a crotchety but demanding sixty-year-old literary lady).

Predictably, for one so committed to his work, Harris died in harness, never letting up from the strenuous labor with his pen. He was hard at work on the magazine when the end came. This conclusion to the humorist's life was appropriate, for his work was his life. It was through his journalistic and literary labor that Harris escaped his poor origins and finally took his prominent place in American literature. He was a man intimately acquainted with trouble and with loss. His shyness was an evidence of the lingering wounds of childhood psychological damage.

Harris's ability not only to survive but to benefit from his troubles was certainly the power that made the sort of flavoring his experience gave him valuable. The vital agent in Harris was his sense of humor. Indeed, Harris's final words to those gathered at his bedside before he lapsed into unconsciousness suggest that the sense of humor that had been with him for a lifetime was still with him as he was leaving this world. Asked by Julian how he felt, Harris responded, "I am about the extent of a tenth of a gnat's eyebrow better."

Through Uncle Remus, Harris's literary achievement will remain as a tribute to a masterful and imaginative creator. Through the evidence of his life, Harris's personal witness to the transforming power of humor will remain to honor that blessed gift.

Summary

Haunted by his illegitimacy, Harris learned his skills at journalism and the art of writing from serving a planter, Joseph Addison Turner, as printer's devil and listening to slave folktales. He moved through jobs at a number of southern papers, finally joining Henry Grady on the *Atlanta Constitution*, a major force for more liberal attitudes and new economic opportunities in the South. Here Harris perfected Uncle Remus, the old black man who retold the tales of Brer Rabbit. The charm of this frame, quite as much as the slave's wish-fulfillment allegory in the tales—the powerless rabbit overcoming far stronger enemies by his wit alone—has given the stories their still-vital life. Harris wrote a wide range of other fiction, including local-color stories, often seeking to improve race relations, and children's stories not based on Brer Rabbit. The folktales remain genuine classics.

Selected Bibliography

Primary Sources

Uncle Remus: His Songs and His Sayings. New York: D. Appleton, 1881.

Nights with Uncle Remus: Myths and Legends of the Old Plantation. Boston: James R. Osgood, 1883.

Mingo and Other Sketches in Black and White. Boston: James R. Osgood, 1884.

Free Joe and Other Georgian Sketches. New York: Charles Scribner's Sons, 1887.

Daddy Jake the Runaway and Short Stories Told After Dark. New York: Century, 1889.

Balaam and His Master and Other Sketches and Stories. New York: Houghton, Mifflin, 1891.

On the Plantation: A Story of a Georgia Boy's Adventures During the War. New York: D. Appleton, 1892.

Uncle Remus and His Friends: Old Plantation Stories, Songs, and Ballads with Sketches of Negro Character. New York: Houghton, Mifflin, 1892.

Sister Jane: Her Friends and Acquaintances. A Narrative of Certain Events and Episodes Transcribed from the Papers of the Late William Wornum. New York: Houghton, Mifflin, 1896.

Tales of the Home Folk in Peace and War. New York: Houghton, Mifflin, 1898.

The Chronicles of Aunt Minervy Ann. New York: Charles Scribner's Sons, 1898.

On the Wing of Occasions: Being the Authorised Version of Certain Curious Episodes of the Late Civil War, Including the Hitherto Suppressed Narrative of the Kidnapping of President Lincoln. New York: Doubleday, Page, 1900.

Gabriel Tolliver: A Story of Reconstruction. New York: McClure, Phillips, 1902.

Wally Wanderoon and His Story-Telling Machine. New York: McClure, Phillips, 1904.

Told by Uncle Remus: New Stories of the Old Plantation. New York: McClure, Phillips, 1905.

The Bishop and the Boogerman: Being the Story of a Little Truly-Girl Who Grew Up; Her Mysterious Companion; Her Crabbed Old Uncle; The Whish-Whish Woods; A Very Civil Engineer, and Mr. Billy Sanders the Sage of Shady Dale. New York: Doubleday, Page, 1909.

The Shadow Between His Shoulder-Blades. Boston: Small, Maynard, 1909.

Uncle Remus and the Little Boy. Boston: Small, Maynard, 1910.

Seven Tales of Uncle Remus. Ed. Thomas H. English. Atlanta: Emory University Sources and Reprints, Series V, No. 2, 1948.

The Complete Tales of Uncle Remus. Ed. Richard Chase. Boston: Houghton Mifflin, 1955.

Secondary Sources

Bibliographies

Bickley, R. Bruce Jr. *Joel Chandler Harris: A Reference Guide.* Boston: G.K. Hall, 1978. The Harris criticism, to the time of each work's publication, is summarized in bibliographies in Stella B. Brookes's work on folklore in Harris, in R. Bruce Bickley's biography, in Paul M. Cousins's biography, and in the Julia Collier Harris biography. In *A Bibliographical Guide to the Study of Southern Literature,* ed. Louis D. Rubin (Baton Rouge: Louisiana State University Press, 1969), pp. 212-214, there is a useful bibliography of secondary sources by Charles A. Ray.

Biographies

Bickley, R. Bruce, Jr. "Joel Chandler Harris." In *Dictionary of Literary Biography.* Vol. 11, Pt. 1. Ed. Stanley Trachtenberg. Detroit: Gale, 1982, pp. 189-201.

Brookes, Stella Brewer. *Joel Chandler Harris: Folklorist.* Athens, Ga.: University of Georgia Press, 1950. The trickster tale and other folk patterns in Remus tales analyzed.

Cousins, Paul M. *Joel Chandler Harris: A Biography.* Baton Rouge: Louisiana State University Press, 1968. Harris's youth, regional background, time learning printing business stressed, as is his positive philosophy. Occasionally overpraising of Harris.

English, Thomas, H., ed. *Mark Twain to Uncle Remus: 1881-1885.* Atlanta: Emory University Sources and Reprints, Series VII, No. 3, 1953. Text of five letters between the two, with critical comment.

Harris, Julia Collier, ed. *Joel Chandler Harris: Editor and Essayist. Miscellaneous Literary, Political, and Social Writings.* Chapel Hill, N.C.: University of North Carolina Press, 1931. Selections from journalism, editorials, 1870 to Harris's death.

Harris, Julia Collier. *The Life and Letters of Joel Chandler Harris.* Boston: Houghton Mifflin, 1918. Thorough, affectionate, if sentimental, account. Interesting personal asides.

Books, Chapters in Books

Bier, Jesse. *The Rise and Fall of American Humor.* New York: Holt, Rinehart, and Winston, 1968. Underscores success-at-any-cost basis of Brer Rabbit ethic, argues that Harris actually relished the chaos and ruthlessness of Brer Rabbit practices.

Blair, Walter. "The Local Colorists." In *Native American Humor.* New York: Chandler, 1960, pp. 143-146.

————, and Hamlin Hill. *America's Humor from Poor Richard to Doonesbury.* New York: Oxford University Press, 1978, pp. 341-342, 371-372.

Bone, Robert. *Down Home: A History of Afro-American Short Fiction from Its Beginnings to the End of the Harlem Renaissance.* New York: G.P. Putnam's Sons, 1975. Surveys literary depictions of the southern plantation. Though Harris is over-tolerant of abuses in slavery system, he helped in legitimizing of black materials in literature.

Buck, Paul H. *The Road to Reunion: 1865-1900.* Boston: Little, Brown, 1937. Long-term standard work on Reconstruction. Honors Harris's empathy with blacks, stresses how his writings in northern magazines helped foster reconciliation.

Budd, Louis J. "Joel Chandler Harris and the Genteeling of Native American Humor." In *Critical Essays on Joel Chandler Harris.* Ed. R. Bruce Bickley, Jr. Boston: G.K. Hall, 1981, pp. 196-209.

Hall, Wade. *The Smiling Phoenix.* Gainesville, Fla.: University of Florida Press, 1965. Considers Civil War in Harris's works, also politics of Reconstruction, feelings of blacks, poor whites.

Hubbell, Jay B. *The South in American Literature 1607-1900.* Durham, N.C.: Duke University Press, 1954. Harris most pleased when he left his reformer persona behind and focused on folk characters, old plantation.

McIlwaine, Shields. *The Southern Poor-White from Lubberland to Tobacco Road.* Norman: University of Oklahoma Press, 1939, pp. 110-124.

Martin, Jay. *Harvests of Change: American Literature 1865-1914.* Englewood Cliffs, N.J.: Prentice-Hall,

1967. Treats Harris's split personality, shyness, and stammering as reflections of his Old South versus New South interior debate, old-time humorist versus reformer journalist.

Skaggs, Merrill M. *The Folk of Southern Fiction.* Athens, Ga.: University of Georgia Press, 1972. Attitude of society to southern "poor white" explored. Feels Harris alone among local colorists was truly sensitive to this group.

Articles

English, Thomas H. "In Memory of Uncle Remus," *Southern Literary Messenger,* 2 (February 1940): 77-83. Stresses Harris's humanizing of blacks to a largely hostile white world in the postwar period.

Flusche, Michael. "Joel Chandler Harris and the Folklore of Slavery," *Journal of American Studies,* 9 (December 1975): 347-363. Black slave's worldview seen as a largely negative image of a place wherein he is unwelcome. Friendly contacts with whites very temporary and fleeting.

Rubin, Louis D., Jr. "Southern Local Color and the Black Man," *Southern Review,* N.S. 6 (October 1970): 1014-1015, 1016-1022. See Harris subscribing to southern racist values in exterior terms. As artist and a poor boy who had to make own way, however, Harris had much feeling for the underdog. Uncle Remus and Brer Rabbit are a unit, the sly creature representing a self of expert scheming to which Remus would never admit.

————. "Uncle Remus and the Ubiquitous Rabbit." *Southern Review,* N.S. 10 (October 1974): 784-804. Harris, the local colorist, was most sensitive to blacks' plight; he was also a writer most antagonistic to materialism of the New South.

Turner, Darwin T. "Daddy Joel Harris and His Old-Time Darkies." *Southern Literary Journal,* 1 (December 1968): 20-41. While Harris's black characters are differentiated in many significant ways, they are still primarily stereotypes.

Wolfe, Bernard. "Uncle Remus and the Malevolent Rabbit," *Commentary,* 8 (July 1949): 31-41. The savage feeling of blacks for whites was only barely concealed behind Uncle Remus' affectionate facade. Brer Rabbit's cruelty, when he gets a chance to hurt another, suggests the depth of spite involved. Harris empathized with blacks, yet never owned to the darker implications of Uncle Remus stories.

St. George Tucker Arnold, Jr.

Hart, Moss

Born: New York City, on October 24, 1904
Education: Formal education concluded after
   he reached the eighth grade
Marriage: Kitty Carlisle, August 10, 1946,
   two children
Died: December 20, 1961

Biography

One of the most influential figures on Broadway
from the 1930s through the 1950s, Moss Hart
was born in the Bronx on October 24, 1904, to
Barnett and Lillian Solomon Hart, Jewish immigrants from London who had come to America
around 1895. His father, a cigar maker, lost the
source of much of his livelihood when the auto-
matic rolling machine was introduced, and the
family, which included a tyrannical grandfather,
an eccentric and overly dramatic Aunt Kate, and
a younger brother, Bernard, was forced to take in
boarders to survive. In his autobiography, *Act
One*, Hart characterized his childhood poverty
as "a living and evil thing," and his career as
a successful playwright was marked by spurts
of ostentatious extravagance in reaction to the
bleakness of his childhood.

Although Hart showed a touching concern
throughout his life for the financial well-being
of his family, he did not feel close to either his
mother or his father. He was drawn, however, to
his Aunt Kate, who was to remind him later of
Blanche Dubois in Tennessee Williams's *A
Streetcar Named Desire*. When money became
so tight that it appeared that even Aunt Kate
would have to work, she, according to Hart,
"blackmailed" her relatives in England to send
her a small monthly allowance. It was partly
because of this allowance that she was able to
take Hart to either the Alhambra or the Bronx
Opera House to see one of their matinee performances every Thursday and Saturday afternoon,
thereby initiating him into a life-long fascination with the theater.

Family finances forced Hart to take a job the
summer he reached the eighth grade, and he
never was to return to public school, a fact that
he always resented. Hart was employed in several menial positions until one day, when he was
seventeen, he went to visit a friend, George
Steinberg, who was an office boy in the theatrical offices of Augustus Pitou, the "King of the
One Night Stands." When Hart discovered that
his friend had recently left the position, he got
the job himself and proceeded to make himself
indispensable. Pitou's chief writer for the six
theatrical companies that he sent out on the road
throughout the country was Anne Nichols, who
left the company when her *Abie's Irish Rose*
became a Broadway smash. Desperate for a re-

placement, Pitou turned to Hart for assistance.
Asked to read through a pile of unsolicited manuscripts, Hart submitted his own work to Pitou,
The Hold-Up Man or the Beloved Bandit, under
the pseudonym of Robert Arnold Conrad. The
deception did not bother Pitou, who was so delighted with the play that he decided to produce
it on Broadway. Despite Pitou's enthusiasm, the
play, which Hart characterized as "a composite
of all the plays Anne Nichols had written for
[the actor] Fiske O'Hara," failed miserably in
tryouts in Rochester and Chicago, lost Pitou
$45,000, and cost Hart his job.

Not wishing to leave the world of drama,
Hart began directing little theater companies
and worked during the summer as a social director for several resorts in the Catskills, where his
inventiveness, his ability to direct amateur theater groups, and his enthusiasm and affability
made him extremely successful. Still, Hart's
heart was with Broadway. For six years he wrote
serious plays in his spare time, only to see them
rejected one by one. Finally, under the prodding
of Richard J. Madden, an agent from the American Play Company, he turned to comedy and,
feeling comfortable only with the satiric style of
George S. Kaufman and Marc Connelly, wrote
Once in a Lifetime, a parody of Hollywood. He
submitted the play to producer Sam Harris and
his general manager, Max Siegel, who liked the
work and suggested that he collaborate with Irving Berlin. At the time Hart disdained musical
comedy and turned down the idea, although he
later was to team up with Berlin, Cole Porter,
Richard Rodgers and Lorenz Hart, and Kurt
Weill, among others. Siegel then suggested he
work with George S. Kaufman, an idea that
appealed to the young Hart and later to Kaufman himself.

After a number of major revisions and mixed
success on the road, the play opened trium-
phantly on Broadway at the Music Box Theatre
on September 24, 1930. Although Kaufman's
friends such as William Allen White and Otto
H. Kahn felt that the play was largely his, Kaufman insisted that Hart receive 60% of the royalties and on opening night announced to a
pleased audience that "80% of this play is Moss
Hart".

Although the pair was to collaborate eventually on seven more shows, they did not get together again until the 1934 production of
Merrily We Roll Along. In the interim, Hart,
showing indefatigable energy, joined Irving Berlin to write the book for *Face the Music* (1932)
and *As Thousands Cheer* (1933). In 1934, he
wrote the light operetta *The Great Waltz*, which
was set to the music of the Strausses. In the same
year he went on a world cruise with Cole Porter
that resulted in the musical revue *Jubilee*. Dur-

ing this period, he also wrote scenarios for two movies, *Flesh* (MGM, 1932) and *The Masquerader* (United Artists, 1933).

Teaming up with Kaufman again, he co-authored *You Can't Take It with You* (1936), which earned the Pulitzer in 1937, *I'd Rather Be Right* (1937), *The Fabulous Invalid* (1938), *The American Way* (1939), *The Man Who Came to Dinner* (1939), and *George Washington Slept Here* (1940).

Hart suffered from periodic bouts of depression and came to rely more and more on the taciturn Kaufman as a surrogate father. He became increasingly convinced that he could not write plays without Kaufman. In 1941, on the advice of his psychiatrist, Dr. Gregory Zilboorg, Hart made a permanent professional break with his collaborator. His theatrical efforts without Kaufman, which included *Lady in the Dark* with Kurt Weill (1941), the blatantly propagandistic *Winged Victory* (1943), *Christopher Blake* (1946), and *The Climate of Eden* (1952), were only moderately successful. However, he became noted for his screenplays, among which were such hits as *Gentlemen's Agreement* (1947), *Hans Christian Anderson* (1952), and the Judy Garland version of *A Star Is Born* (1954). His autobiography, *Act One* (1959), became a best seller, selling over 740,000 copies, and he received the Antoinette Perry Memorial Award ("The Tony") for his direction of *My Fair Lady* in 1957. He served as president of the Authors' League (1955-1961) and the Dramatists' Guild (1947-1955), and took a leading position against the blacklisting of certain writers by Hollywood.

He married actress Kitty Carlisle in 1946 and had two children with her, Christopher and Cathy. He died from a heart attack on December 21, 1961, on his way to the dentist in the same year that his former partner, Kaufman, also died from a heart problem.

Literary Analysis

Moss Hart's first hit, *Once in a Lifetime* (1930), a collaborative effort with George S. Kaufman, very nearly did not make it to Broadway. Feeling that there were insoluble problems in the second and third acts, Kaufman walked away from the play after it flopped in Atlantic City. Some quick but extensive revisions by Hart renewed his interest, but the third act was still characterized by producer Sam Harris as being "too noisy." Hart, accordingly, quieted down the play at the last minute by eliminating a scene costing $20,000 in props that took place in the interior of a Hollywood night club called the Pigeon's Egg, where the patrons sat at tables encased in large cracked eggs and the waitresses were attired in feathers. The description of the resulting success of the play when it finally opened at the Music Box

Theatre in September served as the climax of Hart's autobiography, *Act One*. *Once in a Lifetime* ran for 401 performances, won the Cooper McGrue Prize, and was made into a movie by Universal Studios in 1932.

Hollywood's interest in *Once in a Lifetime* was, perhaps, surprising since the play was conceived as a satire on the garish opulence, lack of creative talent, and the generally fickle and arbitrary nature of the movie industry. However, the humor, while heavy handed, is gentle enough not to offend. The play centers on the three members of an out-of-work vaudevillian team, George Lewis, Jerry Hyland, and May Daniels, who, with the advent of the "talkies," decide to go to Hollywood to set up an elocution school for established actors in the silent pictures who have not had to use their voices hitherto. The trio is aided in their scheme by the unwitting Helen Hobart, an obnoxious gossip columnist presumably modelled after Louella Parsons. Their plan fails miserably, but George, a likeable dim-wit, somehow manages to get himself into the good graces of Herman Glogauer, a movie industry mogul, and produces a picture for him. Despite the fact that George inadvertently uses the wrong script, casts the untalented Susan Walker as the female lead, forgets to turn on the lights during the filming, and ruins the movie's sound track by cracking and eating nuts while it is being recorded, the picture receives rave reviews from the critics. George's other blunders, such as buying 2,000 aeroplanes from a clever salesman, also turn out well, and at the end of the play, he orders the dismantling of the entire studio, much to the approval of the astonished Glogauer, who feels that somehow all will turn out well.

Sam Harris's comment that the work was "noisy" was an appropriate observation, even after the play's revision. It hinges less on plot than on a rapid series of satirical encounters with Hollywood types, including Lawrence Vail, a Broadway dramatist brought to California to write for the movies and subsequently forgotten about even though he draws a weekly check. The part of Vail was originally played on Broadway by Kaufman in his first acting role. The three vaudevillians are really not developed as characters although May has traces of the slightly acerbic wit and commonsense approach to life that in general characterize Kaufman and Hart heroines. She is in love with Jerry, and as is also typical of their heroines, she, the woman, is the strong one in the relationship. The critic Brooks Atkinson, among others, dismissed Kaufman and Hart's love scenes as "nothing more than dutiful gestures to the conventions of the stage," but the pair's reliance on witty one-liners, bizarre situations, eccentric personalities, and fast-paced movement generally precluded the portrayal of any deep relationships.

The next Kaufman and Hart production, *Merrily We Roll Along*, was, despite its title, not a comedy but an intense look at a talented playwright, Richard Niles, who abandoned his career as a serious dramatist to write trivial and careless, albeit highly successful, comedies. The action begins in the present and moves back in time through nine successive scenes to 1916. The play was successful financially, running for 155 performances (at a time when a run of 100 or more performances was characterized as "long") and costing only $60,000 to produce. Ultimately, however, audiences had difficulty in accepting the premise that writing comedies that make a lot of money is inherently bad, particularly since the play's authors were famous for their comedic wit. As playwright Herman Mankiewicz commented about Niles in an oft-quoted remark: "Here's this playwright who writes a play and it's a big success. Then he writes another play and it's a big hit, too. All his plays are big successes. All the actresses in them are in love with him, and he has a yacht and a beautiful home in the country. He has a beautiful wife and two beautiful children, and he makes a million dollars. Now the problem the play propounds is this: How did the poor son of a bitch ever get into this jam?" Two of the characters in the play, Sam Frankel, a brash composer, and Julia Glenn, a sharp-tongued alcoholic writer, were presumed by audiences to be modelled after George Gershwin and Dorothy Parker.

The early 1930s saw Hart as independent of his mentor, Kaufman, as he would ever get until the pair broke up in 1940. He teamed with Berlin in 1932 and 1933, wrote an operetta, *The Great Waltz*, and collaborated with Porter to write *Jubilee*, a light-hearted depiction of a British royal family who decides to escape from the austere life of the aristocracy and mix it up briefly with the common folk.

When Hart united with Kaufman again in 1936, it was for their most successful Broadway venture, *You Can't Take It with You*, which opened December 14 at the Booth Theatre and ran for 837 performances. The movie version, which had its debut on September 6, 1938, won Academy Awards for Best Picture and Best Director (Frank Capra). Both Kaufman and Hart had originally wanted to do a play based on Dalton Trumbo's novel *Washington Jitters in Hollywood*, but they abandoned that idea in favor of a situation about a wild and funny household in which everyone could do what he or she wanted. The original draft took but five weeks to write and revisions only another two for the ordinarily careful and meticulous pair, whose main problem this time was not in the play's composition but in selecting its title. At various times it was called *Money in the Bank*, *Foxy Grandpa*, *The King Is Naked*, and *Grandpa's Other Snake* before they made their final choice.

The central character in the play is seventy-five-year-old Martin Vanderhof who thirty-five years before started up to his office in the elevator, decided he wasn't happy, and came back down again. Since then he has spent his time collecting snakes and stamps, playing darts, dodging the I.R.S., and going to commencement exercises at nearby Columbia University. Others in the household include: his daughter, Penny, who has written a series of unproduced plays with such titles as *Sex Takes a Holiday* after a typewriter had been mistakenly delivered to their house eight years ago; Penny's husband, Paul, who plays with erector sets and makes fireworks with Mr. De Pinna, their former iceman, who quit his job to move in with the family; Penny and Paul's daughter, Essie, who sells homemade candies called "Love Dreams" and performs execrable ballets under the tutelage of a volatile Russian named Kolenkhov; and Essie's husband, Ed, who innocently prints up subversive Trotskyite slogans on his printing press and distributes them with his wife's candies.

The conflict in the play arises when Vanderhof's other granddaughter, Alice, who does not seem to be affected by the mild strain of insanity that runs in the family but who is devoted to them nevertheless, falls in love with Tony Kirby, her boss's son. Despite the fact that Tony wants to marry her, Alice has her doubts about continuing the relationship because of the disparate natures of their families; the Kirbys are Wall Street, formal, and upper class. Alice reluctantly agrees to give a dinner party to see if everyone can get along, but the Kirbys arrive on the wrong night to find Vanderhof playing darts, a drunken actress sleeping on the sofa, snakes crawling about in a terrarium, and Alice's mother painting a picture of Mr. De Pinna as a Roman discus thrower. During the course of the evening, the cook's boyfriend goes out for food and brings back pickled pigs' feet for dinner, Kolenkhov wrestles Mr. Kirby to the ground and breaks his glasses, Penny plays a word game in which Mrs. Kirby reveals her boredom with her sex life, and the entire dinner party is arrested for treason as the result of Ed's broadsides. Although the future looks bleak for the two lovers, Vanderhof convinces the elder Kirby at the play's climax that "you can't take it with you" and that the purpose in life is to enjoy yourself. Kirby, who once played the saxophone and wanted to become a trapeze artist, is won over, approves his son's marriage, and stays for a dinner of cheese blintzes served by the Grand Duchess Olga Katrina, who is now a waitress in Child's Restaurant at Columbus Circle.

Like most of Kaufman and Hart's comedies, *You Can't Take It with You* is essentially plotless; the humor derives from the eccentricities of its characters and the absurdity of its situations. The initial stiffness of Tony's parents serves as a foil for the uninhibited naturalness of the Vanderhof household, and their reserve finally softens when the central problem of the play, the proposed marriage between Alice and Tony, needs to be resolved. Alice, unlike other Kaufman and Hart heroines, does not have a sharp tongue, and her essential goodness along with Vanderhof's ultimate common sense, sets the play's tone. There really are no villains, only stuffed shirts and I.R.S. agents who can either be won over or ignored.

The play won the Pulitzer Prize for 1937, a fact that disturbed many critics who thought the prize should have gone to Maxwell Anderson for *High Tor* on the assumption that comedy is an inferior art form to serious drama. Inferior or not, the play sold to the movies for $200,000, which, at that time, was the highest price ever paid for a story property.

In 1937, Hart and Kaufman tossed around a variety of ideas including one for a revue entitled *The Curtain Going Up*, which fell through when Groucho Marx declined to serve as emcee. They worked instead on a musical, originally called *Hold Your Hats, Boys* but retitled *I'd Rather Be Right*, a shortened form of Henry Clay's famous aphorism. The musical was designed to be a hard-hitting spoof of the New Deal, but both Hart and Kaufman were apprehensive about portraying a living president, Franklin Roosevelt, on stage, although they felt that if they could coax George M. Cohan out of semi-retirement, the public would accept it. Cohan was delighted to work with the team, but he objected to the score by Richard Rodgers and Lorenz Hart, whom he sneeringly referred to as "Gilbert and Sullivan." Production almost came to a halt when Cohan left out some lines of a song about a political hero, Al Smith, and added a few of his own. With Hart and Kaufman spending much of their energies keeping the peace, the musical opened at the Alvin Theatre on April 2, and ran for 266 performances.

Hart and Kaufman departed from comedy for their next two plays, *The Fabulous Invalid* (1938), a tribute to Broadway, and *The American Way* (1939), a patriotic cavalcade that told the story of a German immigrant and his family, the character of the immigrant based in part on the first Kaufman to come to America.

On October 16, 1939, Hart and Kaufman's penultimate play as a team, *The Man Who Came to Dinner*, opened at the Music Box Theatre and ran for 739 performances, making it their second biggest hit. The central character of the play, Sheridan Whiteside, was modelled upon Alexander Woollcott, critic and professional curmudgeon. The idea for the comedy came after Hart had suffered through the experience of having Woollcott as a houseguest. Recalling to Kaufman what Woollcott had written in his guestbook upon leaving—"This is to certify that I had one of the most unpleasant times I ever spent"— Hart speculated on how awful it would have been if his guest had broken a leg and been forced to spend the summer with him.

That premise became the central idea of the new play. The portly Whiteside, critic, lecturer, wit, and radio orator, badgered into having dinner with the Stanleys, an upper-middle-class family of Mesalia, Ohio, slips and falls outside their home and fractures his hip. While recuperating, he sets up his office in the Stanley house, forbids the family to use the telephone or come in by the front door or even eat in their own dining room, and receives an odd assortment of well-known guests and their presents, including an octopus, an Egyptian mummy case, four penguins, and a cockroach farm (species *Periplaneta Americana*). His delightful friends include Banjo, an irrepressible comedian (modelled after Harpo Marx) and brother to Wacko and Sloppo; Beverly Carlton, a charming English playwright with more than a faint resemblance to Noel Coward; and Lorraine Sheldon, a beautiful but unscrupulous actress. Harpo Marx was later to play the part of Banjo in a road show, speaking lines for the first time in 25 years of show business.

The minimal plot begins when Maggie Cutler, long-suffering aide and secretary to Whiteside, falls in love with a local journalist, Bert Jefferson, and announces her desire to marry him. Whiteside, not wishing to be inconvenienced by having to break in a new secretary, brings in Lorraine Sheldon to vamp Maggie's boyfriend. Once Whiteside realizes, however, how much the relationship means to Maggie, he relents and with Banjo's help has Lorraine spirited off to Nova Scotia in the mummy case. Whiteside, then, does have a soft spot in his heart even though his constant badgering of his nurse, Miss Preen, causes her to quit her profession and seek work in a munitions factory for the express purpose of being able to exterminate as much of the human race as possible.

Like most successful Hart and Kaufman comedies, *The Man Who Came to Dinner* succeeds through witty dialogue, absurd situations, and unusual characters. The personality of Whiteside, played on Broadway by Monty Woolley, a bearded ex-Yale professor, makes the play.

In addition to Preen, his foils include Dr. Bradley, an incompetent doctor who mixes up his x-rays and who presents to Whiteside a thick manuscript entitled *Forty Years an Ohio Doctor: The Story of a Humble Practitioner*, and his hosts, the Stanleys. The Stanleys are long suffering, but Mr. Stanley is that most unpardonable sinner in the comic world, a stuffed shirt. His punishment is not Whiteside's threatened law suit, which we cannot quite believe will ever come off, but rather seeing his two children run off into the world under Whiteside's guidance to pursue their dreams and to have Whiteside trip outside his house once again after he has finally recuperated only to be brought back inside for another lengthy stay.

Maggie is a typical Hart and Kaufman heroine, capable of using the barb against those who really deserve it such as Lorraine Sheldon, but, in essence, homespun and traditional. She is the strong one in her relationship with Jefferson, and she knows that if he spends three weeks alone in a cabin with the actress working on his play, she will lose him. And, as is also typical with the playwrights' other works, love and sex do not quite mix. Maggie loves Jefferson and wants to settle down with him, but as far as sex is concerned, she seems above it all. Sex, if anything, for her is seen as a weakness and a source of amusement. The play contains a number of deliciously catty remarks about Lorraine's bedroom romps, and we learn that Banjo once placed a microphone under her mattress and played back his tape the next day for guests at lunch.

The team's next comedy, *George Washington Slept Here*, which opened at the Lyceum Theatre on October 18, 1940, to mixed reviews, was their last play together. Hart found himself becoming dangerously dependent on the shy and insecure Kaufman and wanted to break away and establish his own identity. The play itself may have disappointed audiences because it lacked the plethora of eccentrics and rapidly paced movement that they had come to expect from Hart and Kaufman, although it did run for 173 performances and was made into a movie starring Jack Benny and Ann Sheridan.

The plot revolves about Newton Fuller's purchase in Bucks County of an abandoned farmhouse that has seen better days (George Washington was rumored to have slept there) and his plans to move in with his reluctant wife, Annabelle, and his daughter, Madge. A large portion of the play deals with the misadventures of the family in trying to fix up the farm, many of which Hart himself experienced when he bought a farmhouse in the same area. The roof leaks, the windows are all broken, the hens won't lay, and all the wells come up dry. In addition, the Fullers are forced to take in Annabelle's horrible nephew, Raymond, while his parents are getting divorced, find that Madge is involved in an unfortunate love affair with a married actor, discover that it was Benedict Arnold and not George Washington who slept at the farm, run out of money, and are in danger of losing the farm that even Annabelle has finally come to love. All turns out well in the end as it invariably does in a Hart and Kaufman comedy. Unlike many of their hits, however, this particular comedy lacks a strong central character such as a Sheridan Whiteside around which the drama can revolve. Annabelle is described in the stage directions as "no fool," but she is not distinctive enough to carry the burden of the play. Sex once again is seen as a weakness: the servant has an ill-timed pregnancy; Annabelle's friend, the actress Rena Leslie, has all she can do to keep her wandering husband in line. Under the influence of alcohol, Annabelle and Newton do kiss and profess to enjoy it in what is probably the most passionate moment allowed to central characters in a Hart and Kaufman comedy.

Hart's plays sans Kaufman tended to be more serious in intent. They include *Lady in the Dark* (1941), which is about the editor of a smart woman's magazine who, like Hart, is plagued with self-doubt and seeks psychiatric help; *Winged Victory* (1943), a play dealing with new recruits in the air force and the training they undergo before they can participate in the war; and *Christopher Blake* (1946), a touching but somewhat obvious play about the trauma that a young boy faces in the courtroom when his parents are obtaining a divorce. Hart's one real solo comedy, *Light Up the Dark* (1948), is about an idealistic playwright who is about to produce his first play but who, like Hart with *Once in a Lifetime*, has difficulty with his second act. Hart's last play, *The Climate of Eden* (1952), was an adaptation of Edgar Mittelholzer's novel, *Shadows Move Among Them*, and concerns a young man, Gregory Hawkes, who seeks refuge with the family of a missionary in the jungles of British Guiana. There are some comic moments early in the play, but it takes a decidedly serious turn when we discover that the mentally ill Gregory had intended to kill his wife, who drowned by accident first. Gregory, however, is restored to mental health when he falls in love with the missionary's daughter, Mabel.

Although Hart abandoned the stage after the failure of *The Climate of Eden* (which ran only 20 performances), he continued to write and was responsible for a number of screenplays as well as one of the finest autobiographies, *Act One* (1959), of the twentieth-century theater. Hart did return to Broadway before he died in 1961, this time to direct *My Fair Lady*, a play that set a record run at that time of 2,717 performances.

Summary

Moss Hart was one of the most talented and versatile figures of contemporary theatre. He authored or co-authored serious plays, comedies, musicals, and screenplays. He produced, directed, and even occasionally acted. Today, however, his name is invariably linked with that of his friend and mentor, George S. Kaufman.

Selected Bibliography

Primary Sources

Hart, Moss, and George S. Kaufman. *Once in a Lifetime*. New York: Farrar and Rinehart, 1930.

Berlin, Irving, and Hart. *I Say It's Spinach. Sam Harris Presents "Face the Music," A Musical Comedy Revue*. New York: Irving Berlin, 1932.

Hart, Moss. *Love Will Find You (The Great Waltz)*. New York: T.B. Harris, 1934.

Kaufman, George S., and Hart. *Merrily We Roll Along*. New York: Random House, 1934.

————. *I'd Rather Be Right; A Musical Revue by George S. Kaufman and Moss Hart; Lyrics by Lorenz Hart*. New York: Random House, 1937.

Hart, Moss, and George S. Kaufman. *You Can't Take It with You*. New York: Farrar and Rinehart, 1937.

————. *The Fabulous Invalid*. New York: Random House, 1938.

Kaufman, George S., and Hart. *The American Way*. New York: Random House, 1939.

————. *The Man Who Came to Dinner*. New York: Random House, 1939.

Hart, Moss, and George S. Kaufman. *George Washington Slept Here*. New York: Random House, 1940.

Hart, Moss. *Lady in the Dark, a Musical Play by Moss Hart with Lyrics by Ira Gershwin and Music by Kurt Weill*. New York: Random House, 1941.

————. *Winged Victory*. New York: Random House, 1943.

————. *Christopher Blake*. New York: Random House, 1947.

————. *Light Up the Sky*. New York: Random House, 1949.

————. *The Climate of Eden*. New York: Random House, 1953.

————. *Act One, An Autobiography*. New York: Random House, 1959.

Secondary Sources

Books

Goldstein, Malcolm. *George S. Kaufman: His Life, His Theatre*. New York: Oxford, 1979. Comprehensive biography of Kaufman that includes some material on Hart throughout.

Kaufman, George S., and Moss Hart. *Six Plays by Kaufman and Hart*. New York: Random House, 1942. Contains an interesting evaluation by Brooks Atkinson of the pair's work along with appreciations by Hart and Kaufman of each other.

Meredith, Scott. *George S. Kaufman and His Friends*. Garden City, N.Y.: Doubleday, 1974. The best of the Kaufman studies in terms of his relationship with Hart. Provides some correctives to *Act One*.

Periodicals

Gardner, Mona. "Byron From Brooklyn." *The Saturday Evening Post*, November 18, 1944, pp. 9–11. Brief portrait of Hart with some biographical details.

Harriman, Margaret Case. "Hi-yo Platinum." *The New Yorker*, September 11, 1943, pp. 29–43. An entertaining close-up feature on Hart that covers many of the details included later in Hart's autobiography.

Kenneth Florey

Harte, [Francis] Bret[t]

Born: Albany, New York, on August 25, 1836
Education: Left school at age thirteen
Marriage: Anna Griswold, 1862, four children
Died: May 5, 1902

Biography

Francis Brett Harte, who used the name Bret Harte, was born in Albany, New York, on August 25, 1836, to Henry Harte and Elizabeth Rebecca Ostrander Harte. His heritage was one half English, one quarter Dutch, and one quarter Jewish. Harte's father was an educated, scholarly man who earned a living by teaching in private schools, lecturing and translating. In an effort to survive economically the family moved frequently. By the time he was nine years old Bret Harte had lived in at least six different cities in the North Atlantic states. In 1845, the elder Harte died, and Mrs. Harte moved herself and her four children to New York City, where they were supported by the mother's family and by the paternal grandfather, Bernard Harte.

During his childhood, Harte displayed his father's love for reading. He particularly enjoyed the novels of Charles Dickens, an important influence throughout his life. His main interest, however, was poetry. At the age of eleven he had his first publication, a poem in the *New York Sunday Morning Atlas*. He continued to think of himself primarily as a poet until he was about thirty years old. Harte's literary penchant suggests that he would have been a good student, but family circumstances did not permit him to continue his education. At the age of thirteen he left school; he was apparently self-supporting by the age of sixteen. (Information about his first few years of work is sketchy.)

When his mother remarried in 1857, she and her new husband moved to California. Harte followed on what was to be his pivotal journey. For the first few years he supported himself as he probably had in the East, through odd jobs, teaching, tutoring, and working in an apothecary shop. Legend has it that he tried mining, but this cannot be substantiated.

His real interest continued to be writing, which he worked at diligently. Some of his early pieces were published in San Francisco's newspaper, *Golden Era*, and in some less prestigious eastern magazines, but he did not receive wide recognition. In 1857, he got his first newspaper job on the *Northern Californian*. Here he was able to see accurate, realistic reporting and to get a feel for the sentiments that appealed to the populace. Undoubtedly, both of these factors shaped his writing.

In the 1860s Harte became a known literary figure. He was one of America's most prolific writers, and many of his best pieces were written during this decade. Among them are a collection of poems, *Outcroppings*, and *Condensed Novels and Other Papers*, both published in 1867. Many of the "novels" had been previously published. The 1860s also brought some stability to Harte's personal life. Despite his family's misgivings, he married Anna Griswold in 1862. By 1865, they had two children; eventually they had two more.

Harte's leap to fame occurred after he became the editor of another California paper, the *Overland Monthly*. In 1867, the newspaper printed Harte's finest short story, "The Luck of Roaring Camp," a humorous tale about a prospecting camp's adoption of an orphan baby. In addition to being a prime example of western humor, the story is thought to be one of the first in the local color genre because of the apparently realistic portrayal of the prospectors' characters and living conditions. For this reason it was extremely popular in the East, where people were curious about frontier life. The acclaimed story, "The Outcasts of Poker Flat," appeared in 1869. In 1870, a poem, "Plain Language from Truthful James," otherwise known as "The Heathen Chinee," was published. Harte himself thought little of this piece, but it became his best-known poem.

Harte's meteoric rise aggravated some problems. He developed an extravagant lifestyle and got heavily in debt, which undoubtedly contributed to his marital difficulties. Within a few years it seemed that California held no more opportunities for him, so in 1871 he left for New York. Harte had secured a contract with *Atlantic Monthly*; for $10,000 he was to write twelve short stories. He fulfilled this contract, but the quality of his work was disappointing. Although his reputation was declining, Harte wrote with his usual perseverance. Some of his more notable works from this period are

"Mrs. Skagg's Husbands" (1873), "Tales of the Argonauts" (1875), and an attempted novel, *Gabriel Conroy* (1876).

After his contract with *Atlantic Monthly* was completed, he began extensive lecture tours and founded *Capitol Magazine*. When this publication folded in 1877, Harte found himself in terrible financial straits with little to hold him in the United States. He accepted a consulate position in Prussia in 1878, leaving his family and America, never to return to either. In 1880, he moved to a consulate post in Glasgow, Scotland, where he remained until 1885. Afterward he lived in England, where he was still renowned and thus could support himself through lecturing. Though he wrote extensively, he produced nothing that added to his reputation. In fact, he became known as a hack in his later years.

In 1901, he was diagnosed as having an ulcerated sore throat, which proved to be cancer. On May 5, 1902, he died in Surrey, England.

Literary Analysis

Bret Harte's early prose influences were Washington Irving and, more importantly, Charles Dickens. Like Irving, Harte tried to imitate eighteenth- and nineteenth-century British styles. Many of his stories mix pathos, sentimentality, and social criticism, as Dickens's work does. Harte's unique contribution was to blend these traits with a realistic portrayal of California life. Because of this latter element, many scholars consider him the inventor of local color writing, writing which vividly portrays a particular region by depicting its dress, values, and dialect. In "Tennessee's Partner" (1869), for example, the partner's speech is distinctly regional: "I play this yer hand alone. To come down to the bed-rock, it's just this: Tennessee, thar, has played it pretty rough and expensive-like on a stranger, and on this yer camp" (*Best of Bret Harte*, p. 24).

Harte's authentic depiction of western life is one element of his humor. Often the comedy in his stories comes from the incongruity of situations and a detached narrator's description of regional life. The piece which launched Harte's success, "The Luck of Roaring Camp," is a prime example of local color writing. In this story a rugged prospecting camp adopts an orphan Indian baby. From the beginning the narrator takes a sardonic look at the prospectors' difficult lives. Readers are told that there was considerable excitement over the novelty of birth in this settlement; death, in contrast, was too common to raise an eyebrow. Similarly, the narrator first speculates on the cause of the excitement: "It could not have been a fight, for in 1850 that was not novel enough to call together an entire settlement."

The humor thus arises from the incongruity

of ruffian prospectors nurturing an infant. That they do so successfully is indicative of the optimism characteristic of Harte's work. Often he deals with roughs or outcasts who, in the course of the story, are transformed. "The Luck of Roaring Camp" depicts the positive changes baby Luck brings. The men give up swearing and eventually even agree to let some families live among them. The story does not have a happy ending; the camp is destroyed by flood, and baby Luck perishes. Yet the prospectors who perish are radically different from the coarse, self-serving men who lived before the baby's arrival. Similarly, in "The Outcasts of Poker Flat" a group of undesirables is expelled from the town. The alcoholic steals their mule, leaving them with limited provisions in the middle of winter to face certain death. In the face of adversity, the outcasts develop noble sentiments. Oakhurst the gambler and a prostitute fall in love. In the evening the group sits around a fire and has "square fun"—without whiskey or other unclean entertainment they laugh and sing "I'm proud to be in the service of the Lord." In these stories people behave as they ideally might. Humor and sentimentality blend in a manner particularly appealing to nineteenth-century popular audiences.

Modern critics, however, often charge Harte with a Dickens-like sentimentality. Often Harte's characters die performing noble deeds, as Kentuck in "The Luck of Roaring Camp" dies in an attempt to save the baby. Sometimes the hold of love or friendship is melodramatized. In "Tennessee's Partner" the partner's health declines rapidly after Tennessee is hung. Finally, the partner rides out at night to meet Tennessee, thus meeting death. It is not only these incidents that are sentimental in themselves but the language used to describe them. The end of "The Luck of Roaring Camp," for example, describes how Kentuck "drifted away into the shadowy river that flows forever into the unknown sea" (p. 16).

Despite their sentimental qualities, "The Luck of Roaring Camp" and "The Outcasts of Poker Flat" brought Harte recognition because they were tightly written, humorous, and filled with local color. Like other local color writers, Harte seemed to offer a slice of regional life without the seriousness or profound social criticism of writers such as William Dean Howells. In later years the verisimilitude of Harte's depiction of California life came into question, but during his lifetime, particularly in the East, he was credited with depicting frontier life accurately.

After his early stories enjoyed great popularity, Harte wisely put his poetry in second place. Although he wrote volumes of poems, there is nothing of exceptional merit. In verse Harte never found the distinctive voice that marked his early fiction. Much of his poetry merely imitates

Robert Browning, Henry Wadsworth Longfellow, and others. His best-known poem, "Plain Language from Truthful James," is a typical nineteenth-century rhyme. It plays to the era's bigotry, which is surprising, since Harte had a social conscience and expressed it in a number of ways. He took an active stand against slavery. In his writing he often poked at society's flaws. For example, in "The Outcasts of Poker Flat" the narrator explains that prostitutes were exiled because their crimes were visible: "it was only in such easily established standards of evil that Poker Flat ventured to sit in judgment" (p. 348).

In his poem about a Chinese gambler, however, Harte utilizes a number of negative racial stereotypes:

> That for ways that are dark
> And for tricks that are vain,
> The heathen Chinee is peculiar,—
> Which the same I am free to maintain.
> (*Plain Truth*, p. 434)

Harte's interest in verse is probably attributable to his fine ear for language and style. Perhaps this quality is best displayed in the *Condensed Novels* (1867), which were parodies of well-known works. For example, in "Stories Three," ostensibly by R-d-y--d K-pl--g, there is a sketch, "Jungle Folk," which includes the dialogue:

> "Why do you say 'ye?'" said the Gee Gees together.
>
> "Because it's more impressive than 'you.' Don't you know all the animals talk that way in English?" said the Moo Kow.
> (p. 185)

Despite Harte's talent with language, however, the potential of the boy poet was never realized. Likewise, Harte's later stories did not live up to the promise of his early ones. Often his later work was not tightly written and not developed thematically. While Harte continued to write pictures of western life that were a mixture of humor and sentimentality, he never did so as well as he had in the 1860s.

His early stories established him as a figure with a unique American voice. It was a voice that seemed certain to be imitated. By far the most important possible influence was upon Mark Twain. The two men met while Harte was working on the *Northern Californian*. Over the years they often worked closely together; Harte is credited with editing *Innocents Abroad*. Twain and Harte even collaborated on a play, *Ah Sin* (1877), which was poorly received. Differences over the play strained their friendship and eventually caused a total, bitter rift.

Critics disagree as to the extent of Harte's influence on Twain. Some maintain that there was virtually none, but in *Mark Twain and Bret*

Harte Margaret Duckett offers convincing evidence that Harte sparked Twain's imagination. Harte's interest in writing about the West possibly inspired *Roughing It*. Also, Harte was interested in writing for and about children; Twain may have acquired a similar interest from him. Finally, other critics have suggested that Harte's characters themselves might have inspired some of Twain's creations. Walter Blair, in his *Mark Twain and Huck Finn*, argues that Twain's Colonel Grangerford is a "blood relation" of Harte's Colonel Starbottle.

Perhaps the most important influence upon Twain and other humorists has been Harte's depiction of the outcast. Many of his humorous figures are people who have either been banished from society or cannot fit in. Huck Finn and to a lesser extent Tom Sawyer are such figures. Throughout the years many American comic figures, down to Woody Allen's star characters, have likewise been societal misfits.

Summary

Bret Harte (1836–1902) wrote his most important work in the 1860s when he lived in California and worked for the *Overland Monthly*. While Harte wrote volumes of poetry, two plays, and a novel, he is best known for his early short stories. These are characterized by a vivid depiction of California life, particularly through dialect, and a blend of humor and sentimentality. Harte is credited by some scholars with being one of the first local color writers and with making the outcast in an incongruous situation a comic figure. Without Harte, western humor as we know it would not exist.

Throughout his life Harte continued to write humorous local color stories. None of his later work, however, matches his early stories. So, although Harte wrote many volumes of work, there are only a handful of noteworthy stories, and his crucial contribution is not in the volume of his work, or even in the craft of his finest stories. Rather, it is in his original regional voice and his depiction of the outcast in incongruous circumstances.

Selected Bibliography

Primary Sources

Short Stories and Sketches
An Heiress of Red Dog and Other Tales. London: Chatto and Windus, 1879.
The Heritage of Dedlow Marsh and Other Tales. Leipzig: Tauchnitz Press, 1890.
Barker's Luck. London: Chatto and Windus, 1896.
Opening in the Old Trail. Boston and New York: Houghton-Mifflin, 1902.

Collections
The Best of Bret Harte. Sel. by Wilhemina Harper and Aimée M. Peters. Cambridge, Mass.: Houghton-Mifflin, 1903; rpt. 1947.

The Best of Bret Harte. Ed. and intro. by Robert N. Linscott. 1894. Rpt. New York: Modern Library, 1947.

Parodies
The Complete Edition of the Condensed Novels. London: Charles Routledge and Sons, 1873.

Poetry
The Poetical Works of Bret Harte. N.p.: James Osgood, 1871. Rpt. Boston and New York: Houghton-Mifflin, 1896.

Lectures
The Lectures of Bret Harte. Comp. by Charles Meeker Kozlan. Folcroft, Pa.: Folcroft Press, 1969.

Letters
The Letters of Bret Harte. Ed. Geoffrey Bret Harte. New York: Houghton-Mifflin, 1926.

Secondary Sources

Books
Blair, Walter. *Native American Humor: 1800–1900*. New York: American Book Company, 1937. Argues that Harte is more important historically than aesthetically.
Duckett, Margaret. *Mark Twain and Bret Harte*. Norman, Okla.: University of Oklahoma Press, 1964. A study of how the friendship developed, its progress, and lasting influence.
Hart, James. *The Popular Book: A History of America's Literary Taste*. New York: Oxford University Press, 1950. Discusses Harte's place in Western humor.
Morrow, Patrick D. *Bret Harte: Literary Critic*. Bowling Green State University: Popular Press, 1979. A study of Harte's criticism—reviews, essays and the *Condensed Novels*.
Rourke, Constance. *American Humor: A Study of the National Character*. Garden City: Doubleday, 1932. Argues that Harte was not a pioneer in regional humor.

Bibliography
Barnett, Linda Diz. *Bret Harte: A Reference Guide*. Boston: G.K. Hall, 1980. The most thorough, up-to-date bibliography of works by and about Harte.

Biography
Merwin, Henry Childs. *The Life of Bret Harte*. Boston and New York: Houghton-Mifflin, 1911. An account of Harte's life that focuses on the nature of California pioneer life.
Pemberton, Thomas Edgar. *The Life of Bret Harte*. 1903. Freeport, N.Y.: Books for Libraries, 1970. A thorough account of Harte's life and work.

Articles
Chesterton, G.K. "American Humor and Bret Harte." *Critic*, 41 (August 1902): 170–174. Argues that Harte's brand of humor is unique in America.
Clemens, Samuel. "The Contributor's Club." *Atlantic Monthly*, 45 (June 1877): 850–851. Praises the accuracy of Harte's California scenery but contends that Harte's rendering of dialect is inaccurate.
Howells, William Dean. "Recent Literature." *Atlantic Monthly*, 35 (February 1875): 234–236. A negative review of Harte's *Echoes of the Foothills*. States that the quality of Harte's work is declining.

Morrow, Patrick D. "Bret Harte, Popular Fiction and the Local Color Movement." *Western American Literature*, 8 (Fall 1973): 123–131. An assessment of Harte's place in this movement.

———. "The Predicament of Bret Harte." *American Literary Realism*, 5 (Summer 1972): 181–188. Overview of Harte's literary reputation and style.

Michelle M. Tokarczyk

Heller, Joseph

Born: Brooklyn, New York, on May 1, 1923

Education: Graduated from Abraham Lincoln High School, 1941; New York University, B.A., 1948; Columbia University, M.A., 1949.

Marriage: Shirley Held, September 3, 1945, divorced, 1986, two children; remarried 1987

Biography

The son of Isaac and Lena Heller, Joseph Heller was born in Brooklyn, New York, on May 1, 1923. After graduation from high school, he joined the Air Force in 1941, achieved the rank of first lieutenant, and flew sixty missions as a B-25 wing bombardier stationed in Corsica. Continuing his education after the war, and following his marriage to Shirley Held in 1945, Heller attended the University of Southern California for a year and then transferred to New York University, where he received his B.A. in 1948. After receiving an M.A. from Columbia University in 1949 and spending a year at Oxford University on a Fulbright Scholarship, he became an instructor in English at Pennsylvania State University. From 1952 to 1961 he worked successively as an advertising writer for *Time* (1952–1956) and *Look* magazines (1956–1958), and as a promotion manager for *McCall's*, a position that he left in 1961 to return to the academic world and become Professor of Fiction and Dramatic Writing at Yale University and the University of Pennsylvania, and then Distinguished Professor of English at City College in New York. Since 1975 he has been a full-time writer.

He worked on his first novel, *Catch-22*, from 1954 (publishing the first chapter in *New World Writing* in 1955) until its publication in 1961. Despite the fact that it has now sold over 10,000,000 copies, *Catch-22* achieved only modest initial success, selling 30,000 copies in the first year. Though the reviews were mixed and

Heller recalls worrying about a particularly unfavorable review written for the *New York Times*, the book eventually caught the particular mood of anti-war and anti-authority protest of the 1960s and early 1970s. Heller was to say that the war described there is a war like Vietnam. History had caught up with him, and in 1970 *Catch-22* was made into a film under the direction of Mike Nichols. In the thirteen years before the publication of his next novel, Heller wrote an anti-war play, *We Bombed in New Haven*, produced at the Yale Repertory Theatre in 1967 and for a brief run on Broadway in 1968, and two dramatizations based on *Catch-22*, *Catch-22: A Dramatization* (1971) and *Clevinger's Trial*, produced in London in 1974. The success of *Something Happened* (1974) gave him the financial security to devote all his time to writing. *Good as Gold* followed in 1979 and *God Knows* in 1984. After the breakup of his marriage of over forty years, Heller contracted Guillain-Barré syndrome, which paralyzed him for several months and affected his speech. He recovered sufficiently to walk unaided, drive a car, and swim, and returned to work. He has written a memoir of his illness, *No Laughing Matter*, a screenplay about a novelist who contracts Guillain-Barré, and is writing his next novel.

Literary Analysis

During his literary career, Joseph Heller has talked a number of times about being a humorist. Sometimes he rejects the term, much like any serious writer who does not want his meaning limited to a single aspect of his art. At other times he talks about using humor, making his readers of *Catch-22*, for example, laugh, and then be ashamed that they have laughed as they realize the sinister implications of what at first appeared only comic. For Heller, humor is never a remedy, a tonic, or escape; it is a means of seeing, of striking a nerve. In an interview printed in *U.S. News and World Report* he described his vision of what humor does achieve: "Humor doesn't represent a value in itself, but it helps in determining a set of values. . . . Humor can be very instrumental in helping to keep things in perspective."[1] Certainly the world of Heller's novels abounds in persons who take themselves deadly seriously and their environment literally. When King David in *God Knows* insists that Solomon really did want to cut the baby in two (in the Biblical account, Solomon determines the true mother as the one who begged the baby should be given to the other woman rather than be cut in half and shared), or when he asks that same Solomon be shown the door and his son responds that he's seen a door, these may seem only comic one-liners. However, they contrast the literal Solomon and his anguished, searching father and thus illustrate the distance from life and one's surroundings that leaves open the possibility of attaining humanly responsible stature. Whether it be the M.P.'s in *Catch-22* who ignore the murdered maid and her killer to arrest Yossarian for being in Rome without a military pass, the executive Horace White who has no values but company values in *Something Happened*, Ralph, the diplomat, who comes to believe his own Washington jargon in *Good as Gold*, or David's son, Solomon, the literalists in Heller's works never rise above the system because they can never distance themselves from it. By contrast, for Heller's characters who are striving to differentiate themselves from an all-encompassing system in which they are caught, humor becomes one lifeline for achieving distance. With the exception of *Something Happened*, where humor and distance fail the central character, Heller's novels not only make us laugh but demonstrate the absolute necessity of corrosive, defiant laughter in a contemporary culture that would otherwise absorb the individual into what is false, mechanical, and destructive. Ultimately, Heller's are moral novels, not despite the wisecracking and the humor, but in part because of them. What Heller said of *Catch-22*, that it deals with "the development, the birth of Yossarian's consciousness of himself as a moral being,"[2] can equally be applied to the central characters in *Good as Gold* and *God Knows* and to the extinguishing of such consciousness in *Something Happened*.

The absurdity of the system in Heller's first novel, *Catch-22*, is caught in Yossarian's response when told that Appleby has flies in his eyes and of course he can't see the flies because he's got flies in his eyes. "It made as much sense as anything else," Yossarian reflects, and this statement is in many ways the key to both the zany humor and final meaning of the work.[3] The world from which Yossarian, an Air Force bombardier in the Italian campaign, must escape is not the great crusade against Hitler's atrocities and Nazi tyranny. Rather, it is a situation in that war in which Yossarian's commander, Colonel Cathcart, keeps "fearlessly" raising the number of missions that his men must fly, not for any patriotic reason, but to advance his own career and, of course, the odds of his men being killed. It is, as Heller explained, really a novel about any organization that regards its personnel not as humans but as abstractions, seemingly helpless pawns in someone else's bid for power or glory. Colonel Cathcart, "a military tactician who calculated day and night in the service of himself," lives in "an unstable arithmetical world of black eyes and feathers in his cap" (p. 186) and regards his subordinates' lives and his superiors' actions only in those abstract terms. This reduc-

tion of the human to statistic is dramatized in a number of wildly and often blackly comic ways. The dead man in Yossarian's tent is not dead because he never officially reported for duty, but Doc Daneeka, though everyone sees him walking around, is dead because he was listed on a plane that was shot down. When parents come to visit a dying son, Yossarian is substituted for him: "One dying boy is as good as another" (p. 181). Form letters are sent to bereaved loved ones, and General Peckham orders an attack on a defenseless village to demonstrate bombing patterns and get good pictures. Moreover, a series of inane regulations protects the power of those on top and debases all meaningful language. Major Major is never in to see anyone unless he is out; the only persons allowed to ask questions at briefings are those who never do; no one has to sign Captain Black's loyalty oath, but those who do not will be refused food. The catch-all regulation is Catch-22, "which specified that a concern for one's own safety in the face of dangers that were real and immediate was the process of a rational mind" (p. 46). Anyone who goes insane in the face of the rising bombing missions has only to ask and he can be grounded; however, as soon as he makes such a request, his desire to avoid imminent death demonstrates his sanity, and he now must fly as many missions as ordered. Later Yossarian discovers that Catch-22 really means "they have a right to do anything we can't stop them from doing" (p. 398). In such a situation, then, the enemy is both sides, "anyone who is going to get you killed" (p. 122). Some of Yossarian's comrades, like Clevinger, accept the circumstances out of a sense of duty; others, like Aarfy, accept because of stupidity; most accept because they do not know what to do. Yossarian, however, decides to live forever or die in the attempt. His bleak humor becomes a litmus test of truth. To Clevinger, who doesn't want to admit that although he was recently a schoolboy, now he is an old man, he explains that anyone inches away from death every time he flies a mission is indeed an old man. When supposedly reassured that there is nothing personal in the German attempt to kill him, for they are trying to kill everyone, he inquires what difference that makes. When asked if his superiors will send a crazy man to be killed, his response inquiring who else would strikes at the lie that is Catch-22. Sanity equals distance from the system, and Yossarian's humor is one means of achieving this.

The implications of such an organization are broadened with the introduction of Milo Minderbinder, who moves from being in charge of a mess hall in Yossarian's unit to heading M and M Enterprises, a giant syndicate with its own air force and personnel. He makes money by buying commodities, controlling the market, and reselling them to himself, while appearing to take a loss. He understands that if he can give virtually everyone a share of the profits, he will be invaluable and builds his syndicate on that principle—to harm him would be to act against self-interest. He contracts with the Germans to bomb his own airfield, defends strafing because it's in the contract, siphons pilots and planes from all countries on both sides (except Russia, for that would be un-American), bribes the American government to buy the unmarketable Egyptian cotton he foolishly invested in, and has German planes working for him landing at Allied air fields, all with impunity. In Milo, Heller satirizes those who make a profit out of war and reminds us how such profit-taking demonstrates the greed that can transcend national boundaries. Moreover, all of Milo's acts are comically exaggerated reflections of the central situation in the book. His claim that what is good for M & M Enterprises is good for the country suggests that Cathcart's unspoken assumption that what is good for him is good for his men; his bombing of his own men is reduction to abstraction run wild, and his use of the jargon of free enterprise is much the same kind of cloak as his superiors use. Given the reduction of the human person to an abstraction, Milo's acts are, indeed, as reasonable as anything else in Yossarian's world.

As Milo's argosies of plenty fill the air, the number of missions rises in proportion to the Colonel's desire to get his picture in a national magazine before Christmas, and his fellow crewmen are killed, Yossarian stages a number of acts calculated to keep him from having to fly more missions. In an insane system only individual acts of counter-insanity can be meaningful. Yossarian spends as much time as possible in the hospital with difficult-to-diagnose complaints, moves the bomb-line, causes an epidemic of diarrhea with soap in the mess food, accepts the Distinguished Flying Cross while nude, walks backward, naked and carrying a gun, and finally goes AWOL to Rome. Though Yossarian has to this point been absorbed in his own self-survival, in his nighttime journey through the eternal city he comes to understand the universality of oppression and feels guilt for not assisting other seemingly helpless victims like himself. He sees a man brutally beating a dog, another knocking a boy down again and again in the midst of an immobile crowd. Worried about attracting the attention of the military police, he refuses to help a woman being attacked and arrives at the officers' apartment to discover that his fellow officer, Aarfy, has raped and killed the ugly, innocent maid who cleaned there and thrown her body out the window. M.P.s arrive,

apologize for bothering Aarfy, and arrest Yossarian for having no pass. Punishing Yossarian, however, might reflect badly on the records of Colonel Cathcart and his subordinate, Colonel Korn, since they had promoted him and given him a medal for flying twice over a target. Instead, they offer him a deal. Since his acts at the base are encouraging rebellion in others, they will send him home—provided he will say good things about them and encourage other boys to enlist. At first Yossarian accepts, but the guilt he feels for not helping the woman in Rome leads to the birth of his moral character, his concern for others. He also understands now the lesson of the death of Snowdon, whose insides had spilled out over the plane when Yossarian had tried to assist the wounded rear-gunner: "Man was matter, that was Snowden's secret. Drop him out a window and he'll fall. Set fire to him and he'll burn. Bury him and he'll rot like other kinds of garbage. The spirit gone, man is garbage" (pp. 429-430). Still, there is a way other than joining forces with the oppressors and thus becoming one himself; there is the example of Orr who had miraculously rowed to Sweden. Though Yossarian had considered Orr a simpleminded gnome who kept ditching his plane, he now understands that everything Orr did was practice for his escape. He determines to follow, and his single act, as Orr's, has a ripple effect. Major Danby defies the system in aiding Yossarian's escape and the well-intentioned but previously ineffective chaplain becomes stronger in his determination to do something about the endless missions. It is an insane journey, almost a geographical impossibility for Yossarian to try to reach Sweden from his base, but to them Yossarian's "insanity" makes more sense than anything else.

Because *Catch-22* is not written in a straightforward style, the reader struggles with Yossarian to discover the possibility of a meaningful act. Like Yossarian we laugh sometimes, only to be horrified a page or two later at our response. Heller's comedy never leaves us comfortable. At first we may be amazed by the machinations of Minderbinder only to be horrified when the logic of his actions leads to the killing of his own men. That is what Heller's humor does: through overt exaggeration it forces us to see and examine the tenets of so much that is impersonal and mechanistic in our world of using rather than respecting others. Heller explains that his "idea was to make ridiculous the things that are irrational and very terrible."[4]

Both the humor and tone of *Something Happened* are much darker than in any of Heller's other books. Instead of the final assertion of a saving characteristic within the hero, as is the case in those other novels, *Something Happened* chronicles the ultimate destruction of such remaining principle. While the other novels show the birth of moral character through a concern for others that emerges from a chaos of self-interest, *Something Happened* concludes with the death of such a principle. It is, therefore, more akin to tragedy than to comedy, and the bleak humor of its major character, Bob Slocum, is much closer to self-pity than to the distance gained through the perspective that humor grants. Though the novel certainly stands on its . own and may indeed be Heller's finest work, its demonstration of the obverse pattern also clarifies both the meaning and the nature of humor in his other works.

The saving grace of Slocum at the beginning of *Something Happened* is that he still maintains the distance to see his situation and occasionally feel love and dignity, even if he knows them only as loss, something that had been before something happened. The dehumanization of his immediate and cultural surroundings and his own failure of nerve lead to his absorption into those surroundings. Slocum is a highly paid executive in a successful company, owns a large, sumptuous home, and has a beautiful wife and three children. He ought to be happy; he would be if he couldn't see or feel, if he were as inhuman as the company that employs him. That corporation is a world of abstraction moving of its own momentum; its sane employees all have abstract names like Brown, Green, Black. What would happen, Slocum asks, if I disobeyed and defied the company? A key punch would be touched behind the closed door of a distant office and his "act of rebellion would be absorbed like rain on an ocean and leave no trace."[5] Similarly, his work is of no interest in itself and its only challenge is "whether it's more boring to do something boring than to pass along everything boring that comes in to somebody else and then have nothing to do at all" (p. 33). The result of reducing people to interchangeable parts is a feeling of inconsequence, fear and, above all, sameness. Slocum's only ambitions are to give the three-minute speech denied him last year at the company's annual convention by his boss, who has the whammy on him, and later to have the job of lame and imperfect Andy Kagle. He knows the company has little pity for failure and no affection and recognizes something cankered inside himself "that wishes to burst out and demolish [Kagle], lame and imperfect as he is" (p. 50). Beyond that Slocum only wants to be safe, protected from the conflict, danger, suffering, and ultimate death that make up human life. He avoids all crippled, deformed, and ill people, refuses to read obituaries or visit sick friends; he fears all closed doors, anything unknown.

These attitudes carry over into the descriptions of family life that constitute the largest portion of the novel. Derek, the mentally retarded son, is, like the insane Martha in the office, the only one who is happy. At home, as at the office, Slocum hides his feelings, slides by problems rather than meeting them, and wonders why his wife is "so afraid of me when I am so afraid of her" (pp. 99-100). Here, too, he feels he can affect or change nothing. His unhappy teen-age daughter, who like Kagle has a poor self-image, will have the statistical number of affairs, abortions, children, and husbands. At first he is proud that his younger son can love things for their own sake, enjoy running rather than just winning and even pass the basketball to a poor, left-out boy on the other team. But Coach Forgione convinces Slocum that his boy needs to acquire a competitive spirit, to be, not good necessarily, but "better than the next fellow" (p. 240). Under Slocum's prodding, the boy who could be "laughing and kidding jauntily all the time if there were not so many of us . . . to inhibit and subjugate him" (p. 340), learns like his father to be "good enough" in tasks that he does not love. The retarded son is potentially an embarrassment and a stumbling block in the path of Slocum's career. As with finished office business, he dreams of sending Derek away so he can "erase him, cross him out, file him away" (p. 118). He likewise fantasizes about divorcing his wife who is unhappy and drinking too much.

Slocum at moments feels pity for his daughter, consternation over Derek, affection for his wife, and great, overwhelming love for his son. For Heller the past is something that we carry inside of us and see reflected in our own relations. Thus, Derek is Slocum's own pre-social being, his boy the little boy inside his social armor, his daughter the irreverent rebel, and his wife the *anima* he struggles to thwart: "I have my wife, my daughter, and my son for reference: I am all their ages. They are me" (p. 399). But such feelings for those beings outside and inside himself make him vulnerable, both at the office where all weakness is frowned upon and nobody "with a limp or a retarded child is ever going to be president" (p. 419), and within himself, since to love is to keep himself open to the possibility of loss. His son understands this relationship and frequently asks if Slocum wants to get rid of him as well as Derek. In an automobile accident in which the boy receives only superficial if bloody wounds, Slocum holds him so tight that he smothers him. The little boy outside and inside Slocum is now dead—killed by his fears—and in the concluding chapter of the novel the perfectly hollow, adaptable man now does everything required of him in his new job at the office.

Something Happened is a blistering satire of our adaptive society and the upwardly mobile persons who fill it, written in the tradition of Mark Twain's "The Man That Corrupted Hadleyburg." In our mercenary social world it is precisely our goodness that stands in our way. To succeed we must destroy not only our presocial being where our dreams and our myths lie but the generous, open child who also resides there, as well as the impish self and shadow side of our nature. "I know at last what I want to be when I grow up," Slocum muses. "I want to be a little boy" (p. 338). By the end of the novel, he has lost all distance from his surroundings and he never will be that little boy.

Good as Gold is Heller's novel about assimilation and independence. Though it deals with the price of Jewish assimilation into the American mainstream—more specifically, the American government—it is also more universal than that, for it traces again the birth of moral character and the distance required to achieve it. Bruce Gold has written a favorable review of the President's book about his first year in office and a government position is dangled in front of him: Secretary of State is not out of the question. Gold has sufficient role models for sellout, chief among them Maxwell "Skip" Lieberman, who edits a neo-conservative journal that wants viewpoints, not facts, Harris Rosenblatt, who "used to be Jewish,"[6] and Henry Kissinger, the former Secretary of State, about whom Gold obsessively collects clippings that he hopes to use in a book proving Kissinger is not Jewish. At first it would seem that there is little in Gold's character to keep him from selling out. Much like Slocum, he says of himself: "I don't love Belle. Family life is a bore. So is writing and teaching.—I don't feel close to anyone in the world. Everything I do is boring. I want to marry money" (p. 137). Unlike *Something Happened*, however, this is a political novel. Gold's stasis reflects ironic disenchantment with liberalism as well as a self-criticism that keeps him at a distance from his own rhetoric. Reflecting, for example, that the receding of imperialism had produced not peace and riches for the former colonies but oppression, conflicts, and warfare, he goes on to identify his own self-interest in fearing "a truculent majority in the United Nations that was now not only anti-American, but anti-Americans like Gold" (p. 60). A longer life span, the major achievement of medical science, has produced the unwanted aged—like his own difficult father. Gold "knew in his heart that he much preferred it the old way, when he was safer. Things were much better for him when they had been much worse" (p. 61). In this mood he pens an essay entitled "Nothing Succeeds as Planned," which is regarded in the highest government circles not as an honest preference for self-interest but as the perfect rationale for doing nothing. Translated by government functionaries like Ralph, Gold's personal analysis becomes the single lesson to be learned from history. If nothing is good for the world and the only predictable outcome of good intentions is failure, then take whatever you can when the chance comes to get it. This becomes the only logic behind the government that Heller portrays with broadly satiric strokes. In it, offices are bargaining pawns and the President's major interest is in the price his yearly memoirs will bring; the essence of Gold's committee work for the Commission on Education is to understand that no one wants to read the report. The only difference between Gold and those he encounters in Washington is that while he admits to selfishness, they cloak theirs in the language of self-righteous virtue encased in doublespeak. Language protects rather than reveals. Ralph, for example, has governmental responsibility for covering everything in his area. When Gold asks what his area is, Ralph replies, " 'Just about everything I cover, Bruce' " (p. 189), and is glad that he has helped Bruce understand. To enter this world is to accept its abstractions and the uncritical assurance of their correctness. Ralph advises Bruce to divorce Belle and take a taller wife, which will give him more stature. Andrea Conover will do. In a brilliant surrealistic dream Gold hears voices telling him that he is not Bruce Gold and his family is not his family; instead he is an object: Van Cleef and Arpels, a Fifth Avenue jewelry store. Having undergone such a metamorphosis, his voices tell him, he is not "even a Jew" (p. 231). The irony, however, is that despite his fantasy that through a new blonde wife and a government position he might escape his roots, he is never in this world of abstraction anything but "the Jew." On the Commission of Education which has representatives from all sections, he is the Jew, and the Governor who chairs the committee promises his help if Gold will write the report without saying anything anyone can take exception to, for "a Jew always needs friends in Washington, because he doesn't really belong here" (p. 177). Andrea's father, Hugh Biddle Conover, taunts Gold with his Jewishness and will consent to the marriage only if it means that he will never have to have anything to do with Gold.

While he is attempting to gain office, divorce Belle, and marry Andrea, Gold is researching his book on the Jewish experience, even though he's not sure that he ever had one. He is also attending the ritualistic, drawn-out family gatherings at which he is always put down. "Nobody who knows me treats me with respect" he muses ruefully (p. 196), and this is certainly true of his family, which, along with his self-criticism, keeps him from wholly believing in his Washington *persona*. No one in the family ever reads what he writes, though they will brag to others about his accomplishments. His father, who dislikes him, refuses to move to a warmer Florida climate; his slightly insane stepmother delights in counting still another screw loose in anything that Gold says. Sisters treat him as if he is a wayward child; his older brother Sid twists all of his words. Yet, there is also much life—real, not abstract—in this family. Real life has warts: disobliging fathers, sibling rivalries, forever unresolved conflict, pain, loss and self-recriminations.

Maybe real life is known finally through its pain and is, like Gussie Gold and the family gatherings themselves, slightly mad. And, despite himself, Gold finds his roots in "the webwork of his origins" (p. 146). In the most memorable scene in the book, Gold goes back over what he sees as the sacrifices Sid made, trying to see if the older brother resents the opportunities opened to him through college. To question after question Sid responds simply that he never thought of it that way. This was just Sid's life, his family. It is this real life that Gold ultimately chooses. Finally, he is "Good as Gold," not in the abstract sense of the riches, the jewelry store that he had dreamed himself being, but in terms of family and origins. Having wheedled an invitation to the Embassy Ball at which he may finally meet the President and secure a government position, Gold is informed of Sid's death and leaves immediately to attend the funeral and sit *shivah*. In so doing Gold puts concern for something outside the self ahead of self-interest and moves from "I want" to "They need." Insight, humor, and family had always helped him identify the fraudulent even as he desired it. Despite Ralph's pleadings, he won't return to Washington; he really wouldn't fit there once his moral character, however tenuous, has been born.

Good as Gold combines a variety of styles and subject matter: the family scenes are realistic; the Washington ones are broadly satiric and wildly exaggerated. Interlocked with both are the attacks on Kissinger and other contemporary figures. Jack Beatty in *The New Republic* called the novel a cultural event: "A major novelist has taken on our greatest celebrity with all the power of wit and language at his command, and perhaps not since Tolstoy eviscerated Napoleon . . . has a central historical figure been so intimately castigated by the Word."[7] Morris Dickstein, and many other critics, found *Good as Gold* "not one but several novels jostling each other, without the unifying stylistic and narrative rhythm of *Catch-22* and *Something Happened*."[8] It can be argued, however, that the parts do coalesce and that some of the jarring is

intentional. Gold is fascinated with Kissinger because there is much in him akin to the book's acid portrait of the man whom he consciously despises. The events in Washington seem wildly exaggerated until we turn the page and read one of Gold's clippings from the *New York Times* which surely must be the broadest satire were it not reporting facts. The strife of the family scenes represents complexity and life, that of the Washington scene over-simplification, jargon, abstraction and brute uses of power. The shifting keeps us aware and makes us, like Bruce Gold, ultimately assert a preference. Most importantly, *Good as Gold* demonstrates how difficult it is to maintain this distance. In a society in which the fraudulent is surrounded by promises of glamour, celebrity, open sexuality, and power, even self-knowledge and awareness of what is fake does little to diminish its appeal. *Good as Gold* may not always work, but it is a daring and significant novel.

The situation of *God Knows* is taken from The First Book of the Kings: "Now King David was old and stricken in years, and they covered him with clothes, but he got no heat." David is dying, looking back over his life and receiving what warmth he can from the beautiful young Shunamite virgin, Abishag, who washes, perfumes herself, and lies naked upon him. But Heller's is no purely Biblical David who accepts the role, rewards, and punishments ordained him by his God. He is also an alternately wisecracking, defensive, accusing, bragging, angstridden modern man, whose mind moves freely through history and distances him from that assigned role. The decision that he must make before he dies is whether to bestow his kingdom upon Solomon, whom Heller portrays as an idiotic literalist, or Adonijah, a pompous narcissist. God is no help, for He has been silent since He killed the first son that David sired by Bathsheba. David wants an apology from God; he also wants a book of the Bible named after him and the credit for all those lines that William Shakespeare, John Milton, William Wordsworth, and others stole from him, as well as for inventing romantic love. He has the beautiful Abishag, but he doesn't want her; he wants to make love one last time to Bathsheba, but she's in the queen-mother business now, pushing the claim of their second son, Solomon. "I hate God and I hate life," David says within the first few pages of the novel, "And the closer I come to death, the more I hate life."[9]

In *God Knows* Heller is describing again the moral growth of an individual in terms of a shift from obsessive self-concern and the consequent despair that comes with the discovery that life may be a grim joke. Concern about others becomes the basis for action; in David's case the decision is to make Solomon king. Beyond that there is also too much instinctive life in David for him to accept the absolute negativism of the opening of the book; this is what the reader and David discover about him as he continues his reminiscing. The humor in the book, David's humor, is one of the unmistakable signs of that life. Undoubtedly that is the reason why, without his rationally understanding it, David so admires Abraham and Sarah. When they heard from God that Sarah in her advanced age was to bear a son, they laughed: "Abraham and Sarah are the only ones I know of who ever got a laugh out of a conversation with God" (p. 50). They named their baby Isaac, which means "he laughs."

David is all too aware of these incongruities—sometimes, as in the case of Abraham and Sarah, benign, and other times from a human perspective, perverse—of the fate of the people chosen by God. To these Heller adds the humor of the mixture of Biblical and modern language and attitudes. "Some Promised Land . . . To people in California, God gives a magnificent coastline, a movie industry, and Beverly Hills. To us He gives sand. To Cannes He gives a plush film festival. We get the P.L.O." (p. 40). Since David has the perspective of all of history, in his energetic roving over his life he can let us in on many secrets. Bathsheba was the first woman to wear false eyelashes and fingernails; she invented the caftan and mini-skirt as well as underwear. We read so much of myrrh, incense, and perfumery in the Bible because the sewage system was terrible. Men like Joseph, Moses, Abraham, Samuel and David himself stand out in the Bible because they have solid English names rather than ones like Jehoshaphat or Hadadezer.

David's lusty humor, his sense of the incongruity in the world, exists along with a sense of a similar incongruity within himself. The heart he knows is deceitful in all things. Clearly David's humor and self-knowledge are cut from the same cloth. Life's contradictions are not separate from him; they are of him as well.

David took Saul as his father and would have loved him. But Saul had been told by the prophet Samuel that God has taken the kingdom from him and given it to another. His jealous suspicions that the hand of God is now upon David are aroused, first, by the knowledge that Samuel had journeyed at the Lord's command to the house of David's father and, second, by David's triumphs over Goliath and other Philistines. Saul's dealings with David are much like God's. They seem an erratic mixture of kindness and cruelty. Yet again and again, at risk to himself, David returns to this father and twice, to the dismay of his general, Joab, refuses to take Saul's life when he comes upon him sleeping and unguarded. "How I loved that man Saul. How I looked up to him even when he drove me away and hunted me; . . . My dreams of Saul are of longing, remorse, and reconciliation" (p. 117).

David's other two recurring memories are of the unnamed son who died in infancy and of his son Absalom who revolted and was killed despite the fact that he urged like a fool that no one harm him. "No, not like a fool, but like a fond doting father who will overlook and excuse everything in the child he loves best and who breaks his heart. And in that singular disparity in our desires abides his lasting victory over me: I loved him and he did not love me" (pp. 97-98).

So, despite his initial statement that he cares for nothing and no one, deep beneath the wisecracking surface which is indeed a way of reconciling himself to himself, the world and God, Heller's David emerges as a man who knows pain, remorse, despair—yes, and life, joy and laughter because his capacity for love is as ravenous as all his other appetites. So it is quite simply that he gives the kingdom to Solomon: "I did it in pique and I did it for love. I decided for Bathsheba because once, for a few years of my life, she had made me happy . . ." (p. 345). And more unselfishly: "I did not like to see her looking so frightened" (p. 346). Moreover in the loss of love, the memory of the defeat and death of his son, David may be reconciled to God, for "I feel nearer to God when I am deepest in anguish. That's when I know he is closing in again, and I yearn to call out to him . . . with those words of Ahab . . . 'Hast thou found me, O mine enemy?'" (p. 338). And David has found too the distance to see his own complicity. In the words which Shakespeare, as so many others, stole from him: "The fault I saw was not in my stars but in myself" (p. 338).

Summary

With each successive novel, the overall vision of Heller's writing becomes more evident. Human life is not as simple or abstract as our culture would make it. To be fully human is to be open to pain and loss, as well as to laughter, love, and joy; these are inseparable. It is also to accept otherness, the existence independent of our use of them, of the being and needs of others. At such moments, almost despite ourselves, our moral character is born in the shift from "I want" to "They need." Yossarian reaches such a moment when he turns from the obsession with saving only his own life, rejects the easy deal with the colonels because it would be good for him and not the others, and opts for the dangerous journey to Sweden. Gold selects his responsibility to the family that he cannot control, which will continue to misinterpret and misunderstand his works and his words, over the glittering promise of Washington which reduces everything to abstractions and rejects all it cannot control. David recognizes that he knows God and life in loss and gives the kingdom to Solomon for Bathsheba's sake, even though he knows that she will never be grateful or give him what he desires. Only Slocum finally rejects that which he cannot control or which opens him to loss and smothers love as he smothers his boy. Obviously such life is too complex simply to laugh at it, but without the perspective, the distance from ourselves and our environment that such laughter provides, we may lose other human qualities as well. In all of his works, Heller sees our earlier selves carried inside us. The laugher, the mocker, the irreverent pre-social or even anti-social being is one of those. We need it to keep our other selves alive. We also need it to separate ourselves from our environment in a time when chaos often masquerades as order.

Notes

1. "Humor and the Ability to Create It Cannot Be Taught: A Conversation with Joseph Heller," *U.S. News and World Report*, November 12, 1984, p. 71.
2. Richard B. Sale, "An Interview in New York with Joseph Heller," *Studies in the Novel*, 4 (September 1972), p. 73.
3. Joseph Heller, *Catch-22* (New York: Simon and Schuster, 1961), p. 46. References in the text are to this edition.
4. Quoted in "Joseph Heller," *Contemporary Authors*, New Rev. Ser., 8 (Detroit: Gale Research Company, 1983), p. 239.
5. Joseph Heller, *Something Happened* (New York: Knopf, 1974), p. 5. References in the text are to this edition.
6. Joseph Heller, *Good as Gold* (New York: Simon and Schuster, 1979), p. 347. References in the text are to this edition.
7. Jack Beatty, "*Good as Gold* by Joseph Heller," *The New Republic*, March 10, 1979, p. 43.
8. Morris Dickstein, "Something Didn't Happen," *Saturday Review*, March 31, 1979, p. 51.
9. Joseph Heller, *God Knows* (New York: Knopf, 1984), p. 9. References in the text are to this edition.

Selected Bibliography

Primary Sources

Catch-22. New York: Simon and Schuster, 1961.
We Bombed in New Haven. New York: Knopf, 1968.
Catch-22: A Dramatization. New York: Samuel French, 1971.
Clevenger's Trial. New York: Samuel French, 1973.
Something Happened. New York: Knopf, 1974.
Good as Gold. New York: Simon and Schuster, 1979.
God Knows. New York: Simon and Schuster, 1984.
(with Speed Vogel.) *No Laughing Matter*. New York: Putnam's, 1986.

Secondary Sources

There is no full-length study of Heller's writing.
Beatty, Jack. "*Good as Gold* by Joseph Heller." *The New Republic*, March 10, 1979, pp. 42–44. Praises *Good as Gold* as an astute political novel.
Dickstein, Morris. "Something Didn't Happen." *Saturday Review*, March 31, 1979, pp. 49–51. Several novels and styles in *Good as Gold* fail to coalesce, and Heller's Jewish material "gnaws on bones other writers have thoroughly chewed over."
Janoff, Bruce. "Black Humor, Existentialism, and Absurdity: A Generic Confusion." *Arizona Quarterly*, 30 (1974): 293–304. Discusses *Catch-22* as part of the black humor movement.
Kiley, Frederick, and William McDonald, eds. *A Catch-22 Casebook*. New York: Crowell, 1973.
Le Clair, Thomas. "Joseph Heller, *Something Happened*, and the Art of Excess." *Studies in American Fiction*, 9 (1971): 245–260. In *Something Happened* Heller uses redundancy to defamiliarize and so renew the reader's sense of an often-discussed social situation. A perceptive analysis of Heller's style.
Medwick, Kathleen. "Man Bites God." *Vogue*, October 1984, pp. 637, 701–702. An interview with Heller and discussion of *God Knows*.
Nagel, James, ed. *Critical Essays on Catch-22*. Encino, Calif.: Dickenson, 1973.
Sale, Richard B. "An Interview in New York with Joseph Heller." *Studies in the Novel*, 4 (September 1971): 63–74. Heller talks about *Catch-22* and *Something Happened*.
Sebouhian, George. "From Abraham and Isaac to Bob Slocum and My Boy: Why Fathers Kill Their Sons." *Twentieth Century Literature*, 27 (1981): 43–52. Traces American writings which deal with the offering of the son from Nathaniel Hawthorne's "Roger Malvin's Burial" to Heller's *Something Happened* in which there is "no patriarch, no promise, and no future."

Francis P. Gillen

Herbert, Henry William
[Frank Forester]

Born: London, England, on August 7, 1807
Education: Eton; Cambridge University, 1830
Marriages: Sarah Barker, 1839–1844, one child; Adela R. Budlong, 1858
Died: May 17, 1858

Biography

Henry William Herbert was born on August 7, 1807, in London, England, one of three children of William Herbert, Dean of Manchester, a classicist and parliamentary orator of some pretension, and Letitia E. Dorethea, the daughter of a viscount. Henry's education at Caius College, Cambridge, completed in the winter of 1829–

1830, was probably intended to fit him for the Church, but characteristic personal and financial indiscretions are supposed to have barred him from that career and from the law. After a year traveling in France, he arrived in New York City in 1831. Brief travels and sporting adventures in New York and Canada led him to abandon plans to settle in the British provinces.

Consequently, he accepted employment as Greek and Latin preceptor with the Reverend R. Townsend Huddart's Classical Institute, remaining there for eight years and maintaining excellent relations with his students, one of whom, Charles A. Bristed, also holds a minor place among American humorists. Attractive, well-dressed, and highly educated, Herbert maintained a social position among sportsmen, educated merchant leaders, and literary men in New York City.

Herbert made his American literary debut through occasional pieces and commentary on New York art and theater as editor of the *American Monthly Magazine*, a journal that he began as a competitor to the *Knickerbocker*, from 1833 through 1835 with Charles Fenno Hoffman as his assistant. His sporting articles for the *American Turf Register* established him as "Frank Forester," the father of American sporting and hunting literature. Herbert was a prolific writer of sentimental romances, histories, translations from the classics, and fugitive poetry; however, his works on hunting, fishing, and horsemanship were major contributions to the American sporting scene. He became semi-reclusive in his retreat, "The Cedars," on the banks of the Passaic River outside Newark, New Jersey, where he wrote during the later period of his life. Herbert married Sarah Barker in 1839, and the couple had one son. When his identity as "Frank Forester" was established through the periodical pieces and *The Field Sports of the United States and British Provinces of North America* in 1848, Herbert expanded on his persona by wearing hunting clothes in public, one of the first American authors to indulge in conscious "image" making. Buffeted by implacable and possibly dishonest creditors and the failure of his second marriage (to Adela R. Budlong) after a few weeks' duration, the emotionally mercurial and possibly manic-depressive Herbert shot himself to death on May 17, 1858.

Literary Analysis

Frank Forester began contributing sporting pieces to the *American Turf Register* in 1839, later collected as *The Warwick Woodlands*. In 1841 after the *Register* ceased publication, he began contributing to *Graham's Magazine*. A novel, *Marmaduke Wyvil; or, the Maid's Revenge* (1843), was the most popular of several romances that Herbert wrote. Ultimately, his sketches appeared as *The Warwick Woodlands, My Shooting Box*, and *The Deerstalkers*—according to one critic works so closely related in form as to be a single extended serial of hunting adventures, and so published in Great Britain in 1849 after their separate American appearances. Harry Archer is the central figure and ideal sportsman in these chronicles.

Herbert barely disguised and made humorous changes in portraits of actual New Jersey and New York sporting figures and local characters in his sketches to the great amusement of his contemporaneous readers. His dialect records and descriptions placed him as a northeastern regional humorist among the contributors to American sporting papers. Unhappily for modern critics, Herbert wrote from an elevated viewpoint and frequently omitted jokes and conversations that he referred to but considered inappropriate to detail for his readers. Amusing local characters and vulgar dialect appear in the books named and dramatized travel sketches such as *The Wigwam in the Wilderness, or, 'Ky Sly and His Companye* (with its "leather-faced, cute-looking long, lean specimen of Western New York humanity" as title figure). A similar light treatment of British fox hunting scenes, *The Quorndon Hounds, or a Virginian at Melton Mowbray*, appeared as sketches in *Graham's* and, like Herbert's other sketches of sporting scenes, was published in England.

Summary

Henry William Herbert was a light humorist who described scenes of northeastern hunting life in the 1830s and 1840s, chiefly under the pen name of Frank Forester. His reputation as a sporting writer outweighs his work as an amusing depicter of the peculiarities of the hunters of the vales of New Jersey and New York, but he deserves modest recognition as a humorous sporting writer, one using a persona before such a practice became common during the Civil War.

Selected Bibliography

Primary Sources

The Warwick Woodlands. Philadelphia: G.B. Zieber, 1845.

My Shooting Box. Philadelphia: Carey and Hart, 1846.

Frank Forester and His Friends; or, Woodland Adventures in the Middle States of North America. London: Richard Bentley, 1849. (Includes *The Warwick Woodlands, My Shooting Box*, and *The Deerstalkers*, all published periodically prior to 1843.)

The Deerstalkers. Philadelphia: Carey and Hart, 1849.

The Quorndon Hounds. Philadelphia: Getz, Buck, 1852.

"The Wigwam in the Wilderness." In *Life and Writings of Frank Forester*. Vol. I. London: Frederick Warne [1882], pp. 110-265.

(N.B.: Jacob Blanck's listings in *Bibliography of American Literature* should be checked for the large number of writings outside the humor category.)

Secondary Sources

"Herbert, Henry William" In *A Critical Dictionary of English Literature*. Vol. I. Ed. S. Austin Allibone. Philadelphia: George W. Childs, 1863, p. 830.

Hunt, William, S. *Frank Forester: A Tragedy in Exile*. Newark, N.J.: Cartaret Book Club, 1933.

International Magazine. Vol. III, pp. 289-291.

Judd, David W. "Introductory." *Life and Writings of Frank Forester*. London: Frederick Warne, [1882], pp. 5-104.

David E.E. Sloane

Hoffenstein, Samuel

Born: Lithuania, on October 8, 1890
Education: Lafayette College, Ph.B., 1911
Marriage: Edith M. Morgan, 1927
Died: October 6, 1947

Biography

The son of Josiah Mayer and Taube Gita (Kahn) Hoffenstein, Samuel Goodman Hoffenstein was born in Lithuania on October 8, 1890. When he was four, the family emigrated to the United States, where they settled in Pennsylvania. After attending the public schools of Wilkes-Barre, he entered and received a Ph.B. in 1911 from Lafayette College in Easton, Pennsylvania. He returned to Wilkes-Barre briefly, where he was first principal of the North Main Street School, then a member of the city staff of the *Wilkes-Barre Times-Leader*.

In 1912, he moved to New York, becoming a reporter for the *New York Sun*; the following year, he was a special writer for the paper, and in 1914-1915, as dramatic critic, he had his own column, "The Playgoer." Starting in 1916 and continuing until 1927, he was press agent for Al Woods, the theatrical producer. His first book, a volume of serious poetry, *Life Sings a Song*, was published in 1916 as well.

From 1923 to 1925, he contributed a column called "The Dome" to the *New York Herald Tribune*. In another column in the paper, he parodied Burton Rascoe's *Daybook*; Rascoe was delighted by it and made Hoffenstein a regular contributor to Rascoe's book section in the *Herald Tribune*. Poems that appeared there, as well as many printed in other magazines, among them the fledgling *New Yorker*, were included in the volume *Poems in Praise of Practically Noth-*

ing, published in 1928, Hoffenstein's first and greatest success both critically and commercially.

Two years later, another volume of verse appeared, *Year In, You're Out*, to a somewhat less positive reception. Shortly after this, he left New York and became a Hollywood screenwriter. He wrote or co-wrote over a dozen screenplays; he received Academy Award nominations for co-writing the screenplays for *Dr. Jekyll and Mr. Hyde* and *Laura*. Although he did not publish more volumes of poetry during this time, his poems appeared on infrequent occasions in various periodicals, including *The New Yorker*.

In 1947, two days before he turned fifty-seven, he died of a heart attack in his Los Angeles home. *Pencil in the Air*, a third volume of verse that he had been preparing, was published only three days after his death.

Literary Analysis

Samuel Hoffenstein's work appeared during what Morris Bishop has called "a joyous outburst of light verse."[1] Indeed, a look at the pages of *The New Yorker* in the first ten years of its publication, 1925-1935, finds it liberally sprinkled with humor in verse by Dorothy Parker, Ogden Nash, E.B. White, Phyllis McGinley, and many others. These poets found a ready audience for their often-barbed wit in the urban, sophisticated readers of the magazine. Hoffenstein both influenced and was influenced in turn by those whose work appeared alongside his; he himself acknowledged particular enthusiasm for Parker and Edna St. Vincent Millay, whose highly cynical tone in *A Few Figs from Thistles* (1920) might well have inspired some of his more trenchant expressions of mankind's folly.

From the first, Hoffenstein wrote not just humorous verse but more serious poetry. Both kinds are found in his portion of *The Broadway Anthology* (1917)—which included some poems reprinted from his little-known first volume of non-comic poetry, *Life Sings a Song* (1916). At one moment he does a comic turn, solving "The Strange Case of the Musical Comedy Star" who is unaccountably popular by explaining that, although this woman cannot sing, dance or act, she does have pretty feet; in the next, his mood turns somber, as he reveals that "The laughter's on my tongue, but my heart is clay" (p. 18). Several of the poems in the anthology, in fact, express a downbeat disillusionment with life.

However, Hoffenstein gained notice in the 1920s not for his serious poetry, but for his witty verses and parodies, which Burton Rascoe and others urged him to collect in book form. Indeed, the critical and financial success of the book that he finally produced, *Poems in Praise of Practically Nothing* (1928), clearly rested on the humorous and satirical verses that dominate it.

Nevertheless, in it and the two later volumes, *Year In, You're Out* (1930) and *Pencil in the Air* (1947), the sentiment, "The laughter's on my tongue, but my heart is clay," seems to underlie much of his comic verse as well as his serious poetry. A good indication of how he viewed his role as comic poet is apparent in another poem in *The Broadway Anthology*, "The Jester":

> *Who's the jester? He is one,*
> *Who behind the scenes hath been,*
> *Caught life with his make-up off,*
> *Found him but a harlequin*
> *Cast to play a tragic part—*
> *And the two laughed, heart to heart!*
>
> (p. 21)

Although not one of Hoffenstein's better poems, "The Jester" does point to his apparent stance as a humorist: in the face of a tragically ludicrous world, one must laugh to avoid cursing or crying. He practiced, as one contemporary critic put it, "the art of humorous pessimism."[2]

In all three of his best-known volumes, he practices this art by employing remarkably similar themes and techniques. Often he expresses comic disillusionment with courtship, love, and the fair sex, as in the poem from the group titled, in typically tongue-in-cheek fashion, "Songs to Break the Tedium of Riding a Bicycle, Seeing One's Friends, or Heartbreak":

> *My luck with the proverbial sex*
> *Should rile, torment me and perplex;*
> *Should turn my simple psyche sour*
> *As, par exemple, Schopenhauer.*
> *It should imbue me with disgust*
> *Of women's misproportioned dust;*
> *Should make me look, with dubious eye,*
> *On every female passerby:*
> *Suspect the sting, mistrust the buzz—*
> *Well, my lad, it does, it does!*
>
> (*Poems in Praise*, p. 16)

He also takes on the modern age, looking with satiric eye on everything from business and advertising ("Oh, how my town-tried heart desires/ To know the peace of Kelly Tires") to science and progress in general ("One day they'll resurrect the dead,/ Who'll die again of colds in the head"). One of his favorite targets is psychoanalysis, which had been popularized and used to help explain any and all of life's difficulties. In one of the "Poems of Passion Carefully Restrained So as to Offend Nobody," he accounts for his insecurity about women in psychological terms:

> *When I achieved the peak of twenty,*
> *Bad breaks with dames I had aplenty,*
> *Who left my burning love behind,*
> *And each, a complex in my mind;—*

> *Now, to these inhibitions true,*
> *I am a-Freud of losing you. . . .*
>
> (*Poems in Praise*, p. 31)

Most of all, though, Hoffenstein expresses comic pessimism about being human and, therefore, fatally flawed and doomed to disappointment. He likens the life of man to that of the city sparrow that flits from tenement to tenement, until "his checkered days to crown,/ A checkered taxi runs him down." Self-disgust is part of his jaundiced view of humanity as well; his proem to *Pencil in the Air* states simply that

> *Wherever I go,*
> *I go too,*
> *And spoil everything.*
>
> (p. 15)

As he concludes in one poem, for him life is "the occupational disease of love" (*Pencil*, p. 62). He is even capable, however, of poking fun at his own pessimistic poetry. In the first poem of *Poems in Praise of Practically Nothing*, he revels at how nice his sorrowful metres look in print and worries that good things might come along to prevent him from writing the kind of verse he does best: "There are always better times/ Waiting to corrupt our rhymes (p. 11)."

Hoffenstein is also noted for his parodies of other poets, from his send-ups of Edna St. Vincent Millay, A.E. Housman, W.B. Yeats, T.S. Eliot and others to his satires of the "sweetness and light" school of children's poetry. Sometimes he takes one well-known line from a poem and pairs it with another, startlingly incongruous one of his own, as in the opening of the final poem in *Pencil in the Air*: "My heart leaped up when I beheld/ A friend of mine named Katzenfeld."

Hoffenstein's techniques range from the simple pun (he says of windows, "To stare at all the suns and rains/ And men, should give them window-panes," *Year In*, p. 84) to the far-fetched rhyme ("So, partly serious, but more in jes',/ I try to find rhymes for oranges," *Pencil*, p. 64). He is especially fond of the last-line surprise:

> *Maid of Gotham, ere we part,*
> *Have a hospitable heart—*
> *Since our own delights must end,*
> *Introduce me to your friend.*
>
> (*Poems in Praise*, p. 206)

Although he uses a variety of verse forms, he leans heavily on the couplet and the quatrain in both his comic and serious verse. And, though he does vary the length of lines as well, one reviewer dubbed him, with some justification, "the star of the octosyllabic line";[3] this relatively short line, combined with the rhyming couplet, gives many of his lighter pieces the sing-song playfulness of children's poetry, a quality that only makes the cynical and worldly sentiments he expresses more pointed by contrast: "If you love me, as I love you,/ We'll both be friendly and untrue" (*Poems in Praise*, p. 207).

Largely on the strength of these arch dissections of modern life and those parodies and satires of other poetic works, *Poems in Praise of Practically Nothing* sold remarkably well— 90,000 copies in the first six months alone—and received generally glowing notices. *Year In, You're Out* fared less well with the critics, and *Pencil in the Air*, although praised by those who reviewed it, failed to garner the kind of attention given his earlier work.

Certainly, by the time of the publication of his last book, the tenor of the times had changed, and one would expect less enthusiasm for his kind of flippant cynicism. However, part of the difficulty with his latter two books stems from the increased space given poems serious in intent and execution. In fact, in terms of Hoffenstein's development as a poet, the enlarged role of serious poetry in his work far outweighs any changes that he might have made in his writing of comic verse. *Poems in Praise of Practically Nothing* does contain some serious lyrical poetry, most of which also deals with the poet's disillusionment, which is treated seriously rather than humorously or satirically. In *Year In, You're Out*, however, many more of the pieces are clearly serious in intent; as Paul Wermuth points out, this gives the book a different and less clear tone.[4] Moreover, in *Pencil in the Air* this trend not only continues, but Hoffenstein for the first time includes a few poems of a personal and autobiographical nature that speak of his childhood, his mother, and his religion. Opinion in his own day was divided among those who felt uncomfortable with the serious verse, those who wished he would develop it further and leave the clowning behind, and those who saw both as legitimate aspects of his poetic personality. In any case, the nearly equal mix of the more public voice of the satirist and the more personal voice of the lyric poet does cause problems for readers of those two latter volumes. Certainly the juxtaposition of serious and comic poems, often with similar themes and messages, does tend to make Hoffenstein's humor seem darker and more feigned; perhaps, indeed, the laughter is just on his tongue, while his heart is clay.

Since his death, Hoffenstein's work has not gone unread or unnoticed, although it has never re-achieved the height of popularity that it had in the late 1920s. Modern Library published his *Complete Poetry* in 1954 (which includes only the material in his latter three books), and his humorous work often appears in anthologies of light verse; in 1981, for example, William Zaranka chose to include several of Hoffenstein's delightful parodies in *The Brand-X Anthology of Poetry*.

Summary

Samuel Hoffenstein is best remembered for his first volume of comic verse, *Poems in Praise of Practically Nothing*. In practicing the art of humorous pessimism, he produced poems that satirized modern life and love and expressed comic disillusionment with human existence as a whole. His sharp wit, last-line comic reversals, and tone of arch cynicism made him popular with the largely urban, sophisticated readers of his own time.

Notes

1. Morris Bishop, "Light Verse in America," *The Comic Imagination in American Literature*, ed. Louis D. Rubin, Jr. (New Jersey: Rutgers University Press, 1973), p. 265.
2. Eda Lou Walton, "Samuel Hoffenstein Squints an Ironic Eye," rev. of *Year In, You're Out*, *New York Times Book Review*, July 13, 1930, p. 2.
3. Thomas Sugrue, "Ave Atque Vale," rev. of *Pencil in the Air*, *New York Herald Tribune Weekly Book Review*, October 19, 1947, p. 12.
4. Paul C. Wermuth, "Samuel Hoffenstein," *Dictionary of Literary Biography*, Vol. 11, *American Humorists, 1800-1950*, ed. Stanley Trachtenberg (Detroit: Gale, 1982), p. 204.

Selected Bibliography

Primary Sources
Life Sings a Song. New York: Wilmarth, 1916.
Poems in Praise of Practically Nothing. New York: Boni and Liveright, 1928; London: Cape, 1929.
Year In, You're Out. New York: Liveright, 1930.
Pencil in the Air. Garden City: Doubleday, 1947.
Complete Poetry. New York: Modern Library, 1954.

Secondary Sources
Allen, Everett S. *Famous American Humorous Poets*. New York: Dodd, Mead, 1968, pp. 53–60. Although part of the series "Famous Biographies for Young People," Allen's book provides a useful sketch of Hoffenstein's life and work.
Rascoe, Burton. "Contemporary Reiminiscences." *Arts and Decoration*, January 29, 1930, p. 56. Rascoe gives us some amusing and revealing personal glimpses of Hoffenstein and relates how *Poems in Praise of Practically Nothing* came to be published.
Wermuth, Paul C. "Samuel Hoffenstein." *Dictionary of Literary Biography*. Vol. 11. *American Humorists, 1800-1950*. Ed. Stanley Trachtenberg. Detroit: Gale, 1982, pp. 202–205. Good general account of Hoffenstein's career, with special emphasis on *Poems in Praise of Practically Nothing*.

David K. Steege

Holley, Marietta ["Josiah Allen's Wife"]

Born: Jefferson County, New York, on July 16, 1836
Education: Rural school, largely self-educated
Died: March 1, 1926

Biography

Marietta Holley was born July 16, 1836 to John Milton and Mary Taber Holley. She was the last of seven children born into a farm family in southern Jefferson County, New York, near the villages of Adams and Pierrepont Manor. When her three surviving older brothers left the small farm to make their fortunes in the West after their father's death in the 1860s, Holley was left to help support the family by selling handicrafts and giving music lessons to young women of more prosperous families. Her formal education in the rural district school ended at age fourteen because there was no more money to support it, although an uncle paid for her own music lessons because she seemed gifted. She continued her education through a program of reading and informal study with a neighbor. At an early age she began making verses with accompanying illustrations, but she maintained secrecy about all her writing until 1857 when she started publishing poetry in the local newspaper, *The Jefferson County Journal*, under the pseudonym "Jemyma." Soon she was publishing fiction, some in dialect, in popular magazines. By 1872 she was bold enough to send a few sketches to Elisha Bliss at American Publishing, Mark Twain's publisher. He immediately commissioned her to write a novel in the mode of the vernacular humorists, and the career of "Josiah Allen's Wife" was launched. Holley had used several pseudonyms during her public career, but none served her so long or well as "Samantha Allen." Holley was shy and suffered from a slight speech impediment that kept her from speaking out in public, although she was often asked to do so to support the various reform movements she espoused in her works. Her conversion to the Baptist faith during adolescence led to a life-long concern with piety and spirituality that, yoked with her feminism, informed most of her adult writing. She barely left the precincts of her farm home before she was forty-five years old, preferring instead to live quietly among the neighbors and let the world come to her. Although she informally adopted a young girl and surrounded herself with faithful friends and servants, she led a circumscribed and solitary life. Even after making a comfortable fortune with her pen, Holley eschewed publicity and fame and settled in a mansion built on her fa-ther's farm property where she lived out her long life.

Literary Analysis

Holley was called "the female Mark Twain," the inheritor of the male tradition of the literary comedians—Twain, Josh Billings, Artemus Ward, and Petroleum V. Nasby. She depended for much of her effect on the upcountry dialect, proverbs, and maxims mixed with the extravagant images that were the stuff of the "crackerbox philosophers." Holley's creative orthography attempted a transcription of New York State's North Country speech. To the native idiom she added the usual comic literary devices: anticlimax, misquoted Scripture, puns, malapropisms, mixed metaphors, comic similes, and language reversals such as "foremothers." In addition, her stories chronicled the homely events and hard work that set the rhythm of life for country women. Thus, her work blended with that of the female local color writers of New England. In fact, Holley melded three American literary traditions in a way no other writer had; most of her stories combined the attention to regional detail of the local colorists with the sentimental conventions of the domestic novelists and the vernacular comedy developed by such earlier humorists as Ann Stephens and Frances Whitcher.

Holley's persona used humor for a new end: it made accessible and palatable the ideals of the temperance and suffrage movements. Holley rejuvenated the traditional character types but reversed the reader's sympathies to undermine the conventions that underlay the roles of women and men and thereby created the first significant female comic protagonist, Samantha Allen. Whereas the earlier comedians had made the woman, particularly the woman's rights advocate, the butt of their comedy, Holley created characters of both genders who embodied the absurdities of intemperance and antisuffrage.

Like the vernacular humorists, Holley fixed her works in the voices of dialect speakers, but to this she added the rootedness of place and an awareness of seasons and landscapes. Holley was a regionalist intent on portraying average Americans who are not particularly colorful and picturesque. Hers was a Whitmanesque democratic and panoramic vision of the nation, yet her work anticipated the New England local colorists such as Harriet Beecher Stowe, Sarah Orne Jewett, and Mary Wilkins Freeman in her depiction of life in a circumscribed area, Jonesville.

Her fiction also drew on the tradition of domestic fiction of writers such as E.D.E.N. Southworth, Caroline Lee Hentz, Susan Warner, and Marion Harland. Combining the notion of home-centeredness and the plot and character conventions that the sentimental or domestic novelists had used, Holley turned these to her own purposes to show the failure of gentility to provide a safe, satisfying life for women.

Holley's work clearly depicted the realities and rigors of country life and thus provided a glimpse of an era and place until then largely unrecorded. Such domestic detail recounted with both humor and irritation made her work enormously popular with women readers, as well as with reformers who were struggling with their own advocacy of woman's rights and temperance. Susan B. Anthony and Frances Willard, for example, sought her support and enjoined her to appear with them and write for them. Holley was often invited to address audiences, including the United States Congress, but always declined.

Her first book, *My Opinions and Betsey Bobbet's* (1873), a collection of sketches loosely hung on a narrative strand, was the first in the nineteen-book Samantha series, the novel that established the characters of Samantha Smith Allen, her husband Josiah Allen, and Betsey Bobbet, the spinster spokeswoman for gentility and antifeminism. In that book Holley adopted the pattern that dominated the remaining books: Samantha is presented with a problem that requires her to travel outside the confines of rural Jonesville; she takes with her a rustic sensibility and common sense which, through her commentary, shows the absurdity of much of life in eastern America, especially the politics and genteel society. *Josiah Allen's Wife as a P.A. and P.I.: Samantha at the Centennial* continued the pattern but also initiated another genre for which Holley was to become well-known: travel writing. Seven of her novels were commissioned books about places or events as viewed through Samantha's spectacles: the Centennial (1887), the World's Fair (1893), the world seen on the Grand Tour (1895), the St. Louis Exposition (1904), and Coney Island and the Thousand Islands (1911). Ironically, Holley herself rarely travelled, writing most of these books entirely from maps and guidebooks (she occasionally visited the sites *after* the publication of the work).

In all her fiction, including the travel books, Holley took on nearly every possible reform women agitated for. *My Wayward Pardner; or, My Trials with Josiah, America, and the Widow Bump, and Etcetery* (1880) attacks the Mormon church for its antifemale underpinnings, a subject that Holley addressed that same year in her book-length poem *The Lament of the Mormon Wife*. Her concern with the relationship of women and organized churches continued in *Samantha Among the Brethren* (1890). Temperance was Samantha's concern in most of Holley's fiction, but it was the central issue in *Sweet Cicely: Josiah Allen as a Politician* (1885), her

most accomplished and well-crafted book, showing her at her best with rustic and dialect humor and the temperance and domestic novel genres. Her most commercially successful book, *Samantha at Saratoga* (1887), followed with its criticism of dress and morals.

Collections of her short fiction include *Miss Richard's Boy and Other Stories* (1883), which was radically different from her other writing in its lack of vernacular humor, although it addressed the social issues tackled in the other works: temperance, suffrage, the failure of gentility. Her collection *Poems* (1887) is a generally disappointing assortment of conventional verses. Holley was clearly at her best with the rustic voices and humor of Samantha and her circle.

Summary

After working as a poet, Holley began her career as a humorist with the publication of *My Opinions and Betsey Bobbet's*. This was immediately successful and led to publication of 24 Samantha books over 41 years, including the best-seller of 1887, *Samantha at Saratoga*. Her novels and sketches drew together three literary traditions: the regional detail of the local colorists, the sentimental conventions of the fiction of the 1850s, and the vernacular comedy developed by earlier humorists and the literary comedians. Her signal contribution was the creation of the first comic female protagonist of significance in American literature.

Selected Bibliography

Primary Sources

Fiction
My Opinions and Betsey Bobbet's. Hartford, Conn.: American Publishing, 1873.
Josiah Allen's Wife as a P.A. and P.I.: Samantha at the Centennial. Hartford, Conn.: American Publishing, 1877.
My Wayward Pardner; or, My Trials with Josiah, America, the Widow Bump, and Etcetery. Hartford, Conn.: American Publishing, 1880.
Miss Richard's Boy and Other Stories. Hartford, Conn.: American Publishing, 1883.
Sweet Cicely: Josiah Allen as a Politician. New York: Funk and Wagnalls, 1885.
Miss Jones' Quilting and Other Stories. New York: J.S. Ogilvie, 1887.
Samantha at Saratoga or Flirtin' with Fashion. Philadelphia: Hubbard Brothers, 1887.
Samantha Among the Brethren. New York: Funk and Wagnalls, 1890.
Samantha on the Race Problem. New York: Dodd, Mead, 1892; republished 1898 as *Samantha Among the Colored Folks*.
Tirzah Ann's Summer Trip and Other Sketches. New York: F.M. Lupton, 1892.
Samantha at the World's Fair. New York: Funk and Wagnalls, 1893.

Widder Doodle's Love Affair and Other Stories. New York: F.M. Lupton, 1893.

Josiah's Alarm and Abel Perry's Funeral. Philadelphia: Lippincott, 1895.

Samantha in Europe. New York: Funk and Wagnalls, 1895.

Samantha at the St. Louis Exposition. New York: G.W. Dillingham, 1904.

Around the World with Josiah Allen's Wife. New York: G.W. Dillingham, 1905.

Samantha vs. Josiah; Being the Story of the Borrowed Automobile and What Became of It. New York: Funk and Wagnalls, 1906.

Samantha on Children's Rights. New York: G.W. Dillingham, 1909.

Samantha at Coney Island and a Thousand Other Islands. New York: Christian Herald, 1911.

Samantha on the Woman Question. New York: Fleming H. Revell, 1913.

Josiah Allen on the Woman Question. New York: Fleming H. Revell, 1914.

Poetry

The Lament of the Mormon Wife. Hartford, Conn.: American Publishing, 1880.

Poems. New York: Funk and Wagnalls, 1887.

Drama

Betsey Bobbet: A Drama. Adams, N.Y.: W.J. Allen, 1880.

Josiah's Secret. Watertown, N.Y.: Hungerford-Holbrook, 1910.

Autobiography

"How I Wrote My First Books." *Harper's Bazaar,* 9, 45 (September 1911): 404.

"The Story of My Life," published serially. *Watertown Daily Times,* Watertown, N.Y., February 5 to April 9, 1931.

Secondary Sources

Blyley, Katherine Gillette. "Marietta Holley." Dissertation, University of Pittsburgh, 1936. Begun within the decade after Holley's death, this is a useful record of impressions and elusive facts, a thorough and mostly reliable source of biographical information.

Butler, Ellis P. "Marietta Holley." *Mark Twain Quarterly,* Fall 1937, p. 13.

Curry, Jane, ed. *Samantha Wrastles the Woman Question.* Champaign-Urbana: University of Illinois Press, 1983. This carefully edited collection of Holley's feminist pieces, with Curry's introduction, makes the material readily available.

———. "Women as Subjects and Writers of Nineteenth-Century American Humor." Dissertation, University of Michigan, 1975.

Graulich, Melody. "'Wimmen is my theme, and also Josiah': The Forgotten Humor of Marietta Holley." *American Transcendental Quarterly,* Summer/Fall 1980, pp. 187-197.

Morris, Linda Ann Finton. "Women Vernacular Humorists in Nineteenth Century America: Ann Stephens, Frances Whitcher, and Marietta Holley." Dissertation, University of California, Berkeley, 1978. Chapters 4 and 5 provide insightful analysis of Holley's style and place in the humorous tradition.

Williams, Patricia. "The Crackerbox Philosopher as Feminist: The Novels of Marietta Holley." *American Humor,* 7, no. 1 (1980): 16-21.

Williamson, Mary Celeste. "Marietta Holley's Samantha." Thesis, Catholic University of America, 1946. This study focuses on the ways in which Samantha represents an era and ethic.

Winter, Kate, H. *Marietta Holley: Life with "Josiah Allen's Wife."* Syracuse, N.Y.: Syracuse University Press, 1984. This critical biography connects Holley's life and work and the literary traditions of the vernacular humorists, local color writers, and sentimental novelists of the nineteenth century.

Kate H. Winter

Hooper, Johnson Jones

Born: Wilmington, North Carolina, on June 9, 1815

Education: Wilmington, North Carolina, public school

Marriage: Mary Mildred Brantley, 1842, three children

Died: June 7, 1862

Biography

Like many antebellum southern writers, Johnson Jones Hooper was an immigrant to the region that he helped to make famous as the "new country" of the Old Southwest. He was born on June 9, 1815, in Wilmington, North Carolina, of impressive forebears; both of his parents, Archibald and Charlotte DeBerniere Hooper, could claim distinguished ancestors from pre-Revolutionary North Carolina. His father, whose sporadic tutoring was the source of Hooper's only formal learning beyond the city's public school, provided the youngest of his six children the opportunity for his most valuable education: as a printer's devil for the *Cape-Fear Recorder,* the Wilmington newspaper that Archibald Hooper bought in 1826. This wide-ranging experience during adolescence gave young Johnson Hooper the perspective from which he would shape his adult career—that of the significant double function of an early regional newspaper in promoting local writing and championing political causes. At fifteen he published a comic poem on the accidental dunking of an unpopular and "pompous British consul" at the launching ceremonies of a schooner, thus in one gesture anticipating the two major interests, authorship and partisan politics, that would consume the greatest energies of his brief life.

By the time he was seventeen and feeling the

effects of his father's financial and professional failures, Johnson journeyed west to eastern Alabama in 1835, joining his lawyer brother, George, in La Fayette, a rawboned community of two hundred. Within four years, having served as apprentice in his brother's law office, Hooper was admitted to the bar. Although he practiced desultorily for a few years in Dadeville, in Tallapoosa County, he was never deeply committed to law as a profession. Like many settlers in the new counties of Alabama and Mississippi during Flush Times, Johnson Jones Hooper tried his hand at several occupations: census taker, newspaperman, lawyer, merchandizing agent, legislative clerk, politician, and finally secretary to the Provisional Congress in the first year of the Confederacy.

In 1842, Hooper married Mary Mildred Brantley, the sixteen-year-old daughter of a well-to-do merchant and Whig politician in La Fayette. In the next seven years she bore him three children. Though he was for a time a law partner with his older brother, eventually Hooper followed his father's inclination and succumbed to the lure of journalism. Becoming editor of the *La Fayette East Alabamian* in 1843 was the first in a sequence of his publishing enterprises throughout the state that focused on his twin talents for writing occasional sketches and taunting Democrats, first as a loyal Whig, then as a Know-Nothing, later as an independent states' rights secessionist. His first humorous piece for the *East Alabamian*, "Taking the Census in Alabama," was quickly reprinted in *The Spirit of the Times* in New York. The *Spirit*'s influential editor, William T. Porter, subsequently nourished Hooper's talent by frequently reprinting his work. In late 1844, Hooper published the first of his sketches featuring Simon Suggs, a quintessential frontier trickster; with the help of Porter (whose Suggs reprints were enormously popular among readers of *The Spirit*), Carey and Hart of Philadelphia in 1845 published a collection of the sketches in the form of a mock "campaign biography" as *Some Adventures of Captain Simon Suggs, Late of the Tallapoosa Volunteers*. By 1856, the volume had gone through eleven editions.

In the meantime, however, Hooper's ambitions for public office had grown. Even after becoming the editor of the *Whig* in Wetumpka, he served as a clerk for the House of Representatives in Tuscaloosa in 1845 and 1846 and was a conspicuous member of the commission to select a site for the new capital in Montgomery, where he moved in 1846, this time as associate editor of the *Alabama Journal*. Returning three years later to La Fayette to resume his law practice, Hooper wrote few new sketches; by the time that he lost his race for state representative in the spring of 1849, he was already sensing that the popularity of his shifty fictional character was damaging his chances for political advancement. Later in 1849, he won the race for solicitor of the ninth circuit, a job that required prosecuting cases in six counties, but he was defeated for reelection in 1853. Although Hooper had an irregular legal practice, he was never really inactive as a newspaperman until the eve of the Civil War. In 1849, he joined the *Chambers County Tribune*, published some more humorous and sporting sketches, and after his term as solicitor went again to Montgomery, this time joining the *Mail*, which in the course of his editorship he transformed into an influential party organ for the Know-Nothings. During this period, Hooper published *A Ride with Old Kit Kuncker* (1849), a collection of twenty sketches, and *The Widow Rugby's Husband* (1851), a reprinting of *Kit Kuncker* enriched with some new pieces deriving from his experiences as solicitor of Alabama's "Bloody Ninth."

Although new editions of *Widow Rugby* appeared in 1853 and 1856, Hooper's creative period was over. Like A.B. Longstreet, he was ambivalent about what he perceived as his frivolous writing, considering it incompatible with his serious political concerns. His literary energy was devoted to projects designed to accentuate his political reliability and gentlemanly avocation: *Read and Circulate* (1855), a satire on the Democrats' strong-arm tactics in the Alabama legislature; and the surprisingly popular *Dog and Gun* (1856), an anthology of practical sporting pieces, some of them borrowed freely from other writers, with such titles as "How to Choose a Good Gun" and "Treatment of the Distemper." Still, Hooper could not shake his reputation as the creator of the shifty Simon Suggs. According to the report of one contemporary, in 1856 the humorist confessed his chagrin that in the public view he was "a mere storyteller, with nothing solid in his composition" and that such a reputation had been a "depressing influence" every time he aspired to "soar . . . to a higher rank" or "move in quite a different channel."[1]

Beginning in 1857, Hooper traveled extensively, often for health reasons, once as a business agent for Alabama investors, occasionally as a reporter for horse races, sometimes as a publicist for the Montgomery *Mail* and other newspapers. In 1860, he was deeply involved in national politics, advocating secession of the southern states. By now weaned away from the Know-Nothings, he supported John Breckinridge of Kentucky, a southern Democrat, for president because of all the candidates he was the strongest advocate of states' rights. When Lincoln's election precipitated the action that he had supported for so long, Hooper was named secretary of the Provisional Confederate Congress by acclamation—though his political seriousness was again undercut by one reporter's bland summary of the new nation's legislative proceedings: "The Southern Congress has met, Howell Cobb of Georgia presiding and Simon Suggs of Montgomery clerk."[2]

That even his newspaper friends continued to think of Hooper more as a jovial companion and public entertainer than as an ideologue is evidenced in their farewell party for him when they toasted him as "a witty, spicey writer" who was resigning from the Montgomery *Mail* to devote more time to his job with the Provisional Congress.[3] The move of the Confederate capital to Richmond ended his long career as a newspaperman, but in that political center Hooper enjoyed the news of the early Southern victories on the battlefield and the lively society of the fashionable set. In the factional infighting that followed the seating of a permanent Congress for the Confederacy, Hooper lost his position as secretary, but as consolation he was commissioned to edit the documents of the now-defunct Provisional Congress. He did not live to complete the task. Stricken, apparently with tuberculosis, Hooper died, a Roman Catholic convert, just before his forty-seventh birthday and was buried in Richmond's Shockhoe Hill Cemetery in a grave that went unmarked until the 1950s.

Literary Analysis

At the time of his death in 1862 Hooper had not been an active contributor to the humorous fiction of his region for eleven years, yet in the obituaries—and in the memories of readers both North and South—the journalist and politician continued to be known best as the creator of a crafty frontier confidence man. Hooper's Simon Suggs is a master of adaptation who makes his mark by making marks of others. Shiftless, cowardly, and canny, he expends his greatest energy in devising schemes for potential victims. Though illiterate, he is unerring in detecting "the *soft spots* in his fellow," and his "quick, ready wit" allows him to extricate himself from tight predicaments. Through his skill in impersonation and adaptation, Suggs moves adroitly through his world, outwitting without mercy or discrimination Creek widows, gentleman gamblers, judges, greedy patronage seekers, camp meeting preachers, and gullible yeoman families who favor Andrew Jackson. As Hooper makes clear, his protagonist is suited to his environment; just as Simon himself invokes "natur'" to excuse his expedient use of others, so his creator establishes a pre-Darwinian metaphor to explain Simon's place in the world. If, "in respect to his moral conformation," nature made

Suggs "a beast of prey, she did not refine the cruelty by denying him the fangs and claws."

Aside from the brilliant characterization of Suggs, what is most impressive about Hooper's famous book is its structural unity. Unlike most collections of such humor during this period, Hooper's is not a haphazard assemblage. *Some Adventures of Captain Simon Suggs* not only features a memorable character, it also chronicles the achievement of a remarkable career. We first see Suggs at seventeen, cheating at cards, his fangs and claws already developed. He steals his mother's roosters to fight them, sneaks out his father's plough-horses to race them, and slips off to join more experienced gamblers and prove himself "tip-top at the game of 'Old Sledge.'" The incorrigible son dupes his hypocritical father, a hard-shell Baptist preacher, by applying the theological doctrine of predestination to "fixin'" the cards in a game that he tricks the pious old man into playing. The father, betrayed into a boastfulness and vanity inappropriate to his office, deserves his comeuppance; not so Simon's doting mother—before leaving home Simon secretly laces the old woman's pipe tobacco with a thimbleful of gunpowder. Both paternal authority and maternal indulgence are simultaneously cast off. Thus, in the beginning Hooper establishes his hero's radical amorality by dramatizing his rebellion against the home, often the only unit of social cohesion on the frontier. In later adventures Simon pits his skill against the court, the church, and the military—those repositories of civilized society that would eventually help to bring order to the back country. Like many legitimate campaign biographies, Hooper's ends by reminding the reader that his candidate is running for office; Suggs's qualifications for sheriff as summarized by the narrator (this former military man is getting old and needs the money) cynically counterpoint the actual adventures of an expedient trickster whose only principle is self-interest. The narrator's cynicism, however, is perfectly matched by the captain's self-congratulatory image of himself as an honest man who accepts the workings of Providence while relying on "his own hook" when he must: "Never despar! I've been hunted and tracked and dogged like a cussed wolf, but the Lord has purvided."

Although in his sketches Hooper retains A.B. Longstreet's use of the sophisticated storyteller for a perspective on his chief vernacular character, he discards the genteel moralism of that figure which the narrator uses as a counter weapon against the vernacular assault on civilized values. His own voice is wry and mocking but also indulgent in its superiority. When Simon finds himself a land speculator without funds, his creator actually admires the zest with which the crafty Simon accepts the challenge: "to buy, to sell, to make profits, without a cent in one's pocket—this required judgment, discretion, ingenuity—in short, genius!" His Alabama of the 1830s is fertile ground for assorted gamblers, grafters, opportunists, and cheats, a primitive society in which only the strongest survive. Unlike the world of the half-horse, half-alligator figures, those self-promoting boasters in some other fiction of the Old Southwest who proclaim their boisterous presence by verbal confrontation, Hooper creates a more subtly treacherous world with a built-in system of rewards and punishments by liberally providing his con man with victims whose vanity, ignorance, greed, and vulnerability often invite their own victimization.

Simon's genius is displayed by his adages—the form of which he has learned from his preacher father, the burden of which he has learned from experience—and his sojourn in the world is represented by his varied adventures. "Mother-wit kin beat book-larnin, at *any* game!" is one of his proverbs. "Human natur' and the human family is *my* books," he says, "and I've never seed many but what I could hold my own with." Simon's overwhelming weakness is gambling, specifically faro, which invariably beats him, but even in the face of defeat the sheer joy of playing the game inspires one of his best schemes. Through impersonating a wealthy hog drover from Kentucky amid comfortable faro players, he satisfies his need to "fight the tiger" even as he plays the genial host of a champagne-and-oyster supper; his pleasure comes not merely from the cash his "nephew" collects for his triumphant send-off but from the exhilaration of an act well played. Whether as repentant sinner at a camp meeting, as elected captain of ragtag "Vollantares" to quell Creek uprisings, or as state legislator willing to dispense patronage for a price, Simon sets great store by his skill in adapting himself to and taking advantage of public expectations. On his own terms he succeeds in domesticating the space he shares with others in the anarchic social jungle of frontier Alabama; through only minimum conformity to community standards, Simon can enjoy the maximum freedom to indulge his own desires and needs.

The career of Hooper's opportunistic protagonist, which was fully developed in *Some Adventures* and a few other Suggs sketches after 1845, is a graphic and detailed account of chicanery pervading all phases of life on the Alabama frontier; in its mixture of rambunctious humor and subtle satire, Hooper's most famous book is a remarkable document for a self-taught writer of thirty. Political battles, especially among the shifting alliances that characterized the 1850s,

gradually darkened Hooper's views of human nature, which, to judge from the Suggs material, had never been sanguine. Though the later sketches resolutely confirm his suspicions of Jacksonian democracy, Hooper never faltered in his appetite both for conducting his spirited brand of journalism, which depended on the clash of noisy factions, and for depicting the visceral pleasures of the common folk, which included the same kind of bouts and frays.

As editor of the *Chambers County Tribune*, Hooper simultaneously championed slaveholder Zachary Taylor while poking fun at the northern "Conscience Whigs" and wrote anecdotes, sketches, fillers, and a "Chambers Gossip" column based on the mutual trickery of rival editors and jokes about pretentious lawyers and commonsensical settlers. Hooper also found time in the late 1840s to contribute pieces to other southern newspapers and to collect his miscellany in *A Ride with Old Kit Kuncker*, in which many of the butts of his jests are Irishmen, Yankees, and ugly women. As late as 1853, Hooper was promising William T. Porter further communications from East Alabama—"such notes of birds, beasts, and men, in this region, as might seem worthy of preservation,"[4] but for these sketches he adopted a new pseudonym, "Number Eight," presumably to distance himself from his lingering association with Simon Suggs. From 1854, when he became editor of the Montgomery *Mail*, to the end of the decade, Hooper devoted most of his energies to improving the physical plant of his newspaper, baiting rival editors who were political opponents, cultivating a circle of congenial friends, and assembling two non-humorous books that might help to erase the public's memory of his shifty captain. *Dog and Gun* reflected the image of a prosperous gentleman sportsman and Thomas S. Woodward's *Reminiscences*, an edited collection of historical essays by an old Indian fighter in early Alabama, suggested regional fidelity untouched by satire. For the rest of his career Hooper was embroiled in partisan politics.

After his death in 1862 Hooper's prominence in sporting and humorous literature before the war receded quickly, in part because of revisionist attitudes among the leaders of the conciliatory New South movement and perhaps, as one scholar has conjectured, because of "Baptist-Democratic influence" during the Civil War and Reconstruction.[5] Shifts in literary fashion in the second half of the nineteenth century also contributed to the near obliteration of Hooper's reputation, although in retrospect his influence on later writers now appears to be considerable. Joseph Glover Baldwin paid his respects in *The Flush Times of Alabama and Mississippi* (1853) by creating an epistolary series of "Simon Suggs, Jr." Since 1932, when Bernard De Voto first observed the connection, most scholars have agreed that the techniques of Mark Twain's famous con men, the King and the Duke of *Adventures of Huckleberry Finn* (1884), are heavily informed by those of Simon Suggs. Others have also speculated that Faulkner's comic characters owe something to Hooper's wily captain.

Summary

Only in recent years has Johnson Jones Hooper's reputation as one of the most skillful and important newspaper humorists of the Old South, a distinctive talent in his own right, been revived—primarily because he is now recognized for his splendid ear and for his accurate transcription of frontier language, for his unsentimental vision of human nature, and, at his best, for his deft handling of memorable figures in impeccably paced brief narratives. Although he wrote a number of sketches featuring a variety of characters, "A Night at the Ugly Man's" and "Daddy Biggs' Scrape at Cockerell's Bend" among others, he is remembered now, as he was by his contemporaries, for having created Simon Suggs, who in complexity and vividness has only one rival among the dozens of comic creations from the Old Southwest—George Washington Harris's Sut Lovingood.

Notes

1. Paul Somers, Jr., *Johnson J. Hooper* (Boston: Twayne, 1984), pp. 103–104.
2. Stanley W. Hoole, *Alias Simon Suggs: The Life and Times of Johnson Jones Hooper* (University, Ala.: University of Alabama Press, 1952), p. 160.
3. Ibid., p. 158.
4. Somers, p. 77.
5. Ibid., p. 104.

Selected Bibliography

Primary Sources

Some Adventures of Captain Simon Suggs, Late of the Tallapoosa Volunteers; Together with "Taking the Census," and Other Alabama Sketches. Philadelphia: Carey and Hart, 1845.
A Ride with Old Kit Kuncker, and Other Sketches, and Scenes of Alabama. Tuscaloosa: M.D.J. Slade, 1849.
The Widow Rugby's Husband, A Night at the Ugly Man's, and Other Tales of Alabama. Philadelphia: A. Hart, 1851.
Read and Circulate: Proceedings of the Democratic and Anti-Know-Nothing Party in Caucus; or the Guillotine at Work, at the Capital, during the Session of 1855–'56. Montgomery: Barrett and Wimbish, 1855.
Dog and Gun; A Few Loose Chapters on Shooting, Among Which Will Be Found Some Anecdotes and Incidents. New York: Orange and Judd, 1856.
Thomas S. Woodward, *Woodward's Reminiscences of the Creek, or Muscogee Indians, Contained in Letters to Friends in Georgia and Alabama,* ed. Johnson Jones Hooper. Montgomery: Barrett and Wimbish, 1859.

Secondary Sources

De Voto, Bernard. *Mark Twain's America.* Boston: Houghton Mifflin, 1932. Somewhat dated but still useful for detailing Hooper's influence on Mark Twain and the general cultural context of frontier humor.
Garrett, William. *Reminiscences of Public Men in Alabama for Thirty Years.* Atlanta: Plantation, 1872. Source of much negative impression of Hooper by a political opponent.
Hoole, W. Stanley. *Alias Simon Suggs: The Life and Times of Johnson Jones Hooper.* University, Ala.: University of Alabama Press, 1952. Thorough, factual biography, much of it based on primary documents.
Hopkins, Robert. "Simon Suggs: A Burlesque Campaign Biography." *American Quarterly,* 15 (Fall 1963): 459–463. Argues that Hooper is satirizing two campaign biographies of Andrew Jackson.
Smith, Howard Winston. "An Annotated Edition of Hooper's *Some Adventures of Captain Simon Suggs.*" Dissertation, Vanderbilt University, 1965. Reliable critical edition of the rare first edition with textual and informational footnotes.
Somers, Paul, Jr. *Johnson J. Hooper.* Boston: Twayne, 1984. Succinct study, especially strong on Hooper's political career.
Wellman, Manly Wade, ed. *Adventures of Captain Simon Suggs, Late of the Tallapoosa Volunteers; by Johnson Jones Hooper.* Chapel Hill: University of North Carolina Press, 1969. Valuable reprint with informative introduction; appendix includes J.G. Baldwin's parody, "Simon Suggs, Jr., Esq."
Williams, Benjamin Buford. *A Literary History of Alabama: the Nineteenth Century.* Cranbury, N.J.: Associated University Presses, 1979. Segment on Hooper is sketchy but valuable in placing him in the context of his contemporaries and other newspaper writers.
Yates, Norris W. *William T. Porter and the Spirit of the Times.* Baton Rouge: Louisiana State University Press, 1957. Standard work that sheds much light on Porter's championing of Hooper.

James H. Justus

Hubbard, Elbert Green

Born: Bloomington, Illinois, on June 19, 1856

Education: Formal education ended about age fifteen

Marriages: Bertha Crawford, 1881, four children, divorced; Alice Moore, 1904, one child

Died: May 15, 1915

Biography

Elbert Green Hubbard, son of Dr. Silas and Juliana Frances Hubbard, was born June 19, 1856, in Bloomington, Illinois, the third of five children. He was raised in a strict Baptist setting, attended local schools, and as a boy hired out as a farm hand. His love of the outdoors, physical labor, and horses first turned him toward farming, but his cousin introduced him to the soap-selling business and he spent twenty years at that work. During his early selling years, he canvassed the Midwest, dressed stylishly, and played the role of a rising young businessman. However, in his hunger for knowledge and culture, and in his search for an identity, he also read widely, attended numerous chautauqua groups, and began writing.

In 1881 Hubbard married Bertha Crawford and moved to Buffalo, New York, where his experience, charisma, and innovative sales techniques helped lead J.D. Larkin & Company, a seller of soap products, to financial success. Bertha was to bear him three sons and a daughter, and by 1884, Hubbard moved his family a few miles to the suburb of East Aurora where he met a young high school teacher named Alice Moore. An example of the age's "new woman," Alice possessed the formal education he lacked and the intellectual stimulation unavailable at home. A secret romance developed and several years later, while he was still married to Bertha, Alice gave birth to his daughter. Eventually the secret became public, resulting in a scandalous divorce. Elbert and Alice were married in 1904.

By 1891, Hubbard had published his first novel under the name of Aspasia Hobbs, and a year later he sold his interest in the successful soap business to become a writer. He attended Harvard briefly, but his background and self-education had not prepared him for what H.L. Mencken was to call "the dull, hollow dignity of the pedants," and at thirty-seven he found himself out of place. He dropped out, worked in the publishing field around Boston, and wrote several mediocre novels. In 1894 he traveled to England and Ireland to gather material for a series of impressionistic biographical sketches that later became his famous *Little Journeys to the Homes of Good Men and Great*. He was to continue publishing these monthly sketches for fifteen years. In England he met and was impressed with the neomedievalism of William Morris and visited his Kelmscott Press and commune at Hammersmith. This meeting, more than anything, influenced the founding of Hubbard's Roycroft Campus in East Aurora, named after two seventeenth-century English bookbinders.

Returning from England in 1895 and unable to find a publisher for his sketches, Hubbard and two friends founded the *Philistine*, a pocket-sized literary magazine printed on hand-made paper and bound in a coarse brown butcher-type wrapping. Hubbard soon took complete control of the publication and it became his soap box. It was published monthly between 1895 and his death in 1915, was one of the most successful of the "little magazines" of the period, and in its later years was written almost entirely by Hubbard.

His most famous essay, "A Message to Garcia," focusing on a heroic Spanish-American War event and glamorizing responsibility and initiative, was published in the March 1899 *Philistine*. This little preachment, typical of many that were to follow, thrust Hubbard and his Roycroft Campus toward national and worldwide attention. During the next several years, his Roycroft enterprises published magazines and handcrafted leatherbound books and created unique furniture, leather goods, copper, and other items popular during the arts and crafts movement. At one time he employed up to five hundred workers and craftsmen, and his campus boasted several buildings, including an inn to house curious visitors. A second magazine, the *Fra*, was published later, but the *Philistine* remained Hubbard's personal vehicle for his own style of philosophical humor and sarcastic wit. Now famous, Hubbard took to lecturing, and during the 1910–1911 season, actually did two shows a day on the Orpheum vaudeville circuit. As he became more a part of the establishment he once criticized, Hubbard often took sides with big business as one of its most potent spokesmen.

Elbert and Alice Hubbard sailed on the *Lusitania* for Europe in the spring of 1915. Hubbard hoped to interview the Kaiser and gather new material for his lectures and writings. When the *Lusitania* was sunk by a German U-boat on May 15, the Hubbards were not among the survivors. Although he is now almost forgotten, the more than forty thousand cards and letters of condolence that poured into the Roycroft Campus and the national and worldwide publicity that accompanied his death attest to Elbert Hubbard's one-time fame and popularity.

Literary Analysis

Between 1900 and 1915, Hubbard's name was so well known and his writings so widespread that it is difficult to understand his obscurity today. To call him a "humorist" would be to neglect the many facets of his complex personality and varied life. He was an actor and publicist at heart, and he played many roles: writer, lecturer, opinion molder, magazine editor and publisher, vaudevillian, popular philosopher, horseman and farmer, utopian prophet, purveyor of public taste, and one of this country's most accepted eccentrics. He was both Fabian socialist and later one of big business's most able defenders; however, in everything he was and did, his philosophical humor and biting wit emerged.

From its beginning, the *Philistine* was a vehicle for Hubbard's special brand of humor. It was subtitled "A Periodical of Protest," and it was boasted that it would be "Printed Every Little While for The Society of The Philistines and Published by Them Monthly." Hubbard later wrote: "We called it the *Philistine* because we were going after the Chosen People in literature. . . . The smug and Snugly Ensconced denizens of Union Square called me a Philistine, and I said, 'Yes, I am one if a Philistine is something different from you!'"

Even its subscription policies were soaked in Hubbard wit. For one dollar a year the reader not only received the magazine but also "Health, Success, and Love vibrations that are sent daily to all subscribers at 4 P.M., Eastern Time. (If shy on vibrations, please advise.)" Soon its pages promoted the formation of The Society of Philistines (International), later dubbed the American Academy of Immortals. It claimed to be an association of "Book Lovers and Folks who Write, Paint and Dream. . . . Organized to further Good-Fellowship among men and women who believe in allowing the widest liberty to Individuality in Thought and Expression." In order to maintain membership, a subscriber's duty consisted of "living up to his highest Ideal (as nearly as possible) and attending the Annual Dinner (if convenient)."

In its early years the *Philistine* attacked and ridiculed not only the Boston Brahmins but also the literary establishment in general. Hubbard went after everyone from William Dean Howells (whom he called W. Dean Howl) to Mark Twain. Of Twain, Hubbard wrote:

> Mark Twain says he is writing Joan of Arc anonymously in *Harper's* because he is convinced if he signed it the people would insist the stuff was funny. Mr. Twain is worried unnecessarily. It has been a long time since any one insisted that the matter he turns out so voluminously was or is funny.

(*Philistine*, June 1895, p. 22)

Later, as self-appointed (ex-officio) "General Inspector of the Universe," Hubbard expanded his territory to include ministers, doctors, lawyers, and anyone or anything expounding "establishment" views. He philosophized and preached on all topics from child labor to conspicuous consumption. He loved attacking higher education, boasting of his degree in what he called the School of Hard Knocks and added to his list of mottos "You can lead a boy to college but you can't make him think." By 1910, the *Philistine* and Hubbard's other publications had a combined circulation that competed with the country's top popular magazines; Hubbard became the "unofficial court jester and elder statesman" to big business and probably one of this country's most recognized eccentrics.

Hubbard encouraged his image as an eccentric not only through his writing but also through his dress. His curly, shoulder-length pageboy hair style blended well with a Buster Brown cravat, baggy corduroys, a flannel shirt, farmer's brogans and a western Stetson. Where the image left off and the real man began was and still is debated by his critics. However, a close friend and associate recalled: "Hubbard was of the earth, earthy—a farmer. That's the key to his character. Unlike the popular conception of a 'genius,' he was neither ascetic, neurotic, nor a sensualist. His hands were scarred, his nails were broken with hard work of his own choosing" (Shay, p. 228). He enjoyed telling farmhand jokes—barnyard humor, he called it—and the rural life became an essential part of his philosophy and humor. Throughout the country he was known as the Fra, or Fra Elbertus (one adversary dubbed him Fra Hell-Burnt-Us), and the Sage of East Aurora.

His use of the vernacular separates him from the literary stylists and occasionally makes him difficult to understand. When Hubbard could not find the proper word, he often invented one. A "gabbyjack" was an over-zealous talker; a "cab-thought" was a witty response, the snappy riposte that you had neglected to say at the party, and "kabojolism" meant to credit someone with a saying he did not say but wished he had. These words and others like them became standard vocabulary for Hubbard. To the uninitiated, some of his sentences are puzzling. Even when not salted with words of his own creation, his writing at least played with the vernacular of his day. Sometimes it was difficult to tell which was which. "I smole a smile," he once wrote.

Initially a collection of essays, poetry, epigrams, and anecdotes by a variety of writers, the most lively and witty column from the *Philistine*'s beginning was the Fra's own "Side Talks with the Philistines." It had such early subtitles as "Being Sundry Bits of Wisdom Which Have

Been Heretofore Secreted, And Are Now Set Fourth In Print"; or "Being Soul Easement . . . And Wisdom Incidently." It ended up as "Heart to Heart Talks with Philistines by the Pastor of His Flock." Within a few years it was not uncommon to find an entire *Philistine* consisting of that one column.

The "Side Talks" often began with a typical Hubbard essay or preachment, perhaps two, leading to gossipy anecdotes centering around the Roycroft Campus and its visitors or trips Hubbard had made and ending with a series of epigrams. His essays covered a variety of topics from imperialism to evolutionary theory, from proper diet and exercise to feminism. He commented on the literary scene and poked fun at writers and magazines. Hubbard's subscription list often contained the very men he lambasted; although his "foes," they silently chuckled and anxiously awaited each issue to see whom he would take on next. A shrewd businessman, Fra Elbertus knew that his critics would have to subscribe in order to learn what he had to say about them. His column printed letters of praise, but it also published jabs from his harshest adversaries.

The New York *Nation* commented, "He says he's not a college graduate, a fact that need not have been stated"; the Oil City *Derrick* noted that "The *Philistine* has been printed for sixteen years. Its editor says that during that time there has never been a day when he has not been able to sit up and take nourishment. This is a great tribute to the patience of the American people." According to the Boston *Herald*, "All these are dead: Bill Nye, Mark Twain, Iconoclast Brann, Bill Barlow; but Fra Elbertus still employs two magazines. Let's see, what was it P.T. Barnum said?" The Milwaukee *Sentinel* observed: "Fra Elbertus states that morality is merely a matter of geography. Then he should lose no time in consulting an atlas to find out where he belongs," and the Chicago *Tribune* remarked, "If Fra Elbertus had a crop of hair similar to that which graces the head of John D. Rockefeller, the Roycroft Shop would only be a hole in the ground."

Hubbard regularly printed such comments, enjoying the publicity and no doubt gloating over the fact that the nation's press was not only contributing humor and wit to his publication but contributing it free of charge. Fra Elbertus kept his spear sharpened while trying to keep his worst critics writing about him. He realized that sometimes bad publicity was better than no publicity. As one Hubbard epigram stated: "Every Knock is a Boost."

Much of the Fra's philosophical humor came in the form of epigrams, typically at the end of his "Side Talks" column. The better ones were then highlighted on the *Philistine*'s covers, front and back, inside and outside. Others were featured under cartoons by W. W. Denslow, an artist who started with Hubbard and later became famous as the illustrator of Frank Baum's Oz books. Many of these epigrams and witty definitions were later collected in *The Roycroft Dictionary*, a similar yet less cynical imitator of Ambrose Bierce's *The Devil's Dictionary*. Some of the more popular sayings were printed on posters. The following are typical:

> Profanity does not consist in saying damn. Profanity consists in writing it d——n.

> Fit yourself for the best society,—and then keep out of it.

> If you want to get the Work done, select the Busy Man—the Other Kind has no time!

> A Little Seriousness is a Dangerous Thing. Too Much is Absolutely Fatal.

> It is a great man who can live up to the creases in his trousers.

> Many a successful man goes through life with a spray of mistletoe pinned to his coat tail. PRITHEE, OMIT IT!

Hubbard's fondness for practical jokes and hoaxes was also an essential part of his humor. A running jest on the Roycroft Campus centered around the Fra's horse trainer and hired hand, Anson A. Blackman, a simple, uneducated, somewhat humorless laborer. Hubbard dubbed him "Ali Baba" and used him as a persona, attributing to him all sorts of philosophical epigrams such as "Art is largely a matter of haircut," "Every man is a damn fool for at least five minutes every day," and "Two in the bush are the root of all evil." Some of Hubbard's more hilarious writings are attributed to Ali Baba. Loyal Roycrofters enjoyed watching unknowing visitors seek out Blackman for some philosophical discussion. Although he probably enjoyed the attention, the rather quiet, regular churchgoer also probably considered himself one of the few sane individuals on the campus.

To insiders, Hubbard was affectionately known as "John." That nickname came from a story about a wealthy visitor who pulled up in a stylish carriage to the Roycroft Inn. He viewed the long-haired Hubbard in work clothes sweating at the wood pile. "Here, John! Hold my horses," he ordered. The willing Fra stopped toiling and obediently held the horses while the visitor dashed across campus in search of the legendary Sage of East Aurora.

Hubbard not only teased pretension on paper, he also toyed with it in person. Once, while dining at his inn, he noticed a bride loudly commenting on his bizarre appearance to her husband. She wondered rather audibly whether the Fra would drink his coffee (probably Postum) from his saucer. Hubbard made a production of drinking all of it from his saucer, then benevolently presented the couple with an autographed book. He is known to have led fashionably dressed visitors on a picnic, taking the long way and purposely fording streams instead of using available bridges. Many of these incidents became a part of his writing and lecturing repertoire. He was to learn, especially the year he played vaudeville, that audiences loved to hear a speaker ridicule himself.

Between 1900 and 1915, Hubbard was one of the most popular lecturers in America. His public performances reached a peak when, during 1910–1911, he did two shows a day on a successful seventeen-week tour of Orpheum Circuit vaudeville. He lectured about the same things that he had written about in the *Philistine*, slipping in jokes and epigrams, yet he was still able to squeeze in serious comments about the theories and philosophies behind his Roycroft experiment. The skill of his showmanship can only be appreciated when one realizes that his popular lecture turns occurred between trained animal acts, jugglers, and song-and-dance teams. In writing his memoirs, Major J.B. Pond, Hubbard's vaudeville booker, classifies the Fra not under "Literary Lecturers," "Orators," "Author Readers and Lecturers," or even "Humorists," but under "Miscellaneous" with the likes of Henry Watterson and P.T. Barnum. Pond apparently agreed with the Hartford *Courant*'s assessment of Hubbard as "The P.T. Barnum of art."

When Elbert and Alice Hubbard went down with the *Lusitania*, the Roycrofters realized that the Fra's singular wit and philosophy could not be successfully carried on by an imitator. In July, the *Philistine* ended with a memorial issue saying: "The *Philistine* had been Hubbard's armor, his shield, his sword for long years. He has left us for a Little Journey, we know not where. He may need his *Philistine*, and so with tears on it we give it to him."

Summary

Most of Elbert Hubbard's humorous writing first saw light in either his *Little Journeys* or in the pages of his *Philistine* and were later used as lectures or perhaps incorporated into pamphlets, books, or anthologies. He attacked pretentious establishment values while advocating his own brand of commonsense philosophy. His genius was in the short essay, the anecdote, the epigram, and his power as a public performer

and popular philosopher influenced more than a generation of Americans.

Selected Bibliography

Primary Sources

"Little Journeys to the Homes of the Great." 25 vols., published in monthly installments between 1895 and 1909, first by Putnam and, after 1899, by Roycroft Press. Many bound editions were later published.

Philistine. First issue: June 1895. Last issue: July 1915. Issued monthly; 6 months per vol.

"A Village Industry: The Story of the Conception and Growth of the Roycrofters—The Most Remarkable Community of Workers on the Co-operative Plan in the Country." In *Wisdom Monthly*, August 1902.

Fra. First issue: April 1908. Last issue: August 1917. Issued monthly; 6 months per vol.

The Complete Writings of Elbert Hubbard. 20 vols. East Aurora, N.Y.: Roycroft, 1908–1914.

The Roycroft Shop: A History. East Aurora, N.Y.: Roycroft Press, 1909.

The Notebook of Elbert Hubbard. New York: William H. Wise, 1923.

N.B. The Elbert Hubbard Museum in East Aurora, New York, probably has the most complete collection of material by or about Hubbard and the Roycroft movement.

Secondary Sources

Books and Articles

Allen, Frederick Lewis. "Elbert Hubbard." *Scribners*, September 1938.

Balch, David Arnold. *Elbert Hubbard: Genius of Roycroft*. New York: Stokes, 1940.

Beer, Thomas. *The Mauve Decade: American Life at the End of the Nineteenth Century*. New York: Alfred A. Knopf, 1926.

Champney, Freeman. *Art and Glory: The Story of Elbert Hubbard*. New York: Crown, 1968.

Elbert Hubbard's Scrap Book. New York: William H. Wise, 1923. A collection of quotations from authors who influenced Hubbard.

Hamilton, Charles F. *As Bees in Honey Drown: Elbert Hubbard and the Roycrofters*. Cranbury, N.J.: A.S. Barnes, 1973.

———. *Roycroft Collectibles*. New York: A.S. Barnes, 1980.

Heath, Mary Hubbard. *The Elbert Hubbard I Knew*. East Aurora, N.Y.: Roycroft, 1929; rpt. 1981.

Jackson, Holbrook. *The Eighteen Nineties: A Review of Art and Ideas at the Close of the Nineteenth Century*. New York: Alfred A. Knopf, 1972.

Mott, Frank L. "The Philistine." In *A History of American Magazines: 1885–1905*. Vol. 4. Cambridge: Harvard University Press, 1957, pp. 639–648.

Shay, Felix (Edward J.). *Elbert Hubbard of East Aurora*. New York: William H. Wise, 1926.

Stott, Mary Roelofs. *Rebel with Reverence: Elbert Hubbard, A Granddaughter's Tribute*. Watkins Glen, N.Y.: Century House American Publishers, 1975.

Dissertations and Theses

Crumrine, Janice G. "Personality Development and Social Change: A Study of the Intersection of History and Biography." Dissertation, State University of New York at Buffalo, 1975.

Hopkins, John Stephen. "Elbert Hubbard and the American Business Creed." Thesis, Brown University, 1970.

Douglas R. Capra

Irving, Washington

Born: New York City, on April 3, 1783
Education: Attended several secondary schools; formal education ended at the age of sixteen
Died: November 28, 1859

Biography

The son of William and Sarah Sanders Irving, Washington Irving was born in New York City on April 3, 1783. The youngest of eleven children, he attended four different schools but did not follow his brothers to Columbia College and concluded his formal education when he was sixteen. His earliest publication, the letters attributed to Jonathan Oldstyle, appeared in 1802 in the *New York Morning Chronicle*, a Democratic newspaper edited by his brother, Peter. In collaboration with James Kirke Paulding, Irving created another pseudonym, Launcelot Langstaff, and wrote *Salmagundi* (1807–1808).

Working as a law clerk for Judge Josiah Hoffman, he became friendly with the family and fell in love with the judge's daughter, Matilda. The girl died of consumption in 1809, and Irving, in deep mourning, finished the book he was then working on, *Diedrich Knickerbocker's History of New York* (1809) and then gave up writing for several years. He worked for the family import business and took an editorial job that he disliked. In 1815, he moved to England to see to the European side of the business, but the firm failed in 1818 and Irving turned once more to writing. *The Sketch Book of Geoffrey Crayon* appeared serially in 1819–1820; it was enthusiastically received in America and abroad and established Irving's reputation as an American man of letters. He immediately followed it up with similar miscellanies, *Bracebridge Hall* (1822) and *Tales of a Traveller* (1824). His appointment in 1826 to the American legation in Madrid, Spain, and a stay in that country till 1829, provided him with the materials for much of his later writings. In 1828, he published *A History of the Life and Voyages of Christopher Columbus*, drawing upon his researches in Spain. *A Chronicle of the Conquest of Granada* appeared in 1829, and Irving made further use of his Spanish materials in *Voyages and Discoveries of the Companions of Columbus* (1831) and *The Alhambra*.

After a long sojourn of 17 years abroad, Irving returned to America in 1832 and immediately took extended tours of the West and South, thus appropriating his own country for literary source materials. His move proved a happy one for his art, for out of his travels he wrote *A Tour on the Prairies* (1835), *Astoria* (1836), and *Adventures of Captain Bonneville, U.S.A.* (1837). He was offered a variety of appointments and political opportunities: nomination as mayoral candidate in New York, the secretaryship of the Navy, and a diplomatic post in Naples, Italy. However, he rejected all of these possibilities to continue his literary life and retired in 1836 to Sunnyside, "a little old fashioned mansion, all made up of gable ends," near Tarrytown. Here he planned a history of Mexico but surrendered his plans when he learned that William Hickling Prescott was writing *The Conquest of Mexico*. Instead, in need of money, Irving contracted to write short pieces for the *Knickerbocker*. From 1842 to 1846, he interrupted his work at Sunnyside in order to serve as Minister to Spain and proved a skillful diplomat.

The writings of Irving's later years were varied in their scope and rather variable in their quality. His biography of George Washington, his namesake, occupied him for years; the fifth and final volume of the study appeared in 1859, only months before the author's death. A biography of Oliver Goldsmith (1849) was an expanded version of a biographical sketch that he had written in 1840 for an edition of Goldsmith's writings. The lengthy *Mahomet and His Successors* appeared in 1850, and the miscellaneous pieces from the *Knickerbocker* and other magazines were collected in *Wolfert's Roost* in 1855. On November 28, 1859, in his seventy-seventh year, Irving died at his home in Sunnyside.

Literary Analysis

Irving began his writing career by imitating the style and substance of his 18th-century precursors, the English periodical writers such as Joseph Addison, Richard Steele, and Oliver Goldsmith; probably he also learned from such American writers as Benjamin Franklin, Joseph Dennie, and Philip Freneau. His earliest publications, the letters that appeared under the name of Jonathan Oldstyle, were printed in 1802 in the *Morning Chronicle*, a newspaper edited by his brother, Peter. They betray the immaturity of their nineteen-year-old author, who creates the old, old-fashioned, cranky, and garrulous character of Jonathan to comment on what does not suit him in early nineteenth-century New York. He complains about the new fashion of slovenly dress and manners. Citing "the degeneracy of the present time," he contrasts the dignified style of past weddings with those of the present. He criticizes the New York theater at some length; six of the nine letters are devoted to finding fault with the plays, the actors, the music, the audience's behavior, the sets, and whatever else comes under Oldstyle's censorious eye. He is fair enough to offer a contrasting view by printing letters from his friend, Andrew Quoz, who defends the theater vigorously without, however, convincing the cranky Oldstyle to change his views.

Irving turned from these conventional publications to something just as conventional but, in the light of all we ever knew about the author, quite different from his usual manner. It was known that Irving had done some political writing in 1804 for *The Corrector*, but the anonymous pieces were not sorted out or attributed to him till 1968, when Martin Roth published them with an excellent introduction. The unusual quality of these pieces is that they show a different Irving than we know, not the genial and genteel humorist but a writer capable of invective and obscenity. The pieces do not seem particularly important as part of Irving's literary works, but they do testify to the great magnetism of Aaron Burr and the vicissitudes of the political campaign of 1804; more importantly, they help to offer a corrective to the usual view of Irving.

By the time that he came to write *Salmagundi* (1807–1808) in collaboration with his brother, William, and his friend and fellow author, James Kirke Paulding, Irving had matured considerably beyond the range of the youthful creator of Oldstyle. It is likely that he profited much from his association with Paulding (1778–1860), a quite distinguished and underrated writer. Paulding had been a contributor to the *Morning Chronicle* as early as 1802. A good five years older than Irving, he brought experience and high spirit to their collaboration, and his qualities mixed well with Irving's own rambunctiousness. At the outset the authors announce their program in a sort of piggish Latin: "In hoc est hoax, cum quiz et jokeses,/ Et smokem, toastem, roastem folkeses." In somewhat more orderly language, the first essay asserts, "Our intention is simply to instruct the young, reform the old, correct the town, and castigate the age; this is an arduous task, and therefore we undertake it with confidence."

The essays that follow justify their name of a "salmagundi," for they do form a hash or gallimaufry of odds and ends. There are poems, letters, comments, theatrical criticisms, and parodies. The mixture is rich to the point of indigestibility unless the pieces are read, as they were meant to be read, singly and at intervals. One of the best comments on the book, William P. Kelly's introduction to the Modern Library selection of Irving's writings, puts the matter tersely:

> Again Irving's humor obscures his intent, but there is a method to the anarchy and madness of *Salmagundi*. By carefully locating the journal within the context of Augustan letters, by invoking the example of Addison, Steele, Fielding, Sterne, Smollett, and their myriad American imitators, Irving is not simply acknowledging a literary debt but is reducing to rubble the props which support that tradition.
>
> (p. xviii)

The mix that Irving and Paulding aim for is successfully achieved, but it fails to become a blend. The book does not have much unity of purpose, tone, or sense. The writers behave as though they are standup comics: whatever is available from week to week is their subject matter. As a result, the effectiveness of *Salmagundi* is often diminished by its topicality; subjects fit for laughter in 1807 soon require heavy footnoting.

All of the skills that Irving labored to bring to perfection and polish in his earlier work are put to their best possible use in *Knickerbocker's History of New York* (1809). The book begins by creating a notably living character in its presumed author, Diedrich Knickerbocker:

> He was a small brisk looking old gentleman, dressed in a rusty black coat, a pair of olive velvet breeches, and a small cocked hat. He had a few grey hairs plaited and clubbed behind, and his beard seemed to be of some four and twenty hours growth.

This description, from the "Account of the Author" that introduces the history, presents the reader with a cranky, eccentric little man who is intent upon producing epic historical writing and defending the writing of history as a creative enterprise. He wants to produce a work that will stand up with the best, with Herodotus, Polybius, Diodorus Siculus, Gibbon, Hume, and Smollett. His intent is a worthy one under any normal circumstances, but Irving undercuts his ambitions by creating not history, but satiric parody. Knickerbocker may be lovable and ambitious, but he is a fool. Fortunately, he is as much a creation of Irving's comic mind as is the history itself. The book presumes to tell the history of the city from the beginning of the world, and the first chapters offer a description and a cosmogony of that vast world. Knickerbocker insists that his book "shall not only delight the learned, but likewise instruct the simple, and edify the vulgar." Hence, we are invited to consider the tragic circumstance that Noah had only three sons for, if there had been a fourth, he might have bequeathed America to that one, and thus its discovery need not have been delayed till the time of Columbus. Knickerbocker learnedly disproves the Italian claims to discovery and forthrightly awards the palm to Hendrick Hudson, in plain defiance of all historical fact. He goes on to create a mythopoeia for the hardheaded Dutch settlers, though no aura of the mythic clings to them, and he devises a fictional golden age for the administration of Wouter Van Twiller.

By the time of the *History*, Irving had learned much about the comic art. In the book he cleverly moves his subjects away from the quotidian toward the universal. When he parodies the pedantry of history, anyone who can read real history in all its pedantry understands the topic of his parody. Instead of satirizing individuals and their quirks, he can make observations that apply to all men and all times: "There are two opposite ways by which some men get into notice—one by talking a vast deal and thinking a little, and the other by holding their tongues and not thinking at all." He divides readers into four classes, in Book III, Chapter iii, and concludes that only the fourth class, who "investigate the operations of the human mind, and watch the gradual changes in men and manners," will properly appreciate his history of placid times. He excoriates the Yankees of Connecticut, who "employed their leisure hours in banishing, scourging, or hanging, divers heretical papists, quakers and anabaptists, for daring to abuse the *liberty of conscience*." The reigns of Wilhelm Kieft, or William the Testy, as Knickerbocker prefers to call him, and Peter Stuyvesant are examined in close detail, together with other earthshaking matters. At least the matters are earthshaking to Knickerbocker; to the ordinary reader they will seem deliciously minor.

It has been said that Knickerbocker is an American Don Quixote, his very enterprise doomed by his choice of subject and his defects of character. The book, much less a potpourri than its predecessors, still suffers somewhat from prolixity and repetitiousness. It is not quite a perfect work of art; indeed, given its origins and intent, it could hardly be one. Still, it is a book of great charm, a genuinely American book, playful in the account it gives of its clownish cast of characters and in the affection the author shows for them and for the lovely wilderness world that they were at such pains to subdue.

The *History* achieved an amazing success at home and abroad. It was widely read and highly praised, and it established Irving as a man of letters. At this point in his career, he might have been expected to follow up such a success with a flood of publications, but he fell more or less silent for most of a decade. One reason might have been the tragic early death of his fiancée, Matilda Hoffman; another, that he had to concern himself with the conduct of his family's business, which was now in poor condition; a third, the lack of appropriate subject matter to write about. No doubt all of these reasons contributed to Irving's singular withdrawal from the literary scene. During these years, he edited a collection of the works of Thomas Campbell and wrote about that poet. He briefly edited a magazine, *The Analectic*, but he appears not to have enjoyed that sort of work. To aid in the management of the family import business, he moved to England in 1815, but, by 1818, the firm had to declare bankruptcy.

Turning back to his first love, Irving quickly wrote *The Sketch Book of Geoffrey Crayon, Gent.* (1819–1820), published first in seven installments and then in a two-volume set. Arguably the first great piece of American literature, *The Sketch Book* was successful on both sides of the Atlantic from its first appearance. It contains thirty-four separate pieces and is, as the title suggests, a miscellanea of easily detachable and independent sketches. These are cast in the familiar mold of the personal essay and treat English topics that an American audience might be expected to read about with pleasure: Westminster Abbey, Christmas, rural life, the country church, a Sunday in London, Stratford-on-Avon. All are delineated in genial and expressive prose. The pieces must have given pleasure at their first appearance, and they still can, though they are not much read nowadays. Any American visitor to Westminster Abbey might well take Irving's essay as his guidebook and compare his impressions with those of his congenial companion. The English countryside and country manners, now vanished, are clearly evoked in Irving's faultless prose.

The creation of another persona, a fictional narrator whose name, Geoffrey Crayon, gives his function away and makes him a somewhat humorous figure from the outset, was in keeping with the practices of the early English and American essayists. Readers were familiar with the convention and readily recognized the countenances of the Spectator, the Rambler, the

Idler, Silence Dogood, and their numerous kin. All of Irving's earlier writings had depended upon such creations—Jonathan Oldstyle, Launcelot Langstaff, and Diedrich Knickerbocker—so that he was once more traversing familiar ground. What was new and pleasurable in this book was his selection of subjects that were more than topical concerns, that did not depend upon passing, quickly exhausted interest. It is to Irving's credit that he shows such a sure hand in choosing subjects that are attractive beyond the limits of 1819. Only a few of the pieces betray the passions of the time. One of these is "English Writers on America," which takes British writers to task for their misdirected criticisms of America, but even this article has its value for the present day in recalling a matter that, in Irving's time, was of some serious concern.

However, *The Sketch Book* derives its immortality from "Rip Van Winkle," which appears early in the volume, and "The Legend of Sleepy Hollow," which closes it. Here, surely, is the center of Irving's art and literary achievement. It might be too much to declare that Irving created the short story as a literary genre. There are, after all, examples of well-constructed short fictions that antedate those in *The Sketch Book*. But, what Irving accomplished should not be underrated. He established the short story as a legitimate vehicle for narrative, literary portraiture and pictorialism, and poetic and lyric modes of composition. He thus shaped this new, somewhat unformed type of literary construct into a formidable competitor to the poem, the drama, the novel, and the essay, and he opened the way for the talented writers who were to learn from his example and who created the long list of remarkable American short stories that have since appeared. He thus initiated a brilliant chapter in American literary history by pointing the way for Edgar Allan Poe, Nathaniel Hawthorne, Herman Melville, Henry James, Stephen Crane, Ambrose Bierce, and their 20th-century successors. It is difficult to imagine what the American short story might have become without Irving. Because of him, it has become a glory of American literary art.

The origins of these two stories may be from the folk tales of other countries, but their chief characters are archetypes of American character portraiture in the humorous style. Rip Van Winkle is eloquently imagined as "one of those happy mortals, of foolish, well-oiled dispositions, who take the world easy, eat white bread or brown, whichever can be got with least thought or trouble, and would rather starve on a penny than work for a pound." The shrewish Dame Van Winkle, only briefly apparent in the story, is the perfect image of the termagant wife.

Even Wolf, Rip's inappropriately named dog, is alive on the page. A courageous animal before anything but the lady of the household, he has quickly learned his place: "The moment Wolf entered the house his crest fell, his tail drooped to the ground, or curled between his legs, he sneaked about with a gallows air." After sleeping for twenty years, Rip is blessed with the life of any good man's fantasy; he has survived his horrific wife, he can indulge his laziness at the local tavern, and he has a fantastic story to tell to an inexhaustible supply of credulous listeners.

Irving has the wit to ascribe this delightful story to his friend, Diedrich Knickerbocker, as a "posthumous writing" of the old gentleman. The story itself is thus framed by a headnote explaining its provenance and an endnote attesting its veracity. Knickerbocker claims to have actually talked to the old Rip Van Winkle. Moreover, he has seen a duly notarized statement, "taken before a country justice and signed with a cross, in the justice's own handwriting"—so the story has to be true. On the other hand, the tale of Ichabod Crane in "The Legend of Sleepy Hollow" also comes from the papers of Knickerbocker, but in his endnote the collector of folkish legends cannot vouch to the truth of the story. After all, the story-teller from whom he heard it scarcely believes one-half of the story. Still, even if it is only a fiction, "Sleepy Hollow" gives the reading public a richly portrayed character in Crane, the schoolmaster. Irving is lavish in his physical description:

> He was tall, but exceedingly lank, with narrow shoulders, long arms and legs, hands that dangled a mile out of his sleeves, feet that might have served for shovels, and his whole frame most loosely hung together. His head was small and flat at top, with huge ears, large green glassy eyes, and a long snipe nose, so that it looked like a weather-cock, perched upon his spindle neck, to tell which way the wind blew. To see him striding along the profile of a hill on a windy day, with his clothes bagging and fluttering about him, one might have mistaken him for the genius of famine descending upon the earth, or some scarecrow eloped from a cornfield.

Crane is the very genius of famine, ambitious and always hungry. Imagining his hoped-for marriage to the luscious Katrina Van Tassel, he can see how it might bring wedded bliss, but, mostly, it conjures up the dream of food:

> In his devouring mind's eye, he pictured to himself every roasting pig running about with a pudding in his belly, and an

apple in his mouth; the pigeons were snugly put to bed in a comfortable pie, and tucked in with a coverlet of crust; the geese were swimming in their own gravy; and the ducks pairing cosily in dishes, like snug married couples, with a decent competency of onion sauce.

Irving has a particular talent for portraying animals. Wolf, as we have seen, is a little masterpiece, and Gunpowder, Ichabod's borrowed horse, is extravagantly depicted:

The animal he bestrode was a broken-down plough-horse, that had outlived almost everything but his viciousness. He was gaunt and shagged, with a ewe neck and a head like a hammer; his rusty mane and tail were tangled and knotted with burrs; one eye had lost its pupil, and was glaring and spectral; but the other had the gleam of a genuine devil in it.

The supernatural elements in the story are skillfully managed so that the reader may feel chilled and then relieved to have the Headless Horseman explained away. Though Irving does not portray Ichabod in a sympathetic manner, as he does Rip, one nevertheless is glad that the schoolmaster suffers no lasting ill effects from his ordeal. In fact, if rumors are true, he profits from his experience, for, fleeing his spectral enemy of Sleepy Hollow, he turns to new and interesting careers and, the last we hear of him, he may have even become a politician and a judge.

In some ways it is a misfortune for Irving and *The Sketch Book* that these two brilliant stories put the rest of the contents so decisively in the shade, for the book as a whole is pleasant and appealing to the reader who will stay with it. As William P. Kelly has pointed out, very helpfully,[1] the book's themes should be examined through the device that Irving conceived. That is, they are filtered through the consciousness and spirit of the carefully designated narrator, Geoffrey Crayon. There is an essential separation between the author and the writing ascribed to his created persona, and, if some of the sketches betray a certain sentimentality, the stance is Crayon's, not Irving's.

The Sketch Book is usually taken to be the best that Irving had to offer, and the volumes of sketches that quickly followed it are generally dismissed as pale imitations. This judgment is too harsh for the imaginative felicities of *Bracebridge Hall* (1822) and *Tales of a Traveller* (1824), however. Crayon is again the narrator in *Bracebridge Hall*. He expresses ironic surprise that his European readers have marveled at his

writing "tolerable English." Announcing that his intention is "to paint characters and manners," he presents over fifty sketches whose titles indicate their fairly limited topics and range: "Wives," "Falconry," "Love-Charms," "Gypsies," "May-Day," "Travelling," and "The Haunted House," among others. These genteel, urbane sketches reflect a temperament unwilling to come to grips with the knottier problems of a contemporary world. They are very similar to the pieces in *The Sketch Book* and hardly inferior. Perhaps the critics looked for some advance, some sharpened point of view, or some further awareness in these slightly later sketches, qualities that they do not possess. What *Bracebridge Hall* really lacks is a couple of stories as brilliant as "Rip Van Winkle" and "The Legend of Sleepy Hollow." The stories that the book does contain, notably "Annette Delarbre" and "Dolph Heyliger," are well-written and excellent. They simply are not of the caliber of the two earlier works, and so they, and the collection, have suffered, perhaps unnecessarily, by comparison. A similar case might be made for *Tales of a Traveller*, a European "sketch book." Irving thought highly of this volume. In a letter of December 11, 1824, he wrote, "I have preferred adopting the mode of sketches & short tales rather than long works, because I chose to take a line of writing peculiar to myself; rather than fall into the manner or school of any other writer; and there is a constant activity of thought and a nicety of execution required in writings of the kind, more than the world appears to imagine" (*Letters*, Vol. II, pp. 90–91). Irving is acutely aware that the sketches must be read in the spirit in which they were considered and written. Readers who go to them with a different set of anticipations are sure to be disappointed, and for several generations most readers have been disappointed by *Tales of a Traveller*. Yet, there is much in the book to give pleasure, and perhaps one needs the enthusiasm of Charles Neider, in his introduction to a recent collection, *The Complete Tales*, to make the book palatable and even pleasurable. Neider points out that most of the volume is made up of stories rather than sketches and offers sympathetic comments upon them, especially upon "Buckthorne: or, the Young Man of Great Expectations," a group of pieces that he considers the "masterpiece of the collection."[2]

The later writings of Irving tend to suffer from various defects and readers' prejudices. The biographies that he laboriously composed were, like most biographies, superseded after the generation for which they were written. No one who needs biographical data on George Washington is likely to go to Irving's multi-volumed study (1855–1859) for it. There have been too many discoveries, books, articles, manuscripts come to light, personal recollections of contemporaries, letters, and public papers published in the intervening years and now easily available, as well as reinterpretations of Washington's character and deeds. Something similar might be said of Irving's lives of Christopher Columbus (1828), Oliver Goldsmith (1840), or Mahomet (1850). A biography usually has a brief life. It can outlive its time only if it offers unique materials, as in James Boswell's indispensable personal recollections of Samuel Johnson, or if it has a vivid and satisfying style so that it may be read with pleasure even if its materials have become outdated. Irving's biographies do not rise to either challenge; they are competently handled and can be pleasant to browse through, but not more. It is true that the life of Margaret Davidson that he composed in 1841 has not been superseded, for the good reason that no one in succeeding generations has thought it worthwhile to do more research upon the subject's life and works. Her life was short and probably tragic, but it makes dull reading, and her lamentable poetry is not worth studying.

Irving proved an industrious seeker after literary materials. His Spanish experience gave him a variable return. His Columbus books have outlived their usefulness. *The Conquest of Granada* (1829) is a somewhat dull account, usually ignored. But *Tales of the Alhambra* is in his best vein and deserves to be read widely. It could be called his Spanish "sketch book." Curiously, Charles Neider, though very appreciative of *Tales of a Traveller*, is not much taken with the folktales and sketches of the Spanish collection,[3] but others have been willing to concede their charm and attractiveness.

Irving's return to America in 1832 and his subsequent tours of the country provided the sources of some of his most successful writing. Absent from his native land for seventeen years, he was able to look at it freshly, and surely he saw it with a different perspective than he might have if he had continued to reside in America from 1815 to 1832. His publications profit immensely from this displaced angle of vision. *A Tour on the Prairies* (1835), as he apologetically notes in his introduction, is a "simple narration of every day occurrences, such as happens to everyone who travels the prairies." While it is true that the occurrences are such as might pass under anyone's eyes, the trained journalistic and artistic impulses of an Irving are needed to recreate them in lively and memorable prose. The descriptions of the "grand prairies," the buffalo hunt, the prairie dogs, and the accounts of bear hunting are all rendered by an observant reporter with a knack for getting down the very feel of the occasion. The result is a unified book,

rather than a series of disconnected sketches. Books like the *Tour, Astoria* (1836) and *The Adventures of Captain Bonneville* (1837) all have the virtue of making America as romantic a landscape for the American readers as any they could find in England or Spain. For readers of the present, these are priceless documents that evoke a vanished landscape and call up a timeless past, though Irving depends very little in these narratives upon the resources of humor.

From 1839 to 1841, Irving wrote a series of short pieces under contract to the *Knickerbocker*, one of the best magazines of the period. In 1855, he published these, together with other sketches, in a volume entitled *Wolfert's Roost and Other Papers, Now First Collected.* Irving made no attempt to impose any unity upon the collection. The title piece is taken from his leftover Diedrich Knickerbocker materials, "Mountjoy" is to be associated with the papers of *The Sketch Book* and "The Creole Village" with *A Tour on the Prairies*, and there are Spanish sketches as well. The collection is a grab bag of later materials. It did receive good reviews upon its first appearance, but, in our time, it has been neglected and sometimes derided. It deserves better treatment, for the pieces, apparently written in haste and left unrevised for their book appearance, do retain much of the charm and interest that Irving was usually able to bring to his writing.

Much of the book is enjoyable to read, and one narrative, "The Early Experiences of Ralph Ringwood," is an important piece of Americana. Once more, Irving brings forth Geoffrey Crayon as his imagined narrator to create the framework of the story. Crayon assures the reader that the tale is based upon events in the life of a real person, William P. Duval (1784–1854), and that he has noted down the essentials of the story from conversations with the hero. Duval really existed and served as governor of Florida; Irving did, in fact, interview Duval in 1833 and took notes of their conversation. When an imagined narrator talks with a real person and then concocts a story about another, fictional character, the complicated mix of fact and fiction is likely to be fascinating. The story concerns the initiation of a boy in wilderness America. Ralph Ringwood is allowed to tell his own story in his own words, and, thus, Irving can experiment with the sound of plain language from an unlettered person. The tale is rich in details of Ralph's travels and his encounters with woodsmen and hunters. He tells of meeting a girl, stealing a kiss, then later courting and marrying her. He is brash enough to become a backwoods lawyer without previous training and wins his first case. Irving has tapped a rich body of American experience in this success story, and he tells it in easy, colloquial prose of the kind that eventually came to dominate the literature devoted to the discovery of self in the New World.

Summary

In a very long career marked by popular success, Washington Irving did much to establish many of the characteristic forms of American prose literature. His essays take the best effects from their British models, but he shapes the materials into something possessing a national character. His parody history of New York is an archetypal illustration of comic hoaxing. He is responsible for the first and best short stories produced in America and thus for the long line of distinguished successors who have become a trademark of this country's literature. As a writer who interpreted Great Britain, Spain, and his own country for his readers, he offered a remarkable collection of folktales and legends, antiquarian lore, vivid descriptions of places, and attractive portrayals of human character.

Notes

1. William P. Kelly, "Introduction," in *Selected Writings of Washington Irving* (New York: Random House, 1984), pp. xxiii–xxix.
2. Charles Neider, "Introduction," in *The Complete Tales of Washington Irving* (New York: Doubleday, 1975), p. xxiv.
3. Ibid., p. xxxi.

Selected Bibliography

Primary Sources

The Complete Writings of Washington Irving. Ed. various hands, 1969–present. Madison: University of Wisconsin Press; New York: Twayne Publishers. Irving saw one collected edition of his works through the press (1849–1851), and there have been numerous new editions and reprints over the years, which make the bulk of the author's works easily available in libraries. This most recent of editions has a strong claim to be the most complete and the most authoritative, for it includes the literary works, journals, notebooks, and letters. Much of it has already appeared; some of the most useful volumes, containing helpful introductions, include: *Astoria*, ed. Richard Dilworth Rust (1976); *Bracebridge Hall*, ed. Herbert F. Smith (1977); *The Sketch Book*, ed. Haskell Springer (1978); *The Crayon Miscellany*, ed. Dahlia Kirby Terrell (1979; includes *A Tour on the Prairies*); *Wolfert's Roost*, ed. Roberta Rosenberg (1979); as well as the books on Bonneville, Columbus, and Washington.

Journals and Notebooks, Vol. I, 1803–1806. Ed. Nathalia Wright. Madison: University of Wisconsin Press, 1969. Indispensable source materials for Irving's life and works. More volumes are forthcoming.

Letters. 4 vols. New York: Twayne, 1978–1982. This massive undertaking includes a rich collection of more than twenty-six hundred letters covering the period 1802–1859.

Washington Irving's Contributions to The Corrector. Introduction and Attribution by Martin Roth. Minneapolis: University of Minnesota Press, 1968. This journalism, written in 1804, provides an interesting view of Irving.

Secondary Sources

Bibliography

Springer, Haskell. *Washington Irving: A Reference Guide.* Boston: G. K. Hall, 1976. An invaluable annotated account of scholarship and criticism from 1807 to 1974.

Tuttleton, James W. "Washington Irving." In *Fifteen American Authors Before 1900.* Ed. Earl N. Herbert and Robert A. Rees. Madison: University of Wisconsin Press, 1984. An excellent bibliographical essay, covering scholarship through 1980; helpful guide through the labyrinth of writings about Irving.

Biography

Wagenknecht, Edward. *Washington Irving: Moderation Displayed.* New York: Oxford University Press, 1962. A brief and very useful biography.

Williams, Stanley T. *The Life of Washington Irving.* 2 vols. New York: Oxford University Press, 1935. Monumental and definitive.

Criticism and Scholarship

Bowden, Mary Witherspoon. *Washington Irving.* Boston: Twayne, 1981. A brief but useful introduction to Irving's life and works with a short annotated bibliography.

Hedges, William L. *Washington Irving: An American Study, 1802–1832.* Baltimore: The Johns Hopkins Press, 1965. The best study of Irving's early career.

Kelly, William P. "Introduction." In *Selected Writings of Washington Irving.* Modern Library College Editions. New York: Random House, 1984. An excellent brief critical study of Irving's whole career.

Myers, Andrew B., ed. *A Century of Commentary on the Works of Washington Irving.* Tarrytown, New York: Sleepy Hollow Restorations, 1976. A fine collection of more than forty essays or excerpts, covering the years 1860–1974.

Neider, Charles. "Introduction." In *The Complete Tales of Washington Irving.* New York: Doubleday, 1975. A useful critical statement in a volume that focuses on Irving's short fiction by separating it from the many nonfiction sketches.

Roth, Martin. *Comedy and America: The Lost World of Washington Irving.* Port Washington, N.Y.: Kennikat Press, 1971. Deals with the early writing, especially *A History of New York*.

Douglas Robillard

Jones, Hamilton C.

Born: Greenville County, Virginia, on August 23, 1798

Education: University of North Carolina, B.A., 1818

Marriage: Eliza Henderson, 1820, ten children, six surviving childhood

Died: September 10, 1868

Biography

Hamilton C. ("Ham") Jones was born in Greenville County, Virginia, on August 23, 1798, and taken to Stokes County, North Carolina, when he was an infant. His father died not long after the move, and his mother, Martha, then married Col. James Martin, a widower and a member of a wealthy and prominent family. The Martins were conservative politically, and in a state with strong Republican sentiments, they supported landed and monied interests. Jones followed the Martins's political beliefs: when he was a university student, he supported the Federalists, and after the demise of that party he was passionately committed to Whig principles.

There was a strong educational tradition in the Martin family, and Jones attended the academy for boys at Chapel Hill and then entered the University of North Carolina, class of 1818, where he received a thorough classical education. He was a serious student, graduating fourth in his class, a distinguished one that included the future president, James K. Polk. He remained at the university for a time as a tutor and then read law in New Bern with William Gaston (1778-1844), the most distinguished attorney in the state.

Given Gaston's brilliance and his standing in the legal profession, Jones chose the right person with whom to study, but the decision was not without its dangers for Gaston was a Catholic in an anti-Catholic state. At that time the state constitution forbade anyone who denied "the Truth of the Protestant religion" from holding civil office. Jones's career did not suffer from his close association with a Catholic, though, and his choice of a teacher shows that Jones was independent and not always conventional.

In 1820, after obtaining his license to practice law, Jones married Eliza Henderson (his stepfather Col. James Martin's granddaughter from his first marriage and the only daughter of Major Pleasant Henderson). The young couple moved to Salisbury, where Jones established a successful law practice, presided over a growing family of ten children (six of whom survived infancy), and built up a plantation which he called "Como." In 1832 he founded *The Carolina Watchman*, a Whig newspaper that vigorously opposed the Republican views of the other village paper, *The Western Carolinian*. Jones's paper had a strong political orientation—he deplored the nullification activities in South Carolina and other southern states—but he also envisioned a paper that would "instruct" and "please." Jones's classical education and legal training contributed to the sharpness and literacy of his editorials; he had good taste in the exchange material he chose to include, and his sharp comic sense was often evident in his pages. His own humorous sketches and the comic pieces picked up from the exchanges lightened the tone of the paper.

Jones's publishing activities were carried on in addition to his law practice and his political career. He spent his adult life around his law office and the courts in the western counties of the state, in the state legislature, and in the state supreme court, where he was the reporter. He heard stories from his clients, he observed the activities of the courts, and he exchanged stories with his fellow attorneys. His humorous stories appeared in his own newspaper, which he published until he sold it in 1839, in *Atkinson's Saturday Evening Post*, and in the famous New York sporting paper of the era, *The Spirit of the Times*.

His most widely published and imitated story was "Cousin Sally Dilliard," and he signed his later stories "By the author of 'Cousin Sally Dilliard.'" His identity was known to many, but he did not attempt to capitalize on his renown as a humorist: he did not go on the lecture circuit, and he did not collect his stories in a book. In fact, he ceased to publish in the years before the Civil War, and by the time of his death in 1868, he was largely forgotten as a humorist.

Literary Analysis

"Scattered through the South and Southwest," Franklin J. Meine wrote in *Tall Tales of the Southwest: An Anthology of Southern and Southwestern Humor 1830-1860*, "there sprang up a picturesque local-color group of humorists who flourished in bar-rooms, on law circuits, on steamboats and in the wide open spaces." One of the most talented of these southern humorists was Ham Jones, the conservative attorney who lived in the Piedmont area of the Old North State. He came from a family of wealth and position; he was an Episcopalian living among fundamentalists. He was university educated, a man of taste and refinement living in a remote area of the state among thousands of ill-educated Tar Heels, many of whom were in need of his legal services. He was a gregarious man, and while he was an aristocrat, he was fascinated by the ways, customs, and speech of the Tar Heels. He was less condescending in his attitude toward the "crackers" (impoverished whites in the South) than many others of his fellow humorists; in fact, Jones's humor is subversive, for in his stories the rational, ordered world yearned for by the well-to-do Whigs is replaced by an irrational world in constant disorder.

His first published story, "Cousin Sally Dilliard," appeared in *Atkinson's Saturday Evening Post* on August 6, 1831. It was an immediate success for its humor comes through easily when it is read, and it is a story that can be told with great comic effect. The setting of the story is rural North Carolina; there had been a fight at Captain Rice's entertainment, brought about, no doubt, by the corn liquor being consumed in great quantities. The characters in the story include a pompous young lawyer whose language is highly inflated and a drunken witness who speaks the rural dialect and seems to know that his rambling testimony is an act of subornation. The humor derives from the characters, their language, and the constant repetition of irrelevant details. The judge is unable to control the garrulous witness. The truth about the "riot" is not discovered, and laughter and disorder, not justice, prevail. William T. Porter reprinted the story several times in *The Spirit of the Times* and in his influential collection, *The Big Bear of Arkansas and Other Sketches*. It was often imitated and adapted in print, but it was a story to be told, and it became, with variations, a staple in the repertoire of nineteenth-century American raconteurs, including Abraham Lincoln.

Jones's next story, "The Lost Breeches," appeared in the *Carolina Watchman* on January 19, 1833. In a lengthy introduction Jones identified the teller of this story, a Captain Kincannon, who had been a Revolutionary war hero. Jones had known Kincannon for many years, and he described in detail the captain's peculiarities of speech and manner, anticipating Mark Twain's belief that the *manner* of telling a comic story is the important thing. The story contains many elements of the traditional folktale: the yokel who makes a fool of himself, is robbed, and learns a lesson. Kincannon adds a moral tag, something that Jones does not do in the stories that he controls. Jones does allow the reader to have some sympathy for the yokel, for after suffering the indignity of losing his breeches, he recognizes the foolishness of his blustering ways and decides to stay at home.

Ham Jones was at his most antic in his short *Carolina Watchman* contributions published under the heading "Salisbury Omnibus." Weekly newspapers in the South in the 1830s were filled with state and national political news, cultural and literary stories from English and American exchanges, poetry, agricultural information, and reprinted anecdotes, and they printed little local news. Jones's "Omnibus" pieces were unusual, for his observations range from comic accounts of life in Salisbury to literary spoofs. Some of his jokes are political, others are racial—in one, which effectively uses black dialect, his intent is to show that Abolitionists did not understand the peculiar institution of slavery. He was contemptuous of a political preacher, and he gleefully exposed the humbuggery of a phrenologist. At their best, these humorous "Omnibus" pieces are similar to today's "The Talk of the Town" items in *The New Yorker*.

Jones also inserted his own anecdotes and humorous sketches into the *Carolina Watchman* at places other than under the "Omnibus" heading. They show him perfecting his use of Southern dialect and pointing out the foibles of mankind. His language is racy, but he generally avoids violence and overtly sexual subjects.

"Cousin Sally Dilliard" was a favorite story of William T. Porter, editor of *The Spirit of the Times*, and he began to publish Jones's other stories. The first original sketch used by Porter was "McAlpin's Trip to Charleston," published in *The Spirit* on July 11, 1846, and then reprinted in *A Quarter Race in Kentucky and Other Sketches*. McAlpin was a rustic sent to the city to negotiate the purchase of a plot of land. He was badly treated in Charleston; when he asked directions from a dandy, his civil request was met with, *"Go to h--l, you fool!"* At Col. Lamar's home, where he had gone about the property, he was greatly impressed by the furnishings and by the beauty of Mrs. Lamar, but he was unnerved when his attempt to carve a turkey ended in a horrible fiasco. Jones reworked the usual tale of the country bumpkin in the city, and the reader laughs at but has sympathy for the unsophisticated McAlpin, as well as for Mrs. Lamar, whose placid world was shattered by McAlpin's attempts at gentlemanly gentility.

Porter next published "Going to Muster in North Carolina" in *The Spirit of the Times* on July 18, 1846. At that time in the state all free white males between the ages of eighteen and forty-five were members of the militia and were required to report for muster at least two times a year. These musters were characterized by heavy drinking, betting, fighting, and little useful military training. Jones has the story told by one of his politician friends, a friend recalling the day that he went to his first muster. The boy watches an old man prepare for the holiday, but the old man's wife forbids him to go, fearing that he will spend all his money, get drunk, and wallow in the dirt. The actual muster itself is not described, but it is clear that Jones is holding up to scorn the institution of the muster. As in many of his sketches, the situation is comic but the story itself is not.

"The Sandy Creek Literary Society," published in *The Spirit of the Times* on August 15, 1846, is a typical piece of southwestern humor. It is obvious that the author of the story is an aristocrat satirizing the pretensions and the religious fervor of the unwashed. Jones did not tamper with the formula, and it is one of his most successful stories. It is a framework story told by Fred Thompson, a tavern keeper who lived near Salisbury. He liked to tell stories about his ignorant neighbors, especially Squire Ben Primm, a man who always pronounced "o" as if it were "a"—thus *harse* for *horse*. The effect of this peculiarity is similar to Victor Borge's monologues with verbal punctuation. In this story, the world is in comic chaos.

"The Round Robin," drawing its form from the Declaration of Independence, was a comic attack on the food, drink, service, and accommodations of taverns and inns. Lawyers on the circuit were at the mercy of the inn keepers, and it is clear that Jones intended his satiric sketch to be an indictment of the appalling conditions that travellers often found on their journeys. The story originally appeared in *The Spirit of the Times* on August 22, 1846.

"The Frenchman and His Menagerie" was published in *The Spirit of the Times* on March 16, 1850. It is Jones's most violent sketch: a group of mountain ruffians, unhappy at the high price of admission to the menagerie and enraged by the lack of wild animals, violently attack the owner, a Frenchman who does not speak English well, and his Yankee partner. The ruffians assault the puma (described as a "tiger" by the Frenchman), instigate a fight between the puma and a monkey, and, when the monkey is killed, engage in a parody of justice, setting up a mock court and trying the puma for murder. The mock trial ends in a "hung" jury, and one of the dispensers of "justice" then steals into the "courtroom" and hangs the puma until it is "dead, dead, dead." Jones shows the dark side of southern life—its suspicion of outsiders, its cruelty and sadism, and its lawlessness, and yet Jones has some sympathy for the ruffians—they will not be made "suckers" by the two con men who own the menagerie. An officer of the court, a stalwart member of the legal profession, Jones presents justice in the courtroom as a travesty.

Jones's last story in *The Spirit of the Times* was "Abel Hucks in a Tight Place," which appeared on August 23, 1851. Abel Hucks tells his own story in a letter to Porter, editor of the paper. Abel had suffered all of his life from a sense of inadequacy—he was short and poor. He had resorted to moonshine, and when he was drunk, he fought with a tall man. Abel was brought into court and sentenced to the stocks, but Union County was only recently organized and did not yet have stocks. The sheriff improvised by putting Abel's legs through the rails of a fence. Abel was humiliated and asked Porter: "I want to know whether it is accordin' to the American constitution to put a fellers legs through a rail fence because they haven't got stocks in a new county." To Abel, *real* stocks would have been tolerable but not a rail fence. Abel has the reader's sympathy when he threatens to move to South Carolina and help make a constitution that forbids such indignities.

Jones was clearly interested in the way a story was told. In those stories with a narrator ("The Lost Breeches" and "The Sandy Creek Literary Society" in particular) the narrator's manner of speaking is highly important, the framework of the story adding yet another level of humor. He liked to experiment with forms; he began his humorous career with a work that was to become a classic—"Cousin Sally Dilliard"—told almost entirely in dialogue. A good story teller, having read "Cousin Sally," could then improvise, work out speech patterns and facial expressions, and present his own version to listeners. At times ("The Frenchman and His Menagerie" and "McAlpin's Trip to Charleston") Jones has an omniscient observer tell the story; the stories read well, but they could easily be adapted for oral telling, as could "Abel Hucks in a Tight Place," cast in the form of a letter to the editor. Jones was concerned with authenticity of speech, and he had a good ear for the language of the people he listened to.

Summary

A man of property and position, Ham Jones used his humor to reflect the life he saw around him in North Carolina before the Civil War. He was aware of the ignorance and violence in his society, but he avoided moralizing. He often subverted the accepted social order for he had sympathy for the vital lives and expressive language of the illiterates and ruffians of North Carolina. His surviving sketches, stories, and anecdotes do not make up a large body of work, but they do capture the vitality of his region in the decades before the war. In his stories he followed the stated object of *The Spirit of the Times*: "To paint 'life as it is,' without the artificial embellishments of romance. . . . For it is certainly no more improper to record the acts of men than to promulgate them morally to the world."

Selected Bibliography

Primary Sources

Carolina Watchman, 1832-1839. Fewer than half of the issues of Jones's newspaper are extant, and many of his stories are lost. Many of the humorous stories are not signed; Richard Walser assigns the unsigned "A Buncombe Story" to Jones, but it is not Jones's style and we have not included it in this discussion.

Meine, Franklin J., ed. *Tall Tales of the Southwest: An Anthology of Southern and Southwestern Humor 1830-1860*. New York: Knopf, 1930. An authoritative collection.

The Spirit of the Times, 1831-1861. This sporting magazine contained much of the best southern and southwestern humor.

Secondary Sources

Walser, Richard. "Ham Jones: Southern Folk Humorist," *Journal of American Folklore*, 78 (October-December 1965): 295-316. Collects Jones's stories and those ascribed to him. The best account, to date, of Jones's life and work.

Yates, Norris W. *William T. Porter and The Spirit of the Times*. Baton Rouge: Louisiana State University Press, 1957. The standard study of this important journal.

Willene Hendrick
George Hendrick

Kaufman, George S.

Born: Pittsburgh, Pennsylvania, on November 16, 1889

Education: Law School at Western University of Pennsylvania (University of Pittsburgh), 1907; Alveine School of Dramatic Arts (New York City), 1910; playwriting courses at Columbia University, 1914 and 1915. Received no degrees

Marriages: Beatrice Bakrow, March 15, 1917, died, 1945, one child; Leueen McGrath, May 26, 1949, divorced, 1957

Died: June 2, 1961

Biography

The son of Joseph Simon and Henrietta Myers, George S. Kaufman was born in Pittsburgh, Pennsylvania, on November 16, 1889. His father held various jobs that took the family from Pittsburgh to New Castle back to Pittsburgh, then to Paterson, New Jersey. George was educated in public schools. He wrote his first play at age fourteen and joined a dramatic society at the family Temple Rodef Shalom, where he showed ability as an actor. After graduating from high school in 1907, he briefly attended law school at Western University of Pennsylvania but withdrew during the first term because of illness. He then worked at numerous jobs: surveyor, clerk, stenographer, and salesman, while continuing to write.

Beginning in 1909, his humorous verses appeared regularly in Franklin Pierce Adams's "Always in Good Humor" column in the *New York Evening Mail*. In 1911, he wrote a similar column for Frank Munsey's *Washington Times*, but this job lasted only one year when Munsey discovered that Kaufman was a Jew. Kaufman then moved to New York to pursue his vocation as a writer, first as a reporter for the *New York Tribune*, a post he gained through Adams's assistance. At first signing his contributions GSK, Kaufman later was given a byline. In 1915, with the recommendation of Adams, he was hired by the *Evening Mail* to establish a new humorous column, another job that proved short-lived when the newspaper changed hands later that year. Kaufman then returned to the *Tribune* as a reporter in the drama department. While trying to make his way in journalism, he attended the Alveine School of Dramatic Arts (1910), took courses in playwriting from Hatcher Hughes and Clayton Hamilton at Columbia University (1914 and 1915), and continued to write plays, penning a one-act, "That Infernal Machine," in 1915, and a three-act, *Going Up,* in 1917.

Kaufman met Beatrice Bakrow in 1916, and after an eight-month courtship they were married March 15, 1917. Within six months, George left the *Tribune* to become a drama reporter for the *New York Times* and within a short period replaced Brock Pemberton as drama editor, a post that he held until 1930. In the same year he was hired by the producer, George C. Tyler, to rewrite a "Crook" play that had experienced problems prior to its New York opening. Kaufman's work was so extensive that he was given author credit. The piece, *Someone in the House,* was not a success but launched his theatrical career and also that of actress Lynn Fontanne. The year did not end happily for George and Beatrice, however, as their first child, a son, was stillborn. This event destroyed their physical relationship, and while they would remain married, they made a practice of extramarital affairs. Kaufman's affair with actress Mary Astor created a front-page scandal in 1936 when newspapermen gained access to her diary.

In 1919, Kaufman met Marc Connelly, also a writer from Pittsburgh, and the two became friends and collaborators. For producer Tyler, Kaufman rewrote a Danish play, which failed to reach New York, and with Connelly created a vehicle for Fontanne, which drew upon one of Franklin Pierce Adams's most popular newspaper characters, the dimwitted but charming Dulcinea. *Dulcy,* as the comedy was titled, was a huge success that ran for 246 performances, establishing both writers as popular playwrights.

Success propelled Kaufman into a highly theatrical lifestyle that included regular lunches at the Algonquin Hotel Round Table with such writers and artists as Alexander Woollcott, Frank Adams, Robert Benchley, Dorothy Parker, and Heywood Broun. Dubbed the "Algonquin Wits" by some and the "Vicious Circle" by others, they set the tone for social discourse in New York City during the 1920s. The actions of members became legendary with the creation of a poker club called "Thanatopsis," and in 1922 with a revue *No Sirree!*, a parody of a Russian revue, *Chauve-Souris*, to which all members contributed material. As the 1920s progressed, the success of Kaufman's plays in New York and on the road, his openings in London, and his sales to Hollywood helped fuel his growing reputation as a playwright and celebrity.

In 1922, Kaufman and Connelly collaborated on *To the Ladies*, which had a respectable run, and *Merton of the Movies*, which became a smash hit, playing for 398 performances. In 1923, their first musical, *Helen of Troy, New York*, lost money, as did *The Deep Tangled Wildwood*, but the following year they achieved success by reworking a minor German expressionistic play into a satire on American materialism entitled *Beggar on Horseback*. Another musical, *Be Yourself*, had a short run the same year, after which Kaufman and Connelly parted company, their different work habits making further collaboration unlikely. A compulsive writer, Kaufman involved himself in multiple projects and could not understand why Connelly lacked the same zeal.

In 1925, Kaufman wrote his only full-length play without a collaborator, *The Butter and Egg Man*, which ran for 241 performances, but he preferred to work with a collaborator and had joined earlier with novelist Edna Ferber to produce *Minick* (1924), a modest success. They would write five more plays together, including hits *The Royal Family* (1927), *Dinner at Eight* (1932), and *Stage Door* (1936). Ferber brought to the partnership a penchant for sentimental, moralistic, and family melodramas.

Morrie Ryskind also wrote six plays with Kaufman, including his anonymous contribution to *The Cocoanuts* (1925), with a score by Irving Berlin, and *Animal Crackers* (1928). Both musical comedies starred the Marx Brothers. In 1930, Ryskind revised Kaufman's book for *Strike Up the Band*, a musical by Kaufman and the Gershwins that had failed in 1927, and it became a modest hit, running for 191 performances. Their most successful collaboration, *Of Thee I Sing*, again featured the score of George and Ira Gershwin, had an extended run of 446 performances, and won a Pulitzer Prize in 1932. Less successful were *Let 'Em Eat Cake* (1933), again with the Gershwins, and a nonmusical satire, *Bring on the Girls* (1934), which closed out of

town. Ryskind found political satire to his liking, unlike Kaufman, who expressed few political views.

Kaufman worked with numerous other writers, including Herman J. Mankiewicz on *The Good Fellow* (1926), Ring Lardner on *June Moon* (1929), Alexander Woollcott on *The Channel Road* (1929) and *The Dark Tower* (1933), Howard Dietz on *The Band Wagon* (1931), and Katherine Dayton on *First Lady* (1935). His most successful collaborator in the 1930s, however, was Moss Hart, beginning with *Once in a Lifetime* (1930), which played for 401 performances. The team of Kaufman and Hart became associated closely in the public mind. Their *Merrily We Roll Along* (1934), a modest success, was followed by the smash hit *You Can't Take It with You* (1936), which won a Pulitzer Prize. In quick succession they wrote a musical, *I'd Rather Be Right* (1937), with musical score by Richard Rodgers and Lorenz Hart, *The Fabulous Invalid* (1938), a history of the American theater, an historical pageant, *The American Way* (1939), and another blockbuster, *The Man Who Came to Dinner* (1939), which played for 739 performances, an extraordinary run for the time. Their last collaboration, *George Washington Slept Here* (1940), was not a hit, after which Hart withdrew from the partnership to establish professional independence. Kaufman would never again enjoy such sustained success, although he crafted hits with other writers, including Howard Teichmann on *The Solid Gold Cadillac* (1953) and Leueen McGrath and Abe Burrows on *Silk Stockings* (1955).

Kaufman acquired fame also as a director, staging twenty-four of his own scripts, plus twenty more from other writers—these included *The Front Page* (1928), *Of Mice and Men* (1937), *My Sister Eileen* (1940), *Guys and Dolls* (1950), and *Romanoff and Juliet* (1957). As a director, his forte was comedy, and he was a master of comic timing. His skills were often called upon to "doctor" plays of friends whose plays were having problems in rehearsals. In 1951, Kaufman won his only Antoinette Perry Award for directing *Guys and Dolls*.

He died June 2, 1961, in New York City.

Literary Analysis

Kaufman owed the beginnings of his career as a humorist to Franklin P. Adams. Not only did Adams publish Kaufman's early humorous verses but *Dulcy* drew upon Adams's fictitious newspaper character, the scatterbrained Dulcinea. Kaufman's penchant for collaboration, however, makes an analysis of his comedies difficult. There is clearly a different tone established with each collaborator: flippant and satirical with Connelly; more serious and melodramatic with Ferber; humorous and whimsical but sentimental with Hart; and fantastic and satirical with Morrie Ryskind. Still, certain characteristics reappear frequently, suggesting if not a distinctive Kaufman style then a preference for similar subjects and plot situations. A brief analysis of his most successful collaborations with Connelly and Hart will provide insight into Kaufman as an American humorist.

Much of the fun in *Dulcy* comes from viewing an old-fashioned child-woman in the age of the suffragette. With the new woman demanding not only the vote but also equality in family and career matters, there were comic possibilities in presenting her as a creature of charm, guile, and intuition rather than logic and reason. Dulcy passes off bromides as gems of wisdom (i.e., "My books are my best friends," "Every cloud has a silver lining," and "A burnt child dreads the fire"). "She has a way of speaking an age-old platitude," the authors note, "as though it were a wise and original thought—a little thing casually tossed off in the course of conversation." Married three months, she has "practically discharged" her husband's secretary and now has involved herself in his business affairs by inviting businessman Roger Forbes and his family for the weekend to help promote a merger. Dulcy makes a mess of everything. She plans 18 holes of golf, an evening of bridge, an eight-reel silent film, and a game of billiards when Forbes has a bad back and hates all such activities. She disrupts the lives of all around her, but with such "bubbling good humor" that she remains loveable and sympathetic. In the end, Dulcy proves effective in disarming her victims by the traditional womanly methods. The men are no match for her machinations and they seem to enjoy being manipulated by such a charming creature.

This plot device also served Kaufman and Connelly well for their next play, *To the Ladies*, which presents another newly married wife in much more modest surroundings. Elsie Beebe lives in an apartment with her husband Leonard, a clerk for a piano company, who is depicted as a middle-class bumpkin stuffed with clichés about Florida real-estate deals, get-rich-quick ads, and self-help exercises in popular magazines. Elsie is the practical and sensible member of the family who allows Leonard the illusion that he makes all of the important decisions when in reality he makes none. Leonard's boss is also manipulated by his own wife, so it is implied that "behind every successful man is a woman."

The authors aim their satirical barbs at the boring rituals of middle-class and business life in America. Their first act lampoons the Beebes' attempt at entertaining the boss at home. In the second act, Leonard competes for the post of head clerk by giving a talk at a company dinner, a self-serving affair ridiculed by Kaufman and Connelly in the play's funniest scene. The young man competing with Leonard speaks first and delivers the same speech that Leonard has memorized from "Five hundred Speeches for All Occasions." Theater insiders would have understood and enjoyed the joke of naming this character Thomas Wood Baker, and his talk Speech 47. Leonard is paralyzed with fright but Elsie comes to the rescue by claiming that her tongued-tied husband "suddenly got laryngitis," and then delivering a low-key talk about the need for humanity in the business world. Leonard accepts the applause and the post.

In the last act, Kaufman and Connelly ridicule the clichés of the American business office with its elaborate system of buzzers, telephones, index files, and pencil sharpeners that do not work. Male egos constantly need perks: secretaries, cigars, Haverfield Bond stationery, haircuts, shoe shines, and the inner sanctum of private offices. These men are incapable of meaningful work, yet Leonard is preparing a memo arguing that men in business are superior to women. In the world of this play, wives make important decisions about hiring and firing, and husbands depend upon them for support and advice. The play ends with Elsie and the boss's wife making plans to lunch with the spouse of a new appointee, who will clearly make the decisions for her husband. The comic situtations are timeless: as old as Aristophanes's *Lysistrata* but as contemporary as George Bernard Shaw's *Man and Superman*.

Kaufman and Connelly then aimed their quips at the silent-movie industry. They turned Harry Leon Wilson's *Merton of the Movies* from a serialized story in *Saturday Evening Post* (1922) into a four-act comedy about the adventures of Merton Gill, a clerk in Gashwiler's General Store in Simsbury, Illinois. Merton saves his money and goes to Hollywood to become a star. Like other Kaufman heroes he is first seen as a naïve but likeable bumpkin who wises up to the real world through the help of the heroine. At the beginning, Merton reads movie magazines and has taken a correspondence course in film acting from a bureau in Kansas. He idolizes silent-film stars Beulah Baxter, "the wonder woman of the silver screen," and Harold Parmalee because he believes that they are serious artists.

In the second act, Merton is hanging around a Hollywood studio lot. Although the authors had not been to Hollywood at this time, they did not shy away from satirizing the silly plots, self-serving and ignorant directors, stupid stars, and the false nature of the motion picture industry.

The movie business is depicted as being filled with absurd rituals and large egos—little different from the businesses portrayed in *To the Ladies* and *Dulcy*. The success of *Merton of the Movies* depended upon a proven conceit: "Flips" Montague, an actress who doubles for Beulah Baxter, takes an interest in Merton and educates him to the ways of movie life. Like Dulcy and Elsie, she manipulates those around her (including Merton) to attain success for him. He discovers that his ideals about movies are misplaced because filmmaking is not an art but a business.

Beggar on Horseback (1924) was suggested by Paul Apel's *Hans Sonnenstossers Hollenfahrt*, a minor expressionistic comedy first performed in Germany in 1912. It includes familiar Kaufman and Connelly ingredients: satirical thrusts at business and middle-class life, and a naive young man assisted by a more knowing young woman. But, there are less familiar elements including unsympathetic characters and disjointed and fragmented action. The plot revolves around Neil McRae's decision to give up sweet Cynthia, the girl next door, for wealthy Gladys Cady. In a dream sequence, Neil marries Gladys and prepares to work for her father. Accompanied by jazz music, the wedding ceremony takes on an unreal quality. Gladys introduces the guests in a "rhythmic chant." Her bouquet consists of banknotes. Her new home consists of marble columns and velvet curtains, and comes with twelve butlers. Neil's father-in-law wears golf attire and a telephone attached to his chest. At a Board of Directors meeting Neil delivers a speech similar to what Leonard Beebe had planned in *To the Ladies*. Board members act and speak in a mechanical manner with the dollar being their only objective.

To gain his freedom, Neil kills Gladys and her family. Newspapers publish sensational headlines, and he is brought to trial in an obvious parody of both the legal and political systems. Found guilty, he is sentenced to write popular music at the Cady Consolidated Art Factory. At the play's end, Neil awakes from this dream to reject Gladys and marry the faithful Cynthia. *Beggar on Horseback* was regarded as innovative because of its expressionistic characteristics. Its form, however, seems as much indebted to American silent films as to German expressionistic plays.

Kaufman's next hit, *The Butter and Egg Man*, was written without a collaborator although in plot and style it closely follows the Kaufman-Connelly formula. The play satirizes the process of producing on Broadway in the 1920s and does to the legitimate theatre what *Merton of the Movies* did to silent films. In the first act, two desperate producers, Joe Lehman and Jack McClure, are soliciting funding for their new production. Lehman's wife Fanny is too smart to invest for she has attended a rehearsal. The play seems doomed until McClure meets Peter Jones from Chillicothe, Ohio, a "butter-and-egg man"—the term denoting an out-of-town sucker with a bankroll. Peter is young and no match for Broadway sharpies Lehman and McClure, who separate him from $20,000 of his inheritance. In truth, Peter needs little persuasion since he has fallen under the spell of the office girl, sweet Jane Weston.

In the second act, the play is undergoing out-of-town tryouts in Syracuse. The producers gather after the opening performance in Peter's room to discuss needed changes. Advice is sought indiscriminately from everyone, including the switchboard operator. Even a play doctor from New York arrives to assist in what seems a parody of Kaufman's own role in such matters. Recognizing that they have a failure on their hands, Lehman and McClure sell the show to an unsuspecting Peter for $10,000, which he raises the next day from the hotel assistant manager, Oscar Fritchie—the new butter-and-egg man.

In act three the play has become a smash hit to everyone's surprise except Peter's. "It's what the public wants—that's all," he lectures Jane; "the reason you mustn't ever be surprised at a play like this being a hit is that it's so full of heart interest. That's what the public wants—heart interest—and menace." When asked by Oscar how he knows what the public wants, Peter replies: "It's easy. They always want the same thing." Kaufman's own career suggests that he closely followed Peter's principles.

Kaufman's collaborations with Connelly together with his *The Butter and Egg Man* offered the public topical, witty, and romantic comedies characterized by satirical attacks upon American business practices, middle-class morality, and the fraud of show business. They struck the right tone in the 1920s, as did the writings of Sinclair Lewis, F. Scott Fitzgerald, Eugene O'Neill, and H.L. Mencken. Small-town life was seen as provincial and dull; the middle classes were perceived as being preoccupied with business and money making; and theater and the new medium of silent films was pictured as businesses masquerading as art. Unlike their colleagues, however, Kaufman and Connelly only challenged traditional values before reaffirming them in the last act. In tone, they were never too far ahead of their audience.

Kaufman's collaborations with Moss Hart in the 1930s caught the spirit and emotions of the country during the Great Depression. *You Can't Take It with You* (1936) suggested that the eccentric characters of the Martin Vanderhof household are happier than the Wall Street Kirbys who work at jobs they dislike in order to pile up wealth that they do not need. Topical references—i.e., Mrs. Roosevelt, the Russian Five-Year Plan, Securities Commission, J-men, Communism, relief rolls, income tax—made the comedy contemporary. The main plot involves the love affair of Vanderhof's granddaughter Alice Sycamore and young Tony Kirby. The lovers are separated after a disastrous social occasion—a favorite Kaufman device—in which the Kirbys come to dinner on the wrong evening. They are reunited at the end of the play through the efforts of Grandpa Vanderhof. Interest is maintained throughout by eccentric characters doing eccentric things: for example, Paul Sycamore manufactures fireworks in the basement; Grandpa Vanderhof faces arrest for evasion of income tax; and federal agents arrest everyone in the house, including the Kirbys, for illegally manufacturing the fireworks. The opposition of the Kirbys to the marriage of Alice and Tony also serves to create dramatic tension.

Grandpa Vanderhof is a new type for a Kaufman play. He resembles the traditional Yankee character in appearing to be naïve when in reality he is crafty and shrewd. Grandpa serves up large doses of wisdom and simple piety, including two stage prayers, while refusing to pay taxes or hold down a regular job. There are no villains in the piece. Even the Kirbys are foolish rather than evil. Eccentric characters including Italians, Russians, and blacks live under the same roof and Grandpa presides as a kind and wise family patriarch. The satire is gentle and the situations humorous although the play's tone is more sentimental than the Kaufman–Connelly plays. *You Can't Take It with You* reaffirms such basic American values as individualism and nonconformity but places these attributes within a warm and understanding community.

The Man Who Came to Dinner (1939), unlike the earlier piece, ignores the Depression and deals with characters who have escaped its ravages. The play puts the eccentric Sheridan Whiteside in the middle-class Stanley home in Mesalia, Ohio, after Whiteside injures himself while on a celebrity visit. Initially, the audience is appalled by his aggressive and selfish behavior and sympathies lie with the Stanleys. As the play progresses, however, it becomes evident that the provincialism of the Stanleys is worse than the selfishness of Whiteside. This comic alazon-eiron convention dates from the Greeks. The alazon is a braggart or pretender to knowledge, while the eiron is one who is thought a fool. In the course of the play their roles are reversed. In *The Man Who Came to Dinner*, the sensualist Whiteside ends up the wise man while the puritanical Mr. Stanley defines himself as a fool.

Kaufman's collaborations with other writers provide a catalog of stylistic variations. Ferber-

Kaufman plays are more realistic and less farcical than others. His *June Moon* with Ring Lardner contains a harder edge than either the Connelly or Hart collaborations, though in treatment it resembles the former. His joint efforts with Morrie Ryskind are political in nature but in tone and style also resemble the Kaufman-Connelly plays. Farce and satire were his forte, and Kaufman at his best cleverly mixes the two.

Summary

George S. Kaufman set the style and tone of American stage comedy between 1920 and 1950 with witty and satirical dialogue that crackled with bon mots. Author or co-author of over 40 plays and musical productions, Kaufman usually worked with a collaborator, the most famous being Moss Hart, Marc Connelly, Morrie Ryskind, and Edna Ferber. At least twenty-five of his plays were hits and two won Pulitzer Prizes, making Kaufman the most commercially successful playwright of his generation. Comedies still revived in the 1980s include Kaufman and Hart's *You Can't Take It with You* and *The Man Who Came to Dinner*; Kaufman and Connelly's *Beggar on Horseback*; and Kaufman and Ferber's *The Royal Family*.

Selected Bibliography

Primary Sources

The Butter and Egg Man. New York: Boni and Liveright, 1926.

(with Marc Connelly.) *Dulcy*. New York: G.P. Putnam's, 1921.

———. *To the Ladies! Contemporary American Plays*. Ed. Arthur Hobson Quinn. New York: Charles Scribner's Sons, 1923, pp. 297–376.

———. *Beggar on Horseback*. New York: Boni and Liveright, 1924.

———. *Merton of the Movies*. New York: Samuel French, 1925.

(with Katherine Dayton.) *First Lady*. New York: Random House, 1935.

(with Edna Ferber.) *Minick*. New York: Samuel French, 1925.

———. *The Royal Family*. Garden City: Doubleday, 1928.

———. *Dinner at Eight*. New York: Samuel French, 1935.

———. *Stage Door*. Garden City: Doubleday, 1936.

———. *The Land Is Bright*. Garden City: Doubleday, 1941.

———. *Bravo!* New York: Dramatists Play Service, 1949.

(with Moss Hart.) *Once in a Lifetime*. New York: Farrar and Rinehart, 1930.

———. *Merrily We Roll Along*. New York: Random House, 1934.

———. *You Can't Take It with You*. New York: Farrar and Rinehart, 1937.

———. *I'd Rather Be Right*. New York: Random House, 1937.

————. *The Fabulous Invalid.* New York: Random House, 1938.

————. *The American Way.* New York: Random House, 1939.

————. *The Man Who Came to Dinner.* New York: Random House, 1939.

————. *George Washington Slept Here.* New York: Random House, 1940.

(with Ring Lardner.) *June Moon.* New York: Charles Scribner's Sons, 1930.

(with Leueen McGrath.) *The Small Hours.* New York: Dramatists Play Service, 1951.

————. *Fancy Meeting You Again.* New York: Dramatists Play Service, 1952.

(with Herman J. Mankiewicz.) *The Good Fellow.* New York: Samuel French, 1931.

(with John P. Marquand.) *The Late George Apley.* New York: Dramatists Play Service, 1946.

(with Morrie Ryskind.) *Of Thee I Sing.* New York: Alfred Knopf, 1932.

————. *Let 'Em Eat Cake.* New York: Alfred Knopf, 1933.

(with Howard Teichmann.) *The Solid Gold Cadillac.* New York: Random House, 1954.

(with Alexander Woollcott.) *The Dark Tower.* New York: Samuel French, 1937.

Secondary Sources

Dorgan, Charity Anne. "George S. Kaufman." *Contemporary Authors.* Vol. 108. Ed. Hal May. Detroit: Gale, 1962-1987, p. 255-264. This highly compact reference contains dates of original productions, an interview with Scott Meredith about Kaufman (by Jean W. Ross) and an invaluable bibliography.

Goldstein, Malcolm. *George S. Kaufman: His Life, His Theater.* New York: Oxford University Press, 1979. This is now the standard reference on Kaufman. In twenty-three chapters it covers his life and career offering valuable insights into his collaborations, his friendships, his love affairs, his life in Hollywood, his directing projects, and his influence upon the American theater. Goldstein writes well and his research efforts are impressive.

Hark, Ina Rae. "George S. Kaufman." *Dictionary of Literary Biography.* Vol. 7. Ed. John MacNicholas. Detroit: Gale, 1982-1985, p. 11-26. An excellent short reference on Kaufman, this entry contains specific dates on productions and published plays and a perceptive analysis of his various collaborations.

Hart, Moss. *Act One.* New York: Random House, 1959. This autobiography is helpful in providing another view of the Kaufman-Hart working relationship.

Meredith, Scott. *George S. Kaufman and His Friends.* Garden City, N.Y.: Doubleday, 1974. This biography covers Kaufman's life and career and was the standard reference until Goldstein's book.

Teichmann, Howard. *George S. Kaufman: An Intimate Portrait.* New York: Atheneum, 1971. This is not a biography but a chatty and informal portrait of the playwright. Teichmann's views are more personal and less objective than either Meredith's or Goldstein's.

Tice L. Miller

Keillor, Garrison

Born: Anoka, Minnesota, on August 7, 1942

Education: University of Minnesota, B.A., 1966

Marriage: Mary Guntzel, 1965, divorced, 1976, one child; Ulla Skaerved, 1986

Biography

Garrison Keillor was born to John P. and Grace R. (Denham) Keillor in Anoka, Minnesota, on August 7, 1942. Keillor always wanted to be a writer, but he did not have an easy time getting to where he could live on what he earned by writing. After finishing high school in Anoka he attended the University of Minnesota where he worked at the university radio station. When he graduated in 1966, he failed to find work in publishing and returned to Minnesota and radio, doing a five-day-a-week early morning classical music show for a public radio station at St. John's University in Collegeville. The program came to be known as the "Prairie Home Morning Show" and moved to the Twin Cities of Minneapolis-St. Paul, where the format was changed. On KSJN he began to play jazz and country music, and deliver fake commercials; Keillor also began to make references to a small town named Lake Wobegon.

Literary Analysis

In 1974, Keillor went to Nashville, Tennessee, to do a piece for *The New Yorker* on the Grand Ole Opry, and from this he got the idea of doing his own evening radio show. His first show was broadcast on July 6, 1974, and "Prairie Home Companion" has been on the air since. (Keillor has recently announced his intention to stop doing the show.) The broadcast takes place every Saturday evening for two hours. About two thirds of the show is given over to music, usually featuring guest musicians, but the distinctive part is the monologue by Keillor in which he gives the news from the small, imaginary Minnesota town of Lake Wobegon.

The first Keillor story that was accepted for publication appeared in *The New Yorker* in 1970, and he has been a regular contributor to that magazine ever since. In 1982, a collection of his stories from *The New Yorker* was published under the title *Happy to Be Here.* These stories are mostly satires on the fads, movements, passing fancies, and slightly lunatic causes fervently embraced by segments of the American people. Keillor pays particular attention to the language his characters use. Needless to say, he has little use for jargon. Among his targets are self-awareness therapy as applied to a losing baseball team in "Around the Horn," the pollsters in "How It

Was in America a Week Ago Tuesday," country and western lyrics in "The Slim Graves Show," food faddists in "The People's Shopper," and minorities' rights movements in "Shy Rights: Why Not Pretty Soon." Reviewers tend to see in these stories a serious moral purpose, though Keillor's presentation is so straightfaced that it is not easy to be certain the irony is there, or just exactly what the basis of the irony is, if it is there. Is he out to purify the language of the tribe, to warn his readers that they must be on their guard against being taken in by the rhetoric of pressure groups so that they end up not being able to think clearly, or is he approving of the clamor of these various eccentricities in that they prevent a mass and perhaps dangerous consensus from overwhelming the individual?

Lake Wobegon Days, his second book, published in 1985, is very different from his first, being the written version of the monologues from his radio show. Lake Wobegon, the setting for his stories, is "the town that time forgot . . . where all the women are strong and all the men are good-looking and all the children are above average." The population is made up of Norwegian Lutherans and German Catholics, and the religious difference, if not the national one, can at times be crucial. These are people to whom the majestic does not appeal. They "like the Grand Canyon better with Clarence and Arlene parked in front of it, smiling." Their town motto is "Sumus quod sumus" (we are what we are), and it adumbrates an attitude, a point of view from which they see themselves and from which Keillor sees and describes them. Most of this volume describes what it is like to grow up in a small town such as Lake Wobegon, and for the most part, Keillor presents the people without rancor. He describes them without patronizing them or talking down to them, without excusing or justifying them. To him they are what they are. God made them that way; take them or leave them.

Perhaps what makes the book and radio program so immediately appealing is Keillor's vivid evocation of the time of childhood—not just his own, but everybody's. This is the childhood that his readers remember when they recall their being their children's ages, when the summers were hotter, the winters colder, and they walked to school through snowdrifts unimaginably deep. It is the romanticized past of midwestern small-town America, a sort of collective past that Americans like to think that they share whether they lived it or not. Memory, for most, begins with childhood, and memory, as William Carlos Williams notes, is itself a kind of accomplishment. It may be the one self-measure that everyone has that is as kind as they want it to be. Nostalgia, that strangely comforting feeling of loss, brings feeling of belonging.

However, it is only at the cost of missing some of Keillor's most astute observations that readers can find in his Lake Wobegon and its people a romanticized rustic paradise. He knows fully the constricting narrowness, the frustration, the secret furies that lie beneath the surface of many of the lives that he chronicles. He may deal in kindly fashion with the people whom he describes, and he may show no trace of any urge to reform them, but he has no illusions about them. They are what they are. And, he has no illusions about the fact that it is easier for him to relish them in a benign fellow-feeling now that he has left the town and returns only for an occasional visit. Most of the children leave, he tells his readers, "to realize themselves as finer persons than they were allowed to be at home."

Some reviewers for religious journals have embraced Keillor as preaching their gospel of Christian fellowship in a disguised fashion to an audience that organized churches might not reach. Perhaps Keillor does this, but while doing so he remains an acid critic of the pretensions and postures of organized churches. He, himself, belonged to a small sect called the Plymouth Brethren. They were strict Fundamentalists who saw in their separateness and difference from the other churches a sign of their election. Of all the aspects of the citizenry of Lake Wobegon that he surveys, only their religious beliefs and practices are treated caustically. Keillor describes the narrow views, rigidly adhered to and fanatically defended against different but equally narrow views derived from the same scripture, all by people who relish the perennial sectarian occupation of deciding who is to be saved and who is not, and how this is to be done.

One feature of *Lake Wobegon Days* that cannot escape comment is an extremely long footnote that goes on for twenty-four pages. It purports to be 95 theses written by a former Wobegonian who had returned for a visit and who intended to nail the document to the door of the Lutheran church. He does not, but instead slips this "dramatic complaint against his upbringing" under the door of the local newspaper office. It seems incontrovertible that it is Keillor, himself, speaking, and the complaints against his parents for the manner of his upbringing are many times little short of peevish. Certainly they lack any note of tolerance or forgiveness.

Summary

Garrison Keillor's fond portrayal of small-town life in America has brought him a great deal of acclaim from his contemporaries. Like Cliff Arquette and Minnie Pearl, he recounts the actions of semi-rustic characters who capture the essence of the lighter side of twentieth-century American life. His first book, *Happy to Be Here*, is a collection of his stories reprinted from *The New Yorker*. His second volume, *Lake Wobegon Days*, is based on his immensely popular radio show.

Lake Wobegon Days is not a book filled with weighty messages, but it is one to return to. Keillor has said many times that he is emulating the story tellers that he grew up among, and in his own words: "I remember Uncle Lew's stories not as coming to a point, really, but to a point of rest, a point of contemplation. As I got older, of course, life was becoming strange. I just looked to those stories of his, and to the history of the family, as giving a person some sense of place, that we were not just chips floating on the waves, that in some way we were meant to be here, and had a history. That we had standing."

Selected Bibliography

Primary Sources
Happy to Be Here. New York: Atheneum, 1981.
Lake Wobegon Days. New York: Viking, 1985.

Secondary Sources
"A Conversation with Garrison Keillor: Radio is 'a Magical Country.'" *U.S. News and World Report*, November 4, 1985, p. 75. Keillor talks about radio, his career, and Lake Wobegon.

Heller, Terry. "Garrison Keillor." In *Beacham's Popular Fiction*. Washington, D.C.: Research Publishing, 1986. Discusses Keillor's themes and techniques.

———. "Happy to Be Here." *Magill's Literary Annual: Books of 1982*. Ed. Frank N. Magill. Englewood Cliffs, N.J.: Salem Press, 1983, pp. 326-330.

———. "Lake Wobegon Days." *Magill's Literary Annual: Books of 1985*. Ed. Frank N. Magill. Englewood Cliffs, N.J.: Salem Press, 1986.

Roback, Diane. "PW Interviews Garrison Keillor." *Publishers Weekly*, 228, no. 11 (September 13, 1985): 138-139. Keillor discusses his writing, his career, and *Lake Wobegon Days*.

Skow, John, reported by Jack E. White. "Lonesome Whistle Blowing." *Time*, November 4, 1985, pp. 68-73. Overview of Keillor's life and works.

Barney Cooney

Kerr, [Bridget] Jean [Collins]

Born: Scranton, Pennsylvania, on July 10, 1923
Education: Marywood College, B.A., 1943; Catholic University, M.F.A., 1945
Marriage: Walter Kerr, August 9, 1943, six children

Biography

Jean Kerr has achieved success in two areas—publishing and the theater. Her collection of short essays, *Please Don't Eat the Daisies*, remained on the non-fiction best-seller list for two years, selling over two million copies in hardcover and paper, while her comedy *Mary, Mary* delighted Broadway audiences for 1,572 performances. Kerr's appeal lies in her seemingly inexhaustible wit and her sharp insight into human nature.

Kerr was born Bridget Jean Collins on July 10, 1923, in Scranton, Pennsylvania. Her father was a building contractor; her mother was a second cousin of Eugene O'Neill. Kerr showed a predilection for the theater at an early age, putting on shows with other neighborhood children. She performed in high school and at Marywood College, from which she received her B.A. in 1943. Two years previously, while working as stage manager for the college production of *Romeo and Juliet*, she met Walter Kerr, a professor of drama at Catholic University. She studied there for three semesters and married Kerr in August 1943. In 1945, she received her M.F.A. from Catholic University, where she has also taught.

Kerr's playwriting career dates back to her university days. With her husband she adapted Franz Werfel's popular novel *The Song of Bernadette* (1944), which had a brief run on Broadway in 1946. This was followed by *Our Hearts Were Young and Gay* (1946), an adaptation of Cornelia Otis Skinner and Emily Kimbrough's book; *The Big Help* (1947); and *Jenny Kissed Me* (1949), Kerr's first solo effort to reach New York.

The musical revue *Touch and Go* (1949), another Catholic University export, featured sketches and lyrics by the Kerrs and ran on Broadway for 176 performances. Kerr also contributed sketches to *John Murray Anderson's Almanac* (1953), including "Don Brown's Body," a hard-boiled detective story presented as a staged reading à la Stephen Vincent Benét's *John Brown's Body*.

Kerr's first notable success, *King of Hearts*, appeared in 1954. Written with Eleanor Brooke, the comedy concerned an egocentric cartoonist who loses his fiancée to the man hired to "ghost" his comic strip. Theater critics found fault with the play but warmed to the authors' humorous and snappy dialogue. The play was later filmed as *That Certain Feeling*.

It was also at this time that Kerr was approached by Allene Talmey of *Vogue*, who asked her to write a short humorous article on her home life. (The Kerrs by now were the parents of four sons; two more children, another son and a daughter, would follow.) The piece that resulted, "Please Don't Eat the Daisies," was the first of a series of articles for such magazines as *McCall's*, *Harper's*, *Ladies' Home Journal*, *Saturday Evening Post*, and *Parents'*. Her first collection of these sketches, also titled *Please Don't Eat the Daisies* (1957), was a huge critical and popular success. Three more collections have since appeared: *The Snake Has All the Lines* (1960), *Penny Candy* (1970), and *How I Got to Be Perfect* (1978). In addition, a film and television series were based on *Please Don't Eat the Daisies*.

In 1950, Walter Kerr left Catholic University for the post of drama critic at *Commonweal*, followed by positions at the *New York Herald Tribune* and *The New York Times*, where he has served as drama critic since 1966. The Kerrs returned to the musical stage with the book and lyrics for *Goldilocks* (1958), a frantic musical comedy set in the early days of motion pictures. Although the music by Leroy Anderson was sprightly and the production elaborate, the show's book was faulted as uninteresting, and *Goldilocks* lasted only 161 performances.

Kerr's first big Broadway success was *Mary, Mary* (1961), a witty boy-has-lost-girl-but-gets-her-back-again comedy. The play ran for three and a half years, was transferred to the screen, and remains popular in summer stock and amateur productions. Three plays followed in the next twenty years: *Poor Richard* (1964), *Finishing Touches* (1973), and *Lunch Hour* (1980). All three were praised for their slickness and literacy, while faulted for outmoded attitudes and familiar material.

Literary Analysis

As a writer of humorous sketches, Jean Kerr follows in the tradition of Betty MacDonald, finding humor in the tribulations of daily existence, and Ruth McKenney, describing a woman's attempts to juggle household, husband, and children with a career. In Kerr's case the career is writing, and her efforts to remain sane in a world of disorder and domestic disaster afford her unlimited source material.

Kerr's humor is gentle, but her wit is sharp. She points out the lunacy in everyday events— writing letters of complaint, buying a house, traveling by airplane, dieting—and evokes nods of recognition from her readers. In Kerr's world

little goes right, but constant catastrophes never mar her good humor; her problems are non-threatening and easily weathered, even if more surprises are always lurking around the corner. Kerr's style is simple, friendly, almost conversational, so that the distance between her and her reader is minimized and she becomes as familiar as a next-door neighbor.

In her humorous plays, Kerr incorporates some of the themes from her sketches, and as a result her most memorable characters are women. (This is not true of *King of Hearts*, a collaborative effort, with the original idea and story furnished by Eleanor Brooke.)

The major problem with *Goldilocks* (premiered October 11, 1958) was a lack of focus on the relationship between the main characters. The characterization is weak, yet the heroine is certainly the most vivid of all the characters. Maggie, a Broadway star who is leaving the theater to marry a wealthy suitor, finds herself obligated to honor a film contract held by the irascible and vain director, Max. Maggie and Max battle, fall in love, battle again, and are in each other's arms in time for the final curtain. As in many other musicals of the period, a slight story was given a pleasant score and a gargantuan production that only emphasized the book's poverty. Still, Kerr's zingy one-liners, which found their way into the songs as well as the dialogue, foreshadowed the monumental hit that was to come a few seasons later.

Mary, Mary (March 8, 1961), Kerr's next play, brought her the huge success in theatrical circles that she had already attained in the literary world. To this simple story of a recently-divorced woman who manages to mend her marriage Kerr brought a level of bright sophistication that her earlier plays had lacked. The great Kerr laughs were in abundance, and the result pleased critics and audiences alike. Mary and Bob McKellaway's divorce is the result of a lack of understanding of each other's needs. Mary wants love and acceptance; yet, unsure of herself and afraid of rejection, she projects a brittle and sarcastic exterior, turning all of her husband's attempts to reach her emotionally into jokes. Bob, on the other hand, is insensitive to anyone else's needs and incapable of fully understanding Mary's behavior. Only when the actor Dirk Winston shows a romantic interest in her does Mary accept her femininity and drop the wisecracks. Bob in turn is delighted by this new side of Mary, and a reconciliation is effected.

Mary could have stepped out of the pages of *Please Don't Eat the Daisies*; she exhibits the same persona that Kerr has created in her sketches. Mary is a far cry from the liberated woman of the 1970s and 1980s, and is content with a life of caring for her rather selfish husband's needs. In this manner her need to take care of someone is fulfilled.

Kerr's next play, *Poor Richard* (December 2, 1964), concerned a hard-drinking, fast-living poet consumed with guilt over his seeming indifference to his late wife's love for him. With the help of his editor's secretary, who loves him, Richard is made to realize that he really had loved his wife. This romantic comedy had fewer laughs than Kerr's earlier plays; the seriousness of the central situation precluded gratuitous comic lines. But, the slightness of the plot was a problem that all of the play's charm and good intentions could not overcome, and *Poor Richard* closed after 117 performances.

Kerr addressed the sexual revolution in her next comedy, *Finishing Touches* (November 29, 1973). The play's main character, Katy Cooper, is Mary McKellaway with family problems: her professor husband thinks he has fallen in love with one of his students; her college senior son has brought his live-in girlfriend home for a visit; and her next door neighbor is all too ready to offer her romantic comfort. By the end of the play all of the problems have been solved in Kerr's usual light and amusing manner. The comedy is pleasant and unforced, and the characters have depth. Katy's attitudes seem identical to those of the author; Kerr, a staunch Catholic, has the Catholic Katy frowning on premarital sex and her son's not attending Mass regularly. Yet, the play is too pleasant and dated; its approach to life is that of *Mary, Mary*, even though twelve years have intervened. Audiences, however, appreciated Kerr's usual flair for humor and warm-heartedness, and kept the play running for the rest of the season.

Kerr's latest play, *Lunch Hour* (November 12, 1980), resembles the brittle romantic comedies of the 1930s, even though it is set in the present-day Hamptons. Carrie Sachs, childlike and insecure, informs Oliver DeVreck, a psychiatrist, that their respective spouses are having an affair. At first maddened by Carrie's neurotic behavior, Oliver is eventually attracted to her as they make plans to get their marriages in order. If Kerr's outmoded approach to the basic premise has not changed, her solution to the characters' problem certainly has. As might be expected in a Kerr play, the straying parties see the error of their ways and return to their proper spouses. However, there is every indication that Carrie and Oliver will continue their liaison under the guise of a doctor-patient relationship with a weekly lunch hour appointment. Critics complained of the inadequacies of the play's supporting characters, and felt that only Carrie and Oliver had dimension. This was true, however, in Kerr's previous works as well; with the exception of *Finishing Touches*, secondary characters

in the plays are usually merely onlookers, or at best catalysts who force the main characters to take action. The difference with *Lunch Hour*'s secondary characters is their lack of appeal; it is difficult to determine what attracted the very mismatched couples in the first place.

Summary

Kerr's dramatic work as a whole embraces a rather limited environment. Her characters are middle-class, literate, and financially comfortable. Crises are domestic in nature, and usually revolve around temporary marital difficulties. Kerr is always witty and highly perceptive, and graced with intelligence and common sense. Her usually light approach to her material should not be misconstrued as shallow, though; she has definite ideas on morality, values, and religion, and her characters reflect her sincerity.

Kerr considers herself somewhat old-fashioned in her art, yet makes no apologies. As a result, critical reaction to her work is generally mixed; she is applauded for her wonderful sense of the absurd and her snappy and very funny dialogue, but accused of holding her literary talent in check and being too gentle and familiar. Nevertheless, her popularity and appeal to readers and theatergoers alike seem to be assured, since in a highly volatile world Jean Kerr holds on to traditional values while chuckling at life's everyday absurdities.

Selected Bibliography

Primary Sources

Essay Collections

Please Don't Eat the Daisies. New York: Doubleday, 1957; Fawcett, 1979.

The Snake Has All the Lines. New York: Doubleday, 1960.

Penny Candy. New York: Doubleday, 1970.

How I Got to Be Perfect. New York: Doubleday, 1978.

Plays

(with Walter Kerr.) *The Song of Bernadette*, produced 1944; Chicago: Dramatic Publishing Company, 1944.

Our Hearts Were Young and Gay, produced 1946; Chicago: Dramatic Publishing Company, 1974.

The Big Help, produced 1947; Chicago: Dramatic Publishing Company, 1947.

Jenny Kissed Me, produced 1949; New York: Dramatists Play Service, 1949.

(with Walter Kerr.) *Touch and Go*, produced 1949.

(contributor.) *John Murray Anderson's Almanac*, produced 1953.

(with Eleanor Brooke.) *King of Hearts*, produced 1954; New York: Doubleday, 1955.

(television adaptation.) *The Good Fairy*, produced 1955.

(with Walter Kerr.) *Goldilocks*, produced 1958; New York: Doubleday, 1959.

Mary, Mary, produced 1961; New York: Doubleday, 1963.

Poor Richard, produced 1964; New York: Doubleday, 1965.

Finishing Touches, produced 1973; New York: Doubleday, 1974.

Lunch Hour, produced 1980; New York: Doubleday, 1982.

Other

Playwrights Talk on Writing: Jean Kerr. Interviewed by Lewis Funke. Cassette. Chicago: Dramatic Publishing Company, 1970. Recorded interview with Kerr.

"Queens of Fun." *Theatre Arts*, 40 (July 1955): 32-33. Very brief, illustrated article about *King of Hearts*.

A Visit with Jean Kerr, at Her Home the "Kerr Hilton." Recorded 1973. Iona College (7½ ips, 7" reel). Recorded interview with Kerr by Doug Cooper and George O'Brien.

"Why Don't I Write More Plays? Well. . . ." *New York Times*, November 9, 1980, sec. 2, p. 3, col. 1. Short humorous piece centered around *Lunch Hour*.

Secondary Sources

"Children Run Longer than Plays." *Time*, April 14, 1961, pp. 82-86. Interesting overview of Kerr's career and lifestyle.

Current Biography Yearbook, 1958. New York: H.W. Wilson, 1958.

Dresner, Zita Zatkin. *Twentieth Century American Women Humorists.* Dissertation, University of Maryland, 1982. Perceptive discussion of Kerr's place among humorists, with fine analysis of the major works.

Gaskill, Gayle. "Jean Collins Kerr." *American Women Writers: A Critical Reference Guide.* Vol. 2. Ed. Lina Mainiero and Langdon L. Faust. New York: Frederick Unger, 1980.

Gehman, Richard. "Jean Kerr." *Theatre Arts*, 46 (March 1961): 14-16, 72-74. An interview with Kerr.

Straub, Deborah A. "Kerr, Jean." *Contemporary Authors.* Vol. 7. New Rev. Ser. Detroit: Gale, 1982.

World Authors 1950-1970. Ed. John Wakeman. New York: H.W. Wilson, 1975.

Eric W. Johnson

King, Grace Elizabeth

Born: New Orleans, Louisiana, on November 29, 1852

Education: Institut St. Louis (New Orleans), Diploma, 1868; Sylvester-Larned Institut; Institut Cénas; private tutors

Died: January 12, 1932

Biography

On November 29, 1852, Grace Elizabeth King was born in New Orleans, Louisiana. Her parents, William Woodson King and Sarah Ann Miller King, resided on Camp Street near Lee Circle. Her father was a lawyer who with his brother owned L'Embarass Plantation; her mother was the daughter of a lawyer from an established local family. During the federal occupation of New Orleans, the family lived in refuge on the plantation. At the close of the war, the family, suffering financially, returned to the city and moved into a poor neighborhood near the federal barracks (now Jackson Barracks). Eventually, they were able to move into the Garden District, an uptown neighborhood.

King studied at private Creole schools after the Civil War. The schools emphasized academic training, especially in literature. Although she completed the Institut St. Louis in 1868, she continued with her study of languages and composition at other schools as well as with a tutor. Never married, she devoted herself to a literary life. In 1885, she published her first story "Monsieur Motte," which three years later she transformed into a novel. She fast became part of the literary scene as she was acquainted with Charles Dudley Warner, Mark Twain, and others.

Her education continued with travel to Europe in 1891-92, the beginning of a miracle decade for her writing. In 1892, *Tales of a Time and Place* and two histories were published. *Balcony Stories* appeared in 1893, followed during the next two years by a history of Louisiana and one of New Orleans. In 1898, *DeSoto and His Men in the Land of Florida* ended that phase of her career.

King made two more trips to Europe prior to the outbreak of World War I. Her reputation grew locally during the early years of the twentieth century with awards from Tulane University and the French Consulate, but it had begun to wane nationally. In 1916, she wrote *The Pleasant Ways of St. Médard*, a novel reflecting her return to New Orleans after the Civil War. From 1921 to her death, she continued to write and publish but at a lesser rate. *Memories of a Southern Woman of Letters* came into print in 1932, a few months after her burial in Metairie Cemetery.

Literary Analysis

During a literary career of some forty-four years, Grace King wrote and published thirteen books and a significant number of pieces for periodicals. Fiction, history, and biography—her major interests—represented her attempts to respond to the spirit of the time and to record the contributing elements of the past. She was, indeed, a daughter of the South and a defender of its images and customs in the aftermath of the Civil War. Yet, her views on women were liberal in contrast to her conservative position on racial matters.

Her principal works are two collections of short stories, *Tales of a Time and Place* (1892) and *Balcony Stories* (1893); a novel, *The Pleasant Ways of St. Médard* (1916); and a history, *New Orleans: The Place and the People* (1895). She began her writing with "Monsieur Motte," a short story designed to present a truthful view of Creoles (descendants of the early colonial families of Louisiana) and to counter the error that she perceived in George Washington Cable's stories on this subject. Her first collection of fiction recalls the Civil War and the post-war period, touches on racial matters, and treats the sense of loss common to survivors. Her second collection, "told" from a woman's point of view (as if on a balcony observing the swirl of life about her), focuses on women in the postwar era and shows a greater expertise in the craft of fiction.

The Pleasant Ways of St. Médard leans toward the loosely structured fiction of the modern period, for a series of stories and sketches is brought into a lyrical coherence by common characters, themes, and settings. Here King's fascination with the years after the war continues. Her history of New Orleans has lively and romantic qualities reflecting the narrative grace of the fiction. From the era of exploration to accounts contemporaneous with the writing, King provides a semi-linear treatment of her subject as she stops frequently to discuss characters, events, or issues.

Although much of her fiction explores the difficulty and disappointment of life in the postwar South, her stories have flashes of wit and humor, and her non-fiction prose often turns on amusing anecdotes. King's humor often gives her works a certain grace and openness, and it qualifies her as a local colorist with humorous overtones. As a child, she listened to stories avidly; their telling was an important part of Creole life. In her mature years she knew the wit and polish of a society in which theater and opera were important activities. She visited European capitals, and in Paris she took part in several salons. These aspects of a genteel life come together to inspire the cultivated sense of play that periodically emerges in her writing.

King's fiction shows the effects of the stage in her use of standard devices to evoke humorous responses. In "Bayou L'Ombre" (1887) there is a wonderful incident of mistaken identity in which Yankee and Rebel soldiers change uniforms, and the confusion of identities causes the wrong soldiers to be released from bondage. A variation of this occurs in "A Drama of Three" (1893): Journel secretly supports and manipulates a former general, his tenant, who always thinks less of those serving him. Champigny, a laughable old fellow in "La Grande Demoiselle" (1893), in a turnabout marries a beautiful young woman who had rejected many "gentlemen callers" before the war. In *The Pleasant Ways of St. Médard*, the dialogue between Mr. Talbot and Mademoiselle Mimi over Catholic and Protestant history comes straight from drawing-room comedy, and the exchange between the *casquette* girl, Annette, and her husband the morning after the mass wedding borders on the burlesque in *La Dame de Saint Hermine* (1924). King's boldest effort comes in *The Chevalier Alain de Triton* (1891), in which Alain and a friend raise money through a mock wake.

In much of her fiction there are traces of the tall tale. An example is the incident of the shoes made from alligator hide in *The Pleasant Ways of St. Médard*, but this element is much more fully realized in anecdotes from the biographies and histories. The Indian chief, Capafi, in *Desoto and His Men* (1898) is so overweight that he can only escape by crawling away. In *New Orleans: The Place and the People* (1895), King describes how the pirate Lafitte, with a reward on his head, passed himself off at a party as a gentleman and later managed to meet Governor Claiborne to offer his services against the British (they were accepted). Barnard Marigny's courtship of Anna Mathilde Morales is recounted in *Creole Families of New Orleans* (1921). After meeting her at a ball and occupying her attentions, Marigny received seven challenges to duels from her suitors; he indicated that he would meet one each morning after breakfast.

King took her career as a writer seriously and saw herself as a defender of the South. Her optimism in the face of the difficulties of her city and region surfaced in the humor of her literary and personal life.

Summary

Grace King, a minor southern author rooted in the local color tradition, wrote novels, stories, biographies, histories, and a memoir among other works. Some of her fiction transcends purely local interest in her development of female characters from youth to maturity. Despite the effects of the disaster of the Civil War, her works—fictional and non-fictional—have elements of humor from the dramatic and oral traditions. As the title of her memoir suggests, she was truly a southern woman of letters.

Selected Bibliography

Primary Sources

Novels

Monsieur Motte. New York: Armstrong, 1888.
The Chevalier Alain de Triton in *The Chautauquan* Vol. 13 (1891).
The Pleasant Ways of St. Médard. New York: Holt, 1916.
La Dame de Saint Hermine. New York: Macmillan, 1924.

Short Story Collections

Tales of a Time and Place. New York: Harper, 1892.
Balcony Stories. New York: Century, 1893.

Biographies and Histories

Jean Baptiste le Moyne, Sieur de Bienville. New York: Dodd, Mead, 1892.
New Orleans: The Place and the People. New York: Macmillan, 1895.
De Soto and His Men in the Land of Florida. New York: Macmillan, 1898.
Creole Families of New Orleans. New York: Macmillan, 1921.

Autobiography

Memories of a Southern Woman of Letters. New York: Macmillan, 1932.

Collected Works

Grace King of New Orleans: A Selection of Her Writings. Ed. Robert Bush. Baton Rouge: Louisiana State University Press, 1973.

Secondary Sources

Books

Kirby, David. *Grace King.* Boston: G.K. Hall (Twayne), 1980. A psychological study.

Biography

Bush, Robert. *Grace King: A Southern Destiny.* Baton Rouge: Louisiana State University Press, 1983. Comprehensive and accurate.

Bibliography

Bush, Robert. "Grace King (1852-1932)." *American Literary Realism,* 8 (1975): 43-49. A comprehensive bibliographical essay with attention to manuscripts and needed research.
Vaughn, Bess. "A Bio-Bibliography of Grace Elizabeth King." *Louisiana Historical Quarterly,* 17 (1934): 752-770. Primary and secondary sources.

Articles

Bush, Robert. "Grace King and Mark Twain." *American Literature,* 44 (1972): 31-51.
Fletcher, Marie. "Grace Elizabeth King: Her Delineation of the Southern Heroine." *Louisiana Studies,* 5 (1966): 50-60. On women and the southern ideal.

Thomas Bonner, Jr.

Knight, Sarah Kemble

Birth: Boston, Massachusetts, on April 19, 1666
Marriage: a sea captain, apparently widowed in 1706, one child
Death: September 25, 1727

Biography

Sermons, devotional poems, and historical narratives dominate American literature in the seventeenth and early eighteenth centuries. Studying the exceptions to the rule enhances our knowledge of the daily lives and customs of the people. *The Private Journal* by Sarah Kemble Knight provides an accurate gauge of the temper of the times. Madam Knight's unique brand of earthy humor and practical wisdom, blended with the vestiges of Puritan dogma, captivated the nineteenth-century audience who first saw its publication and continues to amuse contemporary readers.

Born in Boston, Massachusetts, on April 19, 1666, the daughter of a Charlestown shopkeeper, Sarah Kemble married an older man whose primary claim to fame is that he was her husband; they had one daughter. Knight, a London agent for an American-based company, spent much time abroad. During his absences, his wife ran a boarding house and taught school. Tradition holds that Benjamin Franklin and the Mather children were numbered among her pupils. After the death of her husband and her father, she successfully engaged in business and legal affairs. Always industrious, Madam Knight also copied court records and other legal documents. Through this work, she apparently gained enough knowledge of the law to become quite adept at tending such matters as settling estates. No doubt she would be designated a paralegal in our modern society. George Perkins Winship characterizes her as independent-minded, energetic, and somewhat of a feminist; and he remarks further that her character "compensated for whatever she may have lacked of fortune." In the 1825 edition of *The Private Journal,* Theodore Dwight called her "a lady of uncommon literary attainments, as well as of great taste and strength of mind." Mrs. Knight died in New London, Connecticut, on September 25, 1727; her *Journal* was published posthumously.

Literary Analysis

On October 20, 1704, the thirty-eight-year-old Madam Knight embarked on an unchaperoned 200-mile journey from Boston to New Haven, Connecticut, in order to settle the estate of a family member. She would proceed to New York and return to Boston in March of 1705. Her account of her daily observations from the trip would be collected into *The Private Journal*, a not-so-pious description of colonial life. From beginning to end Mrs. Knight entertains her readers with her wry spontaneous wit. Her listening to her guide John's embroidering his previous dangerous trips prompts her to observe:

> Hee entertained me w/ the Adventures he had passed by late Rideing, and eminent Dangers he had escaped, so that, Remembering the Hero's in Parismus and the Knight of the Oracle, I didn't know but I had meet with a Prince disguis'd.

This early passage reveals two distinctive features of the writer: her knowledge of mythology and her keen insight into human nature. Surely if this guide fails to impress his fellow-traveller, Mrs. Knight can face the challenges of her journey and handle legal matters.

Mrs. Knight does not, however, restrict herself to humorous prose. When she and her guide lodge at Mr. Haven's, and are kept awake by a rambunctious gathering in the next room, she resorts to poetry to describe the situation:

> *I ask thy aid, O potent rum!*
> *To charm these wrangling tapers dumb.*
> *Thou has their giddy brains possessed—*
> *The man confounded with the beast—*
> *And I, poor I, can get no rest.*
> *Intoxicate them with thy fumes*
> *O still their tongues 'til morning comes!*

Obviously, Mrs. Knight's real talent is prose, yet one does well to juxtapose these lines with the prevailing verse of the day. For an age dominated by devotional poems, these lines—with the invocation to rum instead of God—demonstrate New England's changing face. One critic properly assesses Madam Knight's makeup: "A lady of good family in respectable society and church standing, who was much too busy with the affairs of daily life to concern herself unduly with the matters of state or of religion." In short Knight was a vital human being.

The Private Journal is, of course, not a purely comic work. It offers a useful social history of New England in the early 1700s: the hardships of travel, the systems of justice, Sabbath observance, the vagaries of the legal system, and the like. Madam Knight blends with this helpful history a fresh wit in which she looks with amusement upon her travelling companions and the individuals whom she meets, the meals she has, and the overnight accommodations between Boston and New York. She observes, for example, that the sauce in a plate of pork and cabbage was "of a deep purple, which I thought was boild in her [the hostess's] dye kettle." Furthermore,

the journalist laughs at herself. When she has to climb a narrow stair-well in a room (she calls it a "Kennelle") at one of the stops en route to New York, she comments: "I had almost stopt by the Bulk of my Body." After her adventures, it is small wonder that she offered thanks to her "great Benefactor" on her safe return to Boston after successfully completing her business.

The Private Journal does not radically depart from the religious orthodoxy of the day. Madam Knight's dogma is there but so is her refreshing wit.

Summary

Sarah Kemble Knight's *The Journal of Mme. Knight* is one of the most accurate and authentic chronicles of colonial life in eighteenth-century America, and one of its main features is the wit which makes the journal enjoyable to read even today.

Selected Bibliography

The Journal of Mme. Knight, 1825; rpt. as *The Journal of Madam Knight*, with an Introductory note by George Parker Winship. New York: Peter Smith, 1935.

E. Kate Stewart

Kuttner, Henry

Born: Los Angeles, California, on April 7, 1915
Education: University of Southern California, B.A., 1954; work toward M.A., until 1958
Marriage: Catherine L. Moore, 1940
Died: February 3, 1958

Biography

The son of Henry and Annie Lewis Kuttner, Henry Kuttner was born in Los Angeles, California, on April 7, 1915. His father, a book dealer, died when the boy was five, and the family moved to San Francisco briefly before returning to Los Angeles. After graduating from high school, Kuttner worked in a literary agency, reading manuscripts.

Kuttner's early reading was greatly influenced by his interest in science fiction, fantasy, and stories of supernatural horror. He discovered the pulp magazines and by 1936 was publishing his own poems and stories in *Weird Tales*. He established contact with other writers for the magazine, corresponded with H.P. Lovecraft,[1] and collaborated on stories with Robert Bloch, C.L. Moore, and Arthur K. Barnes. A prolific writer, he adoped pseudonyms for many of the stories that he was publishing in *Thrilling Wonder Stories, Startling Stories, Astounding Science Fiction, Unknown,* and other magazines of the time.

In 1940 Kuttner married Catherine L. Moore, a popular author of fantasy and science fiction whose earliest stories had appeared in *Weird Tales* in 1933. They formed a close collaboration in the writing of fiction and published under a variety of pseudonyms, including Lewis Padgett, Lawrence O'Donnell, C.H. Liddell, and Hudson Hastings.

The couple lived in New York, a period interrupted by military service (1943-1945) for Kuttner. After the war they settled in Los Angeles, where they continued to write science fiction and fantasy and also wrote a number of detective novels. They offered courses in creative writing and earned degrees by taking courses at the University of Southern California. After being awarded a B.A. in 1954, Kuttner continued with graduate work at Southern California; he had completed all his course work and was apparently working on an M.A. thesis when he died suddenly of a heart attack on February 3, 1958.

Literary Analysis

Some of the stories that Kuttner wrote would grace any anthology of American literature. But, the kinds of fiction that he chose to write and the magazines in which his stories were published have placed him at a disadvantage that his career and his posthumous reputation could do little to overcome. The "pulp" magazines—so-called because they were printed on cheap, rough pulpwood paper rather than on the treated smooth stock adopted by national magazines with large circulations—were, for the most part, a poor showcase for an author's literary talents. They catered to a popular audience and often their contents were subliterary, their covers gaudy and sensational, and their general appearance unpleasing. Payment from editors was low and slow in coming, so that a writer was likely to be driven to compose too much and too quickly and to adhere to formula stories that could sell. An author might achieve a parochial fame, limited to the readership of a magazine, but this did not often translate into a national reputation and good earnings. Some writers made the transition from the pulps to book publication, enormous circulation, and earned fortunes—Edgar Rice Burroughs and Dashiell Hammett, for example—but many were not nearly so fortunate.

In his brief career Kuttner wrote more than two hundred stories, including a fair number of novel-length tales. Kuttner's earliest stories were tales of horror in the tradition of Edgar Allan Poe and his successors. "The Graveyard Rats" (1936), his first published story, is about an unscrupulous gravedigger's losing battle with the huge rats that infest his cemetery. In 1937 there were further stories in *Weird Tales*: one, "The Black Kiss," was written in collaboration with Robert Bloch, a friend who was later to gain much fame as the author of *Psycho*, the Alfred Hitchcock horror thriller; another, "Quest of the Star Stone," was a collaboration with C.L. Moore, whom Kuttner would later marry.

During the next four years, Kuttner wrote more than forty stories, including several short novels, often publishing more than one story in each issue of a pulp magazine and using a pseudonym to conceal that fact. Many of these stories do not rise above the routine. "Hollywood on the Moon" (*Thrilling Wonder Stories*, 1938) shifts a conventional plot to an exotic setting; "We Guard the Black Planet" (*Super Science Stories*, 1942) is a science fantasy that accounts for the legends of the Valkyries. However, as Kelvin Kent, Kuttner developed a series of humorous science fiction stories about Pete Manx, a con artist. Pete's consciousness is sent back into the past by means of a gadgety time machine, and he assumes the body and identity of a person of that time. Given his contemporary point of view and ignorance of history, he manages to get into various scrapes. The titles of the stories, with puns and allusions, telegraph the humor: "The Comedy of Eras" settles the question of whether William Shakespeare or Francis Bacon wrote the plays ascribed to Shakespeare. "Dames Is Poison" is about Lucrezia Borgia, and "World's Pharaoh" is set in ancient Egypt where Pete, inspired by the 1939 New York World's Fair, builds an equivalent. The stories offer a farcical view of history. In "The Comedy of Eras," for instance, Pete, drawing upon his own inaccurate knowledge of the Shakespearean plays, offers advice to Shakespeare about plots. Serious stories of time travel wrestle with problems of anachronism and paradox, but Kuttner introduces anachronisms liberally for his humorous effects. Living in Shakespeare's time, Pete invents the phonograph and teaches Queen Elizabeth and the Elizabethans songs like "Minnie the Moocher." Though it is clear from the story that Shakespeare has indeed written his own plays, he accepts help from Pete, who, it develops, had assumed the identity of Bacon.

Kuttner's marriage to Moore was to have a profound effect upon his writing. Moore, an experienced and skillful writer, had been publishing longer than her husband and, during her career, published stories of considerable distinction—"Shambleau" (1933), "No Woman Born" (1944), and "Vintage Season" (1946), among others. The two writers pooled their talents; as Moore has said, "we collaborated on about everything we wrote, but in varying degrees."[2] It should be clear that any discussion of the fiction published under any of the names Kuttner used during the 1940s and 1950s must always imply that the stories are collaborations with his wife.

During the decade of the forties, the pseudonym used to best effect by the collaborating authors was Lewis Padgett, all of whose stories appeared in *Astounding Science Fiction*, the best of the science fiction magazines of the period. Many of the stories published during this decade in *ASF* have been rightly regarded as the best in the genre and included work by Robert Heinlein, Isaac Asimov, A.E. Van Vogt, Fredric Brown, and Fritz Leiber. The Padgett stories were a notable addition to this roster. Many of them have a nightmarish quality. In "Open Secret" (1943) a man inadvertently sees a floor of his office building given over to robots assuming control of the world. He is unsuccessful in attempts to deter them and his reports are not believed; feeling helpless and futile, he must let things happen. In "The Cure" (1946) a man has a terrible recurrent dream of being entombed. Psychiatric help enables him to learn the truth, that he is from the future, from a world being destroyed and declining into madness. A series of stories, later collected in book form as *Mutant* (1953), deals with life in the world after nuclear catastrophe. The Baldies, a minority of telepathic mutants, must adjust to a suspicious and intolerant world of normal humans. In "The Piper's Son," for instance, Ed Burkhalter, a Baldie, must wear a toupee to cover his identifying baldness, is careful not to react to adverse opinions that he intercepts from the minds of the normal men, and, in a world where duels are regularly fought, is scrupulous about demonstrating that he would have an unfair advantage. As a connected series, the stories are persuasive in advancing the thesis that mankind is capable of growing beyond its destructive potential.

One of the earliest of the Padgett stories, "The Twonky" (1942), has a deserved fame as a science fiction horror story of a future invention introduced into the present with disastrous effects. A man from the future, marooned in our time and suffering from temporary amnesia, builds a device that is apparently common to his own time. It is capable of doing chores but, in a darker way, exerts censorship and can even change patterns of thought, blanking out attempts at individualism. Kuttner leaves some fascinating questions unanswered: From what kind of society could such a machine come? Will our own technology lead us to some fearsome future? In spite of its seriousness, the story has touches of humor in its development, as in the introduction of this fantastic device into our time. After the traveler from the future has made the "twonky," his mind clears, and he comes to understand what has happened to maroon him in the past. "I ran into a temporal snag," he explains, in a delightful metaphor. Apparently, time is a river, and time travelers are like the big river boats that must make their way cautiously up and down stream, trying to avoid dangerous snags.

The device of telling a serious story with touches of humor carries over into some of Padgett's best work. In "Mimsy Were the Borogoves" (1944) some children's toys from the remote future come into our time. The toys teach children and alter them till they leave our world, a serious matter, but much of the early development is handled in a light, humorous manner. In "When the Bough Breaks" (1944) little men from the future come to announce to the fearful parents of their infant, Alexander, that their son will become *the* Alexander, master of the world, and that he has sent them into the past to attend to his early education. Learning the super science of the future, the infant makes life miserable for his parents, till, by a miscue, he destroys himself and the future he was preparing for.

At the same time Padgett was writing a series of overtly comic stories, later collected in the volume, *Robots Have No Tails* (1952). The five stories, first appearing in *ASF* from 1943 to 1948, concern a scientist, Gallegher, who spends most of his time drunk because liquor releases his subconscious inventive genius. The result is that he takes commissions for inventions and invents devices that, sober, he cannot fathom; the stories are devoted to working out the complications and mysteries to a satisfactory conclusion.

Gallegher's inventive concoctions add humor to the stories. In "The Proud Robot" he has made Joe, a humanoid robot that can think and act autonomously and possesses an outsized ego. This device seems to have no function beyond being troublesome, snappishly short-tempered, and self-regarding, and Gallegher spends most of the story trying to figure out why he invented such an irritating, though amusing companion machine. It turns out that Joe was invented to be a can opener, but with his additional skills, he is able to take care of the commissions and clear up the story's mysteries. Joe is at the center of another story, "Ex Machina," which brings up the question of whether a robot can give evidence at a trial; this leads to the further question of whether a mechanical being can have a soul and believe in a supreme being.

One of the most attractive stories in the series is "The World Is Mine." Gallegher has invented a time machine and brought three Lybblas, rabbity little Martians from the future, to Earth. Like other Martians of science fiction renown, they want to conquer the Earth; but unlike H.G. Wells's hateful monsters, these polite creatures gratefully take milk and cookies and tend to cry over spilt milk. After conquering our planet and destroying our cities, they will "capture pretty girls and hold them for ransom or something." This particular aberration sounds as if they have been reading *Huckleberry Finn*. As a further complication to the story, the time machine keeps producing murdered corpses of Gallegher, each older than the living scientist; it is obvious that the future will be depressing for him. The story makes light of one of the major paradoxes of time travel, that of parallel worlds, and it takes a considerable amount of unraveling to rescue Gallegher from any one of several horrifying futures.

The plots of the Gallegher stories are farcical, but science fiction is a literature of ideas, and Kuttner uses the stories to criticize a world that has trouble adjusting its social structures to a runaway technology. The law is one of his targets:

> The legal profession had become so complicated that batteries of experts needed Pederson Calculators and the brain machines of Mechanistra to marshal their farfetched arguments, which went wildly into uncharted realms of symbolic logic and—eventually—nonsense. A murderer could get off scot-free provided he didn't sign a confession. And even if he did, there were ways of discrediting solid, legal proof.[3]

A weaker series of humorous stories, appearing in *Thrilling Wonder Stories* (1947–1949), concerned the Hogbens, a mutant family of hillbillies. In Druidic Britain, the great-grandfather, a tin miner, had been affected by a radioactive plague; as a result his descendants have a variety of unnatural talents—longevity, the ability to fly, be invisible, or read minds. Naturally, their talents attract the attention of normal people and make trouble for all.

Several of Kuttner's more than twenty novels are of high quality: *Earth's Last Citadel* (1943), *The Fairy Chessmen* (1946), *Fury* (1950), and *The Well of the Worlds* (1953). During the earlier part of his career, there was not much encouragement for writing novels, since book publishers almost never considered science fiction a viable commercial venture. By 1950, this situation had changed favorably and, as a result, many of the best of Kuttner's stories are available either in collections of his own stories or in anthologies.

Summary

Henry Kuttner was a prolific writer who has contributed distinguished fiction to the literature of America though his achievement is not yet generally recognized. His humorous science fiction is based on the proposition that science, gone wild, has to be tamed to human proportions. In the comic stories this does happen, though in the serious and often dark tales, science often has a fearsome effect upon fragile humans.

Notes

1. H.P. Lovecraft, *Selected Letters, 1934–1937*, ed. August Derleth and James Turner (Sauk City, Wisc.: Arkham House, 1976), Vol. 5, p. 226.
2. James Gunn, "Henry Kuttner, C.L. Moore, Lewis Padgett et al.," in *Voices for the Future, Vol. I*, ed. Thomas D. Clareson (Bowling Green, Ohio: Bowling Green Popular Press, 1976), p. 189.
3. Lewis Padgett, *Robots Have No Tails* (New York: Gnome Press, 1952), p. 82.

Selected Bibliography

Primary Sources

Fury. New York: Grosset & Dunlap, 1950.
A Gnome There Was (by Lewis Padgett). New York: Simon and Schuster, 1950.
Robots Have No Tails (by Lewis Padgett). New York: Gnome Press, 1952.
Ahead of Time. New York: Ballantine, 1953.
Mutant (by Lewis Padgett). New York: Gnome Press, 1953.
Line to Tomorrow (by Lewis Padgett). New York, Bantam Books, 1954.
Bypass to Otherness. New York: Ballantine, 1961.
The Best of Henry Kuttner. New York: Doubleday, 1975.

Secondary Sources

Bibliography

Contento, William. *Index to Science Fiction Anthologies and Collections*. Boston: G.K. Hall, 1978. Lists appearances of Kuttner's stories in anthologies.
Day, Bradford M. *An Index on the Weird and Fantastica in Magazines*. Ozone Park, N.Y.: Bradford M. Day, 1953. This bibliography, itself almost inaccessible, lists appearances of Kuttner's fiction in *Weird Tales*.
Day, Donald B. *Index to the Science-Fiction Magazines, 1926–1950*. Portland, Oregon: Perri Press, 1952. Lists appearances of Kuttner's fiction in science fiction magazines.

Articles and Chapters in Books

Briney, R.E. "Henry Kuttner." In *Twentieth-Century Science-Fiction Writers*. Ed. Curtis C. Smith. New York: St. Martin's, 1981. A brief account.
Gunn, James. "Henry Kuttner, C.L. Moore, Lewis Padgett et al." In *Voices for the Future*. Vol. I. Ed. Thomas D. Clareson. Bowling Green, Ohio: Bowling Green Popular Press, 1976. Excellent critical study.
Kelly, William P. "Henry Kuttner." In *Dictionary of Literary Biography*. Vol. 8. 2 vols. *Twentieth-Century American Science-Fiction Writers*. Ed. David Cowart and Thomas L. Wymer. Detroit: Gale, 1981. Useful brief account.
Lovecraft, H.P. *Selected Letters, 1934–1937*. Ed. August Derleth and James Turner. Sauk City, Wis.:

Arkham House, 1976. Contains letters from Lovecraft to Kuttner.

Moskowitz, Sam. *Seekers of Tomorrow.* Cleveland: World, 1966. An important study of science fiction with a good chapter on Kuttner.

Shroyer, Frederick. "C.L. Moore and Henry Kuttner." In *Science Fiction Writers.* Ed. E.F. Bleiler, ed. New York: Charles Scribner's Sons, 1982. Interesting essay in an invaluable reference work.

                                        Douglas Robillard

Lardner, Ring[gold Wilmer]

Born: Niles, Michigan, on March 6, 1885

Education: Niles, Michigan, privately tutored; graduated from Niles High School, 1901

Marriage: Ellis Abbott, June 28, 1911, four children

Died: September 25, 1933

Biography

As he was growing up in small-town Michigan, Ring Lardner had no ambition to become a journalist nor did he envision the day when he would regularly interact with the baseball players that were his heroes. He was born March 6, 1885, in Niles, Michigan, a small town just five miles north of the Indiana state line. His parents, Henry and Lena Phillips Lardner, were at the top of the Niles social scale. Henry, a gentleman farmer, was descended from Lynford Lardner, a British immigrant who became a leading citizen of Pennsylvania in colonial times. Lena Bogardus Phillips was the daughter of the Reverend Joseph Phillips, the rector of the Trinity Church, the Episcopal church where anyone who was anyone in Niles worshipped on Sunday morning. The Lardners had six children, spaced in two groups of three. The youngest three, Reginald (called Rex), Anna (called Anne), and Ringgold Wilmer (called Ring), were educated in the insular Lardner home by a private tutor. Though Ring did not escape the isolation of the family home until age twelve, his experience there was far from restrictive. His mother taught him that life should be lived with zest and enjoyment even as she was teaching him the social manners of his caste.

After graduation in 1901 from Niles High School with the distinction of being class poet, Ring meandered through a series of jobs. He went to Chicago, Illinois, where he briefly found various kinds of employment, but returned to Niles to work as a freight hustler for the Michigan Central Railroad. Following a short, disastrous tenure at the Armour Institute of Technology in Chicago (his father thought that he should be a mechanical engineer) and a short stint at the Niles Gas Company, Ring fell into a job at the *South Bend Times* in 1905. His brother Rex was, by then, working for the *South Bend Tribune*, the competing newspaper, and the *Times* editor visited the Lardner home to offer Rex a job. Rex was not home, but Ring was, and he convinced the editor that he could write just as well as Rex—Ring was hired. The experience in journalism that began in South Bend in 1906 would give him the basic education in sports wrting that he would build upon and refine throughout his career. In covering the Class B minor league clubs, he would learn to make quotidian events exciting and fun for his readers. He first experimented with colloquial speech in his newswriting in July 1906, an experimental style that he would combine with sports subjects in his best works.

Ring moved to Chicago in 1907. He first took a job at the *Inter-Ocean* and then in 1908 covered the White Sox for the *Examiner.* While at the *Examiner,* he created the character of Jack Gibbs, a ballplayer for the White Sox who could not read. This character, along with the voice that he developed for Hub Perdue, a Boston pitcher, melded in 1914 into Jack Keefe, the narrator of the *You Know Me Al* stories.

Ring's physical health began to deteriorate in the last half of the 1920s as a result of his demanding work schedule and a lifetime of heavy smoking and drinking. He was hospitalized in late 1924 after he and Ellis had visited the Fitzgeralds in France. Then, in the summer in 1926, he learned that he had contracted tuberculosis. In 1928, the Lardners decided to leave the hubbub of Great Neck society for a more secluded life at East Hampton, Long Island, in a house Ring appropriately called "Still Pond."

In these last years, Lardner wrote several pieces for *The New Yorker,* including radio reviews from 1932 to 1933. In a portion of these reviews Ring mounted a campaign to clean up song lyrics, listing those songs the lyrics of which he found offensive. Beginning in 1931, he wrote a column for Bell Syndicate titled "Night Letter from Ring Lardner," a column of short pieces similar to, but not as strong as, those he had written for "In the Wake of the News." With his finances strained by the Depression and his health rapidly failing, Ring pushed himself to write as much as he was able. Ellis and he spent summers at East Hampton and winters in the South. The remainder of the year he stayed in various hotels where he could be free from interruptions, working intently on his writing.

By September 1933, Ring's condition had weakened to the point that he frequently had to be helped or carried from bed to chair. On the night of September 24, he suffered a heart attack and became unconscious. He died the next day, September 25, 1933, at East Hampton at the age of 48.

Literary Analysis

Lardner reached the top of Chicago journalism in 1908. From 1908 to 1910, Ring alternately covered the Cubs and White Sox for the *Chicago Tribune,* the major Chicago newspaper. His style quickly shaped itself in his articles during these years, and he humanized the Chicago baseball heroes, showing them to be ordinary people just like their fans. It is this element of the Lardner style that Virginia Woolf identifies as the central reference point at which the diffuse American public could come together.

1911 was an important year for Ring. After a four-year courtship, mostly by letter, with Ellis Abbott, who was attending Smith College, the couple married on June 28 at her parents' home in Goshen, Indiana. During the next eight years, Ring and Ellis became the parents of four sons, John, James, Ringgold, Jr., and David, all of whom Ring mentioned often in his various columns. 1911 was also the year that the Lardners left the Midwest for the first time. Ring, following an unhappy three months as editor of *The Sporting News* in St. Louis, accepted an offer with the *Boston American* for which he, as sporting editor, covered the National League's Boston Rustlers. In his Boston sporting features he created the cocksure voice of Hub Perdue, a Boston pitcher, that he later transferred to the fictional Jack Keefe.

Ring's major work at this point in his career appeared from 1913 to 1919 in the *Chicago Tribune* column, "In the Wake of the News." The long-time author of the column, Hugh E. Keough, died in 1913, and Ring, who had returned to Chicago with his small family in 1912, stepped in to more than fill Keough's place. While writing the "Wake" column, a miscellany of short stories, satires, sports gossip, and poems about his children, Lardner refined the character of the "wise boob" and found the Midwestern idiom with which to animate him. This was writing that the ordinary reader understood and identified with. In 1914, the "wise boob" debuted as Jack Keefe, the egotistical, semi-literate baseball player who authored the *You Know Me Al* letters. "A Busher's Letter Home," the first of six stories collected in 1916 under the title *You Know Me Al*, appeared in the Sunday *Tribune* feature section in 1914.

The epistolary form of the "Busher" letters (which eventually numbered twenty-six) was natural to the journalistic medium. Ring, as mentioned above, had already used this form to create fictional letters from real Chicago baseball players. In developing the character and vernacular idiom of Jack Keefe, however, he progressed beyond his previous efforts, creating a language (commonly called "Ringlish") that reflects the character flaws, psychological makeup, and lifestyle of the character who uses it. Keefe, in his semi-literate letters to his friend, Al Blanchard, in Bedford, Indiana, simultaneously produces for the reader two versions of himself, one intended and one completely unintended. The image that he intends to project to Al is that of a brash, swaggering, worldly wise star athlete. The unconscious image of Jack that emerges from between the lines, however, shows him at base to be an arrogant, vain, gullible, bush-league fool— a "wise boob."

Moreover, the language that Lardner puts in Jack's mouth reinforces the readers' understanding of his character. Common words rather than complex ones are inconsistently misspelled, often phonetically, since Jack would check the spelling of only the difficult words on the assumption that he knew how to spell the others. The cadence of the letters, however, is consistent since Jack is simply transcribing his oral language onto paper. In short, though critics have often denigrated Lardner's "wise boob" characters as overly static, his contribution of a unique American character who speaks in a true American idiom in large part outweighs such criticism.

Lardner's first collection, *Bib Ballads*, poems about his son from the "Wake" column, was published in 1915. These poems detail the universal human experience of child and parent. Following the appearance of this collection and the Jack Keefe letters, magazine offers flooded in from around the country. Ring had produced enough short stories, many of them among his best, by 1921 to comprise eight more collections: *Gullible's Travels, Etc.* (1917), satiric pieces narrated in Midwestern vernacular by the semi-literate Gullible; *Treat 'Em Rough* (1918) and *The Real Dope* (1919), the second and third volumes of the Jack Keefe stories; *My Four Weeks in France* (1918), a collection of the eight articles that Ring wrote for *Collier's* when he viewed World War I in France; *Own Your Own Home* (1919), four stories of middle-class life in the suburbs; *Regular Fellows I Have Met* (1919), a series of satiric portraits of socially prominent Chicagoans; *The Young Immigrunts* (1920), a parodic account of the Lardners' move East told from a child's point of view; and *The Big Town* (1921), a collection of connected stories about the peregrination of Tom Finch, his wife, and his sister-in-law from South Bend, Indiana, to New York City.

The Big Town collection more closely resembles a novel than any other of Lardner's writings. All five stories center around the Finches' primary reasons for going to New York: 1) to find a husband for Katie, the sister-in-law, and 2) to temporarily experience the life of the *nouveau riche.* The stories are told from the ironic first-person point of view of Tom Finch, a character whose language in a way resembles Jack Keefe's. The principal difference between the two characters' languages is that Jack's is a complete, direct rendering of his speech, both misspellings and fractured grammar, in written form, whereas Tom's speech is indirect in the sense that only the tortured grammatical forms remain since the misspellings would contribute little to the effect of the story.

While on the surface Tom Finch glibly narrates the events of the story, leaving little doubt as to the self-serving motives that inform all the characters' actions, under the surface Lardner is constructing a coherent indictment of the ridiculous pretentiousness of a whole class of people, social aspirants who are unprincipled but not essentially immoral. He exposes the emptiness of their gains and the insincerity of their acts. For example, Katie goes through a host of suitors, becoming involved and uninvolved with them, with little show of caring for them. Here are people who are utterly human and are flawed in a way that precludes them from ever measuring up to a higher standard.

In 1919, Ring covered the legendary World Series between the Chicago White Sox and the Cincinnati Reds. When the Sox lost the Series to the weaker Cincinnati club in eight games, Ring was sure that the Series was fixed. Sure enough, eight White Sox players, dubbed the Black Sox, were indicted in 1920 for fixing the Series. Ring seems to have compressed his anger and disillusionment into a terse, intelligent piece published in 1922, "Sport and Play." In it, he berates sports fans (i.e., all Americans) who would rather watch sports than participate in them. Hero worship, he contends, is the source of Americans' apathy; they would rather sit for two hours and cheer their idols than exercise and improve their own health.

The last "Wake" column ran in the June 20, 1919, *Chicago Tribune.* Ring had signed a contract in New York to produce a nationally syndicated column, "Ring Lardner's Letter," which ran until 1927. The Lardners, all four boys in tow, moved to Greenwich, Connecticut, in order to be close to New York City; they would never again live in the Midwest.

The 1920s were boom years for the Lardners. Ring's national popularity was at an all-time high, and his short story fee was steadily increasing. Eventually, his yearly income would mount to nearly $100,000. Lardner wrote many of his most famous pieces during this period: "Some Like Them Cold" (1921); "I Gaspiri" (1924), one of his best nonsense plays; *How to Write Short Stories* (1924), his first Scribner's collection; "Haircut" (1925); "The Love Nest" (1925), one of his few stories written in the third person; *The Story of Wonder Man* (1927), a collection of autobiographical pieces from the "Weekly Letter" column; "I Can't Breathe" (1927); and *Round Up* (1929), a collection of 35 stories for the Literary Guild series. He creates such an acute sense of ironic detachment in these writings that critics have often labeled him a misanthrope. Walton Patrick, however, expresses a more moderate view, proposing that Lardner was actually "an acutely sensitive idealist disturbed by the deviations of the real world in which he lived from a better or more ideal world that might be possible if human beings were less prone than they are to self-delusion, pretentiousness, and hypocrisy."[1]

In early 1921, the Lardner family moved into a splendid new home (which Ring christened "The Mange") in Great Neck, Long Island, gaining such illustrious neighbors as F. Scott and Zelda Fitzgerald. Lardner's biographer, Jonathan Yardley, surmises that Ring and Scott formed a mutual bond because they were both, for different reasons, outsiders in the opulent Great Neck society. Scott, a Princeton graduate, preferred the established old money to the lavish new money of Great Neck while Ring accumulated his money for his family's use rather than for ostentatious show.[2] Nonetheless, Lardner still served as a kind of absentee leader of the Algonquin Round Table, a group of such notables as George S. Kaufman, Dorothy Parker, Robert Benchley, Harold Ross, and Franklin P. Adams among others. This group of "wits" met at the posh Algonquin Hotel in New York City to exchange chitchat. Though he often missed these gatherings, his influence was ever present.

Stage plays and musicals were also among Lardner's productions of the 1920s, though he achieved only modest success in the theater. During the period from 1919 to 1928, he wrote five musical comedies and one play, but none of these efforts was received as well as *June Moon,* a stage adaptation of "Some Like Them Cold" written in 1930 in collaboration with George S. Kaufman, that gave Lardner the kind of literary legitimacy that he seems to have believed his journalistic writing could not.

Summary

Critics from 1923 to the present have consistently regarded Ring Lardner's short stories and satiric pieces as praiseworthy for their precise portrayals of uniquely American character types.

Though these works delineate types that were prevalent in the America of the 1920s and 1930s, a frequent critical comment used to show the narrowness of Lardner's writing, they also possess a universal quality that is applicable to Americans of all time periods. Lardner viewed his focus on the worth of the individual and his biting portraits of those types of Americans who threatened that worth as his principal contribution as a satirist. He was concerned with criticizing human conduct that differed from a commonly accepted ideal as well as with implicitly valorizing human conduct that upheld the same ideal. It is this implicit rather than explicit statement of the ideal, the concentration on the deviation from the standard rather than on the standard itself, which has aroused unfavorable critical apppraisals of Lardner's writing.

In the 1930s, Clifton Fadiman and Ludwig Lewisohn made prevalent the view, which has only recently been refuted, of Lardner as the angry misanthrope, the writer whose contempt for humanity and perhaps for himself bubbles to the surface in his writing. The present critical consensus, which, as Jonathan Yardley notes, amounts to inattention to rather than rejection of Lardner's work, is far more objective, pointing up Lardner's lasting contributions to American letters while recognizing his self-proclaimed status as a minor American writer. Though his brand of popular fiction was often labeled as not intellectually "serious," his astute satire of American life and his precise rendering of American speech in written form constitute a valuable legacy.

Notes

1. Walton R. Patrick, *Ring Lardner* (New York: Twayne, 1963), Preface.
2. Jonathan Yardley, *Ring: A Biography of Ring Lardner* (New York: Random House, 1977), p. 259.

Selected Bibliography

Primary Sources

Bib Ballads. Chicago: P.F. Voland, 1915.
You Know Me Al. New York: George H. Doran, 1916.
Gullible's Travels, Etc. Indianapolis: Bobbs-Merrill, 1917.
Treat 'Em Rough. Indianapolis: Bobbs-Merrill, 1918.
The Real Dope. Indianapolis: Bobbs-Merrill, 1919.
Own Your Own Home. Indianapolis: Bobbs-Merrill, 1919.
Regular Fellows I Have Met. Chicago: B.A. Wilmot, 1919.
The Big Town. Indianapolis: Bobbs-Merrill, 1921.
How to Write Short Stories. New York: Charles Scribner's Sons, 1924.
The Love Nest and Other Stories. New York: Charles Scribner's Sons, 1926.
Round Up. New York: Charles Scribner's Sons, 1929.
(with George S. Kaufman.) *June Moon*. New York: Charles Scribner's Sons, 1930.

The Portable Lardner. Ed. Gilbert Seldes. New York: Viking, 1946.
The Ring Lardner Reader. Ed. Maxwell Geismar. New York: Charles Scribner's Sons, 1963.
Some Champions. Ed. Matthew J. Bruccoli and Richard Layman. New York: Charles Scribner's Sons, 1976.

Secondary Sources

Berryman, John. "The Case of Ring Lardner." *Commentary*, 21 (November 1956): 416–423. Criticizes Lardner's writing in terms of its structure, style, and range of invention. Berryman believes that Lardner's successful pieces were "the accident of talent."

Bruccoli, Matthew J., and Richard Layman. *Ring Lardner: A Descriptive Bibliography*. Pittsburgh: University of Pittsburgh Press, 1976. A well-organized, indispensable record of Ring Lardner's work presented in easy-to-use categorical form.

Elder, Donald. *Ring Lardner*. Garden City: Doubleday, 1956. A thorough, useful account of Ring's life and work which incorporates first-hand information gathered from family, friends, and ballplayers who were close to Lardner.

Fadiman, Clifton. "Ring Lardner and the Triangle of Hate." *Nation*, 136 (March 22, 1933): 315–317. Advancing the argument of Lardner's misanthropy, an argument that influenced the critical view of Ring's work for many years, Fadiman identifies the hatred between Lardner and his characters and between the characters themselves as stemming from Lardner's hatred of himself.

Geismar, Maxwell. *Ring Lardner and the Portrait of Folly*. New York: Crowell, 1972. Views the deep-rooted bitterness beneath Lardner's humor as the result of Lardner's morality and innocence being "violated by the materialistic aspects of American society and of mature life."

Layman, Richard. "Bibliographical Information for a Life of Ring Lardner." Unpublished Ph.D. dissertation, University of South Carolina, 1975. A remarkably useful index of Lardner's journalistic career.

Patrick, Walton R. *Ring Lardner*. New York: Twayne, 1963. A superb biography that presents an unbiased view of Ring Lardner.

Smith, Leverett T., Jr. "'The Diameter of Frank Chance's Diamond': Ring Lardner and Professional Sports." *Journal of Popular Culture*, 6 (Summer 1972): 133–156. An excellent critical inquiry into the nature of the relationship between Lardner and sports games.

Van Doren, Carl. "Beyond Grammar: Ring W. Lardner, Philologist Among the Low-Brows." *Century*, 106 (July 1923): 471–475. Shows how Lardner's sure ear for the vernacular contributes to precise characterization.

Webb, Howard W., Jr. "The Meaning of Ring Lardner's Fiction: A Re-Evaluation." *American Literature*, 31 (January 1960): 434–445. Focuses on "the problem of communication" as the primary theme in Lardner's fiction.

Woolf, Virginia. "American Fiction." *The Moment and Other Essays*. London: Hogarth Press, 1952. Argues that Lardner uses games as the central reference point for a diffuse American population.

Yardley, Jonathan. *Ring: A Biography of Ring Lardner.* New York: Random House, 1977. An extensive, carefully researched biography, especially strong on the details of Lardner's journalistic career.

Rebecca S. Blair

Leacock, Stephen Butler

Born: Swanmoor, Hampshire, England, on December 30, 1869

Education: Upper Canada College, Toronto; University of Toronto, 1891; University of Chicago, Ph.D., 1903

Marriage: Beatrix Hamilton, August 7, 1900, one child

Died: March 28, 1944

Biography

Stephen Butler Leacock was born in Swanmoor, Hampshire (or Hants), England, on December 30, 1869, one of eleven children born to Peter and Agnes (Butler) Leacock. His parents migrated to Canada in 1876, when Stephen was seven years old.

Leacock's father became a farmer in Ontario near Lake Simcoe, in the township of Georgina, county of York. Leacock writes that because of economic hardships on the farm "my brothers and I were inevitably driven off the land, and have become professors, business men, and engineers instead of being able to grow up as farm laborers" (Preface, *Sunshine Sketches,* p. xiii).

Leacock received his high school education at Upper Canada College in Toronto, from which he graduated with high honors in 1887. He was awarded his B.A. from the University of Toronto, again with distinction, in 1891. Of his high-school and college educations Leacock wryly wrote: "I spent my entire time in the acquisition of language, living, dead, and half dead; and knew nothing of the outside world" (*Sunshine Sketches,* p. xiii). It was perhaps natural, then, that Leacock returned to Upper Canada College to teach modern languages and to serve as a house master from 1891 to 1899. This experience as a teacher left him with a "profound sympathy" for the "many gifted and brilliant men who are compelled to spend their lives in the most dreary, the most thankless, and the worst paid profession in the world" (*Sunshine Sketches,* p. xiv).

In 1899, inspired by the presence of Thorstein Veblen on its faculty, Leacock went to the University of Chicago to study economics and political science. He soon won a fellowship there and earned his doctorate in 1903. In 1903, he joined the faculty of McGill University in Montreal and was made chairman of its Department of Economics and Political Science in 1908; he retired in 1936. His memory is honored on its campus by the Stephen Leacock Building and by the Leacock Room in the University's McLennan Library. This oak-panelled room contains Leacock's desk, many original manuscripts, and 81 Leacock first editions, as well as his articles in nearly two hundred periodicals. Facing the books and manuscripts is a portrait of the author in old age, painted by Fred Taylor.

Starting in 1910 with *Literary Lapses,* which the author published himself, Leacock turned out almost a book a year for over thirty years. Although many of these were collections of humorous sketches and essays originally written as magazine pieces or as lectures, he somehow found time to also write biographies (*Mark Twain* and *Charles Dickens*), history, and autobiography, as well as books on economics, literature, and language. Particularly successful was his 1906 textbook, *Elements of Political Science,* which was translated into 18 languages and adopted as a standard text by 34 colleges and universities in the United States.

Leacock was married to Beatrix Hamilton on August 7, 1900. Beatrix, an actress, had a small part on the New York stage at the time, so the couple was married in New York City's "Little Church Around the Corner." In 1915, their only child, Stephen Lushington Leacock, was born. Then, in 1925, tragedy struck: Beatrix Leacock died of cancer in Liverpool, England, where Leacock had taken her for treatment. The death of his wife, which had come with very little warning, was a great shock to Leacock, and some critics feel that it affected the quality, if not the quantity, of his humorous writing.

Leacock greatly enjoyed his summer home at Orillia, Ontario. It was to the The Old Brewery Bay, as he called his place on Lake Couchiching, that he retired in 1936, and it was there that he died on March 28, 1944. In 1957, the town of Orillia purchased The Old Brewery Bay and established it as museum, a place where, in the words of the Leacock Memorial Committee, the public may savor "the charm and vitality and personality of the man" (Curry, p. 343). The Orillia Public Library contains an extensive Leacock Memorial Collection as well as a fine portrait bust by Elizabeth Wyn Wood. Of all the honors he received during his lifetime and after death, Leacock might best have liked the Leacock Memorial Medal, which is awarded annually—and with much laughter—for the best book of humor written by a Canadian.

Literary Analysis

In his preface to *Sunshine Sketches of a Little Town* (1912), Leacock wrote: "Many of my friends are under the impression that I write these humorous nothings in idle moments when the wearied brain is unable to perform the serious labors of the economist." He goes on to say that the exact opposite is true and that the writing of humor is "an arduous contrivance only to be achieved in fortunate moments, few and far between" (*Sunshine Sketches*, p. xv).

To be funny, Leacock felt, was to be able to point out the disparity between our aspirations and our achievements and the incongruity between our illusions and reality. In *Sunshine Sketches of a Little Town*, Leacock's masterpiece, the characters' dreams and activities are often in humorous conflict with provincial realities. Pathos is, of course, the other side of the coin, but sadness never gets the better of his characters. They are endowed with enough common sense to see them through the mild disasters incurred by their flights of fancy.

A case in point is the character of Jeff Thorpe, the dreamy and slow-speaking barber of Mariposa. He has absorbed all of the contemporaneous enthusiasm for speculation in stocks and has become the town's Carnegie and Rockefeller rolled into one. But, before he can endow the local poor with his $40,000 fortune, he sends the money off to New York to a mail-order promoter of "Cuban" lands and loses it all. Knocked temporarily speechless, Jeff soon recovers his sense of reality and goes back to raising hens and selling eggs for extra money. He had never given up his barbershop business, so he kept both his good sense and his livelihood intact throughout the crisis.

Leacock believed that humor must be kind. As a corollary, he felt that true humor is possible only in a decent and sympathetic society. This is why the town of Mariposa is itself an important character in *Sunshine Sketches*. Like its inhabitants, it has an inner core of sanity that redeems its follies and provides the necessary social framework for the harmless foolishness of its characters. For Leacock there could be no true humor in satirizing a world gone seriously wrong.

In *Humor: Its Theory and Technique* (1935) Leacock traced the evolution of humor from its lowest point in the barbarous laughter at the mishaps of others to its highest in the civilized discovery and depiction of what is amusing in individual human characters. Is there a contradiction between Leacock's insistence on kindliness as the essential ingredient in humorous creation and his belief that humor's highest expression lies in the description of the foibles, vanities, and other amusing ambiguities of the human personality? Is it really possible to analyze human character, which, when it is funny, is usually ridiculous, without a touch of ridicule? That Leacock himself was not completely able to do so accounts for the fact that the people of Orillia, the real-life model for Mariposa, initially resented his portrait of their town and of themselves in *Sunshine Sketches*. Nor could Leacock completely solve the dilemma by pointing out the pathetic in his characters, for here he would be in danger of taking on the patronizing air of a superior being who "sees all and understands all."

With his love for characterization it is not surprising that the writings of Dickens, especially *Pickwick Papers*, provided Leacock with inspiration and were a great influence on his own humorous writing. *Sunshine Sketches* has a cast of characters that could have stepped from the pages of a Dickens novel: Josh Smith, proprietor of Smith's Hotel, who opens a "Ladies' and Gents' Caff" and a "Rats Cooler" to circumvent the local liquor laws; The Reverend Mr. Drone, a gentle soul whose sermons revolve around translations from his beloved Greek, his single trip outside of Canada (to Mackinaw Island), and his mechanical inventions; Judge Pepperleigh, with his "judicial temper" and peppery readiness to "pass sentence"; Peter Pupkin, a junior bank teller madly in love with the romantic Zena Pepperleigh and hero of the Great Mariposa Bank Robbery.

However, Twain exerted a far greater influence on Leacock than did Dickens or any other English writer. He was almost literally the successor to Twain, for 1910, the year of Twain's death, was also the year of Leacock's first humorous publication, *Literary Lapses*.

In *Humor: Its Theory and Technique* (1935), Leacock stated that Twain was "beyond anybody in the world a technical humorist" (p. 100). In his analysis and appreciation of Twain's techniques of exaggeration, understatement, anticlimax, juxtaposition of incongruities, and other tools of the humorist's trade, Leacock might have been describing his own work. Beyond technique, Leacock admired Twain's "easy flow of language." Like his predecessor, Leacock was an excellent conversationalist and a public lecturer, with the result that he seems to talk *to* rather than write *at* his readers. Both, too, were masters of the short, pithy comparison (as in Leacock's descriptive "eyes like puddles of molasses") and short pithy statements ("Mark Twain did for American humor what Shakespeare did for English drama and Milton did for Hell," Curry, p. 214).

An anti-romantic to the core in his own writing, Leacock adored what he called Twain's "irreverence." Whatever his targets—romantic literature, health fads and the "back to nature" movement, the writing profession, economics, spiritualism—Leacock's own irreverence was, as he wrote of Twain's, "as wholesome as the sweeping of a fresh wind through a dismal swamp" (Curry, p. 279).

Although *Innocents Abroad* was among Leacock's favorite books, he was much annoyed when one critic labeled his own *My Discovery of England* "watered down Mark Twain." Leacock replied that no one has a monopoly on themes such as the American innocent abroad, which is only one aspect of a subject that many humorists use again and again—that of the innocent individual confronting complex and confusing social conventions.

As a great enjoyer of literature, Leacock found much inspiration for humor in its many forms and follies. *Behind the Beyond; and Other Contributions to Human Knowledge* (1913) has as its title piece a blow-by-blow parody of a contemporary "problem play." Through a detailed account of the wholly predictable plot and hilarious asides on the egotistical characters, Leacock not only amuses us but also provides serious food for thought on the silliness of drawing-room dramas.

In "Homer and Humbug; an Academic Suggestion" (also in *Behind the Beyond*), Leacock apologizes for the lies that he has told about his appreciation of classical literature:

> When I reflect that I have openly expressed regret . . . for the missing books of Tacitus and the entire loss of the Abracadabora of Polyphemus of Syracuse I can find no words to beg for pardon. In reality, I was just as much worried over the loss of ichthyosaurus. More indeed; I'd have liked to have seen it; but if the books Tacitus lost were like those he didn't, I wouldn't.
>
> (p. 121)

Leacock then treats us to a witty word-for-word translation of Homer's description of Ajax's dash into battle as well as a sample paragraph of the *Iliad*'s "Catalog of Ships," which he compares to the New York Central's official listing of their locomotives. As in "Behind the Beyond," there is an underlying seriousness to Leacock's humorous approach to the humbug generated by the classics. He concludes this essay:

> This is what I would like to do. I'd like to take a large stone and write on it in very plain writing. "The classics are only primitive literature. . . . They belong in the same class as primitive machinery and primitive music and primitive medicine," and then throw it

through the windows of a University and hide behind a fence to see the Professors buzz.

(p. 125)

In "Outline of Shakespeare" (*Winnowed Wisdom*, 1926), Leacock delights in reducing great literature to the vague and garbled fragments by which it is "known" by most of us:

> Hamlet (not to be confused with *Omlette* which was written by Vollaire). Hamlet, Prince of Denmark, lived among priceless scenery and was dressed all in black. . . . Either because he was mad, or because he was not, Hamlet killed his uncle and destroyed various other people whose names one does not recall. . . . In the end Hamlet kills Laertes and himself, and others leaped into his grave until it was quite full when the play ends. People who possess this accurate recollection rightly consider themselves superior to others.
>
> (p. 5)

Further Foolishness (1916) contains several parodies of popular fiction. In "A Compressed Old English Novel" Swearword and an authentic Anglo-Saxon "have at one another" over the way Swearword murders old Anglo-Saxon speech. In the fight, "Swearword threw . . . his hauberk, his haldrick, and his needlework on the grass." He is then killed; "Thus luckily the whole story was cut off on the first page and ended" (p. 20). What Leacock did for historical fiction in "A Compressed Old English Novel" he did for realistic fiction in "A Condensed Interminable Novel; From the Cradle to the Grave; or a Thousand Pages for a Dollar." Condensing the 250,000 words of Edward Endless's life story into 106 words of blank verse, Leacock gives us this first stanza:

> Edward Endless lived during his youth
>   in Maine
>   in New Hampshire
>   in Vermont
>   in Massachusetts
>   in Rhode Island
>   in Connecticut.
>
> (p. 20)

Woman's magazine fiction is Leacock's target in "The Snoopopaths." The stock characters, The Man, who is always "clean-shaven," and The Woman, who is always "beautifully groomed" and "exquisitely gowned," do and say preposterous things while the narrator points out the disparity between their behavior and the conduct of real life. In "Foreign Fiction in Imported Installments: Serge the Superman; A

Russian Novel," much of the fun lies in such malapropisms as "moujik driving a three-horse tarantula" and in the use of such "Russian" words as *knob* for head, *mugg* for face and *boob* for father. The outcome of the very Russian story is completely absurd: the police inspector, Papoff, was murdered not by the Beautiful Olga, but by Yump The Cook, who did the deed not with a bomb but by sitting on his victim.

As noted before, Leacock found much inspiration for humor in the encounters between the individual and impersonal and overbearing forces. In "My Financial Career," a timid man gets so rattled in banks that he deposits and then immediately withdraws his $56.00 in two humiliating and consecutive transactions. In "The Laundry Problem; A Yearning for the Good Old Days of the Humble Washerwoman," Leacock contrasts the treatment accorded clothes by the washerwoman and the Amalgamated Laundry Company: "Where the poor washerwoman was hopelessly simple was that she never destroyed or injured the shirt. . . . In other words, modern industrialism was in its infancy!" (*Laugh*, p. 21).

Leacock's "Letter to a Plumber" delights anyone who has been at the mercy of one:

> My very dear Sir,
>   It is now four hours since you have been sitting under the sink in my kitchen smoking. You have turned off the water in the basement of my house. And you have made the space under the sink dry and comfortable.
>
> (*Laugh*, p. 144)

In one of his most popular essays, "How We Kept Mother's Day; As Related by a Member of the Family," Leacock shows how social conventions like holidays can get the better of us. In the case of "Mother's Day," Mother is the victim of her own celebration and ends up with all of the work and none of the fun.

Leacock also had great fun with the humor found in the description of the typical, or average, thing or person. One of the most successful of these sketches is his analysis and description of a typical backyard of the 1920s for a "Social Encyclopedia of a Hundred Years Hence." And, just as *Sunshine Sketches* depicted the typical in small-town life and character, so *Arcadian Adventures with the Idle Rich* (1914) typified the manners and morals of the city. Through this kind of caricature Leacock could reduce the follies of life to a pleasant kind of absurdity.

A few of Leacock's pieces are in a more fanciful and literary vein. In "A, B, and C; The Human Element in Mathematics," for instance, he gives flesh and blood to those "characters," A, B, and C, whom we have encountered on the pages of math books:

> A is a full-blooded blustering fellow. . . . It is he who proposes everything, challenges B to work . . . he has been known to work forty-eight hours at a stretch. . . . A mistake in the working of a sum may keep him digging for a fortnight without sleep. A repeating decimal in the answer may kill him. B is a quiet easy-going fellow, afraid of A . . . but very gentle and brotherly to little C. . . . Poor C is an undersized frail man. . . . Constant walking, digging and pumping has broken his health and ruined his nervous system. . . .
>
> (*Literary Lapses*, 1957, p. 143)

English by birth and American by adoption, Leacock had close ties with both cultures. It was from the United States that he derived much of his income as a writer and lecturer. He also influenced such American humorists as Robert Benchley and S.J. Perleman, and, as we have seen, was deeply influenced by Twain. On the other hand, he lectured and published in Great Britain also and was, moreover, a staunch believer in the British Empire and the importance of Canada's remaining a part of it.

As a Canadian, however, Leacock was able to remain somewhat aloof from both powerful nations. His heart and his humor remained firmly planted in Mariposa, for which we might read "Canada" in this excerpt from "The Marine Excursions of the Knights of Pythias" (*Sunshine Sketches of a Little Town*):

> In Mariposa practically everybody belongs to the Knights of Pythias just as they do everything else. . . . You should see them on the seventeenth of March . . . when everybody wears a green ribbon and they're all laughing and glad. . . . On St. Andrew's Day every man in town wears a thistle and shakes hands with everybody else, and you see the fine old Scotch honesty beaming out of their eyes.
>
> (*Sunshine Sketches*, pp. 37-38)

Summary

Like his Mariposans, Leacock belonged to everything. He was a university professor, a lecturer, a writer, a clubman, a generous host, a fisherman and sailor, a linguist and a political orator. He was interested in a multitude of things and knowledgeable about most of them. Leacock's enthusiasm for life in all its confusion and variety found its way into nearly sixty books and countless articles and lectures. Most numerous are the "funny pieces" that he wrote for the magazines of his time and that were collected into yearly books for the Christmas trade (for instance, in his 1915 *Moonbeams from the Larger Lunacy*, Leacock acknowledges permission to republish from *Vanity Fair, The American Magazine, The Popular Magazine, Life, Puck, The Century,* and *Methuen's Annual*). Although somewhat dated in subject matter, these pieces are almost all written in the excellent Leacock style, featuring brief sentences, simple well-chosen words, and the rhythms of conversational speech. In *Sunshine Sketches of a Little Town* and *Arcadian Adventures of the Very Rich*, Leacock produced books of humor that are close to novels and which leave a single and strong impression upon the reader. Balanced between the absurdity of much English humor and the satire of American humor, they bring to their readers a characteristically Canadian point of view. Leacock's writing also has a universal scope and a richness, derived from his knowledge of and interest in all sorts of things.

Selected Bibliography

Primary Sources

Literary Lapses. Toronto: McClelland and Stewart, 1910; rpt. 1957.

Nonsense Novels. London: John Lane, 1911.

Sunshine Sketches of a Little Town. Toronto: McClelland and Stewart, 1912.

Behind the Beyond and Other Contributions to Human Knowledge. London: John Lane, 1913.

Arcadian Adventures with the Idle Rich. London: John Lane, 1914.

Moonbeams from the Larger Lunacy. New York: John Lane, 1915.

Essays and Literary Studies. London: John Lane, 1916.

Further Foolishness: Sketches and Satires on the Follies of the Day. London: John Lane, 1916.

Frenzied Fiction. London: John Lane, 1918.

The Hohenzollerns in America; with the Bolsheviks in Berlin and Other Impossibilities. London: John Lane, 1919.

My Discovery of England. London: John Lane, 1922.

The Garden of Folly. Toronto: Gundy, 1924.

Laugh with Leacock. An Anthology of the Best Work of Stephen Leacock. New York: Dodd, Mead, 1930.

Mark Twain. London: Peter Davies, 1932.

Charles Dickens: His Life and Work. London: Peter Davies, 1933.

Humor: Its Theory and Techniques, with Examples and Samples: A Book of Discovery. London: John Lane, 1935.

Humour and Humanity: An Introduction to the Study of Humour. London: Thornton Butterworth, 1937.

My Remarkable Uncle and Other Sketches. London: John Lane, 1942.

Secondary Sources

Curry, Ralph. *Stephen Leacock: Humorist and Humanist.* New York: Doubleday, 1959. Biography.

Legate, David M. *Stephen Leacock: A Biography.* Toronto and New York: Doubleday, 1970. Biography.

John W. Baer

Lebowitz, Fran[ces Ann]

Born: Morristown, New Jersey, on October 27, 1950

Education: 3 years of public high school, dropped out of Wilson in Mountain Lakes, New Jersey, after three additional months, has passed graduate equivalency examination

Biography

Favorably compared to Dorothy Parker and Oscar Wilde, Fran Lebowitz uses few words to attack nearly all things, with a background of common sense and reasonableness to all her assaults. She expresses attitudes toward popular trends that many average, middle-class persons would themselves espouse. She hates it when others force their opinions, attitudes, and habits upon her, as when there is a dinner party and no meat dish is served. One must avoid assuming, though, any philistinism on her part, even though her bitter words can be misinterpreted as crude when pulled out of context.

Born on October 27, 1950, in Morristown, New Jersey, Fran is the daughter of Harold and Ruth Lebowitz, who run a furniture store in Morris Plains. Fran also has a younger sister, said to be a magician's assistant. Fran wrote a mystery novel in her elementary school years and considered herself an outspoken, difficult child.[1]

Lebowitz had only a limited high school education, but she has a virtual addiction to reading. She was expelled from the private school her parents sent her to, Wilson in Mountain Lakes, New Jersey, but did eventually pass the GED certificate examination.

Her lack of training should not be mistaken for a lack of sophistication, however. She admitted for *Contemporary Biography* that she did not think that college was necessary for what she wished to do in her work and sarcastically included preparation for the David Susskind show as a legitimate reason for attending college.[2]

After she left private school, she did not immediately go out on her own. Sent to live with an uncle in Poughkeepsie, whom she called "a German military engineer," she worked in a Head Start program until she became eighteen and felt that she could escape to New York City. She did almost anything to make her $121.00 per month budget, facing all of the petty humiliations of working people head on: as a maid, a street vendor, a waitress in costume, an envelope stuffer, an usher to a gay review, and a hand bill street drummer.

Lebowitz held poetry readings in small clubs, though she had no prospects for publication. Her first submission was a collection of verse to

Grove Press, but her poetry has never been published. When *Changes*, an "alternative culture" music-focused magazine was launched, Lebowitz convinced the editors to hire her as a book and film critic. Her bitter reviews would eventually lead to her being ostracized from press screenings by movie producers fearing her blasts, but her work on the short-lived *Changes* recommended her to Andy Warhol's *Interview*. A flashy, newsprint magazine, *Interview* appeals to the "fast lane" crowd. While her "Best of the Worst" column froze her out of screenings, it allowed her to turn to writing her broader "I Cover the Waterfront" pieces in the early 1970s.

The *Interview* selections impressed Mary Cantwell, senior editor of *Mademoiselle*, who hired Lebowitz for eighteen months to create the "Lebowitz Report" pieces for that publication. Lebowitz was fired from *Mademoiselle* for not meeting deadlines, but she was given a contract for a book by E.P. Dutton's Laurie Colwin.

Metropolitan Life, characteristically submitted a year late to Dutton, was only given a limited, 6,000-copy, first printing in 1978. Reviewers, delighted with the bite of the hard-boiled, down-to-earth, aphoristic sentences, gave the anthology rave reviews. Lebowitz later suggested that the book had been a "John Leonard" success, showing more the cultural influence of the *New York Times* than her talent or insight.[3] By October 1978 the book had sold 90,000 copies in hard cover, and Lebowitz received a $150,000 contract for the paperback rights. In spite of tempting offers, Lebowitz refused to sell the rights to *Metropolitan Life* to any movie studio. She felt that her impact would be dissipated rather than enhanced by movie versions.[4] She also admits to some "immature" desire to control her work completely and not see it affected by other hands.

Fame has added only one dark corner to her life; her hate mail has increased due to her appearances on television, but she now has this as an excuse to not read *any* of her "fan" mail. Sadly, she reports that the mail runs heavy with anti-Semitic comments, but she brushes this off as a common event for anyone "recognizably Jewish" who appears on television. She also has a prison following, but again says that any woman who appears on television is bound to get letters from male prisoners.[5]

With the income from *Metropolitan Life* Lebowitz attempted to improve her living conditions and she gained enough insights into Manhattan life for her second anthology, *Social Studies* (1981). Promoting her first volume, she also traveled throughout America, gaining grist for her mills from the poor hotel food, airline inefficiency and incompetence, and the fleets of salesmen swarming in airports. Her essays on apartment hunting and servant hunting in the second volume prove that common sense—along with low rents—has long since departed from Manhattan.

Lebowitz is now writing a novel with the working title *Exterior Signs of Wealth* about the cruel behavior of the rich. She suggests that she will need decades to complete the work but now knows, particularly with two volumes in paperback and many appearances on television, that her next book will have a college audience. Her earlier "Notes on 'Trick'" essay contains many of the themes that she will include in her new work, particularly the treatment of the artistic by the wealthy.

The main quality of Lebowitz as a person is her street-urchin sense of helplessness in the face of life and authority figures. She sees adults as self-deceiving when they assume that they are less helpless than the chldren whom they control, and her quiet dread of college campuses and presidents suggests some of the little girl in her past never died.

Literary Analysis

In *Metropolitan Life* Lebowitz satirizes not only her journalistic outlets, but also things like Conan Doyle's stories and even linguistic notes worthy of the *New York Times* or *American Speech*. Her "Notes on 'Trick'" could qualify as an update on H.L. Mencken's essay on Veblen and *Theory of the Leisure Class*: she discussed the nonsense of "kept" men and women, and then provides a nice punch line at the close. The twists at the end, which often amount to an epigram or plot twist, are reminiscent of O. Henry's methods, which Mencken had added to the editorial pages of newspapers long before. Another connection between Mencken and Lebowitz is that while superficially both are undemocratic, they do not spare their social "betters" either. Often the two authors make fun of the seriousness and serious tone of editorials or longer journalistic human interest pieces.

Lebowitz spares no one, including journalism itself. Her essay on an unexpected outbreak of heterosexuality in New York City reads like a mock-serious psychological report that one might find in straight versions in the middle of the road pages of *Time* and *Newsweek*. Besides journalism, though her writing covers such topics as New York landlords. Her satire helps to make Lebowitz one with both the middle class and the lower classes. Her audience can identify with someone whose landlord provides 4,000 roaches per tenant.

Lebowitz's stance and understandably mean-spirited tone juxtaposed with the cleverness of her epigrammatic punch lines make her style appealing. The Yuppies are not spared in their lofts, and the trivial raised on high can be wonderfully funny. It is refreshing to see the idiotic mighty brought low.

Lebowitz's subject matter often seems to parallel that of Calvin Trillin, with its sense of the absurd, but Trillin's material seems more relaxed, less urgent, and it is not written by an author subsisting in the midst of luxury. One of her most ironic pieces involves the all-night diner that serves wine and salads instead of coffee, hamburgers, and eggs. To a Midwesterner, the diner that still serves American fried potatoes and eggs can be a social focal point, so the description of a trucker stopping for wine and veggies produces an unforgettable image. Lebowitz functions for the middle class as its gadfly, poking at the wealthy, doing for the average reader what Tom Wolfe often attempts on a different level.

Social Studies expands Lebowitz's major themes and includes an account of an actual trip to Los Angeles for a close look at the entertainment industry. Travel for her includes the New Yorker's and *The New Yorker's* traditional views of the country, including advice, such as "bring food" and "wait until you get back home to get a haircut." Coach travel on airlines is described as involving any number of crying infants smoking domestic cigars, or Cuban cigars in first class. Her aphorisms are pithy, biting, and accurate:

Polite conversation is rarely either.

Original thought is like original sin: both happened before you were born to people you could not possibly have met.

Great people talk about ideas, average people talk about things, small people talk about wine.

The opposite of talking isn't listening. The opposite of talking is waiting.

Another memorable piece describes her selling personal possessions as if she were English nobility or one of the Rockefellers. She even has measurements and pictures of the "Collection." Other assaults on the new rich and old rich include satirical looks at other aspects of American culture: Anita Loos is inverted in "How Not to Marry a Millionaire: A Guide for the Misfortune Hunter," which includes advice on what the rich should not say to the poor but beloved:

"Oh, a uniform. What a great idea."

"I'll call around noon. Will you be up?"

"Don't believe it for a minute—these waiters make an absolute fortune."

Lebowitz further targets the wealthy when she sets up charity appeal texts for them in a piece titled "The Four Greediest Cases: A Limited Appeal," and in "Lives" of the modern saints, she satirizes classic New York types—the heiress, the make-up man, the film critic. What Lebowitz suggests again in her second book, then, is that social status and wealth are no indication of the character of a person. She paints the contemporary diminished, appearance-over-reality, Philistine era in America with deceptive ease with one- or two-word comparisons that show what has been lost. She uses a chart to illustrate the difference between an "idea" and a "notion."

Ideas:	Notions:
Literature	The Nonfiction Novel
Light Bulbs	Light Beer
Thomas Jefferson	Jerry Brown

Another juxtaposition of lists shows how institutions have gone wrong:

Trial by Jury	of your peers
Adult	Education
Hero	Worship
Popular	Culture
Sexual	Politics
Immaculate	Conception

Summary

Lebowitz's experiences have given her rich material for her urban satire. Coming from a middle-class background, only completing three years of high school, she has been persistent in her efforts to create her own life in New York City. In her essays she presents a simple but unforgettable foil composed of common sense and a love of simple pleasures to counter the frivolities and superficialities of the wealthy and powerful. She never rises to true political satire, never presumes to intellectualism, but instead lobbies for quiet joys and leisure unencumbered by pretension.

Notes

1. Charles Moritz, ed., *Current Biography Yearbook* (New York: H.W. Wilson, 1982), p. 222.
2. Ibid.
3. Ibid., p. 283.
4. Ibid., p. 223.
5. Margaret Mazurkiewicz and Jean W. Ross, "Lebowitz, Fran(ces Ann) 1951(?)–," *Contemporary Authors*. New Rev. Ser., ed. Linda Metzger and Deborah A. Straub, Vol. 14 (Detroit: Gale, 1985), p. 284.

Selected Bibliography

Primary Sources

Anthologies
Metropolitan Life. New York: Dutton, 1978.
Social Studies. New York: Random House, 1981.

Anthologized Essays

"Notes on 'Trick.'" *The Best of Modern Humor*, ed. Mordecai Richler. New York: Knopf, 1983, pp. 526-532.

Secondary Sources

Axthelm, Pete. "The Cookie Monster." *Newsweek*, April 10, 1978, p. 59.

Broyard, Anatole. Review of *Social Studies*. *New York Times*, September 2, 1981, Section C, p. 26.

Collins, Glenn. "The Sour Cream Sensibility." *New York Times Book Review*, August 8, 1981, pp. 7, 20. Review of *Social Studies*.

Davies, Russell. "Joinery." *New Statesmen*, February 19, 1982, pp. 22-23. Review of *Social Studies*.

Day, Ingeborg. *Ms.*, May 1978, p. 35. Review of *Metropolitan Life*.

Lubow, Arthur. "Screw You Humor." *New Republic*, October 21, 1978, pp. 18-22.

Mazurkiewicz, Margaret, and Jean W. Ross. "Lebowitz, Fran(ces Ann) 1951(?)-." *Contemporary Authors*. New Rev. Ser. 16 vols. Vol. 14. Ed. Linda Metzger and Deborah A. Straub. Detroit: Gale, 1985.

Moritz, Charles, et al., eds. *Current Biography Yearbook*. New York: H.W. Wilson, 1982, pp. 221-224.

Robinson, Jill. "Swift and Cranky." *New York Times Book Review*, March 26, 1978, p. 9. Review of *Metropolitan Life*.

Sheppard, R.Z. "She Wits and Funny Persons." *Time*, May 29, 1978, pp. 92-96.

Patrick William Merman

Lehrer, Tom

Born: New York City, on April 9, 1928

Education: Harvard, B.A., 1946; M.A., 1947; postgraduate work at Harvard, 1947-1953, 1960-1965; at Columbia, 1948-1949

Biography

Thomas Andrew Lehrer was born in New York City on April 9, 1928. His parents were James and Anna (Waller) Lehrer. During his years in grade school and high school, Tom Lehrer was an outstanding student; early on, he showed all the promise of a prodigy at the piano, composing his own songs at the age of seven. He enrolled at Harvard University in 1943 at the age of fourteen, took his B.A. in mathematics three years later, and then received the M.A. in the following year, while teaching in the graduate school. Lehrer apparently established a record for length of time in graduate study, variously at Harvard and Columbia.

Lehrer's teaching career unfolded at Harvard, where he taught calculus in the Business School (1961) and geometry in the Education School (1963-65), and at Wellesley, where he taught statistics in the Psychology Department. Easily juggling careers, he taught concurrently at M.I.T. from 1962 to 1971. Since 1972, he has divided his lecturing duties equally between Cambridge and the University of California at Santa Cruz, where he has taught courses in mathematics and in American musical theater. Despite his considerable success as a song writer and an entertainer, and aside from his reputation as a wicked humorist, Lehrer seems to have mainly defined himself as a teacher. In an interview with Jeremy Bernstein in the early 1980s, from which comes most of the biographical data available on the reclusive Lehrer, he said, "I'm not really a mathematician, I'm a *teacher* of mathematics."[1]

During the early years of the Korean War, Lehrer was employed in a Cambridge firm, Baird-Atomic; the nature of his work there required him to spend some time at Los Alamos, New Mexico, in 1952. Later, he was drafted into the U.S. Army (1955-1957), most of that time working in the National Security Agency in Washington, D.C. It was, however, his work as occasional entertainer and composer of satiric songs that endeared him to a large segment of the American public.

Literary Analysis

Lehrer's reputation as a humorist survives principally because of his cabaret and television performances in the 1950s and the early 60s and, perhaps even more, because of his wickedly comic recordings which now enjoy classic status. In both the performing and the recording he may owe much to his genius for being in strange places at the right times.

Lehrer has been called "One of the most popular performers on the coffee house and campus circuit of the 1950s and early '60s."[2] While it is true that Lehrer was popular in those years, it is not enough to call him a "performer." He was an innovator of a style of performing. A reviewer for *Saturday Review* in 1954 recognized this innovation when he wrote that Lehrer's "area" of performing offered "Abe Burrows and very little else."[3] Lehrer himself has admitted that his kind of concert did not exist when he first began performing: "If you said that you were going to do a concert, people assumed that you were going to play the piano or something. The only humorous concerts then were given by Anna Russell or Victor Borge. The idea of a George Carlin or a David Steinberg giving a concert just didn't exist."[4] Lehrer's mode of performing helped prepare the times for the stand-up comedy routines that were to start appearing. Jesse Bier's "library" of these stand-up comedians includes Shelley Berman, Mort Sahl, Jonathan Winters, Nichols and May, Woody Allen, and Bob Newhart, all entertainers who followed in the wake of Lehrer.[5]

Lehrer's first public performance in a continuing series occurred in 1951 on a weekly television satire program which aired in the Boston area for four weeks and was hosted by Al Capp, the cartoonist. However, his performing career began almost by accident in 1950 when the Harvard Law School sponsored a quartet contest; as part of the successful group that won the contest, he began to sing his own songs at smokers and dance intermissions.[6] Well before the end of the 1950s Lehrer's appearances at places like the Blue Angel in New York City were being reviewed in the popular press. About one of his Blue Angel concerts *Newsweek* reported on April 22, 1957 that "Every night at 11 and again at 1, a lanky figure supporting a thatch of collegian cropped hair, horn-rimmed glasses, and a blandly amiable expression sits down at the piano at the Blue Angel in New York and unlooses a burble of gleefully sardonic songs. In the course of each half-hour stint, 29-year-old Tom Lehrer chants and thumps his way through a repertory which offers 'something for every depraved taste.'" After a Hunter College concert in that same year he began touring and for the next three years performed often in European countries.

The British television program "That Was the Week That Was" came to the United States in 1964, and Lehrer was invited to perform his songs on that show. Though he wrote a number of songs for public television's *The Electric Company*, including "Silent E" and "L-Y" in 1971-1972, he made his last public concert appearances at the hungry i in San Francisco in 1965 when he was trying out the material for an album, *That Was the Year That Was*. In 1980 a retrospective of Lehrer's work, *Tomfoolery*, directed by Cameron Mackintosh, opened in London; two productions ran in America in 1981. In the same year Pantheon Books released *Too Many Songs by Tom Lehrer with Not Enough Pictures by Ronald Searle*, a near-definitive songbook of Lehrer's work.

The true definition of the nature of Tom Lehrer's work is to be found in the three collections of his songs: *Songs by Tom Lehrer, An Evening Wasted with Tom Lehrer,* and *That Was the Year that Was,* and in the variant reprints. The famous Lehrer luck seems to have been at work on the first album, for its fortune and its influence were both unexpected. Lehrer recorded *Songs by Tom Lehrer* in 1953, using

the facilities of a local recording company which he located in the Yellow Pages. Both expectations and cost were minimal. "The total cost of everything—studio, tape, engineer, microphone, piano, everything—was fifteen dollars," he recalled in the Bernstein interview. The run was four hundred records; however, the music critic for the *San Francisco Chronicle* praised the album in a column, and the album ultimately sold in the thousands.

Songs by Tom Lehrer pretty well established the composer's style of writing and his type of humorous content. Sardonic humor was to be his forte, as indicated in the liner notes of the first album: "Now at last some of the songs with which he has been revolting local audiences for years are available to all, and it is no wonder that a great deal of public apathy has been stirred up at the prospect." The album cover was illustrated with a drawing of a satanic Lehrer, horned and tailed, playing a piano keyboard in the midst of flames. Inside, his compositions are devilish versions of stereotyped song styles: folk, traditional, and popular tunes.

Lehrer's artistic intent was to provide black humor framed in parodies of popular song styles, and to examine a few of his songs is to define his characteristic art. "The Irish Ballad," Lehrer's folk song, a genre that he describes on the album cover as a "form of permissible idiocy of the intellectual fringe," is a ballad "complete with modal tune, simple story line, and inane refrain, but it differs from other ancient ballads in that it was written in 1950." Thus, on the one hand, "The Irish Ballad" reflects a genuine underlying ballad structure. But, "the simple story line" out-ballads anything that ever came from the dark imagination of the folk. It tells the story of an Irish maid who went well beyond the notorious actions of the American ax murderer Lizzie Borden in "doing in" her family. Lizzie only axed mother and father; the Irish maid continues through the baby, sister, and brother:

> She weighted her brother down with stones,
>   Sing rickety-tickety-tin,
> She weighted her brother down with stones,
> And sent him off to Davy Jones.
> All they ever found were some bones,
>   And occasional pieces of skin, of skin,
>   Occasional pieces of skin.

The song itself is as much of a shock treatment as anything Ambrose Bierce ever wrote, even bearing some kinship to a story like "Oil of Dog," for example. Despite the macabre tone, the song, when performed in the wry voice of Lehrer, is funny. Besides, in the final stanza Lehrer puts the responsibility for the song on the audience by singing, "And if you do not enjoy my song,/ You've yourselves to blame if it's too long,/ You should never have let me begin, begin." Clever and wry, the lyrics and the voice tame the ugly content, though the parody of the folk song still exists.

Both of Lehrer's songs on the first album that promise to harken back to some golden era in the past, "The Wild West Is Where I Want to Be" and "I Wanna Go Back to Dixie," contain more ire than nostalgia. Both the West and the South in popular songs, whether out of B-movies or Disney, are golden places in the popular imagination. Though the titles of Lehrer's parodies suggest that the singer wants to return to the golden West and the dewy South, the lyrics clearly identify the irony in the titles. Neither singer nor audience could ever long for such inhospitable environments. In the West "the scenery's attractive," but "the air is radioactive." Even though the times in Dixie are "not forgotten," it is mainly because of "Whuppin' slaves and sellin' cotton." The West, in short, seems to have been projected into some crazy future where guided missiles and mushroom clouds have invaded the "desert's hush." In the case of Dixie, the singer can only conclude after all the talk of pellagra, hominy, and boll weevils that "what the hell, it's home." Clearly, Lehrer sings such lyrics with a cheeky tongue; clearly also, the parodies are vehicles for Swiftian satire.

Songs from the later albums are no less biting, no less clever. As the titles of Lehrer's songs indicate, his subjects for satire are universal: "We Will All Go Together When We Go," "National Brotherhood Week," "Smut," "Send the Marines," "Poisoning Pigeons in the Park." Lehrer's lyrics, as well as his targets, remain alive. Part of the second stanza of "National Brotherhood Week" unfortunately seems to bear enough of the message of truth about human experience that it can operate as something like a key to Lehrer's message and intent:

> *Oh, the poor folks hate the rich folks,*
> *And the rich folks hate the poor folks.*
> *All of my folks hate all of your folks,*
> *It's American as apple pie.*

Within the cleverness and comic appeal of Lehrer's art lies the cutting edge of a message about the human species that is as old and as new as Jonathan Swift.

Summary

Tom Lehrer's career as a comic satirist began early enough at the beginning of the 1950s to provide an example for the stand-up comics who gained fame in the 1960s. That Lehrer defined himself as a teacher and not as an entertainer probably explains his early retirement from performing. That he thought of himself as a teacher may also explain his motives for the three albums of dark, comic satires that he issued between 1953 and 1965. That his objects of satire proved to be universal human weakness may also account for the classic status of his work.

Notes

1. Jeremy Bernstein, "Tom Lehrer: Having Fun," *The American Scholar*, Summer 1984, p. 299.
2. Irwin Stambler and G. Landon, *Encyclopedia of Folk, Country and Western Music* (New York: St. Martin's, 1969), p. 170.
3. "Meet Tom Lehrer," *Saturday Review*, August 28, 1954, p. 65.
4. Bernstein, p. 299.
5. Ibid., p. 328.
6. Ibid., p. 298.

Selected Bibliography

Primary Sources

Book

Too Many Songs by Tom Lehrer with Not Enough Drawings by Ronald Searle. New York: Pantheon Books, 1981.

Discography

Songs by Tom Lehrer. Lehrer TL 101, 1953; Reprise RS-6216, a reprint, 1966; U.K.: Decca LF 1311, 1958.

An Evening Wasted with Tom Lehrer. Lehrer TL 202, 1959; U.K.: Decca LK 4332 and SKL 4097 (mono and stereo), 1959.

That Was the Year That Was. Reprise RS-6179, 1965; U.K.: Pye R-6179, 1965.

Secondary Sources

Bernstein, Jeremy. "Tom Lehrer: Having Fun." *The American Scholar*, Summer 1984, pp. 295-302.

"Imp of the Blue Angel." *Newsweek* April 22, 1957, p. 70.

"Meet Tom Lehrer." *Saturday Review*, August 28, 1954, p. 65.

Stambler, Irwin, and G. Landon. *Encyclopedia of Folk, Country and Western Music.* New York: St. Martin's, 1969.

Lonnie L. Willis

Levenson, Sam

Born: New York City, on December 28, 1911

Education: Brooklyn College, B.A. 1934; Columbia University, M.A. 1938

Marriage: Esther Levine, December 27, 1936, two children

Died: August 27, 1980

Biography

Samuel Levenson was born in New York City on December 28, 1911, the son of Hyman Levenson, a tailor, and Rebecca (Fishelman) Levenson, and the youngest of eight children. The family's income was small, but the children had a wholesome and happy upbringing, due largely to their mother's tolerant yet firm philosophy of childrearing. Levenson attended high school in Brooklyn, where his family had moved, and graduated from Brooklyn College in 1934 with a B.A. in Spanish. Later he earned a master's degree in Romance Languages at Columbia University. On December 27, 1936, he married Esther Levine; they were to have two children. He began a teaching career and, in 1938, was assigned to Brooklyn's Samuel J. Tilden High School; he remained there for the next eight years.

Levenson broke into show business in 1940 as a master of ceremonies for a group of teachers who had organized an orchestra to perform in the Catskills. He learned the art of timing and perfected his own style of delivery during these engagements. By 1942, he was advertising himself as a "folk humorist" willing to entertain at a wide variety of social functions. Personal recollections as well as jokes were now an important part of his routines. In 1946, Levenson chose to become a full-fledged entertainer. Night club bookings led to his appearance on Ed Sullivan's television program, *Toast of the Town*, in the spring of 1949. During the next eighteen months, Levenson made four successful appearances on Sullivan's program and was guest entertainer on *This Is Show Business*, *Cavalcade of Stars*, and the Rudy Vallee and Milton Berle shows. He was hired by Jack Benny when Benny began his CBS-TV series in October of 1950 to talk about such subjects as sending a child to summer camp and the dangers of a home with children and a TV set. Critical acclaim led to his own program, *The Sam Levenson Show*, first seen on CBS-TV in January of 1951. This kids' show with a sense of humor established Levenson's reputation was a shrewd and witty observer of the American scene. The program ran until June of 1952.

From 1951 to 1954, Levenson was a regular panelist on *This Is Show Business*. Hired in the summer of 1955 to substitute for humorist Herb Shriner as moderator on *Two for the Money*, he continued with the show in 1956. Levenson rejected offers extended him for educational programs by NBC and CBS in 1958 because he believed that the networks wasted TV as an aid to education. He appeared as a regular panelist on *Masquerade Party* in 1956, and in April of 1960, *The Sam Levenson Show* was selected to succeed *Arthur Godfrey Time* when Godfrey underwent treatment for cancer. A regular panelist on *To Tell the Truth* from 1961 to 1963 and on *The Match Game* in 1965, he continued to make guest appearances on a variety of television and radio programs. Levenson died in New York City on August 27, 1980.

Literary Analysis

A gentle and homespun nightclub and television monologist and writer, Sam Levenson used his experiences growing up in a large Jewish immigrant family and teaching in a Brooklyn high school as grist for his brand of folk humor. Stressing the happy, wholesome side of being poor in the good old days, he delighted TV and nightclub audiences as well as his readers with humorous reminiscences of his boyhood and comments on the everyday problems of youth and family life. His family chronicles, which struck a chord with audiences of varied backgrounds, constituted what he considered to be an intelligent form of comedy that gave him an opportunity to say something about the American scene. Laughing heartily and infectiously at his own jokes, Levenson was no deadpan humorist, but he did believe that it was difficult for a comedian to meet a weekly schedule without tiring his audience.

Levenson's first book, *Meet the Folks: A Session of American-Jewish Humor* was published in 1948. The volume is a compilation of his original anecdotes and jokes about life in American-Jewish homes. His *Everything but Money* appeared in 1966. A witty and warm book, it is an account of Levenson's life from boyhood in a crowded East Harlem tenement to his successful career as a television personality and humorist. The early pages constitute a memoir of a family rich in everything but money. In a section entitled "Off My Chest," Levenson discourses on the American educational system as he has observed it and as he would like to see it changed for the better.

Of his *Sex and the Single Child* (1969), Levenson observes that "that is not a book for children, but about children, innocent children."[1] Illustrated by Whitney Darrow, Jr., it is by turns funny and touching as it treats such topics as "Where Did I Come From? . . .," "He Learns by Observation," "Birds, Bees, Ants, Eggs, Seeds, and Other Ploys," amd "Teacher Said. . . ." In his *In One Era and Out the Other* (1973), Levenson discusses such topics as time, work, love, marriage and the family, freedom, and sex education—as he perceived these subjects when he was young and later. With his straightforward, low-key narration, he presents a plain, old-fashioned menu of humor.

In *You Can Say That Again, Sam* (1975), Levenson reflects on youth and age, about raising children and the beating many marriages take as a result of this endeavor, and about the difference between growing up a generation or more ago and growing up in the 1970s. His humor is universal as he looks back through the past with rose-colored glasses and confronts the present with underplayed naiveté. Particularly well done is his homey satire on modern business and advertising. Levenson's *You Don't Have to Be in Who's Who to Know What's What* (1979) touches upon a number of universal themes that have concerned humanity forever—birth, death, love, prejudice, war, God, sex, and money. Hundreds of quips are strung together by Levenson's witty commentary, giving the whole the flavor of a humorous dissertation.

Summary

Sam Levenson's humor had wide appeal, both on television and the printed page. No matter where he went, he was often going home, taking his audiences back comfortably to an older time. When he examined contemporary manners, he focused on excess and the folly that comes from an underdeveloped self-awareness.

Note

1. Sam Levenson, *Sex and the Single Child* (New York: Simon and Schuster, 1969), p. 13.

Selected Bibliography

Primary Sources

Meet the Folks: A Session of American-Jewish Humor with Sammy Levenson. New York: Citadel Press, 1948.

Everything But Money. New York: Simon and Schuster, 1966.

Sex and the Single Child. New York: Simon and Schuster, 1969; Simon and Schuster in 1976 as *A Time for Innocence: A Kid's-eye View of the Facts of Life.*

In One Era and Out the Other. New York: Simon and Schuster, 1973.

You Can Say That Again, Sam! The Choice Wit and Wisdom of Sam Levenson. New York: Pocket Books, 1975.

You Don't Have to Be in Who's Who to Know What's What. New York: Simon and Schuster, 1979.

Secondary Sources

Freedman, Morris. "Comedian in a Business Suit: Jewish Experience, Everybody's Humor."

Commentary, 20 (September 1955): 255–261. An analysis of Levenson's humor emphasizing its broad appeal.

Herrmann, Helen Markel. "Folk Humorist from Brooklyn." *New York Times Magazine*, December 17, 1950, pp. 14, 26–28, 30. Good account of Levenson's life and career to 1950.

Smith, Ronald Lande. *The Stars of Stand-Up Comedy.* New York: Garland Publishing, 1986, pp. 123–124. Brief treatment of Levenson's career as a humorist.

L. Moody Simms, Jr.

Lewis, Charles Bertrand

Born: Liverpool, Ohio, on February 15, 1842

Education: The Agricultural College of Lansing, Michigan

Marriage: Married, one child

Died: August 21, 1924

Biography

Charles Bertrand Lewis was born on February 15, 1842 in Liverpool, Ohio. His father, a successful building contractor and man of notable education, moved the family to Michigan when Charles was quite young. There the boy received a public education and pursued a course of study at the Agricultural College of Lansing, Michigan. He found his true calling, however, in the composing rooms and editorial offices of small newspapers. As early as fourteen, he began an apprenticeship at the Pontiac, Michigan, *Jacksonian* and continued in newspaper work, with time out for a stint in the Union Army during the Civil War, for the next sixty-eight years of his life.

In 1869, Lewis was hired by the *Detroit Free Press* as a legislative reporter, in which capacity he served for five years before turning to humor. During this period, he developed his narrative craft by writing dime novels for Beadle and Adams, George Munro, and *Ballou's Magazine*. Success came when he published in the *Free Press* an account of his experiences several years earlier aboard the Ohio River steamer *Magnolia*. Lewis had been traveling to Jonesboro, Tennessee, to assume an editorship there when the boat exploded, seriously injuring Lewis and killing many passengers. Lewis's droll narration of the catastrophe and of his subsequent recuperation in a Cincinnati, Ohio, hospital, titled "How It Feels to Be Blown Up" (later included in his collected works as "Up Among the Splinters"), was flavored with a liberal dose of grisly details combined with an insouciant narrative voice in the manner of the popular western humorists of the period. "Blown Up" was quickly picked up by the newspaper exchange and became something of a phenomenon, earning the *Free Press* a national reputation and making Lewis a recognized figure in humor circles. From that point he concentrated on humor, writing filler paragraphs and daily columns that he intermittently collected into book form. Financial success followed. Lewis became part owner of the *Free Press* and enjoyed large sales of his books during the 1870s and 1880s. Though he remained a humorist for the rest of his career, he did sustain his journalistic interests with occasional serious projects, including a volume of Civil War history (*Field, Fort and Fleet,* 1885). Lewis also had a lifetime interest in the theater. He wrote five plays, one of which, *Yakie,* was produced in 1884.

Lewis moved to New York in 1891 to join the staff of the *World* and *Evening World,* for which he wrote six humor columns a week. Lewis's last years were not happy. He outlived his popularity and suffered severe rheumatism in spite of which he was able to continue writing until his death on August 21, 1924. There is scant public record of his family life. He did marry and had a son, A.D. Lewis.

Literary Analysis

On the basis of "How it Feels to be Blown Up," Lewis earned an early reputation as a western humorist similar in style to Mark Twain and Bill Nye. Some materials in his popular early volume *Quad's Odds* (1875) sustained this view. *Odds* was a lengthy folio of pieces from the *Free Press* with little to unite them beyond a common format. Most were brief character sketches or comic vignettes told in a flat voice by a self-effacing narrator. Occasionally Lewis touched on subject matter—Indians and Mormons, for example—popular with western writers. Yet unlike the western humorists, Lewis never really developed a comic persona. He did write under the pseudonym M. Quad, a play on "'em quad," the printing term for a blank slug in a line of type, and he made sporadic attempts in *Quad's Odds* to give the figure a genealogy and family, including a son named Small Pica, but the persona never evolved into a character. Lewis was far more successful with the styles of humor associated with eastern popular theater and the journalistic humor of the literary comedians. He wrote dialogue well and preferred to develop vivid characters—many of them ethnic stereotypes from the popular stage—around whom he could construct jokes. In this respect he fit into the school of humor associated with Robert Burdette and

James M. Bailey, who were developing the conventions of suburban domestic comedy in their newspaper pieces.

Lewis was at his best and most popular with materials that were tied together by an extended community of regular characters, such as the members of the Lime Kiln Club, a black fraternal lodge in Detroit presided over by Brother Gardener, a paternally sanctimonious figure given to windy philosophy and sermonizing lectures bestowed upon his brethren at the start of each lodge meeting. Lewis wrote the Lime Kiln pieces in the form of proceedings of the lodge meetings and developed literally dozens of supporting characters with names like Waydown Beebe, Giveadam Jones, Pickles Smith and Elder Toots, whose function was to provide bulesque committee reports and whose antics gave Brother Gardener opportunities to deliver pointed homilies on such subjects as comfortable shoes and chicken stealing. Though blatantly racist, the Lime Kiln materials did accomplish some telling satire of fraternal lodges and were highly popular for the non sequiturs, malapropisms, and labored puns of the characters' broad minstrel show dialects.

Lewis's main accomplishments as a humorist were his stories of the Bowsers, a childless, middle-aged, middle-class couple confronted with the tribulations of urban domestic life. Lewis developed the characters after moving to New York, and he published four volumes of their stories between 1899 and 1911. Mr. Bowser was older than his wife, childlike, impractical, bombastic, and overweight. He was a catastrophizer and sucker for fads. She, in contrast, kept a clean and modest house and was resourceful, long suffering, and only occasionally outspoken. Most of the Bowsers' escapades involved misguided attempts on his part at home economy. Given to tyrannically infantile burst of temper, Mr. Bowser always blamed his wife for the consequences of his own mistakes, which took the form of an endless stream of do-it-yourself schemes that invariably caused household destruction and led to bitter arguments with Mrs. Bowser culminating in moments of icy calm in which he announced his intentions of divorcing her. "My lawyer will see your lawyer in the morning," served as a signature line for most of the pieces. Contemporaries of Lewis improved the various elements of his Bowser sketches. Robert Benchley, for example, softened and polished the husband's childlike incompetence in his own narrative persona, and comic domestic warfare served as a staple of newspaper comics in the teens and 1920s, but not until the combination reoccurred in *The Honeymooners* was Lewis surpassed in this vein.

Summary

Charles Bertrand Lewis, writing as M. Quad, was a leading literary comedian of the last quarter of the nineteenth century. He influenced the conventions of domestic urban comedy and it was on his early works that the reputation of the *Detroit Free Press* primarily depended.

Selected Bibliography

Primary Sources

Bugler Ben; or, The Scout of the Delaware. New York: G. Munro, 1872.

The Hunter's Vision: The Search for the Cave of Gold. Boston: Office American Union and Ballou's Magazine, 1872.

Mad Dan, the Spy of 1776: A Centennial Story. New York: Beadle and Adams, 1873.

Goaks & Tears. Boston: H.L. Shepard, 1875.

Quad's Odds. Detroit: R.D.S. Tyler, 1875.

Bessie Baine; or, The Mormon's Victim. Boston: G.W. Studley, 1876.

Ben and Dot; a Comedy in 3 Acts. Detroit: n.p., 1879.

Deacon Jackson; a Comedy in 4 Acts. Detroit: n.p., 1879.

The Comic Biography of James A. Garfield. New York: n.p., 187-.

Bijah; a Comedy in 1 Act and 3 Scenes. Detroit: n.p., 1880.

Brother Gardener's Lime Kiln Club. Chicago: Belford, Clark & Co., 1882.

Sawed Off Sketches. New York: G.W. Carleton & Co., 1884.

Field, Fort and Fleet. Detroit: Free Press Publishing, 1885.

Sparks of Wit. Detroit: R.D.S. Tyler, 1885.

Tennessee; a Three Cast Play in One Act. Brooklyn: n.p., 1898.

Under Five Lakes; or, Cruising in the Submarine Boat "Destroyer." New York: George Munro's Sons, 1898.

Mr. and Mrs. Bowser and Their Varied Experiences. New York: J.S. Ogilvie, 1899.

Trials and Troubles of the Bowser Family. New York: J.S. Ogilvie, 1899.

The Life and Troubles of Mr. Bowser. New York: Charles C. Thompson, 1902.

The Humorous Mr. Bowser. New York: J.S. Ogilvie, 1911.

Secondary Sources

Coyle, William. *Ohio Authors and Their Books 1796-1950.* Cleveland: World, 1962, p. 383.

Dictionary of American Biography. Vol. 6. New York: Scribner's, 1961, pp. 207-208.

Kunitz, Stanley, and Howard Haycraft. *American Authors 1600-1900.* New York: H.W. Wilson, 1938, pp. 465-466.

The National Cyclopedia of American Biography, Vol. 6. Ann Arbor, Michigan: University Microfilms, 1967, p. 30.

New York Times, August 23, 1924, p. 9.

Who's Who in America, 1920-21, p. 1711.

Gary Engle

Lewis, Henry Clay

Birth: Charleston, South Carolina, on June 26, 1825
Education: Louisville Medical Institute, M.D., 1846
Death: August 5, 1850

Biography

Henry Clay Lewis, known to contemporary readers of his humorous sketches as "Madison Tensas, M.D., the Louisiana Swamp Doctor," lived a short but interestingly varied life.[1] The seventh of nine children, Lewis was born in Charleston, South Carolina, on June 26, 1825, and was named for his grandfather, Henry Lewis, whose wife, Judith D'Israeli, was related to Benjamin Disraeli, a future prime minister of England. Lewis had lived in Charleston for only four years when his father, David Lewis, a furniture merchant, moved his family to Cincinnati, Ohio. Two years later, in 1831, his mother, Rachel, died, and Lewis was sent to live with his married brother, Alexander, who also resided in Cincinnati. In his brother's home he seems to have been compelled to perform menial tasks by his sister-in-law and was denied the opportunity for formal education.

Finding this situation intolerable, Lewis ran away in 1835, escaping aboard an Ohio River steamboat. During the next year, he engaged in a series of odd jobs on Ohio and Mississippi riverboats, finally securing a position as a cook's assistant and cabin boy on a Yazoo River steamer packet, running between Vicksburg and Manchester, Mississippi (the name of the latter town was subsequently changed to Yazoo City). This experience provided him with a practical education of observing people and hearing stories, both important to his later development as a writer of humorous sketches.

Highly motivated to get ahead in the world, Lewis soon gave up his river life. His older brother, Joseph, who lived in Manchester, the chief port on the Yazoo River, persuaded Lewis to live with him and his wife, promising to finance the long-awaited education that Henry hoped for. Lewis remained in Manchester for the next ten years. After he had been there for only a short time, however, his brother experienced financial disaster, a consequence of the economic panic of 1837. Because of Joseph's financial problems, Henry's formal education had to be postponed indefinitely, and he was compelled to work in the cotton fields for the next five years. Even so, he found time to acquaint himself with some of the squatters of the Yazoo swamps, notable raconteurs of tall-talish hunting stories, an experience that likely influenced the composition of some of his own later humorous hunting sketches such as "The Indefatigable Bear Hunter," which initially appeared in William T. Porter's *The Spirit of the Times* on April 20, 1850.

In 1841, when Lewis was sixteen, Joseph arranged for him to be apprenticed to Dr. Washington Dorsey, a Yazoo City physician under whom he could learn the rudiments of medicine through practical experience and thereby gain the background and training preparatory to entering the medical profession. During his medical apprenticeship, Lewis became notorious as a prankster and practical joker. In one of his apparently autobiographical sketches, "The Day of Judgment," included in *Odd Leaves from the Life of a Louisiana "Swamp Doctor,"* Lewis recounts how he had once made a handsome profit by deceptively inoculating persons against smallpox. To carry out his stratagem, what he calls "a pious fraud," he used a supply of fluid from the back of his horse. Despite such occasional pranks, most of the time Lewis performed the tasks of his apprenticeship diligently and responsibly. While still an apprentice with Dorsey, he also began to write, contributing several poems under the pseudonym "Ion" to the *Yazoo City Whig*. Two of these appeared in the *Whig* in 1844: "A Vision of Pandemonium," a satirical attack on Democrats, and "An Acrostic," a celebratory poem about Henry Clay.

Upon completing his medical apprenticeship in 1844, Lewis began his formal medical studies at the Louisville Medical Institute, which had been founded only eight years earlier. In 1845, after completing his first term of study, he returned to Yazoo City for the summer to continue his practical training under Dorsey's tutelage. In August of that same year, Lewis anonymously published in *The Spirit of the Times* his first and subsequently one of his best-known humorous sketches, "Cupping on the Sternum," an autobiographical work that seems to have been based on an incident that occurred in 1842 during his medical apprenticeship. This sketch was reprinted in William T. Porter's anthology, *A Quarter Race in Kentucky and Other Sketches* (1846).

In March 1846, several months before his twenty-first birthday, Lewis completed his medical studies at the Louisville Medical Institute and returned to Yazoo City to establish a practice. A scarcity of patients, however, prompted him to move his practice to Madison Parish, an area in the remote and primitive swamp country of northeastern Louisiana on the Tensas River. The inhabitants of the area were mainly large and small planters who owned slaves, farmers without slaves, swampers, and bear hunters—the prototypes of characters that he would later incorporate into his humorous sketches. Between 1846 and 1849, the period of his sojourn in the swamps and canebrakes on the Tensas, Lewis treated many varied diseases and established a busy and lucrative medical practice. He also published in *The Spirit of the Times*, under the pseudonym "Tensas," five sketches focusing on his medical apprenticeship, his medical school experience, and his practice. Subsequently, the sketches that Lewis submitted to the *Spirit* bore the pseudonym, "Madison Tensas." "A Leaf from the Life of A 'Swamp Doctor,'" appearing in *The Spirit of the Times* in May 1847, was the first sketch in which Lewis actually used the "Swamp Doctor" pen-name, a fact suggesting that he had already begun to ponder the possibility of developing a series of humorous tales using this character.

Near the end of 1848, when Lewis decided to leave the Tensas River region, he had probably already started a book based on his previously published sketches. In 1849 he moved to Richmond, Louisiana, a prosperous cotton-growing region and the seat of Madison Parish, where he would reside for the rest of his life. In Richmond he set up a joint practice with a prominent physician, a fortuitous move enabling him to prosper and to gain access to the prominent social circles of the community. His professional and social activities in Richmond, however, seem to have prevented Lewis from doing any additional writing. His book, *Odd Leaves from the Life of a Louisiana "Swamp Doctor,"* which he had been working on before his move to Richmond, was published by A. Hart of Philadelphia in March 1850.[2] In the summer of this same year, a cholera epidemic plagued Madison Parish, and on August 5, 1850, after visiting a cholera patient, Lewis drowned when his horse apparently became entangled in submerged willows.

Literary Analysis

Lewis's fame as a humorist rests on an incredibly small body of work: a total of twenty-five sketches, twenty-two of which appear in his only book, *Odd Leaves from the Life of a Louisiana "Swamp Doctor."* Adopting as his persona "Madison Tensas," an old swamp doctor, Lewis amusingly recounts under the guise of partially distorted autobiography some of his experiences as a medical apprentice, medical student, and frontier doctor. As a humorist, Lewis belongs to the southwestern school of Augustus B. Longstreet, Johnson Jones Hooper, Thomas Bangs Thorpe, and George Washington Harris, writers, Arlin Turner has pointed out, who were using "materials outside the bounds of polite literature."[3] His typical sketches employ some of the features commonly associated with southwestern humor: the framework, dialect, elements of folklore, tall-talish exaggeration, and incongruous juxtaposition of fantasy and reality. Yet, the feature of his work of primary interest to modern critics is what Hennig Cohen and William B. Dillingham have called "the element of cruelty and degradation . . . the underside of comedy."[4]

This particular aspect of humor—what we commonly refer to as the grotesque—characterizes many of Lewis' sketches. And, in such sketches, as Charles Israel has noted, "there is a pervasive atmosphere of cruelty and victimization," the victims being the "guilty" as well as the "innocent."[5] In "How to Cure Fits," for instance, Lewis describes a black woman who feigns sickness to evade working in the fields. When the vigilant Tensas discovers her scheme, he threatens to throw her from a bridge into the bayou and thereby quickly "cures" this woman of her aversion to work, and to assure that his "remedy" would be permanent, Tensas discloses that "a liberal flagellation completed the cure, and she has never been troubled with fits since!"[6] Other sketches in this vein, such as "The Curious Widow," treating a landlady who becomes temporarily insane when her medical student boarders carry out a grim prank to cure her of her obsessive nosiness, and "Valerian and the Panther," in which a boy has three of his fingers bitten off when he tries to steal a plug of tobacco from the jaw of his sleeping swamp squatter father, also display Lewis's shocking and realistically sardonic brand of humor.

Farce is another dominant feature of Lewis's comic strategy. In "A Tight Race Considerin'," one of the more skillfully crafted tales in *Odd Leaves*, a backwoods storyteller chronicles a lively tale concerning how he tricked his mother and a parson into a horse race. In concluding his yarn the storyteller, maintaining a deadpan pose, reports that although his mother won the race, her horse pitched her "like a lam for the sacryfise" through the meeting house window and into the midst of the bewildered congregation. In reacting to her rapid and unexpected arrival on the scene, "The men," the teller continues, "shot their eyes and scrambled outen the house, an' the women gin Mam so much of their close that they like to put themselves in the same fix" (p. 102).

In addition to slapstick Lewis attempted to generate humor in some of his sketches through exaggerated, incongruous comparisons, a stylistic device that John Q. Anderson broadly classifies as "folk language."[7] The dialect portions of *Odd Leaves* frequently exhibit graphic examples of humorous frontier tall talk, principally in the form of comic similes. In "A Tight Race Considerin'" the bewildered parson's "face [is] as pale as a rabbit's belly" (p. 99); in "The 'Mississippi Patent Plan' for Pulling Teeth" the neck of a Kentucky backswoodsman strapped in an operating chair to have his tooth extracted is described as "gradually extending itself like a terrapin's emerging from its shell" (p. 110); in "My First Call in the Swamp" one of the patients the doctor visits has hair "whiter than the inside of a persimmon seed" (p. 197); and in "Cupping on the Sternum" grease flows from the posterior of a black woman who has been cupped there "like molasses out of a worm hole" (p. 91).

A further dimension of Lewis's humorous manipulation of language is in his conscious use of wordplay. In "Cupping on the Sternum," for example, after Tensas mistakenly applies a scarificator to a black woman's posterior, he observes that "the cups were too *infat*uated to draw blood from that quarter" (p. 91). Moreover, the victim of the medical apprentice's malpractice foolishness is quite funny as the following dialogue containing a clever malapropism demonstrates: "'I does feel 'mazing bad—the mis'ry in my bosom, almost broke my heart; I can scasely perspire'" (p. 90). To be certain that the reader will not overlook the humor of her response, Lewis interjects that Chaney meant to say "respire" rather than "perspire"; but even without his overt editorializing, Chaney's word choice humorously epitomizes her predicament and how she feels about it.

Like many of the other writers of the Southwestern humor tradition, Lewis also turned his attention to what Walter Blair calls the "mock oral tale,"[8] using it as another mechanism for humorous expression. The best example of this mode in *Odd Leaves* and a work that is probably the most widely known of Lewis's sketches is "The Indefatigable Bear Hunter," which in part derives from the legendary exploits of Mike Hooter, a Mississippi bear hunter and lay preacher.[9] An amalgam of bizarre realism and entertaining fantasy, Lewis's tale focuses on a larger-than-life backwoodsman named Mik-hootah, whose sole ambition is to become the best "bear-hunter of Ameriky" (p. 239). Mik, to be sure, is in a class by himself. As Lewis states, when his "horn sounded—so tradition ran—the bears began to draw lots to see who should die that day" (p. 234). Subsequently, when one of Mik's legs is seriously maimed in a fight with a bear and has to be amputated, the hunter, in confronting another bear sometime later, uses as a weapon to kill the brute a piece of the wooden leg that the swamp doctor had made for him. And, in describing his triumph over the bear, Mik does so in his own coarse, uninhibited vernacular, thereby creating a zestful and vividly exaggerated tale. In his account of this incredible hunt, Mik acknowledges that he became so angry because his wooden leg prevented him from pursuing the bear that "I cust till the trees cummenst shedding their leaves and small branches" (p. 241). Mik employs the same kind of humorous tall talk in detailing the appearance of the place where he successfully subdued the bear. It gave the impression, he remarks, that "'stead of a bar fight that I had been cuttin' cane and deadenin' timber for a corn patch, the sile wer so worked up" (p. 244).

Summary

Among the best of the subversive contingent of southwestern humorists, Henry Clay Lewis has been aptly designated as "a native absurdist who thrived upon the absurd ambivalence of the comic-horrible life."[10] He wrote a series of humorous sketches, the majority collected in *Odd Leaves from the Life of a Louisiana "Swamp Doctor."* Focusing on the foibles and frailties of his characters and using as his authorial persona, "Madison Tensas, M.D.," who serves both as a conveyor and target of his satire, Lewis presents grimly amusing and sometimes disturbingly realistic accounts of life on the lower southern frontier before the Civil War. In exposing the unsavory side of the medical profession of his times, he employs with skillful competence the familiar techniques of southwestern humor to create a gallery of unforgettable and eccentric character types and humorous situations. In acknowledging his achievement, one must recognize that Lewis, along with several other humorists of the Old Southwest, helped to initiate the revolt against some of the widely popular literary conventions of antebellum America, forms characterized by gentility (both of language and subject matter), mawkish sentimentality, and obtrusive didacticism. Accordingly, Lewis and some of his compeers among the frontier yarnspinners were important precursors of the earthy and grotesque humor found in selected works of Erskine Caldwell, William Faulkner, and Flannery O'Connor and, therefore, as Turner has noted, they "pointed modestly but clearly in the direction of the homely matter, the frankness, and the elemental qualities which have supplied so much of the distinctness and the vitality of the best American writing."[11]

Notes

1. All biographical information on Lewis has been taken from John Q. Anderson's *Louisiana Swamp Doctor: The Life and Writings of Henry Clay Lewis* (Baton Rouge: Louisiana State University Press, 1962), pp. 3–59.
2. *Odd Leaves* was subsequently reissued in 1852, 1854, 1855, 1856, 1858, and 1881.
3. Arlin Turner, "Seeds of Literary Revolt in the Humor of the Old Southwest," *Louisiana Historical Quarterly*, 39 (1956): 145.
4. Hennig Cohen and William B. Dillingham, eds.,

Humor of the Old Southwest, 2nd ed. (Athens: University of Georgia Press, 1975), p. 337.
5. Charles Israel, "Henry Clay Lewis's *Odd Leaves*: Studies in the Surreal and Grotesque," *Mississippi Quarterly*, 28 (Winter 1974–1975): 64.
6. Anderson, *Louisiana Swamp Doctor*, p. 216. Subsequent references to Lewis's works will be to this edition, and page numbers will appear parenthetically in the text.
7. Ibid., p. 67.
8. Walter Blair, *Native American Humor* (San Francisco: Chandler, 1960), p. 89.
9. John Q. Anderson, "Mike Hooter—The Making of a Myth," *Southern Folklore Quarterly*, 19 (1955), 99.
10. Richard Boyd Hauck, *A Cheerful Nihilism: Confidence and "The Absurd" in American Humorous Fiction* (Bloomington: Indiana University Press, 1971), p. 44.
11. Turner, p. 151.

Selected Bibliography

Primary Sources

Odd Leaves from the Life of a Louisiana "Swamp Doctor." Philadelphia: A. Hart, 1850.

Secondary Sources

Bibliography

Anderson, John Q. "Henry Clay Lewis (1825–1850)." In *A Bibliographical Guide to the Study of Southern Literature.* Ed. Louis D. Rubin, Jr. Baton Rouge: Louisiana State University Press, 1969, pp. 240–241. A selected, briefly annotated list of sources about Lewis and his work.

Biography

Anderson, John Q. *Louisiana Swamp Doctor: The Life and Writings of Henry Clay Lewis.* Baton Rouge: Louisiana State University Press, 1962. Meticulously researched, this biographical account assembles all the known facts about Lewis's life; also reprints all of Lewis's extant humorous sketches and a poem.

Articles

Anderson, John Q. "Folklore in the Writings of 'The Louisiana Swamp Doctor.'" *Southern Folklore Quarterly*, 19 (December 1955): 243–251. Examines Lewis's handling of the elements of the mock oral tale, folk language, and folk medicine.

———. "Henry Clay Lewis, Alias 'Madison Tensas, M.D., the Louisiana Swamp Doctor.'" *Bulletin of the Medical Library Association*, 43 (January 1955): 58–73. Discusses Lewis's autobiographical sketches which treat his medical apprenticeship and training as well as his experiences as a physician.

———. "Henry Clay Lewis, Louisville Medical Institute Student, 1844–1846." *Filson Club Historical Quarterly*, 32 (January 1958): 30–37. Explores the five sketches in *Odd Leaves* that were based on Lewis's experiences at the Louisville Medical Institute.

———. "Louisiana 'Swamp Doctor.'" *McNeese Review*, 5 (Spring 1953): 45–53. Uses three of the sketches from *Odd Leaves* to illustrate how "Madison Tensas" employed devices common to southwestern humor.

———. "Mike Hooter—The Making of a Myth." *Southern Folklore Quarterly*, 19 (1955): 90–100. Demonstrates the influence of the materials of the "Mike Hooter legend" on Lewis's "The Indefatigable Bear Hunter."

Israel, Charles. "Henry Clay Lewis' *Odd Leaves*: Studies in the Surreal and Grotesque." *Mississippi Quarterly*, 28 (Winter 1974-1975): 61–69. Focuses on Lewis's "conscious artistic use of violence, grotesque episodes and images, and surreal humor to create a consistent world view.

Keller, Mark A. "'Aesculapius in Buckskin'—The Swamp Doctor as Satirist in Henry Clay Lewis's *Odd Leaves*." *Southern Studies*, 18 (Winter 1980): 425–448. Views *Odd Leaves* as a light-hearted satire as well as a serious defense of the medical profession.

Mace, Jennings R. "Henry Clay Lewis." In *Antebellum Writers in New York and the South*. Ed. Joel Myerson. Detroit: Gale, 1979, pp. 202–203. Brief overview of Lewis's life and work.

Rickels, Milton. "The Humor of the Old Southwest in London *Bentley's Miscellany*." *American Literature*, 27 (January 1956): 557–560. Notes that sketches of Southwestern humorists were reprinted in this magazine, including nine selections from Lewis's *Odd Leaves*.

Rose, Alan H. "The Image of the Negro in the Writings of Henry Clay Lewis." *American Literature*, 41 (May 1969): 255–263. A psychoanalytic study demonstrating that Lewis's sketches portraying the "demonic Negro" can be attributed to the author's own alienation from the dominant society of his time. In treating his own psychological tensions, Lewis seems to have expressed the covert fears of his fellow southerners.

Turner, Arlin. "Seeds of Literary Revolt in the Humor of the Old Southwest." *Louisiana Historical Quarterly*, 39 (1956): 143–151. Treats Longstreet, Thorpe, Hooper, Harris, and Lewis as participants in the "revolt" against genteel literature.

Edward J. Piacentino

Liebling, A[bbott] J[oseph]

Born: New York City, on October 18, 1904

Education: Entered Dartmouth College, 1920; expelled in 1923 for failure to attend chapel; Columbia University School of Journalism, B. Litt., 1925

Marriages: Anne Beatrice McGinn, July 28, 1934, divorced, 1949; Lucille Hille Spectorsky, 1949; divorced, 1959; Jean Stafford, April 3, 1959.

Died: December 28, 1963

Biography

Abbott Joseph Liebling was born in New York City on October 8, 1904, the son of Joseph Liebling, a prosperous furrier, and Anna Slone Liebling. He attended Dartmouth College and the School of Journalism at Columbia University, from which he graduated in 1925. Joining the sports department of the *New York Times*, he worked there for eight months before being fired. In 1926, Liebling went to Paris and studied at the Sorbonne for a brief time. He learned about French cooking, which engaged his interest and appetite from then on. Returning to the United States in 1927, he was employed by the *Providence Journal* and the *Evening Bulletin* as a reporter and feature writer for three years. Liebling worked on the *New York World-Telegram* from 1931 to 1935; he wrote more than one thousand feature articles. When he was refused a raise, he quit and worked for a time for King Features' *Evening Journal Magazine*.

In 1935, Harold Ross, who liked Liebling's irreverent and unpretentious style, hired him to work at *The New Yorker*. Liebling remained with the magazine until his death. In the early years, he wrote profiles and articles on figures ranging from jockey Eddie Arcaro to General George Marshall. Liebling was sent to Paris in October of 1939 to report on the first phases of World War II. Having returned to New York in 1940, he flew to England in July, 1941, to cover the activities of the Royal Air Force. He later covered American air strikes from England, the African campaign, and D-Day. In August 1944, he was in Paris when the city was liberated.

Soon after the war, Liebling began writing "The Wayward Press," a *New Yorker* department begun in the 1930s by Robert Benchley. With a characteristic biting humor, he fought to preserve the integrity of journalism by lambasting and lampooning the shortcomings of editors, publishers, reporters, politicians, and the public alike. To Liebling, nothing in the world of journalism was sacred. In addition to writing his regular column, Liebling was a leading contributor to *The New Yorker*, producing articles in prodigious numbers. Prominent among his many interests were language, food, boxing, New York's lowlife characters, horse racing, France, and colorful politicians. He was married three times, to Anne Beatrice McGinn in 1934, to Lucille Hille Spectorsky in 1949, and to the novelist Jean Stafford in 1959. His first two marriages ended in divorce, the first in 1949 and the second in 1959. Still reacting to life with great gusto, Liebling died in new York City on December 28, 1963.

Literary Analysis

Earning laurels as the gadfly of American journalism with his "The Wayward Press" column for *The New Yorker*, A.J. Liebling left behind an awesome body of work characterized by Raymond Sokolov as "learned without heaviness, funny, stylish, verbose, rebellious and, finally, heroic."[1] Witty in a serious way, Liebling's journalism is cheerful and defiant. The knowing tone of a humane skeptic runs through much of his work.

Liebling was primarily a magazine writer; nearly all of his books are composed of collected *New Yorker* pieces, sometimes extensively rewritten. In *Back Where I Came From* (1938), his first book, which contained pieces from the *World-Telegram* as well as *The New Yorker*, Liebling describes New York, clearly his first love, with amused affection. With indefatigable verve and humor, he provides portraits of his favorite Broadway sharpsters and antic con men. Another collection of lowlife pieces appeared in 1942 as *The Telephone Booth Indian*. As one absurdity follows another, the reader shares an enclosed world swarming with tricksters. Much of Liebling's war correspondence for *The New Yorker* is collected in *The Road Back to Paris* (1944), *Normandy Revisited* (1958), and *Mollie and Other War Pieces* (1964). Two wartime reviewers of the first work declared Liebling to be the intellectual's Ernie Pyle.

Liebling's first collection of "The Wayward Press" pieces appeared in 1947 as *The Wayward Press*. Dour commentaries are mixed with humorous and incisive quotations and analyses as he wittily exposes the vagaries and shortcomings of newspapers and newspapermen. In his *Chicago: The Second City* (1952), some of Liebling's sharpest barbs are aimed at Colonel Robert McCormick of the *Chicago Tribune*. Ties with Rabelais and the American tall-tale tellers can be seen in *The Honest Rainmaker* (1953), a study of Colonel John R. Stingo (alias James A. Macdonald), a somewhat fabulous, though real, figure of the contemporary sporting world. Sokolov sees Stingo as "an early version of the half-fictional picaro so common in the avant-garde fiction of the sixties and seventies."[2]

In his collection of boxing pieces, *The Sweet Science* (1956), Liebling writes in a style that is a pastiche of orotund and slangy prose. In 1961, another collection of his "The Wayward Press" columns appeared as *The Press*. The same year saw the publication of *The Earl of Louisiana*, in which Liebling portrays Louisiana governor Earl Long as a southern version of the fast-talking con men he had met elsewhere. In 1962, another collection of Liebling's lowlife pieces, *The Jollity Building*, appeared, as well as his *Between Meals: An Appetite for Paris*. The latter work focuses on two of Liebling's favorite subjects: food and France; throughout, he describes his gargantuan eating habits with the same zest that he uses to portray the sights and sounds of Paris.

Summary

Much of A.J. Liebling's work is humorous and skeptical in a generally warm-hearted way. His humor is sharp, but it springs from an understanding of and kindliness toward human beings of all sorts and conditions. Liebling's work found a natural outlet in the pages of *The New Yorker*, well-known for its intellectual satiric bent.

Notes

1. Raymond Sokolov, *Wayward Reporter: The Life of A.J. Liebling* (New York: Harper's, 1980), p. 320.
2. Ibid., p. 253.

Selected Bibliography

Primary Sources
Back Where I Came From. New York: Sheridan House, 1938.
The Telephone Booth Indian. Garden City: Doubleday, Doran, 1942.
The Road Back to Paris. Garden City: Doubleday, Doran, 1944; London: M. Joseph, 1944.
The Wayward Pressman. Garden City: Doubleday, 1947.
Chicago: The Second City. New York: Knopf, 1952.
The Honest Rainmaker: The Life and Times of Colonel John R. Stingo. Garden City: Doubleday, 1953.
The Sweet Science. New York: Viking, 1956; London: Gollancz, 1956.
Normandy Revisited. New York: Simon and Schuster, 1958.
The Earl of Louisiana. New York: Simon and Schuster, 1961.
The Press. New York: Ballantine Books, 1961; rev. ed., 1964; second rev. ed., with an introduction by Jean Stafford, 1975.
Between Meals: An Appetite for Paris. New York: Simon and Schuster, 1962.
The Jollity Building. New York: Ballantine, 1962.
The Most of A.J. Liebling. Sel. William Cole. New York: Simon and Schuster, 1963.
Mollie and Other War Pieces. New York: Ballantine, 1964.

Secondary Sources
Midura, Edmund M. *A.J. Liebling: The Wayward Pressman as Critic*. Lexington, Ky.: Association for Education in Journalism, 1974. Contains an anno-

tated bibliography of Liebling's principal works on the press.

Sokolov, Raymond. *Wayward Reporter: The Life of A.J. Liebling.* New York: Harper and Row, 1980. The standard work on Liebling's life and career as a writer.

L. Moody Simms, Jr.

Locke, David Ross

Born: Vestal, New York, on September 20, 1833

Education: Primary school, Marathon, New York, 1840–1845

Marriage: Martha H. Bodine, 1855, three children

Died: February 15, 1888

Biography

David Ross Locke was born in Vestal, Broome County, New York, near Binghamton, in 1833. His father, Nathaniel Reed Locke, was a laborer, tanner and shoemaker. His mother, Hester Ross Locke, died when he was six, and he was subsequently raised by a stepmother, Phila Amelia Taft Locke. David was deeply influenced by his father's belief in the value of hard work and faith in the rightness of temperance and abolition as preached in the hell-fire and damnation theology of the Methodist Episcopal church to which Nathaniel Locke belonged. For a brief period, between the ages of seven and twelve, David attended a one-room school in Marathon, New York.

In 1845 David Locke went to work as an apprentice in the editorial offices of the *Courtland* (New York) *Democrat*, where over the next seven years he learned the nuts and bolts of the newspaper trade. There followed a period as an itinerant printer during which time he worked as a compositor and occasional reporter for such papers as the *Corning* (New York) *Journal* (where he formed a lifelong friendship with Marcus "Brick" Pomeroy), the *Cleveland Plain Dealer*, and the *Pittsburgh Chronicle*. In 1853 he founded, with James G. Robinson, the *Plymouth* (Ohio) *Advertiser*. Thus began a career as publisher and editor of Ohio newspapers that saw him affiliated in rapid succession with the *Mansfield Herald*, the *Bucyrus Journal*, the *Hancock Jeffersonian* in Findlay, and, eventually, the *Toledo Blade*.

The 1850s were crucial in shaping Locke's life. There were personal milestones, including a marriage to Martha H. Bodine of Plymouth, Ohio, in 1855 and the birth of their first child. Locke's keen business sense revealed itself in the consistent success of his newspaper ventures. He also published his first humor during the period, a series of sketches now known as "The Sniggs Articles." These included thinly veiled accounts of his own riotous drinking binges and so offended his in-laws that Locke later had them suppressed. Locke's politics and social values coalesced around certain events of the period. In 1857 he joined the Republican party in Bucyrus. He interviewed Abraham Lincoln the following year. News of the Harper's Ferry incident in 1859 deeply affected him and served to confirm him in the role of a Republican spokesman. Locke emerged from the decade with two unshakeable addictions that were to shape the course of his future: the Republican party and alcohol.

In March 1861 Locke responded to the news of South Carolina's secession from the Union by publishing a letter in the *Hancock Jeffersonian* announcing the secession of Wingert's Corners, Ohio. The letter was signed with the name Petroleum V. Nasby and marked the beginning of one of the most prolific careers in the history of American humor. Locke wrote Nasby letters on an almost daily basis for most of the rest of his life, earning him the reputation of America's most famous and brutally effective satirist during the period of the Civil War and its aftermath.

In an effort to capitalize on the popularity of Nasby, Locke turned to public speaking, beginning in 1867, and was for a period of three years one of the most popular and highly paid performers on the lyceum circuit. His first and most famous lecture, delivered in the character of Nasby, was "Cussid Be Canaan," a straightforward polemic on racial equality whose opening line—"We are all descended from grandfathers"—became a slogan of the day. A year of touring "Canaan" was followed by two other lectures: "The Struggles of a Conservative with the Woman Question," in which he offered a qualified endorsement of the women's suffrage movement, and "In Search of the Man of Sin," in which he surveyed the moral climate of America and found it wanting, thus producing one of the earliest indictments of the Gilded Age. Locke's success as a lecturer earned him the respect and friendship of Mark Twain with whom he frequently travelled and caroused during the period.

Locke's home life was not happy. His alcoholism merely exacerbated a serious personality conflict with his wife. The lengthy separations necessitated by his speaking schedule resulted in an estrangement that lasted for most of the 1870s, during which time he lived in New York working on the staff of the *Evening Mail*. His wife remained in Toledo, where their eldest son, Robinson, oversaw an increasingly complex family business empire that included majority ownership in the Toledo *Blade* Corporation and numerous real estate and manufacturing interests. Private unhappiness, however, was matched to an extent by public success. Nasby made Locke a national figure; hard work made him a wealthy and influential man.

The New York years marked an increase in the variety of Locke's literary endeavors. Besides continuing the Nasby materials, Locke wrote short fiction and essays, some pseudonymously. He wrote a great deal of verse, the most successful being a long narrative poem titled *Hannah Jane* (1871). Locke scored well in the theater with *The Widow Bedott, or A Hunt for a Husband*, adapted from materials by Frances M. Whitcher. Two novels were completed during the decade: *A Paper City* (1879), about a real-estate investment scheme, and *The Demagogue*, published posthumously and now considered one of the better examples of the social protest fiction of the era, addressing with a skeptical eye the motives of the businessmen and politicians of the Gilded Age. Locke produced all of this in addition to the literally thousands of anonymous editorials churned out during his career. While in New York, Locke underwrote the publication of the *Index*, a magazine edited by the controversial Unitarian minister Francis Ellington Abbot, which was committed to the principles of free religion and social reform. The New York years were also witness to marathon bouts of dissipation.

In 1881, in an effort to come to grips with his alcoholism, Locke set out on what was planned as an extended tour of Europe with Robinson, for whom he had ambitions in the diplomatic corps. The tour resulted in a wealth of travel materials published in 1882 as *Nasby in Exile*. Locke returned to Toledo after only six months and spent the rest of his life suffering increasing ill health. The last years were marked by a personal temperance campaign waged from the editorial chair of the *Blade* and known by the catch phrase "Pulverize the Rum Power." So deeply committed was he to reducing the influence of the brewing industry and liquor dealers in Toledo that he ran successfully for alderman in 1886. Locke died of tuberculosis on February 15, 1888.

Literary Analysis

Though a celebrated jokester and raconteur, Locke was more a propagandist and satirist than a humorist. His wit was never sharper than when used to further a cause, and the causes he favored were those of the Republican party: abolition of slavery and preservation of the Union. His finest accomplishment was the creation of Petroleum Vesuvius Nasby, one of the most vividly drawn grotesques in all of American humor. Nasby was an offensively racist drunk, marginally literate yet cunning, cowardly, and lazy, whom Locke intended as a caricature of the supporters of the Copperheads, that wing of the Democratic party sympathetic to the Southern cause. The vividness of the caricature resulted from Locke's first-hand experience with the type in the villages and backwoods of Crawford County, Ohio, during his years with the Bucyrus *Journal*.

Locke's satiric technique was simple. Any position taken by Nasby was irretrievably tainted by the association. Thus, Nasby spoke on behalf of slavery and states' rights and campaigned for select politicians such as Ohio congressman Clement Laird Vallandigham, a national leader of the Copperheads and supreme commander of the notorious Order of the Sons of Liberty. Locke couched the caricature in background details and provided a cast of secondary characters sufficient to make Nasby live in the minds of the nation's readers, eventually settling him as postmaster in the fictional village of Confedrit X Roads, Kentucky, where the loafer wheedled what liquor he could on credit and occupied himself with writing letters to the editor of the *Blade* expressing his outrageous political and social views.

In 1864 Locke began reprinting the Nasby letters in book form. The earliest of these volumes, including *The Nasby Papers* (1864), *Divers Opinions and Prophecies* (1865), *Swingin Round the Cirkle* (1867), and *Ekkoes from Kentucky* (1868), are now regarded as containing his sharpest satire. So popular were the early Nasby letters that Lincoln, a devoted fan as early as 1863, invited Locke to Washington for a visit. Lincoln's love of the Nasby materials was legendary, producing numerous stories of his habit of reading from them at cabinet meetings. There is, in fact, evidence that *The Nasby Papers* was the last book from which Lincoln read before his assassination. Lincoln offered Locke a political appointment, which he turned down, as he did a subsequent offer of an ambassadorship by President Ulysses Grant.

Among the early volumes, *Swingin Round the Cirkle* deserves particular attention. It was the first of Locke's books illustrated by Thomas Nast and marked the beginning of a long collaboration between them. It was also one of the few Nasby volumes with a unified structure. Locke had accompanied President Andrew Johnson on a political tour of the western states in 1866. Though originally sympathetic to Johnson, Locke gradually became discouraged by the president's willingness to sacrifice emancipation as a means of achieving national reunification, and he found himself increasingly in the camp of the radical wing of the Republican party. *Swingin* recorded this shift as Nasby became a more and more ardent Johnson advocate during the course of the tour, much to the embarrassment of the president.

The farther removed Locke became from the war and its aftermath, the less effective was his satire. He did find a likely target in the money policies of the Grant administration, which resulted in the 1875 collection *Inflation at the X Roads*, but for the most part the post-Reconstruction Nasby materials were marked by a gradual decrease in venom and humor. Still, the figure remained immensely popular. Over the years Locke toned down the comic misspellings and grammatical atrocities with which he had begun the caricature in an effort to make Nasby more urbane. By the time of *Nasby in Exile* the figure was a realistically drawn American middle-class portrait, characterized by a general skepticism wedded to cultural naivete. In effect, the personalities of Nasby and Locke merged, resulting in little of interest save some penetrating sketches of the drinking habits of the English and numerous passages of forceful descriptive writings. Much more successful as humor was Locke's one non-Nasby volume, *The Morals of Abou Ben Adhem, or Eastern Fruits on Western Dishes* (1875), which contained a series of satirical sketches on human nature presented in the guise of parables told to simple folk seeking wisdom by one Zephaniah Scudder, a counterfeiter and con man who presented himself as a Persian sage.

Summary

David Ross Locke was a versatile talent. A humorist, poet, novelist, editor, publisher, lecturer, and businessman, he succeeded at virtually everything to which he applied his hand. The early Petroleum V. Nasby letters made him politically influential and earned him the popular reputation of having been a major factor on the North's winning of the Civil War. Charles Farrar Browne (Artemus Ward) and Henry Wheeler Shaw (Josh Billings) were the only humorists of his generation to rival him in the effective use of deformed grammar and comic non sequiturs, and only Mark Twain, whose Pap Finn and scurrilous Dauphin of *Huckleberry Finn* reveal the influence of Nasby, exceeded him in popularity.

Selected Bibliography

Primary Sources

The Nasby Papers. Letters and Sermons Containing the Views on the Topics of the Day, of Petroleum V. Nasby. Indianapolis: Perrine, 1864.

Divers Views, Opinions, and Prophecies of Yoors Trooly Petroleum V. Nasby. Cincinnati: R. W. Carroll, 1866.

"Swingin Round the Cirkle." By Petroleum V. Nasby. Boston: Lee and Shepard, 1867.

Ekkoes from Kentucky. By Petroleum V. Nasby. Boston: Lee and Shepard, 1868.

The Impendin Crisis uv the Dimocracy . . . By Petroleum V. Nasby. Toledo: Miller, Locke & Co., 1868.

The Struggles (Social, Financial and Political) of Petroleum V. Nasby. Boston: I. N. Richards & Co., 1872.

The Morals of Abou Ben Adhem, or Eastern Fruits on Western Dishes. Boston: Lee and Shepard, 1875.

Inflation at the X Roads. New York: American News, 1875.

Nasby in Exile: or, Six Months of Travel in England, Ireland, Scotland, France, Germany, Switzerland and Belgium, with Many Things Not of Travel. Toledo: Locke, 1882.

The Nasby Letters. Being the Original Nasby Letters, as Written During His Lifetime. Toledo: The Toledo Blade Co., 1893.

Secondary Sources

Austin, James C. "David Ross Locke (1833–1888, pseud. Petroleum V. Nasby)." *American Literary Realism*, 4, no. 2 (Spring 1971): 192–200. The most thorough bibliography available.

———. *Petroleum V. Nasby* (David Ross Locke). New York: Twain, 1965. Treats Locke as a political satirist rather than as a humorist.

Clemens, Cyril. *Petroleum Vesuvius Nasby.* Webster Groves, Mo.: International Mark Twain Society, 1936. The first attempt at scholarly biography. Limited by its reliance on unauthenticated sources.

Harrison, John M. *The Man Who Made Nasby, David Ross Locke.* Chapel Hill: University of North Carolina Press, 1969. The standard biography. Looks beyond Nasby to assess Locke's influence as a businessman, journalist, and spokesman for liberal causes.

Gary Engle

Longstreet, Augustus Baldwin

Born: Augusta, Georgia, on September 22, 1790

Education: Waddel School, Willington, South Carolina, 1808–1811; Yale College, 1811–1813; Reeve and Gould Law Institute, Litchfield, Connecticut, 1813–1814

Marriage: Frances Eliza Parke, 1817, three children

Died: July 9, 1870

Biography

Augustus Baldwin Longstreet's parents moved from New Jersey to Augusta, Georgia, only four years before he was born on September 22, 1790. Although his father, William, was an unsuccessful inventor and speculator, young Longstreet grew up with a solid sense of his family's stature among the neighbors, one so strong that a rebelliousness born of snobbery threatened to interfere with his earliest education. But, by the time he was admitted to the bar in 1815 after having completed his legal training under Judge Tapping Reeve in Litchfield, Connecticut, Longstreet had established himself as a potential civic leader with political aspirations. After his marriage to the well-to-do Frances Parke in 1817, he moved to her hometown, Greensboro, where he was elected judge of the Superior Court in Georgia's Ocmulgee District. His duties on the judicial circuit provided Longstreet with ample opportunities to observe a wide spectrum of country and village life, observations that would serve him well for writing the anecdotes in *Georgia Scenes* (1835).

He may have written as early as 1830 some sketches, and in 1833–1834 he published eight in the *Southern Recorder* of Milledgeville. After the death of his first child, Alfred, in 1824, Longstreet entered a period of depression, giving up his political plans to run for Congress and downplaying what he increasingly came to see as his frivolous writing. Becoming gradually more conservative, he saw the utility of freely mixing his religious and political views and in finding platforms for expressing them. He bought an Augusta newspaper in 1834 and renamed it the *State Rights' Sentinel*, where he reprinted the earlier pieces and published several new ones. His most famous book, a collection of 19 sketches issued from his own newspaper office, listed only "A Native Georgian" as its author. He was ordained a Methodist minister in 1838, accepting the junior pastorate of an Augusta church until a more opportune position arose. In 1839 he took up the presidency of Emory College with considerable missionary zeal. From this post, which he held until 1848,

Longstreet defended the southern branch of his church against abolitionist attacks from the northern branch; his most effective polemical writing was a series of pro-slavery letters from "Georgia" to "Massachusetts," collected as *A Voice from the South* (1847). As a strict anti-abolitionist and moralist, Longstreet continued his professional career by becoming, in succession, president of Centenary College in Louisiana (1849), the University of Mississippi (1849–1856), and South Carolina College (1858–1861). His only other significant work of fiction, *Master William Mitten* (1864), is a didactic novel about deficient methods of child-rearing. When the Civil War began, Longstreet moved his family back to Mississippi, only to see his home burned by federal troops; for the rest of the war years he lived with his daughter and son-in-law, L.Q.C. Lamar, in Georgia. His wife of fifty-one years died in 1868. Most of his final years, before he died peacefully in 1870, were occupied with scholarly study of the Bible and belated defenses of John C. Calhoun.

Literary Analysis

Longstreet's only memorable work remains *Georgia Scenes*. This first collection of semi-fictional sketches inaugurated the literary phenomenon now popularly known as humor of the Old Southwest. The volume not only established the literary standard by which succeeding books in the genre would be measured, it also initiated the conventions—of language, characterization, and structure—that would be regularly employed by other amateur writers who followed Longstreet. He set the tone for the characteristically ambivalent attitudes of the educated man toward the plain folk whose often-rowdy adventures became the chief subject matter of the writing, and he devised the distancing technique of the frame tale and narrator to protect the author's own social integrity as satiric observer. He calculated the effects of a double language—the slightly stuffy English of the gentleman and the racy colloquialisms of the backwoodsman—for both dramatic contrast and social commentary. Almost from the beginning Longstreet denied that he had intended *Georgia Scenes: Characters, Incidents &c., in the First Half Century of the Republic* to be a book of humor; his anecdotes were meant, he said, to allow posterity "to see us *precisely as we are*" in "all ranks of society."[1] Many of the writers and editors of the 1840s and 1850s would make similar claims.

In order to give his picture the variety that the time and place required, Longstreet in effect divided himself into two narrators—Hall, who is attracted to the most rambunctious events preferred by cruder Georgian males, and the more sedate Baldwin, whose satiric eye and ear deflate the pretentiousness and shallow fashions of middle-class Georgians, especially females. What both narrators share is a realistic appraisal of a people whose recent transition from the frontier stage of society had left little room for the gracious plantation life of wealthy planters and their ladies, the romantic stuff of earlier southern fiction. In the hands of both Hall and Baldwin, however, the persona's studied detachment from his subject matter lends Longstreet's sketches a greater formality than the regional writings that followed *Georgia Scenes*. The narrating voice is consistently that of an educated observer whose tendency to moralize on the defective manners of his fellow Georgians is sometimes balanced by a wry indulgence that sees all humanity flawed. The sketches generally show the influence of the *Spectator* essayists filtered through Washington Irving's romantic adaptations more than they do that of Davy Crockett and the full-fledged exploitation of regional vernacular.

In "The Dance" Baldwin encounters an old sweetheart, now a matron supervising a country ball for young people, who fails to remember him; the adjustment of a sophisticated amateur to rural rigors and contests is the topic of "The Fox Hunt" and "The Shooting-Match"; and the inept imitation of urban music tastes among Georgian hostesses is the target of "The Song." Even in the more kinetic sketches that make use of backwoods violence and the dialects appropriate to its perpetrators, the vigor of the subject matter (gander-pullings, fights, horse-swaps) is always implicitly glossed by a distancing sensibility whose learned idioms reflect the region's planter class—the author's social and political perspective. Though the rough-and-tumble democracy of a rawboned society may be both amusing and shocking, its potential for anarchy is also faintly troubling for Longstreet. In his finest sketch, "The Fight," a rollicking account of two rival village bruisers egged into a confrontation by a spindly poor white, Longstreet suggests the ease with which the institutions of order can be subverted by the mischief of the lower classes and the boredom of ordinary villagers. The process that leads to the fight is masterfully paced; the psychological needs of Ransy Sniffle are cannily set against the masculine punctilio of the rivals who actually respect each other; the unpretentious code of the two males honorifically sets in relief the competitive pride of their wives, who when provoked quickly drop their refined mode of address copied from their betters for the direct insults that come more naturally to gutter harridans; and in Squire Loggins, the conventional figure of sage village wisdom is genially deflated. Only at the end of the tale does Longstreet articulate his moral disapproval: "Thanks to the Christian religion, to schools, colleges, and benevolent associations, such scenes of barbarism and cruelty, as that which I have been just describing, are now of rare occurrence: though they may still be occasionally met with in some of the new counties. Wherever they prevail, they are a disgrace to that community."[2]

Longstreet's final paragraph of "The Fight" reveals his divided feelings about his subjects throughout *Georgia Scenes*. The judicial moralist condemns all those "peace-officers who countenance" such eruptions of violence, but Longstreet the writer is sufficiently enamored of primitive vitality and excess that he allows the robust figures to dominate the scenes and their crude vernacular to subvert his own style, which modulates between the measured and rational and the sentimental and romantic. As representative of those civilizing institutions—the church, the school, and the court—Longstreet must reprove the society that has not yet been brought fully under their sway, but, he also suggests that when such influences are victorious, the more homogeneous life that emerges will be as dull as it is righteous and orderly.

Realizing with some chagrin that the "moral darkness" of his time and place has inspired his book, Longstreet feels compelled to stress the gradual improvement that has followed the advance of the newer counties of Georgia "from vice and folly to virtue and holiness." Yet, this declaration (in "Georgia Theatrics") is laced with the wit inherent in the stock situation in which the yokel bests the gentleman: what the narrator assumes to be a vicious fight in the bushes turns out to be a rehearsal for a fight by a youth who "had played all the parts." When the narrator, duped by his senses, protests the violence, his is the voice of moral enlightenment, but his erroneous conclusions are carried by a language that is heavily static and prissy; on the other hand, the theatrical youth, a product of "moral darkness," speaks in an idiom that is guileless and fresh—and resonantly metaphorical: "You needn't kick before you're spur'd. There a'nt nobody there, nor ha'nt been nother. I was jist seein' how I could 'a' *fout*." The imagery of the narrator, when Hall describes the battle site of "Georgia Theatrics," is by contrast derivative and stately: "the ground around was broken up as if two stags had been engaged upon it" (*Georgia Scenes*, pp. 5–8).

Longstreet brings to bear on his picture of backwoods society a long tradition of older satire and humor. Giving characters such names as Mr. Flirt, Mr. Crouch, and Mrs. Mushy is too conventional to enliven "The Ball," a sketch on cotillion etiquette, and the attack on legalese in "The Debating Society" loses much of its force from attenuation, the price that so much specialty humor pays. Like the eighteenth-century essayists, Longstreet is a self-conscious stylist writing in balanced sentences, with arch asides, literary and historical allusions, Latin tags, apostrophes, and direct addresses to the "gentle reader." The linguistic energy of the cultivated narrators throughout *Georgia Scenes* is anemic. Both Hall and Baldwin—as well as Crabshaw, who relates "The Militia Company Drill," a sketch borrowed from one of Longstreet's lawyer friends—are patronizing observers whose language is correct, formal, and ponderous, particularly when it is directly juxtaposed against the linguistic raciness of the country characters.

Longstreet was a reluctant humorist. Uncomfortable with the popular success of *Georgia Scenes*, he declared in 1840 that however much it had been entertained, the public had misread his intentions. By this time he was already a Methodist minister and a college president. Ignoring the pleas of William Tappan Thompson, his friend and journalist colleague, to enrich future editions of *Georgia Scenes* with sketches already written but unpublished—"there is nothing in the unpublished numbers which can savor of immorality," Thompson noted[3]—Longstreet would henceforth publish only works that would be received as unambiguously serious: orations on education and defenses of slavery based on biblical study and historical precedent. His only other sustained fiction was *Master William Mitten*, a novel that he began writing as president of Centenary College in 1849 but that was not published until six years before his death. The posthumous *Stories with a Moral: Humorous and Descriptive of Southern Life a Century Ago* (1912), originally published in a Charleston newspaper, was collected and edited by a nephew.

Longstreet was not only a reluctant humorist, he was only inadvertently the father of the entire school of backwoods humor that flourished in the three decades before the Civil War. What *Georgia Scenes* importantly documents, however, is not the narrow mode known as Southwestern Humor; it is, instead, one of the earliest attempts to depict faithfully a region in all its social and cultural moods. Although Longstreet was not by theory a pre-Howellsian realist, both his stated intentions and his actual practice reveal him to be primarily a social and cultural historian but one with an unusual gift for narrative pace, discriminating characterization, and sophisticated manipulation of point of view. Like the ambivalent drama of change and human progress that Cooper enacted in *The Pioneers*, Longstreet surveyed the costs of civilization and the rule of law with a profound appreciation of human and social weakness; the purpose of *Georgia Scenes*, he maintained, was "to exhibit Georgia just as it is . . . so that those who come after us may know not only the changes which have taken place in the character and dialect of the people, but in the face of the country."[4] If he is repulsed by the penchant for violence and folly that he perceives as lying just beneath the surface of human, not merely regional, character, Longstreet also is curiously drawn to such unvirtuous behavior. Ned Brace, the socially well-placed wit of two of the sketches, is a lord of misrule who instigates as much social disorder and enjoys it as grotesquely as the little "five feet nothing" dirt-eater, Ransy Sniffle. As Kimball King has observed, Longstreet describes two Georgias, the older one with its vital pioneering heritage and the newer one of prospering towns; the first is crude and opportunistic, the second materialistic and pretentious. The fact that Hall and Baldwin tell their stories with different emphases in *Georgia Sketches* is a tacit admission that "the synthesis of the two orders is impossible."[5]

Summary

In *Georgia Scenes* the Piedmont South for the first time was depicted in detail and with accuracy and perception. While Longstreet clearly admired the vitality and simple integrity of the sturdy yeomanry that contributed to Georgia's agrarian society, his patrician perspective committed him to preferring the greater benefits of those civilizing institutions that would in time neutralize the more grotesque examples of backwoods communities. The innovation of his book was in capturing the actuality of social complexities by translating the kind of yarn common to oral tale-telling into an effective written form. The pioneering literary efforts of this judge, educator, and moralist led directly first to the work of a whole generation (notably Joseph Glover Baldwin, William Tappan Thompson, and Johnson Jones Hooper) and later to such local colorists as Joel Chandler Harris and Charles Egbert Craddock. Also in Longstreet's line of descent in the twentieth century is, most memorably, the William Faulkner of *As I Lay Dying* and *The Hamlet*. It is a coincidence, but an appropriate one, that Faulkner is buried not far from Judge Longstreet's grave in St. Peter's Cemetery in Oxford, Mississippi.

Notes

1. James B. Meriwether, "Augustus Baldwin Longstreet: Realist and Artist," *Mississippi Quarterly*, 35 (Fall 1982): 356.
2. Fitz R. Longstreet, ed., *Stories with a Moral: Humorous and Descriptive of Southern Life a Century Ago* (Philadelphia: John C. Winston, 1912), p. 66.
3. Meriwether, p. 356.
4. Ibid., p. 357.

5. Kimball King, *Augustus Baldwin Longstreet* (Boston: Twayne, 1984), p. 139.

Selected Bibliography

Primary Sources

Georgia Scenes, Characters, Incidents, &c., in the First Half Century of the Republic: By a Native Georgian. Augusta, Ga.: S.R. Office, 1835.

A Voice from the South: Comprising Letters from Georgia to Massachusetts, and to the Southern States: With an Appendix Containing an Article from the Charleston Mercury on the Wilmot Proviso. Baltimore: Western Continent, 1847.

Master William Mitten: Or, a Youth of Brilliant Talents Who Was Ruined by Bad Luck. Macon, Ga.: Burke, Boykin, 1864.

Stories with a Moral: Humorous and Descriptive of Southern Life a Century Ago. Ed. Fitz R. Longstreet. Philadelphia: John C. Winston, 1912.

Secondary Sources

Blair, Walter, and Hamlin Hill. *America's Humor: From Poor Richard to Doonesbury.* New York: Oxford University Press, 1978. Emphasizes the subversive aspects of Longstreet's priggish narrators.

Fitzgerald, Oscar P. *Judge Longstreet, A Life Sketch.* Nashville: Methodist Church South, 1891. Pioneering biography by a friend of Longstreet who collected all available information, some of it erroneous.

King, Kimball. *Augustus Baldwin Longstreet.* Boston: Twayne, 1984. Most substantial bio-critical study yet done; excellent critical evaluations of both *Georgia Scenes* and *Master William Mitten.*

Meriwether, James B. "Augustus Baldwin Longstreet: Realist and Artist." *Mississippi Quarterly*, 35 (Fall 1982): 351-364. Argues that Longstreet was an early realist, not a humorist; excellent interpretation of Hall and Baldwin as narrators.

Phillips, Robert L. "The Novel and the Romance in Middle Georgia Humor and Local Color." Ph.D. dissertation, University of North Carolina, 1971. Treats the vacillation between romance and realism in Longstreet and his fellow Georgian authors.

Scafidel, J.R. "The Letters of Augustus Baldwin Longstreet." Ph.D. dissertation, University of South Carolina, 1977. Both biographically and bibliographically essential.

Wade, John Donald. *Augustus Baldwin Longstreet: A Study of the Development of Culture in the South.* New York: Macmillan, 1924; new edition, ed. M. Thomas Inge, Athens: University of Georgia Press, 1969. More important for its insights into the cultural contexts than for its accuracy in biographical details.

James H. Justus

Loos, Anita

Born: Sissons, California, on April 26, 1888
Education: High school in California
Marriage: Frank Pallma, Jr., June 1915, annulled one day later; John Emerson, 1919
Died: August 18, 1981

Biography

Anita Loos lived—and wrote—for most of the twentieth century. The first of her scenarios to be turned into a motion picture appeared in 1912 and the last book that she supervised through publication appeared sixty-seven years later, in 1979. Moreover, in those seven decades it was her fortune to be in the right place at the right time, meeting many notable people: Los Angeles at the birth of the motion picture industry, New York in the roaring twenties, Hollywood again at the height of its golden studio years, and later New York again at the height of its Broadway musical years. In between, literally on a trip between Hollywood and New York, she concocted one of the most enduring characters in American humorous fiction, Lorelei Lee of *Gentlemen Prefer Blondes.*

Born in Sissons (now Mount Shasta), California, to Minnie Smith and a roving, roguish newspaperman/theater producer, R. Beers Loos, Anita early began meeting the creative, offbeat kind of people whom she attracted all of her life. Loos became a child actress (she was one of the children in the first American production of Henrik Ibsen's *A Doll's House*), but her real love from an early age was writing. While acting in her father's amateur stock company, she sent off a one-page scenario to American Biograph Studios, whose address she found on the canister of a one-reeler being shown between acts of one of her father's productions. That scenario, or perhaps a later one (Loos's memory is not totally reliable), was made into a picture by D.W. Griffith, the head of American Biograph. *The New York Hat* (1912), featuring Mary Pickford, Lionel Barrymore, and Lillian and Dorothy Gish, was the first of many films using scenarios that Griffith bought from Loos. When Griffith moved his operations from New York to California, he invited Loos to join his studio. The diminutive Anita, about five feet and ninety pounds, astounded Griffith, who found it difficult to believe that this child-like creature could be the author of the sophisticated scenarios that he had been buying. Somewhere in her career, Loos apparently parlayed the advantage of her youthful looks into becoming five years younger: at her death, according to the *New York Times*, friends reported that she was really ninety-three, making her birth year 1888, not 1893, as most sources indicate.

Literary Analysis

In the next few years after Griffith purchased her first effort, Loos wrote over a hundred scenarios. Few survive, but Loos reports that most were slapstick comedies. Her contemporaries indicate that much of the verbal humor of these scenarios was lost when they were placed on the silent screen. However, when Loos met New York director John Emerson, who used one of her scenarios for a movie starring newcomer Douglas Fairbanks, he suggested that she use subtitles to express that humor. When the picture captivated a New York audience, Griffith, who had earlier rejected the idea of making an audience read, now turned to Loos to create titles for the pictures he directed, even non-comedies. Years later, viewing *Intolerance*, she was delighted to learn that one of her titles still drew laughs: "When women cease to attract men, they often turn to reform as a second choice."

Despite the enormous popular and commercial success of the Emerson-Loos-Fairbanks movies (eight in all), Loos welcomed the chance to move to New York. There Loos wrote and Emerson directed for Joe Schneck thirteen movies that starred either Constance or Norma Talmadge. There also Loos and Emerson married, and Loos met the literati and intelligentsia of the day. Though never a member of the Algonquin Club, she became friends with many of the members, including her idol, H.L. Mencken. Contrary to her expectations, however, she discovered that even learned, witty men like Mencken could be turned into jelly by a good-looking blonde. In mock revenge, she wrote the diary of one such blonde, Lorelei Lee, and sent it off to Mencken. He loved it, but thought it too risqué to publish in *American Mercury*. Eventually, augmented by chapters chronicling Lorelei's "education" in Europe, the diary appeared serially in *Harper's Bazaar*. A popular sensation when it came out in book form in 1925 (eventually achieving eighty-five printings and being translated into fourteen languages), *Gentlemen Prefer Blondes* drew praise from every quarter, including H.G. Wells, Aldous Huxley, George Santayana, and James Joyce; Edith Wharton called it *the* American novel. *Gentlemen* has seldom left the consciousness of the American public since. It became a stage play with June Walker in 1926, a movie with Ruth Taylor in 1928, a Broadway musical with Carol Channing in 1949, and a movie musical with Marilyn Monroe in 1953. An updated version of the Broadway musical was produced in 1974, and the latest edition of the book is copyrighted 1983.

After the stock market crash put an end to the life of theater and clubs and luncheon dates and speakeasy nights in New York (with Palm Beach winters), Loos accepted a bid from Irving Thalberg to return to Hollywood, this time to work for Metro-Goldwyn-Mayer. There she wrote, adapted, or collaborated on over twenty scripts. They included *Red-Headed Woman* (1932), written for Jean Harlow; *Biography of a Bachelor Girl* (1934), from the S.N. Behrman stage play; *San Francisco* (1936), written as a tribute to Wilson Mizner, whom she identifies in her memoirs as her one true love; *The Women* (1939), an admired adaptation of the Clare Boothe play; and *I Married an Angel* (1942), a Jeanette MacDonald/Nelson Eddy musical satire.

By 1942, after Thalberg's death, Loos was ready to return to New York. Though her never-smooth marriage to Emerson continued, after this return she maintained her own household. Indeed, in her memoirs Loos reports that she supported Emerson from the time of the stock market crash. Moreover, she indicates that his name appeared on their co-authored works to appease Emerson's ego and not because he did anything more than proofread her writing.

Back in New York, Loos continued to write, creating a comedy, *Happy Birthday* (1946), specifically for her friend Helen Hayes, with whom she later collaborated on a tour guide to New York (*Twice over Lightly*, 1972). Loos also adapted many works for the stage, most notably *Gigi* (1951) and *Cheri* (1959) from Colette's novels, and the musical versions of *Gentlemen* (1949, 1974) from her own novel. Turning to the notebooks that she had kept during her Hollywood years, Loos transformed some of the material into fiction—*A Mouse Is Born* (1951) and *No Mother to Guide Her* (1961)—and some into non-fiction. First came her autobiography, *A Girl Like I* (1966), and later several volumes of memoirs, primarily concerning famous people whom she had known. These memoirs include *Cast of Thousands* (1977), *Kiss Hollywood Good-by* (1974), and *The Talmadge Girls* (1978). In the last decades of her life, though she still wrote, she was, perhaps, better known as a personality, appearing at parties, fashion shows, and theater openings, and sometimes on talk shows, where she recounted anecdotes about the old Hollywood.

Loos many times confessed to her love of the wisecrack, both her own and other people's. Her friend Paulette Goddard's comment, modified, became Lorelei's guide: "kissing your hand may make you feel very very good but a diamond and safire bracelet lasts forever." The chief wisecracker in *Gentlemen* is Lorelei's traveling companion Dorothy, with whom Loos identified. About the corpulent Germans they meet in a theater lobby, Dorothy says, "You can say what you want about the Germans being full of 'kunst,' but what they are really full of is delicatessen." Dorothy finds Henry Spoffard, Lorelei's target for matrimony, much less than desirable: "Dorothy says the only thing she could stand being to Henry, would be his widow at the age of 18."

Still, *Gentlemen* is far more than a collection of wisecracks. In *Gentlemen* Loos's figure of an innocent traveling abroad and experiencing picaresque adventures in a less-than-innocent world is brought together with an Horatio Alger-like climb from obscurity to fame and fortune. However, Loos turns these traditions on their head. The innocent is a Ritz-kept mistress who began her climb from the obscurity of Little Rock, Arkansas, where she was acquitted of murdering her first protector: "it seems that I had a revolver in my hand and it seems that the revolver had shot Mr. Jennings." Her trip abroad, sponsored by Chicago's button king, Gus Eisman, is ostensibly made to improve her mind, though there is some question about her capacity to absorb much since to her the historical sights of Paris are the buildings housing Coty and Cartier. Furthermore, it is Lorelei who does the teaching; when she discovers that the notorious penny-pincher Sir Francis Beekman is her only hope to attain the diamond tiara that she has her heart set on, she uses every strategy to teach him, successfully, of course, how to treat "a girl like I."

Yet, for all her adventuring and gold-digging, Lorelei has a middle-class sense of security—and of propriety. She chastises Dorothy for her use of slang and is prim in her own language, even if she does get the wrong word or the wrong spelling, to say nothing of the wrong syntax and pronoun. Moving this fresh-eyed, anything-but-innocent heroine through foreign lands, Loos can make fun not only of the gullibility of the men everywhere who become Lorelei's victims but also of the foibles of other types whom she meets—characters who exhibit the smugness of the English aristocracy, Gallic gallantry coupled with miserliness, German eating, and Austrian work habits. She satirizes especially the hypocrisy of the American upper-middle class, illustrated particularly by Henry, who likes to watch "over and over" the portions of films that he and a censorship society have deleted to protect the morals of the public. This mixture, the happy joining of an uneduated innocent adventuring in the world with the American dream of making it big in fame and fortune, sprinkled with wisecracks and saturated in satire, remains as fresh today as it was in the twenties.

Summary

Toward the end of her life, Loos thought that *Gentlemen Prefer Blondes* was the best of her works. Most critics would agree. That she spent so many years reviewing her Hollywood memories instead of continuing to see America through fresh but not-so-innocent eyes is our loss. Nevertheless, her prodigious output in silent and talking pictures, in comedic and musical theater, and in essays and novels ensures Loos a place among notable American humorists. Since Loos introduced a timeless style of verbal comedy into movies and created the enduring figure of Lorelei Lee, her place should be secure.

Selected Bibliography

Primary Sources

Fiction

Gentlemen Prefer Blondes: The Illuminating Diary of a Professional Lady. New York: Boni and Liveright, 1925. Also published with *But Gentlemen Marry Brunettes.* New York: Vintage, 1983.

But Gentlemen Marry Brunettes. New York: Boni and Liveright, 1928. Also published with *Gentlemen Prefer Blondes.* New York: Vintage, 1983.

A Mouse Is Born. Garden City, N.Y.: Doubleday, 1951.

No Mother to Guide Her. New York: McGraw-Hill, 1961.

Nonfiction

(with J. Emerson.) *How to Write Photoplays.* New York: McCann, 1920.

———. *Breaking into the Movies.* New York: McCann, 1921.

A Girl Like I. New York: Viking, 1966.

(with Helen Hayes.) *Twice over Lightly: New York Then and Now.* New York: Harcourt Brace Jovanovich, 1972.

Kiss Hollywood Good-by. New York: Viking, 1974.

Cast of Thousands. New York: Grosset and Dunlap, 1977.

The Talmadge Girls: A Memoir. New York: Viking, 1978.

Plays/Musicals

(with J. Emerson.) *The Whole Town's Talking,* premiered, New York, Bijou Theatre, August 29, 1923; published New York: Longmans, Green, 1925.

———. *The Fall of Eve.* New York, Booth Theatre, August 31, 1925.

———. *Gentlemen Prefer Blondes.* New York, Times Square Theatre, September 28, 1926.

———. (one sketch.) *Nine Fifteen Revue.* New York, George M. Cohan Theatre, February 11, 1930.

———. *Cherries Are Ripe.* Wilmington, Del., October 13, 1930.

———. *The Social Register.* New York, Fulton Theatre, November 9, 1931.

Happy Birthday. New York, Broadhurst Theatre, October 31, 1946; published New York: S. French, 1947.

(with Joseph Fields.) *Gentlemen Prefer Blondes.* Music by Jule Styne, lyrics by Leo Robin. New York, Ziegfeld Theatre, December 8, 1949. Adapted from her novel of the same name.

Gigi. New York, Fulton Theatre, November 24, 1951; published New York: Random House, 1952. Adapted from the novel by Colette.

The Amazing Adele. Philadelphia, Shubert Theatre, December 26, 1955.

Cheri. New York, Morosco Theatre, October 12, 1959. Adapted from the novel by Colette.

Gogo Loves You. Music by Claude Leveille, lyrics by Gladys Shelley. New York, Theatre de Lys, October 9, 1964.

The King's Mare. London, Garrick Theatre, July 20, 1966; published London: Evans Plays, 1967. Translated and adapted from Jean Canolle's play.

Lorelei, or Gentlemen Still Prefer Blondes. Music by Jule Styne, lyrics by Betty Comden and Adolph Green. New York, Palace Theatre, January 27, 1974.

Periodicals

"Heredity and Nella: A Fable with an Awful Moral for Eugenists." *Vanity Fair,* February, 1915, p. 43.

(with J. Emerson.) "Photoplay Writing." *Photoplay,* February, 1918, pp. 51-52; March, 1918, pp. 53-54; April, 1918, pp. 81-82, 122; May, 1918, pp. 81-82, 118; June, 1918, pp. 78-79; July, 1918, pp. 88-89, 121.

"A Dissertation on the Mink." *New York Times Magazine,* October 29, 1950, pp. 16, 29.

"History of the Preferred Blonde." *New York Times Magazine,* April 26, 1953, pp. 22, 46, 48.

"To Charlie." *Theatre Arts,* June, 1957, pp. 82-83. On Charles MacArthur.

"The New Vamp." *Vogue,* March 1, 1958, p. 128.

"Aldous Huxley in California." *Harper's,* May, 1964, pp. 51-55.

"Unfogettable Tallulah." *Reader's Digest,* July, 1969, pp. 130-134. On Tallulah Bankhead.

"Ode for Anybody Aged Ten." *McCall's,* April, 1973, p. 118. A poem.

"Greatest Actress in Motion Pictures." *Vogue,* September, 1981, pp. 374, 377, 379. On Louise Brooks.

Fate Keeps on Happening: Adventures of Lorelei Lee and Other Writings. Ed. Ray Pierre Corsini. New York: Dodd, Mead, 1984. A collection of forty-three fiction and non-fiction articles, thirty-one of them previously published. No article duplicates any listed above.

Motion Pictures

The New York Hat (Biograph, 1912), scenario.

The Power of the Camera (Biograph, 1913), scenario.

A Hicksville Epicure (Biograph, 1913), scenario.

A Cure for Suffragettes (Biograph, 1913), scenario.

The Wedding Gown (Biograph, 1913), scenario.

His Picture in the Paper (Triangle Film, 1916), scenario.

Macbeth (Lucky Film Producers, 1916), titles.

Intolerance (D.W. Griffith, 1916), titles.

(with J. Emerson.) *Reaching for the Moon* (Artcraft Pictures, 1917), scenario.

——. *A Virtuous Vamp* (First National, 1919), scenario.

——. *Learning to Love* (First National, 1925), scenario.

——. *Gentlemen Prefer Blondes* (Paramount Famous Lasky, 1928), screenplay.

Red-Headed Woman (Metro-Goldwyn-Mayer, 1932), screenplay.

Biography of a Bachelor Girl (MGM, 1934), screenplay.

San Francisco (MGM, 1936), screenplay.

(with Jane Murfin.) *The Women* (MGM, 1939), screenplay.

Susan and God (MGM, 1940), screenplay.

(with Edwin Justin Mayer and Leon Gordon.) *They Met in Bombay* (MGM, 1941), screenplay.

(with S.K. Lauren.) *When Ladies Meet* (MGM, 1941), screenplay.

I Married an Angel (MGM, 1942), screenplay.

Note: Loos wrote over a hundred scenarios and filmscripts. For a more complete list, see Loos, *Kiss Hollywood Good-by,* above, which, besides studio and date, includes the source of the film, its length, what Loos was paid for the film, the director, the stars, and *New York Times* review information.

Published Motion Pictures

(with J. Emerson.) *The Love Expert.* In their *How to Write Photoplays* (see in Nonfiction above).

San Francisco: A Screenplay. Ed. Matthew G. Bruccoli. Carbondale: Southern Illinois University Press, 1979.

(with Jane Murfin.) *The Women. Twenty Best Film Plays.* Ed. John Gassner and Dudley Nichols. New York: Crown, 1943, pp. 61-130.

Secondary Sources

Blom, T.E. "Anita Loos and Sexual Economics: *Gentlemen Prefer Blondes.*" *The Canadian Review of American Studies,* 7 (Spring 1976): 39-47. Blom finds *Gentlemen* "a classic send-up of the American myth in which a nobody from nowhere defeats the old European values of class and education, and wins all that is thought worth winning—money and fame." Like the people around her, Lorelei dedicates herself to the pursuit of wealth. Beginning passively, she becomes increasingly aware of the necessity of taking her future into her own hands, and so learns to manipulate her image in order to bring off her marriage to wealthy Henry Spoffard. Her progress in self-education allows Loos to satirize the hypocrisies of contemporary society.

Bruccoli, Matthew J. "Anita Loos." *Conversations with Writers. II.* Ed. Vance Bourjaity. Detroit: Gale Research, 1977, pp. 124-140. Loos answers questions about her early days in Hollywood, particularly about working with D.W. Griffith and Irving Thalberg. Unsentimental about those days, the movie industry, or herself, she considers *Gentlemen* the best of her work and herself "just a girl out there trying to get a fast buck."

Carey, Gary. "Prehistory: Anita Loos." *The Hollywood Screenwriters: A Film Comment Book.* Ed. Richard Corliss. New York: Avon, 1965, pp. 37-50. Calling Loos the first screen "practitioner of the wise-crack," Carey credits her with introducing verbal humor into film "singlehandedly." He reviews in some detail her early career writing scenarios and subtitles. He also recounts briefly the later films for Metro-Goldwyn-Mayer. Included is a list of films from 1912 to 1955, which includes directors, stars, and sources of the filmscripts.

Douglas, George H. "Anita Loos." *Women of the 20s.* Dallas: Saybrook, 1986, pp. 193-218. This mainly biographical account of the life and works of Loos also includes an assessment of her view that male-female relations, including romance, cannot be taken seriously, that such relationships are a game to be enjoyed. Douglas also notes the probable influence of her own rather strange marriage and her many male friendships.

Everett, Barbara. "The New Style of *Sweeney Agonistes*." *English Satire and the Satiric Tradition.* Ed. Claude Rawson. Oxford: Basil Blackwell, 1984, pp. 243-263. Everett finds Eliot's new style in "Sweeney" distinctly American: Doris and Dusty are specimens of the Dumb Blonde and the verse play is full of wisecracks. Everett notes the possible sources for this style in Loos's *Gentlemen* and in the works of Ring Lardner.

Grant, Thomas. "Anita Loos." *Dictionary of Literary Biography.* Vol. 11. *American Humorists, 1800-1950.* Ed. Stanley Trachtenberg. Detroit: Gale, 1982, pp. 283-291. Discussion of Loos's major works, in a biographical context.

Hotchner, A.E. "Gentlemen Still Prefer Blondes." *Theatre Arts*, July, 1953, pp. 26-27, 93-94. Hotchner reviews the origin and the impact of *Gentlemen*, including the various movie versions. He also includes material on Loos's early years as a screenwriter.

Nasso, Christine, ed. "Anita Loos." *Contemporary Authors.* Vols. 21-24. 1st Rev. Ser. Detroit: Gale, 1977, p. 548. Brief overview of life and works.

Schmidt, Karl. "The Handwriting on the Screen." *Everybody's*, 36 (May, 1917): 622-623. This interview with Loos notes her skill as "an expert subtitle writer" and scenarist, the earliest such acknowledgment.

Walker, Nancy. "'Fragile and Dumb': The 'Little Woman' in Women's Humor, 1900-1940." *Thalia: Studies in Literary Humor*, 5 (Fall and Winter, 1982-83): 24-29. Walker notes that the little woman figure is sometimes used as a source to satirize other targets. The most popular such figure is Lorelei Lee.

Wittman, Livia Z. "Erfolgschancen eines Gaukelspiels: Vergleichende Beobachtungen zu *Gentlemen Prefer Blondes* (Anita Loos) und *Das kunstseidene Mädchen* (Irmgard Keun)." *Carleton Germanic Papers* 11 (1983): 35-49. Despite the similarities of the Keun novel and the Loos novel which influenced it, the differences are striking. While Lorelei succeeds in securing a rich husband, Keun's heroine fails, partly because of the grim economics of the thirties (*Das Mädchen* was published in 1932) and partly because she allows her feelings to influence her actions. Though both books provide amusing criticism of the times, Loos uses caricatures and satire, while Keun uses a realism ("Neue Sachlichkeit") that leaves a lump in the throat.

Phyllis R. Randall

Lowell, James Russell

Born: Cambridge, Massachusetts, on February 22, 1819

Education: Harvard College, B.A., 1838; Dane College Law School, law degree, 1840

Marriage: Maria White, December 26, 1844

Died: August 12, 1891

Biography

Born at Elmwood in Cambridge, Massachusetts, on February 22, 1819, James Russell Lowell was a poet and humorist in a Brahmin dynasty of clergymen, lawyers, and college presidents. He inherited much of his literary talent and interest in ballad lore from his mother, Harriet Traill Spence. Lowell's father, the Reverend Charles Lowell, pastor of West Church in Boston, was praised by his congregation for his oratory gifts from the pulpit. The youngest of six children, James Russell heard many tales and ballads from his hypersensitive mother, and his childhood relations with his brother, Charles, were very close. In his early years, he was thoroughly trained in Greek and Latin at the private school near his home. At fifteen, Lowell entered Harvard College. Well-read in English literature, he soon showed his talent as a humorist by contributing comic pieces to the college magazine *Harvardiana*. In the meantime, his carefree attitudes were judged unacceptable, and he was temporarily exiled to Concord in 1836, though he graduated that year. His ingrained irreverence prompted him to write satiric poems in which he directed his shafts at the prevailing intellectual modes such as transcendentalism, abolitionism, temperance, women's rights and vegetarianism. When Lowell met Maria White, the sister of one of his classmates, in December 1839, he suddenly turned from skepticism to enthusiasm over humanitarian causes, owing to Maria's deep involvement in the antislavery movement. They became engaged in 1840.

Lowell remained undecided as to the choice of a profession although he graduated from the Dane College Law School in Cambridge in 1840. In 1842, he was admitted to the bar and opened his own office, but practiced law with little success. Prompted by Maria, who had recognized his literary talent, he soon published poems and prose essays in such renowned magazines as *The Southern Literary Messenger, The Dial*, and the *Boston Miscellany*. At the end of 1842 he decided to give up law. His first editorial venture was the founding of the *Pioneer* in January 1843. The magazine was intended as a "rational substitute" for the sentimental fiction of the popular press. Although Lowell enlisted Edgar Allan Poe and Nathaniel Hawthorne as contributors, the experience was shortlived and only three issues appeared. A few days after their marriage on December 26, 1844, Lowell and Maria went to Philadelphia, Pennsylvania, where he was to work for the *Pennsylvania Freeman*, but his income proved too meager to support a family. In May 1845, they returned to Elmwood where their first daughter Blanche was born on December 31 of the same year. Relying on the modest inheritance that Maria received from her father's estate, Lowell wrote occasional poems until he became a regular contributor to the *National Anti-Slavery Standard*. In March 1847, Blanche died and in September a second daughter, Mabel, was born. She was the only one of four children to live to adulthood.

1848 was Lowell's *annus mirabilis*. He published *The Fable for Critics* and *The Biglow Papers, First Series*, in which he lampooned the supporters of the Mexican War. In 1849, he became corresponding editor of the *Anti-Slavery Standard*. A third daughter, Rose, was born on July 16, 1849, and Lowell's only son was born in December 1850. About this time, Maria's health began to fail, and Lowell decided to take the family in quest of a warmer climate. They visited Italy, Switzerland, France, and England between 1851 and 1852. Lowell's son died in April 1852, and a year after the family returned to New England Maria died, on October 27, 1853. Mabel, the only member left to him of the family, was then the source of his greatest comfort.

After the publication of his travel writings in *Putnam's Magazine* and *Graham's Magazine*, Lowell prepared lectures on English poets, a series that he delivered at the Lowell Institute of Boston during the season of 1854-1855. He was then appointed Smith Professor of French and Spanish Languages and Literatures at Harvard, where he succeeded Henry Wadsworth Longfellow. Beginning in September 1856, he taught for sixteen years, with occasional interruptions for travels in Europe. In 1857, Lowell married Frances (Fanny) Dunlap, a friend of the family who had been in charge of Mabel after Maria's death. In 1857, Lowell became the first editor of the *Atlantic Monthly*. This prominent position acquainted him with the most illustrious writers of the time. As a member of the Saturday Club, started in 1859 in Boston, Lowell knew Longfellow, Ralph Waldo Emerson, Hawthorne, and William Dean Howells. His editorial work with the *Atlantic Monthly* came to an end in May 1861 when the publisher decided to assume the editorship. In January 1864, Lowell and Charles Eliot Norton became joint editors of the *North American Review* and gave this somewhat severe magazine much of the pleasant flavor of the *Atlantic Monthly*. During the Civil War, Lowell

contributed many articles, essays, and poems in support of Lincoln and the Union, yet his most significant work was the second series of the *Biglow Papers*. He left New England again in 1872 for a two-year stay in Europe, received honorary degrees in Oxford and Cambridge and spent several months in France, Italy, Germany, and Switzerland. On his return to Harvard, he became active in politics. A delegate to the Republican Convention in Cincinnati, he was chosen a presidential elector in 1876. Lowell then shifted from teaching to diplomacy.

His first mission was his assignment in 1877 to the American legation in Madrid. He owed his position to Howells, who served as Rutherford Hayes's messenger. Lowell had turned down an offer to become Minister to Austria and lightly suggested to Howells that he would enjoy watching some of Calderon's plays. While in Madrid, Lowell was welcomed by King Alfonso XII, who already knew about the *Biglow Papers*. This diplomatic experience would have been thoroughly satisfactory had not Fanny contracted typhus in the summer of 1879. It took her months to recover, and she was never in good health again. In January 1880, Lowell was appointed as Minister to the Court of St. James. While staying in London from 1882 to 1885 he was on very friendly terms with Lord Granville, Gladstone's Foreign Secretary, and the two men solved many problems related to Irishmen on both sides of the Atlantic when the Feinian organization caused serious disturbances. Meanwhile, Lowell was received with great warmth by the British public and asked to give lectures about the literatures of the new and the old continents. As much as Lowell enjoyed his years in England, the election of Grover Cleveland in 1884 resulted in his return to America. Fanny died in February 1885, only a few months before his departure. When Lowell left for the United States in June, he decided to go to his daughter's home at Southborough, Massachusetts. He had been abroad seven years and needed the peacefulness of the New England country and the comfort of the only child left to him. In the winter of 1889 he stayed with his sister in Boston, where he renewed some old friendships, especially with Howells, but many of his former acquaintances were now dead. At last he returned to Elmwood where he resumed his activities as scholar, poet, and lecturer. He was asked to deliver speeches at the Centennial celebration of George Washington's Inauguration at Harvard in 1889. During the winter of 1889-1890, Lowell was busy preparing the uniform edition of his works in ten volumes. Soon after the publication of this definitive edition, he suffered a severe illness. He was an invalid for a long period and finally died on August 12, 1891, at Elmwood.

Literary Analysis

Although Lowell is remembered today as a dedicated Abolitionist and a Yankee humorist, he wished to be recognized as a poet more than anything else. He published four volumes of verse in addition to such better-known works as the two series of the *Biglow Papers*, "The Vision of Sir Launfal," "The Cathedral," and the "Fable for Critics." Yet the poet could never be totally reconciled with the scholar. Lowell's sophisticated inspiration estranged him from the spontaneous overflow of powerful feelings in Romantic poetry. His innate sense of humor often induced him to adorn his writing with allusions and digressions that soon made his style more attractive than his themes. In terms of Lowell's humorous production, the "Fable for Critics" established his reputation as humorist in 1847. Intended as "A Glance at a Few of our Literary Progenies from the Tub of Diogenes," this long satiric poem portrayed prominent American writers of the time. Lowell's irrepressible impertinence prompted him to single out the mannerisms of such major figures as James Fenimore Cooper, Poe, Emerson, Margaret Fuller, Nathaniel P. Willis, and John Neal among many others, though his introspective habits also led him to turn his ironic shafts to self-mockery:

> There is Lowell, who's striving Parnassus to climb
>
> With a whole bale of isms tied together with rhymes,
>
> He might get on alone, spite of brambles and boulders,
>
> But he can't with that bundle he has on his shoulders,
>
> The top of the hill he will ne'er come near reaching
>
> Till he learns the distinction 'twixt singing and preaching;[1]

A *jeu d'esprit*, The "Fable for Critics" generally revealed Lowell's critical acumen. Of Cooper, he said:

> His Indians, with proper respect be it said,
>
> Are just Natty Bumppo, daubed with red,
>
> And his very Long Toms are the same useful Nat,
>
> Rigged up in duck pants and a sou'wester hat. . . .[2]

Margaret Fuller's portrait was undoubtedly the harshest owing to Lowell's urge to revenge for her cruel treatment of his poetry in an earlier period. The "Fable for Critics" met with immediate success although such writers as William Gilmore Simms and Poe responded indignantly. Lowell had seen in the latter "three fifths . . . genius and two fifths sheer fudge" while generally slighting southern authors.

The first *Biglow Paper*, a satire in Yankee dialect on the campaign to recruit troops in Massachusetts for the war with Mexico, appeared in the *Boston Courier* on June 17, 1846. At that time Lowell did not intend to write an extended series of comments on the Mexican War, but the pressure of events induced him to publish nine *Papers* within a few months. Most pieces were presented as if from the pen of Hosea Biglow, a young Yankee farmer antagonistic toward slavery who mailed letters from Jaalam, a mythic Down East village. Two other Yankees complete the cast: Increase D. O'Phace, whose name is ironically derived from the "dough faces" who in the North were tolerant of slavery, and Birdofredum Sawin, a volunteer in the war who, like General Scott, ultimately wants to take advantage of alleged military feats on the Mexican front by running for President. In 1849, Lowell collected the papers into a volume and introduced as "editor" the figure of Parson Wilbur, Jaalam's scholarly minister.

Lowell viewed "Mr. Polk's war" as a cynical attempt to extend slavery under the guise of Manifest Destiny. For him, smug Yankees, especially politicians, were just as guilty as southern planters when they tolerated warmongers, provided their own security was not threatened. Biglow embodies the stern morality inherited from the Puritan colony; in his opinion, New England has too readily submitted to the claims of the planter class.

The first *Biglow Paper* is a letter from Ezekiel Biglow, Hosea's father, to the editor of the *Boston Courier*. It relates how Hosea met a recruiting agent who tried to get him to join up for service in the war. Then follows a letter from Birdofredum, a volunteer in the Massachusetts regiment who complains about his situation. In the third and fourth papers, Lowell satirizes all of those Yankees who are easily bought off by "slavocracy," such as Caleb Cushing, the colonel of the Massachusetts Regiment of Volunteers, and O'Phace, a spokesman for the Yankee turncoats who shift from zealous support of the Whigs to the side of the Democrats. "The Debate in the Sennit, sot of Nursry Rhyme" is a satire on the stir caused by Captain Drayton in rescuing 77 slaves from Washington in the Schooner *Pearl*. After the slaves were recaptured, Drayton was sentenced to a long prison term. When Senator Hale from New Hampshire publicly sympathized with the slaves and their saviour, both "Cotton Whigs" and southern planters abused him. *Papers* Number VII and VIII lampoon the shifting loyalties of Zachary Taylor, who claims:

Ez to my princerples, I glory
In heving' nothin' o' the sort;
I ain't a Wig, I ain't a tory,
I'm just a canderate, in short;
Thet's fair an' square an' parpendicular
But, ef the Public care a fig
To hev me an'thin' in particler
Wy, I'm a kind o' peri-Wig[3]

Birdofredum, a Yankee *picaro*, then echoes Taylor's cynicism. He is back from the war, having lost one leg, one eye, and one arm. He plans to run for president, and he realizes that one must come from the South to have a reasonable chance. In the last of the *Biglow Papers*, Sawin further develops his conception of American parties: "They're like two pickpockets in league fer Uncle Samwell's pus;/ Each takes a side an' then they squeeze the ole man in between 'em,/ Turn all his pockets wrong side out an' quick ez lightnin' clean 'em."[4]

Many years separated the first *Biglow Papers* from the second. During the Civil War, Lowell was asked by J.T. Fields to publish more of Hosea's poems in the *Atlantic*. The first of the new series appeared in January 1862, but the papers were discontinued in June of the same year. Lowell himself admitted that the comic muse was failing him and declared, "better no crop than small potatoes." After the lapse of a half-year, the "Latest Views of Mr. Biglow" appeared in February 1863. Two more papers followed in 1865 ·and in the autumn of 1866, the entire Second Series was published in book form.

The Second Series's "Mason and Slidell; a Yankee Idyll" was one of Lowell's most entertaining pieces. Mason and Slidell, two agents sent by Jefferson Davis to England and France to represent the southern cause, were caught by Captain Wilkes of the man-of-war *Jacinto* while they were sailing on the *Trent*, a British mail steamer. At the request of Lord Russell they were finally released. This was an occasion for Lowell to evoke the tumultuous love idyll between Jonathan and John Bull:

God means to make this land, John,
Clear thru, from sea to sea,
Believe an' understand, John,
the wuth of being free.[5]

In another letter, Sawin tells how he was converted at a southern camp meeting and eventually married to a widow who would not have him without religion. A refreshing mood pervades "Sunthin' in the Pastoral Line." Hosea has a dream that includes nostalgic visions of his forebears when New England was the mainspring of power and faith. In another poetic interlude, "The Courtin'," Lowell returns to the tradition of the Yankee pastoral by staging two country lovers in comic scenes reminiscent of the folk humor of "husking bees."

The rest of the papers are comic comments on topical issues. Most of the dramatic events of the time are seen in the light of Yankee idiosyncrasies, but their treatment often lacks thematic unity. Sometimes the papers come close to low parody of national crises, and during the Civil War, Lowell's jocular tone and apparently casual use of the Yankee dialect often seemed inappropriate to people who were too much in earnest to appreciate mock-heroic satire.

The Second Series was more episodic and fragmentary than the First. Lowell no longer had the impetus of the earlier years and imagined his favorite characters from a consistently humorous distance. It was certainly less challenging than before for the Harvard professor to characterize such a variety of Down East types in an accurate Down East dialect.

If Lowell's intention is clearly satirical in both series, his choice of three major Yankee characters reveals how indebted his inspiration is to the New England rustic environment. Hosea Biglow, Parson Wilbur, and Birdofredum Sawin assume points of view that create comic incongruities. The range of Lowell's humor extends from wisecracks to sheer buffoonery. Through his personae, he refers to the solid values of the past—which he opposes to the inconsistencies of the present. He likes to deride the foibles of his Down East figures, which gives him additional credibility when he ironically castigates John C. Calhoun and his Yankee supporters. Confronted with contemporary issues, his characters either retain their Yankee heritage or spurn it, and their actions and statements are valued in accordance to their faithfulness to a secular vision that links the Pilgrim Fathers to Jonathan and Yankee Doodle. Lowell's humor is therefore consistently didactic. As he states:

> If I put on the cap and bells and made
> myself one of the court-fools of King
> Demos, it was less to make his majesty
> laugh than to win a passage to his royal
> ears for certain serious things which I
> had deeply at heart. I say this because
> there is no imputation that could be
> more galling to any man's self-respect
> than that of being a mere jester.[6]

By alternating dialect humor and incisive irony, Lowell provides both comic entertainment and moral teaching. By borrowing several voices he communicates indirectly with his reader. Such indirection is a bulwark against fanaticism for Lowell. Biglow is a shrewd crackerbox philosopher, Homer Wilbur a pedantic parson encumbered with his profuse quotations from the classics, and Birdofredurn a Yankee rogue in the image of the peddler. Each represents part of ancestral New England, and their juxtaposed comments symbolize the contradictions of a troubled age.

Biglow plays the part of the clever ignoramus who disguises his thoughts so that he may not be tricked by strangers. His character is indebted to the crackerbarrel tradition of native American humor. He especially delights in homespun metaphors while discussing political issues, as when he calls a gossip "a two-legged gab machine," a skunk, "an essence peddler," and describes average citizens faced with devious politicians as "Mis'ble roosters in a rain, heads down an' tails half-mast." When talking of the war, he exclaims:

> *Wut's the use o' meetin'-goin'*
> *Every Sabbath, wet or dry,*
> *Ef it's right to go amowin'*
> *Feller-men like oats an' rye?*[7]

Biglow's inventive monologue is a Yankee yarn in verse in which the greenhorn learns quickly from his mishaps and soon unmasks humbugs and twisted rhetoric.

As editor of the *Biglow Papers*, Homer Wilbur burlesques a scholarly tradition that dates back to Cotton Mather. He delights in the minutiae of learned allusions and biographical mentions. An imitation of Oliver Goldsmith's *Vicar of Wakefield*, Doctor Primrose, Wilbur undoubtedly amounts to a comic self-portrait of Lowell himself and his interest in philology makes him a reliable transcriber of Down East dialect. The combination in the *Biglow Papers* of the New England vernacular with highbrow disquisitions also constitutes a parody of the tension between the backcountry and Boston, and thus provided Lowell with a way to accept himself as a Brahmin without betraying age-old Puritan pragmatic idealism. This is illustrated in his evocation of the Yankee character:

> A strange hybrid, indeed, did circumstances beget, here in the New World, upon the old Puritan stock, and the earth never before saw such mystic-practicalism, such niggard-geniality, such calculating-fanaticism, such cast-iron-enthusiasm, such sourfaced-humor, such close-fisted-generosity. . . . Jonathan is conscious still that he lives in the world of the Unseen as well as of the Seen. To move John, you must make your fulcrum of solid beef and pudding, an abstract idea will do for Jonathan.[8]

Wilbur is a dignified oracle whose bookish serenity makes him an eccentric but trustworthy observer of the American scene. With him the Yankee spirit remains a safeguard against the so-called "Manifest Destiny" claimed by Southern expansionists.

Sawin is a self-deluded *picaro* whose confused mind makes him act like a buffoon. A perverted Yankee, he lacks the faith in man that Wilbur maintains. Thus, in self-defense, Sawin becomes a rustic Lucifer who subverts the ideals of the Yankee community while deriving no advantage from his betrayals. Military propaganda has been so efficient with him that he says, "I had a strong persuasion/ That Mexicans worn't human beans—an ourang-outang nation,/ A sort o' folks a chap could kill an' never dream on't arter,/ No more 'n a feler'd dream o'pigs thet he hed hed to slarter."[9] Instead of Montezuma's palace, he finds horror on the battlefields. Sawin's comic discomfiture is illustrated in his concern about the incapacity of his wooden leg to assimilate the amount of liquor that his body normally consumes in large quantities. Emulating southern planters, Sawin decides to buy himself a slave, whom he calls Pomp. One day the latter unfastens the wooden leg of his owner, who has dozed off, and runs away, then comes back to capture the powerless master and compel him to be his servant. On his return from Mexico, Sawin seems to have lost his mind since he wants to run for president like Scott or Taylor. Naturally, his vagaries lead him to further disasters. In the clashes between Sawin and the world, nothing impels him to question his own version of reality. In both series of the *Biglow Papers*, the episodes involving Sawin constitute a sustained picaresque yarn in verse. In the first series, the episodes are intended to show the danger of the Unionism-at-all-costs stance by suggesting the moral damage caused by expansionist propaganda among vulnerable New Englanders. The second series reveals that Lowell has turned from pacifism to Yankee jingoism as Hosea blesses his son who goes to war.

Throughout the *Biglow Papers*, Lowell's characterization of comic Yankees is more elaborate than those offered in popular yarns and tall tales of the mid-nineteenth century. Although they talk like the stock figures of Yankee folk humor, Biglow, Wilbur, and Sawin express views that transcend trickster tales concerning horse swapping, bundling, husking, clockpeddling, or New England primer teaching. Lowell was aware that he could satisfy his didactic purpose by using comic dialect rather than by formally expounding on elusive abstract concepts.

Summary

James Russell Lowell's contributions to the tradition of American humor served as a significant link between Yankee lore and the comic fiction of the late nineteenth century. He satirized the self-centered cautiousness of his fellow Yankees when he was fully committed first to abolition-ism and then to the saving of the Union. Thanks to his introspective habits, he was able to turn his vehemence into self-mockery. His deliberate choice of Yankee dialect to make fun of contem-porary humbug at the time of the Mexican War and the Civil War resulted in a comic presenta-tion of dramatic events intended to defuse vio-lent antagonisms among his readers. Averse to the rhetorical devices that obscured plain truths, in an age of abstract idealism the Boston Brah-min trusted the vernacular of his Yankee bump-kins more than the elaborate concepts of the Transcendentalists. The object of Lowell's dia-lect humor was to tone down the instinctive, sarcastic irony that he was tempted to express as a militant Abolitionist or Unionist. He could not refrain from holding up politicians to ridicule whenever their attitudes exemplified hypocrisy or personal ambition, but the self-righteous Pu-ritan in him submitted to the jocular Yankee. He actually wished to stand halfway between the common man and the intellectual elite. Since no single voice could easily express such a point of view without being by turns aggressive or conde-scending, he relied on indirection and adopted several masks. Lowell's scholarly didacticism was unobtrusive while his fairly strictly controlled comic spirit always remained.

Notes

1. *The Complete Poetical Works of James Russell Lowell* (Boston: Houghton, Mifflin, 1897), p. 145.
2. Ibid., p. 164.
3. *The Biglow Papers, First Series, A Critical Edition.* Ed. Thomas Wortham (DeKalb: Northern Illinois University Press.), p. 114.
4. Ibid., p. 137.
5. *The Complete Poetical Works*, p. 239.
6. *The Writings of James Russell Lowell in Prose and Poetry*, Riverside Edition. 10 vols. (Boston: Houghton, Mifflin, 1890), Vol. 7, p. 57.
7. *The Complete Poetical Works*, p. 203.
8. Ibid., p. 137.
9. Ibid, p. 207.

Selected Bibliography

Primary Sources

The Writings of James Russell Lowell in Prose and Poetry. Riverside Edition. 10 vols. Boston: Houghton, Mifflin, 1890.

The Complete Poetical Works of James Russell Lo-well. Cambridge Edition. Ed. H.E. Scudder. Boston: Houghton, Mifflin, 1897.

The Complete Writings of James Russell Lowell. Elm-wood Edition. 16 vols. Boston: Riverside Press, 1904.

The Biglow Papers. Ed. Thomas Wortham. DeKalb: Northern Illinois University Press, 1977.

Secondary Scources

Beatty, Richmond Croom. *James Russell Lowell*. Nashville: University of Tennessee Press, 1942.

Blair, Walter. "A Brahmin Dons Homespun." In *Horse Sense in American Humor*. Ed. Blair. Chi-cago: The University of Chicago Press, 1942.

Duberman, Martin. *James Russell Lowell*. Boston: Houghton Mifflin, 1966.

Howard, Leon. *A Victorian Knight Errant, a Study of the Early Career of James Russell Lowell*. Berkeley: University of California Press, 1952. Indispensable.

McGlinchee, Claire. *James Russell Lowell*. New York: Twayne, 1967. Overview.

Royot, Daniel. *L'Humour Américain, des Puritains aux Yankees*. Lyon: Presses Universitaires de Lyon, 1980.

———. "James Russell Lowell: Un Humoriste Yankee Face au Sud et à l'Esclavage." *Etudes Anglaises*, 39,1 (1986): 26-36.

Wagenknecht, Edward. *James Russell Lowell, Portrait of a Many-Sided Man*. New York: Oxford Univer-sity Press, 1971.

Daniel G. Royot

McGinley, Phyllis

Born: Ontario, Oregon, on March 21, 1905
Education: University of Utah, graduated 1927
Marriage: Charles L. Hayden, June 1937, two children
Died: February 22, 1978

Biography

The daughter of Daniel and Julia Kiesel McGin-ley, Phyllis Louise McGinley was born in On-tario, Oregon, on March 21, 1905. Her family soon moved to a ranch near Iliff, Colorado, where McGinley attended a small country school and read voraciously. She was writing verse by the time she was six, though her talent for humor did not emerge until she was an adult. With her father's death in 1917, she moved to her mother's family home in Ogden, Utah, where she attended Sacred Heart Academy and Ogden High School. At the University of Utah, from which she graduated in 1927, she won prizes for her essays, short stories, and poetry. While teaching school, she sent her work to New York magazines, and some of her poems were accepted. She moved in 1929 to New Ro-chelle, New York, where she taught junior high school and continued to write. *New Yorker* fic-tion editor Katharine White encouraged her to inject more humor into her work. When *The New Yorker* responded enthusiastically to the light verse that she began to write in the early 1930s, McGinley resigned her teaching position and moved to New York City, where she worked as a poetry editor and advertising copywriter while trying to establish herself as a free-lance writer.

McGinley's first collection of verse, *On the Contrary*, appeared in 1934. In June of 1937, she married Charles L. Hayden; they would have two children. In addition to publishing numerous volumes of verse, McGinley also used her humorous talents to write children's books, beginning with *The Horse Who Lived Upstairs* in 1944. *The Love Letters of Phyllis McGinley* won the Edna St. Vincent Millay Award in 1954, the first in a series of honors that included election in 1955 to the National Institute of Arts and Letters. Much of her later work, which sold well, was published originally in *The New Yorker*, though her pieces began appearing more frequently in women's magazines such as *Mademoiselle* and *Good Housekeeping*. In 1961, McGinley was awarded the Pulitzer Prize for *Times Three* (1960), a collection of nearly 300 of her poems, 70 of which had not been collected previously. During the 1960s, she became known as an important spokesman for traditional motherhood—a role that occasionally made her uncomfortable—based on essays in which she defended the role of housewife and mother. McGinley died on Feburary 22, 1978.

Literary Analysis

Phyllis McGinley was one of the most prolific and widely known American writers of light verse in the twentieth century. She was often praised for the technical proficiency of her verse, for a workmanship that keeps even her most emotional poems from seeming mawkish. Sometimes her poetry and prose had a direct tie with newspaper headlines—war, poetry, progressive education; often her writing related only to her own world as woman, wife, and mother. In both cases, she was responding to topics recognizable to most of her readers. Her message was often nostalgic. Depending on the significance of the subject, her tone varied accordingly from lighthearted mirth to incisive wit.

McGinley's first three collections of light verse—*On The Contrary* 1934), *One More Manhattan* (1937), and *A Pocketful of Wry* (1940)—have urban themes. She playfully satirizes department stores, shopping, and fashions while reflecting on the details of city life. Such topical subjects as newspaper items, radio programs, and films provide inspiration for her poems. In all of this work, McGinley reveals that she had early mastered the various techniques of light verse—wordplay and rhyme in conventional yet polished form.

Husbands Are Difficult (1941) is a collection of many of McGinley's early poems dealing with the battle between the sexes. Light in tone, this verse reveals that McGinley is content with her life as a housewife and mother. As is the case in other of her collections, many of the poems in *Stones from a Glass House: New Poems* (1946) utilize parody and consistent patterns of meter and rhyme to survey subjects of broad popular appeal. Pro-suburban sentiments are expressed in such poems as "The 5:32," "Confessions of a Reluctant Optimist," and "Occupation: Housewife." *A Short Walk from the Station* (1951) continues the defense of suburban life.

Most of the poems in *The Love Letters of Phyllis McGinley* (1954) celebrate rather than satirize; the humor is gentle. McGinley's Pulitzer Prize-winning *Times Three* (1960) contains nearly 300 poems, arranged by decades in reverse chronology. Though most ephemeral and topical verses are excluded, the volume nonetheless reveals the development of McGinley's techniques and themes. Some of the essays collected in *The Province of the Heart* (1959) defend suburbia and the role of housewife and mother, while some of the semi-autobiographical pieces brought together in *Sixpence in Her Shoe* (1964) range in tone from sarcastic to nostalgic and were seen by her publisher as a rebuttal of Betty Friedan's *The Feminine Mystique* (1963).

Summary

During her long career as a writer, Phyllis McGinley was widely known for her witty and often satiric poems and essays. She became a public voice and virtually a public institution. For decades, she dissected with humor and understanding a variety of topics familiar to her many readers.

Selected Bibliography

Primary Sources

On the Contrary. Garden City: Doubleday, Doran, 1934.

One More Manhattan. New York: Harcourt, Brace, 1937.

A Pocketful of Wry. New York: Duell, Sloan and Pearce, 1940.

Husbands Are Difficult; or, The Book of Oliver Ames. New York: Duell, Sloan and Pearce, 1941.

The Horse Who Lived Upstairs. Philadelphia: Lippincott, 1945.

The Plain Princess. Philadelphia: Lippincott, 1945.

Stones from a Glass House: New Poems. New York: Viking, 1946.

A Name for Kitty. New York: Simon & Schuster, 1948; London: Muller, 1950.

All Around the Town. Philadelphia: Lippincott, 1948.

The Most Wonderful Doll in the World. Philadelphia: Lippincott, 1950.

Blunderbus. Philadelphia: Lippincott, 1951.

The Horse Who Had His Picture in the Paper. Philadelphia: Lippincott, 1951.

A Short Walk from the Station. New York: Viking, 1951.

The Make-Believe Twins. Philadelphia: Lippincott, 1953.

The Love Letters of Phyllis McGinley. New York: Viking, 1954; London: Dent, 1955.

The Year Without a Santa Claus. Philadelphia: Lippincott, 1957; Leicester, U.K.: Brockhampton Press, 1960.

Merry Christmas, Happy New Year. New York: Viking, 1958; London: Secker and Warburg, 1959.

Lucy McLockett. Philadelphia: Lippincott, 1959; Leicester, U.K.: Brockhampton Press, 1961.

The Province of the Heart. New York: Viking, 1959; London: Catholic Book Club, 1963.

Times Three: Selected Verse from Three Decades, with Seventy New Poems. New York: Viking, 1960; London: Secker and Warburg, 1961.

Sugar and Spice: The ABC of Being a Girl. New York: Watts, 1960.

Mince Pie and Mistletoe. Philadelphia: Lippincott, 1961.

Boys Are Awful. New York: Watts, 1962.

The B Book. New York: Crowell-Collier, 1962; London: Collier-Macmillan, 1968.

A Girl and Her Room. New York: Watts, 1963.

How Mrs. Santa Claus Saved Christmas. Philadelphia: Lippincott, 1963; Kingswood, Surrey, U.K.: World's Work, 1964.

Sixpence in Her Shoe. New York: Macmillan, 1964.

Wonderful Time. Philadelphia: Lippincott, 1966.

A Wreath of Christmas Legends. New York: Macmillan, 1967.

Wonders and Surprises: A Collection of Poems. Philadelphia: Lippincott, 1966.

Saint-Watching. New York: Viking, 1969; London: Collins, 1970.

Christmas Con and Pro. Berkeley: Hart Press, 1971.

Confessions of a Reluctant Optimist. Ed. Barbara Wells Price. Kansas City, Missouri: Hallmark Editions, 1973.

Secondary Sources

McCord, David. "She Speaks a Language of Delight," *Saturday Review,* 43 (December 10, 1960): 32. Brief but perceptive discussion of McGinley's work from the late 1920s to 1960.

"The Telltale Hearth," *Time,* 85 (June 18, 1965): 74–78. Good interview with McGinley.

Wagner, Linda Welshimer. *Phyllis McGinley.* New York: Twayne, 1971. The standard treatment of McGinley's work.

L. Moody Simms, Jr.

McGuane, Thomas Francis, III

Born: Wyandotte, Michigan, on December 11, 1939

Education: University of Michigan; Olivet College; Michigan State University, B.A., 1962; Yale University, M.F.A., 1965

Marriages: Portia Rebecca Crockett, 1962, divorced, 1975, one child; Margot Kidder, 1976, divorced, 1977, one child; Laurie Buffet, 1977, one child

Biography

Thomas McGuane's life has a quality of myth to it; like Hemingway, whom he resembles in several ways, he seems at times to live more excitingly than he writes or at least to live excitingly in order to accumulate a rich store of experience about which to write. He comes from an upper-middle-class, Irish-American family in Michigan. After a private secondary education in Bloomfield Hills, Michigan, he attended the University of Michigan, where he flunked out. He graduated from Michigan State University, where he was the editor of the literary magazine and worked on his own writing. In an interview he has said that at this point of his life, he was a "sociopath." He has also attended not only Yale, from which he received an M.F.A. in 1965, but Stanford University.

The two most important constants in McGuane's life seem to have been writing and outdoor sport—usually of a solitary and non-competitive sort, such as hunting, fishing, riding, roping and other cowboy work. The writing and the sport have identified him with three parts of the United States also common to Hemingway: Michigan, Key West and the waters around it, and the American West, specifically Montana. His celebrity derives from his suitability as a counter-cultural hero, based on his first three novels; his involvement with the movies, most notably the peculiar 1976 film *The Missouri Breaks,* written by McGuane, starring Jack Nicholson and Marlon Brando; and his fairly well-documented and Hollywoodesque marital career, dotted with three marriages, an affair with actress Elizabeth Ashley celebrated in her autobiography, and children born out of wedlock. McGuane's friendships with other celebrities such as singer Jimmy Buffett, actor Peter Fonda (who is married to McGuane's ex-wife), director Sam Peckinpah, and writers Jim Harrison and the late Richard Brautigan have helped him to a nonliterary celebrity. All of this sometimes obscures the unique strengths of McGuane's writing.

Literary Analysis

McGuane's funniest novel is also probably his best, his second book, *The Bushwhacked Piano.*

Published in 1971, it is the unsettlingly pica-resque story of Nicholas Payne, an intelligent, consistently absorbing character who has more than a trace of his creator in him. Payne devotes himself to travel, to the pursuit of Ann Fitzge-rald, and to cross-country adventures, usually with Ann. Beginning in Michigan, he moves to Montana and ends up in South Florida. Along the way he offends decorum in a variety of ways. Payne's life is "aimless"—until he begins work-ing with C.J. Clovis, a visionary, a man who builds and sells bat towers, or batriums, for in-sect control. Clovis, aside from his unusual cal-ling, is an original character; sorely tested by overweight and disease, he is slowly snipped away during the novel.

The Bushwhacked Piano dramatizes the occa-sionally bizarre but always honest behavior of Nicholas Payne, partly by contrasting it with that of his rival for Ann Fitzgerald, a buttoned-up junior executive named George Russell. The book ends with Payne's defeat, in most ways: the collapse of the batrium business, the death of C.J. Clovis, Payne's mutilation in a botched hemor-rhoid operation, Ann's predictable defection in favor of George—but his indomitable spirit lives. The novel ends with a sort of Sisyphean triumph; robbed of dignity and everything else, Payne nevertheless insists: "I am at large."[1] The humor of the novel is of two sorts: verbal felici-ties, or wit, and the characters' involvement in outrageous events. In the following passage, C.J. Clovis is discussing bats with Nicholas Payne, particularly whether they gobble bugs:

> I could take a Western Pipestrel and have the little son of a bitch eating his weight in June bugs night after night. This here is a question of style, a ques-tion of class. I want a classy bat! And I don't want something that has to be near running water or has to live in a narrow slot or within two miles of euca-lyptus or that sucks the wind for rabies. What's the difference. The Little Brown is okay. That goes for the Silverhaired. But no one is going to pretend they're class bats by a long shot.
>
> (pp. 96–97)

The outrageous situations typically involve Ann's parents, sometimes in a confrontation with Payne, whom they hate, sometimes in a confrontation with each other caused by the un-welcome presence of Payne. Once, drunk, he breaks into their house and wanders through it drinking brandy and trailing toilet paper. In the Fitzgeralds' bedroom, he silently watches them sleep, and holds the muzzle of a shotgun to Mrs. Fitzgerald's face:

> He remembered too—looking at her laid out like this—that Saint Francis Borgia had been impelled to his monk-hood through horror at the sight of the corpse of Isabella of Portugal. Beside her, and invisible in a ledge of shadow, her husband rotated in the blankets and unveiled his wife. Wearing only a pair of floppy prizefighter's trunks labeled *Everlast*, her gruesome figure was re-vealed. It upset Payne to see such a thing.
>
> (p. 30)

One more scene, this time between the two Fitz-geralds, conveys the manic tone of this novel. Edna speaks first.

> "I'll pragmatize you, you wheezing G.M. cretin."
> "Your pills, Edna, your pills. You're getting balmy."
> "Show me that little trick with your hand, where it tells me I'm talking too much."
> "Get your pills, Edna."
> "Go on, show it to me."
> He showed her the blabbing motion with his hand at the same time he told her, "Get the pills, Edna." She slapped his hand open. He made the blabbing motion again. "Get your pills I said!" Then she nailed him in the blaring red mug and ran for it. He galloped after her grunting and baying as he hauled her away from the desk. She turned then and raked his chest with a handful of ballpoint pens and a protractor.
>
> (p. 72)

In addition to the humor, and the variety of interesting characters, this novel has a number of elements that recur in McGuane's fiction. One is a mordantly despairing point of view about modern American civilization, called here "sni-velization," and called in *Ninety-two in the Shade* (1973) "Hotcakesland." Another is a con-tinuing theme of men testing themselves. Payne, despite his drifting, countercultural style and his occasional mild madness, is competent and knowing; he can handle himself; he is a good carpenter, a competent rodeo cowboy, a wily fighter. McGuane's men are usually like this. They are involved, either by profession or by way of recreation (*serious* recreation—proving themselves) in deep sea fishing (*Ninety-two in the Shade*), hunting (*The Sporting Club*, 1969), or ranching (*Nobody's Angel*, 1982; *Something to Be Desired*, 1984). The hero of *Nobody's Angel* is, he often reminds us, a captain of tanks, though this is never made entirely credible or tangible, like the horseriding and fence mending. McGuane, reminiscent of Hemingway, is deeply *knowing*; he writes casually about the steady performance of tasks in a way that radiates authority. His protagonists are knowing men, competent men. The exception is Chet Pomeroy of *Panama* (1978), a drugged, lost casualty of modern America and his own publicity, a rock star adrift in Key West. He experiences a sort of free-floating angst, rails against fate, snuffles up cocaine from a city sidewalk; he nails his own hand to his wife's door (requiring, admittedly, a good deal of competence), but otherwise lacks the *savoir faire* expected from McGuane's protagonists.

A final McGuane characteristic is a weakness in creating women characters. The concentration on "a man's world" limits these women; McGuane's men love women, and they are usually believably desirable, but they are two-dimensional, usually, not really reliable, lacking in the complexity that the men show, and finally not to be trusted like men. The abandoned wife in *Something to Be Desired* comes closest to being something more than a *belle dame sans merci* (in the Ann Fitzgerald mode) or the woman too limited to comprehend the hero.

In *The Sporting Club* the plot involves an unspoken struggle between two men, a test of strength and courage and unflappability marked by dangerous behavior, outrageous impositions on the rest of the world, and really adolescent, but nonetheless funny stunts. The fiancée of the dominant man watches from the sidelines, sadly uncomprehending. The struggle is finally inconclusive.

Summary

In *The Sporting Club* or, better yet, *The Bushwhacked Piano*, readers see the essential McGuane novel: a plot of man against man and man against nature, with something elemental in the struggle, combined with a texture of outrageous self-expression and sometimes wild humor. Donald Katz, writing of the first three McGuane novels, sums up what is best about his work—and the source of what is funniest in the fiction: "the sheer romanticization of a lunacy verging on mild sociopathy and the contention that the observation of the secret beauty of one's impending madness is almost worth the pain."[2]

Notes

1. Thomas Francis McGuane, *The Bushwhacked Piano* (New York: Simon and Schuster, 1971), p. 220.
2. Donald Katz, "Thomas McGuane: Heroes in 'Hotcakesland,'" *The New Republic*, 181 (August 18, 1979): 38.

Selected Bibliography

Primary Sources

Novels
The Sporting Club. New York: Simon and Schuster, 1969.
The Bushwhacked Piano. New York: Simon and Schuster, 1971.
Ninety-Two in the Shade. New York: Farrar, Straus and Giroux, 1973.
Panama. New York: Farrar, Straus and Giroux, 1978.
Nobody's Angel. New York: Random House, 1982.
Something To Be Desired. New York: Random House, 1984.

Other
An Outside Chance. New York: Farrar, Straus and Giroux, 1980. Sports essays.
Screenplays for *Rancho Deluxe* (1975), *Ninety-Two in the Shade* (1975; also director), *The Missouri Breaks* (1976), and *Tom Horn* (1980).

Secondary Sources
Carter, Albert Howard, III. "McGuane's First Three Novels; Games, Fun, Nemesis." *Critique*, 17 (1975): 91-104. Good overview of these three books and their interplay of humor and pathos.
Katz, Donald R. "Thomas McGuane: Heroes in 'Hotcakesland.'" *The New Republic*, 181 (August 18, 1979): 38-39. Uncommonly perceptive treatment of the first three novels, identifying them as important cultural artifacts of the late 1960s, early 1970s.
Martin, Russell. "Writers of the Purple Sage." *New York Times Magazine*, 131 (December 27, 1981): 18-22, 40-41. About McGuane and other western writers.

Merritt Moseley

McKenney, Ruth

Born: Mishawaka, Indiana, on November 18, 1911
Education: Shaw High School, Cleveland, Ohio; Ohio State University (two years)
Marriage: Richard Bransten, August 12, 1937, three children
Died: New York City, July 25, 1972

Biography

Although Ruth McKenney preferred to think of herself as a sociologist and labor activist, her fame rests largely on her talents as a humorist. McKenney's sketches of her childhood and adventures with her younger sister Eileen became the basis for several books, two Hollywood films, three Broadway plays and a television series, all of which left audiences all over the world chuckling at the girls' antics. Yet her humorous sketches masked what McKenney maintained to be an unhappy childhood.

McKenney was born in Mishawaka, Indiana, on November 18, 1911, the daughter of John Sidney and Marguerite Flynn McKenney. When Ruth was six, the family moved to Cleveland, where Mrs. McKenney, an ardent Irish Nationalist and schoolteacher, died two years later. Living with the McKenneys were Ruth's maternal grandfather and several other family members, who provided her with unending source material for her humorous books. As a child she was plump, smart, and unpopular, in contrast to her attractive sister Eileen, whom she idolized.

At age 14, McKenney became an apprentice printer at the O.E. Thomas Print Shop in Cleveland. Her writing career began a few years later when she entered Ohio State University. There she became first a reporter for the *Ohio State Lantern*, and then campus reporter for the *Columbus Dispatch*. She dropped out of college in her junior year to chaperone a former roommate through Europe and never graduated. McKenney later used these experiences when she became a contributor to *The New Yorker*.

On her return to the United States, McKenney became a reporter for the Akron *Beacon Journal* and won statewide awards for feature writing. In 1933 she accepted a job offer from a Newark newspaper, and she and Eileen moved east. Unfortunately the paper was on strike when she arrived in Newark, but she quickly found a job as feature writer with the *New York Post*. The sisters shared an apartment in Greenwich Village while Ruth worked at the *Post* from 1934 to 1936.

In 1936, following other journalistic endeavors, McKenney began to write stories for *The New Yorker* based on her experiences as a child in Ohio and as a working girl in New York. She interrupted her humorous writing with a trip to Akron to gather material for a book about the Goodyear rubber strike and the formation of the C.I.O., *Industrial Valley*. After completing her research and returning east, she met and married Richard Bransten, an editor and historian who wrote under the pseudonym Bruce Minton.

Despite the success of her Eileen stories, which appeared as a book, *My Sister Eileen*, in 1938 and a play two years later, McKenney always preferred her serious writings. She considered *Industrial Valley* (1939) her best work. In general the critics reacted favorably to this semi-fictionalized account of recent American labor history, while faulting her leftist approach and borderline propagandism. Through excerpts

from newspaper headlines, statistical data, and editorial comments, the feelings and emotions of American workers in a time of industrial foment were depicted with skill and heartfelt intensity. The book won an award in 1939 at the Writers' Congress.

Following the publication of a short work entitled *Browder and Ford: For Peace, Jobs and Socialism* (1940), endorsing the Communist Party candidates in the presidential campaign of 1940, a second book with a labor theme, *Jake Home*, appeared in 1943. This story of a miner who becomes a labor leader and Communist received negative reviews from critics who found the title character unbelievable and McKenney's wide-eyed ideology dated. McKenney herself later stated that she had erred in creating such a heroic but generally implausible character.

By this time McKenney and Bransten had moved to Washington, D.C., and become members of the Communist party. Ruth was writing a column, "Strictly Personal," for the Communist weekly *New Masses*. Eileen had moved to California and married the novelist Nathanael West in 1940. In December of that year, a few days before the opening of the play *My Sister Eileen*, she and West were killed in an automobile accident while returning from Mexico. The Branstens adopted Eileen's only child Patrick, and in December 1942 Ruth gave birth to a daughter, whom the Branstens named Eileen.

Beginning with the war years, the Branstens lived in a variety of cities—Washington, D.C.; Hollywood (where they wrote screenplays for a year); Westport, Connecticut; Brussels; London; New York; and finally, France. The Branstens were slowly growing disillusioned with left-wing activities and were thrown out of the Communist party in 1946 for departing from party doctrine. During this peripatetic period McKenney produced *The Loud Red Patrick*, a book of stories about her grandfather (1947); *Love Story*, the chronicle of her married life (1950); *Here's England*, an unconventional but readable guidebook mixing history, tourism, and personal narrative, which she wrote with her husband (1950); *All About Eileen*, a collection of old and new stories about her late sister (1952); and *Far, Far from Home*, which detailed life with the Branstens in Brussels (1954).

After her husband's death in 1955, McKenney published only one more book. *Mirage* (1956) told the story of a chemist who took part in Napoleon's Egyptian campaign, an odd choice of subject in light of her other works. Reviews were mixed, but critics agreed that, despite its inaccuracies and anachronistic dialogue, the book was far from dull.

Ruth McKenney died in New York City on July 25, 1971, from complications brought on by a heart ailment and diabetes.

Literary Analysis

Even in her serious writings, McKenney could not help but include touches of the humor from which she gained fame. Part of the success of *Industrial Valley* is due to the inclusion of satire in an otherwise somber and serious history. This technique could also work against her, as *Jake Home* proved; the combination of earnestness and satire turned the title character into what the *New York Times* reviewer called a "burlesque hero."

No such problem of technique existed in her lighter writings, however. The best, and most widely read, are the Eileen stories, which began life in magazines and were published in three separate collections: *My Sister Eileen* (1938), *The McKenneys Carry On* (1940), and *All About Eileen* (1952). Yet for all the emphasis on Eileen in the ensuing play and film versions, most of the stories focus on Ruth herself, her childhood as "Eileen's sister," and her problems in making the transition from a small town to a big city.

The contrast between the girls provides much of the humor in the situations. Eileen—beautiful, popular, unconcerned—is usually exasperated with her level-headed, brainy, not-so-beautiful older sister, while Ruth cannot refrain from trying to protect Eileen from the vicissitudes of the world. The fact that the resourceful Eileen can take care of herself, except possibly financially, and that much of Ruth's worrying is needless provides extra humor to zany situations, such as the girls' attempts to evade the amorous advances of the Brazilian navy.

Some of the situations occur when Ruth and Eileen are children; their attempts at music and elocution are detailed, as are adventures in bird-watching at Camp Hi-Wah, lifesaving at Red Cross swimming lessons (with Ruth as victim), and emotional afternoons spent sobbing into popcorn at the local movie theater. Later on, Ruth's career in journalism is foreshadowed by an unnerving interview with Randolph Churchill, while the girls' introduction to New York life is described in the hilarious "Mr. Spitzer and the Fungus" and "Beware the Brazilian Navy," the primary sources for all ensuing stage, film, and television adaptations.

Taken together, and stripped of their madcap antics, the Eileen stories tell of two small-town young ladies typically trying to achieve success in the big city. Ruth's leftist philosophy, which altered as the years passed, has no place in these tales; her intent is to entertain, a goal she certainly achieves. The humor is not subtle, and many of the adventures border on the slapstick. But readers were enthusiastic enough about *My Sister Eileen* to occasion the two subsequent volumes about the sisters.

The stories that make up *The Loud Red Patrick* focus on McKenney's maternal grandfather. A Democrat in a Republican neighborhood, Patrick was loud and gruff and opinionated but also generous and sentimental. As with many of Ruth's family stories, it is not so much the tale as the telling that provides the hilarity. Critics noted that occasionally her plots were thin, but McKenney's sense of the ridiculous and her honesty in depicting family members saved the Patrick stories from becoming either too sentimental or too unbelievable. They, like *My Sister Eileen*, were turned into a Broadway play in 1956.

Honesty is prevalent in *Love Story*, in which McKenney describes the first twelve years of her marriage. Ruth's view of Eileen changes subtly from that of her earlier works; she still obviously adores her sister and is crushed by her sudden and tragic death but sees Eileen's somewhat self-centered personality with a more realistic eye. McKenney is forthright in discussing her relationship with her husband Richard, their political beliefs and their work for the *New Masses*, their screenwriting efforts in Hollywood, and the illnesses that almost claimed her life and that of her only daughter. Much humor is still present, but it is the humor of an older, maturer Ruth, who has become a wife, mother, and successful author, survived the death of a loved one, and softened her once rock-hard political beliefs.

Summary

Ruth McKenney's stories seem very much a part of their era, and today her popularity has waned. The various stage and screen treatments of her stories kept two generations laughing at the antics of Ruth and Eileen, yet the New York she describes as so overwhelming to the sisters seems as quaint as the midwestern towns of her childhood. Ironically, McKenney's reputation as a writer may rest on *Industrial Valley* rather than her family reminiscences, but she will still hold a place in American humor as a minor but cherished chronicler of the mad doings of the McKenney clan.

Selected Bibliography

Primary Sources

My Sister Eileen. New York: Harcourt, Brace & Co. 1938.

Industrial Valley. New York: Harcourt, Brace & Co., 1939.

Browder and Ford: For Peace, Jobs and Socialism. New York: Workers Library Publishers, Inc., 1940.

The McKenneys Carry On. New York: Harcourt, Brace & Co., 1940.

Jake Home. New York: Harcourt, Brace & Co., 1943.

The Loud Red Patrick. New York: Harcourt, Brace & Co., 1947.

Love Story. New York: Harcourt, Brace & Co., 1950.

(with Richard Bransten.) *Here's England: A Highly Informal Guide.* New York: Harper & Brothers, 1950; rev. ed., 1955.

All About Eileen. New York: Harcourt, Brace & Co., 1952.

Far, Far from Home. New York: Harper & Brothers, 1954.

Mirage. New York: Farrar, Straus, 1956.

Secondary Sources

Contemporary Authors. Vols. 93-96. Detroit: Gale, 1980.

Current Biography, 1942. New York: H.W. Wilson Company, 1943.

Klein, Kathleen G. "Ruth McKenney." *American Women Writers.* Ed. Lina Mainiero. 4 vols. New York: Frederick Ungar, 1979-1982. Very brief overview of McKenney's life and works; includes erroneous publication dates for two of her works.

New York Times, 27 July 1972, p. 34, col. 1. McKenney's obituary notice.

Twentieth Century Authors. Ed. Stanley J. Kunitz and Howard Haycraft. New York: H.W. Wilson Company, 1942.

Twentieth Century Authors, First Supplement. Ed. Stanley J. Kunitz. New York: H.W. Wilson Company, 1955.

Eric W. Johnson

McNutt, Alexander Gallatin

Born: Rockbridge County, Virginia, on January 3, 1802

Education: Washington College, 1821

Marriage: Married, no children

Died: October 22, 1848

Biography

Alexander Gallatin McNutt, the eleventh governor of Mississippi, was born in Rockbridge County, Virginia, the seventh child in a family of thirteen children. His father died when he was ten, and he made his own way in the world thereafter. He taught country school in Virginia and completed his studies at Washington College in 1821. After reading law in Lexington, Virginia, he joined the tide of westward immigration, reaching Jackson, Mississippi, in 1823. He later moved to Vicksburg where in time he developed a lucrative legal practice.

In 1835 McNutt was elected to the state legislature as a Democrat, and in 1837 and 1839 he was elected governor of Mississippi. He was a controversial figure in Mississippi politics, championing the poor farmers in the northern part of the state against the bankers and plantation owners in the south. In his second term as governor he repudiated the bonds of a major Vicksburg bank in order to stop speculation, thereby causing a financial crisis in the state. McNutt was a very powerful man in his later years, and he refused to duel or fight with his challengers, which led to the charge of personal cowardice against him. Duelling was still a frontier custom in Mississippi then, and a man was expected to defend his "honor." Serious charges were made against him by a leading political rival, Henry S. Foote, who accused him of conspiring in the murder of his business partner and of then marrying the widow to get control of the whole property. It was while campaigning for Foote's seat in the U.S. Senate that McNutt became ill and died at the age of 46.

Literary Analysis

McNutt belongs to the school of amateur writers known today as humorists of the Old Southwest. During the last few years of his life, McNutt sent a series of humorous sketches to the popular sporting weekly, William T. Porter's *The Spirit of the Times,* in New York. He used a pen name, "The Turkey Trotter," following the contemporary custom of most of the contributors of popular tales, and he adopted the form and style from similar stories that he had read in *The Spirit of the Times* and other papers.

McNutt's stories usually concern two frontier characters who lived on his plantation, Jim and Chunkey, who are among the most original and funniest rustic characters to emerge in this genre of humor. They are hunting and fishing pals, frontiersmen of the "ring-tailed roarer" variety, and their dialect accounts are full of irrelevant ramblings, exaggerations and homemade words. They tell their adventures to the "Capting," who introduces most of the tales and acts as interlocutor, his own urbane language providing an incongruous contrast to the garrulous dialect of his friends.

In "Scenes on Deer Creek and the Sunflower," for example, Capting asks Jim to tell him about a certain bear hunt. Characteristically, Jim begins on a tangent, explaining how a bear differs from an office seeker:

> A bar, Capting, an old *he* bar, ain't no candidate or other good-natured greenhorn to stand gougin and treating. Oh no, *he* ain't, but he's as ramstugenous an animal as a log-cabin loafer in the dog

days, jist about, and if a stranger fools with him he'll get sarved.

In the same tale Jim describes his own plight when he nearly drowns after diving into a river after a deer:

> Chunk! my head went agin a log, and then I knowed the thing were *irrefrangably out*, but I div agin, still workin' on my oars smartly, until I hung agin! "Good by, Chunkey!—farewell, Governor," says I. But Capting, I were all the time tryin' to do *something*. Things had begun to look speckled, green, and then *omniferous*.

While watching his struggle to get out of the river, Jim's pal, Chunkey, had been overcome by thirst and had gone back to the house to get a drink, but Jim did not resent being abandoned, as he tells the Capting: "When Chunkey wants a drink, if his daddy was drounin', Chunkey would go to the licker gourd."

In "Chunkey's Fight with the Panthers" the protagonist describes the attack of a large panther who caught him unarmed:

> Lightin close to me, it squatted to the ground and commenced creepin towards me—its years laid back, its eyes turnin green, and sorter swimmin round like, and the end of its tail twistin like a snake. . . . I seen her commence slippin her legs under her, and knew she were gwine to spring.

After a ferocious bare-handed battle, Chunkey drives the panther off. "When I sorter come to myself, I war struttin' and thunderin' like a big he-gobler," he says.

Summary

McNutt seems to have written only eight frontier sketches, but they are frequently included in anthologies of frontier humor as examples of the very best of that genre.

Selected Bibliography

Primary Sources

"Scences on Deer Creek and the Sunflower" (sometimes called "Swim for a Deer"). *The Spirit of the Times*, April 20, 1844, p. 91.

"Chunkey's Fight with the Panthers!" *The Spirit of the Times*, May 18, 1844, p. 139.

"Hunting in the Swamps and Bayous of Mississippi." *The Spirit of the Times*, June 1, 1844, p. 163.

"Falling Off a Log in a Game of 'Seven-Up.'" *The Spirit of the Times*, September 14, 1844, p. 343.

"Catching Buffalo with a Gig." *The Spirit of the Times*, September 21, 1844, p. 349.

"The Chase in the Southwest." *The Spirit of the Times*, July 12, 1845, p. 225.

"Another Story of Jim and Chunkey." *The Spirit of the Times*, October 18, 1845, p. 399.

"A Frightful Adventure in Mississippi: My First and Last Day on Dismal Lake." *The Spirit of the Times*, April 3, 1847, p. 67.

Secondary Sources

Foote, Henry S. *Casket of Reminiscences*. Washington, D.C.: The Negro University Press, 1874. Autobiography of a contemporary politican, a bitter rival of McNutt in political contests, and a source of unflattering comments about him.

Howell, Elmo. "Governor Alexander G. McNutt of Mississippi: Humorists of the Old Southwest." *Journal of Mississippi History*, 25 (May 1873): 153-165. Brief biographical sketch, including some of Foote's charges, and summary of McNutt stories.

Moss, Warner. "Governor Alexander G. McNutt (1802-1848)." *Journal of Mississippi History*, 42 (August 1980): 244-257. A self-serving autobiographical sketch inserted by McNutt in a Natchez newspaper in 1837 as a campaign device.

Yates, Norris W. *William T. Porter and the Spirit of the Times: A Study of the Big Bear School of Humor*. Baton Rouge: Lousiana University Press, 1957, pp. 81-82. Summary of biographical data and comment on stories.

Raymond C. Craig

Marquis, Don

Born: Walnut, Illinois, on July 29, 1878
Education: Knox College, 1898, no degree
Marriages: Reina Melcher, June 8, 1909, two children, died, 1923; Marjorie Vonnegut, February 2, 1926, no children (two from Vonnegut's previous marriage)
Died: December 29, 1937

Biography

Don Marquis (pronounced "Mar-kwiss"), most of whose humor grew out of the American urban experience, was born on July 29, 1878, in the small Midwestern town of Walnut, Illinois. His parents, Dr. James Stewart and Virginia Whitmore Marquis, were advocates of a strict Calvinism, a faith whose hell-fire severity their religiously undogmatic son was quick to repudiate.

To the exasperation of his father, Marquis's early years lacked direction. He read extensively, dabbled in poetry, attended Knox College for a few months, and skipped aimlessly from job to job before deciding on a career in the newspaper business. He wrote first for a small paper in the

Walnut area, an experience that introduced him to the creative possibilities of column-writing; among other material, his columns included apocryphal tales of Abraham Lincoln, some of which, according to Marquis himself, were accepted into the historical record. He then moved to Washington, D.C., where he worked for the Census Bureau while unsuccessfully trying to get a column of his own. Following an equally unsuccessful stay in Philadelphia, he became associate editor of the *Atlanta News*, a position that allowed him to indulge his love of column-writing.

The Atlanta experience was important for a number of reasons. It introduced Marquis to the young Grantland Rice, the great sportswriter, and to veteran journalist Frank L. Stanton, Atlanta's premier columnist, both of whom encouraged his writing endeavors. It brought him into association with Joel Chandler Harris, who added Marquis to the staff of *Uncle Remus's Magazine*, thereby providing him with an invaluable apprenticeship in humor. Finally, it brought him a wife, Reina Melcher, to whom Marquis was married on June 8, 1909, and who would bear him two children, Robert and Barbara, before her sudden, untimely death on December 2, 1923.

With Reina's blessing, Marquis moved to New York City in late 1909 in hopes of becoming a columnist as admired as Franklin P. Adams. Free-lancing plus rewrite work for the *New York American* paid room and board for a time, but when the *American* fired Marquis in March 1910, he and Reina endured three months of near starvation. Conditions soon improved, but it was not until 1912 that Marquis was assigned his own column, an opportunity that he fully exploited. During its appearance from 1912 to 1922 in the *New York Evening Sun*, "The Sun Dial" made Marquis a nationally recognized figure and introduced the public to a fascinating gallery of characters, including the immensely popular Archy and Mehitabel. When he left the *Sun* to write "The Lantern" for the *New York Herald Tribune* from 1922 to 1925, his success continued.

In addition to ushering in his career as a New York columnist, 1912 witnessed the publication of the first of Marquis's more than two dozen books, the novel *Danny's Own Story*, a work that bears witness to its author's lifelong fascination with Mark Twain. *Dreams and Dust*, a collection of poems, was published in 1915, after which Marquis produced novels, plays, poetry, and sketches in almost bewildering profusion. In the 1920s alone, eighteen books, varying widely in genre and quality, appeared over the Marquis name. Although he shared Twain's ambition of succeeding both as a comic and as a "serious"

writer, most of Marquis's books are humorous, with much of his very best work drawn directly from "The Sun Dial" and "The Lantern."

A combination of imaginative ebullience and financial exigency inspired Marquis's prolific creative output, an output that might have been qualitatively more consistent if his need for money had been less pressing. Beginning in 1916, his sisters, Maud and Neva, depended on him for financial support. Maud, who has been suspected by some of having abused drugs, was especially troublesome. Her moody, abrasive personality caused continual family discord. Neither of Marquis's wives could cope with her, but out of generosity and a sense of familial duty, Marquis refused, despite the catastrophic drain on his emotions and his finances, to push her aside.

Income from his columns, from the publication of his books, from the staging of a number of his plays, and, during the late 1920s and early 1930s, from intermittent screenwriting in Hollywood (a city he came to despise) allowed Marquis to maintain some semblance of financial solvency, but other problems gradually overwhelmed him. His son Robert died on February 15, 1921. On December 2, 1923, Reina collapsed on the bathroom floor of their Forest Hills home and was dead within minutes. His daughter Barbara, a precociously creative child, concern for whom was partially responsible for his various migrations to the healthier climate of California, died on October 26, 1931. His second wife, Marjorie, a successful actress whom Marquis had married on February 2, 1926, died unexpectedly on October 25, 1936. Marquis's own health had been deteriorating for several years before Marjorie's death. Heart and kidney problems had plagued him during the 1920s, and during the 1930s, he was increasingly incapacitated by strokes. He was hardly able to speak or to move during the months before death came on December 29, 1937.

Literary Analysis

Marquis was one of New York's finest columnists during an era of great column-writing. Raised on the columns of Eugene Field and the sketches of George Ade, Marquis was a respected colleague of Franklin P. Adams, Christopher Morley, Alexander Woollcott, and others of comparable talent. His columns differed from theirs, however, in the greater use he made of created characters to draw his satiric points. Furthermore, as Walter Blair and Hamlin Hill point out, these characters and the worlds they lived in are "closer to the native tradition in American humor than anything the other" columnists were producing,[1] an unsurprising fact given Marquis's small-town upbringing and his years with Joel Chandler Harris. Indeed, it is difficult to do justice to Marquis's lasting significance to American humor without organizing the discussion around the memorable characters who emerge from the columns. Preeminent among these are Hermione, the Old Soak, and the incomparable Archy and Mehitabel.

Like many another American humorist, Marquis hated intellectual and artistic pretension, especially of the sort he found in the clubs and coffee houses of Greenwich Village, and in Hermione, he embodied all the pompous shallowness of the fad thinker. Hermione is constantly "taking up" things "in a serious way" and discovering how "wonderful" they are. Russians, purification through suffering, the exotic in poetry and art, prison reform—all are "fascinating" to this universal dilettante, but no interest produces a single significant idea, and the shortness of Hermione's attention span is exceeded only by the extent of her hypocrisy:

> I'm taking up Bergson this week.
> Next week I'm going to take up Etruscan vases and the Montessori system.
> Oh, no, I haven't lost my interest in sociology.
> Only the other night we went down in the auto and watched the bread line.[2]

The columns that comprise *Hermione and Her Little Group of Serious Thinkers* were gathered into book form in 1916, but Hermione's crack-brained enthusiasms often seem disconcertingly contemporary, as in the following account of what a particularly attractive man had to say about auras:

> This man had the most interesting eyes and the silkiest beard, and he said his aura was pink.
> If he should meet a girl, you know, with an aura just the shade of pink that his aura is, why then they would know they were in psychic harmony.
> Simple, isn't it? But then all truly great ideas *are* simple, aren't they?
> But if his aura was blue, and her aura was yellow, then, of course, they would quarrel. That's what makes so much domestic unhappiness.
> But he said something that gave me the most frightfully insecure feeling.
> He said the aura *changes* its color as the soul progresses.
> Two people may be in harmony today, and both have pink auras, and in a year hers may be green and his golden.
> What desperate chances a woman takes when she marries, doesn't she?[3]

The apparent contemporaneity of this passage may surprise us, but its continuing timeliness would not have surprised Marquis himself, who recognized that the Hermiones of this world are "deathless":

> She will not die—in Brainstorm Slum
> Fake, Nut and Freak Psychologist
> Eternally shall buzz and hum,
> And Spook and Swami keep their tryst
> With Thinkers in a Mental Mist.
> You threaten her with Night and Sorrow?
> Out of the Silences, I wist,
> More Little Groups will rise tomorrow![4]

The Old Soak possesses a continuing vitality, too, although his creation is linked more directly with a particular period of American history, the era of Prohibition. The Old Soak, Clem Hawley by name, originated in "The Sun Dial" and then appeared in *The Old Soak, and Hail and Farewell* (1921), *The Old Soak's History of the World* (1924), *The Old Soak: A Comedy in Three Acts* (1926), and *Everything's Jake* (performed, 1930; published, 1978). The 1926 comedy was especially popular, managing a Broadway run of 423 performances.

A veteran drinker who often swore off demon liquor, Marquis had ample knowledge of the hypocrisy and corruption associated with Prohibition, a subject replete with comic possibilities. Nor did he lack models, including himself, for the garrulous, eccentric Clem Hawley, a character whose creation was strongly influenced, too, by the dialect humor of the Old Southwest. If Twain or the writers from whom Twain learned his craft had written of home brew, for example, they might have offered an anecdote like the following, from the earliest of the Hawley books:

> Hope is what these here fellows has got that is tryin' to make their own with a tea-kettle and a piece of hose. That's awful stuff, that is. There's a friend of mine made some of that stuff and he was scared of it, and he thinks before he drinks any he will try some of it onto a dumb beast.
> But there ain't no dumb beast anywheres handy, so he feeds some of it to his wife's parrot. That there parrot was the only parrot I ever knowed of that wasn't named Polly. It was named Peter, and was supposed to be a gentleman parrot for the last eight or ten years. But whether it was or not, after it had drunk some of that there home-made hootch Peter went and laid an egg.
> That there home-made stuff ain't anything to trifle with.[5]

Prohibition, then, has brought a new danger into the world, a danger that the barroom drinker never had to face.

The passing away of the legal barroom brought spiritual dangers, too, since the Salvation Army lady and her fund-raising compatriots disappeared from the drinker's life. Because of the constant solicitation for dimes and quarters, Hawley tells us, "you kept in touch with religions and it made a better man out of you . . . ," but where is the drinker to get his sense of morality now? The barroom fostered gentility as well, because "if a gent would forget to be genteel after he took too much . . . and imbue himself with loud talk or rough language," his presence would no longer be tolerated. The Old Soak had often "seen such throwed out on their ear, for the better class places always aimed to be decent and orderly and never to have an indecent reputation for loudness and roughhouseness."[6] Furthermore, the barroom was a place where "you could keep in touch with politics," and that "made a better citizen out of you for every man ought to vote for what his consciousness tells him is right and to abide in politics by his consciousness."

With a touch of the exuberance of the Wife of Bath's arguments against chastity, Clem Hawley's comments on Prohibition are framed as the pronouncements of a cracker-barrel social historian with extensive first-hand knowledge of his subject. This is not to say that Hawley was any more reluctant than Huck Finn to speak expertly about subjects with which he had no more than a nodding acquaintance. For instance, in *The Old Soak's History of the World*, we learn that "Sampson . . . never liked to work none but use to loaf around with his hair long and show how stout he was and as far as taking a drink was concerned it never hurt him none but he would liquor up and slay more Phillipines drunk than one of these here Prohibitionists was ever man enough to do sober." Nor would the results have been different if Sampson had come up against evolutionists instead of Phillipines:

> If you had said to him he was descended off of a monkey he would of beaned you with anything that was handy. And in my history of the World it will be proved that men is not descended off of monkeys for if so why did not all the monkeys turn into men. You can't get back of the Good Book in them things, and for my part I don't hanker to.[7]

Hawley also teaches us that "Caster and Pollus" "growed up" to "found Roam and become the first umpires," that the "massiker of Saint Barthollomew" occurred when the saint killed "King Looey" on the roof of "the Basteel," and

that the statue of "Maree Antonette," who was apparently "killed . . . piece meal" at the "Eyefull Tower" and elsewhere, stands in "the Loov" nearly naked and without arms.

If the Old Soak's mangling of language and history places him firmly in the tradition of dialect humor perfected by Twain and others, elements of Marquis's mentor Harris's Americanized beast fable are clearly to be found, as several critics have suggested, in the tales of Archy and Mehitabel. However, the settings for the tales are urban rather than rural, and Marquis's characters are the struggling denizens of the northern streets rather than the deadly rivals of the southern countryside.

Marquis long recognized that he might be remembered primarily for creating "a Goddam Cockroach," and the date of Archy's first appearance in "The Sun Dial," March 29, 1916, is the most important in Marquis's career. Hamlin Hill has pointed out that the idea for Archy may have begun developing as early as January 1908 when Marquis published a passage entitled "Literary Cockroaches" in *Uncle Remus's Magazine*. Referring to Upton Sinclair, he wrote,

> Of course there was another way open to him; if it was absolutely necessary for his literary purposes to crawl around the kitchen sinks of other people, to pry into their wardrobes, to scramble along their pantry shelves, to scurry from under their beds, and so forth, he might have cast aside disguises altogether and gone as a cockroach.[8]

An incident in Marquis's office at the *Sun* may also have helped inspire Archy's creation. Describing the incident to Frink Dana Burnet at Lipton's Bar, a favorite hangout of the newspaper crowd, Marquis said, "Frink, this morning there scampered across my desk the goddam biggest cockroach you ever saw. I believe he could damn near play my typewriter."[9] Archy, of course, would have just that capacity.

With his very first words in "The Sun Dial," Archy establishes his identity:

> *expression is the need of my soul*
> *i was once a vers libre bard*
> *but i died and my soul went into the body of a*
>   *cockroach*
> *it has given me a new outlook upon life*
> *i see things from the underside now*[10]

A frustrated poet who taps out his works letter by letter by diving headfirst onto the keys of Marquis's typewriter, Archy sees life from a perspective that reverses Hermione's; he sees it from the point of view of the lowly and the powerless. His inability to hit the capital key is a satiric reference to E.E. Cummings's poetic technique, but the contents of his writings have little to do with what interested Cummings. Archy writes of the troubled lives of the suffering but indomitable creatures who dwell in New York's tenements and back alleys. Most importantly, he writes of Mehitabel.

Possessed of the same vitality as the free-spirited flapper, Mehitabel is forever telling us that she is "toujours gai" and that "there's a dance in the old dame yet." Her "past is shady/ but wotthehell"; she is still "a lady/ and class will tell." She knows that she will "end down the bay" and that "the garbage scow's dirty" that will carry her out of this existence, but life, nevertheless, is to be lived to the full. Her infectious arrogance is a manifestation of democratic pride, and her toughness is representative of the sometimes amoral vigor that assures the survival of the common people.

Mehitabel's boundless energy shows itself most frequently in her sexual activities. Although an account of the sexual adventures of a liberated woman might have brought Marquis into conflict with the staid guardians of public morality, tales of the promiscuity of an alley cat caused him no such problems. The sexual mores of Marquis's New York were not those of the small-town America of his upbringing, and in Mehitabel he was able to embody the differences. Mehitabel is not a one-tom feline. Males enter and leave her life with surprising rapidity, and more than one litter of unwanted kittens has appeared to remind her of an evening's bliss. Although the abortions and adoptions that human females may use to solve such difficulties are not available to Mehitabel, a providential shower can always be relied on to wash away the mistakes of a passionate night. On one such occasion, after declaring her love for her latest unwanted litter, she mentions that the kittens are living in a garbage can, and she worries aloud that a rainstorm might drown them. Later, Archy comments sardonically that

> we had a heavy rain
> right after she spoke to me
> but probably that garbage can
> leaks and so the kittens
> have not yet
> been drowned[11]

Mehitabel possesses all of the resilience of a character from *Candide*, and her temper, when she feels betrayed, is wondrous. When an aristocratic tomcat turns on her in order to please his master, Mehitabel lays for the "slob/ for two days and nights" and proceeds to teach him how to treat a lady:

> i caught the boob in the shrubbery
> pretty thing i said

> it hurts me worse than it does you
> to remove that left eye of yours
> but i did it with one sweep of my claws
> you call yourself a gentleman do you
> i said as i took a strip out of his nose
> you will think twice after this before
> you offer an insult
> to an unprotected young tabby[12]

Mehitabel, despite her constant protests to the contrary, lacks refinement, but she possesses an uncompromising toughness that is difficult not to admire.

If Mehitabel exhibits the raw physical energy that gives urban America so much of its vitality, Archy displays the complementary urges toward artistic and intellectual fulfillment. Seeing the world "from/ the underside," however, Archy has become "a pessimistic/ guy," and much of what he writes has a satiric edge to it. Although he occasionally shows a touch of self-importance himself, he cannot abide self-importance in others:

> i once heard the survivors
> of a colony of ants
> that had been partially
> obliterated by a cow s foot
> seriously debating
> the intention of the gods
> towards their civilization[13]

Nor does he put great faith in human benevolence, as is suggested by the following lines from an anecdote about the rescue of a lamb from a wolf:

> gently he cut her throat
> all the while inveighing
> against the inhuman wolf
> and tenderly he cooked her
> and lovingly he sauced her
> and meltingly he ate her
> and piously he said a grace
> thanking his gods
> for their bountiful gifts to him[14]

Sounding a bit like a Pudd'nhead Wilson or like a Gulliver in a Brechtian universe, Archy does his best to reform mankind, but his "influence is limited" because "a prophet . . . is not/ without honor save on his own/ planet."[15]

Most of the "honor" still bestowed upon Marquis is the result of continuing interest in Archy and Mehitabel. He himself never entirely understood their popularity, but he gathered the Archy and Mehitabel columns into three of his most successful books, *Archy and Mehitabel* (1927), *Archy's Life of Mehitabel* (1933), and *Archy Does His Part* (1935). The posthumous collected edition, *the lives and times of archy and mehitabel* (1940), with illustrations by George

Herriman, creator of Krazy Kat, is one of the few Marquis books still readily available.

Summary

Christopher Morley has described his friend Don Marquis as a writer "alert to the bewildering absurdity of life," who wrote best about "anyone on the losing side of society."[16] Although he learned his craft in the Midwest while doing newspaper work in and around Walnut, Illinois, and in the South while writing for Joel Chandler Harris's *Uncle Remus's Magazine*, he came to national prominence as a New York City columnist. "The Sun Dial" appeared in the *New York Evening Sun* from 1912 to 1922, and "The Lantern" followed from 1922 to 1925 in the *New York Herald Tribune*. Both addressed topics of concern to an urban audience but made use of humorous techniques perfected largely by the writers of America's Old Southwest. The columns produced an impressive cast of characters, a number of whom reappeared in Marquis's more than two dozen books: Hermione, the Old Soak, and Archy and Mehitabel. Only Archy and Mehitabel retain some measure of their original popularity.

Notes

1. Walter Blair and Hamlin Hill, *America's Humor: From Poor Richard to Doonesbury* (New York: Oxford University Press, 1978), p. 406.
2. From *The Best of Don Marquis* (Garden City: Doubleday, 1946), p. 565 (excerpt from the "Soul Mates" section of *Hermione and Her Little Group of Serious Thinkers*).
3. From *The Best of Don Marquis*, pp. 566–567 (also excerpted from "Soul Mates").
4. From *The Best of Don Marquis*, p. 583 (excerpt from the "Envoy" section of *Hermione and Her Little Group of Practical Thinkers*).
5. From *The Best of Don Marquis*, pp. 181–182 (excerpt from the "Introducing the Old Soak" section of *The Old Soak, and Hail and Farewell*).
6. From *The Best of Don Marquis*, p. 191.
7. From *The Best of Don Marquis*, pp. 223–224 (excerpt from the "Men Are Not Descended Off of Monkeys" section of *The Old Soak's History of the World*).
8. Lynn Lee, "Archy and Uncle Remus: Don Marquis's Debt to Joel Chandler Harris," *Georgia Review*, 15 (Spring 1961): 80–81.
9. Edward Anthony, *O Rare Don Marquis: A Biography* (Garden City: Doubleday, 1962), p. 142.
10. From *The Best of Don Marquis*, p. 4 (excerpt from "the coming of archy" section of *Archy and Mehitabel*).
11. From *The Best of Don Marquis*, pp. 54–55 (excerpt from the "mehitabel and her kittens" section of *Archy and Mehitabel*).
12. From *the lives and times of archy and mehitabel*, p. 60 (excerpt from the "mehitabel has an adventure" section of *Archy and Mehitabel*).
13. From *the lives and times of archy and mehitabel*,

pp. 54–55 (excerpt from the "certain maxims of archy" section of *Archy and Mehitabel*).
14. From *the lives and times of archy and mehitabel*, p. 90 (excerpt from the "aesop revised by archy" section of *Archy and Mehitabel*).
15. Christopher Morley, "Introduction," *The Best of Don Marquis* (Garden City: Doubleday, 1946), p. xiii.
16. From *the lives and times of archy and mehitabel*, pp. 123–124.

Selected Bibliography

Primary Sources

Hermione and Her Little Group of Serious Thinkers. New York: Appleton, 1916.

The Old Soak, and Hail and Farewell. Garden City: Doubleday, Page, 1921.

The Old Soak's History of the World. Garden City: Doubleday, Page, 1924.

The Old Soak: A Comedy in Three Acts. New York: French, 1926.

Archy and Mehitabel. Garden City: Doubleday, Page, 1927.

Archy's Life of Mehitabel. Garden City: Doubleday, Doran, 1933.

Archy Does His Part. Garden City: Doubleday, Doran, 1935.

the lives and times of archy and mehitabel. New York: Doubleday, Doran, 1940.

The Best of Don Marquis. Garden City: Doubleday, 1946.

Everything's Jake. Tacoma: Non-Profit Press, 1978.

Secondary Sources

Anthony, Edward. *O Rare Don Marquis: A Biography.* Garden City: Doubleday, 1962. Although Anthony's admiration for Marquis sometimes interferes with his critical objectivity, this is the definitive biography. Anthony makes especially good use of Marquis's "egobiography."

Blair, Walter, and Hamlin Hill. *America's Humor: From Poor Richard to Doonesbury.* New York: Oxford University Press, 1978. Blair and Hill emphasize the influence of traditional American humor on Marquis's comic technique.

Jaffe, Dan. "Don Marquis." In *Dictionary of Literary Biography.* Vol. 11, Part 2: M–Z. *American Humorists, 1800–1950.* Ed. Stanley Trachtenberg. Detroit: Gale Research, 1982, pp. 309–317. Jaffe's article contains an excellent bibliography of Marquis's books and gives a concise account of his life and career.

Lee, Lynn. *Don Marquis.* Boston: Twayne, 1981. Contains some of the most detailed analyses of Marquis's work.

Morley, Christopher. "Introduction." *The Best of Don Marquis.* Garden City: Doubleday, 1946, pp. xiii–xxx. Morley's essay is an articulate appreciation of Marquis's career, although it sometimes slips too far toward eulogy. His comparison of Marquis and Twain is especially insightful.

Robert H. O'Connor

Mayer, Orlando Benedict

Born: Pomaria, Newberry County, South
Carolina, on February 24, 1818

Education: Classical Academy of the Lutheran Theological Seminary, Lexington,
S.C., ca. 1834; South Carolina College,
B.A., 1837; Medical College of South Carolina, M.D., 1840; studied medicine at
Edinburgh, Paris, and Berlin, chemistry
at Giessen, and German at Heidelberg,
1844–1847

Marriages: Mary Davis, 1839–1840; Caroline N. DeWalt, 1851–1861, six children; Louisa Kinard, 1870(?)–1891

Died: July 16, 1891

Biography

Orlando Benedict Mayer was born in 1818 in an
area of central South Carolina called the Dutch
(Deutsch) Fork, a community settled by German
and Swiss Protestants in the mid-1700s.[1] During
the author's childhood, the German language,
customs, folklore, and Lutheranism were all the
community knew, but when Mayer was a young
man, these traditions began to weaken somewhat with interaction with surrounding English
and Scotch-Irish settlements. Mayer was born
and raised in the heart of this Teutonic island at
his grandmother Eve Margaret Summer Mayer's
farm. Here, he listened to her and her old friend,
Ommee Lohner, carry on lively German conversations and tell tales of the old days. Many were
stories about witches, wizards, and practices that
had their origins in pre-Christian German myth,
and he would use them as the basis for many of
his own stories, like "Aberhot Koselhantz, the
Wizard Gunsmith."

As a barefoot farmboy in a homespun linen
shirt with great old-fashioned ruffles, Mayer visited the state capital some thirty miles distant
and was made fun of by the town boys. His
characters who venture from their community
are likewise constantly aware of their separateness. One character, for example, who had always been proud of the rich intonation of his
German name, is hurt to find that in another
district a family and its friends of English background ridicule his strange, foreign-sounding
name. In Mayer's work, as in his life, the son of
the Dutch Fork is ill at ease until he returns
home.

The home itself, however, was undergoing a
great cultural change. During Mayer's coming of
age, English replaced the German language in
the pulpits of the churches in his area, and English likewise became the preferred language for
speaking and writing in the schools. Non-Ger-
man Carolinians praised the Dutch Forker's industry, neatness, honesty, and loyalty to friends
but found their way of speaking and their superstitions and customs very peculiar. Mayer must
have become acutely aware of all this when at
South Carolina College at Columbia and the
Medical College at Charleston he had to come to
terms with an English world.

At South Carolina College, he studied literature (classical, sacred, and modern), but his exposure to the arts had already begun in 1824
with his first studies at the school run by
St. Johannes (now St. John's) Lutheran Church.
Here he had been particularly adept at language
and literature. Here also Mayer studied alongside his friend and kinsman, Adam Geiselhardt
Summer, who would himself become an author
of humorous sketches and an editor who would
figure largely in Mayer's career.

After graduation from the Medical College in
1840, Mayer returned home to Pomaria to practice. His young wife from nearby Monticello, in
Fairfield County, died the following year, and
Mayer decided to renew his studies for three
years in Europe: first, Edinburgh, Scotland; then
Paris, for a stay of fifteen months; and finally
thirteen months in Heidelberg, studying German; Giessen, where he attended the lectures of
the famous chemist, Leibig; and Berlin, where he
again studied medicine. In 1847, he once again
returned to Pomaria, where, for the next two
years, he continued the medical practice begun
seven years earlier. Wishing to extend his practice, he moved to the neighboring village of
Newberry in 1849, where, according to one of
his biographers, "he lived, honored and useful,
for nearly forty-five years."

Mayer achieved an eminent reputation as a
doctor. His personality seemed especially well
suited for practicing medicine among the rural
and small-town inhabitants of his native region,
for, as one commentator on his life has observed,
Mayer was "a jolly extrovert who enjoyed practical jokes."[2]

Literary Analysis

Upon his return from Europe in 1847, O.B.
Mayer began publishing fiction based on his European travels. His first known sketch is entitled
"A Sunday Evening in Germany," which appeared in the *South Carolinian* on November 5,
1847. Other stories with European settings appeared over the next decade, but, while exhibiting considerable artistic merit, they are in the
popular Gothic-Romantic mode, with its attendant intrigue, mystery, and suspense, reminiscent
of works by Washington Irving and Edgar Allan
Poe. There is little or no humor in them, and as
good as they are, they fall short of the fiction in
which Mayer utilizes this strength.

Mayer's literary reputation rests primarily on

his humorous tales with Dutch Fork settings and character types that he wrote for the Columbia *South Carolinian*, Paul Hamilton Hayne's *Russell's Magazine* and *Southern Bivouac*, and other magazines and newspapers. Like his contemporary, Henry Clay Lewis of Louisiana, a country doctor and frontier humorist of some renown, Mayer managed to balance the demanding responsibilities of a physician with his avocation as an author of comic backwoods tales.

Mayer's most important and representative literary works generally place him in the school of southern frontier humor. His first known humorous stories were published in the Columbia *South Carolinian*, a weekly agricultural newspaper edited by his friend, Adam G. Summer, who also wrote humorous tales, several of which were published in the New York-based *Spirit of the Times*. During his tenure as editor of the *South Carolinian*, between 1845 and 1848, Summer, who has been called "a kind of Southern William Trotter Porter,"[3] not only published rustic tales of South Carolina humorists like Mayer but also reprinted some of the sketches of many of the well-known humorists of the 1840s, including Johnson Jones Hooper, William Tappan Thompson, Thomas Bangs Thorpe, George Washington Harris, Sol Smith, Joseph Field, and John S. Robb.[4] As one of the *South Carolinian*'s contributors, it is likely that Mayer read some of these humorists. In fact, Mayer knew Thompson, whom he and Summer entertained in Columbia in 1848, the same year that Mayer published his first humorous tale.[5]

The first of Mayer's comic sketches of a subliterary, backwoods variety, "The Innocent Cause, Or How Snoring Broke Off a Match," appeared in the *South Carolinian* on January 25, 1848 under the pseudonym "Haggis" and exhibits most of the ingredients familiarly associated with the frontier tall tale: the frame device, lively and earthy dialect, exaggerated descriptions, graphically animated action, incongruous situations, and an eccentric rustic prankster. Employing the epistolary format that Thompson skillfully used in *Major Jones's Courtship* (1843) and a rogue whose traits were soon to suggest a close literary kinship to Harris's Sut Lovingood, Mayer creates in his chief character, Belt Seebub, more commonly and humorously known as Belzebub, a likable prankster-fool whose antics provide an entertaining and engaging story of rural courtship.[6] Incongruities abound, the most humorous being in some of Belt's exaggerated figurative renderings of character and incident. For instance, in describing a snoring Kentucky hog driver, whom he regards as a meddlesomely unwanted competitor in his quest for a country girl's affections and a man with whom he must share a room for the night, Belt resorts to unflattering hyperbole to create a comic effect: "He lay flat upon his back, with his hed berried in the piller, his eyes sot and half open, and his under jaw hung down tel his tongue could be seen as dry as a swinged pig tail. In fact, his mouth looked like a steel trap set for a otter and baited with a piece of dried beef" (*Fireside Tales*, p. 41). When the Kentuckian's snoring becomes so loud that Belt cannot sleep, he expediently places the end of a stove-pipe over the man's face. The resulting noise, which Belt ludicrously asserts "was sumthin between the howl of lettin off steam and the scream of a circular saw cuttin through a hard pine-knot" (p. 42), causes fright and pandemonium among the farm animals and the soot blown through the stove-pipe soils the clean white petticoats drying on the clothes line.

"Snip—A Tale," Mayer's second humorous work of short fiction and his first to employ a discernible Dutch Fork setting and German dialect, was likewise published under the signature of "Haggis" in the *South Carolinian* on September 5, 1848. It delineates with genial humor the character of a horse named "Snip" and the role that he plays in a rural family—focusing on a Dutch Fork wedding and the customs that it involves. In part the tale's humorous incongruity depends on the juxtaposition of Dr. Haggis's (the frame narrator) allusive and stilted rhetoric, sometimes even approaching lyricism, and the vividly unrestrained, realistic dialect of the rural characters of the Dutch Fork. Yet Haggis, a native Dutch Forker, does not exhibit, as do A.B. Longstreet and other genteel raconteurs of southern frontier humor, a conspicuously condescending attitude toward these characters or their eccentricities. Following the manner of backwoods comedy, Mayer includes several slapstick situations. At the outset, when a wagon belonging to the Wimples, a local farm family, becomes bogged down in the mud, Snip, their horse, a steed more reliable for courting purposes than for strenuous work, refuses to pull it out of the mire. Attempting to coerce the horse to pull, young Joe Wimple falls "flat upon his back, leaving an impression in the mud, from which a very correct cast of his proportions could have been taken" (*Fireside Tales*, p. 60). The story is at once backwoods humor and local color but rises above both genres with its universal characters. In fact, these three characteristics, with a strong predilection for the latter, mark all of Mayer's humorous works. His approach to character almost always comes through a good-natured realization that man is often a foolish, even absurd creature owing to his vanity, stubbornness, pride, selfishness, and hypocrisy. Unlike Mark Twain, Mayer was never to denounce bitterly the whole damned human race but instead pointed out its foibles and laughed at them.

Mayer's love of humanity is never in doubt. As a physician, he was always praised for his kind-heartedness, patience, and unselfishness, and these qualities show through his warm humor. However, he was never blind to men's faults, and as a result, Mayer never idealizes. While possessing endearing traits, Mayer's characters can also be incredibly pig-headed.

This focus on character, particularly on the humorous and absurd aspects thereof, seemed to grow during his career. Another story of the southwestern variety and exhibiting humorous incongruity in characterization, "The Easter Eggs" is a lengthy piece that first appeared in the *South Carolinian* on October 27, 1848. Focusing again on Dutch Fork courtship customs and featuring comic incongruity by contrasting the vernacular and formal literary stylistic modes, the tale's humor is most graphically exemplified by the reenactment of the "big brag" or "ring-tailed roarer" motif involving a conflict between two rival suitors of a rural lass. Interestingly, this scene, including the use of accentuated gesture and phrasing (one of the suitors remarks to the other, "'my mammy is as good a man as ever trod shoe leather!'" and then springs into the air, striking "his heels together three times before he touched the earth," *Fireside Tales*, p. 112) anticipates a similar confrontation between two raftsmen in that renowned episode that Twain had originally composed for inclusion in *Huckleberry Finn*.

Two months after the appearance of "The Easter Eggs," Mayer published another long story in the *South Carolinian* entitled "The Corn Cob Pipe," which exhibits several close parallels to Irving's "The Legend of Sleepy Hollow." Indeed, Irving has been called one of the most important literary influences on southern backwoods humor as a whole,[7] and there is little doubt Mayer was conforming to the pattern of his genre in this tale. "The Corn Cob Pipe," which has been acclaimed Mayer's "single best work of short fiction,"[8] is another story of courtship characterized by frequent comic incongruity. While the modern reader may condemn the frame narrator's editorializing as antiquated, the plot of the tale, appropriate to situation comedy, centers around a conflict between a young Dutch Fork farm girl and her parents regarding whom she should marry. Whereas they desire that she marry the genteel schoolmaster, Isom Jones, her own personal preference is Abram Priester, a young farmer "of athletic proportion." To accomplish her objective, the girl contrives a scheme for blowing up her father, a stratagem which when executed results in the schoolmaster's being erroneously blamed as the culprit and his subsequent rapid disappearance "from the neighborhood like the pedagogue

of Sleepy Hollow" (*Fireside Tales*, p. 131). As one recent critic has written, in "The Corn Cob Pipe" Mayer's "ability to deal frankly and humorously with the violent power struggles that sometimes occur between children and parents" is central to an understanding of his art. Mayer's story, while indeed delineating customs, actually concerns the lengths to which a young woman will go to get the man whom she has chosen. This critic continues that the story goes beyond its model and that "Surely, the rubric of 'local color' can only become a pejorative term when applied to a story such as this."[9]

"Aberhot Koselhantz, the Wizard Gunsmith" was published in the May 1857 issue of *Russell's*. Part of the tale's humor derives from Koselhantz's supernatural ability to cast immobilizing spells on persons attempting to harm his family. When British soldiers attempt to harm Koselhantz and his wife and to molest his daughter, Mayer shifts the tale into the fantastic mode with the gunsmith casting a devious spell that makes the intruders "as cold and stiff as so many statues" (p. 149). Once the gunsmith frees them from their fixed state of enchantment, the fantasy of their immobility is abruptly transformed into semi-farcical movements, veritably a comedy of errors, with the soldiers unsuccessfully attempting to complete their sinister actions.

Mayer's finest work of long fiction, *John Punterick, A Novel of Life in the Old Dutch Fork*, written in 1860, was not published until 1981.[10] In *John Punterick* Mayer's native cultural influences run strong. At the novel's beginning, set in 1847, several friends, among them Mayer and Summer, have gathered to swap stories of character, of past community events that have shaped the present, and of changing times. The tradition is of the oral narrative—relaxed, discursive, sometimes episodic, but always redolent of good common sense, friendly humor, and frank realistic observation of character. Fritz, one of the characters in the frame, proposes to read a manuscript in his possession, a semi-humorous satire of the Horatian ilk that mildly ridicules the foibles and frailties of the society in transition. Though most of the novel's characters, including John Punterick, are near caricatures, they nonetheless reveal Mayer's shrewd insights into human nature. His title character is a representative man of the modern era, of the new American society that is replacing the old traditional culture to which he stands in marked contrast. He is materialistic, hedonistic, and self-centered. Unlike the typical man of the old German community, he does not care about tradition, communal ties, or neighbors. Money and self-indulgence are his aims. Mayer provides a humorous view of a host of less serious human foibles in his minor characters, who suffer variously from hypocrisy, superstition, stubbornness, obsession with trivial matters, meddlesomeness, and monomania, to name only a few. Yet Mayer does not fail to portray their strengths, so the novel provides a rounded study of human nature.

Mayer's literary realism seems to have been most closely influenced by Henry Fielding. Like that novelist, whom he quotes occasionally, he depicts his characters' vanity and folly as the true source of the ridiculous with tolerance and understanding. Jonathan Swift is another literary forebear, but Mayer never uses Swift's bitter invective. Mayer was remarkably well-read; a quick survey of his literary allusions provides rather staggering results. His favorites were Burns, Byron, Chatterton, Swift, Irving, Poe, Shakespeare, Scott, Pope, Milton, Dryden, Fielding, folk ballads, Virgil, Homer, Goethe, Gray, Cowper, Cervantes, Spenser, Goldsmith, and Dickens, but these represent only a few of his antecedents. His chief influences in humor remain Fielding, Irving, Swift, and the oral and written southern backwoods humor tradition.

During the decade of the War Between the States Mayer produced little fiction; he taught chemistry, botany, mineralogy, and geology at the Lutheran college in Newberry. He published many humorous stories in the local newspapers, among them "Old Nick," "Jes Middlin, Mass Ben," and "Polly Pompernickel." These and others will no doubt turn up in extant newspaper files, and such investigation is presently the most crying need for research on the author.

Several significant works of fiction appeared in Mayer's last years. "The Two Marksmen of Ruff's Mountain" (published in *Southern Bivouac* in November 1886) is set in the Dutch Fork during the Revolution. A quasi-humorous work with a plot centering around the vengeance of two brothers against a villainous British murderer, the tale indicates that Mayer was still consciously influenced by the frontier tall tale. He portrays two rustics, one superbly skillful in rifle marksmanship and the other incredibly adept at throwing stones, displaying "such power and dexterity that he could, without fail, strike a bullock dead, at the distance of twenty-five paces" (p. 362). Both of these characters resemble such archetypal demigods of the frontier tradition as Davy Crockett.

In the final years of his life Mayer undertook several other literary projects, one of which was a novel based on a strange apparition in the form of a man and a woman on a white horse that he had observed near Stonehenge in England in 1885. This book, *Malladoce, the Briton. His Wanderings from Druidism to Christianity*, was completed by Mayer's friend, John A. Chapman, and published posthumously in 1891. Employing a conventional travel-book structure and using the Gothic mode of some of Mayer's European stories of the 1850s, *Malladoce* is of little significance in the Mayer canon.

Another project to which Mayer turned his attention in his last days was a series of endearing, nostalgic sketches published serially in the Newberry *Herald and News* in 1891. They focus, he writes in the preface, on "the most prominent events occurring in the Dutch Fork within my recollections . . . and what I have gathered from legends coming down through many years preceding my early boyhood" (*The Dutch Fork*, p. 1). Celebrating the past as a simpler and better time, these sketches, while providing entertaining reading, exploit some of the same subject matter—social customs, folklore, and superstitions as well as the contrast between the genteel and rustic and the new and the traditional—found in Mayer's earlier humorous fiction. In his last days, Mayer also wrote the Dutch Fork story "Little Dassie," a humorous work that reveals that while he had drifted toward sentimentality his old love of realistic characterization was still with him. Death was much on his mind during the 1880s. The loss of a wife, two children, and his three closest friends (including Summer) had deepened a melancholy that had always been a facet of his character. Mayer's personality shows a dichotomy: he was a jolly humorist who cultivated melancholy and a doctor who often faced death yet found its reality difficult to accept.

Although a local historian wrote that during his day Mayer "acquired celebrity as a writer," his fame must have been almost entirely limited to his community. He made no impression on the literary establishment of his day. This did not concern Mayer; his indifference to notoriety is perhaps explained in one of his favorite poems, Gray's "Elegy," which stresses the short and simple annals of the little man. With all his accomplishments as a celebrated physician, he remained close to his rural community and her folk traditions. His abiding interest in character might best be expressed in the words of a figure in Mayer's last story. In "Little Dassie," Big Dave, the gentle rustic, is fond of saying, "Human natur, Doc, is more amazin than the seasins" (*Fireside Tales*, p. 150). In this same story, Mayer recommends the keeping of a diary by country doctors, who would each, by the age of forty, thereby become "a wise acre and warm hearted humorist" (*Fireside Tales*, p. 142). This phrase describes Mayer and is a fitting summation of his career and its wellspring.

Summary

Based on a relatively small quantity of comic writing—a novel, eight extant short stories, and a series of reminiscences of life in the Dutch Fork of bygone days—it may be premature to assess O.B. Mayer's significance as a humorist. After all, some of his published comic works have yet to be discovered. But, if they are eventually found and interest in Mayer increases, he may be elevated to a more prominent position in the ranks of the southern frontier humorists than he now enjoys. Until that happens, however, any evaluation of Mayer's contributions as a humorist must remain tentative and incomplete. Certainly his humorous novel, *John Punterick*, is a work of reputable literary merit, and several of his humorous stories—"The Innocent Cause," "Snip—A Tale," "The Corn Cob Pipe," "The Easter Eggs," and "Aberhot Koselhantz"—are of the first rank and therefore may be favorably compared with similar tales penned by some of the more prominent humorists of the antebellum southern frontier school. As these works attest, Mayer was an entertaining and technically competent storyteller with a keen ear for dialect and fond appreciation for the quaint and rustic customs and traditions of his "little postage stamp of native soil." Because he never aspired for literary eminence, at the time of their initial publication his works were never widely disseminated, and Mayer has remained virtually anonymous. Interest in Mayer's work has recently been stimulated with the publication of editions of *John Punterick* and some of his stories. With the likelihood that still more of his work will be reissued, Mayer may in time receive a well-deserved reevaluation.

Notes

1. Biographical information on Mayer has been taken from the following sources: "Dr. Orlando Benedict Mayer," in *Cyclopedia of Eminent and Representative Men of the Carolinas of the Nineteenth Century* (Madison, Wis.: Brant and Fuller, 1892), pp. 323-324; John A. Chapman's addition to John Belton O'Neall, *The Annals of Newberry* (Newberry, S.C.: Aull and Houseal, 1892), pp. 567-568; and James E. Kibler, Jr., "O.B. Mayer," in *Antebellum Writers in New York and the South*, Vol. 3, *Dictionary of Literary Biography* (Detroit: Gale, 1979), pp. 213-218.
2. Kibler, "O.B. Mayer," p. 214.
3. Jim Kibler, "'The Innocent Cause, Or How Snoring Broke Off a Match': A Sketch from the Dutch Fork School of Humor," *Studies in American Humor*, 2 (Winter 1983-1984), p. 185.
4. Kibler, "O.B. Mayer," p. 214.
5. Kibler, "'The Innocent Cause,'" p. 185.
6. Ibid., p. 186.
7. Hennig Cohen and William B. Dillingham, "Introduction," *Humor of the Old Southwest*. Ed. Cohen and Dillingham (Boston: Houghton Mifflin, 1964), p. xvi.
8. Kibler, "O.B. Mayer," p. 215.
9. Leland Cox, "Realistic and Humorous Writing in Ante-Bellum Charleston Magazines," *South Caro-*

lina Journals and Journalists. Ed. James B. Meriwether (Spartanburg, S.C.: Reprint Co., 1975), p. 184.
10. James E. Kibler, Jr., "Introduction," *John Punterick, A Novel of Life in the Old Dutch Fork* (Spartanburg, S.C.: Reprint Co., 1981), pp. ix-x.

Selected Bibliography

Primary Sources

Short Stories and Sketches

"A Sunday Evening in Germany," Columbia *South Carolinian*, November 5, 1847.

"'The Innocent Cause, Or How Snoring Broke Off a Match.' A Tale of Hog-Killing Time," Columbia *South Carolinian*, January 25, 1848. Reprinted with an introduction in *Studies in American Humor*, 2 (Winter 1983-1984): 185-194, and *Fireside Tales* (Columbia, S.C.: Dutch Fork Press, 1984), pp. 35-44, 160-161.

"Batchelor's Hall—A Glimpse." Columbia *South Carolinian*, February 15, 1848.

"Snip. A Tale." Columbia *South Carolinian*, September 5, 1848. Reprinted in *Fireside Tales*, pp. 59-73, 163-166.

"The Easter Eggs; A Tale of Love, Poetry, and Prose." Columbia *South Carolinian*, October 27, 1848. Reprinted in *Fireside Tales*, pp. 99-115, 172-175. A revised version appeared in Newberry *Herald and News*, April 2, 9, and 16, 1891.

"The Corn Cob Pipe: A Tale of the Comet of '43." Columbia *South Carolinian*, December 8, 1848. Reprinted in *Fireside Tales*, pp. 117-131, 175-177. A revised version appeared in *Russell's*, 3 (May 1858): 155-164. A second revised version appeared in Newberry *Herald and News*, May 28, June 4 and 11, 1891, which is reprinted in Mayer's *The Dutch Fork*, pp. 39-60.

"The Music Girl of the Rue de la Harpe." *Russell's*, 1 (April 1857): 27-36. Revised in Newberry *Herald* (January 7, 1874).

"Aberhot Koselhantz, the Wizard Gunsmith. Story of the Dutch Fork." *Russell's*, 1 (May 1857): 144-152. Revised in *The Dutch Fork*, pp. 89-98.

"The Voice, the Hand, and the Silhouette, Being the Title of a Manuscript Found in a Stove." *Russell's*, 1 (August 1857): 455-460; (September 1857): 521-533; 2 (October 1857): 69-78; (November 1857): 144-151.

"My Landlady's Story." *Russell's*, 3 (August 1858): 437-441.

"A Stroll in Dutch Fork." Newberry *Herald*, January 7, 1874. Reprinted in *The Dutch Fork*, pp. 100-108.

"The Two Marksmen of Ruff's Mountain." *Southern Bivouac*, 2 (November 1886): 361-367; (December 1886): 417-423; (January 1887): 469-474. Mayer had first published this story in an as-yet-unlocated issue of the Newberry *News* sometime before 1884.

"Little Dassie, or 'The Burning Pine-Knot's Fitful Flare.'" Newberry *Herald and News* (1891), reprinted in *Fireside Tales*, pp. 141-153, 179-180.

Novels

John Punterick. A Novel of Life in the Old Dutch Fork, Ed. James E. Kibler, Jr. Spartanburg, S.C.: Reprint Company, 1981.

Malladoce, the Briton. His Wanderings from Druidism to Christianity (co-authored with John A. Chapman). Richmond, Va.: Everett Waddey, 1891.

Essays and Sketches

"Letters from Europe." Columbia *South Carolinian*, May 8, 15, June 19, July 3, August 14, 1845.

"Do de Woders of Lexington." Columbia *South Carolinian*, July 28, 1848.

"Obituary of Thomas Jefferson Summer." Columbia *South Carolinian*, March 1852.

"Report on the Endemic Diseases of Newberry, Read Before the Newberry Agricultural Society." *Southern Agriculturist*, 1 (June 1853): 165-167.

"Fireside Revisitings." Newberry *Conservatist*, April 6, 13, 20; May 4, 11, 25; June 8; July 6; August 3, 17, 1858.

"Johnston's New Map of the Republics of North America." Newberry *Rising Sun*, October 13, 1858.

"Obituary of Adam G. Summer," unidentified newspaper clipping ca. July 6, 1866.

"Obituary of Mrs. Mary Margaret Summer," unidentified newspaper clipping, ca. December 1871.

"Obituary of Henry Summer." Newberry *News*, October 18, 1878.

Luther and the Children, South Carolina Lutheran Synod, 1883.

"Pinnacles of Remembrance: Being Recollections of Travel in Europe Forty Years Ago." Newberry College *Stylus*, 1 (January, February, March, April, May, June, October, November 1884).

The Dutch Fork, Newberry *Herald and News* (April 23, 30; May 7, 14, 21, 28; June 4, 11, 18, 25; July 2, 9, 1891). Rpt. Columbia, S.C.: Dutch Fork Press, 1982. Ed. James E. Kibler, Jr.

"Dr. Jacob H. King and Nicholas Summer, Esq.," "The Physicians of the County," and "Rev. Herman Aull." In John B. O'Neall, *The Annals of Newberry*. Newberry, S.C.: Aull and Houseal, 1892, pp. 453-454, 557-562, 658-664.

Secondary Sources

Cox, Leland. "Realistic and Humorous Writings in Ante-Bellum Charleston Magazines." *South Carolina Journals and Journalists*. Ed. James B. Meriwether. Spartanburg, S.C.: The Reprint Co., 1975, pp. 177-205. A short critical appraisal of Mayer's *Russell's Magazine* stories.

Kibler, James E., Jr. "O.B. Mayer." In *Antebellum Writers in New York and the South*. Vol. 3. *Dictionary of Literary Biography*. Ed. Joel Myerson. Detroit: Gale, 1979, pp. 213-218. A critical overview of Mayer's life and extant work.

———. "Introduction." *John Punterick. A Novel of Life in the Old Dutch Fork*. By O.B. Mayer. Spartanburg, S.C.: The Reprint Co., 1981, pp. ix-xix. Recognizes that *John Punterick* is "one of the comparatively few antebellum Southern novels of literary merit which avoid excesses of romantic sentimentality, style, and diction, while providing a realistic look at human nature"; the novel presents a veritable rendering of the "lives, language, customs, folklore, and traditions" of the Dutch Fork community.

———. "Introduction." *The Dutch Fork*. By O.B. Mayer. Spartanburg, S.C.: The Reprint Co., 1982, pp. vii-xv. Assesses these sketches as being more

properly "folk myth" than history, "a delightful affirmation of traditional values."

———. "The Dutch Fork of Mayer's Fiction." *Names in South Carolina*, 30 (Winter 1983): 24-31. A listing of important place names in Mayer's fiction which have been keyed to a map of the Dutch Fork.

———. "'The Innocent Cause, Or How Snoring Broke Off a Match': A Sketch from the Dutch Fork School of Humor." *Studies in American Humor*, 2 (Winter 1983-1984): 185-194. Establishes several parallels between Belt Seebub and Harris's Sut Lovingood.

———. "Preface." *Fireside Tales: Stories of the Old Dutch Fork*. Ed. James E. Kibler, Jr. Columbia, S.C.: Dutch Fork Press, 1984, pp. 1-4. Sees these stories by Mayer, Summer, and others as products of oral tradition.

O'Neall, John B. *The Annals of Newberry*. Newberry, S.C.: Aull and Houseal, 1892, pp. 567-568. A brief laudatory biographical sketch of Mayer.

"Orlando Benedict Mayer." In *Cyclopedia of Eminent and Representative Men of the Carolinas of the Nineteenth Century*. Vol. 1. Madison, Wis.: Brant and Fuller, 1892, pp. 323-324. A biographical sketch focusing primarily on Mayer's professional and civic achievements.

James E. Kibler, Jr.
Edward J. Piacentino

Mencken, H[enry] L[ewis]

Born: Baltimore, Maryland, on September 12, 1880

Education: Baltimore Polytechnic Institute, 1896

Marriage: Sara Haardt, August 27, 1930

Died: January 29, 1956

Biography

Of Henry Louis Mencken it is wistfully said perhaps more often than of any other writer in our history: if only he were here today! The "Sage of Baltimore" knew how to expose with unrelenting satire the shallow arts of America's public figures, the vacuousness of its intellectual life, and the folly of its most hallowed national and private ideals. The preeminent journalist of his era, Mencken is most often linked with the Baltimore *Sunpapers* although he worked for or contributed material to a number of other Eastern newspapers as well. Mencken's career was actually composed of three careers, for in addition to his newspaper work he edited or co-edited two major magazines and a number of minor ones, and he authored or co-authored more than twenty books. In his heyday, the decade of the 1920s, Mencken was much admired and much disdained but rarely ignored. As viewers in the 1980s would later say of a popular television character, he was a man you loved to hate. Mencken himself, critic James L. Kilpatrick notes, hated very well: scarcely any object of his disapproval was spared his cutting invective,[1] and his virtuosity with language enabled him to hate, or occasionally adore, exquisitely.

Louis D. Rubin, Jr., remarks that H.L. Mencken enjoyed posing as one to whom nothing mattered[2]; he had great fun acting as the American iconoclast *par excellence*, shattering sacred cows often, it would seem, for the pure joy of doing so. Yet, somehow the converse is also true: to Mencken, in one sense, everything mattered. How else can the drive of a man who wrote so much and so passionately be explained? As much as he claimed to dislike idealists of any kind, Mencken was himself one of their number. In this fundamental contradiction lay the source of Mencken's humor: nothing, except everything, meant anything.

That Mencken would become a rebel of rebels no one who knew him as a youngster would likely have predicted. Born September 12, 1880, to August and Anna Mencken, middle-class Baltimoreans of German descent, "Harry" lived the first two decades of his life in near-idyllic, traditional American surroundings. His father and uncle ran a successful cigar factory, his paternal grandfather governed all family matters, his mother guided and protected her children lovingly, and his brothers, sister, and next-door cousins joined him in playfully terrorizing the servants and neighbors. Mencken himself counted his father's influence the strongest in his life, for it was August Mencken's essentially conservative, bourgeois values that the son came to inherit—and to write much about, defending them in some respects, attacking them in others. From August, too, Henry may have derived his sense of humor; the elder Mencken loved a good laugh and an occasional practical joke. Only one serious conflict, over Henry's career preference, seems to have divided father and son. To his mother he was unabashedly devoted. Not until five years after the death in 1925 of Anna Abhau Mencken did her eldest son leave the warm home that she had fashioned for his family at 1524 Hollins Street, and to it he returned when his own wife died five years after that. All of his life Mencken remained deeply attached to the stable family life that had nurtured him and to the comfortable, preindustrial Baltimore that had grown up with him.

Although his family spent some very enjoyable summer vacations outside the city, Mencken was never truly drawn to any but an urban setting. The scenes of everyday human life and business, with their ceaseless variety of color, sound, and smell, enchanted him. Late nineteenth-century Baltimore was large enough that it offered such variety, yet small enough that it suffered few of the ills attending urbanization. Mencken would later assert, tongue in cheek, that all he needed to be happy was good food, a source of amusement, and a sense of his own superiority to most other human beings. Evidently Baltimore gave him all of these, for in seventy-five years Mencken never left.

Very early in his life Mencken acquired the habit of educating himself. As an adolescent, he read an unusually wide range of the English classics, preferring William Makepeace Thackeray to T.S. Eliot and Chaucer to Milton or Spenser. Of Americans he read Henry James, Stephen Crane, and William Dean Howells, among others. The literary experience of his life was Mark Twain's *Adventures of Huckleberry Finn*, to which he returned time and again. As he grew into a young man, he also read the works of such iconoclasts as Thomas Huxley, George Bernard Shaw, Friedrich Nietzsche, and the American critic James Gibbons Huneker. This last group was especially crucial to the shaping of Mencken's thought. A seedling iconoclast himself, he found that the works of those who made it their business to challenge conventional ideas and behavior were his models of free-thinking, independent expression.

Mencken's formal schooling began at F. Knapp's Institute, a German establishment that he very much liked, and ended at Baltimore Polytechnic Institute, which he did not like at all. Nevertheless, he graduated at the top of his class. Science and journalism attracted him, but when he finally settled on journalism, his father stood firmly in the way. He could go to college or he could learn the family business. Reluctantly, he chose the latter, for although he enjoyed reading and writing immensely, formal education left him cold. He did not wish to oppose his father—yet. The two years Mencken spent making and selling cigars were among the few unhappy ones of his life. When August Mencken died suddenly in January 1899, young Henry lost no time in presenting himself at the office of Max Ways, city editor of the *Baltimore Morning Herald*. Unwilling to employ a novice, Ways told him to come back another time. Mencken did go back, night after night, and his persistence was rewarded with odd reporting assignments but no pay (for that, he continued to work days at the factory). By late spring the editor was impressed by Mencken's determination and hired him. Thus began Mencken's real education. He later wrote:

It was the maddest, gladdest, damndest existence ever enjoyed by mortal youth. At a time when the respectable bourgeois youngsters of my generation were college freshmen, oppressed by simian sophomores and affronted with balderdash daily and hourly by chalky pedagogues, I was at large in a wicked seaport of half a million people, with a front seat at every public show . . . getting earfuls and eyefuls of instruction in a hundred giddy arcana, none of them taught in schools. . . . If I neglected the humanities I was meanwhile laying in all the worldly wisdom of a police lieutenant, a bartender, a shyster lawyer, or a midwife.

(*Newspaper Days*, p. ix)

Mencken and the new century got under way together, and he would see and help to shape a full half of it. The record of his work dominated that of his entire adult life, for he was married only five years and never fathered children. Mencken died January 29, 1956, seven years after a severe stroke had silenced the public man.

Literary Analysis

The speed with which Mencken advanced through the ranks of the *Baltimore Herald* evidenced his enterprise and aptitutde for the newspaper trade. Competence was the trait that he most admired in others and the one that he strove hardest to nurture in himself. Thus, within a year of his start at the *Herald* he was doing less routine reporting and more human interest writing; by March 1901 he was covering local politics and contributing an occasional editorial; the following autumn he began a column, "Rhyme and Reason," the first of many such outlets for humor and opinion that he would employ. The *Herald* also sent him to cover important stories beyond Baltimore—the Jacksonville, Florida, fire to begin with. The bumbling relief efforts that he witnessed there helped to render Mencken unsympathetic to most causes of "Service," a feeling that would never leave him. Mencken honed an ability to present his material clearly while simultaneously signing it with his own lively personality. If news for a given issue was scant, he was not above inventing some for spice. Eventually he was promoted to each of the paper's editorial posts until the Great Fire of Baltimore (1904) seriously crippled the *Herald*. By spring 1906 there was no longer a *Baltimore Herald*.

Mencken was not long finding a job with the *Baltimore Evening News*, nor was he long leaving it for the Baltimore *Sunpapers*, whose offer of the Sunday editorship he preferred. When the publisher created the *Evening Sun* Mencken became its associate editor. Biographer Carl Bode notes that the beginning of Mencken's long connection with the *Sunpapers* promised little, for he did not enjoy writing the drama criticism or editorials expected of him. The plays that he was to review were second rate, and, although politics very much amused him, editorials did not really give him the freedom to say exactly what he thought of the vaudeville performances that politics continually provided,[3] but a column did, and this he began in April 1910. Eventually called the "Free Lance," its author ("H.L.M.") made bold pronouncements on topics ranging from politics to language to popular culture. Literary historian Alfred Kazin correctly asserts that Mencken's lifelong approach to writing was meant to "[invert] conventional prejudices"[4]; the "Free Lance" was perhaps the first time that he set out to do so, and with irreverent zest. Not yet thirty, Mencken emerged as a distinct personality in Baltimore.

However, as rising tensions in Europe turned into war and Mencken openly sided with Germany (to some extent, this stance resulted from his intense anti-British sentiment), Baltimoreans grew less patient with the "Sage's" antagonistic heterodoxy. By late 1915 the disfavor into which Mencken and his "Free Lance" had fallen suggested the wisdom of sheathing the sword. Accordingly, the *Sun* sent him to Germany as a war correspondent. From there he reported on the situation in Europe, and by the time he came back to the States in the early spring of 1916 he had also covered a revolution in Cuba to which he had been inadvertently taken during his return voyage.

Their relationship now strained beyond endurance as a result of dissimilar political views, Mencken left the *Sunpapers* to write for the somewhat less prestigious *New York Evening Mail* (he did not, however, leave Baltimore). For two years his contributions on various topics appeared; these were some of the most famous essays that Mencken ever wrote. There was "A Neglected Anniversary," for instance, Mencken's history of the bathtub, well received from the outset and frequently cited over the years despite its utter untruth! No other of Mencken's hoaxes ever succeeded quite as that one did. Here also he first published the notorious "Sahara of the Bozart," in which he denounced the South for its (apparently) utter lack of cultural refinement. Still, the *Evening Mail* let him go during a change of management, so Mencken turned away from newspapers for a short while to work on his books.

After the war Mencken found that his readership still included Baltimore, despite the "silence" which the *Sunpapers* had asked of him.

Early in 1920 he returned to its pages with a series that was to run for nearly twenty years, the "Monday Articles." In these essays America's rowdiest journalist would eventually cover every national political convention held between 1920 and 1948, excepting 1944. These conventions were part of the "carnival of buncombe" that Mencken so delighted in, for although he often disparaged the mass of common American humanity, nothing thrilled him more than to jump into the thick of it. And what better occasion could he choose than that of a political convention, when "Boobus americanus" was in his best form? Mencken's stocky, crumpled figure with a perpetually wide-eyed look on its lumpy face from which protruded a cheap cigar ("Uncle Willies") became a familiar sight at these public circuses. He was frequently seen at his typewriter, joyfully hammering out the sum of his observations and predictions regarding all manner of issues, votes, speeches, personalities, and events.

Mencken did more for the *Baltimore Sun* than write for it. In 1934 he was elected to its board of directors, and four years later he served a short stint as acting editor of the evening paper. Both his writing and his abundant advice gave the *Evening Sun* a strong Menckenian flavor; for a long while it became the organ of open, unconventional—sometimes highly charged—speech that Mencken hoped it would remain.[5] Toward the end of the thirties, however, the *Sun* and its most famous personage again became disenchanted with one another, and with the onset of World War II Mencken once more receded into the background. They would never really be done with each other, though, until late 1948, when Mencken's stroke would leave him unable to read and write.

Although he always thought of himself chiefly as a newspaperman, Mencken by no means confined himself to this role. As early as 1908 he began reviewing books for a flashy magazine called *The Smart Set*, thus launching a long association not only with magazine journalism but also with George Jean Nathan.

Mencken had been reviewing books for *The Smart Set* for a year when Nathan became its drama critic; by 1914 he and Mencken were co-editing the magazine. In the next two decades their friendship became one of the country's most famous, their faces appearing together in fashionable New York night spots nearly as often as their names appeared together in print. Nathan was a sophisticate, an esthete, and doubtless this quality, along with his sense of humor, was what attracted Mencken. Both men were in the habit of looking about for whatever modicum of artistic ability and taste might be found in their own country; Europe (excluding Great Brit-

ain, in Mencken's view) plainly had the edge over the United States in cultural development, they felt, and America's persistent mediocrity exasperated them, particularly Mencken. The two men set out to encourage experiment among young American writers and dramatists. *The Smart Set* had already been fairly open to new names before Mencken and Nathan took over, but these two went in search of talent. With *The Smart Set* they intended to attack and to seriously undermine the forces of genteel, Victorian Puritanism, an influence that Mencken, Nathan, and many contemporary journalists believed a serious stumbling block to the development of a viable national literature.

But, by the time these men controlled *The Smart Set*, its potential as a medium of serious argument had been weakened by its reputation as a light, somewhat sleazy publication. Mencken and Nathan could not entirely reverse this situation, nor did they altogether wish to, for the magazine gave them an outlet for much of their own light satire. Of similar literary tastes and humor, they proved able associates, their ten-year editorship of *The Smart Set* doing them as much good as it did the magazine. The rewards were strictly personal and professional, however, not financial. As a moneymaker, *The Smart Set* was never successful, so its editors dabbled in the publication of a few "pulp" magazines that sold well. By 1923 the two men were planning a new magazine that would not only better suit their tastes but also prove profitable.

With the new year in 1924 came the first issue of *The American Mercury*, Mencken and Nathan's brainchild that their friend Alfred A. Knopf had agreed to publish. Despite its coeditors' conflicting ideas regarding the magazine's range, tone, and goals, the *Mercury* began impressively, attracting the attention of young writers and intellectuals across the country. Nathan preferred that the magazine emphasize the arts; Mencken saw it as having a much broader scope—that of the entire American scene, including medicine, education, and politics. It was not long before the *Mercury* took this broader direction, Nathan and his objections gradually fading into the background, and the latter half of the 1920s responded as cordially to the magazine as Mencken could have hoped. As in the days of *The Smart Set*, he worked hard to publish new, talented writers with fresh ideas, in fiction and non-fiction alike, for his old crusade against staid and stuffy orthodoxy was always foremost in his mind. So bold was he that his liberal editorial policy actually resulted in his arrest once when in 1926 a Boston anti-vice group tried to suppress the magazine for having published a story about a prostitute. At his trial Mencken was acquitted, and although it took time for public opinion to come to his defense, eventually the notorious "Hatrack" case brought him acclaim as an important American spokesman for freedom of speech and of the press. For this reason, and by virtue of the high standards that the magazine maintained in the quality of its writing, the *Mercury* sailed into the 1930s among the ranks of the nation's most prestigious and influencial periodicals. Mencken remained its editor a full ten years before he grew tired of the enterprise, ready to move on to something else.

His last few years with *The American Mercury* were significant in another way, for they were the period of his marriage to Sara Haardt. In 1930 the newspapers had a field day when Mencken's engagement was announced, since he had long been the wittiest and most outspoken defender of the single life ("Bachelors have consciences. Married men have wives"). Mencken had little trouble adjusting, however, to the changes marriage brought to his life, and his brief time with Sara by all accounts was very happy indeed. An Alabama teacher, Sara Haardt had been one of the many young fiction writers whom Mencken had advised in his capacity as magazine editor. Her premature death in 1935 left him empty and dejected, but his love of work served to pull him through the trying aftermath.

All of his life Mencken was a man of unflagging energies which even years of newspaper and magazine journalism could not sap. Books, then, became yet another outlet for him, though some of them were merely collections of material he had first published elsewhere. His first book was actually a volume of poetry (*Ventures into Verse*, 1903), and although he also tried writing short stories, a novel, and a few plays (co-authored with Nathan), the genre for which he showed the most interest and gift was that of the essay. Many of his contemporaries thought him its modern American master.

Essayist and dramatist George Bernard Shaw attracted Mencken very early on, so much so that Mencken made him the subject of his first prose work in 1905, *George Bernard Shaw: His Plays*. Not long after its appearance he set to work on another study, *The Philosophy of Friedrich Nietzsche* (1908). He had found both Shaw and Nietzsche as interesting for their prose styles as for their ideas, and in writing about them Mencken further developed the clear, bracing style that was to become his hallmark. In 1916 *A Little Book in C Major* and *A Book of Burlesques* attracted notice for their now-recognizable, thoroughly Menckenian satire. Although a small travel piece co-authored with Nathan and Willard Huntington Wright (*Europe After 8:15*, 1914) failed miserably, Mencken's *Book of Prefaces* (1917) did not, for it collected some of his best literary criticism. *Damn! A Book of Cal-*

umny, another gathering of essays, these on various aspects of American culture, soon followed in 1918. Of greater substance was his *In Defense of Women* (1918) in which Mencken set himself the task of illustrating that the "weaker sex" in America was no such thing; for women Mencken generally had the utmost respect and admiration.

In 1919, the astonishing Mencken published yet another full-length work, the first version of what he would come to consider his greatest achievement. *The American Language*, its subsequent three editions (each revised and enlarged, running to several hundreds of pages), and its final two supplements established the author as more than just a newspaperman, more than a magazine editor, more than a critic of American ideas and culture, and above all, more than a humorist: he was also a scholar. It should be remembered that Mencken never went to college, and when Mencken's literary criticism had begun to attract attention (when he joined *The Smart Set*), many university scholars had been unwilling to credit him with scholastic or critical ability, often because they themselves had been the objects, individually and collectively, of his attacks on the American intelligentsia. Now, even they had to admit that Mencken was among the best students of American English that the nation could boast. This group was small, to be sure, and the fact nettled Mencken: where if not in our very speech could it be more plain that the United States was not a "little England"? Why did not the academicians leave their musty "tomes" from ages past in favor of the more useful study of the life (social as well as artistic) around them, beginning with the language? If today the idea that "American" is a strain of English unto itself seems commonplace and scholarly journals devote page upon page to the subject, then much of the credit for this belongs to Mencken.

Prejudices: First Series also appeared in 1919. The title was well chosen, for these essays, some of them revised versions of book reviews, represent the opinions of the most opinionated American writer of the day. That all six volumes of the *Prejudices* series coincided with the 1920s (the last one appearing in 1927) seems in retrospect entirely appropriate. With these works and with *The American Mercury* the era became as much that of "gay and mocking" Mencken, as Kazin called him,[6] as it was of raunchy politics, jazz, and Hollywood. The "Lost Generation" of American novelists and poets may have been struggling to understand the times, but Mencken was only out to make his readers understand the times as he did.

In 1926, Mencken brought out *Notes on Democracy* it order to elaborate on the criticisms of

American government and politics that he had often set forth in various articles. As much as he believed in the sanctity of freedom of speech, Mencken thought most other principles of democracy inane, for such a system proceeded from the fallacious idea that all humans are equal. To Mencken it was clear that some people are more valuable than others; he advocated an aristocracy of the mind, leadership that could be trusted to govern rationally—exactly what he believed officials elected by the masses were incapable of doing.

Other topics that had similarly absorbed him, religion (particularly Christianity) and morality, led him to write *Treatise on the Gods* (1930) and *Treatise on Right and Wrong* (1934); to both of these works the author attempted to bring a scholarly perspective as well as the customary, intensely personal one. They did not bring him the acclaim, however, that his next project would: *Happy Days* (1940), *Newspaper Days* (1941), and *Heathen Days* (1943) represent Mencken's three-volume autobiography, the consequence of a series of *New Yorker* magazine sketches. The *Days* books remain highly esteemed among American autobiographies, for in them the author's style is fresh and clear, the humor is gentler than most Menckenian satire, and the picture of bygone America is a fond one in the national memory. During his last years, Mencken also collected his own favorite essays and aphorisms in *A Mencken Chrestomathy* (1949), and he was in the process of compiling some previously unpublished notes for *Minority Report* when his stroke disabled him. With the help of a secretary, however, he did manage to complete the book, published shortly after his death in January 1956.

While at work on his books on Shaw and Nietzsche, Mencken formed ideas that would change very little over the years: middle-class man was fundamentally an absurd little creature in body, mind, and heart; his systems of religion and government were fascinating but overrated; and history was far from being the story of progress that most people had come to believe. But, turn-of-the-century iconoclasts did not convert Mencken to their ranks so much as they confirmed in him a way of approaching the world, a particular mindset that he had already begun to cultivate. Emerging into adulthood during an era when everything from shoe polish to education to politics was touted as "progressive," Mencken brought to all that he encountered a skepticism inherited from his father. When the young writer found that this skepticism and his blithe sense of humor suited one another well, he was off like a horse out of the starting gate, and in thirty-five years the satire never entirely let up. A self-proclaimed critic of ideas, Mencken

was not always taken seriously, and sometimes he was taken too seriously, but he usually managed to make himself heard.

The range of ideas, attitudes, trends, books, public figures, and American institutions that Mencken attacked throughout his career was astonishingly wide. He preferred to denounce (and he was better at it) rather than defend; his flair for the polished insult actually had a winning charm about it that attracted rather than repelled readers.[7] Swedenborgians, Socialists, Scotsmen, stockbrokers, businessmen of any kind, farmers in general and Southern farmers in particular, homeopaths, osteopaths, Prohibitionists, social workers, psychologists, pedagogues and "schoolma'ams," college presidents, theologians, Holy Rollers, archbishops, Methodists, Marxists, Anglo-Saxons in general and the American "booboisie" in particular, Rotarians, Y.M.C.A. members, Congressmen, and every American president since the first Roosevelt: Mencken tossed barbs at these and many other figures. Indeed, it soon became clear that much of him was pure though delightful bombast. Woodrow Wilson was "a typical Puritan. . . . Magnanimity was simply beyond him." William Jennings Bryan was riddled with ambition, "the ambition of a common man to get his hand upon the collar of his superiors, or, failing that, to get his thumb into their eyes." Henry James's "painful psychologizings, when translated into plain English, turn out to be chiefly kittenishness— an arch tickling of the ribs of elderly virgins— the daring of a grandma smoking marijuana." Mencken ridiculed so many people and things American that he was sometimes asked why he chose to remain here, to which query he would respond, "Why do men go to zoos?" No critic of the American scene was ever so completely infatuated with it as was Mencken.

But, when the rollicking, irresponsible fun of the 1920s gave way to the very grave problems of the 1930s and 1940s, Americans looked upon Mencken's persistent satire with much less favor. How does one remain patient with a man who ignored or even denied the threats of the Great Depression and Nazi Germany? Rather than alter his views in the face of changing public opinion, Mencken simply and wisely slipped into the wings and worked at updating his *American Language*.

In his heyday, however, the one issue that had continually occupied him proved to be the one that readers were always willing to hear Mencken address; here his influence probably reached its height, and we may yet be feeling it sixty years later. Mencken was so thoroughly anti-Puritan as to be in danger of becoming a puritan of sorts himself. Christianity had done this country far more harm than good, he felt, for its heavily Puritanical emphasis had repressed aesthetic sensibility to the point of leaving America culturally barren. His crusade against the forces of the genteel, Puritan tradition began with literature, for in all his prodigious reading Mencken rarely found any mainstream American fiction that approached intellectual truth or emotional power without yielding to the temptation to moralize at worst or to sentimentalize at best. Contemporary fiction was "thin and watery," suffering from "a dearth of intellectual audacity and of aesthetic passions." Despite his technical virtuosity, the typical American writer remained "a Presbyterian first and an artist second," which to Mencken was "just as comfortable as trying to be a Presbyterian first and a chorus girl second." Many contemporary critics and writers shared this view—but many did not. For a long while traditionalists gave Mencken and his fellow libertarians just the sort of lively fight he so enjoyed.

Acting, therefore, in the interests of a new literature unfettered by misguided morality or shallow gentility, Mencken came to the very vocal defense first of Theodore Dreiser and later of James Branch Cabell, Sinclair Lewis, Willa Cather, and Sherwood Anderson, among others. *The Smart Set* and *The American Mercury* gave Mencken his best weapons, for in them he not only could roar loud and long about the state of American letters, he could actually publish those writers trying to usher in the modern age. Under Mencken and Nathan's management, for instance, *The Smart Set* was the first to publish F. Scott Fitzgerald and Eugene O'Neill, and it also published some early James Joyce. In *The American Mercury* appeared early work by Ruth Suckow, Edgar Lee Masters, Carl Sandburg, Countee Cullen, and William Faulkner. Although authors in the twenties did not always find in Mencken their shrewdest critic, they did have in him their staunchest ally.

He could certainly be flip about his cause— "Puritanism [is] the haunting fear that someone, somewhere, may be happy"—but generally Mencken decried its influence in any sphere in the bitterest of terms. When fundamentalist America, for instance, produced such figures as the Midwest's populist leader William Jennings Bryan, Mencken was more certain than ever that Puritanism and democracy together would be the nation's undoing ("Democracy is the theory that the common people know what they want, and deserve to get it good and hard"). The undoing of Bryan was a task Mencken undertook with relish when in 1925 he traveled to Dayton, Tennessee, to cover the famous Scopes "monkey" trial. Bryan led the pro-Creationism forces that wanted to prosecute a young science teacher, John Thomas Scopes, for defying a state law

banning the teaching of the theory of evolution in public schools. Mencken had much earlier decided that Darwin's explanation of species development far outshone Biblical accounts in Genesis for simple logic and credibility; thus, he thought Bryan and his fellow evangelicals the quintessence of American "boobery," always quick to cast its lot with whatever was "palpably untrue." Scopes was convicted, but when Bryan died just days after the trial, Mencken used the occasion to proclaim that the advocates of liberal enlightenment would eventually win the war against ignorance, despite the recent loss of a single battle.

It was one thing for muddled, Puritan politics to concern itself with legislation regarding evolutionist teaching; it was quite another for the "Bible-thumpers" to finally win legal permission to tell Mencken that he could not, whenever he so desired, take a drink. Prohibition: the word sent a shudder through his frame and ceaseless invective through his pen. Mencken had often quipped, "I am ombibulous"—that is, he considered himself a connoisseur of the grape, though he was always careful not to drink if any work remained to be done. Prohibition tried his patience mightily, but in this matter as in all things his sense of humor sustained him. To a friend Mencken wrote in January 1919: "All is lost, including honor. But I have enough good whiskey, fair wine and prime beer secreted to last me two solid years—and by then I hope to be far from these Wesleyan scenes."

Rebel though he was regarding things Puritan, most of Mencken's ideas were actually quite conservative, a fact often overlooked. Moreover, few of them could now be considered in any way extraordinary. Still, "H.L.M." was a phenomenon unto himself, not in what he said but in how he said it. Although most of the issues that he addressed are now dated, people will continue to read Mencken primarily for his prose style; indeed, it was only for his style that people ever read him at all, for without it he would have been just another loud voice issuing from an era of many loud voices. Even very early on his work was lucid and fluent to a degree that precious little journalism ever is. Advocates and detractors alike came to admire several traits of Mencken's writing, but the author himself maintained that clarity was absolutely its chief hallmark. Like Thomas Huxley, the British writer from whom Mencken claimed to have learned much, Mencken could immediately make himself understood, a feat many beginning writers have been surprised to find is not easy to achieve, and as a journalist, Mencken had to write quickly, under the constant pressure of deadlines. Extensive revision was not often possible, a fact that renders the quality of his writing all the more remarkable. Mencken's own words on the subject of style exemplify his gift for clarity, here accomplished through sharp images and smooth syntax:

> The essence of a sound style is that it cannot be reduced to rules—that it is a living and breathing thing, with something of the demoniacal in it—that it fits its proprietor tightly and yet ever so loosely, as his skin fits him. It is, in fact, quite as securely an integral part of him as that skin is. It hardens as his arteries harden. It is gaudy when he is young and gathers decorum when he grows old. . . . In brief, a style is always the outward and visible symbol of a man, and it cannot be anything else.
>
> (*Prejudices: Fifth Series*, p. 197)

If style was the man and the man the style in the case of Mencken, then perhaps the same is true of the man and his humor. Apart from his writing, Mencken's friends knew him as an enormously funny and energetic person. He was given to slapstick one-liners (as when the country's most famous atheist signed his personal letters, "Yours in Christ") and elaborate practical jokes and hoaxes (for example, he once had stationery printed with the fabricated name of a Negro country club, on which paper he wrote to his racist acquaintances in the South, inviting them to join him for golf).

Among the special characteristics of Mencken's style and humor is his sense of cadence, for which his love of classical music may have been largely responsible. An amateur pianist himself, Mencken thought music the most beautiful of "languages," and he claimed to do his best thinking first in music, second in words. A master of English prose, he could yet lament, "I shall die an inarticulate man, for my best ideas have beset me in a language I know only vaguely and speak only like a child." However musically gifted he may or may not have been, his prose nevertheless reveals a solid sense of rhythm. Under Mencken's direction compound sentences glide rather than lumber along; strong verbs and their object complements carry much of the meaning; and parallel constructions fall neatly into single file.

Smooth though Mencken could be, Kilpatrick notes that he was a show-off, a ham, a "smart-ass,"[8] able to give readers a good time primarily because he was having great fun doing his job. One of his special provinces was that of word choice. He sought exaggerated effects, sometimes with Latinized words (as in "cerebelli" and "umbilicarii," terms he invented for thirdrate intellectuals), sometimes with fabricated titles ("Herr Professor-Doktor") prefacing a name, frequently that of an American president. Words that had previously enjoyed little use—or indeed, had never before existed—seemed to sparkle with life when Mencken penned them: a victim of his satire was likely to be a "wowser," one of the "chautauqua," a "mountebank," a "charlatan," a purveyor of "flapdoodle," "flummery," "pother," "hooey," "buffooneries," "buncombe," "balderdash," or "brummagem" nonsense; Mencken might accuse someone of trying to "bamboozle" everyone with his "rhodomontades," "laparotomies" or "pronunciamentoes." Even if other characteristics of his writing do not immediately give him away as the author of a piece, one can usually spot the "Menckenese" which no writer since has been able to imitate, though many have tried.

He drew comparisons between the most unlikely of images and ideas, producing hilarious similes and metaphors: seeing an awful verb in the London *Times* "affected [him] like seeing an archbishop wink at a loose woman"; Abraham Lincoln's writing was "as bare of rhetorical element and the niceties of professors as a yell for the police"; writing of any kind other than that to which he was accustomed would be for him "as false as an appearance of decency in a Congressman." Such incongruities are, of course, the essence of humor.

And, incongruity caught his attention everywhere. Probably Mencken's humor will best be remembered for its penetrating insight into the discrepancies presented by the times in which he lived. In "H.L.M." the country had a discriminating judge, able to see where the real did not match the professed ideal. He was the one most likely to point out to us that who we actually were usually did not dovetail with who we said we were. In particular his observations on relations between the sexes yielded some of his most pithy remarks:

> A man always remembers his first love with special tenderness. But after that he begins to bunch them.

> Bachelors know more about women than married men. If they didn't they'd be married, too.

> In every woman's life there is one real and consuming love. But very few women guess which one it is.

> When a woman says she won't, it is a good sign that she will. And when she says she will it is an even better sign.

A few similarly incisive comments concerning other subjects are worth noting:

Archbishop—A Christian ecclesiastic of a rank superior to that attained by Christ.

Christian—One who is willing to serve three Gods, but draws the line at one wife.

Creator—A comedian whose audience is afraid to laugh.

Remorse—Regret that one waited so long to do it.

After all, it was the way that Mencken overturned even the most ordinary notions that Americans had about themselves and their culture that both endeared readers to him and created for him countless enemies. Although he took several of his crusades very seriously, ultimately it appears that he wished to be remembered not as a belligerent force but as a humanizing one; the epitaph he wrote for himself reads, "If, after I depart this vale, you ever remember me and have thought to please my ghost, forgive some sinner and wink your eye at some homely girl."

Summary

Newspaperman, magazine editor, and author Henry Louis Mencken received more public attention than any other American journalist of his day. His reputation as an iconoclast, an exploder of conventional wisdom and pieties, reached its height during the "roaring twenties" although his career had been well under way for two decades; it continued to thrive, somewhat less publicly, into the 1940s. Mencken cofounded *The American Mercury*, a prestigious magazine of Americana, and he wrote for or advised the *Sunpapers* of his native Baltimore off and on for more than forty years. Although most of his books are collections of essays, Mencken is also credited with several critical works and with a major scholarly contribution to the field of linguistics. As a humorist, he is best known for cutting satire, frequently achieved through comic exaggeration, outlandish diction, and incongruous juxtapositions of ideas and images. These techniques served him well in his war against the forces of Puritanism in American literature, politics, and culture.

Notes

1. James L. Kilpatrick, "The Writer Mencken," *Menckeniana*, 79 (Fall 1981), p. 6.
2. Louis D. Rubin, Jr., ed., *The Comic Imagination in American Literature*, (New Brunswick, N.J.: Rutgers University Press, 1973), p. 225.
3. Carl Bode, *Mencken* (Carbondale and Edwardsville: Southern Illinois University, 1969), pp. 41-42.
4. Alfred Kazin, *On Native Grounds: An Interpretation of Modern American Prose Literature* (New York: Reynal and Hitchcock, 1942), p. 202.
5. Bode, p. 193.
6. Kazin, p. 200.
7. Ibid., p. 201.
8. Kilpatrick, p. 4.

Selected Bibliography

Primary Sources

Books

Ventures into Verse. Baltimore: Marshall, Beck, and Gordon, 1903.
George Bernard Shaw: His plays. Boston: Luce, 1905.
The Philosophy of Friedrich Nietzsche. Boston: Luce, 1908; rev. ed., 1913.
A Little Book in C Major. New York: Lane, 1916.
A Book of Burlesques. New York: Lane, 1916.
A Book of Prefaces. New York: Knopf, 1917.
Damn! A Book of Calumny. New York: Philip Goodman, 1918.
In Defense of Women. New York: Knopf, 1918.
The American Language: An Inquiry into the Development of English in the United States. New York: Knopf, 1919; rev. eds., 1921, 1923, 1936; *Supplements I* and *II*, 1945 and 1948, respectively.
Prejudices: First Series. New York: Knopf, 1919; *Second Series*, 1920; *Third Series*, 1922; *Fourth Series*, 1924; *Fifth Series*, 1926; *Sixth Series*, 1927; all published by Knopf.
Notes on Democracy. New York: Knopf, 1926.
Treatise on the Gods. New York: Knopf, 1930.
Treatise on Right and Wrong. New York: Knopf, 1934.
Happy Days, 1880-1892. New York: Knopf, 1940.
Newspaper Days, 1899-1906. New York: Knopf, 1941.
Heathen Days, 1890-1936. New York: Knopf, 1943.
A Mencken Chrestomathy. New York: Knopf, 1949.
Minority Report: H.L. Mencken's Notebooks. New York: Knopf, 1956.

Co-authored Books

Men Versus the Man: A Correspondence Between Rives La Monte, Socialist, and H.L. Mencken, Individualist. New York: Holt, 1910.
(with George Jean Nathan and Willard Huntington Wright.) *Europe After 8:15*. New York: Lane, 1914.
(with George Jean Nathan.) *The American Credo: A Contribution Toward the Interpretation of the National Mind*. New York: Knopf, 1920.

Secondary Sources

Books

Bode, Carl. *Mencken*. Carbondale and Edwardsville: Southern Illinois University, 1969. Probably the most objective and most complete picture of Mencken available, of the many biographies published.
Fecher, Charles A. *Mencken: A Study of His Thought*. New York: Knopf, 1978. A judicious study of Mencken the philosopher, literary critic, political analyst, and stylist.
Williams, W.H.A. *H.L. Mencken*. Boston: G.K. Hall, 1977. An insightful look at the contradictory facets of the satirist.

Bibliographies

Adler, Betty. *H.L.M.: The Mencken Bibliography*. Baltimore: Johns Hopkins Press, 1961. An invaluable list of Mencken's works, accompanied by a selective list of secondary materials. This secondary bibliography is kept up to date by the journal *Menckeniana*, which Adler also founded.

Menckeniana: A Quarterly Review. Baltimore: Enoch Pratt Free Library, since 1962. Includes articles on Mencken and abstracts of articles published elsewhere as they appear; attempts to keep up with even the slightest of references to the humorist.

Articles

Fitzpatrick, Vincent. "The Elusive Butterfly's Angry Pursuer: The Jamesian Style, Mencken, and Clear Writing." *Menckeniana*, 59 (Fall 1976): 13-17. An examination of Mencken's style with reference to his remarks on James.

Kilpatrick, James L. "The Writer Mencken." *Menckeniana*, 79 (Fall 1981): 2-10. A useful catalog of some of Mencken's stylistic traits; should be read critically, however, for Kilpatrick suggests that Mencken used few metaphors and similes—but even a superficial reading of Mencken proves otherwise.

Lippmann, Walter. "H.L. Mencken." *Saturday Review of Literature*, 3 (December 11, 1926): 413-414. Begins with a review of *Notes on Democracy*; includes several penetrating observations on Mencken as an "outraged sentimentalist."

Wilson, Edmund. "H.L. Mencken." *New Republic*, 27 (June 1, 1921): 10-13. An interesting sketch of Mencken the idealist and the anti-Puritan.

Other

Kazin, Alfred. *On Native Grounds: An Interpretation of Modern American Prose Literature*. New York: Reynal and Hitchcock, 1942. A picture of Mencken much less flattering than those usually offered by literary historians; emphasizes the bombast over the influence.

Mott, Frank Luther. *A History of American Magazines, 1905-1930*. Cambridge: Harvard University Press, 1968. Includes comprehensive profiles of *The Smart Set* and *The American Mercury*.

Rubin, Louis D., Jr., ed. *The Comic Imagination in American Literature*. New Brunswick, N.J.: Rutgers University Press, 1973. Rubin's chapter on Mencken provides a thorough introduction to him as a journalist, critic, and humorist.

Yates, Norris W. *The American Humorist: Conscience of the Twentieth Century*. Ames, Iowa: University of Iowa Press, 1964. Rpt. New York: Citadel, 1965. Analyzes the various poses Mencken maintained in his humor.

Allison Bulsterbaum

Morton, Thomas

Born: c. 1575-1590, place unknown
Marriage: Alice Miller, 1621
Died: 1647

Biography

Next to nothing is known about the forty-plus years that Thomas Morton lived before he arrived in Massachusetts, threw up a maypole, and became the hobgoblin of Pilgrims and Puritans. Morton was born as early as around 1575 or 1579, according to Donald F. Connors, in the West Country of England and as late as 1590, according to the *Encyclopedia Britannica*; he was perhaps the son of a soldier. He studied law at Clifford's Inn, one of the Inns of Chancery in London, and later practiced in the West Country. In 1621 he married a widow named Alice Miller, and, in the public record for the next few years, Morton's name appears as a party in lawsuits with his new son-in-law over certain property rights. In 1624 Morton landed in Massachusetts with a party of fur traders and indentured servants who, led by a Captain Wollaston, established Mount Wollaston on the present site of Quincy, Massachusetts. According to Pilgrim governor William Bradford's *History of Plymouth Plantation*, the captain soon found New England not what he expected and so transported part of his servants to Virginia where he sold them "at good rates." His plans to do the same with the rest were frustrated by Morton's leading the servants to revolt and establish a plantation where, according to Bradford, he promised all would "be free from service, and we will converse, plant, trade, and live together as equals and support and protect one another." Mount Wollaston was renamed. According to Morton it became Ma-re Mount, or hill by the sea; according to Bradford, Merry Mount.

From the start Morton's community found itself in conflict with its neighbors. Not only were they economic competitors, they were politically, theologically, and temperamentally antagonistic. For the Separatists, Merry Mount seemed the most terrifying of nightmares made flesh. "They fell to great licentiousness," wrote Bradford, "and led a dissolute life, pouring out themselves into all profaneness. And Morton became Lord of Misrule, and maintained (as it were) a School of Atheism. . . . They also set up a maypole, drinking and dancing about it many days together, inviting the Indian women for their consorts, dancing and frisking together like so many fairies, or furies rather." The Pilgrims feared that like plague Morton's "anarchy" would "spread over all, if not prevented" and that the Plymouth colonists "should keep no servants for . . . all the scum of the country or any discontents would flock to him from all places, if this nest was not broken. And they should stand in more fear of their lives and goods in short time from this wicked and debased crew than from the savages themselves." The Pilgrims were also terrified by Morton's trading guns to the Indians, who, they believed, were their technological superiors and consequently likely to surpass them soon in the maintenance of weapons and the manufacture of powder and bullets.

In 1628, Plymouth joined with other plantations in bringing charges against Morton. Merry Mount was "stormed" by a party under the command of Miles Standish. Morton was arrested, tried, and shipped back to England after being marooned for a month on an island where, he claimed, friendly Indians kept him alive. Morton departed from America in August; in September Salem was settled by Puritans led by John Endicott, who pulled down the maypole of Merry Mount. In England, meanwhile, the charges against Morton were dismissed.

In 1629 Morton returned to his plantation and very quickly fell into conflict with the Salem Puritans over questions of civil law, religious law, and the rights of independent fur traders. In 1630, he was arrested once again, tried, and sentenced to the stocks. His goods were seized and his house burned to the ground; then he was sent back to England. During this second exile from America, Morton wrote *The New English Canaan*, a book intended partly as an expression of his love of the New World and partly as self-justification. It was also intended to serve the political ends of Ferdinando Gorges and Bishop Laud, old adversaries of the Puritans who were engaged in a struggle with them over control of the Bay colony. Gorges and Laud for a time championed Morton and used him, but finally threw him aside.

In 1643, six years after the publication of the book which Governor Bradford pronounced "an infamous and scurrilous book against many godly and chief men of the country: full of lies and slanders and fraught with profane calumnies against their names and persons and the ways of God," Morton returned to Massachusetts. He was arrested the next year and brought to trial on the charge that while in England he had himself lodged a charge against the Puritan government. He was also, it is generally believed, being tried for writing his book. After spending a year in jail, Morton was fined £100 and released. He was freed because, in the words of John Winthrop, the Puritan governor, "he was a charge to the country, for he had nothing and we thought it not fit to inflict corporal punishment upon him, being old and crazy." Morton made his way to Maine and two years later died.

Literary Analysis

New English Canaan or New Canaan was published in Amsterdam in 1637. It is divided into three parts: an account of the Indians of New England; a catalogue of plants, animals, fish, fowl, and other natural endowments of the New World; and a brief history of Pilgrim and Puritan settlements and Morton's difficulties with them. Parts one and two fit neatly into the tradition of optimistic visions of America and promotional tracts. Morton accepted the dream made fact by many writers that the New World presented humankind with an opportunity to return to the paradise of the Golden Age—a time without war, law, or excessive labor. Set within the temperate zone, New England was, according to Morton, a land of the golden mean, a rich country in "nothing inferior to Canaan of Israel but a kind of parallel to it in all points." Here a natively noble people had created, or recreated, Plato's commonwealth. These people, the Indians were, Morton claimed, not Asiatics as some believed but the descendants of dispersed Trojans, a fact proved by the many Greek and Latin words in their language. Humane, virtuous, gentle, they were the antithesis of the selfish, dishonest Calvinist hypocrites who attempted to exploit them.

The land, according to Morton, was bountiful. It overflowed with beast, fish, and fowl. It was a place of laughing streams that jet "most jocundly where they do meet and hand in hand run down to Neptune's court." It was a place of pleasure where drinking from certain springs could cure melancholy and eating beaver tail could increase "priapic virtues." Contradictions in Morton's vision suggest, however, that his America was shaped partly by literary convention, partly by wishful thinking, and partly by a desire to prove the land and people were antithetical to the Pilgrims and Puritans. In the end, Morton concluded that the paradise he had discovered had been intended for the English by the God who sent plagues to destroy the lost Trojans who were, in spite of their virtues, governed by the Devil and standing in the way of the newly chosen people, the party of King and established Church.

Morton's small reputation rests on Part III, the mocking account of the Separatists and Morton's adventures with them. As Charles Francis Adams, the nineteenth-century editor of *New English Canaan*, wrote: "It is, indeed, the author's sense of humor . . . which gives to the *New Canaan* its only real distinction among the early works relating to New England. In this respect it stands by itself." Like his picture of the new world, Morton's comedy seems to have been shaped by the pursuit of two linked goals—the denigration of Pilgrims and Puritans and the celebration of the author himself as their nemesis. Morton, or "Mine Host" as he refers to himself, is presented as an open, cheerful, witty, and intelligent man. He is of the party of life; his descriptions of the New World reveal his curiosity and his interest in all aspects of human experience: in the intellectual, the spiritual, the sensual. Intended as the embodiment of civilization, Morton's prose is filled with his time's agreed-upon signs of intelligence, rationality, and education. His playful style is made up of learned words, ornate phrases, allusions, witty and often cryptic puns. As Adams said, Morton "took a positive pleasure in concealing what he meant to say under a cloud of metaphor." Part III of *New English Canaan* contains allegorical stories and poems which, to Morton's delight, completely befuddled his antagonistic neighbors who almost automatically assumed some tended to "lasciviousness and others to the detraction and scandal of some persons." A poem that Morton affixed to his maypole is typical of his writing both in its form and in the Pilgrims' reaction to it.

> *Rise Oedipus, and, if thou canst, unfold*
> *What means Charybdis underneath the mold,*
> *When Scylla solitary on the ground*
> *(Sitting in form of Niobe) was found,*
> *Till Amphitrite's Darling did acquaint*
> *Grim Neptune with the Tenor of her plaint,*
> *And caused him send forth Triton with the*
>   *sound*
> *of Trumpet loud, at which the Seas were found*
> *So full of Protean forms that the bold shore*
> *Presented Scylla a new paramour*
> *So strong as Samson and so patient*
> *As Job, himself, directed thus, by fate,*
> *To comfort Scylla so unfortunate.*
> *I do profess by Cupid's beauteous Mother,*
> *Here is Scogan's choice for Scylla, and none*
>   *other;*
> *Though Scylla's sick with grief, because no sign*
> *Can there be found of virtue masculine.*
> *Aesculapius come; I know right well*
> *His labor's lost when you may ring her Knell.*
> *The fatal sister's doom none none can withstand,*
> *Nor Cytharea's power, who points to land*
> *With proclamation that the first of May*
> *At Ma-re Mount shall be kept holiday.*
>   (*Canaan*, pp. 277-278)

Solving this rhymed riddle depended upon being able to translate into American experience Morton's complicated and ingenious play with classical and Biblical allusions. That was beyond the Pilgrims, as in fact comprehending Morton's more cryptic writing has been beyond readers of ensuing generations. Nevertheless, for Morton the Pilgrims' reading into his riddle some reference to a carpenter in their party named Samson Job and assuming that the poem attacked them

was emphatic illustration of their characteristic stupidity, their egoism, their almost instinctive assumption of the worst about everyone and everything outside their group, and the aggressive anti-intellectualism by which they isolated themselves from the real world. Just as revealing for Morton was his antagonists' conclusion that his maypole

> was in memory of a whore not knowing that it was a trophy erected at first in honor of Maia, the Lady of Learning, which they despise, vilifying the two universities with uncivil terms, accounting what is there obtained by study is but unnecessary learning, not considering that learning does enable men's minds to converse with elements of a higher nature than is to be found within the habitation of the mole.
>   (*Canaan*, pp. 281-282)

Morton was much more straightforward in describing his enemies' inferiority than in demonstrating his superiority. Ironically, Morton saw in the Pilgrims and Puritans exactly what they saw in him—chaos. His antagonists, he believed, defied not only King and Church but Nature. He gave them many of the characteristics that modern writers attribute to "fringe cults": repressive internal government, hostility toward the outside world, closed minds, "the neglect" of "father mother and all friendship" for "the general good of their church and commonwealth." For Morton, no order could exist in a church without hierarchy where "not any . . . though he be but a Cowkeeper, but is allowed to exercise his gifts in the public assembly so as he do not make use of any notes" and where the most admired speakers are likely when taken by religion to fall "into a fit (which they term a zealous meditation.)" (*Canaan*, p. 322).

Luckily for both his book and reputation, Morton's fear and loathing were set within the context of a comic vision. So, instead of monsters or demons, his Pilgrims and Puritans became buffoons, dullards, and humorously obvious hypocrites. Morton gives Miles Standish, John Winthrop, and unknown others names like "Captain Shrimp," "Ananais Increase," "Captain Littleworth," and "Master Bubble." When Winthrop arrives in Massachusetts protecting the colony's charter by carrying it in a specially made case, Morton's Separatists assume that he is a musician. When their debts to an outsider fall due, they remit letters filled with good advice instead of money. They hang a known innocent to demonstrate their zeal for justice to the Indians. Their doctor keeps the overall health of the community at a high level by killing all of his patients. "They wink when they pray because they think themselves so perfect in the high way to heaven that they can find it blindfolded," Morton asserts. When stirred into action, they naturally become the characters of farce. While on a trading expedition, for example, Master Bubble has an attack of inflamed imagination suggesting to himself that he was:

> pressed by a company of Indians and their shafts were let fly as thick as hail at him, he puts off his breeches and puts them on his head, for to save him from the shafts that flew after him so thick that no man could perceive them, and crying out, avoid Satan what have ye to do with me! thus running on his way without breeches he was pitifully scratched up with the brush of the underwoods, as he wandered up and down in unknown ways: The savages in the mean time put up all his implements in the sack he left behind and brought them to Wessaguscus where they thought to have found him.
>
> (*Canaan*, 271)

During his second imprisonment, Morton escaped from his captors by walking out of their jail. Then, he wrote, "the word, which was given with an alarm, was, oh he's gone, he's gone, what shall we do, he's gone! The rest (half asleep) start up in a maze, and, like rams, ran their heads one at another full butt in the dark." The reaction of Pilgrim and Puritan to all of this has been noted; Morton's antagonists were not amused. It is interesting to at least consider the idea, however, that at least one of them may have attempted to retaliate in kind. Bradford's account of the storming of Merry Mount contains one of the few examples in Pilgrim or Puritan literature of what might be taken for conscious humor. The passage in question very much resembles Morton's slapstick and has no counterpart in his account. Bradford wrote: "Neither was there any hurt done to any of either side, save that one was so drunk that he ran his own nose upon the point of a sword that one held before him, as he entered the house; but he lost but a little of his hot blood" (Bradford, II, 57).

Morton was not a great writer. Nor was he in any way an influential one. His image of Pilgrims and Puritans has certainly not become part of the American mythology. Even when treated negatively, the two groups are given the grave dignity of terror. They are sometimes pictured as fanatics but seldom as dullards and buffoons. *New English Canaan* is read today primarily by only a few specialists in early American literature. The imaginations of later American writers have at times been struck by Morton's story, or perhaps, more precisely, by his maypole and the free community surround-

ing it. They and Morton have appeared in stories, poems, and opera by Lydia Maria Child, Catherine Sedgewick, John Lothrop Motley, Stephen Vincent Benét, Howard Hanson, Robert Lowell, and Richard Stokes. Ironically, Nathaniel Hawthorne's "The Maypole of Merry Mount," the best known literary use of Morton's plantation, does not include him among its characters. Most literary allusions to Morton seem to follow a traditional line and picture him as a villain or a knave—at best a reprobate, at worst a cavalier subversive attempting to undercut the Anglo-Saxon Protestant progress of our New England forebears. Occasionally, a more favorably inclined writer will wonder, as did Leslie Fiedler, "What would have happened if it had survived, this beatnik colony in the seventeenth-century New England woods, presided over by university Bohemians—full of classical quotations, rum and deviltry" (Fiedler, 380)?

Perhaps even Morton sensed that his only significance was as an adversary. Perhaps his seemingly mad returns to New England signalled that he knew that he had a special identity only there. As Charles Francis Adams, Jr., wrote, in England Morton was indistinguishable from many who fit "the Alsatian Squire and Wild Rake type." But, again, according to Adams, "Morton chanced to get out of place. He was a vulgar Royalist libertine, thrown by accident into the midst of a Puritan community. He was unable to take himself off; and hence followed his misfortunes and his notoriety" (*Canaan*, 92).

Summary

Thomas Morton probably deserves better than a short paragraph in American literary history. Certainly, he is important to American humor. He was one of our first comic writers. His account of a lively, sensual humorist thrown into the center of a stiff, repressive, sober, single-minded, materialistic and, for him, dangerous community that has no sense of humor, no perception of the ludicrous, discovers a comic situation and set of antagonisms that reoccur throughout our culture in the works of Artemus Ward, Mark Twain, Buster Keaton, the Marx Brothers, Ring Lardner, Sinclair Lewis, Preston Sturges, Anita Loos, and Peter DeVries, just to name a few. Arguably, Morton's tale is the American comic story, or a very strong nominee. On the other hand, the sanest assessment of Morton and his book may well be that of Charles Francis Adams, Jr., himself a descendant of Puritans and by no means an enthusiastic admirer of their old adversary:

> Such solemnity, such everlasting consciousness of responsibility to God and man is grand and perhaps impressive; but it grows wearisome. It is pleasant to

have it broken at last, even though that which breaks it is in some respects not to be commended. A touch of ribaldry becomes bearable. Among what are called *Americana*, therefore, the *New Canaan* is and will always remain a refreshing book. It is a connecting link. Poor as it may be, it is yet all we have to remind us that in literature, also, Bradford and Winthrop and Cotton were Englishmen of the time of Shakespeare and Jonson and Butler.

(*Canaan*, 98)

Selected Bibliography

Primary Source

Morton Thomas. *The New English Canaan*. Ed. Charles Francis Adams, Jr. Boston: The Prince Society, 1883.

Secondary Sources

Bradford, William. *The History of Plymouth Plantation*. Boston: Houghton Mifflin, 1912.
Connors, Donald F. *Thomas Morton*. New York: Twayne, 1969. A full-length study of the author's life and writings.
Fiedler, Leslie, and Arthur Ziegler. *O Brave New World*. New York: Dell, 1968.

Michael D. Butler

Nash, Ogden

Born: Rye, New York, on August 19, 1902
Education: Harvard University, 1920–1921
Marriage: Frances Rider Leonard, 1931, two children
Died: May 19, 1971

Biography

The son of Edmund and Mattie Chenault Nash, Frederick Ogden Nash was born in Rye, New York, on August 19, 1902. After completing his secondary education at St. George's School in Newport, Rhode Island, he attended Harvard University for one year, then dropped out "to earn a living." Several attempts at careers followed: as a secondary school teacher at St. George's, a bond salesman, an advertising copy writer, and, briefly, an editorial writer at *The New Yorker*. Establishing himself as a popular author quite early in his career, he was able to give up other forms of employment and devote himself to his writing.

The earliest of Nash's publications were children's books; in 1925 he collaborated with Joseph Alger in *The Crickets of Carador*. Begin-

ning in 1931, his work appeared in the large-circulation general magazines, with many of his poems being printed in *The Saturday Evening Post*, and others appearing in *The New Yorker*, *Cosmopolitan*, *American Magazine*, *The Saturday Review of Literature*, *Harper's Bazaar*, and a wide variety of other periodicals. Solo book publication began early with *Hard Lines* and *Free Wheeling*, both volumes appearing in 1931, the same year that Nash married Francis Rider Leonard (the couple produced two children). During the 1930s and much of the 1940s, he concentrated upon poetry for adult readers, but, by 1947, he was again writing for children, and he continued this important part of his creative activity for the rest of his life. Over a period of years, he edited several anthologies and, in the theater, collaborated with S.J. Perelman on *One Touch of Venus*. This musical play, with an excellent score by Kurt Weill, opened in 1943 and had a successful Broadway run of 567 performances. He died on May 19, 1971, in Baltimore, Maryland. The extremely popular author of over 40 volumes, Nash was elected to both the American Academy of Arts and Sciences and the National Institute of Arts and Letters.

Literary Analysis

Although Nash published more than fifteen books for children, served as editor of some collections, and even worked briefly on Broadway, his chief contribution to American literature is the large body of humorous poetry written and published over a span of forty years. His poems have been immensely popular with the reading public, but they have suffered from a considerable critical injustice.

A strange dichotomy exists between what many critics believe to be "poetry" and "light verse." Poetry is said to be serious, tragic, lyrical, descriptive, amorous, political, and, somehow, worthy of one's most earnest attention. It is, plainly, "the best that has been thought and said." On the other hand, light verse is likely to be thought of as poetry only in unguarded moments. Nash's books were often reviewed as "a volume of humorous verse," and he was sometimes called "an essayist in verse" who wrote "jingles" or "comic verse." Whether or not he was a poet hardly seemed debatable. His work has eluded criticism or, perhaps, criticism has eluded him. In more than fifty years, there have been many reviews of his books, some "literary portraits" and miscellaneous pieces on the man and his writings, but critical assessment has been limited to a few pages by Morris Bishop, an excellent article by Louis Hasley, and an attractive introduction by Archibald MacLeish. Critics who have written incessantly about Robert Frost, Wallace Stevens, T.S. Eliot, or Hart Crane have avoided Nash. The horses of critical instruction—Marxist, psychoanalytic, phenomenological, deconstructive—have all trotted past Nash's elegant poetry with averted eyes.

Still, Nash has certainly written poetry, and his poems cannot all be lumped together as "light verse." In fact, within his large and impressive body of work there is great variety. True, some of the pieces are actually examples of light verse, so light as to be nearly airborne. There are brief characterizations of animals: "The cow is of the bovine ilk;/ One end is moo, the other, milk." Some animals are fixed within the reader's imagination by such lines as "He who attempts to tease the cobra/ Is soon a sadder he, and sobra." A charming bestiary, with appropriate drawings, could easily be culled from Nash's observations about our inhuman friends.

Some brief poems that tend toward homely, philosophical admonitions appear as reflections upon their topics. In his "Reflection on Caution," Nash observes that affection is a fine quality to have, "But it also leads to breach of promise/ If you go around lavishing it on red-hot momise." In another reflective poem, "Song of the Open Road," Nash begins promisingly by misquoting Joyce Kilmer: "I think that I shall never see/ A billboard lovely as a tree." But, after considering the situation, he concludes, with some gravity, "Indeed, unless the billboards fall/ I'll never see a tree at all."

Nash's longer poems often have as much weight as wit. In 1969 he assembled a thematic collection drawn from his entire body of work. The title made the theme clear: *Bed Riddance, A Posy for the Indisposed.* The poems are about illness, insomnia, dieting, discomfort, doctors, germs, and even getting well. In his introduction, the poet clearly identifies the stance taken by the poems: "I like to think that they are not altogether bitter, that they may even stir in you who are temporarily inactivated at home or in hospital some healing sense of the ludicrous aspect of human frailty." He has the very last word on women's diets: "Oh, often I am haunted/ By the thought that somebody might some day discover a diet that would let ladies reduce just as much as they wanted." He celebrates the powerful germ, "smaller than a pachyderm," and expresses annoyance with the summer cold, as "Nostrilly, tonsilly,/ It prowls irresponsilly."

A generous serving of quotations would easily reveal Nash's typical poetic devices. In his article, Hasley summarizes them succinctly:

> the irregularities are wild, the clichés
> are altered, the inversions are extreme;
> and the rhymes, elaborately contrived,
> often become outrageous word distor-

tions. Bonus additions are redundancy and vernacular grammar.[1]

To Hasley's analysis might be added Nash's penchant for making a rhymed couplet of a very long line jammed against a short one, as in "Oh, sometimes I sit around and think, what would you do if you were up a dark alley and there was Caesar Borgia,/ And he was coming torgia." Archibald MacLeish contends that a Nash poem "has *no lines* in the verse sense; the line's end is a typographical accident with Nash and it is the sentence—the infinitely extensible sentence—which bears the burden." Nash's delight in those distorted rhymes, always a visual shock, is another characteristic device: "foible/enjoible," "lioness/ your hioness," "King Midas/tonsilidas," and "laundry/double entendry," for example.

The anonymous article in *Current Biography 1941* appropriately dubbed Nash's inventive wordplay as *bouffe rime* and went on to add, justly, that he "comes out against" all of the things that readers are afraid to come out against; it might be added that he courageously praises things that readers might be afraid to praise. Head on, he attacks ganders, grackles, Philo Vance, current news, Lord Byron, cold bath water, parsnips, and wasps. But, on the other hand, he has good things to say about monsters, wealth, smelts, the ocean, turtles, and Hippolyte Adolphe Taine. He especially dislikes little boys who might grow up to marry one's favorite daughter. Perhaps he complains more than he praises; one of his last books is appropriately titled, in a quotation from Robert Frost, *The Old Dog Barks Backwards* (1972).

In reading through Nash's work, incidental pleasures abound. His titles are often miniature comments, or epigrams, or tiny poems. Consider the joys of "At Least I'm Not the Kind of Fool Who Sobs, What Kind of Fool Am I?" or "Speak to Me Only with Thine Eyes, and Please, Not Too Fast" or "Pix Sheets Top Keats Feats." For a single volume that gives the most comprehensive picture of Nash's writing, one must turn to the posthumously published *I Wouldn't Have Missed It: Selected Poems of Ogden Nash* (1975). The book offers the usual pleasures, several hundred pages of Nash's best concoctions, and some unusual pleasures as well. One is MacLeish's pertinent and affectionate introduction. Another is the section of notes appended to the volume to tell readers things that they are not at all sure they wanted to know. It informs readers, authoritatively, that the title of one of their favorite poems, "Reflection on Ice-breaking," should be "Reflections on Ice-breaking" and carefully lists variant readings in other poems. The "Index of First Lines," a useful and pleasurable addition to any large collection of a poet's works, especially for readers who like to read first lines, is followed by an inspired "Index of Last Lines," just about as readable as anything else in the volume. This index reveals much about Nash's poetic techniques. For instance, he enjoys ending poems with lines beginning with the words *and, because, I,* and *if;* the trademarks of lesser poets, *the* and *a,* are somewhat skimped. Indeed, the last lines offer genuine motivation for going back to read or reread the poems. No inquiring reader could resist "Down with the kiddies," "I hardly ever repent," or "Don't anther."

Nash's poems have not been properly recognized for what they really offer, a perceptive view of contemporary life, delivered with equanimity and aplomb, in poised, sophisticated compositions. Unfortunately, anthologists of modern American literature still neglect him. His satire is gentle, a form of badinage rather than caustic ridicule. Unlike Molière or Jonathan Swift, he does not actually hope that his raillery can change humanity. But, reading his poetry, humanity, if it has any humanity in it, might almost wish to change.

Summary

Ogden Nash is the creator of a large body of wise and fastidious poetry that deals with the often diverting aberrations of the human and inhuman animal. He points out flaws, offers advice (for whatever it is worth), celebrates, and anathematizes his subjects. Despite his levity, many of his poems possess seriousness and a genuine flair for the didactic, though he is usually successful in suppressing that side of his nature. Finally, then, Nash's popularity both during his lifetime and to the present rests on his ability to express his lessons and observations in lyrics (that sometimes convey a message and sometimes do not) that is in itself amusing because of its preposterous play with sound and startling conceptual juxtapositions and imagery. He remains the foremost creator of light verse in American literature.

Note

1. Louis Hasley, "The Golden Trashery of Ogden Nashery," *Arizona Quarterly*, 27 (Autumn 1971): 241.

Selected Bibliography

Primary Sources
Hard Lines. New York: Simon and Schuster, 1931.
I'm a Stranger Here Myself. Boston: Little, Brown, 1938.
Good Intentions. Boston: Little, Brown, 1942.
Versus. Boston: Little, Brown, 1949.
You Can't Get There from Here. Boston: Little, Brown, 1957.
Verses from 1929 On. Boston: Little, Brown, 1959.

Bed Riddance: A Posy for the Indisposed. Boston: Little, Brown, 1970.
The Old Dog Barks Backwards. Boston: Little, Brown, 1972.
I Wouldn't Have Missed It. Boston: Little, Brown, 1975.

Children's Books
(with Joseph Alger.) *The Cricket of Carador.* Garden City: Doubleday, Page, 1925.
Parents Keep Out: Elderly Poems for Youngerly Readers. Boston: Little, Brown, 1951.
The Christmas That Almost Wasn't. Boston: Little, Brown, 1957.
The Cruise of the Aardvark. New York: Evans, 1967.

Secondary Sources
Arnold, St. George Tucker, Jr. "Ogden Nash." In *Dictionary of Literary Biography.* Vol. 11. *American Humorists, 1800-1950.* Vol. 2. Ed. Stanley Trachtenberg. Detroit: Gale, 1982, pp. 331–344. A good summary account of Nash's life and career.
Axford, Lavonne B. *An Index to the Poems of Ogden Nash.* Metuchen, N.J.: Scarecrow Press, 1972. A helpful bibliographic volume.
Bishop, Morris. "Light Verse in America." In *The Comic Imagination in American Literature.* Ed. Louis D. Rubin, Jr. New Brunswick, N.J.: Rutgers University Press, 1973, pp. 259–273. Only a few pages are about Nash, but they contain perceptive insights.
Gale, Steven H. *S.J. Perelman: A Critical Study.* Westport, Conn.: Greenwood, 1987. Includes brief commentary on Nash's contributions to *One Touch of Venus.*
Hasley, Louis. "The Golden Trashery of Ogden Nashery." *Arizona Quarterly,* 27 (Autumn 1971): 241–250. An excellent article.
MacLeish, Archibald. "Introduction" to *I Wouldn't Have Missed It: Selected Poems of Ogden Nash.* Ed. Linnel Smith and Isabel Eberstadt. Boston: Little, Brown, 1972. A fine brief comment on Nash.
Sanders, Ronald. *The Days Grow Short: The Life and Music of Kurt Weill.* New York: Holt, Rinehart and Winston, 1980. A brief account (pp. 323, 324, 331) of Nash's role in *One Touch of Venus.*

Douglas Robillard

Newell, Robert Henry

Born: New York City, on December 13, 1836

Education: Private academy, New York

Marriage: Adah Isaacs Menken, September 24, 1862, divorced, 1865

Died: July 1901

Biography

Robert Henry Newell, familiar to mid-nineteenth-century readers as Orpheus C. Kerr, grew up in a comfortable middle-class home in New York in the 1840s and 50s. He was born in New York City on December 13, 1836. His father, Robert, Sr., was an inventor of bank locks whose successes earned gold medals at fairs and exhibitions in London and Vienna. The private schooling that the Newells were able to provide for their son ended in 1854 with the father's death. Robert Henry was forced by the family's straitened circumstances to forego college. Shortly after his father's death, he began writing for a variety of New York newspapers and quickly earned a position as assistant editor with the *Mercury*, one of the city's largest dailies. From 1858 to 1876 Newell worked as a correspondent and editor for several New York publications, including the *Herald, World, Daily Graphic,* and *Hearth and Home.*

With the outbreak of the Civil War, Newell achieved celebrity as the author of a series of fictional letters from Washington, D.C., that spoofed the hordes of office seekers whose appearance in the capitol at the beginning of the Lincoln administration was a national joke. *The Orpheus C. Kerr Papers,* as the letters came to be known, were widely read in the Northeast and appeared in collected form in three volumes between 1862 and 1865. His success during the period was capped by a marriage in 1862 to the celebrated actress Adah Isaacs Menken, who divorced him three years later.

Newell thought of himself as a *litterateur* rather than as a humorist and so turned his full energies following the end of the war to writing poetry and serious fiction: two volumes of verse—*The Palace Beautiful* (1865) and *Versatilities* (1871)—fared poorly, as did *Avery Gliburn; or, Between Two Fires* (1867), a romance; *The Cloven Foot* (1870) was an effort to complete Dickens's *The Mystery of Edwin Drood* in an American setting; and *The Walking Doll; or, the Asters and Disasters of Society* (1872) was a novel of manners. Newell's output diminished in the early 1870s because of severe ill health. As early as 1864, a nervous disorder had led to a year's leave of absence from his newspaper work (during which time he traveled in California) and no doubt contributed to the breakup of his marriage. By 1876, he was unable to work at all and spent the next quarter century in obscure retirement interrupted only by *Studies in Stanzas* (1882) and *There Was Once a Man* (1884), a satirical novel on the Darwinian theme of the descent of man. Newell died at his home in Brooklyn, New York, during the first week of July in 1901.

Literary Analysis

As a humorist, Newell's major accomplishment was the *Orpheus C. Kerr Papers,* a series of over one hundred Chesterfieldian letters addressed to a correspondent identified only as "my boy," which detail the adventures of an office seeker in Washington, D.C. Failing to gain an appointment, Kerr spends his days on horseback observing the affairs of a Union regiment called the Mackeral Brigade. The brigade's efforts to defend the capitol and the follies and shenanigans of its officer corps make up the subject matter of the majority of the letters. On the basis of these materials, Newell has consistently been placed by critics and historians in the company of the Civil War satirists, David R. Locke (Petroleum V. Nasby) and Charles Henry Smith (Bill Arp) in particular, and has suffered by comparison. Where Locke and Smith were pointed, even vicious, Newell seldom went beyond a flabby criticism of the political climate in Washington, of the patronage system, and of the neutral or "no party" men on whose ineptitude or indecisiveness Newell placed the blame for the slow prosecution of the war. Few specific personalities or events could be identified as targets of Newell's wit, at least in part a result of his approaching his subject second hand through published newspaper accounts of the war. His consistent objective was a broad picture of incompetence characterized by a poorly guided and ill-equipped army sloshing about month in and month out in the mud of the Potomac River basin.

The *Papers* are far more interesting, particularly the first series (1862), if read from a literary rather than historical perspective. What Newell accomplished, apart from whatever satirical intentions he may have had, was a seamless combination of most of the conventions of humor familiar to the theater-going and reading public of New York. Among the characters whom Kerr meets in Washington are Irish volunteer firemen in the "Mose the B'howery B'hoy" mold, blacks modeled on minstrel clowns, Down East Yankees patterned after James Russell Lowell's rustics, and drunks and roughnecks all of whose antics are held together by the witty erudition and fatuous urbanity of the author. Kerr was no Nasby or Arp but rather a comic portrait in the gallery of New York humor that included Washington Irving's Jonathan Oldstyle and Mortimer M. Thompson's Q.K. Philander Doesticks. With a degree of mock heroic hyperbole drawn from the tradition of the English comic novel, particularly Dickens, and with a gift for Pickwickian-styled caricature, Newell sent Kerr to the front lines aboard his "gothic steed Pegasus," accompanied by his "frescoed dog Bologna," who, like the old guard of France, was "always around the bony parts thrown." Kerr's letters were at all points erudite and witty, revealing Newell's wide reading in the classics and his mastery of comic devices spanning the gamut from dialect humor to polyglot puns. Newell even included examples of his own bathetic poetry and achieved some of his most striking humor in several literary burlesques. These include a truncated romance by Gushalina Crushit, a parody of Edgar Allan Poe's "The Raven" called "Baltimore," and an account of a national anthem writing contest with entries from such American poets as Henry Wadsworth Longfellow, James Greenleaf Whittier, William Cullen Bryant, Oliver Wendell Holmes, Ralph Waldo Emerson, Richard Henry Stoddard, and Thomas Bailey Aldrich.

Summary

Robert Henry Newell, writing as Orpheus C. Kerr, produced a series of comic letters satirizing Union incompetence during the Civil War and created one of the wittier comic personae in the school of humor associated with mid-century New York literary circles.

Selected Bibliography

Primary Sources
Reconstruction. New York: The American News Company, n.d.
The Orpheus C. Kerr Papers. New York: Blakeman and Mason, 1862.
The Orpheus C. Kerr Papers, Second Series. New York: Carleton, 1863.
The Orpheus C. Kerr Papers, First-Third Series. New York: Carleton, 1864–1865.
The Martyr President. New York: Carleton, 1865.
The Palace Beautiful and Other Poems. New York: Carleton, 1865.
Comicalities. New York: J.C. Haney, 1866.
Avery Gliburn; or, Between Two Fires. New York: G.W. Carleton, 1867.
Smoked Glass. New York: G.W. Carleton, 1868.
The Cloven Foot: Being an Adaptation of the English Novel "The Mystery of Edwin Drood" to American Scenes, Characters, Customs and Nomenclatures. New York: Carleton, 1870.
Varsatilities. New York: Lee, Shepard and Dillingham, 1871.
The Walking Doll; or, the Asters and Disasters of Society. New York: F.B. Felt, 1872.
Studies in Stanzas. New York: The Useful Knowledge, 1882.
There Was Once a Man. New York: Fords, Howard and Hulbert, 1884.
Secondary Sources
Butler, Michael. "Robert Henry Newell." In *Dictionary of Literary Biography.* Vol. 11. *American Humorists, 1800–1950.* Ed. Stanley Trachtenberg. Detroit: Gale, 1982, pp. 350–359. An overview of Newell's writing, in a biographical context.
Dictionary of American Biography. New York: Scribners, 1962. Vol. 7, pp. 458–459.
The National Cyclopedia of American Biography. Vol. 11. Ann Arbor, Mich.: University Microfilms, 1967, p. 528.
Tandy, Jennette. *Crackerbox Philosophers in American Humor and Satire.* New York: Columbia University Press, 1925, pp. 118–120.
Trent, W.P. "A Retrospect of American Humor," *Century Magazine,* November, 1901, pp. 45–64.
Who's Who in America, 1901–02, p. 826.

Gary Engle

Noland, Charles Fenton Mercer

Born: Loudoun County, Virginia, in August 1810
Education: West Point, 1823–1825
Marriage: Lucretia Ringgold, 1840
Died: June 23, 1858

Biography

Charles Fenton Mercer Noland, Virginia gentleman and friend of presidents, was at the same time a teller of tall tales and a legendary desperado of the Old Southwest. His life encompassed both Tidewater Virginia and the Ozarks of Arkansas. Ted R. Worley of the Arkansas Historical Association has said, "Noland never became a Pete Whetstone mountaineer, nor did he remain an Old Dominion aristocrat."[1]

Noland was born in Loudoun County, Virginia, in 1810, the child of Catherine Callender and William Noland. Although little is known of his childhood, most of the information concerning his parents suggests that he was reared among the socially elite. His father was a prominent churchman, a member of the Virginia Legislature,[2] and a friend of at least two presidents, Monroe and Tyler.[3] Catherine Callender was a descendant of the very prominent Gibson family of Pennsylvania with whom Major André of Revolutionary War notoriety had visited.[4]

Fenton Noland's first venture outside of his home came in 1823 when he accepted C.F. Mercer's appointment to West Point. Records of his performance at the academy are scant; those that are available indicate that he performed poorly in his two years there, that his bearing was "more vivacious than military."[5] In 1825, Noland was dismissed from the academy for deficiency in drawing and mathematics and soon thereafter joined his father who had accepted President Monroe's appointment to the Arkansas Land Office in Batesville. Fenton was put to work immediately studying law in the office of Judge Woodson Bates, who, as first territorial delegate to Congress, was heavily involved in the politics of Arkansas.

In the fall of 1827 the elder Noland returned to his family in the East, but Fenton, only 17 years old at that time, remained in Arkansas in the home of Judge Bates. In the absence of his father, Fenton soon became very close to several of the old settlers who passed along a great store of backwoods knowledge that allowed him to identify even more completely with the life of the frontier.

Noland's political interests began to draw him into Arkansas Territory politics. Partisan political connections eventually led Noland to write scorching attacks on the opposition in the *Arkansas Advocate* that culminated in a duel with Governor Pope's nephew in which Noland fatally wounded the young man.[6] Noland remained in Batesville as the deputy clerk of the Circuit Court until June 15, 1831, when after Pope's death he left Arkansas Territory—most probably in an attempt to remove himself from the area of the fatal shooting.

He returned to his home at Aldie, Virginia, but the life of the Southwest was too much a part of him for him to remain away from it for long. Upon returning to Arkansas he entered law and was confirmed as a member of the bar in 1836. At the time of the Constitutional Convention for the newly born state, he was selected by his friend C. P. Bertram (editor of the *Advocate*) to carry the State Constitution to Washington.[7] It was this trip to Washington that brought forth Noland's first-known contribution to William T. Porter's *The Spirit of the Times*. He remained in Virginia until the middle of June, during which time several of his letters were printed in Porter's magazine.

Soon after his return to Arkansas in September he was elected to the state legislature as the representative from Independence County and continued to write as a correspondent for Porter's paper. By 1840 his reputation with the New York periodical had grown sufficiently that he became America's first reporter for the *London Sporting Magazine* (April 11, 1840). That same year he married Lucretia Ringgold, the daughter of "the most prominent of the early settlers of Batesville," and withdrew from his law practice to assume duties as land agent and editor of the *Batesville Eagle*.[8] His position as editor of this Whig paper kept his attention focused on politics and, together with his special correspondence and other outside interests, began to reduce his correspondence with *The Spirit of the Times*. His ability as a newspaper editor is not known, but some measure of his success can be seen in his move in 1845 to the *Arkansas Gazette* and a later offer he received, but declined, from a Memphis paper.[9]

In 1842, sickness, which had dogged him through a long part of his life, forced him to almost abandon his correspondence with *The Spirit of the Times*. He was elected once again to the legislature in 1846, but was not returned thereafter. While in Little Rock he served as receiver of the bank, but the weakening effects of tuberculosis left him unable to work and on June 23, 1858, he died.[10]

Literary Analysis

Noland's place in the newspaper literature of his own day was substantial. His first sketches, beginning in 1836, were apparently the earliest of the original humorous contributions for which *The Spirit of the Times* became celebrated; his constant communication from 1836 to 1858 made him the most frequent correspondent Porter's paper ever had. He was variously labeled as "our favorite correspondent" (Vol. 6, p. 341, December 10, 1936), a "household word" (Vol. 28, p. 291, July 31, 1858), and the "most popular correspondent of the *Spirit of the Times*" (Porter, *Bear*, 143).

His work and reputation were not confined to that periodical; his correspondence was printed in the *London Sporting Magazine*, where he was noted as "the only American writer who figures to manifest advantage in the English Sporting Magazines." He was also included in humor collections such as *Thorpe's Scene in Arkansas*, which featured his "Playing Poker in Arkansas."[11]

Noland was the product of an aristocratic Virginia heritage, but he spent over half his life on or near the frontier. This combination of eastern heritage and frontier experience shaped his writing, establishing him as a part of the tension-ridden genre of Southwestern humor. Horse racing was the vehicle that first won Noland attention as a correspondent for *The Spirit of the Times*; in his first letters he referred to famous horses, fashionable breeders, and genteel life in the South. But, his more raucous sketches drawn from his frontier experience established his reputation. He created Van Swanrigen, who took a cow into dangerous Indian country, and Major Mason, who killed a "rabbit running and partridge flying with one shot." Even in these earliest pieces, descriptions of Arkansas as a place where "Derringers and big knives are fashionable" and the "people are occasionally rough in their manners" are balanced with good feelings for the "kind, warm-hearted, generous people." As he continued to write, he became adept at producing correspondence that cast a genteel eye toward the track and other sketches that celebrated the free-wheeling life of the new territory. His divided loyalties could not be integrated into single pieces of writing. Some pieces were written under the heading, "From a Virginia Correspondent" but signed "N. of Arkansas." It was not until he began to concentrate on character development with a zestful delight in the voice and manner of the rustic heroes that some integration began to be realized. His keen ear for authentically rough oaths and his mastery of their tall tales and humorous sketches allowed him to fashion his best-realized character, Pete Whetstone. His brash persona was a major accomplishment in that Pete was the first character of the frontier in a series of tales to speak as an entity separate from his creator. This unique persona was Noland's means of channeling his voice and ideals through another personality and thereby expressing his new-found devotion to southwestern life. This creation allowed him to write as C.F.M. Noland, the Whig, and then speak through the voice of Pete Whetstone, the frontier man. His Whetstone letters were so authentic in voice and event that many local Arkansas readers took the pose to be fact rather than fiction. These early pieces were notable in that Noland was able to develop a sustained voice, multiple characters, interior dialogue, the beginnings of a sophisticated story line, and a clear sense of place. His tales were peppered with undermined authorities, bullies and braggarts, rough customers and pretentious Easterners, and endless fights. As the Whetstone series continued, Noland's techniques matured. He developed a good sense of dramatic action, a shrewd use of repetition, and a nice control of exaggeration. To this body of correspondence he added Pete's attacks on local Jacksonian Democrats as phony frontiersmen. This politization of Pete undermined some of his duality, but Noland was still celebrating the very ideals which the Whigs distrusted through Pete's essential personality. Thus, the tension was continued even in these most partisan sketches.

Two early humorists seem to have been major influences on Noland: Augustus Baldwin Longstreet and Davy Crockett. From Longstreet he adopted a spectator style that contrasted an intentionally high-toned language with the raw dialect of the Southwest. Like Longstreet he effectively exaggerated both styles to develop contrast. From Crockett, he copied almost directly the use of a frontier pose for political gain. His attacks on Campbell and other Democrats were clearly inherited from Crockett's merciless political style.

Noland's influence possibly radiates to the work of his contemporaries Thorpe and Hooper, and to Mark Twain, who brought the talents of all of the southwestern humorists to their perfection, and may even be found in modern literature's best representative of the region, William Faulkner.

Summary

Charles Fenton Mercer Noland was a Virginia gentleman who moved to the Arkansas Territory and became captivated by the unsettled life of the frontier. The letters that he wrote to *The Spirit of the Times* about the robust life the old Southwest had great appeal for eastern readers. Noland's Whig politics and Virginian gentility flow out of his letters, but an equal zest for the raucous folk of the new settlement is embedded in his work. The characters he included in his early writing began to gain more attention and grew to be bigger than life as his reputation as a correspondent grew. The most notable of these creations was Pete Whetstone. He was full of fun and frontier wisdom, and as Noland let Pete's voice become dominant his fame in *The Spirit of the Times* increased. Noland's numerous entries were so popular that he was the best-known contributor to that important periodical. His fame was such that he was asked to contribute to the *London Sporting Magazine* as well, and his work provides a foretaste of Twain and Faulkner. He was a truly significant early American humorist.

Notes

1. Ted R. Worley, "An Early American Sportsman: C.F.M. Noland," *Arkansas Historical Quarterly*, 11 (Spring 1952): 14.
2. William Meade, *Old Churches, Ministers, and Families of Virginia* (Philadelphia: J.B. Lippincott, 1857), Vol. I, p. 278.
3. Josiah H. Shinn, "The Life and Public Services of Charles Fenton Mercer Noland," *Publications of the Arkansas Historical Association* (Vol. I, ed. John H. Reynolds, Fayetteville, Ark., 1906), p. 332.
4. Ibid., p. 331.
5. Worley, p. 3.
6. William J. Pope, *Early Days in Arkansas* (Little Rock: Allsopp, 1895), p. 119.
7. Alfred Arringon, *The Lives and Adventures of the Desperadoes of the South-West* (New York: W.H. Graham, 1849), pp. 73–74.
8. I.N. Barnett, "Early Days of Batesville," *Arkansas Historical Quarterly*, 11 (Spring 1952): 15–16.
9. James R. Masterson, *Tall Tales of Arkansaw* (Boston: Chapman and Grimes, 1943), p. 32.
10. Worley, p. 16.
11. Ed. William T. Porter (Philadelphia, 1858), p. 18.

Selected Bibliography

Primary Sources

"Playing Poker in Arkansas." *Colonel Thorpe's Scenes in Arkansas.* Ed. William T. Porter. Philadelphia, 1858.

Secondary Sources

Arkansas Gazette, January 1–February 1, 1831.

Arkansas, *Journals of the Special Sessions of the General Assembly of the State of Arkansas,* 1836.

Arrington, Alfred. *The Lives and Adventures of the Desperadoes of the South-West.* New York: Graham, 1849. A romantic if not mythic account of frontier folk that includes an overblown account of Noland as a desperado rather than a duelist.

Baldwin, Joseph Glover. *The Flush Times of Alabama and Mississippi.* New York, 1853.

Barnett, I.N. "Early Days of Batesville." *Arkansas Historical Quarterly,* 11 (Spring 1952): 15–23.

Blair, Walter. *Native American Humor (1800–1900).* New York: American, 1937. An important account of the literary antecedents of Twain. Blair pays particular attention to the historical context of this humor.

Brinley, Francis. *The Life of William T. Porter.* New York: Appleton, 1860. A contemporary account of the life of the famous sportsman–editor.

Gilman, Daniel C. *James Monroe.* Boston: Houghton, 1899.

Lynn, Kenneth. *Mark Twain and Southwestern Humor.* Boston: Little, Brown, 1960. A consideration of the political intentions of Twain and the humorists who predated him. Lynn claims that they all wrote in a spirit of Whig condescension.

Masterson, James R. *Tall Tales of Arkansaw.* Boston: Chapman and Grimes, 1943.

Meade, William. *Old Churches, Ministers, and Families of Virginia.* Vol. I. Philadelphia: Lippincott, 1857. A glowing account of the famous ecclesiastical forefathers of the Old Dominion.

Newberry, Farrar. "Some Notes on Robert Crittenden." *Arkansas Historical Quarterly,* 16 (Autumn 1957): 243–256.

Pope, William F. *Early Days in Arkansas.* Little Rock: Allsopp, 1895. An account of the political wars of Arkansas's days as a territory.

Porter, William T., ed. *The Big Bear of Arkansas and Other Sketches.* Philadelphia: Carey and Hart, 1845.

———. *A Quarter Race in Kentucky and Other Sketches.* Philadelphia: Carey and Hart, 1847.

Rickels, Milton. *Thomas Bangs Thorpe.* Baton Rouge: Louisiana State University Press, 1962. The best assessment of Thorpe's life and literary contributions.

Seager, Robert. *and Tyler too.* New York: McGraw-Hill, 1963. A good review of the Van Buren–Tyler years.

Shinn, Josiah H. "The Life and Public Services of Charles Fenton Mercer Noland." *Publications of the Arkansas Historical Association.* Vol. I. Ed. John H. Reynolds. Fayetteville, Ark., 1906.

White, Lonnie J. "The Pope Noland Duel of 1831." *Arkansas Historical Quarterly,* 22 (Summer 1963): 117–123.

Worley, Ted R. "An Early American Sportsman: C.F.M. Noland." *Arkansas Historical Quarterly,* 11 (Spring 1952): 25–39. A short account of Noland's life and literary efforts.

———. "The Story of Alfred W. Arrington." *Arkansas Historical Quarterly,* 14 (Winter 1955): 315–339.

Yates, Norris B. *William T. Porter and the "Spirit of the Times."* Baton Rouge: Louisiana State University Press, 1957. The best account of the brilliant editor of the important newspaper *The Spirit of the Times.*

Joseph O. Milner

Nye, Edgar Wilson [Bill]

Born: Shirley, Maine, on August 25, 1850
Education: Elementary school in Hudson and River Falls, Wisconsin
Marriage: Clara Frances Smith, 1877, four children
Died: February 22, 1897

Biography

Born to poor Yankee farm folk in Shirley, Maine, Edgar Wilson (Bill) Nye was two years old when the family moved and ultimately settled near the town of Hudson, Wisconsin, where the family again began to farm. Twenty-three years later, frustrated by a lack of career opportunities, Nye traveled west as far as Cheyenne where his money ran out. He turned for help in finding a job to John T. Jenkins, a friend who formerly practiced law in Wisconsin. Aware of Nye's journalistic experience, Jenkins introduced him to J.H. Hayford, editor of the *Daily Sentinel* in nearby Laramie.

Nye had received a modest formal education, first at an academy in Hudson and then at a military school in River Falls, the village nearest the family farm. He learned something about farming, of course, and spent some time working for a local miller. He also tried teaching school at thirty dollars a month, reading for the law, and writing for newspapers. He worked for the Hudson *Star* and the Chippewa Falls *Weekly Herald,* as well, but he tried without success to get full-time employment on midwestern newspapers.

Not quite a decade old, Laramie was in need of professional people when it gave Nye immediate opportunities in both journalism and law. His first full-time newspaper job came from Hayford who, in May 1876, hired him as assistant editor of the *Sentinel* for twelve dollars a week. On the *Sentinel* Nye could display the gift for humor that helped to make him one of the best-known men in the territory. His articles on the weather, landscape, western customs, mining, and miners revealed a genuine fondness for his new home, and the people of the territory responded in kind. The humorist was discovering himself and being discovered. Among the honors Laramie bestowed upon its most popular wit was the chairmanship of the Forty Liars Club.

For all of his popular success as a newspaperman, Nye clung to the family's ambition that the sons achieve distinction in the law. (Two brothers became distinguished judges in Minnesota, one serving for a time in Congress.) Within his first year in Laramie, Nye passed the bar examination and sought to establish a law practice. While he never achieved financial success as a lawyer, he did become a notary public, a justice of the peace, and a United States land commissioner. A favorable turn in political fortunes made him postmaster of Laramie.

Although he left the *Sentinel* to take his chances as a lawyer, Nye continued to write for the *Laramie Times*, the *Cheyenne Sun*, and the *Denver Tribune* (which paid him seven dollars for each "Letter" he contributed). By 1881 he was certain that his future lay in journalism. Financed by Republicans who shared his political views, Nye was cofounder and first editor of another newspaper in Laramie which he named after his mule, Boomerang. The *Boomerang* enjoyed an influence and popularity as a daily and a weekly that far exceeded its peak daily circulation of 300. Nye wrote humor columns for the daily which he combined and printed on the first page of the weekly. These columns contributed importantly to the paper's success, won subscribers for the weekly from many parts of the nation, and provided the substance of Nye's first three books.

Four years earlier, Bill Nye had married Clara Frances Smith of Illinois, endowing her, as he remarked, with his poverty. Fortunately, by 1881 their prospects for a reasonably good life had substantially improved. With income from the postmastership and other newspapers (irregularly from the *Boomerang*) and with the two of four children born to them who reached adulthood, the Nyes seemed destined to remain in Laramie. However, Nye was felled by cerebrospinal meningitis in 1883. He recuperated in Greeley, Colorado, but never fully regained his health and strength. On the advice of his doctor, he moved back to the lower elevations of Hudson, Wisconsin, where he remained for three years in a house that he jovially named Slippery-elmhurst.

Nye came back to Wisconsin a budding celebrity. The Laramie years, which ended with a comic "Resign" from the postmastership, had given him a most rewarding apprenticeship and early maturity as a writer. It had also given him his first two books, *Bill Nye and Boomerang* (1881) and *Forty Liars and Other Lies* (1882), and the material for a third book completed in Wisconsin, *Baled Hay* (1884).

At Slipperyelmhurst Nye capitalized upon opportunities that came with increasing public recognition. He also developed new materials, including a series of "Dear Henry" letters containing the humorous philosophical notions of an old-fashioned farmer and his newfangled son. In addition, there were such adventures as getting caught in a cyclone and being tossed violently about and injured. After recovering from this brush with disaster, Nye wrote another comic resignation piece: "My position as United States Cyclonist for this Judicial District is now vacant. I resigned on the 9th day of September, A.D. 1884." While claiming the "necessary personal magnetism to look a cyclone in the eye and make it quail," he confessed that "when a Manitoba simoon takes me by the brow of my pantaloons and throws me across Township 28, Range 18, West of the 5th Principal Meridian, I lose my mental reserve and become anxious and even taciturn."

Nye's first taste of performing as comic lecturer came during the Wisconsin interlude. In the spring of 1885 he performed in Duluth, Superior, and Cumberland. "The Bronco Cow" was especially well received, demonstrating that the Laramie material would serve him well. In May of that year he went east at the urging of Charles H. Taylor of the Boston *Globe* to perform in New York and Boston. He arrived in the latter city carrying a letter from George Parsons Lathrop introducing him to William Dean Howells.

During the years at Slipperyelmhurst, Nye made his first attempts to write plays. He wrote two, *Gas Fixtures* and *The Village Postmaster* (1886). The latter play drew upon Nye's experiences as postmaster and contained some of his Laramie friends as characters. In 1891 this play was revised, renamed *The Cadi*, and put on the stage in New York City where it ran for 125 performances, a long run for that time. (In 1895 *The Stag Party*, coauthored by Paul M. Potter, lasted 12 performances at New York's Garden Theater.)

But, the most spectacular success of the Slipperyelmhurst years, and a harbinger of successes to come, was Nye's appearance in Indianapolis with old friend Eugene Field of the Denver *Tribune* and the Hoosier poet James Whitcomb Riley. To a standing-room-only audience Field presented the "Romance of a Waterbury Watch," Riley recited "Deer Crick" and "Fessler's Bees," and one of Nye's comic successes was a recollection of his earlier brush with disaster, "Robust Cyclones." Thereafter, Riley and Nye—billed as the "Twins of Genius"—made one of the most successful and profitable lecturing teams of the era.[1]

A record-breaking snowstorm in North Carolina where the Nye family wintered in 1886 inspired Nye to send a letter, "In My Sunny Southern Home," to the New York *World* (circulation 252,000, then the largest in America). It so took the fancy of John Cockerill and Joseph Pulitzer that they published it and offered Nye $150 per week for a weekly humor column. Three years later the *World* would pay Nye a thousand dollars a week and expenses to cover the Paris Exposition. After a modest start Nye and Riley were also doing handsomely with Major James B. Pond's Lyceum Bureau. The "Twins of Genius" had remarkable success from 1888 through 1890, with Nye earning up to $30,000 per year. Tired of the exhausting tours, Riley quit in 1890, but Nye continued to perform.

Many of Nye's experiences as traveler and observer found their way into his books. His developing skills and broadening perspectives are reflected in the pieces that he published in *Remarks* (1887).[2] His identification with the growing masses of Americans who travel is expressed in the popular *Nye and Riley's Railway Guide* (1888). *Bill Nye's Chestnuts Old and New* is, like *Remarks*, a book made up of previously published newspaper columns. Like the *Railway Guide*, *Thinks* (1888) consists of an often droll variety of short pieces for the amusement of the traveler. The second article, "A Patent Oratorical Steam Organette for Railroad Stumping," has fun with both politics and railroad traveling.

Nye's most enduring popular works came toward the end of his life. They are *Bill Nye's History of the United States* (1894) and *Bill Nye's History of England from the Druids to the Reign of Henry VIII* (1896). The latter book was produced at the urging of J.B. Lippincott, who sought to capitalize on the success of the first history. It succeeds less well because Nye's death prevented its completion and because the subject did not excite the full range of Nye's interests and comic abilities. In the *History of the United States* Frederick B. Opper's illustration of a bemused Uncle Sam confronting Bill Nye in fool's cap and motley richly suggests the attitude that Nye took toward American history. The comic perspective at work is indicated by bogus bibliographies (for instance, "The Crow Indian and His Caws, by Me") and bogus historical notes. But, it is more vividly suggested by such incongruous juxtapositions as that of Balboa with Kope Elias, "who first discovered in the mountains of North Carolina what is now known as moonshine whiskey." A final volume of sketches and essays, *A Guest of the Ludlow* (1897), was in press when Nye died.

Literary Analysis

Critics differ as to whether Nye wrote his best humor during the Laramie, Wyoming, years (1876–1883) or surpassed those early efforts with a more varied, more sophisticated humor during the last years of his life.[3] The question of when he excelled aside, Bill Nye was always funny and always prolific. His son Jim estimated that the humorist wrote more than three million words for publication, the greater number of them during his twenty years of newspaper writing. There were also two plays and a collaboration on a third, two comic histories, an almanac, a novel, and some verse.[4] Scholars agree that the West was an important influence on Nye's work, tempering the outlook and seasoning the wit that made him one of the most popular humorists of the late nineteenth century. Even the name "Bill" was a gift of the West, an insistence of Wyoming citizens who associated him with the Bill Nye of Bret Harte's poem "Plain Language from Truthful James."

Had they intuited the emerging comic abilities of Nye, westerners would have emphasized the word "language" in Harte's title more than the name "Bill," for language is a major source of Nye's humor. He seizes the catchy "pop" phrases of the day—as in "olive oil" (*au revoir*). He yokes Biblical language with the deflating commonplace: "Pride goeth before destruction and a haughty spirit before a plunk." In a playful mood he conjures up Vaseline Tubbs, who catches a cold in her first name. Though sparing with malapropisms, he enjoys the lady emerging from the public bath "covered with ermine." It was as humorist as well as justice of the peace in Laramie that he took the measure of robbers: "They were disagreeable men in some respects and yet they did much to elevate the stage, especially the Rock Creek and Black Hill stages." He loved tomfoolery with Latin and other languages. Amused by sumptuous carriages in Central Park, he envisions them with appropriate crests, including one crest that "consisted of a towel-rack penchant, with cockroach regardant, holding in his beak a large red tape-worm on which was inscribed 'spiritus frumenti, cum homo tomorrow.'" He delighted as well in mixing technical and lay terms in writing bogus assays. The report on ore specimen no. 35832 contains a note cataloging various rocks, including malachite and schist; it ends with the assayer's advice to quit the claim: "I think that would be schist about as good as anything you could do."

The West loved such playfulness with language and encouraged Nye to make it a lifelong interest. But, for all his playing with words, Nye was a disciplined writer who usually eschewed the comic misspellings and clots of substandard language resorted to by other literary comedians (but not the mixed metaphors, anticlimaxes, and comic catalogs). Most of his humor comes in the voice of a somewhat zany but literate man. How does one get to Ludlow Street jail?—"fire a shotgun into a Sabbath-school." "I like Washington," President Cleveland remarks in a sketch, "where respectability is not a hobby." Some Nye witticisms were on everyone's lips—for example, "Yesterday I made New Year's calls, I am told."

Nye's popularity continued after his death. Publishers reprinted various volumes, issued new collections of his work, and included selections in volumes containing works by other writers of humor. *The Funny Fellow's Grab Bag* (1903) is one such posthumous volume that includes some of Nye's work, along with that of other humorists. Thirty years after his death, his son Frank Wilson (Jim) Nye could truthfully write that Bill Nye was so well remembered that a book depicting his career had a ready audience. It did indeed. *Bill Nye: His Own Life Story, with Continuity by Frank Wilson Nye* was warmly received in 1926.

More than a century has passed since Bill Nye published his first squib (1876) in the *Sentinel* about a worker who fell off the roof of a building in Laramie and landed hard—but kept his pipe from going out. By the time of his death in 1896, Nye had achieved a popular status equal to that of any other American humorist, and he was linked with Mark Twain in the public mind. As Midwesterners who went west to discover their pen names and initiate their careers as humorists, they had much in common. They corresponded in friendly fashion as equals, revealing mutual respect and appreciation. They dined together with mutual friends. On occasion they appeared together at such functions as the meeting of the International Copyright League (New York, November 28–29, 1887). Furthermore, Twain introduced Nye and Riley when the twins of genius first appeared together in Boston.

Today, Twain clearly transcends the era more successfully than Nye. In this respect it is significant that Nye's first and last books are compilations of previously published newspaper columns. Most of Nye's *oeuvre* consists of such material, pieces that respond to the interests and events of the day. Unlike Twain, Nye is thus limited to the daily or weekly newspaper column—a limitation of quotidian perspective, of size, and hence of imaginative possibilities. As the events which inspired Nye to write fade in interest and immediacy, the humor, however scintillating, loses its impact, in contrast to Twain's humor which is often found in contexts of sustained and ever-increasing interest.

Another important difference is that Twain had the ability to create a host of immortal characters—Simon Wheeler, Tom Sawyer, Huck Finn. By contrast, Nye has but one substantial character and that is "Bill" Nye. Nye uses "Bill" well, often brilliantly, to expose follies by making him, like the naive Mark of *Roughing It*, the butt of jests and the victim of mishaps. Yet, Sam Clemens would have a far different reputation in literary history if Mark Twain had been his one major character. As Mark Twain, for example, Clemens could never have told the adventures of Huck Finn and thereby changed the course of American literature.

Summary

His limitations notwithstanding, Bill Nye repays those who read him. He is a gifted humorist whose fresh and lively prose holds up very well. Editions of selected works continue to be issued, especially by university presses, and rightly so. It is frequently the office of the talented, lesser writer to reveal more of his times than does the major figure. If that is to be Nye's office, he performs it with abundant good humor. His interests were broad; his prejudices, blatantly faithful reflections of his era. Hence, he continues to interest scholars. His still popular *History of the United States* has been republished. All of this continuing interest reflects his importance to American humor. Any man who would post a sign inviting visitors to climb the stair to his office or to "twist the tail of the iron-gray mule and take the elevator" is not simply an inveterate humorist, he is also a man who commands attention.

Notes

1. Eyewitness accounts describe Nye as an exceptional stage performer. Tall and comically bald, he adopted a solemn look and a sepulchral voice when he said something funny. Audiences found the visual and aural effects of his presentations irresistible. "Nye is simply superb," Riley wrote his friend George Hitt, "and no newspaper report can halfway reproduce either the curious charm of his drollery—his improvisations—inspirations and so forth." *Bill Nye: His Own Life Story, with Continuity by Frank Wilson Nye* (New York: The Century Company, 1926), p. 146.
2. The most representative of Nye's books is *Remarks* (later known as the *Red Book*). Walter Blair cites it as "Nye's most typical collection" in *Native American Humor* (New York: American Book Company, 1937), p. 108, note 1. New readers of Nye would do well to begin with *Remarks*.
3. T.A. Larson believes that Nye's best work was done in Laramie. See the "Introduction" to *Bill Nye's Western Humor* (Lincoln: University of Nebraska Press, 1968). However, David B. Kesterson finds that Nye's best work came in later years. See his *Bill Nye (Edgar Wilson Nye)*. Boston: Twayne, 1981.
4. None of the plays is extant. The manuscript of Nye's novel, *Thelma*, was lost at sea in February 1895.

Selected Bibliography

Primary Sources

Books

Bill Nye and Boomerang: or, The Tale of a Meek-Eyed Mule, and Other Literary Gems. Chicago: Belford, Clarke, 1881.

Forty Liars and Other Lies. Chicago: Belford, Clarke, 1882.

Baled Hay: A Drier Book Than Walt Whitman's "Leaves of Grass." Chicago and New York: Belford, Clarke, 1884.

Remarks. Chicago: A.E. David, 1887. Rpt. as *Bill Nye's Redbook,* 1891, 1906.

Nye and Riley's Railway Guide, by Bill Nye and James Whitcomb Riley. Chicago: Dearborn, 1888. Retitled and republished as *Nye and Riley's Wit and Humor* 1896, and as *On the "Shoestring Limited,"* 1905.

Bill Nye's Thinks. Chicago: Dearborn, 1888. Republished as *Sparks from the Pen of Bill Nye,* 1891, 1892.

An Almanac for 1891. New York: Privately printed, 1890.

Bill Nye's History of the United States. Philadelphia: Lippincott, 1894; London: Chatto and Windus, 1894.

Bill Nye's History of England from the Druids to the Reign of Henry VIII. Philadelphia: Lippincott, 1896.

A Guest of the Ludlow and Other Stories. Indianapolis and Kansas City: Bowen-Merrill, 1897.

Articles

"The Autobiography of a Justice of the Peace." *Century,* 43 (November 1891): 60–67.

"The Autobiography of an Editor." *Century,* 45 (November 1892): 156–159.

"'Bill Nye' on the Art of Lecturing." *Century,* 80 (June 1910): 316–319.

Autobiography

Bill Nye: His Own Life Story, with Continuity by Frank Wilson Nye. New York and London: The Century Co., 1926. Still the best single source of primary material on Bill Nye.

Secondary Sources

Blair, Walter. *Native American Humor 1800–1900.* New York: American Book Company, 1937; Chandler, 1960. No study places Nye so authoritatively among his fellow humorists as this book.

Kesterson, David B. *Bill Nye (Edgar Wilson Nye).* Boston: Twayne, 1981. Kesterson is the best scholar-critic of Nye and his works today.

Kesterson, David B. *Bill Nye: The Western Writings.* Boise: Boise State University, 1976.

Larson, T.A. "Introduction" to *Bill Nye's Western Humor.* Lincoln: University of Nebraska Press, 1968. A concise and useful introduction to Bill Nye as man and writer.

Clyde G. Wade

Parker, Dorothy [Rothschild]

Born: West End, New Jersey, on August 22, 1893

Education: Miss Dana's, a private girls' school, 1911

Marriages: Edwin Pond Parker II, 1917, divorced, 1928; Alan Campbell, 1933, divorced, 1947; remarried, 1950

Died: June 7, 1967

Biography

Dorothy Parker was born Dorothy Rothschild on August 22, 1893, the daughter of a Jewish father and a Catholic mother who died shortly after her birth. The family was fairly well off, and Dorothy attended Catholic and private schools. She was reared by a stepmother whom she hated and who tried to bleed the Jewishness out of her, and she was terrified of her father; for the most part she led a very lonely childhood, growing up alienated and ashamed of her half-Jewishness.

Dorothy learned early on that humor could be her best defense. She started writing poetry at Miss Dana's, a private girls' school, from which she graduated in 1911. From this strict, conservative background she emerged with a sense of who she was and who she could be. Her father's death a year after her graduation forced her to go out, get a job, and fend for herself. She soon took a position at *Vogue* writing clever captions. Her first verse, "Any Porch," was published in 1915 in *Vanity Fair, Vogue*'s sister publication.

In 1917, Dorothy met, fell in love with, and married that same year, Edwin Pond Parker II, a well-to-do, handsome Wall Street stockbroker. The war separated them, and during that time, her marriage to Parker failed. They were divorced in 1928.

Dorothy Parker suffered from periods of alternating highs and lows. She attempted suicide on three occasions, once after warning friends. She became sentimental and self-pitying and often drank to excess. Always the party girl, she frequented the social scene with young gay and bisexual escorts. Soon she started living with Alan Campbell, an actor. She was forty; he, twenty-nine. They married in 1933 and formed a partnership as screenwriters.

After a stint in Hollywood, they moved back to New York briefly where Parker lent her efforts to help found the Anti-Nazi League. She and Alan bought a farm in Bucks County, Pennsylvania, a center for many of the literati of the day, including S.J. Perleman, Nathanael West, and George S. Kaufman. There the couple retreated and worked on scripts. She was hopefully beginning a new and better life. She was forty-three years old and pregnant; her hopes were dashed, though, when she miscarried in her third month.

When the United States entered World War II, Alan, a graduate of the Virginia Military Institute, enlisted in the Army Air Force. Dorothy accompanied Alan for his ground school training and tried to enlist as a WAC, but she was too old. She then tried to go abroad as a war correspondent but found to her surprise that her early antifascist involvements branded her as a possible subversive, and she could not get a passport. She began to throw herself into political efforts again, working for the Emergency Conference to Save the Jews of Europe and becoming active in the National Council of American-Soviet Friendship.

Dorothy was also an active "feminist." This overused word has lost its original meaning, but when there really was a fight for the emancipation of women, Parker was involved. She cut her hair, got out the vote, and competed with men professionally. She was herself—an uncompromising woman who knew what she wanted to do and did it with a few setbacks.

When the war was finally over, Alan did not come home; he stayed in London. Angry and hurt, Parker blamed his decision on a homosexual affair and began to drink heavily again. In 1947, Alan sued her for divorce based on their separation by the war, but he later let her sue him, and they were divorced on May 27, 1947.

In June 1949, Parker found herself blacklisted by the California State Senate Committee on Un-American Activities. She did, however, enjoy a brief happiness when she and Alan were reunited and remarried in 1950. But, then, in 1951, screenwriter Martin Berkeley recited before the House Un-American Activities Committee a list of Hollywood Communists. Dorothy and Alan were named, and the Joint Anti-Fascist Refugee Committee she helped found was named as a Communist front organization. She was then subpoenaed before the McCarthy committee, and, when asked if she was a Communist, she pleaded the Fifth Amendment.

Because of the "witchhunts," Alan could not get any work in Hollywood. The couple began to fight and drink and finally, only two years after their remarriage, they separated. Parker left for New York and settled in the Hotel Volney. Alan remained in Hollywood.

On June 15, 1963, Alan died of an accidental overdose of sleeping pills. Parker was devastated. On June 7, 1967, Parker died of a heart attack. Lillian Hellman and Zero Mostel delivered the brief eulogies. She left $10,000, the bulk of her estate, to the Rev. Dr. Martin Luther King, Jr., with the remainder going to the NAACP upon his death. She had never met Dr. King but had admired his work. To the end, she always remained sympathetic to liberal causes.

Literary Analysis

Who is Dorothy Parker? Many know her as "Constant Reader," a tireless reviewer of often tired books. Others know her as the mistress of the witty remark. "Men seldom make passes at girls who wear glasses" is perhaps her most famous quip. More importantly, she was the writer of short stories, such as "Big Blonde," which recently aired on PBS, and of filmscripts.

Dorothy Parker was a writer of short stories and light verse from the start. She began writing captions for *Vogue* and then moved to *Vanity Fair*, where she formed a lasting friendship with Robert Benchley. Her biographer, John Keats, erroneously records her first published verse as being for *Vogue* in 1916. Actually, she had published three earlier poems in 1915, all for *Vanity Fair*.

Parker's magic is at work when it comes to her verse, which exemplifies the "smart" generation of young people with a perceptive eye and an equally quick tongue and pen. Brad Darrach has commented that "Dorothy Parker did more than anyone else to make wise-guy a prevailing American style."[1] Her "Hate Songs" (1921-1924), in which she attacks men, actresses, slackers, bohemians, college boys, and all the other vulnerables, are more than just funny verses: they are brilliant, alive and sparkling with the wit of a woman who understood both how to use language and the times in which she lived. J. Donald Adams, in a *New York Times* book review in 1944, said, "Dorothy Parker, both in her prose and her poetry, might almost be used as a symbol (so far as American literature goes) for that kind of exceedingly clever and polished writing which derives from an attitude."[2] It is this attitude that set Parker apart and made her the perfect barometer of her times.

While at *Vanity Fair*, Parker worked for Frank Crowninshield; it was under his direction that the magazine turned into a sophisticated, satirical review of literature, theater, the arts, and society. Parker was in her element, and her talent took wing. She soon became a permanent by-line in the publication and often attended parties as Crowninshield's date at the home of Condé Nast.

Her keen interest in drama soon led to her succeeding P.G. Wodehouse (in April 1918) as *Vanity Fair*'s drama reviewer. Crowninshield remarked that "though she was full of prejudices, her perceptions were so sure, her judgment so unerring, that she always seemed certain to hit the center of the mark."[3]

Two Harvard graduates were hired at *Vanity Fair*; they were Robert Benchley and Robert E. Sherwood. Together with Parker they formed a fast friendship and often met at the Algonquin

Hotel, which served the best food in the city, to continue the witty conversations that they had begun while at work. They were soon joined by Alexander Woollcott, Franklin P. Adams, and Harold Ross; these six became the beginnings of a regular luncheon club of literary and theater people that came to be known as the Round Table. Adams often recorded Parker's best and wittiest remarks in his newspaper column, "The Conning Tower," and so helped make her famous. In 1935, *Scholastic* magazine wrote: "Her fame as a satirist and deadly wit [had] reached the point where any particularly vitriolic phrase that happened to be going around town at the moment [got] attributed to her."[4]

At *Vanity Fair*, Parker used her talent for turning a phrase in her play reviews. Unfortunately, though her points may have been correct, they were rendered too sharply for the powers that be, and she ruffled too many feathers. When she was told by Crowninshield that she would soon be replaced as the drama reviewer, she resigned. Benchley resigned with her.

Parker and Benchley rented a small office out of which they did free-lance projects until he got a job with *Life* and she landed one with *Ainslee's*. This began one of her most prolific periods. There were no restrictions placed on her at *Ainslee's* or at *Life*, where she was a frequent contributor. She was able to use whatever irreverence suited her fancy. Besides her many verse contributions, she also began writing character sketches and essays for *Saturday Evening Post*, *Ladies' Home Journal*, and *Everybody's*. This was the first step in her preparation for her fiction writing.

Parker suffered from continual bouts of depression that could be attributed to her acute, perceptive intelligence, and she developed a serious drinking problem that turned into permanent alcoholism. She often seemed to wallow in her unhappiness and frequently turned to autobiographical writing, as in "Mr. Durant," (1924) a short story about an abortion.

In 1924, she collaborated with Elmer Rice on a play, first called *Soft Music* and then *Close Harmony*, about two frustrated people who start an adulterous affair. The work did not provide an adequate outlet for Parker's wit, and it closed after a four-week run, having been gently panned by the critics—no doubt a bitter pill for Parker.

With the publication of *Enough Rope* (1926), a collection of her poems, Parker's fame spread further, though few took the content value of her verse seriously—even those such as the one entitled "Resume" from which John Keats drew the title of his Parker biography:

> *Razors pain you;*
> *Rivers are damp;*
> *Acids stain you;*
> *And drugs cause cramp.*
> *Guns aren't lawful;*
> *Nooses give;*
> *Gas smells awful;*
> *You might as well live.*

Parker's career was helped enormously with the emergence of *The New Yorker*. She was one of the magazine's "Advisory Editors," and her prominence helped Harold Ross gain financial backing for the journal (he hoped to meld the sophistication of New York City with the wit of the Round Table). In return for the use of her name, she got a steady job and artistic freedom. It was at *The New Yorker* that she began her book review column, "Constant Reader," in 1927. The acidity that she had found at *Vanity Fair* and had strengthened at *Ainslee's* now provided *The New Yorker* with some of its most quoted lines. She praised Ernest Hemingway, but after reading the work of A.A. Milne, she claimed that the "Tonstant weader fwowed up."[5]

During this period, she also published her second volume of verse, *Sunset Gun* (1928). She also began drinking more heavily and missing deadlines, though she managed to publish a collection of her short stories, *Laments for the Living*, in 1930. In 1931, Parker collected her last poems in a volume entitled *Death and Taxes*. All these volumes were met almost without exception by fine reviews. Her second volume of short stories, *After Such Pleasures*, appeared in 1933. This collection contained some of her best-known narratives, such as "The Waltz," which delve into the shallowness of society, as well as more sympathetic portraits, such as that of a fading actress in "Glory in the Daytime."

It was at this time that Parker emerged as a political and social activist. She was among a group of writers arrested for protesting the execution of Sacco and Vanzetti. She also won her first literary award, the O. Henry Prize, for her short story, "Big Blonde" (1929), an autobiographical tale of Hazel Morse, a victim of alcoholic depressions, ill-fated love affairs, and attempted suicides. Like Parker, Hazel was terrified of her loneliness and despair, but she was thought by her friends to be a party girl always up for a good time and full of jokes. This is, perhaps, Parker's best short story and one that shows her talent in a new light. The tale established her not only as a great wit, but as a great writer as well.

As it did for many writers of the time, Hollywood attracted good scenario writers, and Parker followed when she was beckoned, though at first for only three months in 1931. She then returned to New York, where she lived off her book sales, drank steadily, and wrote when and where she could. Not much was published. She collected the three volumes that included most of her verse and published them as *Not So Deep As a Well* in 1936. Reviews were mixed but hardly encouraging. Parker herself even began to grow discontented with her stories.

After marrying Alan Campbell, she moved to the West Coast where they signed with Paramount Studios and worked on scripts like *Paris in Spring* and *Big Broadcast of 1936*. The money was ample, but as usual she spent it as quickly as it came in. Campbell and Parker's most famous collaboration was on *A Star Is Born*, written for David Selznick and starring Fredric March and Janet Gaynor. Other pictures for which they wrote the screenplay included the sentimental *Sweethearts*, which featured Nelson Eddy and Jeanette MacDonald, and *Trade Winds*, which starred Fredric March and Joan Bennett.

By now Parker no longer wrote verse and only completed a few short stories. She did find a renewed sense of purpose in the liberal movements of Hollywood, however. Even during her days at Miss Dana's, she had been drawn to social causes. She had always felt sorry for the underdog, and her writings often mirrored her sympathy for the suffering and the needy. Like many in Hollywood she faced the skepticism of others who would hardly consider her limousine consonant with her liberal philosophies, but her involvement and dedication were evidence of the depth of her sincerity.

Along with Lillian Hellman and Dashiell Hammett, Parker became a chief organizer of the Screen Writers Guild. She also joined a committee of authors working for President Franklin Delano Roosevelt's reelection. Again her writing turned autobiographical with the story, "Soldiers of the Republic" (1938), which recorded her meeting with some American soldiers in Spain during a trip with Campbell; she was an ardent supporter of the Loyalists.

In 1939, Parker gathered her fiction, added "Soldiers of the Republic" and "Clothe the Naked" (1938), and wrote a new story about an aging woman's affairs with young men called "The Custard Heart." She published these collected stories under the title *Here Lies*. Interestingly, her obsession with funereal titles went back to the days when she shared an office with Robert Benchley—they subscribed to various undertaking journals and publications from which they found macabre spurs to their creative minds.

Parker's involvement with liberal causes made her husband fear that they might have trouble getting work. He was right. They were given no script assignments in 1939 or 1940. While Campbell was in the service, Dorothy tried to bury herself in her work, writing a scathing portrait of a war supporter, "Song of the Shirt, 1941," which was published in *The New Yorker*. In 1942, the Modern Library published her *Collected Stories*, a reprint of *Here Lies*, which she dedicated to Lillian Hellman.

Viking published *The Portable Dorothy Parker* in 1944. Included was a new poem dedicated to Alan Campbell:

War Song

Soldier, in a curious land
All across a swaying sea,
Take her smile and life her hand—
Have no guilt of me.
Soldier, when were soldiers true?
If she's kind and sweet and gay,
Use the wish I send to you—
Lie not lone till day!
Only, for the nights that were,
Soldiers, and the dawns that came,
When in sleep you turn to her
Call her by my name.

For those who always thought that Parker was a writer of frivolous, satiric verse, here is a poem of sentiment and substance that has often been overlooked by the critics.

After the war, Parker returned to Hollywood where she scripted *Smash Up*, a film that starred Susan Hayward as an alcoholic, a part that helped make her famous. In 1949, Parker collaborated with Ross Evans on *Lady Windemere's Fan* for Otto Preminger. The pair also wrote a play, *The Coast of Illyria*, based on the life of Charles and Mary Lamb, which opened in Dallas in April 1949. Though her affair with Evans gave her renewed hope, the failure of the play to go to Broadway, coupled with a lack of offers from Hollywood, left her in despair. She soon broke with Evans—actually he ran off with another woman during a trip to Mexico—and returned to New York. Her reunion with Campbell was marred by the McCarthy witchhunts that caused the couple to be blacklisted; she split again with Campbell and remained in New York.

She was soon back to writing, collaborating with Arnaud d'Usseau on her last play, *The Ladies of the Corridor*. Again autobiography came into play in this drama of lonely people living in a hotel. The play opened on October 21, 1953, and starred Betty Field, Edna Best, and Walter Matthau. It was deemed to be her best play. In 1954, Alan and she got back together and scripted *A Star Is Born*; in 1957 *The New Yorker* published "The Banquet of Crow," a story about a separated couple and the woman's hopes for a reconciliation. This time it was for real; Alan had moved away in 1956.

Parker was in demand again. *Esquire* asked her to do a monthly book review along the lines of "Constant Reader." Her first review appeared in December 1957, but her subsequent contributions were irregular. Writing was becoming difficult for her, and she had trouble meeting deadlines.

On April 30, 1958, she received a standing ovation from the National Institute and American Academy of Arts and Letters when she received the Marjorie Peabody Waite Award for her fiction and poetry. In November of the same year, she took part in a symposium on the role of the writer in America held by *Esquire* and the Columbia University Writers Club. Saul Bellow, Wright Morris, and Leslie Fiedler also participated. She also succeeded Christopher Isherwood as the Distinguished Visiting Professor of English at California State College in Los Angeles.

In the fall of 1963, Dorothy Parker moved back to New York for the last time. In November 1964, she published her last work for the magazines, "New York at Six-thirty P.M.," for *Esquire*. She was out of money, but would not accept any help. After Parker's death Lillian Hellman found several checks for large amounts that had never been cashed. She was alone and lonely, save for the company of her poodle; she drank quite a bit, often remaining drunk for days. She ate little and lost much weight, wasting away.

Around one hundred and fifty friends gathered for her funeral in June 1967. Perhaps Hellman, her friend and executrix, best summed up the specialness of Dorothy Parker:

> She was part of nothing and nobody except herself, and it was this independence of mind and spirit that was her true distinction.[6]

Summary

Dorothy Parker was a survivor. She lived life as it had to be lived. She withstood many acute changes in her life; in fact, she saw the world change. When she started writing, women wore dresses to the floor and did not have the vote. She lived through the "Roaring Twenties," Prohibition, the Depression, World Wars I and II, the McCarthy trials, and the civil rights movement. She was a writer, and her craft changed with the times.

At first, her witty, epigrammatic barbs fit perfectly into the "smart" set of the 1910s and 1920s. But, as the frivolity of the time began to wear thin into the Depression, so did her verse. But, it changed too. Her writing became a social as well as a literary barometer.

She turned her perceptive mind and her talented pen to commentary—book reviews, theater reviews, and miscellaneous essays on topics from bobbed hair to Ernest Hemingway. Through reading her criticism, one gets a real feel for the period as well as some valuable insights into the literary figures of the time.

Ultimately, Parker's lasting reputation as an artist will lie in her prose writing. Short stories such as "Big Blonde," "Horsie," and "Mr. Durant," to name a few, not only capture the tenor of the times and the life of Dorothy Parker, but also firmly establish her as a talented prose writer (and an award-winning one). In addition, there is a mass of verse that ranges from the satiric—as characterized by her series of "Hate Songs," where the strength lies in distanced tone and clever observations—to the more serious side, such as in "War Song." Again, these poems mirror a time as well as being the literary outlet of a talented woman with a penchant for perceptive humor.

Notes

1. Brad Darrach, "Tragedy of Backchat and Bons Mots," *Life*, 69 (October 16, 1970), p. 69.
2. J. Donald Adams, "Speaking of Books," *New York Times Book Review*, June 11, 1944, p. 2.
3. Frank Crowninshield, "Crowninshield in the Clubs Den." *Vogue*, September 15, 1944, pp. 197-198.
4. *Scholastic*, 26 (March 23, 1935), p. 5.
5. Dorothy Parker, "Reading and Writing—Mr. Morley Capers on a Toadstool—Mr. Milne Grows to Be Six" (Constant Reader), *New Yorker*, (November 12, 1927), pp. 112-113.
6. "Dorothy Parker Recalled As Wit," *New York Times*, June 10, 1967, p. 33.

Selected Bibliography

Primary Sources

Enough Rope (poems) New York: Boni and Liveright, 1926.

Sunset Gun (poems) New York: Boni and Liveright, 1928.

(with Elmer L. Rice.) *Close Harmony*; or, *The Lady Next Door* (play in three acts). New York: Samuel French, 1929.

Laments for the Living (short stories). New York: Viking, 1930.

Death and Taxes (poems). New York: Viking, 1931.

After Such Pleasures (short stories). New York: Viking, 1933.

Not So Deep as a Well. The Collected Poems of Dorothy Parker. Decorated by Valenti Angelo. New York: Viking, 1936.

Here Lies. The Collected Stories of Dorothy Parker. New York: Viking, 1939. Rpt. as *Collected Stories*. New York: Modern Library, 1942.

Dorothy Parker. The Viking Portable Library. New York: Viking, 1944.

(with Arnaud d'Usseau.) *The Ladies of the Corridor* (play). New York: Viking, 1954.

Constant Reader. New York: Viking, 1970.

The Portable Dorothy Parker. Revised and enlarged with a new Introduction by Brendan Gill. New York: Viking, 1973.

Secondary Sources

Books

Gaines, James R. *Wit's End. Days and Nights of the Algonquin Round Table.* New York: Harcourt Brace Jovanovich, 1977, pp. 25-39, 50, 58-60, 66, 70, 76-81, 94, 100, 107, 113-116, 120, 124, 130, 132, 152, 156, 158, 160-163, 166-167, 170, 172, 174, 182, 200, 208-213, 224-226, 228, 232, 235-239. Journalistic study of the Round Table, with special attention given to Parker from the *Vanity Fair* days through her marriage to Campbell.

Hellman, Lillian. *An Unfinished Woman.* Boston: Little, Brown, 1969, pp. 212-228. An incisive but affectionate personal memoir of Parker from 1935 until her death in 1967.

Keats, John. *You Might As Well Live; The Life and Times of Dorothy Parker.* New York: Simon and Schuster, 1970. The standard, popular biography though unauthorized. No literary judgments.

Kinney, Arthur F. *Dorothy Parker.* Boston: Twayne, 1978. Only biographical and critical study of Parker's life and work.

Kline, Virginia W. *Dorothy Parker. An Annotated Bibliography.* New York: Garland, forthcoming. Annotated bibliography.

Articles

Capron, Marion. "The Art of Fiction. XIII. Dorothy Parker," *Paris Review*, 13 (Summer, 1956): 72-87. Interview, mainly biographical in nature. Focuses on the *Vogue* and Hollywood years, the reasons she wrote, and the "lost generation of the 20's." Also includes manuscript page from the short story, "I Live on Your Visits."

Cooper, Wyatt. "Whatever You Think Dorothy Parker Was Like, She Wasn't." *Esquire*, 70 (July, 1968): 56-57, 61, 110-114. Glowing account of her life, including past interview with quotes by Parker and including examples of her great wit. Also mentions her relationship with F. Scott Fitzgerald and Ernest Hemingway. Cooper also reminisces about Parker's life with Alan Campbell. Puts her life in perspective.

Ephron, Nora. "Women." *Esquire*, 80 (October, 1973): 58, 86. Good article about Ephron's heroine; trying to assess who Dorothy Parker really was and considering her work in general: "Dorothy Parker had not been terribly good at being Dorothy Parker either."

Luhrs, Marie. "Fashionable Poetry." *Poetry*, 30 (April, 1927): 52-54. Refers to Parker's brand of verse as poetry that is "smart" in the fashion designer's sense of the word.

Matthews, T.S. "Fiction by Young and Old." *New Republic*, 77 (November 15, 1933):24. "Like other American humorists . . . Dorothy Parker is never purely funny; she makes more sense than nonsense, and gets her laughs by exaggerating the tragic grimace. . . ."

Sokolov, Raymond A. "Wittiest Woman." *Newsweek*, 76 (October 12, 1970):124, 126. "She was the most lethal of literary critics . . . . Though most of the hacks she attacked have to be brought back from oblivion by footnotes, her verbal rapiers have not diminished." Review of *Constant Reader*.

Whitman, Alden. "Dorothy Parker, 73, Literary Wit,

Dies." *New York Times*, June 8, 1967, pp. 1, 38. Lengthy tribute to Dorothy Parker as short story writer, poet, critic, sardonic humorist, and literary wit. Includes examples of her work: "A Very Short Song," "De Profundis," "The Flaw in Paganism," "Bohemia," "Conjecture," and "Resume."

Virginia Kline

Paulding, James Kirke

Born: Pleasant Valley, New York, on August 22, 1778

Education: Formal education concluded at age eight or nine

Marriage: Gertrude Kemble, November 15, 1818, seven children, four surviving to adulthood

Died: April 6, 1860

Biography

The son of William and Catherine (Ogden) Paulding, and of Dutch descent, James Kirke Paulding was born north of Tarrytown, in Pleasant Valley, New York, on August 22, 1778. Effects of the American Revolution—his father's poverty resulted from using personal resources to supply troops and his cousin John Paulding's assistance in capturing Major John André, who conspired to deliver West Point to Benedict Arnold in 1780—inspired Paulding's lifelong nationalism. Given little formal education, he learned, nevertheless, to love reading, and his great penchant for eighteenth-century writers like Henry Fielding and Oliver Goldsmith promoted his own overall Neoclassic leanings, which, in turn, influenced the irony and satire frequent in his writings. Thence, too, sprang Paulding's skepticism toward what he saw as frequent emotional excesses in contemporary Romanticism.

A clerk's post in the United States Loan Office at New York City led to friendship with the Irving family. During the first decade of the nineteenth century, Paulding's initial literary ventures, spurred by Washington Irving, were comic and topical. In the next fifteen years more satires in all genres issued from Paulding's pen, but full-time authorship was deferred when he enlisted in the New York militia, was soon appointed Secretary of the Board of Navy Commissioners (1815), and moved to Washington, D.C., from whence he journeyed the next year through Virginia, and on November 15, 1818 married

Gertrude Kemble. Of their seven children, four sons survived the parents.

During the 1820s and 1830s Paulding served as Navy Agent for New York, was awarded an honorary M.A. by Columbia (1824), published a life of George Washington (1835) and *Slavery in the United States* (1836), and was made Secretary of the Navy (1838–1841). He lost his wife in 1841. During the 1820s and through the 1840s, he gained fame as critic, poet, novelist, playwright, and short-story writer. In 1842, he travelled into the South and West with Martin Van Buren, visiting such famous Americans as Joel Poinsett in North Carolina, Andrew Jackson in Tennessee, and Henry Clay in Kentucky. Paulding's delight in this trip is evident in three travel sketches published in the 1840s. In 1845, he retired to a farm, "Placentia," near Hyde Park on the Hudson River, where he lived quietly, writing little, until his death on April 6, 1860.

Literary Analysis

Even in the earliest of his published letters currents of humor course through Paulding's writings. His humor divides into three principal types: irony and satire derivative from Neoclassical origins; a more rough, frontier variety; and (much neglected) barrages of anti-Gothic sentiments. Overlapping often blurs the perimeters of these modes of amusement.

Paulding's earliest work ran in Peter Irving's *Morning Chronicle*, under the pseudonym "Walter Withers" (1802–1805), soon to be succeeded by more significant contributions to *Salmagundi*, serial pamphlets that appeared from January 24, 1807, through January 25, 1808. Salmagundi means "medley" or "potpourri," and the combined efforts of Washington and William Irving, along with Paulding, made it just that indeed. The topical satire upon follies in fashions then current in New York (including swipes at dandies, tailors, dancing, and general pretentiousness) has faded, but *Salmagundi* remains signal for American humor because it depicts eccentric characters, emphasizes realistic language (running into the abrupt and colloquial for effect) in contrast to the overblown, stilted expression then so common, and alludes to well-known comic writers and their work, e.g., in the *Tatler* or *Spectator* or, from America proper, the Hartford Wits. Furthermore, character sketches such as "Mine Uncle John" and "The Little Man in Black" adumbrate stories like Paulding's "Cobus Yerks" or Irving's "The Stout Gentleman." *Salmagundi* paved the way for comedy that gave underpinnings to much "Knickerbocker" literature (written about New York City and New York State by inhabitants). The Mustapha letters prepare for Irving's comic methods in the *Knickerbocker History of New York* (1809). A

related, but more broadly proportioned humor that persisted from *Salmagundi* through Irving's and Paulding's writings is that involving "Orientalism" (which denoted Near rather than Far Eastern phenomena through much of the nineteenth century). This feature had grown popular from the first translations, in the early 1700s, of the *Arabian Nights* and similar fiction.

Satiric elements peppered the books that express Paulding's American nationalistic attitudes toward England. *The Diverting History of John Bull and Brother Jonathan* (1812) allegorically outlines the differences between John Bull (England) and his child Jonathan (America) as the parent attempts to control this self-sufficient child. A condensation of the essentials in this book appears in "Brother Jonathan," a sketch in the *New-York Mirror* (1825). Paulding later revised his book, incorporating ridicule of Mrs. Frances Trollope's well-known travel account, *Domestic Manners of the Americans* (1832), which presented Americans and their customs as barbarous. *The Lay of the Scottish Fiddle* (1813), a poem in Popean couplets, burlesqued the verse narratives of Sir Walter Scott, taking occasion as well to denounce the British burning of Havre de Grace, Maryland, during the War of 1812. A savage notice of Paulding's poem and C.J. Ingersoll's *Inchiquin's Letters* (1810) by the prestigious British *Quarterly Review* in 1814 elicited satiric rebuttal in Paulding's *The United States and England* (1815). *A Sketch of Old England by a New England Man* (1822) continued this vein, though feebly, and *John Bull in America* (1825) closed the series in strong comedy. Its method of an "editor" working over the manuscript of the "author" prefigures the framing technique in many later American yarns, as do the tall tales included.

Turning to Paulding's frontier humor is appropriate at this juncture, because *John Bull in America* was by no means his initial effort in this vein. Actually, his first such piece is the decidedly non-comic "The Adventures of Henry Bird," a narrative outlining brutal torture by hostile Indians. In *Letters from the South* (1817), however, the stories about the snakes anticipate much of the "ring-tailed roarer" yarn-writing that surfaced during the 1830s and flourished through the early 1860s. Such comic fiction reaches later eminence in work by Mark Twain, crops up in other later nineteenth-century writers like Joel Chandler Harris, Mary N. Murfree, Virginia Frazier Boyle, and again reaches high peaks in William Faulkner's fiction in the twentieth century.

In a first novel that demonstrates heterogeneous comic aspects, *Koningsmarke* (1823), Paulding's interest in the frontier (this time in the Swedish settlement of Elsinburgh in America) teams with his skepticism toward the historical fiction of Sir Walter Scott. The book divides into nine sections, each opening with a humorously critical disquisition on historical fiction and other current theories about literature. An allusion to the genial and sprightly Diedrich Knickerbocker, Washington Irving's much-celebrated comic, should not lull us; grim incidents darken *Koningsmarke*. Irony in regard to historical romance grows uncertain, however, and so readers sometimes have difficulty distinguishing sober from parodic Gothicism in certain sections. As the novel concludes, Paulding's admission that he has been fooling readers about certain circumstances within the story may seem gratuitous flummery. The love scenes involving Koningsmarke and Christina, daughter to testy old governor Peter Piper (he of the pickled peppers), and amusing characterizations of several others in this novel provide a sly, satiric tone that adds zest. Paulding's second and most popular novel, *The Dutchman's Fireside* (1831), adds no great dimension to his reputation as a humorist. Depicting Dutch life on the Hudson River during the 1750s, it is better historical fiction than *Koningsmarke*, but the comedy of the bashful lover, Sybrandt Westbrook (who is otherwise a plausible hero), and the coquettish Catalina Vancour cloys, as does racial and male-chauvinistic humor elsewhere.

Paulding also showed an interest in dramatic writing, as evidenced by his *The Bucktails, Or Americans in England* (written around 1816, published in 1847) and *The Lion of the West* (1830-1831, published 1954). Both of these comedies contrast unsophisticated American ways with those of high society, foreign or American. *The Bucktails* reverses ideas from contemporaneous travel accounts by Europeans that imply that barbarism pervades American life, which must be treated condescendingly. Paulding's central focus, however, lighted upon individual characters' oddities rather than national traits. More decided, and more significant, humor in *The Lion of the West* contrasts American primitivism with the sophistication (or, more accurately, pseudo-sophistication) of established society, both in America and from Europe. The character of Colonel Nimrod Wildfire, Kentucky frontiersman and self-proclaimed "half horse and half alligator" (also the "lion of the West"), although not strikingly original at the date of his creation, took the American and British public by storm when performed by the popular American comedian, James H. Hackett. Hackett had run a contest for the best American play, Paulding's submission won, and the enthusiasm for the drama stemmed in large part from audiences' identification of Wildfire with Davy Crockett, who was the untamed frontiersman in

the minds of many. Thence sprang a host of figures in comic yarns, those "ring-tailed roarers" from the Old Southwest.

Paulding's preoccupation with characters like Colonel Wildfire shows also in his next novel, *Westward Ho!* (1832). The sinking fortunes of Colonel Dangerfield necessitate moving his family from Virginia to Kentucky. Captain Samuel Hugg, who conducts the Dangerfields over the water toward their new home, is another frontier story-teller. His tall tales recall those in *Letters from the South*, and his talkativeness is more dramatically presented than that, say, of Lob Dottrell in *Koningsmarke*. Thus, he anticipates many later spinners of yarns. More central, and more fully developed, Ambrose Bushfield, a North Carolinian who moved to Kentucky for the spatial freedom of a wilderness settlement, seems a recasting of Nimrod Wildfire. Having joined Daniel Boone, engaged in many hunting escapades, and suffered torture by Indians, Bushfield is a much-valued neighbor to the Dangerfields in Kentucky. The second portion of *Westward Ho!* centers upon the mental derangement of Dudley Rainsford, who in the end marries Virginia Dangerfield, and so comedy yields to portraiture of abnormal psychology. Bushfield, we later learn, though, had sought the unconfining wilds yet again, moved to Missouri, and at last died just after shooting a buffalo. Although Paulding's later novels, *The Old Continental; Or, the Price of Liberty* (1846) and *The Puritan and His Daughter* (1849), reveal flashes of humor, the flashes stand as flickering candles in comparison with the comic passages of the earlier books.

Paulding's volleys upon the Gothic tradition recur throughout his career, and they often appear to greatest advantage in his short stories. These he turned out in quantity, seventy in number and uneven in quality. Unfortunately, too, much of Paulding's short fiction remains uncollected. Before turning to the short fiction proper, some attention to Paulding's small respect for Gothicism elsewhere may provide pertinent background. As early as 1818, he lambasted "Marmions, Rokebys, Brides of Abydos, giaours, ghosts, spiritualism, devils, saints, crosses, crescents, magic, witchery, spiritualism, infernalism, hobgoblinism, and bug-a-booism."[1] This list encompasses fashionable verse-narratives by Walter Scott and Lord Byron, plus the staples of supernatural literature. These, and like materials, remained Paulding's nemeses insofar as his critical pronouncements went, although he frequently incorporated such paraphernalia into his own imaginative writings.

For example, the Prophet in *The Backwoodsman* in his seeming superhumanness bears kinship with Gothic figures and Byronic hero-villains. *Koningsmarke*, despite its ties to Fielding, turns repeatedly to lurid scenes (the Indians torturing whites, the execution of Cupid, the prefatory critical observations opening each "Book"). Demonic traits in Cupid and in old Bombie of the Frizzled Head, an obvious takeoff from Scott's Norna of the Fitful Head, in *The Pirate* (1822) are undercut by the racist tone toward and/or comic handling of them in many passages. The pair nonetheless are forerunners of those types in whom race is used to signify violence and murderous impulses, as is evident in the writings of Edgar Allan Poe, Herman Melville, and other American authors. The mystery surrounding the hero himself proves at the last to be nothing Faust-like although earlier he seemed a veritable Cain.

A pair of stories written close together reveal a better integration of horror and humor. "The Little Dutch Sentinel of the Manahadoes" (1827) and "Cobus Yerks" (1828), the latter probably Paulding's best tale, use the same New York Dutch materials that Irving had made so popular in *The Sketch Book* (1819). Supernaturalism in the former proves to be no ghostly being at work after all; instead, a drunken vision assumes apparent otherworldly implications. "Cobus Yerks" recalls Irving's "The Legend of Sleepy Hollow" in its preparation by means of telling ghost stories for a "spectral" visitation upon Cobus, who is gullible and who also gives ready credence to horrifics. Tim Canty, an Englishman, fiddler, and man of the world who regales the company assembled at the local tavern with a tale about a poisoning and the ensuing departure of a black bulldog with a cloven hoof, stands as an antagonist to little Dutch Cobus. As Yerks later journeys homeward, he is presumably set upon by the very demonic dog that had given interest to Canty's recital. Cobus is discovered the next day, battered from being pitched out of his wagon and also recovering from considerable drunkenness, although his state is left, calculatedly on Paulding's part, ambiguous. Readers, of course, are permitted to assume that intoxication mingles with Cobus's attempt to rationalize in his recounting his pursuit by a ghostly dog. This adventure nevertheless is reminiscent of that terrible hound legend central to Sir Arthur Conan Doyle's story of Sherlock Holmes in *The Hound of the Baskervilles* (1902).

Although Paulding evidently considered the day of ghosts and melodramatic characters amidst mysterious locales on the wane, he could not altogether relinquish them, witness *John Bull in America*. A British traveller, thinking himself beset by demonic powers, suggests to the captain of an American steamboat the expedience of conducting a witch hunt, only to learn that Americans think that witches, vampires, and ghosts "went away about the time the race of giants and mammoths disappeared" (pp. 327–328). Paulding echoes these sentiments years later in a letter to Rufus W. Griswold (1843): "the Public I think is quite tired of raw-head-and-bloody-bones, romance."[2] He more jocularly remarks in *The Puritan and His Daughter* (1: 109) that abridgingly omitting the connecting links from Mrs. Radcliffe's renowned Gothic novels would improve them. As late as 1845, however, in "The Vroucolacas," a tale in *Graham's Magazine*, Paulding spoofed once again the lore of the undead within an Eastern setting—fitting, perhaps, because Lord Byron and his acquaintance Dr. Polidori had previously set their more gruesome vampire tales in the Near East. What is viewed as supernatural occurrence is discovered to have very natural explanations, and the ending is happy for the young lovers. Many similar comments about the baneful effects of Gothic tradition occur in Paulding's writings and just as often they occur within contexts sufficiently comic to inform us that he holds no absolute abhorrence toward such materials.

Summary

Paulding's comedy shows best in his works containing what was to be developed with greater sophistication by such writers as George Washington Harris, Thomas Bangs Thorpe, Mark Twain, William Faulkner. Using in many of his creative writings what he championed in critical dicta (though he was not always consistent in bridging the two), he pioneered in frontier themes (tall tales) and character types ("half horse and half alligator"). Thus, he stands as a transition figure between the genial comedy of Washington Irving and the more somber variety of humor effected by later authors. Paulding's own failure to maintain a high quality in such achievements relegates him to the second rank in terms of "major" American literary production. In his inherited satiric and ironic modes, he also but again imperfectly attained high peaks. Generally overlooked, his forays upon the extravagances in Gothicism and Byronic horrors furnish not merely another significant context for Paulding the humorist, they add to a chapter in our national literary history by throwing light on American attitudes toward and practices with Gothic materials. Gothic tradition was often dismissed by early historians of American literature as an inferior sort of work and consequently Paulding's treatments of it have been neglected. He will be remembered mainly as a writer who mined the same Dutch materials as those used by Washington Irving and other Knickerbockers and as a forerunner of Southwestern humor.

Paulding's humor overall, however, merits revaluation.

Notes

1. Review of *The Bridal of Vaumond. American Monthly Magazine and Critical Review*, 2 (1818): p. 254.
2. *The Letters of James Kirke Paulding*, ed. Ralph M. Aderman (Madison, Wis.: University of Wisconsin Press, 1962), p. 325.

Selected Bibliography

Primary Sources

(with W.I. Paulding.) "The Bucktails," *American Comedies*. Philadelphia: Carey and Hart, 1847. Rpt. *American Plays*. Ed. A.G. Halline. New York: American Book Co., 1935, pp. 77-115.

"Cobus Yerks." *The Atlantic Souvenir*. Philadelphia: Carey, Lea, and Carey, 1828, pp. 192-206. Rpt. *Minor Knickerbockers: Representative Selections*. Ed. Kendall B. Taft. New York: American Book Co., 1947, pp. 42-52.

The Dutchman's Fireside: A Tale. 2 vols. New York: Harper and Bros., 1831. Rpt. Ed. Thomas F. O'Donnell. New Haven: College and University Press, 1961. Introduction excellent for overview; text is of first edition and is better than later, revised versions.

Koningsmarke, The Long Finne: A Story of the New World. 2 vols. New York: Charles Wiley, 1823. Author's first novel, aimed at satirizing historical fiction, notably Sir Walter Scott's, in genial manner of Henry Fielding. Also employs but hits at Gothicism.

"Legend of the Ancient Tile-Roofed Cottage." *New-York Mirror*, November 20, 1830, p. 156.

The Letters of James Kirke Paulding. Ed. Ralph M. Aderman. Madison, Wis: University of Wisconsin Press, 1962. Contains much information significant for Paulding's humor.

The Lion of the West. Ed. James N. Tidwell. Stanford: Stanford University Press, 1954. Published from the acting copy [revised from the original version by Paulding] deposited at the Lord Chamberlin's Office for British performance, and thereafter placed in the British Library.

"National Literature," *Salmagundi, Second Series*. 3 vols. Philadelphia and New York: M. Thomas; J. Haly and C. Thomas, 1819-1820, Vol. 3, pp. 264-288; revised in *Salmagundi, Second Series*. New York: Harper and Bro., 1835. 2 vols. Vol. 2, pp. 265-272.

"The Vroucolacas. A Tale." *Graham's Magazine*, 28 (1846): 271-277.

Westward Ho! 2 vols. New York: J. and J. Harper. Rpt. Gross Point, Mich.: Scholarly Press, 1968.

The Works of James Kirke Paulding. 15 vols. New York: Harper and Bros., 1835-1839. The most extensive edition, although materials pertinent to Paulding the humorist are more conveniently collected in the 4-volume edition prepared by W.I. Paulding, New York: C. Scribner, 1867-1868.

Secondary Sources

Aderman, Ralph M. "James Kirke Paulding's Contributions to American Magazines," *Studies in Bibliography*, 17 (1964): 141-151. Enlarges our knowledge of Paulding's writings overall.

Arpad, Joseph J. "John Wesley Jarvis, James Kirk[sic] Paulding, and Colonel Nimrod Wildfire." *New York Folklore Quarterly*, 21 (1965): 92-106.

Cohen, Hennig, and William B. Dillingham, eds. *Humor of the Old Southwest*. 2nd ed. Athens, Ga.: University of Georgia Press, 1975, pp. xiii, 8-14, 424-425. Places Paulding with frontier humorists. Good secondary bibliography on his comic work.

Conklin, Willet Titus. "Paulding's Prose Treatment of Types and Frontier Lore Before Cooper." *University of Texas Studies in English*, 19 (1939): 163-171. Paulding should receive some of the acclaim that typically goes to Cooper.

Fisher, Benjamin Franklin, IV. "The Residual Gothic Impulse, 1824-1873." *Horror Literature: A Core Collection and Reference Guide*. Ed. Marshall B. Tymn. New York: R.R. Bowker, 1981, pp. 176-184, 214-215. Notes Paulding's mixed views about Gothicism.

Gerber, Gerald E. "James Kirke Paulding and the Image of the Machine." *American Quarterly*, 22 (1970): 736-741. Good critique of Paulding's social and economic criticism through satire.

Griswold, Rufus W. "James Kirke Paulding." *The Prose Writers of America*. 4th ed. Philadelphia: Parry and McMillan, 1846, 1847, pp. 143-144. Estimate by the most famous anthologist of Paulding's day, who thinks that his humor often runs to the coarse and vulgar.

Herold, Amos L. *James Kirke Paulding: Versatile American*. New York: Columbia University Press, 1926. Rpt. New York: AMS, n.d.

Pritchard, John Paul. *Literary Wise Men of Gotham: Criticism in New York, 1815-1860*. Baton Rouge: Louisiana State University Press, 1963. Places Paulding within critical currents in his day and analyzes his literary nationalism as it impinged upon others.

Reynolds, Larry J. *James Kirke Paulding*. Boston: Twayne Publishers, 1984. The first full-length study of Paulding since Herold with more current critical judgments.

Wilson, James Grant. *Bryant and His Friends: Some Reminiscences of the Knickerbocker Writers*. New York: Fords, Howard, and Hulbert, 1886, pp. 129-156, 377. Sketches Paulding's life and literary career. Defines "Knickerbocker Literature" as that written in New York City and State during the first half of the nineteenth century. Paulding and Irving pioneered in this mode, beginning with *Salmagundi*.

Benjamin F. Fisher IV

Perelman, S[idney] J[oseph]

Born: Brooklyn, New York, on February 1,
    1904
Education: Brown University, 1921–1925,
    no degree
Marriage: Laura West, July 4, 1929, two
    children
Died: October 17, 1979

Biography

S.J. Perelman was born in Brooklyn, New York,
on February 1, 1904, to Joseph and Sophia
Charra Perelman. The son of a Jewish chicken
farmer, he grew up in Providence, Rhode Island,
where he attended Brown University and edited
the campus humor magazine. In 1925, he joined
our national version of the Left Bank existence
in Manhattan's Greenwich Village and over the
next few years contributed cartoons and prose
sketches to *Judge, College Humor,* and kindred
publications, and co-authored with Quentin
Reynolds, Jr., a comic novel called *Parlor, Bedlam and Bath.* On July 4, 1929, he married Laura
West, the sister of the novelist Nathanael West,
and they would eventually have two children,
Adam and Abby Laura.

Perelman's career began to ascend when he
and Will Johnstone co-authored the screenplay
for the Marx Brothers' hit movie *Monkey Business* in 1931, and during that same decade Perelman's short comic sketches began to be published in *The New Yorker* (where 278 would
appear during the next 45 years); he also wrote
for Broadway and Hollywood. His work for the
stage included the revues *The Third Little Show,
Walk a Little Faster,* and a comedy called *All
Good Americans* about pseudo-bohemian expa-
triates in Paris. Screenwriting in Hollywood included another Marx Brothers movie, *Horse
Feathers.* "Easy, pleasant work," Perelman
quipped after enduring for the second time the
shenanigans and chaos that always surrounded
the Marxes, "It's comparable to shaving with a
piece of glass or removing a coat of tar and
feathers."

Other films that Perelman wrote or co-wrote
were B-level potboilers, the equivalent of today's
weekly television, and he never pretended that
he had any motive other than getting his hands
on some studio money. Perelman found Hollywood repulsive and ridiculous, "a dreary industrial town controlled by hoodlums of enormous
wealth, the ethical sense of a pack of jackals and
taste so degraded that it befouled everything it
touched." He and Laura flogged out screenplays
for *Florida Special* (1936), *Ambush* (1939), and
The Golden Fleecing (1940), and wrote a play
called *The Night Before Christmas* later made
into a film (*Larceny, Inc.*) starring Edward G.

Robinson, about bumbling safecrackers. In 1943,
Perelman enjoyed his only Broadway triumph as
the creator of the book for the musical comedy
One Touch of Venus (music by Kurt Weill, lyrics
by Ogden Nash), a starring vehicle for a very
young Mary Martin which ran for 567 performances. Perelman was to claim ever afterward
that the excitement of the theater provided the
"keenest distilled satisfaction a writer can get."

Collections containing selections of Perelman's almost 500 short "casuals" which were
culled from *The New Yorker* and other journals
were published about every two or three years in
the 1940s, '50s, and '60s. These included *Strictly
from Hunger* (1937), *Look Who's Talking*
(1940), *Crazy Like a Fox* (1944), *Keep It Crisp*
(1946), *Acres and Pains* (1947), *Westward Ha!*
(1948), *The Swiss Family Perelman* (1950), *The
Ill-Tempered Clavicord* (1952), *Perelman's
Home Companion* (1955), *The Rising Gorge*
(1961), *Chicken Inspector No. 23* (1966), and
Baby, It's Cold Inside (1970). The two most
important anthologies are *The Best of S.J. Perelman* (1947) and *The Most of S.J. Perelman*
(1958).

In 1955, Perelman was hired by Mike Todd to
adapt Jules Verne's *Around the World in Eighty
Days* for the screen, a project that was eventually
to culminate in a New York Film Critics Award
and Oscar for Best Screenplay for his effort. The
most extravagant of all of Hollywood's supercol-
ossal schemes to win back its audience from the
home screen, *Around the World in Eighty Days*
was conceived by Todd as a kind of filmic assault
on *The Guinness Book of World Records*:
46 major stars in cameo roles, 34 directors for
shooting in 112 locations, 140 full-scale sets, and
74,685 costumed actors, and the whole epic captured in the new 70 millimeter wide-angle
Todd-AO process that Todd, who had nothing to
do with its invention, modestly named after
himself. The film was a box-office smash and
Perelman won the Academy Award, but he was
done with Hollywood for the rest of his career.

He continued to write for his first love,
though, the stage and journals. In 1962, Perelman's comedy *The Beauty Part,* starring Bert
Lahr, reached Broadway just as the International
Typographical Union closed down all of the
metropolitan New York newspapers for 114
days, and neither the excellent notices earned by
the play (the critics could only publish them
outside New York City) nor the mail-order advertising essential to Broadway survival could
reach the play's potential audience. Lahr, who
had been in show business from 1910, told a
New Yorker interviewer that "I quite honestly
feel that it's the funniest show I've ever been in,"
but Perelman's madcap satire about cultural
prostitution folded after two months. Sheer bad

luck had destroyed a great potential success, and Perelman never forgave the fates.

Perelman's efforts for television were lucrative, energetic, and disappointing. In 1957, he had served as a staff writer for NBC's semi-highbrow *Omnibus* series, and in 1959 a spoof on Hollywood that he wrote called *Malice in Wonderland* and a salute to burlesque starring Bert Lahr called *The Big Wheel* were aired. Perelman collaborated with Cole Porter in the creation of a CBS musical spectacular, *Aladdin* (the media critics loathed it), and he wrote the continuity for a glamour-documentary, *Elizabeth Taylor's London*, but he noted with wry distaste that in the realm of television the verb "to polish" indicates a ritual in which every interested party with money riding on a script gets to have a go at it, and "anything that might be construed as amusing is painstakingly removed."

Laura Perelman died in the summer of 1970. Perelman moved to England later that year, but after two years of living in England, he returned to New York City in 1972. In 1978, he received the first Special Achievement Award conferred by the National Book Awards, the loftiest "official" recognition that he ever received for his prose. Perelman died of cardiac arrest on October 17, 1979, alone in his apartment at Manhattan's Gramercy Park Hotel.

Literary Analysis

Speaking roughly, there are four points of departure for Perelman's comic flights in prose: (1) most often they were stimulated by other people's writing, whether James Joyce's *Ulysses*, Jules Verne's *Twenty Thousand Leagues Under the Sea*, Edgar Rice Burroughs's *Tarzan of the Apes*, an advertising fatuity in *Vogue*, or a Schrafft's restaurant menu; (2) the show-biz scene; (3) the routine terrors of owning a home and the land it stands upon, with all of the comic possibilities inherent in the world of maids, cooks, hired hands, domestic animals, plumbing, and visiting relatives; and (4) travel.

Travel provided Perelman with the simplest comic springboard, and his persona in those pieces is that classic figure of fun, the innocent abroad, a bedeviled narrator who finds himself a victim whose revenge on the natives who have taken advantage of and degraded him can come only through words. All writers inherit a tradition; good ones perfect it. It is no exaggeration to say that Perelman perfected the comic travel piece, once and for all. And, if his formula is changeless and stylized as a Chaplin two-reeler, it is no less a model of the type.

"I really do love to travel," Perelman told Roy Newquist, "and I find, as far as copy is concerned, that the stresses and strains one encounters with customs officials and hotel capers and all that sort of thing is highly productive of the kind of situation I can write about." Although Perelman spoke only for himself, it can be hypothesized that travel is in its essence one of the richest mines of all for a writer of the comic persuasion. Tobias Smollett, Jonathan Swift, Dr. Samuel Johnson, Lewis Carroll, Mark Twain, Jules Verne, Evelyn Waugh, and Vladimir Nabokov have all found travel, real or imaginary, peculiarly suited to their genius and created out of its juxtapositions and contrasts some of the most entertaining comic prose in our language.

For Perelman's purposes, travel not only created comic difficulties and contretemps, but also offered him the opportunity of reporting the chemical reduction of his own romantic expectations in the universal solvent of observed reality: "From bar mitzvah on," he said, "I had longed to qualify as a Jewish Robert Louis Stevenson." Thus, the wry humor in his travel writing is created out of the poignant contrast between an N. C. Wyeth-illustrated edition of Stevenson's *Treasure Island* read under the covers by flashlight and the very humdrum locales that a grown-up Perelman discovered lying in wait to disappoint him behind the very romantic Technicolor versions of some place names. In every case, the aesthetic distance between boyhood illusion and adult fact is about the same as that from a Wagnerian overture to a dial tone. Thus, a Malaysian rubber plantation is nothing more than a vast inland sea of rubber trees and, "unless your name is Harvey Firestone, it is doubtful if the sight of twelve thousand acres of future hot-water bottles will affect you as the Grecian urn did Keats." The night life of Bombay conjures up that of "Schwenksville, Pennsylvania," and, furthermore, of all the "lethargic, benighted, somnolent fleabags this side of Hollywood, the port of Georgetown on the island of Penang is the most abysmal." The food is usually terrible everywhere they dock, and sometimes Perelman even gets to see it again; enduring a spell of very dirty weather in the Indian Ocean, Perelman renders the experience of seasickness with lyrical precision: "Liver and colon, lung and lights, all the shiny interior plumbing I had amassed so painstakingly in dribs and drabs over the years, fused into a single hard knot and wedged in my epiglottis." Every cabman, waiter, and bellhop is out to gouge the tourist; every meal east of Suez is an act of masochism (complete with items such as "a dab of penicillin posing as a potato"), and the temperature always seems to be in three figures—climaxing with a nice, round 119° F. at the Sphinx, where the brain-boiling heat is accompanied with a living cloud of sand-flies and the vista is defiled by the presence of a soda-pop stand.

While travel and show business offered obvious targets for Perelman's comedy, his most distinctive efforts were always more literary in origin. For sheer comic delightfulness, of all of the hundreds of pieces that Perelman wrote using someone else's prose as a springboard, none surpasses the series that he called "Cloudland Revisited," and although after writing twenty-two of them he came to feel that he had exhausted the device, the "Cloudland" pieces constitute some of the finest comic writing in American literature. As art, they are, like many brilliant inventions, at once so inevitable as to seem startlingly fresh. Perelman simply reads again or sees again a book or movie that had thrilled him when he was young. Obviously, the experience is not the same. No one could believe otherwise. The moths of time, indifference, and disillusion will have gotten into the magic carpet of childhood's ability to believe, and the return to the anticipated thrill will inevitably be saturated with anticlimax and melancholy. Speaking of his rereading of George Barr McCutcheon's *Graustark*, for example, Perelman notes rather poignantly that "our reunion, like most, left something to be desired"; that comment might be used as a caption for each and every "Cloudland" piece. But, of course, the longing to reenter the past is not in itself the stuff of comedy, and it is really Perelman's witty and acerbic commentary on the work that he is revisiting that gives each piece its charm.

It is also important to see that this frame of ironic commentary is not just simple mockery, either, although Perelman sometimes pretends that it is. Readers are enchanted in part because Perelman's wit and intelligence, his imaginative energy, manage to evoke a sort of campy participative exhilaration, a touch of the original adolescent thrill itself. Good comic writing frequently creates a sort of perverse affection for its objects, no matter how vehement its rhetorical disapproval of those objects may be, and in the "Cloudland" pieces readers experience once more a little of what it felt like when they discovered Verne, Edgar Rice Burroughs, or Sax Rohmer for the first time, but with this return now poignantly shadowed by a valedictory sense of seeing from the outside those excitements that can be experienced from the inside only once. Even if the gremlins of experience and sheer living (always something of a disappointment) have gotten at the book or movie, "curdled the motivation, converted the hero into an insufferable jackanapes, drawn mustaches on the ladies . . . and generally sprinkled sneeze powder over the derring-do," Perelman demonstrates that there is a little wobbly flight still left in the old magic carpet even if it takes a comic incantation to conjure it out.

Perelman discovers that "crow's-feet and wrinkles" have come to disfigure the resurrected visage of *The Mystery of Dr. Fu-Manchu*, for example, but at least that famous melodrama offers him one of his finest comic opportunities. Sax Rohmer (the pen name of Arthur Sarsfield Ward) began publishing his accounts of "the most malign and formidable" evil genius in the annals of American literature just before World War I, an era characterized by a degree of racial chauvinism in the American public arts that is startling and embarrassing today. "The cruel cunning of an entire Eastern race" is one of Rohmer's favorite adjective clusters to describe Dr. Fu-Manchu's malignity, and this Mephistophelian creature is again and again characterized as "the yellow peril incarnate in one man," an apocalyptic threat to "the entire white race." And, of course, Rohmer's plot contrivances are irresistibly silly, especially in retrospect after Perelman's wit has had its flattening way with them. Thus, after the malignant doctor's assistant, Kâramanéh, saves some British detectives from drowning in the Thames by extending to them her false pigtail, Perelman caps his summary of the incident with this drollery: "It is at approximately this juncture that one begins to appreciate how lightly the laws of probability weighed on Sax Rohmer. Once you step with him into Never-Never Land, the grave's the limit, and no character is deemed extinct until you can use his skull as a paper-weight."

Technically, the mode and tone here are elements of what is classified as "Horatian satire"; the speaker's persona is urbane, witty, and tolerantly amused by the child's play that he sees enacted down there beneath his elevated and quasi-aristocratic vantage point. There is a negligible amount of passion or indignation (compared, say, with Jonathan Swift's underlying fury and disgust in "A Modest Proposal," which would be classified as "Juvenalian satire"). The tone in Perelman's piece is relaxed, gentlemanly, playful, cosmopolitan. Social and moral correction are not being advocated; in fact, nothing strenuous or serious is even remotely at issue. Almost all of Perelman's work is in this mode, and it might also be emphasized that the reader is implicitly flattered to be included in the disdainful irony reflected in the tone which is, essentially, a *courtly* tone, the wave-length of a privileged minority. This last point, central to the reader's appreciation of Perelman, can be made clearer by contrast with the manner in which the reader identifies with the narrative voice in Mark Twain's *Huckleberry Finn* or James Thurber's "You Could Look It Up," or with Holden Caulfield's voice in J. D. Salinger's *The Catcher in the Rye*. In these instances the creator and the reader wink conspiratorially at each other over the heads of the narrators, above the level of discourse established by the narrative persona, for the writer and reader are a bit more sophisticated and aware than is the narrator who mediates between them.

"Farewell, My Lovely Appetizer," one of Perelman's most famous pieces, might serve as a specimen illustration for his constant concern with technique. This "casual" is a straight parody of Raymond Chandler's famous detective stories—indeed, Chandler himself was delighted with it—and the narrator's voice here is a strict comic impersonation rather than a series of comments delivered from the outside. Mimicry, not just irony, is part of the performance:

> I could go for you, sugar," I said slowly. Her face was veiled, watchful. I stared at her ears, liking the way they were joined to her head. There was something complete about them; you knew they were there for keeps. When you're a private eye, you want things to stay put.

Like any great caricaturist from Daumier to David Levine, Perelman reduced and intensified the salient features of his model until he had created an imitation that was at once exaggerated enough to be funny and yet accurate enough to be recognized. The kernel of the comic device is created when "veiled, watchful," which catches the pseudo-poetic diction so much favored by the tough-guy detective novelists of the 1930s, is fused with the Bogartian insouciance in the anatomical assessment but that assessment is directed toward the *wrong* features. The mock-profound street-wisdom that rounds out the paragraph—"When you're a private eye, you want things to stay put"—is a miniature masterpiece of comic imitation: the private detective, weary of the sordid underside of it all, would indeed yearn for "things to stay put" (at least this is the literary convention), but that the "things" that he would yearn for to "stay put" are his secretary's "ears" is, to speak pedantically, not quite what the reader expects. "The sudden transformation of a strained expectation into nothing," Immanuel Kant called humor, and later commentators such as M.H. Abrams have amended and amplified that insight to a more accurate equation: "the sudden satisfaction of an expectation, but in a way we did not in the least expect."

"I consider myself purely traditonal," Perelman told an interviewer, "a disciple of people like George Ade, Ring Lardner, Stephen Leacock, Robert Benchley, and Frank Sullivan." He also praised Dorothy Parker, whose taste and intelligence allowed her to keep her "standards very high." Ambrose Bierce and H.L. Mencken were other antecedents.

Perelman's influence can be seen in the work of several writers associated with *The New Yorker* and is perhaps more apparent in sophisticated magazine journalism than in fiction. For example, Roger Angell's baseball pieces gleam with a vocabulary and wit that is reminiscent of Perelman's style, and Red Smith's sportswriting for the *New York Times* was an obvious beneficiary. Woody Allen's comic prose owes a debt to Perelman's, and a comic novelist like Peter De Vries might not write quite like he does without Perelman's example. When Paul Theroux and John Updike write as reviewers or parodists, Perelman can be detected in their DNA. John Barth obviously developed under his influence, too.

Satire is a weapon, but parody is a toy. Whatever his private feelings might have been, as a professional writer Perelman was a one-man F.A.O. Schwartz, a Santa's workshop of prose comedy. He was disgusted and angry over what he considered the Vietnam stupidities, but aside from the few stray comments that he made to interviewers, there is nothing about the war, satiric or otherwise, in his professional prose. Watergate was not a target, nor did Richard Nixon's actions appeal to Perelman as having comic possibilities. There were occasional side comments in passing, but nowhere did he go after Joseph McCarthy, the Bay of Pigs, the CIA, or South Africa. The drug culture and feminism lay untouched, not the subjects of even a single piece. These are remarkable omissions, made more remarkable by comparison. In "The Schmeed Memoirs," Perelman's disciple Woody Allen satirizes the good German, the little man who only did his job and was neither expected to exert moral discrimination or choose against evil. Schmeed, Hitler's barber, assures the reader that he was never "aware of the moral implications of what I was doing," and that "when I finally did find out what a monster Hitler was, it was too late to do anything, as I had made a down payment on some furniture. Once, toward the end of the war, I did contemplate loosening the Fuhrer's neck-napkin and allowing some tiny hairs to get down his back, but at the last minute my nerve failed me." Here the humorist's irony hardly conceals the humanistic outrage that drives it forward, but this is the sort of irony seldom found in Perelman. Style, not substance, was always his target—and by "style" one indicates style in a relatively narrow sense: literary style, verbal style, style in the visual arts, the debased styles of Madison Avenue and television. Although he responded with great irritation to interviewers who might tacitly recall him to the higher purposes of satire—"I regard *my* comic writing as serious"—Perelman's work (if one must judge it as an instrument of correction) does indeed lie outside the tradition of militant satire and wit in the service of humanity. Perelman refused to engage the larger targets, and he loathed the bandwagon of social virtue.

Summary

"I don't believe in the importance of scale," Perelman once said with exasperation, "To me the muralist is no more valid than the miniature painter." Thus, the reader will look long and in vain for redeeming social value or Freudian significance in the miniatures of Perelman's wit; if that wit needs justification, it will have to be that of the comic catharsis as a therapeutic end in itself. Don Quixote's windmills seemed to the old mad knight to be the powers of darkness; if Perelman's targets were evil, it was evil reduced to the size of a pinwheel. To try to justify his charm by pointing to its social importance is to miss the point. Perelman's devotion to style as a value in and of itself must finally be regarded as the source of his enduring appeal—early and late, Perelman the miniaturist knew what he wanted to do, and he did it more than well, he did it once and for all. Alan Brien indeed may be right when he predicts that "School boys and girls yet unborn, studying the origins of the twenty-first century's dominant tongue, Anglo-American, may find in Perelman its first assured master, fusing the heritage of Twain and Hazlitt." There is truth in Auden's famous observation that Time loves words and forgives all those who live by them, and there is no doubt that Perelman's ingenious and superbly crafted work will be cherished as one of the most unique and durable comic achievements of twentieth-century America.

Selected Bibliography

Primary Sources

Collections
The Best of S.J. Perelman. New York: Modern Library, 1947.
The Most of S.J. Perelman. New York: Simon and Schuster, 1958. Contains 123 pieces.

Books, Plays, and Films
Dawn Ginsbergh's Revenge. New York: Liveright, 1929.
(with Quentin Reynolds, Jr.) *Parlor, Bedlam, and Bath.* New York: Liveright, 1930.
Monkey Business. Paramount Publix, 1931. Screenplay by Will Johnstone and Perelman.
Horse Feathers. Paramount, 1932. Screenplay by Harry Ruby, Bert Kalmar, and Perelman.
Florida Special. Paramount, 1936. Screenplay by David Boehm, Marguerite Roberts, and S.J. and Laura Perelman, based on a story by Clarence B. Kelland.
Ambush. Paramount, 1939. Screenplay by S.J. and Laura Perelman, based on a story by Robert Day.
The Golden Fleecing. MGM, 1940. Screenplay by Marion Parsonnet and S. J. and Laura Perelman, from a story by Lynn Root and Frank Fenton.
Larceny, Inc. Warner Brothers, 1942. Screenplay by Everett Freeman and Edwin Giblert, from the play

The Night Before Christmas, by S.J. and Laura Perelman.
The Dream Department. New York: Random House, 1943.
Crazy Like a Fox. New York: Random House, 1944.
One Touch of Venus. Boston: Little, Brown, 1944.
Keep It Crisp. New York: Random House, 1946.
Acres and Pains. New York: Reynal, 1947.
One Touch of Venus. Universal-International, 1948. Screenplay by Hurry Kurnitz and Frank Tashlin, based on a stage musical by Ogden Nash and Perelman.
Westward Ha! or Around the World in Eighty Clichés. New York: Simon and Schuster, 1948.
Listen to the Mocking Bird. New York: Simon and Schuster, 1949.
Look Who's Talking. New York: Random House, 1949.
The Swiss Family Perelman. New York: Simon and Schuster, 1950.
The Ill-Tempered Clavicord. New York: Simon and Schuster, 1952.
Perelman's Home Companion. New York: Simon and Schuster, 1955.
Around the World in Eighty Days. United Artists, 1956. Screenplay by Perelman, James Poe, and John Farrow, based on the novel by Jules Verne.
The Road to Miltown. New York: Simon and Schuster, 1957.
The Rising Gorge. New York: Simon and Schuster, 1961.
The Beauty Part. New York: Simon and Schuster, 1966.
Chicken Inspector No. 23. New York: Simon and Schuster, 1966.
Baby, It's Cold Inside. New York: Simon and Schuster, 1970.
The Four Marx Brothers in "Monkey Business" and "Duck Soup." New York: Simon and Schuster, 1972.
Vinegar Puss. New York: Simon and Schuster, 1975.
Eastward Ha! New York: Simon and Schuster, 1977.
The Last Laugh. New York: Simon and Schuster, 1981. Material collected after Perelman's death includes bits of an autobiography.
For the best available, limited list of the separate publications of Perelman's "casuals" see Steven H. Gale, "S.J. Perelman: Twenty Years of American Humor," *Bulletin of Bibliography,* 29 (January–March 1972): 10–12, an invaluable listing of the books and 171 short essays between 1940 and 1960. Gale's *S.J. Perelman: An Annotated Bibliography* (New York: Garland, 1986) updates this to include virtually all of Perelman's writings in all genres throughout his career.

Secondary Sources

Alter, Robert. "Jewish Humor and the Domestication of Myth." In *Veins of Humor.* Ed. Harry Levin. Cambridge: Harvard University Press, 1972, pp. 255–279. Intelligent and persuasive.
Bier, Jess. *The Rise and Fall of American Humor.* New York: Holt, Rinehart and Winston, 1968. Admirable research, ambitious (and highly suspect) theoretical approach; notes that Perelman's devotion to style has preserved the freshness of his work for more than a generation.

Blair, Walter. *Horse Sense in American Humor, from Benjamin Franklin to Ogden Nash.* Chicago: University of Chicago, 1942. An attempt to place Perelman in the context of the American humorous tradition.

Cole, William, and George Plimpton. *Writers at Work: The Paris Review Interviews: Second Series.* New York: Viking, 1963, pp. 241–256. Funny and fascinating glimpses of the artist in the toils of creative agony.

Fowler, Douglas. *S.J. Perelman.* Boston: G.K. Hall, 1983. Bio-critical study with some attention to Perelman's relationships to American-Jewish sensibility.

Gale, Steven H. *S.J. Perelman: A Critical Analysis.* Westport, Conn.: Greenwood, 1987. Examines Perelman's journal writing, films, and plays. Analyzes style and themes.

————. *S.J. Perelman: An Annotated Bibliography.* New York: Garland, 1986. The standard bibliography. Includes over 650 listings of Perelman's individual publications and 380 entries of critical and scholarly reactions to Perelman's oeuvre.

Hasley, Louis. "The Kangaroo Mind of S.J. Perelman." *South Atlantic Quarterly*, 72 (Winter 1973): 115–121. Good article stressing Perelman's underlying reasonableness.

Martin, Jay. *Nathanael West: The Art of His Life.* New York: Farrar, Straus and Giroux, 1970. The definitive biography of Perelman's brother-in-law includes a good deal of material on Perelman and Laura.

Newquist, Roy. *Conversations.* New York: Rand McNally, 1967, pp. 275–286. Interesting and detailed interview in which Perelman stresses his sense of tradition, his literary admirations (Twain, Ade, Lardner, Benchley, et al.), and reaffirms his "sole ambition" to write as well as he can in the form of the short comic essay.

Pinsker, Sanford. "Jumping on Hollywood's Bones, or How S.J. Perelman and Woody Allen Found It at the Movies." *Midwest Quarterly*, 21, no. 3 (Spring 1980): 371–383. Interesting affinities noted.

Shenker, Israel. *Words and Their Masters.* New York: Doubleday, 1974, pp. 18–20, 202–204, 364–368. Three interviews, conducted before and after Perelman's flight to England.

Theroux, Paul. "Marxist." *New Statesman*, 96 (April 9, 1976): 476. Excellent short analysis of Perelman's affinity for James Joyce by a brilliant contemporary writer.

Yates, Norris W. "The Sane Psychoses of S.J. Perelman." *The American Humorist: Conscience of the Twentieth Century.* Ames: Iowa State University, 1964, pp. 331–350. Doctrinaire effort to show that Perelman's comic efforts are good medicine.

Zinsser, William. "The Perelman of Great Price is 65." *New York Times Magazine*, January 26, 1969, pp. 25–26, 72–74, 76. Invaluable interview-article on Perelman's career.

Douglas Fowler

Reed, Ishmael

Born: Chattanooga, Tennessee, on February 22, 1938

Education: State University of New York at Buffalo, B.A., 1960

Marriages: Priscilla Rose, 1960, separated, 1963, divorced, 1970, one child; Carla Blank, 1970, one child

Biography

Ishmael Scott Reed was born to working-class parents; his father, Henry Lenoir, was a fundraiser for the YMCA, and his mother, Thelma Coleman, was a sales clerk in a local department store. A short time after Ishmael's birth, she married Bennie Reed, an auto worker. At age four, Reed and his mother moved to Buffalo, where he would live for the next twenty years, attending public schools and sharpening his powers of observation, noting the injustices suffered by the lower class and disadvantaged. Reed attended Buffalo Technical High School between 1952 and 1954, but graduated from East High School in 1956. He began his college education in the night school division of the University of Buffalo at Millard Fillmore College; he worked days as a clerk in the public library system but was forced to withdraw from the university for lack of funds in 1960.

While a student, Reed's gift for satire and storytelling became apparent to several of his professors in the English Department and linguistics division. They encouraged him to actively pursue a career in writing and, perhaps more importantly, revealed to Reed the untapped potential of the Afro-American vernacular as a literary source, a vital yet widely ignored language. Upon leaving the university, Reed moved into the infamous Talbert Mall, a lower-class black housing project. While he admitted that it was a "horrible experience," the move provided him with an insight into life outside the sheltered and artificial academic environment. The experience also fueled his growing desire to define himself and his place as a black American writer within the traditions of the dominant white Western culture.

During the early 1960s, affected by the oppressive and seemingly inescapable poverty of large numbers of people for whom the American Dream seemed a nightmare, Reed became politically active, both in the civil rights and black power movements. He secured a position as a staff writer for the *Empire Star Weekly*. In the summer of 1961, along with his editor, Reed cohosted a controversial talk show for the WVFO radio station. His guests on "Buffalo Community Roundtable" included such figures as black nationalist Malcolm X. Reed also met and married his first wife, Priscilla Rose (with whom he had a daughter), during this period, and tried his hand at acting, performing in several plays (Edward Albee's *The Death of Bessie Smith*, Tennessee Williams's *Camino Real*, and Lorraine Hansberry's *A Raisin in the Sun*).

In 1962, Reed made a key move to New York City, enabling him to participate more freely in black culture and the arts, along with various political interest groups. A period of intense creative energy followed, during which he produced his first novel, *The Free-Lance Pallbearers*. In 1967, Reed moved to Berkeley, California, and began teaching in the English Department at the University of California. He has also taught at the University of Washington (1969), the State University of New York at Buffalo (1975), Yale University (1979), and Dartmouth College (1980). Although denied tenure in 1977, Reed continues to teach at Berkeley, where he resides with his second wife, Carla Blank, and their daughter.

Literary Analysis

Among post-modern American writers, as his name suggests, Ishmael Reed is viewed as an outcast of sorts, a nonconformist, a literary maverick. Novelist, poet, essayist, and editor, Reed finds himself caught between the desire to firmly establish the black American literary voice within the accepted canon of American literature and his urge to attack the establishment with a "savage indignation" that wavers between high comedy and deadly seriousness. Armed with words and a wry wit, Reed battles like a Kongo satirist, who, in the African tradition, is feared by his enemies for his ability to put their names "in song." He attacks the "Zombies of Ideology," the "straight," "square," "upright" "nATiOnaLIStS" who claim the novel is dead and champions the common man in his struggle against the cultural elite, turning their conventional beliefs upside-down and inside-out for a sustained comic effect.

In his view, it is the monocultural establishment, populated by rationalist technocrats, political "gliberals" and "talking androids" who place science and technology ahead of human concerns, that has prevented the black American writer from attaining his deserved place in literary history. Gifted with a sardonic voice, which he has steadily perfected over the years in six novels and numerous poems, Reed finds it necessary to return to the cultural artifacts and vital language of the aesthetic he calls "Neo-Hoo-Dooism" in his efforts to fight the breakdown of communication between races and generations. In his "Neo-HooDoo Manifesto," originally published in the *Los Angeles Free Press* (September 1970, pp. 18–24), Reed attempts to define the ancient Afro-American HooDoo as a contemporary art form, one in which "every man is an artist and every artist is a priest." It is, he said, the thing that brought him as close to a revelation as he'll ever come.

While the influences on his style and sensibility are diverse, ranging from his interest in music (and its legendary figures such as King HooDoo Zulu Louis Armstrong) to popular culture in its variety of forms and genres (science fiction, detective fiction, the western), Reed points out that he uses the techniques of comic literature and satire (particularly those of the Afro-American literary corpus that includes Rudolph Fisher, George Schuyler, Wallace Thurman, and Zora Neale Hurston). Another writer whose novels served as models for Reed's fiction is William S. Burroughs; Reed's *Mumbo Jumbo* (1972), like Burroughs's *Naked Lunch*, utilizes a fragmented, non-linear narrative in his experimentation with the novel form. In reference to his use of Afro-American culture and language patterns in his works, Reed denounces those "sullen humorless critics" who confuse his use of folklore with an unsophisticated and uncouth interpretation of human experience.

In his attempts to stretch the novel form, to incorporate within it his own poetic, energetic language, Reed does with fiction what "painters, dancers, film makers, musicians in the West have taken for granted for at least fifty years, and the artists of many cultures, for thousands of years." As he states in the introduction to his collection of autobiographical essays, *Shrovetide in Old New Orleans* (1978), "Time past is time present. This is why writing is good to me." Believing this, Reed resurrects old cultures and makes them contemporary, deliberately stepping out of time (according to critic Henry Louis Gates, Jr., in the *Dictionary of Literary Biography*) because his "fictional concerns are not directed at his contemporaries but at his antecedents and heirs . . . the traditional apologia of the satirist" (*Dictionary of Literary Biography*, p. 220).

Like many of his fictional characters, such as Bukka Doopey-Duk in his first novel, *The Free-Lance Pallbearers* (1967), the Loop Garoo Kid in his second novel, *Yellow Back Radio Broke-Down* (1969), and Raven Quickskill in his fifth novel, *Flight to Canada* (1976), Reed is deeply involved in a quixotic quest to become master of himself, his language, and his world, a world that consistently resists new art forms and ignores or misuses its precious cultural artifacts and treasures, imprisoning them in places such as the Centers for Art Detention in *Mumbo Jumbo* (1972):

> America, Europe's last hope, the protector of the archives of "mankind's"

achievements had come down with a bad case of Jes Grew and Mu'tafikah too. Europe can no longer guard the "fetishes" of civilizations which were placed in the various Centers of Art Detention, located in New York City. Bootlegging Houses financed by Robber Barons, Copper Kings, Oil Magnets, Tycoons and Gentlemen Planters.

Giving his characters such colorful and bizarre comic names as Flinch Savage, Jamaica Queens, and Nance Saturday (all in his recent novel *The Terrible Twos*, published in 1982), Reed places them in settings past and future, moving as easily between the two as he does between biting social satire and high comedy. Whereas in *Flight to Canada* Reed's hero is the runaway slave, Raven Quickskill, who provides us with his view of the Civil War, in *The Terrible Twos*, Reed gives us his vision of America in the near future, satirizing its economic state in the decade between 1980 and 1990.

Though better known for his novels, Reed confesses in *Shrovetide in Old New Orleans* that "I get the most kicks out of writing poetry, fiction is the second most fun; the essay is the ditch-digging occupation of writing." Yet, dealing with words and "untrodden things" isn't easy. In his poem "Jacket Notes," from the volume *Chattanooga* (1973), Reed writes:

> *Being a colored poet*
> *Is like going over*
> *Niagra Falls in a*
> *Barrel . . .*
> *But what really hurts is*
> *You're bigger than the*
> *Barrel.*

Reed's poetry is characterized by the same playful experimentation with words and the urge to subvert reason and order through language as are his novels. This is obvious in the titles of many of his poems ("There's a whale in my thigh," "off d pig," "Al Capone in Alaska") and in their ironic tone, such as that found in "dress rehearsal #275," from *Conjure* (1972):

> *in san francisco they are*
> *taking up a collection. if*
> *the earthquake won't come*
> *they'll send for it.*

His irreverence for historical figures, great and small, is also a characteristic of some of his best humorous works, as in "Mystery 1st Lady" in *Chattanooga* (1973):

> *franklin pierce's wife never*
> *came downstairs. she never*
> *came upstairs either.*

Reed's contribution to American humor is unique, although he has been compared to a number of writers, including Juvenal and Jonathan Swift. Rather than merely repeat or imitate the established patterns of parody and satire, Reed pushes the conventions of comic literature to new boundaries. Indeed, more often than not, literary convention itself is his prime target. One need only look at the comic Partial Bibliography that he attaches to the end of *Mumbo Jumbo* to affirm his opinion of pedantry and outworn attitudes in literary circles. While his ironic stance often shades into a Dadaistic spirit of anarchy and mockery when confronting the dehumanizing effects of economic exploitation, racism, and sexism, Reed's work conveys an underlying optimism. His tragicomic heroes and characters, though irrational and chaotic, are nonetheless genuine in their beliefs and actions that enable them to transcend their oppressive surroundings: "I see life as mysterious, holy, profound, exciting, serious, fun. The so-called 'humor' which appears in my works is affirmative, positive. It teaches people, institutions, and me to be humble, not to take ourselves too seriously." Part scholar, part stand-up comic, Reed exposes the stupidity of stereotypical attitudes, ridiculing past traditions, present authority, and spurious sentimental emotions. He is a trickster; like the ritual clown figure who exists in all cultures, he is both a social critic and the victim of criticism for his violation of our sacred taboos; a redeemer of sorts, he points out the shame in our social order so that we may rectify the problems, making us laugh along the way.

Summary

Ishmael Reed's place in American literature has yet to be fully measured, though his reputation at home and abroad continues to grow. Having produced seven novels, four volumes of poetry, two collections of essays, and numerous articles, he is at the forefront of the post-modern black American writers' movement. In his attempts to reinvent the novel form, he has drawn his inspiration from folklore, American popular culture and history, and the aesthetics of Afro-American culture. He promises to continue in this satiric tradition as evidenced by his latest novel, *Reckless Eyeballing* (1986). Alternately sly and irreverent, controversial and comedic in his view of America, Reed continues to blend philosophy, politics, parody, and Afro-American HooDoo to challenge the establishment in the name of the underdog, the common man. Employing a variety of techniques, Reed is most comfortable with social satire; he reworks history, creates new myths and shatters old stereotypes, and revives language in wildly innovative novels that experiment with words, pictures, photos, songs, and advertisements to break the narrative into significant episodes and fragments. Engaged in reconstructing the body of American literature so that it will include all "hyphenated Americans," Reed has also actively supported a number of multi-cultural programs aimed at cutting across racial/racist barriers. In 1973, he received nominations for the National Book Award in poetry and fiction as well as a Pulitzer Prize in poetry; in 1974, he received a National Endowment fellowship for creative writing and a year later, a Guggenheim Memorial Foundation award for fiction. Described by *The Nation* as "the brightest contribution to American Satire since Mark Twain," Ishmael Reed seeks, as he says in the introduction to *Shrovetide in Old New Orleans*, to "wake America from its easy chair and can of beer," even though his vision is "still strange, often frightening, peculiar and odd to some, ill-considered and unwelcome to others."

Selected Bibliography

Primary Sources

Books

The Free-Lance Pallbearers. Garden City: Doubleday; London: MacGibbon and Kee, 1968.
Yellow Back Radio Broke-Down. Garden City: Doubleday; London: Allison and Busby, 1971.
Mumbo Jumbo. Garden City: Doubleday, 1972.
The Last Days of Louisiana Red. New York: Random House, 1974.
Flight to Canada. New York: Random House, 1976.
The Terrible Twos. New York: St. Martin's/Marek, 1982.
Reckless Eyeballing. New York: St. Martin's, 1986.

Poetry

Catechism of D Neoamerican HooDoo Church: Poems. London: Paul Bremen, 1970.
Conjure: Selected Poems 1963-1970. Amherst: University of Massachusetts Press, 1972.
Chattanooga: Poems. New York: Random House, 1973.
A Secretary to the Spirits. New York: NOK Publisher's Intl. Ltd., 1977.

Essays

Shrovetide in Old New Orleans. Garden City: Doubleday, 1978.
God Made Alaska for the Indians: Selected Essays. New York: Garland, 1982.

Editings

The Rise, Fall, And . . . ? of Adam Clayton Powell. New York: Bee-line Books, 1967.
19 Necromancers from Now. Garden City: Doubleday, 1970.
Yardbird Reader. Vols. 1-5. Berkeley: Yardbird Pub. Cooperative, 1972-1976.
Yardbird Lives! With Al Young. New York: Grove Press, 1978.
Calafia: The California Poetry. Berkeley: Y'Bird Pub., 1979.

Shorter Works

Numerous articles and short reviews—over 70 between 1965 and 1982.

Drama

"Hell Hath No Fury"—unpublished play (presented by the Playwrights and Directors Project of the Actor's Studio, Sunday, June 1, 1980, New York).

Records/Video Tapes

San Francisco Poetry Center Videotape Library. San Francisco State University, 1973-1974.
Ishmael Reed Reading His Poetry. Cornell University, April 23, 1976.
Ishmael Reed and Michael Harper Reading in the UCSD New Poetry Series. Winter. University of California, San Diego, 1977.

Interviews

Fred Beauford. "A Conversation with Ishmael Reed," *Black Creation*, 4 (1973): 12-15.
John O'Brien. "Ishmael Reed.' In his *Interviews with Black Writers*; New York: Liveright, 1973, pp. 165-183.

Secondary Sources

Bibliography

Ishmael Reed—A Primary and Secondary Bibliography. Ed. Elizabeth and Thomas Settle. Boston: G.K. Hall, 1982. This helpful volume includes writings by Reed, writings about Reed, and a quick-reference index. Fully annotated.

Articles

Gates, Henry L., Jr. "The 'Blackness of Blackness': A Critique of the Sign and Signifying Monkey." *Critical Inquiry*, 9 (June 1983): 685-723.
———. "Ishmael Reed." *Dictionary of Literary Biography*. Volume on Afro-American Writers. Excellent, detailed, thorough analyses of Reed's life, career, aesthetics to date; he is described as "one of the cardinal figures in the Afro-American literary tradition."
Johnson, Lemuel A. "'Aint's,' 'Us'ens,' and 'Mother Dear': Issues in the Language of Madhubuti, Jones, and Reed." *Journal of Black Studies* 10, no. 2 (December): 139-166. A lengthy article that examines Reed's style and experimentation with language in his novels and poetry, and the function of certain elements of Afro-American speech and language.
Nichols, Charles. "Comic Modes in Black America." In *Comic Relief: Humor in Contemporary Literature*. Ed. Sarah B. Cohen. Urbana: University of Illinois Press, 1978, pp. 105-126. A discussion of Reed's comedic novels and their structure; analyzes his use of farce, satire, and conventional modes adapted for comic effects.
Scruggs, Charles. "*Shrovetide in New Orleans* by Ishmael Reed." *Arizona Quarterly* 35, no. 3 (Autumn 1979): 275-277. A short article that classifies Reed's collection of autobiographical essays as his *apologia pro vita sua* disguised as a tossed salad; that Reed makes serious assertations about human foibles and behavior beneath his satiric pose is evident, and Scruggs likens Reed to Swift, moved to write satire by the same sense of outrage at the injustices of society.
Turan, Kenneth. "Voodoo Man Versus the Moochers." *New West* 4 (April 23, 1979): 63. A commentary on Reed's career up to that point, focusing on Reed's joyously sardonic literary voice.

Paula Uruburu

Richler, Mordecai

Born: Montreal, Quebec, on January 27, 1931

Education: Sir George Williams College, 1948–1950

Marriages: Catherine Boudreau, 1954, divorced; Florence Wood, 1959, five children

Biography

Although most of his novels were written in Europe, and although he is known for his acerbic and unpitying attacks upon all things Jewish, Mordecai Richler identifies himself proudly as both a Canadian and a Jew. "No matter how long I continue to live abroad," he wrote in 1970, "I do feel forever rooted in Montreal's St. Urbain Street. That was my time, my place, and I have elected myself to get it right."[1]

Richler, the son of Moses and Lily Richler, was born on January 27, 1931, in the Jewish ghetto of Montreal, Quebec. Growing up in an isolated enclave of orthodoxy within the larger French-Canadian community, Richler received a traditional Jewish education and was expected to become a rabbi; instead, he began at an early age to fight the rigidity and parochialism of his environment. His limited contact with the non-Jewish world (provided primarily by his teachers at Baron Byng High School) further fueled his desire to escape the ghetto and produced a spirit of restlessness that was to remain with him throughout his young adulthood.

In 1948, Richler entered Sir George Williams College, his hopes of attending McGill University dashed by his unspectacular high school record. He found college life only intermittently interesting and after two years thought seriously of leaving school to become a writer. True, he was already writing professionally as a part-time reporter for the *Montreal Herald*, but he yearned for a less confining career—specifically, the romantic life of the world-traveling novelist. By 1951, Richler (then only nineteen years old) had become thoroughly tired of college and Canada and, in quest of the milieu of Ernest Hemingway's "lost generation," moved to Europe. In Paris, he joined ranks with other expatriate writers, including Terry Southern, James Baldwin, and Allen Ginsberg, and began to write in earnest. His first publication, a short story entitled "Shades of Darkness," appeared in the Paris magazine *Points* in 1951. He also started work on his first novel, *The Acrobats*, a rather humorless portrait of the romantic frustrations and death of a Canadian artist living in Spain.

In 1952, Richler returned to Canada, penniless and exhausted but with his finished manuscript in hand. He found work with the Canadian Broadcasting Corporation as a news editor and began the arduous task of peddling his novel to publishers. Although Andre Deutsch agreed to purchase *The Acrobats* in 1953, the novel required extensive rewriting and was not published until 1954. Richler, homesick for Europe, left Canada for London later that year, this time in the company of Catherine Boudreau, whom he married and, shortly afterward, divorced. Apart from occasional and short-lived returns to Canada, England was to remain his home for almost two decades. It was there that he married Florence Wood in 1959 and there that his children spent their early years.

In 1959, after writing two moderately well-received novels, *Son of a Smaller Hero* and *A Choice of Enemies*, Richler published what was to become his most celebrated book, *The Apprenticeship of Duddy Kravitz*. The novel, a scathing but not entirely unsympathetic portrait of a young man consumed by his need for material success, brought Richler critical acclaim and a variety of awards, among them a Canada Council Junior Arts Fellowship and a Guggenheim Foundation Fellowship in Creative Writing.

In 1963, *The Incomparable Atuk*, at that time Richler's most imaginative and comic novel, was published. *Atuk*, which details the rise of an Eskimo poet from obscurity to social prominence and his eventual death at the hands of a manipulative Canadian tycoon, combined caricature, fantasy, and social commentary. Richler's facility for satire and fantasy became even more apparent with the publication of the grotesquely flamboyant *Cocksure* in 1968. Although *Cocksure* was denounced by some critics as a pornographic potboiler, it earned Richler *Paris Review*'s Humour Prize and, in Canada, the Governor-General's Literary Award.

The publication of *St. Urbain's Horseman* in 1971 marked Richler's movement away from fantasy and toward semi-autobiographical reminiscence. Regarded by many critics as Richler's best work, this narrative of a Jewish-Canadian film director living in London won the Governor-General's Literary Award. In his next novel, *Joshua Then and Now* (1980), Richler continued to explore his attitudes toward Canada, Jewishness, and the creative process. An episodic account of the life of a Jewish-Canadian journalist from boyhood through adulthood, it was similar in tone and style to *St. Urbaine's Horseman* and was highly praised by critics.

Although the novel is clearly Richler's favorite medium, he has not been afraid to dabble in a variety of other fields. Richler branched out into scriptwriting in 1959, adapting one of his own stories, "The Trouble with Benny," for British television. Throughout his career he has continued to rework his own and other authors' stories for radio, television, and film; in addition, he has composed such original scripts as "The Bells of Hell," which appeared on CBC television in 1974. His most successful screenplay, the film treatment of *Duddy Kravitz*, was nominated for an Academy Award in 1974; it did not win the Oscar competition but was voted best comedy screenplay of the year by the Screenwriters Guild of America. Richler entered the field of juvenile literature in 1975 with the publication of *Jacob Two-Two Meets the Hooded Fang*, which won the Canadian Bookseller's Award for children's literature the following year.

Richler has also remained active as a journalist and editor. His articles and reviews, which comment upon topics as diverse as Canadian book awards, Jewish athletes, and comic book heroes, have appeared in British, American, and Canadian periodicals. Many of his best essays can be found in three collections: *Hunting Tigers Under Glass* (1968), *Shoveling Trouble* (1972), and *Notes on an Endangered Species and Others* (1974). As an editor, Richler has compiled two anthologies of modern writing: *Canadian Writing Today* (1970) and *The Best of Modern Humor*, a 1983 anthology of essays, short stories, and book excerpts by British, Canadian, and American humorists. He is currently working on a ninth novel, *Solomon Gursky Was Here*.

Literary Analysis

For Mordecai Richler, effective comic writing is fundamentally incompatible with niceness:

> Truly good humor, charged with outlandish hooks and unexpected sharp jabs, is bound to offend, for, in the nature of things, it ridicules our prejudices and popular institutions. Alas, people have become so touchy that to be irreverent these days is to invite an outraged retort from some pompous organization or another.[2]

Richler should know. His satiric attacks on Canadian society have been dismissed as "the hit-and-miss, insubstantial chitchat of a pseudointellectual tea party."[3] His essays (such as his tongue-in-cheek review of *The Encyclopedia of Jews in Sport*), have provoked furious letters denouncing him as a Jew-hating know-it-all. His novels have been criticized as anti-Canadian, anti-Semitic, *and* obscene.

Like most satirists, Richler aims his barbs at what he knows best. As a Jewish-Canadian novelist/screenwriter/professor, it is not surprising that he is pointedly critical of Canada, Jews, writers, show business, and academe. It is also not surprising that his books and essays, coupled with his physical isolation from Canada,

have led to Richler's being labeled by some critics as an arrogant, unpatriotic, anti-Semitic writer with few real ties to the targets of his satire. Such critics overlook the possibility that Richler's writings are motivated not by meanspiritedness but rather by his own genuinely unresolved feelings about his background, values, and ambitions.

A typical example of Richler's ambivalence toward his roots is his fourth novel, *The Apprenticeship of Duddy Kravitz*. The protagonist, an ambitious but morally directionless young man yearning to escape the Jewish ghetto of Montreal, is the embodiment of the stereotypical money-hungry, ruthless Jew. Duddy, intent upon "being somebody," (which, he believes, is entirely dependent upon owning property), monomaniacally directs his energies toward making (or, when necessary, taking) money. As one coworker, Irwin Shubert, observes disgustedly, "It's the cretinous little money-grubbers like Kravitz that cause anti-Semitism."[4]

At the same time, Duddy is a strangely endearing figure. He lusts after land, it is true, but his ambitions are largely driven by his love for his grandfather, who yearns to own a farm. He resents his brother Lenny, who, as a medical student, symbolizes the kind of success that Duddy so desperately wants, but unhesitatingly saves him from professional and personal ruin after he performs an illegal abortion.

More than anything else, however, it is Richler's comic exaggeration of Duddy's ill-founded arrogance that makes Duddy at once detestable and likeable. Duddy's cocky self-assuredness is so inflated, so wildly inappropriate, that it cannot help but provoke laughter as well as disgust. In the movie version of the novel (the screenplay was also written by Richler) Duddy laments, not his own lack of resourcefulness, but the diminishing number of opportunities left open for such a talented entrepreneur as himself:

> I have a lot of ideas. I'm a real comer. The only trouble is, there were a lot of comers before me. I mean, Toni Home Permanent's already been invented . . . some other guy already thought up Kleenex![5]

Richler's comic embellishment of his protagonists' shortcomings is a common thread throughout his novels, as is his characters' desperately felt need to be highly regarded. Most, like Duddy, choose grossly inappropriate means for attaining their goals. Just as Duddy believes that he can become "somebody" only by becoming a landowner, Atuk (the Eskimo-poet-turned-media-star of *The Incomparable Atuk*) believes that he can become a financial and social success only by exploiting his own ethnicity. In the ironically titled *Cocksure*, Mortimer Griffin is tormented by doubts about his heterosexuality and ethnic background and conceals his uneasiness by ostentatiously purchasing sexual paraphernalia and brandishing documentation of his Gentile roots. Jake Hersh, the protagonist of *St. Urbain's Horseman*, idolizes his cousin Joey (the Horseman) and places his faith exclusively in him as the source of moral truth. In their warped senses of self and their surface bravado, Duddy, Atuk, Jake, and Mortimer may be caricatures of Richler himself, who, as an ex-patriate Jewish-Canadian, must surely have suffered similar crises of identity.

If the protagonists in Richler's novels are characterized by insecurity and failed ambition, the villains are noteworthy for their manipulativeness and seductive self-assurance. In *The Apprenticeship of Duddy Kravitz*, Duddy does not derive his moral values from his grandfather, but from a morally corrupt wheeler-dealer known as the Boy Wonder. In *Cocksure*, Mortimer Griffin is both fascinated and repelled by the Star Maker, an obviously insane Hollywood producer who literally creates his movie stars out of rubber and, to repair his own aging body, demands organ and limb donations from his underlings. These mock paragons of success, with their impersonal nicknames and their seeming invulnerability to failure, are strikingly similar to comic book characters, a pop-culture phenomenon that has preoccupied Richler in his nonfiction as well as his novels. In one essay, in fact, Richler explores his boyhood feelings toward comic book heroes and sounds more than a little like the insecure but starry-eyed Duddy Kravitz:

> Superman, The Flash, The Human Torch, even Captain Marvel, were our *golems*. They were invulnerable, all-conquering, whereas we were miserable, puny, and defeated. They were also infinitely more reliable than real-life champions.[6]

The themes of self-doubt and misdirected ambition are also prominent in Richler's more serious essays, which explore the writer's uneasy relationships with Canada, Judaism, and the academic community. Richler seems particularly concerned about his dual identity as writer and scholar. At once estranged from and a member of the academic world, Richler's equivocal attitude toward university life is no doubt rooted in his years at St. George Williams College; as a young, restless student, he was both thankful to the school for introducing him to poetry and literature and resentful of its duller required courses. When Richler returned to the college as Writer-in-Residence in 1968, fresh from his relatively unfettered career as a free-lance writer, he found the constrictions and conventions of academic life almost laughable. In a 1970 essay (written after leaving St. George Williams) he says:

> I now realize, after having ridden the academic gravy train for a season, that vaudeville hasn't disappeared or been killed by TV, but merely retired to small circuits, among them, the universities. . . . If stand-up comics now employ batteries of gag writers because national TV exposure means they can only use their material once, then professors, playing to a new house every season, can peddle the same one-liners year after year, improving only on timing and delivery. For promos, they publish. Bringing out journals necessary to no known audience, but essential to their advancement.[7]

In a typically ambivalent move, Richler, in the same essay, undercuts this blast at his abandoned career by characterizing his current profession, fiction writing, as a dying art and gloomily predicting its imminent demise. In one oddly prescient paragraph (demonstrating, if nothing else, that the satire of today is the reality of tomorrow), Richler laments the decline of the novel and sarcastically suggests an alternative to reading that (in 1970) must have seemed ridiculous:

> Sooner or later, somebody's bound to turn to the cassette. No need to bruise your thumbs turning pages. You slip the thing into a machine and listen to Raquel Welch read it.[8]

One can only wonder how Richler felt when that dark vision became fact.

Summary

Frequently attacked, often misunderstood, but gamely carrying on, Richler continues his search for the "one novel that will last, something that will make me remembered after death."[9] If one mark of a successful satirist is his ability to provoke virulent criticism, Richler has already achieved more success than many of his contemporaries. Given that even the harshest criticism of Richler's work is tempered with praise for its insightfulness and comic inventiveness, Richler's place as an accomplished satirist seems assured. As Larry Zolf said in his review of *Hunting Tigers Under Glass*, "Richler . . . is a bad Jew and a worse Canadian, but he tells it as it is."[10]

Notes

1. Mordecai Richler, "Why I Write," *Shovelling Trouble* (Toronto: McClelland and Stewart, 1972), p. 19.
2. Richler, "Foreword," *The Best of Modern Humor* (New York: Knopf, 1983), p. xvii.
3. Nathan Cohen, "Heroes of the Richler View," in G. David Sheps, ed., *Mordecai Richler* (Toronto: McGraw-Hill/Ryerson, 1971), p. 55.
4. Richler, *The Apprenticeship of Duddy Kravitz* (Toronto: Collins, 1959), p. 71.
5. Richler, *The Apprenticeship of Duddy Kravitz* (screenplay, Paramount, 1974).
6. Richler, "The Great Comic Book Heroes," *Notes on an Endangered Species and Others* (New York: Knopf, 1974), p. 119.
7. Richler, "Why I Write," *Notes on an Endangered Species and Others* (New York: Knopf, 1974), p. 43.
8. Ibid., p. 39.
9. Richler, "Why I Write," in *Shovelling Trouble*, p. 19.
10. Larry Zolf. "Why, Why Should Mordecai Bother with Us at All?," ed. G.D. Sheps, *Mordecai Richler*, p. 112.

Selected Bibliography

Primary Sources

Novels

The Acrobats. Toronto: Ambassador, 1954.
Son of a Smaller Hero. Toronto: Collins, 1955.
A Choice of Enemies. Toronto: Collins, 1957.
The Apprenticeship of Duddy Kravitz. Toronto: Collins, 1959.
The Incomparable Atuk. Toronto: McClelland and Stewart, 1963.
Cocksure. Toronto: McClelland and Stewart, 1968.
St. Urbain's Horseman. Toronto: McClelland and Stewart, 1971.
Jacob Two-Two Meets the Hooded Fang. Toronto: McClelland and Stewart, 1975.
Joshua Then and Now. Toronto: McClelland and Stewart, 1980.

Nonfiction

Hunting Tigers Under Glass: Essays and Reports. Toronto: McClelland and Stewart, 1968.
The Street: A Memoir. Toronto: McClelland and Stewart, 1969.
Shovelling Trouble. Toronto: McClelland and Stewart, 1972.
Notes of an Endangered Species and Others. New York: Knopf, 1974.
(with Peter Christopher.) *Images of Spain*. Toronto: McClelland and Stewart, 1977.
Home Sweet Home. New York: Knopf, 1985.

Edited by Mordecai Richler

Canadian Writing Today. Harmondsworth: Penguin, 1970.
The Best of Modern Humor. Toronto: McClelland and Stewart, 1983.

Scripts

The Apprenticeship of Duddy Kravitz. Paramount, 1974.

"The Wordsmith." Canadian Broadcasting Company, 1979.

Secondary Sources

Bevan, A.R. "Introduction." *The Apprenticeship of Duddy Kravitz*. Toronto: McClelland and Stewart, 1969. A description of the novel as a pitiless and bitter attack upon Jewish-Canadian society.
Metcalf, John. "Black Humour: An Interview with Mordecai Richler." *Journal of Canadian Fiction*, 3 (Winter 1974): 73–76. An interview concerning Richler's increasing use of humor in his later novels.
Myers, David. "Mordecai Richler as Satirist." *A Review of International English Literature*, 4 (January 1973): 47–61. Examines Richler's simulltaneous use of satire and sentimentality.
Northey, Margot. "Satiric Grotesque: *Cocksure*." Chapter 12 of Northey, *The Haunted Wilderness: The Gothic and Grotesque in Canadian Fiction*. Toronto: University of Toronto Press, 1976.
Ower, John. "Sociology, Psychology, and Satire in *The Apprenticeship of Duddy Kravitz*." *Modern Fiction Studies*, 22 (Autumn 1976): 413–428. A Freudian analysis of the character of Duddy Kravitz.
Ramraj, Victor. *Mordecai Richler*. Boston: Twayne, 1983. Extensive biographical information about Richler, as well as thorough critical analyses of the novels and a very good selected bibliography.
Sheps, G. David, ed. *Mordecai Richler*. Toronto: Ryerson-McGraw-Hill, 1971. An anthology of critical articles.
Warentin, Germaine. "Cocksure: An Abandoned Introduction." *Journal of Canadian Fiction*, 15 (1975): 81–86. Defends *Cocksure* against charges of frivolity and unredeeming grotesqueness.
Woodcock, George. *Mordecai Richler*. Toronto: McClelland and Stewart, 1970.

General References

Contemporary Authors. Detroit: Gale Research. Vols. 65–68, pp. 488–490.
Contemporary Literary Criticism. Detroit: Gale Research Co., 1976. Vol. 5 (1975), pp. 371–378.
Contemporary Novelists. Ed. D.L. Kirkpatrick. 4th ed. London and Chicago: St. James Press, 1986, pp. 708–710.

C.J. Bartelt

Riley, James Whitcomb

Born: Greenfield, Indiana, on October 7, 1849
Education: Grade school
Died: July 22, 1916

Biography

James Whitcomb Riley has been the one poet in American literary history to rival Henry Wadsworth Longfellow in both public approbation and financial success. Like the older poet, Riley gained the affectionate esteem of people from all walks of life. Even fellow writers thought well of him: James Russell Lowell referred to him as a "true poet"; William Dean Howells praised the poetry and the man whom he called "one of the honestest souls"; British author Rudyard Kipling paid tribute with a poem "To JWR"; and Mark Twain, appreciating his talent as a humorist, regarded him as a performer par excellence, a narrator who in telling a story could create "art" that is "fine and beautiful." Universities gave him honorary degrees (Wabash College, Yale University, the University of Pennsylvania, Indiana University). In 1910, October 7 was set aside as "Riley Day" in Indiana schools. Five years later the National Commissioner of Education issued a directive that "Riley Day" be observed in all public schools in the United States. In that same year President Woodrow Wilson praised him "for the many pleasures he has given me, along with the rest of the great body of readers in English."[1] In light of such popular appeal, it is not surprising that the six volumes of poetry published in his lifetime—1044 poems—sold well. One poem, in eighteen, four-line stanzas, "An Old Sweetheart of Mine," brought Riley about $500 per word before the year 1902.

The man who experienced such respect and success was born October 7, 1849, in Greenfield, Indiana, the second son and third child of Reuben and Elizabeth Marine Riley. Five of the six Riley children reached maturity: John Andrew, James, Elva May, Humboldt Alexander, and Mary. Riley was named after James Whitcomb, who served as governor of Indiana during his father's term in the state legislature. Though Greenfield was but a village of only a few hundred souls and Riley was born in a log cabin, Greenfield was no isolated hamlet; nor were the Rileys—who loved music and poetry—rude backwoods folk. The National Road over which travellers made their way west to the gold fields of California ran through Greenfield. It was planked in 1852, the year after the Indiana Central Railroad came to the town. A prosperous lawyer, Reuben Riley edited a local newspaper for a few months, gained local acclaim as an orator, and published poetry in local newspapers. Elizabeth Riley was also a frequent contributor of poems in the same papers. James, often called Bud, was thus brought up in a stable, happy, literate environment. He came to love the good life of rural and small-town America. Its outlook and values provided substance and perspective for his literary work. Indeed, it was his life-long celebration of rural America that made him loved and famous.

Riley was an avid student of the life swirling about him, but he was not a particularly willing school boy. He was unevenly educated at home and in local schools, in part because of the limited opportunities for disciplined education in private and public schools but mostly because he preferred reading Beadle and Munro dime novels in class and playing hooky. However, Captain Lee O. Harris, the schoolmaster of his teenage years, began to choose his books and thus introduced him to good literature. An Englishman, Tom Snow, brought a full set of Charles Dickens novels to Greenfield, and Riley feasted upon them and also upon some 300 volumes donated to the village by a philanthropist. Among the authors whom Riley read were Washington Irving, James Fenimore Cooper, and a number of poets. His favorite book was the *Arabian Nights*, but a more influential one was the five-volume *The Lives of Eminent British Painters and Sculptors*.

Reuben Riley wanted his son to earn a living at something, so he apprenticed him to a sign painter. Thereafter, Riley tried his hand at many things, including selling Bibles, painting signs, and travelling with a medicine show, Dr. McCrillus's Standard Remedies, in 1872. His father was able to persuade him to read law for a time in the mid-1870s, but the experiment was short lived because in 1874 Riley made his first solo appearance as a recitationist in Monrovia, Indiana. The following year he sold a poem, "A Destiny," and joined the Wizard Oil Company, another patent medicine show. Travelling and selling patent medicine gave the emerging "humorist and recitationist" opportunities to perform "The Bear Story," "Father Whipple, Bachelor," and "Dot Leedle Boy." Soon his career included newspaper work. In 1877, he became editor of the Anderson, Indiana, *Democrat*. Within four months the sketches, poems, and jingles that emerged from his lively wit helped increase the paper's circulation from 400 to 2400. By the end of the first month, his salary had jumped from $40 to $60 per month.

Prosperity notwithstanding, the urge to win recognition as a poet, especially in the East where literary reputations were made, was partly responsible for his abandoning editorial work. He wrote a poem, "Leonainie," after the manner of Edgar Allan Poe and published it in the *Kokomo Dispatch* (August 2, 1877) as a newly discovered work by Poe. The hoax was partly inspired by Riley's curiosity to know if his work under a famous name could rouse the interest of the eastern literary establishment. The ruse worked too well. When the hoax was exposed at the end of the month, negative public reaction hurt Riley. However, the episode helped to make him well known. His poetry was in demand, and the *Indianapolis Journal* hired him as resident poet and humorist. Thus Riley acquired both a steady income and an outlet for his poetry. In 1881, he joined the Redpath Lyceum Bureau circuit to capitalize on the popular craze for humorists. When he gave his first reading in Boston in 1882, he had already begun to impress the eastern establishment. While in Boston he met Longfellow; it was a mutually satisfying experience for both poets. Five years later he began to perform with Bill Nye, and his fame reached new heights. The humorists were perfect foils for one another, and theirs was a long and rewarding professional and personal relationship. When Riley read "The Frost is on the Punkin'" before the International Copyright League in New York on November 28, 1887, he was embraced by the major literary figures of his day. Thereafter Riley was a poet of national importance, a reputation that he enjoyed until his death on July 22, 1916.

Literary Analysis

In recent decades Riley has been neither very popular with readers nor highly regarded by writers and critics. For example, in 1961 Louis Leary lumped him with Oliver Wendell Holmes, Longfellow, and James Greenleaf Whittier as one of the "short-order cooks" of literature—that is, a writer of simple fare that is easily consumed and easily forgotten.[2] Peter Revell echoed Leary's judgment in a conscientious study of Riley published in 1970. Such judgments readily apply to Riley's prose (collected in Volume VI of the Biographical Edition of his work), for most of it has proven perishable. Among the better prose pieces is "The Old Soldier's Story" which Mark Twain admired and which he praised in the essay "How to Tell a Story."

A number of Riley's poems in standard English merit consideration. Most, however, share the fate of his prose. Collected in 1911 in a volume entitled *The Lockerbie Book, Containing Poems Not in Dialect*, these poems reveal Riley's opinion that his genteel poems are superior to the vernacular poems that he collected in the *Hoosier Book, Containing Poems in Dialect* (1916). Today it is obvious that his best work was done in the rustic speech of his native region. A recent volume by Donald C. Manlove, *The Best of James Whitcomb Riley* (1982), contains some of Riley's best poetry in standard English and dialect as well as a few of his better prose pieces. This edition demonstrates that Riley was capable of impressive range and variety in his verse making, as demonstrated by the virtuoso effect with odd-syllable lines (seven alternating with five) in the brief but expressive "The Prayer Perfect" and the intricate pattern of internal and external rhyme in "The Circus-Day Parade." The refrain, not always the best of Riley's repetitive devices, works well in the terse advice of Pap in "Pap's Old Sayin'": "Shet up, and eat yer vittels!" More vivid are the exuberant refrains of such poems as "The Man in the Moon": "Whee!/ Whim!; Whee!/ Whing!" Probably the best—and certainly the most memorable—refrains express the delight of children in such poems as "Little Orphant Annie": "An' the Gobble-uns 'at gits you/ If you/ Don't Watch/ Out!"

Another notable characteristic of Riley's verse is an abundance of expressive images. In "A Sudden Shower" the entire poem is elevated above the ordinary by one striking image: "Without, beneath the rose-bush stands/ A dripping rooster on one leg." The poem "Knee-Deep in June" contains a perfect summertime image: "Mr. Bluejay, full o'sass,/ In them baseball clothes o' his. . . ." In "Out to Old Aunt Mary's," a poem crowded with local color, Riley writes of "sunshine spread/ As thick as butter on country bread." Some of Riley's best images occur when he is possessed by a spirit of pure whimsy: "So remarkably deaf was my Grandfather Squeers/ That he had to wear lightning rods over his ears/ To even hear thunder—and oftentimes then/ He was forced to request it to thunder again."

A work that exemplifies some of the best attributes of Riley's humorous poetry is "The Bear Story," a verse narrative that contains a tale "That Alex 'Ist Maked Up His-Own Se'f." As a young man, Riley remembered the story and made a successful recitation piece of it for the medicine shows. The poem succeeds because Riley focuses upon his little brother's struggle to sustain a narrative which taxes his fledgling powers of concentration and invention, for Alex is no more than six years old, as the speaking voice suggests: "wite" (right), "*grea'-big Bear*," "an' nen" (and then). The desire to inform his tale with terror collides with his youthful lack of knowledge about real bears and real hunts. Still, Alex proves to be resourceful, finding his terror in another species of narrative. The Little Boy hears the bear before he sees it. It neither growls nor snarls but makes ghostly sounds: "Wooh! And Woo-ooh!"

Problems arise because Alex is beset by conflicting ambitions. On the one hand, he is inspired to improve upon the dangers encountered by the Little Boy. On the other, he occasionally realizes a need to maintain verisimilitude. Ambitious to impress an audience of children who are implicitly present in the poem, Alex abruptly discards the one *"grea'-big shore-nuff Bear"* in favor of two huge bears which he even more abruptly exchanges for one big and one small bear. Other marvelous developments follow. The tree the Little Boy climbs to escape the bears is a "sicka-*more* tree." With limbless trunks and smooth bark, big sycamores will be climbed by few, if any, little boys and by no bears. However, Alex's Little Boy not only climbs the tree, he brings along his gun—and the bears clamber up after him. Other problems for Alex derive from his fascination with "the nicest gun." The Little Boy shoots first one and then the other bear with it. Belatedly Alex recalls that after the first bear is killed, "They uz no load in the gun/ . . . anymore." Faced with this sudden realization, Alex creates additional marvels to extricate himself. The big bear is promptly resurrected. The chase up the tree is resumed. In the "teeny-weeny tip top" of the tree, the Little Boy discovers in the trunk a hole big enough to hide in (the gun is "too tall" to take into the hole). From this hiding place the Little Boy darts out with an axe (totally unaccounted for), chops through a limb, and sends the big bear crashing to his death. The gun also falls, smashing to bits. Apparently safe, the Little Boy descends, only to discover that miraculous happenings also occur on the ground. The big bear is only injured by the fall, not killed. Trapped in the sycamore and unable to go home to supper, the Little Boy dines on apples harvested from nearby limbs. At daylight the bear finds the unloaded gun which is not broken after all and tries to shoot the Little Boy with it, but happily for the Little Boy the bear confuses one end with the other and shoots himself instead. Then the Little Boy kills both bears dead again, hauls them home, and cooks and eats them. No half-horse, half-alligator frontiersman ever concluded a hunt with a more triumphant flourish.

The perfectly realized narrator and Hoosier voice, the blank verse that accommodates the oral tale with perfect naturalness, and the artful artlessness of the poem all contribute to the enduring humor of "The Bear Story." The successful embodiment of humor in the poem depends upon a complete lack of awareness by Alex and his childish audience that there is anything humorous in the story. In this way Riley avoids cuteness and creates farce. For it *is* farce, with the logic of illogic that characterizes the genre grounded in the psyche of little Alex

(hence in life itself) and fully realized as superior farce in a work of art. The humor of it has significance. The brave little hunter, the adventure and excitement of the hunt in the woods, the richly imagined and arduous life-and-death struggle, the fascination with guns, the humor itself emerging via Alex from the ethos of a folk, and above all the joys of yarning off a story—all of these things express important cultural values of rural nineteenth-century America.

Riley's earliest attempts to express those values appear in his first volume of poems, *The Old Swimmin' Hole an 'Leven More Poems* (1883). Riley creates a spokesman, Benjamin F. Johnson of Boone County, an uneducated but thoughtful old farmer with a fondness for writing verse in his native Hoosier speech. Two of Johnson's poems treat death, "On the Death of Little Mahala Ashcraft" and "To My Old Friend, William Leachman." The other Johnson poems in the volume indicate the kind of humor Riley was to write for the rest of his life. Poems like "In Wortermelon Time" and "When the Frost is on the Punkin'" celebrate a ceaselessly bountiful nature, and they demonstrate via nature's abundance reasons for a contented life in the rural heartland. By implication they criticize the emerging urban environment, just as poems like "The Old Swimmin' Hole" lament the loss of community established by early settlers even while they are expressing the pleasures of youth in the country. The vernacular "A Summer's Day" is a notable companion poem treating the joys of life in the country. Both poems counter the nostalgic mood with dialect, the rhythms of oral speech, and homely figures that create a comic effect.

Through such poems Riley creates an Edenic sense of the past. The Johnson persona provides a comic, albeit genuine, pioneer perspective through which Riley can bring the past to life. Nevertheless, it is a view of the past that, by implication, requires defending. In "Thoughts for the Discouraged Farmer," "My Philosofy," and "A Hymb of Faith," Johnson espouses the theme of contentment in the rural life. Good humor plays lightly through these poems, implying that humor itself is a necessary, positive response to life. Some of Riley's best homely figures are to be found in these poems. In "Thoughts for the Discouraged Farmer," for example, there are drunken bees: "And they been a-swiggin' honey, above board and on the sly,/ Tel they stutter in theyr buzzin' and stagger as they fly." The verb *ooze* energizes one of the best comic lines in Riley: "Don't the buzzards ooze around up thare just like they've allus done?" Amid certainties about life's values, it is permissible to make extra demands upon God with gentle good humor, as Johnson does in "A Hymb of Faith": "So knock the Louder, Lord, without/ And we'll unlock the door." What these poems demonstrate is directly stated in "My Philosofy": "My doctern," says Johnson, "is to lay aside/ Contensions, and be satisfied."

Riley, then, presents a paradisal world in the Johnson of Boone County poems. It is a land of plenty in which contentment is the only sensible attitude to take. Riley has transformed the actualities of farm and small town life into an Eden or at least a happy land of Cockaigne. As Peter Revell observes, Riley created "what was virtually a new form in American poetry, the Middle western pastoral," a vision "of a settled and abundantly prosperous rural life."[3] Within this milieu Riley wrote his best humorous verse about farm folk, bee hives, watermelon patches, and hired hands. His poems of rural gossip, folk tales, courtship, and marriage constitute a pleasant rural comedy of manners, the humor of which depends more upon language than character and event. While Johnson and Alex are exceptions, most of Riley's characters are like the hired man of his poems, a voice more than a character. Because the humor depends so heavily upon language, it finds its most delightful expression in poems that a child or the Raggedy Man narrates.

Editions that contain Riley's best humorous work are *The Old Swimmin' Hole and 'Leven More Poems* (1883), *Neighborly Poems* (1891), and the *Hoosier Book* (1916), but when Riley's humor is spoken of, many of the poems of childhood must also be taken into account—*Rhymes of Childhood* (1890), *A Child's World* (1897), and *The Book of Joyous Children* (1902). Among the best pieces are the dialect poems that treat the Raggedy Man and the Hired Girl; probably the best known humorous poem is "Little Orphant Annie."

Summary

A study of James Whitcomb Riley's humorous poems inevitably raises questions. First, why are the vernacular poems better than his conventional verse? They are better because they contain greater imaginative power and range and greater emotional depth. They also possess a spontaneously natural expression that Riley seldom attained in poems written in the approved language of the genteel establishment. Writing in the Hoosier voice, he revealed a surer, more intimate grasp of the joys and sorrows of common folk and the richly imaginative world of children. Moreover, he found an expressive vehicle for his delightfully playful sense of humor. He was, after all, a whimsical man inclined to sign his letters James Popcorn Riley, Old E.Z. Mark, An Adjustable Lunatic, and James Hoosier Riley, the Whitcomb poet. Most important, it was Riley's mastery of Hoosier speech that made

possible his effective celebration of small town and rural life, and it is this celebration of common folk that provides his strongest claim to a place of note in American literary history.

Second, what is Riley's reputation as a humorist today? It has declined steeply. A judicious selection of his best humorous verse published in a single volume would undoubtedly enhance his status. Furthermore, such a volume would help to assure that Riley will continue to be read, for his best work *is* the humorous poems. He created no outstanding characters in his many narrative poems, no Hosea Bigelow or Huck Finn. Much of his poetry is quite poor. In emphasizing the ideal pastoral world, Riley too often limited his subject matter to Greenfield, Indiana, as he liked to remember it. His contemporary, Twain, gave a similar portrait of Hannibal as St. Petersburg in *Tom Sawyer*, yet Twain also presented the meanness and hypocrisy of small-town life in Dawson's Landing and Hadleyburg. Thus Twain could and did use other modes of humor such as irony and satire. The ideal pastoral world that Riley created allowed few such opportunities. Even so, his was the authentic voice of rustic folk at a time when the nation was changing from a predominantly rural to a predominantly urban culture. Though his perspective was narrow and selective, he has nevertheless written an impressive comedy of rural manners, capturing for all time a significant amount of the human comedy of his age. For these reasons, he has earned a lasting, if minor, place in the history of American humor.

Notes

1. Lowell is quoted in Marcus Dickey, *The Maturity of James Whitcomb Riley* (Indianapolis: Bobbs-Merrill, 1922), p. 221; Howells's remark appears in *Harper's Magazine* (May 1891), p. 965; Kipling wrote "To JWR" in appreciation for *Riley's Rhymes of Childhood*; Twain's remarks appear in "How to Tell a Story" (1895). Wilson's letter is quoted in Dickey's *The Maturity of James Whitcomb Riley*, p. 409.
2. Lewis Leary, *John Greanleaf Whittier* (New York, 1961), p. 80.
3. Peter Revell, *James Whitcomb Riley* (New York, 1970), p. 19.

Selected Bibliography

Primary Sources
The Old Swimmin' Hole and 'Leven More Poems. Cincinnati: George C. Hitt, 1883; second ed., Indianapolis: Merrill, Meigs and Co., 1883.
Rhymes of Childhood. Indianapolis: Bowen-Merrill, 1888.
A Child's World. Indianapolis: Bowen-Merrill, 1897.
The Book of Joyous Children. Indianapolis: Bobbs-Merrill, 1902.
The Lockerbie Book, Containing Poems Not in Dialect. Idianapolis: Bobbs-Merrill, 1911.

The Hoosier Book, Containing Poems in Dialect. Indianapolis: Bobbs-Merrill, 1916.

The Complete Works of James Whitcomb Riley. 6 vols. Biographical Edition. Ed. Edmund H. Eitel. Indianapolis: Bobbs-Merrill, 1913. Definitive text with invaluable notes.

The Complete Poetical Works of James Whitcomb Riley. Indianapolis: Bobbs-Merrill, 1937. Contains text of biographical edition without notes.

The Best of James Whitcomb Riley. Ed. Donald C. Manlove. Bloomington: Indiana University Press, 1982. Useful.

Secondary Sources

Bibliography

Russo, Anthony J., and Dorothy R. Russo. *A Bibliography of James Whitcomb Riley.* Indianapolis: Indiana Historical Society, 1944.

Biography and Criticism

Crowder, Richard. *Those Innocent Years: The Legacy and Inheritance of a Hero of the Victorian Era, James Whitcomb Riley.* Indianapolis: Bobbs-Merrill, 1957.

Dickey, Marcus. *The Youth of James Whitcomb Riley.* Indianapolis: Bobbs-Merrill, 1919.

————. *The Maturity of James Whitcomb Riley.* Indianapolis: Bobbs-Merrill, 1922.

Revell, Peter. *James Whitcomb Riley.* New York: Twayne, 1970.

Clyde G. Wade

Robb, John S.

Born: Philadelphia, Pennsylvania (?), 1813
Died: 1856

Biography

Like most of the humorists of the Old Southwest, John S. Robb was not primarily a professional literary man. Very little is known about Robb's life, but he seems to have been born in Philadelphia, Pennsylvania, in 1813 and trained, like his father, as a printer. His career as a printer, journalist, and newspaper editor took him throughout much of the United States. He was in Detroit in 1839 and later "may have worked on the *Picayune* in New Orleans, Louisiana" (McDermott, *Streaks*, p. vi). He also worked in newspaper offices in Philadelphia, Sacramento, California, and St. Louis, Missouri. In this last city he edited the *Ledger* in 1842 and later served as a printer for the *Missouri Republican.* By 1845, he was employed as a printer for the *St. Louis Reveille*, founded in 1844 by Charles Keemle, Matthew Field, and Joseph M. Field. This paper became one of the nation's

most important outlets for Southwestern humor (along with the New York *Spirit of the Times* and the *New Orleans Picayune*), and Robb became one of its most important contributors in this genre. In addition to his humorous writing, Robb frequently wrote feature stories for the paper or served as a special correspondent. In 1848, for example, "when the making of moving panoramas of the Mississippi became the rage . . . Robb went north by excursion steamboat to Fort Snelling, spent ten days visiting Captain and Mrs. Seth Eastman at that post and looking at 'Indian land,' and then accompanied Henry Lewis in his sketching boat down the river— reporting all these scenes and actions in the *Reveille*" (McDermott, *Streaks*, p. vii).

In 1846, Robb moved from working as a printer for the *Reveille* to an editorial position, in which he continued until 1849. In that year Robb went west to cover the gold rush for the paper, something he did in a series of letters. Although expected to return, Robb elected to stay in California, where he later edited the *Journal* in Stockton in 1850 and became involved in Whig politics. Later, he turned to the Know-Nothing Party, whose candidates he supported in the *Sacramento Age*, a paper of his editing (Cohen and Dillingham, p. 142). He died in San Francisco in 1856.

John S. Robb's importance to American humor lies in his sketches and stories of the Old Southwest, that area comprising what is now Georgia, Alabama, Mississippi, Tennessee, Arkansas, Louisiana, and Missouri. Most of his tales and sketches appeared first in the *St. Louis Reveille* and then in the New York *Spirit of the Times*, whose editor, William T. Porter, did much to encourage and foster the development of frontier humor. Many of Robb's stories were collected in a volume called *Streaks of Squatter Life, and Far-West Scenes*, published by Carey and Hart in its "Library of American Humorous Works," a series that included many of the classic works of Southwestern humor. Like most of the frontier humorists, Robb wrote under a pseudonym; his was "Solitaire."

Literary Analysis

John S. Robb first became known as a writer of humorous sketches when he published "Swallowing an Oyster Alive" in the *St. Louis* (Missouri) *Reveille* in 1844. This sketch was very widely reprinted, so much so in fact that many of Robb's later sketches were identified as being "by the author of 'Swallowing Oysters' alive." The tale makes use of a stock situation in frontier humor, a hoax played upon an innocent country man, and also a typical structure in which a sophisticated narrative voice is set in contrast to vernacular dialect. The "hero" is introduced in the opening paragraph as a Sucker, one from Illinois, who appeared "the other night [at] the door of an oyster house in our city [i.e., St. Louis]" (Cohen and Dillingham, p. 143). The quality of the narrative voice is suggested by the description of the Sucker's clothing: "His outer covering was hard to define, but after surveying it minutely, we came to the conclusion that his suit had been made in his boyhood, of a dingy yellow linsey-wolsey, and that, having sprouted up with astonishing rapidity, he had been forced to piece it out with all colours, in order to keep pace with his body." In lively contrast to this formal prose is the Sucker's own vernacular, as represented in his comment on the difficulty of removing oysters from the shell: "I never seed any thin' hold on so—takes an amazin' site of screwin, hoss, to get 'em out, and aint they slick and slip'ry when they does come?" (p. 143).

The Sucker has, of course, never eaten oysters before, which makes him a prime target for a wag who has been amusedly observing him. When the Sucker swallows his first oyster, the wag sings out, "Swallowed alive, as I'm a Christian!" (p. 144). Dismayed, the Sucker asks whether he's in danger, to which the wag replies, "You're a dead man! . . . the creature is alive, and will eat right through you." Frenzied, the Sucker first calls for a "pizen pump" to pump the oyster out and then, at the wag's urging, swallows half a bottle of strong pepper sauce in an effort to kill it. The Sucker "fairly squealed from its effects, and gasped and blowed, and pitched, and twisted, as if it were coursing through him with electric effect" (p. 144). When asked whether he had killed the oyster, the Sucker replies, "Well, I did, hoss'—ugh, ugh o-o-o my inards. If that *ister* critter's dyin' agonies didn't stir a 'ruption in me equal to a small arthquake, then 'taint no use sayin' it—it squirmed like a sarpent, when that killin' stuff touched it" (pp. 144-145). The story concludes, then, with the Sucker's leaving the bar and the beginning of laughter from the more sophisticated crowd.

Although Robb pokes fun at the Sucker and characters like him in many of his stories, he does not hold them in contempt. In the "Preface" to *Streaks of Squatter Life*, he carefully distinguishes between two types of characters living on the frontier, "the actual settler and the *border harpy*." The harpy, Robb continues, "is generally some worthless and criminal character, who, having to flee from more populous districts, seeks refuge at the outskirts of civilization, and there preys alike upon the red man and unsuspecting settler" (p. ix). The squatter, on the other hand, "is a free and jovial character, inclined to mirth rather than evil, and when he encounters his fellow man at a barbecue, elec-

tion, log-rolling, or frolic, he is more disposed to join in a feeling of hilarity on the occasion, than to participate in wrong or outrage" (p. ix). Robb's "streaks" are of "squatter life," of life as lived by members of this latter class. His sketches lack the darker vision of the frontier that emerges at times in the work of George Washington Harris or Henry Clay Lewis. For the most part, Robb's subjects are the hilarities of such frontier pastimes as drinking, courting, and politicking rather than the more macabre aspects of frontier life.

Frontier drinking provides the humor of "Not a Drop More, Major, Unless It's Sweeten'd," a tale about an old couple who come to visit a Major who keeps an inn in southern Missouri "famous for its *sweeten'd drinks*" (*Streaks*, p. 56). On one occasion the Major coaxes this couple into taking several of his "sweeten'd" drinks, in part by complimenting the "Missus": "What'll you take Missus? shall I *sweeten* you a little of about *the* best Cincinnati rectified that ever was *toted* into these 'ere parts?—it jest looks as bright as your eyes!" (*Streaks*, p. 57). Later as the couple is riding home, the husband in front of his wife, she lauds the Major: "Sich another man as that Major . . . ain't nowhere . . . and sich a mixtur' as he *does* make, is temptin' to temperance lecturers. He is an amazin' nice man, and, if any thing, he sweetens the last drop better than the first" (*Streaks*, pp. 57-58). Soon thereafter the husband hears a jolt from his wife's mare as they are passing a small stream, but he thinks nothing of it and begins to upbraid her for her "*rayther* unbecomin'" conduct with the Major. When he reaches home, the husband finds he is alone, the Major is charged with abduction, and a search party goes out to find the old woman. She is found lying by the small stream, where she has fallen from her horse. Its waters lave her lips and she softly murmurs, "Not a drop more, Major, *unless it's sweeten'd!*" (*Streaks*, p. 59).

The danger of frontier courtship is the subject of "Nettle Bottom Ball," in which Jim Sikes tells of his adventures in courting Betsy Jones. Dressed in a "bran new pair of buckskin trowsers" with "stirrups to 'em to keep 'em down" (*Streaks*, p. 61), Jim calls at the Joneses', where he is met by old Tom Jones's greeting, "What the h-ll are you doin in disgise . . . are you comin' down here to steal?" Continuing in this vein, the old man tells Jim that it is good that he has not come to steal, for "I'd make a hole to light your innards, ef you did" (*Streaks*, p. 62). After Jim asks to take Betsy to the ball at Nettle Bottom, she goes upstairs to dress. While she is doing so, Jim and the father sit at the supper table, on whose center sits "a whappin' big pan of *mush*" (*Streaks*, p. 61). Soon some of the loose floor boards of the second floor give way, and Betsy, "without any thin' on yearth on her but one of these *starn cushins*," drops through and "sot herself, *flat into the pan of mush!*" (*Streaks*, p. 63). At this point chaos is come again: Jim dashes a pan of milk on Betsy to cool her, the mother knocks Jim sprawling, his stirrups give out, the old man reaches for him, and Jim "lent him one with my half-lows, on the smeller, that spread him, and maybe I didn't leave *sudden!*" (*Streaks*, p. 63).

What is perhaps Robb's most successful sketch focuses on a staple subject in frontier humor, the political barbecue. "The Standing Candidate" presents Old Sugar, who while not running for office is nevertheless an everpresent figure at these political gatherings. Dressed in his "coarse suit of brown linsey-woolsey" and patched pants, shirt tied at the neck with twine, and "woollen cap, of divers colors," Sugar appears at "the scene of political action," bearing a "keg of *bran new whiskey*, of his own manufacture" (*Streaks*, p. 92). Sugar has "long been the *standing candidate* of Nianga county," Missouri, having "founded his claim to the office upon the fact of his being the first 'squatter' in that county—his having killed the first *bar* there, ever killed by a white man, and, to place his right beyond cavil, he had '*stilled* the first keg of whiskey.'" (*Streaks*, pp. 92–93). Sugar yields his claim to office, however, at every canvass, after selling his fluid to a liberal purchaser. He thereupon announces himself "a candidate for the *next* term" (*Streaks*, p. 93).

The delight of this sketch derives from Robb's skillful handling of old Sugar's language. In touting his whiskey, Sugar claims, "this mixtur' of mine will make a fellar talk as iley as goose-grease,—as sharp as lightnin', and as *per*suadin' as a young gal at a quiltin'" (*Streaks*, p. 94). Later, when one of the candidates refuses to drink, Sugar dismisses him thusly: "He's got an *a*-ristocracy stomach, and can't go the *native licker*" (*Streaks*, p. 95). But, Old Sugar's triumph is reserved for the stump speech that he delivers at the end of the story. In this speech he tells a tale explaining why he has remained a bachelor. Once he was very taken by a Tennessee girl, Sofy Mason, and he and a neighbor, Jake Simons, engaged in competitive courting of her. Because both Sofy and her father had an eye to the main chance, Sugar and Jake sought to outdo one another in possessions. Both originally owned three slaves. Each acquired a fourth. Then each bought a cow. Sugar considered that he was about even with Jake until one day at church he saw his rival "sittin' close bang up agin Sofy, in the same pew with her daddy!" Subsequently, Sugar understood why he lost out:

> Passin' by Jake's plantation I looked over the fence, and thar stood an explanation of the marter, right facin' the road, whar every one passin' could see it—his consarned *cow* was tied to a stake in the gardin', *with a most promisin' calf alongside of her*! That *calf* jest soured my milk.
> (*Streaks*, pp. 99–100)

When Jake lets it be known that he had borrowed the calf, Sugar finds himself something of a joke in the settlement. He thus faces a choice, and the decision that he makes determines his bachelorhood: "I'd a shot Jake, but I thort it war a free country, and the gal had a right to her choice without bein' made a widder, so I jest sold out and travelled!" (*Streaks*, p. 100).

Summary

Printer, journalist, and writer of humorous sketches, John S. Robb is important to American literature as a representative of the humorists of the Old Southwest. Making extensive use of vernacular dialect, his tales provide a comic record of the customs and characters of the settlements on the edge of the frontier. The uniquely American genre of writing to which he contributed is important not only in its own right but also for its influence on such major works of the American imagination as Mark Twain's *Huckleberry Finn* and William Faulkner's "The Bear."

Selected Bibliography

Primary Sources

Streaks of Squatter Life, and Far-West Scenes. Philadelphia: Carey and Hart, 1847. Rpt. Scholars' Facsimiles and Reprints, 1962, with editing and introduction by John Francis McDermott.

"Swallowing an Oyster Alive" and "Smoking a Grizzly," not part of *Streaks*, appear in *Humor of the Old Southwest*. Ed. Hennig Cohen and William B. Dillingham. Athens: University of Georgia Press, 1975, pp. 143–145, 153–155. Includes a brief biographical sketch of Robb and an excellent introduction to frontier humor.

McDermott, John Francis, ed. "Gold Fever: The Letters of 'Solitaire,' Goldrush Correspondent of '49." *Missouri Historical Society Bulletin*, 5 (1948–1949): 115–126, 211–223, 316–331; 6 (1949–1950): 34–43.

———. "A Journalist at Old Fort Snelling: Some Letters of 'Solitaire' Robb." *Minnesota History*, 31 (1950): 209–221.

Secondary Sources

Barrett, Mary Helen. "A Study of John S. Robb, a Southwest Humorist." M.A. Thesis, University of Missouri, 1950. A good general study of Robb's life and writings.

Blair, Walter, ed. *Native American Humor*. San Francisco: Chandler, 1960. Revision of 1937 edition. A standard anthology, with an excellent introduction to southwestern humor by one of the pioneer scholars in the field.

Oehlschlaeger, Fritz. "A Bibliography of Frontier Humor in the St. Louis *Daily Reveille*, 1844-1850." Forthcoming in two parts in *Studies in American Humor*. Contains publication information on Robb's many contributions to the *Reveille*.

Spotts, Carl Brooks. "The Development of Fiction on the Missouri Frontier." *Missouri Historical Review*, 29 (1935): 100-108, 186-194. Gives a basic account of Robb's career.

Yates, Norris W. *William T. Porter and the Spirit of the Times*. Baton Rouge: Louisiana State University Press, 1957. A fine historical and critical study of the most important outlet for the humor of the Old Southwest.

Fritz Oehlschlaeger

Rogers, William Penn Adair [Will]

Born: Near Claremore, Oklahoma, on November 4, 1879

Education: Did not complete secondary school

Marriage: Betty Blake, November 25, 1908, four children

Died: August 15, 1935

Biography

Three-sixteenths Cherokee, William Penn Adair (Will) Rogers was born on November 4, 1879, at his parents' ranch near Claremore, Oklahoma, in what was then Indian Territory, the home of the Cherokee nation after its forcible removal from Georgia along the "Trail of Tears" during the winter of 1837-1838. The youngest of seven children, by his own account he grew up wild. Though his father was a successful rancher, Rogers always considered "riding and roping" as play. He attended a number of schools, continuing his education for about ten years, but he claimed never to have gone beyond McGuffey's fourth reader. In 1898, he ran away from the Kemper Military Institute in Missouri, ending his formal education.

Between 1898 and 1902, Rogers moved from job to job. He was a ranch hand in the Southwest, then managed his father's ranch briefly before travelling to South America and then South Africa to work as a ranch hand again. He left this exploration of "frontiers" for jobs that brought his frontier experiences before urban audiences. His show business career began in 1903 when he joined Texas Jack's Wild West Show in South Africa as a trick rider and roper. He later joined Colonel Mulhall's Wild West

Show, performing in the United States, and eventually gained a vaudeville contract in New York. He married Betty Blake on November 25, 1908, and the couple had four children.

Rogers's career advanced as he rather casually moved from silent to verbal performance and as the news media discovered him. His first vaudeville act was composed simply of rope tricks, though these were by no means simple as can be seen in his silent film *The Roping Fool* (about 1920), parts of which are shown at the Will Rogers Memorial in Claremore. When he added humorous comments to his tricks, his popularity increased. Florenz Ziegfeld hired him for the Midnight Frolics in 1915. Forced to produce new material for each show, Rogers followed his wife's suggestion, turning to the newspapers and to his famous opening line, "All I know is what I read in the papers." This approach was well received, and as he improved his technique, his popularity grew until Ziegfeld gave him a place in the Follies in 1916.

In 1919, Rogers broke into print, where he published collections of his remarks about Prohibition and the Versailles Peace Conference. Moving to Hollywood, he made a number of films first with MGM, then on his own. When his own ventures failed, he returned to the Follies in New York City and also joined the lecture circuit, where his success attracted the attention of V.V. McNitt of the McNaught Newspaper Syndicate. McNitt offered Rogers a column in 1922. Rogers quickly established himself in this new medium. In 1926, he began a series of Daily Telegrams, short comments on current events, which were also syndicated and, along with his weekly columns, continued to appear until his death.

During this most productive period, Rogers continued to publish books and to lecture. He travelled throughout the world, appeared in plays and in such popular films as *A Connecticut Yankee in King Arthur's Court* (1931) and *State Fair* (1933), and was active in humanitarian relief for victims of natural and economic disasters. When he died in a plane crash with famed aviator Wiley Post on August 15, 1935, at Point Barrow, Alaska, he was generally considered the most popular man in America. This popularity is attested to by the impressive memorial which was established largely through donations and dedicated on November 4, 1938, just three years after his death.

Literary Analysis

When Donald Day edited *The Autobiography of Will Rogers* (1949), he said, "When all of Will's writings are published they will constitute the best *blow-by-blow* history of a period ever written" (p. xv). Day went on to argue that such a history would be unique in that it could be a common man's history, expressing the views of "the big Honest Majority" of Americans alive between 1922 and 1935. This argument reveals both the strength and the weakness of Rogers's humor. Because it was essentially topical and because it deliberately and wittily expressed the ideas of an American majority at a particular period in American history, his humor was very important in its time and place. For these same reasons, his writing has lost much of its power since World War II. Without a detailed knowledge of the period, readers find that most of his humor is inaccessible.

Still, one cannot deny Rogers's importance. He was probably the last humorist to hold virtually the whole nation as an audience. He came along at the moment when the mass media of print, film, and radio were unifying America through communication and when forces as various as the movement for racial equality and the vicissitudes of being a world power seemed to be dividing the nation into sometimes narrow interest groups. Rogers is often viewed as the first and the last media personality to express what might legitimately be called a general "American viewpoint."

Rogers is usually placed in the line of great "crackerbox philosophers," which includes such figures as Benjamin Franklin, Abraham Lincoln, and Mark Twain. As they did, Rogers distilled folk wisdom into wit, punctured the pompous, and extolled common sense as a cure for the "bunk" that so often seemed to pass for intelligence in American social life. Unlike them, Rogers was essentially a commentator; he did not establish an enduring reputation by means of political or literary achievement and, therefore, will probably become less widely read in the future.

Rogers's literary career began with his two collections on the Versailles Treaty and Prohibition, *The Cowboy Philosopher on the Peace Conference* (1919) and *The Cowboy Philosopher on Prohibition* (1919). Because these volumes were well received, he continued to publish selections from his columns and speeches. *The Illiterate Digest* (1924) was selected from his syndicated column. The pieces included in this collection dealt humorously and often ironically with daily events. Sometimes the irony was painful: "If your Hog has the Cholera the whole State knows it and everybody is assisting in stamping it out. You can have 5 Children down with the Infantile Paralysis . . . and see how many Doctors they send out from Washington to help you." Throughout his career, Rogers expressed anger at a government that generally ignored the human sufferings of its citizens while zealously protecting property. In *Letters of a Self-Made Diplomat to His President* (1926) and *There's Not a Bathing Suit in Russia* (1927), he collected *Saturday Evening Post* articles that he had written on a European tour.

Ether and Me (1929) is probably the one book that Rogers published that remains easily readable for today's audience. It amply reflects the personal Will Rogers, and, because it is more autobiography than commentary, it has not become dated. His jokes about doctors, nurses, and hospitals, and his jokes about himself remain funny, as when he describes the doctor completing his diagnosis: "Then he turned and exclaimed with a practiced and well-subdued enthusiasm, 'It's the Gall Bladder—just what I was afraid of.' Now you all know what that word 'afraid of,' when spoken by a doctor, leads to. It leads to more calls." In the hospital, he feels that he is always giving blood: "I was beginning to think that some of them were keeping a friend who might be anaemic." He inquires minutely into the nature of gallstones and learns their true causes: "Republicans staying in power too long will increase the epidemic; seeing the same endings to Moving Pictures is a prime cause; a wife driving from the rear seat will cause Gastric juices to form an acid, that slowly jells into a stone as she keeps hollering."

In addition to *Ether and Me*, Day's selections in the posthumous *The Autobiography of Will Rogers* and *Sanity Is Where You Find It* (1955) are likely to remain the most widely read of Rogers's literary works. Though much of the material in these selections is dated, enough remains available to contemporary audiences to make these volumes enjoyable reading. They capture well Rogers's characteristic approaches to humor and his attitudes toward the main social and political issues of his period.

Critics have noted that Rogers makes use of most of the familiar devices of literary humor in the American tradition, including humorous spellings, dialect, witty aphorisms, puns, exaggeration, and understatement. Critics agree that Rogers stands out because of his popularity and the resultant power he achieved over public opinion. No other humorist before or since seems to have so acutely gauged the public mind and so accurately spoken on its behalf. William R. Brown suggests that this unique power may have resulted in part from Rogers's command of irony. Rogers often creates a persona who presents an absurd position. When the reader or listener penetrates this mask, he feels a sense of communion with the "real" Will Rogers. This communion helps to move the reader to an understanding of Rogers's real position while simultaneously establishing an intimacy and trust between Rogers and his audience.

During the Depression, Rogers found ample

opportunity to practice irony. In one of his columns, he described a combine to city dwellers as one giant machine that makes just one trip over the ground. It begins by making "a deal to take over the ground (from the bank that is holding the present mortgage)," then it performs a number of functions including plowing, planting, and harvesting. The threshed grain is poured "into sacks and into a big Grain Elevator that is fastened onto the thing." Finally, "on near the back end is a stock Market board where a bunch of men that don't own the farm, the wheat, or the Combine, buy it back and forth from each other. This is if you have threshed a thousand bushels why they sell each other a million bushels of this thousand bushels which was actually threshed, then they announce to the farmer that on account of supply and demand, the wheat is only worth two bits." Obviously, Rogers is describing the economic machine rather than the harvesting machine, accounting for the harvest of poverty and suffering which he deplored in the Depression. As soon as his readers see through the mask's "naive mistake," they join their ally behind the mask in condemnation of the forces that victimized so many.

Summary

Though perhaps more important as a molder of public opinion between the World Wars, Will Rogers was an accomplished humorist in print, on stage, on radio, on the lecture platform, and in film. Because he spoke for the majority of Americans in his usually genial, yet telling commentary on the American scene, he was widely loved and admired. In addition to speaking forcefully on behalf of the unfortunate, he often worked directly for victims of disasters, establishing a reputation as a humanitarian. In his material and technique, he is related to the tradition of crackerbox humorists, but he made irony his special trademark. At his death, as "Unofficial President of the United States," he was probably the most popular man in America. The epitaph that he wrote for himself suggests why he was so beloved: "When I die, my epitaph . . . is going to read: 'I joked about every prominent man of my time, but I never met a man I didn't like.' I am proud of that. I can hardly wait to die so it can be carved and when you come 'round to my grave you'll find me sitting there proudly reading it."

Selected Bibliography

Primary Sources

The Cowboy Philosopher on the Peace Conference. New York: Harper, 1919.

The Cowboy Philosopher on Prohibition. New York: Harper, 1919.

The Illiterate Digest. New York: A. and C. Boni, 1924.

Letters of a Self-Made Diplomat to His President. New York: A. and C. Boni, 1926.

There's Not a Bathing Suit in Russia. New York: A. and C. Boni, 1927.

Ether and Me. New York and London: Putnam, 1929.

The Autobiography of Will Rogers. Ed. Donald Day. Boston: Houghton Mifflin, 1949.

Sanity Is Where You Find It. Ed. Donald Day. Boston: Houghton Mifflin, 1955.

The Writings of Will Rogers. Ed. Joseph A. Stout, Jr., and James M. Smallwood. Stillwater: Oklahoma State University Press, 1973.

Secondary Sources

Books

Alworth, Paul E. *Will Rogers.* New York: Twayne, 1974. The only full-length study of Rogers with chapters on the background, development, and the techniques of his humor.

Biography

Croy, Homer. *Our Will Rogers.* New York: Duell, Sloan, and Pearce, 1953. A good full biography with special attention to Rogers's life in California and work in the movies.

Day, Donald. *Will Rogers.* New York: David McKay, 1962. The standard biography. Complete and accurate, it captures fully Rogers's personality and the flavor of his humor.

Essays

Brown, William R. "Will Rogers: Ironist as Persuader." *Speech Monographs,* 99 (1972): 183–192. Though somewhat muddied with jargon, this essay helpfully explains and illustrates the special quality of Rogers's irony.

Yates, Morris. *The American Humorist.* Ames: Iowa State University Press, 1964, pp. 118–127. A chapter on Rogers as humorist and opinion maker.

Terry Heller

Rooney, Andrew Aitken [Andy]

Born: Albany, New York, on January 14, 1919

Education: Albany Academy; attended Colgate University

Marriage: Marguerite Howard, April 21, 1942, four children

Biography

The son of Walter S. and Ellinor (Reynolds) Rooney, Andrew Aitken Rooney was born in Albany, New York, on January 14, 1919. He graduated from Albany Academy and attended Colgate University in Hamilton, New York, until the end of his junior year when he was drafted into the army to serve during World War II. Prior to shipping overseas as a battery clerk he married Marguerite Howard on

April 21, 1942. He later became a reporter for *Stars and Stripes*, the London-based GI newspaper. He and his wife would raise four children, Ellen, Martha, Emily, and Brian.

Although he had dreamed of being a writer since he was twelve, had worked a summer as a copy boy for the *Albany Knickerbocker News*, and in college edited a literary-humorous magazine, he received his intensive training in journalism working for the *Stars and Stripes*. On assignment he flew some ten bombing raids and covered the French invasion, landing on the beach just four days after D-Day in June, 1944. During his stint in the army, he also collaborated on several books based on wartime experiences with fellow reporter Oram C. "Bud" Hutton.

Immediately after the war, Rooney and Hutton went to Hollywood, California, writing a screenplay and other assignments. Returning to Albany a year later, Rooney tried his hand as a free-lance magazine writer, publishing in *Look, Esquire, Life, Saturday Review, Harper's,* and *Reader's Digest* among others. His unpredictable income convinced him that there must be a better way to be a writer, and in 1949 he began his career in radio and television with the Columbia Broadcasting System. From 1949 to 1955, he wrote for Arthur Godfrey, and in the following years he wrote for Victor Borge, Herb Shriner, Sam Levenson, and Garry Moore. From 1962 to 1968, Rooney, as writer-producer, teamed with Harry Reasoner, as narrator, for news specials. The half-hour and hour documentaries touched on such ordinary subjects as doors, bridges, hotels, automobiles, and women. Rooney wrote whatever was needed at CBS, working on television documentaries and an occasional segment for CBS's weekly newsmagazine, *60 Minutes.*

In 1970, Rooney switched to the Public Broadcasting Service where he first appeared on television reading his own words. The following year he worked for ABC, but returned to CBS in 1972, continuing with the essay style that had worked so successfully with Reasoner. Now used to appearing on camera, he narrated his own hour specials. In 1978, he began appearing on *60 Minutes* with a short essay at the end of the show and, in 1979, he became a regular feature, delighting audiences with his three-minute essays. Also in 1979 he began writing a three-times-a-week syndicated newspaper column, expounding on the little things in life that affect people most. In the 1980s he published four books. The first was based on his TV essays, the last three were collections taken from his newspaper column.

Andy Rooney is a stocky man (5'9" and 200 lbs.), which adds to his self-promulgated image as the average man. He enjoys woodworking, browsing in hardware stores on Saturday mornings, baking bread, playing tennis, and being with his family. He shuns fame, never promoting his books and rarely appearing on the lecture circuit. He and his wife still live in the house in Rowayton, Connecticut, where they raised their four children.

Literary Analysis

Andy Rooney does not consider himself a humorist, but his dry sense of humor, his tongue-in-cheek delivery, and his wry wit argue otherwise. He is a folksy philosopher, ruminating over the ordinary things of everyday life. He approaches a subject, turns it inside out, flips it over and back again, gives it a couple of twists, puts it back together and presents an essay on it from a fresh perspective, all angles covered. Louis Grossberger, writing for *New York* magazine, put it best: "He doesn't do many jokes as such. Instead of 'Ha!' he goes for the 'Huh!'—that grunt of recognition and pleasure evoked when you hit somebody with a homely truth."[1]

Rooney's identification with the ordinary man runs through all of his writings. Even his early pieces on World War II focus on individuals and insights into the mind of the common man. With "Bud" Hutton, he wrote *Air Gunner* (1944), sketches of American soldiers in England who operated the guns on the planes flying missions over Europe. In 1946, Rooney and Hutton wrote *The Story of the Stars and Stripes*, combining the history of the GI newspaper with lively anecdotes about the staff and previously unrevealed details of World War II events. When Metro-Goldwyn-Mayer bought the screen rights to *The Story of the Stars and Stripes*, three weeks after Rooney and Hutton were honorably discharged from the army, both men went to Hollywood to write the screenplay. On another assignment the two returned to postwar Europe together and examined their findings in *Conqueror's Peace: A Report to the American Stockholders* (1947). In straightforward reporting they revealed how the Europeans felt toward the American occupation troops, the effect of war on the landscape, and looked at American cemeteries.

After the completion of his joint venture with Hutton, Rooney launched a short-term career as a free-lance writer. In March 1947, he published a now-it-can-be-told piece in *Harper's*, "Did They Try to Bomb New York?" The essay recounted the rumors of the robot bomb that hit New York City in 1944, his efforts to track down the story, and his interview with a German who was on a refueling ship for the submarine that launched one bomb before being captured. Even in this piece of historical reporting, Rooney becomes Everyman by describing his emotions: his curiosity at hearing the rumor, his frustration at being given the runaround from various government officials, and his satisfaction at sorting it all out when he talked to the German.

Finding the free-lance business too unpredictable, Rooney turned to radio and television and began his long association with the Columbia Broadcasting System in 1949. For over six years he wrote clever lines for Arthur Godfrey. In his article for *Look* magazine in 1959, "The Godfrey You Don't Know," Rooney discussed what he felt made Godfrey the popular entertainer that he was. Godfrey understood that people are lonely and they respond to being part of the group of mankind: "Godfrey, in his seemingly aimless talks, touches on basic elements of likeness in superficially unlike individuals, and every listener recognizes something of himself and feels he 'belongs.'"[2] Rooney could have been describing the characteristic that dominates his own writing. Perhaps he learned from Godfrey, or perhaps Godfrey learned from him.

Rooney later wrote for other CBS personalities, and from 1959 to 1964 he wrote for the *Garry Moore Show*. During this time, he also researched and wrote for the CBS News documentary programs *The Twentieth Century* and *Adventure*. In fact, research for one program led to his history, *The Fortunes of War: Four Great Battles of World War II* (1962). This book presents clear pictures of the battles of Tarawa, Stalingrad, D-Day, and the Bulge, combining straight military history with the story of individual soldiers at war in a readable manner. A History Book Club selection of 1962, it is one of Rooney's best works. While it is not humorous, humorous events are recalled and the personal element runs throughout.

As awards began to flow in during the six years that writer-producer Rooney teamed with narrator Harry Reasoner, Rooney came more into the public eye. Each of the television essays focused on single topics, but they expounded on all that touched the subject. "The Great Love Affair," on Americans and their cars, earned Rooney his first Writers Guild of America Award in 1966. Also in that year his "An Essay on Women" won a Peabody Award. The piece begins with his characteristic tongue-in-cheek manner: "This broadcast was prepared by men, and makes no claim to be fair. Prejudice has saved us a great deal of time in preparation."[3]

A serious essay on the misrepresentation of blacks in the media and history books, narrated by Bill Cosby, won Rooney a second Writers Guild of America Award in 1968. Another award-winning piece, "An Essay on War," was originally written as a segment for the CBS newsmagazine *60 Minutes*. When it was cut from a half-hour to fifteen minutes and rearranged considerably, Rooney rebelled. He bought the piece from CBS and walked directly to the Public Broadcasting Service. The essay aired on "The Great American Dream Machine" in 1971. Since everyone on the program read his own material, Rooney faced the camera for the first time. He did fifteen more pieces for the program before it went off the air.

When asked back to CBS, Rooney accepted. Now a veteran in front of the camera, he not only wrote and produced his hour-long specials but narrated them as well. "In Praise of New York City" captured the diversity of the city. "The Colleges" expanded on his 1969 essay "Burn, Bursar, Burn" which had appeared in *Life*, and suggested that parents supporting college students had reason to become campus militants. He criss-crossed the country to research "Mr. Rooney Goes to Dinner," analyzing restaurant decor, checks, and menus, and sampling the best and worst cuisine, putting on fourteen pounds in the process. He interviewed employees and employers in "Mr. Rooney Goes to Work," surprising himself with his conclusion that Americans are working hard and seem to like their jobs.

Rooney won another Peabody Award and Writers Guild of America Award for "Mr. Rooney Goes to Washington." Again he utilized the essay style and personal interview for a candid picture of life at the hub of our government: "The joke in government is that before you throw anything out, you Xerox it so you'll have a copy."[4]

Besides his essays, Rooney also wrote straight news segments for *60 Minutes*, but he argued that there was a place for a short essay somewhere at CBS. He was given a chance as a 1978 summer replacement for the "Point-Counterpoint" segment of *60 Minutes*. His essays were so successful that he became a regular, alternating weeks with "Point-Counterpoint" that fall. A year later "Point-Counterpoint" was out and Rooney was in, his popularity soaring.

His essays are videotaped in his office at CBS. Behind a cluttered desk, shelves in the background jumbled with books, papers and various important items, and with his two 1920 Underwood typewriters upon which he has written all his work from *Air Gunner* to the present at hand, he sits and talks to the camera. Occasionally he uses a prop or two—license plates, sunglasses, large packaging boxes for small products, or catalogues. His raspy voice complains, but the viewer understands that he has a legitimate complaint because his exasperation and disgust come through in his delivery, and his commentary is insightful.

The best of his television essays, both the three-minute pieces for *60 Minutes* and his longer specials, have been compiled in the best-selling book *A Few Minutes with Andy Rooney* (1981). "The Mr. Rooney Goes to . . ." series is included, even the dialogue is transcribed, so that it does not come across as quite smooth; some places need the intonation of his voice, the quizzical raising of a bushy eyebrow. His shorter essays stand on their own. Most are lighthearted: on political debates, ". . . we are, after all, electing a First Lady, too. So the last debate will be different. For half an hour, each candidate will argue with his wife" (p. 126); on a feminist changing her name from Goodman to Goodperson, "Well, I'm not going to say whether I think that was right or wrong. I have absolutely no opinion about that kind of idiocy" (p. 187). His "Essay on War" is moving and honest, philosophizing on the good and bad of war and the characteristics that it brings out in people. The serious essays contrast with his humorous ones, lending a balance to the book that makes it readable in one sitting, instead of being palatable just a couple of essays at a time.

Frustrated that he did not have sufficient outlets for his many ideas, Rooney began writing a syndicated column in 1979 that now appears three times a week in over 300 newspapers. The variety of subjects in his essays has led editors to argue—in some papers his column is on the editorial page, in others it is placed with the comics.

And More by Andy Rooney (1982), *Pieces of My Mind* (1984), and *Word for Word* (1986) are collections of the writer's finest newspaper essays. These books contain more polished pieces than his television essays, since they rely exclusively on the written word and do not depend on help from audiovisual equipment. These essays, like his television essays, are based on Rooney's personal prejudices and experiences. The reader is not bored by personal glimpses into the humorist's home or office. Instead, the reader understands and relates to his position because Rooney points out things that the reader knew but did not know that he knew or did not think that anyone else knew, too.

And More by Andy Rooney touches on many ordinary subjects: hangers, "A doorknob has a lot of advantages over the standard wire hanger" (p. 8); dictionaries, "The trouble with dictionaries is, they tell you more about words than you want to know without answering the questions you have" (p. 19); Christmas, "Someone always thinks something has been thrown out with the wrappings, but it turns out not to be true. It was under something else" (p. 150); memory, "The trouble with people with good memories is that they keep wanting to show it off to you by remembering things you don't want to hear" (pp. 212–213).

Pieces of My Mind continues in the same pattern. Rooney analyzes things in his simple, I'm-talking-to-you style and supplies a sampling of his dislikes (the flu, broken ribs, coughing, flies, elevators) and an equal number of his favorite things (friendship, rainy days, dogs, Henry Fonda). His common sense dominates his writing. Even if the reader disagrees with an opinion, he understands why Rooney has it.

Rooney's fans clamored for another book and in 1986 *Word for Word* was published. Again Rooney tackles a variety of subjects: the annoyances and pleasures that affect the reader, from spaghetti and doctors to gardening and grandfatherhood. He believes that Congress should rescind an old law every time it passes a new one and that it might be cheaper and more devastating to drop money on the Soviets instead of investing so much money in bombs. Of course he has a few words about his nemesis, the repairman. "It doesn't matter what job you want done, it's always the same. Things are worse than you thought" (p. 40).

Rooney believes that "Writing a column is one of the most satisfying things a writer can do and anyone who gets to write one is lucky."[5] Although he views his television work as an extension of his writing, because of the fleeting nature of fame, he realizes that if he is to be remembered, it will be for his work in print. Since there is plenty of material, his fans will probably be getting still another volume of his best newspaper essays soon.

Summary

Andy Rooney is a modern American Everyman. His humor comes from looking at ordinary things from a thoroughly analytical and often literalist point of view. His is truly American wit, built around middle-class American values and attitudes. He complains, he whines, but he hits homely truths that make his readers identify with him and thus feel a stronger bond with the family of man.

Notes

1. Lewis Grossberger, "A Few Minutes with Andy Rooney," *New York*, 13 (March 17, 1980), p. 47.
2. Andrew A. Rooney, "The Godfrey You Don't Know," *Look*, 23 (December 22, 1959), p. 82.
3. Ann Evory and Linda Metzger, eds., *Contemporary Authors* (Detroit: Gale, 1983), vol. 9, p. 425.
4. Andrew A. Rooney, *A Few Minutes with Andy Rooney* (New York: Atheneum, 1981), p. 151.
5. Andrew A. Rooney, "Column Writers Learn a Lot As They Go Along," *The Joplin Globe* (October 21, 1986), p. 4.

Selected Bibliography

Primary Sources

Books

The Fortunes of War. Boston: Little, Brown and Company, 1962.

A Few Minutes with Andy Rooney. New York: Atheneum, 1981.

And More by Andy Rooney. New York: Atheneum, 1982.

Pieces of My Mind. New York: Atheneum, 1984.

Word for Word. New York: Putnam, 1986.

Rooney and Oram C. Hutton. *Air Gunner*. New York: Farrar and Rinehart, 1944.

———. *Conqueror's Peace: A Report to the American Stockholders*. New York: Doubleday, 1947.

———. *The Story of the Stars and Stripes*. New York: Farrar and Rinehart, 1946; rpt. Westport, Conn.: Greenwood Press, 1970.

Rooney and Dickson Hartwell, eds. *Off the Record: The Best Stories of Foreign Correspondents*. New York: Doubleday, 1952.

Articles

"Did They Try to Bomb New York?" *Harper's*, 194 (March 1947): 274–276.

"A Place for Everything." *Saturday Review*, 42 (July 18, 1959): 31.

"The Godfrey You Don't Know." *Look*, 23 (December 22, 1959): 80–92.

"Fish." *Saturday Review*, 43 (August 20, 1960): 4, 6.

"Burn, Bursar, Burn." *Life*, 66 (June 13, 1969): 20.

"Life on the List, or My Struggle with 'Moses the Kitten.'" *The New York Times Book Review*, March 17, 1985, p. 3.

"Column Writers Learn a Lot as They Go Along." *The Joplin Globe*, October 21, 1986, p. 4.

Secondary Sources

Articles in Magazines and Books

"Bookends." *Time*, 128 (November 3, 1986): 84. Applauds Rooney's easy style in *Word for Word*. "Rooney is always good company" (p. 84).

Davis, Annie. "Book Review." *Library Journal*, 106 (November 1, 1981): 2135. Davis believes that Rooney is optimistic and favorably reviews *A Few Minutes with Andy Rooney*.

———. "Book Review." *Library Journal*, 107 (November 15, 1982): 2169. Davis like the combination of serious and humorous essays in *And More by Andy Rooney*.

Evory, Ann, and Linda Metzger, eds. *Contemporary Authors*. Vol. 9. Detroit: Gale, 1983, pp. 424–428. A good biography of Rooney, listing his awards and including a question-and-answer interview.

"A Few Seconds with Andy Rooney." *New Yorker*, 58 (February 7, 1983): 31–32. Presents a clear picture of the man, his opinions on being rich, the lecture circuit, and fame.

Grossberger, Lewis. "A Few Minutes with Andy Rooney." *New York*, 13 (March 17, 1980): 41+. This interview with Rooney captures his personality.

Harris, R.R. "And More by Andy Rooney." *The New York Times Book Review*, December 19, 1982, pp. 14–15. Harris favorably reviews Rooney's second collection of essays.

"The Man Behind Harry." *Time*, 94 (July 11, 1969): 68. A candid look at the man behind the Reasoner essays.

Miller, Holly G. "Sixty Minutes with Andy Rooney." *The Saturday Evening Post*, 256 (March 1984): 64+. Miller's interview with Rooney emphasizes his background and concludes that Rooney can

evoke emotions from the readers by describing his own.

Moritz, Charles, ed. *Current Biography Yearbook*. New York: H.W. Wilson, 1982, pp. 364–367. Good biographical portrait of Rooney.

Peer, Elizabeth. "The Lamentations of Rooney." *Newsweek*, 100 (December 6, 1982): 157. A brief biography of Rooney with a favorable critique of his work.

Reed, J. D. "Suburban Sage." *Time*, 120 (November 1, 1982): 82. This favorable review of *And More by Andy Rooney* is well done. Reed claims that "No one should suffer the minutiae of another person's life. Unless that person happens to be Andy Rooney" (p. 82).

"Rooney Tunes." *Time*, 116 (July 21, 1980): 62–63. A favorable review of Rooney's television spot on *60 Minutes*.

Teachout, Terry. "Books in Brief." *National Review*, 34 (October 1, 1982): 12–34. Teachout enjoyed Rooney's collection of television essays but thought that the transcripts of the "Mr. Rooney Goes to . . ." series were too rough and needed to be edited. Those portions needed the voice and camera to be effective.

Who's Who in America, 1984–85. Chicago: Marquis, 1984, p. 2787. Very brief biography of Rooney.

Veda Jones

Rosten, Leo[nard Calvin] [pseudonym Leonard Q. Ross]

Born: Lodz, Poland, on April 11, 1908

Education: University of Chicago, Ph.B., 1930, Ph.D., 1937; post-graduate studies, London School of Economics and Political Science, 1934; travel study in Europe, 1928, 1934, 1951, 1953; DHL, University of Rochester, 1973

Marriages: Priscilla Mead, March 30, 1935, deceased, three children; Gertrude Zimmerman, January 5, 1960

Biography

Born in Lodz, Poland, on April 11, 1908, Leonard C. Rosten was taken to Chicago by his parents at the age of three. He attended grammar school in Chicago, and later entered the University of Chicago. By 1930 he had completed his Ph.B. and taken his first of many trips to Europe. During this time he supported himself by teaching night school English to immigrants—the primary source of his material for the Hyman Kaplan stories.

By 1932 he had enrolled in the Graduate School of Political Science and International Relations at the University of Chicago. In 1934 he entered the London School of Economics and Political Science, graduating with a Ph.D. in 1937. The ensuing wartime years saw Leo Rosten serving the U.S. government and, later, several corporations in a variety of high-level defense-related government posts, working as a consultant, advisor, and administrator. This service was interspersed with a number of prestigious teaching positions at such institutions as Stanford, New York University, Yale, UCLA, and Berkeley, among others. He is presently a faculty associate at Columbia University and is engaged in research on communications and symbolism.

In addition to his work as an economist and political scientist, Rosten haş served a number of literary and educational organizations: the National Book Committee, the Author's Guild of America, the Author's League of America, and the Education Association Education Policies Commission. He has also received the Freedom Foundation award, the Commonwealth Club, San Francisco, Silver Medal for Literature, and the George Polk Memorial Award.

In 1935, to pay debts incurred through the illness of his newly wed wife, Priscilla Ann Mead, he began to write humorous sketches for *The New Yorker* that resulted in the later publication of his most notable works of humor, the Hyman Kaplan stories. This success was followed by an offer from Hollywood to do screen writing. By 1941 he had written three sociological books based on his Hollywood experience, his ideas about films, and his experience with filmmaking: *Hollywood, The Movie Colony,* and *The Movie Makers.* During his involvement with Hollywood, Rosten made over ten movies under the pseudonym Leonard Ross. In addition, *The Education of H*Y*M*A*N K*A*P*L*A*N* was adapted as a musical and opened at the Alvin Theatre, New York, in April 1968.

Rosten has become best known as a writer of stories, satires, social commentary, and essays. Yet while his most noted books have been the two volumes of humorous sketches published under the pseudonym Leonard Q. Ross, *The Education of H*Y*M*A*N K*A*P*L*A*N* (1937), and *The Return of Hyman Kaplan* (1938), his remarkable versatility as a writer is displayed best in the Rosten anthology, *The Many Worlds of Leo Rosten* (1964).

Literary Analysis

In his Preface to *The Return of Hyman Kaplan,* Rosten defines his own humor as "the affectionate communication of insight." He goes on to point out that for any writer, the genre of humor is the subtlest and most difficult of forms and cites as evidence of this the fact that there are a thousand novelists, essayists, poets, and journalists for each humorist in American literature. His quantitative contribution to American humorous literature is confined to five small volumes and miscellaneous pieces, but his significance is suggested by Sir Isaiah Berlin, who has written that Hyman Kaplan is "one of the great comic creations of the twentieth century." Louis Untermeyer gives both Kaplan books high praise, while Charles Rolo calls Kaplan "a Shakespeare of broken English."

Writing in the comic traditions of Josh Billings, Artemus Ward and Mark Twain, S. J. Perelman, Ring Lardner, James Thurber, and to a degree, Dorothy Parker, Rosten relies heavily on comic dialect, the solecism, the pun, the malapropism, blasé quips, slang, *faux pas,* genteelisms, oxymoron, metathesis, litotes, synecdoche, polyopton, mimesis, paranomasia, "malaprintism" and metonymy. In fact, his absolute relish for such verbal miscegenation is Elizabethan in its sophistication and glee.

The Hyman Kaplan stories depend for their primary effect on these techniques learned from a variety of sources in English, American and classical literature. But the primary effect is certainly derived from the "antic" spelling of Hymie Kaplan's phonetically rendered Eastern European pronunciation and verbal goofs, something Rosten learned much about from Ring Lardner's genius at depicting eccentric characters through their idioms.

With his own Eastern European parentage and experience teaching English at a night school for adult immigrants, Rosten has developed a fine ear for the nuances of mispronunciation, lexicon, and idiomatic usage common to a variety of immigrants from the Mediterranean to the Baltic. He portrayed them in the humorous setting of the pedantic and earnest Mr. Parkhill's beginners' class in American English. Through Mr. Parkhill's classroom parades not only the expansive and buoyant H*Y*M*A*N K*A*P*L*A*N, but the Goldbergs, Tomasics, Mitnicks, Kowalskis, Weinsteins, Feigenbaums, Rodrigueses, Rubins, Plonskys, and Moskowitzes who represent a cross-section of the European immigrants of the 1920s and 1930s. His humor derives from the depiction of his chief comic creation, Hyman Kaplan, and the mock heroic situation comedy of the adult night school students' attempts to learn English grammar, idiom, and usage.

Both books are written in the third person, and interspersed generously with the direct "misspeak" of numerous students who come up against the beleaguered pedantic and proper Mr. Parkhill, their beloved teacher. Blessed with an abject earnestness and kindliness of purpose, Mr. Parkhill is most frequently seen flailing, at best ironically, at worst, helplessly, under the explosions of exotic personality, international conflict, wrenched syntax, comic mispronunciation, and hilarious verbal incapacity of his students. A kind of Don Quixote in his mock heroic attempts to correct each and every error of usage and pronunciation, he become a perfect straight man for the central protagonist.

Philosophical, full of *noblesse oblige* and sophistry, Hyman Kaplan is a buoyant, expansive individual possessed of an imperishably bland smile and a flamboyant habit of writing his name on both blackboard and homework exercise—H*Y*M*A*N K*A*P*L*A*N—in colored crayons. He is further distinguished by his grand oratorical style, his enthusiastic "Hau Kay's," his joy in rushing to the front of the classroom to orate on any pretext, and his ingenious rationalizations for his linguistic havoc with synonyms, antonyms, superlatives, comparatives and the full gamut of English usage. Above all, he is possessed of a great and gracious humanity.

The tone of Rosten's humor is warm and accepting as he depicts Mr. Parkhill's gentleness of spirit, lack of imagination, and verbal skills in tandem with Hyman Kaplan's noble spirit, excess of imagination and limited linguistic universe. In addition, he presents a whole galaxy of national stereotypes including Mrs. Moskowitz with her limited mental capacities and her "Cimmerian sufferings," Mrs. Rodrigues with her "Latin temperament," Mr. Plonsky with his exasperated back turnings, Mrs. Tarnova with her Dosteoevskian Russian passions, and Miss Mitnick with her infuriating prissy correctness and abject shyness.

Those sensitive to the ethnic stereotyping that inevitably erupts from the depiction of the respective dialects of numerous European nationals will find much to complain of in these sketches written during the Depression years of the 1930s. However, Rosten has provided as fine a map of the linguistic potpourri of major eastern American cities during that wave of European immigration as Twain did with his nineteenth-century Pike County dialects in *Huckleberry Finn*. Rosten's faithful linguistic rendering preserves the speech and language problems of a whole era of new Americans.

Perhaps next to the Hyman Kaplan stories, Leo Rosten is best known for his immensely popular volume, *The Joys of Yiddish* (1968), reprinted numerous times. One reviewer comments, "Leo Rosten does for the Yiddish language what Cezanne did for the apple—gives it a body and soul, and typically he adds an affectionate and witty wisdom." Certainly the funniest

piece of dictionary building and annotation in the American language, *The Joys of Yiddish* is both remarkably erudite and remarkably funny with its teasingly eccentric insights into both the Yiddish language and the Jewish culture and history from which it arose. It is a superb exercise in comic lexicography.

Less well known than the Hyman Kaplan stories are four other works of humor by Leo Rosten. *Rome Wasn't Burned in a Day: The Mischief of Language* (1972) delightfully illustrated by Robert Day, contains a collection of verbal bloopers and misquoted adages that demonstrate Rosten's hilarious sense of humor and sophisticated grasp of the structure of language. His most "Elizabethan" sortie into the realms of verbal humor, this work is remarkably cultured and erudite by comparison with the Hyman Kaplan stories, and less endearing. It reads more like a series of *Punch* cartoons with captions than a story.

Dear "Herm": With a Cast of Dozens (1974) consists of a series of letters, some of which are purportedly written by Leo Rosten, the noted humorist, and Herm, a rather hapless boyhood friend; and others are written to various correspondents. Their humor rests on Rosten's acute perception of the mental habits of Herm and his inimitable wife, Flo, along with the rest of the cast. The humor is at the expense of the ebullient but uneducated Herm, or is self-satire, but much more is general social criticism. Once again, Rosten evokes the revealing spelling, editing, typing, and linguistic habits of his correspondents in a visual form, as he did in the Hyman Kaplan stories. The typeface is that of a manual home typewriter; the formats are the memo, the personal letter, the business letter, the advertising circular, the letter to the editor, inscribed letterhead, and desk-pad letterhead. They show the mental, social and written language habits of our post-war era American bureaucracy.

The Power of Positive Nonsense (1977), Rosten's most recently published work of humor, takes its title from Norman Vincent Peale's *The Power of Positive Thinking*. Section One contains a format borrowed from Benjamin Franklin and entitled "Poor Rosten's Almanac." Full of well-known saws, truisms, and proverbial wisdom such as "A picture is worth a thousand words," this section contains funny short annotations designed to debunk the "nonsense," "twiddle," and "flapdoodle" people believe without questioning. Other sections include "It Just Aint So," which examines commonly misunderstood facts: a section called "Quiz on Quotes," annotating the circumstances surrounding the original quote; a further section called simply "Fanmail," and a final section on eccentric trivia.

This book has not been as acclaimed as the Hyman Kaplan stories.

Summary

Economist, political scientist, researcher, prominent lecturer, government adviser and humorist, Leo Rosten (pseudonym Leonard Q. Ross) is mostly remarkable for the diversity of his expertise, as reflected in his anthology *The Many Worlds of Leo Rosten.* Primary among his contributions to American humor are his three volumes of Hyman Kaplan stories and perhaps his more enduring work, *The Joys of Yiddish.* Rosten, along with S.J. Perelman, is a significant twentieth-century American humorist and an important figure in post-war American-Jewish literature.

Selected Bibliography

Primary Sources (Humorous Works)

The Education of H*Y*M*A*N K*A*P*L*A*N. New York: Harcourt, Brace and World, 1937.

The Return of Hyman Kaplan. New York: Harper and Row, 1938; rpt. 1959.

The Joys of Yiddish. New York: McGraw-Hill, 1968.

Rome Wasn't Burned in a Day. New York: Doubleday, 1972.

Dear Herm. New York: McGraw-Hill, 1974.

O Kaplan, My Kaplan. New York: Harper and Row, 1976.

The Power of Positive Nonsense. New York: McGraw-Hill, 1977.

Secondary Sources

Foell, Earl W. "English Without Tears." *Christian Science Monitor,* September 17, 1959, Books Section. Review of *The Return of H*Y*M*A*N K*A*P*L*A*N.*

Golub, Ellen. "Leo Rosten." In *Dictionary of Literary Biography.* Vol. 11. *American Humorists 1800–1950.* Ed. Stanley Trachtenberg. Detroit: Gale, 1982, pp. 410–418. Overview of Rosten's life and works.

Rolo, Charles. "Reader's Choice," *Atlantic,* 204, no. 5 (November 1959): p. 176. Review of *The Return of H*Y*M*A*N K*A*P*L*A*N.*

Untermeyer, Louis. "A Naturalized Natural." *Saturday Review of Literature* 26, no. 17 (August 21, 1937): 5. Essay-review of *The Education of H*Y*M*A*N K*A*P*L*A*N.*

Van Gelder, Robert. "A Mr. Malaprop in the Bronx Idiom," *New York Times Book Review,* August 29, 1937, p. 11.

Gloria L. Cronin

Royko, Mike

Born: Chicago, Illinois, on September 19, 1932

Education: Wright Junior College, 1951–1952

Marriage: Carol Joyce Duckman, November 7, 1954, she died September 1979

Biography

Mike Royko was born in Chicago, the city where he has spent all of his career, and the city that has fed him the stories and characters that he has reported, enlarged, and invented in the course of his writing career. He was born September 19, 1932, the son of Michael and Helen Zak Royko.

Royko attended Wright Junior College before entering the United States Air Force in 1952. After serving a four-year hitch, he went to work as a reporter for Chicago's North Side Newspapers briefly before joining Chicago's legendary City News Bureau where he worked for three years as a reporter and eventually as assistant city editor.

Royko left the City News Bureau in 1959 to join the paper with which he has so far had the longest association, *The Chicago Daily News.* He became a reporter and then a columnist for the *Daily News* and was named associate editor for the paper in 1978, the year before it folded.

Chicago had been America's greatest newspaper city in its heydey, but the number of papers had dwindled by the late 1970s. With the closing of the *News,* Royko moved to the *Chicago Sun-Times* and stayed for six years, until the paper was purchased by Australian media magnate Rupert Murdoch in 1984. Royko publicly confessed to a dislike for Murdoch, and he moved to Chicago's other remaining daily, *The Chicago Tribune.*

Royko's columns were frequently collected in books, and they were nearly always best-sellers: *I May Be Wrong, But I Doubt It* (1968), *Slats Grobnick and Some Other Friends* (1973), and *Sez Who? Sez Me* (1983). Despite his other titles, such as associate editor, Royko prefers being called a reporter. As such, he has had few peers, as exemplified by *Boss* (1971), his vivid portrait of Mayor Richard J. Daley. He won the 1972 Pulitzer Prize for commentary for columns that were eventually collected in *Slats Grobnick.* Royko also won the Heywood Broun Award in 1968 and the Medal for Service from the University of Missouri School of Journalism in 1979; he was inducted into the Chicago Press Club's Hall of Fame in 1980.

Literary Analysis

As Tom Wolfe wrote in his memoir of the early days of "New Journalism," the concept of the newspaper column was defined by "snore-mongers" such as Walter Lippmann and Arthur J. Krock. "The usual practice," Wolfe wrote, "was to give a man a column as a reward for outstanding service as a reporter. That way they could lose a reporter and gain a bad writer." Royko, along with Jimmy Breslin in New York, changed the concept of the newspaper column and created new models to follow. Gone was the cud-chewing and rumination over what it all *meant*; the new model consisted of reporting and a different sort of wizened commentary. Royko was among those who pioneered this new form of column-writing in the 1960s. His domain was Chicago, and he was to that city what Damon Runyon had been to New York.

Royko may have used a few "stretchers" (as Mark Twain would have called them) but the demands of the newspaper column required him to relate stories that were essentially true. His skill is in finding the comic scene within the ordinary. As a photographer develops an eye to see pictures that others cannot, Royko manages to find the humor in everyday life that many miss.

Even on a slow day, when the ideas might appear to have vanished, Royko still has to meet the demands placed on all journalists; he must produce. It was on such a slow day that he decided to attack the alleged imbecility of residents of a neighboring state—Indiana. When he received an overwhelming response to his column, he commented on the mail, noting that most of the letters were written with Crayolas.

Royko's writing style has been imitated by a number of columnists, but as *Harper's* noted in 1982 in a review of *Sez Who? Sez Me*: "If he isn't the dean, Mike Royko is certainly one of the more distinguished faculty members in the school of beer-and-a-shot journalism."

Not all of Royko's columns are humorous. He earned his daily spot in the newspaper and he often uses it to ruminate, though with more entertaining results than Walter Lippmann. While most of Royko's books are collections of columns, *Boss* is a more sustained work about Mayor Richard J. Daley of Chicago. Though it contains a good deal of humor, it also shows how Royko got to the top of the journalism profession. He applies the techniques used by good reporters in writing his columns to produce effective, often humorous, and credible characters and situations for his commentaries.

Summary

Mike Royko's tough-talking characters from Chicago have earned him a place in the top rank of American newspaper columnists. He is something akin to a Damon Runyon for the latter part of the twentieth century.

Selected Bibliography

Primary Sources

Up Against It. Chicago: Regnery, 1967.
I May be Wrong But I Doubt It. New York: Dutton, 1968.
Boss. New York: Dutton, 1971.
Slats Grobnick and Some Other Friends. New York: Dutton, 1973.
Sez Who? Sez Me. New York: Dutton, 1982.
Like I was Sayin'. New York: Dutton, 1984.

Secondary Sources

S., D. B. "Sez Who? Sez Me." *Harper's*, 265, no. 1590 (November 1982): 76–77.
Who's Who in America. 44th ed. Vol. 2. Wilmett, Ill.: Marquis Who's Who, 1986.
Wolfe, Tom, *The New Journalism.* New York: Harper, 1973.

William McKeen

Runyon, [Alfred] Damon

Born: Manhattan, Kansas, on October 8, 1880

Education: Formal education concluded at sixth grade when he was expelled

Marriages: Ellen Egan, May 1911, died, 1931, two children; Patrice Amati, July 7, 1932

Died: December 10, 1946

Biography

The son of Alfred Lee and Libbie (Damon) Runyan, Alfred Damon Runyan was born in Manhattan, Kansas, on October 8, 1880. Young Al was moved from town to town in Kansas as his father, a printer and sometime newspaper editor, changed jobs. When the family ended up in Pueblo, Colorado, Al started his education at Hinsdale School. After his mother died when he was nine, he was left alone with his father, who was not particularly paternal. Al became a boy of the streets, attending school only often enough to keep out of the truant officer's hands. Always into mischief, in the sixth grade he was expelled and began hanging around saloons, listening to the tales of his father and the other men, and working as an errand boy for local newspapers, where he picked up the newspaper fever. That same year he published his first two stories in the *Pueblo Colorado Advertiser*, which was temporarily being edited by his father. He was thirteen years old. By the age of fifteen he was hired as a full-time reporter by the *Pueblo Evening News*. When a typesetter misspelled his last name, changing the "a" to "o," Al liked the way it looked and from then on went by "Runyon."

The next decade of Runyon's life was one of turmoil—traveling, hard drinking, carousing with women of the night, and listening, always listening, to the people around him. At eighteen he enlisted in the army and was shipped to the Philippines during the Spanish-American War. In 1900, he was discharged, spent all of his money on a drinking binge in California, and lived as a hobo for six months before riding the rails back to Pueblo. There he found a job as a reporter on the *Chieftain* and wrote verse as leads to his stories, which gained him the moniker "The Colorado Kipling." His first published poem, "Song of the Bullet," was printed by *Collier's Magazine* in 1904. Runyon's heavy drinking cost him the *Chieftain* job and several others in Colorado towns, including Denver. For a brief time he reported sports for the *San Francisco Post*, then returned to Denver to write for the *Rocky Mountain News*.

In 1907, his first short story, "Two Men Named Collins," was published in *Reader* magazine. Other stories and poems followed in *McClure's*, *Lippincott's*, *Harper's* and *Everybody's*. This success prompted Al to move to the nation's publishing capital, New York, to become a writer. He had quit drinking, because a doctor had told him that his heart could not stand any more blackout binges, and because he knew that drinking stood in the way of success. To compensate, he drank coffee, somewhere between twenty and forty cups a day. Al was still producing short stories, but after a year in New York, needed a steady job. When a friend got him an interview at William Randolph Hearst's *New York American* in 1911, he began a career with the Hearst newspapers that continued for 35 years. He was assigned to the sports desk, where the editor took one look at his three name by-line, said "too long," and cut the Alfred.

Damon married Ellen Egan, a former society editor from Denver, in May 1911, and began making a name for himself as a reporter. He covered sporting events—baseball, horse racing, boxing—and as the need arose, he covered political conventions and trials. By 1914, his colorful commentary had won him his own column, "The Mornin's Mornin'," which covered any subject that happened to catch his fancy. His short stories were featured in the Sunday section in the *New York American*, and they also were syndicated by the Hearst newspaper chain across the country as well. He also began writing short stories for magazines again. Subjects for both his column and his stories came from his years of listening to the people around him, both Broadway gangsters and the people back in his home town.

Ellen died in 1931, leaving Damon with two children. Since they had been separated three years before her death, he continued in the lifestyle that he had set for himself, hanging out in Broadway bars (drinking coffee) and coming in to sleep when the sun came up. The children were sent to Ellen's relatives. On July 7, 1932, Damon married a twenty-five-year-old showgirl, Patrice Amati. They had an apartment in New York, a house in Florida, and another in California, where Damon worked on movies. Sixteen of his stories were made into movies during his lifetime, an achievement of which he was very proud. This was perhaps his happiest period, but it did not last long. He and Patrice were divorced after fourteen years of marriage.

Two years before his death on December 10, 1946, Damon was diagnosed as having cancer of the throat. His larynx was removed, leaving him voiceless and able to communicate only by mouthed words or by scribbled notes. Still, he continued to write his column. These pieces were some of his more somber works but also some of his best.

Walter Winchell, a radio commentator and newspaperman, was so moved by his friend's death that he started the Damon Runyon Cancer Fund for research. He expected to make $50,000 from contributions from Damon's readers, but millions poured in. The Damon Runyon–Walter Winchell Cancer Fund, renamed after Winchell died of the same disease, is still in existence, funding fellowships for research.

Literary Analysis

Damon Runyon was a writer, but first and foremost, he was a newspaperman. He learned his trade from his father, his early editors at small-town Colorado newspapers, and from the yellow journalistic press of the Hearst newspaper empire. He also learned by listening—listening to the men spin yarns in the Pueblo saloons, listening to soldiers' conversations during the war, and listening to the underworld figures talking on Broadway. He understood that people wanted to hear the human element of a story, and that is exactly what he added to straight news. In his sports reporting, he told anecdotes about the players, sometimes not getting to the point of who won the contest until the fifth or sixth paragraph. Embellishment added length to his pieces, and many times he had several articles and columns in the same edition; that he was a prolific writer is not disputed, but it is difficult to believe he could have written the ninety million published words attributed to him.

Runyon's first two published volumes, *The Tents of Trouble* (1911) and *Rhymes of the Firing Line* (1912), were collections of verse. A later volume, *Poems for Men* (1947), was published posthumously and reprints some rhymes about hobos and soldiers from the first two volumes and some new ones about gamblers and athletes. In his poems, Runyon used slang, described the common man, and many consider the verses Runyon's addition to the genre of American folk tales. He reflects on emotions Everyman can understand—loneliness, failure, and disappointment—but always ends with an optimistic note. Many times he introduced a newspaper sports story with a light verse. Most famous is his "A Handy Guy Like Sande," about jockey Earl Sande, which was reprinted several times between 1922 and 1940. Runyon wrote new stanzas when the jockey would bring winning horses across the finish line. Although more light rhymes than serious poetry, several of his poems have become familiarly quoted, but his authorship is usually not acknowledged. Runyon himself said that he gave up poetry because there was no money in it, and money was very important to him.

There was a great deal of money for Damon Runyon in writing short stories. In July of 1929, his first Broadway story appeared in *Cosmopolitan.* "Romance in the Roaring Forties" sent his popularity soaring, and it was said by one editor that a Damon Runyon story touted on the cover boosted a magazine's circulation by 60,000. Runyon had been writing vignettes for his column about his nightly haunts on Broadway using the same style that he employed in his stories, but it was the short stories, printed in *The Saturday Evening Post, Liberty, Cosmopolitan,* and *Collier's,* that made sixteen blocks of Broadway, from Times Square to Columbus Circle, famous.

The Broadway stories featured gangsters and gamblers and the underworld society that flourished during Prohibition. Narrated in the first person by a nameless, innocent bystander, the stories were told almost entirely through conversation. Using the historic present tense, the narrator parleys with "I say" and "He says," the speech pattern that Runyon heard from the less-educated people who prowled Broadway through the wee hours of the morning. Runyon embellished the slang he heard and developed his own particular dialect that came to be called "Runyonese." He called men "guys" and women "dolls," "sweethearts," "broads," and "pancakes," affectionate but condescending terms. Nicknames were important and oftentimes employed alliteration. Dave the Dude, Hot Horse Herbie, and Tobias the Terrible were all members of the Broadway set. Runyon coined words by adding suffixes such as -enroo, -aroo, -ola, and -us. Phonus balonus was a small alteration of phony baloney. He used gangsters' terms: guns were rods, betsys, old equalizers, rooty-toot-toots; a yes-man was a nod guy; a tongue

was a lawyer. Set expressions were also a part of Runyonese. "No little and quite some" and "more than somewhat" were Runyon trademarks.

The Broadway stories were sentimental, humorous, and often ended with a twist, not unlike those of O. Henry, but social comment was hidden among the humor. The underworld code of ethics and loyalty was based on trust, and Runyon often hinted at the difference between appearance and reality. Society actually lived with one set of values while advocating another.

The Broadway stories were collected in several anthologies. The first two, *Guys and Dolls* (1931) and *Blue Plate Special* (1934), were enormous successes. Fourteen movies were made from these stories during his lifetime. After his death, his most famous, *Guys and Dolls,* was adapted first as a play and later as a movie.

Damon Runyon's columns, "The Mornin's Mornin," "As I See It," "Damon Runyon Says," and "The Brighter Side," provided material for several books. *My Old Man* (1939) contains vignettes that remind one of Runyon's father in his Pueblo days. Told by narrator A. Mugg, the dialogue is generally in the past tense. Although A. Mugg repeats "my old man said" too many times, the home-spun philosophy about ordinary human behavior makes interesting and amusing reading.

My Wife Ethel (1939) was based on a series of columns about a middle-American couple. Joe Turp, the narrator, writes letters about life with his wife and her opinions. This time Runyon used the present tense, lower-class speech patterns, and very little punctuation. These vignettes reflect the working-class ideals held by the law-abiding people who work within the system. A short story that Runyon wrote about the Turps, "A Call on the President," was made into a movie.

In Our Town (1946) received overall favorable reception, which surprised Runyon because the sketches had not caused much of a stir when they were originally published in his column. These stories are told in the past tense by an innocent bystander, and Runyon's typical slang and pat expressions are missing as he attempted to create a terse, closely woven story. The good guy does not necessarily win in these vignettes, which reflect a bitter outlook. Yet, humor, present in irrelevant comments or absurd situations, breaks the tense moods Runyon sets.

Runyon's *Trials and Other Tribulations* (1948) includes some of his best reporting. The newspaper accounts of five trials plus one Senate subcommittee hearing were colored with descriptions of not only the accused and the accuser but the spectators as well. Although made humorous through Runyon's sports analogies and other descriptive slang expressions, the emotional reaction of the people comes through, and the reader feels that he was present at the trial.

Runyon collaborated with Howard Lindsay on one play, *A Slight Case of Murder*. It was a typical Broadway tale, about a bootlegger and a corpse. Although it did not meet with great success, closing after seventy performances, it was later made into a movie.

Damon Runyon anthologies have been printed in nine foreign languages, and thirteen of his volumes were published in England, where his works were enormously popular. Although most of his books are out of print, library circulation attests that he still has a following in the United States.

Summary

Damon Runyon was a newspaperman. He had an eye for detail and an understanding of the human emotions that make up a story. Although he wrote poetry and one play, his newspaper columns and his short stories were what won him immense popularity in the United States and abroad. A British critic has commented that Runyon made an outstanding contribution to humorous writing, with his use of the present tense, his exaggerations, and his Runyonese. American critics were not as kind. Popularity was considered a negative element by American critics, and they called Runyon's work simple, stylized, and sentimental. It may have been, but his humorous columns were read by millions of people daily, and when one mentions a specific Damon Runyon character, a vivid mental image immediately fills one's mind.

Selected Bibliography

Primary Sources

Poetry

The Tents of Trouble, Ballads of the Wanderbund and Other Verse. New York: Desmond Fitzgerald, 1911.

Rhymes of the Firing Line. New York: Desmond Fitzgerald, 1912.

Poems for Men. Garden City, N.Y.: Permabooks, 1951.

Short Stories

Guys and Dolls. New York: Frederick A. Stokes, 1931.

Blue Plate Special. New York: Frederick A. Stokes, 1934.

Money from Home. New York: Frederick A. Stokes, 1935.

Take It Easy. New York: Frederick A. Stokes, 1938.

The Best of Damon Runyon. New York: Frederick A. Stokes, 1938.

The Damon Runyon Omnibus. Garden City, N.Y.: Sun Dial Press, 1944.

Runyon a la Carte. Philadelphia: J.B. Lippincott, 1944.

The Three Wise Guys and Other Stories. New York: Avon, 1946.

Runyon, First and Last. Philadelphia: J.B. Lippincott, 1949.

More Guys and Dolls. Garden City, N.Y.: Garden City Books, 1951.

Newspaper Columns

My Old Man. New York: Stackpole Sons, 1939.

My Wife Ethel. Philadelphia: David McKay, 1939.

In Our Town. New York: Creative Age Press, 1946.

Short Takes, Reader's Choice of the Best Columns of America's Favorite Newspaperman. New York: Somerset Books, 1946.

Trials and Other Tribulations. Philadelphia: J.B. Lippincott, 1948.

Plays

(co-authored with Howard Lindsay.) *A Slight Case of Murder*. New York: Dramatists Play Service, 1940.

Secondary Sources

Books

D'Itri, Patricia Ward. *Damon Runyon*. Boston: Twayne Publishers, 1982. A critical review of Runyon's style.

Hoyt, Edwin P. *A Gentleman of Broadway*. Boston: Little, Brown, 1964. An excellent biography and critical analysis.

Mosedale, John. *The Men Who Invented Broadway*. New York: Richard Marek Publishers, 1981. A well-documented and very readable account of Damon Runyon, Walter Winchell, and their times.

Runyon, Damon, Jr. *Father's Footsteps*. New York: Random House, 1953. A son's view of his famous father and their struggle to understand each other.

Weiner, Ed. *The Damon Runyon Story*. New York: Longmans, Green, 1948. Biography with contemporary information.

Articles in Books and Magazines

Block, Maxine, ed. "Damon Runyon." In *Current Biography 1942*. New York: H.W. Wilson, 1942, pp. 723–725. Good biographical portrait of Runyon.

Grant, Thomas. "Damon Runyon." *Dictionary of Literary Biography*. Vol. 11, Part 2. *American Humorists, 1800–1950*. Ed. Stanley Trachtenberg. Detroit: Gale Research Company, 1982, pp. 419–429. A condensed biography and analysis of Runyon's best-known works.

"Hand Me My Kady." *Time*, 48 (December 23, 1946): 57–58. Obituary of a true newspaperman.

"My Old Man." *New York Times*, November 19, 1939, p. 26. Favorable review of Runyon's book. Says his "humor is human and unforced."

Peterson, Ralph. "Short Takes." *Christian Science Monitor*, May 18, 1946, p. 16. Peterson compares Runyon's philosophy to Will Rogers's and Mark Twain's.

"Runyon with the Half-Boob Air." *Time*, 47 (June 24, 1946): 70–71. Reviews Runyon's review of his own book, *Short Takes*.

Veda Jones

Schisgal, Murray Joseph

Born: Brooklyn, New York, on November 25, 1926

Education: Long Island University, New York; Brooklyn Law School, LL.B., 1953; New School for Social Research, New York, B.A., 1959.

Marriage: Reene Schapiro, on June 29, 1958

Biography

The son of an immigrant, Murray Schisgal was born November 25, 1926, in Brooklyn, New York. Although Schisgal became a full-time writer in 1960, his prior experiences vary widely, ranging from a stint in the U.S. Navy to a five-year stay teaching English in an East Harlem high school.

Leaving Thomas Jefferson High School at age sixteen, Schisgal served as a radioman in the navy from 1944 until 1946. After this, Schisgal began to earn his high school diploma at night; he also worked odd jobs, among them playing saxophone and clarinet as a jazz musician. Writing short stories all the while, Schisgal left New York to travel, first taking a bus to Miami, Florida, and then hitchhiking to New Orleans, Louisiana, Houston, Texas, and Canada. Returning to New York, Schisgal spent two years at Long Island University, after which he started law school on the G.I. Bill. He earned his LL.B. from Brooklyn Law School in 1953, hoping to use his law degree to sustain him while he wrote. After spending several years attempting to balance the practice of law and the discipline of writing, Schisgal gave up his law practice. Working at another string of odd jobs—including typing and teaching English in a Chassidic Yeshiva—he eventually earned a B.A. at the New School for Social Research in New York. During this time, roughly from 1955 until 1960, he also taught English at James Fenimore Cooper High School in East Harlem, and in 1958 he married Reene Schapiro.

Having written numerous short stories and three novels, none of which were published, Schisgal turned to writing plays. When he and his wife stopped in London in 1960 on their way to Spain, where they were planning to live briefly so that Schisgal could write uninterruptedly, a London producer optioned and produced three of Schisgal's plays—*The Typists*, *The Tiger*, and *A Simple Kind of Love Story*. It was not until 1963, however, that Schisgal saw the first New York production of his work, when a double bill of the one-act plays *The Typists* and *The Tiger* was produced Off-Broadway. While *The Tiger* earned Schisgal both a Vernon Rice Award and an Outer Circle Award for best play

in 1963, his greatest popular success came with *Luv*, which opened in London in 1963 and in New York the following year. The success of *Luv*, chosen by Otis L. Guernsey as one of the Best Plays of 1964, was later followed by *All Over Town*, a Best Play of 1974. Although prolific in the intervening years, Schisgal received little critical attention during this decade; in fact, critics panned *Jimmy Shine* in 1968 although the play marked the beginning of a long association between Schisgal and Dustin Hoffman, who made his Broadway debut in the title role.

Schisgal also wrote the screenplay for *The Tiger Makes Out*, the 1967 film version of *The Tiger*, and in 1980 co-authored the screenplay for the immensely successful *Tootsie*. His television credits include the plays *The Love Song of Barney Kempenski* (1966) and *Natasha Kovolina Pipishinsky* (1976). In 1980, Schisgal published a novel, *Days and Nights of a French Horn Player*.

Literary Analysis

When *Luv* appeared on Broadway in 1964, theater critics hailed Schisgal as an incisive and humorous satirist of the by-then stale themes and conventions of absurdist farce—existential despair and loneliness, the ultimate emptiness and inadequacy of language as a gauge of human feeling, the problematic and often destructive relationship between the sexes, and so on. Playwrights such as Edward Albee explored notions of the meaninglessness of language and action, especially in contemporary American life. In *The Zoo Story*, *The Sandbox* (later *The American Dream*), and *Who's Afraid of Virginia Woolf?*, Albee dissects empty human relationships and motivations and the human search for satisfaction and understanding, underscoring the characters' aggression and hostility. Schisgal, however, takes aim at these conventions, depicting them as humorously narcissistic and self-serving. At the same time, Schisgal incorporates into his work well-worn comic situations (almost always in an urban setting), primarily those involving spouses attempting, with varying degrees of success, to be unfaithful to each other.

The Typists and *The Tiger* (1960), while less ambitious both in comedic and thematic scope than the more successful *Luv*, exemplify Schisgal's enduring fascination with relationships between men and women. *The Typists* is essentially a comedy of thwarted love and ambition. The play concerns the ineffectual love of Sylvia and Paul, who age as they make abortive attempts to realize their love for one another, each claiming that life is incomplete while ultimately (and sadly) doing nothing significant to alter their situations. *The Tiger*, on the other hand, offers more comic potential, centering on the growing relationship between a clumsy and ineffectual kidnapper and his victim. A frustrated pseudo-intellectual and pseudo-revolutionary, Ben works as a postman and harbors a deep sense that he has been abused by the world; Gloria, a housewife and mother, is deeply dissatisfied with her middle-class routine. The two fall in love; they plan to continue their assignations after the "kidnapping." What began as a "threatening" scenario ends in "true love"; "the tiger," erstwhile rapist and rebel-without-a-cause, is revealed to be a frustrated academic whose principal grudge against the world is that he could not pass the French test on his graduate school entrance exam. A parody of the dangerous misfit (à la Jerry in *The Zoo Story*, perhaps), Ben finally emerges as a bumbling postman whose secret desire is to be "a professor of epistemology and linguistics."

This parody of the desperate act of a desperate man appears again in *Luv*, as does the comic version of a love-hate relationship between man and woman. In fact, *Luv* seems to be a comic echo of Albee in several ways, most obviously in the presence of a sandbox on stage (see *The Sandbox*) and in the various knives wielded by the odd trio of characters, Harry, Milt, and Ellen (see *The Zoo Story*). In the course of the play, however, Schisgal manages to deflate a number of existentialist poses. Harry, Milt, and Ellen all plan to commit suicide, and Harry complains, "Despair. Debilitation. The works. It hit me all at once." Seemingly the butt of one great cosmic joke, Harry is a failure at all that he attempts to accomplish; in the final scene of the play, a dog urinates on his pants leg.

During this merry-go-round of suicide attempts, ironically it is Harry who saves the lives of the other two, and eventually Harry and Ellen marry; Milt and his mistress marry, and finally Milt and Ellen remarry. The crux of the play is, after all, "love"—or what passes for love—in all of its manifestations. When asked about the spelling of *love* in the title, Schisgal commented that he was exploring ways in which the idea of love "has been perverted and misused" and wielded as a self-serving tool;[1] love, as is all too apparent in this play, is primarily a word, not a deeply felt emotion. The ease with which Milt and Ellen divorce and remarry—and Harry's infantile dependence on Ellen (she is more a caretaker than a wife)—suggest the casualness with which the idea of love is bandied about.

This concern with superficiality and role-playing as opposed to honest emotional commitment is played out in Schisgal's subsequent works. In *A Need for Brussels Sprouts* (1982), he again creates a situation in which a man and woman—Leon and Margaret—struggle through a humorously hostile encounter to attempt to communicate. Margaret is a tough policewoman, Leon an out-of-work actor who lives in the apartment below her, and the action of the play depends on her complaints that he plays his stereo too loud. Like George and Martha in *Who's Afraid of Virginia Woolf?*, Margaret and Leon are antagonists, but where Albee's characters achieve emotional "connection" through mutual destruction, Schisgal plays this antagonism for laughs to show that it need *not* lead to destruction. As in *The Tiger* and in the companion piece to *Brussels Sprouts, A Need for Less Expertise*, there seems to be significant authorial approval of an attempt, bumbling and funny though it may be, at an honest, unidealized relationship.

In *Jimmy Shine* (1968) and *All over Town* (1974), Schisgal expands both the size of his cast and the scope of his comedy and satire. Still focusing on the foibles of people who claim to be searching for love and self-fulfillment, Schisgal continues to examine the definitions of "love" that underlie the often glib use of the word. At the same time, he analyzes the various roles that individuals assume as they pursue success in love, sex, and friendship.

Jimmy Shine is Schisgal's quintessential "starving artist"; where cliché would have the artist striving (and starving) in his garret as a martyr to his art, Schisgal's artist is a mediocre painter who has stumbled into this role accidentally. Similarly, Jimmy is unable simply to "put on" the role of romantic artist-lover. When the girl he silently worships marries his best friend, Jimmy turns to prostitutes, but even here he is ineffectual—in his first encounter with Sally Weber, a seedy local madam, he is robbed; Rosie, the anemic prostitute who begins and ends the play with Jimmy, repeatedly asks him to pay for services rendered. Further, it becomes clear that Jimmy is not a victim of circumstance; his assumption of a role that is clichéd, empty, and totally unsuited to his (nonexistent) talents is a form of self-paralysis. When in the second act Elizabeth, his erstwhile love, actually proposes that they run away together, he refuses, and although he perceives that she wants to use him as a weapon against her husband, he is also refusing an opportunity of which he has dreamed for years. The play ends problematically, with a glimmer that in refusing Elizabeth (and his romantic dreams) Jimmy has shed himself of the past and his failures, yet he is left with the mundane reality of Rosie and her wig, both of which Jimmy is trying to sketch and to turn into art.

What Jimmy calls *love* is, however, almost purely sex; thus Rosie and not Elizabeth is his match. In *All Over Town* Schisgal goes further in debunking romantic and intellectualized notions of love, notions that obscure the simple reality of physical and emotional needs. A complex sex farce, *All Over Town* has as its central joke the question of what allows a man—one Louie Lucas—to be so sexually prolific that he has fathered nine illegitimate children. The answer is simple: he uses the old standard, "I love you very much and as soon as I get a little bread together, we'll get married." The ornate counterpoint to this straightforward come-on constitutes the comedy of the play—mistaken identity, unfaithful spouses, inept burglars, plentiful sexual innuendo, and so on. At the bottom, however, is the notion that for better or worse, self-interest, animal magnetism, greed, or any one of a host of essential motivations underlie slick pseudo-intellectual rationalizations.

Yet, Schisgal is still a comic playwright. Assuring us that these issues should not paralyze us, that we should not take ourselves and our problems (and his plays) too seriously, he deftly intertwines verbal comedy and slapstick with careful parody. The way questions of gender and sexual roleplaying are enacted in *Tootsie* is a case in point. Satirizing fetishes of despair, loneliness, and abandonment, Schisgal creates such memorably comic moments as the exchanges in *Luv* between Harry, Milt, and Ellen (in varying combinations) in which they one-up each other telling stories of deprived childhoods and bad marriages. Milt comes to jump from the bridge, like Harry, but in another parodic twist, he brings a knife in order to stab himself. Later in the play, Schisgal orchestrates a slapstick routine in which Milt inadvertently leaps over a bridge railing while trying to push Harry over instead.

Similarly, the comedy of *All Over Town* derives in large part from physical comedy and standard comedic, farcical situations—mistaking a black man for a white man, having a streetwise black man gleefully and successfully manipulate white liberals, using a myopic burglar, to name a few devices. Yet at the same time, Schisgal parodies the American fetish for emotional crutches and external panaceas for emotional inadequacy; the epitome of this impulse is Dr. Morris, a bumbling and ineffectual psychiatrist. One of Schisgal's most recent plays, *Closet Madness*, continues the comic exploration of roleplaying and emotional dependency; the play deals with the attempts of two men to "become" homosexuals because of their failure to find happiness in heterosexual relationships.

Summary

Murray Schisgal's comedy derives both from traditional comedic devices of farce and slapstick and from his parody of the voguish existential posturing of the 1950s and 1960s. Although his satire and comedy touch on the self-absorbed poses of the social "misfit"—loneliness, despair, rage—Schisgal is most concerned with human relationships and the nature of love and friendship between men and women.

Note

1. Ira Peck, "Interview with the Author," in *Luv*, intro. Walter Kerr (New York: Coward-McCann, 1965), pp. xiv–xv.

Selected Bibliography

Primary Sources

Plays

The Typists, and The Tiger. Produced London, 1960. New York: Coward-McCann, 1963.

Ducks and Lovers. Produced London, 1961. New York: Dramatists Play Service, 1972.

Luv. Produced London, 1963; New York, 1964. New York: Coward-McCann, 1965.

Fragments, Windows and Other Plays. New York: Coward-McCann, 1965.

Five One Act Plays. New York: Dramatists Play Service, 1968.

Jimmy Shine. Produced New York, 1968. New York: Atheneum, 1969.

The Chinese, and Dr. Fish. New York: Dramatists Play Service, 1970.

An American Millionaire. New York: Dramatists Play Service, 1974.

All Over Town. Produced New York, 1974. New York: Dramatists Play Service, 1975.

The Pushcart Peddlers, The Flatulist, and Other Plays. New York: Dramatists Play Service, 1980.

Luv and Other Plays. New York: Dodd, Mead, 1983.

Twice Around the Park. New York: French, 1983.

Closet Madness and Other Plays. New York: French, 1984.

Popkins. New York: Dramatists Play Service, 1984.

Jealousy, and There Are No Sacher Tortes in Our Society! New York: Dramatists Play Service, 1985.

Screenplays

The Tiger Makes Out, 1967.

Tootsie (co-writer), 1980.

Television Plays

The Love Song of Barney Kempenski, 1966.

Natasha Kovolina Pipishinsky, 1976.

Novel

Days and Nights of a French Horn Player. Boston: Little, Brown, 1980.

Secondary Sources

Articles and Chapters in Books

Arlen, M.J. "Murray Schisgal: Portrait of the Playwright in the Catbird Seat." *Show*, April 1965, pp. 69–71. This is a glowing article predicting success for Schisgal in the wake of *Luv*. Arlen's is not a scholarly piece, but it offers a glimpse of contemporary enthusiasm for *Luv* and for Schisgal which is especially interesting in light of the fact that Schisgal has remained a steadily productive but seldom acclaimed playwright.

"An Interview with Murray Schisgal." In *The American Theater Today*. Ed. Alan S. Downer. New York: Basic Books, 1967, pp. 124–135. Contains some biographical background but focuses on Schisgal's thoughts about the economic difficulty involved in producing plays in America and Europe as well as his feeling that American and European theater are closely connected. Schisgal also talks at length of the necessity of maintaining audience interest and involvement in a play, commenting on his disaffection with the Brechtian technique of holding an audience at arm's length. Schisgal finds such labels as "comic," "absurdist," and "existentialist" restrictive.

Simon, John. *Uneasy Stages*. New York: Random House, 1975, pp. 66–68. In a scant two pages Simon scathingly criticizes *Luv* as "Beckett in bobbysox . . . Ionesco on a bagel with lox," labelling *Luv* a slim vaudeville version of Theatre of the Absurd.

Theses

Gilbertson, John Lawrence. "A Director's Prompt Book and Directorial Notes for a Staged Production of Murray Schisgal's *Luv*, with an Analysis of the Play's Meaning as Conveyed through Offbeat Comedy." M.A. Thesis, Mankato State University, 1973.

Lowell-Lewis, Sherry Susan. "A Prompt Book for *The Typist and The Tiger*." M.A. Thesis, University of Texas at El Paso, 1982.

LuAnne Clark Holladay

Shepherd, Jean

Born: Chicago, Illinois, on July 26, 1925[?]
Education: Studied at Indiana University after World War II, leaving in 1949 without taking a degree

Biography

The son of Jean P. and Anne Heinrichs Shepherd, Jean Parker Shepherd was born in Chicago, Illinois. Though it is certain that his birthday is July 26, the year of his birth is elusive, with published estimates ranging from 1923 to 1929. Growing up in Hammond, Indiana, Shepherd worked as a mailboy in a steel mill, then began his radio career at age sixteen, doing weekly sports broadcasts for a local radio station in Hammond. Juvenile roles on network radio in Chicago soon followed, including the part of Billy Fairchild in the *Jack Armstrong, the All-American Boy* serial. Shepherd served in the Signal Corps during World War II, installing radar. Utilizing the GI Bill after the war, he studied psychology and engineering at Indiana University and acting at the Goodman Theater School in Chicago. After leaving Indiana University in 1949, he took radio jobs in Ohio and Pennsylvania before joining the staff of radio station WLW in Cincinnati, where he also hosted *Rear Bumper*, a popular late-night comedy show on WLW-TV.

The mid-1950s found Shepherd in New York City, where he began a long association with radio station WOR. With his show *Night People*, he discovered his natural audience—in twenty-seven states and as far north as Canada and as far south as Bermuda—in the midnight and pre-dawn hours. With a centerpiece story but no script, Shepherd would launch into a rambling, stream-of-consciousness discourse punctuated by whispers, cackles, and explosive laughter. The popularity of the show overcame early problems with WOR's management caused by Shepherd's irreverent handling of commercials and his committing other breaches of broadcasting orthodoxy. It has been suggested that Shepherd may have inspired an important scene in the 1976 movie *Network* when he exhorted his listeners on one occasion to put their radios in their windows and turn up the volume to flood the eastern half of the United States with shouts of "Excelsior, you fatheads!" and "Oh my God, this is fantastic!"

Shepherd's first book was published in 1961; it was followed by numerous stories, which appeared in such magazines as *Playboy*, and a number of books. In the late 1950s and early 1960s, Shepherd appeared in many off-Broadway productions, began doing one-man stage shows and stand-up nightclub appearances, and presided over jazz concerts sponsored by the *Village Voice*, for which he was then writing. During 1960 and 1961, he hosted *Inside Jean Shepherd* on WOR-TV; the following television season, he played a character on the soap opera *From These Roots* and made regular appearances on the *Today* show. For three seasons, beginning in 1969, PBS television aired *Jean Shepherd's America*, a highly personalized guided tour of the United States (new episodes followed in the mid-1980s). A second television series, *Shepherd's Pie*, and several of Shepherd's full-length plays were also aired on PBS. Shepherd co-wrote and narrated the 1983 theatrical film, *A Christmas Story*, which received mixed reviews but did well at the box office.

Literary Analysis

An American humorist in the midwestern tradition of Mark Twain and George Ade, writer and multimedia performer Jean Shepherd is a storyteller with a keen imagination, a maverick wit, and an eye for authenticating detail. Calling him "a radical in the best sense of the word," longtime fan Martin A. Jackson maintains that Shepherd "switched on bulbs in the heads of a whole generation by simply explaining America" to them.[1] Using his fables—which are loosely drawn in part from his experiences in Middle America—to place the rituals of everyday life in this country in the perspective of a futile human condition, he shows his audiences that they might as well laugh because there is little else that they can do. Shepherd also wants to preserve in humor the way most Americans live so that future readers of today's literature will not believe that everybody was wealthy and lived in Westchester County.

Beginning in the mid-1950s, Shepherd attracted a large cult following on the eastern seaboard as an innovative, free-form radio raconteur who mocked American fads and foibles. His following grew through recordings, syndication, books, television dramatizations of his stories and the travelogue/monologue series *Jean Shepherd's America* on PBS, the theatrical film feature *A Christmas Story* (adapted from one of his stories), and personal appearances, especially on college campuses. Much of this work draws upon Shepherd's fictionalized, anti-nostalgic recollections of the 1930s and 1940s in Hammond. The tough, industrial town becomes "Hohman" in Shepherd's stories about the childhood and adolescence of "Ralph Parker." As Hohman, Hammond is universalized to represent industrial America and is populated with characters who are amalgams of people whom Shepherd has known. In story after story, Ralph Parker goes on blind dates, cleans fish on the back porch, undergoes trial-by-prom, treks through winter gales to Warren G. Harding School, and listens to the radio serial *Little Orphan Annie* with his secret decoder ring in hand.

In 1961, Shepherd edited *The America of George Ade*, a selection of Ade's fables, short stories, and essays. Shepherd stresses in his introduction the elements of loneliness in Ade's life and humor. Seven chapters of Shepherd's 1966 work, *In God We Trust; All Others Pay Cash*, originally appeared in *Playboy*. The narrator is Ralph Parker, now a successful writer who returns to Hohman to visit his home and old friends. The whole book consists of a description of an afternoon that Ralph spends in a bar reminiscing with Flick, a childhood crony. Shepherd reveals a fine eye for absurdity and idiocy as he renders each incident recalled as a world in microcosm.

Wanda Hickey's Night of Golden Memories, and Other Disasters (1971) brought together eight pieces that had appeared earlier in *Playboy*. Shepherd sees the book as a succession of open-ended occurrences rather than a collection of stories. The title piece tells about a prom date that degenerates into disaster. In "Daphne Bigelow and the Spine-Chilling Saga of the Snail-Encrusted Tinfoil Noose," the young hero gets a date with the most sought-after girl in school, a blue-blood, only to learn painfully the reality of the barriers of social class. The young protagonist's romantic illusions regarding Polish girls from East Chicago lead him to the brink of an all-too-early marriage in "The Star-Crossed Romance of Josephine Cosnowski."

All of the humorous pieces in *The Ferrari in the Bedroom* (1972) were originals, with the exception of three that first appeared in *Car and Driver* and in one reprinted from the *National Lampoon*. Shepherd explains in the introduction that the book had its origin in magazine and newspaper items and ads, a "Vast File of Dynamic Trivia," that he had accumulated over the years. The trivia items grew into fantasies that targeted such subjects as the reversal of sex roles, wealthy left-wing folk singers, the oppressive nature of modern urban life, and anti-drunk-driving crusades and automation (this last combination leads to the invention of a driverless automobile).

In *A Fistful of Fig Newtons* (1981), Shepherd delivers more of his unstructured musings on American culture. A number of the stories are mental flashbacks set off by urban situations encountered by the narrator. In the title episode, "A Fistful of Fig Newtons, or the Shootout in Room 303," a carload of beer-guzzling college students causes the narrator to recall the dire consequences of a college dorm party. A slow journey through the Lincoln Tunnel triggers recollections of misadventures in the Signal Corps and a summer as a child at Camp Nobba-WaWa-Nockee. Charting an inner landscape familiar to many, all of these pieces—with their aural dimensions—demonstrate Shepherd's ability to transpose his radio persons into print.

Summary

Throughout his work, Jean Shepherd has shown that he understands one of the primary requirements of a humorist: affection for his subjects. His needling is not unkind as he fondly and wittily reminisces about the quirky habits of people and the embarrassing moments that we have all known. "It is Shepherd's gift and burden to be addicted to America," writes Martin A. Jackson. "He's a piece of flypaper upon which the dust and flotsam of this peculiar situation have been accumulating for years."[2]

Notes

1. Martin A. Jackson, "Jean Shepherd," *New York Times Book Review*, February 28, 1982, p. 12.
2. Ibid., p. 13.

Selected Bibliography

Primary Sources

Editor. *The America of George Ade, 1866–1944: Fables, Short Stories, Essays.* New York: Putnam, 1961.

Introduction to *The Night People's Guide to New York*. New York: Bantam Books, 1965.

In God We Trust; All Others Pay Cash. Garden City, N.Y.: Doubleday, 1966.

Wanda Hickey's Night of Golden Memories, and Other Disasters. Garden City, N.Y.: Doubleday, 1971.

The Ferrari in the Bedroom. New York: Dodd, Mead, 1972.

The Phantom of the Open Hearth: A Film for Television. New York: Doubleday, 1978.

A Fistful of Fig Newtons. Garden City, N.Y.: Doubleday, 1981.

Secondary Sources

Bier, Jesse. *The Rise and Fall of American Humor.* New York: Holt, Rinehart and Winston, 1968, pp. 308–309. Focuses on Shepherd as a radio humorist, "a descendant of the satiric Henry Morgan of the prewar period and the same metropolitan area" (p. 309).

Godfrey, Stephen. "Jean Shepherd's World of Everyday Rituals." *Toronto Globe and Mail*, November 18, 1983, Entertainment Section, p. E5. Contains biographical material on Shepherd.

Jackson, Martin A. "Jean Shepherd." *New York Times Book Review*, February 28, 1982, pp. 12–13, 20. A perceptive view of *A Fistful of Fig Newtons* and of Shepherd's role as a humorist. Jackson calls Shepherd "one of our major humorists" who has helped his readers "to understand this odd nation a bit more" (p. 12).

Zorn, Eric. "Jean Shepherd's Jaded Journey Home." *Chicago Tribune*, April 21, 1982, Section 3, pp. 1, 11. Contains biographical material on Shepherd, who is quoted as saying that he writes about "Industrial Town America . . . Newark, Gary, Detroit . . . kind of like Faulkner used his mythical county to represent the South" (p. 11).

L. Moody Simms, Jr.

Shillaber, Benjamin Pendleton

Born: Portsmouth, New Hampshire, on July 12, 1814

Education: West School in Portsmouth until 1830

Marriage: Ann Tappan de Rochemont, August 15, 1838, died, 1883, eight children

Died: November 25, 1890

Biography

Born in Portsmouth, New Hampshire, on July 12, 1814, Benjamin Pendleton Shillaber was one of six children of William Shillaber and his second wife Sarah. His ancestors were involved in the Revolutionary War, and his paternal grandfather served on John Paul Jones's *Bonhomme Richard*. Portsmouth always remained dear to the heart of the humorist, who later incorporated many of his youthful memories in his books for boys. At sixteen, Shillaber left the West School in Portsmouth to become an apprentice on the *New Hampshire Palladium* in Dover. In 1833 he moved to Boston, Massachusetts, where he lived in boardinghouses for several years; a number of the comic anecdotes he published later used such a setting. Shillaber first worked for Tuttle and Weeks where he met editors and authors of the publishing firm of John Allen and William D. Ticknor, among them James T. Fields, who was to become a lifelong friend. Shillaber was an ardent Democrat; he was also a Universalist, which may explain his cheerful vision of human nature and his indomitable faith in the destiny of the country. In 1835 Shillaber met Ann Tappan de Rochemont, who later became his wife. Nevertheless, he left Boston the same year upon the advice of his physician after a severe nasal hemorrhage and settled for two years in Demerara, British Guiana, where he worked as a compositor on the *Royal Gazette*. Shillaber returned to Boston in July 1837, and married Ann on August 15, 1838. They had eight children, four of whom died at a young age. In 1840, he joined the Boston *Post* as a printer and within a few years was promoted to journalist thanks to the support of the editor, Charles Gordon Greene. By 1847, Shillaber was in charge of a column titled "All Sorts of Paragraphs" in which he defended his democratic principles.

The first quips about his most famous comic character, Mrs. Partington, appeared on February 26 and June 5, 1847. Within a few weeks, they were reprinted by newspapers all over the country. Shillaber then added other burlesque figures to his anecdotes, such as Old Roger, Wideswarth, and Ike Partington. He continued to work on the *Post* until 1850, then joined the

Pathfinder and Railway Guide, which published humorous sketches in addition to railroad schedules. A year later he became coeditor of the *Carpet Bag*, the first exclusively comic magazine in the United States. This weekly was claimed by the editors, Charles G. Halpine, John Trowbridge, Silas W. Wilder, and Shillaber, to be instructive and entertaining with a "variety of things necessary for the comfort and happiness of the highways of life."[1] The first issue appeared on March 29, 1851. Among the best-known contributors were John Townsend Trowbridge and Tobias H. Miller (Uncle Toby). It also published anecdotes and yarns by Mark Twain, Artemus Ward, and John Phoenix. Yet, the *Carpet Bag* never had a wide circulation and its publication was discontinued on March 26, 1853. Its failure may be explained by the rising tide of sectional chauvinism. When Ensign Jehiel Stebbings, a native of Spunkville and veteran of the Aroostook "War" was invented by the *Carpet Bag* to parody the presidential campaigns of Taylor and Scott, the burlesque treatment of military heroes aroused the anger of many jingoistic readers. Shillaber returned to the Boston *Post* as local editor, shortly after the demise of the *Carpet Bag*. He reintroduced the sketches involving Mrs. Partington and published *The Life and Sayings of Mrs. Partington and Others of the Family* (1854), anthologizing the humorous pieces from his column and anecdotes from the *Carpet Bag*. In 1856, Shillaber left the *Post* to become the associate editor of the Boston *Saturday Evening Gazette*, a Sunday weekly. All of his previous comic characters reappeared in "Melange," a column that was for ten years the main attraction of the paper. In 1859, Shillaber published *Knitting Work: A Web of Many Textures, Wrought by Ruth Partington*, a collection of humorous tales that proved to be a great success. Repeated attacks of gout compelled him to relinquish his editorial task on the *Saturday Evening Gazette* in 1867. For two decades he earned a living as contributor to several papers and magazines, among them the *Hartford Post*. He published *Partingtonian Patchwork* in 1873 and *Ike Partington, or, The Adventures of a Human Boy and His Friends* in 1879. In the meantime, he wrote a volume of verse and gained immense popularity as lecturer. He also worked on his autobiography (published posthumously in serial form as "Experiences During Many Years" by *New England Magazine* in 1893). The last decade of Shillaber's life was plagued with sickness and poverty. He spent his last decade in a wheelchair and constantly sought financial assistance from friends. When Shillaber died in 1890, Mark Twain was America's most popular humorist. Forty years earlier, the Yankee editor had welcomed the latter to the columns of the *Carpet Bag*, thus bridging the gap between Down East humor and its southern counterpart.

Literary Analysis

James Russell Lowell noted that in the 1840s every possible form of intellectual and physical dyspepsia brought forth its gospel, and even swearing had its evangelists. Everybody had a mission to attend to everybody else's business. Some had an assurance of instant millennium and conventions were held for every purpose.[2] The "Apostles of the Newness," so named by Emerson, were innumerable. The feminists, perfectionists, suffragists, and temperance men not only introduced brand-new "notions" into Yankeeland but also invented lifestyles. Shillaber was one among many popular humorists who responded to intellectual fads with provocative attacks, and after Seba Smith and Thomas Chandler Haliburton, his use of Yankee dialect contributed to the development of the vernacular tradition as a distinctive prose style.

Mrs. Partington first appeared in the *Post* on February 26, 1847. Her name was borrowed from Sydney Smith, the English essayist who had used it in a speech to upbraid the harsh conservatism of British aristocrats who were against the reform movement and who were fighting a losing battle for their privileges. Smith's Mrs. Partington attempted to sweep back the Atlantic Ocean with her broom during a storm. The idiosyncrasies of Shillaber's comic female character were similar, but she also voiced the feelings of the people, thus reflecting Shillaber's democratic beliefs. A commensensical eccentric, his Mrs. Partington spoke in monologues filled with malapropisms and her own special language, a comic character in an urban environment and not a country bumpkin.

Descended from the Puritans, Ruth Trotter, later Mrs. Partington, lived first in the small village of Beanville, Massachusetts. When her husband, Paul, died she took charge of her nephew Ike. They moved to Boston when their home was pulled down to make way for the Beanville Railroad. In the stronghold of the genteel tradition, Mrs. Partington was a candid philistine whose folk wisdom readily found fault with Brahmin language and culture. Unlettered and parochial, she ignored the conventions of genteel society and played the role of the wise fool. Unlike most other Yankee types, she was neither sly nor ambitious but rather a feminine replica of the traditional crackerbox philosopher. Through his persona, Shillaber explored the comic potentialities of malapropisms, yet Mrs. Partington was not merely an imitation Mrs. Malaprop. Confronted with the sophistication of city life, she interpreted the experiences of people around her and created a poetic universe that substituted for the harsh facts of life as described in papers and magazines. In her, ignorance combined with commonsense and imagination, thus providing the old widow with a vision of life that sheltered her from intellectual vagaries. Whatever her comments, she eventually fell back on her daily chores with renewed self-reliance. The following anecdote illustrates her peculiar rhetoric.

> "Adulterated tea!" said Mrs Partington, as she read in the *Transcript* an account of the adulteration of teas in England, at which she was much shocked. "I wonder if this is adulterated?" and she bowed her head over the steaming and fragrant decoction in the cup before her, whose genial odors mingled with the silvery vapor, and encircled her venerable poll like a halo. "It smells virtuous," continued she, smiling with satisfaction, "and I know this Shoo-shon tea must be good, because I bought it of Mr. Shoo-shon himself, at Redding's. Adulterated!" she meandered on, pensively as a brook in June, "and it's agin the commandment, too, which says—don't break that, Isaac!" as she saw that interesting juvenile amusing himself with making refracted sunbeams dance upon the wall, and around the dark profile, and among the leaves of the sweet fern, like yellow butterflies or fugitive chips of new June butter. The alarm for her crockery dispelled all disquietude about the tea, and she sipped her beverage, all oblivious of dele-tea-rious infusions.[3]

The stylistic devices used to construct the linguistic world of Mrs. Partington are based on connotation, syllepsis, and truism.

Shillaber often parodies dogmatic assertions through his persona:

> "I've always noticed," said Mrs. Partington on New Year's Day, dropping her voice to the key that people adopt when they are disposed to be philosophical or moral; "I've always noticed that every year added to a man's life is apt to make him older, just as a man who goes a journey finds, as he jogs on, that every mile he goes brings him nearer where he is going, and farther from where he started. I am not so young as I was once, and I don't believe I ever shall be, if I live to the age of Samson, which, Heaven knows as well as I do, I don't want to, for I wouldn't be a centurian or an octagon, and survive

my factories, and become idiomatic, by any means. But then there is no way of knowing how a thing will turn out till it takes place; and we shall come to an end someday, though we may never live to see it."[4]

Through Mrs. Partington, Shillaber also satirizes the intellectual fads of the period and unmasks the snobbery of pseudoreformers and cultists. Although a self-proclaimed Democrat, he generally takes a mild stand on local political issues. A staunch opponent of slavery, he nevertheless blames antislavery Northerners who teach moral lessons to the southern planters, as Mrs. Partington states: "I knew a poor old colored man here in Boston that they treat jest like a nigger. People an't no better than scribes, pharisees, and hippogriffs, that say one thing and do another."[5] Implicit moral conclusions emerge from Mrs. Partington's strings of absurdities as though her confused mind is the mainspring of superior wisdom. When reporting on her vision of society, the narrator sometimes suggests his own perplexity about her homespun philosophy as in her quaint syllogisms, evidence is often suspended and postulates become useless when applied to everyday experience. Mrs. Partington's instinctive anti-intellectualism is especially obvious in her gossip on the literary scene. She confuses "the humor of Hawthorne" with a syrup of buckthorne."[6] Averse to evasive connotations, she trusts only the literal meaning of words:

> "When I lent her the eggs," said Mrs. Partington, "she said she would be eternally indebted to me, and I guess she will. How can people do so?"[7]

Deeply rooted in Down East values, Mrs. Partington's wisdom is durable though apparently archaic. In the age of the New England Renaissance, Transcendentalist idealism often became obtrusive to unsophisticated observers of the cultural environment. Despite his attachment to the spirit of reform, Shillaber opposed intellectual pursuits that are not based upon a sincere confrontation of the facts of life. Thus, Mrs. Partington challenges Brahmin rhetoric. Seemingly regressive and eccentric, her attitudes finally prove serene, stubborn, and valuable under closer scrutiny. In her own way, she mediated between age-old Down East culture and the urban refinement of the Boston intellectual circles.

Other comic characters surround Mrs. Partington. If these were primarily intended to confront the old widow's whims with their eccentricities, they gradually assumed an independent existence. None speak in Yankee dialect or express the oracular wisdom of the crackerbox philosopher. Old Roger and Doctor Spooner are burlesque figures reminiscent of eighteenth-century English humor in the tradition of the *Spectator*, but they also evoke Dickensian idiosyncrasies.[8] An upper-middle-class Bostonian, Old Roger indulges in utopian projects in company with his friends Philanthropos and Poo-Poo. The three of them are dedicated Brahmins who live in the cozy atmosphere of a boarding-house. Old Roger loves puns and spoonerisms. He suffers from dyspepsia, which prompts him to pass severe judgments on his fellowmen whenever they do not come up to his expectations. Doctor Spooner also displays the abstract generosity of the Brahmins. For instance, he imprudently advises manual workers to take time for contemplation:

> "I love to see people industrious," remarked Mr. Plane, the carpenter, giving a finishing knock at a clapboard nail he was driving, as though he were putting it as a period to his sentence. "So do I," said Dr. Spooner, "but perhaps we would not agree with regard to our definition of the word industry. I do not believe that industry is slavish devotion to work, that never allows a moment's respite from toil, that from early morning to night devotes itself, might and main, hammer and tongs, speaking after the manner of men, to one pursuit—that is not my idea of industry. There is an old saying that it is better to wear out than rust out, but, between you and I, I think I shall allow myself to rust a little." "I think I shall," said the carpenter, laying down his hammer. "I like your theory, sir, and as you are so kind, I shall leave clapboarding your barn for this afternoon and go fishing." "Ah," replied the Doctor, "that alters the case materially, and if the work is not done by tomorrow night, you will receive no dimes therefor. In this particular case a little industry is a great virtue." The Doctor turned away, and the carpenter, with an expressive wink at his journeyman, resumed his hammer and the work was done.[9]

Wideswarth and Blifkins are blundering scapegoats who express contemporary foibles.[10] Wideswarth epitomizes upperclass smugness. His devotion to English romantic poets, as his name suggests, impels him to write lyrical verse. But, totally ignorant of nature, he falls back on poetic diction: "On rushing wings the fairy snow-flake flies,/ Urged by the breath of the onhurrying gale."[11] Shy and cowardly, Wideswarth also wants to emulate frontier heroes and even deludes himself into believing that he has participated in the Mexican War. He is pathetic and grotesque, and his experiences invariably result in discomfiture.

Another of Shillaber's burlesque characters, Benjamin Blifkins, foreshadows James Thurber's Little Man. A storekeeper and henpecked husband, he is constantly frustrated by his own inadequacies. Attempting to cope with a variety of domestic problems, Blifkins always fights a losing battle while his wife undermines his confidence with continuous harassment, although sometimes he rebels against Mrs. Blifkins's domination. Every event in Blifkins's life substantiates his alienation. Disappointed by reality, he sometimes takes refuge in daydreaming like Walter Mitty and sees himself involved in a romance with the lady next door, but his wife soon awakens him. While Blifkins generally accepts humiliation in order to live in peace, he remains a delinquent hedonist. Innocent, passive, and resigned, he embodies hilarious confusion in an urban environment submitted to social pressure.

The character of Ike Partington was created by Shillaber in 1848 to introduce some variety in the *Boston Post* anecdotes involving Mrs. Partington. Ike soon appeared as a comic counterpart to the typical heroes of boys' books when such fiction was highly moralistic and didactic. Whereas Dickens's young heroes adjusted to the requirements of Victorian society after a painful education, Shillaber's replica was a reversed *Bildungsroman*.

Ike acts like a youthful Sut Lovingood. He plagues everybody with his practical jokes, lies, steals, and tortures cats. He is also endowed with vitality and inventiveness; the humorist conceived him as an "imitation of the universal human boy."[12] Unlike Dickens's young heroes, Ike hardly ever thinks like an adult. Mrs. Partington's conception of education is avowedly permissive and her mischievous nephew takes full advantage of this. In "Paul's Ghosts," for instance, he dresses in the uniform of his deceased uncle with such skill that Mrs. Partington believes that her late husband is back.[13] Like Tom Sawyer, Ike is an expert in imagining devices to trick his aunt, and enjoys playing pirate. He shares with Huckleberry Finn the attitudes of the bad boy who refuses to be "sivilized" even though Mrs. Partington has nothing in common with Miss Watson or Widow Douglas. A born prankster, Ike takes his place in a long line of American practical jokers. Yet Shillaber does not see him as a rebel against the social order. Whereas Tom Sawyer takes refuge in the world of romance and retrospectively stands for a bygone southern culture, Ike embodies the resourcefulness of a nascent business culture. With Mrs. Partington and Ike, the humorist suggests that pastoral nostalgia can coexist with youthful attitudes. Such a comic presentation of social tensions enabled readers to maintain equilibrium during the troubled years that constituted a transition between antebellum and postbellum America.

Summary

In his creation of Ruth Partington in 1847, Benjamin Pendleton Shillaber adapted the tradition of the crackerbox oracle to an urban environment. His treatment of Yankee characters at odds with the cultural environment of Boston is based upon a set of incongruities between popular and genteel attitudes. Patterned upon Benjamin Franklin's Silence Dogood, Mrs. Partington embodied sterling feminine qualities. As an old widow, she was totally immune to the lures of the flesh and represented a vision of life that appeared unpolluted by the evils of city life. Shillaber created a shrewd ignoramus who was also a benevolent, self-reliant old lady in a period when the women's rights' movements were often judged self-seeking, subversive, and morally ominous. His manifold contributions to the tradition of American humor can be seen in his ability to transmute rural Yankee humor into a new comedy of manners, in his association, especially through the *Carpet Bag*, of the Down East oracle with the southern rogue, and finally, in his anticipation of two significant figures. Ike Partington was clearly a model for Huckleberry Finn and Tom Sawyer, and Benjamin Blifkins foreshadowed the Little Man of a comic tradition that includes Walter Mitty and Charlie Chaplin.

Notes

1. "To the Reader," *Carpet Bag*, 1 (March 29, 1851): 5.
2. *The Writings of James Russell Lowell in Prose and Poetry.* Vol. 1 (Boston and New York: Houghton, Mifflin, 1890), p. 362.
3. "Mrs. Partington at Tea," *The Life and Sayings of Mrs. Partington* (New York: J.C. Derby, 1854), p. 79.
4. "Oracular Pearls," *Partingtonian Patchwork* (Boston: Lee and Shepard, 1872), p. 168.
5. "A Home Truth," *Sayings*, p. 162.
6. "Mrs. Partington's Idea of Humor," *Sayings*, p. 129.
7. "Eternal Indebtedness," *Sayings*, p. 246.
8. Many of the sketches that appeared in the *Post* and the *Gazette* were later collected in book form. Old Roger and Spooner are to be found in *Partingtonian Patchwork*.
9. *Mrs. Partington's Knitting Work and What Was Done by the Plaguy Boy Ike; a Web of Many Textures, as Wrought by the Old Lady Herself* (Philadelphia: Potter, 1868), pp. 42–43.
10. Blifkins appears in *Partingtonian Patchwork* and

Wideswarth in *Rhymes with Reason and Without* (Boston: Abel Tompkins and B.B. Mussey, 1853), *Lines in Pleasant Places: Rhymics of Many Moods and Quantities, Wise and Otherwise* (Cambridge: Moses King, 1882), and *Wideswarth. Embracing Lines in Pleasant Places and Other Rhymes Wise and Otherwise* (Cambridge: Moses King, 1882).
11. *Rhymes with Reason and Without* (Boston: Abel Tomkins and B.B. Mussey, 1853), p. 305.
12. *New England Magazine*, 9 (October 1893): 153.
13. "Paul's Ghost," *Sayings*, pp. 51, 53.

Selected Bibliography

Primary Sources
Rhymes, with Reason and Without. Boston: Abel Tompkins and B.B. Mussey, 1853.
Life and Sayings of Mrs. Partington and Others of the Family. New York: J.C. Derby, 1854.
The Sayings and Doings of the Celebrated Mrs. Partington. London: James Blackwood, 1854.
Knitting-Work: A Web of Many Textures, Wrought by Ruth Partington. Boston: Brown, Taggard and Chase, 1859.
Mrs. Partington's Ridicule: A Collection of Wit and Humor, Which the Old Lady Offers to Her Friends. Boston: Thomes and Talbot, 1863.
Mrs. Partington's Knitting Work: and What Was Done by Her Plaguy Boy Ike. A Web of Many Textures, as Wrought by the Old Lady Herself. Philadelphia: John E. Potter, 1868.
Partingtonian Patchwork. Boston: Lee and Shepard, 1872.
Lines in Pleasant Places; Rhythmics of Many Moods and Quantities, Wise and Otherwise. Chelsea, Mass.: The Author, 1874.
Lively Boys! Lively Boys! Ike Partington, or, The Adventures of a Human Boy and His Friends. Boston: Lee and Shepard, 1879.
Wide-Swarth: Embracing Lines in Pleasant Places and Other Rhymes Wise and Otherwise. Cambridge: Moses King, 1882.
Mrs. Partington's New Grip Sack, Filled with Fresh Things. New York: J.S. Ogilvie, 1890.
"Experiences During Many Years." *New England Magazine*, 8 (1893): 511–525, 618–627, 719–724; 9 (1893): 88–95, 153–160, 529–533, 625–631; 10 (1894): 29–36, 247–256, 286–294.

Secondary Sources
Austin, James C. *Artemus Ward.* New York: Twayne Publishers, 1964. Discusses Shillaber and the *Carpet Bag.*
Blair, Walter. *Horse Sense in American Humor from Benjamin Franklin to Ogden Nash.* Chicago: University of Chicago Press, 1942. A study of Shillaber in the context of the crackerbox tradition.
———. *Mark Twain and Huck Finn.* Berkeley: University of California Press, 1960. Discusses the influence of Shillaber on Clemens.
———. *Native American Humor.* New York: American Book Company, 1937. An excellent appraisal of Shillaber's achievement as native humorist.
———, and Hamlin Hill. *America's Humor, From Poor Richard to Doonesbury.* New York: Oxford University Press, 1978.
Clemens, Cyril. "Benjamin Shillaber and His 'Carpet

Bag.'" *New England Quarterly*, 14 (September 1941). More factual than analytical.

———. *Shillaber*. Webster Groves, Mo.: International Mark Twain Society, 1946. A biography.

Meine, Franklin J. "American Comic Periodicals. No. 1—The Carpet Bag." *The Collector's Journal*, 4 (October, November, December 1933): 411–413.

Reed, John Q. *Benjamin Pendleton Shillaber*. New York: Twayne Publishers, 1972. The only full-length study of Shillaber. Indispensable.

Rourke, Constance. *American Humor: A Study of the National Character*. New York: Harcourt, Brace and Company, 1931.

Royot, Daniel. *L'Humour Américain, des Puritains aux Yankees*. Lyon: Presses Universitaires de Lyon, 1980. A study of Shillaber's achievement as Yankee humorist of the urban age.

Tandy, Jennette. *Crackerbox Philosophers in American Humor and Satire*. New York: Columbia University Press, 1925.

Daniel G. Royot

Smith, Charles Henry ["Bill Arp"]

Born: Lawrenceville, Georgia, on June 15, 1826

Education: Gwinnet County [Georgia] Manual Labor Institute; attended Franklin College (later the University of Georgia), but did not graduate

Marriage: Mary Octavia Hutchins, 1849, thirteen children

Died: August 24, 1903

Biography

The son of Asahel Reid and Caroline Ann Maguire Smith, Charles Henry Smith was born in Lawrenceville, Georgia, on June 15, 1826. One of ten children, he attended the Gwinnet County Manual Labor Institute and clerked in his father's store. In 1844, Smith entered Franklin College (later the University of Georgia), but he left in 1847 before completing his degree. His father's illness forced him to return home and manage the family store. Smith married sixteen-year-old Mary Octavia Hutchins in 1849; they eventually had thirteen children, ten of whom lived to adulthood. After briefly studying the law, Smith was admitted to the bar and became a lawyer traveling for the Georgia Circuit Court. Moving his growing family to Rome, Georgia, in 1851, he formed a law partnership with John W.H. Underwood. A respected member of the Rome community, he became clerk of the city council in 1852 and city alderman in 1861.

When the Civil War began, Smith enlisted as a private in the Rome Light Guards. In July 1861, he joined the Eighth Georgia Regiment where he served as a supply commissioner with the rank of major. Smith was reelected city alderman in 1863, and the following year he was made a first lieutenant in the Forrest Light Artillery Company. He again became city alderman in 1864 and also was appointed a judge advocate in Macon. Setting up a store in Rome in 1865, he was soon elected to the new Georgia senate. Between 1867 and 1877, Smith spent much of his time on politics, serving as the mayor of Rome in 1867 and for four terms as city alderman. In 1878, he began giving public lectures and contributing a weekly letter to the *Atlanta Constitution* (the letters would continue until 1903). Smith died in Cartersville, Georgia, on August 24, 1903.

Literary Analysis

Between 1861 and 1903, under the pseudonym of "Bill Arp," Charles Henry Smith published more than 2,000 humorous letters, most of which first appeared in such Southern newspapers as the *Atlanta Constitution*. With Bill Arp, Smith joined the ranks of a new breed of literary comedians produced by the Civil War, a group of humorists—including Henry Wheeler Shaw ("Josh Billings"), David Ross Locke ("Petroleum V. Nasby"), and Charles Farrar Browne ("Artemus Ward")—who capitalized on caricatures, with the tortured dialects of illiterate individuals, and comic misquotations and misspellings.

The work of Smith also stands as a link between the antebellum and postbellum humor of the South. Though his Bill Arp letters lack much of the crudity, blood, and ugliness of earlier writers, Smith undoubtedly looked back to the work of such pre–Civil War figures as Augustus Baldwin Longstreet. Longstreet's "The Fight" is recalled in several of Bill Arp's adventures. Yet, Smith's careful descriptions of local customs look forward to the Southern local colorists. As Jay B. Hubbell has pointed out, Billy Sanders, Joel Chandler Harris's cracker humorist and philosopher, "is almost like a reincarnation of Bill Arp."[1]

Smith sent the first letter signed "Bill Arp" to a Rome, Georgia, newspaper, the *Southern Confederacy*, in April 1861. Addressed to Abraham Lincoln ("Abe Linkhorn") and written by a supposedly almost illiterate Georgia cracker, it appeared shortly after the taking of Harpers Ferry by Union forces. Arp's second letter to Lincoln appeared in January 1862; his third and fourth such letters were published in December of the same year. For the most part Smith's Bill Arp maintains a tone of skeptical inquiry, satirizing such subjects as high taxes, corrupt offi-cials, and draft dodgers. These dialect letters are quite unlike those of George Washington Har-ris's Sut Lovingood that attack Lincoln and all Yankees in a vicious manner.

Published in New York in 1866, Smith's *Bill Arp, So Called: A Side Show of the Southern Side of the War* contains the four letters to Lincoln and other wartime sketches. An imme-diate success, it was followed in 1873 with *Bill Arp's Peace Papers*. Each new Arp volume con-tained some newer material and reprints of early letters. *Bill Arp's Scrap Book; Humor and Phi-losophy* was published in 1884; *The Farm and the Fireside: Sketches of Domestic Life in War and in Peace* in 1891; and *Bill Arp: From the Uncivil War to Date, 1861-1903* in 1903. The latter volume is the most complete collection of Arp letters.

When he first wrote for the newspapers, Smith was clearly influenced by Charles Farrar Browne, the creator of Artemus Ward. Arp's initial letters to Lincoln are reminiscent of Ward's earlier interviews with Lincoln and Jef-ferson Davis. At the beginning of their writing careers, both Smith and Browne pulverized grammar and spelled horribly. Neither could avoid puns. Much of Smith's pun play is derived from mispronunciation, as in Arp's "Abe Link-horn" or "Mack C. Million." Arp also joined Ward in misquoting classical authors. Misquo-tation combined with mispronunciation was used to produce comic redundancy. Smith, like Browne, also frequently ridiculed *belles-lettres* and pompous oratory. In time, both Arp and Ward became more literate. When the Arp let-ters were collected in book form—with the ex-ception of *Bill Arp's Peace Papers* (1873)— Smith dropped the humorous misspellings, hav-ing come to see it as detrimental to the English language.

After writing the first letter to Lincoln, Smith apparently read it aloud to several friends on a Rome, Georgia, streetcorner. Among the listeners was the town wag, one William Arp. The following exchange ensued between the real-life Arp and Smith:

> "'Squire, are you gwine print that?"
>
> "I reckon I will, Bill," said I.
>
> "What name are you gwine to put to it?" said he.
>
> "I don't know yet," said I; "I haven't thought about a name."
>
> "Well, 'Squire," said he, "I wish you would put mine, for them's my senti-ments."[2]

Smith's greatest popularity among his con-temporaries and his most lasting fame came from the Bill Arp letters that he wrote during

and at the conclusion of the Civil War. Natu-rally, the main object of Arp's satire was the North and its conduct of the war. According to Arp, the actions of Yankee soldiers were fre-quently despicable, and northern versions of ac-complishments by the Union army were often exaggerated. Yet, Arp's letters made it clear that Southerners were never unanimously behind the Confederacy. He attacked those who did not sup-port or mismanaged the war. A favorite target was the governor of Georgia, Joseph Brown. Shirkers and draft dodgers came in for criticism from Arp's pen. He ruminated on the fluctua-tions of Confederate money, the currency bill, and the suspension of *habeas corpus*. Though Arp could still see some hope for success when the war was going against the South, he was occasionally more realistic about the South's chances, especially toward the war's end. In spec-ulating on a Union victory, though, he usually became defiant, thus setting the stage for Recon-struction. Through it all, Arp exhibited a keen eye for the weaknesses in human nature and the dogged courage of the isolated small farmer. Smith's picture of the war mellowed with time. Though he still preferred the South, he came to see, for example, that not all Yankee soldiers had been villains.

Arp's letters of the Reconstruction period were the most bitter Smith ever wrote. Many of them appeared in *Bill Arp's Peace Papers* (1873) but were not published in later collections of Arp letters. During Reconstruction, Smith, who remained a staunch and unreconciled Democrat, was much involved in politics; not surprisingly, many of Arp's letters deal with the contempo-rary political scene. In various letters of the late 1860s and early 1870s, Arp approved of Presi-dent Andrew Johnson's efforts to implement Lincoln's policy of moderation toward the South, attacked ex-Governor Joseph Brown when he counseled compromise with the Reconstruction-ists in Georgia, revealed bitter feelings toward the "black Republicans," and deplored the politi-cal scandals of the Grant administration. By Smith's last year as a Rome alderman, 1873-1874, he was apparently losing interest in poli-tics. A certain political disengagement can be seen in the Arp letters of the 1870s. In 1877, at the age of fifty-one, Smith gave up the law, storekeeping, and politics to become a farmer. He would supplement his negligible farm in-come by contributing Arp letters to the *Atlanta Constitution*.

The character of Smith's post-1877 Arp let-ters is different from that of the earlier ones. The later letters are less satirical, more sentimental. The "new" Arp is an industrious, good-humored farmer who chats about his family, farm life, friends, and social conditions in Georgia. Now a genial, homely philosopher, he advocates reconciliation between North and South. As James C. Austin has observed, Smith "the timely satirist had become the country sage."[3] The publication of *The Farm and the Fireside* in 1891 and *A School History of Georgia* in 1893 reveals the pleasure he derived from hearth and home. Keeping alive memories of regionalism and secession had given way to emphasizing the unity of family, state, and nation.

Summary

As a literary comedian, Charles Henry Smith compares favorably with Henry Wheeler Shaw, Charles Farrar Browne, and other "Phunny Phellows" who rose and prospered between 1855 and 1895. His Bill Arp is best remembered as a simple and strong Georgia cracker whose letters provide a unique record of the hopes and frustrations, the successes and failures of the ordinary Southerner during the Civil War, Reconstruction, and the Gilded Age.

Notes

1. Jay B. Hubbell, *The South in American Literature, 1607-1900.* (N.p.: Duke University Press, 1954), p. 686.
2. Charles Henry Smith, *Bill Arp's Scrap Book; Humor and Philosophy* (Atlanta: J. P. Harrison, 1884), p. 8.
3. James C. Austin, *Bill Arp* (New York: Twayne, 1969), p. 69.

Selected Bibliography

Primary Sources

Bill Arp, So Called: A Side Show of the Southern Side of the War. New York: Metropolitan Record Office, 1866.
Bill Arp's Peace Papers. New York: Carleton, 1873.
Bill Arp's Scrap Book; Humor and Philosophy. Atlanta: J.P. Harrison, 1884.
The Farm and the Fireside: Sketches of Domestic Life in War and in Peace. Atlanta: Constitution, 1891.
A School History of Georgia: Georgia as a Colony and a State, 1733-1893. Boston: Ginn, 1893.
Bill Arp: From the Uncivil War to Date, 1861-1903. Atlanta: Byrd Printing, 1903.

Secondary Sources

Book

Austin, James C. *Bill Arp.* New York: Twayne, 1969. A sound study of Smith's life and work. Contains extensive quotations from the Bill Arp letters.

Articles and Chapters in Books

Christie, Anne M. "Civil War Humor: Bill Arp." *Civil War History,* 2 (September 1956): 103–119. Good brief assessment of the Bill Arp letters. Based on the dissertation cited below.
Ginther, James E. "Charles Henry Smith, Alias Bill Arp." *Georgia Review,* 4 (Winter 1950): 313–321. Concise treatment of Smith's life and the Bill Arp letters.
———. "Charles Henry Smith, the Creator of Bill Arp." *Mark Twain Journal,* 10 (Summer 1955): 11–12, 23–24. Similar to preceding article but with a few additional details.
Hall, Wade H. *Reflections of the Civil War in Southern Humor.* Gainesville: University of Florida Press, 1962, Chapter One. Contains an estimate of Smith as a realistic interpreter of the Civil War. Based on the dissertation cited below.
Hubbell, Jay B. *The South in American Literature, 1607-1900.* N.p.: Duke University Press, 1954, pp. 683–686. Good estimate of Smith in relation to southern society.

Dissertations

Christie, Anne M. "Charles Henry Smith: 'Bill Arp': A Biographical and Critical Study of a Nineteenth Century Georgia Humorist, Politician, Homely Philosopher." Ph.D. dissertation, University of Chicago, 1952. An authoritative study of Smith's life and writings. Contains an exhaustive bibliography and a list of all of Smith's known lectures.
Hall, Wade H. "A Study of Southern Humor, 1865–1913." Ph.D. dissertation, University of Illinois, 1961. A sound assessment of Charles Henry Smith's place in post-Civil War Southern humor.

L. Moody Simms, Jr.

Smith, H[arry] Allen

Born: McLeansboro, Illinois, on December 19, 1907

Education: Completed eighth grade at St. Mary's Parochial School, Huntington, Indiana

Marriage: Nelle Mae Simpson, April 14, 1927, two children

Died: February 24, 1976

Biography

The son of Henry and Adeline (Allen) Smith, H. Allen Smith was born on December 19, 1907, in McLeansboro, Illinois. The large family (he was one of nine children and the first boy) made several moves in Illinois and Ohio before settling in Huntington, Indiana, in 1919. In many ways Smith retained his upper-Middle-Western roots, finding there a source of anecdotes for his autobiographical works and of colorful language and characters for his novels.

He left school after eighth grade and held a variety of jobs—chicken plucker, hair sweeper in a barber shop, shoeshine boy. At fifteen he became a proofreader for the *Huntington Press,* and eventually a reporter and the creator of an occasional humorous column by "Miss Ella Vator." His career on the *Press* and in Huntington itself ended abruptly when, at seventeen, he was arrested and convicted for writing and distributing a "lewd, licentious, obscene, and lascivious" off-color tale, "Stranded on a Davenport."

For the next few years, Smith was an itinerant newspaperman in Kentucky, Florida, Oklahoma, and Colorado. At the age of nineteen, he was editor and chief writer for a Sebring, Florida, daily, *The American*. There he met Nelle Mae Simpson, his future wife, who was the writer for the woman's page. They were married April 14, 1927, in Texas. In the following years they had two children, Allen Wyatt, born in 1928, and Nancy Jean, born in 1929. In 1927, Smith joined the *Denver Morning Post* as a reporter, and in 1929, he moved to New York as a feature writer for United Press. In 1936, he became a rewrite man for the *New York World-Telegram*, a position that he kept until 1941.

His first book, the biographical study *Robert Gair* (1939), was reviewed as "spirited and informal." It was followed by a humorous novel, *Mr. Klein's Kampf* (1939). *Low Man on the Totem Pole* (1941), however, was the work that established Smith's reputation. This assortment of childhood reminiscences and yarns and characters from his newspaper days became a best seller, as did the succeeding collections, *Life in a Putty Knife Factory* (1943) and his tales of Hollywood, *Lost in the Horse Latitudes* (1944). *Rhubarb* (1946), the story of a large, irascible and very rich cat, remains his most popular novel; it was made into a movie by Paramount in 1951. Among his better-known later works are *Larks in the Popcorn* (1948), *The Compleat Practical Joker* (1953) and *How to Write Without Knowing Nothing* (1961). An anecdotal autobiography, *To Hell in a Handbasket*, was published in 1962. Smith remained an active writer until his death in San Francisco, California, on February 24, 1976.

Literary Analysis

One key element to Smith's success as a humorist was his commitment to an honest reporting of the world as he saw it. "I am generally classified as a humorist," he wrote in *To Hell in a Handbasket*, "but I don't particularly care for the designation. I prefer to think of myself as a reporter, a reporter with a humorous slant. I am funny only in the sense that the world is funny" (p. 4). Objectivity was his conscious goal: a political independent, an agnostic tending towards atheism, sentimental but without sentiment, Smith placed himself in the tradition of cynical critics and commentators upon American life, such as Mark Twain and H.L. Mencken. The attitude came early; as he wrote in *To Hell in a Handbasket*, "By the time I hit Louisville [at seventeen] I had already been indoctrinated in the principles of free-press cynicism and callos-

ity. Nothing was anywhere close to sacred. Misery and suffering was a matter of type-size" (p. 127). Smith's approach was supremely democratic; he particularly enjoyed puncturing the pretensions of the rich, but the poor could be equally absurd. His portraits included members of the New York and Los Angeles literary/theatrical set but he dealt also with characters from his past in Indiana and with friends of his father. "I told the plain truth," he said of his anecdotes about his hometown, "and the people of McLeansboro came close to burning my birth certificate in the public square" (*To Hell*, p. 19). Pomposity, egotism, and self-importance were, however, the special objects of Smith's attention, no matter at what social level they might be found. He detested overblown pride and the sort of adulation that feeds that pride and delighted in lampooning it.

More often, though, Smith's works were marked by a gentler humor as he recounted the oddities and quirks of his contemporaries. Even in his first job in Huntington he had "Miss Ella" "dabbling in personalities" (*To Hell*, p. 97). His ability to find humor in the ordinary and extraordinary doings of people generated much of his writing and interview work, both during his newspaper years and later when he had turned to books and magazine articles: "For better or for worse I had what is known around newspaper shops as The Light Touch. . . . All week long I used to get stories tossed at me with the abrupt order, 'Make it funny.'" Being put on all the "'get-rid-of-the-nut-at-the-door' jobs" became his stock in trade, but "in the course of getting rid of many such nuts," he wrote, "I listened to them, and I began writing about them" (*To Hell*, p. 315).

A distinctive feature of Smith's work was the clear, direct, and often colloquial straightforwardness of his diction and phrasing. He was, as he had said of his father, "profane but seldom obscene" (*Life in a Putty Knife Factory*, p. 15) and he could capture the various dialects of the country with an accurate ear. For example, in *Life in a Putty Knife Factory*, he reconstructed his father's tale of making a kite:

> Maybe you don't remember this, but when you was about four er five years old I made you a kite. Be god damn if I didn't work half a day on it. Made the best damn kite I ever saw in my life. . . . Well you run a little ways and the kite started goin' up and got up about fifty foot and, 'y God, you stopped and turned around to look at it. . . . I was cussin' you and tellin' you to keep runnin', but you'd only run a little ways and then you'd stop and turn around to look. Fin'ly the

kite come down and I was so god-damn
mad I walked up to it and stomped it to
pieces and went on home and cussed
every step of the way.

(p. 16)

His books often were loose and disjointed in
structure, with a rambling, conversational tone.
Like his collections of anecdotes, his novels often
seemed to be a miscellany of yarns and characters as quirky as those he described from life. Yet
if the structure as a whole was loose, individual
portraits were often well wrought. In *Son of
Rhubarb* (1967), he describes Judge Andrew
Bippus thus:

It was not difficult for Judge Bippus to
achieve a pained expression; Nature had
given him a head start over most people.
He was tall and quite bony, with a long
face, a long pointed nose, and eyebrows
consisting almost entirely of wild hairs.
He somehow managed to retain the look
of a man with a constant stabbing tooth-
ache. That, or a sour stomach.

(p. 59)

This Dickensian eye for detail is one of the
constants in Smith's ability to create characterizations.

Summary

Ultimately, H. Allen Smith will be best remembered for the anecdotes, yarns, interviews, and
reminiscences of a reporter with an eye for the
humorous collected in *Low Man on a Totem
Pole, Life in a Putty Knife Factory, Lost in the
Horse Latitudes*, and *The Compleat Practical
Joker*. His humor lay, as he said, in presenting
people as they were, clearly, frankly, often affectionately, and sometimes, when the occasion demanded, sarcastically. Whether recounting a
practical joke, poking fun at a celebrity, or recalling an experience from his newspaper days,
Smith had the ability, as a newsperson would
say, to "get it right."

Selected Bibliography

Primary Sources

Robert Gair: A Study. New York: Dial, 1939.
Mr. Klein's Kampf; or, His Life as Hitler's Double.
New York: Stackpole, 1939.
Low Man on a Totem Pole. New York: Doubleday,
1941.
Life in a Putty Knife Factory. New York: Doubleday,
1943.
Lost in the Horse Latitudes. New York: Doubleday,
1944.
Desert Island Decameron. New York: Doubleday,
1945.
Rhubarb. New York: Doubleday, 1946. Rpt. Pocket
Books, 1977.

Larks in the Popcorn. New York: Doubleday, 1948.
Rpt. Greenwood Press, 1974.
The Compleat Practical Joker. New York: Doubleday,
1953. Rev. ed. Morrow, 1980.
The World, the Flesh, and H. Allen Smith. Ed. Bergen
Evans. Garden City: Garden City Books, 1954.
*How to Write without Knowing Nothing: A Book
Largely Concerned with the Use and Misuse of
Language at Home and Abroad*. Boston: Little,
Brown, 1961.
To Hell in a Handbasket. New York: Doubleday, 1962.
Low Man Rides Again. New York: Doubleday, 1973.
Return of the Virginian. New York: Doubleday, 1974.

Secondary Sources

Contemporary Authors. New Rev. Ser., Vol. 5. Ed.
Ann Evory. Detroit: Gale, 1982, pp. 497–498.
Current Biography. Ed. Maxine Block. New York: Wil-
son, 1942, pp. 773–775.
Curtis, Gregory. "The Dream House of H. Allen
Smith." *Texas Monthly*, February 1976.
Evans, Bergen, ed. *The World, the Flesh, and H. Allen
Smith*. Garden City, N.Y.: Hanover House, 1954,
pp. ix–xvi.
Miles, Elton, ed. *The Best of H. Allen Smith*. New
York: Trident, 1972, pp. 1–3.
Nawrozki, Joe. "Humor Was Serious Stuff for Smith."
Baltimore News-American, February 29, 1976.
Obituary and brief overview.
Obituary. *New York Times*, February 25, 1976, p. 42.
Simms, L. Moody, Jr. "H. Allen Smith." In *Dictionary
of Literary Biography*. Vol. 11. *American Humor-
ists, 1800–1950*. Ed. Stanley Trachtenberg. Detroit:
Gale, 1982, pp. 452–458. Overview of Smith's
writing, in a biographical context.
Van Gelder, Robert. "An Interview with Mr. H. Allen
Smith." *New York Times Book Review*, August
24, 1941, pp. 2, 22.

Malcolm Hayward

Smith, Seba

Born: Buckfield, Maine, on September 14,
1792

Education: Bowdoin College, 1818

Marriage: Elizabeth Oakes Prince, March
6, 1823, six children, four surviving to
adulthood

Died: July 28, 1868

Biography

Seba Smith, the creator of Major Jack Downing,
the character who provided the model for many
a Yankee sharper as well as Uncle Sam himself
and who personified in his age the rising common man of Jacksonian Democracy, was born in
a log cabin on what was then the frontier. His
ancestors were Massachusetts people, and his
grandfather and father moved to Turner, Maine,

in 1780. After marrying Apphia Stevens, his father (also named Seba Smith) moved back to the wilderness, helping to establish the settlement of Buckfield in Oxford County, Maine. On the fourteenth of September, 1792, Seba Smith was born.

Before settling down, the family moved to several places in Maine. When Smith was six years old they returned to Turner, a town which would be the model for the fictional Downingville. Four to five years later the Smiths again moved, this time to Bridgton in Cumberland County, about forty miles north of Portland. At the age of eighteen young Smith had mastered an education in depth enough to teach in the district schools of the Bridgton area. In 1815, after teaching two years at the newly opened Bridgton preparatory school, Smith (with the help of a wealthy philanthropist in the town) entered Bowdoin College as a twenty-three-year-old sophomore. A few years later, Henry Wadsworth Longfellow and Nathaniel Hawthorne would enroll as students. At Bowdoin Smith received a solid education, but one without the sophistication of a school such as Harvard.

Smith, in an effort to manage expenses, prepared his own meals and returned to teaching during vacations. He seems to have taken his studies seriously, since he was one of five class members elected to Phi Beta Kappa and was also a member of Peucinian (Bowdoin's first literary society), which required him to read several papers at student meetings. Although his health failed in his final year, Smith graduated with distinction and delivered the valedictorian oration at the commencement in 1818.

After graduating, Smith obtained a position in a private school near Portland and began writing poetry, some of which was published in *Eastern Argus*. At the completion of one year of teaching, Smith decided to take a vacation to improve his health. He traveled through the Atlantic states as far south as Charleston, South Carolina, and booked passage on a freighter to Liverpool. Evidently during his trip to Europe, Smith decided to give up teaching and to concentrate on publishing. Upon his return he found that the owner of *Eastern Argus* had died and left the paper in confusion; Smith promptly became assistant editor and purchased a half interest in the paper.

Finding himself in a comparatively comfortable position at the age of thirty-one, Smith married Elizabeth Oakes of Cumberland, Maine, on March 6, 1823. Their marriage was to last until Smith's death forty-four years later. Elizabeth bore Seba six sons (four of whom lived to adulthood) and cooperated with him on a number of literary ventures. She did, however, maintain a separate career as a writer and lec-

turer, which at the time overshadowed Smith's own. She knew and corresponded with many prominent people of the day, including Edgar Allan Poe, Ralph Waldo Emerson, and Longfellow. She often left on lecture tours while Seba tended the children and did household chores. Perhaps the point that disturbed Seba the most was his wife's changing her name, as well as the children's, to Oaksmith.

In October 1829, Smith established the weekly *Family Reader* and the daily *Portland Courier*; the latter soon contained the letters of Jack Downing from Downingville. Smith first began publishing the letters in an attempt to show the ridiculousness of a legislature whose extreme partisanship worked to paralyze the governing body. By discussing current political policies through the words of an ignorant country boy, Smith was able to satirize state politics without choosing a side. The following three years Smith experimented with folk humor through the vernacular language and rural values in the Downing letters. The letters became so popular that they were imitated by many writers, the most famous being Charles Augustus Davis, although these imitations (distinguished by the signature J. Downing, Major) lack the richness of Smith's work.

The 1830s were both the most profitable, as far as Smith's reputation was concerned, and the most economically devastating for the author. The Downing letters were combined in a book, but the expected wealth never materialized due to the failure of Smith's publishers, Lilly, Wait, Colman, and Holden. After this setback, Smith tried land speculation, which further depleted his savings, and in 1839, he moved to South Carolina where he was involved in a short and dismal attempt at marketing a machine that cleaned cotton fibers. Having sold their interest in the *Portland Courier*, the family moved to New York and was forced to take in boarders to pay expenses. Smith published a new batch of letters from a new character named John Smith in the *New York Mirror* and afterward published his book *John Smith's Letters with Picters to Match* (1839). These are similar to the Downing letters, but John Smith is a more intelligent commentator.

During the 1840s and 1850s, Smith contributed to many journals and papers, including *The Knickerbocker*, *Graham's Magazine*, and Horace Greeley's *New Yorker*, doing editing when the work was available. Sporadically in the years to follow, Smith published several other books, but never again did he approach the rich mixture of humor and social commentary found in the Downing letters. These later works include a volume on mathematics entitled *New Elements of Geometry* (1850), which seems to have been met with little encouragement. Suffering from paralysis, deafness, and a variety of illnesses, Smith retired to Patchogue, Long Island, where he died July 28, 1868. Strangely enough, his epitaph mentions nothing of his accomplishments in American humor; the tombstone reads "Poet and Scholar," two things that Smith approached with vigor but never accomplished successfully.

Literary Analysis

As has been already stated, the Downing letters are Smith's greatest achievement, and this is so for a number of reasons. Through Jack Downing's ignorance and innocence, Smith portrays the senselessness of many political events. Since Jack also represents the common man in America, in essence, this provides a study in contrasts as well. Downing's qualities allow him to see the process of Jacksonian control objectively and, therefore, he does not cover up what supporters of the movement hope would go unnoticed. On the other hand, Downing's honesty turns into foolishness when personal gain is concerned, causing him to fall into bad habits easily, sometimes verging on dishonesty, yet always rationalizing his actions with comments on the actions of others. By being presented this way, he cannot be judged as good or bad, honest or dishonest, and so epitomizes characters involved in the political process, from the country bumpkin to the political manipulator.

Because Smith gives the whole Downing family a voice (at times letters are presented from Cousin Ephraim, Uncle Joshua, Cousin Nabby, and Jack's mother, each supplying a separate point of view), the reader is exposed to a number of perspectives. Sometimes, Jack himself gives the reader several perspectives as in his response to authority. In the early letters, Jack comments on the confusion concerning a law that provided a replacement in the event of a governor's death, epitomized by a situation that arises in which it is possible for the state to have as many as two ruling governors or none at all due to a technicality.

Milton Rickels comments in his study of Smith that Jack is filled with a "fantasy of release," thinking that he now has the chance to revenge a wrong done him by an enemy back home. He sees the situation in reference to his own personal gain, not in terms of the state's welfare. This "upsurge of joy and aggressive power," asserts Rickels, is a necessary part of a person's fulfillment and can be witnessed in society as a whole as well as in the myths which the society creates.[1] Jack also sees himself as a figure of authority when he writes home that he may run for public office. He sees the office of governor as being above the law, a fact that is illustrated often by the masses who idolize polit-

ical figures in the real world. Smith often satirizes state and local politics as he leads Downing through an initiation of shrewdness toward deceit. It must be admitted, however, that Smith's later Downing letters are heavy-handed with reform and that lessens their effectiveness.

After the publication of the Downing letters in book form, Smith turned his energies to other literary endeavors. The first to appear was a 200-page poem entitled *Powhatan: A Metrical Romance*, published in 1841. It is a rendering of the meeting of Captain John Smith and Pocahontas (known as Metoka in the poem). The poem also concentrates on the chief of the tribe who shows himself as the archetypal noble savage. Smith's effort has been seen as a failed epic, the very historical accuracy of which dooms it to failure. In 1845, Smith resurrected Downing in a small volume entitled *May-Day in New-York; or House-Hunting and Moving* with a twenty-eight-page preface in mock literary style discussing Downing literature and the shortcomings of several impostors. In these letters Jack is no longer a bumpkin with a unique eye for politics; he has become a middle-class city dweller and father of two. Downing makes yet another appearance in *My Thirty Years out of the Senate* (1859), this time as friend and advisor to President James Polk. Downing satirizes manifest destiny, slavery, and the presidential campaign of 1852. This volume virtually ended the career of Downing as character and Smith as creator.

Summary

Smith is noted as the originator of a type of folk humor whose protagonist, by communicating through letters written "back home," proves himself to be a conscientious yet naive representation of the common man, voicing his feelings concerning a system of government that is moving toward alienating him. Smith's writings not only brought him recognition in his day, perhaps because it broke with the traditional portrayal of the Yankee as an impossibly stupid character, but also influenced Artemus Ward, Henry Wheeler Shaw, Mark Twain, and other later humorists. Like that of all originators, Smith's work is at times difficult for the modern reader, having become obscured by the passage of time; yet, his work is worth careful study in itself, and is the egg from which late nineteenth-century humor hatched.

Note

1. Milton and Patricia Rickels, *Seba Smith* (Boston: Twayne Publishers, 1977).

Selected Bibliography

Primary Sources
The Life and Writings of Major Jack Downing, of Downingville, Away Down East in the State of

Maine. Written by Himself. Boston: Lilly, Wait, Colman, & Holden, 1833. Reprinted from original, New York: AMS Press, 1973.

John Smith's Letters with "Picters" to Match. New York: Samuel Colman, 1839.

Powhatan: A Metrical Romance, In Seven Cantos. By Seba Smith. New York: Harper and Brothers, 1841.

May-Day in New-York: or House-Hunting and Moving; Illustrated and Explained in Letters to Aunt Keziah. By Major Jack Downing. New York: Burgess, Stringer and Company, 1845.

New Elements of Geometry. New York: George P. Putnam, 1850.

'Way Down East; or, Portraitures of Yankee Life. By Seba Smith. The Original Major Jack Downing. New York: Derby and Jackson, 1854; Boston: Samson and Phillips, 1854.

My Thirty Years out of the Senate. By Major Jack Downing. New York: Oaksmith and Company, 1859.

Secondary Sources

Biographies

Rickels, Milton, and Patricia Rickels. *Seba Smith.* Boston: Twayne Publishers, 1977. Good overall study of Smith's life with a considerable discussion of his work.

Wyman, Mary Alice. *Two American Pioneers: Seba Smith and Elizabeth Oakes Smith.* New York: Columbia University Press, 1927. A full, factual study with an in depth bibliography.

General Criticism

Bier, Jesse. *The Rise and Fall of American Humor.* New York: Holt, Rinehart, and Winston, 1968, pp. 60–65. Gives general information concerning Smith and Downing with a casual analysis of the latter.

Blair, Walter. *Horse Sense in American Humor.* Chicago: University of Chicago Press, 1942, pp. 55–65. Attempts to place Jack Downing in the forefront of the folk humor tradition.

———. *Native American Humor.* San Francisco: Chandler, 1960, pp. 58–60, 203–228. Originally printed in 1937. Includes a good bibliography along with a discussion of Smith and selections from the Downing letters.

Rourke, Constance. *American Humor: A Study of the National Character.* New York: Harcourt, Brace, 1931, pp. 29–33. Comments on Jack Downing as a representation of the common man.

Sloane, David E.E. *The Literary Humor of the Urban Northeast 1830-1890.* Baton Rouge, La.: Louisiana State University Press, 1983, pp. 122–137. Gives a brief discussion of Smith and Elizabeth Oaksmith with examples from the works of both.

Tandy, Jennette. *Crackerbox Philosophers in American Humor and Satire.* New York: Columbia University Press, 1925, pp. 25–31. This study of the naive philosopher analyzes the work of Smith and also compares it to that of his imitators.

Michael Pettengell

Smith, Solomon Franklin

Born: Norwich, New York, on April 20, 1801

Education: Little formal education

Marriages: Martha Therese Matthews, 1822, died, June 4, 1838, six children; Elizabeth Pugsly, 1839, three children

Died: February 14, 1869

Biography

Solomon Franklin Smith, known more generally as "Sol" or "Old Sol," had the varied kind of career typical of the humorists of the Old Southwest. Smith was, at one time or another, a lawyer, printer, newspaper editor, actor, and theater manager. The center of his life, however, was the theater, to which he first became attracted as a young man in New York state. The son of Levi Smith, a goldsmith who had been a piper in the Revolutionary War, and the former Hannah Holland, Smith lived most of his early life in a log house in Solon, New York. In 1817 he tried to join an acting company at Albany, but the company dissolved before he had a chance to act. Over the next several years, he worked at various occupations—as an apprentice printer in Louisville, Kentucky, as a printer in Vincennes, Indiana, and in Nashville, Tennessee, as an actor in Vincennes, and as a prompter in a Cincinnati, Ohio, theater. In Cincinnati he also studied law and began the *Independent Press* newspaper in 1822. During that year, he married Martha Therese Matthews, the principal soprano in the local Haydn society, of which Smith was likewise a member. She later acted occasionally with some of his troupes.

After 1823 Smith followed what he calls in his autobiography "the precarious occupation of a Theatrical Manager." He opened the Globe and Columbia Street theaters in Cincinnati that year, and learned just how precarious the life of a manager could be, as he comments in *Theatrical Management*:

> My funds ran out, and most of my actors scattered, as actors generally do when they find no money is to be had—and they are right, for they can not live on air—though *I* have almost done so on several occasions. At the close of the theatre I found myself in debt eleven hundred and fifty dollars. Rather an unfortunate beginning.
>
> (p. 29)

Nevertheless, Smith took his company on the road to West Virginia and to Pittsburgh, Pennsylvania, thus beginning a pattern of itinerant trouping that he continued for much of the next twelve years. About 1825 he toured Canada; in

1827 he was touring Kentucky; in 1829 he and his brother, Lemuel, formed a company to play Mississippi and western Tennessee; and in the early 1830s he was again on the road through Tennessee, Alabama, and Georgia. During this time, Smith not only managed various companies but also acted himself, his forte being low comedy. He must have been especially adept at playing the roles of old men, for he received his nickname "Old Sol" "in consequence of the many old men roles he acted." He seems to have been well, and even affectionately, received nearly everywhere he played and by 1835 had become sufficiently well known to be invited to play starring engagements at the Park Theatre in New York City and the Walnut Street Theatre in Philadelphia, Pennsylvania.

The year 1835 also marked the beginning of Smith's partnership with Noah Miller Ludlow in the theatrical company of Ludlow and Smith. William G.B. Carson, historian of the frontier theater, has called this firm "one of the most important in the West, if not in the country." The partnership was formed in Mobile, Alabama, where the company played from 1835 to 1840 and again from 1843 to 1848. From 1836 to 1851 "it dominated the St. Louis stage, and in that city built the first real theatre west of the Mississippi." From 1840 to 1853 it also operated in New Orleans, Louisiana, where it built the new St. Charles Theatre in 1842. Of the company's contribution to the American theater, Arthur Tees has commented justly:

> The firm of Ludlow and Smith . . . raised the standards of the early American theatre. As a result of their labors, the great stars of the time were seen not only in the more favored Eastern seaboard cities, but in the lower Midwest as well. The plays of Shakespeare, as well as many other works of less enduring merit, were professionally acted more frequently, to a wider audience, than is true today in those cities.

In 1853 Smith's partnership with Noah Ludlow was dissolved, and Smith retired from the stage. Between 1853 and 1868 he performed only about a dozen times, frequently in benefits for his friends or for charitable purposes. After the dissolution of the acting company, Smith settled in St. Louis, where he practiced law. In 1861 he was elected to the State Convention of Missouri, called by the Legislature to take the state out of the Union. Smith, however, was ardently pro-Union and, despite what he calls "dire threats," did his part to keep Missouri from secession "by dissolving the Legislature, deposing the governor and executive officers, and erecting a provisional government for the

state." Smith died on February 15, 1869, after suffering a paralytic stroke.

Literary Analysis

Smith's importance to American humor lies in his contribution to the frontier humor of the Old Southwest. During the twenty-five years before the Civil War, numerous non-professional literary men—lawyers, physicians, planters, judges, actors—developed a distinctively masculine brand of humor, the sources of which lay in the folk heritage of the region. Typical subjects of the frontier humor sketches and tales were hunting, fighting, racing, electioneering, gambling, drinking, and swindling. The life of the legislature, courtroom, camp meeting, riverboat, and stage also frequently provided the subjects of frontier humor, as did depictions of dandies, bumpkins, and eccentrics of all kinds. Much of the work in this genre appeared in a single periodical based in New York, *The Spirit of the Times*, which described itself as "A Chronicle of the Turf, Agriculture, Field Sports, Literature, and the Stage," and claimed a circulation as large as 40,000 in 1856. Its editor, William Trotter Porter, played an exceedingly important role in the development of the genre for he "was sympathetic to the southern humorists, sought their sketches, and helped them to get their books published." Many of Smith's sketches appeared in this important periodical, though quite a few others came out in one of the important regional outlets of Old Southwest humor, Joseph M. Field's St. Louis *Reveille*. Smith's humorous pieces were then gathered in a series of autobiographical volumes: *Sol. Smith's Theatrical Apprenticeship* (1845), which covered the first seven years of his professional life; *The Theatrical Journey-Work and Anecdotical Recollections of Sol. Smith* (1854), devoted to the second seven years; and *Theatrical Management in the West and South for Thirty Years* (1868), which incorporated material from both the earlier volumes in a full record of Smith's life and career. The first of these volumes, *Theatrical Apprenticeship*, is of special bibliographic note, too, for it was reprinted in 1849 as the first volume in the popular Carey and Hart series, "Library of American Humorous Works."

In his humorous writing, Smith never develops as sustained a narrative as Thomas Bangs Thorpe does in his classic, "The Big Bear of Arkansas," nor does he create a fully wrought fictional character in the manner of Johnson Jones Hooper's Simon Suggs or George Washington Harris's Sut Lovingood. Smith's works are more properly sketches or anecdotes of life on the frontier, frequently that of the theatre. He excels in stories about hoaxes or swindles, odd or eccentric characters, and cases of mistaken identity, often involving himself (he seems to have been taken for a preacher or doctor occasionally). The artistry of these tales typically depends upon what Walter Blair long ago pointed out to be the basic structural device of Southwest humor: the use of a frame or "box-like structure" to establish the circumstances of a tale's telling and the character of its teller before the actual narrating of the tale. Such a structure creates comic possibilities through incongruity: between the grammatical, literary language of the frame and the dialect of the story; between the "situation at the time the yarn was told and the situation described in the yarn itself"; and between the realism of the frame and the sometimes fantastic quality of the tale itself.

One of Smith's best tall tales, "Slow Traveling by Steam," illustrates both his artistic methods and typical subject matter. The story begins with the frame, Smith asking in his own voice whether anyone remembers the *Caravan*, a steamboat that "would now be considered a slow boat; *then* she was regularly advertised as the 'fast-running' etc." Just how slow this boat was he intimates by saying, "A voyage from New Orleans to Vicksburg and back, including stoppages, generally entitled the officers and crew to a month's wages." Having thus established his own voice and the general premise of the tale, the *Caravan*'s slowness, he turns to his specific circumstance: night drawing on, the boat moving upstream against the current, the wood supply low, and the captain and one of his pilots involved in an intense game of "brag" (a form of poker).

The first humor in the tale results from the satirical folk wisdom of the owner of a wood-yard where the *Caravan* stops for wood. When the captain objects to the price of the wood, the merchant responds:

> Why, capting . . . wood's riz since you went down two weeks ago; besides, you are awar' that you very seldom stop going *down*; when you're going *up* you're sometimes obleeged to give me a call, becaze the current's against you, and there's no other wood-yard for nine miles ahead; and if you happen to be nearly out of fooel, why—.

(p. 68)

The comedy here results in part from the incongruity between this dialect voice and the more formal, literary language of the narrative voice. As the story proceeds, Smith follows the captain through a night of brag in which he and one pilot play against two passengers who are "anxious to *learn the game*." The boat has two pilots who alternate between playing and steering the boat, and Smith sets up his comic conclusion by asking,

"'*When did they sleep?*'" The wood taken on at the wood-yard is very poor quality cottonwood, and several times during the night the boat must stop for more wood. Each time additional fuel is purchased, the captain is too busy with his game to do more than negotiate the price by shouting to a voice on shore. Each time the price is "Three *and* a quarter," the exorbitant charge to which the captain had objected at the first yard.

All of the elements are thus in place for the tale's resolution, which reveals a pair of swindles. First, we learn that the captain has been in league during the brag with his pilots, "with whom he had been on very bad terms during the progress of the game." To the pilot, he winks, saying, "Forty apiece for you, and I, and Jemes [the other pilot] is not bad for one night." But, soon the captain is made to change roles, as he is revealed to be the mark for the wood dealer. Again the boat needs wood, and the captain calls out to a wood-yard that the boat is apparently nearing. A woman calls out that the price is "'Three and a qua-a-rter!'" and when the captain objects, she says that she will let him talk to the old man. Out comes the same backwoodsman encountered the previous night for the deflation of the "bragging" captain: "'Why, darn it all, capting, there is but three or four cords left, and *since it's you*, I don't care if I *do* let you have it for THREE—*as you're a good customer!*'" So lacking in power that it could not break the cables fastened when it first stopped, and unsupervised by the pilots, who slept when they were not playing cards, the *Caravan* "HAD BEEN WOODING ALL NIGHT AT THE SAME WOOD-YARD!" Thus, the tale ends with a fantastic new meaning given to the originally realistic premise of the *Caravan*'s slowness.

Incongruity between narrative and vernacular voices also provides the humor of two sketches deriving from Smith's travels as a theater manager. In "The Consolate Widow" he comes upon a terrible scene, where a crowd has collected around the bodies of a horse and rider killed in a quarter race for a gallon of whisky. The rider's body is particularly ghastly for he has an enormous gash in his throat. Immediately the narrator sets about finding out what happened, but without stirring much response from the crowd. Finally he interviews a woman standing near:

> "He has a wife, then?" I remarked. "What will be her feelings when she learns the fatal termination of this most unfortunate race?"
>
> "Yes," sighed the female, "it *was* an unfortunate race. Poor man! he lost the whisky."

(*Theatrical Management*, p. 102)

And, as the story moves to its conclusion, the difference between the two levels of language becomes specifically an issue:

> "You, madam! *You* the wife of this man who has been so untimely cut off?" I exclaimed, in astonishment.
>
> "Yes, and what about it?" said she. "Untimely cut off? His throat's cut, that's all, by that 'tarnal sharp end of a log; and as for it's being *untimely*, I don't know but it's as well now as any time— *he warn't of much account, no how!*'

(p. 103)

In "A Tennessee Door-Keeper" Smith and his company play Greenville in East Tennessee for two nights to nearly empty houses. Attributing the lack of attendance to competition from a nearby camp-meeting, Smith plays one more night, after the meeting has concluded, and the house is packed. The performance goes on and on, as the audience simply will not allow it to end. When it finally does, Smith and the door-keeper go into another room to count the receipts, the manager obviously expecting a healthy profit. Finding only seven tickets, he begins to interrogate the door-keeper, sparking a comic interchange that ends with the door-keeper's advising Sol about the habits of East Tennessee crowds:

> "You employed me as *door-keeper*— mark the distinction—I had nothin' at all to do with the WINDERS—*and thar's where your hundred and eighty people came in*, you 'tarnal fool to leave 'em open when there was sich a crowd comin' from camp-meetin'!"

(Cohen and Dillingham, p. 73)

Many of the stories in Smith's autobiographies deal with similar vicissitudes of his life as an actor and theater manager. Indeed, these tales constitute his most distinctive contribution to the genre known as the humor of the Old Southwest.

Summary

Author of *Theatrical Apprenticeship* (1845), *Theatrical Journey-Work* (1854), and *Theatrical Management in the West and South* (1868), Sol Smith played an important role in the development of the humor of the Old Southwest. This distinctively American school of humor is significant both in itself and for its influence on such major American writers as Mark Twain and William Faulkner. Smith's writings are typical of frontier humor both in their subject matter and style. His tall tales and stories of hoaxes, swindles, and eccentric characters make extensive use of frame narration to create incongruity, especially between the correct language of the narrator and the racy dialect of the vernacular characters. An actor and theater manager himself, Smith made a distinctive contribution to the genre as the author of sketches dealing with the comic aspects of frontier theater.

Selected Bibliography

Primary Sources

Sol. Smith's Theatrical Apprenticeship. Philadelphia: Carey & Hart, 1845.

The Theatrical Journey-Work and Anecdotical Recollections of Sol. Smith, Comedian, Attorney at Law, etc., etc. Philadelphia: T.B. Peterson & Brothers, 1854.

Theatrical Management in the West and South for Thirty Years. New York: Harper & Brothers, 1868. Reprinted, with an introduction by Arthur Thomas Tees, by Benjamin Blom, 1968.

Sol. Smith Papers, Missouri Historical Society, St. Louis, Missouri.

Secondary Sources

Books

Arnold, Wayne William. "Sol Smith: Chapters for a Biography." M.A. Thesis, Washington University, 1939. An excellent biographical study.

Blair, Walter, ed. *Native American Humor.* San Francisco: Chandler Publishing, 1960. Revision of 1937 edition. A standard anthology with an excellent introduction to Southwest humor by one of the pioneer scholars in the field.

Carson, William G.B. *Managers in Distress: The St. Louis Stage, 1840-1844.* St. Louis: St. Louis Historical Documents Foundation, 1949. Based on manuscript material on the Ludlow-Smith partnership from the Missouri Historical Society; Carson sides with Smith in his account of the conflict with Ludlow.

——. *The Theatre on the Frontier: The Early Years of the St. Louis Stage.* Chicago: The University of Chicago Press, 1932. Excellent theater history with much on Ludlow and Smith.

Cohen, Hennig, and William B. Dillingham, eds. *Humor of the Old Southwest.* Athens: The University of Georgia Press, 1975. Revision of 1964 edition. Includes selections from Sol Smith, a brief biographical sketch, and an excellent general introduction to frontier humor.

Ludlow, Noah M. *Dramatic Life As I Found It.* 1880. Rpt. New York: Benjamin Blom, 1966. By Smith's partner in Ludlow and Smith. Abounds in information about their stage managing but is marred by a hostile bias against Smith with whom Ludlow quarreled over money.

Articles

Carson, W.G.B. "Solomon Franklin Smith." *Dictionary of American Biography.* Vol. 17. Ed. Dumas Malone. New York: Charles Scribner's Sons, 1935, pp. 346-347. A useful brief sketch.

Oehlschlaeger, Fritz. "A Bibliography of the St. Louis *Reveille*, 1844-1846." Forthcoming in *Studies in American Humor.* Contains publication information on Smith's contributions to the *Reveille*.

Fritz Oehlschlaeger

Smith, Thorne

Born: Annapolis, Maryland, in 1892
Education: Dartmouth College
Marriage: Celia Sullivan, two children
Died: June 21, 1934

Biography

James Thorne Smith, Jr., was born in 1892 on the grounds of the Naval Academy at Annapolis, Maryland; his father James, Sr., was a commodore in the United States Navy. Thorne Smith attended private schools and Dartmouth College, entering the advertising business after graduation. During World War I, he served in the Navy, editing the Naval Reserve magazine, *Broadside*, for which he wrote a series of comic stories of the misadventures of a hapless seaman. These were collected after the war in the volumes *Biltmore Oswald* (1918) and *Out O' Luck* (1919). Smith returned to advertising after the war and contributed a serious chapter on advertising to a volume titled *Civilization in the United States* (1922). His other serious writing included *Haunts and By-Paths* (1919), a book of poems; *Dream's End* (1927), a novel; and *Lazy Bear Lane* (1931), a children's book.

Topper, published in 1926, was Smith's first big success. It and the comic novels that followed at the rate of about two a year enabled him to leave advertising and live on his writing. He worked briefly in Hollywood in 1933, contributing dialogue to other writers' scripts. Smith died of a heart attack in Sarasota, Florida, on June 21, 1934, leaving a wife and two daughters. One completed novel, *The Glorious Pool*, was published later that year, and a partial manuscript was completed by Norman Matson and published as *The Passionate Witch* in 1941. Three of Smith's novels were turned into successful films: *Topper* (1937), *Topper Takes a Trip* (1939), and *Turnabout* (1941). There was also a non-Smith sequel, *Topper Returns* (1941). Later, *Topper* was the basis for a popular television series in 1953–1956 and a television film in 1979; *Turnabout* was an unsuccessful television series in 1979.

Literary Analysis

Smith said that the inspiration for *Topper* came from watching a small dog move almost invisibly through tall grass. This led to the idea of an invisible dog, then invisible people. What began as a short story grew into the novel in which Cosmo Topper, a staid banker, encounters the ghosts of George and Marion Kirby, a newly deceased socialite couple who decide to earn their way into heaven by bringing a little joy into Topper's life. The process involves a variety of confusing and embarrassing escapades, since the irresponsible Kirbys can make themselves invisible at will, leaving Topper to explain whatever prank they have just indulged in. Their project eventually succeeds as Topper begins to loosen up and enjoy the adventures.

The success of *Topper* gave Smith a formula to work variations on for the rest of his short career: a successful but somehow unfulfilled businessman has his life touched by magic in a way that leads to an escalating series of embarrassing and Rabelaisian adventures, generally involving supernatural transformations, impossible-to-explain situations, uninhibitedly amorous young ladies with a propensity for losing or shedding their clothes, vast quantities of bootleg liquor, totally confused policemen and judges, a gradual liberation of the hero's spirit, and a happy ending, often in the arms of the secretary, model, or shopgirl who has loved him from afar.

In *The Bishop's Jaegers* (1932), for example, a preternatural fog sends a commuter ferry off course and into a nudist colony with inhibition-destroying results. In *Skin and Bones* (1933) the hero finds himself likely to turn into a walking skeleton without warning; after a while he begins to enjoy the effect that this has on others. The hero of *The Stray Lamb* (1929), on the other hand, keeps metamorphosing into various animals, while in *Turnabout* (1931) a married couple wake up one morning to find their minds in each other's bodies. In *The Night Life of the Gods* (1931) the classical statues in a museum come alive and decide to make up for centuries of lost debauching, involving a hapless mortal in their adventures, and in *Rain in the Doorway* (1933) the hero takes refuge from a storm in a mad department store that has the air of a bawdy *Alice in Wonderland*.

What might seem to be Smith's most original quality—his magical plots—in fact follows earlier models. Magic-in-everyday-life stories represented a recognizable genre of fabulist fiction in the first quarter of the century. Among its practitioners was the British satirist F. Anstey (Thomas Anstey Guthrie, 1856–1934), whose *Vice Versa*, in which a conservative old man changes bodies with his rakehell son, and *The Tinted Venus*, in which a statue comes alive, might be thought the inspirations for *Turnabout* and *Night Life* respectively, if such plot premises were not fairly standard for the genre.

Smith's major contributions to the genre, and to the entertainment of his readers, are three. First, by setting his novels in the Prohibition era and the world of the well-to-do, he captures a spirit of "anything goes" that enables his characters to adjust to their bizarre adventures with remarkable aplomb. When Mr. Bland in *Skin and Bones* first becomes a skeleton he is in a speakeasy, and both he and those around him are at a level of tipsiness that is willing to accept the experience with comical calm:

> "Do you mind?" asked Mr. Bland.
> "Not at all," replied the man. "I'm relieved you're not a pink monkey or a blue dragon or a flock of loathsome reptiles. . . ."
> "What do you use for eyes, Mr. Bland?" asked Pauline. "There isn't one in your head."
> "Search me," replied Mr. Bland.
> "That wouldn't be hard," put in Whittle, "but it would be damned unpleasant."
>
> (p. 46)

In the same spirit and spirits, the characters in *Rain in the Doorway* decide impulsively to buy a stuffed whale. Then, having trucked it around town for a while, they offer it to passers-by and are genuinely surprised that anyone finds this noteworthy. This happy nonconformity frequently rises to the level of Marx Brothers anarchy as the less-inhibited characters take a perverse delight in creating confusion:

> "Don't say one word," he commanded. "I have eyes in my head, haven't I? Am I a fool? A driveling idiot?"
> "Yes," replied Tim. . . .
> "What!" shrilled the judge. "You call me a fool and an idiot—a driveling one?"
> "No," said Tim hastily. "I was saying 'yes' to something else."
> "What were you saying 'yes' to?"
> "I was merely saying 'Yes, you have.'"
> "Yes, I have? Speak up, you ninny. Yes, I have what?"
> "Yes, you have eyes in your head."
>
> (*Turnabout*, p. 252)

Only the sober people in Smith's novels cannot cope with the bizarre goings-on. Among them are the heroes' unsympathetic wives and the judges in the inevitable courtroom scenes:

> "Well, your honor," began Jo easily, "it was like this. You see, there was a fog and—"
> "What fog?" interrupted the magistrate.
> Jo looked puzzled.
> "How do you mean, what fog?" she asked. . . .
> "Where and when was this fog?" he demanded.
> "All over," said Jo. "I forget just when."
> Magistrate Wagger looked thoroughly disheartened.

> "Tell it your way," he muttered. "I won't believe you anyhow."
>
> (*The Bishop's Jaegers*, p. 297)

This mildly antisocial tone encourages the reader to share the delight in Rabelaisian naughtiness.

The Rabelaisian tone is Smith's second great quality and the basis of much of his humor. He has the knack of making mildly bawdy scenes and lines seem more naughty than they are, and there is scarcely a page without its wicked giggle:

> "Will you make a clean breast of it?" he demanded.
> "Why, your honor," said Sandra, dropping her eyes. "What a thing to ask!"
>
> (*The Stray Lamb*, p. 274)

In *Rain in the Doorway* the hapless hero finds himself behind the department store's book counter, where customers keep demanding to know if he has "The Sex Life of the Flea." In *Turnabout* a secretary offers her boss a drink from her secret flask:

> "Very old and rare," [he] gasped. "The person who drinks that should never suffer from baldness of the chest."
> "I don't suffer from that disease," the girl replied. "I glory in it."
>
> (p. 119)

Added to these are the scenes, almost as obligatory as the courtrooms, in which the hero tries to protect his honor from what seems like hordes of naked women:

> "Hello!" cried Mr. Owen. "Room clerk? Good! I've got two beds and two baths, and there is a naked woman in each. . . ."
> "I don't know about you," said the clerk, "but if I was fixed up as you are, I'd either go to bed or take a bath. You can't lose."
> "Something has to be done about all these women," fumed Mr. Owen. "And that without further delay."
> "I should say so," agreed the clerk. "The night isn't getting any shorter."
>
> (*Rain in the Doorway*, p. 184)

The third source of Smith's popularity and effectiveness, and perhaps the one most making him worthy of serious study, is the wish-fulfillment quality of his fantasies. Depression readers must have taken special delight in imagining orgiastic goings-on among the well-to-do, but beyond that there is a deeper fantasy level. Smith's tales of bawdy and liberating magic speak directly to the successful businessman who finds no pleasure in his work or what it buys him, and who longs for something more, even as he fears that he is unequipped to appreciate it. As fantasies, Smith's novels promise such a reader that the world can change suddenly, releasing him from the rat race, that the woman of his dreams will appear and guide him toward the ability to feel and express his emotions openly, and that some unpredictable adventure awaits him. The novels could only be as popular as they were in a society where the hunger for such a magical escape lay just beneath the surface. The distance between Smith's heroes and Jay Gatsby is not great, and Smith's comic romps capture the secret emptiness of the 1920s as surely as do the serious novels of F. Scott Fitzgerald.

Summary

Thorne Smith was the author of several very popular comic novels during the 1920s and 1930s. Typically, a lonely businessman would be touched by magic, meeting ghosts or goddesses, or turning into a skeleton or an animal, and have a string of bawdy and comic adventures that loosened his inhibitions and left him free-spirited and happy. Much of the humor came from the wit and ribaldry inspired by large quantities of alcohol and from the confusion caused to wives, police, and other staid figures.

Selected Bibliography

Primary Sources

Biltmore Oswald. New York: Frederick A. Stokes, 1918.

Out O' Luck. New York: Frederick A. Stokes, 1919.

Haunts and By-Paths. New York: Frederick A. Stokes, 1919.

Topper. New York: R.M. McBride, 1926.

Dream's End. New York: R.M. McBride, 1927.

The Stray Lamb. New York: Grosset and Dunlap, 1929.

Did She Fall? New York: Cosmopolitan Book Corporation, 1930.

Turnabout. Garden City: Doubleday, Doran, 1931.

Lazy Bear Lane. Garden City: Doubleday, Doran, 1931.

The Night Life of the Gods. Garden City: Doubleday, Doran, 1931.

Topper Takes a Trip. Garden City: Doubleday, Doran, 1932.

The Bishop's Jaegers. Garden City: Doubleday, Doran, 1932.

Skin and Bones. Garden City: Doubleday, Doran, 1933.

Rain in the Doorway. Garden City: Doubleday, Doran, 1933.

The Glorious Pool. Garden City: Doubleday, Doran, 1934.

(completed by Norman Matson.) *The Passionate Witch.* Garden City: Doubleday, Doran, 1941.

Secondary Sources

Jitomir, Howard Steven. "Forgotten Excellence: A Study of Thorne Smith's Humor." Dissertation, St. John's University, 1983. Argues among other points that Smith's bawdry keeps him from the respect accorded contemporary humorists such as Robert Benchley and James Thurber and that Smith offers interesting insights into such subjects as the battle of the sexes.

Obituary. *New York Times*, June 22, 1934, p. 33.

Thorne Smith: His Life and Times. New York: Doubleday Doran, 1934. A promotional booklet issued by Smith's publisher, including an autobiographical essay by Smith.

Neilson, Keith. "Thorne Smith." *Supernatural Fiction Writers: Fantasy and Horror.* Ed. E.F. Bleiler. New York: Scribner's, 1985. Discusses Smith's narrative characteristics in his "fantasy" novels.

Scheetz, George H., and Rodney N. Henshaw. "Thorne Smith." *Bulletin of Bibliography*, 41, no. 1 (March 1984): 25–37. Bibliography of primary and secondary sources.

Gerald M. Berkowitz

Southern, Terry

Born: Alvarado, Texas, on May 1, 1928

Education: Northwestern University, B.A., 1948; Sorbonne, Paris, 1948–1950

Marriage: Carol Kaufman, July 14, 1950, one child

Biography

Terry Southern, perhaps the hippest of the hip black humorists of the 1960s, is a shy, somewhat retiring gentleman whose manners border on the courtly. It is no surprise, then, to discover that he was born in a small southern town. He was raised in Alvarado, Texas, about 40 miles south of Fort Worth.

Southern was schooled at Northwestern and the Sorbonne, and was living in Switzerland in the mid-1950s when he and a friend, Mason Hoffenberg, conspired to write an entry in Maurice Girodias's "Traveller's Companion" series for the Olympia Press. Southern outlined the heroine of the short novel in this way: she is a "sensitive, progressive-school humanist who comes from Wisconsin to New York's lower East Side to be an art student, social worker, etc., and to find (unlike her father) 'beauty in a mean place.' She has an especially romantic idea about 'minorities' and of course gets raped by Negroes, robbed by Jews, knocked up by Puerto Ricans, etc.—though her feeling of 'being needed' sustains her for quite a while, through a devouring gauntlet of freaks, faggots, psychiatrists and aesthetic cults."

"She," of course, was the heroine of *Candy*. The novel, published under the pseudonym of Maxwell Kenton, finally appeared in the summer of 1958. It was largely Southern's work, and Girodias tried to persuade him to publish the book under his own name. Southern demurred. He had a children's book under consideration, he wrote Girodias, and "any news linking me with a book 'in questionable taste' would irreparably shatter my chances. . . ." Instead, the book was credited to a disenchanted atomic scientist whom Southern invented. It made a much greater splash than was usually the case for a "d.b." (Girodias's shorthand for a dirty book). In New York, Southern wrote his publisher that the book was having an underground success, but Girodias said the book was "too hip to enjoy normal sale as a d.b.," and it took longer to unload than the usual Olympia titles.

Meanwhile, Southern was pursuing a legitimate, above-ground career. He published *Flash and Filigree* in 1958 and *The Magic Christian* (with Random House) in 1959. He also began an association with *Esquire* to which he was to contribute some outstanding journalism in the 1960s. Still, *Candy*'s fame continued to grow in the early years of the decade and, after a long series of publishing squabbles and copyright battles, the book was finally published under the Southern-Hoffenberg byline by Putnam in 1964. Three paperback publishers rushed out copies under the Kenton name, claiming to be in violation of no copyright.

The film world had beckoned, and it was to be 10 years between novels for Southern. Southern's first produced script was *Dr. Strangelove*, which he and Stanley Kubrick concocted from Peter George's straight-faced novel, *Red Alert*. Southern earned a screenwriter's award and an Academy Award nomination in 1964.

Hollywood kept Southern busy for the rest of the 1960s. He was well known as a script doctor and worked in collaboration on a number of the decade's best films: *The Loved One* (with Christopher Isherwood), 1964; *The Cincinnati Kid* (with Ring Lardner, Jr.), 1965; *Barbarella* (with Roger Vadim), 1967; *Candy*, 1968; *The End of the Road*, 1968; *Easy Rider* (with Peter Fonda and Dennis Hopper), 1969; *The Magic Christian*, 1970; and *Blue Movie*, 1970. Southern's work on *Easy Rider* earned him his second Academy Award nomination. His major contributions to that script include Jack Nicholson's memorable "stoned" monologues.

Blue Movie, in 1970, was Southern's return to the novel after a ten-year absence. He also published a collection of journalism and tales titled *Red-Dirt Marijuana and Other Tastes*.

Southern's output has dropped off since the early 1970s, though he remains a popular college speaker. Perhaps he is amused that his book, *Candy*, so controversial on many campuses 25 years ago, is now enshrined in rare book collections of university libraries.

Literary Analysis

Introducing Southern to a college audience once, Clemson University professor Raymond Merlock said: "When I was in high school, I got ahold of a copy of *Candy*, and I learned to laugh about sex. Then I saw *Dr. Strangelove* and I learned to laugh about nuclear war. Then I saw *The Loved One* and I learned to laugh about death. Then I saw *Barbarella* and fell in love with Jane Fonda. Then I saw *Easy Rider* and sold my motorcycle. I guess Terry Southern has had a great influence on my life."

Southern seemed to influence a lot of lives in the 1960s, and his work forms an important cultural record of the decade. It is difficult to judge who contributed what to a multi-author screenplay, but the fact that Southern's name is credited as a coauthor of some of the most important films in the 1960s indicates the sizable role that he played in their creation.

Southern's early work met with much negative criticism. *Flash and Filigree*, the adventures of a "pretty but puerile" nurse and the world's foremost dermatologist, featured some of the wild black humor that would characterize his screenplays. The nurse is pursued by a "wolfish pharmacy student" and the doctor is hounded by a transvestite named Felix who "winds up as a cadaver for all his trouble" (descriptions taken from the *New York Times*). At one point, there is even a game show called "What's My Disease?" *The New Yorker*, in a brief review, said that Southern "ignored all the intimations of reality without which such spoofing cannot function. The writing is no less eccentric and here and there is downright unintelligible." *Time* was more generous. The reviewer said that the book "lacks weight and discipline, but it also has an unfailing sense of the ridiculous, heightened by a deadpan delivery." Few critics were as kind as the *Time* reviewer, who saw a similarity between Southern's writing and that of an author he was destined to adapt for the screen: "Author Southern's California of wide-screen girls, cultists, simpletons and satyrs has been seen before in Evelyn Waugh's *The Loved One*."

Southern's next novel, *The Magic Christian*, was let loose upon bewildered reviewers in 1960. The book told the story of Guy Grand, the world's richest man. Blessed with a sense of the absurd, Grand went to Africa and hunted with howitzers, manufactured a convertible longer than a Greyhound Bus, and published a newspaper composed solely of letters to the editor. *The Spectator* said that the book was "in the worst possible taste." *The Times Literary Supplement* said that Southern had failed to lay the "foundation of ordinary sanity and decent values" on which good satire must be based.

But, people seemed to be catching on to Terry Southern's humor. Nelson Algren, writing in *The Nation*, called *The Magic Christian* "the most profoundly satiric and wildly comic account of our life and times." And, in *Commonweal* Edward Kenneback said, "we have nightmares of our own, true enough, but Mr. Southern's can be a lot of fun."

One appreciative reader of *The Magic Christian* was British actor Peter Sellers, who eventually bought the screen rights. His interest in Southern first involved Sellers's upcoming participation in a new film by Stanley Kubrick, however. Sellers and Kubrick, who were bringing Nabokov's *Lolita* to the screen, were also working on adapting a novel called *Red Alert* by Peter George. Kubrick had read over 70 books on the subject of nuclear war, and was a subscriber to *The Bulletin of the Atomic Scientists*. He and Southern took George's melodramatic plot and fashioned a nightmare comedy. There was a base in reality, this time. In fact, the film had a near-documentary look. But, it was a skewed reality: although a nuclear war is imminent, a hardened sergeant (Sgt. Bat Guano) will not vandalize a Coke machine for change to make a pay-phone call to the president that could save the world. He is worried about "answering to the Coca Cola company." Audiences liked Southern's black comedy, and so did his colleagues. It was a strong, tight script blending verbal and visual comedy. In some ways, it set the tone for the 1960s: he had audiences laughing through the apocalypse, to borrow a phrase from *Esquire*.

Southern's next project, adapting Waugh's *The Loved One*, was similar in some respects. It was an attempt to get the mass-market audience laughing about another grim subject: death. Waugh was not pleased with the results, as Southern embellished the story with satirical jabs at almost anything on the American landscape. The film was a hit with some critics, but not with the popular audience.

The Cincinnati Kid, a taut drama with some elements of comedy, is perhaps the most sane film to bear Southern's name. His contributions to *Barbarella* were obscured by the somewhat scandalous (though tame by later standards) nudity. Southern's monologues for Nicholson in *Easy Rider* were the brightest part in a script composed largely of grunts and groans by the two dope-dealing heroes.

Candy was finally published "above-ground" in 1964 and enjoyed wide success. Though the film version of it four years later (Marlon Brando, Richard Burton, and Ringo Starr were in it) was financially successful, the filmmakers seemed to miss the point of the book.

Southern, after adapting works by other authors, turned his talents to his own work. Working with Sellers again, he returned to *The Magic Christian*. The screenplay credits Southern, but he disavows much of the film, which had become a series of sight gags about the lust for money. The finale featured Sellers and Starr (as Guy Grand's adopted son) sprinkling money over a vat of blood, excrement, and urine, and watching bowler-hatted businessmen leaping in to retrieve the dollar bills.

Southern's last screenplay was the unproduced *Blue Movie*. His novel version, published in 1970, was not well received. It told of the making of an "art" pornographic film and included prolific sex scenes, including a "little necrophilia thrown in for good measure" (*New York Times Book Review*). *Book World* said that the book contained "the usual kerosene-on-the-cat sort of humor." Southern was "not the dirty writer he aspires to be, and there is little else to recommend this book."

Red-Dirt Marijuana and Other Tastes, a collection of stories and articles published in 1967, shows Southern's talent as a journalist. Tom Wolfe included Southern's 1962 *Esquire* article, "Twirling at Ole Miss," in his anthology, *The New Journalism*. Wolfe gives Southern credit for exploring and establishing an unusual style of personal reportage that was later perfected by Hunter S. Thompson, and Wolfe considers Southern the real father of Gonzo Journalism.

"Twirling at Ole Miss" may be the best short work Southern has done. It is a comical account of playing reporter in Oxford, Mississippi, during a pre-pubescent baton-twirling workshop. Southern repeatedly sets up serious-sounding situations, then deflates the highfalutin' effect with one-liners. In the midst of his humor is a commentary on race relations; Oxford was the town that saw the bloodbath following the enrollment of James Meredith at the University of Mississippi:

> High-style (or "all-out") Strutting is to be seen mainly in the South, and what it resembles more than anything else is a very contemporary burlesque-house number—with the grinds in and the bumps out. It is the sort of dance one associates with jaded and sequin-covered washed-out blondes in their very late thirties—but Ole Miss, as is perhaps well known, is in "the heartland of beautiful girls," having produced two Miss Americas and any number of runners-up, and to watch a hundred of

their nymphets practice the Strut, in bathing suits, short shorts, and other such skimp, is a visual treat which cuts anything the Twist may offer the viewer. It is said, incidentally, that the best Strutting is done at the colored schools of the South, and that of these the greatest of all is to be seen at Alabama State Teachers College. That jazz trends have decisively influenced the style of Strutting in recent years is readily acknowledged, and is highly apparent indeed.

(Excerpt from *Red-Dirt Marijuana and Other Tastes* © 1967, Terry Southern. Originally appeared in *Esquire*)

Southern may have fallen out of favor with Hollywood filmmakers, and his manuscripts might not be commercial enough for today's publishers, but in the 1960s, there were few humorists who could match Southern. He documented the spirit of the 1960s and was himself a large part of it, recording America's obsessiveness and obsessions.

Summary

Terry Southern was at his peak in the 1960s, and his irreverence and dark world view seemed, in that decade, to coincide with much of the national conscience. He is perhaps best-known as a screenwriter for *Dr. Strangelove, The Loved One,* and *Easy Rider,* and for creating *Candy,* an underground classic that became an aboveground bestseller.

Selected Bibliography

Primary Sources

Books

(with Mason Hoffenberg; as Maxwell Kenton.) *Candy.* Paris: Olympia, 1958.
Flash and Filigree. New York: Coward-McCann, 1958.
The Magic Christian. New York: Random House, 1960.
(with Mason Hoffenberg.) *Candy.* New York: Putnam, 1964.
Red-Dirt Marijuana and Other Tastes. New York: Random House, 1967.
Blue Movie. New York: World, 1970.

Screenplays

(with Stanley Kubrick and Peter George.) *Dr. Strangelove,* released in 1964.
(with Christopher Isherwood.) *The Loved One,* 1964.
(with Ring Lardner, Jr.) *The Cincinnati Kid,* 1965.
(with Roger Vadim.) *Barbarella,* 1967.
(with Peter Fonda and Dennis Hopper.) *Easy Rider,* 1969.
Blue Movie, 1970.
(with Joseph McGrath.) *The Magic Christian,* 1971.

Secondary Sources

Girodias, Maurice. *The Olympia Reader.* New York: Grove, 1965.

Kagan, Norman. *The Cinema of Stanley Kubrick.* New York: Holt, Rinehart and Winston, 1972.
Mitford, Jessica. *Poison Penmanship.* New York: Knopf, 1979.
Who's Who in America.

William McKeen

Streeter, Edward

Born: Chestertown, New York, on August 1, 1891
Education: Pomfret School; Harvard University, A.B., 1914
Marriage: Charlotte Warren, 1919, four children
Died: March 31, 1976

Biography

Edward Streeter was born on August 1, 1891, in Chestertown, New York, a remote village in the Adirondacks. He was the son of Harvey and Frances (Chamberlain) Streeter and was brought up in Buffalo, New York. During childhood, Streeter developed a love for books. His family had a large library and encouraged his reading. He began a novel when he was nine years old but only wrote a few chapters before losing interest in the project.

His literary interests reappeared at Pomfret School where he edited the school paper and the class book. While he was at Harvard he edited the *Lampoon* and wrote the script for the Hasty Pudding show. After he graduated in 1914 he worked as a reporter on the *Buffalo Express,* where he was paid by the column-inch pay scale. At the same time, he had a second job with a building supply business in Buffalo. Within a short time, the *Express* hired him as a regular reporter, and he gained experience in what has come to be known as "investigative reporting."

Streeter kept his connection with the newspaper when he served with the New York National Guard (Troop I, First Cavalry, Twenty-Seventh Division) on the Mexican border from June 1916 to March 1917. The Twenty-Seventh Division had a local newspaper, and soon Streeter was assigned a column called "The Incinerator." He had already been toying with the idea of writing about his experiences in the National Guard and decided to try his hand at a series of satirical letters from an imaginary soldier to his girl friend and placed one in the column.[1] Fellow rookies were enthusiastic about

"Dere Mable," the title Streeter gave his letter, and he wrote a second one. In 1917 the division was sent on active duty to Camp Wadsworth in Spartanburg, South Carolina. Richard Connell, editor of the camp magazine there (and a former classmate of Streeter's at Harvard), persuaded the writer to continue his series of letters. Streeter described the way his letters came into book form, saying: "just before the Division sailed for France I received a five-day leave. It occurred to me that . . . I might stumble on some editor optimistic enough to turn my manuscript into a book."[2]

He dashed to a publishing house, threw the manuscript and his camp address on the desk of the treasurer of the firm, and ran to a train. Alfred Harcourt at Henry Holt and Company, to whom Streeter submitted that manuscript, turned the work over to William Morrow at Frederick A. Stokes and Company; Morrow was another Harvard man who was appreciative of Streeter's work.[3]

In 1918, the volume appeared in print under the full title of *Dere Mable: Love Letters of a Rookie* and won immediate acclaim as one of the few humorous works to come out of World War I. It was followed by two other volumes: *That's Me All Over, Mable* and *Same Old Bill, Eh Mable*.

During his service in Europe, Streeter was promoted to first lieutenant in the field artillery. When he came home in 1919, he married Charlotte Lockwood Warren and continued his writing on a freelance basis but soon joined the Bankers Trust Company in New York City. He worked there as an assistant vice president until 1929 when he became a partner in the firm of Blake Brothers, members of the New York Stock Exchange. Two years later he moved to the Fifth Avenue Bank as a vice president. That bank later merged with the Bank of New York, and Streeter remained there until his retirement in August 1956.[4]

During those years, he and his wife had four children: Claire, Edward, Jr., William, and Charlotte. Mrs. Streeter died in 1965. Streeter died of cancer on March 31, 1976, at the age of 84.[5]

During his first years with the bank, Streeter published no books, but he did write short stories and articles that appeared in the *Saturday Evening Post* and *Redbook*. In later years he contributed to *McCall's* and *Good Housekeeping*. In 1938, another book, *Daily Except Sunday* (Simon and Schuster, 1938), was published, and he began a period of productivity that continued until some time after his retirement.

His writings included (in addition to the *Dere Mable* series and *Daily Except Sunday*): *Beany, Gangleshanks and the Tub*, New York and London, Putnam's, 1921; *Father of the Bride*, Simon and Schuster, 1949; *Skoal Scandinavia*, Harper, 1952; *Mr. Hobbs' Vacation*, Harper, 1954; *Merry Christmas, Mr. Baxter*, Harper, 1956; *Mr. Robbins Rides Again*, Harper, 1957; *Window on America*, Bank of New York, 1957; *Chairman of the Bored*, Harper, 1961; *Along the Ridge: From Northwestern Spain to Southern Yugoslavia*, New York: Harper and Row, 1969; and an address at the dinner for new members of the Century Association delivered on October 5, 1961, at Stamford, Connecticut, published by Overbrook Press, 1962.

Literary Analysis

Edward Streeter combined a career as banker and broker with that of humorist. At first glance, the combination seems strange, but Streeter found his humor in the fact that men and women who lived their lives in the staid conventional pattern of upper-middle-class society were often beset with the unexpected crises of life with which the so-called "common man" could identify.

His first writing exposed readers to his way of regarding the hard, confining, regimented, and often dull life in the army. Streeter shared his experiences with his imaginary girl friend in such a way that readers were able to see humor in the situations. *Dere Mable* originally included nineteen undated letters from Camp Wadsworth, written by Pvt. Bill Smith to his girl friend Mable Gimp in "Philopolis," New York. The letters were illustrated by Corporal "Bill" Breck's drawings. Misspelled words, malapropisms, and strange French phrases added to the humor of the letters. In one he wrote, "They say Cleanliness is next to Godliness. Mabel. I say it's next to impossible." In another epistle, he wrote: "Our guns is pointed at some woods. We been shootin' at 'em for a week and haven't hit 'em yet. We always seem to go over 'em."[6] While the humor was mild, readers delighted in the books. Since the letters had a special appeal to soldiers and sailors, the material was reprinted in 1941 and provided chuckles to World War II servicemen and women. Streeter confined most of his writing to articles for magazines between 1921 and 1938. In 1938, *Daily Except Sunday* was the first of his books to be illustrated by Gluyas Williams, and Streeter's work began to show the mixture of urbane satire and down-to-earth mellowness that became his trademark.

Readers reveled in his description of the adventures that befall a father whose daughter is getting married in style in *Father of the Bride*. The attitudes and emotions were described in an understated manner. The book was bought by Metro-Goldwyn-Mayer and became a successful film with Spencer Tracy and Elizabeth Taylor in the leading roles. Since Streeter's two daughters had married, he undoubtedly wrote from personal experience, as he had in *Dere Mable.*

His next novel, *Mr. Hobbs' Vacation* (1954), was also made into a movie, starring James Stewart and Maureen O'Hara. Although the book and the film added to Streeter's popularity, the movie did not capture the charm of the book. *Merry Christmas, Mr. Baxter* (1956) was illustrated by Dorothea Warren Fox. The style resembled that of *Father of the Bride,* and the plot centered around the preparations and activities for the celebration of Christmas. Like most American men, Mr. Baxter wanted to reduce the fuss and expense of Christmas activities. Mrs. Baxter had an entirely different idea. The clash of ideas transformed the final celebration from a budgeted simple activity into a comic event. As critic Dan Wickender described the book, "In the hands of a satirist less benign than Edward Streeter, all this might have become a sort of horror story. As it is, by the time Christmas (as usual) is completely out of control, Mr. Baxter (as usual) himself falls prey to the spirit of the occasion. Beneath the commercialized uproar and vulgarity, the old magic still exists, and Mr. Streeter ends by expressing some simple truths that bear reiteration."[7]

With the publication of *Chairman of the Bored* in 1961, Streeter entered another phase of his career as a humorist. The first two sections of the work center on a serious study of the trauma of retirement; the last sections deal with the protagonist's inept attempts to fit into country living and his satisfying return to the city and the life that is familiar to him. While the work's style was criticized, the philosophy leaves a reader with something more than a laugh at the adventures of Graham Crombie. When Crombie got back into the business world, he asked his former secretary if she was surprised to see him back. "Not a bit," she told him. "I've lived so long with top brass that I guess I've learned to know it better than it knows itself."[8] Later she said, "If I'd said to you, 'Don't go to the country, it's not your dish. Work is your dish'—if I'd said that, you wouldn't have paid any attention to me. You had to dig it out yourself." When he asked if there shouldn't be a place when a person stops working, she said: "Your interest is business. Why should you have to take up travel or golf or rug-hooking as your life work just because you're sixty-five? Why shouldn't people go right on doing what interests them?"[9]

In the book, *Ham Martin, Class of '17,* a secretary plays a significant part once again—a reflection of Streeter's own experience in the banking world. The plot deals with a talented young man whose plans for a literary career are changed by his decision to devote himself to earning enough money for that career. When he gets into the business world, he finds himself completely involved there. His parents, wife, and children do not understand that absorption, for they still think of him as making money so he can write. They take his love of business as a selfish action, never realizing that they had wanted him to be a literary figure and that their desire had not been truly his personal wish. Once again Streeter's development of the plot brings out a serious philosophy that expresses itself through his work.

The humorist's travel literature and serious philosophical writing did not bring the acclaim that his earlier humorous works did.

Summary

The period from 1910 to 1920 has been characterized by some critics as a time during which the reading public became more sophisticated.[10] That sophistication was apparent in the humorous writing of the time. Edward Streeter was one of the writers who was able to look at himself and at his peers and chuckle over the foibles of those who prided themselves on their culture, education, and acceptance of material values. From the months of his military service up through the 1960s, he was part of the establishment, yet he could stand to the side and laugh at himself and his adventures—adventures that were also part and parcel of the life of his peers.

Notes

1. John Wakeman, ed., *World Authors, 1950-1970.* New York: H.W. Wilson, 1975, p. 1386.
2. Roy Arthur Swanson, "Edward Streeter." *Dictionary of Literary Biography,* Vol. 11, Part 2, M–Z, *American Humorists, 1800-1950,* ed. Stanley Trachtenberg (Detroit: Gale Research Co., 1982), pp. 474–475.
3. Ibid.
4. Lewis Nichols, "Edward Streeter, Humorist, Dies at 84," *New York Times,* April 2, 1976, p. 34.
5. Ibid. See also *Contemporary Authors,* Vol. II (Detroit: Gale Research Co., 1981), p. 614.
6. Ibid.
7. Dan Wickender, *Christian Science Monitor,* August 1, 1956, p. 539. Quoted in *Book Review Digest,* March 1956 to February 1957, p. 903. New York: H.W. Wilson, 1957.
8. Lewis Nichols, *New York Herald Tribune,* July 1976, p. 4.
9. Edward Streeter, *Chairman of the Bored.* New York: Harper & Brothers, 1961, pp. 272-274.
10. Norris W. Yates, *The American Humorist—Conscience of the Twentieth Century.* Ames, Iowa: Iowa State University Press, 1964, p. 140.

Selected Bibliography

Primary Sources

Dere Mable: Love Letters of a Rookie. New York: F.A. Stokes, 1918.

Same Ole Bill, Eh, Mable. New York: F.A. Stokes, 1919.

That's Me All Over, Mable. New York: F.A. Stokes, 1919.

Love Letters of Bill to Mable (contains *Dere Mable: Love Letters of a Rookie, That's Me All Over, Mable,* and *Same Old Bill, Eh, Mable*). New York: F.A. Stokes, 1919.

Daily Except Sunday. New York: Simon & Schuster, 1938.

Father of the Bride. New York: Simon & Schuster, 1949.

Skoal Scandinavia. New York: Harper, 1952.

Mr. Hobbs' Vacation. New York: Harper, 1954.

Merry Christmas, Mr. Baxter. New York: Harper & Brothers, 1956.

Mr. Robbins Rides Again. New York: Harper, 1957.

Window on America. New York: Bank of New York, 1957.

Chairman of the Bored. New York: Harper & Brothers, 1961.

Along the Ridge. New York: Harper, 1964.

Ham Martin, Class of '17. New York: Harper, 1969.

Contributed to popular magazines.

Secondary Sources

Books

"Streeter, Edward, 1891–1976." In *Contemporary Authors.* Vol. II. Detroit: Gale, 1981.

Swanson, Roy Arthur. "Edward Streeter." In *Dictionary of Literary Biography.* Vol. 11, Part 2, M–Z. *American Humorists, 1800–1950.* Ed. Stanley Trachtenberg. Detroit: Gale, 1982.

Wakeman, John, ed. *World Authors, 1950–1970.* New York: H.W. Wilson, 1975.

Yates, Norris W. *The American Humorist—Conscience of the Twentieth Century.* Ames, Iowa: Iowa State University Press, 1964.

Newspapers and Magazines

Newsweek. Obituary, April 12, 1976, p. 111.

Nichols, Lewis. "Edward Streeter, Humorist, Dies at 84," *New York Times,* April 2, 1976, p. 34.

Wickender, Dan. "*Merry Christmas, Mr. Baxter* Reviewed." *Christian Science Monitor,* August 1, 1956, p. 539. Quoted in *Book Review Digest,* March 1956 to February 1957, p. 903. New York: H.W. Wilson, 1957.

Irma R. Cruse

Sullivan, Francis John [Frank]

Born: Saratoga Springs, New York, on September 22, 1892

Education: Cornell University, B.A., 1914

Died: February 19, 1976

Biography

Francis John Sullivan, the son of Dennis and Catherine Shea Sullivan, was born in Saratoga Springs, New York, on September 22, 1892. The family home (in which Sullivan lived for all but 16 years of his life) was two blocks from the celebrated Saratoga racetrack, and it was there, among the horses and the jockeys, that Sullivan spent most of his childhood. For a boy living in pre-Depression America, the racetrack was a dream come true; at the age of ten, Frank made ten to fifteen dollars a day working at the track's betting ring.

Sullivan began his writing career as an occasional contributor to the Saratoga High School *Recorder.* While still in high school he was also hired by the city newspaper, the *Saratogian,* as a cub reporter. Sullivan left the *Saratogian* in 1910 to enter Cornell University but returned after his graduation in 1914 and continued to work there until the First World War.

In 1919, after serving two years in the U.S. Army, Sullivan moved to New York City. There he worked for the New York *Herald* before succeeding Don Marquis as a daily columnist for the *Evening Sun* in 1922. Later that same year Sullivan moved to a third newspaper, the *World,* at the invitation of editor Herbert Bayard Swope.

At the *World,* Sullivan's facility for humor (and his unfitness for factual reporting) quickly became evident. One of the young reporter's first stories, a front-page obituary for a society matron, was accurate in every respect but one: the woman had not died. This inauspicious start was followed shortly by a second blunder during Sullivan's coverage of the Democratic Convention. Finding himself short of copy on a slow news day, Sullivan filled out his column with a paragraph about one Aunt Sarah Gallup, a feisty, 104-year-old delegate who had spent her last dime traveling from Holcomb Landing in Ticonderoga, New York, to cheer for Al Smith. Competing newspapers and the Associated Press attempted to follow up on Sullivan's story, but neither the lady nor the landing existed, and the embarrassed Sullivan was forced to admit that the story was a hoax. Fortunately for Sullivan's readers, this was not the end of Aunt Sarah, who in even more exaggerated form continued to appear in Sullivan's columns and books.

When the *World's* star columnist, Franklin P. Adams, left on a two-week honeymoon in

1925, Swope's instincts told him to install the imaginative Sullivan as temporary helmsman of "The Conning Tower," a position for which the young reporter felt totally inadequate. However, due to the help of his friends (including an uncharacteristically generous Dorothy Parker, who submitted two poems with the note, "If you can't use these, given them to some poor family") and his own fast thinking, Sullivan was a hit. It was during this time that Sullivan, again finding himself short of material, impulsively fabricated the character of Martha Hepplethwaite, the eccentric secretary/Arctic explorer who, like Sarah Gallup, was to become a fixture in his future pieces.

Sullivan continued to serve as a regular replacement for Adams and also Heywood Broun until 1925, when Swope ordered him to write a thrice-weekly humor column under his own byline. This column, "Out of a Clear Sky," covered topics from politics to opera and was the source of material for Sullivan's first book, *The Life and Times of Martha Hepplethwaite* (1926). In addition to the continuing saga of Sullivan's fictitious secretary, the book featured Sullivan's first seriocomic pieces on the loneliness and frustrations of urban life, a natural topic for the homesick, unmarried Sullivan.

These themes were repeated in a second collection, *Innocent Bystanding* (1928), which also contained gentle jabs at the enterprise of writing, another recurring topic in Sullivanian humor. In the book's mock foreword, Sullivan effusively thanks everyone remotely connected with the writing, production, and editing of his opus, including:

> Sir John Weether Brakemore, professor of philatotemy and don of Ephraim College, Ufton University, England, who was kind enough to read the chapter on "Gladstone, Man or Myth?" and suggest a few changes, one of which was that the chapter be omitted.[1]

The proud author also makes special note of the book's design:

> The paper is white. The ink used is a special new color which we are tentatively calling black, until a better name can be found.[2]

Sullivan's literary success was accompanied by rapid improvement in his social life. During the 1920s, he established lasting friendships with James Thurber, Robert Benchley, Corey Ford, and many other New York-based humorists. The Beekman Place apartment that he shared with Ford served as a haven for struggling writers (William Faulkner was one temporary lodger) and became a frequent meeting place for members of the Algonquin Round Table, which by this time had accepted Sullivan as a full-fledged if somewhat timid member.

It is to Sullivan's credit that he was so readily accepted and admired by the so-called "Vicious Circle," a group not particularly known for its benevolence, modesty,or psychological adjustment. Unlike many of the people he knew, the chubby, cherubic Sullivan (known variously as "Sully," "The Sage of Saratoga," "Ford's Ugly Roomer," and, to Alexander Woollcott, "that timorous little omadhaun") was fiercely loyal to his friends and unstinting in his praise for fellow humorists. Marc Connelly called Sullivan "a generous personality, the least bitter man I ever knew."[3]

Sullivan was not, however, without his own personal quirks, chief among them this profound and ineradicable fear of traveling. Apart from his occasional "oscillation," as he put it, between Saratoga Springs and New York City, Sullivan rarely went anywhere. On the advice of a physician, he once attempted a train journey to St. Louis, Missouri, but even with a nurse in attendance he found the experience too terrifying to repeat. This reluctance to travel had at least one good consequence; it was probably responsible for Sullivan's heavy reliance on letter-writing as a means of keeping in touch with his far-flung friends.

Sullivan worked for the *World* for over eight years, until the paper's demise in 1931. He then joined the staff of *The New Yorker* and in 1932 wrote the first of his forty-two annual Christmas poems for the magazine. These poems, adapted from a shorter version that Sullivan had composed for the *World*, consisted of holiday greetings to as many of the year's newsmakers as Sullivan could fit comfortably into his rhyme scheme. Since Sullivan's friends frequently lobbied for inclusion in the poem and publicly harassed him if they were omitted, the number of personalities Sullivan was expected to include often became overwhelming, as he hinted in his 1932 effort:

> *I greet you all, mes petits choux,*
> *I greet the whole goddam Who's Who.*[4]

It was in 1932, too, that Sullivan's third collection of pieces, *Broccoli and Old Lace*, was published. While some reviewers considered many of the pieces overworked and repetitive, the book was immensely popular with the public. In one sense, the book even made it to Broadway; producers Lindsay and Crouse reworked the title to fit the hit play, *Arsenic and Old Lace*.

In One Ear, which appeared the following year, introduced a new character to the Sullivan menagerie, a stay-at-home traveler whose bizarre accounts of exotic locales were completely uncontaminated by factual material. *In One Ear* also contained more of Sullivan's characteristic essays on the irritations of life in the big city. Typical of these pieces is "Yvonne," in which Sullivan, the urban victim, is driven to distraction by a young girl who stands on a street corner near his apartment building and screams "Yvonne!" every afternoon precisely at three o'clock.

Although his early books were both popular and critically well received, it was not until 1934 that Sullivan made his most lasting contribution to American humor. In September of that year he created the unforgettable Mr. Arbuthnot, better known to *The New Yorker* readers as The Cliché Expert. This individual, whose self-assured testimony on an astounding array of topics consisted entirely of platitudes and banalities, was an instant sensation. Particularly appealing was the character's utter calm and unflappability. Only occasionally did Mr. Arbuthnot's robot-like recitation give way to honest emotion, as it did when he was asked to explain a newly acquired black eye: "A silvery birch whose image was mirrored in the cool green depths below sprang back and damn near knocked my eye out."[5] Among the subjects tackled by the Cliché Expert over the years were vacations, Franklin Delano Roosevelt, love, cooking, drinking, the atom, politics, Christmas, health, radio, literary criticism, and politics.

Despite his growing personal and professional popularity, Sullivan, never comfortable with urban life, returned to Saratoga Springs in 1935 and thereafter limited his contact with New York City to infrequent visits. He continued to write, however, contributing articles to *The New Yorker, Town and Country, PM, Good Housekeeping*, and the *Saturday Evening Post*. Two more collections of his pieces were published in the late 1930s—*A Pearl in Every Oyster* (1938) and *Sullivan at Bay* (1939), a collection tailored for British readers. These volumes, featuring slapstick pieces on subjects ranging from race horses to Joan Blondell's face, successfully repeated many of the themes in Sullivan's earlier books. Mr. Arbuthnot, however, was undoubtedly the star attraction and remained so for the rest of Sullivan's career. In the 1940s Sullivan even portrayed the Cliché Expert on the radio.

The Cliché Expert's short foray into radio was Sullivan's only involvement with show business. Unlike many of his colleagues, Sullivan steadfastly resisted the urge to "sell out" and become a Hollywood scriptwriter. He answered one obsequious job offer, a 500-word telegram from an over-eager producer, with a three-word cable of his own: "DON'T BE SILLY." Part of Sullivan's reluctance to move to California may

be attributable to his fear of traveling, but more likely it reflected a genuine hostility toward Hollywood. In the 1940s Sullivan had seen Samuel Goldwyn transform Thurber's "The Secret Life of Walter Mitty" into a muddled, thoroughly un-Thurberish screenplay. Although Sullivan angrily formed a Walter Mitty Association in protest and wrote menacing letters to Goldwyn, he was unable to prevent the film's production and eventual release. (Years later, Thurber dedicated *The Years with Ross* to Sullivan, writing, "To Frank Sullivan, master of humor, newspaperman, good companion, friend to Ross, this book is dedicated with the love and admiration I share with everybody who knows him."[6])

Sullivan followed *A Pearl in Every Oyster* with the more ominously titled *A Rock in Every Snowball* in 1946. While this volume continued Sullivan's tradition of exaggerated nonsense (it contains Sullivan's justifiably famous parody of excessive footnoting and the Cliché Expert on radio, health, the atom, football, Christmas, and politics), it also featured unabashedly sentimental and nostalgic essays, the first pieces to present the author's genuine fears and regrets in an undisguised format. Sullivan's tendency to replace slapstick and wordplay with emotional reminiscences continued in 1953's *The Night the Old Nostalgia Burned Down*, but the volume also contained large enough doses of Aunt Sarah Gallup and Mr. Arbuthnot to win over the critics.

Sullivan's literary output decreased dramatically after 1953. His last two books were slim volumes featuring none of the familiar Sullivan characters: *Sullivan Bites News* (1954), a collection of off-beat news stories, and *A Moose in the Hoose* (1959), a critically acclaimed but commercially unsuccessful children's book. In the 1960s Sullivan retired permanently, refusing to leave Saratoga Springs for any reason and devoting his life to his garden, the Saratoga racetrack, and his unending correspondence with friends. He steadfastly resisted his colleagues' entreaties to produce more pieces, insisting that, apart from his annual *New Yorker* Christmas poem, he had nothing more to offer the public. George Oppenheimer collected many of Sullivan's personal letters and classic pieces into a final Sullivan volume, *Frank Sullivan Through the Looking Glass* (1970), but this book was also a commercial failure.

After several years of declining health, Sullivan died on February 19, 1976, in Saratoga Springs.

Literary Analysis

Although Sullivan often feigned indifference or even hostility toward his profession, his love for writing is obvious in both his humorous pieces and his copious correspondence. At their best, Sullivan's pieces are understated, relaxed, and impish. Unlike humorists who are compelled to belabor their pieces with gag after gag, or those who telegraph each punchline to ensure that their readers won't miss a joke, Sullivan wrote with confidence in and respect for his readers—a luxury that he could afford, perhaps, because of his association with *The New Yorker.* Indeed, some of his gems (e.g., "Crazy or not—I like quilts") are so casually dropped into his pieces that the inattentive reader can easily miss them on first reading. It is not surprising that Sullivan was fond of British humor, of which he said, "[It is] all very quiet and understated. The English do that much better than we; we have to throw custard pies to make our point."[7]

While puns do not make up a substantial part of Sullivan's humor, his appreciation of clever wordplay and his fascination with unusual names (Hepplethwaite, Arbuthnot, and so forth) are clearly evident in his writings. Some critics have been tempted to read significance into Sullivan's use of particular names, but such speculations ignore Sullivan's fundamental playfulness and are probably far off the mark. Betsy Erkkila has suggested that the Cliché Expert's name "probably represents a nod in the direction of eighteenth-century physician wit Dr. Arbuthnot,"[8] but it was more likely plucked randomly from the large and prized collection of odd names that Sullivan, Stanley Walker, and Nunnally Johnson compiled as members of Sullivan's informal "Nomenclature Club." Sullivan customarily signed his own correspondence with such specimens from the collection as "Havelock Frothingham" or "Augustine Whitpenny."

Sullivan's humor, while playful, is also unquestionably pointed. As satire, Sullivan's prose is effective precisely because of its indirect approach. As critic Richard Maney put it in his review of *A Rock in Every Snowball,* Sullivan attacks his targets "gently when a more headlong if not more malicious sufferer would have at them with daggers, puns, and mixed metaphors. His is the delayed rather than the surface malice."[9]

One of Sullivan's most effective devices is to filter his words through the mouths of other characters, most of whom are exaggerations of commonly encountered personality types. They include Mr. Arbuthnot, the fussy expert whose "knowledge" is reducible to vapid aphorisms; Miss Hepplethwaite, Sullivan's exasperating, volatile secretary; Aunt Sarah Gallup, the blustery old gal from the Adirondacks; and the unnamed homebody whose total lack of traveling experience does not deter him from writing highly detailed tourist guides of foreign lands. All have highly recognizable flaws, all believe

that they have their lives under control, and all are fundamentally likable.

This likability is absolutely crucial to Sullivan's style of kindly exaggeration. The Cliché Expert is funny not because he provokes genuine loathing for himself or the institutions he describes but because he spews out the same banal overgeneralizations that we all use when original thought escapes us. In "The Cliché Expert Testifies on Love," Mr. Arbuthnot rattles off his description of the ideal woman as mechanically as an accountant tabulating profits and losses:

> Q: Describe the Only Girl in the World.
> A: Her eyes are like stars. Her teeth are like pearls. Her lips are ruby. Her cheek is damask, and her form divine.
> Q: Haven't you forgotten something?
> A: Eyes, teeth, lips, cheek, form—no, sir, I don't think so.
> Q: Her hair?
> A: Oh, certainly. How stupid of me. She has hair like spun gold.[10]

Of course, not all of Sullivan's alter egos are as grossly exaggerated as Mr. Arbuthnot. The *persona* of Sullivan's more sober pieces is the anonymous city dweller who, like Sullivan, is continuously besieged by the major and minor irritations of modern urban life. This character, intimidated by the forces of nature as well as the technology of man, has been described by critics as Sullivan's "Little Man" or "Everyman," and comes perhaps the closest to Sullivan's own view of himself and of contemporary man in general. (Similar characterizations of the beleaguered urban male also appear in the works of Sullivan's contemporaries, James Thurber and Robert Benchley.) The "Little Man" was overshadowed by Sullivan's more comic characters in the 1920s and 1930s, but he became the dominant personality in Sullivan's later works.

Like other humorists of his generation (most notably, James Thurber), Sullivan grew more pessimistic and cynical with middle age. His prose became sentimental, at times almost mawkish, and he frequently pondered the value and relevance of humor to modern society. While Sullivan generally applauded humor as worthwhile on its own merits (one of his most famous serious essays is entitled, "Well, There's No Harm in Laughing"), he increasingly felt that humorists had a social responsibility to "tell the truth, which, though it shall make you free, may also make you uneasy."[11] A good part of Sullivan's brooding was undoubtedly provoked by the events of the day—anti-Communist hysteria, nuclear proliferation, the Cold War—but another factor may have been the commonly felt need of aging humorists to make a "serious" contribution to society during their lifetimes. Not surprisingly, it occurred to Sullivan during the 1950s to turn Mr. Arbuthnot loose on McCarthyism—an idea that Harold Ross discouraged, probably wisely. "I don't think so," Ross wrote Sullivan. "I can't see it myself, and if I can't see a thing, I'm usually right."[12]

Sullivan also became increasingly concerned with the declining number of American humorists and blamed this development on his old nemesis, Hollywood. In "Well, There's No Harm in Laughing," he wrote:

> Could it be what we may call the Moola factor, by which promising young humorists . . . are lured into writing for radio, television or Hollywood by the promise of vast sums of moola, bigger messes of pottage, more imposing gastric ulcers and anxiety neuroses designed to astound psychoanalysts at a distance of thirty couches?[13]

It is ironic that Sullivan should lament the paucity of American humor at the very time that his friends were begging him to continue writing. However, convinced that his whimsical, benign satire was no longer in vogue, Sullivan withdrew from public life in the 1960s, long before his considerable talents had diminished. In the opinion of his many fans, it was a premature retirement.

Summary

Frank Sullivan's impact upon American humor was remarkable, particularly considering the relative shortness of his career; almost all of his best writing was done in the sixteen short years he lived in New York City. His facility for creating bizarre but lovable characters was unmatched, and the benevolence apparent in even his most pointed essays was a refreshing change from the overt misogyny, misanthropy, and cynicism common among his Algonquin compatriots. Many of Sullivan's pieces are timelessly funny, and his most beloved creation, Mr. Arbuthnot, is unquestionably one of the most imitated characters in contemporary humor.

Notes

1. Frank Sullivan, "Foreword," in *Innocent Bystanding* (New York: H. Liveright, 1928), p. xi.
2. Ibid., p. x.
3. "Frank Sullivan," *Contemporary Authors: A Bio-Bibliographical Guide to Current Authors and Their Works* (Detroit: Gale Research, 1967), Permanent Series, Vol. 2, p. 502.
4. Sullivan, "Greetings, Friends!" *The New Yorker*, December 24, 1932, p. 16.
5. Sullivan, "The Cliche Expert Testifies on Vacations," *A Pearl in Every Oyster* (Boston: Little, Brown, 1938), p. 232.
6. James Thurber, *The Years with Ross* (Boston: Little, Brown, 1959), dedication.
7. Sullivan, *Frank Sullivan Through the Looking Glass* (New York: Doubleday, 1972), p. 127.
8. Betsy Erkkila, "Frank Sullivan," *Dictionary of Literary Biography*, Vol. 11, *American Humorists, 1800-1950*, ed. Stanley Trachtenberg (Detroit: Gale Research), pp. 481-482.
9. Richard Maney, "Gay, Urbane, Flecked with Irony," *New York Times Book Review*, August 8, 1946, p. 4.
10. Sullivan, "The Cliche Expert Testifies on Love," *A Pearl in Every Oyster*, p. 16.
11. Sullivan, "Well, There's No Harm in Laughing," *Frank Sullivan Through the Looking Glass* (New York: Doubleday, 1972), p. 4.
12. Thurber, *The Years with Ross*, p. 172.
13. Sullivan, "Well, There's No Harm in Laughing," *Frank Sullivan Through the Looking Glass*, p. 6.

Selected Bibliography

Primary Sources

The Life and Times of Martha Hepplethwaite. New York: Boni & Liveright, 1926.

Innocent Bystanding. New York: H. Liveright, 1928.

Broccoli and Old Lace. New York: H. Liveright, 1931.

In One Ear. New York: Viking Press, 1933.

A Pearl in Every Oyster. Boston: Little, Brown, 1938.

Sullivan at Bay. London: J.M. Dent & Sons, 1939.

A Rock in Every Snowball. Boston: Little, Brown, 1946.

The Night the Old Nostalgia Burned Down. Boston: Little, Brown, 1953.

Sullivan Bites News: Perverse News Items. Boston: Little, Brown, 1954.

A Moose in the Hoose. New York: Random House, 1959.

Frank Sullivan Through the Looking Glass. Ed. and Afterword by George Oppenheimer. Introd. by Marc Connelly. New York: Doubleday, 1972.

Well, There's No Harm in Laughing. Ed. and Afterword by George Oppenheimer. Introd. by Marc Connelly. New York: Doubleday, 1972. [First published in 1970 under the title *Frank Sullivan Through the Looking Glass*.]

Edited by Frank Sullivan

Cannon, James J. *The Sergeant Says*. New York: A.A. Knopf, 1943.

Introduction by Frank Sullivan

Benchley, Robert. *Chips Off the Old Benchley*. New York: Harper, 1949.

Secondary Sources

Bernstein, Burton. *Thurber*. New York: Arbor House, 1975.

Bryan, J., III. "Well, There's No Harm in Laughing." *New York Times Book Review*, October 22, 1972, p. 31.

Clark, Edwin. "Madcaps and Moralists, Too." *New York Times Book Review*, December 12, 1926, pp. 2, 18.

Contemporary Authors. Permanent ser. Vol. 2. Detroit: Gale Research, 1965, pp. 501-502.

Ford, Corey. *The Time of Laughter*. Boston: Little, Brown, 1967.

Harriman, M.C. *The Vicious Circle*. New York: Rinehart, 1951.

Hutchens, John K. "The Happy Essence of Frank Sullivan." *Saturday Review*, 53 (September 12, 1970): 88–89.

Keats, John. *You Might As Well Live: The Life and Times of Dorothy Parker*. New York: Simon & Schuster, 1970.

Kunitz, Stanley, ed. *Authors Today and Yesterday*. New York: H.W. Wilson, 1933.

Kunitz, Stanley J., and Haycraft Howards, eds. *Twentieth Century Authors*. New York: H.W. Wilson, 1942.

Kunitz, Stanley J., ed. *Twentieth Century Authors, First Supplement*. New York: H.W. Wilson, 1955.

Maney, Richard. "Gay, Urbane, Flecked with Irony." *New York Times Book Review*, August 8, 1946, p. 4.

Sherman, Beatrice. "Bravo Once More, Frank Sullivan!" *New York Times Book Review*, November 27, 1938, p. 5.

Thurber, James. *The Years with Ross*. Boston: Little, Brown, 1959.

Trachtenberg, Stanley, ed. *Dictionary of Literary Biography*. Vol. 11, Part 2. *American Humorists, 1800-1950*. Detroit: Gale Research, 1982, pp. 478–485.

Yates, Norris. W. *The American Humorist; Conscience of the Twentieth Century*. Ames: Iowa State University Press, 1964.

Who's Who in America, 1976-1977. 39th ed. Vol. 2, p. 3060.

Obituaries
The New Yorker, March 8, 1976.
Newsweek, March 1, 1976.
Time, March 5, 1976.
Variety, February 25, 1976.

C.J. Bartelt

Taliaferro, H[ardin] E[dwards]

Born: Surry County, North Carolina, in 1811

Education: Early schooling unknown; one year (1833) at Madisonville Academy in Tennessee

Marriage: Elizabeth Henderson, 1834, three children

Died: November 2, 1875

Biography

H.E. Taliaferro, as he was to be known throughout his life, was born in Surry County, North Carolina, in 1811, the eighth child and sixth son of Charles Taliaferro and Sallie Burroughs. Charles Taliaferro (pronounced Toliver) was a prominent landowner and public figure who had represented the county in the state legislature for three terms. The family was of Virginia origins; Charles's father, a Revolutionary War surgeon, had moved from Pittsylvania County, Virginia, into North Carolina in 1779.

Surry County is located in the northwestern corner of the state, bordering the Blue Ridge mountains, and in 1811 it was sparsely populated by small, yeoman farmers and a few "gentry" such as the Taliaferros. It was an isolated area and life was slow-paced there, the families closely knit through intermarriage. Surry County became the source for many of the tales and sketches later recorded by Taliaferro in his *Fisher's River* collection.

In 1829, at the age of eighteen, Taliaferro travelled to Roane County, Tennessee, a few miles below Knoxville, to join three of his brothers who had settled there, farming and operating a tanyard. His oldest brother, Charles, was also pastor of the local Baptist church, and Taliaferro was soon baptized there and shortly afterward licensed to preach. After serving in small pulpits in the area for about a year, he moved to Madisonville, Tennessee, to attend the Academy. In Madisonville he met and married Elizabeth Henderson, the daughter of a local printer.

In the fall of 1835 Taliaferro and Elizabeth moved 250 miles further south, to a small claim in Alabama on the outskirts of Talladega, then little more than a settler's house chosen for court meetings because it had a good spring for watering the horses. In addition to farming, he became pastor for several small Baptist churches which he served in rotation, a pattern of weekend preaching that he continued for the rest of his life.

Over the next few years Taliaferro rose to some prominence in the Baptist church of Alabama, doing important work in the state association and corresponding with Baptist newspapers in adjoining states. In 1855 he moved to Tuskegee to join his brother-in-law, Sam Henderson, as co-publisher of the *South Western Baptist*, an influential weekly paper published there. For the most of the next twenty years Taliaferro was editor of this paper during the week and pastor to local rural churches on weekends.

As a prominent Alabama Baptist, Taliaferro played a part in the affairs that led to the split of the Baptist church into northern and southern conventions in 1845. He was a stout defender of the South and of slavery, and his newspaper condemned the North before and during the War. But, Taliaferro was also an independent man, living by his own conscience and principles. When, shortly after the War, the northern church undertook to help the newly freed blacks in the South in training black ministers, Taliaferro was one of only three Baptist ministers in

Alabama who offered to help. He was hired in 1869 by the Northern Mission Society to help train black ministers in the vicinity of Tuskegee and to help them establish their state organization. At one time he had thirty young blacks in training for the pulpit. Taliaferro's stand was not popular among his peers; in his obituaries by brother ministers and in the histories of the Baptist church of the period, no notice is taken of this work.

The *South Western Baptist* was banned by the Union Army after the war, but Taliaferro and his brother-in-law used the same presses to publish *The Tuskegee News* for several years, a look-alike to their religious paper. Taliaferro continued to serve his rural churches, too, but his prominence in state Baptist affairs declined and in 1873 he moved with his wife and one widowed daughter back to Loudon, Tennessee, to be among his many relatives there. He opened a general store, continued preaching, and lived quietly. He died there on November 2, 1875, at the age of sixty-four. He is buried in the small cemetery beside the Good Hope Baptist Church, where he had first declared his faith as a boy more than forty years earlier.

Literary Analysis

Taliaferro is an important member of the Old Southwest humor school of writers which flourished on the frontier from about 1830 to 1870. Taliaferro often livened the pages of his newspaper with short humorous pieces, anecdotes about the comical, rustic frontier people he met in his travels as editor and church leader. Such stories were widely circulated in the frontier press, often submitted anonymously by professional men living on the frontier. Following a visit to Surry County in 1857, Taliaferro began a serious effort to record the humorous stories from that region, and in 1858 he published a collection of short pieces with Harper and Brothers, using the pen name "Skitt" to protect his dignity as a Baptist leader in Alabama. During the next four years, he published more "Skitt" sketches in *The Southern Literary Review*, but by then the ordeal of the Civil War in Alabama had overwhelmed him, and Taliaferro did not return to humor writing after the war. The frontier had moved further west by then, and the Old South was preoccupied with other affairs.

Taliaferro's body of work consists of one small volume of humorous pieces, *Fisher's River (North Carolina) Scenes and Sketches, By "Skitt" Who Was Raised Thar*, published in 1859, nine sketches published in *The Southern Literary Review* from 1860 to 1863, and scattered anonymous humorous pieces in the pages of the *South Western Baptist*. Some of the Fisher's River sketches appeared in altered form in the *South Western Baptist* during the 1850s. No manuscripts or papers have survived, so the authority for texts rests on the earliest published versions of his writings. In all there are about fifty separate sketches or stories.

Fisher's River is in Surry County, North Carolina, near where Taliaferro grew up, and many of the stories and characters that he records are from that area. Storytelling was a principal form of recreation among the mostly illiterate neighbors, and the community boasted a number of expert narrators, each a "character" in his own right, with his own style of storytelling. What sets Taliaferro's treatment of the humor of these storytellers apart is that he identifies them by name—they are real people identifiable in census and courthouse records of the period—and tries to capture their storytelling styles as well as their best tales.

The degree of realism is almost literal, as Taliaferro blends the people, the customs, and the oral literature into a picture of the whole backwoods community in which these stories are told. Eighty-six persons from the county are named in *Fisher's River*, and thirty-three places named, including most of the nearby mountains and passes, river forks, creeks, and camping locations. Even the names of favorite horses, guns, dogs, and pocket knives are included.

The storytellers themselves are the stars of the community, and there were many of them, odd and colorful characters, each with his proprietary repertoire of stories—Uncle Davy Lane, the local gunsmith, lazy, garrulous, rarely separated from his hunting rifle; Old Bucksmasher; poor gullible Uncle Billy Lewis, who got into trouble for shooting horses instead of deer on a night hunt and who was duped into preaching a wild sermon at the Baptist church about a flying snake on Bald Rock; Oliver Stanley, who had been to sea and told tall tales and lies without a blink; and Bob Snipes, Josh Hash Head Jones, and a whole string of Snows—Larkin, Dick, Johnson, Frost, John—each good for a story.

Among the stories they told or were featured in were "Famus or No Famus," concerning a nearly disastrous military muster at which the only "knock-'em-stiff" available had been contaminated with the corpse of a local dog, Famus; "The Chase," in which Davy Lane, being chased by a rolling hoop snake, runs so fast that his skin starts to shed; "The Escape from the Whale," in which Oliver Stanley coolly retells the Jonah story as a personal experience; and "Dick Snow's Courtship," in which Dick becomes so flustered while closing a rail fence that he puts the fence back with his own horse on the wrong side, leaving his rival to ride away with his Sally.

As a Baptist preacher himself, Taliaferro

loved anecdotes about preachers and camp meetings and recorded more of them than any other frontier humorist. His favorite target is Parson Bellows, the local "Mathodiss" preacher, but Taliaferro's laughter is much gentler and more indulgent than that of most of the frontier humorists of this period. His stories treat women, blacks, cripples, and other popular targets of frontier humor with kindness, and he is a unique source of the earnest but comic sermons of the illiterate black preachers he encountered.

The oral literature collected by Taliaferro often contained elements of traditional folklore which have since been catalogued. The storytellers would add these motifs to their stories, telling them in the first person, of course, without hesitation, as something they had "hearn." Their favorite stories concerned hunting, courtships, religions, fights, quiltings, weddings, and their own embarrassing encounters with the manners of "quality" folks. Animals sometimes were personified and made to speak, but part of the fun in those stories was the patent lying of the narrator in a community of strong moral ethic.

Storytelling was deadpan and deliberate, and audience response and occasional interference was part of the art. Taliaferro describes the attitude of Uncle Davy Lane, the most competitive of the Surry County storytellers, thusly: "After a lazy laugh, in which he cared not whether you engaged or not—at least his looks would so indicate—Uncle Davy would straighten himself, fetch a long breath, charge his mouth with a fresh chew of tobacco, and would proceed." Such storytellers could go one for a whole day, and their storytelling called forth their most colorful language, strongly metaphorical, full of local sayings and dialect. Indeed, their language became part of their character. "I'll be smashed inter piecrust—yes, inter a million giblets, afore I'll be as ignunt as some jewkers!" declares Johnson Snow, who offers to fight a whole congregation in church and who loves hogs gullicks (throats) and the local "knock-'em-stiff." Oliver Stanley, who has a taste for elegant words of his own, begins one story, "On the shank ov one monstracious nice evenin'," and regularly offers words such as "qualmy" (uneasy) and "tetotatiously." Their stories frequently end with a peculiar indifference and pointlessness that adds immensely to the fun for a seasoned audience who already knows the stories by heart.

Summary

Hardin E. Taliaferro is a unique contributor to the school of Old Southwest humor, with his transcriptions of actual storytellers' tales, his anecdotes about frontier religion, and his sympathetic portrayal of frontier social life. He is among America's early realists in his faithful use of settings, characters, and language from the lower social classes, and one of the most credible sources of folklore about those classes. As a devout Baptist preacher in Alabama and a prominent Baptist publisher, he preferred to keep his identity as a humorist concealed, but he is increasingly recognized as one of the most important of those writers who recorded the oral literature and folkways of the frontier between 1820 and 1855. His humor is gentle and low-key, the writings of an indulgent preacher chuckling over the quaint language and eccentric characters of his frontier contemporaries.

Selected Bibliography

Primary Sources

Fisher's River (North Carolina) Scenes and Characters. By "Skitt," "Who Was Raised Thar." New York: Harper & Brothers, 1859.

Carolina Humor: Sketches by Harden [sic] *E. Taliaferro.* Ed. David K. Jackson. Richmond: The Dietz Press, 1938.

The Grace of God Magnified: An Experimental Tract. Charleston: The Southern Baptist Publication Society, 1857.

Secondary Sources

Dissertations

Bettich, Heinrich R. "Hardin Edwards Taliaferro: Life, Literature, and Folklore." Dissertation, University of North Carolina, 1983. Thorough treatment of folklore aspects of *Fisher's River.*

Craig, Raymond C. "An Edition of the Major Writings of H.E. Taliaferro." Dissertation, University of Illinois, 1983. Biographical sketch and facsimile copy of all known writings with commentary.

Articles

Boggs, Ralph Steele. "North Carolina Folktales Current in the 1820's." *Journal of American Folklore*, 47 (1934): 269–288. Calls attention to folklore types and motifs contained in *Fisher's River.* Article became the source for several entries in Ernest Baughman's landmark *Type and Motif Index* published in 1966.

Coffin, Tristan P. "Harden E. Taliaferro and Use of Folklore by American Literary Figures." *South Atlantic Quarterly*, 64 (1965): 241–246. Argues that Taliaferro is more folklorist than humorist.

Walser, Richard. "Biblio-biography of Skitt Taliaferro." *The North Carolina Historical Review*, 15 (1978): 375–392. Gathers all that was known to that date of life of Taliaferro.

Raymond C. Craig

Taylor, Bayard

Born: Chester County, Pennsylvania, on
January 11, 1825
Education: Bolmar's Academy, West Chester, Pennsylvania
Marriages: Mary Agnew, October 24, 1850,
died, December 21, 1850; Marie Hansen,
October 1857, one child
Died: December 19, 1878

Biography

Bayard Taylor was born in the village of Kennett Square, Chester County, Pennsylvania, in 1825, the fourth child of Joseph and Rebecca Taylor, of Quaker stock. At 17, financially unable to enter college, he was apprenticed to a printer of West Chester and by 1844 had written and published (privately) his first book of poems, *Ximena*. An adventurous youth, Bayard, at 19 and with little money, began a two-year trip to Europe that took him through England, Ireland, Scotland, Belgium, Germany, Austria, Switzerland, Italy, and France, largely on foot. Returning home in 1846, he published the first of his many travel books, *Views A-Foot*, which became a best-seller. In 1848, he joined Horace Greeley's *New York Tribune* and was sent to California in 1849 to report on the gold rush. His letters to the newspaper became *Eldorado, or Adventures in the Path of Empire* (1850), one of his best travel books.

Taylor married Mary Agnew on October 24, 1850; she died of tuberculosis just two months later, on December 21. His second marriage, to Marie Hansen of Germany in October 1857, produced one child, a daughter, Lillian, born the following year.

Although he enjoyed great success as a journalist and travel writer, in his own eyes Taylor remained primarily a poet, publishing *Rhymes of Travel, Ballads and Poems* in 1849, *Poems of the Orient* in 1854, and many later volumes. Popular and critically well received in their own time, today Taylor's poems seem the least interesting of his writings, belonging so completely to the genteel tradition of the middle and later 19th century in America. The only exceptions to this are the poetic parodies he composed for the *Atlantic Monthly* in 1872. In any case, Taylor relied on his travel writings and the popular lectures that he gave in connection with them as the chief sources of his income. His most ambitious trip was to Africa, the Near East, and finally to India and Japan, out of which he wrote *A Journey to Central Africa* (1854), *The Lands of the Saracen* (1854), and *A Visit to India, China, and Japan* (1855). The African book, written in response to the intense interest in that region at the time, is perhaps the best of all his travel writings. In later years Taylor visited

Europe again, the Scandinavian countries, Russia, Greece, Egypt, Iceland, and the American West (this last is recorded in *Colorado: A Summer Trip*, 1867). *At Home and Abroad* (two volumes, 1859 and 1862) combines accounts of his European and American travels.

In the 1860s Taylor wrote his four novels: *Hannah Thurston* (1863), *John Godfrey's Fortunes* (1864), *The Story of Kennett* (1866), *Joseph and His Friend* (1870), and most of the stories collected as *Beauty and the Beast* (1872). His marriage to his second wife in 1857 and a general fascination with things German led to Taylor's translation of Goethe's *Faust* (1871), the labor of many years and still considered a creditable version of the original. In his later years Taylor lectured widely on German literature in general and became the foremost interpreter of German culture for Americans. His *Studies in German Literature* (1879), lucid and wide-ranging, was published posthumously. Taylor was appointed minister to Germany in May 1878, and died in Berlin on December 19, 1878. His body was returned to Kennett Square, Pennsylvania, where it lies not far from Taylor's beloved mansion, Cedarcroft, completed in 1860 with the income from his travel writing and popular lectures.

Literary Analysis

Bayard Taylor was a good-humored, vastly energetic man, and humor in its literary sense plays a significant part in his written work. It is, however, almost entirely absent from his poetry, where the high-mindedness, the quasi-religious view of nature, and the idealized conception of women characteristic of the genteel tradition leave little room for a humorous treatment of any subject. Even when writing of California, Taylor's poetic eye is drawn to scenes of love or honor among the Mexican inhabitants rather than to the humors of the mining camp that absorbed Mark Twain.

The prose of the travel books is another matter. Taylor writes with an appealing mixture of down-to-earth factuality and realism (telling exactly how he got from here to there, and often the precise cost), poetic appreciation of landscape and place, and humorous anecdotes, although the latter are not frequent. He never adopts the purely comic mode of Twain's *Innocents Abroad* or *Roughing It*. His humorous passages are good-natured and mild, never wild or extravagant, and often at his own expense. On the road toward Calcutta, for example, in 1853 (*India, China, and Japan*, 1855), Taylor is overtaken and passed by two unlikely racers:

> During the forenoon I was overtaken by
> a green garree, in which sat two ladies.

> As it approached, I heard a shrill voice urging on the driver, who lashed his horse into a gallop, and as the vehicle passed, the elder lady thrust her head out of the window, and nodded to me with an air of insolent triumph. She had a decidedly red face, diversified with freckles, keen gray eyes, a nose with a palpable snub, and a profusion of coarse hair, of a color, which I will charitably term auburn. It was rather humiliating to be passed in the race by a female of that style of beauty, but I did not dispute her triumph.

The humor here is delicate but distinct, arising largely from the poet's adroit choice of individual words, and certainly at Taylor's own expense—the gentleman in defeat but restraining his wrath. The passage is characteristic of the humor in the travel books.

Taylor turned to prose fiction in the 1860s largely because his income from giving lectures was drastically curtailed with the outbreak of the Civil War. His first novel, *Hannah Thurston* (1863), is a humorous account of the movement for women's rights somewhat resembling Alfred Lord Tennyson's poetic *The Princess* (1847). The heroine, Hannah, is well drawn and sympathetic, but her involvement in the movement is pictured as the error of an otherwise appealing woman, an error that she corrects at last by marrying her conventional suitor and taking her proper place in the home. Thus, Taylor's view of women's rights is retrogressive, but his main character is strong and attractive (till the end, at least), and the narrative lively. The novel incidentally satirizes other reform movements of the time: spiritualism, temperance, and even abolitionism. The satiric impulse continues in *John Godfrey's Fortunes* (1864), which is loosely autobiographical and charmingly humorous, but chiefly notable for its disillusioned and often quite funny picture of the New York City literary scene. Parts of the main plot are weak (the story of Godfrey's fall into poverty, and his eventual recovery), but Taylor's acid portraits of the self-proclaimed lady poet gushing about Inspiration, the Whitman-like bard of the people, and the buying and selling of good reviews are cutting and amusing even today, and the early chapters on Godfrey's youth are mild and literate humor in the manner of William Makepeace Thackeray. Taylor's other novels, *The Story of Kennett* (a rural idyl of life in the nineteenth century) and *Joseph and His Friend* (a deeply flawed but interesting celebration of male friendship as opposed to romantic love), do not have significant humorous elements.

Among the short stories of *Beauty and the Beast* (1872), "Experiences of the A.C." (Arcadian Club) delightfully tells of the organization and early collapse of a utopian community committed to "the natural life," vegetarian food, and total candor. The characters soon betray all of these ideals and return to normal life. "Mrs. Strongitharm's Report" concerns the women's movement of the 1860s but is more ambivalent than *Hannah Thurston*; there is satire in it (as when the ardent feminist is offered marriage by the governor of the state, accepts at once, and leaves the movement), but Taylor seems to take the whole idea more seriously than he had in the novel.

In the same year that Taylor published *Beauty and the Beast*, he also wrote the series of poetic parodies by which his name is chiefly remembered today (these appear in Dwight Macdonald's anthology of *Parodies*). Taylor first printed the parodies in the *Atlantic Monthly* in 1872, then collected them in a volume, *The Echo Club and Other Literary Diversions* (1876). The format is a series of nightly meetings in a beer cellar during which four literary men choose names from a hat, make up parodies on the spot, and offer critical comment on their contemporaries (although John Keats is sneaked in too, in "Ode on a Jar of Pickles" with its "Odors unsmelled are keen, but those I smell/ Are keener"). Several of the targets are forgotten figures, but Edgar Allan Poe, Robert Browning, Ralph Waldo Emerson, John Greenleaf Whittier, William Cullen Bryant, Henry Wadsworth Longfellow, Tennyson and Walt Whitman are parodied, as is Taylor himself. Emerson takes a hit in "All or Nothing": "Whoso answers my questions/ Knoweth more than me;/ Hunger is but knowledge/ In a less degree." The best parodies are of poets Taylor did not know personally and could thus risk offending. He parodies Whitman in "Camerados":

> Everywhere, everywhere, following me;
> Taking me by the buttonhole, pulling off my boots, hustling me with the elbows;
> Sitting down with me to clams and the chowder-kettle;
> Plunging naked at my side into the sleek, irascible surges;
> Soothing me with the strain that I neither permit nor prohibit . . .
> Everywhere listening to my yawp and glad whenever they hear it
> Everywhere saying, say it, Walt, we believe it.

Summary

Bayard Taylor's claim to a significant place in American literary history is supported not by his serious poetry (as he himself desired) but by his prose works, his translation of *Faust*, and his parodies. His reputation as a humorist is also secure, resting firmly on his two satirical novels, *Hannah Thurston* and *John Godfrey's Fortunes*, some of his short fiction, his skillful poetic parodies, and, to a lesser extent, on the humorous passages in his many travel books.

Selected Bibliography

Primary Sources

Travel

Views A-Foot, or Europe Seen with Knapsack and Staff. New York: Wiley and Putnam, 1846.

Eldorado, or Adventures in the Path of Empire. London: Bohn; New York: Putnam, 1850.

A Journey to Central Africa. New York: Putnam, 1854.

The Lands of the Saracen. New York: Putnam, 1855.

A Visit to India, China and Japan in the year 1853. New York: Putnam, 1855.

At Home and Abroad. New York: Putnam, 1860; Second Series, 1862.

Colorado: A Summer Trip. New York: Putnam, 1867.

Egypt and Iceland in the Year 1874. New York: Putnam, 1874.

Poetry

Ximena and Other Poems. Philadelphia: Hooker, 1844.

Rhymes of Travel, Ballads and Poems. New York: Putnam, 1849.

Poems of the Orient. Boston: Ticknor and Fields, 1854.

Poems of Home and Travel. Boston: Ticknor and Fields, 1855.

The Picture of St. John. Boston: Ticknor and Fields, 1866.

The Golden Wedding: A Masque. Philadelphia: J.B. Lippincott, 1868.

The Ballad of Abraham Lincoln. Boston: Fields, Osgood, 1870.

Lars: A Pastoral of Norway. Boston: J.R. Osgood, 1873.

The Prophet: A Tragedy. Boston: J.R. Osgood, 1874.

Poetical Works of Bayard Taylor. Boston: Houghton, Osgood, 1880.

Dramatic Works of Bayard Taylor. Ed. Marie H. Taylor. Boston: Houghton Mifflin, 1880.

Fiction

Hannah Thurston. London: Low and Son; New York: Putnam, 1863.

John Godfrey's Fortunes. London: Low and Son, 1864.

The Story of Kennett. New York: Putnam, 1866.

Joseph and His Friend. New York: G.P. Putnam, 1870.

Beauty and the Beast, and Tales of Home. New York: G.P. Putnam, 1872.

Criticism, Translation, and Parody

Johann Wolfgang von Goethe. *Faust, A Tragedy.* Trans. Bayard Taylor. Boston: Fields, Osgood, 1870.

The Echo Club and Other Literary Diversions. Boston: J.R. Osgood, 1876.

Studies in German Literature. London: Sampson, Low; New York: Putnam, 1879.

Secondary Sources

Biography

Beatty, Richmond Croom. *Bayard Taylor: Laureate of the Gilded Age.* Norman: University of Oklahoma Press, 1936. Taylor is seen as a victim of his time.

Hansen-Taylor, Marie, and Horace Scudder. *Life and Letters of Bayard Taylor.* 2 vols. Boston: Houghton Mifflin, 1884. Pious, but a valuable source for its letters.

Smyth, Albert H. *Bayard Taylor.* American Men of Letters Series. Boston and New York: Houghton Mifflin, 1896. Genteel but accurate. Good bibliography.

Stoddard, Richard Henry. *Recollections, Personal and Literary.* New York: A.S. Barnes, 1903. Assessment by Taylor's close friend.

Van Doren, Carl. "Bayard Taylor." In *Dictionary of American Biography* (1943–1958). Excellent brief account.

Criticism

Cary, Richard. *The Genteel Circle: Bayard Taylor and His New York Friends.* Ithaca, N.Y.: Cornell University Press, 1952.

Krumpelmann, John T. *Bayard Taylor and German Letters.* Hamburg: Cram, De Gruyter, 1959. A thorough account of its subject.

Martin, Robert. "Bayard Taylor's Valley of Bliss." *Markham Review* 9 (1979): 13–17. Taylor had a "homosexual sensibility" expressed in many poems and in *Joseph and His Friend.*

Rose, Alan. "Sin and the City: The Uses of Disorder in the Urban Novel." *Centennial Review*, 16 (1972): 203–220. Discussion of *John Godfrey* with *Sister Carrie*, *Gatsby*, and other novels.

Schwartz, Thomas. "Bayard Taylor's *The Prophet.*" *Brigham Young University Studies*, 14 (1974): 235–247. Taylor broke the taboo against writing about Mormons.

Thorp, Willard. "Defenders of Ideality." In *Literary History of the United States.* New York: Macmillan, 1959.

Wermuth, Paul C. *Bayard Taylor.* Twayne's United States Authors Series. New York: Twayne, 1973. Good brief survey, rather harsh. Bibliography.

James Hazen

Tenn, William [Philip Klass]

Born: London, England, on May 9, 1920
Education: Abraham Lincoln High School,
    Brooklyn, New York, 1936; courses at
    City College of New York, New York
    University, North Carolina State, Uni-
    versity of Pittsburgh, The New School,
    Hunter College
Marriage: Fruma   Breecher,   1957,   one
child

Biography

The son of Aaron-David and Millie Fisher Klass,
Philip Klass was born in London on May 9,
1920. His father had emigrated from Eastern
Europe to England and married an English girl.
The family moved to America, where the father
worked as a sheet-metal worker and later owned
a sheet metal specialty shop. Troubles over political affiliations led to difficulties about natural-
ization, and it was only after the Second World
War that the son became a citizen of the United
States.

Before the war Philip completed his high
school education in Brooklyn, but, not interested
in seeking a degree, he took a wide variety of
courses in a number of different colleges. His
brother, Morton, taking a more usual academic
route, became a professor of anthropology at
Barnard College. Klass read science fiction and
was especially interested in *Wonder Stories* and
the Tarzan novels of Edgar Rice Burroughs,
though he did not care for Burroughs's Martian
series. He wrote for a college magazine and for
radical publications and composed, as he has
said, "much expressionist poetry." In 1942 he
commenced a three-year term of service in the
armed forces and was in the Quartermaster
Corps, the infantry, and the combat engineers.
Discharged in 1945, he commuted from Brooklyn to a job as technical writer for the Watson
Laboratory in Red Bank, New Jersey, and began
his first professional writing. Not caring for
other genres, he turned to science fiction as an
ideal "literature of ideas" and published his first
story in *Astounding Science Fiction* in 1946,
quickly following up with sales to *Planet Stories*,
Weird Tales, and *Thrilling Wonder Stories*.
During the next decade or so, *Galaxy* seemed
one of his best markets among the magazines
for the satirical fiction he was writing, but he
sold to many of the other magazines as well.

Klass lectured to fan groups and at universities, and, in 1961 read a paper at the Modern
Language Association session on science fiction.
In 1966 he was invited to teach writing for a year
at Pennsylvania State University, and he has
stayed on and had an exemplary career as an
academic, rising in rank to full professor. A popular and effective teacher, he received the All
University Teaching Award in 1976.

For complex reasons, including the very low
pay for stories and some disappointment with
the world of science fiction, he virtually stopped
producing SF after the late 1960s. Fortunately,
he expects to have a novel ready for publication
soon.

Literary Analysis

In the introductory "Author's Note" to his story
collection, *The Wooden Star* (1968), Tenn explains his literary approach: "Most of these stories are social satires, thinly disguised as science
fiction. They have generally encountered what
satire deserves: trouble—occasionally they have
effected what satire attempts: change." Since
satire derides the follies it exposes and tries to
change, a broad range of humor from wit to
farce informs many of Tenn's stories. The first
of his published SF stories, "Alexander the Bait"
(1946), contains elements that will be found in
much of his later work. The development of
interplanetary travel is its subject. In order to
stimulate the greed of those in a financial position to make travel to the moon possible, Alexander Parks organizes a careful hoax to make
them believe that the moon contains radioactive
materials. Ironically, successful in his trickery, he
is then banned from interplanetary travel.

One of Tenn's best and most famous stories,
"Child's Play" (1947), might well have been
written by Henry Kuttner and uses one of the
devices that Kuttner was fond of, the dangerous
invention from the future that can have a devastating effect upon the present. Sam Weller receives a gift-wrapped package sent by error from
the year 2353 A.D. and it turns out to be a child's
biochemistry set. The "Bild-A-Man Set #3" has
been assembled to teach youngsters of the future
about the mysteries of biology and the creation
of life. Sam, an ordinary character, is elevated to
the position of a kind of deity by the gift. He
creates "a primitive brown mold that, in the
field of the microscope, fed diffidently on a piece
of pretzel, put forth a few spores and died in
about twenty minutes." Encouraged, Sam creates
a monster that has to be disassembled; then, still
learning, he creates a baby girl without a navel
and has to abandon her on the steps of a found-
ling home. Tenn has a fine time with creating a
language of the future. Money is calculated in
"slunks" and unexplained terms appear—
"phanphophlink," "chrondromos," "yokekkled,"
and "demortoned." Sam is tracked down by a
guardian from the future, mistaken for the du-
plicate he has just made of himself, and messily
disassembled.

There is a different future in "Time Waits for

Winthrop" (1947), in which ordinary citizens from our time are sent for a brief visit to the year 2458 and the aged Winthrop does not want to return to his own time. This future is bizarre and broadly comic. Floors ripple like endless escalators under one's feet and an amiable ceiling extrudes a purple hump that acts as a polite receptionist. Winthrop may be happy with the future, but his companions are unhappy with an Oracle Machine, designed to solve all problems, or a shriek session on Panic Field, designed to rid the psyche of its troubles. There are parodies of standard science fiction themes as when an official of the Temporal Embassy goes off on a micro-hunt in a drop of water that contains a culture of intestinal amoebae and adventurously attacks them with a sword, like an infinitesimal Conan.

The satire is often directed toward political themes. In "Null-P" (1951) there are dire predictions about the destiny of mankind, an obsessive science fiction theme. As early as *The Time Machine* (1895), H. G. Wells had predicted that mankind would have no future at all, but that humankind would simply degenerate and then cease to exist, supplanted by other species. Something similar happens in Tenn's story when the world discovers George Abnego, the absolutely average man. Abnegism becomes a way of life and eventually a way of death, for, instead of evolving and improving, the human species retrogresses into mediocrity. The name of the story's anti-hero is appropriate, for abnegation is rejection, and what the world seems to reject is its humanity. It is only fitting that the human race is eventually supplanted by ambitious and intelligent Labrador retrievers. The dogs breed men to throw sticks for them to retrieve, prizing pets with long arms, or short, sinewy arms, or arms with specially induced rickets. But, when the dogs invent machines that can outdo their pets, humanity disappears, except in the most backward of canine communities.

Comedy in the political satires is dark. In "The Liberation of Earth" (1953), a story inspired by the Korean War, Earth is made virtually uninhabitable by its frequent "liberation" by the alien races that fight over it. "Brooklyn Project" (1948) offers the science fiction theme of a present altered by time travel that introduces changes into the past; it is also about censorship, in a government where the Secretary of Security is a cabinet post and the phrase "reasons of security" is full of dread for newsmen. "Eastward Ho" (1958) reverses historical fact by portraying a post-catastrophe America in which the adaptable Indians have regained control of most of the country and their tribes rule all but a thin strip of New Jersey and New York.

Two of Tenn's best stories deal with the perverse artistry of the confidence game. In "Bernie the Faust" (1965) the narrator is drawn into a scheme to sell ridiculous items to an apparently odd and naive stranger who wants to buy the Golden Gate Bridge, the Sea of Azov, and, finally, the whole planet. Bernie is obliging as long as he can make a profit, but the stranger, a sophisticated extraterrestrial, is only bankrolling the repair of his damaged space ship. The title of "Betelguese Bridge" (1951) alludes to the trick of selling the Brooklyn Bridge to the unaware. Slick, highly civilized extraterrestrials sell a tricky rejuvenation device to our planet in return for its entire stock of radioactive materials. Earth is left stripped and poor, and cheated as well, because the devices need radioactives to operate. Luckily, human ingenuity is able to save the world from itself.

To date, Tenn has published only two novels. *A Lamp for Medusa* (1968) is brief and lightweight, but *Of Men and Monsters* (1968) is a serious treatment of alien invasion of our planet with some ironic inversions. The monsters that usually invade Earth are of comfortably manageable size (Wells's Martians, for instance), but Tenn's extraterrestrials are so huge that, to them, terrestrials are not opponents to battle, but verminous little creatures, like roaches or mice, to be disposed of or endured. The first section of the book appeared in *Galaxy* in 1963 under an appropriate title, "The Men in the Walls." Humans burrow into the insulation in the walls of the alien houses, come out of mouseholes, dodge around clifflike slabs of huge furniture, and steal crumbs of food. Captured, some of them are taken to a pest control center where the aliens dissect, experiment with, and kill them in various ways in hopes of finding a workable pesticide. One of the encouraging aspects of alien invasion stories has always been that humans can, somehow, stand up to their invaders and eventually conquer them. Tenn offers no such hope. The best his humans can manage is to plan to conceal themselves on the enormous cargo ships of the aliens, live like vermin there, and spread their seed to all of the alien-controlled planets in the galaxy. He displays a keen novelistic sense in plotting and developing his longer tales and now believes that it would have been wise for him to compose more booklength stories. One story, "Firewater" (1952), was designed as a novel, but he was discouraged from proceeding with it and it exists only in a truncated form.

Human-alien relations form a backbone for science fiction plotting, and Tenn is much taken with the lighter side of the subject. In "Party of the Two Parts" (1954) he satirizes the complexities of the law and the nature of pornography.

An extraterrestrial, in ameboid shape, has obscene photos of his species to sell on earth. Amusingly, what passes for lewd pictures for a society of ameboid beings serves well on earth as a set of illustrations for an elementary biology textbook. In addition, the complications of galactic law give rise to insoluble legal entanglements. Another story, "The Flat-Eyed Monster" (1955), simply upends the usual horror story of the creature from another world who comes to Earth, does massive damage, frightens the citizenry while dealing out death to assorted groups, and finally succumbs to the brawny hero bent on saving his beautiful lover. Brought to a planet whose inhabitants resemble suitcases with tentacles, Clyde Manship is a monster. He is powerful enough to break out of the paper bag in which he has been incarcerated. The search for him parodies scenes from popular monster movies, as he throws the populace into a panic. When he attempts to escape on an alien space ship, he unfortunately abducts the fiancee, if that is what she is, of the brave alien hero, who rescues his lady by blasting poor Clyde, the "flat-eyed monster," to death. The reader ends up with ambiguous feelings about the story, as the author intended: the farcical takeoffs on monster stories develop sympathy for the harmless figure who is so ill-treated. The satirist Tenn usually nourishes the hope that humanity is reasonable enough to see its foolishness if it is presented with corrosive wit; that it desires to better itself; and that it can be changed.

Summary

In a brief writing career, William Tenn has published short stories that amuse and disturb through their pictures of human failings. His comic effects range from subtle wit and irony to broad farce and slapstick in well-mixed proportions. Taking over the standard topics of science fiction for his plots, he turns them inside out in order to offer pointed commentary upon the human condition.

Selected Bibliography

Primary Sources

Of All Possible Worlds. New York: Ballantine, 1955.
The Human Angle. New York: Ballantine, 1956.
Time in Advance. New York: Bantam Books, 1958.
A Lamp for Medusa (novel). New York: Belmont Books, 1968.
Of Men and Monsters (novel). New York: Ballantine, 1968.
The Wooden Star. New York: Ballantine, 1968.
The Square Root of Man. New York: Ballantine, 1968.
The Seven Sexes. New York: Ballantine, 1968.

Secondary Sources

Bibliography

Contento, William. *Index to Science Fiction Anthologies and Collections.* Boston: G.K. Hall, 1978. A valuable listing of book appearances of Tenn's stories in. the most readily available collections. A 1984 volume by Contento updates his listings.

Day, Donald B. *Index to the Science-Fiction Magazines, 1926–1950.* Portland, Ore.: Perri Press, 1952. A listing of magazine appearances of Tenn's stories during this period.

Lewis, Anthony. *Index to the Science-Fiction Magazines, 1966–1970.* Cambridge, Mass.: New England Science Fiction Association, 1971. A continuation of Day.

Strauss, Erwin S. *MITSFS Index to the SF Magazines 1951–1965.* Cambridge, Mass.: MIT SF Society, 1966. A continuation of Day.

Tuck, Donald H. *The Encyclopedia of Science Fiction and Fantasy Through 1968.* 3 vols. Chicago: Advent Publishers, 1974, 1978, 1983. Valuable listing of contents of Tenn's collections of short stories, as well as foreign editions.

Articles

Edwards, Malcolm. "William Tenn." In *Science Fiction Writers.* Ed. E.F. Bleiler. New York: Charles Scribner's Sons, 1982, pp. 525–530. A useful summary of Tenn's career.

Rutledge, Amelia A. "William Tenn." In *Twentieth-Century American Science-Fiction Writers.* Ed. David Cowart and Thomas Wymer. Detroit: Gale, 1981, pp. 165–167. Helpful, but contains factual errors.

Stableford, Brian M. "The Short Fiction of William Tenn." In *Survey of Science Fiction Literature.* Ed. Frank N. Magill. New Jersey: Salem Press, 1979, pp. 2065–2069.

Zebrowski, George. "William Tenn." In *Twentieth-Century Science-Fiction Writers.* Ed. Curtis C. Smith. New York: St. Martin's, 1981, pp. 530–531. A brief, perceptive commentary.

Douglas Robillard

Tenney, Tabitha Gilman

Born: Exeter, New Hampshire, on April 7, 1762
Marriage: Samuel Tenney, September 1788
Died: May 2, 1837

Biography

Tabitha Gilman was born in Exeter, New Hampshire, on April 7, 1762, into a family whose members since 1638 had been notable for their civic and military contributions to the community. She was the first of seven children born to Samuel Gilman and his second wife, Lydia Robinson Giddings.

According to the biographical sketch in *Notable American Women,* "nothing is known of Tabitha Gilman's education"; therefore, the reader must rely upon hints derived from her "mature work," which "suggests a cultured background, wide reading, and training beyond what a small-town schooling of that date might have afforded."[1]

In September 1788, her marriage intention was filed, and in the same month she married Dr. Samuel Tenney, who was fourteen years her senior. The account of Tenney in Charles Henry Bell's *History* indicates a satisfactory marital and community life: "His domestic and social relations were of the happiest character."[2] Although the Tenneys had no children of their own, an account in the Gilman genealogy notes that Anne, an orphaned relative, spent most of her life at the Tenney home.[3]

After serving as an army surgeon in the Revolutionary War, Dr. Tenney returned to Exeter but discontinued medical practice. He entered politics, and from 1800 to 1807 he lived in Washington, D.C., as a member of the United States Congress. His wife spent several winters in Washington with him.

Mrs. Tenney achieved notice in her community and beyond in 1799 with her compilation of "elevating selections from the poets and from classical authors"[4] into an anthology titled *The Pleasing Instructor*, a book intended to uplift the minds of young women. In 1801, her popular *Female Quixotism: Exhibited in the Romantic Opinions and Extravagant Adventures of Dorcasina Sheldon* was published, and in 1808, *Domestic Cookery* appeared. There are no known copies of either *The Pleasing Instructor* or *Domestic Cookery* in existence today.

After her husband's death in 1816 it appears that Mrs. Tenney occupied the remainder of her life performing charitable deeds and executing elegant needlework. In 1837, following a brief illness, she died in Exeter. She and Dr. Tenney are buried there in the Winter Street Graveyard.

Literary Analysis

Dorcasina Sheldon, the heroine of *Female Quixotism*, is a plain-looking, impressionable woman whose imagination, fueled by her permissive father's novels, has led her to believe that she is irresistible to men and that she is destined for passionate romance. By humorously depicting Dorcasina's misconceptions and misadventures, Tenney responds to the spate of late eighteenth-century sentimental literary romances, particularly those imported from England. Thus Tenney joins the chorus of declaimers against what they considered the corruptive influences of that subversive fiction. However, instead of employing her contemporaries' somber and fearful puritanical cry against immorality, Tenney uses a usually lighthearted, Horatian, sometimes even

racy, ridiculing approach that places her novel in the ranks of such early American satire as Hugh Henry Brackenridge's *Modern Chivalry*. Occasional sportive Gothic episodes which mock the machinery of the current popular Gothic novels suggest still another literary influence in her work.

Although Dorcasina displays the harmful effects of her "novel mania" to an extreme, Tenney's frequent allusions to works such as Samuel Richardson's *Sir Charles Grandison* and Tobias Smollett's *Roderick Random* that have distorted Dorcasina's senses show clearly that Tenney herself was intimately familiar with those works. Obviously considering herself immune to their deleterious effects, she was, to a certain extent, mocking the fears of those who inveighed against romantic novels. However, Tenney's primary satiric purpose was to expose the dangers of reading sentimental fiction.

This satiric purpose reflects directly the influence of Miguel de Cervantes's *Don Quixote* and almost certainly that of Charlotte Lennox's derivative *The Female Quixote*, although Dorcasina lacks the mad grandeur of Quixote and the exquisite beauty of Lennox's Arabella. In spite of frequent borrowings from foreign works, though, *Female Quixotism* remains decidedly nationalistic. Although a tone of tolerance generally prevails throughout the novel, there are occasional hints of racial condescension, ridicule of fervent abolitionism, and the rejection of foreigners, especially Roman Catholic Irish. More vehemently Tenney assails certain ideologies that were alien to turn-of-the-century New Englanders. Responding to the fear of the subversive effects of Illuminationism, Jacobinism, and atheism, Tenney echoes the conservative factions in religion and politics that strived to ward off foreign influences and to maintain, in their opinion, an uncorrupted Protestant society in America.

In spite of those attempts to ward off corruption, Tenney recognized the persistence of fundamental human weakness in society. Her observation that "it is a mortifying truth that perfection is not to be found in human nature"[5] clearly states one of the major themes of the novel and provides a key to her satiric techniques. No character is exempt from her probing wit, nor does even the reader escape her barbs. Additionally, Tenney proceeds a long step beyond her creation of imperfect characters by assailing the very quest for perfection, a point that she manifests in her ridicule of the idealistic drive inherent in Dorcasina's own novel mania.

Tenney employs a number of techniques to achieve her satiric humor. Thus, *Female Quixotism* emerges in refreshing contradistinction to the sugary, overemotional fabrications of much of the prevailing contemporary American as well as imported fiction. Exploring a realism grounded in a deliberately distorted vision, Tenney has created a gallery of comical characters in order to illustrate the effects of affectation, a cast running the gamut of errors from Dorcasina's extreme vanity to the hypocrisy of O'Connor and Seymore, two of her false suitors.

Openly mocking the conventions of sentimental fiction that depict a heroine of ideal beauty, Tenney describes the young Dorcasina as an ordinary woman "of a middling stature, a little enbonpoint, but neither elegant nor clumsy. Her complexion was rather dark; her skin somewhat rough; and features remarkable neither for beauty nor deformity" (Vol. I, p. 8). Toward the end of the novel, Dorcasina has moved so far from any concept of the romantic heroine that she truly has become grotesque. Aging and grey-haired, she presents a "lean withered form, sallow complexion, and toothless mouth" (Vol. III, p. 150). Nevertheless, she continues to entertain notions that men are vulnerable to her beauty and becomes involved in increasingly ridiculous attachments to unprincipled, sometimes young, fortune hunters who are willing to subordinate any fastidiousness about physical appearance and age differences to the attractions of Dorcasina's money.

Just as Dorcasina's foolishness is striking, the situations in which she embroils herself are memorable and provide an often-uproarious parody of the extravagant actions that dominated much of the current fiction. For instance, anticipating her first meeting with Lysander, her first suitor, Dorcasina regrets keenly that she cannot arrive in some dramatic fashion, such as becoming wounded, rescuing her on a runaway horse, or saving her from one whose smitten heart has driven him to abducting her. Deflating the sensational events of fiction, Tenney reduces Dorcasina's expectations of quixotic escapades to mere expression of emotions: "But as none of these romantic adventures, with which she had been so delighted in novels, had ever happened to her, she thought she must be satisfied, if at their first interview, he beheld her with raptures of delight" (Vol. I, p. 12).

Lysander, the suitor whose steady character promises a satisfactory marriage grounded in solid reality, disappoints Dorcasina with his dearth of rapturous zeal. On the other hand, O'Connor, whose barefaced fortune-hunting conniving threatens to destroy Dorcasina's future happiness and security, employs for his dishonest ends the very language and romantic scenes that she believes are essential to her marital felicity. Having arranged a "chance" first meeting in Dorcasina's favorite arbor, he casts "such languishing glances" upon her and heaves "such amorous sighs from his apparently enraptured bosom" that he wins her heart immediately (Vol. I, p. 53). Later, when the two "lovers" hold a forbidden tryst, with mock modesty Tenney diminishes the momentousness of its romantic nature by sarcastically alluding to another writer: "It would require the pen of a Richardson to describe the ecstacy and raptures of this meeting; but as mine pretends to no such powers, they shall be passed over in silence" (Vol. I, p. 175).

Tenney's repeated use of mistaken identity and masquerade heightens her portrayal of the ridiculousness inherent in "these enchanting books" and provides the reader with abundant boisterous humor. O'Connor's carefully rehearsed courtship of Dorcasina disintegrates ignominiously into farce when the woman he has mistaken for the object of his pursuit turns out to be Moll, a comparative newcomer to the ranks of the village prostitutes. When Dorcasina attempts to simulate the scene of her own meeting with O'Connor and compels her maid Betty to serve as proxy for the Irishman by donning Mr. Sheldon's large-sized clothes and wooing her with extravagant phrases, the burlesque increases in hilarity in proportion to the inflation of Dorcasina's seriousness and Betty's embarrassed despair.

Betty herself, however, is subject to certain amusing weaknesses that sometimes appear in sportive Gothic episodes. When she, dressed in Mr. Sheldon's clothes, waits in the grove until dusk so that she might return home without detection, she becomes terrified by a violent thunder and lightning storm. Fleeing from the grove, she senses that she is being followed and looks around. At first she beholds "a creature all in white, with saucer eyes flashing fire, like a very devil." When she looks a second time, it has "increased to the bigness of a calf; and the third time, to that of a large horse." Finally she believes that it is "the evil one himself, come to take her off bodily" (Vol. I, p. 209). After she escapes, she reports to her fellow servants that she has "seen a ghost, or the devil, who run after me till I got into the house" (Vol. I, pp. 210–211).

Later Betty, when she visits the same grove with Dorcasina, becomes apprehensive as darkness falls and again imagines the presence of spectres and ghosts. When she tells her mistress of her fears, Dorcasina chides her: "Your head is filled with ridiculous notions of ghosts and spirits"; however, Dorcasina's commonsense admonition breaks down when she indicates that her own head is filled "with good substantial flesh and blood, in the form of lovers, sighing at my feet" (Vol. I, p. 226). Tenney thus cleverly jabs both at sentimental romances through Dorcasina's illusions and Betty's commonsense rejoinders and at the Gothic tradition through Betty's apprehensions of eerie, ghostly terrors and Dorcasina's unexpectedly clearheaded realism.

In addition, Tenney employs Betty's ignorance to produce a comic distortion of the language of romance. When Dorcasina compels her servant to adopt a masculine masquerade, Betty disappoints and irritates her mistress with the incoherence of her speech: "Dear soul, intosticating charmer, celestial deity; Mars, Junos, and Venis; my very marrow is burnt up from the fire of your dazzling eyes" (Vol. I, p. 203). Betty's failure, however, cannot be attributed wholly to her ignorance. While it is true that she characteristically slaughters the English language, in this scene there is an element of humor in her rebelliousness. Determined never to repeat the mortifying experience, she speaks as outlandishly as possible while bowing ridiculously and squeezing Dorcasina's hand firmly enough to produce pain. Clearly Tenney builds multiple avenues of humor radiating from the center of her satire, including the ridicule of falsely romantic utterance in novels.

Attacks against the language of romances, however, is not Tenney's only satiric use of the spoken word. Perhaps to the modern reader the most surprising element of *Female Quixotism* is the occasional appearance of coarse language. Tenney was the church-going wife of a judge in the little New Hampshire community of Exeter, her robustious episodes and occasionally indelicate dialogue, particularly in juxtaposition to her prevailing refinement of expression, accomplish her satiric intention to startle, even shock, the reader. Although Tenney (or the publisher) discreetly followed the convention of using only the first letter, followed by a dash, of a word of dubious taste, the reader can play a reasonably accurate guessing game and receive the full flavor of Tenney's humor. For instance, there can be no question about the meaning when O'Connor expresses his vexation about Mr. Sheldon's recovery from an illness which the Irishman had hoped would be fatal: "The devil he is [recovered] . . . why, what stuff is the old fellow made of? I'll be d——d if he has not as many lives as a cat" (Vol. I, p. 93).

Thus Tenney exploits dialogue ranging from elaborate protestations of love to obscene vituperation. Compounding her derision of self-importance and personal affectation, she introduces roisterous episodes calculated to strip human beings of their complacency and dignity. In the process she mocks basic aspects of both the sentimental and the Gothic traditions.

Summary

From a literary perspective, *Female Quixotism* falls far short of being a great novel. Nevertheless, it has many qualities that recommend it as a book worth reading, for pleasure as well as for information, for Tenney's satirical tone pervades her entire work and dominates her purpose. In sum, then, *Female Quixotism* emerges as a novel that, in spite of its exaggerated ridiculousness, deserves the attention of today's reader and scholar because of its great popularity in the first half of nineteenth-century America, its significance as a satiric and nationalistic response to late eighteenth-century imported sentimental fiction, the vivid exposure of human foibles, and its enduring powers of description and humor.

Notes

1. Ola Elizabeth Winslow, "Tabitha Tenney," *Notable American Women 1607-1950: A Biographical Dictionary*. Vol. 3. Ed. Edward T. James (Cambridge, Mass.: Belknap Press of Harvard University Press, 1971), p. 439.
2. Charles Henry Bell, *History of the Town of Exeter, New Hampshire* (Boston: Press of E.E. Farwell, 1888), p. 383.
3. Arthur Gilman, *The Gilman Family Traced in the Line of Hon. John Gilman, of Exeter, N.H. with an Account of Many Other Gilmans in England and America* (Albany, N.Y.: Joel Munsell, 1869), p. 130.
4. Bell, p. 383.
5. Tabitha G. Tenney, *Female Quixotism: Exhibited in the Romantic Opinions and Extravagant Adventures of Dorcasina Sheldon*, 3 vols. (Boston: George Clark, 1841), Vol. I, p. 7. Subsequent references to *Female Quixotism* are from this text.

Selected Bibliography

Primary Sources

The Pleasing Instructor. 1799.
Female Quixotism: Exhibited in the Romantic Opinions and Extravagant Adventures of Dorcasina Sheldon. 2 vols. Boston: Thomas and Andrews, 1801; 2 vols. Newburyport: Thomas & Whipple, 1808; 2 vols. Boston: J.P. Peaslee, 1825, 1829; 3 vols. Boston: George Clark, 1841.

Secondary Sources

Bell, Charles Henry. *History of the Town of Exeter New Hampshire.* Boston: Press of E.E. Farwell, 1888. Provides factual references to Samuel Tenney within the historical context of Exeter.
Brown, Herbert Ross. *The Sentimental Novel in America 1789-1860.* Durham, N.C.: Duke University Press, 1940. Refers to Tenney's burlesque of the stock seduction-elopement formula, "elegant epistolarians," prejudice against maiden ladies, dangers of reading romances, and zealous, visionary heroines.
Cowie, Alexander. *The Rise of the American Novel.* New York: American Book Company, 1951. Summarizes the plot of *Female Quixotism* and stresses the book's freshness, humor, and longevity.
Davidson, Cathy. *Revolution and the Word: The Rise of the Novel in America.* New York: Oxford University Press, 1986. Discusses *Female Quixotism* in terms of the female picaresque novel.
Duyckinck, Evert A., and George L. Duyckinck. *Cyclo-*

paedia of American Literature. Vol. I. Philadelphia: Wm. Rutter & Co. 1854. Provides a biography of Tabitha Tenney and a summary, with several excerpts, from *Female Quixotism.*

Freibert, Lucy M., and Barbara A. White, eds. *Hidden Hands: An Anthology of American Women Writers, 1790-1870.* New Brunswick, N.J.: Rutgers University Press, 1985. Provides a biography of Tenney and excerpts from *Female Quixotism.*

Gilman, Arthur. *The Gilman Family Traced in the Line of Hon. John Gilman, of Exeter, N.H. with an Account of Many Other Gilmans in England and America.* Albany, N.Y.: Joel Munsell, 1869. Includes Tenney in this genealogical account.

Loshe, Lillie Deming. *The Early American Novel.* New York: Columbia University Press, 1907. Compares *Female Quixotism* to Charlotte Lennox's *Female Quixote* and notes the influence of cruelty as drawn from Tobias Smollett's writing.

McNall, Sally Allen. *Who Is in the House? A Psychological Study of Two Centuries of Women's Fiction in America, 1795 to the Present.* New York: Elsevier, 1981. Devotes several pages to a discussion of Tenney.

Notable American Women 1607-1950: A Biographical Dictionary. Vol. 3. Ed. Edward T. James. Cambridge, Mass.: Harvard University Press, Belknap Press, 1971. Contains Ola Elizabeth Winslow's biographical and critical sketch of Tabitha Tenney.

Petter, Henri. *The Early American Novel.* Columbus: Ohio State University Press, 1971. Devotes an entire chapter, as well as later references, to a discussion of *Female Quixotism.*

Tenney, Martha Jane. *The Tenney Family or the Descendants of Thomas Tenney of Rowley, Massachusetts, 1638-1904.* Rev. Concord, N.H.: The Rumford Press, 1904. A genealogical account that focuses primarily on Dr. Samuel Tenney but also refers to his marriage to Tabitha Gilman and to her accomplishments.

Sally C. Hoople

Thompson, William Tappan

Born: Ravenna, Ohio, on August 31, 1812
Education: Formal education concluded when Thompson was orphaned at the age of fourteen
Marriage: Caroline Amour Carrie, 1837, ten children
Died: March 24, 1882

Biography

The son of David and Catherine Kerney Thompson, William Tappan Thompson was born in Ravenna, Ohio, on August 31, 1812. Orphaned at the age of fourteen, he ended his formal education and moved to Philadelphia, Pennsylvania, where he worked in the office of the *Daily Chronicle.* Named private secretary to James D. Wescott, Secretary of the Territory of Florida, Thompson went to Tallahassee in 1830. Moving to Augusta, Georgia, in 1834, he was employed the following year by Augustus Baldwin Longstreet on the *States' Rights Sentinel.* When Longstreet gave up the *Sentinel* in 1836, Thompson joined a militia unit called "The Richmond Blues" and served briefly in the Seminole campaign in Florida.

Returning to Augusta in 1837, he married Caroline Amour Carrie; they would have ten children, four surviving to adulthood. In March 1838, he reentered the world of journalism, founding a semimonthly magazine, the Augusta *Mirror.* Early in 1842 Thompson merged the *Mirror* with the Macon *Family Companion,* owned by Benjamin Griffin and edited by his wife Sarah, to form the *Family Companion and Ladies' Mirror.* He and Mrs. Griffin were not compatible editors, and he left the magazine in August 1842. The same month, Thompson assumed the editorship of the *Southern Miscellany* in Madison, Georgia, a position he held until February 1844.

In 1846, Thompson moved to Baltimore where he joined Park Benjamin in editing a newspaper called the *Western Continent.* He returned to Georgia in 1849. In 1850, he founded the *Savannah Morning News,* a newspaper that he actively edited until his death. Thompson left Savannah for a short time in 1864, joining the Confederate forces attempting to defend the area against Sherman. He travelled to Europe in 1867. In 1868, he served as a delegate to the national Democratic convention, and in 1877, he was a member of the convention that shaped a new state constitution for Georgia. Thompson died in Savannah on March 24, 1882.

Literary Analysis

During the 1830s, Augustus Baldwin Longstreet's *Georgia Scenes,* Seba Smith's Major Jack

Downing, and stories about Davy Crockett were very popular. Such stories and characters provided Thompson with models for humorous sketches of rustic life. Present at the publication of Longstreet's *Georgia Scenes* by the *Sentinel* press, Thompson remained an enthusiastic supporter of Longstreet's writing and political views.

Thompson's first Pineville story appeared in the *Family Companion and Ladies' Mirror* in March 1842; in June his first Major Jones letter was published in the same magazine. Thompson thought so little of the Major Jones letter that he published it anonymously. Surprised by the attention that it attracted, he soon began writing more letters. Some 30 Jones letters appeared in the *Southern Miscellany* between August 20, 1842, and February 9, 1844. The first 16 letters were collected in 1843, as *Major Jones's Courtship*, a pamphlet offered as a subscription premium by the *Southern Miscellany*. In 1844, an enlarged edition of *Major Jones's Courtship*, containing 26 letters and 12 illustrations by F.O.C. Darley was published in Philadelphia. Fifteen thousand copies of this edition were sold that year. Another revised and augmented edition appeared in 1872. The work was reprinted nearly 30 times by 1900.

With the character of Major Joseph Jones, Thompson expressed from a humorous and realistic perspective and in native dialect, the morals and tastes of a whimsical upper-middle-class planter from Pineville, Georgia. The original for Major Jones was said to have been a man named Wall who lived in Pineville. Like "Bill Arp" and Joel Chandler Harris's Billy Sanders, the Major is a crackerbox philosopher. He is a Whig like his creator, and he names his first-born Henry Clay. Thompson makes him a medium for Whig propaganda and for satire on such subjects as women's fashions, the dress of dandies, and heavy drinking.

Thompson's Major is a believable figure, and most of the other characters in his tales are likewise convincing. As the title suggests, *Major Jones's Courtship* makes light-hearted fun of the rituals of flirting, proposing, and marrying. Settled and respectable enough by the 1840s, Pineville could delight in a brand of humor that reaffirmed the prevalent social code in a world where the word "stocking" caused proper young ladies to blush. Longstreet and Thompson were the only outstanding southwestern humorists who concerned themselves much with the more tender domestic scenes. Yet, unlike Longstreet's *Georgia Scenes*, *Major Jones's Courtship* contains nothing coarse or brutal. There are good-natured high jinks and practical jokes—but no eye gouging—in Jones's Pineville.

Major Jones was as prolific a letter writer as Major Jack Downing. He believed deeply in the underlying morality of the universe that his letters reflected. The respectability of Jones's opinions was influenced by his moderate affluence and the fact that he had enough education to intersperse foreign phrases and quotations from the classics throughout his letters; the mixing of these erudite quotations with illiterate spelling reveals the Major's contradictory traits and the quaintness of regional peculiarities.

F.O.C. Darley's twelve illustrations for the 1844 edition of *Major Jones's Courtship* depict the Major in top hat, cravat, waistcoat, and tails. Jones's attire is strikingly similar to that of Major Jack Downing. Undoubtedly, Seba Smith's congenial, bumbling Yankee was a model for the picturesque speech and homespun wit of Major Jones. Thompson's debt to Longstreet's *Georgia Scenes* is also apparent. Still, his format is different. Longstreet used the frame tale, giving him distance between his refined narrator and the rustics. By letting Jones ramble on in his colorful dialect, Thompson keeps the focus on Pineville's homely virtues.

When the courting rites, parlor games, and tricks described in *Major Jones's Courtship* won ready acceptance with his readers, Thompson quickly prepared another collection of sketches for publication. *Chronicles of Pineville*, which appeared in 1845, is much closer in format to Longstreet's *Georgia Scenes*. In the preface to *Chronicles of Pineville*, Thompson stated that *Major Jones's Courtship* was an attempt "to depict some of the peculiar features of the Georgia backwoodsman." His second book contained "other stories illustrative of a similar character . . . [designed] to present a few more interesting specimens of the genus Cracker." The Cracker, he continues, has "strongly marked" lineaments, easy for even a beginner to catch. The author has tried "to catch his 'manners living as they rise' . . . to afford the student of human nature a glance at characters not often found in books, or anywhere else, indeed, except in just such places as 'Pineville,' Georgia."[1] Because the earlier Pineville was a different place, even less refined than the Pineville of his own day, Thompson claimed—as had Longstreet—that he wished to record rapidly vanishing historical phenomena, yet the sketches of *Chronicles of Pineville* lack the immediacy of Major Jones's voice. The language is often forced and gives evidence of hasty composition. Apologies abound regarding the haphazard direction of the narration.

Thompson used the pages of the *Western Continent* to continue his Major Jones letters. Called "Major Jones on his Travels" and representing a return to the epistolary format, this series was collected as *Major Jones's Sketches of Travel* in 1848. The domestic flavor of Pineville is absent in these letters. Thompson had recognized the value of having an insular character like the Major take trips and relate in comic fashion his responses to new sights, including metropolitan scenes. *Major Jones's Sketches of Travel* relates scenes, incidents, and adventures on a tour from Georgia to Canada. Though on occasion Jones makes an ass of himself, more often than not he sees through big city sham. Going north also allows him an opportunity to deliver satirical pronouncements on national politics and to defend the institution of slavery. Like Major Downing before him, Jones even drops in to chat with the president, who, unfortunately, is tied up in a cabinet meeting. The revival of Major Jones's voice in *Major Jones's Sketches of Travel* gave Thompson's prose more authority than that exhibited in *Chronicles of Pineville*.

Major Jones became a meal ticket for Thompson. He wrote a version for the stage; called *Major Jones's Courtship; Or, Adventures of a Christmas Eve*, it had a successful run in Baltimore. Thompson's popularity continued after the Civil War and interest in his work was given new life by the posthumous republication, with additional sketches, of *John's Alive; Or, The Bride of a Ghost, and Other Sketches* in 1883. Nonetheless, his work was out of print by the turn of the century.

Summary

As a humorous writer, William Tappan Thompson's skill is represented best by his Major Jones's letters. His first selection of letters remained the most popular, and his best attempts afterward were efforts to exploit the colloquial voice of Major Jones. Through the garrulous and well-meaning Major, Thompson sought to delineate and defend the values of a society he knew well, one which emphasized the virtues of family ties, respect for women, and community stability.

Note

1. William Tappan Thompson, *Chronicles of Pineville* (Philadelphia: Carey and Hart, 1845), preface.

Selected Bibliography

Primary Sources

Major Jones's Courtship: Detailed, with Other Scenes, Incidents, and Adventures, in a Series of Letters, by Himself. Madison, Ga.: R. Hanleiter, 1843; augmented, Philadelphia: Carey & Hart, 1844; revised and augmented, New York: Appleton, 1872.

Chronicles of Pineville: Embracing Sketches of Georgia Scenes, Incidents, and Characters. Philadelphia: Carey and Hart, 1845.

John's Alive: Or, The Bride of a Ghost. Baltimore: Taylor, Wilde, 1846; posthumously republished, with additional sketches, Philadelphia: D. McKay, 1883.

Major Jones's Sketches of Travel, Comprising the Scenes, Incidents, and Adventures in His Tour from Georgia to Canada. Philadelphia: Carey and Hart, 1848.

Major Jones's Courtship; Or, Adventures of a Christmas Eve: A Domestic Comedy in Two Acts. Savannah, Ga.: E.J. Purse, 1850.

Rancy Cottem's Courtship. Detailed, with Other Humorous Sketches and Adventures. Philadelphia: T.B. Peterson and Brothers, 1879.

Secondary Sources

Articles and Chapters in Books

Ellison, George R. "William Tappan Thompson and the *Southern Miscellany, 1842-1844. Mississippi Quarterly*, 23 (Spring 1970): 155-168. Analyzes the content of the *Southern Miscellany* with an emphasis on Thompson's contributions.

Hubbell, Jay B. *The South in American Literature, 1607-1900.* Durham, N.C.: Duke University Press, 1954, pp. 669-672. Calls Major Jones "that most representative of Southern comic figures" (p. 669).

Miller, Henry Prentice. "The Background and Significance of *Major Jones's Courtship*." *Georgia Historical Quarterly*, 30 (December 1946): 267-296. Good account of Thompson and his work, based upon the author's University of Chicago dissertation, cited below.

Osthaus, Carl R. "From the Old South to the New South: The Editorial Career of William Tappan Thompson of the *Savannah Morning News*." *Southern Quarterly*, 14 (April 1976): 237-260. Finds more continuity than change in Thompson's long editorial career. Thompson maintained his beliefs in white supremacy, the sanctity of the Democratic Party, and the need for the South to be economically self-sufficient.

Theses and Dissertations

Holbrook, Laura Doster. "Georgia Scenes and Life in the Works of the William Tappan Thompson." M.A. thesis, University of Georgia, 1967. Explores the Georgia milieu of Thompson's works.

Miller, Henry Prentice. "The Life and Works of William Tappan Thompson." Ph.D. dissertation, University of Chicago, 1942. Most extensive treatment of Thompson's life and overview of his work.

L. Moody Simms, Jr.

Thomson, Mortimer Neal

Born: Riga, New York, on September 2, 1831

Education: University of Michigan, 1849–1850

Marriages: Anna H. Van Cleve, October 24, 1857, one child; Grace Eldredge, July 1861, one child

Died: June 25, 1875

Biography

Mortimer Neal Thomson, better known during the height of his popularity in the 1850s as Q.K. Philander Doesticks, P.B. (for Queer Kritter and Perfect Brick), was born to Edwin and Sophia Hall Thomson in Riga, New York, a small town near Rochester, on September 2, 1831.[1] Ten years later his family moved to Ann Arbor, Michigan, where his father practiced law. In the fall of 1849 Thomson entered the University of Michigan but was expelled in the winter of his freshman year because of his membership in Chi Psi, a secret fraternity whose existence the University had never officially authorized.

Few details of any consequence are known about the period in Thomson's life immediately following his expulsion. For a while, apparently, he joined a traveling dramatic troupe; however, becoming disenchanted, he returned home to Ann Arbor. In the early 1850s, he visited Niagara Falls, an excursion that provided the background for "Doesticks on a Bender," his first humorous sketch which appeared in 1854 and was widely reprinted in newspapers throughout the country. By 1854 Thomson moved to New York City where he was employed as a clerk in a jewelry store. At about the same time he started writing a series of letters, also under the Doesticks pseudonym, for the *Detroit Advertiser*, a paper where his younger brother, Clifford, was employed. Between September 22, 1854, and May 30, 1855, the *Advertiser* published 29 of the Doesticks letters. Several others were published in the *New York Daily Tribune* and the New York *The Spirit of the Times*. Most of these letters were subsequently reprinted in Thomson's first book, *Doesticks: What He Says* (1855). At about the time this book appeared, Thomson joined the *New York Tribune* as a reporter and wrote a series of popular police-court sketches that he later incorporated into *The History and Records of the Elephant Club* (1856), a collaboration with Edward Fitch Underhill, "Knight Russ Ockside, M.D." In the spring of 1856, Thomson published a 261-page poetic burlesque of Longfellow's *Song of Hiawatha*, entitled *Plu-ri-bus-tah*. He was also writing for the original *New Yorker* and the *New York Picayune*, the latter being the most prominent comic weekly in America at this time.

Early in 1857 Thomson wrote 16 feature articles for the *Tribune*, the product of his investigations into the subject of New York fortune tellers. These sketches were collected and published under the title *The Witches of New York* (1858). In the autumn of 1857 he also published a 306-line poem, *Nothing to Say*, with the subtitle, "A Slight Slap at Mobocratic Snobbery," a parody of William Allen Butler's popular poem on women's fashions, "Nothing to Wear." Thomson also became editor of the *New York Picayune*, a paper to which he had been contributing sketches for about a year. As editor, a position that he held until the early fall of 1858, he doubled the paper to quarto size.[2] In late October 1857 he married seventeen-year-old Anna H. Van Cleve, a Minnesotan. Barely a year later, on December 22, 1858, Anna died after giving birth to a son, Marco. Throughout 1858, Thomson wrote drama reviews for the *Tribune* and continued to do so until the outbreak of the Civil War. In March 1859 the *Tribune* sent Thomson to Savannah, Georgia, to investigate an auction sale of slaves. The product of his investigations, printed in the March 9, 1859, issue of the *Tribune*, was an anti-slavery story that one newspaper claimed to be so powerful that it "rang through the North like an alarm bell."[3]

During the Civil War, Thomson served as a correspondent for the *Tribune* and as a chaplain to a regiment. In June 1860 his only play, *The Lady of the Lake*, a parody of Sir Walter Scott's poem of the same title, premiered. In 1862 Thomson married for a second time. His new wife, Grace Eldredge, was the daughter of "Fanny Fern" (Sara Payson Willis Parton), a minor nineteenth-century writer. This marriage, like Thomson's first marriage to Anna Van Cleve, ended tragically; twenty days after giving birth to their daughter, Ethel, in December 1862, Grace died of scarlet fever.

Between 1862 and 1869 Thomson wrote for the *New York Weekly* and lectured, and in the early 1870s he served briefly as an associate editor of the *Minneapolis Tribune*, a paper with which Clifford was associated. Then, in 1873, he returned to New York City to serve as editor of *Leslie's Illustrated Magazine*, a position that he held until his death on June 25, 1875. After his death *The Adventures of Snoozer, A Sleepwalker* (1876), a short burlesque featuring the ludicrous and rollicking exploits of a somnabulist, was published by J.L. Winchell.

Literary Analysis

The literary career of Mortimer Neal Thomson was relatively short-termed, his major works appearing between 1855 and 1860. While virtually unknown today, except among few specialists of American humor, Thomson enjoyed wide popularity among his contemporaries and was regarded at the time of his death as one of the leading literary humorists of the 1850s, "the authorized New York agent of King Momus," according to an obituary notice in the *New York Herald*.[4]

Thomson's first and probably most significant work, *Doesticks: What He Says*, published in 1855, was composed of sketches principally drawn from those that he had written for the *Detroit Advertiser*. The subject matter was what one contemporary reviewer called "the many-colored absurdities of metropolitan life."[5] Presented from the perspective of a "traveling naif,"[6] these sketches—that Thomson himself labeled "A Series of Unpremeditated Literary Extravagances"—burlesque a broad range of subjects, most focusing on contemporary aspects of New York City life in the 1850s. Spiritualism and witchcraft, various amusements and curiosities (including P.T. Barnum's famed museum), the living conditions in boarding houses, fire fighting companies, the Millerites, the theater, stagecraft, charity balls, the municipal police, politics, travel, social customs and festive occasions, hypocrisy under varied guises, religious fanaticism, secret societies, and patent medicine remedies comprise the kaleidoscopic range of contemporary concerns that Thomson satirizes. In portraying the tenderfoot who comes to the city as both an object and vehicle for his satire, Thomson employed a literary type that anticipates some of the innocent-eyed personae that Marietta Holley, Artemus Ward, and Mark Twain would similarly use after the Civil War.[7]

Much of the satire in *Doesticks* is double-edged. Thomson's comic strategy was not only to repeatedly debunk his persona's abject simplicity and gullibility but many of the outlandish events and persons whom he observes as well. Moreover, his satiric thrust is typically ironic and unidealistic. For instance, in a sketch entitled "An Evening with the Spiritualists—Rampant Ghostology," Doesticks and two of his friends visit a spiritual medium, caricatured as "a vinegar-complexioned woman, with a ruby nose, mouth the exact shape of a sound-hole to a violin, who wore green spectacles, and robes of equivocal purity" (p. 255). During the ensuing seance the men unexpectedly discover the spirits of notable historical personages to be excessively worldly, materialistic, and undignified, a sharp disparity between the anticipated ideal and banal actuality: "I learned that Sampson and Hercules have gone into partnership in the millinery business. Julius Caesar is peddling apples and molasses candy. . . . Noah is running a canal boat" (pp. 258–259).

Other humorous techniques abound in *Doesticks*, including jumbled syntax, jerky, frag-mented sentences (sometimes characterized by witty and ironic turns), comic lists (amplified by ludicrous, often slangy exaggeration and exhibiting disparagingly incongruous comparisons), sarcastic asides, farcical descriptions, and comic names such as Damphool, Bull Dogge, Rantan-rave Hellitisplit. In addition, seven illustrations by John McLenan—who incidentally illustrated all of Thomson's books except one—pictorially complement the verbal humor of the sketches.

This anti-idealistic focus likewise characterizes Thomson's second principal work, *Plu-ri-bus-tah, A Song That's-By-No-Author*, a burlesque social history of the United States in which, as David Sloane observes, "the natural, sublime, and the ideal are consistently dragged down to the vulgar."[8] Regarded as Thomson's "most original work,"[9] *Plu-ri-bus-tah*, published on May 7, 1856, and embellished with 156 illustrations by McLenan, employs the monotonous trochaic meter of Longfellow's *Hiawatha* throughout. In "The Author's Apology" to *Plu-ri-bus-tah*, Thomson boldly asserts: "When I began this work, I assumed the right to distort facts, to mutilate the records, to belie history, to outrage common sense, and to speak as I should please, about all dignitaries, persons, places, and events, without the slightest regard for truth or probability" (p. ix). And, indeed, he does just that in the form of a satiric allegory debunking the American love of money and attendant socio-political issues. Thomson burlesques many facets of American history in the poem. The hero, Plu-ri-bus-tah, who represents one of the original Pilgrim settlers, relentlessly and recklessly pursues the materialistic ethic, the "Potent and ALMIGHTY DOLLAR/ Dirty, filthy, greasy, DOLLAR!" [which] "he would have loved as truly,/ Hugged as closely, kissed as fondly,/ Had the female image on it/ Been a dog, or been a jackass" (pp. 119–121). In the pursuit of his goal he soundly defeats Johnny Taurus, the son of Ruhl Brittania (Great Britain) in a war, ironically diminished to a seven-year prize fight, a thinly disguised travesty of the Revolutionary War. Thomson treats other events in *Plu-ri-bus-tah* in a similar mock-heroic manner. For instance, in the first section he juxtaposes the mythological and the contemporary, ironically presenting the god Jupiter as a hideous American urban type who withdraws to his woodshed where he sits "on the slop-pail,/ In his slippers and his shirt-sleeves,/ With one leg across the other/ In the style of Mrs. Bloomer,/ At the Woman's Rights Convention" (pp. 29–30). When the goddess America appears to him soon after, he lustily embraces her, an action unnoticed by his wife, Juno, who "was in the parlor,/ With her hair put up in papers,/ With her feet in ragged slippers,/ With a torn and dirty dress on,/ Studying the latest fashions" (pp. 32–33). Again, Thomson employs ironic reversal, reducing the mythological Juno to a common, unappealing urban housewife with banal interests. In *Plu-ri-bus-tah* Thomson extends his burlesque to include many social issues of contemporary concern as well, including political issues surrounding slavery, Barnum's museum, spiritualism, free love, excessive greed, hypocrisy and corruption, the dissolution of the Union, the failures of the Atlantic cable and the Pacific railroad, and the Civil War (he predicts defeat for both the North and the South). The plot of the poem culminates on a pessimistic note. In surroundings of devastation and ruin, Yunga-Merrakah (the son of Plu-ri-bus-tah), an irresponsible libertine, is overthrown by Cuffee, his father's former slave, and is crushed when an enormous dollar falls on him.

Thomson's next work, *The History and Records of the Elephant Club*, his only collaboration, was published in November 1856. Though Edward F. Underhill was his collaborator, Thomson authored the major portions of the book, parts of which consisted of police-court sketches he had published in the *New York Tribune*. Underhill presumably shaped the various episodes into a unified work.[10] The plot centers around the burlesque accounts of members of the Elephant Club, whose objective is to view New York City, the "Metropolitan Elephant," from many and varied angles, "surveying him in all his majesty of proportion, by tracing him to his secret haunts, and observing his habits, both in his wild and domestic state" (p. 39). The misadventures of the club's members take them to a shooting gallery, a bowling alley, a Turkish smoking house, and an oyster bar. Also, they encounter a drunken "gutter snipe" who "sleeps anywhere and everywhere" (p. 57), and two competing hose companies rushing to a fire, the latter incident enhanced by farcical humor. The most ludicrous episodes, however, are several of the police-court sketches that the members recount. One involves a drunken sailor who is unable to converse coherently since he cannot answer one question until another has been asked, the result being a series of amusing non sequiturs. In another sketch when the judge asks a man, aptly named Wallabout Warbler, who has been arrested for public drunkenness for standing in a garbage barrel "extemporizing doggerel to an imaginary audience" how he got drunk, Warbler responds in highly affected, nonsensical, lyrical effusions (p. 242). These and other sketches typify Thomson's burlesque strategy and help to reinforce the claim of a contemporary reviewer that *The History and Records of the Elephant Club* is "a ludicrous satire upon the manners and customs of the community."[11]

In 1857 Thomson published his fourth book, *Nothing to Say*, a poetic parody of William Allen Butler's widely popular satire on women's clothing, "Nothing to Wear" (1857). The decision to write *Nothing to Say* turned out to be a successful commercial enterprise for Thomson. He completed his 306-line poem in less than a week, and for his efforts his publisher, Rudd and Carleton, paid him $800. Whereas Butler's poem ridicules the rich who actually possess large wardrobes but lament of having "nothing to wear," *Nothing to Say* is, according to Thomson, "a new home-made allegorical fable" (p. 16). Moreover, it is a work, one reviewer noted, that "abounds in clever, downright hits at fashionable society, and shows a thorough acquaintance with certain phases of New York life."[12] Again using an iconoclastic approach, although the burlesque is less pronounced than in his earlier works, in *Nothing to Say* Thomson employs a journey motif involving two unappealing allegorical characters, the Spirit of Cant, portrayed as demonic and impish, and his female guide, Charity. Their excursions carry them not only to several familiar New York City landmarks, the Cooper Institute and the Astor Library—both of which offer their services to the poor—but to the North Pole, where they view the Grinnell Expedition searching for survivors "who have perilled their lives in these Northern snows" (p. 47). Finally, Cant and Charity travel to Norfolk, Virginia, where Charity shows him strangers nursing the victims of a pestilence. Cant responds to all of these revelations in the same manner: he simply has "nothing to say," perhaps an indication that the rich, contrary to expectations, have tried to assist the poor and unfortunate through "noble charities."

Published in December 1858, *The Witches of New York*, Thomson's next major work, is a collection of detailed satirical portraits of fortune-tellers, sorceresses, and clairvoyants, reprinted from articles written for the *Tribune* in 1857. Using his familiar Doesticks persona, Thomson presents an unrestrained satiric examination of the notorious and disreputable activities of New York fortune-tellers, exposing not only their hypocritical and deceptive tactics to dupe the unwary but their practice of hideous crimes, ranging from abortion and prostitution to counterfeiting of currency and infanticide. The same unifying pattern is followed throughout. Doesticks, posing as an over-eager naif looking for a wife, visits the fortune-teller, caricatures her, her habitation, and her assistant (if she has one), engages in a dialogue with her and has his fortune told (the latter always resulting in preposterous predictions), and finally departs, usually disillusioned by what he has seen and heard. Burlesque is the prevalent humorous technique, and although the satire focuses on Gotham's fortune-telling industry, Thomson also occasionally disparages Doesticks himself. In summing up the various prognostications made to him during the course of his visits, Doesticks ironically notes that he had been promised thirty-three wives and ninety children, informed that he had been "born under nearly all the planets known to astronomers," had "passed through so many scenes of unexpected happiness and complicated misfortune in his past life, that he must have lived fifty hours to the day and been wide awake all the time" and had "so many fortunes marked out for him that at three hundred and fifty years old his work will not be half done" (pp. 404–405).

The Great Auction Sale of Slaves at Savannah, Georgia (1859), Thomson's sixth book, is a work of propagandistic social criticism, a caustic and sentimental Abolitionist tract leveled against the cruel and inhumane treatment of southern slaves. Initially published in the *Tribune* under the title "A Great Slave Auction," it was widely circulated in northern newspapers. Reprinted as a pamphlet by the American Anti-Slavery Society, it was reissued in England, Ireland, and Scotland.[13] The auction sale on which the work was based took place on March 2 and 3, 1859. Disguised as a southern planter, Thomson traveled to Savannah to observe the proceedings firsthand and described them in painstaking detail. Thoroughly iconoclastic, *The Great Auction Sale* disparages the insensitive slave buyers while at the same time it evokes sympathy for the 436 hapless and pitiful slaves of Pierce M. Butler, a well-to-do Philadelphian who was compelled to sell them to pay his debts. Thomson intensifies his satire through caricature. For instance, in describing Mr. Walsh, the auctioneer, he observes that "not only is his face red, but his skin has been taken off in spots by blisters of some sort, giving him a peely look; so that, taking his face all in all, the peeliness and the redness combined, he looks much as if he had been boiled in the same pot with a red cabbage" (p. 14). The work culminates on a bitterly ironic note: Butler gives each of his former slaves, before their forced separation from their loved ones, a dollar "fresh from the mint, to give an additional glitter to his generosity" (p. 27).

Thomson's only play and most inferior work, *The Lady of the Lake*, which opened on June 21, 1860, at Niblo's Garden in New York City, is a travesty of Sir Walter Scott's 1810 poem. Preserving the original names of the characters and the plot line of Scott's poem, *The Lady of the Lake* consists of one act in eight scenes. Heavily melodramatic and dependent on caricature, the play generates much of its humor through puns, of which there are approximately 119. The artifi-

cially contrived resolution, with the Spirit of the Lake functioning as a *deus ex machina* and emerging through the stage floor to resurrect all the dead characters, accentuates the play's burlesque impression. The play enjoyed a very short run, the final performance taking place on June 30, 1860.

Thomson's final work, *The Adventures of Snoozer, A Sleepwalker*, with illustrations by Thomas Worth, was completed six months before the author's death, although it did not appear in print until 1876. Only 47 pages in length, the work episodically chronicles, under the guise of an abbreviated confessional autobiography, the outrageous escapades of an indefatigable sleepwalker named Abijah Jeremiah Skillibob Snoozer. Heavily laden with puns like *The Lady of the Lake*, *Snoozer* employs the same recurring humorous pattern throughout: Snoozer dreams and then attempts to act out his fantasies through his somnambulism, a behavioral response that usually gets him into trouble and at the same time causes chaos for everyone with whom he comes in contact. Although Thomson's portrait of his sleepwalker is self-deprecating, he extends his burlesque to encompass several social issues of the contemporary urban scene. While described by the publisher as "the culminating effort of Doesticks's genius and . . . universally accepted as his masterpiece," *The Adventures of Snoozer, A Sleepwalker* does not measure up to this prediction.

Summary

Although highly regarded in the 1850s, his major period of creativity, and singled out more recently "as a spokesman for the 'American' viewpoint of the Northeast . . . [prefiguring in works such as "Doesticks on a Bender"] the traveler's irony of other American humorists after the Civil War,"[14] Mortimer Neal Thomson and his work have been largely forgotten by contemporary students of American literature. Nevertheless, in his works set against the background of a recognizable social milieu, he introduced a gallery of humorous urban types whom he portrayed from an unidealized, ironic, usually burlesque perspective. In addition, "he brought to American humor terse, vigorous, quick-moving phrases and vivid slang," as Franklin J. Meine has observed.[15] A skillful and hilariously witty social satirist and a major humorist of the nineteenth-century urban Northeast, Thomson may, indeed, deserve the generous accolade accorded to him at the time of his death in 1875, when it was recognized that during the heyday of his popularity he was "the king of American humorists."[16]

Notes

1. The biographical data in this essay principally come from Fletcher D. Slater, "The Life and Let-

ters of Mortimer Thomson," M.A. thesis, Northwestern University, 1931. Selected details are from Franklin J. Meine's entry on Thomson in the *Dictionary of American Biography*, Vol. 18, ed. Dumas Malone (New York: Charles Scribner's Sons, 1936), pp. 487–488.

2. David E.E. Sloane, "Mortimer Thomson (Q.K. Philander Doesticks, P.B.)," in *Dictionary of Literary Biography*, Vol. 11, *American Humorists, 1800-1950*, ed. Stanley Trachtenberg (Detroit: Gale, 1982), p. 495.

3. Obituary, *New York Herald*, June 26, 1875, p. 10.

4. Ibid.

5. Review of *Doesticks: What He Says*, by Q.K. Philander Doesticks, P.B., *New York Tribune*, July 23, 1855, p. 3.

6. Sloane, p. 491.

7. Sloane, "Introduction," *The Literary Humor of the Urban Northeast, 1830-1890*, ed. Sloane (Baton Rouge: Louisiana State University Press, 1983), p. 31.

8. Sloane, "Mortimer Thomson," p. 492.

9. Slater, p. 74.

10. Ibid., p. 117.

11. Review of *The History and Records of the Elephant Club*, by Knight Russ Ockside, M.D., and Q.K. Philander Doesticks, P.B., *The Spirit of the Times*, December 20, 1856, p. 530.

12. Review of *Nothing to Say*, by Q.K. Philander Doesticks, P.B., *Ballou's*, October 24, 1857, p. 27; quoted in Slater, p. 153.

13. Review of *The Great Auction Sale of Slaves at Savannah, Georgia*, by Mortimer Thomson, *Atlantic Monthly*, 4 (September 1859): 387.

14. Sloane, "Introduction," *The Literary Humor of the Urban Northeast*, p. 31.

15. Meine, p. 488.

16. Obituary, *New York Herald*, p. 10.

Selected Bibliography

Primary Sources

Prose

Doesticks: What He Says. New York: Edward Livermore, 1855.

The History and Records of the Elephant Club, by Thomson (Doesticks) and Edward F. Underhill (Knight Russ Ockside, M.D.), New York: Livermore and Rudd, 1856.

The Witches of New York. New York: Rudd and Carleton, 1858.

The Great Auction Sale of Slaves at Savannah, Georgia. New York: American Anti-Slavery Society, 1859.

The Adventures of Snoozer, A Sleepwalker. New York: J.L. Winchell, 1876.

Poetry

Plu-ri-bus-tah, A Song That's-By-No-Author. New York: Livermore and Rudd, 1856.

Nothing to Say. New York: Rudd and Carleton, 1857.

Drama

The Lady of the Lake. New York: French, 1860. Performed in New York, Niblo's Garden, June 21, 1860.

Secondary Sources

Books

Sloane, David E.E. "Introduction." *The Literary Humor of the Urban Northeast, 1830-1890*. Ed. David E.E. Sloane. Baton Rouge: Louisiana State University Press, 1983, pp. 1–48. Sloane regards Thomson as a "dominant figure in American humor" in the 1850s, an anti-idealist especially skillful at burlesquing contemporary subjects. In his anthology Sloane includes 25 pages of excerpts from two of Thomson's works.

Articles

Kuethe, J. Louis. "Q.K. Philander Doesticks, P.B., Neologist." *American Speech*, 12 (April 1937): 111–116. Provides a generous sampling of Thomson's urban word coinages.

Lorch, Fred W. "'Doesticks' and *Innocents Abroad*." *American Literature*, 20 (January 1949): 446–449. Lorch speculates that Mark Twain may have been familiar with some of the Doesticks letters that were reprinted in the St. Louis *Evening News* in 1854 and that they may have provided a paradigm for *Innocents Abroad*.

Meine, Franklin J. "Thomson, Mortimer Neal." In *Dictionary of American Biography*. Vol. 18. Ed. Dumas Malone. New York: Charles Scribner's Sons, 1936, pp. 487–488. A brief but critically astute overview of Thomson's life and literary career.

Obituary. *New York Daily Tribune*, June 26, 1875, p. 7. Brief biographical sketch.

Obituary. *New York Herald*, June 26, 1875, p. 10. A biographical sketch and laudatory appraisal of Thomson's stature as a humorist.

Slater, Fletcher D. "The Life and Letters of Mortimer Thomson." M.A. thesis, Northwestern University, 1931. This thoroughly researched thesis provides the most comprehensive treatment of Thomson and his work yet to appear.

Sloane, David E.E. "Mortimer Thomson (Q.K. Philander Doesticks, P.B.)." In *Dictionary of Literary Biography*. Vol. 11. *American Humorists, 1800-1950*. Ed. Stanley Trachtenberg. Detroit: Gale, 1982, pp. 491–497. An engaging critical essay on Thomson's life and art.

Edward J. Piacentino

Thorpe, Thomas Bangs

Born: Westfield, Massachusetts, on March 1, 1815

Education: Wesleyan University, Middletown, Connecticut, 1834–1836; awarded an honorary M.A. degree by that school, 1847

Marriages: Anne Maria Hinckley, probably 1838, widowed, 1855, three children; Jane Fosdick, 1857, one child

Died: September 20, 1878

Biography

Born March 1, 1815, at Westfield, Massachusetts, Thomas Bangs Thorpe was of English descent.[1] His ancestors settled in Connecticut sometime before 1639. His father, a circuit-riding Methodist minister in Connecticut and Massachusetts, died at an early age. After his father's death, Thorpe resided as a young man in Albany and in New York City. In this latter city, under the tutelage of John Quidor, he studied painting, a field that he pursued intermittently throughout his life. Thorpe attended Wesleyan University in Middletown, Connecticut, from 1834 to 1836, when he withdrew because of poor health. At the urging of some college friends from the South, he travelled to Louisiana for a period of recuperation and made that state his home for most of the time from 1837 to 1854.

Thorpe married Anne Maria Hinckley of Maine soon after his move to Louisiana. He struggled financially at first, apparently earning a living by painting portraits for wealthy plantation owners. In July 1839, he published his first literary work, "Tom Owen, the Bee-Hunter," in the popular sporting paper the New York *Spirit of the Times*. This comic character sketch was reprinted widely by other newspapers of the day, and it inaugurated a successful writing career of nearly forty years for Thorpe, during which he published a total of six books, as well as over 150 stories, essays, and editorial pieces in many distinguished American magazines and in newspapers. From 1843 to 1847, he owned, edited, or worked for at least five newspapers, three of them in New Orleans. During the Mexican War, Thorpe secured a temporary commission as a colonel of the Louisiana Volunteers and journeyed to the war scene, where he collected material for future non-fiction writings. Subsequently, he became involved in Whig politics and waged an unsuccessful campaign for a state office in Louisiana in 1854.

Thorpe moved back to New York that year, where he devoted most of his time to writing and painting. His wife died the following year, leaving him a widower with one son and two daughters. In the fall of 1857, he became a member of the editorial staff of *Frank Leslie's Illustrated Newspaper* and took another wife, Jane Fosdick of New York, by whom he would have a daughter. From 1858 to 1862, Thorpe served as a clerk in the New York Custom House, but during this period he also practiced law briefly, after qualifying through an examination, and became a part-owner and coeditor of *The Spirit of the Times* for two years.

Following the conquest of New Orleans by Union forces during the Civil War, in June 1862, Thorpe transferred from the New York Custom House to become a customs officer there. After only two weeks in this position, he received an appointment as Surveyor of the new city government. In implementing a program devised by the area commander, Thorpe distinguished himself in bringing relief to the defeated New Orleans populace. From 1864 to 1866, he held another position in the New Orleans Custom House and turned to Republican political activity. Little is known about his life for the next few years, but by 1869 he had returned to New York and taken a position as a clerk in the Custom House there. He continued to work in various positions with that agency for the remainder of his life, although he apparently resigned from a job as weigher in December 1877, under threat of firing for alleged shady business transactions. During these Custom House years, he resumed writing literary works for national magazines, mainly essays concerning natural history and art. Thorpe died on September 20, 1878, as a result of Bright's disease.

Literary Analysis

Thomas Bangs Thorpe is usually associated today with the humorists of the Old Southwest, a group of writers of comic and realistic backwoods stories who produced most of their literature from 1835 to 1860. His one masterpiece, "The Big Bear of Arkansas," is the most famous story created by these writers and is primarily responsible for Thorpe's literary reputation today. However, his early training as an artist and his educational background seemed to equip him much better for serious expository writing than for humorous short fiction. He published a prodigious number of essays during his lifetime but only a relatively few stories of a purely comic vein. Some of Thorpe's sketches display a stilted prose style and a sentimental tone more typical of the popular romantic literature of his day than of the southern humorists' writings, which emphasized comic realism and often made use of vernacular speech.

Thorpe's body of work includes two collections of stories in the southwestern humor tradition—*The Mysteries of the Backwoods* (1846) and *The Hive of 'The Bee-Hunter'* (1854); an undistinguished novel (written under the pseudonym "Logan") titled *The Master's House; A Tale of Southern Life* (1854); and three nonfiction books resulting from his brief exposure to the Mexican War—*Our Army on the Rio Grande* (1846), *Our Army at Monterey* (1847), and *The Taylor Anecdote Book* (1848).

His best writing is contained in *The Hive of 'The Bee-Hunter,'* described in the full title of the book as "A Repository of Sketches, Including Peculiar American Character, Scenery, and Rural Sports." The volume is composed of twenty-four sketches (including 13 of the 16 selections published in the earlier *Mysteries of the Backwoods*), among which are his most famous backwoods humor pieces. In the preface Thorpe stated that the two main goals of the volume were "to give to those personally unacquainted with the scenery of the southwest, some idea of the country, its surface, and vegetation,"[2] as well as to describe "the great original characters national to these localities,"[3] characters "truly American."[4]

In "Tom Owen, the Bee-Hunter," his most widely published sketch in his own day, Thorpe achieved these goals. This comic character study described real-life Louisiana backwoodsman Owen. Tom's profession of "topping trees" was a truly dangerous one, but Thorpe perceived the comic possibilities by emphasizing instead Tom's favorite pastime of "hunting" bees for their honey. Thorpe employed a mock-heroic tone throughout the sketch in describing the "courageous" backwoodsman and his fierce "battle" with the bees. While the character and setting are distinctly southern, the style is more reminiscent of Washington Irving, whose *Sketch Book* and *Knickerbocker's History* Thorpe reportedly admired greatly as a youth. Thus, "Tom Owen, the Bee-Hunter" stands as an important transition piece bridging the genteel humor of early nineteenth-century America and the later more realistic, racy type of humor promoted by the humorists of the Old Southwest such as George Washington Harris.

The *Hive of 'The Bee-Hunter'* also contains "The Big Bear of Arkansas," published originally in *The Spirit of the Times* in March 1841. This story is generally considered the best single short work produced by the southwestern humorists. It served as the title story for the first anthology of humor in this tradition, *The Big Bear of Arkansas, and Other Sketches* (1845), compiled by William T. Porter, the editor of *The Spirit of the Times.*

The plot of "The Big Bear of Arkansas" is a simple one, but the story is richly layered with symbol, myth, and sophisticated literary techniques. The passengers aboard the steamboat *Invincible,* in traveling up the Mississippi River from New Orleans, are entertained with a tale told by a fellow passenger, Jim Doggett, a backwoodsman of the ring-tailed-roarer variety. In prefatory remarks to the yarn proper, Doggett uses exaggeration in describing Arkansas as the "creation State," where the land is so fertile that corn can shoot up full-grown overnight and the smallest wild turkeys can weigh forty pounds. Doggett's story focuses on a particular bear that he hunted in his home state once, a huge "creation bear" that eludes him on several occasions, seemingly through superior cunning, until it *chooses* to die at his hands.

Most literary critics have viewed the backwoods life described in the story as an Eden-like environment from which man—represented by the hunter Doggett—is destined to fall.[5] The killing of the "unhuntable" bear is usually seen symbolically as the passing of the wilderness, a microcosmic action that foretold what would occur all across America in the years following, as the forces of civilization confronted those of the frontier.

The structure and style of "The Big Bear of Arkansas" are noteworthy also. In the sketch Thorpe offers a "story within a story," framing Doggett's yarn within introductory and concluding commentary by another steamboat passenger, an unnamed gentleman narrator whose polished speech contrasts sharply with the backwoods vernacular employed by Doggett. Much of the humor of the story comes from incongruities within it, the most prominent being the contrast in language of the two characters and the contrast between the realistic setting of the steamboat described by the gentleman narrator and the fantasy setting of Arkansas described by Doggett.

The theme of "The Big Bear of Arkansas"— the passing of the wilderness from the American scene—reflects Thorpe's ecological concerns as expressed in other sketches in the *Hive of 'The Bee-Hunter.'* For instance, in the essays "Wild Turkey Hunting," "Alligator Killing," and "Buffalo Hunting," he laments, through brief didactic comments, the thinning out of these species as men advanced into their habitats. Ironically, in these sketches and in others in the *Hive* volume, at the same time that he is decrying the destruction of wildlife and the environment by man, Thorpe offers specific advice to sportsmen in their hunting ventures. For example, in "Wild Turkey Hunting," he tells how to make an effective turkey-caller; in "Summer Retreat in Arkansas" and "Grizzly Bear-Hunting," he describes where to place a shot to be assured of killing rather than wounding a bear; and in "Arrow-Fishing," he discusses how to detect fish below the surface of the water and how to use a bow and arrow in killing them.

The stories and essays in the *Hive of 'The Bee-Hunter'* reveal Thorpe's ambivalent attitude in trying to define the American character: he clearly admired the remarkable self-reliance and resourcefulness that the backwoodsmen and first settlers of an area demonstrated, but he recognized that communities of men could dilute or pervert such values in the name of progress. In "The Mississippi," Thorpe noted that aspects of nature, whether in the form of the Mississippi River or the forests lining its banks, could teach "lessons of strength and sublimity," lessons that were lost as civilization advanced and nature retreated. His reservations about the American character and the consequences for the country's future are expressed in the last sketch of the volume, "The Way That Americans Go Down Hill," in which he contrasts the European and the American character.

Another interesting element of the *Hive* sketches is Thorpe's attitude toward the Indians, who were being displaced by the inexorable westward movement of white society. While reminding the reader occasionally of the savage nature of some of them, Thorpe for the most part depicts the Indians sympathetically. In "Place de La Croix" a dying white man lost in the wilderness is nursed back to health by a kind Indian maiden (though he ultimately loses his life at the hands of her jealous suitor). In "Mike Fink, the Keel Boatman" (titled "The Disgraced Scalp-Lock" in the *Mysteries of the Backwoods*), even a renegade Indian scorned by his tribe is shown by Thorpe to possess an admirable code of conduct requiring him to endure many hardships in order to avenge his humiliation at having his scalp-lock shot off by Mike Fink. And, in "Familiar Scenes on the Mississippi," in describing an incident that he witnessed involving the harsh treatment of four hundred Seminoles, Thorpe makes clear his disdain for the forced removal of Indians from their homes to territories west of the Mississippi by the U.S. government.

There is one other notable production by Thorpe in addition to the *Hive* and the *Mysteries* volumes. From August 1843 to February 1844, when he was editing the *Concordia* (Louisiana) *Intelligencer*, Thorpe published a delightful series of twelve letters burlesquing Matthew C. Field's reports in the New Orleans *Picayune* of a five-month hunting expedition in the Rocky Mountains. Field had accompanied the Scottish sportsman Sir William Drummond Stewart on the expedition; his *Picayune* letters offered an idealized view of their western experience. Thorpe's "Letters from the Far West" mainly satirize the romantic notions of "sport" in the West by having the narrator "Little Woeful" recount his activities on the hunting trip. Woeful, a "green" sportsman, has difficulty even staying astride his horse and encounters trouble at every turn in his adventures. In addition to ridiculing the inexperienced sportsman, Thorpe's series satirizes aspects of earlier travel and sporting literature such as romantic metaphors in descriptions, prairie artifact collecting, eastern views of Indians, and "marvelous" animals and hunts. Illustrative of this last category is an episode in which a buffalo's carcass rolls down a hill, impales two wolves on its horns, and crushes a buzzard so flat that its remains are wafted away by a breeze. Thorpe also satirizes James Audubon and natural history enthusiasts who viewed western wildlife from what he considered an overly intellectual stance. The "Letters from the Far West" were reprinted by many newspapers across the country, a number of which did not recognize the satiric intent.

Summary

Thomas Bangs Thorpe (1815–1878) is truly an American literary phenomenon. There was little evidence in his early years that he would become an established southern humorist in his own day or would gain lasting fame for such work in the future. He published his first short story in 1839, "Tom Owen, the Bee-Hunter," that became one of the most popular works ever published by *The Spirit of the Times* and started Thorpe on a literary career that spanned nearly forty years, during which time he published six books (three of them non-fiction works), as well as numerous essays, hunting sketches, and comic backwoods stories in such distinguished magazines as *Harper's* and *Graham's*. Thorpe's reputation today as a humorist may be attributed mainly to one story, "The Big Bear of Arkansas," the most famous and most frequently anthologized story of the humorists of the Old Southwest.

Notes

1. All biographical information for this study is from Milton Rickels, *Thomas Bangs Thorpe: Humorist of the Old Southwest* (Baton Rouge: Louisiana State University Press, 1962), and Stanton Garner, "Thomas Bangs Thorpe in the Gilded Age: Shifty in a New Country," *Mississippi Quarterly*, 36 (Winter 1982–1983): 35–52.
2. *The Hive of the 'The Bee-Hunter,' A Repository of Sketches, Including Peculiar American Character, Scenery, and Rural Sports* (New York: D. Appleton & Co., 1854), p. 5.
3. Ibid.
4. Ibid., p. 6.
5. The sources for critical approaches to the themes and techniques in this story and in Thorpe's other works are given in the annotated bibliography that follows.

Selected Bibliography

Primary Sources

Books

The Mysteries of the Backwoods; or Sketches of the Southwest: Including Character, Scenery, and Rural Sports. Philadelphia: Carey and Hart, 1846.

The Hive of "The Bee-Hunter," A Repository of Sketches, Including Peculiar American Character, Scenery, and Rural Sports. New York: D. Appleton, 1854.

Articles

"Letters from the Far West." A series of twelve letters published originally in the *Concordia* (Louisiana) *Intelligencer* during the period from August 1843 to February 1844. Collected, edited, and reprinted by Leland H. Cox, Jr., in *Gyascutus: Studies in Antebellum Southern Humorous and Sporting Writing*, ed. James L.W. West, III. *Costerus*, N.S., Vol. 5–6. (Atlantic Highlands, N.J.: Humanities Press, Inc., 1978), pp. 115–158.

Secondary Sources

Books

Cohen, Hennig, and William B. Dillingham, eds. *Humor of the Old Southwest*. Athens, Ga.: University of Georgia Press, 1975. The introduction gives a helpful, concise overview of the literature in this tradition. Reprints three of Thorpe's stories, including "The Big Bear of Arkansas."

Rickels, Milton. *Thomas Bangs Thorpe: Humorist of the Old Southwest*. Baton Rouge: Louisiana State University Press, 1962. A first-rate biography and critical study by one of America's foremost humor specialists. Also provides an extensive bibliography of Thorpe's writings.

Articles

Blair, Walter. "The Technique of 'The Big Bear of Arkansas.'" *Southwest Review*, 28 (1943): 426–435. A seminal study of Thorpe's rhetorical techniques in the story.

Cox, Leland H., Jr. "T.B. Thorpe's Far West Letters." In *Gyascutus: Studies in Antebellum Southern Humorous and Sporting Writing*. Ed. James L.W. West, III. *Costerus*, N.S., Vol. 5–6. Atlantic Highlands, N.J.: Humanities Press, Inc., 1978, pp. 115–158. Introduces, edits, and reprints these letters.

Garner, Stanton. "Thomas Bangs Thorpe in the Gilded Age: Shifty in a New Country." *Mississippi Quarterly*, 36 (Winter 1982–1983): 35–52. Provides much new information about Thorpe's career after 1858, with an emphasis on his shady dealings as an employee of the New York Custom House.

Keller, Mark A. "T.B. Thorpe's 'Tom Owen, The Bee-Hunter': Southwestern Humor's 'Origin of Species.'" *Southern Studies: An Interdisciplinary Journal of the South*, 18 (1979): 89–101. Assesses the significance of this sketch in the history of American humor and discusses the role it played in the success of the New York *Spirit of the Times*. Also reprints an 1859 article by Thorpe that gives biographical information about the Louisiana backwoodsman Tom Owen.

Lemay, J. A. Leo. "The Text, Tradition, and Themes of 'The Big Bear of Arkansas.'" *American Literature*, 47 (1975): 321–342. A potpourri of information about the story. Contrasts the three texts, relates the story to colonial promotion tracts, reviews motifs, symbols, and mythical elements in it, and offers an extended interpretation.

Littlefield, Daniel F., Jr. "Thomas Bangs Thorpe and the Passing of the Southwestern Wilderness." *Southern Literary Journal*, 11 (1979): 56–65. Offers a thorough examination of Thorpe's ecological concerns.

Simoneaux, Katherine G. "Symbolism in Thorpe's 'The Big Bear of Arkansas.'" *Arkansas Historical Quarterly*, 25 (1966): 240–247. Presents the standard view that the death of the bear symbolizes the passing of the frontier from the American scene.

Mark A. Keller

Thurber, James Grover

Born: Columbus, Ohio, on December 8, 1894

Education: Ohio State University, 1913–1918 (no degree)

Marriages: Althea Adams, May 20, 1922, divorced, 1935, one child; Helen Wismer, June 25, 1935

Died: November 2, 1961

Biography

Thurber, christened James Grover, was born December 8, 1894, in Columbus, Ohio. His parents were Mary Fisher and Charles L. Thurber. In 1901 the family moved to Washington, D.C., and it was there that Thurber suffered the eye injury that instantly destroyed vision in his left eye and was later to cause his total blindness. He and his brother, William, were playing a modified game of "William Tell." In turn each faced away from the direction of the shooter with an object on his head. William took a long time getting ready and Thurber turned around just in time to be hit in the left eye by the arrow.

In 1903 the family returned to Columbus where Thurber eventually became a student at Ohio State University, which he entered in 1913. He made his difficulties with focusing a microscope and learning to drill with the R.O.T.C. a part of the national culture in his quasi-autobiographical essay entitled "University Days." At Ohio State Thurber met Elliott Nugent, with whom he later collaborated on the play *The Male Animal* (1940). Thurber blossomed under the tutelage of Nugent, who introduced him to campus activities including pledging him to a fraternity. From an eccentric and unnoticed student, Thurber became active in numerous campus organizations. He wrote for the campus paper and the magazine and was active in drama until his college career ended in 1918 without his completing the requirements for a degree.

Briefly, he worked for the United States State Department as a code clerk, first in Washington, D.C., and then in Paris. Because Thurber used his own experiences, exaggerated for comic purposes, in much of his writing, it is difficult to separate fact from fiction, but he claimed that the Paris office of the State Department had merely asked for forty code books and was considerably surprised when they received forty clerks instead. In 1920 he was back in Columbus where he worked as a reporter for the *Dispatch*. On May 20, 1922, he married Althea Adams, whom he had met at Ohio State University, and with whom he was to have a daughter, Rosemary. After unsuccessfully attempting to do free-lance writing as a means of earning his livelihood, he took on several newspaper jobs, including one in France for the Paris edition of the *Chicago Tribune*.

In 1926 he was back in the United States; Althea had elected to remain in France, thus presaging the difficulties that would later end this marriage. Thurber settled in New York City where he started as a reporter for the *New York Evening Post*. The next year he began work as an editor for *The New Yorker*, which had begun publication under the general editorship of Harold Ross. Apparently because Thurber mentioned the name of E.B. White, Ross got the idea that they were old friends although they had just met. Ross immediately appointed Thurber to the post of editor. This experience and the difficulties resulting from such an inappropriate assignment were later explored by Thurber in his book *The Years with Ross* (1959).

Thurber's first book, *Is Sex Necessary?* was written in collaboration with E.B. White and appeared in 1929. Thurber had been relieved of his duties as editor, a job for which he was ill suited, and had found his real strength in writing the casual essays and stories in a light ironical tone for which *The New Yorker* was to become famous. His book was a spoof of the self-help and marriage counseling books that were proliferating in American publishing at this time. By 1931 his cartoons and drawings began to appear in *The New Yorker*, rescued, so the legend goes, from the wastepaper basket by his collaborator and colleague at *The New Yorker*, White. At first Ross could not believe that the crude drawings were to be taken seriously or used in the form that Thurber left them. He was finally persuaded to publish them after similar drawings had been published by Harper in *Is Sex Necessary?*

In 1935 Thurber divorced Althea (the marriage had been a troubled one since their days in France and there had been a lengthy separation) and on June 25 he married Helen Muriel Wismer. In the same year he gave up his staff job with *The New Yorker* for free-lance writing. His short pieces of writing and his drawings continued to appear in *The New Yorker* and in other periodicals. In addition, collections were issued from time to time in book form. During his career, he published some twenty-eight books, largely made up of previously published work but sometimes with new material added. His play *The Male Animal* and several of his short stories were produced as motion pictures; they included "The Secret Life of Walter Mitty," "The Unicorn in the Garden," and "The Catbird Seat" (which was retitled *The Battle of the Sexes* when it was translated into a motion picture).

Thurber received many honors during his later lifetime, including honorary doctoral degrees from Kenyon College, Williams College, and Yale University; he declined to accept a doctorate from Ohio State University in 1951 because he felt that the trustees were not protecting academic freedom from McCarthy-era restraints. He gave one-man shows of his drawings and received numerous awards for both his writing and his drawing.

As his sight continued to worsen, Thurber tried various devices intended to permit him to continue to draw his famous nondescript dogs, stern women, and intimidated men. In 1951 his sight failed almost entirely and he was forced to give up drawing, though he continued to write and to publish books over the following ten years. Thurber collapsed on October 4, 1961, as a result of a stroke. He had surgery for a blood clot on the brain, and after four weeks he died from pneumonia on November 2, 1961, in New York City.

Literary Analysis

Thurber's contribution as one of America's great humorists began with his work in establishing the manner and tone of the "Talk of the Town" section of *The New Yorker*, a task he shared with several other writers including E.B. White and Robert Benchley. He received recognition with the publication of his first two books, *Is Sex Necessary?* and *The Owl in the Attic* (1931). After Thurber's drawings were used as illustrations in his book, *Is Sex Necessary?*, they became a regular feature in *The New Yorker*, and he became as well-known for his drawings as for his writing.

His second book, *The Owl in the Attic*, consisted of the eight Mr. and Mrs. Monroe stories, the Pet Department (reprinted from a regular feature of *The New Yorker* which was a comic spoof of question-and-answer columns in the newspapers), and the "Guide to Modern English Usage," a parody of writing manuals. The Monroe series introduced several central Thurber characters and themes. Mr. Monroe was typical of the bewildered and frustrated "little" man from whose unfocused perceptions much of the later Thurber was developed. This figure was in sharp contrast with earlier characters developed in American humor. He lacked the gusto and exuberance of the tellers of tall tales and the frontier braggarts of nineteenth-century humorists. The "little" man was clearly timid and unsure where his predecessors were brash and confident. The figures in earlier humor dealt comically with the most serious issues—hardship, sexuality, and death; Thurber's characters seemed overwhelmed by trivial concerns. In his "Preface" to *My Life and Hard Times* (1933), Thurber says of the persona of the humorist that

> [h]is gestures are the ludicrous reflexes of the maladjusted; his repose is the momentary inertia of the nonplussed. He pulls the blinds against the morning and creeps into smokey corners at night. He talks largely about small matters and smally about great affairs. His ears are shut to the ominous rumblings of the dynasties of the world moving toward a cloudier chaos than ever before, but he hears with an acute perception the startling sounds that rabbits make twisting in the bushes along a country road at night.

The Monroe stories were all based on actual incidents that had happened to Thurber and his former wife Althea, in keeping with his practice of making humor out of exaggerated versions of his own experience. Mr. Monroe was an impractical dreamer married to the prototypical Thurber wife, a confident and practical realist who was always contemptuous of her incompetent and dreamy mate. Similar characters peopled the stories and essays that followed and they identify the major conflicts—the battle of the sexes, the clash of romantic idealism with cold reality, and the inability of comic males to cope with machinery and other complexities of modern living.

Between 1932 and 1935, Thurber published *My Life and Hard Times, The Seal in the Bedroom,* and *The Middle-Aged Man on The Flying Trapeze.* Collections, mainly of *The New Yorker* pieces, these books were based on his memories of growing up in Columbus with a family reputedly already eccentric, but whose adventures were enhanced and exaggerated for comic effect. Some of his best-known and most popular pieces were presented in the format of a Thurber-like narrator who recounted his experiences with a mother given to practical jokes, a grandfather who often confused the time in which he was living with his Civil War past, and aunts and uncles with their own peculiarities as well. These sketches had a flavor of turn-of-the-century, mid-western life and were often bittersweet below the comic events of the surface in that life moved unpredictably and the characters were often seriously out of touch with the contemporary world.

During his long association with *The New Yorker* magazine, Thurber worked with and became friends with some of the brightest and wittiest of twentieth-century American writers. The humor of Thurber, under Ross's watchful eye and ever active blue pencil, was most often in the form of a short piece of informal writing that Ross termed a "casual." Both Thurber and White constantly feared that the pieces that they were currently working on had already been done better by Robert Benchley. The narrator or spokesman was generally a middle-aged, middleclass white collar worker insufficiently equipped to cope with the complications of a technological civilization. The figure was often characterized as "the little man," a person victimized by salesmen, executives, and by his own family—especially his wife. He was a bungler, a dreamy impractical character who was frustrated both by mechanical devices, bureaucratic regulations, and the commonplace duties necessary for getting through the day, and by natural phenomena—particularly when this urban person attempted some rural pursuit. For instance, in Thurber's sketch, "University Days," the narrator was unable to focus a microscope properly in biology class and ended up drawing his own eye. Thurber's short stories followed a pattern that condemned the perplexed little man to defeat as he encountered everyday experiences; the most famous example is that of "The Secret Life of Walter Mitty." The fame of this story is attested to by an anecdote about two American pilots each unknown to the other who were flying their respective planes when one pilot began to murmur into his open microphone the famous tag-line from Mitty's day-dream life, "ta-pocketa pocketa" and the other promptly responded, "Come in, Walter Mitty." Only in a few stories ("The Catbird Seat" and "The Unicorn in the Garden" are examples) was the little man able to reverse the situation and triumph over a female tormentor and then only by shifting his own insanity to his antagonist.

Thurber's characteristic manner can be seen

in "The Dog That Bit People," which first appeared in his book *My Life and Hard Times*. The piece begins typically with the first person narrator, a strangely inept and confused man, talking about a matter that purports to be a bit of autobiography. The dog that bit people was an "Airedale named Muggs" who has given the narrator more trouble than any other of the fifty-four or fifty-five dogs that he has owned put together. The first paragraph turns to a digression, never completed, about a "Scotch terrier named Jeannie, who had just had four puppies in the shoe closet of a fourth-floor apartment in New York, had the fifth and last at the corner of—" Here the account breaks off, but not before Thurber has recounted the event with a specificity more appropriate to testimony in a murder trial than to a whelping. The inappropriate use of language leads the reader to a recognition of the comic loss of dignity stemming from an inescapable triviality.

Thurber takes an ordinary situation and by treating it with mock seriousness, imposing an arcane vocabulary, and indicating the involvement bordering on obsession by his speaker, transforms it into a ludicrous scene. The situation includes more or less eccentric relatives and neighbors who seem strangely unaware that their behavior violates community norms. Certain recognizable commonplace reactions or phrases tend to place the bizarre behavior of Thurber's participants in a down-to-earth ambience belied by what is actually going on. His "mother," for instance, says of Muggs that he was always sorry after he bit someone, though the narrator cannot fathom the grounds for this belief since the dog never appears to be sorry. Several devices are utilized in this account: the use of a cliché to excuse the vicious behavior of the dog, for instance, and the suggestion that dogs do not only experience the feeling of sorrow, but have the means of expressing it—all expressed in a matter-of-fact tone that in itself is an assertion of validity.

The narrator continues to use the device of over-specificity, not very helpfully telling the reader that "old Major Moberly fired at him [Muggs] once with his service revolver near the Seneca Hotel in East Broad Street." He then proceeds by association, apparently random, to describe scenes in which the dog "moodily chewed up the morning paper," "bit a congressman who had called to see my father on business," and the "time my mother went to the Chittenden Hotel to call on a woman mental healer who was lecturing . . . on the subject of 'Harmonious Vibrations.'" Muggs manages to defeat each attempt to control his biting, but the attempts are obviously self-defeating. The congressman was not to be trusted because "he was

Saturn with the moon in Virgo," and the bitten iceman has failed because he *thought* the dog would bite him, thus spoiling the vibrations.

Sometimes the humor arises from an arcane reference. In "The Dog That Bit People" the narrator reports with his customary dead-pan manner that "my mother's Uncle Horatio boasted that he was the third man up Missionary Ridge." The upshot of Uncle Horatio's involvement with the dog is that he, too, is defeated, but the narrator adds that if Horatio had had Muggs to contend with, he might have been the first man up Missionary Ridge. The situation becomes extreme, the chaos created by the dog spreads until neither the garbage man, the iceman, nor the laundryman will come near the house, and the narrator's mother has been forced to employ a sheet of metal to create the sound of thunder, which brings the dog cowering into the house.

The death of Muggs leads to more inappropriate behavior. Mother wants to bury him in the family plot with an inscription such as "Flights of angels sing thee to thy rest," but is persuaded to drop the idea. The narrator gets his final revenge by putting a board over a remote grave which reads, "*Cave Canem.*" He reports that "Mother was quite pleased with the simple, classic dignity of the old Latin epitaph." Just as do the other parts of the piece, the ending imparts an almost legendary (though comic) quality to the career of Muggs, but it also portrays a family and surroundings in which the trivial overcomes more significant concerns and finally spreads chaos in an ever-widening circle. Echoes of familiar lines or phrases place the events in a context that is bizarre but strangely evocative of reality. While few of Thurber's readers might put up with the long-term predations of a Muggs, all have been close enough to the ludicrous dominance of some trivial matter for the essay to effect recognition. There are other stylistic devices in Thurber's pieces, from pure nonsense to non-sequiturs, but they, too, share with "The Dog That Bit People" the ability to make his audience feel that control is limited and that often in commonplace events there lurks a malign spirit that threatens human dignity.

Thurber's gift for pure nonsense can be seen in the essay "How to Name a Dog," in which he claims that "[n]ames of dogs end up in 176th place in the list of things that amaze and fascinate me," although he will spend several thousand words on the topic in this essay. He refers to "canine cognomens" and discusses several varieties, citing examples as he goes including a "roving Airedale named Marco Polo, . . . and a Peke named Darien, . . . and "Poker, alias *Fantome Noir*," who was entered in the American Kennel Club. The owners' youngest child wanted to know, "if he belongs to that club, why doesn't he ever go there?" The narrator speaks of the resulting nervous crack-up of a seeing-eye dog when his owner regained his sight. Thurber uses an occasional misapplied metaphor in creating the comic confusion of his pieces as, for instance, when "names of dogs . . . have a range almost as wide as that of the violin." He comments on the category "Cynical" in the naming of dogs, citing Mussolini, Tojo, and Adolf. The "Coy" category he illustrates with Bubbles, Twinkies, and Sugarkins. A sub-branch of "Coy" consists of names selected by self-styled "Wits" who characteristically own two dogs and give them names like Pitter and Patter, Willy and Nilly, or Pro and Connie. Thurber's narrator never gets around to indicating how to name a dog, and the piece ends with a rambling anecdote about a dog named Christabel.

In "A Snapshot of Rex" the same narrator remembers a dog that he owned in his youth, an "American" bull terrier of legendary strength and fighting ability. The anecdotes of Rex are indicative not only of the persistence of the dog in his activities but also of the affection entertained for him by the youth, now remembered by a middle-aged speaker. The events and feelings of the past era are treated with gentle humor, not patronization, and a sense of poignancy is created by the report of the death of the dog. The tone is subdued and while the comic possibilities of the situation are exploited there is no sense of burlesque; the feelings of the boy are illustrated, not sentimentalized. This tone was one that Thurber often achieved in his *New Yorker* pieces and is fully as characteristic as the befuddlement of the narrator in an uncontrollable, but folly-laden circumstance that is his manner in the best-known works.

Thurber's drawings, rescued from the wastepaper basket for publication, came to illustrate his books as well as the pages of *The New Yorker*. It is a commonplace description in American conversation to refer to a "Thurber" dog or man, so familiar have his line drawings become. The manner of the drawings is cartoon-like and they are not filled in but consist of an outline of broad strokes that lend a fanciful unreality to the situations depicted. The well-known Thurber dog has the body of a bassett and the head of a blood hound. Thurber's male figures are harassed and timid and usually smaller than his females. The latter often appear both purposeful and forbidding; they are shapeless, except for an occasional siren (who is equally, though for different reasons, terrifying to the Thurber man). Many of the drawings have a surreal quality that is established by the bizarre juxtaposition of incongruous but recognizable items. The title *The Seal in the Bedroom*

derives from a Thurber drawing that shows a man and woman in bed; above the headboard is the emerging upper half of a seal. The woman is saying: "All right, have it your way—you heard a seal bark." Neither the males nor females in the drawings are particularly attractive; they appear bemused or fixed in special problems or attitudes that an outsider would hesitate to intrude upon. Thurber's animals, however, often have an appealing innocence and lovableness about them that is uncharacteristic of his human beings.

While the ironic overtones of Thurber's writing (and sometimes his drawings) often contribute to the sense of a mild satire against a technological civilization and its inevitable frustrations, he is generally more interested in the resulting humor than in social commentary. An exception to the rule can be found in the play *The Male Animal*. Here there are two plots, one involving a possible rival for the wife of a college professor and the other involving the professor's reading Sacco's "Letter to the Court" to a class. The first plot is an adaptation of a convention of romantic comedy and concerns itself with a typical conflict; there are rivals for the lady's favor, one obviously extremely masculine and the other a mild-mannered English professor. The second plot explores the question of academic freedom and the different kind of courage that it took to persist in reading the letter to a class despite the threat of being fired.

Thurber wrote two collections of pieces in the tradition of Aesop and La Fontaine, *Fables for Our Time* (1940) and *Further Fables for Our Time* (1956). They are parodies of the earlier fables in that they have a witty rather than an appropriate moral, but they also serve as fables through an implied moral arising from their structure. The familiar form of the fable—an animal story intended to illuminate human behavior—is present in Thurber's tales which in addition are characterized by elaborate wordplay and gentle irony. In keeping with the tone established by *The New Yorker*, from which these fables were reprinted, the emphasis of the writing is on wit rather than morality. The wry turn of the inappropriate moral at the end of the fable redirects the reader's attention to the real observation that Thurber wishes to make. (This pattern of the somewhat askew moral at the end of a comic fable had been established by George Ade, an earlier humorous writer.)

During his writing career, Thurber also produced five books ostensibly for children; however, these volumes have a charm and wittiness about them that appeals to adults without lessening their appropriateness for children. As he does in the fables, Thurber means for each of his books to tell a story while at the same time demonstrating a dilemma of contemporary life. Comic incongruity is achieved through depiction of situations and settings of the traditional Romance, told in the language and reflecting the attitudes of the twentieth century. Phraseology used by the characters makes them figures in a Romance as well as characters from the present. Two themes running through all five books are the failure of power and scientific knowledge to satisfy the needs of mankind and the saving grace that comes from love and imagination. The stores are stylistically mixed as Thurber's characteristic wordplay intermingles with passages of lyrical beauty.

In most of his later collections, including *The Thurber Album* (1952), *Thurber Country* (1953), *Alarms and Diversions* (1957), *Lanterns and Lances* (1961), and *Credos and Curios* (1962), Thurber continued to develop themes introduced in his earlier books. As his eyesight failed and his health deteriorated, his wit and comic sense remained, but they were tempered by an emerging despair not characteristic of his previous works. It is true that on occasion he was capable of a mordant drawing such as the one showing people hurrying past a cemetery with the simple caption, "Destinations." At times his feeling that the present generation was not worthy of an ideal past (which Thurber placed at the turn of the century) led him to overt statement rather than irony. Some of his later pieces are dominated by a melancholy that had remained peripheral or subdued in earlier writing; they express his sense of an American civilization diminished by a lack of the individualism of the earlier period.

Perhaps his delight in the strong eccentrics who peopled the sketches of his youth in Columbus was a part of his interest in describing the career of his long-time boss and friend, Harold Ross. *The Years with Ross* (1959) described Thurber's experiences at *The New Yorker* with particular emphasis on anecdotes that illustrated Ross's character. The series of articles, first published in *The Atlantic Monthly*, showed the struggles that Ross had in establishing *The New Yorker* against what must have seemed impossible odds. Thurber concentrated his attention on presenting Ross as a unique and strong individual who, for all of his eccentricities and limited education, was a genuine hero of his time. The sketches show Ross's often ludicrous encounters with staff members who were creative and clever but undisciplined. In keeping with his role of humorist, Thurber included much that is comic, but his book on Ross also reveals the inner character and personality of its subject.

In his time Thurber wrote in a number of different forms—the play, the sketch, the fable, the short story, the children's book, and the unconventional biographic study of Ross. His output included twenty-eight books and numerous uncollected pieces from a long career in journalism. He produced many drawings that served to illustrate the collections of his work; he has left unforgettable characters including the "Thurber" woman, the unmistakable "Thurber" dog, and the "little" man of which Walter Mitty is the best known example. His humor touches vividly on aspects of modern American life—our encounters with complicated mechanical devices, our frustrations with bureaucratic complexity, and our self-conscious attempts at scientific analysis of our own behavior. His bewildered urban figures, beset by their frustrations with the trivia of getting through the day, are the prototypes for comic characters who have proliferated in movies and television. In Thurber's word they represent a "jumpiness" that characterizes our neurotic, middle-class, middle-brow culture. His social criticism is most often muted and his major goal is to amuse, but underlying the down-trodden little man of his drawings and the complex verbal play in his writing is his conviction of the primacy of the individual and the efficacy of the creative imagination.

Summary

James Grover Thurber was born in Columbus, Ohio, in 1894 and died in New York City in 1961. He enjoyed a long career in journalism during which he wrote for numerous newspapers and was a constant contributor to several magazines, particularly *The New Yorker*. Many of his casual pieces from these sources were collected in twenty-eight bound volumes. He became equally famous for his drawings, for which captions were often supplied by his friend and colleague, E.B. White. He was twice married; as he used the experiences of growing up in Columbus as sources for his writing, he also drew exaggerated accounts of his marital relationships. Many of his works have appeared as motion pictures, including his uncharacteristic venture into social commentary, the play, *The Male Animal*. As much as any other comic writer, he set a new tone in humor in that he was a major contributor to the movement away from the humorous personae of traditional American humor and toward such urban characters as the neurotic "little man" in contemporary writing. Thurber employed an elegant prose style that was often characterized by elaborate wordplay. His fables delight adults and children alike; his sometimes surrealistic drawings can express a zany exuberance for living as well as occasionally expressing a somber commentary on a contemporary dilemma. He was a major American humorist and no description of twentieth-century work in the field can fail to give him a prominent place.

Selected Bibliography

Primary Sources

(with E.B. White.) *Is Sex Necessary?* New York: Harper and Brothers, 1929.

The Owl in the Attic and Other Perplexities. New York: Harper and Brothers, 1931.

The Seal in the Bedroom and Other Predicaments. New York: Harper and Brothers, 1932.

My Life and Hard Times. New York: Harper and Brothers, 1933.

The Middle Aged Man on the Flying Trapeze. New York: Harper and Brothers, 1935.

Let Your Mind Alone! New York: Harper and Brothers, 1937.

The Last Flower. New York: Harper and Brothers, 1939.

Cream of Thurber. London: Hamish Hamilton, 1939.

Fables for Our Time. New York: Harper and Brothers, 1940.

My World and Welcome to It. New York: Harcourt, Brace, 1942.

(with Elliott Nugent.) *The Male Animal.* New York: Random House, 1943.

Many Moons. New York: Harcourt, Brace, 1943.

Men, Women, and Dogs. New York: Harcourt, Brace, 1943.

The Great Quillow. New York: Harcourt, Brace, 1944.

The White Deer. New York: Harcourt, Brace, 1945.

The Thurber Carnival. New York: Harper and Brothers, 1945.

The Beast in Me and Other Animals. New York: Harcourt, Brace, 1948.

The 13 Clocks. New York: Simon and Schuster, 1950.

The Thurber Album. New York: Simon and Schuster, 1952.

Thurber Country. New York: Simon and Schuster, 1953.

Thurber's Dogs. New York: Simon and Schuster, 1955.

A Thurber Garland. London: Hamish Hamilton, 1955.

Further Fables for Our Time. New York: Simon and Schuster, 1956.

Alarms and Diversions. New York: Harper and Row, 1957.

The Wonderful O. New York: Simon and Schuster, 1957.

The Years With Ross. Boston: Little, Brown, 1959.

Lanterns and Lances. New York: Harper and Brothers, 1961.

Credos and Curios. New York: Harper and Row, 1962.

Selected Letters of James Thurber. Ed. Helen Thurber and Edward Weeks. Boston: Little, Brown, 1981.

Secondary Sources

Bernstein, Burton. *Thurber: A Biography.* New York: Dodd, Mead, 1975. The official biography, which was written with the cooperation of Helen Thurber although she did not approve of everything in the completed book.

Bowden, Edwin T. *James Thurber: A Bibliography.* Columbus, Ohio: Ohio State University Press, 1968. A complete bibliography of Thurber's writings and drawings.

Holmes, Charles S. *The Clocks of Columbus: The Literary Career of James Thurber.* New York: Atheneum, 1972. An analysis of Thurber's work based on an interpretation of his Ohio background.

Kenney, Catherine McGehee. *Thurber's Anatomy of Confusion.* Hamden, Conn.: The Shoe String Press, 1984. Criticism and analysis of Thurber's work.

Morsberger, Robert E. *James Thurber.* New York: Twayne, 1964. Contains details of the life, an analysis of the work, and a bibliography.

Tobias, Richard C. *The Art of James Thurber.* Athens, Ohio: Ohio University Press, 1964. An analysis of the methods Thurber used in creating his humor.

F. William Nelson

Toole, John Kennedy

Born: New Orleans, Louisiana, in December 1937
Education: Tulane University, B.A., 1958; Columbia, M.A., 1959
Died: March 1969

Biography

John Kennedy Toole was born in New Orleans, Louisiana, in December 1937, and spent most of his short life in that city. Something of a child prodigy, he wrote his first novel, *The Neon Bible*, when he was 16. (The book is still unpublished.) His reputation as a humorist rests on his one published work, the massive novel, *A Confederacy of Dunces*, in which he celebrates the rich life of his hometown. The book was published a full decade after Toole's suicide, and he was posthumously awarded the Pulitzer Prize for fiction in 1981.

The rich comedy of *A Confederacy of Dunces* is overshadowed by its author's tragedy. Toole wrote the book from 1962 to 1963, while serving with the United States Army in Puerto Rico. He continued to work on the manuscript after leaving the service, while teaching at Dominican College in New Orleans. Having finished the manuscript, Toole attempted to sell his book to a New York publisher. One publisher showed interest, requested numerous revisions, then decided against publication. Depressed over the rejection of his book, Toole committed suicide by carbon monoxide poisoning in Biloxi, Mississippi, in March 1969.

Thelma Toole, his mother, decided not to rest until she saw her son's book in print. "I've been reading since I was a young girl," Mrs. Toole told *The New York Times.* "I knew John's book was good. When he came back from the Army, he gave it to me and I finished it the next night. It was great, I told him." Mrs. Toole spent the first five years after her son's death mailing the manuscript to publishers and getting it back in the mail. In all, she tried nine houses before she decided to take the book to novelist Walker Percy in 1976.

Percy, author of *The Moviegoer*, was teaching at Loyola University in New Orleans when Mrs. Toole began to pester him. "I began to get telephone calls from a lady unknown to me," Percy wrote in his foreword to *A Confederacy of Dunces*. "What she had proposed was preposterous. It was not that she had written a couple of chapters of a novel and wanted to get into my class. It was that her son, who was dead, had written an entire novel during the early sixties, a big novel, and she wanted me to read it. Why would I want to do that? I asked her. Because it is a great novel, she said."

Percy finally agreed to read the shabby, smudged manuscript. Percy read, "first with the sinking feeling that it was not bad enough to quit, then with a prickle of interest, then a growing excitement, and finally an incredulity: surely it was not possible that it was so good." Percy took a section of the book and had it published in *The New Orleans Review*. When that appeared, he clipped the excerpt and sent it to the Louisiana State University Press, with a note to L.E. Phillabaum, the director, asking if LSU Press would like to consider publishing the whole book. In 1978, the LSU Press had decided to include more fiction in its program, and one of the first manuscripts to arrive after that decision was Toole's.

The initial printing of the book was 2,500 copies. It has since gone through eight printings. The paperback edition was published by Grove Press and the film rights were sold. In addition to the Pulitzer Prize, the book was nominated for the PEN/Faulkner Award and the *Los Angeles Times* Book Award. Acclaim for the book pleased Thelma Toole. "I don't like fame," she said, "but I'm happy for my son."

Literary Analysis

A Confederaccy of Dunces was as good as Walker Percy recognized, but it caught on because of timing. John Irving's *The World According to Garp*, another book with wild, colorful characters and bizarre occurrences, was published in 1978 and was hugely successful. When *A Confederacy of Dunces* was published two years later, reviewers noted the similarity of tone and recommended the book.

The novel tells the story of Ignatius J. Reilly, a character at odds with the modern age. Toole's description of his protagonist in the first paragraph of the novel is characteristic:

> A green hunting cap squeezed the top of the fleshy balloon of a head. The green earflaps, full of large ears and uncut hair and the fine bristles that grew in the

ears themselves, stuck out on either side like turn signals indicating two directions at once. Full, pursed lips protruded beneath the bushy black moustache and, at their corners, sank into little folds filled with disapproval and potato chip crumbs. In the shadow under the green visor of the cap Ignatius J. Reilly's supercilious blue and yellow eyes looked down upon the other people waiting under the clock at the D.H. Holmes department store, studying the crowd of people for signs of bad taste in dress. Several of the outfits, Ignatius noticed, were new enough and expensive enough to be properly considered offenses against taste and decency. Possession of anything new or expensive only reflected a person's lack of theology and geometry; it could even cast doubts upon one's soul.

Toole's colorful New Orleans characters make *A Confederacy of Dunces* a delightful glimpse into a way of life unknown to out-of-towners. In fact, Percy feared it might be *too* special. "I felt it was a book that would only have regional appeal," Percy told the *New York Times*. "Frankly, I was astonished at the national response."

The book was greeted with enthusiastic reviews. Brad Owens, writing in *The Christian Science Monitor*, said, "I am the kind of surly reader who doesn't laugh out loud at books, even at passages I find genuinely funny. I found myself laughing out loud again and again as I read this farcical, ribald book." Phelps Gay, in *The New Republic*, wrote, "[This is,] without question, one of the funniest books ever written. And by funny I don't mean merely witty. I mean that it will make you laugh out loud until your belly aches." Alan Friedman, in *The New York Times*, complained that the "relentless concentration" on hilarious dialogue resulted in pages that read like a TV situation comedy. In the end, though, Friedman admitted that the novel "resists the corrosions of our criticism." He called it "a masterwork of comedy" and "nothing less than a grand comic fugue."

In the end, the story of the book's publication nearly overshadows the wealth of Toole's talent. *The New York Times* noted on the front page of its April 14, 1981, edition: POSTHUMOUS PULITZER GIVEN TO WRITER WHO COULDN'T GET NOVEL PUBLISHED. Toole's story is a tragedy. The story he tells is hilarious.

Summary

A Confederacy of Dunces, by John Kennedy Toole, is a masterwork of modern American humor. Toole committed suicide at age 32 after his novel was rejected by publishers. It was finally published after his relentless mother finally found a champion in novelist Walker Percy. Toole became only the second individual to be awarded the Pulitzer Prize posthumously.

Selected Bibliography

Primary Sources

A Confederacy of Dunces. Baton Rouge: Louisiana State University Press, 1980.

The Neon Bible (unpublished).

Secondary Sources

Friedman, Alan. "A Sad and Funny Story." *The New York Times Book Review*, June 22, 1980, pp. 7, 27.

Gay, Phelps. "Brief Review: 'A Confederacy of Dunces.'" *The New Republic*, 183, no. 3 (July 19, 1980): 34-35.

Kihss, Peter. "Posthumous Pulitzer Given Writer Who Couldn't Get Novel Published." *The New York Times*, April 14, 1981, pp. 1, B5; April 15, 1981.

Owens, Brad. "Farce in a Southern Drawl." *The Christian Science Monitor*, 72, no. 134 (June 4, 1970): 17.

Phillabaum, L.E. *Memo from the Publisher*. Baton Rouge: Louisiana State University Press, 1985.

S., D.B. "Review: 'Sez Who? Sez Me.'" *Harper's*, 265, no. 1590 (November 1982): 76-77.

William McKeen

Trumbull, John

Born: Westbury, Connecticut (near Waterbury, now Watertown), on April 24, (new style) 1750

Education: Yale, B.A., 1767, M.A., 1770; Honorary Doctor of Laws, 1818

Marriage: Sarah Hubbard, November 21, 1776; seven children

Died: May 11, 1831

Biography

Born to an illustrious Connecticut family on April 24, 1750, John Trumbull very early demonstrated an astonishing scholastic precocity. Before he was four he had read the entire Bible, and at age seven, having studied widely in the classics, he passed the entrance examination at Yale, where he matriculated six years later. As both an undergraduate and a graduate student, Trumbull broadened his reading and whetted his poetic skills, experimenting with various verse forms in a number of spirited burlesques that gained him a reputation among his classmates.

Collaborating with Timothy Dwight, a fellow student at Yale, Trumbull also proved his competence in the Addisonian essay, contributing the larger share of the installments in two published series appearing between 1769 and 1773, "The Meddler" and "The Correspondent." After taking the Master of Arts degree at Yale in September of 1770, he endured a bleak year of teaching at Wethersfield, Connecticut, before returning to his alma mater as a tutor. In the two years of his tutorship, Trumbull worked with Dwight, Joseph Howe, David Humphreys, and others in an attempt to reform the Yale curriculum, which in their view slighted English composition, oratory, theater, and modern literature. Trumbull's dissatisfaction with contemporary education was given literary form in his first major poetic effort, *The Progress of Dulness* (published 1722-1773), a three-part satire aimed at the pedantry, irrelevance, and misapplication of conventional higher learning. Shortly after completing the work, Trumbull moved to Boston, Massachusetts, where he studied law with John Adams for a year before returning to practice in New Haven, Connecticut, and later Hartford, until 1825. The British Port Bill, effected while Trumbull was in Boston, prompted him to write *An Elegy on the Times* (1774), a stern but not inflammatory condemnation of British conduct, and the following year, one of growing revolutionary fervor, saw the composition of the anti-Tory first canto of *M'Fingal* (1776), Trumbull's most famous work. Not completed until 1783, the poem, which also satirized Whig excesses, was the most popular American poetic effort until the publication of Henry Wadsworth Longfellow's *Evangeline* in 1847.

On November 21, 1776, the same year that the first canto of *M'Fingal* appeared, the author married Sarah Hubbard; the couple were to have seven children. Although he held a number of public offices and wrote sheaves of political prose, Trumbull is better known among students of literature for his affiliation with a group of luminaries known variously as the Hartford Wits or Connecticut Wits. With three members of this group, David Humphreys, Joel Barlow, and Lemuel Hopkins, Trumbull collaborated in the composition of *The Anarchiad* (1786-1787), a satire attacking democratic liberalism. Devoting more time to judicial and legal matters, Trumbull produced only slight belletristic efforts in the remaining forty years of his life. He died on May 11, 1831.

Literary Analysis

John Trumbull's literary reputation rests chiefly on two satiric poems, *The Progress of Dulness* and *M'Fingal*. Both are written in octosyllabic couplets—"Hudibrastic" verse, so named for Samuel Butler's seventeenth-century satire in the same verse form. In *The Progress of Dulness* Trumbull directed his satire at a conventional system of higher education that inculcated knowledge for its own sake, coddled incompetent students, and failed, in its broader social responsibility, to address the intellectual needs of women. Each of the poem's three parts focuses on a product of this system: Part First concerns Tom Brainless, an accomplished rural dunce; Part Second, Dick Hairbrain, a free-thinking roué; and Part Third, a vacuous flirt, Miss Harriet Simper. Tom, whose father has freed him from farm chores to pursue an education for the ministry, takes his college preparatory instruction from an ignorant clergyman: "So to the priest in form he goes,/ Prepar'd to study and to doze" (I, 33-34). With much labor and much help from his Latin dictionary, Tom gains admission to college, where he often pleads illness to avoid study but nonetheless cultivates "The dulness of a letter'd brain" (I, 126). He learns to despise "English grammar, phrase and style" (I, 128) and joins his fellow students who "Read antient [sic] authors o'er in vain,/ Nor taste one beauty they contain" (I, 131-132). The education that Tom receives neither disciplines his intellect nor refines his powers of communication, and so he graduates a clod:

> Four years at college doz'd away
> In sleep, and slothfulness and play,
> Too dull for vice, with clearest conscience,
> Charg'd with no fault, but that of nonsense . . .
> He passes trial fair, and free,
> And takes in form his first degree.

(I, 231-238)

After a turn at schoolteaching, Tom undertakes to learn "the art of preaching," which involves punditic doctrinal hashing and the development of an obsolete mode of expression unaffected by modern prose style. He is forthwith licensed,

> though his learning be so slight,
> He scarcely knows to spell or write;
> What though his skull be cudgel-proof!
> He's orthodox, and that's enough.

(I, 353-356)

The narrator warns clergymen and educators that such incompetence in the ministry threatens to discredit the profession entirely if measures are not taken to better train its aspirants and purge the dimwits among them. Part First concludes with Tom's halting delivery of a sermon in which he "Deals forth the dulness of the day" (I, 444) and puts his auditors to sleep.

Perhaps in an effort to conciliate those whom his satire had touched in his pointed attack on modern education, Trumbull turned his satire on more conventional types in the final two parts of *The Progress*. A country clown turned city fop, Dick Hairbrain spends his college years cultivating disdain for established religion and improving his card game. He runs with a "mob" of coxcombs who learn "by rote, like studious play'rs,/ The fop's infinity of airs" (II, 343-344), and after he has received his degree *pro meritis* he goes abroad, only to return an even more egregious fop who scoffs at "*College-educations*." Ultimately, Dick's rioting catches up with him, and he sinks into pitiful self-contempt.

Whereas Dick, rather than the educational system, is primarily responsible for making a farce of his college years, society must bear a large share of the responsibility for molding the character of Harriet Simper. A good bit of the satire in Part Third comes at the expense of this stereotypical coquette, but the narrator indicts society as a whole—which holds that "'Tis quite enough for girls to know,/ If she can read a billet-doux" (III, 36-38)—for debasing through negligence the character and intellect of women. Harriet's marriage to Tom Brainless at the conclusion of the poem fitly unites these two products of misguided education.

None of the three central characters in *The Progress of Dulness*, however, is fleshed out; all seem more incidental than integral to Trumbull's satire, and the narratives of their "adventures" thus can barely support the poem's lengthy expositional passages. Trumbull's stylistic strengths in *The Progress* are to be found not so much in his use of the Hudibrastic multiple rhyme or in an Alexander Pope-like cleverness and density of expression (though he has been justly praised for these elements of his style), but in an unassuming fluency of statement, a flair for droll anticlimax, and a generally sustained high quality of verse.

M'Fingal, begun in 1775 (perhaps at the prompting of some members of the Continental Congress who desired a work that would rouse colonial spirits), has accrued a somewhat erroneous reputation as a patriotic Revolutionary poem. Trumbull actually levelled the satire in this mock-epic, completed in 1782, at both the Tories and those Whigs whose democratic fanaticism, Trumbull feared, would lead to chaos. But, it was Trumbull's devastating satire of the British that caught the American imagination and propelled *M'Fingal* and its author to fame.

Cantos I and II, which together in slightly different form made up the original first canto published in 1776, feature a debate, divided into morning and afternoon sessions, between the Tory M'Fingal and the Whig Honorious. In the morning debate Honorious condemns Britain, which "Sent fire and sword, and called it, Len-

ity,/ Starv'd us, and christen'd it, Humanity"
(I, 263-264). M'Fingal, whose arguments are
usually self-defeating, retorts that "hell is theirs,
the scripture shows,/ Whoe'er *the pow'rs that
be* oppose" (I, 503-504), and concludes ridiculously: "Nor need we blush your Whigs before;/
If we've no virtue you've no more" (I, 693-694).
After "dinner done in epic fashion," M'Fingal
resumes the debate by illustrating Britain's magnanimity toward the colonies:

> *Did not the deeds of England's Primate*
> *First drive your fathers to this climate,*
> *Whom jails and fines and ev'ry ill*
> *Forc'd to their good against their will. . . .*
> *Did [England] not send you charters o'er,*
> *And give you lands you own'd before*
>
> (II, 37-40, 45-46)

Honorious interrupts to deride Britain's strategic ineptitude and Thomas Gage's notorious
proclamations, and M'Fingal rejoins with a defense of British conduct, asserting that their numerous retreats are sincere efforts to prevent
civil war. He warns that the true wrath of Britain will descend on the colonies and its soldiers
will "Display their glory and their wits,/ Fright
unarm'd children into fits" (II, 517-518). Invok-
ing his gift of "second sight," M'Fingal foresees
an America of titles and estates, a vision disputed by Honorious before the debate adjourns
in chaos.

In Canto III, M'Fingal addresses the patriot
rabble, now gathered around a liberty pole. In
both the pole (which he likens to the Tower of
Babel) and the disorderly assembly of Whigs, he
sees an emblem of the democratic extremism
that must follow a Whig victory. Echoing the
worst fears of Trumbull, himself an advocate of
strong central government, M'Fingal derides the
crowd:

> *Ye dupes to ev'ry factious rogue,*
> *Or taverprating demagogue,*
> *Whose tongue but rings, with sound more full,*
> *On th'empty drumhead of his skull. . . .*
> *For Liberty in your own by-sense*
> *Is but for crimes a patient licence [sic];*
> *To break of law th'Egyptian yoke,*
> *And throw the world in common stock,*
> *Reduce all grievances and ills*
> *To Magna Charta of your wills*
>
> (III, 63-66, 69-74)

A mock epic battle ensues, wherein the Tories
are routed and M'Fingal is tarred and feathered.

In the final canto, M'Fingal, addressing the
fugitive Tories from a turnip bin in his cellar,
relates a vision in which his friend Malcolm,
upon a gallows, has clarified his second sight and
revealed to him the future events of the war.

Turgidly embellished with classical and biblical
allusions, this vision depicts the course of British
defeat (attended by British atrocities), the subsequent decline of the British empire, and the
ascendence of America (after a period of
anarchy) to "glory, wealth and fame" (IV, 1033).
A final mock-heroic tussie precedes M'Fingal's
escape at the poem's conclusion.

In its style and sensibility, *M'Fingal* looks
back to the British Augustan age rather than
forward to the Romantic. Trumbull's stylistic
models were Samuel Butler, Pope, Jonathan
Swift, Matthew Prior, and John Churchill; his
adoption of the mock epic, with its array of
classical allusions, afforded him the protocol for
an attack on all brands of fanaticism, while it
provided him a means of displaying his considerable learning and his talent for satire. A Connecticut conservative who distrusted the democratic impulse, Trumbull was anything but a
Revolutionary firebrand like Paine or Philip
Freneau; still, despite the comparatively less
partisan satire of *M'Fingal,* the poem found
favor among patriots, especially those whose education enabled them to appreciate its sophistication, and it has become a part of America's
Revolutionary myth.

Summary

Though temperamentally a conservative, John
Trumbull is best known for two satiric poems
associated with revolutionary activities. In *The
Progress of Dulness* (1772-1773) he advocated
(among other things) the renovation of the Yale
curriculum; in *M'Fingal* (1775-1782) he satirized the conduct of Britain in the Revolutionary
War, but he attacked as well some Whig excesses. By profession a lawyer and public servant, Trumbull was the unofficial leader of the
Connecticut Wits, a group of Hartford illumi-
nati. After his collaboration with members of
this coterie on *The Anarchiad* (1786-1787),
Trumbull virtually ceased writing poetry.

Selected Bibliography

Primary Sources
The Poetical Works of John Trumbull. 2 vols. 1820.
    Rpt. Grosse Pointe, Mich.: Scholarly Press, 1968. A
    facsimile.
The Satiric Poems of John Trumbull. Ed. Edwin T.
    Bowden. Austin: University of Texas Press, 1962.
    Contains texts of *The Progress of Dulness* and
    M'Fingal, a preface, and valuable notes.

Secondary Sources
Books
Cowie, Alexander. *John Trumbull: Connecticut Wit.*
    Chapel Hill: University of North Carolina Press,
    1936. Useful, documented, groundbreaking critical
    biography.
Gimmestad, Victor E. *John Trumbull.* Twayne's
    United States authors series, No. 240. New York:

Twayne Publishers, 1974. Contains much new research and an excellent selected bibliography of Trumbull's published and unpublished works.

Howard, Leon. *The Connecticut Wits.* Chicago: University of Chicago Press, 1943. An engaging study that provides good intellectual and cultural background.

Parrington, Vernon Louis, ed. *The Connecticut Wits.* New York: Harcourt, Brace, 1926. An anthology of representative works, with an introduction providing social and historical background.

———. *Main Currents in American Thought: An Interpretation of American Literature from the Beginnings to 1920.* Vol. I. *The Colonial Mind.* New York: Harcourt, Brace, 1927, 1930. Includes valuable section on Trumbull's life and work.

Article

Granger, Bruce I. "Hudibras in the American Revolution." *American Literature*, 27 (1956): 499–508. Places *M'Fingal* in the context of other Hudibrastic poems of the Revolution.

Kris Lackey

Ward, Nathaniel

Born: Haverhill (Suffolk), England, c. 1578
Education: Emmanuel College, Cambridge,
   B.A., 1600; M.A., 1603
Marriage: Married, wife's name unknown,
   three children
Died: 1652

Biography

Nathaniel Ward, son of minister John Ward, was born in Haverhill, England, circa 1578. Ward attended Emmanuel College, Cambridge, and received a B.A. in 1600 and an M.A. in 1603. After studying law for a time, he traveled extensively on the Continent, met theologian David Pareus at Heidelberg, and was persuaded to enter the ministry. In 1618, Ward took holy orders and from 1620 to 1624 served as chaplain to a colony of British merchants in Elbing, Prussia. After a brief period as curate of St. James, Piccadilly, he was granted the living of Stondon Massey, Essex, but soon came into conflict with later Archbishop William Laud and was ordered to stop preaching because he objected to the Anglican service and rituals.

Ward left England in 1634 and settled as minister at Agawam (later Ipswich), Massachusetts. In 1636, due to impaired health and the rigors of frontier life, he resigned his cure, but was soon set to work, because of his legal background, on the creation of a code of laws for New England. This seminal work of American constitutional history was published by the General Court in 1641 as "The Body of Liberties." Although granted 600 acres of land near Haverhill, Massachusetts, he was forced by illness to return to Boston, where, in 1645, he wrote *The Simple Cobler of Aggawam.* The *Cobler* was published in London in 1647 and went through four editions before the end of the year.

In 1646, with Oliver Cromwell now in power, Ward returned to England and was invited to preach the Fast Day sermon before Parliament in June 1647. He continued to press for a free Parliament and strict control of religion. Ward was appointed, early in 1648, to a living in Shenfield, Essex, and died in 1652, leaving two sons and a daughter.

Literary Analysis

Although satire and humor, conscious and unconscious, occasionally surfaced in early colonial literature, Nathaniel Ward's *The Simple Cobler of Aggawam* can justly be considered the first sustained prose satire to appear in New England. Published in London during the English Civil War (January 29, 1647), *The Simple Cobler* employs the persona of an irascible yet good-hearted shoemaker intent upon sending his plea across the Atlantic to save a beleaguered England. The problems facing the motherland are clear: license rather than Reformed religion is in the ascendant; men and women are far more concerned with fashion than with truth; the state totters while the King, bizarre sects, political parties, and Parliament maneuver for power. The solution is equally clear: true religion must be established and maintained as an absolute; all interested parties must set partisan concerns aside for a compromise that will protect everyone from the horrors of irreligion and civil war.

Once Ward moves beyond introductory material to the substance of his attack he hardly bothers to sustain the persona of the cobbler. He writes with the manifold verbal skill of a true child of Renaissance polemic, employing elaborate tropes, classical allusions, and theological subtleties—the world's state is precarious, but fortunately the author has the true solution to the problem that he will force the reader to recognize through traditional satiric means.

Ward divides his satire into three rough divisions. The first assails the dangerous innovation of state toleration of every blasphemous sect and opinion: "Wee have beene reputed a Colluvies of wild Opinionists, swarmed into a remote wildernes to find elbow-roome for our phanatick Doctrines and practises: I trust our diligence past, and constant sedulity against such persons and courses, will plead better things for us. I dare take upon me, to bee the Herauld of *New-England* so farre, as to proclaime to the world, in the name of our Colony, that all Familists, Antinomians, Anabaptists, and other Enthusiasts shall have free Liberty to keepe away from us, and such as will come to be gone as fast as they can, the sooner the better" (p. 6).

Another open scandal—women's fashions and effeminacy in long-haired men—is addressed in the second part of the *Simple Cobler.* Fashion represents a degradation of true womanhood and cannot fail to affect society as a whole, Ward claims: "To speak moderately, I truly confesse it is beyond the ken of my understanding to conceive, how these women should have any true grace, or valuable vertue, that have so little wit, as to disfigure themselves with such exotick garbes, as not only dismantles their native lovely lustre, but transclouts them into gant-bar-geese, ill-shapen-shotten-shell-fish, Egyptian Hyeroglyphicks, or at the best into French flurts of the pastery, which a proper English woman should scorne with her heels: it is no marvell they weare drailes on the hinder part of their heads, having nothing as it seems in the fore-part, but a few Squirrils brains to help them frisk from one ill-favour'd fashion to another" (p. 26).

The concluding portion of the *Cobler* concerns the potential political ruin involved in a nation turning against itself—King against Parliament and people. Ward supports the Parliament and the right of the people to revolt against unjust actions by the King. This is far from a democratic sentiment, however, and his hopes include "composition," a King willing to correct wrongs in light of the sincere affection of his loyal subjects. The result must be a strong state bound by mutual respect and love: "Prosecutions of Warres between a King and his Parliament, are the direfull dilacerations of the world, the cruell Catastrophes of States, dreadfull to speak of; they are *nefanda & n'agenda*: I known no grounds can be given of them but two: Either upon Reason founded upon some surmisall of Treason, which my reason cannot reach: I could never conceive why a rationall King should commit Treason against a reasonable Parliament; or how a faithful Parliament against their lawfull King: the most I can imagine, is a misprision of Treason, upon a misprision of Reason. He that knows not the spirit of his King, is an Atheist. Our King is not *Charles le simple* sometime of *France*: he understands not our King that understands him not to bee understanding. The Parliament is supposed Omniscient, because under God they are Omnipotent: if a Parliament have not as much knowledge and all other Vertues, as all the kingdome beside, they are no good Abridgement of the Commonwealth. I beleeve Remonstrances have demonstrated enough concerning this point of Reason,

to give satisfaction to such as satisfaction will satisfie" (p. 59).

Ward's *Cobler* is the stylistic descendant of a century and a half of Reformation polemic. As such, it employs the full satiric artillery accessible to men with solid classical backgrounds and great verbal sensitivity. Puns, extended analogies, parallelism, classical and Biblical quotation mixed heterogeneously, doggerel verse, and recondite allusion blend into each other and almost achieve a life of their own apart from the original issues. Two celebrated pamphlet explosions of the sixteenth century might have served as direct examples for Ward: the Marprelate tracts (1588–1590) and the works of Thomas Nashe (several pamphlets, 1589–1599). The Marprelate tracts attempt to gradually force the opposition into surrender by rendering all associated with the object of attack totally ridiculous. Nashe, employing many of the verbal techniques of the Marprelate tracts, carried the tradition of the flyting—endless, railing denunciation utilizing incredible catalogs of invective—to new heights of venom and verbal virtuosity. Ward seems to benefit from both of these examples as well as from the older tradition of Cynic humor, of which Robert Burton's Democritus in *The Anatomy of Melancholy* is perhaps the best representative in English.

Summary

The traditions of the Cynics, of Martin Marprelate, and of Thomas Nashe were translated effectively by Nathaniel Ward into the first sustained work of humor produced in New England—*The Simple Cobler of Aggawam*, which satirically comments on religious sects, English politics, and women's fashions.

Selected Bibliography

Primary Source

The Simple Cobler of Aggawam in America. Ed. P.M. Zall. Lincoln, Neb.: University of Nebraska Press, 1969. A solid, careful, convenient edition and as close to a definitive edition as is likely considering the interest in Ward.

Secondary Sources

Béranger, Jean. *Nathaniel Ward.* Bordeaux, France: Société Bordelaise de Diffusion de Travaux des Lettres et Science Humaines, 1969. An exhaustive stylistic analysis that nicely incorporates biographical and historical background.

Bohi, Mary J. "Nathaniel Ward, Pastor Ingeniosus." Ph.D. dissertation, University of Illinois, 1959. A systematic biography of Ward stressing his English background, especially his pastoral activities.

Tyler, Moses Coit. *A History of American Literature.* New York, N.Y.: G.P. Putnam's Sons, 1890, pp. 229–241. This pioneering classic viewed Ward as a genial transplanted Elizabethan, a pattern most literary histories follow.

Daniel O'Bryan

Warren, Kittrell J.

Born: Clarke County, Alabama, on October 6, 1829

Education: Brownwood classical school

Died: December 28, 1889

Biography

Kittrell J. Warren, whom modern scholars have usually recognized as one of the last and least known of the humorists of the Old Southwest, was born in Clarke County, Alabama, on October 6, 1829, the youngest of three sons of the Reverend Kittrell Warren, a frontier Baptist minister.[1] During his early youth, the Warren family moved to Houston County, Georgia, where they resided until his father's death. In 1837 or 1838, Kit Warren and his mother migrated to Lee County, Georgia, where his older brother, E. W. Warren, practiced law. His only known formal education was at Brownwood, a classical school for boys under the direction of the Reverend Otis Smith near La Grange, in Troup County, Georgia. Sometime later Warren studied law under his brother and apparently resided in Lee County until about 1883.

Loyal to the Confederate cause, on July 3, 1861, Warren joined Company B of the Eleventh Georgia Volunteers, and in 1863 after leaving the service, he published a brief commemorative account of his military company's war experiences, a pamphlet entitled *History of the Eleventh Georgia Vols., Embracing the Muster Rolls, Together with a Special and Succinct Account of the Marches, Engagements, Casualties, Etc.* Two years earlier he had published *Ups and Downs of Wife Hunting,* "a comic pamphlet on courtship, a sort of jokebook for Confederate soldiers."[2] Like the hero of this pamphlet, Warren never married.

After returning from the war Warren was elected to the Georgia Legislature from Lee County but because of illness was forced to relinquish his seat temporarily in December 1863. When he recovered he returned to the Legislature in 1864 to serve two more terms. In 1865 he published anonymously the volume *Life and Public Services of an Army Straggler,* his only work that still elicits occasional attention from modern literary critics.

In the twenty years following the Civil War, Warren channeled his interests primarily into politics and legal affairs and wrote no works of major importance. In 1866 he became solicitor general, and from 1877 to 1884, he served as judge of the county court for Lee County. But, in the last few years as county court judge, he seems to have renewed his interest in writing, chiefly of a journalistic variety. During this time, he held positions on various newspapers and maga-

zines, beginning with the Leesburg *Telephone* in 1882. A year later he became managing editor of the Sumter, South Carolina, *Republican* and afterwards served a brief stint with the Chattanooga, Tennessee, *Evening Dispatch,* a position that he held until the paper's demise. Returning to Georgia, probably in 1884, he accepted a position as associate editor of *The Sunny South,* an Atlanta-based, mass-circulation, weekly newspaper-magazine, a periodical "devoted to Literature, Romance, the News, and Southern Development," and contributed a column entitled "Kit Warren's Musings," which appeared irregularly from November 1884 to July 1886. Among his more interesting contributions to *The Sunny South* were a series of three humorous sketches about Confederate Army life which were printed in June 1885. The best of the three, the first sketch in the series, exhibited the frame device, colloquial dialect, and tall-tale exaggeration, and featured an inveterate backwoods liar, echoing the familiar strategies and subject matter of the antebellum southwestern humorists.

Having been a lawyer, state legislator, county judge, managing editor of a newspaper, associate editor of a magazine, author of two pamphlets and a short book, and an occasional contributor to newspapers and magazines, Warren continued to dabble in journalistic endeavors during the last years of his life. In 1886, he was recruited for and accepted a position as editor of the *Macon* (Georgia) *Evening News,* and in October 1887, he served briefly as managing editor of the *Atlanta Evening Capitol.* A year later, after the demise of the *Evening Capitol,* he worked for a short time with the Swift Specific Company, but, afflicted with declining health, he returned to Atlanta to live with his niece, remaining in her care until his death on December 28, 1889.

Literary Analysis

Published initially in August 1861, Warren's first work, a 31-page pamphlet, the *Ups and Downs of Wife Hunting: Or, Merry Jokes for Camp Perusal,* seems generally indebted to the familiar subject matter of comical courtship previously treated in southwestern humor, most notably in such widely popular works as William Tappan Thompson's *Major Jones's Courtship* (1843), a book that Warren likely had read. Written pseudonymously, *Ups and Downs* employs a persona, Jezebel Huggins, who is obsessively determined to find himself a wife but whose dedicated and persistent attempts or "trials," as he calls them, to accomplish his goal always end unsuccessfully. In his candid self-portrait, Jezebel gives in the second chapter of his retrospective narrative what is perhaps the primary reason that his repeated quests to obtain a wife have not succeeded. Using pompous literary language, such as one frequently finds among the genteel narrators in the frame in southwestern humorous sketches, he writes:

> It seems that Dame Nature, in assorting the ingredients with which to set me up, made up her mind to do her 'level prettiest' to construct a queer and hard-looking specimen of masculinity. In that effort she didn't bungle: I am five feet nine in my stockings (or anybody's else's,) have black hair, heavy red whiskers, squint pop eyes, sharp cheek bones, one club foot, and a nose which describes the arc of a parabola.[3]

In a later chapter Jezebel's hideously comical appearance is openly exposed when one of the women, whom he hopes to marry, stares at him, a look that he ironically misinterprets as one of physical attraction. Then, after his inquiring of her why she has been watching him "so intently," she unexpectedly exclaims: "'bekase . . . you was so tarnashun ugly, I couldn't help it'" (p. 19).

Huggins's deficiencies in wife hunting extend beyond his unattractive appearance. He is also a fool, but likable, as his misadventures in courtship readily demonstrate. Moreover, in his unflagging efforts to find a suitable spouse, Jezebel is deceived by his own enthusiasm, nurtured in part by his reading of romantic novels, which stand in stark contrast to the uncertain conditions and practical considerations of wooing women in the real world. Typical of the reversals he experiences in wife hunting and one of the more humorous episodes in *Ups and Downs* is his description of his attempt to elope with Betsy Barron, a farmer's daughter. Mounted on a donkey, Jezebel arrives at Betsy's house at midnight, the hour of their prearranged rendezvous; however, his donkey brays, arousing her father's dogs. The situation that ensues is farcical, a veritable comedy of errors with fast-moving antics reminiscent of the coarse slapstick exemplified in some of the yarns of George Washington Harris's Sut Lovingood. Mistaken for a thief by Betsy's father, Jezebel, upon finding his donkey "to be spur-proof" when he tries to effect an escape, becomes the victim of numerous dog bites, but even worse is his humiliation, when, at the height of the pandemonium, he is unable to explain intelligibly to Betsy's father why he has come to his farm in the first place.

While humorous situations, such as a foiled elopement, must have seemed amusing to Warren's Confederate comrades-in-arms, the modern reader of *Ups and Downs of Wife Hunting* probably finds as much humor in Jezebel's highly affected language and his occasional use of incongruous figurative descriptions. His flowery, pretentious, and pedantic rhetoric is well illustrated in an excerpt from a letter that he writes to his Uncle Tim, informing him of his intentions to marry. This letter, which his uncle finds utterly unintelligible, requires three days for a school teacher to "translate" into comprehensible English. In it, Jezebel writes:

> I deem it an imperative duty to apprise you, without deferring, but with great deference, of the illimitably important communication about to be most devoutly perpetrated. I am now upon the giddy verge of committing connubiation. I am about to pluck from its parent stem one of the loveliest flowers that ever bloomed in pristine gorgeousness outside of the garden of Paradise. . . . A very Ganymede, my fidelity shall remain unabated until the lamp of life wavers in feebly-flickering corruscations, preliminary to its extinguishment.

(p. 10)

Jezebel's diction is not always so grandiloquent. Sometimes his manner is noticeably informal, his monologues containing exaggerated figurative language. On one occasion he casually remarks concerning "two clever, buxom, illiterate lasses" whom he has been visiting that he "had about as much love [for them] as a frog has for mint juleps" (p. 14).

Although reissued in two more editions, the third appearing in 1879 and expanded to 95 pages with the addition of several autobiographical sketches, *Ups and Downs of Wife Hunting* apparently did not enjoy widespread popularity. Even so, according to Floyd C. Watkins's accurate appraisal, the pamphlet "succeeds best in its presentation of comic situations sometimes almost ridiculous enough to be appropriate to the yarns of the Old Southwest humorists, in occasional brief passages of true rural dialogue, and in a few natural and backwoods characters."[4]

Published in Richmond, Virginia, in 1863, Warren's next work, also a pamphlet, the *History of the Eleventh Georgia Vols., Embracing the Muster Rolls, Together with a Special and Succinct Account of the Marches, Engagements, Casualties, Etc.*, contains 22 pages of muster rolls of the Eleventh Georgia Regiment, the unit in which the author himself served in the Civil War, followed by a brief, selectively dramatic chronicle of some of their hardships and military engagements. Although Warren promised to write "a revised and expanded edition" of his *History*, he never carried out this intention. The object of the *History*, Warren wrote, was "to travel along with the regiment, and record, not embryo plans, purposes and processes of the army, but acts and facts pertaining to the eleventh Georgia, as they are moulded into stubborn practical realities."[5]

Not intended as a comic or burlesque work, Warren's *History*, while mainly a eulogistic account to promote patriotism for the Confederate war effort, does exhibit a few flashes of humor that relieve an otherwise staid and monotonously factual chronicle. One instance is found in a brief dialogue, which, although relegated by Warren to a footnote, reflects an earthy zest commonly featured in the colloquial dialect of southwestern humor. In it Warren recounts a humorous situation in which a Yankee cavalier self-confidently rides into an outpost formerly held by his comrades and attempts to make a Confederate officer his prisoner. Unknown to the Yankee, however, the Confederate's men now hold the outpost, and one of them, upon emerging from his hiding place with gun in hand, delivers a stern warning to the surprised intruder in humorously folksy dialect: "See here mister, ef you don't quit yer foolishness and gin up shotly, this here old gally nipper fuzee o' mine haint got no better sense 'an to bore a auger hole thu' that dodrotted Yankee camp chist of your'n" (p. 39).

In addition, Warren occasionally emerges from behind his mask of formality and literary rhetoric in *History of the Eleventh Georgia Vols.* to interject memorably exaggerated figurative descriptions. For example, in describing the tributaries of the Shenandoah River, Warren observes that "the water [was] cold enough to have given a whetstone the cramp" (p. 56). And, as was the case in *Ups and Downs of Wife Hunting*, the modern reader of Warren's *History* finds amusement in Warren's stilted, overly lyricized prose. Evidence of this self-conscious overstraining can be seen in a purple passage in which he pictures the imminent siege of Richmond, the Confederate capital, by northern troops: "The fate of Richmond now seemed pendant and trembling in doubtful scales. The 'flower' of the Northern army stood knocking at the gate. The coil of the anaconda was being pressed more closely, more crampingly around the capital, and the great heart of the nation swelled and throbbed under the suffocating embrace" (p. 39).

Aptly labeled "one of the last remnants of Old Southwest humor,"[6] Warren's most ambitious and significant work, *Life and Public Services of an Army Straggler*, was published in 1865, several months after the Confederate surrender at Appomatox, by J. W. Burke and Company, Phoenix Printing House, in Macon, Geor-

gia. No records have survived to indicate that *An Army Straggler* achieved a popular success, and by the time of Warren's death in 1889, his small book had been virtually forgotten. Published pseudonymously under the appellation Chatham, *An Army Straggler* episodically chronicles the misadventures of Billy Fishback, a Confederate deserter and confidence man, a despicable rapscallion and conscienceless *picaro*, who desires to escape from the war and return to Georgia. A malicious opportunist and thoroughgoing prevaricator and hypocrite, Fishback is a likely literary descendant of two earlier and well-known rogues of southern frontier humor—Johnson Jones Hooper's Simon Suggs and George Washington Harris's Sut Lovingood. Yet, Fishback is even more odious than either of these celebrated sharpers; in fact, Fishback, as well as most of the other characters in *An Army Straggler*, exemplifies what Warren refers to in his Preface as "the grosser elements of human nature."[7]

Ignorant, unpatriotic, and persistently deceitful, Fishback, in an effort to survive and ultimately to escape from the dangers and uncertainties of the Civil War, fabricates numerous lies and stratagems to serve his materialistic desires. For instance, in one episode he manages to win the confidence of Captain Smith, his commanding officer, who had already been warned that Fishback is the "very soul of treachery, dissimulation, and villainy" (p. 31), by getting him drunk and stealing $500 from him, eventually manipulating the situation so skillfully that an innocent man, to whom Fishback has entrusted the Captain's pocketbook which still contains $460, is accused of being a thief. Fishback's temporary triumph is unique, though, for throughout most of the narrative his insidious schemes are foiled before they are carried to completion, the end result usually being his own victimization. In short, the rapacious Fishback is a bungler. In Chapter V of *An Army Straggler*, he manages to dupe a greedy and hypocritical Virginia family by pretending to be a rich Georgia planter. Through this deception he hopes to persuade the family to allow him to marry one of their daughters. The family has land and other valuable assets that they agree to sell well below market value because he has falsely promised that when they move to Georgia after his marriage to their daughter, they will be able to purchase twice as much prime land. The amoral Fishback intends to abandon his new wife, sell the slaves, retain the money from the land sale, and go "to parts unknown." Fishback's knavery seems to be working out as planned until the day of the appointed wedding when an elder brother of the bride arrives. Fishback recognizes him as the man who had terrified him in an earlier episode and absconds empty-handed. The culminating blow, the ultimate victimization of Fishback, occurs near the end of *An Army Straggler* when Warren's antihero dies of smallpox which he contracts while posing as a doctor, his ploy to obtain a seat beside a sick man on a crowded train.

Fishback's rascality knows no bounds. In treating his escapades, Warren draws freely from the well-established lode of southwestern humor using most of the key conventions of this subliterary form, including the frame, folksy dialect, and the confidence-man stock character, but with several new variations and exaggerated incongruous comparisons. First, the frame, as in representative southwestern humorous sketches, affords the author a ready-made device for establishing aesthetic distance between himself and the notorious Fishback. While the authorial narrator of the frame is a genteel user of standard literary, bombastic, and occasionally pedantic language and an advocate of a strictly proper moral code (the latter he espouses in frequent "dear reader" passages that frame the various episodes), Fishback is uncouth, dishonorable, a user of non-standard, backwoods dialect, and thoroughly immoral.

Fishback's colorful dialect, characterized by exaggerated figures of speech, demonstrates another comic convention borrowed from the southwestern humorists. Near the outset of *An Army Straggler*, after feigning sickness to obtain leave from his regiment, Fishback soliloquizes about his real motive for departure: "Cuddent stand to be a marchin along when all them waggins is a beatin the rode into the safest kind of batter, stickin myself in the ground every step like a darnd liberty pole, slippin down every time I go to go up and down hill, which the hills is slippier than a ingyun with the peelin off, and havin a officer all the time devlin me to close up" (pp. 6–7). Later, in reflecting on Captain Slaughter's grandiloquent and unintelligible language, Fishback exclaims: "Sich a dod-dratted fool. Wonder what creek he catcht them big words outen?" (p. 67) On another occasion, hoping to rejoin his regiment but finding that Captain Smith, his commanding officer, no longer trusts him, Fishback brags to a fellow soldier that he will dispel the Captain's suspicion, confidently remarking that "a trout cuddent pull a fishin line no strater'n I'll have him agin night" (p. 88).

Lastly, in Billy Fishback, Warren creates an unprincipled rogue lacking any redeemable qualities. Billy exhibits a closer kinship to scoundrels like William Faulkner's Flem Snopes than to most of the shrewd, roguish tricksters—his immediate literary predecessors—from the tradition of southwestern humor. Furthermore, in

Captain Slaughter (who is actually a private), a charlatan and user of conspicuously high-flown, abstract, and elaborately pretentious language, a sometime accomplice in Fishback's flim-flam activities, Warren introduced a character quite unlike the backwoods sharpers found in earlier works of frontier humor. As one commentator has observed, when Fishback and Slaughter "work together (or against each other), they seem to anticipate the pair who spoil Huck's quiet existence on the raft."[8]

Although the conventions of southwestern humor provide the principal basis for the comic texture of *An Army Straggler*, it has been pointed out recently that the book is an admixture of realism, sentiment, and frontier humor.[9] The realism may be accounted for in part by the fact that Fishback is a fictional representative of a large number of soldiers who actually deserted from the Confederate Army.[10] Regarding the sentiment in *An Army Straggler*, William E. Lenz indicates that "the return of the lover thought dead, the trapping of the fiend in his own trap, and the appropriately agonizing death of the deceiver are traditional sentimental motifs."[11]

Summary

"One of the last of the Southwestern humorists,"[12] Kittrell J. Warren is principally remembered today for one work, *Life and Public Services of An Army Straggler*, which employs many of the devices and techniques introduced and popularized by earlier practitioners of southern frontier humor. Warren's handling of the character, Billy Fishback, the degenerate hero of the book, represents a step forward in the evolution of the confidence man stereotype in American humor. Concerning the overall importance of *An Army Straggler*, Floyd C. Watkins succinctly notes, "it looks backward to Davy Crockett, Hooper, Harris, and Longstreet and vaguely forward to later uses of frontier humor by such diverse writers as Mark Twain, William Faulkner, and Robert Penn Warren."[13] Therefore, while Warren's two earlier pamphlets, *Ups and Downs of Wife Hunting* and *History of the Eleventh Georgia Vols.*, should be viewed as of little consequence in assessing his reputation as a humorist, *An Army Straggler* should not be overlooked by anyone seriously interested in the picaresque hero in American literature, for it provides a transitional link on which later and better American writers would build in shaping some of their own more challengingly complex and artfully rendered portraitures of disreputable, inimical tricksters.

Notes

1. No standard biography on Kittrell J. Warren exists; therefore, the biographical information I have

included in this essay has been taken from an obituary notice, "Kit Warren Dead," Atlantic *Constitution*, December 29, 1889, p. 17, and the more reliable overview of his life, Floyd C. Watkins's "Introduction" to his edition of Warren's first published pamphlet, *Ups and Downs of Wife Hunting* (Atlanta: The Emory University Library, 1957), pp. v–vi.

2. Floyd C. Watkins, "Introduction," *Life and Public Services of an Army Straggler* (Athens: University of Georgia Press, 1961), p. x.
3. *Ups and Downs of Wife Hunting*, 2nd ed., p. 6. Subsequent references will be to this edition, and page numbers will appear parenthetically in the text.
4. Watkins, "Introduction," *Ups and Downs of Wife Hunting*, p. viii.
5. Kittrell J. Warren, *History of the Eleventh Georgia Vols., Embracing the Muster Rolls, Together with a Special and Succinct Account of the Marches, Engagements, Casualties, Etc.* (Richmond: Smith, Bailey & Co., Printers, 1863), p. 44. Subsequent references will be to this edition, and page numbers will appear parenthetically in the text.
6. Watkins, "Introduction," *An Army Straggler*, p. xi.
7. *Life and Public Services of an Army Straggler*, p. 3. Subsequent page references will appear parenthetically in the text.
8. Richard Boyd Hauck, *A Cheerful Nihilism: Confidence and "The Absurd" in American Humorous Fiction* (Bloomington: Indiana University Press, 1971), p. 67. The Huck alluded to here is, of course, Mark Twain's Huckleberry Finn.
9. William E. Lenz, *Fast Talk & Flush Times: The Confidence Man as a Literary Convention* (Columbia: University of Missouri Press, 1985), p. 142.
10. Watkins, "Introduction," *An Army Straggler*, p. x.
11. Lenz, p. 143.
12. Hennig Cohen and William B. Dillingham, eds. *Humor of the Old Southwest*, 2nd ed. (Athens: University of Georgia Press, 1975), p. 360.
13. Watkins, "Introduction," *An Army Straggler*, p. xi.

Selected Bibliography

Primary Sources

Prose Fiction

Ups and Downs of Wife Hunting: Or, Merry Jokes for Camp Perusal. 2nd ed. Augusta, Ga.: Printed at the Office of *The Constitutionalist*, 1861.

Life and Public Services of an Army Straggler. Macon, Ga.: J. W. Burke, Phoenix Printing House, 1865.

"Recollections of Scenes, Incidents and Characters Around the Camp-Fire in the 'Happy Days Gone By.'" *The Sunny South*, June 1885. The first sketch in this series has been reprinted, with a brief introduction, in Floyd C. Watkins's "A Tall Tale of the Civil War," *Emory University Quarterly*, 13 (March 1957): 48–54.

History

History of the Eleventh Georgia Vols., Embracing the Muster Rolls, Together with a Special and Succinct Account of the Marches, Engagements, Casualties, Etc. Richmond: Smith, Bailey, 1863.

Secondary Sources

Hauck, Richard Boyd. *A Cheerful Nihilism: Confidence and "The Absurd" in American Humorous Fiction.* Bloomington: Indiana University Press, 1971, pp. 66–70. Treats Warren's *An Army Straggler* as the portrayal of an antihero who is "caught forever in absurd circles, many of his own making."

"Kit Warren Dead." Atlanta *Constitution*, December 29, 1889, p. 17. An obituary notice providing a brief and partially erroneous overview of Warren's life.

Lenz, William E. *Fast Talk and Flush Times: The Confidence Man as a Literary Convention.* Columbia: University of Missouri Press, 1985, pp. 137–145. Sees Warren's *An Army Straggler* as an amalgam of realism, sentiment, and southwestern humor, noting, moreover, that the author's "narrative ambivalence, the various languages he employs, and the almost sadistic yet moralistic ending . . . suggest the competing and often contradictory pressures under which *Straggler* was written" and offer testament to his own "doubts and fears" about the country divided by war.

Watkins, Floyd C. "Introduction." *Ups and Downs of Wife Hunting.* Atlanta: The Emory University Library, 1957, pp. v–viii. Presents a short biographical sketch of Warren and states that *Ups and Downs* is historically significant "as a record of manners among early Georgians."

———. "Introduction." *Life and Public Services of an Army Straggler.* Athens: University of Georgia Press, 1961, pp. ix–xiv. Calls *An Army Straggler* "one of the last remnants of Old Southwest humor," a work anticipating "later uses of frontier humor" by better writers, most notably Mark Twain and William Faulkner.

Edward J. Piacentino

Weeks, Raymond

Born: Tabor, Iowa, on January 2, 1863
Education: Phillips Academy, Andover; Harvard University, A.B., 1891, M.A.; Université de Paris; Universität Berlin; Harvard University, Ph.D., 1897
Marriage: Mary Arnoldia, 1885
Died: 1954

Biography

Raymond Weeks was born in Tabor, Iowa, the son of Joseph Van Rennsselaer and Imogene Cookson, on January 2, 1863. At age three he traveled by covered wagon with his parents to Jackson County, Missouri. The family lived on the farm of Walter and Eva Beach whose son, Rex Beach (1877–1949), later became a successful novelist who wrote about his experiences in the Klondike. After a year the family moved to Kansas City, then a frontier town. After graduating from Kansas City High School, Weeks attended Phillips Academy in Andover, Massachusetts. In 1885, he married Mary Arnoldia. Weeks received a degree in Romance Languages from Harvard in 1891 and for two years taught French at the University of Michigan. He later studied at the universities in Paris and Berlin for an additional two years as a Harvard Traveling Fellow. Returning home he taught at the University of Missouri in Columbia, where he was professor of Romance Languages. Harvard awarded him the Ph.D. in 1897. In 1908, Weeks accepted a position at Columbia University, and retired to his farm, "Rochambeau," near Manakin, Virginia, in 1929.

Raymond Weeks was the author of both scholarly articles and short stories. His scholarly work mainly concerned medieval French literature and phonetics.[1] Weeks was very active in his profession as president of the Spelling Reform Association, the American Dialect Society, and the Modern Language Association. His most important humorous writings are gathered in a volume entitled *The Hound-Tuner of Callaway*, first published in 1927 and reprinted in 1971. Weeks's literary work appeared in John T. Frederick's *Midland* magazine, the earliest and probably the most important Midwest regional magazine to achieve a national readership.

Literary Analysis

Raymond Weeks was a man of great erudition and humanity who chose to write about the "remembered happenings and imaginings of the time of the later pioneers in the Missouri Valley" where he grew up. His stories are incisive but loving satires of earlier generations and their way of life, of horses, leisure, hospitality, week-long visits, servants, eccentric inventors, wagon trains leaving for the West, hypocrites, rogues, and difficult courtships. Referring no doubt to Rex Beach, who wrote of Alaskan wilds, Weeks's disclaimer in his preface underscores his intention to stick to the familiar but fantastic ground of his own Missouri where excitement is more likely to be found in a family scandal, a notorious murder, or a ghost story recounted during a mid-summer thunderstorm. His book, *The Hound-Tuner of Callaway*, Weeks writes, "should not, however, be denied the humble virtues of its limitations. No one is obliged to read it" (p. vii). Weeks writes about the "Kingdom of Callaway," a county midway between St. Louis and Kansas City that has traditionally held itself aloof from its neighbors after its voluntary secession from the Union during the Civil War. Like most of Weeks's writing, this is a tale of whimsical humor yet clear-eyed appreciation of human vanity and perfidy.

Weeks's characters are ordinary people familiar to us from Midwestern realistic fiction. But Weeks views them from an entirely different angle, thus expanding the scope of comic possibility. The Midwest has produced a rich and memorable tradition of humor, despite its reputation for novels of dreary realism. Towering above all other American humorists is, of course, Mark Twain. A significant body of humor also has appeared in newspapers, magazines such as *Midland*, in collections such as Jack Conroy's *Midland Humor* (1947), and more recently in Garrison Keillor's contributions to *The New Yorker*. A certain debunking spirit is a familiar element in midwestern humor, together with a respect for the common life and a fascination with eccentricity in speech habit and character.[2]

The inhabitants of Callaway, Weeks tells us in "The Hound-Tuner of Callaway," are a very proud people. The baying of their hounds is more melodious than in adjoining counties, owing to the genius of one man whose tuning fork mesmerizes hunting dogs, placing them entirely within his power. His one great misfortune is to lose a beautiful daughter named Peggy who runs away with "a graceless fellow named Sam Black, who was not even born in Callaway!" (p. 7). Abandoning his work, the Hound-Tuner, accompanied by his hounds, heads west in search of his daughter. He eventually locates the runaways in a farmhouse near Kansas City. The "King's" epic search is told by Joe Holloway, a black born of a slave. Joe, Weeks tells us in an aside, was a great source of tales about the "old times" when Weeks was a boy: "Then, too, it was a pleasure just to hear him talk. His dialect walked upright, unaided and unashamed" (p. 14).

Despite the difficulties of transcription, Weeks renders Joe's story in dialect, a task for which Weeks was eminently suited, given his training in phonetics and his familiarity with Missouri speech and its variants. The device of the second narrator in "The Hound-Tuner" derives from the long-established "frame" tradition. Its effect is to draw attention to the oral style of the black storyteller, for a great part of the interest in Weeks's tales lies in the language of the telling.

The problem of phonetic transcription of dialect for humorous purposes sometimes baffled Weeks. In "The Snakes of Boone" he writes:

> It would be impossible to write phonetically or otherwise the pronunciation of Mr. Tutt when he sang this well-known dialect song. Such words as "girl," "unconcerning," "stingers," "yearning," which occur in "Little Girl," defy transcription, as does the intonation.
>
> (p. 259)

By pointing out the limitations of transcription, Weeks enlists the reader's imaginative involvement in the telling of the story. Weeks loved the "rich, beautiful dialect which crept up the rivers of Missouri in the first quarter of the nineteenth century and was as much superior to the inane, schoolmarm English now to be heard as persimmon to pawpaw!" (p. 259). Weeks satirizes the ungrammatical discourse of certain

> pioneers of the Missouri valley, who were all men of gigantic intellect. . . . These giants inherited a feeling for superior English. They knew, for example, that it is more expressive to say: "I done it," "I ain't said nothing" than to say flabbily and ineffectually: "I did it," "I haven't said anything."
>
> (p. 208)

These same "giants" are unhinged, however, when a man from Ohio introduces a strange locution. He has come to Westport, Missouri, planning to join a caravan west but changes his mind. To the "intellectual giants" stationed before a tavern he says enigmatically: "Thou canst not say 'I did it.'" All Westport is subsequently confounded by these words. After six months of conjecture the meaning is finally resolved. "Do you wonder," Weeks concludes, "that no families from Ohio were to be found among the early settlers of Westport?" (p. 210).

Weeks's humor is characterized by good feeling and high spirits, as for instance in "Arkansas." Like certain medieval French fabliaux, "Arkansas" is a burlesque tale of a "noble" quest. It tells the story of Alphonse Turgeon who, consumed with the desire to regain his family's past triumphs in the annual hog show at the county fair, challenges his rival to a race between their fastest squealers. Having made the challenge, Alphonse goes to the wilds of Arkansas to find a razorback hog. Alphonse captures and tames a piglet who becomes his companion, naming it "Arkansas"—"There was on the farm only one animal with which Arkansas refused to have anything to do, and that was the pigs" (p. 146). "Arkansas" has a special advantage: the legs on one side are shorter for having been raised on a mountainside, which aids her in navigating the circular track. Alphonse's razorback easily outdistances its competitor, but nearing the end of the race she veers off toward her native state in "a vast curve, which turned gradually toward the south, with all the inevitability of mathematics!" (p. 154). Trailing behind her are "her beloved master and Bonny, his horse" (p. 155).

False piety and hypocrisy are targets of several of Weeks's humorous tales, most notably in "The Fly-Catcher to the Harris House." The satire of this tale is aimed directly at intolerance and cruelty. A strange box is suspended from the ceiling of the Harris House dining room where travelers and important people of Westport are served. The box is propelled from within by a small negro boy, Sylvester. The purpose of the contraption is to sweep the heads of the diners with streamers to brush away flies. Sylvester's job is made awkward by the sneers of the Reverend Job Limner, a predecessor of Sinclair Lewis's Elmer Gantry. Sylvester takes his revenge when he polishes the Reverend's boots with honey. Hoping to make a favorable impression upon the members of his new parish, in particular a young woman named Becky Wells, the Reverend has prepared an eloquent sermon. While sitting next to the pulpit awaiting his moment he is suddenly enveloped by a swarm of black flies attracted to his boots. He makes for the door while the church-goers, including Becky, double up in laughter. Hieing out of town on a horse, unwittingly he passes "A small, bareheaded black boy standing in the shade" who watches him "jolting down the road on the back of the big, mean sorrel that Bud [the livery owner] hired to persons whom he did not like" (p. 277).

Weeks's gentle but pointed satire also focused on another target, the state university in Columbia, Missouri, where he once taught. According to Weeks's story, "Snakes of Boone," six counties "had secretly bought the legislature" so that the university would be built in one of them. Boone County, however, bought the judges who made the final decision. In revenge the other counties, according to Harry Tutt, Weeks's storyteller, drove their snakes into Boone County. "Talk of snakes! Boone was nothing but snakes!" (p. 262). Concluding his "lesson in history" Tutt says (with obvious allegorical implications): "Columbia was buried under snakes—buried so deep that the minds of its inhabitants will see nothing but snakes for a thousand years" (p. 263). The story makes a great impression on the young boys who are guests of Colonel Jack Avidon in his new home, the setting for Harry Tutt's evening of impromptu storytelling. "What is a university?" one of the boys timidly inquires at the finish of the narrative:

> A university, my boy, is a perpetual circus. It has a group of performing animals quite wonderful to observe, and a collection of fossils which are fascinating to examine and whose remembrance is a joy forever. These fossils are self-perpetuating and never disappear. . . . Young men go and pass four years listening to them, so as to learn to become fossils in turn.
>
> (p. 264)

Many of Weeks's tales concern the difficulties with which vigorous and successful men of action court and win the women they desire. One such story is "The Disappearing Hen's Nest," in which a young woman, after renouncing her engagement over a trivial slight, finally returns to her senses. It is a story of the "old times," of odd contraptions, and post–Civil War boom and crisis. The tone is a mixture of gentle irony, quiet laughter, and subtle character analysis.

These characteristics are even better displayed in "The Bucking Palfrey," Weeks's longest and best-developed short story. The opening sentence is an allusion to Daudet's famous "La Chevre de M. Seguin," Weeks explains in a footnote: "It is not known who related to Daudet the affairs of Leonidas Segwin" (p. 185). Mr. Segwin is the protagonist of Weeks's story who, like M. Seguin's goat-keeper, loses what he seeks most fervently to guard. Segwin is a successful farmer who has married a succession of wives, each one of whom has run away from him leaving no explanation. In desperation Segwin looks for eligible young women leaving Westport in wagon trains for the West. He finally convinces a dying widower to give his daughter, Sylvia, to Segwin as a bride. Bored and restless, Sylvia develops a passion for riding a bucking horse named Rosebud and makes a close friend of Sophronia, an older, unmarried woman who lives nearby. Sylvia becomes ill with typhoid and nears death. When Segwin brings her an epitaph which he has composed, "Sacred to the memory of Sylvia Segwin, wife of one of nature's noblemen," the reader glimpses one of the reasons that Segwin's wives have abandoned him.

Sylvia suddenly grows well again in response to the epitaph; but "she was much changed. . . . She went about doing things in a melancholy way" (p. 198). Sylvia takes French leave, leaving a letter to Sophronia, making her promise not to open it for two years. While she was sick she had made her husband promise not to remarry as long as Rosebud is not bucking. Anxious to remarry after Sylvia's disappearance, Segwin attempts in vain to get Rosebud to buck. The letter to Sophronia discloses the secret to Rosebud's bucking: a horse-chestnut placed between the saddle and felt on the horse's back. Segwin sees Sophronia riding the bucking horse, his "cheeks wet with tears of gratitude and inarticulate joys, his eyes fixed on the slowly advancing cloud of dust, which meant happiness for him" (p. 207). Weeks leaves us to speculate on the arrangement Sylvia has made.

Most of Weeks's stories first appeared in John T. Frederick's *Midland* magazine, one of the earliest and most important attempts to create a market for midwestern writers in the face of eastern dominance of publishing. Frederick preferred stories like Weeks's, full of laughter and "quiet optimism,"[3] though not all of Weeks's stories are cheerful any more than are all of the contributions to *Midland*. Melancholy and bittersweet recollection characterize "Jessie's Friend" and "The Deep Sleeper." "Sport for White Men" is a compelling and eerie story of human cruelty. Nonetheless, tenderness is generally the main literary quality of Weeks's writing, as Frederick points out;[4] moreover, this quality has no necessary connection with sentimentality. Weeks was an enormously learned man with a keen wit and a firm possession of literary standards (according to which mere sentimentality ranked very low). What in the eyes of one critic passes as "folk humor" in Weeks's writing is in fact very clever satire with antecedents in dialect humor, French literature, and literary realism.[5]

Weeks's other contribution to American humor occurs in an unlikely field—mathematics. Problems in arithmetic, he advises in his *The Boy's Own Arithmetic* (1924), should be turned into stories, thus making them springboards for the imagination rather than dreaded exercises of rote memorization. A further defect, he says, in the instruction of mathematics is the demand that questions always have answers. "What is life but a matter of oddments and remainders," Weeks asks. "Have you ever known anything in life to come out even?" (p. vii). Weeks proceeds to illustrate his method of teaching arithmetic by offering a series of "stories" containing problems which young people will feel the urge to solve. A cat chases a mouse into a grandfather's clock; the mouse gnaws the strands of the rope attached to the weights; the weight falls and kills the cat. What time of day did this event occur? (More details are given in the story.) Weeks was proposing no less than a revolution in teaching, based upon the uses of laughter. He had a large tolerance toward human foible. Nonetheless, his stand against suffering by precept, as evidenced in his arithmetic primer, reveals a man of strong conviction.

A greater fault than dogmatism in human character, and one that he would not tolerate, was inhospitality. Weeks reveals in his stories another side of the frontier with its reputation for violence and rude manners. Kindness and generosity also existed, and although these virtues are often occasions for humor in his stories, there is no doubt in the reader's mind that Weeks purposely chose to represent them rather than the violence of the frontier mind. Weeks's stories do not ignore the darker side of human behavior; rather they turn to subtler forms of comedy, employing linguistic tools and psychological insights, and should be valued as counterparts to the figures of ring-tailed roarers and half-alligator, half-men.

Summary

Raymond Weeks grew up in Westport (Kansas City) when wagon trains were still leaving for the West. His short stories are based upon his recollections of the "old time" in Missouri. They are gentle satires of earlier generations and their way of life, neither ignorant of the coarseness and violence of frontier life nor fascinated by these characteristics. His satire targets hypocrisy, vanity, dogmatism and perfidy. Weeks was interested in eccentricities in speech habit and character. An expert in phonetics, he experimented successfully with transcriptions of Missouri speech. Humor, he shows us, lies not only in what is said but how it is said. The difficulties of phonetic transcription, of transforming oral to literary text, are formidable. Nonetheless, his stories manage to convey the subtle flavor of speech localisms together with the ironies inherent in situations which he dramatizes through the use of a second narrator. While most frontier humorists made comic use of exaggerated behavior, Weeks preferred to illustrate other aspects of the frontier mind through gentle irony, quiet laughter, and subtle character analysis. John T. Frederick, editor of *Midland*, published many of Weeks's stories in his magazine, praising them for their tenderness. Tolerant of human foible, Weeks's stories nonetheless poke fun at moral blindness and obsessionary behavior, raising American humor to a level of subtle analysis.

Notes

1. For instance, Weeks's article entitled "Origin of the Covenant Vivien" is a scholarly study of a poem from the heroic period of the Old French epic. It appeared in *The University of Missouri Studies*, 1 (1902). Weeks also authored a book on French phonetics.
2. See Conroy's valuable prefaces in *Midland Humor* (New York: Current, 1947).
3. Frederick Hoffman et al., *The Little Magazine* (Princeton, N.J.: Princeton University Press, 1947), p. 129.
4. *The Midland*, 14 (1928): 266.
5. See Reigelman's valuable study of *The Midland* (Iowa City: University of Iowa Press, 1975), in which he gives a brief treatment of Weeks. Reigelman places "folk humor" in quotation marks without explaining in what ways Weeks's writing differs from genuine folk humor.

Selected Bibliography

Primary Sources

Books

Ode to France. New York: Oxford University Press, 1918.

The Boy's Own Arithmetic. New York: Dutton, 1924.

The Hound-Tuner of Calloway. 1927. Freeport, N.Y.: Books for Libraries, 1971.

Articles (not included in The Hound-Tuner)

"Linwood." *The Midland*, 4 (1918): 263–267.

"Two Sketches of the War." *The Midland*, 7 (1921): 253–257.

"Two Poems." *The Midland*, 14 (1928): 259–265.

"The Two Hands." *The Midland*, 14 (1928): 259–265.

Secondary Sources

Books

Conroy, Jack, ed. *Midland Humor.* New York: Current, 1947. See Conroy's note on Weeks as well as his prefaces to other Midwestern humorists.

Frederick, John T., ed. *Out of the Midwest.* New York: Whittlesey House, 1944. Frederick reprints Weeks's "Arkansas" and adds a valuable note on Weeks's work. Frederick was Weeks's editor for many years.

Hoffman, Frederick H., Charles Allen, and Carolyn F. Ulrich. *The Little Magazine.* Princeton, N.J.: Princeton University Press, 1947. See Chapter 7 on "regionalism," as well as a valuable discussion on *The Midland*, pp. 141–147.

Reigelman, Milton M. *The Midland, a Venture in Literary Regionalism.* Iowa City: University of Iowa Press, 1975. See Reigelman's discussion of Weeks, pp. 93–95. This is an important book for those interested in Frederick's enormous contribution as well as his unfailing eye for talent such as Weeks.

Who Was Who Among North American Authors 1921-1939. Detroit: Gale, 1976, p. 1493. Brief note on Weeks.

Wimberly, W. C., ed. *MidCountry: Writings from the Heart of America.* Lincoln, Neb.: University of Nebraska Press, 1945. Biographical note on Weeks, pp. 509–510.

Douglas C. Wixson

Wells, Carolyn

Born: Rahway, New Jersey, on June 18, 1869

Marriage: Hadwin Houghton, April 2, 1918, no children

Died: March 26, 1942

Biography

Carolyn Wells was a prolific writer of light, whimsical, and nonsense verse, parodies of both verse and prose, and games, riddles, and other diversions. While many of her pieces have been anthologized, much more remains uncollected and is printed only in the magazines for which she wrote, including *Puck, The Chap Book, The Lark*, the old *Life, The Philistine, The Bibelot, The Yellow Book, Scribners*, and *Outlook*. Her best humorous verse was composed in the 1890s and early 1900s, at times in collaboration with such friends as Gelett Burgess, the illustrators Peter Newell and Wallace Morgan, and her favorite collaborator, Oliver Herford. With Herford as illustrator, she published *The Jingle Book* (1899), *Idle Idylls* (1900), *A Phenomenal Fauna* (1902), and *Baubles* (1917). She was also noted as an editor of humorous verse. *A Nonsense Anthology* (1902) was an immediate success and has remained her most popular book, going through 17 separate printings in her lifetime. This was followed by her *Parody Anthology* (1904), *Satire Anthology* (1905), *Whimsey Anthology* (1906), *A Vers de Society Anthology* (1907), and *The Book of Humorous Verse* (1920). In 1923 she published *An Outline of Humor* (reissued in 1933 as *The World's Best Humor*), which provided a theory of humor and analysis of selections of humor from the Greeks and Romans to the present. While in her later years she devoted much time to writing mysteries, including 46 Fleming Stone detective novels, and several series of children's and young people's books, these, too, are marked by her gaiety and wit.

Wells was born June 18, 1869, in Rahway, New Jersey, the daughter of William and Anna (Woodruff) Wells. In her autobiography, *The Rest of My Life* (1937), she proudly traced her ancestry to Thomas Welles, the fourth governor of Connecticut. Raised in a suburban home, not quite an estate but graced with "broad lawns, big trees, flower gardens and pleasant verandas,"[1] by well-to-do and supportive parents, her early life was unmarred except for a bout of scarlet fever at age six that affected her hearing.

She was blessed with a "leaping mind." As she said, "If I begin a book or if a friend begins to tell me a story, my thoughts leap to the inevitable or probable denouement. Anything that happens to me causes a rapid run of the gamut of consequences, pausing only at the very end."[2] This quickness, together with a certain precociousness—she was reading by the age of three and wrote her first "book" at six—made her dissatisfied with the dull rigidity of schools. She attended no college for, "since school was wasted motion, college would be the same thing raised to the nth power."[3] Instead, she relied on private lessons from family friends and acquaintances and her own voluminous reading in a variety of fields, including botany, entomology, history, and geography, as well as English and American literature, particularly the novelists Charles Dickens and William Makepeace Thackeray, Sir Walter Scott, Thomas Hardy, Anthony Trollope, Jane Austen, and the Elizabethan poets and dramatists.

In the early 1890s Wells became librarian for the Rahway Public Library. The situation was ideal: "Every book worth having, we bought; every periodical worth reading we subscribed to, and the librarian sat in the middle and read her way out."[4] Her reading together with the habit of keeping a commonplace books prepared her for her series of humor anthologies.

Wells's writing career began in 1892 with contributions of verse to *Puck* and other humor magazines. Her work found ready acceptance and she became a frequent contributor. In fact, so many poems were accepted for the special numbers of the *World's Fair Puck* of 1893 that some were printed anonymously or under her initials. While at Amherst taking a summer Shakespeare class under William Rolfe, she discovered the charade books of William Bellamy. At Rolfe's suggestion she put together a book of her own charades; *At the Sign of the Sphinx*, her first book, was published in 1896 and was a popular success. Meanwhile, she continued to write verse for a number of magazines, including, particularly at this time, *The Century Magazine*, *The Youth's Companion*, *The Delineator*, *Judge*, and *St. Nicholas* (through which she met Oliver Herford, who illustrated her jingles in 1895).

Although her literary successes in the 1890s tied her closely to the New York social and publishing world, she continued to live in Rahway until her marriage, in 1918, to Hadwin Houghton, a friend she had known for some years. (Although the son of Bernard Houghton, of the Boston publishing family, he was not connected with the firm.) After their marriage they moved to an apartment at the Hotel d'Artistes, 1 West 67th Street, in New York City. Their marriage, which Wells described as a time of "joyful interest," was cut short by his untimely death in 1919. Remaining in the New York apartment after his death, Wells pursued her writing, editing, and other interests, including book collecting, gathering significant collections of Walt Whitman and Edward Lear materials. Though her apartment was noted as a center for lively gatherings and she herself was known for her effervescent wit, in her later years she was invalided by several long illnesses and her increasing deafness. She died in New York on March 26, 1942.

Literary Analysis

Carolyn Wells was most accomplished in her nonsense and whimsey, and parodies and light satires, published in numerous magazines and collected in *Folly in the Forest* (1902), *Folly for the Wise* (1904), *Fluffy Ruffles* (1907), and other works. Her verse was often based upon her skill in metrical manipulations and logological play, as in her well-known tautonymic limerick, "The Tutor":

A Tutor who tooted the flute,
Tried to teach two young tooters to toot;
Said the two to the Tutor,
"Is it harder to toot or
To tutor two tooters to toot?"[5]

The limerick was a favorite form of hers and her anthology, *Carolyn Wells' Book of American Limericks*, was published in 1925. Nonsense might also grow from puns or other plays on words, such as the punning portmanteau limerick, "The Stone Walrus," which shows the influences of Lewis Carroll and Edward Lear:

This Stone-Walrus is used as a guard
To keep people out of the yard.
It sighs for the sea,
And gets mad as can be,
And I must say I think it is hard.[6]

A similar cleverness may be seen in the poem "One Week," which has been classified as a "catalogue whimsey":

The year had gloomily begun
For Willie Weeks, a poor man's SUN.
He was beset with bill and dun
And he had very little MON.
"This cash," said he, "won't pay my dues,
I've nothing here but ones and TUES."
A bright thought struck him, and he said,
"The rich Miss Goldrocks I will WED."
But when he paid his court to her,
She lisped, but firmly said, "No, THUR!"
"Alas!" said he, "then I must die!"
His soul went where they say souls FRI.
They found his gloves, and coat, and hat;
The Coroner upon them SAT.

(*Whimsey Anthology*, pp. 120-121)

The humor lies in the absolute appropriateness of the weekdays to the lines and in the irony that informs this and many of her whimseys and nonsense verses—the frying of the unfortunate Weeks's soul and the casual indifference of the coroner to Willie's last effects.

Such turns of phrase and plays on language typify many of her poems, ostensibly for children, such as "The Experiences of Gentle Jane." In the section "The Rude Train," though the humor arises partially from the pun, the greater effects are from the off-handed and light manner in which the train's rudeness is treated:

Last week Tuesday, gentle Jane
Met a passing railroad train;
"Ah, good afternoon," she said;
But the train just cut her dead.

(*Folly for the Wise*, p. 83)

This morbidity is seen also in the quatrains making up "Our Polite Parents":

Bobby with the nursery shears
Cut off both the baby's ears;
At the baby, so unsightly,
Mamma raised her eyebrows slightly.

(*Folly for the Wise*, p. 81)

The wit, which a later generation termed "sick," is cool and detached; the absurd is never far beneath the superficial whimsey or nonsensicality.

Even Wells's riddles show a kind of strength and power in this type of humor, as in number 12 from her *Book of Charades* (1927):

Beneath the sharp ax Queen Mary knelt,
And often its blows my first has dealt
To kings and queens and chickens.
The hour for my whole to each must come,
My first of my second is thought by some
The finest work of Dickens.

(p. 27)

(The answer is "Deathknell.") Number 43 again captures the irony of a violence hidden not too deeply beneath a placid scene:

I walked across my first,
With my second in my arms,
In hopes that I might find my whole
At one of the nearby farms.
Success my efforts crowned,
My whole came at my beck;
I left my one and two, and said,
"Be sure to wring its neck."

(p. 58)

(The answer is "Laundress.")

Her technical skill in poetry and quick grasp of the absurd made her an excellent parodist. The essence of parody is, as she says in the introduction to *A Parody Anthology* (1904), "sense rendering [which] . . . utilizes not only the original writer's diction and style, but follows a train of thought precisely along the lines that he would have pursued from the given premises" (p. xxi). This is seen in her imitation of Kipling redoing "Peter, Peter, Pumpkin Eater" as a ballad (from "A Symposium of Poets" in *An Outline of Humor* [1923]):

In a great big Mammoth pumpkin
Lookin' eastward to the sea,
There's a wife of mine a-settin'
And I know she's mad at me.
For I hear her calling, "Peter!"
With a wild hysteric shout;
"Come you back, you Punkin Eater,—
Come you back and let me out!"

(p. 757)

Occasionally, she used parody to satirize contemporary life, as in "The Poster Girl," her imitation of Gabriel Rossetti, which satirizes modern art, and "The Whist Player's Soliloquy" ("To trump or not to trump,—that is the question") on the rigors of bridge—one of her favorite diversions. She also parodied longer literary forms, including *Abeniki Caldwell* (1902), a burlesque historical novel, and *Ptomaine Street* (1921), a parody of *Main Street*.

Much of Wells's humor seems to lie on the surface, in the entanglements of language and the intricate wit of wordplay. This wit lies behind the games of her *Rainy Day Diversions* (1907), *Pleasant Day Diversions* (1909), *All for Fun Brain Teasers* (1933), and the precursor to Trivial Pursuit, *Ask Me a Question* (1927), a game based on "2000 questions and answers on interesting and informative subjects." Ultimately, however, the strength of Carolyn Wells's humor is the irony in her satires, parodies, and nonsense verse. She sets the language that we use to guide our lives against the realities that face us and finds that conventional wisdom scarcely meets the needs of the world. Thus, her "Mixed Maxims" and "Mixed Morals" provide better guidance than ordinary wise sayings:

> *A word to the wise is the root of all evil.*
> *The course of true love waits for no man.*
> *It's an ill wind that sweeps*
> *A friend in need is the thief of time.*
> *Uneasy lies the head that has no turning.*
>
> (*Folly for the Wise*, p. 108)

In a world of whimsey and nonsense, we are close to a recognition of the world as absurd. "Mixed Morals" are short fables providing contradictory conclusions. In "The Two Automobilists," for example, one "Bold and Audacious" young man drives his car "like a Red Dragon Pursuing his Prey," crashes, and is killed. The other "Timorous and Careful" young man drives slowly and cautiously, is run into from behind by two automobiles and an ice wagon—and is killed. She concludes, "This Fable teaches Us, The More Haste The Less Speed and Delays Are Dangerous" (*FW*, pp. 147-148). The voice is strikingly modern, as Wells's wit lies on the narrow verge between nonsense and the absurd, between whimsey and irony. The closing lines to her autobiography encapsulate this well:

> *When I think of Life as a—well, as a subject to think of, I begin to laugh.*
> *A bystanding friend said, "Stop your laughing!"*
> *But I said, "I don't see anything to stop laughing at."*

(p. 287)

Summary

Nonsense is always in danger when it is taken too seriously, but it is equally in danger when it is not taken seriously enough. Carolyn Wells solidified the position of nonsense and whimsey in American humor. Her verse in the 1890s and early 1900s and her collaborations with Gelett Burgess and Oliver Herford made her the most prominent and probably the most prolific writer of light verse in those decades. Her poetry is noted both for its technical merit and its verve, wit, and imaginative word play. Through her own work and the anthologies of nonsense, whimsey, parody, and satire, published between 1902 and 1906, which brought together hitherto uncollected works by major writers, anonymous and ephemeral works, and works by her contemporaries, Carolyn Wells helped to define the genre of light verse.

Notes

1. Carolyn Wells, *The Rest of My Life* (Philadelphia: Lippincott, 1937), p. 233.
2. Ibid., p. 24.
3. Ibid., p. 36.
4. Ibid., p. 193.
5. Wells, ed., *A Whimsey Anthology* (New York: Scribner's, 1906), pp. 264-265.
6. Wells, *Folly for the Wise* (Indianapolis: Bobbs-Merrill, 1904), p. 17.

Selected Bibliography

Primary Sources

Humor

At the Sign of the Sphinx. New York: Stone and Kimball, 1896.
The Jingle Book. New York: Macmillan, 1899.
Folly for the Wise. Indianapolis: Bobbs-Merrill, 1904.
Rubaiyat of a Motor Car. New York: Dodd, Mead, 1906.
Ptomaine Street. Philadelphia: Lippincott, 1921.
A Book of Charades. New York: George Doran, 1927.

Edited Anthologies

A Nonsense Anthology. New York: Scribner's, 1902.
A Parody Anthology. New York: Scribner's, 1904.
A Satire Anthology. New York: Scribner's, 1905.
A Whimsey Anthology. New York: Scribner's, 1906.
The Book of Humorous Verse. New York: George Doran, 1920.
An Outline of Humor. New York: Putnam's, 1923.

Autobiography

The Rest of My Life. Philadelphia: Lippincott, 1937.

Secondary Sources

"Carolyn Wells." *Wilson Bulletin*, April 1930, p. 366.
Dresner, Zita Zatkin. "Carolyn Wells." *Dictionary of Literary Biography*. Vol. 11. *American Humorists, 1800-1950.* Ed. Stanley Trachtenberg. Detroit: Gale, 1982, pp. 556-560. Overview of Wells's life and works.
Masson, Thomas L. *Our American Humorists.* New York: Moffat, Yard, 1922, pp. 303-323.

Malcolm Hayward

Whitcher, Frances Miriam Berry

Born: Whitesboro, New York, on November 1, 1811
Education: Local schools
Marriage: Benjamin W. Whitcher, one child
Died: January 4, 1852

Biography

Frances Berry Whitcher was one of the most popular American humorists of the nineteenth century. Partly because her career was so short that her complete works fill only two books—*The Papers of the Widow Bedott* (1856) and *Widow Spriggins, Mary Elmer, and Other Sketches* (1867)—Whitcher's reputation has declined over the years. However, to contemporaries her Yankee pieces were among the best ever written; for some they were the best.

One of the thirteen children of Lewis Berry, a tavern owner, and his wife Elizabeth Wells, Frances Berry was born in Whitesboro, New York, on November 1, 1811. Her life seems to have been relatively retired and uneventful; at least that is the impression conveyed by her friends. Official biographies and eulogies published after her death amount to little more than collections of loosely related anecdotes in which Whitcher remains a shadowy figure. According to one, "So singularly modest and unobtrusive were her habits, that her life might safely yield in variety of incident, to the humblest champion of woman's rights, or the most obscure victim of woman's wrongs" (*Spriggins*, pp. 11-12).

Nevertheless, to judge from hints sprinkled through her sister's recollections as well as her own writings, Frances's childhood was not a particularly happy one. In "Letters from Timberville," a late series of sketches related in a voice presumably near her own, the narrator discusses a "wild boy" with a penchant for jokes and caricature who has been written off by family and friends as unmanageable and who believes that people "don't treat me like a human being. "To tell the truth," the passage runs, "I had a sort of sympathy for the child, to which, perhaps, certain recollections of my own juvenile experience contributed in some degree" (*Spriggins*, p. 314). Elsewhere Whitcher described herself as "a lonely child almost without companionship; wandering alone, for hours, in the woods and fields, creating for myself an ideal world, and in that ideal world I lived for many years" (*Bedott*, p. xiv).

Whitesboro was a Presbyterian community, and although, as an adult, Whitcher found the tenets of Calvinism oppressive enough that she became an Episcopalian, her childhood poems reveal a melancholy particularly characteristic of nineteenth-century America's backwater Calvinist settlements. Indeed, she never escaped the fundamental pessimism of her childhood religion; it remained in her work until the end of her life. Frances Berry was taller than most women; perhaps that was one reason for her being very shy with strangers. In later life this habitual reserve was often mistaken for arrogance.

Frances was educated in Whitesboro, first at the village school and then at a local classical academy. Her first teacher was, according to her sister, "a sour-faced woman who knocked the alphabet into the heads of a little group of unruly children"; her second—at the academy—was "the kindest-hearted and most indulgent of pedagogues . . . but the younger fry were left to take care of themselves." Consequently Frances largely educated herself in the local library reading romantic novels, histories, and the works of approved writers such as Joseph Addison, William Goldsmith, and Sir Walter Scott. At around eighteen she was tutored by a "rarely gifted woman" of Utica (*Passages*, pp. 50, 52). She learned French well enough to converse fluently in that language. Although her sketches of American provincial life suggest a familiarity with French writers—particularly Honoré de Balzac—because of her characteristic "horror of affectation and display" in life and literature, she "never allowed herself to use a French phrase in writing or conversation, unless it were in such common use as to be in a measure Anglicized" (*Passages*, p. 53). In similar fashion she always prized an English "style . . . plain and homely." "I have," she wrote specifically of a late work, "been so anxious to avoid the grandiloquent style of many of our female story writers, that I may have gone too far the other way" (*Spriggins*, p. 34).

She wrote and recited poetry from a very early age and was extremely skilled at drawing. Her most notable characteristic, however, was a sense of humor appreciated by neither her neighbors nor herself. "I received at my birth," she wrote, "the undesirable gift of a remarkably strong sense of the ridiculous. I can scarcely remember the time when the neighbors were not afraid that I would make fun of them. For indulging in this propensity, I was scolded at home, and wept over and prayed with, by certain well-meaning old maids in the neighborhood; but all to no purpose."

Frances Berry became a professional writer in her thirties. Her first pieces, the Widow Spriggins sketches, were done for the entertainment of a local literary society, one of whose members urged her to publish them in a Rome, New York, newspaper. There they drew enough attention that in 1846 Joseph C. Neal asked her to write for his *Saturday Gazette and Lady's*

Literary Museum. For that magazine, Berry created the Widow Bedott papers, which were in turn so great a success that in 1847 Lewis Godey asked her to contribute to *Godey's Lady's Book,* one of America's most popular periodicals.

In the meantime Berry married B.W. Whitcher, an Episcopal minister, and the Aunt Maguire papers that she wrote for *Godey's* detail the problems of ministers and their wives— particularly those thought by parishioners to be publishing humorists. In 1849, she gave birth to a daughter. Shortly afterwards her health began to fail. She left her husband's parish in Oswego, New York, and returned to Whitesboro where she died of consumption in 1852.

Literary Analysis

Whitcher's writings fit neatly into the vernacular tradition that evolved during the first half of the nineteenth century and was known as "Down East humor," "Yankee humor," or "the literature of misspelling." Her style, techniques, and themes are those of contemporaries working the same vein. Whitcher's is a comedy of the provinces, detailing the characters and activities of small New England towns undergoing great economic, social, political, and intellectual changes. Her earliest pieces are essentially monologues in dialect. The commentaries of Permilly Ruggles Spriggins, the Widow Bedott, and Aunt Maguire are filled with the comic misspellings, malapropisms, coined words, and indecorous combinations of lofty diction and slang characteristic of vernacular humor. The sketches contain "i" for "e" as in "gintel," and "poitry," dropped final "g's," misspellings of words seen but never heard—for example "billy dux (that are's the French for love-letter)"—as well as plenty of "eny's," "agins," "heerds," "knowds," "kinders," and "enufs." Permilee Ruggles, the belle of Podunk, who is "of Dutch distraction on the mother's side, and New England consent on the father's," "jackleates" in a moment of passion: "O! if there is a minnit when the heart-broken sperrit feels as if it would go off the handle with joy, 'tis when long severcatid frinds onexpectedly meets!" (*Spriggins*, p. 127). In a poem celebrating her second marriage, the Widow Bedott writes:

> O Shadrack, my Shadrack! Prisilla did speak,
> While the rosy red blushes surmantled her
>   cheek,
> And the tears of affection bedoozled her eye,
> O Shadrack, my Shadrack! I'm yourn till I die.
>   (Bedott, p. 114)

In general, Whitcher used standard comic devices very intelligently. Her dialect revealed both her characters and their society instead of merely isolating them from an educated norm. Malapropisms, for example, often look more like translations than funny words created in igno-

rance. That is, they suggest a process of popular etymology by which the half-educated citizens of Whitcher's America attempt to bring the exotic, the elevated, the yearned-for into their lives. The choices they make as to the meaning of an unfamiliar word, the equivalent local context to fit it into, and its shape or sound tell a great deal about their values, processes, attitudes, and conventions. Permilee is transforming herself into a lady like those in the novels she reads and so she always "condescends" the stairs. She refers to the males chosen as heroes in her largely imagined romantic adventures as "swine," not "swain." Because she has learned from books that the primary characteristic of a lady is insufferable arrogance and because her lovers turn out to be jokers cruelly mocking her literary fantasies, her word is the correct one for Podunk. In like fashion, the Widow Bedott's translation of the semi-French "religious devoirs" into the all-Wiggletown "devours" suggests the voracious egotism in all her activities—not just the religious. When she attends a literary "swearee," the posturing, back-biting, and raving she encounters make her version of the word more accurate than "soirees."

Much of the humor of Whitcher's dialect writing comes, therefore, from the appropriateness rather than the inappropriateness of all variation from standards. In her work such shifts are not jack-in-the-box absurdities; they make sense contextually. They suggest a people characterized not only by their ignorance of what ought to be but by their being in the process of creating something new but not necessarily admirable or attractive. That is also true of the many examples of "poitry" by which the Widows Spriggins and Bedott distinguish themselves. Their art has nothing to do with truth, beauty, or literary tradition—Bedott, for example, has never heard of Shakespeare. Rhythm, rhyme, and "fine" words and phrases serve solely to identify the work as real "poitry." The main formal criterion of this art is that the poem be long enough to give the reader "his money's worth." The subject of a verse is always—even when submerged—the writer and its purpose the realization of the writer's desire to celebrate herself, send a very specific message to a particular person, or show off her remarkable talent and sensitivity. Typical is Bedott's self-consuming "K.K.—Can't Calculate," a card played in her wooing of the Baptist minister, Elder Sniffles:

> What poor short-sighted worms we be—
>   For we can't calculate
> With any sort of sartinee,
>   What is to be our fate.
>
> These words Prisilla's heart did reach
> And caused her tears to flow,

When first she heard the Elder preach
  About six months ago.

How true it is what he did state,
  And thus affected her,
That nobody can't calculate
  What is gwine to occur.

When we retire, can't calculate
  But what afore the morn
Our housen will conflaggerate
  And we be left forlorn.

. . .

Can't calculate with no precision
  On naught beneath the sky;
And so I've come to the decision,
  That ain't worth while to try.
                    (*Bedott*, pp. 93-94)

Similar evidence of self-involvement is to be found in the rambling organization of Spriggins' and Bedott's monologues. In "Hezekiah Bedott," perhaps the most frequently anthologized of Whitcher's works, the widow begins: "He was a wonderful hand to moralize, husband was, 'specially after he begun to enjoy poor health. He made an observation once when he was in one of his poor turns, that I shall never forget the longest day I live" (*Bedott*, p. 7). Then follow several pages of observations seemingly unrelated to the main point and seemingly carrying the sketch away from the emphasis of its opening to an inevitable anti-climax. Finally the widow concludes: "Says he to me, says he, 'Silly.' I says to him, says I, 'What?' He says to me, says he, '*We're all poor critters!*'" On one hand the narration of "Hezekiah Bedott" reveals the lack of any intellectual discipline or system in the mind and imagination of the teller. The widow is, like some of Edgar Allan Poe's and Mark Twain's story-tellers, unable to resist any association or analogy and compulsively pursues digression after digression. On the other hand, the widow's memories of her husband's health, the marriages of other townspeople, her initial reaction to her husband's name, and the day that she and he got stuck in the snow in retrospect do seem to have been made coherent by that concluding observation. Instead of no organization, "Hezekiah Bedott" seems to possess a new and unorthodox one in which—in Emersonian fashion—thought discovers its own shape and in which the organizing agent is a perverted version of Self Reliance. Whereas narrators like Twain's tellers of "The Celebrated Jumping Frog" or "Grandfather's Ram" completely lose themselves in their admiration for the characters of their stories and the fascinating things

they do, Whitcher's widows cannot forget themselves long enough to relate a complete story about someone else. They are tempted into digression by anything that allows them to talk about themselves. They shape their stories and ultimately their realities, constructing and reconstructing them to fit their desires. They are amusing but quite mad.

Ruggles introduces herself:

> I was born in Podunk, a charming and sequesterated villidge on the banks of the Morantic and meanderin' Mohawk . . . I was the flower of the family. I've heern my mother tell that I was a wonderful cretur from the time I was knee high to a hop-toad . . . My figger was oncommon graceful, and I had a great deal of dignity. But more'n all that, I writ poitry of the first order, and was called the biggest genyus in Podunk. I was a touch above the vulgar as I said before, and so I kept myself putty scerce.
>   (*Spriggins*, p. 39)

Later, describing her preparations for a grand occasion, she writes:

> I unlocked my chist, and took out a white dimity with a long short with a blue ribbin' found the bottom on't, and put it on, and tied a red sash round my waist; then I took and tied a yaller ribbin round my head and stuck a number of mornin' glories in it; then I huv a pink silk long shawl round my neck, and my twilight was completed. So you see I didn't depart from the elegant simplicity always conspicuous in my dress.
>   (*Spriggins*, p. 60)

In her earliest pieces, Whitcher varied from common practice by using neither a frame nor a "civilized" narrator to evaluate her characters or guide the reader's reactions to them. She let her characters reveal themselves and trusted readers to reach correct conclusions about them. She must either have been uncomfortable with unadorned monologue or felt restricted by it, however, for her later work became more conventional in formal point of view. Some of the later Bedott papers experiment with a dramatic form; they contain dialogue with speakers identified as in a playscript and stage directions set in parentheses. Others contain intrusive letters of comment from "superiors," that is, from better educated, more rational people. The Aunt Maguire papers written for *Godey's* utilize a different kind of narrator altogether. Although still a vernacular character, Aunt Maguire is less self-centered than her sister, the Widow Bedott. She is also not a performer but an observer who sits at the edge of action, watching and recording. In "Letters from Timberville," the last series of comic pieces published in her lifetime, Whitcher dropped a vernacular narrator and spoke through a well-educated minister's wife, presumably a character much like herself. The narrative voice of "Mary Elmer, or Trials and Changes," a "more serious" work left unfinished at her death, is that of an unidentified omniscient.

These changes may have been responses to success. As a result of the popularity of her writings and perhaps of her widening experience of the world, Whitcher may have grown more confident of her values and asserted them more in her work. The changes in narrative strategy may also have reflected the pressure traditionally applied to our best humorists by themselves and others to become "more serious." Early in her career Whitcher did consider giving up writing comedy. She was dissuaded by Joseph Neal's reassurance that her humor served a very moral purpose. The reminiscences published after her death suggest that friends and relatives seldom let her forget that they considered her capable of better than Bedott and Maguire—capable of "more sensible matter" and "the exercise of a higher and purer taste." It is possible, however, that changes in her narrative form were the consequences of changing attitudes toward her comic creations. Her early works are farcical; the later ones more realistic. The early works concentrate on isolated literary eccentrics; the later ones resemble genre pictures of groups of people lodged uncomfortably together in what is presumably "the actual world." Whitcher, therefore, may have come to believe that while a few imaginary Permilly Ruggles or Silly Bedotts may be amusing, a living nation of them is not. Her shift in point of view may have signified a desire not only to separate herself from her vernacular characters but to make clear how much she hated them and feared the values that they embody.

The egotism of Permilly Ruggles is relatively harmless. As "the biggest genyus in Podunk," she attempts to improve herself by using a romantic novel, *The Children of the Abbey*, as her guide to life. She seeks to be a heroine, but in rejecting the real world for a literary one, she becomes a looney grotesque. She writes "sensitive poitry." She creates a language half slang, half book-borrowed, that is impressive and incomprehensible. When her parents urge her to marry a successful but un-pale, un-thin merchant, she "jackleates": "You may manure me in the most gloomiest dunjin in Podunk . . . but you will never conduce me to giv my willin consent except against my inclination." There are only a few traces of darkness in Whitcher's portrait of Permilly. The girl's self-absorption approaches

the monstrous when she composes an elegy on the death of her mother and in the catalog of her emotional responses barely mentions her parent. The potential effect on a democratic society of such a character is briefly suggested when Permilly establishes a "Simminary" for girls at which students' questions draw responses like "I guess ye ha'nt been under very good deseplyne in the schools ye've ben to afore yit, or ye wouldn't darst to ax yer school marm questions, and sich questions! Want to know the meanin' of Nommi, Possimine', Onjine! Why it's grammar—that's the meanin' on't—so shet yer head." Community opinion is divided on Ruggles. "Is the young lady deranged?" asks one man. "No . . . only she's rather smarter'n common folks," replies her Aunt Huldy. Witcher did not, we can infer, intend that the girl be taken as a dangerously representative type. Furthermore, just as Permilly is not greatly touched by reality, she does not, Whitcher implied, touch it. She has little effect on society; if anyone is victimized by her behavior it is she.

The Widow Bedott is essentially Ruggles grown older and portrayed with either more restraint or a shifted emphasis. Literary satire is more muted in the Bedott sketches. Like Permilly, Persilly is, however, a great hand at "poitry" and does occasionally incorporate literary conventions into her own life—as when she wanders lonely in the woods reciting a poetic lament of her unrequited love for Parson Sniffles. There is more of a point to her behavior, though; she knows that he will overhear her. Bedott is more conscious than Spriggins. She is "innocently selfish" and self-absorbed (a letter to a daughter announcing her second marriage contains no information about the groom) but she is more interested in the immediate world and much more active in it.

Bedott is saved from being thoroughly reprehensible and perhaps unfunny by her energy, ingenuity, and shrewdness, by a disinterested kindness when her ambitions or social anxieties are not aroused, and by a commonsensical ability to survive in "this changing kind of a world." She is saved, in other words, by the attractive animal qualities of the vernacular hero. In addition, she is not made the representative of the dark possibilities of American democracy. Like Permilly, she is an isolated case. Her relatives are sensible and attractive. At the same time, far worse people than she live in the world of her sketches. The clumsiness of her pretensions and the transparency of her deceptions give her an unintended honesty not as evident in more practised hypocrites. The widow tricks Sniggles into marrying her by saying nothing to discredit a rumor started by her nephew that she is rich, but when after her marriage he angrily confronts her with the truth, she asks: "Which was most to blame, me for lettin' you think I was rich, or you for marryin' me *because* you thought I was rich? For my part, I think *that* was ruther incompatible with *your* professions. *Ministers* had ought to have their affections sot above transiterry riches" (*Bedott*, p. 138). Finally, like Permilly, the widow is her own victim. Her triumph is her defeat. In winning the Parson she has, Whitcher made clear, locked herself into an ill-matched and loveless combat of a marriage. And so, once again like Permilly, to survive she must retreat into fiction. She lies to her diary. After the argument, for example, she writes: "O that I may be truly thankful for the blessins I injoy, especially for such a pardner!" (*Bedott*, p. 139).

The Aunt Maguire Papers that Whitcher wrote for *Godey's* included more changes in the style of her comic writing. To begin with, their narrator, Silly Bedott's Sister, Aunt Maguire, is more sensible and less selfish than the widow; consequently, she provides a normative identification within the stories. As a watcher rather than a doer, she also acts as a buffer between readers and the worst excesses of the vernacular. In addition to reflecting *Godey's* demand for gentility, these alterations in the narrative character and strategy may suggest Whitcher's growing desire to cage her characters. The new point of view of the *Godey* pieces is accompanied by a widening in the scope of Whitcher's satire; her attention seems to have been transferred from individuals to society. In describing a donation party that is intended to supplement a minister's pitifully small salary but which turns into a rich free-loaders' riot that nearly ruins him, or the formation of a sewing circle that proposes to earn money for the renovation of a community church but spends more on its own entertainment, or the persecution of a minister's wife thought to be a *Godey's* humorist, or the badgering of Deacon Bedott by a self-appointed guardian of public morality who is told by a joker that the Deacon was seen "half-shaved on cider," Whitcher detailed the fear, envy, ambition, and hypocrisy characterizing the social tyranny in America's Podunks, Scrabble Hills, and Slabtowns. Democratic in profession but "rastocratical" in practice and desire, the populations of these towns seem made up mostly of bullies, toadies, and victims. The relatively innocent-seeming egotism of Spriggins and Bedott here developed into something nastier, more virulent, and more pervasive. The towns have their good, intelligent, and humane people but these are distinctly in the minority. Society as described by Aunt Maguire is organized around hatred and resentment, as Whitcher reveals in Scrabble Hill's version of the American Dream realized, the rise of the Savage family. Mr. Sav-

age's success results in a big stone house filled with furniture shipped all the way from Philadelphia and his wife's setting up for a lady:

> She made up her mind she'd rule the roast, no matter what it cost—she'd be the first in Scrabble Hill . . . Of course, them that thinks money's the main thing (and there's plenty such here and everywhere), is ready to flatter her and make a fuss over her, and approves of all her dewin's. If there's anybody that *won't* knuckle tew her, I tell ye they have to take it *about east.* She abuses 'em to their faces and slanders 'em to their backs. Such conduct wouldent be put up with in a poor woman; but them that would be for drummin' *me* out of town if I should act so, is ready to *uphold* Miss Samson Savage, and call it *independence* and *frankness* in her.
>
> (*Bedott*, p. 183)

The Whitchers were threatened with a lawsuit by a stranger who believed Mrs. Savage a portrait of his wife, and they were essentially driven out of their parish after the publication of the *Godey* letters. No doubt these events must at the very least have strengthened a suspicion in Whitcher that she was describing not just the eccentricities of one small New England town but the general conditions of American life.

The shift from vernacular to educated narrator in Whitcher's last works, "Letters from Timberville" and the unfinished "Mary Elmer," not only continued the widening of her satirical attack, it also distanced the writer from her material and, by placing the stories in a more serious context (in the case of "Mary Elmer" sentimental melodrama) cut off the reader's ability to evade Whitcher's observations with the laughing dismissal of "It's only a joke." These are developments characteristic of America's dark humor, as is the attitude toward change that becomes prominent in Whitcher's later writings. Timberville, according to the letters' narrator, is a place "neither city nor country, but, as it were, in a state of *betweenity*, aping the former yet possessing many of the peculiarities of the latter, but in nothing resembling those old-fashioned, stationary country villages, in one of which I had the happiness to be born and reared" (*Spriggins*, p. 323). Timberville is a "new *enterprising*" American community.

Getting rich is the chief ambition of Timberville; "rich and poor" the "chief distinction." The world of "Mary Elmer" is even darker. Husbands abandon their wives to actual poverty as they rush to California in search of wealth. When the eminent ladies of the town hear of illness in a distressed family, they talk about warning the landlord who might have trouble rerenting his house after evicting the sick. They suggest that the afflicted be quickly committed to the poorhouse, where their disease can do no harm. Within this society religion has been distorted into the prop of self-centered materialism; Scripture has been twisted into a gospel of self-justification. The new Golden Rule reads: "Everyone must look to their own interest, you know."

Widow Spriggins, Mary Elmer, and Other Sketches contains one last letter from Aunt Maguire, "Account of the Mission to Mufflete-gawny," that suggests what Whitcher thought was the next step for the new American civilization—its export. The letter describes the attempts of a pair of married missionaries to give away their children before returning to labor in heathen lands. "Scripter commands us," they say, "to leave all and foller the Lord" (*Spriggins*, p. 349). Their holiness and sacrifice are praised by the townspeople who will not help the needy of their own community but will gladly contribute to carrying light into the dark. In a sense, Whitcher here touched the center of hypocrisy, greed, materialism, and idealism perverted beyond recognition at the heart of the mad community of self that was her comic world.

Although Whitcher's career was short and her comic techniques, values, and character types remained fundamentally the same throughout, her writing shows considerable technical and intellectual development. As she wrote she seems to have become more and more aware of both her art and the world it described. Her earliest pieces are mixtures of literary parody and comic characters; her last, biting social criticism. In some ways, Whitcher's work suggests what might be called a "female perspective." Women and their activities dominate the stories. Whitcher touched on the exploitation of daughters by parents, the absolute necessity for a woman to marry, the dangerous dependence of married women on unstable men, and the victimization of women by the thoughtless jokes of men. (Interestingly enough, only men are allowed to be humorists in her fictive world. Women can be funny but only men are conscious jokers.) Nevertheless, it would be a mistake to isolate Whitcher from American humor in a small category labeled "Oddities: American Women Humorists." Her work is fundamentally like that of all her contemporaries and descendants. Her techniques, subjects, and attitudes are either those said to be characteristic of Down East and Southwestern humor or variations of them. Her characters are the *eirons*, *alazons*, swindlers, bullies, blusterers, rubes, newly rich squires and squiresses of mainstream comic writing. Her humor is less physical but just as pointed, angry, nasty, and, intellectually at least,

violent. The assaults of fools on social and artistic decorum reported in her work may be less excessive than those found in others' comedy, but in their way they are just as grotesque. At the end of her life, her humor was becoming increasingly political.

Summary

As Clyde G. Wade has rightly stated, the brevity of Frances Whitcher's career and her limited literary output will no doubt prevent her ever being considered more than a minor figure in American literature. Nevertheless, the popularity of the Widow Bedott papers, which went through around twenty-four editions in the nineteenth century and were dramatized in 1879 long after her death by David Ross Locke, one of the best known of our vernacular humorists, as well as the foreshadowings of writers like Twain, Ring Lardner, and Sinclair Lewis one finds in her work all suggest that her influence on the shaping of at least one strand of American humor may have been considerable. Although Whitcher's consignment to the small world of scholarly footnotes seems unfair and unfortunate, it would not matter much if it did not prevent the tales of the Widows Spriggins and Bedott, Aunt Maguire, and the rest getting into the hands of modern readers. Unlike much nineteenth century humor, Whitcher's work is still amusing, pertinent, thought-provoking, and readable. Frances Whitcher was one of nineteenth-century America's most interesting humorists and, arguably, one of American literature's best.

Selected Bibliography

Primary Sources

The Widow Bedott Papers. New York: J.C. Derby, 1856.

Widow Spriggins, Mary Elmer, and Other Sketches, Ed. M.L. Ward Whitcher. New York: Charleton, 1867.

Secondary Sources

Neal, Alice B. "Introductory." *The Widow Bedott Papers*. New York: Oakly and Mason, 1869, pp. i–xix.

"Passages in the Life of the Author of Aunt Maguire's Letters, Bedott Papers, Etc., in Two Parts. By Her Sister." *Godey's Magazine and Ladies Book*, 47 (July and August, 1853): 49–54; 109–115.

Wade, Clyde G. "Frances Miriam Whitcher." *Dictionary of Literary Biography*. Vol. 11, part 2. *American Humorists, 1800–1950*. Ed. Stanley Trachtenberg. Detroit: Gale Research, 1982, pp. 560–567.

"Whitcher, Frances Miriam." *Dictionary of American Biography*. Vol. 20. New York: Charles Scribner's Sons, 1936, p. 82.

"Whitcher, Frances Miriam." *National Cyclopedia of American Biography*. Vol. 6. New York: James T. White, 1892, p. 30.

Michael D. Butler

White, E[lwyn] B[rooks]

Born: Mount Vernon, New York, on July 11, 1899
Education: Cornell University, B.A., 1921
Marriage: Katharine Sergeant Angell, 1929, one child
Died: October 1, 1985

Biography

Elwyn Brooks "Andy" White has long been regarded as one of America's finest essayists. He has been credited with rejuvenating the informal essay as a genre.[1] He has also written poetry, short stories, editorials, children's books, and even cartoon captions, but the form that he made truly his own is the "casual," the apparently off-handed, gently humorous essay with which he got his start in *The New Yorker.* Although he began as a newspaper man, magazine writing launched his literary career. Even readers unfamiliar with his work for *The New Yorker* or *Harper's Magazine* will remember him for the children's books that he gave them—*Stuart Little, Charlotte's Web, The Trumpet of the Swan*—and for "the little book" that he gave them as college students, a revised version of William Strunk, Jr.'s *The Elements of Style.* At various times White has commented wryly on the American scene and has defended human values and aspirations, always with a grace and precision that set his style apart from that of his contemporaries.

Born July 11, 1899, in Mt. Vernon, New York, Elwyn was the youngest of six children born to Samuel Tilly White and Jessie Hart White. As president of a prosperous piano-manufacturing company in New York City, Samuel was able to give his family a comfortable, secure home in Mount Vernon, then about a half hour's train ride from the city. At his birth Elwyn's parents were approaching middle age and his brothers and sisters were five or more years older than he, so before he finished grammar school he was the sole child occupying a large Victorian home that was governed firmly but lovingly. Respected within the family and without, his parents nurtured in their children such traditional American values as love of home, church (the Whites were Protestant), and country, regard for honest and decent behavior, and reverence for the natural world. In adulthood their youngest son abandoned only one of these values, the love of church, and then more from lack of interest than lack of belief.

The Whites also encouraged learning, although Elwyn most appreciated the informal schooling afforded him by the world just beyond his door; books and teachers were secondary to neighborhood stables and ponds, and school was among the places that he least enjoyed. Of slight build but of energetic spirits, he was shy and awkward with girls, active and well liked among boys. Even as a youngster White counted writing almost as important a pursuit as bicycling, skating, and boating; by his fifteenth year he had already won three literary prizes, two of them from the *St. Nicholas Magazine*, which liked to encourage young talent. The Mount Vernon High School *Oracle* published his poems, sketches, and stories, and even his biology lab notes were written with the spare, graceful style that was to become his hallmark.[2] Though perhaps he was not yet aware of it, White's vocation as a writer was probably decided by the end of his freshman year at Cornell University, where he had already become a reporter for the university newspaper.

A freshman in 1917, White expected to be drafted, but the end of World War I in 1918 insured that he would complete four uninterrupted years of school. There he distinguished himself through his work for the *Cornell Daily Sun*, becoming editor-in-chief his junior year. One of only two college dailies printed in America when White entered Cornell, the *Sun* provided him with valuable journalistic and editorial experience, and the good humor and honesty of his personality began asserting itself in print. Association with such astute and inspiring professors as George Lincoln Burr (history) and William Strunk, Jr. (English) and involvement with the Manuscript Club, a weekly gathering of students and faculty who met to share their writing, also contributed to White's development as a thinker and a writer.

After college, "Andy," as his friends had dubbed him following a tradition relating to a former president of the college, lacked a firm sense of direction; he knew that he wanted to write, but he was unsure of his format. He quickly tired of reporting for the United Press, his first job after graduation (excepting a summer stint as a counselor at a Canadian boys' camp). He tried public relations work for various firms but found it unengaging. The spring of 1922, White and a college friend, Howard Cushman, set out on a rambling journey west in a Model T Ford nicknamed Hotspur, purchased for the trip. Supporting themselves any way that they could manage, from selling poems to local papers to selling roach powder door-to-door, the two young men thoroughly enjoyed their road's-eye-view of America, a view that subsequently informed, if only subtly, much of White's writing. They eventually landed in Seattle, Washington, where White was able to get a job reporting for the *Seattle Times.* Once again, routine reporting did not suit him, and although White's editor allowed him to venture into feature stories and his own small column, he was eventually fired. In the summer of 1923, White headed north for, as he recalled forty years later, "there is a period near the beginning of every man's life when he has little to cling to except his unmanageable dream, little to support him except good health, and nowhere to go but all over the place."[3] With only enough money for one-way passage, he boarded a steamer bound for Alaska. The trip proved memorable for the exciting experiences it afforded him, deepening his sensitivity to people of all classes and types. He continued to fill the pages of a journal he had begun keeping in his teens, recording impressions, feelings, memories, and experiments with verse.

By autumn 1923, White was back in Mount Vernon, where he lived with his parents and worked in advertising in New York City. He soon moved to the city, although he had no steady job during the next eighteen months because advertising proved as uncongenial to him as reporting had. It was a significant period for him as he thoroughly acquainted himself with the city that had already become one of the loves of his life. Since his return from the west, he had begun publishing a few poems in Christopher Morley's column, "Bowling Green," in the *New York Post* and in Franklin Pierce Adams's ("F.P.A.") prestigious "Conning Tower" in the *New York World*, trying to earn his living as a writer. In February 1925, a new magazine appeared in the city, aptly named *The New Yorker*. Acting on a friend's suggestion that this periodical might appreciate White's brand of humor, Andy began to contribute light sketches ("casuals") which brought him a job the following year as a *New Yorker* staff writer. Editor Harold Ross and his assistant, Katharine Sergeant Angell, had some difficulty securing White's full-time services, however, for by this time he so cherished his personal freedom that a desk job with regular hours, it seemed to him, might as well be his death warrant. Finally, he agreed to a part-time arrangement. White's attachment to the magazine grew in both a professional and an emotional way and was sealed in 1929 when he married the recently divorced Katharine Sergeant, herself one of *The New Yorker*'s greatest editorial assets.

From 1929 to 1938, the Whites spent most of each year in New York, leading professionally and personally rewarding lives as their magazine passed through the Depression virtually unscathed and as their family expanded with the birth late in 1930 of a son, Joel (by her previous marriage Katharine had two other children, Nancy and Roger). In 1933, White bought a saltwater farm in Maine, a state where he had enjoyed vacationing off and on since boyhood. For five years he supervised, largely by mail, the running of his farm by hired hands until he was able to move his family there in the spring of 1938. White did not altogether abandon *The New Yorker*'s pages when he took up farming, but he began writing a monthly column for *Harper's Magazine*. In March 1943, however, he gave up the column to resume the writing of weekly editorials for *The New Yorker*, for he felt that more frequent publication in a weekly periodical was necessary to keep up with the progression of World War II.

This return to *The New Yorker* meant the Whites' return to New York City for another fourteen years, and although they moved back to the Maine farm permanently in 1957, White's contributions to *The New Yorker* continued until 1982. Katharine White died in 1977; E.B. White died on October 1, 1985.

Literary Analysis

Throughout boyhood and his college days, White's friends appreciated his warm wit, and very likely no one was surprised when his sense of humor began to infect his writing, especially while he served as editor-in-chief of the *Cornell Daily Sun*. White's and the century's twenties coincided, and although they both had their share of restless high spirits, the young man never succumbed to the era's most enticing invitations—a life of playboyish glamour at the one extreme or of disillusionment and self-imposed exile at the other. Similarly, in his *Sun* editorials, in his journals, in the poetry and sketches he published in various periodicals, and in the early writing he did for *The New Yorker*, White's humor was rarely slapstick, nor was his serious comment particularly biting, though it sometimes became so later. Certainly he could be hilarious, as in a cartoon caption for a dinnertime scene in which a mother says to her child, "It's broccoli, dear," and the child replies, "I say it's spinach and I say the hell with it." Moreover, he sometimes approached pointed satire, as in his comment regarding the widespread commercialization of the Lindbergh transatlantic flight: "We noted that the *Spirit of St. Louis* had not left the ground ten minutes before it was joined by the Spirit of Me Too."[4] Still, the words that readers most often use to describe his work are "gentle," "modest," "lyric," and "honest." Early in his career White's style became what it remained: colloquial but precise, his tone assuring readers that he was one of them, an ordinary fellow trying to find his bumbling way in the world.

Of literary influences, there were very few. Never very bookish, White quickly outgrew whatever youthful aspirations he may have had for writing "great" literature, so he did not spend much time reading it. He professed admiration for Sinclair Lewis and Carl Sandburg, known for their penetrating portraits of midwestern people and places, and for such journalists as Christopher Morley, S.J. Perelman, Don Marquis, Ring Lardner, F.P.A., and H.L. Mencken. If he ever came close to following a literary tradition, it was that of Henry David Thoreau, with whom White is often compared. The two writers share certain appealing themes: interest in living simply in a world gone complex; interest in life's cyclical progressions, especially as they are manifested in nature; and above all, interest in themselves. Their styles are also similar, exhibiting a common desire to write informally and without pretense, a concern for clarity and conciseness, an appreciation for the well-chosen word or figure of speech, and a gift for the striking contrast or juxtaposition. Both men also enjoy the potential lyricism and elasticity of the English language but rarely let themselves be carried away from the ordinary truth of experience into the obscure realms of abstraction.

Closer to him, others who helped in their way to shape White's work were his somewhat eccentric professor, William Strunk, Jr. ("'Omit needless words! Omit needless words! Omit needless words!'"),[5] his editors, Harold Ross and Katharine Sergeant, and his comrade-at-pens, James Thurber. The lighthearted, bantering spirit pervading *The New Yorker*'s offices during its early years undoubtedly played a part in the development of White's humorous writing, although it is generally acknowledged that White was himself the source of much of that spirit.

White's job with *The New Yorker* marked the beginning of the most formative phase of his career. Editing and composing tag-lines for "newsbreaks" sharpened his wit, and "paragraphing" for the "Notes and Comment" section at the front of the magazine honed his insight into daily experience—public and private—while it simultaneously taught him to make the most of a small block of print. White had already tried his hand at similarly brief, amusing anecdotes and incisive comments in his "Personal Column" in the *Seattle Times* but with limited success.

Newspapers and magazines of the 1920s and earlier commonly turned to newsbreaks when columns were left unfilled by regular articles or features. The idea was to reprint headlines or portions of newspaper accounts, material that was comic by virtue of grammatical, typographical, or editorial errors; if these items were not quite funny in themselves, then it was the job of a staff writer to supply a line or two to make them so.[6] White proved one of the ablest of newsbreak editors, as demonstrated in the following examples:

MONDAY AND TUESDAY—"Up in Mabel's Room." Notice: An officer will be at the door to take the slingshots from the children. They shoot at the screen.—*Theatre adv. in the Largo (Fla.) Sentinel*

Criticism, trying to come into its own.

Dr. Pammel said persons and animals eating cowbane frequently have conclusions.—*Des Moines (Ia.) Tribune*

Send us fifty cowbane.

Waitress wanted with wonderful personality. Apply Teenie Weenie Tavern, So. Franklin.—*Adv. in Saginaw (Mich.) Daily News*

And div us a dwate big Porterhouse steak, peese.

GENT'S laundry taken home. Or serve at parties.—*Pittsburgh Sun Telegraph*

Oh, take it home.

Eventually White learned how to introduce some newsbreaks with "department headings" so that the excerpt nearly spoke for itself; he would preface an item with something like "Department of Understatement," "Neatest Trick of the Week," or "How's That Again? Department."

White invented another column-filler called "Answers to Hard Questions," a device that he also included with comic effect in a book that he co-authored with James Thurber, *Is Sex Necessary? Or Why You Feel the Way You Do* (1929):

Q. My youngest boy, age 28, turned against love because in a book he was reading, where the writer meant to say, "A woman in love is sacred" there was a misprint and it came out, "A woman in love is scared." How would you go about this?

A. We do not regard the case as typical. Presumably your boy is badly frightened himself, or he wouldn't be reading books; he would be out somewhere. The way to overcome this is to build up his general health.

(p. 180)

Besides filling columns, White's job at *The New Yorker* required him to compose "paragraphs," short editorial pieces that comprised the magazine's "Notes and Comment." Like the newsbreak, the paragraph was an old journalistic technique by which editors and columnists set forth remarks, often funny or cutting, on public issues or events. As a matter of magazine policy, "Notes and Comment" paragraphs had to employ the editorial "we," but White saw to it that his readers remembered to distinguish the writer from his editor. He used the word "ourself" to indicate that his own voice and the official voice of the magazine were separate, but "united in a common cause": "We [meant here as 'I'] write as we please, and the magazine publishes as *it* pleases. When the two pleasures coincide, something gets into print."[7] This distinction was important to White, for earlier he had made one of the most valuable discoveries of his career, "that the world would pay a man for setting down a simple, legible account of his own misfortunes."[8] He had found that he could make a living writing about the subject of greatest interest to him, himself. Hence, he found the editorial "we" constricting and felt that he had to compromise with "ourself."

Every Day Is Saturday represents a collection of some of White's early "Notes and Comment" paragraphs, and shortly after its publication in 1934 the author tried to win permission from *The New Yorker* editor, Ross, to drop the third person pronoun in favor of the first person "I." Although he lost his case, White was allowed to arrange the order in which his subsequent paragraphs would appear so that there soon evolved loosely organized essays fashioned out of paragraphs that could stand alone but which also elaborated a single theme.[9] Alongside the "casuals" and a couple of short stories, these essays are among the best writing that White ever did.

His magazine writing did not prevent White from pursuing other projects, such as collaborating with Thurber on a book of humor. *Is Sex Necessary?* successfully parodied contemporary, quasi-scientific works regarding sexual attitudes and behavior, books and pamphlets that began to flood the publishing world in the 1920s. *The New Yorker*'s two funniest men shared not only a similar sense of humor but also a single cramped office so it happened that White was the first to "discover" Thurber's now-famous drawings. Andy salvaged his friend's doodles as they drifted from his desk to the floor, and with the publication of some of them in *Is Sex Necessary?* in 1929, Thurber's reputation as a cartoonist-writer was established.

Earlier the same year White's first book, *The Lady Is Cold*, had appeared. A collection of poems, most of which had been previously published in *The New Yorker* or in F.P.A.'s "Conning Tower," the volume demonstrated that White could have fun in verse, as in his "definitions":

CRITIC

The critic leaves at curtain fall
To find, in starting to review it,
He scarcely saw the play at all
For watching his reaction to it.

(p. 51)

He could comment wryly upon himself, too, as a twentieth-century urban dweller, as a lover, or as a writer:

WORDS

Words are not a proper thing
For a lad to play with;
Thoughts are best upon the wing,
Not to spend the day with.

Thoughts are moths that go at night,
Flying at a taper;
Never hold them to the light
Pinned upon a paper!

Words but catch the moment's tint,
Though their meaning rock you;
Never one shall fly to print
Will not live to mock you.

(p. 86)

Some of the selections in this volume hint at the more serious poetry to come in *The Fox of Peapack and Other Poems* (1938), but that book also contains some of White's best light verse.[10] Although contemporary poets such as Ezra Pound and T.S. Eliot were setting conventional forms and meters aside, White never joined the poetic avant-garde, preferring to address the ordinary rather than the intellectual reader. His poetic voice actually informs his prose more successfully than it does his verse, although writing poetry was always something of a compulsion with him.

Perhaps the greatest significance of *The Lady Is Cold* lies in the themes that it sets forth, for they are among those that White returned to throughout his career.[11] Even had his style been less readable and attractive than it was, the subjects that he chose and the positions that he took might well have assured White's popularity. He appeals to those who share his fear that too much that is good in life passes too quickly. He spoke out eloquently on behalf of the individual's right to freedom and privacy. In a city sprouting steel and concrete, he was the one who reported with sincere, wide-eyed appreciation that the pigeons were adjusting just fine, for the durability of nature in the face of urbanization always fascinated him. When advertising and moving pictures had begun to cast a glossy sheen across the image of American life, White was happy to identify himself with the unbeautiful and the inadequate, for everyone and everything seemed always to get the best of him—from servants to geese, from gold-framed mirrors to dachshunds, from real bouts with hay fever to imagined confrontations with the chairman of the House Committee on Un-American Activities.

White's essays on these and other subjects were periodically collected and reprinted (most of them having first appeared in magazines) in *Quo Vadimus?* (1939), *The Second Tree from the Corner* (1954), *The Points of My Compass* (1962), *An E.B. White Reader* (1966), *Essays of E.B. White* (1977), and *Poems and Sketches of E.B. White* (1983). In a book he co-edited with his wife, *A Subtreasury of American Humor* (1941), a few of White's pieces were reprinted alongside those of other writers. *The Wild Flag* (1946) is a collection of excerpts from "Notes and Comment" in which White addresses international problems of government and peace, issues that he had begun considering very seriously while writing his column for *Harper's*. This column was entitled "One Man's Meat," and its essays were brought together in a book by the same name in 1942. The collection became so popular that it was enlarged in 1944, eventually running through eight editions and several foreign translations.

White brought the informal essay to a new level of finesse. He knew how to begin an essay by writing lightly about himself or about someone close to him, and he knew how to relate his own experience to that of others, even to that of the entire natural or human world. In doing so he might cross the thin line separating humor from pathos. Wit and sobriety mingle by the end of his essays so that the reader has seen into not one life but many, into the delicate balance of thought, emotion, and experience integral to life itself. In "Death of a Pig," for example, a farmer (White) is caught in the somewhat ludicrous position of having to nurse an ailing porker originally destined for the family dinner table; in the aftermath of the experience, however, the farmer discovers that the pig "had evidently become precious to [him], not that he represented a distant nourishment in a hungry time, but that he had suffered in a suffering world."[12]

White's ability to establish connections between apparently unrelated objects, people, events, or ideas is at the root of his humor, for where there is incongruity there is the potential for laughter. To read White is to encounter an arrogant, "vile old dachshund" who "suffers greatly from arthritis . . . and [who] would be bedridden if he could find anyone willing to serve him meals on a tray";[13] an earnest but inept reporter (the young Andy White) trying to keep up his courage while riding in a railway car "conceived in malice" by a building janitor—

atop the building, five stories high;[14] and a housekeeper named Antoinette who White believes will remain in his home even until his dying moment at which time she will likely be found "performing some grotesquely irrelevant act like ironing a dog's blanket."[15] By juxtaposing unrelated matters such as a man's death and a dog's blanket, White effectively uses contrast, an artistic technique guaranteed to engage an audience, whatever the medium.

Here as elsewhere White works in the best tradition of American humor, for the battle between the real and the ideal, between a man who would be the dignified master of his household and the actual household that masters him, has been and remains basic to the American experience.[16] It took an H.L. Mencken to throw the discrepancies created by the modern scene into sharp, satirical relief, but it was White who more gently tapped the individual American on the shoulder, directing his attention toward the folly and beauty of his own humanity.

Summary

Roughly spanning the decades between 1920 and 1980, much of E.B. White's career was closely associated with writing he did for *The New Yorker* and *Harper's Magazine*. He also co-authored a book with James Thurber, co-edited with his wife, Katharine, a collection of American humor, revised his former college professor's slim book on writing, and wrote three popular children's books. Through such comic devices as parody, satire, understatement, splashes of colloquial dialogue, and the attribution of human characteristics to animals, White became one of this century's most admired humorists, although his reputation as a thoughtful, serious defender of human values is equally if not more significant. On various occasions he criticized, worried over, or poked fun at the natural and human worlds—but he never ceased to love and celebrate them.

Notes

1. Warren Beck, "E.B. White," *College English*, 7 (April 1946): 368.
2. Scott Elledge, *E.B. White: A Biography* (New York: W.W. Norton, 1984), p. 26.
3. "The Years of Wonder," *Essays of E.B. White* (New York: Harper and Row, 1977), p. 169.
4. *The New Yorker*, May 28, 1927.
5. E.B. White, *Essays of E.B. White*, p. 259.
6. Elledge, p. 120.
7. *The New Yorker*, March 4, 1944.
8. E.B. White, "The Hotel of the Total Stranger," *Poems and Sketches of E.B. White* (New York: Harper and Row, 1983), p. 5.
9. Elledge, pp. 192–193.
10. Edward C. Sampson, *E.B. White* (New York: Twayne Publishers, 1974), p. 41.
11. Ibid., p. 40.

12. *The Second Tree from the Corner* (New York: Harper and Brothers, 1954), p. 244.
13. "Death of a Pig," *Second Tree*, pp. 247-249.
14. "Speaking of Counterweights," *Second Tree*, p. 14.
15. "Memoirs, *"Poems and Sketches*, p. 80.
16. Louis D. Rubin, Jr., ed. *The Comic Imagination in American Literature* (New Brunswick, N.J.: Rutgers University Press, 1973), p. 12.

Selected Bibliography

Primary Sources

Books

The Lady Is Cold: Poems by E.B.W. New York: Harper and Brothers, 1929.

Ho Hum: Newsbreaks from the "New Yorker." New York: Farrar and Rinehart, 1931.

Another Ho Hum: More Newsbreaks from the "New Yorker." New York: Farrar and Rinehart, 1932.

Every Day Is Saturday. New York: Harper and Brothers, 1934.

The Fox of Peapack and Other Poems. New York: Harper and Brothers, 1938.

Quo Vadimus? Or the Case for the Bicycle. New York: Harper and Brothers, 1939.

One Man's Meat. New York: Harper and Brothers, 1942.

The Wild Flag. Boston: Houghton Mifflin, 1946.

The Second Tree from the Corner. New York: Harper and Brothers, 1954.

The Points of My Compass. New York: Harper and Row, 1962.

An E.B. White Reader. Ed. William W. Watt and Robert W. Bradford. New York: Harper and Row, 1966.

Letters of E.B. White. Dorothy Lobrano Guth, ed. New York: Harper and Row, 1976.

Essays of E.B. White. New York: Harper and Row, 1977.

Poems and Sketches of E.B. White. New York: Harper and Row, 1983.

Children's Books

Stuart Little. New York: Harper and Brothers, 1945.

Charlotte's Web. New York: Harper and Brothers, 1952.

The Trumpet of the Swan. New York: Harper and Row, 1970.

Books Co-authored, Edited, and Co-edited

(with James Thurber.) *Is Sex Necessary? Or Why You Feel the Way You Do.* New York: Harper and Brothers, 1929.

(edited with Katharine S. White.) *A Subtreasury of American Humor.* New York: Coward McCann, 1941.

Strunk, William Jr. *The Elements of Style: With Revisions, an Introduction, and a New Chapter on Style by E.B. White.* New York: Macmillan Company, 1959.

White, Katharine S. *Onward and Upward in the Garden.* Ed. E.B. White. Farrar, Straus and Giroux, 1979.

Secondary Sources

Books

Elledge, Scott. *E.B. White: A Biography.* New York: W.W. Norton, 1984. Very informative and readable; the only existing biography, with some critical attention given White's work.

Sampson, Edward C. *E.B. White.* New York: Twayne Publishers, 1974. Fullest discussion of White's thought available to date; emphasizes his serious writing over his humor.

Bibliography

Hall, Katharine Romans, comp. *E.B. White: A Bibliographic Catalogue of Printed Materials in the Department of Rare Books, Cornell University Library.* New York: Garland Publishing, 1979. Thorough and accessible, although subsequent White publications render it incomplete.

Dissertations

Fuller, John Wesley. "Prose Styles in the Essays of E.B. White." University of Washington, 1959. Complete analysis of characteristic diction, sentence patterns, and related matters of White's style.

Articles

Beck, Warren. "E.B. White." *College English*, 7 (April 1946): 367-373. Appreciative, insightful review of White's early career and the enduring qualities of his work.

Plimpton, George, and Frank H. Crowther. "The Art of the Essay I: E.B. White." *Paris Review*, 48 (Fall 1969): 65-88. One of the most interesting interviews of White available, especially valuable for his remarks on humor.

Thurber, James. "E.B.W." *Saturday Review of Literature*, 18 (October 15, 1938): 8-9. An informal, witty profile of Thurber's friend and mentor on *The New Yorker* staff.

Weales, Gerald. "Not for the Old Lady in Dubuque." In *The Comic Imagination in American Literature*. Louis D. Rubin, ed. New Brunswick, N.J.: Rutgers University Press, 1973. Valuable not only for its discussion of White's humor but also for observations on the humor of other *New Yorker* writers.

Other

Blair, Walter. *America's Humor.* New York: Oxford University Press, 1978, pp. 437-440. Some interesting remarks on the "homespun quality" of White's thought; places him within the larger context of American humor of this century and earlier.

Rubin, Louis D., Jr., ed. *The Comic Imagination in American Literature.* New Brunswick, N.J.: Rutgers University Press, 1973. Introductory and concluding chapters are good on the main currents that have developed in American humor.

Allison Bulsterbaum

Whittier, Matthew Franklin

Born: East Haverhill, Massachusetts, on
July 18, 1812

Marriages: Abigail Poyen, August 1836,
two children; Jane Vaughan, 1841, three
children; Mary Waite Tolman, 1863

Died: January 7, 1883

Biography

Matthew Whittier's achievements as humorist
were overshadowed by the literary fame of his
brother, John Greenleaf Whittier. Matthew expressed the outspoken, romantic, and funmaking
potentialities of his family environment by a
lack of respectability apparently incompatible
with his Quaker background.

Born on July 18, 1812, at the ancestral farmhouse of the Whittiers in East Haverhill, Massachusetts, Matthew Franklin grew up in rural
surroundings. The youngest son, he shared the
limited schooling of his elder brother, John
Greenleaf, and his sister, Elizabeth. When their
father died in 1830, the two brothers tried to
keep the farm. Already active in politics, John
Greenleaf served as member of the Massachusetts legislature in 1835 and was often away
from Haverhill. He decided to sell the property
in 1836 and went to live with his mother and
younger sister in a cottage at Amesbury, a neighboring village. In August 1836, Matthew married Abigail Poyen, born in 1817, the attractive
daughter of a French refugee from the island of
Guadeloupe. The young couple lived near Haverhill where Matthew conducted a writing
school during the Depression of 1837. Already
self-taught in English literature and an insatiable reader of the *Arabian Nights*, classical legends, and American history, he worked for some
time on the staff of the *Amesbury News and
Courier*. The first child of Matthew and Abigail,
Joseph, born on August 20, 1837, died less than
a year after his birth. Shortly afterward, Matthew considered going West but despite John
Greenleaf's encouragements, soon cancelled his
plans. Meanwhile, his erratic behavior together
with his intemperance made him notorious in
his neighborhood. In 1839, he moved to Portland, Maine. Thanks to John Greenleaf, he became a clerk with John Winslow and Sons, a
Quaker firm dealing in general merchandise.
Matthew soon joined with Hugh Montgomery
and purchased the concern. In 1844, the firm
dissolved, probably owing to the partners' drinking and subsequent neglect of their business. In
July 1840, a daughter, Sarah Greenleaf, was born,
but she died a few months later. Matthew's wife
did not survive the shock and died in March
1841. About a year after her death, Matthew
married Jane Vaughan, a native of St. John, New

Brunswick. During the next six years, they had
three children, Charles Franklin, Elizabeth and
Alice. Elizabeth was to become the wife of Samuel Pickard, John Greenleaf Whittier's first biographer.

Until 1860, Matthew had a variety of occupations and changed his residence several times.
He was by turns an employee of commission
merchants, a clerk in the Portland post office
during the Whig administration of Tyler, a city
clerk, and an employee of Union Wharf. In the
meantime, he found an outlet to his vicissitudes
by writing the Ethan Spike Letters. The first of a
long series was printed in the *Portland Transcript* in January 1846. Others appeared in the
Boston Carpet Bag, the *Boston Weekly Museum*,
and the New York *Vanity Fair* until the 1860s.
Although sporadic, the letters had a nationwide
circulation as they were reprinted in many periodicals over two decades. Matthew's elder
brother was then a prominent figure as poet and
abolitionist. By 1860, Matthew's satire of pro-
slavery leaders in the Ethan Spike letters had
won him the sympathy of Republican politicians. Thanks to John Greenleaf's support, he
obtained an appointment in the Boston Customs
House from Charles Sumner. In 1863, he met
Mary Waite Tolman and probably married her,
although no record of the marriage has ever
been found.

The couple lived successively in Medford,
Boston, and Brookline. In 1877, John Greenleaf
had to intervene several times to keep his
brother in office. However, the latter suffered
drastic reductions in his salary. In the late 1870s,
Matthew's health steadily declined and although
his condition became critical, he refused to give
up his clerkship at the Customs House despite
his brother's offer of financial assistance. In
1881, Matthew had a severe attack of rheumatism and could not return to his duties. He retired in 1882 and spent the fall at Peterboro,
New Hampshire, with Mary. He died in Boston
on January 7, 1883, at the age of 70 and was
buried in the family plot at Amesbury.

Literary Analysis

Most of the Ethan Spike letters appeared in the
Portland Transcript between January 10, 1846,
and November 7, 1863. A dozen others were
contributed to the *Carpet Bag* in 1851 and the
New York *Vanity Fair* in 1862–1863. Ethan
Spike, Matthew Whittier's persona, is a citizen
of the mythical town of Hornby, Oxford County,
Maine. A young man in his twenties at the beginning of the series, he is too old to be drafted
during the Civil War. Both actor and narrator,
he exemplifies the Yankee bumpkin's responses
to contemporary issues by involving himself in
the major events of his times. Throughout his

picaresque adventures he suffers many hardships, and his misfortunes leave their marks on him; he loses his scalp and a toe on his journey to the California gold fields in 1849. When he goes South, a decade later, irate planters mistake him for an abolitionist while he is trying to buy two slaves. He is tarred and feathered, then almost lynched by a mob in Virginia. Ultimately, they tear off one of his ears and put a ring in his nose. On his return to the North he is offered a dollar to appear in Barnum's New York museum.

Spike is keenly aware of his own failures but, undaunted, retains his optimism. Constantly deceived by propaganda, he flaunts a self-defeating jingoism despite his own personal wretchedness. For instance, he advocates the annexation of Cuba in 1853 and has a row with a Canadian who calls him a "white-livered Yankee ass." During the Civil War, he plans to sink the Confederate ship *"Merrimuck"* if she happens to reach Hornby. A professional office seeker, Ethan allies himself with the "dimmercratic party" and emulates Seba Smith's Jack Downing, first when campaigning to become postmaster in his native village, then to be a member of the Maine legislature.

The Down Easter from Hornby also appears as a confused supporter of slavery while helping to catch a fugitive slave on the Boston streets in 1851. A year later he organizes a filibustering expedition to Cuba to obtain a "kokkernut plantation and a hull full of West-ingy niggers." In 1861, Spike persuades the inhabitants of his native village to join the Confederacy and goes to Charleston, lobbying for his friend, "Kellup Cushion" (Caleb Cushing), a well-known "dough face."

Through the character of Ethan Spike, Whittier satirizes the Copperheads and, more generally, northern pro-slavery politicians who for various reasons adopt a mild stand toward the "Patriarcal institution." Like all the members of the Whittier family, Matthew was schooled in Quakerism. Unlike John Greenleaf, who viewed all aspects of life from a spiritual plane, he could hardly repress his indignation, so chose the tone of sarcastic humor and donned a comic mask to voice his opinions. As picaro, his protagonist, Spike, has little in common with the crackerbox oracle of Yankee humor. Instead of the innocent pose, he assumes the boastful, cynical attitudes of the southern ringtailed roarer. Rejecting the patterns of behavior provided by religion and education, this Yankee *picaro* resolutely places himself outside the community. An easy prey for swindlers and pettifoggers, he immerses himself in the world with indomitable energy. Like Sut Lovingood, George Washington Harris's southern rogue, Spike hates law and order. He enjoys mistreating the innocent whenever he has the opportunity. For example, he bites off the finger of an Indian woman who feeds him when he is sick on his California trek. A hedonist, he never fails to celebrate his liberation from social restraints by his heavy absorption of punch, rum, and rye.

The Ethan Spike letters express a consistently hilarious nihilism. In a mock-heroic tone, Matthew Whittier suggests through an inverted epic that American ideals have been perverted. For him the pursuit of happiness, Manifest Destiny, and the Jacksonian rise of the common man amount to absurd jokes. Ethan's imagination enables him to transfigure fateful experiences into burlesque scenes with the bold imagination of a Mississippi keelboatman, and his braggadocio seems to foreshadow an episode that appears in Mark Twain's *Life on the Mississippi* when a group of Southerners, having "kept the jug moving," get into a quarrelsome mood:

> I peeled off clean down to shirt an trowsis, stomped on my hat, and squared away against England.
> "Kim on," says I, "brung out yer redcoats—yer infernal biled lobsters! Who keeps a brumagen cuss for yer lion! He's a super-moonerated old critter that orter go to a dentist. Why bless yer silly old soul, John! We manyfacters tomcats in this hum of the braves that'll lick yer wild beasts an beastesses, an holler for more."[1]

Ethan loves fighting, gambling, and women, although he has no luck with such entertainments. In his account of a calico ball, he recaptures the mood of the traditional Yankee frolic:

> I skersly say that S.S. stands for Salewbrity Skillins. Salewbrity is awful pooty at any time, but on this orspicious occasion, she did look good enough to eat. She had on the blewest gaown ever seen in this imparfact state of existence, with hoops into it, was the yallerest, pettiGet aout! What am I talking abaout—the yallerest onmentionable—an below that ere a pair of white stockings wich wouldn't have hurt a bit. Her tows was dreadful fantastical. She danced like a syrup. As she glided an bobbed abaout, she looked jest like an aingill, an put me in mind of that sublime stansis beginnin:
> "Here she goes an there she goes."[2]

As a true-born Yankee, Spike should have an intimate knowledge of sparking, yet his paramours happen to be ruthlessly deceitful. Nancy Biglow, a Hornby poetess, is just a bigoted bluestocking. His dealings with Patience Pillsbury make him think that he has been fighting a match "with a wild cat and come second best." Nancy Pike he soon forgets, however, when he is confronted with temptation in the shape of a scarlet woman in New York. Such mishaps substantiate Ethan's misogyny, and he concludes:

> I've done with em naow. The Queen of Sheber, the sleepin beauty, Keopatry's needle, Pompey's pillow and Lot's wife with a steam ingine to help em couldn't seduce me. The very sight o a bunnit riles me.[3]

Spike's apocalyptic destiny is reflected in chaotic imagery. A Yankee Sisyphus, he creates his own absurd logic to describe his experiences. His language is based on eye-dialect, substitutions, misspellings, and puns. For instance, he says "paws" for "pause," "catarrh" for "guitar," and "pot in tates" instead of "potatoes." The New England drawl can be found in such words as "draown," "bile," or "keer." Ethan's similes expand into wild hyperboles: "it will make your hairs stand on eend like quills on the frightened konkerbine." Whittier also incorporates the tall tale element that clearly smacks of Southern humor:

> I was ollers considered a few in the way of running, having once beat a great she bear that wanted me properly for supper, in a race of ten miles.[4]

Describing the Hornby river, Spike exclaims that it is "a crooked river which is so darned crooked that to this day, nobody knows which way it runs."[5]

A corrosive misanthropist, Spike revenges his alienation by excoriating the community that snubs him, as when he describes Boston before causing havoc in the city:

> The popperlation is to be a leetle risin 47362462, partly hewman beeins, an the balance composed of niggers, furriners, cats and dogs. The people is mostly idolaters, worshippin as a gineral thing the Golden Calf—though some serve the Devil. The people never cheat onless they have a chance, an drink nothin stronger as a gineral thing—than whisky, except when they're dry.[6]

Matthew Whittier's style thus combines the exuberance of frontier humor with deadpan sarcasm. A shrewd observer of his environment, he voices comic potentialities that his brother John Greenleaf's dedication to moral causes was bound to repress owing to his public role, but his uninhibited virulence and racy comments on antebellum America constitute a significant landmark in the history of American humor.

Summary

Raised in a Quaker family, Matthew Whittier lived through many hardships while retaining a sense of humor that was instrumental in expressing his own personality. Unlike his brother, John Greenleaf, he did not explore holiness and spiritual truth, but his castigation of American society through the character of Ethan Spike reveals his independent mind. By no means a negative figure, Ethan embodies a life force. His attitude anticipates the feigned misanthropy of comic antiheroes such as Huckleberry Finn who know that freedom results in solitude. The Ethan Spike letters reveal that by the midnineteenth century there was no great dividing line between the various brands of regional humor.

Notes

1. *Portland Transcript*, August 23, 1862.
2. Ibid., March 13, 1858.
3. Ibid., February 9, 1856.
4. Ibid., August 12, 1848.
5. Ibid., October 1, 1859.
6. Ibid., August 24, 1861.

Selected Bibliography

Primary Sources

The Ethan Spike letters appeared in the *Portland Transcript*, January 10, 1846–November 7, 1863; the *Boston Weekly Museum*, November 30, 1850–January 4, 1851; the *Boston Carpet Bag*, May 10, 1851–November 8, 1851; and *Vanity Fair*, June 7, 1862–May 9, 1863.

Secondary Sources

Blair, Walter. *Native American Humor (1800-1900)*. New York: American Book Company, 1937, p. 42.
———. "Burlesques in Nineteenth-Century American Humor." *American Literature*, 2 (November 1930): 236–237.
———. "The Popularity of Nineteenth-Century American Humorists," *American Literature*, (May 1931): 175–194.
Blair, Walter, and Hamlin Hill. *America's Humor, From Poor Richard to Doonesbury*. New York: Oxford University Press, 1978, p. 280.
Griffin, Lloyd Wilfred. "The Life and Works of Matthew Franklin Whittier." Unpublished M.A. thesis, University of Maine, Orono, 1941.
———. "Matthew Franklin Whittier, Ethan Spike." *The New England Quarterly*, 14, no. 4 (1941).
Pickard, John B. *John Greenleaf Whittier*. New York: Holt, Rinehart and Winston, 1961.
Pickard, Samuel T. *The Life and Letters of John Greenleaf Whittier*. Two vols. Boston: Houghton, Mifflin, 1894.
Reed, John. *Benjamin Penhallow Shillaber*. New York: Twayne, 1972.
Royot, Daniel. *L'Humour americain, des Puritains aux Yankees*. Lyon: Presses Universitaires de Lyon, 1980.

Daniel G. Royot

Contributors

St. George Tucker Arnold, Jr.

Professor Arnold received his B.A. from Van-derbilt University and his Ph.D. from Stanford University. Arnold is an Associate Professor of English at Florida International University in Miami. He has published articles on archetypal patterns in Eudora Welty's fiction, and the de-piction of animals in the works of Mark Twain, George Washington Harris, Joel Chandler Har-ris, Don Marquis, and James Thurber, as well as other subjects in American southern literature and humor in journals such as *Southern Folklore Quarterly* and *Thalia*.

John W. Baer

Professor Baer received a B.A. degree in sociol-ogy from Harvard College, an M.B.A. from Co-lumbia Graduate Business School (Columbia University), and a D.A. (in economics) from Catholic University in Washington, D.C. Baer is Professor of Economics at Anne Arundel Com-munity College. Like Stephen Leacock, he has spent most of his life as an economics professor and, like Leacock, he spent most summers in the 1930s and early 1940s vacationing in Orillia, Ontario, Canada. Baer's publications include arti-cles on "The Great Depression Humor of Gal-braith, Leacock, and Mencken" in *Studies in American Humor* and on H.L. Mencken in *Menckeniana*.

Grady W. Ballenger

Professor Ballenger received an M.A. from Co-lumbia University and a Ph.D. from the Univer-sity of North Carolina at Chapel Hill. He teaches American and British literature and creative writing at the Louisiana School for Math, Science, and the Arts. His dissertation was a study of James Thurber's humor.

C.J. Bartelt

C.J. Bartelt received her B.A. in English from the University of Chicago and her M.S. in journal-ism from Columbia University; she is currently writing her doctoral dissertation on "Parapsy-chology and the Demarcation between Science and Pseudoscience" in the Department of His-tory and Philosophy of Science at Indiana Uni-versity. Bartelt is a free-lance author and has contributed to the *Chicago Tribune* and *The Na-tional Lampoon*, as well as to school and com-munity newspapers. Her current project is a comic novel, tentatively titled *The Logic of Pur-suit*. She has also worked in an editorial capacity at the University of Wisconsin at Madison, was an assistant editor at Garland Publishing, and a research editor for *The National Lampoon*.

Lawrence I. Berkove

Professor Berkove received a B.A. from the Uni-versity of Illinois, an M.A. from the University of Minnesota, and a Ph.D. from the University of Pennsylvania. Berkove is Professor of English at the University of Michigan-Dearborn, where he specializes in American literature of the nine-teenth and early twentieth centuries. He served as Visiting Professor of English and American Literature at Rikkyo University in Tokyo and later was invited to return to Japan to give a series of lectures on American literature. Ber-kove's dissertation was on Ambrose Bierce, and he has published a highly rated book on Bierce, *Skepticism and Dissent*; another book on Bierce's fiction is forthcoming. Berkove has also published articles on Bierce and other American writers in *Mark Twain Journal, Nathaniel Haw-thorne Journal, Huntington Library Quarterly*, and *Southern Quarterly*.

Gerald M. Berkowitz

Professor Berkowitz received an M.A. from Columbia University and a Ph.D. from Indiana University in 1969. Berkowitz is Professor of English at Northern Illinois University. He is the author of *New Broadways: Theatre Across America, 1950-1980* and two other books on the theater, as well as numerous scholarly articles. He is also listed in the *Guinness Book of Records* as the world's champion theatergoer for having seen 145 plays in a span of 35 consecutive days.

Rebecca S. Blair

Rebecca Blair is Associate Instructor at Indiana University, where she is working on her disser-tation, "The Other Woman: Women Authors and Cultural Stereotypes in American Litera-ture," and where she teaches composition and American literature. She has written essays on a wide range of topics in American literature and in composition studies.

Thomas Bonner, Jr.

Professor Bonner received his Ph.D. in English from Tulane University. He teaches at Xavier University of Louisiana, where his specialty is southern literature. Bonner is the author of *William Faulkner: The William B. Wisdom Collection* and *A Kate Chopin Companion*. He has contributed to *The History of Southern Literature, Southern Writers: A Biographical Dictionary*, and *In Old New Orleans* and has published in *American Literary Realism, Bulletin of Bibliography, Mississippi Quarterly,* and *Southern Quarterly*. He is also the editor of the *Xavier Review*.

Allison Bulsterbaum

Professor Bulsterbaum received her B.A.E. and her M.A. from the University of Mississippi. She is currently a doctoral student in English at the University of North Carolina at Chapel Hill, where she also teaches composition and criticism. Bulsterbaum has published articles on Toni Morrison, William Faulkner, and several nineteenth-century magazines, and she is currently completing *H.L. Mencken: A Research Guide*, which is to be published by Garland.

Michael D. Butler

Professor Butler received his B.A. from Stanford University and his Ph.D. from the University of Illinois. He is currently Associate Professor of English at the University of Kansas, where he specializes in American literature. Butler's publications include articles on nineteenth-century American fiction, American humor, and western American literature in *American Literature, Studies in American Fiction, Western American Literature, The Kansas Arts Reader, Dictionary of Literary Biography* (Robert Henry Newall), and *American Comic Periodicals and Humor Magazines*, and he is an assisting compiler of the "Annual Bibliography of Midwestern Literature" in *Midamerica*.

Douglas R. Capra

Capra received his B.A. in English literature from Northeastern University and has pursued independent studies in Europe in ancient history and medieval architecture. He teaches at a high school in Alaska. Capra has worked as a free-lance writer, newspaper reporter, and photographer, and in the professional theater as both an actor and a director. His publications include articles on Rockwell Kent, and he is an expert on the customs of sleighs and sleighing in America.

Barney Cooney

Barney Cooney, a native of Ireland, received an M.A. in theology from Notre Dame University. An independent scholar, he taught history in Dublin for some years, and has been associated with Marquette University and Southwest Missouri State University.

Raymond C. Craig

Professor Craig received his B.A. from William Jewell College, his M.A. from Vanderbilt University, and his Ph.D. from the University of Illinois. He is presently chairman of the English Department at Marian College, where he teaches nineteenth-century American literature. His publications include *The Humor of H.E. Taliaferro* (University of Tennessee Press, 1987).

Gloria L. Cronin

Professor Cronin received her B.A. from Canterbury University in New Zealand and her Ph.D. from Brigham Young University. She is Associate Professor of American Literature at Brigham Young University, where she teaches courses on American modernism, contemporary American literature, American women writers, and Jewish-American literature. She is also the Executive Director of the Saul Bellow Society and Associate Editor of the *Saul Bellow Journal*, and she is preparing an annotated bibliography on Bellow. Her publications include a number of articles on Bellow and other Jewish-American authors of the postwar period.

Irma R. Cruse

Irma Cruse received her B.A. in journalism from the University of Alabama, and M.A.s in both English and history from Samford University. An independent scholar and free-lance writer, Cruse has published articles on a variety of subjects in numerous journals, served as a journal editor, and received several honors for her writing.

Wheeler Dixon

Professor Dixon received his B.A., M.A., M.Phil., and Ph.D. from Rutgers University in New Brunswick. He has taught at Rutgers University, the New School for Social Research, Douglas College, and Livingston College, and he is currently an associate professor in the departments of English and art at the University of

Nebraska at Lincoln, where he specializes in film studies. Dixon is the author of *The "B" Directors: A Biographical Directory* (Scarecrow, 1985), *Producers Releasing Corporation: A Comprehensive History* (McFarland, 1986), *The Cinematic Vision of F. Scott Fitzgerald* (UMI Research Press, 1986), and *Freddie Francis and Terence Fisher: The Critical Reception* (Scarecrow, forthcoming). He has also published articles in a number of journals, including *Interview, Films in Review,* and *Film/Literature Quarterly,* and in the Modern Language Association guide to teaching *Frankenstein.* In addition, Dixon's films have been shown at the Whitney Museum, the Jewish Museum, and the Museum of Modern Art in New York, and he has received filmmaking grants from the Royal Film Archive (Belgium), the Rockefeller Foundation, the National Endowment for the Humanities, and the New Jersey State Arts Council.

Gary Engle

Professor Engle received his B.A. from Northwestern University and his M.A. and Ph.D. from the University of Chicago. He is Associate Professor of English at Cleveland State University. Among his more than 100 publications are articles in *Resources for American Literary Study, Journal of Popular Film, Film Criticism, Dialogue, Gamut,* and *Contemporary Literary Criticism,* and he has published *This Grotesque Essence: Plays from the American Minstrel Stage* (Louisiana State University Press, 1978) and *Superman at Fifty: The Persistence of a Legend* (Octavia, 1987). Engle has read papers at the Popular Culture Association of America Conference, is a contributing editor for *Northern Ohio Live Magazine,* and is a member of the Board of Contributors for *Comic Periodicals Bibliography* (Greenwood Press, 1984).

Mark W. Estrin

Professor Estrin received his B.A. from Amherst College, his M.A. from Columbia University, and his Ph.D. from New York University. He is Professor of English and Director of Film Studies at Rhode Island College. Estrin is the author of *Lillian Hellman: Plays, Films, Memoirs* (G.K. Hall, 1980) and the editor of *Critical Essays on Lillian Hellman* (Hall, 1987). His essays and reviews have appeared in *The International Dictionary of Films and Filmmakers* (St. James Press), *Contemporary Dramatists* (St. Martin's Press), *Modern Drama, Literature/ Film Quarterly, Journal of Narrative Technique,* and *Resources for American Literary Study,* and others. Among the awards that Estrin has re-

ceived are a National Endowment for the Humanities Summer Research Fellowship and his college's Distinguished Teaching Award.

Benjamin Fisher, III

Professor Fisher received his B.A. from Ursinus College and both his M.A. and Ph.D. from Duke University. He is Professor of English at the University of Mississippi, where he specializes in teaching American writers of the nineteenth century, the Victorian era, and Gothic and detective fiction. The author or editor of six books on Edgar Allan Poe, Gothicism, and detective fiction, Fisher is the editor of *The University of Mississippi Studies in English* and serves on the editorial boards of *Poe Studies, Gothic, English Literature in Transition,* and *Victorian Poetry.* He is a past president of the Poe Studies Association and the American vice-president of the Housman Society.

Martha A. Fisher

Professor Fisher received her B.A. in classical languages from Willson College and her M.A. in English from The Pennsylvania State University. She is Associate Professor of English at the Mont Alto Campus of The Pennsylvania State University, where she teaches composition, literature, Latin, and linguistics. She has published the authorized English translation from German of Herbert Reinecker's *Nachtzug,* as well as various articles on American humor and teaching grammar and composition.

Kenneth Florey

Professor Florey received his B.A. from Lafayette College and both his M.A. and Ph.D. from Syracuse University. He is Professor of English and chairman of the Department of English at Southern Connecticut State University, where he teaches Anglo-Saxon literature, medieval literature, history of the English language, and mythology. Florey's publications include "Stability, Chaos, and Dramatic Design in Anglo-Saxon Poetry," "*Huckleberry Finn* and the Nineteenth Century Tradition of Black Dialect in Literature," and "Chickens and Poetry in *Uncle Tom's Cabin.*"

Douglas Fowler

Professor Fowler received a B.A., an M.F.A., and a Ph.D. from Cornell University. He is Professor of English at Florida State University, where his emphasis is on twentieth-century literature. Fowler is the author of *Reading Nabokov* (Cornell University Press, 1974), *A Reader's Guide to Gravity's Rainbow* (Ardis, 1980), *S.J. Perelman* (G.K. Hall, 1983), and *Ira Levin* (Starmont, 1987). He has also published articles in the *Yeats-Eliot Journal, South Atlantic Quarterly, Extrapolation,* and *The Journal of Narrative Technique,* and contributed an essay to a forthcoming book on teaching the work of T.S. Eliot (Modern Language Association).

Steven H. Gale

Professor Gale received his B.A. from Duke University, his M.A. from the University of California at Los Angeles, and his Ph.D. from the University of Southern California, and he has studied at Oxford University. He has taught a wide range of subjects at the University of Southern California, the University of California at Los Angeles, the University of Puerto Rico, the University of Liberia (as a Fulbright Professor), the University of Florida, and Missouri Southern State College (where he served as head of the department and is currently director of the campus-wide honors program). Author of over 60 articles on a diversity of topics, he has published two books on S.J. Perelman (*S.J. Perelman: An Annotated Bibliography,* Garland, 1985, and *S.J. Perelman: A Critical Analysis,* Greenwood, 1987). He has also published three volumes on contemporary British dramatist Harold Pinter and a composition textbook; he is currently working on three books on Pinter (two for Greenwood and one for G.K. Hall), four books on American playwright David Mamet (two for Greenwood, one for Garland, and one for the University of Missouri Press), and a business writing textbook (for Charles Merrill). Gale is also series editor for Peter Lang Publishing's "Contemporary American and British Drama and Film" series, president of the Harold Pinter Society, and co-editor of *The Pinter Review.*

Francis P. Gillen

Professor Gillen received his M.A. and Ph.D. from Fordham University. He is Professor of English and Director of the Honors Program at the University of Tampa. Gillen's extensive publications include studies in both modern fiction and drama—essays on E.M. Forster, Henry James, Virginia Woolf, Donald Barthelme, Mary McCarthy, Tennessee Williams, Anthony Shaffer, and Harold Pinter. He is currently working on a book-length study of Pinter and is co-editor of *The Pinter Review.*

Kalman Goldstein

Professor Goldstein received his Ph.D. in American history from Columbia University. He is Professor of History at Fairleigh Dickinson University. Goldstein has written on various aspects of eighteenth-, nineteenth-, and twentieth-century America. His present interest is in the relationships among politics, humor, and art. Goldstein is a member of the editorial board of Fairleigh Dickinson University Press.

Thomas Grant

Professor Grant received his B.A. from Gonzaga University and his M.A. and Ph.D. from Rutgers University. He has taught at Seattle University and he is currently Associate Professor of English at the University of Hartford. Grant has authored a book on George Chapman, was a contributor to the *Dictionary of Literary Biography* volume on *American Humorists, 1800-1950,* and has published articles on Mark Twain and other humorists, as well as on modern drama and western film.

Malcolm Hayward

Professor Hayward received his B.A. from Drew University, and his M.A. and Ph.D. from Tulane University. He is currently Professor of English at Indiana University of Pennsylvania, where he specializes in composition theory and nineteenth-century British literature. Hayward is the editor of *Studies in the Humanities.*

James Hazen

Professor Hazen received his Ph.D. from the University of Wisconsin-Madison. He is Professor of English at the University of Las Vegas-Nevada, where he specializes in Victorian and early modern British literature. Hazen has published articles in *Victorian Poetry, Texas Studies in Literature and Language, Blake Studies, American Transcendental Quarterly,* and *Essays on Graham Greene,* and he wrote the entry on John Henry Newman for the *Dictionary of Literary Biography.*

Terry Heller

Professor Heller received his B.A. from North Central College and his M.A. and Ph.D. from the University of Chicago. He has taught at the University of Missouri at St. Louis, was a Fulbright lecturer at the University of Turin in Italy, and is currently Associate Professor of

English at Coe College, where he has served as chairman of the department and where he specializes in fiction of the nineteenth and twentieth centuries. Heller's publications include *The Delights of Terror: An Aesthetics of the Tale of Terror* (University of Illinois Press, 1987) and articles on William Faulkner in *Arizona Quarterly, Thalia, Coe Review,* and *Gothic.*

George Hendrick

Professor Hendrick received his B.A. from Texas Christian University and his M.A. and Ph.D. from the University of Texas. He has taught at Southwest Texas State University, the University of Colorado, the University of Frankfurt, and the University of Illinois at Chicago. He is currently Professor of English at the University of Illinois at Urbana-Champaign, where he has served as head of the department and associate dean of the graduate college. Hendrick has published extensively on figures in American literature such as Henry David Thoreau, Carl Sandburg, Mark Van Doren, and Mark Twain, and he recently published jointly with his wife, Willene, *On the Illinois Frontier: Dr. Hiram Rutherford, 1840-1848.* The Hendricks will soon publish a revised edition of *Katherine Anne Porter* (Twayne).

Willene Hendrick

Willene Hendrick received her B.S.N. from the University of Colorado. She has published articles in professional nursing journals and recently published jointly with her husband, George, *On the Illinois Frontier: Dr. Hiram Rutherford, 1840-1848.* The Hendricks will soon publish a revised edition of *Katherine Anne Porter* (Twayne).

LuAnne Clark Holladay

LuAnne Clark Holladay is completing her Ph.D. in English at Indiana University. Her primary area of interest is nineteenth-century American and British literature. Holladay has published an article on George Meredith in *The Journal of Pre-Raphaelite Studies.*

Sally C. Hoople

Sally C. Hoople received her B.A. and M.A. in English Education from Syracuse University, an M.A. in English from New York University, and a Ph.D. in English from Fordham University. She taught at White Plains High School for many years and currently teaches composition and humanities at the Maine Maritime Academy.

Eric W. Johnson

Eric W. Johnson is the head of the Reference Department at the University of Bridgeport Library in Connecticut. He has previously held library positions at Yale University and the University of New Haven. Johnson has contributed to *The Reference Librarian* and *American Humor Magazines and Comic Newspapers,* and he is a regular book reviewer for *Library Journal.*

Veda Jones

Veda Jones received her A.A. from Crowder College, her B.A. in history from Pittsburg State University, and her M.A. in history from the University of Arkansas. She is a free-lance author and independent scholar. Jones's publications include an article on Harold Bell Wright in *Popular Fiction in America.*

James H. Justus

Professor Justus received his B.A. and M.A. from the University of Tennessee and his Ph.D. from the University of Washington. He is Professor of English at Indiana University, where he specializes in southern American literature, particularly that of the nineteenth and twentieth centuries. Justus is the author of *The Achievement of Robert Penn Warren* (Louisiana State University Press, 1981) and editor of Joseph G. Baldwin's *The Flush Times of Alabama and Mississippi* (Louisiana State University Press, 1987). He has also published articles in *American Literature, Southern Literary Journal, Sewanee Review, Southern Review, Mississippi Quarterly, Kenyon Review,* and elsewhere.

Mark A. Keller

Professor Keller received his B.S. and M.A. from Mississippi State University and his Ph.D. from Auburn University. He is currently Associate Professor of English at Middle Georgia College, where he specializes in antebellum American humor, particularly that published in the New York *Spirit of the Times.* Keller's publications include about twenty-five articles in *American Literature, Papers of the Bibliographical Society of America, New England Quarterly, Southern Folklore Quarterly, Encyclopedia of Southern*

Culture, and *American Humor Magazines and Comic Newspapers.*

James E. Kibler, Jr.

Professor Kibler received his Ph.D. from the University of South Carolina. He is Professor of English at the University of Georgia. Kibler is the author and editor of several books on southern literature, including the standard study of O.B. Mayer.

Virginia White Kline

Virginia Kline received her M.A. in English literature from the University of Maryland, College Park. She is an independent scholar and free-lance writer. Kline will soon publish *Dorothy Parker: An Annotated Bibliography* (Garland, forthcoming).

Stuart Kollar

Stuart Kollar has been Director of Publications at Case Western Reserve University and managing editor of *Veterinary Economics Magazine* and *Sign and Display Industry Magazine.* He is currently Director of Publications at Cleveland State University. Kollar's publications include contributions to *The Gamut, History of American Periodical Literature,* and *Cleveland Magazine.*

Kris Lackey

Kris Lackey is Instructor of English at Auburn University. He has published in *Melville Society Extracts* and *Victorian Poetry.*

Carmela McIntire

Professor McIntire received her Ph.D. from Michigan State University. She teaches literature and composition at Florida International University. McIntire is currently working on a book-length study of Josephine Lawrence.

William McKeen

Professor McKeen received a B.A. in history and an M.S. in journalism from Indiana University, and a Ph.D. in education from the University of Oklahoma. The recipient of several teaching awards, he has taught at the University of Oklahoma, and he currently teaches journalism at the University of Florida. Among McKeen's publications are pieces in *The Saturday Evening Post, Holiday,* and several regional magazines and newspapers, and his fiction has appeared in American and Canadian literary reviews. McKeen was assistant editor of *The American Story* (Curtins, 1975) and a contributor to *A Biographical Dictionary of American Journalism* (Greenwood Press, 1985). He is currently writing a study of the Beatles and their contribution to popular culture.

James H. Maguire

Professor Maguire received his B.A. from the University of Colorado and his Ph.D. from Indiana University. He is currently Professor of English at Boise State University, where he specializes in western American literature. Maguire's publications include *Mary Hallock Foote* (in the Boise State Western Writers Series), and he is the editor of *The Literature of Idaho: An Anthology* (Boise: Hemingway Western Studies, 1986) and an editor and contributor to *A Literary History of the American West* (Fort Worth: Texas Christian University Press, 1987).

Patrick William Merman

Patrick William Merman received his B.A. in English from the University of Notre Dame and an M.S. in industrial relations from the University of Michigan. He has worked at the American School in Chicago and is currently studying at the University of Chicago. Merman served as a research assistant on the *Linguistic Atlas of the Middle and South Atlantic States* and he prepared the notes for the final bibliography of Raven I. McDavid, Jr.'s scholarship for *The Journal of English Linguistics.*

Tice L. Miller

Professor Miller received his Ph.D. from the University of Illinois. He is currently Professor of Theatre at the University of Nebraska-Lincoln. Miller is the author of *Bohemians and Critics: Nineteenth-Century Theatre Criticism* (1981; nominated for the George Freedley Award) and has published in *Theatre History Studies, Nineteenth-Century Theatre Research, Theatre Studies, Theatre Survey, Southern Speech Communication Journal, Theatre Journal,* and *Central States Communication Journal.* He is associate editor and a contributor to *Shakespeare around the Globe; Notable Postwar International Revivals* (1986) and co-editor and contributor to the *Cambridge Guide to World Theatre* (forthcoming). He is also Vice-President for Research and Publication of the Association for Theatre in Higher Education.

Joseph O. Milner

Professor Milner received his B.A. from Davidson College, and his M.A. and Ph.D. from the University of North Carolina at Chapel Hill. He has taught at North Carolina State University and the University of North Carolina, and is currently chairman of the Department of Education at Wake Forest University. Milner is also Director of the North Carolina Writing Projects and a member of the National Humanities Faculty. He has published critical essays on Wallace Stevens and James Agee and pedagogical essays in *English Journal, English Education, Children's Literature*, and other journals, and research studies in the *Journal of Genetic Psychology*. He has also served as editor of a journal affiliated with the National Humanities Faculty and has been coordinator of the Curriculum at the North Carolina Governors School and Director of the Teachers Training Institute of North Carolina.

Merritt Moseley

Professor Moseley received his M.A. and his Ph.D. in English from the University of North Carolina at Chapel Hill. He is Associate Professor of Literature at the University of North Carolina at Asheville, where he specializes in nineteenth- and twentieth-century American and British literature and the history and poetics of fiction. Moseley has published on Victorian literature and American humor in *South Atlantic Review, College Literature, Studies in Contemporary Satire*, and *Sewanee Review*, and he is a contributor to *Fifty Southern Writers Before 1900* and *The Ungar Encyclopedia of American Literature*.

F. William Nelson

Professor Nelson received his B.A. from the University of Texas, his M.A. from Columbia University, and his Ph.D. from the University of Oklahoma. He has taught at the University of Wichita. He is currently Professor of American Studies at Wichita State University. Nelson's publications include articles on the comic, on crime stories, and on popular fiction in *Clues: A Journal of Detective Fiction, Thalia, Twentieth-Century Literature, Modern Fiction Studies*, and *Critical Survey of Long Fiction* and has edited a casebook on William Golding's *Lord of the Flies*.

Laura Niesen de Abruña

Professor Niesen received her B.A. from Smith College and her M.A. and Ph.D. from the University of North Carolina at Chapel Hill, and has studied at the Université de Paris-Sorbonne and Yale University. She has taught at the University of North Carolina, the University of Texas, and the University of Puerto Rico and is currently Assistant Professor of English at Ithaca College, where she specializes in modern American and British literature. Niesen has published articles in *South Atlantic Review, The Explicator, British Women Writers, Engendering the Word: Feminist Essays in Psychosexual Poetics, The Journal of the Midwest Modern Language Association, The Women's Studies Encyclopedia*, and *World Literature Written in English*, and she is working on *The Refining Fire: Herakles and Other Heroes in T.S. Eliot's Works* (forthcoming from Peter Lang). She is also on the editorial board of *Mid-Hudson Language Studies*.

Don L.F. Nilsen

Professor Nilsen received a B.A. in French from Brigham Young University, an M.A. in applied linguistics from American University, and a Ph.D. in linguistics from the University of Michigan. He is Professor of English at Arizona State University, where he specializes in humor studies. Nilsen is the author of *Language Play: An Introduction to Linguistics* (Newbury House), *Semantic Theory: A Linguistic Approach* (Newbury House), *Syntactic and Semantic Tests for the Instrumental Case in English* (Mouton), *Toward a Semantic Specification of Deep Case* (Mouton), and *English Adverbials* (Mouton). He is the co-editor, with Alleen Pace Nilsen, of *World Humor and Irony Membership Serial Yearbook (WHIMSY)* (Arizona State University, Volumes 1-5). He also serves in an advisory capacity with Workshop Library on World Humor (WLWH) and World Humor and Irony Membership (WHIM).

Daniel W. O'Bryan

Professor O'Bryan received his B.A. from the University of Nevada, Reno, his M.A. from the University of California at Berkeley, and his Ph.D. from the University of Washington. His specialty is sixteenth- and seventeenth-century English literature, and his most recent position was as Dean of Humanities and Professor of Language and Literature at Old College, Reno.

Robert H. O'Connor

Professor O'Connor received his B.A. from Cornell University, his M.A. from the State University of New York at Binghamton, and his Ph.D.

from Bowling Green State University. He has taught at Southwest Texas State University and is currently Assistant Professor of English at North Dakota State University, where he specializes in British Romantic literature. O'Connor's research interests include Gothic literature and nineteenth-century British drama; his publications include articles in *The Wordsworth Circle, The Lamar Journal of the Humanities, Notes on Contemporary Fiction,* and *Gothic.* He has also contributed to *The Dictionary of Literary Biography: American Poets, 1915-1945, The Magill Critical Survey of Drama,* and *The Magill Literary Annual.*

Fritz Oehlschlaeger

Professor Oehlschlaeger received his B.A. from the University of Michigan and his Ph.D. in American literature from the University of Illinois. He is Associate Professor of English at Virginia Polytechnic Institute and State University. Oehlschlaeger has contributed articles on American literature to *American Literature, Modern Fiction Studies, American Literary Realism, Essays in Literature,* and *Western American Literature.* He co-edited *Toward the Making of Thoreau's Modern Reputation* (University of Illinois Press, 1980) and is presently completing an edition of frontier humor published in the *St. Louis Reveille.*

Thomas C. Parramore

Professor Parramore received his B.A., M.A., and Ph.D. (in English history) from the University of North Carolina at Chapel Hill. He teaches at Meredith College, where his specialty is North Carolina history. He is the recipient of numerous historical association awards. Parramore's publications include *Carolina Quest* (Prentice-Hall, 1978), *North Carolina: The History of an American State* (Prentice-Hall, 1983), *Express Lanes and Country Roads,* Volume 5 of *The Way We Lived in North Carolina* (University of North Carolina Press, 1983), and *Southampton County, Virginia* (University Press of ·Virginia, 1978). He is the co-author of *The North Carolina Experience: A Documentary History* (University of North Carolina Press, 1984) and has authored numerous articles.

Michael Pettengell

Michael Pettengell received both a B.A. and a B.S.E. in English at Arkansas State University and is currently working on an M.A. at the University of Mississippi. He has contributed to *History of American Newspapers* (1978) and *Bibliography of the Blues* (University of Mississippi Center for Southern Study, 1987), and he is writing a study of *The Arkansas Thomas Cat.* Pettengell is a program director for Mississippi Public Radio's blues program, "Highway 61."

Edward J. Piacentino

Professor Piacentino received his B.A. from the University of North Carolina at Chapel Hill, his M.A. from Appalachian State University, and his Ph.D. in American literature from the University of North Carolina at Chapel Hill. He is Professor of English and Director of the Honors Program at High Point College, where he specializes in American literature. He has contributed to *Mark Twain Journal, Mississippi Quarterly, Southern Literary Journal, The Markham Review, Studies in Short Fiction, Notes on Modern American Literature, American Quarterly, Poe Studies,* and *Studies in American Humor.* His book, *T.S. Stribling: Pioneer Realist in Modern Southern Literature,* is forthcoming.

Thomas Pribeck

Professor Pribek received his B.S. from the University of Wisconsin-LaCrosse, his M.A. from the University of Minnesota-Twin Cities, and his Ph.D. from the University of Wisconsin-Madison. He is Assistant Professor of English at the University of Wisconsin-LaCrosse. Pribek's publications include articles in *Philological Quarterly, Nineteenth-Century Fiction, Hawthorne Society Newsletter, Studies in American Fiction, Studies in the American Renaissance, Arizona Quarterly, Papers on Language and Literature, American Literary Realism, Poe Studies, Journal of Evolutionary Psychology, Massachusetts Studies in English, College Language Association Journal,* and *Melville Society Extracts.*

Phyllis R. Randall

Professor Randall received her B.A. from Juniata College, her M.A. from the University of Pennsylvania, and her Ph.D. from the University of North Carolina at Chapel Hill. She is currently Professor of English at North Carolina Central University, where she specializes in twentieth-century British and American drama, women's studies (particularly women's communication), and sociolinguistics. Randall has published, with Mary E. Jarrard, *Women Speaking: An Annotated Bibliography of Verbal and Nonverbal Communication, 1970-1980* (Garland, 1982), and articles on David Storey in *Essays in Contemporary British Drama* (1981) and *Essays on the Contemporary English Novel* (1986), as well as essays in *Women's Studies in Communication* and *Communication Education*. She is also Assistant Editor of *American Speech*.

Joanna E. Rapf

Professor Rapf is Associate Professor of English and Film at the University of Oklahoma. Her publications include articles on screenwriters, adaptation, and film comedy in *Literature/Film Quarterly, Studies in English Literature, The Western Humanities Review, Post Script*, and *Studies in American Humor*, and her books include *Buster Keaton: A Bio-Bibliography* (Greenwood Press).

Douglas Robillard

Professor Robillard received a B.S. and an M.A. from Columbia University and a Ph.D from Wayne State University. He is Professor of English at the University of New Haven, where he specializes in American literature. Robillard is the editor of *Poems of Herman Melville* (College and University Press, 1976), he contributed to *Supernatural and Fantasy Fiction* and *The Penguin Encyclopedia of the Supernatural*, and he has published articles in *Victorian Newsletter, English Language Notes, Southern Quarterly, South Dakota Quarterly, Studies in the Literary Imagination, Essays in Arts and Sciences*, and the *North Carolina Historical Review*. He also served as an assistant editor for this *Encyclopedia of American Humorists*.

Daniel G. Royot

Professor Royot received his Licence d'anglais and his DES anglais from the Université de Dijon and his Doctorate d'Etat from the Université de Lyon. He has taught at the Université de Clermont-Ferrand and is currently Professor at the Université Paul Valéry in Montpellier, France. Royot also has been a visiting professor at San Diego State University, California State University-Los Angeles, Southern Illinois University, and the University of Texas, and he was the Tallman Professor of French Civilization at Bowdoin College. He is the author of *L'Humour Americain, des Puritains aux Yankees* (Presses Universitaires de Lyon, 1980) and *Hollywood, Reflexions sur l'Ecran* (GRENA, 1984), and he has co-authored or edited a number of volumes: *American Trails, An Anthology of Representative Writers* (Armand Colin), *Histoire et Civili-sation des Etats-Unis, Textes et Documents commentes du XVIIe siècle à nos jours* (Fernand Nathan, 1974), *La France et l'Esprit de 76* (1976), *The American Puzzle* (Armand Colin, 1982), *Le Commentaire de Civilisation Anglaise et Americaine* (Armand Colin, 1982), *Interface: Essays on History, Myth and Art in American Literature* (Université de Montpellier, 1985), and *Images des U.S.A., de l'Icone populaire à l'Oeuvre d'Art* (Alei, 1985). Currently, he is completing two studies, *Le Folklore des Etats-Unis* (Aubier) and *Frances Whitcher (The Widow Bedott)*. Royot has also contributed to a number of scholarly journals and books, and served as guest editor for special issues of *Thalia* and *Revue Française d'Etudes Americaines*.

Richard Alan Schwartz

Professor Schwartz received his Ph.D. from the University of Chicago. He is currently Associate Professor of English at Florida International University, where he specializes in American humor, twentieth-century literature, and creative writing.

L. Moody Simms, Jr.

Professor Simms received his B.A. in history from Millsaps College and his M.A. and Ph.D. from the University of Virginia, where he was a Woodrow Wilson Fellow and concentrated on American history. He is Professor of History and former chairman of the department at Illinois State University. Simms has published widely on the social, cultural, and intellectual history of the South, on southern literature and art, and on American popular culture in *American Humor, Mississippi Quarterly, Southern Studies, Resources for American Literary Study, American Literary Realism 1870-1910*, and *Mid-South Folklore*, and he contributed essays on Joseph Glover Baldwin and H. Allen Smith to the *Dictionary of Literary Biography: American Humorists, 1800-1950*.

David E.E. Sloane

Professor Sloane received his B.A. from Wesleyan University and both his M.A. and Ph.D. from Duke University. He taught at Lafayette College and Rutgers University and is presently Professor of English at the University of New Haven. Sloane's publications include *Mark Twain as a Literary Comedian* (1979) and *The Literary Humor of the Urban Northeast, 1830-1890* (1983). He is the editor of *American Humor Magazines and Comic Periodicals*

(Greenwood Press, 1987) and the author of a number of articles on northeastern humorists, realism, Poe studies, and business writing and linguistics. Sloane also served as assistant editor for this *Encyclopedia of American Humorists*.

David K. Steege

David Steege received his B.A. from Pomona College and his M.A. from the University of North Carolina at Chapel Hill, where he is currently working on his doctorate. He teaches composition at the University of North Carolina. Steege has served as an editorial assistant for *The Southern Literary Journal*.

E. Kate Stewart

Professor Stewart received her Ph.D. from the University of Mississippi. She is currently Visiting Assistant Professor of English in the Humanities Department of Worcester Polytechnic Institute. Stewart specializes in nineteenth-century American literature and is the author of *Arthur Sherburne Hardy: Man of American Letters* (1986). She has also published on Edgar Allan Poe in *Poe Studies, University of Mississippi Studies in English*, and *Poe and His Times*, and on literary magazines.

Thomas H. Stewart

Thomas H. Stewart is working on his doctorate at the University of Mississippi. He has taught at the University of Mississippi. Stewart has published on early American literature in the *University of Mississippi Studies in English* and *The Tennessee Folklore Society Bulletin*.

George A. Test

Professor Test received his B.A. from Swarthmore College and his M.A. and Ph.D. from the University of Pennsylvania. He taught at Allegheny College and National University in Santiago, Chile, as a Fulbright Lecturer, and he is presently Professor of English and former chair of the Department of English at the State University of New York at Oneonta, where he specializes in American literature and studies in satire. Test has published articles in *American Quarterly, CEA Critic, American Notes and Queries, Carleton Miscellany, Thalia, Studies in Contemporary Satire, Scholia Satyrica, American Humor: An Interdisciplinary Newsletter/ Studies in American Humor*, and other journals; he has edited papers from conferences on James Fenimore Cooper and contributed to *American*

Humor Magazines and Comic Periodicals and *Ritual and Ceremony in Popular Culture*, and he was the founder and editor of *Satire Newsletter*. He also served as an assistant editor of this *Encyclopedia of American Humorists*.

Michelle M. Tokarczyk

Professor Tokarczyk received her B.A. from Herbert Lehman College (CUNY) and her M.A. and Ph.D. from the State University of New York at Stony Brook. She has taught at Douglass College and Hofstra University, and she is currently Assistant Professor and Associate Director of Composition at Rutgers University. Her specialty is American literature, with an emphasis on contemporary literature, women's literature, and interdisciplinary approaches in literature. Tokarczyk's publications include articles in *Women's Quarterly Review*. She is currently working on *E.L. Doctorow: An Annotated Bibliography* (forthcoming from Garland Publishing), she has published poetry in several small magazines, and she is a consulting editor for *Belles Lettres* and the poetry editor for *Women's Quarterly Review*.

Paula Uruburu

Professor Uruburu received her Ph.D. in English from the State University of New York at Stony Brook. She is currently Assistant Professor of English at Hofstra University, where she specializes in American literature, women's studies, and the grotesque in literature. Uruburu's publications include *The Gruesome Doorway: A Definition of the American Grotesque* (Peter Lang, 1987).

Clyde G. Wade

Professor Wade received his Ph.D. from the University of Missouri-Columbia. Currently, he is Associate Professor of English at the University of Missouri at Rolla. Wade has published essays in British and American literature, including articles on B.P. Shillaber and Frances Miriam Whitcher in *Dictionary of Literary Biography: American Humorists, 1800–1950*. He is presently working on a study, *Continuities in American Humor*.

Ritchie D. Watson, Jr.

Professor Watson received his B.A. and his Ph.D. from the University of North Carolina at Chapel Hill. He is Professor of English at Randolph-Macon College and was a Lilly Foundation Visiting Scholar at Duke University. His publications include *The Cavalier in Virigina Fiction* (Louisiana State University Press, 1985) and fourteen journal articles on subjects in his area of specialization, antebellum southern fiction. He has also served as co-editor of the North Carolina-Virginia College English Association *Newsletter* and the *Ellen Glasgow Newsletter*.

Stephen Watt

Stephen Watt is Assistant Professor of English and Victorian studies at Indiana University. He has published essays on modern drama and Irish culture in *Eire-Ireland, The Journal of Irish Literature, Comparative Drama*, and *Perspectives on Contemporary Literature*. He has co-edited, with Judith Fisher, a collection of essays on nineteenth-century theater history, and at present he is at work on a book-length study of Irish drama and theater at the beginning of the twentieth century.

Kenny Williams

Professor Williams received a B.A. from Benedict College, an M.A. in English from DePaul University, an M.A. and a Ph.D. in American civilization from the University of Pennsylvania. She is currently Professor of English at Duke University. In addition to articles and reviews, Williams's publications include *They Also Spoke: An Essay on Negro Literature in America, 1787-1930* (1970), *In the City of Men: Another Story of Chicago* (1974), *Prairie Voices: A Literary History of Chicago from the Frontier to 1893* (1980), and *A Storyteller and a City: Sherwood Anderson's Chicago Years and Urban Vision (1896-1925)* (forthcoming). With Bernard Duffey she published *Chicago's Public Wits: A Chapter in the American Comic Spirit* (1983). Williams received the 1986 Mid-America Award for "distinguished contributions to the study of midwestern literature." She served as an assistant editor of this *Encyclopedia of American Humorists*.

Lonnie L. Willis

Professor Willis received his M.A. from the University of Texas and his Ph.D. from the University of Colorado, Boulder. He is Professor of English at Boise State University, where his specialty is American literature, particularly that of the first half of the nineteenth century, contemporary fiction, and popular culture, including film. Among his publications are articles on Henry David Thoreau, Richard Brautigan, Harry Crews, Larry McMurtry, and pornography in *Critique, Notes on Contemporary Literature, The Thoreau Society Bulletin, Western American Literature, cold drill*, and *Rocky Mountain Review*.

Kate H. Winter

Professor Winter received her B.A. from the State University of New York at Geneseo, her M.A. from the State University College at Cortland, and her Ph.D. from the State University of New York at Albany. In addition to teaching high school English, she has taught at Tompkins-Cortland Community College and Skidmore College; she is currently a lecturer at the State University of New York at Albany, where she specializes in nineteenth-century American literature, narrative theory, and the teaching of writing. Winter's publications include a prize-winning essay, "North Country Voices," which appeared in *Upstate Literature*, and *Marietta Holley: Life with "Josiah Allen's Wife"* (Syracuse University Press, 1984), which won the John Ben Snow Prize and the RCHA Award for 1984.

Douglas Charles Wixson

Professor Wixson received degrees from M.I.T. and Stanford University, and his Ph.D. from the University of North Carolina at Chapel Hill. He also studied at the Universität Göttingen. Presently Associate Professor of English at the University of Missouri at Rolla, he has also taught at the University of North Carolina at Chapel Hill, the University of North Carolina at Greensboro, and at universities in St.-Étienne and Chambéry in France, and he has received several fellowships and other awards. Wixson edited Jack Conroy's *The Weed King and Other Stories* (Lawrence Hill, 1985). He has published on Conroy, Bertolt Brecht, Thornton Wilder, Shakespeare, George Orwell, Charles Juliet, and Henry Miller in *Modern Drama, Shakespeare Studies, Mid-America, North Dakota Quarterly, Studies in the Humanities*, and *The French-American Review*. Currently, he is completing of study of Conroy and midwestern literary radicalism.

Index